2016 Principles of Business Taxation

AUTHORS

David L. Gibberman, J.D.

Geralyn A. Jover-Ledesma, LL.B., LL.M., CPA

Editorial Staff

Production . . . . Linda Kalteux

ISBN: 978-0-8080-4077-4

Printed in the United States of America

Preface

Most business students enrolled in the first federal income tax course at a four-year university, or in an associate degree program, do not pursue a career in tax. Moreover, upon graduation from a university, more accounting majors are employed as auditors or corporate accountants than as tax practitioners. The vast majority of students who take the first tax course are not going to be tax practitioners at all but they do need to understand how the tax law works and the impact taxes have on business. What is the best approach for the first tax course that can insure relevant and beneficial coverage for all students?

More traditional tax textbooks and undergraduate tax courses focus on individual income taxation and offer coverage of personal items, such as who qualifies as a dependent, the rules regarding filing status, vacation homes, and qualifying for the earned income credit. Perhaps the rationale in this approach is that all students, whether destined for tax practice or not, can walk away with helpful information on individual income tax. Those students going into tax practice would have some basics to build on in future tax classes, and those who were not destined for tax practice could have some helpful information for their own financial future.

However, tax practice has changed and individual income tax preparation is no longer the major cornerstone of accounting services. Moreover, business tax planning goes beyond individual tax planning concepts so that a student pursuing business interests after graduation will benefit more from a basic knowledge of business tax concepts and planning rather than from exposure only to individual tax planning. Today, business tax planning and practice is more central to the modern accounting firm than individual tax compliance. The AICPA and others have posited for over a decade that a better starting point for teaching taxes is a business approach. Individual income taxation software has also taken much of the sting from individual income tax preparation, so the average business major is more likely to benefit from a good understanding of how business decisions, planning, and operations are affected by taxes than a crash course on the hundreds of tax rules that relate to their own individual taxes. Just as all business and finance majors are expected to understand the time value of money, so it is also critical that these students understand basic tax principals and how various tax considerations and strategies can result in substantial tax savings. Business decisions are based on the after-tax implications of decisions and the true cost of investment and risk.

Principles of Business Taxation focuses on the central concepts that build our tax framework from a business perspective. The book approaches the study of taxation from the perspective of the business person faced with business decisions. Among all factors that must be considered in making business decisions, tax consequences are critical and the impact must be considered and understood. *Principles of Business Taxation* provides students with the necessary technical material to address common, everyday tax questions. It accomplishes this by presenting the material in an easy-to-read and straight-forward manner.

Principles of Business Taxation is divided into six parts: Overview of Taxes and the Federal Income Tax System; Federal Taxation of Business Income and Deductions; Transactions Involving Business Property; Calculating Tax Liability and Taxes Owed; Business Entity Issues and U.S. Taxation of International Transactions. Part one provides students who want to expand their technical knowledge with the skills to do so by introducing them to tax research early in the book and then providing one research question in the homework for each subsequent chapter. This perspective leads to a very different coverage in this textbook, coverage that is useful for accounting, finance, and general business majors. It encourages students to ask questions and to engage in research to discover the answers.

Although many of the exclusions, deductions, and credits in the tax system apply equally to individual and corporate taxpayers, this book focuses on the business perspective of these items. In some cases, this means covering an item not available to individuals (e.g., the dividends received deduction and the concept of earnings and profits and how it relates to corporate distributions). In other cases it means making the business, rather than the individual, aspects of the tax rules the primary focus of the topic. While the focus is on concepts and how taxes affect business decisions, taxation of sole proprietorships and other passthrough entities is not abandoned. After all, many core tax concepts apply to individuals as well as businesses, and the book is not shy in pointing out such application. When charitable contributions are introduced, the general rules for deductibility are described, and then the limitations that apply to corporate and individual taxpayers are discussed separately. An advantage to this approach is that most of the students who take only one course in taxation will learn how businesses are taxed and, in turn, have a better appreciation for how taxes affect business decisions. Another advantage to this approach is that the topics dovetail into other business, finance, and accounting coursework.

Students using *Principles of Business Taxation* have access to the complete and comprehensive Fundamental Tax Topics library on CCH Study MATE, an online site that can be used to review any and all fundamental tax topics. (A special card with access code is bound into this book.) In this way, we believe *Principles of Business Taxation* offers a tremendous opportunity for students of taxation to experience a course and text that truly offers the most useful approach for the future, and they can access these online courses for additional information that their instructor may deem helpful based on individual circumstances and objectives.

We hope *Principles of Business Taxation* will serve you well as you consider the implications of our tax law on business decisions and development. We welcome your comments, criticisms, and questions.

Wolters Kluwer Tax Law Editors

TABLE OF CONTENTS

Chapter 3: Tax Accounting

PART II: FEDERAL TAXATION OF BUSINESS INCOME AND DEDUCTIONS

Chapter 4: Federal Income Taxes and Gross Income

Chapter 5: Business Deductions: Ordinary and Necessary Business Expenses

Chapter 6: Business Deductions: Employment-Related Expenses

Chapter 7: Depreciation, Depletion, and Amortization

PART III: TRANSACTIONS INVOLVING BUSINESS PROPERTY

Chapter 8: Property Transactions: Realized and Recognized Gains and Losses

Chapter 9: Property Transactions: Character of Gain or Loss

PART IV: CALCULATING TAX LIABILITY AND TAXES OWED

Chapter 10: NOLs, AMT, and Other Business Taxes

Chapter 11: Tax Credits

PART V: BUSINESS ENTITY ISSUES AND TAX PLANNING

Chapter 12: Corporate Formation, Distributions, and Other Corporation-Related Tax Issues

Chapter 15: Income Tax Planning for Business

PART VI: U.S. TAXATION OF INTERNATIONAL TRANSACTIONS

Chapter 16: Taxation of International Transactions

Appendix

Finding Devices

PART I:

Overview of Taxes and the Federal Income Tax System

CHAPTER 1

Introduction to Taxation

CHAPTER CONTENTS

LEARNING OBJECTIVES

1. Explain a government's need to tax.
2. List the various taxes U.S. residents and businesses pay and describe how the taxes are calculated.
3. Describe the factors governments take into consideration in deciding how to allocate the tax burden.
4. Explain why taxes are a transaction cost that should not be ignored when making decisions and why having a basic understanding of how the tax laws operate is important.

¶ 100 Introduction

But in this world nothing is certain but death and taxes. –Benjamin Franklin

This famous quote by Benjamin Franklin sums it up—there is just no way to avoid taxes. Sales taxes, property taxes, excise taxes, income taxes. It is hard to make it through the day without taxes affecting our lives. Thinking about taking on a second job to help pay your bills? Keep in mind that a portion of those extra earnings will go to the government to cover your payroll and income taxes. Have some money to invest? Depending on the type of investment you choose, you could end up sharing anywhere from zero percent to over 40 percent of the investment income with the government. Looking to buy a new car? The government could reimburse you if you buy the right model at the right time of the year. Thinking about adopting a child? Depending on your income level, you can reduce your income taxes in 2015 by up to $13,400 of the cost if the adoption is finalized by the end of the year. Heading to the grocery store? San Francisco debated a $.17 tax on grocery bags (not the groceries, just the bag itself). Many other cities followed suit on imposing tax on plastic grocery bags.

So just how important are taxes to modern businesses? Major corporations employ dozens of tax specialists and pay tens of thousands of dollars each year for tax assistance from international and national accounting firms. Those accounting firms employ thousands of individuals who specialize in business taxation. Very few significant transactions occur in major corporations without their tax departments first analyzing them. For example, a business considering where to locate its new manufacturing facility will have cities, states, and even foreign countries lined up to discuss the tax incentives they can offer the company. Regardless of the aspect of business you plan to specialize in, eventually you will need to interact with the personnel in the tax department. Therefore, it is essential that business students, especially those majoring in accounting, have a basic understanding of how the tax laws operate.

This chapter describes the major role that taxes play when making decisions. It begins with a discussion of why governments tax and introduces some of the more common types of taxes that individuals and businesses frequently encounter. The chapter also discusses the various factors governments take into consideration when deciding whom and what to tax. It concludes with a discussion of why taxes are an important element to consider when making decisions.

¶ 101 Why Governments Must Tax

Taxes, after all, are dues that we pay for the privileges of membership in an organized society. – Franklin D. Roosevelt

Why governments exist and the appropriate scope of government activities are philosophical and political questions. Within the United States, a broadly accepted role of government has been to protect the individual rights of citizens from threats within and outside its geographical boundaries. Accordingly, the federal government provides homeland security and national defense. Federal, state, and local governments all share responsibilities for enforcing laws protecting individual rights. Governments also fund the development of economic infrastructure, including roadways, water supply, and air traffic control. Modern governments also fund public services such as providing and maintaining schools, hospitals, and emergency response systems. They also provide benefits to the poor, elderly, and disabled. These are only a few of the many types of services that persons living in the United States have come to expect from the government. Still, the list is sufficient to illustrate that governments must spend tremendous amounts of cash to fund the goods and services they provide. Like any business, governments must generate revenues in order to pay for their expenditures. Taxes are the primary mechanism by which funds are transferred from the private sector (individuals and businesses) to the government.

¶ 102 Allocating the Tax Burden

The point to remember is that what the government gives it must first take away. –John S. Coleman, address, Detroit Chamber of Commerce, 1956

Although the need for revenues may be evident, the tax systems governments use to raise tax revenues are more complicated. To illustrate the dilemma governments face when deciding whom and what to tax, take as an example a neighborhood community where the residents have concerns about security. The community has voted to pay a security firm to patrol its streets between 10 p.m. and 6 a.m. each night, and now it must decide how to pay the $50,000 annual fee for these services. One option would be to divide the cost only among those in the community who want the security service. However, those who claim not to want the security service (perhaps to avoid paying for it) will still enjoy the benefits. Economists refer to this as a free-rider problem. In this case, the security service is a **public good**. A distinguishing characteristic of a public good is that there is no effective means of limiting the enjoyment of the good.

To avoid the free-rider problem, the community could divide the costs equally among all residences. This approach has the benefit of simplicity. Of course, this is not the only way to allocate the costs. For example, some community members might argue that residents with more expensive homes have more to gain from a security service and, therefore, should contribute more toward the costs. These members suggest that the cost should be spread among residences unequally, based on the assessed value of the homes. Although admittedly this approach would be more complicated, they believe it would be a much more equitable method of allocating the costs.

Now contrast the above situation with a community that wants to add a recreation center to the neighborhood. The community has agreed all homeowners would share in the cost of constructing the facility, and it is now in the process of deciding who should pay the annual costs of operating and maintaining the facility. Unlike the previous situation where providing security benefits the entire community, in this scenario, the community is able to control access to the facility and thus has the option of charging user fees to those who use it. However, the presence of a recreation center may make the community a more attractive place to live, which could cause property values to increase. Accordingly, the community needs to decide whether it would be appropriate to require only those who use the recreation center to bear the entire cost of maintaining it. These are the types of issues governments face when deciding whom and what to tax in order to raise revenues to fund government-provided goods and services.

When two parties enter into a transaction (including situations in which the government provides goods and services), the transaction may positively or negatively affect third parties. When the transaction affects persons or businesses unrelated to the transaction, economists refer to the situation as an **externality**. A negative externality results in a cost unwillingly borne by someone other than the parties involved in the transaction. An example of a negative externality is the pollution a factory generates during the manufacturing process. The costs neighboring residents and businesses bear in the form of poorer air quality, lower property values, etc., are a negative externality.

A positive externality, on the other hand, results when third parties derive benefits from the transaction. Public transportation is an example in which persons enter into transactions with the government to use a government-provided service. When individuals choose to use public transportation rather than drive their own vehicles, roadway congestion decreases and air quality improves. In addition, property values tend to be higher in areas that offer public transportation. Because public transportation provides benefits that extend beyond those who use it, governments generally charge a reduced user fee and find other ways to finance the remainder of the costs.

¶ 103 Deciding on a Tax Structure

When the government provides goods or services that are not public goods, it has the option of imposing a user fee on those who utilize the goods or services. Typically user fees are a flat amount. Examples of the government's use of user fees are the tollbooth charges drivers pay to use the Florida turnpike, entrance fees those who visit the Grand Canyon National Park pay, or the cost of postage for those who use the U.S. Postal Service to mail letters and packages.

If the amounts collected from user fees are not sufficient to cover the entire costs or if a public good is involved, the government raises the necessary revenues by imposing other taxes. This involves applying a tax rate to a tax base. Deciding on a **tax base** involves determining whom and what to tax. The tax base might be the amount of an employee's wages, the value of property, or the retail sales price of an item. However, many other tax bases could be used. Once the tax base has been established, it is multiplied by a tax rate to determine the amount of tax. Three types of tax rate structures are regressive, proportional, and progressive.

To illustrate the differences among these three tax rate structures, assume that a government needs to raise $12,000 in revenues from its residents. To keep things simple, the tax can be raised from two residents: Tom Johnson and Jane Smith. The government has decided that its tax base will be based on employee wages, and it now must decide upon a tax rate.

Under Proposal A, a tax rate of 7.65 percent would be imposed on the first $94,200 of employee wages. All wages in excess of that amount would be subject to a 1.45-percent tax. During the current year, Tom and Jane earn wages of $120,000 and $60,000, respectively. Their tax liabilities would be computed as follows:

Tom's tax liability under Proposal A

$94,200 × 7.65%	$ 7,206
($120,000 – $94,200) × 1.45%	374
	$ 7,580

Jane's tax liability under Proposal A

$60,000 × 7.65%	$ 4,590

Total taxes raised ($7,580 + $4,590)	$12,170

Under the tax structure in Proposal A, Tom would pay more taxes than Jane. However, Tom's $7,580 tax liability on his $120,000 tax base means that his average tax rate is only 6.32 percent ($7,580 ÷ $120,000), as compared to Jane's 7.65-percent average tax rate ($4,590 ÷ $60,000). By calculating the **average tax rate** (total tax liability ÷ the tax base) for each taxpayer, one can see what portion of each taxpayer's tax base is used to finance the tax burden. Although Tom would pay more tax than Jane, a smaller portion of his wages would be used to pay his share of the taxes. A tax structure in which the *average tax rate decreases as the tax base increases* is called a **regressive tax**.

Under Proposal B, a single tax rate of 6.75 percent would apply to all employee wages. A tax structure in which the *average tax rate stays constant as the tax base fluctuates* is called a **proportional tax**. This type of tax is also commonly called a **flat tax**.

Tom's tax liability under Proposal B

$120,000 × 6.75%	$ 8,100

Jane's tax liability under Proposal B

$60,000 × 6.75%	$ 4,050

Total taxes raised ($8,100 + $4,050)	$12,150

Under Proposal C, the first $20,000 of wages would be taxed at two percent. Wages in excess of $20,000 but less than or equal to $40,000 would be taxed at four percent, wages in excess of $40,000 but less than or equal to $80,000 would be taxed at eight percent, and all wages in excess of $80,000 would be taxed at 12 percent. Under Proposal C, Tom and Jane's tax liabilities would be computed as follows:

Tom's tax liability under Proposal C

$20,000 × 2%	$ 400
($40,000 – $20,000) × 4%	800
($80,000 – $40,000) × 8%	3,200
($120,000 – $80,000) × 12%	4,800
	$ 9,200

Jane's tax liability under Proposal C

$20,000 × 2%	$ 400
($40,000 – $20,000) × 4%	800
($60,000 – $40,000) × 8%	1,600
	$ 2,800

Total taxes raised ($9,200 + $2,800)	$12,000

Under Proposal C, Tom would not only pay more tax dollars than Jane would, but he would also pay a greater percentage of his gross wages in tax ($9,200 ÷ $120,000 = 7.67% versus Jane's $2,800 ÷ $60,000 = 4.67%). A tax structure where the *average tax rate increases as the tax base increases* is called a **progressive tax**.

Although each of these three proposals achieve the government's goal of raising the $12,000 of revenues needed to finance government operations, the distribution of the tax burden differs among the three tax rate structures. Thus, in addition to deciding upon a tax base, governments must also decide which tax rate structure to use. A proportional (flat) tax rate has the advantage of simplicity because each taxpayer is subject to the same single rate of tax. Although somewhat more complicated to calculate, a progressive tax allows governments to collect a greater portion of the tax liability from those who have higher tax bases. In the section that follows, the more commonly encountered taxes imposed by federal, state, and local governments in the United States are discussed. For each type of tax, pay special attention not only to the tax base employed but also to the tax rate structure used to calculate the tax. Governments use a variety of tax bases and rate schedules.

¶ 104 Major Types of Taxes

The federal government generates most of its revenues from income taxes and payroll taxes. In contrast, a main source of revenues for most local governments is property taxes; for state governments, sales taxes and income taxes are the main sources of revenues. Taxes affect everyday transactions. They directly affect the amount we pay for merchandise (sales tax) and certain items like gasoline, tobacco, and alcohol (excise taxes). They also reduce the amount employees take home from their paychecks (income taxes and payroll taxes) as well as affect the amount people pay to own property (property taxes). Businesses are affected by taxes when they hire employees (employment taxes), own property (property taxes), or generate profits (income taxes). Because taxes represent additional costs to individuals and businesses, they need to understand the various types of taxes they may encounter during the normal course of business. Although not every tax is discussed in this chapter, the more commonly encountered taxes are introduced.

.01 Property Taxes

State and local governments raise a significant portion of their revenues by collecting property taxes from property owners. In the second quarter of 2014, 29.7 percent of all state and local revenues came from property taxes.[1] Most property taxes are *ad valorem* **taxes**, which means the value of the property is used as the tax base. The tax rate used for computing property taxes is typically a single tax rate, making it a proportional or flat tax. In deciding what property to tax, governments realize that unless they can keep track of the owners of the property, low compliance will result. Thus, the most common property taxes are levied on real estate and personal property for which ownership records are kept.

Real estate taxes. The most common property tax the government collects is the annual tax imposed on owners of land and buildings. Since land and buildings are **real property,** this type of tax is commonly called a "real estate tax." Local (county) governments keep records of the owners of real property, thereby allowing them to collect real estate taxes with relatively low administrative and compliance costs. The tax base for real estate taxes is the property's value (or some percentage thereof). Since the true value of real property can only be ascertained upon its sale to an unrelated party, using value as a tax base requires that the real estate be periodically appraised. The appraisal process for real estate varies, but a commonly used method involves having a government worker research recent sales of comparable property along with other relevant data to establish the property's value. The appraised value (or portion thereof) is then used to calculate the amount of property tax the real estate owners must pay. Many states calculate the real estate tax using a millage system. With a millage system the property tax rate is called the "millage rate" and is expressed in "mills." A mill is $1 per $1,000 of property value. So, for example, a millage rate of 15 mills would mean you would pay $1,500 per $100,000 of the property's taxable value.

Example 1: Stanford, Inc. operates a storefront in a county that imposes an annual real estate tax equal to one percent of the appraised value of the property. During 2014, Stanford's building was appraised at $300,000. Thus, its 2014 real estate taxes were $3,000 ($300,000 × 1%). During 2015, the building is appraised for $317,000, and accordingly, its real estate taxes for 2015 increase to $3,170 ($317,000 × 1%). If this tax had been expressed in "mills," the tax rate would have been stated as 10 mills representing a tax of $10 per $1,000 of appraised value.

 Spotlight: Over the years, real estate taxes have become less of a source of revenue for state governments, but they are still a primary source of revenue for local governments. Local governments, which include cities, counties, townships, and school districts, often use the revenues from real estate taxes to finance the construction and operation of public schools (kindergarten through 12th grade). Because real estate tends to appreciate over time, using value as the tax base allows governments to generate an increasing source of revenues without having to alter the tax rate.

Personal property taxes. Real property is not the only type of property subject to property taxes. Some states impose a tax on certain items of personal property. **Personal property** is all property other than real estate. Individuals can own real property for their own personal use, like personal residences or vacation homes. They can also own personal property that they use in their personal lives, like clothing, automobiles, and home furnishings. Businesses too can own both real and personal property. Office buildings, factories, and warehouses are examples of real property a business might own. Automobiles, office furniture, and machinery are examples of personal property used in a trade or business. It is important to distinguish between the general use of the term personal property and the specific use of that term as it relates to taxation. For tax purposes, personal property is any type of property that is not real estate.

Personal property can be tangible or intangible. Tangible property has physical characteristics; intangible property does not. Examples of **tangible personal property** include automobiles,

---

[1] U.S. Census Bureau. Federal, State, and Local Governments.
Quarterly Summary of State and Local Government Tax Revenue
for 2014: Q2, released Sept. 23, 2014.

jewelry, clothing, and equipment. States that impose a tax on tangible personal property generally tax property that taxpayers register with the state, like motor vehicles, boats, and aircraft. This allows the government to levy property taxes in conjunction with the annual registration or licensing of the property. Unlike real estate taxes, which are frequently used as a revenue source by local governments, personal property taxes are more likely to be assessed and collected by state governments.

Example 2: Under State of Florida statutes, anyone owning tangible personal property on January 1, who has a proprietorship, partnership, corporation, is a self-employed agent or a contractor, must file a tangible personal property return with the Property Appraiser by April 1 each year. Property owners who lease, lend, or rent property must also file. The appraised value of the tangible property is taxed at a millage rate established by the County in which the tangible property resides. As an example, if the tangible property had been appraised at $100,000 for 2015 and the millage rate imposed is 125 mills, the tax imposed upon the tangible property would be $12,500 ($100,000 × 125 mills (.125)).

Although it is not as common, some states impose a tax on intangible personal property. **Intangible property** has no physical characteristics; it includes copyrights, patents, goodwill, and other intangible assets frequently mentioned in financial accounting textbooks. For tax purposes, intangible personal property also includes stocks, bonds, mutual funds, and money market accounts. Since ascertaining the value of certain types of intangibles is easier than determining the value of other types of intangibles, states that impose an intangible personal property tax usually use as the tax base the current market value of stocks, bonds, mutual funds, and money market accounts the taxpayer owns.

Fair market value (FMV) is the price that a willing seller and a willing buyer would agree to with respect to the sale of property, provided neither party was compelled to enter into the transaction. In the case of intangible property like stocks, bonds, and mutual funds, market quotations are an acceptable measure of FMV, provided the quantity being valued is not so great as to significantly influence the market price as a result of the sale.

Example 3: Martin Vanderbilt lives in a state that imposes an intangibles tax on the value of stocks, bonds, mutual funds, and money market accounts as of January 1 of each year. The tax rate is $.50 for each $1,000 of intangibles valued in excess of $250,000. As of January 1, the value of Martin's intangible property is $700,000. Thus, Martin's intangible tax equals $225 ($700,000 − $250,000 = $450,000/$1,000 × $.50).

.02 Sales and Use Taxes

Sales tax is a broad-based tax on the consumption of goods and services. The federal government does not impose a sales tax, but most state and local governments rely on sales taxes as a source of revenues. For the second quarter of 2014, general sales tax and gross receipts tax generated 28.4 percent of all state and local revenues.[2] Sales tax is added to the purchase price of goods and therefore it is levied on consumers but collected by the vendor, who is then responsible for remitting the tax amounts to the appropriate government agencies. Currently all states except Alaska, Delaware, Montana, New Hampshire, and Oregon impose a sales tax on the purchase of various goods. Although the sales tax rate is typically a flat rate, the rates vary not only from state to state, but also among various local governments.

The state of Florida provides for a state sales tax of six percent statewide and for a local government sales tax levied at the discretion of County government (referred to as a discretionary sales surtax). The discretionary sales surtax, also called a county tax, is imposed by many Florida counties and applies to most transactions subject to sales tax. A taxpayer responsible for the collection of tax must collect the discretionary sales surtax in addition to Florida's general sales tax

---

[2] *Id.*

of six percent. The discretionary sales surtax is based on the rate in the county where you deliver taxable goods or services. A few counties do not impose the surtax.

Example 4: Santiago Hardware Store operates in Alachua County, Florida. Based upon the Discretionary Sales Surtax for Alachua County, Santiago must collect the statewide six percent sales tax plus a County surtax of .25 percent. Based upon a taxable sale of $1,000, Santiago would be required to collect $60 in state sales tax and $2.50 in surtax.

In addition to state and local sales taxes, some states impose an additional sales tax on certain items. For example, Minnesota has a 6.875-percent state sales tax, but it imposes a 9.375-percent sales tax on beer and liquor. Vermont's general sales tax is six percent, but it imposes a nine-percent sales tax on restaurant meals and hotel room rentals. New Hampshire does not have a sales tax, but it imposes a nine-percent tax on lodging and on meals served in restaurants.

Services are not usually subject to sales tax, and almost every state that imposes a sales tax exempts the purchase of prescription drugs. In many states, food is either exempt from sales tax or taxed at a significantly reduced rate. A few states exempt clothing from their tax base.

Example 5: Karen's Entertainment Complex provides a wide variety of items for parties and entertainment including party favors, souvenirs and pony rides. The party favors and souvenirs that she sells are subject to sales tax, but the pony rides offered are exempt from sales tax. If the sales tax rate is six percent and Wayne purchased $500 in party favors and souvenirs and $1,000 in pony rides, he would have to pay $1,530 ($1,000 plus $500 plus the sales tax of $30 on the party favors and souvenirs).

Because sales tax rates vary from state to state, it is possible for residents of states with a higher sales tax to purchase their goods from states that have lower or no sales taxes. States combat this potential loss of revenues by levying a use tax. A **use tax** is a tax on the consumption, use, or storage of goods and services otherwise not subject to sales tax. Any goods purchased that are not subject to sales taxes because the transaction occurred outside of the state are likely to be subject to use taxes when brought back into the state for use, consumption, or storage. Accordingly, use taxes complement sales taxes by ensuring that the appropriate revenues are collected on all goods used, consumed, or stored in the state.

 Reason for the Rule: Use taxes ensure that states collect the appropriate sales taxes from residents who order merchandise from online companies. They also prevent residents from avoiding paying their state's full sales tax rate by making purchases in other states. For example, Tennessee's general sales tax rate is seven percent; Georgia's is four percent. If a Tennessee business purchases merchandise from a merchant in Georgia and pays a four-percent sales tax, the business then owes the Tennessee government a three-percent use tax. Use taxes not only raise state revenues but they also protect local merchants (who are required to collect the sales tax from their customers) from unfair competition from out-of-state merchants who do not charge the same rate of sales tax.

.03 Excise Taxes

An **excise tax** is a tax on the production or consumption of specific goods and services. Most excise taxes are assessed on a per-unit basis and are a source of revenue for all levels of government. For example, the federal government levies a $.39 excise tax on a pack of cigarettes. In addition to tobacco products, the federal government levies excise taxes on the sale of alcohol, gasoline, firearms, tires, telephone services, and air travel. It also imposes excise taxes on activities such as wagering or highway usage by trucks. Most states and many local governments levy excise taxes on gasoline, alcohol, and tobacco; however, the tax rates can vary greatly. For example, the state excise tax levied on a pack of cigarettes is $.07 in South Carolina but it is $2.46 in Rhode Island. Local taxes may range anywhere from $.01 to $1.50 a pack.

 Spotlight: Some local governments levy excise taxes on hotel occupancy and car rentals. These taxes are popular because they raise revenues to fund local services by taxing customers who typically live outside the local area.

Excise taxes are usually included in the price of the product. However, the tax can be levied on the producer of the product (for example, the refiner or importer of gasoline). When excise taxes are levied on the producer, the cost is usually passed on to the retailer and then again to the consumer. Thus, regardless on whom the excise tax is levied, the consumer typically bears the economic burden of the excise tax. Many excise taxes are **indirect taxes** because they are levied on an intermediary who is not the one who ultimately bears the economic burden of the tax. In contrast, a **direct tax** is levied on the party who bears the economic burden of the tax. Sales taxes and property taxes are examples of direct taxes.

Example 6: Meredith Majors paid $2.45 a gallon for gasoline. Included in the purchase price were $.184 a gallon for federal excise tax and $.291 a gallon for state and local excises taxes. Thus, of the amount paid, $.475 was for excise taxes, and just under $2 a gallon covered the retail sales price of the gasoline and any sales tax imposed by the state and local governments.

 Spotlight: When an excise tax is imposed on a per-unit basis, the amount of revenue generated from excise taxes does not vary as the price for the good changes. Thus, to increase revenues from excise taxes, either the demand for the product or the tax rate must increase.

Severance taxes. A "severance tax" is an excise tax levied on the extraction of natural resources, like oil, gas, timber, ore, and coal. Common tax bases used to compute severance taxes are the value or number of units extracted. Severance taxes are a source of revenue for many state governments, as 39 states currently levy severance taxes on the extraction of at least one natural resource.

The Alaskan government levies a severance tax on oil and gas extracted in the state. Although the severance tax is levied on the oil companies, the additional cost is passed along and ultimately borne by consumers across the country. In fiscal year 2013, the Alaskan government generated almost $4 billion in revenue from severance taxes, which comprised around 78.5 percent of the general fund unrestricted revenues collected that year.[3] As a result of the revenues generated from this tax, Alaska is the only state that does not levy either personal income taxes or state sales taxes. In fact, the amount of revenues the Alaskan government raises from excise taxes on oil and gas is so substantial that each spring the government mails out checks to its residents from the surplus of revenues.

.04 User Fees

A **user fee** is a tax the government charges those using government-provided goods and services. User fees are an appropriate form of taxation only when the government can control the use of the goods or services it provides. For example, the federal government provides and operates a postal delivery service. Since it is easy to identify the users of this service, the government can generate a portion of the revenues it needs to operate the U.S. Postal Service by charging postage

---

[3] Alaska Department of Revenue—Tax Division, Spring 2013 Annual Report.

each time the service is used. As previously discussed in the chapter, most governments impose user fees on persons who use their public transportation services as a way of financing part of the cost of providing the service. Other examples of governments' use of user fees include admission fees to museums and various government-provided performing art productions, like the ballet, opera, or symphony.

.05 Wealth Transfer Taxes

The federal government and several states tax the transfer of wealth either during a person's lifetime or at death. When the transfer occurs during a person's lifetime, the transfer is a gift, and any tax owed on the transfer is **gift tax**. Gift taxes are always levied on the transferor (donor). When the transfer occurs upon a person's death, the transfer is an inheritance and the tax owed is **estate tax** (when levied on the transferor) or an **inheritance tax** (when levied on the recipient).

The tax base for wealth transfer taxes is the FMV of the property transferred. In regard to real estate, a professional real estate appraisal can be used. Personal property appraisers can be useful in obtaining the value of tangible personal property. In the case of intangible property, like stocks, bonds, and mutual funds, market quotations are an acceptable measure of FMV, provided the quantity is not so great that it would significantly influence the market price if sold.

Federal gift tax. During a person's lifetime, the federal government taxes transfers of wealth. Attempting to tax all transfers between persons would be nearly impossible to administer because people customarily make gifts to one another on special occasions such as birthdays, holidays, graduations, and marriages. Thus, the tax laws specifically do not tax transfers up to a certain amount each year, and they allow unlimited transfers between spouses. As long as total transfers during the year to any one person (other than one's spouse) do not exceed this amount, the government does not require the transfers to be disclosed. During 2015, a person can transfer up to $14,000 to another individual without any federal gift tax consequences.

Example 7: Ted Walters and his wife Lynne have two children and five grandchildren. Ted can make unlimited transfers to Lynne without any gift tax consequences. He can also gift up to $14,000 to each of his children and grandchildren, thereby effectively transferring $98,000 ($14,000 × 7) of his wealth to other family members without reporting the gifts to the federal government. Likewise, Lynne can gift up to $14,000 to each of her seven descendants without any gift tax consequences.

Example 8: In January 2015, Frieda Smith gifts $14,000 to her best friend and then in October gifts the same friend property worth $200,000. Since Frieda's gifts to her friend during 2015 exceed $14,000, the $200,000 excess constitutes a taxable gift.

Persons who transfer amounts in excess of the annual exemption amount during a calendar year must report the gifts they make during the year to the federal government. A gift tax is imposed on all "taxable gifts" (gifts made to individuals in excess of the annual exclusion amount). The federal gift tax rates are progressive and, during 2015, range from 18 to 40 percent. As the amount of taxable gifts a person makes over one's lifetime accumulates, the tax rate assessed on taxable gifts increases. However, each person is currently allowed a reduction against his or her gift tax that is equivalent to a $5,000,000 lifetime exemption against taxable gifts, adjusted for inflation; $5,430,000 for 2015. Accordingly, in 2015, only taxable gifts in excess of the $5,430,000 lifetime exemption ever result in the actual payment to the federal government for gift taxes owed.

Example 9: Continuing with the previous example, Frieda's $200,000 taxable gift must be reported to the federal government. If this is the first year in which Frieda made any taxable gifts, she will not pay tax on the transfer. However, her $5,430,000 lifetime exemption for taxable gifts will be reduced to $5,230,000.

Federal estate tax. When a person dies, the value of all of the property owned at the time of death is referred to as the "decedent's estate." After reducing the value of the estate by amounts owed to creditors, certain expenses paid by the estate, and bequests made to the spouse and qualified charitable organizations, the remainder of the estate is added to the decedent's cumulative taxable gifts, and the entire amount of taxable wealth transfers is subject to estate tax. To avoid the need to file an estate tax return on a small estate, the federal government allows a reduction against the estate tax of an amount equivalent to $5 million, adjusted for inflation after 2011, of taxable wealth transfers for persons who die during 2011 and thereafter. Thus, for a decedent who has made taxable gifts during his or her lifetime, this $5 million estate exemption must be used to cover both taxable gifts and the decedent's taxable estate.

 Spotlight: The Tax Relief, Unemployment Insurance Reauthorization, and Job Creation Act of 2010 reinstated federal estate and generation-skipping transfer (GST) taxes to apply until December 31, 2012. The reinstatement will result to a higher applicable exclusion amount of $5 million, subject to inflation adjustment beginning in 2012 and lower tax rates with a maximum rate of 35 percent.

 Spotlight: The American Taxpayer Relief Act of 2012 (ATRA; P.L. 112-240) increased the maximum tax rate to 40 percent.

Example 10: Mark dies in 2015, leaving his entire estate with a net worth of $5,000,000 to his son. In the same year, he also made a gift to the son amounting to $200,000. The entire $5,000,000 plus the $200,000 taxable gift is subject to estate tax. However, once the $5,430,000 estate tax exemption is taken into consideration, none of his estate is actually subject to federal estate tax.

State wealth transfer taxes. Only a handful of states tax transfers made during a person's lifetime. These states provide for annual and lifetime exemptions similar to those allowed by the federal government. Although the state gift tax rates are progressive, they are significantly lower than those imposed by the federal government. Currently 15 states levy an estate tax in addition to the federal estate taxes imposed on the decedent's estate, and 10 states impose an inheritance tax, which taxes beneficiaries on their inheritances. Among the states that impose wealth transfer taxes, all allow tax-free transfers to the decedent's spouse, and many have reduced tax rates on transfers to close family members.

 Spotlight: The state wealth transfer tax has been tied to the federal estate taxes in terms of the calculation of the tax due in certain states. For example, the Wisconsin estate tax is based upon the federal credit for state death taxes after December 31, 2007. Under federal law there will be no federal credit for state death taxes for deaths occurring in 2008 through 2010. Therefore, there is no Wisconsin estate tax for deaths occurring between January 1, 2008, and December 31, 2010. In the absence of a change in the federal or Wisconsin law, both the federal and Wisconsin estate tax will be restored for deaths occurring on or after January 1, 2011.

 Spotlight: The Tax Relief, Unemployment Insurance Reauthorization, and Job Creation Act of 2010 extended the sunset provision of the Economic Growth and Tax Relief Reconciliation Act of 2001 (EGTRRA). Thus, the state death tax credit allowed for estate, inheritance, legacy, or succession taxes actually paid to any state or the District of Columbia with respect to any property included in a decedent's gross estate will be restored for the estates of decedents dying after December 31, 2012. Further, the state death tax deduction will no longer be available to the estates of decedents dying after

> December 31, 2012. Thus, the estates of decedents dying after 2012 will not be able to deduct estate, inheritance, legacy, or succession taxes actually paid to any state or the District of Columbia from the value of the gross estate.

.06 Employment Taxes

There are two types of federal employment taxes: **FICA (Federal Insurance Contributions Act)** and **FUTA (Federal Unemployment Tax Act)**. FICA taxes consist of two parts: (1) social security taxes (also known as old-age, survivors, and disability insurance (OASDI)) and (2) Medicare taxes. FICA taxes are used to finance Medicare benefits paid to eligible beneficiaries and monthly payments made to the elderly and disabled. FUTA taxes, on the other hand, help finance the payment of unemployment benefits to those who have lost their jobs and are in the process of seeking gainful employment.

Social security and Medicare taxes. FICA tax is imposed on employees' wages at a combined 7.65-percent tax rate, which consists of a 6.2-percent tax for social security (OASDI) plus a 1.45-percent tax for Medicare. Both the employee and the employer pay FICA taxes. For 2015, the OASDI portion of the FICA tax applies only to the first $118,500 of an employee's wages.[4] There is no limit on the amount of wages subject to the 1.45-percent Medicare tax. Thus, for the first $118,500 of an employee's wages, a total contribution of 15.3 percent (7.65 percent by the employee plus 7.65 percent by the employer) is made to the social security and Medicare systems. For wages in excess of $118,500, only a total rate of 2.9 percent is contributed to the Medicare system.

 Spotlight: The employee's portion of the OASDI tax rate under the payroll tax is reduced by two percentage points to 4.2 percent for 2011 and 2012. Similarly, the OASDI portion of the self-employment tax is reduced by two percentage points to 10.4 percent for 2011 and 2012. A similar reduction applies to the railroad retirement tax. This rate went back to 6.2 percent in 2013 and thereafter.

Example 11: Sara Jenkins's wages for 2015 are $50,000. From this amount, her employer withholds $3,100 for social security taxes ($50,000 × 6.2%) and $725 for Medicare taxes ($50,000 × 1.45%). Her employer matches these amounts and remits a total of $6,200 ($3,100 × 2) and $1,450 ($725 × 2), respectively to the Social Security Administration. The employer OASDI tax rate remains at 6.2 percent.

 Spotlight: In 2015, only the first $118,500 of an employee's wages is subject to the full 7.65-percent FICA tax rate. Wages in excess of this amount are subject to the 1.45-percent Medicare tax only. Therefore, as employees' wages exceed $118,500, the average tax rate decreases. For wages up to $118,500, FICA is a flat tax. For all subsequent levels of income, it is regressive.

A self-employed business owner acts both as an employee and as an employer of the business. Therefore, these business owners, known as **sole proprietors**, are required to contribute both the employer and employee portions of FICA. When FICA tax is paid on the profits of a sole proprietorship, it is called a **self-employment tax**. For 2015, the self-employment tax rate is 15.3 percent on all *net earnings from self-employment* up to $118,500. After that, the self-employment tax rate drops to 2.9 percent.

Example 12: Judd Hampton operates his business as a sole proprietorship. During 2015, Judd's net earnings from self-employment were $45,000. Since that amount is less than

---

[4] *www.ssa.gov.*

CCH Study**MATE**™
Your Personal Online Tax "Tutor"—24/7!

If you find taxes difficult, you're not alone!

Now you have CCH StudyMATE™, a personal online "tutor." With StudyMATE you can plug into online learning any time of day or night. CCH StudyMATE walks you through the most important concepts covered in your textbook using individual learning sessions designed to make learning as easy as possible.

CCH Study MATE is easy to use, and since you've bought our book, you have free access to our Fundamental Tax Topics Library for a full year! CCH StudyMATE courses are designed with web learning in mind, so you can navigate your way through them independently. They are relatively short, but each course covers a substantial amount of material—including the top concepts covered in your textbook. These are student-centered courses with presentations that are different than those found in the text, so they give you another voice—another opportunity for concepts to sink in.

How Many Courses Do I Take?

Your instructor may want you to access all the courses in the fundamental series, you may be asked to take selective courses on certain topics, or your instructor may leave it up to you to use StudyMATE as you choose.

Access CCH Study MATE at www.cchstudymate.com

For your records, print your User ID and Password below:

User ID: _____

Password: _____

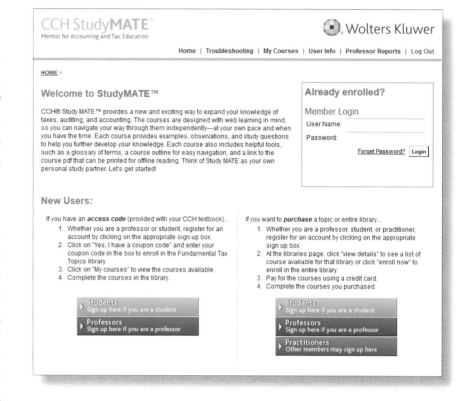

So, How Do I Get In?

Getting started is easy.

1 Go to www.cchstudymate.com and follow the instructions for New Users with an ACCESS CODE to sign up for a free account. Fill in the information on the registration page including a user ID and password of your choice.

2 Continue following the online instructions to enter your access code (provided below).

3 Click on MY COURSES to view the list of online courses, then click on the course title to begin.

ACCESS CODE:

CCHSM_15_TACL_1_797949

Technical Support: 866-798-5897 • support@learning.net

Wolters Kluwer

Wolters Kluwer • 4025 West Peterson Ave. • Chicago, IL 60646-6085

Take advantage of all the CCH StudyMATE courses offered!

The Fundamental Topics library covers the most important federal tax concepts typically covered in a one- or two-semester tax course.

- Accumulated Earnings and Personal Holding Company Taxes
- Alternative Minimum Tax
- Business Deductions
- Calculating Gain or Loss Realized from a Disposition of Property
- Characterization of Gain or Loss from a Disposition of Property
- Deductions for Losses and Bad Debts
- Deductions for an Individual's Personal and Investment Expenses
- Distributions Liquidating a C Corporation
- Distributions by C Corporations to Their Shareholders
- Education Savings Plans and Other Tax Breaks for Educational Expenses
- Estate Tax
- Federal Income Taxation—An Overview
- Federal Tax Practice and Procedure
- Generation-Skipping Transfer Tax
- Gift Tax
- Gross Income
- Gross Income—Exclusions
- Income Tax Credits
- Income Taxation of Trusts, Estates, and Their Beneficiaries
- Multijurisdictional Taxation: International and State and Local Transactions
- Nonrecognition of Gain or Loss from a Disposition of Property
- Organization and Income of C Corporations
- Partnerships-Distributions to Partners and Sales of Partnership Interests
- Partnerships—Formation and Operation
- Qualified and Nonqualified Retirement Plans (Including IRAs)
- Reorganization of a C Corporation
- S Corporations
- Tax Accounting

www.cchstudymate.com

$118,500, Judd's self-employment tax for 2015 is $6,885. The calculation of the amount is as follows:

Self-employment net earnings	$45,000
Tax rate on self-employment income	15.3%
Self-employment tax for 2015	$6,885

Example 13: Consider the same facts as in the previous example, except that Judd's 2015 net earnings from self-employment are $126,700. Since this amount exceeds $118,500 by $8,200, Judd's self-employment tax for 2015 is $18,130.50 ($118,500 × 15.3%) plus $237.80 ($8,200 × 2.9%) or $18,368.30.

Employers' responsibility for withholding and contributing FICA taxes is discussed in Chapter 6. Self-employment taxes, including the calculation of net earnings from self-employment, are further discussed in Chapter 13.

Unemployment taxes. FUTA is a federal tax that was enacted so states could provide unemployed workers with a portion of their regular income during periods of temporary unemployment. Although FUTA taxes are imposed by the federal government, the amounts collected are distributed to the states, which then add the FUTA tax amounts to any unemployment tax amounts they collect. Unlike employment taxes, FUTA taxes are levied only on employers. In 2015, FUTA taxes will be assessed at a rate of 6.2 percent, which is reduced to an effective rate of .8 percent if the employer pays state unemployment tax on the wages and does so in a timely manner. The tax rate for the employer is then applied to the first $7,000 of an employee's wages paid during the year. Most states also impose unemployment taxes on employee wages. States may use a different maximum amount for employee wages that are subject to the state unemployment compensation tax than does the federal government. State tax rates range anywhere from zero percent to just over 10 percent. For example, the Pennsylvania unemployment compensation tax rates are based upon a standard tax rate adjusted for several factors including the amount of unemployment claims made by former employees. The standard unemployment compensation tax rates in Pennsylvania range from 5.9632 percent to 9.9836 percent. In addition, the unemployment compensation tax rate is applied to the first $8,000 of employee's wages. An employer's responsibility for paying FUTA and state unemployment taxes is discussed further in Chapter 6.

Example 14: Jackson Industries operates a business in Pennsylvania where they employ several employees, all of whom make more than $10,000 per year. Pennsylvania has assigned Jackson an unemployment compensation tax rate of seven percent for 2015. Jackson filed timely all Pennsylvania unemployment compensation tax returns paying $560 ($8,000 × 7%) in state unemployment tax per employee for the 2015 tax year. In addition, Jackson will be liable for $56 ($7,000 × .8%) per employee in FUTA taxes for 2015. The FUTA rate of .8 percent applies because Jackson paid state unemployment taxes on all the wages on a timely basis.

 Reason for the Rule: Sole proprietors are required to pay unemployment taxes on their employees' wages, but they do not pay unemployment taxes on their business profits. Accordingly, sole proprietors are not eligible to receive unemployment benefits through their businesses.

.07 Federal Income Taxes

The federal government's primary source of revenues comes from income tax, which uses taxable income as its tax base. Simply put, **taxable income** is income that the government taxes minus any allowable deductions. The formula for computing taxable income is shown in Figure 1-1.

Figure 1-1 Taxable Income Formula

Income	$ xx,xxx
Less: Exclusions	(xx,xxx)
Gross Income	$ xx,xxx
Less: Deductions	(xx,xxx)
Taxable Income	$ xx,xxx

The tax laws define **income** broadly and suggest it includes all increases in wealth. Accordingly, a decrease in amounts a taxpayer owes causes wealth to increase; therefore, when a taxpayer's debt is forgiven, it constitutes "income" for purposes of computing taxable income. Along similar lines of reasoning, income would include appreciation in the value of property. However, mere appreciation in value is difficult to tax for several reasons, the most obvious is the difficulty in measuring the amount of appreciation. For most property, the true value can only be ascertained upon its sale to an unrelated party. In addition to the measurement issues, governments recognize that appreciation in value does not necessarily mean that the taxpayer has the resources available from which to pay the tax on the resulting income. Thus, the tax laws omit appreciation in value from income and instead operate under the **realization principle,** whereby income is realized only upon the disposal of property. The realization principle follows the **wherewithal-to-pay concept,** which recognizes that mere appreciation in value does not necessarily mean that the owner has the resources (wherewithal) to pay the tax associated with the appreciation. This wherewithal-to-pay is assured when the property is disposed of and the proceeds can be used to pay the necessary taxes.

In addition to the realization principle, the **capital recovery doctrine** ensures that when taxpayers dispose of property, the amount of proceeds that allows them to recover their investment in the property will not be taxed. Thus, only the excess of the proceeds over their investment is taxed. The capital recovery doctrine applies to all sales of property, including inventory. Therefore, only gross profit, computed as the excess of sales price over cost of goods sold, is included in income.

Despite the fact that the tax laws define income broadly, some income is exempt from taxation. Income that the government does not tax is called an **exclusion**. An example of an exclusion in the calculation of federal taxable income is the interest earned on investments in state and local government bonds (also called "municipal bonds"). Like corporate bonds, municipal bonds pay interest semiannually; however, the interest bondholders receive from municipal bonds is income that the federal government chooses not to tax. After exclusions are subtracted from total income, the amount remaining is known as **gross income**. Thus, gross income is all income that the government has decided to tax. The income tax laws are written such that all items of income are subject to tax unless a tax law exists that specifically states that they are not subject to tax. This is known as an **all-inclusive approach** to defining income. Therefore, in order to properly report the correct amounts of gross income on the federal tax return, it is necessary to study the tax laws to learn about all exclusions the government makes available to taxpayers. Gross income used in the calculation of federal taxable income is discussed in Chapter 4.

In addition to excluding certain types of income from tax, the federal government also allows most business expenditures to be deducted in arriving at taxable income. Ordinary and necessary expenses incurred in the operation of a business are allowed as a **deduction** to offset business income, as are losses on the sale of business and investment property. However, special rules may control the timing or the amount allowed as a deduction. Business deductions allowed in computing federal taxable income are the focus of Chapters 5, 6, and 7.

Once taxable income is computed, tax rates are applied to determine the taxpayer's tax liability. The federal government uses a progressive tax rate structure in which the average tax rate increases as taxable income increases. Corporate and individual income tax rates are discussed in Chapter 4 at ¶ 405. A progressive tax rate structure might look something like this:

Tax base over—	But not over—	Tax rate
$ 0	$ 10,000	1%
10,000	50,000	4%
50,000	100,000	8%
100,000		10%

Example 15: Jamie Rivers has taxable income of $150,000. Using the above tax rate schedule, Jamie computes the tax liability on her taxable income as follows.

$10,000 × 1%	$ 100
($50,000 – $10,000) × 4%	1,600
($100,000 – $50,000) × 8%	4,000
($150,000 – $100,000) × 10%	5,000
	$10,700

From tax liability, taxpayers subtract out tax credits, including prepayments, to arrive at the amount of taxes owed or refund due back from the government. Most **tax credits** are incentive-based items that taxpayers obtain by investing or participating in certain activities. Unlike deductions, which reduce taxable income, tax credits directly reduce tax liability. Accordingly, the tax savings derived from a $1 tax credit equals $1. The tax savings derived from a $1 deduction depends on the taxpayer's marginal tax rate. The **marginal tax rate** is the rate of tax that the taxpayer pays on the last dollar of income, or stated another way, the tax savings that a taxpayer derives by reducing taxable income by $1. If in Example 15 Jamie were to decrease her taxable income from $150,000 to $149,999, her tax liability would decrease by $.10. Therefore, Jamie's last dollar of taxable income is taxed at 10 percent, which is her marginal tax rate. Dollar-for-dollar, tax credits are always preferred to tax deductions. Tax credits are discussed in Chapter 11.

Example 16: Jamie Rivers from the previous example has the option of receiving a $1,000 deduction or a $1,000 credit. If Jamie chooses the deduction, her tax liability will be reduced by $100 ($1,000 × 10%). If she chooses the tax credit, her tax liability will be reduced by $1,000. Thus, all other things being equal, Jamie would prefer the $1,000 tax credit.

Tax credits can be refundable or nonrefundable. A **refundable tax credit** is one for which the credit not only reduces the taxpayer's tax liability but also results in a refund of any excess to the taxpayer when the credit exceeds the tax liability. A **nonrefundable tax credit** can only reduce the taxpayer's tax liability. Most tax credits are nonrefundable credits. A few personal tax credits available to individuals and a couple of business credits are refundable credits.

Example 17: Janice Hartman's tax liability is $1,300 and she reports a $2,000 tax credit on her tax return. If the tax credit is a nonrefundable credit, it will reduce her tax liability to $0. If it is a refundable credit, it will reduce her tax liability to $0 and she will be entitled to receive a $700 ($2,000 – $1,300) refund from the government.

Prepayments are amounts that the taxpayer has paid to the government during the year to cover the current year's tax liability. Employees prepay the government when they have amounts withheld from their paychecks during the year. Taxpayers that generate taxable income from sources other than wages are required to make quarterly estimated payments to the government to cover the corresponding tax liability. If the amount of prepayments the taxpayer makes during the year exceeds the amount left over after subtracting nonrefundable tax credits from tax liability, the excess is refundable. Thus, prepayments are considered a refundable tax credit. The calculation of taxes owed (refund due) is illustrated in Figure 1-2.

Figure 1-2 Calculation of Tax Owed or Refund Due

Tax liability	$ xx,xxx
Less: Nonrefundable tax credits	(xx,xxx)
Remaining tax liability (not less than $0)	$ xx,xxx
Less: Refundable tax credits, including prepayments	(xx,xxx)
Tax owed (refund due)	$ xx,xxx

Federal income tax is imposed on the taxable income of individuals and corporations (referred to as **C corporations**). When a business is operated as a sole proprietorship, the owner is personally responsible for the debts and activities of the business, and the profits from the business are taxed on the sole proprietor's personal income tax return. In contrast, profits from a C corporation are taxed on the corporation's income tax return and then again when distributed to shareholders in the form of a dividend. Although corporate profits may be taxed twice, one advantage of operating a business as a corporation is that the shareholders are not responsible for the liabilities of the business, a concept known as **limited liability**. Shareholders are only at risk for losing the amounts they have invested in the corporation (that is, amounts paid for their shares of stock). The treatment of corporate distributions and the impact of the double taxation of corporate profits are discussed in Chapter 12.

Businesses can also choose to operate as partnerships. A **partnership** is a business entity that must always have at least two owners (partners). Partnerships do not pay taxes, but they must file an annual tax return reporting the business's activities for the year. A partnership is a **flow-through entity**, which gets it name because throughout the year it gathers information about gross income, deductions, and credits generated during the year and at the end of the year it files a tax return and passes this information along to the partners. The partners then report on their own income tax returns their respective shares of income, deductions, and credits. Thus, one advantage of choosing to operate a business as a partnership is that the profits of the business are taxed directly to the owners. However, a disadvantage of operating a business as a partnership is that at least one partner must be personally liable for the debts of the partnership. The taxation of partnerships is discussed in Chapter 13.

An **S corporation** is a special type of business entity that shares features of both the corporate and partnership entities. Like the owners of a C corporation, the owners of an S corporation are shareholders, and as such, they are protected from the liabilities of the S corporation. However, S corporations are similar to partnerships in that they are flow-through entities whose profits are passed through (and taxed one time) to the shareholders. The advantage of operating as an S corporation should be obvious—the owners enjoy limited liability and a single layer of taxation. Like

C corporations, S corporations can have just one shareholder, thereby making this business entity an attractive alternative to businesses with a sole owner. However, restrictions exist as to the number and type of shareholders an S corporation can have, which make it an entity choice only for certain smaller businesses. The taxation of S corporations is discussed in Chapter 14.

All states now allow businesses to operate as a **limited liability company (LLC)** or **limited liability partnership (LLP)**. Although state laws govern the rules of operation for LLCs and LLPs, the federal government allows these business entities to be taxed as partnerships. Accordingly, LLCs and LLPs are required to file an annual income tax return reporting the entity's activities for the year and to pass along to the owners their respective shares of income, deductions, and credits. The advantage of operating a business as an LLC or LLP is that while profits can be taxed a single time to the owners (similar to a partnership), the owners are sheltered from the general liabilities of the business (similar to a corporation). In addition, LLCs can have a single owner, making them attractive choices for businesses with a sole owner. Although some restrictions may apply to LLCs and LLPs, the restrictions are not as severe as those imposed on S corporations. LLCs provide their owners with more protection from liabilities of the business than LLPs; however, neither LLCs nor LLPs are required to have an owner that is personally responsible for the general liabilities of the business. For these reasons, LLCs and LLPs have become popular entity choices in recent years. LLCs and LLPs are discussed in Chapter 13.

Individual income tax. Many tax laws apply equally to all taxpayers; however, a few rules exist that apply solely to individual taxpayers. The tax laws that apply to individual taxpayers as sole proprietorships is one area of focus in Chapter 13. The business activities of a sole proprietorship are reported on the proprietor's individual income tax return, so it is important to understand the basics of the federal individual tax rules. Accordingly, this section summarizes some of the more basic features regarding the calculation of taxable income for individual taxpayers.

When individuals compute taxable income, deductions are separated into three categories: deductions for **adjusted gross income** (AGI), above the line deductions and deductions from AGI. Thus, the taxable income formula for individuals is expanded as shown in Figure 1-3.

Figure 1-3 Taxable Income Formula for Individual Taxpayers

Income	$ xx,xxx
Less: Deductions for AGI	(xx,xxx)
Gross Income	$ xx,xxx
Less: Above the line deductions	(xx,xxx)
Adjusted gross income (AGI)	$ xx,xxx
Less: Deductions from AGI	(xx,xxx)
Taxable Income	$ xx,xxx

The primary distinction between deductions for AGI and deductions *from* AGI is that the latter are primarily nonbusiness deductions. Expenditures that can be deducted as deductions for AGI include business deductions that are used to offset the business income from a sole proprietorship, rental expenses that are used to offset rental income reported by the landlord, and losses on the sale of business and investment property. In contrast, deductions taken from AGI involve expenditures that are personal in nature such as: (1) the *greater* of a standard deduction or the taxpayer's itemized deductions, and (2) the taxpayer's personal and dependency exemptions. Above the line deductions are deducted from gross income to get to AGI. Above the line deductions vary from year to year but for the past few years some of the mainstays are: student loan interest, self-employed retirement contributions, self-employed health insurance deductions, tuition and fees and moving expenses. So this is really a mix of both personal and business deductions.

Itemized deductions are the accumulation of various personal expenditures that the federal government allows individuals to offset against AGI. The most commonly deducted itemized deductions include charitable contributions, state and local income taxes or general sales taxes, home mortgage interest, and real estate taxes taxpayers pay in conjunction with owning a personal residence. Other itemized deductions include unreimbursed medical expenses in excess of 10 percent of the taxpayer's AGI and uninsured casualty and theft losses in excess of 10 percent AGI.

Unlike itemized deductions, which involve actual personal expenditures that taxpayers incurred during the year, the **standard deduction** is an amount that the federal government allows each individual taxpayer to deduct in lieu of deducting itemized deductions. The amount is based on the taxpayer's filing status (for example, single and married filing a joint return are two of five possible filing statuses). For 2015, the standard deduction for single taxpayers is $6,300 for married couples who file a joint return, the standard deduction is $12,600. Additional amounts are allowed if the taxpayer is blind or over age 64. Individuals deduct from AGI the *greater* of their itemized deductions or the standard deduction.

Example 18: Bruce Collins is unmarried. In 2015, Bruce's total itemized deductions are $2,400. Since this amount does not exceed the $6,300 standard deduction for single taxpayers in 2015, Bruce will subtract from AGI the $6,300 standard deduction in computing his 2015 taxable income.

Example 19: Tim and Diane Raines file a joint return. In 2015, the Raines have itemized deductions totaling $14,800. Since this amount exceeds the $12,600 standard deduction provided to married taxpayers in 2015, they will deduct $14,800 from AGI in computing their 2015 taxable income.

The second deduction from AGI is for the taxpayer's **personal and dependency exemptions.** For 2015, each exemption results in a $4,000 deduction in arriving at taxable income. Each taxpayer is entitled to one personal exemption; therefore, a married couple filing a joint tax return would be entitled to claim two personal exemptions. In addition to the personal exemption, individuals are allowed to take an exemption for each person who qualifies as their dependent. The taxpayer's minor children generally qualify as dependents, but others may qualify as well. Although the rules for who qualifies as a dependent are beyond the scope of this discussion, "dependents" are usually persons who either live with or are related to the taxpayer and for whom the taxpayer provides the majority of support during the year.

Corporate income taxes. The tax laws treat a C corporation as a tax-paying entity, separate and apart from its shareholders. As is true for individuals, the corporation's tax base is taxable income. Taxable income equals gross income minus all allowable deductions. A corporation's gross income is its gross profit (net sales minus cost of goods sold) plus other income earned, such as dividends, interest, rents, royalties, and gain from the sale of property other than inventory. From this amount, the corporation subtracts all deductions allowed by the law, such as depreciation, salaries, rent, property taxes, and loss on the sale of property. These deductions are similar to those allowed an individual taxpayer, except that all deductions are presumed to be business-related and a corporation is not entitled to a personal exemption. Taxes on corporate taxable income are determined through the use of a graduated progressive tax rate structure. See ¶ 405.01.

At the end of each fiscal year, all publicly-traded corporations are required to issue audited financial statements prepared in accordance with **generally accepted accounting principles (GAAP).** The federal income tax laws are a compilation of the Internal Revenue Code, Treasury Regulations, IRS rulings, and case law. In many instances the tax laws used in computing federal taxable income and GAAP (used to compute net income) follow the same or similar rules. However, because different governing bodies are responsible for writing these two sets of rules, the calculation of taxable income may be different from the calculation of net income that is taught in financial accounting textbooks. As part of the annual tax filing process, larger C corporations are required to reconcile net income and taxable income, documenting where differences between the two exist. Accordingly, as the tax laws are presented throughout this textbook, any differences between the tax laws and financial accounting rules will be highlighted and discussed. Chapter 2 provides an overview of the various sources of the U.S. federal income tax laws.

 Spotlight: An IRS study of 38,516 corporate tax returns for the year 2005 revealed that the difference between taxable income and GAAP income was $130.9 billion. $129.2 billion of the difference was the result of timing differences and $1.7 billion reflected permanent differences.[5]

.08 State and Local Income Taxes

Most state governments impose an individual income tax, and many "piggyback" on the federal tax systems by modifying federal taxable income to compute their own versions of state taxable income. However, New Hampshire and Tennessee only tax interest and dividend income. Cities that impose an income tax typically use employees' wages as their tax base; however, some, like New York City, use a modified version of federal taxable income. Tax rates for state and local income taxes can be flat or progressive.

 Spotlight: In fiscal 2003, the city of Philadelphia generated over half of its revenues by imposing a "wage tax" on nonresidents' wages earned while working within the city limits as well as on all of the wages of its residents, regardless of where those wages were earned. Because all wages earned within the city limits are subject to the Philadelphia wage tax, visiting professional athletes are subject to the wage tax on the portion of their wages earned while playing their away games against Philadelphia's professional sports teams.

Although many states have a corporate income tax, some choose to levy a franchise tax on businesses. A **franchise tax** is an annual tax on the privilege of doing business in the state. It differs from an income tax in that the tax base is typically some combination of the value of the corporation's capital stock and its annual earnings. For example, Pennsylvania levies a franchise tax on corporations that do business in the state and uses the value of the corporation's allocable capital stock as its tax base. Texas also levies a franchise tax, but it uses the value of the corporation's allocable contributed capital and taxable earned surplus (defined as net income with a few adjustments) in computing its franchise tax. Although S corporations and LLCs are treated as flow-through entities for purposes of federal income tax, many states levy franchise taxes on these business entities.

¶ 105 The Makings of a "Good" Tax

Most everyone would agree that a good tax is one that is both equitable and efficient. An equitable tax system is one that fairly distributes the tax burden. An efficient tax is one that minimizes both the compliance costs to the taxpayer and the administrative costs to the government. Unfortunately, establishing a system of taxation that meets those criteria is more challenging than it may seem. One problem is the difficulty of arriving at a consensus as to what constitutes an equitable sharing of the tax burden. In addition, lawmakers have found that many factors that add to a tax system's fairness often increase its complexity, thereby adding to administrative and compliance costs.

---

[5] Charles Boynton, Portia DeFilippes, and Ellen Legel; "A First Look at 2005 Schedule M-3 Corporate Reporting," *http://* *www.irs.gov/pub/irs-utl/schm-32005firstlookboynton-defilippes-legel11_03_08.pdf.*

.01 Make It Fair

An equitable tax is one that is *perceived* as being fair to all who are affected by the tax. However, perception is a subjective observation, and as such, it is virtually impossible for everyone to come to a consensus as to what constitutes a fair tax. An example earlier in the chapter illustrated this point. It involved a government that needed to raise $12,000 in revenues from its two residents: Tom Johnson and Jane Smith (see ¶ 103). The tax base was determined to be the employees' wages, and the government was in the process of considering three tax rate structures. The distribution of the tax burden under each tax rate structure is summarized below.

	Tax Liability		Tax Base		Average Tax Rate	
	Tom	Jane	Tom	Jane	Tom	Jane
Regressive	$7,580	$4,590	$120,000	$60,000	6.32%	7.65%
Proportional	$8,100	$4,050	$120,000	$60,000	6.75%	6.75%
Progressive	$9,200	$2,800	$120,000	$60,000	7.67%	4.67%

Because Tom's wages are more than Jane's, a tax that requires Jane to pay more taxes than Tom unarguably would be perceived as an unfair tax. Under each tax rate structure, Tom would pay more taxes than Jane, so one might initially conclude that any of these tax rate structures was an equitable way to distribute the $12,000 tax burden. However, under the regressive tax rate structure, Tom would pay considerably more taxes than Jane ($7,580 versus $4,590), but the amount represents a *smaller portion* of his wages (6.32% versus Jane's 7.65%). Thus, few would conclude that a regressive tax was an equitable way to distribute the tax burden.

Under a proportional tax, Tom and Jane would pay the same 6.75-percent rate of tax; under a progressive tax, Tom would pay a greater percentage of his gross wages in tax (7.67 percent versus 4.67 percent). Those who support the position that a proportional tax is the fairest tax might believe that Tom, who earns twice as much as Jane, should pay twice the amount of taxes Jane pays, and accordingly, he would be contributing his fair share toward the overall tax burden. On the other hand, those who feel that a progressive tax structure is more equitable may feel that as two single individuals, Tom and Jane have the same basic needs for food, shelter, clothing, etc. After they each finish paying for these basic needs, Tom should have more left over than Jane because his wages are double Jane's wages. Hence, Tom's ability to contribute to the tax system is greater than Jane's and therefore he should pay a greater portion of his wages in taxes. Regardless of which tax rate structure one believes to be more equitable, this example demonstrates that not everyone will perceive fairness the same way. Accordingly, governments attempting to enact a "fair" tax must recognize this fact.

.02 Make It Efficient

Inarguably, a good tax is one that minimizes compliance costs to the taxpayer and administrative costs to the government. The best way to accomplish this is to create a tax system in which the tax base is easy to identify and compute. A tax system with which taxpayers can comply with little personal effort would be preferred to one that requires extensive personal effort or requires the taxpayer to hire and pay for professional assistance. From an administrative standpoint, running a tax collection agency costs money. Inevitably, additional costs are incurred with a more complicated tax system. As we saw in the example involving Tom and Jane, the calculation of a flat tax is by far the easiest, but many believe that the more complicated progressive rate structure results in a more equitable distribution of the tax burden.

Too often, equity and efficiency are rivals when it comes to creating a tax system. Another example involves the role of the standard deduction and personal exemptions in the federal income tax system. The purpose behind these two deductions is to prevent lower-income taxpayers from having any taxable income. However, whenever exclusions, deductions, or credits are introduced into the tax system, the complexity of the system increases. Thus, any attempt to fairly allocate the tax burden usually sacrifices efficiency.

 Spotlight: In 2005, taxpayers paid approximately $265.1 billion in their efforts to comply with the federal income tax system. This was just under $.22 for each $1 of federal revenue collected. It is estimated that taxpayers will spend over 6 billion hours complying with the federal income tax laws when filing their tax returns. This number of hours is equivalent to a workforce of 2,884,000 individuals working 40 hours per week for one year, which is staggering considering that number of people is larger than the populations of Dallas, Detroit, and Washington, D.C. combined. The number is also larger than the number of workers in the automotive, airline, computer manufacturing, and steel industries combined.[6]

¶ 106 Factors Taken Into Consideration When Creating a Tax

The art of taxation consists in so plucking the goose as to get the most feathers with the least hissing. –Jean Baptiste Colbert, French Economist and Minister of Finance under King Louis XIV of France (1619–1683)

Although raising revenues is the primary reason governments impose taxes, governments consider several factors when deciding whom and what to tax. The government must first decide whether it is possible to control usage of the goods or services. If so, then charging user fees would be feasible. However, when offering goods or services results in externalities, assessing user fees to cover the entire cost may not be appropriate. Public transportation is an example of a government-provided service for which usage can easily be controlled. As previously mentioned, when individuals use public transportation, roadways are less congested and air quality improves. Consequently, governments that provide public transportation generally charge a reduced user fee and find other means to finance the remainder of the costs.

To the extent that raising revenues through user fees is not feasible or appropriate, other factors are considered, including how to equitably spread the tax burden among taxpayers. Other issues may be contemplated as well. For example, many tax laws are enacted with the intention of eliciting certain types of behavior; others are enacted to redistribute wealth or to minimize administrative and compliance costs. Some tax laws are enacted purely for political reasons. Because it is often helpful to understand why a particular law was enacted, the various factors governments use in deciding how to allocate the tax burden are discussed below. As specific tax laws are presented throughout this textbook, these factors will be discussed in a boxed area called "Reason for the Rule."

.01 Equity Concerns

While no one likes paying taxes, taxpayers who believe that taxes are assessed and collected fairly to meet our nation's needs are more likely to comply with the tax laws. The Internal Revenue Service (IRS) estimates that a one-tenth of one percentage point (0.1 percent) improvement in compliance would increase federal revenues by more than $1 billion annually.[7] In response, governments often strive to collect taxes from those who have the greatest ability to pay taxes. Common measures of a taxpayer's ability to pay are income or wealth. Among the three tax rate structures, the progressive tax rate structure best illustrates the **ability-to-pay concept**. With progressive tax rates, the taxpayer's average tax rate increases as the tax base increases. Accord-

---

[6] J. Scott Moody, Wendy P. Warcholik, and Scott A. Hodge, "The Rising Costs of Complying with the Federal Income Tax," *Tax Foundation Special Report*, No. 138 (December 2005).

[7] "IRS Moves to Ensure Fairness of Tax System: Research Program Works to Increase Compliance Program Effectiveness, Reduce Burdens on Taxpayers," IRS News Release, IR-2002-05, January 16, 2002.

ingly, those with higher tax bases (presumably those in a better position to pay taxes) pay a greater percentage of their tax bases toward the overall tax burden.

Earlier in the chapter, the concept of marginal tax rate was introduced as a way of measuring the tax savings derived from deductions. Tax deductions become more valuable as the taxpayer's marginal tax rate increases. A $1,000 deduction to a taxpayer in the 15-percent tax bracket results in $150 of tax savings ($1,000 × 15%), whereas that same $1,000 deduction is worth $310 to a taxpayer in the 31-percent tax bracket ($1,000 × 31%). Since the tax rates increase as the tax base increases, deductions favor higher-income taxpayers under a progressive tax structure. Accordingly, governments that employ a progressive rate structure often enact tax laws that allow for tax credits rather than tax deductions, thereby providing the same tax savings to higher- and lower-income taxpayers.

When a proportional tax rate is used, other methods of addressing the ability to pay issue must be examined. Many state and local governments rely heavily on property taxes as a source of revenues. Since real estate taxes are *ad valorem,* real estate taxes increase as real estate values rise. Elderly persons tend to live on fixed incomes, and accordingly, often have more difficulty keeping up with increasing property taxes. Many state and local governments that impose taxes on real estate provide some mechanism in their tax systems that allows elderly homeowners to pay reduced real estate taxes.

For example, Nevada imposes an annual real estate tax on 35 percent of the FMV of real property, but it allows homeowners over age 61 who earn no more than $27,863 to receive tax rebates the amount of which may not exceed the amount of the accrued property tax paid by homeowner or $500, whichever is less. In Kentucky, homeowners over age 64 can exempt the first $31,400 of the assessed value of their homes from the property tax base. Thus, a 70-year-old Kentucky homeowner with a home valued at $75,000 would only be subject to real estate taxes on an assessed value of $43,600 ($75,000 – $31,400), or 58 percent of its full market value ($43,600/$75,000). Compare this to a 70-year-old homeowner with a $200,000 home that would be subject to real estate taxes on an assessed value of $168,600 ($200,000 – $31,400), or 84 percent of its full market value ($168,600/$200,000). Kentucky's $31,400 exemption provides the greatest benefit to elderly residents with more modestly valued homes. These residents are presumably those less able to afford higher-priced homes, and they thus have less ability to pay taxes. It should be noted that when states enact special rules for certain taxpayers, the system can become more difficult to comprehend and administer, and consequently, efficiency may decrease.

Sales tax is also a proportional tax, and many state and local governments address the issue of ability to pay by exempting certain goods from sales tax or by imposing reduced tax rates on certain goods. The elderly often live on fixed incomes, but they are more likely to purchase prescription drugs. Hence, most every state and local government that imposes a sales tax exempts prescription drugs from the tax base. In addition, some states either exempt food and clothing or impose reduced tax rates on these items because they are considered necessities. For example, Pennsylvania imposes a six-percent sales tax on most goods, but it exempts food, clothing, textbooks, heating fuel, and prescription and nonprescription medications from its sales tax base. In Vermont, where the state sales tax is also six percent, both prescription and nonprescription drugs are exempt from tax, but only clothing and shoes costing less than $110 are exempt from sales tax. These examples illustrate how various state governments have considered the issue of equity when enacting their tax laws. However, when they impose different rates on different goods, they introduce complexity and compromise efficiency.

.02 Social and Economic Considerations

If you want more of something, subsidize it; if you want less, tax it. –Unknown

In addition to enacting tax laws aimed at achieving an equitable distribution of the tax burden, governments frequently use taxes in an attempt to alter taxpayer behavior. This is typically done by providing tax incentives to taxpayers who make certain choices that they otherwise might not make.

Taxes used as a means to encourage certain activities. The federal government frequently enacts tax laws to elicit certain types of behavior. For example, some tax laws offer tax benefits to businesses that provide housing for low-income persons and families. By offering these tax incentives, the government hopes businesses will find low-income housing a worthwhile investment, thereby alleviating the government's need to construct and maintain such housing. To ensure that these businesses continue to offer low-income housing on a sustained basis, the low-income housing credit is taken over a 10-year period, and it is taken back if at any time during the first 15 years the percentage of low-income tenants falls below a specified level.

In 1996, the federal government enacted tax legislation allowing tax credits to businesses that employ certain groups of economically disadvantaged individuals, including welfare recipients, qualified ex-felons, and veterans. Normally employers are allowed a tax deduction for wages paid to their workers. The tax savings from this deduction depend on the employer's marginal tax rate. The work opportunity credit now allows employers to take a tax credit for a portion of the wages paid to qualified workers during their two years of employment (in the case of a qualified welfare recipient) or during their first year of employment (in the case of all other qualified workers). By offering a tax credit rather than a tax deduction for a portion of these employees' wages, businesses can generate greater tax savings by hiring specific workers who might otherwise have difficulty finding employment. This tax credit was enacted to encourage businesses to hire and retain workers from certain targeted groups. By allowing the credit to be taken over two years (in the case of a qualified welfare recipient) and by increasing the credit in the employee's second year, the tax law encourages businesses not only to hire, but also to retain, welfare recipients.

Example 20: Jacobs Enterprises is in the process of hiring a new worker. The worker will earn $16,000 during his first two years of employment. Jacobs's marginal tax rate is 25 percent. If Jacobs hires a qualified welfare recipient, it can take a work opportunity credit equal to 40 percent of the first $10,000 of the employee's first year wages and 50 percent of the first $10,000 of his second year wages. Any wages not taken as a credit would be deductible from gross income. If a qualified welfare recipient is hired at a salary of $16,000 per year, over the first two years of the worker's employment, Jacobs will be allowed to take a tax credit equal to $9,000 ($10,000 × 40% plus $10,000 × 50%). Jacobs will also be able to deduct the remaining $23,000 ($16,000 for two years minus $9,000) as a wage expense. The tax savings from this deduction equals $5,750 ($23,000 × 25%), and Jacobs's total taxes would be reduced by $14,750 ($9,000 + $5,750) during the worker's first two years of employment. Compare this to the total tax savings Jacobs would realize if the company hired a worker that was not from one of the targeted groups. In that case, Jacobs Enterprises could only deduct $8,000 ($16,000 deduction for wage expense × 2 years × 25%).

Another example of the federal government using income tax laws to encourage certain types of decisions involves hybrid automobiles. These automobiles generally cost a few thousand dollars more than their nonhybrid counterparts. For example, the Ford Escape Hybrid costs approximately $3,500 more than the Ford Escape XLT. Since hybrid cars are powered by a combination of gas and battery, they are more fuel efficient and emit less pollution than standard automobiles. Hybrid automobiles have been around since 1999; however, the additional costs associated with the purchase of a hybrid automobile typically outweigh the savings that would be realized from increased fuel efficiency. As a result, relatively few hybrid automobiles have been sold.

From 2002–2005, the federal government allowed taxpayers a $2,000 deduction from gross income in the year they purchased a hybrid automobile to help offset the higher costs associated with acquiring hybrid vehicles. The intent behind enacting this tax law was to encourage Americans to buy hybrid cars, thereby protecting the environment and decreasing dependence on oil from the

Middle East. However, because the tax incentive was offered as a deduction, the actual tax savings ranged anywhere from $200 for taxpayers in the 10-percent tax bracket to almost $800 for those in the highest tax bracket. Although rising gasoline prices during 2005 increased demand for hybrid automobiles, they continue to comprise a small portion of new cars sold each year. In 2005, fewer than 200,000 new hybrid vehicles were sold in the United States, representing 1.2 percent of the total number of vehicles sold that year.[8]

For 2009, the federal government offered tax credits ranging anywhere from $400 to $3,400 to taxpayers that purchased hybrid automobiles. The exact amount depended upon a combination of the vehicle's fuel economy and its total expected lifetime fuel savings. By increasing the tax incentives in two ways from how it was structured prior to 2006—changing a deduction to a credit and increasing the amount now available to all taxpayers—the federal government hoped to encourage consumers to consider purchasing hybrid automobiles over standard models, with the intended results of decreasing demand for gasoline and improving air quality.

 Spotlight: The Internal Revenue Code also requires that the qualified hybrid motor vehicle credit begin to phase out after a manufacturer sells a specific quantity of qualifying vehicles. Toyota Motor Sales, U.S.A., Inc., manufacturer of Toyota and Lexus automobiles reached the 60,000 unit mark to initiate the phase out of the credit for their hybrid vehicles in the second quarter of 2006. Thus, Toyota and Lexus hybrids placed into service on or after October 1, 2006, will only qualify for 50 percent of the certified credit amount; hybrids placed in service on or after April 1, 2007, will only qualify for 25 percent of the certified credit amount; and hybrids placed in service on or after October 1, 2007, will be ineligible to claim any credit amount. The behavior that the government sought to encourage, utilizing hybrid automobiles, met the government's expectation and the limit placed upon the credit came into play. Currently, no domestic automobile manufacturer of certified hybrid motor vehicles has entered the phase out period.

 Spotlight: In 2009, Congress modified the credit for qualified plug-in electric drive vehicles purchased after December 31, 2009. The vehicles must be newly purchased, have four or more wheels, have a gross vehicle weight rating of less than 14,000 pounds, and draw propulsion using a battery with at least four kilowatt hours that can be recharged from an external source of electricity. The credit is $2,500 to $7,500, depending on the battery capacity and will be reduced after at least 200,000 vehicles are sold. Another tax credit was created for certain low-speed electric vehicles (including those with two and three wheels). The vehicle must be either a low speed vehicle propelled by an electric motor that draws electricity from a battery with a capacity of 4 kilowatt hours or more or be a two- or three-wheeled vehicle propelled by an electric motor that draws electricity from a battery with the capacity of 2.5 kilowatt hours. A taxpayer may not claim this credit if the plug-in electric drive vehicle credit is allowable. This law also created a tax credit for plug-in electric drive conversion kits. The maximum amount of the credit is $4,000. A taxpayer may claim this credit even if the taxpayer claimed a hybrid vehicle credit for the same vehicle in an earlier year.

Taxes used as a means to encourage growth in certain industries. The cost of business property whose usefulness extends beyond the current year must be deducted over a number of years. Examples include machinery, equipment, and buildings. The tax laws involved in the calculation of this deduction, known as "depreciation," have been used to stimulate capital invest-ment and economic growth. Prior to 1981, the number of years over which the cost of an asset was

---

[8] "Sales Continue to Speed Up," *News & Features*, Hybrid-cars.com (December 28, 2005).

deducted corresponded closely with the estimated useful life of the asset, which is similar to how depreciation is calculated in financial accounting. In 1981, Congress enacted the Accelerated Cost Recovery System (ACRS), for recovering capital costs using accelerated methods over predetermined recovery periods that were much shorter than the properties' useful lives. Under ACRS, automobiles were depreciated over three tax years; buildings were depreciated over 18 years. By allowing these assets to be written off over shorter periods, the government intended the tax savings from the depreciation deduction (equal to the amount of the deduction times the taxpayer's marginal tax rate) to be realized earlier, thereby accelerating cash flows into the earlier years. One of the principal reasons for enacting ACRS was to provide faster tax savings to businesses in an attempt to stimulate capital formation and the growth of the economy.[9] In 1986, Congress enacted the Modified Accelerated Cost Recovery System (MACRS), which extended the depreciation periods for most depreciable assets, thereby slowing down the pace at which depreciation is deducted, but still allowing much shorter cost recovery periods than the actual useful lives of the assets. MACRS continues to be the depreciation system in effect today. The depreciation rules are discussed in Chapter 7.

The federal government also used the tax system to encourage businesses to acquire new property in the aftermath of the events of September 11, 2001. The provision allowed businesses to deduct "bonus" first-year depreciation on all purchases of new tangible personal property placed in service between September 11, 2001, and December 31, 2005. The remainder of the cost was depreciated using MACRS. By allowing larger tax deductions in the first year, businesses that purchased new machinery, equipment, and other tangible personal property were able to generate much greater tax savings (and greater cash back from their investments) in the first year than they would have without this provision.

Example 21: Kendell, Inc. purchased new machinery in 2005 for $800,000. Kendell is in the 35-percent tax bracket. By taking the bonus depreciation, Kendell was allowed to deduct 50 percent, or $400,000, of the cost of the machine in 2005 and to deduct the remaining $400,000 over the next eight years, starting in 2005. Because of the bonus depreciation provision, Kendell's 2005 taxes were reduced by $140,000 ($400,000 × 35%) plus the tax savings from the portion of the remaining $400,000 that was deducted in 2005 under MACRS. Without this provision, Kendell would have been required to deduct the $800,000 over the next eight years. Although the entire $800,000 would be deducted over an eight-year period in both scenarios, by allowing bonus depreciation in the first year, Kendall accelerated the timing of the deduction, thereby increasing cash flows in 2005. The cash savings could then be used to pay expenses, pay down debt, etc. Alternatively, the additional cash savings could be invested and could earn investment income for the company beginning in 2005.

In enacting the bonus depreciation rules, the federal government hoped that by providing businesses with the opportunity to accelerate the timing of the cash flows, demand for new tangible personal property would increase. In turn, job growth would ensue, as companies that manufacture these assets would need to increase their workforces to meet the increased demand.

Congress continues to view bonus depreciation as an important tool for stimulating the economy. The *American Recovery and Reinvestment Act of 2009*, signed into law in February 2009, extends bonus depreciation through 2010.

 Spotlight: The Creating Small Business Jobs Act of 2010 (P.L. 111-240) extended the 50-percent bonus depreciation for one year to apply to qualifying property acquired by a taxpayer after December 31, 2007, and placed in service before January 1, 2011. Further,

---

[9] Staff of the Joint Committee on Taxation, 97th Cong., General Explanation of the Economic Recovery Tax Act of 1981, at 75–76 (Comm. Print 1981).

the Section 179 annual dollar limit is increased to $500,000 for tax years beginning in 2010 and 2011 while the investment limit is increased to $2 million for tax years beginning in 2010 and 2011. The ability to revoke an expensing election without the IRS's consent has also been extended to tax years beginning in 2011. Similarly, the allowance of expensing for off-the-shelf computer software is extended for software placed in service in tax years beginning in 2011.

 Spotlight: The 50-percent bonus depreciation allowance is further extended for two additional years to apply to qualifying property placed in service before January 1, 2013 (or before January 1, 2014, in the case of property with a longer production period and certain noncommercial aircraft) by the Tax Relief, Unemployment Insurance Reauthorization, and Job Creation Act of 2010. Further, the bonus depreciation rate is increased from 50 percent to 100 percent in the case of qualifying property acquired after September 8, 2010, and before January 1, 2012, and placed in service before January 1, 2012 (or before January 1, 2013, in the cases of property with a longer production period and certain noncommercial aircraft).

Taxes used as a means to encourage socially desirable behavior. Shortly after Hurricane Katrina, the federal government passed tax legislation that contained many provisions aimed at encouraging and rewarding certain behavior. For example, businesses that became inoperable due to the hurricane but continued to pay wages to their employees were allowed to take a tax credit equal to 40 percent of up to $6,000 of each employee's wages paid through the end of 2005. By offering this tax incentive, the government hoped businesses would continue to pay their employees while they looked for temporary employment. This action would then postpone or possibly avoid the need for those workers to file for unemployment benefits, thereby reducing state and federal governments' responsibilities to pay such benefits.

Another provision in this legislation allowed taxpayers an additional $500 exemption against taxable income for each qualified displaced Katrina person for whom they provided rent-free housing for a period lasting at least 60 consecutive days. This provision was intended to encourage and reward taxpayers who provided temporary housing to persons displaced by the hurricane.

Another example of tax laws enacted to encourage socially desirable behavior involves the deduction allowed in arriving at taxable income for contributions made to qualified charities. In addition to encouraging and rewarding this behavior, the government attempts to enhance contributions to religious, charitable, educational, scientific, and literary organizations (among others) through its definition of what constitutes a qualified charity. These activities are deemed important to society, but they usually cannot be supported in the marketplace without at least some government assistance. Thus, to the extent that the tax laws encourage individuals and businesses to provide support for these activities, they help alleviate the government's responsibility to provide funding for the activities.

Example 22: Norton Industries is in the 35-percent tax bracket. Norton donates $1,000,000 to a qualified charity. This donation is deducted in arriving at Norton's taxable income and reduces its tax liability by $350,000 ($1,000,000 × 35%). Thus, of the $1 million donation, $650,000 ($1,000,000 – $350,000) came from Norton, and $350,000 came from the federal government. Even though the federal government is subsidizing $350,000 of the contribution, the charitable organization receives a $1,000,000 donation that the federal government might otherwise have been required to fund.

Taxes used as a means to discourage certain behavior. In addition to enacting tax laws that attempt to encourage certain types of decision-making behavior, the government may also enact tax laws that discourage certain types of behavior. For example, excise taxes on tobacco and alcohol are often referred to as "sin taxes," because of the negative connotation associated with the products being purchased. Governments use sin taxes to limit consumption of these goods. Although gasoline is not known as a sin tax, by increasing gasoline excise taxes (and therefore increasing the retail price of gasoline), the government encourages motorists to conserve fuel by carpooling, using public transportation, or purchasing more fuel-efficient vehicles.

In 1978, the federal government enacted a gas guzzler excise tax. This tax penalizes companies that manufacture passenger automobiles whose fuel economy is below 22.5 miles per gallon. The tax is imposed on manufacturers and importers of automobiles, but presumably some (if not all) of the tax is passed along to consumers through higher retail prices. Thus, the intent behind the gas guzzler tax is to discourage automakers from manufacturing and consumers from buying the less fuel-efficient automobiles.

 Spotlight: Congress created a $1 billion cash-for-clunkers program as part of the Consumer Assistance to Recycle and Save Act of 2009 (CARS Act) to encourage taxpayers to trade in old vehicles for new, higher fuel-efficient models. The widely popular program began running out of funds less than a week after it began, prompting the White House and Congress to seek additional funding; thus an additional $2 billion was appropriated to keep the program running. Program vouchers, worth $3,500 or $4,500, are given to dealers when consumers trade in old vehicles for ones with higher fuel efficiency.

San Francisco city officials considered a proposal that would charge grocery shoppers $.17 for every paper or plastic bag they took home. The $.17 user fee was determined based on the city's estimate of the costs it incurs to clean up and dispose of the thousands of plastic bags left on city streets during the year. Thus, San Francisco planned to pay for the entire cost of providing grocery bags by charging user fees. Those who were in favor of the bag tax cited environmental concerns, in particular, the number of trees cut down each year in the manufacture of grocery bags and the growing amount of plastic in the ocean that is choking marine life.[10] In commenting on the proposal, the San Francisco Commission vice-president said, "We're not trying to just charge a user fee; we're trying to make a change in behavior."[11] It appears that the Commission's plan has some merit, as in 2002 Ireland passed a $.22 per bag tax on plastic bags and found that within weeks, plastic bag use dropped 94 percent.[12]

As mentioned earlier in the chapter, the federal income tax system allows a deduction against business income of all ordinary and necessary expenses incurred in the regular course of a business. Accordingly, professional truck drivers may argue that speeding fines are an ordinary and necessary business expense in the trucking industry. The government, not wanting to reward this and similar types of behavior, specifically enacted tax laws that prohibit the deduction of expenses that are deemed to be in violation of public policy. Similar laws have been enacted to disallow the deduction of bribes and kickbacks a business may make, even if they are incurred in the ordinary course of business.

 Spotlight: Every deduction the government allows to reduce taxable income reduces the taxpayer's tax liability by the amount of the deduction times the taxpayer's marginal tax rate. Therefore, by allowing a particular deduction, the government is subsidizing the expenditure. This, in turn, could be construed as the government endorsing any behavior that results in a tax deduction. For this reason, governments may enact tax laws that specifically disallow certain types of deductions.

---

[10] Traci Watson, "S.F. Considers 17-Cent Tax on Grocery Bags," *USA Today*, November 22, 2005.

[11] Wyatt Buchanan, "17-Cent Fee on Bags Okd by Environment Panel," *San Francisco Chronicle*, January 26, 2005.

[12] "With Tax, Plastic Bags Disappear in Ireland," *The New York Times*, Saturday, February 2, 2008.

.03 Redistribution of Wealth

The art of government consists of taking as much money as possible from one class of citizens to give to the other. –Voltaire

Some tax laws are enacted for the sole purpose of redistributing wealth from one group of taxpayers to another. The best example of this is wealth transfer taxes. Most property an individual owns at the time of his or her death has been previously taxed through any one of a number of means. All income earned was subject to income tax; most property was subject to sales tax at the time it was purchased. Less than two percent of the people who died in 2002 had estates large enough to pay any estate tax. Even though the estate tax comprises very little of the federal government's total revenues collected, and despite the fact that the tax laws surrounding the estate tax are extremely complicated, it nonetheless continues to exist and to serve as a means of redistributing wealth.

Other examples of the government's use of taxes to redistribute wealth involve the enactment of refundable personal tax credits. The tax laws allow a $1,000 tax credit for each child under the age of 17 claimed as a dependent on the taxpayer's income tax return. Because this credit is intended to help taxpayers with modest levels of income, the full credit is only available for taxpayers with an AGI below certain levels ($75,000 for unmarried taxpayers; $110,000 for married couples filing a joint return). However, when the amount of the child tax credit exceeds the taxpayer's tax liability, the excess may result in a refund. In such a case, not only does the taxpayer pay zero income taxes during the year, but he or she may also be entitled to a tax refund from the government. The funding for these refunds comes from other taxpayers, and the result is a redistribution of wealth.

Example 23: Nancy and David Clark are married and have two children, ages seven and nine. In 2015, the Clarks' taxable income is $16,500. Although taxes will be calculated on the $16,500 of taxable income, the Clarks will be allowed to reduce their taxes by $2,000 ($1,000 child tax credit for each child). If the amount of the credit exceeds the Clarks' tax liability, the excess may result in a refund.

Another tax credit the government makes available to lower-income taxpayers is the earned income credit (EIC). The EIC is a refundable credit that reduces the tax liabilities of low-income taxpayers and provides a tax refund for any excess credit. However, in order to generate any EIC, the taxpayer must report earned income on the tax return. Because only taxpayers with earned income qualify for this credit, not only is this tax provision used as a means of redistributing wealth, but it also encourages lower-income taxpayers to work so they can receive a refund from the federal government when they file their income tax returns.

Example 24: Samantha and Daniel Wright claim their two children as dependents. Because of the available deductions from AGI, the Wrights have zero taxable income and no income tax liability. However, because Samantha and Daniel both work and report earned income in 2015, they are entitled to a maximum of $5,548 EIC, depending on their income. Although the Wrights have no income tax liability, they will receive a maximum of $5,548 refund from the federal government when they file their tax return.

.04 Administrative Convenience

A tax law enacted to reduce either administrative or compliance costs is enacted for **administrative convenience**. As previously discussed in this chapter, the federal government does not require persons to file a gift tax return in 2015, provided that gifts to persons other than one's spouse do not exceed $14,000 per person. Subjecting every gift to a gift tax would be a difficult administrative task, and compliance would probably be very low. Allowing certain *de minimis* amounts of transfers between persons to occur each year without any tax or reporting consequences is one example of tax laws enacted for administrative convenience.

Another example of administrative convenience is the option given to taxpayers to deduct from taxable income the *greater of* the standard deduction or itemized deductions. Taxpayers who itemize report the total amounts spent for each type of expenditure; they are required to retain the receipts documenting their deductions for at least three years. The presence of the standard deduction allows taxpayers with limited amounts of itemized deductions to avoid having to keep track of these smaller expenditures, thereby minimizing their compliance costs as well as the government's administrative costs.

.05 Political Considerations

If you have been voting for politicians who promise to give you goodies at someone else's expense, then you have no right to complain when they take your money and give it to someone else, including themselves. –Thomas Sowell, syndicated columnist

Politicians strive to be re-elected; lobbyists strive to please their constituents. As a result, some tax laws are enacted solely because they are popular or for other political reasons. For example, tax laws have been enacted to provide tax breaks to specific industries. It was previously mentioned in this chapter that the excise taxes on a pack of cigarettes vary from state to state, ranging anywhere from $.07 a pack in South Carolina to $2.46 a pack in Rhode Island. In addition to seeking a source of revenues, governments impose excise taxes on tobacco products to discourage individuals from purchasing those products. Because the economy in tobacco-producing states depends heavily on the demand for tobacco products, imposing higher excise taxes on such products could hurt the state's economy. North Carolina, Kentucky, Tennessee, South Carolina, and Virginia are five of the largest tobacco-producing states in the United States. Therefore, it is not surprising that the excise taxes on a pack of cigarettes in those five states are among the seven lowest in the nation.

The elderly comprise a large percentage of voters, and consequently, it is not unusual to find tax breaks throughout the various tax systems to accommodate elderly taxpayers. Most local governments that impose real estate taxes allow a reduced tax base to elderly homeowners. The federal government allows taxpayers over age 64 an additional standard deduction when computing their taxable income, and state and local governments exempt prescription drugs from their tax bases for sales tax purposes. However, anytime a special exemption, deduction, or credit is incorporated into the tax laws, complexity is introduced into the tax system. Consequently, most special provisions that have been added to the tax laws for political reasons have contributed to their complexity and have reduced the efficiency of the U.S. tax system.

Sometimes tax laws are passed because of their popularity. Hotel occupancy taxes and rental car "surcharges" have become popular taxes for local governments. They provide local governments with a source of revenue, and the tax is usually levied on persons who do not live (and do not have a vote) in the community. Severance taxes are also a very popular means of increasing state revenues because the costs incurred by businesses that extract natural resources from the state are passed along to consumers in other states.

¶ 107 The Importance of Studying Federal Income Tax Laws

Taxes are transaction costs that must be considered when making business decisions. Since most sources of revenue a business generates will be subject to tax, only a portion of each dollar earned is retained by the business. Similarly, any expenditure a business makes that qualifies as a deduction results in less taxes owed. The taxpayer's marginal tax rate is used in determining the amount of the transaction costs when revenues and expenditures are involved. When determining a taxpayer's marginal tax rate, it is important to consider taxes imposed by all levels of government, not just the federal government.

Example 25: Speedy Services, Inc. operates in a state that imposes a flat 7.3-percent tax on taxable income. Speedy is in the 35-percent tax bracket for federal income tax purposes. Thus, when determining the tax savings from an additional dollar of deduction or the cost for an additional dollar of revenue, Speedy's marginal tax rate is 39.75 percent $(35\% + (7.3\% \times (100\% - 35\%)))$.

Tax credits also often arise from expenditures; however, $1 of tax credit results in $1 of tax savings. Accordingly, the tax consequences of receiving income or making expenditures must be considered in order to make the best possible decisions.

Example 26: In Example 20, Jacobs Enterprises (whose marginal tax rate was 25 percent) had the opportunity to save $14,750 in taxes ($9,000 tax credit plus $5,750 from deducting $23,000 as wage expense) over a two-year period by hiring a qualified welfare recipient. If Jacobs hires someone who is not a qualified welfare recipient, it will deduct the $32,000 of wages paid during the first two years, but the corresponding tax savings would be only $8,000 ($32,000 × 25%). Accordingly, the cash savings of hiring a person who is a qualified welfare recipient over one who is not would be $6,750 ($14,750 – $8,000) over a two-year period.

Some tax laws do not alter the amount of the deduction, but instead accelerate the timing of the deduction. Although in the end, the same amount will be deducted, deductions that can be taken in earlier years (as opposed to later years) result in less taxes paid today. Those accelerated tax savings constitute cash flows that can be invested today to generate additional cash flows in future years. Alternatively, the accelerated cash flows can be used to pay the company's current expenditures, thereby eliminating the need to find other sources from which to pay for those costs. Through tax planning, taxpayers can arrange their affairs to minimize taxes. However, proper tax planning involves a thorough understanding of the tax laws. U.S. Supreme Court Justice Learned Hand once said,

> Over and over again courts have said that there is nothing sinister in arranging one's affairs so as to make taxes as low as possible. Everybody does so, rich or poor, and do right, for nobody has any public duty to pay more taxes than the law demands. Taxes are enforced exaction, not voluntary contributions.

Tax avoidance is the art of using existing tax laws to pay the least amount of tax legally possible. **Tax evasion**, on the other hand, involves paying less than the full amount of taxes rightly owed to the government, whether through intentional disregard of the tax laws, through willful neglect, or for any other reason. Practicing tax avoidance is not illegal. It fact, it should be every taxpayer's goal when it comes to paying taxes.

Whereas tax planning was once an exclusive game for the rich, it is now the pursuit of everybody except the foolish. –Charles Adams

As discussed in this chapter, the federal income tax laws allow businesses to deduct a wide array of expenditures related to the generation of business revenues. They also allow many types of income to be exempt from taxation and provide opportunities to generate tax credits that reduce taxes. Understanding which types of income the government taxes and which types of expenditures can be used to reduce taxable income (or perhaps tax liability) is essential in making the best business decisions. This book provides the foundation for understanding how the federal government taxes income its residents and businesses earn. As a Morgan Stanley advertisement once read, "You must pay taxes. But there's no law that says you gotta leave a tip."

 Planning Pointer: Businesses need to consider all types of taxes when making decisions. This textbook focuses on the tax laws that are pertinent to the federal income tax system, which is one of the primary taxing bodies that businesses encounter.

¶ 107

¶ 108 Summary

Although raising revenues remains the primary reason behind our tax laws, social, economic, and political considerations play important roles in deciding how to allocate the tax burden. All governments, from the federal government to townships to local school districts, generate revenues by imposing taxes, and they have a variety of tax bases and tax rate structures from which to choose. Because taxes represent a transfer from the private sector to the government, minimizing taxes owed to the government results in increased private wealth. A solid understanding of how tax laws operate is crucial to achieving this goal.

The primary focus of this book is on the federal income tax laws that pertain to businesses. Regardless of the type of entity used to operate the business—sole proprietorship, partnership, S corporation, LLP, LLC, or C corporation—the rules in this textbook will allow the reader to gain a better understanding of how the federal income tax laws affect business decisions. This chapter introduced the federal taxable income formula and the concepts of income, deduction, and tax credit. These topics are covered more thoroughly in upcoming chapters. The final chapters of the book take a closer look at each type of entity choice and discuss the particular tax laws that pertain specifically to that type of entity.

GLOSSARY OF TERMS INTRODUCED IN THE CHAPTER

Ability-to-pay concept. Taxes are imposed on taxpayers that are in the best position to pay the taxes by having them pay a greater share of their tax bases toward the tax burden.

Administrative convenience. When a tax law is enacted because it reduces administrative costs or taxpayers' compliance costs.

Ad valorem **tax.** A tax that uses the value of property as the tax base.

Adjusted gross income (AGI). An intermediate step between gross income and taxable income that individuals calculate. Only deductions for AGI are subtracted from gross income in computing AGI.

All-inclusive approach. The method used to define income. Under this approach, all income is subject to income tax unless a provision in the tax laws allows it not to be taxed.

Average tax rate. The total tax liability divided by the tax base. Used in determining the portion of the tax base that is paid in taxes.

C corporation. An incorporated business entity other than an S corporation that is treated as a separate tax entity from its shareholders. The income of a C corporation is subject to two layers of taxation.

Capital recovery doctrine. When taxpayers dispose of property, in determining the amount of gain included in gross income (or loss deductible from gross income) they are allowed to recover their investment in the property.

Deduction. Expenditure made by a taxpayer that the government allows the taxpayer to use to reduce taxable income.

Direct tax. A tax levied on the party who ultimately bears the burden of the tax.

Employment tax. A tax imposed by the government on employee wages (FICA and FUTA) and on net earnings from a sole proprietorship (self-employment taxes).

Estate tax. A wealth transfer tax assessed on a decedent's taxable estate.

Excise tax. A tax on the production or consumption of specific goods or services, like tobacco products, alcohol, and gasoline.

Exclusion. An item of income that according to the tax laws is not subject to taxation.

Externality. The positive or negative effect of a transaction that occurs to persons or businesses that are not part of that transaction.

FICA (Federal Insurance Contributions Act). The combination of social security (OASDI) and Medicare taxes shared equally by the employee and the employer.

Fair market value (FMV). The amount that would induce a willing seller to sell and a willing buyer to buy certain property.

Flat tax. *See* Proportional tax.

Flow-through entity. A business entity that does not pay taxes, but files a tax return reporting the amounts of gross income, deductions, and credits generated by the business during the year, and passes information along to its owners regarding their respective shares of such items. Examples include partnerships, S corporations, limited liability corporations, and limited liability partnerships.

Franchise tax. An annual tax on the privilege of doing business in the state.

FUTA (Federal Unemployment Tax Act). A federal tax imposed on employers. The tax base is employee wages up to $7,000; the tax rate equals 6.2 percent.

GAAP (Generally Accepted Accounting Principles). The set of rules publicly-traded companies must adhere to when preparing financial statements.

Gift tax. A wealth transfer tax the government imposes upon the transferor for transfers to nonspouses in excess of a certain amount each year.

Gross income. All income from whatever source derived, except as specifically excluded by a provision in the Internal Revenue Code or other tax law. Represents the income the government has chosen to tax. Equals income minus exclusions.

Income. Broadly defined as increases in wealth that the taxpayer has realized.

Indirect tax. A tax levied on someone other than the one who ultimately bears the burden of the tax.

Inheritance tax. A tax levied on the beneficiary upon receipt of inherited property.

Intangible property. Personal property that has no physical characteristics. Examples include goodwill, patents, copyrights, mutual funds, stocks, and bonds.

Itemized deductions. A deduction from adjusted gross income that consists of various personal expenses that the federal government allows individuals to deduct in lieu of a standard deduction.

Limited liability. When an owner's liability with respect to the business is limited to the amount the owner has invested in the business.

Limited liability company (LLC). A business entity that can be treated as a partnership for tax purposes and whose owners enjoy limited liability.

Limited liability partnership (LLP). A business entity that can be treated as a partnership for tax purposes, but whose owners enjoy some aspects of limited liability.

Marginal tax rate. The rate of tax on the last dollar of taxable income or the amount of taxes saved on an additional dollar of deduction.

Nonrefundable tax credit. A tax credit that can only reduce a taxpayer's income tax liability.

Partnership. A flow-through entity that has at all times at least two owners, at least one of whom is responsible for the debts of the business.

Personal and dependency exemptions. A deduction from adjusted gross income the government allows to individual taxpayers. A deduction is allowed for the taxpayer, the taxpayer's spouse (if filing a joint return), and the taxpayer's dependents.

Personal property. Property that is not real estate. *See* Tangible personal property and Intangible property.

Progressive tax. A tax structure in which the average tax rate increases as the tax base increases.

Property tax. A tax assessed on property, including real property, tangible personal property, and intangible personal property.

Proportional tax. A tax structure in which the average tax rate does not change as the tax base changes (also referred to as flat tax).

Public good. A government-provided good or service for which enjoyment of the good cannot be limited.

Real property. Land and buildings (also referred to as real estate).

Realization principle. Gains and losses on property are not reported on the tax return until the year in which property is disposed of in a taxable transaction.

Refundable tax credit. A credit that can reduce a taxpayer's tax liability to zero and produce a refund for any amount of the credit in excess of the taxpayer's tax liability.

Regressive tax. A tax structure in which the average tax rate decreases as the tax base increases.

S corporation. A flow-through business entity that does not pay income taxes. An S corporation gets its name because it is a corporation that has elected to be taxed under Subchapter S of Chapter 1 of the Code. Only corporations that satisfy certain requirements can elect to be taxed as S corporations.

Sales tax. A broad-based tax on the consumption of goods and services.

Self-employment tax. The employee and employer portions of FICA tax that are imposed on net earnings from self-employment.

Sole proprietor. The owner of an unincorporated business.

Standard deduction. A deduction from adjusted gross income that the federal government allows individual taxpayers to deduct in lieu of itemized deductions.

Tangible personal property. Property that has physical characteristics but is not real estate.

Tax avoidance. The art of reducing tax liability through legitimate means.

Tax base. Used in computing tax liability. It represents the amount subject to tax. The tax base is multiplied by the tax rate to determine the taxpayer's tax liability.

Tax credit. Amount that reduces a taxpayer's tax liability. Can be either refundable or nonrefundable.

Tax evasion. Understating taxes due to the government through unlawful means.

Taxable income. The difference between a taxpayer's gross income and the total deductions a taxpayer is allowed. The tax base used in the regular income tax system.

Use tax. A tax charged by states on the consumption, use, or storage of goods and services that are not subject to sales tax.

User fee. A tax charged to those that use a government-provided good or service.

Wealth transfer tax. The tax a government imposes on transfers of wealth between two individuals. *See also* Estate tax, Gift tax, and Inheritance tax.

Wherewithal-to-pay concept. The principle that taxes income at the point at which the taxpayer has the greatest ability to pay the tax on such income.

CHAPTER PROBLEMS

The following questions and problems relate to the discussion in Chapter 1, Introduction to Taxation, which begins at ¶ 100 in *Part I: Overview of Taxes and the Federal Income Tax System*.

Chapter 1 Discussion Questions

1. Government-provided goods and services can be categorized as public goods or nonpublic goods. Provide examples of each. For which goods and services is it appropriate to consider a user fee to raise revenues associated with the costs incurred in providing those goods and services? When the opportunity exists to cover the costs of those goods and services through user fees, why do governments often choose to raise taxes for those goods and services partly through other means?

2. What is the difference between a taxpayer's average tax rate and the taxpayer's marginal tax rate? Which of these rates is most useful in determining the benefits derived from additional deductions? Which of these rates is most useful in determining whether a tax rate structure is regressive, progressive, or proportional? Which of these rates is most useful in determining the benefits derived from a tax credit?

3. Tax rate structures can be regressive, proportional, or progressive. Provide an example of a tax that uses each of these tax structures.

4. All property owned can be categorized either as real property or as personal property. What is the distinction between these two types of property? Provide examples of each.

5. All personal property can be categorized either as tangible personal property or as intangible personal property. What is the distinction between these two types of property? Provide examples of each.

6. Are an individual's personal belongings always personal property? Explain.

7. FICA and FUTA are two types of unemployment taxes. Are FICA and FUTA regressive, proportional, or progressive taxes? Explain.

8. Some taxes are direct taxes, whereas others are indirect taxes. Among the taxes discussed in this chapter, which ones are direct taxes? Which ones are indirect taxes? Who bears the economic burden of these taxes? Explain.

9. What is the distinction between sales taxes and excise taxes?

10. Estate taxes and inheritance taxes are sometimes referred to as "death taxes" because the tax levied on the transfer of wealth is triggered by someone's death. On whom are these

death taxes levied? Which levels of government levy these wealth transfer taxes? What tax base is used?

11. What is gross income and how is it computed?

12. Both exclusions and deductions reduce taxable income, so why do the income tax laws make a distinction between the two?

13. The income tax laws use an all-inclusive approach to defining income. What does this mean?

14. How does a tax credit differ from a tax deduction?

15. What is the difference between refundable and nonrefundable tax credits?

16. Tax avoidance and tax evasion are two ways a taxpayer can reduce the amount of taxes owed to the government. What is the important distinction between these two terms?

17. Fairness and efficiency are two goals of every tax system. Give an example that shows why it is difficult to achieve both at the same time.

18. In addition to using taxes for raising revenues, governments use them for a variety of other purposes. Name the other factors governments consider when deciding whom and what to tax. Provide examples of each.

19. Discuss the importance of taxes when making business decisions.

20. Explain why being able to accelerate the timing of a business deduction is valuable to a business.

Chapter 1 Problems

1. A major city recently entered into an agreement for a professional sports team to build its new stadium in the city. In exchange, the city will exempt the owners of the team from property taxes for the next 10 years. The mayor of the city is lauding the transaction because of all the positive externalities that building the stadium in the city will bring. Discuss some of the possible positive externalities from this transaction. Can you think of any negative externalities from this transaction?

2. If a taxpayer in the 25% marginal tax rate bracket is given the choice between a $1,000 deduction and a $300 tax credit, which would result in more tax savings?

3. Taxpayer A pays taxes of $3,000 on a $10,000 tax base. Taxpayer B pays taxes of $5,000 on a $15,000 tax base. Is this tax rate structure regressive, proportional, or progressive? Explain.

4. Taxpayer C pays taxes of $4,000 on a $10,000 tax base. Taxpayer D pays taxes of $4,800 on a $15,000 tax base. Is this tax rate structure regressive, proportional, or progressive? Explain.

5. Taxpayer E pays taxes of $3,500 on a $10,000 tax base. Taxpayer F pays taxes of $5,000 on a $15,000 tax base. Is this tax rate structure regressive, proportional, or progressive? Explain.

6. Taxpayer G pays taxes of $3,000 on a tax base of $10,000. If the tax rate structure is regressive, what is the maximum amount of taxes Taxpayer H would pay on a tax base of $15,000?

7. Taxpayer I pays taxes of $2,000 on a tax base of $10,000. If the tax rate structure is proportional, what is the amount of taxes Taxpayer J would pay on a tax base of $15,000?

8. Taxpayer K pays taxes of $2,500 on a tax base of $10,000. If the tax rate structure is progressive, what is the minimum amount of taxes Taxpayer L would pay on a tax base of $15,000?

9. Which entity choice(s) protect the owners from the general obligations of the business?

   a. Sole proprietorship

   b. C corporation

   c. S corporation

   d. Partnership

e. LLC

f. LLP

10. Which entity choice(s) only tax the profits of the business one time?

    a. Sole proprietorship

    b. C corporation

    c. S corporation

    d. Partnership

    e. LLC

    f. LLP

11. Which entity choice(s) are available for businesses with a single owner?

    a. Sole proprietorship

    b. C corporation

    c. S corporation

    d. Partnership

    e. LLC

    f. LLP

12. Which entity choice(s) are required to file an annual income tax return?

    a. Sole proprietorship

    b. C corporation

    c. S corporation

    d. Partnership

    e. LLC

    f. LLP

13. Julie and Ron Johansson are interested in making tax-free gifts to each of their six children and 14 grandchildren during 2015. What is the maximum amount that the Johanssons can transfer to their descendents tax free during 2015?

14. Eric Robertson died during 2015 leaving a taxable estate worth $5,000,000. During his lifetime, Eric made taxable gifts totaling $800,000, but since they did not exceed the $5,430,000 lifetime exemption amount, he never paid any gift tax. Will an estate tax be imposed on Eric's estate? Explain.

15. The federal government currently allows tax credits to consumers who purchase hybrid automobiles. What externalities do purchases of hybrid automobiles produce that are driving the federal government to provide this tax incentive?

16. In recent years, a debate has arisen over replacing the incredibly complex income tax system and the payroll tax with a simpler flat tax on all income. If the government were able to accomplish this, how might this affect the various equity, social, and economic issues that governments often consider when deciding how to raise revenues?

17. What is the primary tax or nontax advantage of operating a business as a C corporation over a sole proprietorship?

18. What is the primary tax or nontax disadvantage of operating a business as a C corporation over a sole proprietorship?

19. If a taxpayer in the 25% tax bracket is able to take a tax credit for 20 percent of the $10,000 of wages it pays a particular employee and deduct the rest as wage expense, how much more tax savings will the taxpayer generate over just being able to deduct the entire $10,000 as wage expense?

20. A single taxpayer has adjusted gross income of $35,000 and itemized deductions of $1,000 in 2015. What is the taxpayer's taxable income assuming no dependency exemptions?

21. A congressman is deciding between proposing a $1,000 increase in the child tax credit or a $5,000 increase in the deduction for the dependency exemption. Calculate the tax savings of the credit versus an increased deduction for a taxpayer in the 15% tax bracket with one who is in 28% tax bracket. Which person benefits most from the tax credit versus the increased deduction?

22. A congressman is trying to determine whether to propose a $1,000 increase in the child tax credit or a $5,000 increase in the dependency exemption. Calculate the tax savings of the credit versus exemption for a taxpayer in the 10% tax bracket with one who is in the 35% tax bracket. Which person benefits most from the tax credit versus the increased exemption?

23. A congressman is trying to determine whether to propose a $750 tax credit or a $4,000 tax deduction for the purchase of a hybrid car. Calculate the tax savings of the credit versus deduction for a taxpayer in the 10% tax bracket with one who is in the 35% tax bracket. Which person benefits most from the tax credit versus the deduction? In making your decision, does it matter that a wealthier individual is more likely to buy a $25,000 Prius than a less wealthy person?

24. A congressperson wants to encourage the establishment of renewable energy business in her state by providing tax incentives dealing with the start-up expenses of these businesses. Among the ideas she is considering are (1) allowing a write-off over 60 month of all start-up expenses; (2) allowing a deduction of $5,000 of start-up expenses with a 180 month write-off for any remaining start-up expenses; and (3) allowing a deduction of all start-up expenses up to $50,000 with no write-off allowed for expenses in excess of $50,000. What are the pros and cons of each option?

25. A congressman is trying to determine whether to propose a nonrefundable $500 tuition tax credit or a $2,500 tax deduction. Calculate the tax savings of the credit versus deduction for a taxpayer in the 10% tax bracket with one who is in the 35% tax bracket. Which person benefits most from the tax credit versus the deduction? If we assume that more students are in the 10% bracket and therefore prefer the tuition tax credit, will this proposed tax law provide them with a lot of assistance? Discuss whether the tuition tax credit should be refundable.

CHAPTER 2
Researching Federal Tax Laws

CHAPTER CONTENTS

LEARNING OBJECTIVES

1. Learn what gives Congress the right to tax income.
2. Learn what sources are available to answer a tax question.
3. Be able to distinguish between primary and secondary sources of tax law.
4. Understand which sources of tax law are more authoritative than others.
5. Be able to locate primary sources of tax law.
6. Learn the steps involved in researching a tax question.
7. Understand the ethical considerations in researching a tax question.

¶ 200 Introduction

Almost all business transactions have tax implications. When revenue is earned, questions are raised as to whether the revenue is taxable, how much is taxable, and when it is taxable. When an expenditure is incurred, businesses must determine whether an amount can be deducted and, if so, how much and when. They also must determine whether any credit is available with respect to the expenditure and, if so, the amount of the credit and when it may be taken. When businesses dispose of property, questions are raised as to the amount of gain or loss realized from the transaction, what amount must be recognized, and when that amount must be reported on the tax return. The answer to these and all other tax questions can be found in the tax laws of the U.S. income tax system.

The underlying foundation for the U.S. income tax laws is the Internal Revenue Code (the "Code"); however, the information in the Code alone may not be sufficient to adequately address the issue at hand. Consequently, taxpayers must consult other sources of legislative, administrative, and judicial authority to determine the tax consequences of a transaction.

The purpose of this chapter is to present the various sources of primary tax law, which include legislative, administrative, and judicial authority. In addition to introducing these various authorities, guidance is provided to help students locate and use these sources. Guidance also is provided to help students understand how ambiguities in the tax law are clarified. The chapter begins with a brief history of where the U.S. income tax laws originate, followed by a discussion of the various sources of tax authority. The chapter concludes with a discussion of the tax research process and ethical standards that are expected to be followed when researching tax issues.

¶ 201 History of the U.S. Federal Income Tax

Prior to the Civil War, the federal government relied primarily on tariffs and excise taxes to generate revenues. Tariffs were imposed on imported goods, and excise taxes were imposed on the consumption of specific goods. The first federal individual income tax was enacted in 1861 to help pay for fighting the Civil War. A three-percent tax was imposed on a person's annual income in excess of $800 (equivalent to approximately $22,150 as of the beginning of 2015). In 1862, a two-tiered rate structure was enacted. Taxable income in excess of $10,000 was taxed at five percent. In 1872, Congress repealed the individual income tax and went back to relying primarily on excises taxes to generate revenue for the federal government.

The repeal of the income tax was short-lived. In 1894, Congress reinstated an individual income tax. However, it was challenged as unconstitutional on the ground that the U.S. Constitution allowed Congress to impose direct taxes only when they could be levied in proportion to each state's population. Because an individual income tax is levied on an individual's income and not collected based on the states' populations, the U.S. Supreme Court agreed with the petitioner and held that the individual income tax was unconstitutional.[1]

Congress recognized that relying heavily on excise taxes resulted in lower-income taxpayers spending a disproportionately higher portion of their income in taxes. Consequently, in the years following the Supreme Court's decision, a great deal of debate ensued about how the government should raise its needed revenues. Industrialized states from the Northeast opposed high excise taxes because they drove up the price of goods and were paid disproportionately by less affluent Americans. Agricultural states feared that revenue lost from reducing excise taxes would be replaced by taxing property, which they owned in abundance.

The problem was resolved when Congress passed the Sixteenth Amendment to the Constitution, which made it possible for the federal government to impose an individual income tax. This amendment became effective on March 1, 1913. The first constitutional income tax rates ranged

---

[1] *Pollock v. Farmers' Loan & Trust Co.*, SCt, 157 US 429, 15 SCt 673 (1895).

from one percent on the first $20,000 of "lawful" taxable income in excess of $3,000 for unmarried individuals ($4,000 for married individuals) to seven percent on "lawful" taxable income in excess of $500,000. The individual income tax return, Form 1040, was introduced as the standard tax reporting form, and, though it has changed significantly over the years, it remains in use today. In 1913, fewer than one percent of individuals were required to pay any income tax.[2]

 Spotlight: An initial problem with the new income tax law was how to define "lawful" income. The problem was quickly addressed in 1915 by eliminating the word "lawful" from the definition of income and replacing it with an all-inclusive definition of "income." By taxing all income, even that which is earned by illegal means, many purported criminals who may have been able to escape justice for their crimes have been incarcerated on tax evasion charges.

¶ 202 The Legislative Process

Income tax laws are enacted when approved by a majority vote in both chambers of Congress and signed by the president (or vetoed by the president and passed by a two-thirds or greater vote of each chamber of Congress). Currently, 435 members of the House of Representatives and 100 members of the Senate comprise the two chambers of Congress. In accordance with the Constitution, changes to the income tax laws originate in the House of Representatives (House), where the responsibility rests with the members of the House who form the House Ways and Means Committee. Any changes to the tax laws initiated by the House Ways and Means Committee are drafted into a House Bill. Once the House Bill is passed with a majority vote by the committee, it is voted on by the House. If the bill passes the House with a majority vote, then the focus turns to the Senate, where changes to current tax laws are considered by the senators who comprise the Senate Finance Committee. This committee is in charge of drafting a Senate Bill that will pass (with a majority vote) in both the Senate Finance Committee and the full Senate. Accordingly, because the Senate Finance Committee is not concerned with the Senate Bill passing in the House, the Senate Bill is almost always somewhat different from the House Bill.

Once the Senate Bill passes the full Senate with at least 51 votes, the legislative process shifts to reconciling the House and Senate bills in the Conference Committee. The Conference Committee, comprised of members of both the House Ways & Means Committee and the Senate Finance Committee, is responsible for generating a single tax bill (Conference Committee bill) that can be passed by a majority vote in both the House and the Senate. Once the Conference Committee Bill is passed with a majority vote by the Conference Committee and each chamber of Congress, it is sent to the president's desk for the president's signature or veto. A tax bill vetoed by the president can still be enacted into law with a two-thirds or greater vote in both chambers of Congress. The five steps in the legislative process are summarized in Figure 2-1.

[2] U.S. Department of the Treasury Fact Sheets: History of the U.S. Tax System, available at *www.policyalmanac.org/economic/archive/tax_history.shtml.*

Figure 2-1 The Legislative Process

Step	Event
1	Passage of a House Bill by the House Ways and Means Committee and then by the House of Representatives
2	Passage of a Senate Bill by the Senate Finance Committee and then by the Senate
3	Creation of a Bill that reconciles the House and Senate Bills and then is passed by the Conference Committee
4	Passage of the Conference Committee Bill by both the House and Senate
5	Signing the bill into law by the president (or override of a presidential veto by both the House and Senate)

.01 Internal Revenue Code

The ultimate source of federal tax law is the U.S. Constitution, which gives Congress the power "to lay and collect taxes, duties, imposts, and excises."[3] Most tax laws enacted by Congress have been codified as the **Internal Revenue Code** (the "Code"), which is published as Title 26 of the U.S. Code. In its most basic form, the provisions in the Code are a collection of sections. Each section contains the tax law for a different topic, and each section is assigned a different number. For example, Section 163 contains the tax laws governing the deductibility of interest paid on loans and other debt obligations. Section 164 describes the various types of taxes that can be deducted against taxable income.

.02 Amendment of the Code

Periodically, Code sections are amended, added, or deleted by a public law (abbreviated as "P.L.") enacted by Congress and signed into law by the President under the legislative process previously described. When a Code section is amended, added, or deleted, Congress specifies when the change will take place (the "effective date"). Congress also may specify a termination date for an amendment, addition, or deletion. For example, a provision in the Jobs and Growth Tax Relief Reconciliation Act of 2003 (P.L. 108-27) added paragraph (11) to Code Sec. 1(h), which taxes an individual's qualified dividend income at the same rate as the individual's net capital gain. This change became effective for tax years beginning after December 31, 2002. Another provision in the Act states that this change will not apply to tax years beginning after December 31, 2008.[4] However, on May 11, 2006, Congress passed the Tax Increase Prevention and Reconciliation Act of 2005 (P.L. 109-222), which extended the provision taxing an individual's qualified dividend income at the same rate as the individual's net capital gain for an additional two years.[5] This tax treatment was extended once again for two years by the Tax Relief, Unemployment Insurance Reauthorization, and Job Creation Act of 2010 (P.L. 111-312).[6] The change was made permanent by the American Taxpayer Relief Act of 2012 (P.L. 112-240).

 Planning Pointer: Whenever taxpayers are using a published version of the Code, they should make certain that the version includes all changes that have been made, including the effective dates.

---

[3] U.S. Const. art. I, § 8, cl. 1.

[4] Act Secs. 302 and 303 of the Jobs and Growth Tax Relief Reconciliation Act of 2003 (P.L. 108-27).

[5] Act Sec. 102 of the Tax Increase Prevention and Reconciliation Act of 2005 (P.L. 109-222).

[6] Act Section 101(a)(1).

¶ 203 Primary vs. Secondary Sources of Tax Law

Although most of the U.S. federal tax law is included in the Code, when writing the tax laws it is virtually impossible for Congress to anticipate every possible situation that taxpayers may encounter. Therefore, many areas of the tax law have to be interpreted and clarified. The provisions in the Code often must be studied in conjunction with other legislative authority, administrative interpretations (administrative authority), and court rulings (judicial authority). The legislative, administrative, and judicial authority comprise the U.S. tax laws and are called **primary sources of authority.**

Because primary sources of authority include a great amount of material, researchers often find it difficult to easily find the materials they need to answer their tax questions. Someone relying solely on primary sources would find it time consuming and highly ineffective to "wade through" all of the primary sources to find answers to a specific tax question. Although computerized tax research and key word searches help narrow down the amount of material that has to be perused, a good portion of irrelevant material may surface during the search for relevant authority.

Secondary sources of authority bring together pertinent primary sources on an area of the tax law and help explain the area in a relatively straightforward manner. Without secondary sources, a taxpayer would have to read all cases and rulings to determine which ones, if any, applied to the taxpayer's situation. Secondary sources of authority are various references that explain and comment on primary sources of authority. Popular examples of secondary sources include tax services, citators, and legal periodicals.

The discussion that follows introduces each of the three primary sources of tax law: legislative authority, administrative authority, and judicial authority. Once these primary sources of authority have been discussed, the tax research process is explained.

LEGISLATIVE AUTHORITY

Legislative authority includes tax law that results from the legislative process. In addition to the provisions in the Code, legislative authority includes committee reports, Blue Books, and treaties.

¶ 204 The Internal Revenue Code

The sections within Title 26 of the U.S. Code are organized by subtitle. There are 11 subtitles within the Code, and they are designated sequentially with capital letters. All income tax laws are set forth in Subtitle A of the Code. The tax laws governing estate, gift, and generation-skipping transfer taxes are set forth in Subtitle B. Employment tax laws are set forth in Subtitle C. Within each subtitle are a series of chapters, each sequentially numbered. For example, in Subtitle A, Income Taxes, there are six chapters. Chapter 1 is titled Normal Taxes and Surtaxes. Chapter 2 is titled Tax on Self-Employment Income.

Each chapter can be broken down into subchapters, which are various topics that fall within the chapter. For example, within Chapter 1, Normal Taxes and Surtaxes of Subtitle A, there are 25 subchapters (shown in Table 2-1).

Table 2-1 Subchapters within Chapter 1, Normal Taxes and Surtaxes

Subchapter	Description	Code Sections
A	Determination of Tax Liability	1-59A
B	Computation of Taxable Income	61-291
C	Corporate Distributions and Adjustments	301-385
D	Deferred Compensation, Etc.	401-436
E	Accounting Periods and Methods of Accounting	441-483
F	Exempt Organizations	501-530
G	Corporations Used to Avoid Income Tax on Shareholders	531-565
H	Banking Institutions	581-597
I	Natural Resources	611-638
J	Estates, Trusts, Beneficiaries, and Decedents	641-692
K	Partners and Partnerships	701-777
L	Insurance Companies	801-848
M	Regulated Investment Companies and Real Estate Investment Trusts	851-860G
N	Tax Based on Income From Sources Within or Without the United States	861-999
O	Gain or Loss on Disposition of Property	1001-1092
P	Capital Gains and Losses	1201-1298
Q	Readjustment of Tax Between Years and Special Limitations	1301-1351
R	Election To Determine Corporate Tax on Certain International Shipping Activities Using Per Ton Rate	1352-1359
S	Tax Treatment of S Corporations and Their Shareholders	1361-1379
T	Cooperatives and Their Patrons	1381-1388
U	Designation and Treatment of Empowerment Zones, Enterprise Communities, and Rural Development Investment Areas	1391-1397F
V	Title 11 Cases	1398-1399
W	District of Columbia Enterprise Zone	1400-1400C
X	Renewal Communities	1400E-1400J
Y	Short-Term Regional Benefits	1400L-1400U-3

Many of the subchapters listed in Table 2-1 discuss topics discussed in this textbook. Most of the tax laws behind the topics introduced in Chapters 3 through 7 are included in Subchapter A, Determination of Tax Liability, and Subchapter B, Computation of Taxable Income. Taxable corporations are often called C corporations because the tax laws applied to these business entities are located in Subchapter C, Corporate Distributions and Adjustments. Tax laws specific to corporate entities are discussed in Chapter 12. As mentioned in the previous chapter, businesses can operate as flow-through entities, which are taxed either as a partnership or S corporation. The partnership tax laws are in Subchapter K. The tax laws governing S corporations are in Subchapter S (hence the name "S corporation").

Subchapters are divided into parts and subparts. Parts are specific topics within a subchapter and are listed in numerical order using roman numerals. For example, Part I of Subchapter C describes the tax laws that govern distributions by a C corporation. These rules are in Code Secs. 301-318. Subparts A, B, and C within Part I contain subtopics on corporation distributions, including the tax consequences to the recipient (Subpart A), the tax consequences to the corporation (Subpart B), and definitions (Subpart C). A list of the various parts within Subchapter C and subparts under Part I of that subchapter are provided in Tables 2-2 and 2-3.

Table 2-2 Parts within Subchapter C, Corporate Distributions and Adjustments

Part	Description	Code Sections
I	Distributions by Corporations	301-318
II	Corporate Liquidations	331-346
III	Corporate Organizations and Reorganizations	351-368
IV	[Repealed]	370-374
V	Carryovers	381-384
VI	Treatment of Certain Corporate Interest as Stock or Indebtedness	385

Table 2-3 Subparts within Part I, Distributions by Corporations

Subpart	Description	Code Sections
A	Effects on Recipients	301-307
B	Effects on Corporation	311-312
C	Definitions; Constructive Ownership of Stock	316-318

The actual tax laws are set forth in sections. For example, the two Code sections within Subpart B from Table 2-3 are Code Sec. 311, Taxability of Corporation on Distributions, and Code Sec. 312, Effect on Earnings and Profits. Each Code section describes very specific tax laws on a particular topic. In these particular Code sections, the tax consequences to both parties affected when a corporation distributes property to its shareholders are discussed. Code sections are organized in outline form, as shown below with Code Sec. 311, which outlines the tax consequences to a corporation when it distributes property to its shareholders.

Code Sec. 311 Taxability of Corporation on Distributions

  (a) **GENERAL RULE.** — Except as provided in subsection (b), no gain or loss shall be recognized to a corporation on the distribution (not in complete liquidation) with respect to its stock of —

    (1) its stock (or rights to acquire its stock), or

    (2) property.

  (b) **DISTRIBUTIONS OF APPRECIATED PROPERTY.** —

    (1) **IN GENERAL.** —If —

      (A) *a corporation distributes property (other than an obligation of such corporation) to a shareholder in a distribution to which subpart A applies, and*

      (B) the fair market value of such property exceeds its adjusted basis (in the hands of the distributing corporation),

    then gain shall be recognized to the distributing corporation as if such property were sold to the distributee at its fair market value.

(2) **TREATMENT OF LIABILITIES.** —Rules similar to the rules of section 336(b) shall apply for purposes of this subsection.

(3) **SPECIAL RULE FOR CERTAIN DISTRIBUTIONS OF PARTNERSHIP OR TRUST INTERESTS.** —If the property distributed consists of an interest in a partnership or trust, the Secretary may by regulations provide that the amount of the gain recognized under paragraph (1) shall be computed without regard to any loss attributable to property contributed to the partnership or trust for the principal purpose of recognizing such loss on the distribution.

To properly comprehend the tax laws described in a Code section, it is important to first understand the various components of a Code section. For example, the citation for the italicized portion of Code Sec. 311 from above is dissected below.

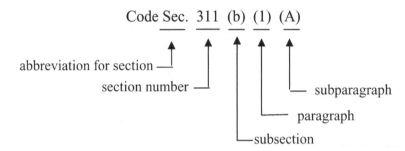

A section of the Code, such as Section 311, may be referred to as Code Sec. 311, Code § 311, or as 26 U.S.C. § 311. In the citation Code Sec. 311(b)(1)(A), the number after the words "Code Sec." designates the Code section, and the letter "b" refers to the second subsection in Code Sec. 311. The number "1" refers to the first paragraph under subsection (b), and the letter "A" refers to the first subparagraph under paragraph 1. After subparagraphs, clauses are designated with small Roman numerals (i, ii, iii, etc.), followed by subclauses, which are designated with capital Roman numerals (I, II, III, etc.).

Subsection (a) of Code Sec. 311 provides a general rule regarding the tax consequences to corporations when they distribute property. Under this general rule, unless otherwise stated in subsection (b), a corporation does not recognize gain or loss when it distributes stock (or rights to acquire its stock) [paragraph (1)] or property [paragraph (2)] with respect to its stock. Subsection (b) contains an exception to this general rule. It provides that when a corporation distributes appreciated property (where the fair market value exceeds the corporation's adjusted basis in the property), the corporation is treated as having sold the property to the shareholder for its fair market value. Accordingly, the corporation will recognize gain.

Print versions of the Code are available from many commercial publishers. Also available from many commercial publishers are CD-ROMs that reproduce the Code and online subscriptions that include the Code. The Office of the Law Revision Counsel of the U.S. House of Representatives prepares and publishes the Code on its website at: *http://uscode.house.gov.*

¶ 205 Committee Reports

Although many tax questions can be answered simply by reading a Code provision, sometimes the language in the Code is ambiguous. In these situations, it is helpful to have access to the discussions that took place when the language in the Code was being written. As tax legislation proceeds through Congress, most bills are accompanied by a committee report. Although these reports are not as authoritative as the provisions in the Code itself, when the language in the Code is ambiguous these reports help explain what Congress intended when it enacted the new legislation. Reports that come from the committee bill that most closely matches the provisions enacted into law are the ones that carry the greatest authoritative weight.

For example, assume that a Senate bill contains a provision that is incorporated into the Conference Committee bill enacted into law. The House bill was silent on this matter. The appropriate committee reports to examine to determine Congressional intent would be the Senate Finance Committee report and the Conference Committee report.

 Planning Pointer: When Congress passes tax legislation, it votes on the provisions and words contained in the Conference Committee bill, not the words contained in any of the committee reports. For this reason, committee reports should never be relied upon when the language in the Code is clear.

As another example: prior to the Tax Reform Act of 1986 (TRA 1986), individuals could deduct personal interest as an itemized deduction. Thus, if individual taxpayers were assessed interest on an underpayment of taxes resulting from an error made on their personal income tax returns, such interest could be deducted from adjusted gross income as an itemized deduction. In TRA 1986, Congress enacted Code Sec. 163(h), which no longer allows a deduction for personal interest. Personal interest is defined as all interest paid or incurred by a taxpayer that is not interest properly allocable to the taxpayer's business (subparagraph A), investment interest (subparagraph B), interest from a passive activity (subparagraph C), home mortgage and other residence-related interest (subparagraph D), certain interest paid in connection with estates (subparagraph E), and student loan interest (subparagraph F). Code Sec. 163(h) is reproduced below.

163(h)

(1) **IN GENERAL.** —In the case of a taxpayer other than a corporation, no deduction shall be allowed under this chapter for personal interest paid or accrued during the taxable year.

(2) **PERSONAL INTEREST.** —For purposes of this subsection, the term "personal interest" means any interest allowable as a deduction under this chapter other than —

    (A) interest paid or accrued on indebtedness properly allocable to a trade or business (other than the trade or business of performing services as an employee),

    (B) any investment interest (within the meaning of subsection (d)),

    (C) any interest which is taken into account under section 469 in computing income or loss from a passive activity of the taxpayer,

    (D) any qualified residence interest (within the meaning of paragraph (3)),

    (E) any interest payable under section 6601 on any unpaid portion of the tax imposed by section 2001 for the period during which an extension of time for payment of such tax is in effect under section 6163, and

    (F) any interest allowable as a deduction under section 221 (relating to interest on educational loans).

Although this Code section clearly states that six types of interest are not considered personal interest, it is unclear whether interest paid to the IRS on a tax deficiency resulting from a failure to report business income on the owner's individual income tax return constitutes business interest (which is not personal interest under Code Sec. 163(h)(2)(A)) or nondeductible personal interest (under the general rule in Code Sec. 163(h)(1)).

The IRS has taken the position that interest paid on an underpayment of individual federal, state, or local income taxes (or on indebtedness used to pay such taxes) is personal interest even though the source of the income generating the tax liability is business income.[7] This regulation has been upheld as a permissible and reasonable construction of the statute.[8]

Congress (at *http://beta.congress.gov/*) makes available committee reports published since 1995. Committee reports published since 1997 also are available from the GPO's Federal Digital System (at *http://www.gpo.gov/fdsys/browse/committeetab.action*). Those committee reports and older committee reports can be found in *U.S. Code Congressional and Administrative News* and are available on CD-ROMs and online subscription services from commercial publishers.

---

[7] Temp. Reg. § 1.163-9T(b)(2)(i)(A).

[8] *D. Miller*, CA-8, 95-2 USTC ¶ 50,485, 65 F3d 687; *J. L. Redlark*, CA-9, 98-1 USTC ¶ 50,322, 141 F3d 936; *R.R. Allen, Sr.*, CA-4, 99-1 USTC ¶ 50,470, 173 F3d 533; *M. McDonnell*, CA-6, 99-1 USTC ¶ 50,556, 180 F3d 721; *N. Kikalos*, 99-2 USTC ¶ 50,823, 190 F3d 791; *E.A. Robinson III*, 119 T.C. 44, CCH Dec. 54,863 (2002).

¶ 206 Blue Books

The Joint Committee on Taxation assists Congress in all stages of the legislative process and works directly with Congress to help research and answer questions as a bill makes its way through the various stages in the legislative process. After a major tax act has been signed into law, the staff of the Joint Committee on Taxation prepares an explanation. These explanations are called *General Explanation of Tax Legislation,* otherwise known as **blue books** because of the color of their cover.

Although written by the staff of the Joint Committee on Taxation, and not by actual members of Congress, the individuals who write blue books can often provide insight into Congress's intent when enacting legislation. Both the IRS and the courts have been known to use information from the blue books in rendering their rulings and decisions.

Blue Books published since 1969 are available on The Joint Committee on Taxation's website (*www.jct.gov*). Older Blue Books are available on CD-ROMs and online subscription services from commercial publishers.

¶ 207 Treaties

Tax treaties are agreements between countries to promote tax enforcement and prevent double taxation of income. In situations where income can be taxed by more than one country, a treaty will specify which country taxes the income.

Treaties usually provide that income received by nonresidents of a treaty party will be taxed at special rates. Treaties between the United States and other countries are authorized by the U.S. Constitution. They are negotiated by the President and approved by the Senate. When the language in the Code and the provisions in a tax treaty conflict, the "later in time" rule applies, which means that the more recently enacted authority is the one that is followed.

 Reason for the Rule: A treaty is enacted with full knowledge of the existing statute. Accordingly, the language in the treaty was intended to override any existing Code provision. Likewise, when Congress enacts new tax legislation, it does so with full knowledge of the existing treaties that the United States has with other countries. Accordingly, if Congress uses language in the statute that conflicts with a provision in a treaty, then it is considered Congress's intent to override the treaty provision.

ADMINISTRATIVE AUTHORITY

Administrative authority is tax law that comes from the Secretary of the Treasury and the Internal Revenue Service (IRS). Its role is to help taxpayers understand what the tax laws mean and how they are to be applied. Administrative authority includes Treasury regulations and various IRS pronouncements.

¶ 208 Treasury Regulations

Treasury regulations are the Secretary of the Treasury's official interpretation of the provisions in the Code and represent an important source of authority to consider when researching federal tax law. Regulations are especially valuable when the language in the Code is vague because regulations interpret and give direction for complying with the Code. Regulations often define terms, clarify language used in the Code, and explain how the tax laws should be interpreted. They often contain examples of how the tax laws should be applied, which make them especially useful sources of authority.

For example, Code Sec. 41 allows businesses to take a tax credit equal to 20 percent of the excess of qualified research expenses over a base amount. Although "qualified research expenses" and "base amount" are defined in the Code, Reg. § 1.41-2 elaborates on the definition of qualified research expenses and provides numerous examples of such expenditures. In addition to defining what the base amount is, Reg. § 1.41-3 illustrates how the amount is calculated.

Like the Code, regulations are divided into parts. The citation for a final regulation might look like this:

> Reg. § 1.301-1, Rules applicable with respect to distributions of money and other property.

The "§" in the citation is the symbol for section. The "301" indicates that the regulation relates to Code Sec. 301. The number preceding the decimal point before "301" provides information as to the type of regulation. The "1" means that this is a regulation that discusses an income tax law. The other types of regulations are listed in Table 2-4. The "1" following the hyphen indicates that this final regulation concerning Code Sec. 301 is numbered "1." Typically there is one or more regulation for each Code provision. Subsequent regulations within Reg. § 1.301 would be numbered -2, -3, etc.

Table 2-4 Regulation Types Used in Citations

Number	Area of Tax Law Discussed
1	Income tax
20	Estate tax
25	Gift tax and valuation issues
26	Generation-skipping transfer tax
31	Employment taxes
40-56	Excise taxes
156-157	Additional excise taxes
301	Procedure and administration
601	Procedural rules

Regulations are published in the *Federal Register*. They are available online from the GPO's Federal Digital System at *http://www.gpo.gov/fdsys/browse/collectionCfr.action?collectionCode=CFR* and also through CD-ROMs and online subscription services offered by commercial publishers.

.01 Stages of Regulations

Regulations are issued by the Secretary of the Treasury under the authority of Congress. To ensure that regulations accurately interpret the provisions in the Code, regulations usually are first issued in proposed form (when guidance is needed quickly, temporary regulations may be issued at the same time as proposed regulations). The IRS publishes a **proposed regulation** in the *Federal Register* as a Notice of Proposed Rulemaking and solicits comments from the public about the regulation. Although a proposed regulation is not binding on a taxpayer, often the provisions contained in a proposed regulation are those that appear in the final regulation.

Planning Pointer: The rules prescribed by a proposed regulation will not necessarily be the same rules included in a final regulation. Neither the IRS nor taxpayers are bound by proposed regulations. However, the IRS increasingly has been authorizing taxpayers to rely on proposed regulations so that they know how a transaction they engage in will be taxed.

Once comments from the public have been taken into consideration, proposed regulations are revised and either reissued again as proposed regulations or issued as final regulations. **Final regulations** are published in the *Federal Register* as Treasury Decisions. The process of evaluating a proposed regulation, revising it, and issuing it as a final regulation can take several years to complete. For example, a proposed regulation[9] pertaining to Code Sec. 280A was originally issued on August 7, 1980. The regulation was revised and released again as a proposed regulation on July 21, 1983. This particular regulation has yet to be released in final form, which suggests that problems in the regulation continue to exist.

Proposed regulations are distinguished from other types of regulations by including "Prop." at the front of the citation. For example, the citation for the proposed regulation referred to above is Prop. Reg. § 1.280A-1.

When Congress enacts major changes to the tax laws, it is often necessary that guidance be issued quickly so that taxpayers can correctly prepare their tax returns for the upcoming year. If the changes are substantial, there may not be time to issue all of the needed regulations in proposed form and wait until the public has a chance to comment on them before issuing them in final form. In these situations, Congress allows the Secretary to issue **temporary regulations**, which have the same force and effect as final regulations, even though they have not been through the proposed stage.[10]

Temporary regulations, also published as Treasury Decisions in the *Federal Register,* provide interim guidance to tax practitioners and the public until final regulations can be issued. The rules contained in temporary regulations can be used as authority pending issuance of final regulations. Temporary regulations issued after November 20, 1988, expire three years after the date that they were issued. Congress requires that all temporary regulations be simultaneously issued as proposed regulations.[11] This allows the Secretary three years to make any necessary changes to the Temporary regulation before issuing it in final form.

The citation for temporary regulations can be distinguished from the citations for other types of regulations because they include the word "Temp." and the capital letter "T" in the citation. The citation for the ninth regulation for Code Sec. 163 is Temp. Reg. § 1.163-9T.

 Reason for the Rule: Prior to the Technical and Miscellaneous Revenue Act of 1988, temporary regulations did not expire. Because temporary regulations are accorded the same authoritative weight as final regulations, there was little incentive for the Secretary to make amendments to temporary regulations. Because temporary regulations are usually issued within a short period of time after major tax legislation is passed into law, Congress felt there needed to be a mechanism in place in the Code to ensure that these regulations eventually go through the proposed stage where potential problems with the regulation can be identified and corrected. Accordingly, Code Sec. 7805(e) was enacted into law, and all temporary regulations issued after November 20, 1988, expire after three years.

---

[9] Prop. Reg. § 1.280A-1.
[10] Code Sec. 7805.

[11] Code Sec. 7805(e).

.02 Interpretive, Legislative, and Procedural Regulations

Guidance provided by regulations can be classified as one of three types: interpretive, legislative, or procedural. Most regulations are **interpretive regulations,** meaning that they interpret the provisions in the Code under the general authority provided to the Secretary under Code Sec. 7805.[12] **Legislative regulations,** on the other hand, define a statutory term or prescribe a method for implementing a Code provision. These regulations are also written pursuant to authority granted by Congress, but through specific language in the Code section to which they relate. For example, in Code Sec. 1502, Congress wrote:

> The Secretary shall prescribe such regulations as he may deem necessary in order that the tax liability of any affiliated group of corporations making a consolidated return and of each corporation in the group, both during and after the period of affiliation, may be returned, determined, computed, assessed, collected, and adjusted, in such manner as clearly to reflect the income tax liability and the various factors necessary for the determination of such liability, and in order to prevent avoidance of such tax liability. In carrying out the preceding sentence, the Secretary may prescribe rules that are different from the provisions of chapter 1 that would apply if such corporations filed separate returns.

The above passage is the only provision in the Code that addresses how corporations in a consolidated group should file a consolidated income tax return. As this section directs, the tax law regarding this issue can be found in the regulations under Code Sec. 1502. Accordingly, taxpayers interested in the tax laws governing consolidated income tax returns need to refer to Reg. §§1.1502-1 through 1.1502-100.

Code Sec. 611 provides that, "in the case of mines, oil and gas wells, other natural deposits, and timber, there shall be allowed as a deduction in computing taxable income a reasonable allowance for depletion and for depreciation of improvements, according to the peculiar conditions in each case; such reasonable allowance in all cases to be made under regulations prescribed by the Secretary." Thus, pursuant to the authority found in the language to Code Sec. 611, legislative regulations Reg. §§1.611-0 through 1.614-8 have been adopted.

 Reason for the Rule: Congress delegates to the Secretary of the Treasury responsibility for writing specified provisions of a tax law either because Congress cannot or prefers not to deal with the details of a tax provision.

A **procedural regulation** is a regulation that establishes procedure or practice requirements (such as prescribing how an election is made). For example, expenses whose useful life extends beyond the current tax year usually must be capitalized and expensed over a number of years. Code Sec. 190 allows businesses to elect to currently deduct up to $15,000 of expenditures incurred to make their trade or business more accessible to the elderly and disabled. Reg. §1.190-3 explains how taxpayers can make this election.

There is no way to distinguish between the three types of regulations by looking at their citations. A distinction can be made only by reading the language of the Code section. If the phrase "under regulations prescribed by the Secretary" or "The Secretary shall prescribe" appears in the Code section, this is indicative of a legislative regulation. If such language or similar language is absent, then the regulation is either an interpretative or procedural regulation.

.03 Authoritative Weight Accorded to Regulations

The IRS is bound by regulations that the Secretary issues. Regulations generally command the court's respect because Congress delegated to the Secretary the task of administering the tax laws.[13] Accordingly, taxpayers cannot ignore regulations.

---

[12] Code Sec. 7805(a).

[13] *Portland Cement Company of Utah,* SCt, 81-1 USTC ¶9219, 450 US 156, 101 SCt 1037.

Prior to the U.S. Supreme Court's decision in *Mayo Foundation for Medical Education and Research*,[14] courts were required to give more deference to a legislative regulation than to an interpretive regulation. Now both types of regulations are analyzed under the standards promulgated by *Chevron U.S.A., Inc. v. Natural Resources Defense Council, Inc.*[15]

Under *Chevron*'s two-step test, courts first ask whether Congress has directly addressed the precise question at issue. If Congress' intent is clear, the court must give effect to that intent. If the statute is silent or ambiguous with respect to the specific question, a court will uphold a regulation if it is a reasonable interpretation of the statute and not arbitrary, capricious, or manifestly contrary to the statute.

Going back to the issue regarding the deductibility of deficiency interest discussed earlier in the chapter, the Secretary issued the following temporary regulation shortly after Congress passed TRA 1986 in regards to this matter.

Temp. Reg. §1.163-9T., Personal interest (Temporary)

(a) ***In general.*** —No deduction under any provision of Chapter 1 of the Internal Revenue Code shall be allowed for personal interest paid or accrued during the taxable year by a taxpayer other than a corporation.

(b) ***Personal interest***

(1) ***Definition.*** —For purposes of this section, personal interest is any interest expense other than —

(i) Interest paid or accrued on indebtedness properly allocable (within the meaning of §1.163-8T) to the conduct of a trade or business (other than the trade or business of performing services as an employee),

(ii) Any investment interest (within the meaning of section 163(d)(3)),

(iii) Any interest that is taken into account under section 469 in computing income or loss from a passive activity of the taxpayer,

(iv) Any qualified residence interest (within the meaning of section 163(h)(3) and §1.163-10T), and

(v) Any interest payable under section 6601 with respect to the unpaid portion of the tax imposed by section 2001 for the period during which an extension of time for payment of such tax is in effect under section 6163, 6166, or 6166A (as in effect before its repeal by the Economic Recovery Tax Act of 1981).

(2) ***Interest relating to taxes***

(i) ***In general.*** —Except as provided in paragraph (b)(2)(iii) of this section, personal interest includes interest —

(A) Paid on underpayments of individual Federal, State or local income taxes and on indebtedness used to pay such taxes (within the meaning of §1.163-8T), regardless of the source of the income generating the tax liability;

(B) Paid under section 453C(e)(4)(B) (interest on deferred tax resulting from certain installment sales) and section 1291(c) (interest on deferred tax attributable to passive foreign investment companies); or

(C) Paid by a trust, S corporation, or other pass-through entity on underpayments of State or local income taxes and on indebtedness used to pay such taxes.

(ii) ***Example.*** —A, an individual, owns stock of an S corporation. On its return for 1987, the corporation underreports its taxable income. Consequently, A underreports A's share of that income on A's tax return. In 1989, A pays the resulting deficiency plus interest to the

---

[14] *Mayo Foundation for Medical Education and Research*, U.S., 2011-1 USTC ¶ 50,143, 131 SCt 704 (2011).

[15] *Chevron U.S.A., Inc. v. Natural Resources Defense Council, Inc.*, 467 US 837, 104 SCt 2778 (1984).

Internal Revenue Service. The interest paid by A in 1989 on the tax deficiency is personal interest, notwithstanding the fact that the additional tax liability may have arisen out of income from a trade or business. The result would be the same if A's business had been operated as a sole proprietorship.

(iii) **Certain other taxes.** —Personal interest does not include interest —

(A) Paid with respect to sales, excise and similar taxes that are incurred in connection with a trade or business or an investment activity;

(B) Paid by an S corporation with respect to an underpayment of income tax from a year in which the S corporation was a C corporation or with respect to an underpayment of the taxes imposed by sections 1374 or 1375, or similar provision of State law; or

(C) Paid by a transferee under section 6901 (tax liability resulting from transferred assets), or a similar provision of State law, with respect to a C corporation's underpayment of income tax.

(3) **Cross references.** —See §1.163-8T for rules for determining the allocation of interest expense to various activities. See §1.163-10T for rules concerning qualified residence interest.

* * *

.01 Historical Comment: Adopted 12/21/87 by T.D. 8168 (corrected 3/18/2003).

In Temp. Reg. §1.163-9T(b)(1), the Secretary merely restates the provisions in Code Sec. 163(h). In Temp. Reg. §1.163-9T(b)(2)(i)(A), the Secretary interprets the provisions in Code Sec. 163(h) to mean that all interest paid by an individual taxpayer on a tax deficiency is personal interest, regardless of the source of the deficiency. This language is almost identical to that found in the Blue Book. The example in Temp. Reg. §1.163-9T(b)(2)(ii) makes it absolutely clear from the Secretary's perspective that this rule applies to a sole proprietor. Because this temporary regulation was originally issued prior to November 20, 1988 (see historical comment), it does not expire and continues to have the same authority as a final regulation. Although several taxpayers have challenged the IRS's position on this matter, the courts concluded that the Secretary's interpretation is, in fact, a reasonable interpretation and, therefore, the temporary regulation is valid and must be followed.[16]

¶ 209 IRS Revenue Rulings and Other Pronouncements

In addition to regulations, the IRS issues rulings and other pronouncements that interpret and apply the tax laws to a specific set of facts. Some rulings are published to provide guidance for all taxpayers. Other rulings are issued specifically for a particular taxpayer. IRS pronouncements disseminate information to taxpayers that is useful in helping them understand and comply with the tax laws.

.01 Revenue Rulings

A **revenue ruling** is an official interpretation of the tax laws by the IRS. It represents the IRS's conclusion as to the application of the tax laws to a specific set of facts. For example, expenses incurred to commute between the taxpayer's residence and the place of business or employment are nondeductible personal expenses. In contrast, expenses incurred in traveling from one business location to another are deductible business expenses. In Rev. Rul. 99-7, the IRS considered whether

---

[16] *J.E. Redlark*, CA-9, 98-1 USTC ¶ 50,322, 141 F3d 936, rev'g 106 TC 31, Dec. 51,104; *D. Miller*, CA-8, 95-2 USTC ¶ 50,485, 65 F3d 687; *R.R. Allen, Sr.*, CA-4, 99-1 USTC ¶ 50,470, rev'g DC N.C., 98-1 USTC ¶ 50,196; *D.V. Alfaro*, CA-5, 2003-2 USTC ¶ 50,715, 349 F3d 225; *E.A. Robinson III*, 119 TC 44, Dec. 54,863; *W.C. Fowler*, 84 TCM 281, Dec. 54,864(M), TC Memo. 2002-223.

transportation expenses incurred between the taxpayer's residence and a temporary work location were deductible business expenses or nondeductible commuting expense. The IRS ruled that such costs are deductible business expenses, provided that the nature of the work is temporary. If the nature of the work is not temporary, then the travel to and from the work location constitutes a nondeductible commuting expense.[17]

Code Sec. 1031(a) provides that no gain or loss is recognized when property held for productive use in a trade or business or for investment is exchanged solely for like-kind property to be held either for productive use in a trade or business or for investment. Although the Code provides some general guidance as to what constitutes "like-kind property," it does not specifically say whether contracts of major league baseball players should be considered an exchange of like-kind property. In Rev. Rul. 67-380, the IRS concluded that when a major league baseball club trades one player contract for another player contract, the trade is treated as an exchange of like-kind property.[18]

Revenue rulings do not have the force and effect of Treasury regulations. Nonetheless, IRS personnel are required to follow the position contained in a ruling because it represents the IRS's position on that area of the tax law. Taxpayers may rely on a favorable revenue ruling, but they are not bound by unfavorable conclusions. However, any disputes between the taxpayer and the IRS may need to be eventually resolved by the courts. Therefore, before taxpayers challenge the IRS's position in a revenue ruling, they should have a well-reasoned argument as to why the IRS's interpretation of the tax law is faulty or otherwise not appropriate to follow.

Revenue rulings are published weekly in the *Internal Revenue Bulletin* and until 2009 were included in a semiannually bound publication called the *Cumulative Bulletin*. Weekly issues of the *Internal Revenue Bulletin* since July 7, 2003, are set forth on the IRS's website at *http://www.irs.gov/irb*. Revenue rulings are available from commercial publishers on CD-ROMs or through online subscription services.

The citation for Revenue Ruling 99-7 is:

Rev. Rul. 99-7, IRB 1999-5, 4 or

Rev. Rul. 99-7, 1999-1 CB 361.

From this citation, one can tell that this revenue ruling was the seventh revenue ruling issued in 1999. It begins on page 4 of the fifth issue of the *Internal Revenue Bulletin* published in 1999 and on page 361 of the first volume of the 1999 *Cumulative Bulletin*.

 Planning Pointer: When evaluating a revenue ruling, subsequent legislation, regulations, court decisions, revenue rulings, and revenue procedures must be considered. Revenue rulings may be modified, amplified, superseded, revoked, or made obsolete by subsequent changes in the law and court decisions. Whether a revenue ruling has been modified, amplified, superseded, revoked, or made obsolete by the IRS can be determined by consulting the index to the most recent issue of the *Internal Revenue Bulletin*. Commercial publishers provide citators for determining the current status of a revenue ruling. Neither the IRS publications nor the commercial citators may indicate whether a revenue ruling has been modified, revoked, or made obsolete by subsequent legislation and/or court decisions.

.02 Revenue Procedures

A **revenue procedure** is an official statement by the IRS of a procedure that affects the rights or duties of taxpayers under federal tax law. Whereas a revenue ruling states the IRS's position on a

---

[17] Rev. Rul. 99-7, 1999-1 CB 361.

[18] Rev. Rul. 67-380, 1967-2 CB 291.

tax issue, a revenue procedure provides tax return filing and other instructions concerning an IRS position. For example, each year the IRS issues a revenue procedure listing inflation-adjusted amounts for the next tax year. In Rev. Proc. 2014-61,[19] the IRS sets forth the tax rate tables, standard deduction, and other inflation-adjusted amounts for tax years beginning in 2015. In Rev. Proc. 2006-45,[20] the IRS outlines specific procedures C corporations must follow if they want to change their tax year. Corporations that comply with the requirements set forth in this revenue procedure automatically will be deemed to have received the IRS's consent to change their tax year.

Revenue procedures do not have the force and effect of Treasury regulations, but they may be relied on as authority. However, like a revenue ruling, they may be amplified, modified, superseded, revoked, or made obsolete by subsequent changes in the law or court decisions. When evaluating a revenue procedure, subsequent legislation, regulations, court decisions, revenue rulings, and revenue procedures must be considered.

 Planning Pointer: Whether a revenue procedure has been modified, amplified, superseded, revoked, or made obsolete by the IRS can be determined by consulting the index to the most recent issue of the *Internal Revenue Bulletin*. Commercial publishers provide citators for determining the current status of a revenue procedure. Neither the IRS publications nor the commercial citators may indicate whether a revenue procedure has been modified, revoked, or made obsolete by subsequent legislation and/or court decisions.

Revenue procedures are published weekly in the *Internal Revenue Bulletin* and, until 2009, were published semiannually in the *Cumulative Bulletin*. Weekly issues of the *Internal Revenue Bulletin* since July 7, 2003, are set forth on the IRS's website at *http://www.irs.gov/irb*. Revenue rulings are available from commercial publishers on CD-ROMs or through online subscription services.

The citation for Revenue Procedure 2003-43 is:

Rev. Proc. 2003-43, IRB 2003-23, 998 or

Rev. Proc. 2003-43, 2003-1 CB 998.

This ruling is the forty-third revenue procedure issued in 2003. It begins on page 998 of the twenty-third issue of the *Internal Revenue Bulletin* for 2003 and on page 998 of the first volume of the 2003 *Cumulative Bulletin*.

.03 Written Determinations

The IRS issues four types of **written determinations**, three of which are issued in response to a taxpayer's specific factual situation: private letter rulings, technical advice memoranda, determination letters, and Chief Counsel Advice.

Private letter rulings. A private letter ruling is a written statement that interprets and applies the tax laws to a specific set of facts presented to the IRS by the taxpayer. For example, under Code Sec. 1031(a), no gain or loss is recognized when property held for productive use in a trade or business or for investment is exchanged solely for like-kind property to be held either for productive use in a trade or business or for investment. However, it is not clear whether an exchange of an interest in old-growth timberlands for reproduction timberlands constitutes a like-kind exchange. In IRS Letter Ruling 200541037, the IRS told one taxpayer that such an exchange of property can qualify as a like-kind exchange.

---

[19] Rev. Proc. 2014-61, 2014-47 IRB 860.

[20] Rev. Proc. 2006-45, 2006-2 CB 851, modified and clarified by Rev. Proc. 2007-64, 2007-2 CB 818.

Letter rulings, which are issued by the IRS's Office of Associate Chief Counsel in response to a written request by a taxpayer, establish the federal tax consequences of a particular transaction. Letter rulings can be issued for open fact situations (where the transaction has yet to be completed) or closed transactions (where the transaction has been completed). In either case, the letter ruling is requested prior to the taxpayer's filing of the tax return that involves the transaction. A user fee ($18,000 for most types of requests) is charged for a letter ruling.[21]

 Planning Pointer: Taxpayers can benefit by obtaining a letter ruling because it lets them know in advance the IRS's opinion regarding a proposed transaction. With that information, taxpayers can decide whether or not to proceed with the transaction. When a requested ruling involves an open-fact situation and the position in the letter ruling is not favorable to the taxpayer, the taxpayer has the opportunity to alter the facts in an effort to achieve a more favorable tax position before entering into the transaction. Alternatively, the taxpayer can decide not to pursue the transaction due to the potential unfavorable tax consequences.

A letter ruling is binding on the IRS with respect to a taxpayer's proposed treatment of an item unless there was a misstatement or omission of a material fact or the facts that subsequently develop are materially different from the facts on which the letter ruling was based. Although taxpayers may rely on a letter ruling issued to them personally as precedent, they may not rely on letter rulings issued to other taxpayers. However, taxpayers can use letter rulings issued to other taxpayers to help them determine the correct tax consequences of a transaction. **Precedent** refers to the principle in law of using past decisions to assist in making current decisions. **Tax authority** is established tax law that can be used to help reach a conclusion about a tax issue.

Example 1: A company requested and paid for a letter ruling from the IRS regarding a planned transaction. The company received a favorable private letter ruling. The ruling is an established precedent for the company that requested it. If the company carries out the transaction as it is described in the ruling, it can follow the IRS's advice in the letter ruling and know with absolute certainty that it cannot be challenged by the IRS, even if at some later date the IRS changes its opinion with respect to the issue.

Example 2: Rushlow Supplies, who is not the taxpayer who requested the ruling in Example 1 above, is in the process of researching the tax consequences of a planned transaction. Through its research efforts, it comes across the letter ruling issued to the taxpayer in Example 1. The facts in the letter ruling describe a transaction that is identical to Rushlow's planned transaction. Although the transactions are identical, Rushlow cannot rely on a letter ruling issued to another taxpayer as an established precedent. The ruling can, however, be used as authority by Rushlow. Accordingly, if Rushlow goes through with the transaction and reports the tax consequences as described in the letter ruling, there is no guarantee that the IRS will accept Rushlow's position. To avoid uncertainty in this regard, Rushlow can request that the IRS issue a letter ruling to it based on its specific fact situation.

 Planning Pointer: Although a letter ruling can be used as precedent only by the taxpayer with respect to which it was issued, taxpayers and tax professionals benefit by reading letter rulings because they provide insight as to how the IRS may apply the tax law to taxpayers in similar situations. Taxpayers may rely on a letter ruling to avoid the penalty for a substantial understatement of income tax. (See ¶ 215.02.)

---

[21] Rev. Proc. 2013-1, 2013-1 IRB 1 (Appendix A).

The contents of a letter ruling are made public after information that can identify the taxpayer to whom it was issued has been removed. Letter rulings that have been available to the public since the beginning of 1999 are available in the IRS's Electronic Reading Room at *http://www.irs.gov/uac/Electronic-Reading-Room*. The full texts of letter rulings are available in print in *IRS Letter Rulings Reporter* (published by CCH, a Wolters Kluwer business) and are available from commercial publishers through their online subscription services and CD-ROMs.

Examples of a citation for a letter ruling are:

Ltr. Rul. 200602045 (October 18, 2005)

Pvt. Ltr. Rul. 200602045 (October 18, 2005)

LR 200602045

The "2006" at the beginning of the citation refers to the year that the letter ruling was issued. The next two numbers "02" signify that the letter ruling was issued during the second week of 2006, and the next three digits "045" signify that the letter ruling was the forty-fifth written determination issued that week. The date in parentheses is the date that the letter ruling was written. Prior to 1999, only two numerals were used to signify the year that a letter ruling was issued. For example, IRS Letter Ruling 9628006 was issued in 1996.

Technical advice memorandum. A technical advice memorandum (TAM) is issued by the IRS's Office of Associate Chief Counsel. Field offices request a TAM when an issue arises during an audit or review of a tax return and lack of uniformity exists within the IRS regarding the treatment of the issue. A TAM also may be requested when an issue is unusual or complex enough to warrant consideration. Accordingly, TAMs are issued only on closed transactions. No fee is charged taxpayers for a TAM.

For example, Code Sec. 1031(a) provides that no gain or loss is recognized when property held for productive use in a trade or business or for investment is exchanged solely for like-kind property to be held either for productive use in a trade or business or for investment. In Technical Advice Memorandum 200602034, the IRS rejected the taxpayer's argument that the exchange of any trademark or trade name for another trademark or trade name can qualify as an exchange of like-kind property.

The advice rendered in a TAM represents a final determination of the IRS's position, but only with respect to the specific issue in the specific case for which the advice is issued. The IRS is bound by its conclusion. However, a TAM that is adverse to a taxpayer does not preclude the taxpayer from litigating the issue.

> **Planning Pointer:** TAMs are useful because they permit taxpayers to settle disputes with the IRS during an audit. Although a TAM can be used as precedent only by the taxpayer with respect to which it was issued, taxpayers benefit from TAMs because they provide insight into how the IRS will apply the law to the particular facts presented and other factual circumstances. Taxpayers may rely on a TAM to avoid the penalty for a substantial understatement of income tax. (See ¶ 215.02.)

TAMs that have been made publicly available since the beginning of 1999 can be found at *apps.irs.gov/app/picklist/list/writtenDeterminations.html*. The full texts of TAMs are available in print in *IRS Letter Rulings Reporter* (published by CCH) and are available from commercial publishers through their online subscription services and CD-ROMs.

The citation for a TAM is similar to that of a letter ruling. Examples of a citation for a TAM are:

Tech. Adv. Mem. 200605011 (September 5, 2005)

TAM 200605011 (September 5, 2005)

This TAM was published in 2006, but it was actually written on September 5, 2005. It was issued during the fifth week of 2006 and was the eleventh written determination issued that week. Prior to 1999, only two numerals were used to signify the year that a TAM was issued. For example, Technical Advice Memorandum 9816007 was issued in 1998.

Determination letters. Determination letters differ from the two other types of written determinations because they are issued by an IRS Director rather than by the Office of Associate Chief Counsel. A **determination letter** applies the principles and precedents previously announced by the IRS to a specific set of facts. A determination letter will be issued only when the question presented is specifically answered by a statute, a tax treaty, the regulations, a conclusion stated in a revenue ruling, or an opinion or court decision that represents the IRS's position. A determination letter will not be issued if a question involves a novel issue. A determination letter will be issued only if it concerns a return that has been filed or is required to be filed. The fee for issuing a determination letter ($275[22]) is significantly less than the fee charged for a private letter ruling. A determination letter has the same effect as a letter ruling issued to a taxpayer. It is binding on the IRS and can be relied on only by the taxpayer to whom it is issued.

 Planning Pointer: Because a determination letter is issued only when the law applicable to a given set of facts is settled, it cannot be requested when a taxpayer needs guidance regarding an unsettled area of tax law. Under those circumstances, a taxpayer must request a letter ruling instead of a determination letter. A determination letter usually is requested with respect to the qualification of a retirement plan or tax-exempt organization.

Chief Counsel Advice. Written advice or instructions prepared by the Office of Chief Counsel and issued to field or service center employees of the IRS or Office of Chief Counsel are referred to as **Chief Counsel Advice (CCA)**. Chief Counsel work product formerly was referred to as Field Service Advice (FSA), Service Center Advice (SCA), Technical Assistance, Litigation Guideline Memoranda (LGMs), and various Bulletins.

CCAs that have been made publicly available since December 21, 2000, can be found in the IRS's Electronic Reading Room at *apps.irs.gov/app/picklist/list/writtenDeterminations.html*. The full texts of CCAs are available in print in *IRS Letter Rulings Reporter* (published by CCH) and are available from commercial publishers through their online subscription services and CD-ROMs.

The citation for a CCA is similar to that of a letter ruling. Examples of citations for a CCA are:

Chief Counsel Advice 200946037 (October 26, 2009)

CCA 200946037 (October 26, 2009)

This CCA was issued during the forty-sixth week of 2009 and was the thirty-seventh written determination issued that week.

.04 Other Pronouncements and Publications

In addition to rulings, the IRS provides other guidance to help people comply with the tax laws. These include notices, announcements, news releases, IRS publications, and actions on decision.

---

[22] Rev. Proc. 2013-1, 2013-1 IRB 1 (Appendix A).

Notices. The IRS issues public **notices** to provide substantive interpretations of the Code. They often are issued to provide taxpayers with guidance about recently enacted legislation or to alert taxpayers about pending regulations. For example, in Notice 2014-36, the IRS published inflation adjustment factors and reference prices for computing the renewable electricity production credit for calendar year 2014.[23] In Notice 2014-32, the IRS announced that it would issue regulations relating to the treatment of property used to acquire stock or securities in certain triangular reorganizations involving one or more foreign corporations.[24]

The IRS normally gives notices the same status as revenue rulings and revenue procedures. Taxpayers can rely on a notice as authority unless the notice itself says otherwise. Notices are published in the *Internal Revenue Bulletin*. They also are available from commercial publishers through their online subscription services and CD-ROMs.

The citation for Notice 93-7 is:

Notice 93-7, 1993-5 IRB 13 or

Notice 93-7, 1993-1 CB 297.

This notice was the seventh notice issued in 1993. The full text of this notice can be found on page 13 of the fifth issue of the *Internal Revenue Bulletin* published in 1993, and on page 297 of the first volume of the *Cumulative Bulletin* for 1993.

Announcements and news releases. Periodically, the IRS issues announcements and news releases. **Announcements** inform the public about matters of general interest. They may provide guidance as to both substantive and procedural matters. **News releases** are issued to the media to announce items of general interest. They often are used to announce that an important new revenue ruling or revenue procedure is going to be released and set forth the text of that ruling or procedure. For example, in Announcement 2013-38, the IRS announced that the U.S. and Belgium had entered into a competent authority agreement pursuant to the U.S.-Belgium Income Tax Treaty.[25] In News Release IR-2014-104, the IRS issued cost-of-living adjustments for various tax code provisions. In IR-2014-94, the IRS gave farmers and ranchers forced to sell livestock due to drought an extension of time to replace the livestock and defer tax on any gains from the forced sales.

Announcements are published in the *Internal Revenue Bulletin*. They also are available from commercial publishers through their online subscription services and CD-ROMs. News releases published since 1997 are available on the IRS's website at *http://www.irs.gov/uac/News-Release-and-Fact-Sheet-Archive*. They also are available from commercial publishers through their online subscription services and CD-ROMs.

The citation for IRS Announcement 2004-9 is:

Ann. 2004-9, 2004-6 IRB 441 or

Ann. 2004-9, 2004-1 CB 441.

This announcement was the ninth made in 2004. It can be found on page 441 of the sixth issue of the *Internal Revenue Bulletin* for 2004 and on page 441 of the first volume of the *Cumulative Bulletin* for 2004.

Acquiescence, nonacquiescence, and action on decision. When a court rules against the IRS on one or more issues, the IRS may announce whether it will follow the court's decision in similar situations. When the IRS acquiesces, it is saying that it will follow the court's decision because it has accepted the court's conclusion, but not necessarily the reasons given by the court for its decision. When the IRS issues a nonacquiescence, it is saying that it does not intend to follow the

---

[23] Notice 2014-36, 2014-22 IRB 1058.
[24] Notice 2014-32, 2014-20 IRB 1006.

[25] Announcement 2013-38, 2013-36 IRB 185.

decision in disputes involving other taxpayers with similar situations. A nonacquiescence puts taxpayers on notice that the IRS will continue to challenge the position and force taxpayers in a similar situation to litigate the issue. The IRS is not bound by its announcement of acquiescence or nonacquiescence and may withdraw it at any time.

When the IRS issues an acquiescence or nonacquiescence to a decision, it announces it in an **Action on Decision (AOD)**. AODs issued since 1997 are available on the IRS's website at *apps.irs.gov/app/picklist/list/actionsOnDecisions.html*. The IRS also announces its acquiescence or nonacquiescence to a court's decision at the beginning of *Internal Revenue Bulletins*. AODs also are available from commercial publishers on CD-ROMs and online subscription services.

An example of a citation for an AOD is:

AOD 2003-03 (October 20, 2003).

This citation tells the researcher that this AOD was the third one issued in 2003. It was issued on October 20, 2003.

IRS publications. The IRS publishes various publications for businesses and the general public. These publications are intended to provide guidance to taxpayers on specific tax topics. Examples of IRS publications include Publication 15, Circular E, *Employer's Tax Guide*; Publication 17, *Your Federal Income Tax (For Individuals)*; Publication 334, *Tax Guide for Small Business (For Individuals Who Use Schedule C or C-EZ)*; Publication 535, *Business Expenses*; Publication 538, *Accounting Periods and Methods*; Publication 541, *Partnerships*; and Publication 542, *Corporations*.

Publications contain explanations of the tax rules based on the Code, regulations, rulings, and important court decisions. Sometimes these publications contain information not found elsewhere. Publications can be obtained by telephoning the IRS or going to its website at *www.irs.gov/Forms-&-Pubs*.

JUDICIAL AUTHORITY

When the IRS disputes an item or items reported on the taxpayer's tax return and the matter cannot be resolved through the appeals process within the IRS, the only recourse for the parties is to have the issue resolved by the courts. The federal court system consists of three trial courts and various appellate courts.

When a taxpayer and the IRS disagree about an interpretation of an area of tax law, the taxpayer may challenge the IRS's decision in the U.S. Tax Court, a U.S. district court, or the U.S. Court of Federal Claims. If either the taxpayer or the IRS is not satisfied with a trial court's decision, the litigant can appeal to the appropriate Court of Appeals. Litigants unhappy with a decision made by a Court of Appeals may request that the U.S. Supreme Court review their case. However, review usually is at the discretion of the U.S. Supreme Court, which accepts only a small percentage of the cases it is asked to review.

Judicial decisions represent a third primary source of federal tax law. The decisions made by federal courts provide additional guidance regarding the tax laws and can be used to determine the correct course of action to be taken on the tax return. However, only court decisions for the taxpayer's jurisdiction are binding on taxpayers. Figure 2-2 shows the hierarchy of the various federal courts.

Figure 2-2 Federal Court System

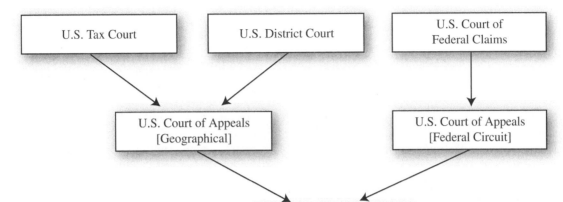

¶ 210 Trial Courts

Disputes between taxpayers and the IRS are first heard in one of three trial courts. Decisions rendered by a trial court can be appealed to the appellate court that has jurisdiction over the court. For example, appeals of decisions rendered by the Tax Court or a district court are heard by the geographical Court of Appeals located in the circuit in which the taxpayer works or resides (see Figure 2-3). The appeal of a decision rendered by the Federal Court of Claims is heard by the Federal Circuit Court of Appeals.

Taxpayers need to know which courts are available to hear their disputes and whether or not any of them have ruled favorably to taxpayers in similar situations. They will want their dispute heard by a court likely to rule in their favor.

.01 U.S. Tax Court

The **U.S. Tax Court** is a special court established to provide a forum to dispute tax deficiencies determined by the IRS. Unlike other federal courts, the Tax Court hears only federal tax cases. Its 19 judges are nominated by the President and confirmed by the U.S. Senate to 15-year terms. The court is located in Washington, D.C., but the judges travel and conduct trials in various cities throughout the United States.

 Spotlight: The U.S. Tax Court was established so that taxpayers could dispute a deficiency assessed against them by the IRS without first having to pay the amount that the IRS claimed they owed. Prior to the establishment of the Tax Court, a taxpayer first had to pay the disputed amount and then file suit for a refund. Not having to pay the disputed amount before appealing the IRS's determination is a big advantage of litigating disputes in the Tax Court. Before litigating a dispute in either of the other two trial courts, a taxpayer must pay the full amount of taxes, interest, and penalties that the IRS has determined that the taxpayer owes before the taxpayer can sue the IRS for a refund.

Example 3: The IRS contends that Hand Shovels, Inc. owes $100,000 in additional income tax and interest because the company improperly characterized certain expenses as currently

deductible business expenses rather than nondeductible capital expenditures. If the company appeals the IRS's determination to the Tax Court, it will not have to pay the $100,000 unless the Tax Court decides that the IRS's decision was correct. If the taxpayer loses in the Tax Court, interest on the $100,000 will be owed to the IRS in addition to the $100,000 currently in dispute. However, before Hand Shovels decides to litigate its dispute in the U.S. district court or U.S. Court of Federal Claims, it first must pay the $100,000. If the IRS loses the case in either the district court or Court of Federal Claims, interest on the $100,000 will be due to Hand Shovels in addition to the $100,000.

The Tax Court issues three types of opinions: regular, memorandum, and summary. Regular opinions are those that the Tax Court considers important or expressive of some new point not previously covered by one of its published opinions. In theory, a memorandum opinion applies well-established principles of law to facts found by the court. However, there are times when memorandum opinions also develop new law. If the taxpayer elects the small tax procedures (available for disputes involving $50,000 or less), a summary opinion is issued by the Tax Court.

Regular and memorandum decisions may be appealed to the Court of Appeals for the geographic area where the dispute was litigated. No appeal may be taken from a Summary opinion issued when a taxpayer has elected to have the case heard in small tax procedures court.[26] Taxpayers may rely on regular and memorandum decisions as precedent but may not treat a summary opinion as a precedent.

Because the Tax Court is a national court, its decisions can be appealed to the Court of Appeals where the taxpayer works or resides (see Figure 2-3). Because decisions of each Court of Appeals are made independent of one another, it is possible that different decisions can be reached by different circuits on the same tax issue. The Tax Court is required to follow decisions made by the Court of Appeals to which its decision can be appealed (the *Golsen* **rule**).[27] As a result, the Tax Court may rule differently on identical factual patterns in two different cases if the taxpayers reside in different circuits and the Courts of Appeals for those circuits have made inconsistent decisions.

The IRS is not required to follow a decision by the Tax Court. The IRS signifies its agreement or disagreement by noting its acquiescence or nonacquiescence to the decision in the *Internal Revenue Bulletin*. The IRS may explain its reasons for acquiescing or not acquiescing to a decision by publishing an Action on Decision (see ¶ 209.04).

Tax Court regular decisions are published by the U.S. Government Printing Office in bound volumes under the title *United States Tax Court Reports* (cited as "TC"). Memorandum and summary opinions are not published by the U.S. Government Printing Office. Regular and memorandum opinions starting September 25, 1995, and summary opinions starting January 1, 2001, are available at the Tax Court's official website: *www.ustaxcourt.gov*. Regular, memorandum, and summary opinions are available in print from commercial publishers (such as CCH and Thomson Reuters/RIA) and as part of CD-ROMs and online subscription services. CCH publishes memorandum opinions under the title *Tax Court Memorandum Decisions* (cited as "TCM"); Thomson Reuters/RIA publishes memorandum opinions under the title *RIA Memorandum Decisions* (cited as "TC Memo").

Citing a Tax Court decision. The citation for the 2005 Tax Court decision involving *Van Der Aa Investments, Inc.* is:

Van Der Aa Investments, Inc., 125 TC 1, Dec. 56,086 (2005).

"Van Der Aa Investments, Inc." is the name of the taxpayer involved in the litigation. "125 TC" signifies that the opinion appears in volume 125 of the *United States Tax Court Reports*. The "1" indicates the page number in the volume where the decision starts. "Dec. 56,086" signifies that the

---

[26] Code Sec. 7463(b).

[27] *J.E. Golsen*, 54 TC 742, Dec. 30,049, aff'd CA-10, 71-2 USTC ¶ 9497, 445 F2d 985.

decision is printed in paragraph 56,086 of CCH's *Tax Court Decisions.* The "2005" is the year that the opinion was filed. Because there is a delay in time between the date a decision is rendered and the date that it appears in the *United States Tax Court Reports*, a temporary citation form is used. An example of that temporary form is: 126 TC No. 6 (2006). This citation indicates that the opinion will be the sixth opinion in volume 126 of the *United States Tax Court Reports.*

The citation for a memorandum decision is slightly different because regular and memorandum decisions are printed by different services. The citation for the 2005 memorandum decision for *S.J. Hauge is:*

> *S.J. Hauge,* 90 TCM 538, Dec. 56,209(M), TC Memo. 2005-276.

The "90 TCM 538" signifies that the opinion begins on page 538 of volume 90 of CCH's *Tax Court Memorandum Decisions.* The "Dec. 56,209(M)" signifies that the opinion is in paragraph 56,209(M) of CCH's *Tax Court Decisions.* The "(M)" signifies that the decision is a Tax Court Memorandum decision. The "TC Memo. 2005-276" signifies that the opinion is printed in paragraph 2005-276 of Thomson Reuters/RIA's *Tax Court Reported and Memorandum Decisions.*

.02 U.S. District Court

Instead of litigating disputes with the IRS in the U.S. Tax Court, taxpayers may pay the amount of taxes, interest, and penalty the IRS says they owe and file a claim for a refund with the U.S. district court where they work or reside. Unlike the Tax Court, **district courts** hear a wide variety of cases; they are not limited to disputes involving federal tax law. Each state has at least one district court.

 Planning Pointer: Taxpayers can request a jury trial when their dispute heard by a U.S. district court involves a question of fact. Juries are not allowed to decide questions of law. The option of a jury trial for tax issues involving questions of fact is not available when taxpayers take their case to the U.S. Tax Court or U.S. Court of Federal Claims.

Example 4: On October 18, 2005, the IRS published proposed regulations reversing its previous position that an owner of a single-member limited liability company (LLC) is personally liable for the company's employment taxes. A taxpayer argued that this regulation should be applied retroactively to him and his single-member LLC. In *E. Kandi,*[28] the U.S. district court for the Western District of Washington decided that the IRS did not abuse its discretion by refusing to apply the proposed regulation retroactively.

Decisions by a U.S. district court may be appealed to the Court of Appeals for the geographic area of the district court. The IRS is not required to follow a decision by a U.S. district court with respect to taxpayers other than those involved in the decision made by the U.S. district court. The IRS may signify its agreement or disagreement by noting its acquiescence or nonacquiescence to the decision in the *Internal Revenue Bulletin.* The IRS may explain its reasons for acquiescing or not acquiescing to a decision by publishing an Action on Decision (see ¶ 209.04).

Many of the decisions made by U.S. district courts are reported in a series of books titled *Federal Supplement.* More recent cases are reported in the third series of the *Federal Supplement.* Tax decisions made by district courts are reported by CCH in its *United States Tax Cases* (cited as "USTC") and by Thomson Reuters/RIA in its *American Federal Tax Reports* (cited as "AFTR").

Citing a district court decision. An example of a citation for the 2000 U.S. district court case of *H.E. Butt Grocery Co.* is:

> *H.E. Butt Grocery Co.,* DC Tex., 2000-2 USTC ¶ 50,649, 108 FSupp2d 709, 86 AFTR2d 2000-5209.

"DC Tex." signifies that the court was a district court for Texas. "2000-2 USTC ¶ 50,649" signifies that the case is published in paragraph 50,649 of the second volume of the *United States Tax Cases* for the

---

[28] *E. Kandi,* DC Wash., 2006-1 USTC ¶ 50,231.

year 2000. The "108 FSupp2d 709" signifies that the first page of the case is located on page 709 of volume 108 of the *Federal Supplement, Second Series*. "86 AFTR2d 2000-5209" signifies that the case has been published at 2000-5209 in volume 86 of the *American Federal Tax Reports 2ⁿᵈ Series*.

.03 U.S. Court of Federal Claims

To have their case heard by the U.S. Court of Federal Claims, taxpayers must pay the amount of taxes, interest, and penalties the IRS says they owe and file a claim for a refund. The court is located in Washington, D.C.; however, its judges periodically hear cases in major cities around the country.

The **U.S. Court of Federal Claims** was created by Congress solely to hear monetary claims against the United States based on the U.S. Constitution, federal statutes, executive regulations, and contracts with the United States. Many cases before the court involve tax refund suits. The U.S. Court of Federal Claims consists of 16 judges nominated by the President and confirmed by the Senate for a term of 15 years.

Decisions by the U.S. Court of Federal Claims may be appealed to the Federal Circuit Court of Appeals. That is the Court of Appeals whose decisions the U.S. Court of Federal Claims must follow, even when the U.S. Court of Federal Claims holds hearings in an area governed by a different (geographical) Court of Appeals.

The IRS is not required to follow a decision by the U.S. Court of Federal Claims with respect to taxpayers other than those involved in decisions made by the U.S. Court of Federal Claims. The IRS may signify its agreement or disagreement by noting its acquiescence or nonacquiescence to the decision in the *Internal Revenue Bulletin*. The IRS may explain why it is acquiescing or not acquiescing to a decision in an Action on Decision (see ¶ 209.04).

Published decisions dating from January 6, 1997, are available on the court's website at *http://www.uscfc.uscourts.gov/aggregator/sources/8*. Unpublished decisions dating from February 18, 2005, can be found at *http://www.uscfc.uscourts.gov/aggregator/sources/10*. Thomson Reuters/RIA publishes court decisions since 1992 in its *Federal Claims Reporter* (cited as "FedCl") and earlier decisions (when the court was named the "Claims Court") in its *U.S. Claims Court Reporter* (cited as "ClsCt").

Decisions by the court's predecessor, the Court of Claims, were published by the U.S. Government Printing Office in its *U.S. Court of Claims* Reports (cited as "CtCls"). West Publishing Co. published decisions of the Court of Claims from May 1960 through establishment of the Claims Court in its *Federal Reporter 2d* Series (cited as "F2d") and published earlier decisions in its *Federal Supplement* (cited as "FSupp"). Tax decisions made by the U.S. Court of Federal Claims and Court of Claims are reported by CCH in its *United States Tax Cases* (cited as "USTC") and by Thomson Reuters/RIA in its *American Federal Tax Reports* (cited as "AFTR").

Citing a Court of Federal Claims decision. The citation for the 2001 Court of Federal Claims of *Marsh & McLennan Companies, Inc.* is:

Marsh & McLennan Companies, Inc., FedCl, 2001-2 USTC ¶ 50,575, 50 FedCl 140, 88 AFTR2d 2001-5381.

The "FedCl" signifies that this is a Court of Federal Claims case. The "2001-2 USTC ¶ 50,575" signifies that the case is published in paragraph 50,575 of the second volume of the *United States Tax Cases* for the year 2001. The "50 FedCl 140" signifies that the first page of the case is on page 140 of volume 50 of the *Federal Claims Reporter*. The "88 AFTR2d 2001-5381" signifies that the case appears at 2001-5381 in volume 88 of the *American Federal Tax Reports, 2ⁿᵈ Series*.

¶ 211 Appellate Courts

There are two types of appellate courts to which trial court decisions can be appealed. The appellate court having jurisdiction over the trial court's decision is the court to which the case can be appealed. Decisions made by the U.S. Tax Court or a U.S. district court may be appealed to the **Court of Appeals** for the geographic area of the trial court. Appeals from the U.S. Court of Federal Claims are made to the Federal Circuit Court of Appeals. Review usually is limited to legal, not factual, issues.

.01 Courts of Appeals

There are 13 Courts of Appeals. Twelve cover specific geographic areas; the thirteenth (the Federal Circuit) hears particular types of cases. The geographical location of these courts, as well as the states that each court covers is depicted in Figure 2-3.

Figure 2-3 Geographical Courts of Appeals

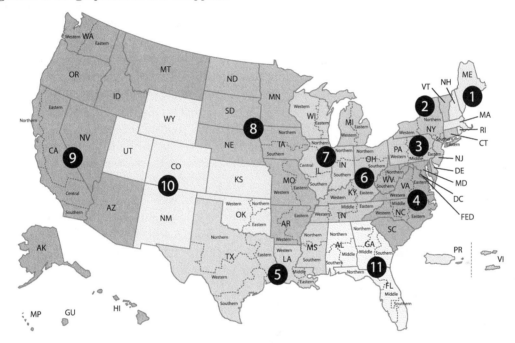

First Circuit:	Maine, Massachusetts, New Hampshire, Rhode Island, and Puerto Rico
Second Circuit:	Connecticut, New York, and Vermont
Third Circuit:	Delaware, New Jersey, Pennsylvania, and the Virgin Islands
Fourth Circuit:	Maryland, North Carolina, South Carolina, Virginia, and West Virginia
Fifth Circuit:	Louisiana, Mississippi, and Texas
Sixth Circuit:	Kentucky, Michigan, Ohio, and Tennessee
Seventh Circuit:	Illinois, Indiana, and Wisconsin
Eighth Circuit:	Arkansas, Iowa, Minnesota, Missouri, Nebraska, North Dakota, and South Dakota
Ninth Circuit:	Alaska, Arizona, California, Hawaii, Idaho, Montana, Nevada, Oregon, and Washington
Tenth Circuit:	Colorado, Kansas, New Mexico, Oklahoma, Utah, and Wyoming
Eleventh Circuit:	Alabama, Florida, and Georgia
D.C. Circuit:	District of Columbia

Source: *http://www.uscourts.gov/court_locator.aspx*

Decisions made by the geographical Court of Appeals for the area in which the taxpayer resides or does business establish precedent for the taxpayer. The IRS is required to follow a decision by a Court of Appeals, but only in the states within that court's jurisdiction. When the IRS acquiesces or nonacquiesces to a court decision, it notes its acquiescence or nonacquiescence in the *Internal Revenue Bulletin*. It explains its reasons for acquiescing or not acquiescing to a decision in an Action on Decision (see ¶ 209.04).

Example 5:   Structural Clay, Inc. conducts its business in Illinois. During the year, Structural paid to have mold removed from one of its buildings. Structural is hoping that it can deduct these costs in the current year, rather than capitalize them. While researching this issue, it found a decision by the Ninth Circuit Court that disagreed with its planned tax treatment of its expenditures. However, a decision by the Seventh Circuit agreed that the costs could be expensed currently. Because Illinois is located in the Seventh Circuit, the Seventh Circuit would have jurisdiction over Structural's case. Therefore, Structural Clay can use that case as precedent and deduct the expenses in the current year.

Example 6:   Assume the same facts as in Example 5, except that Structural Clay is located in Texas, which is located in the Fifth Circuit. Because neither of these cases establishes precedent for Structural, both cases can be used as authority in determining the course of action Structural should take with respect to these costs.

Example 7:   Under the Code's all-inclusive approach to defining income, self-employment earnings are subject to income tax. In addition, these earnings are subject to self-employment taxes. Usually rental income from real estate is not considered self-employment income; however, an exception is made for farm rental income if the lessor materially participates in farm production. In *M. McNamara*,[29] the Eighth Circuit decided that the IRS must prove a nexus between the rents received by a taxpayer and the arrangement that requires the taxpayer's material participation. In AOD 2003-03, the IRS announced that it would not acquiesce to *McNamara*. Therefore, the IRS is bound by the Eighth Circuit's decision in the states making up the Eighth Circuit (Arkansas, Missouri, Iowa, Minnesota, Nebraska, South Dakota, and North Dakota), and, accordingly, *McNamara* establishes precedent to taxpayers located in those states. For taxpayers living in states outside of the Eighth Circuit, the appellate court's decision in *McNamara* can be used as authority for avoiding substantial understatement penalties. (See ¶ 215.) However, the IRS has put these taxpayers on notice that it intends to exercise its right to challenge the issue and litigate again in another circuit.

Federal Circuit Court of Appeals. The Federal Circuit Court of Appeals hears appeals of tax and other cases from the U.S. Court of Federal Claims. It also hears appeals from a variety of other courts and government agencies.

Decisions made by a Court of Appeals carry great weight because each Court of Appeals is independent from the others and can be overruled only by the U.S. Supreme Court, which agrees to hear very few tax cases each year. The Federal Circuit Court of Appeals is a national court. Consequently, all taxpayers that choose to have their tax case heard initially by the U.S. Court of Federal Claims can use decisions rendered by the Federal Circuit Court of Appeals as established precedent.

---

[29] *M. McNamara*, CA-8, 2001-1 USTC ¶ 50,188, 236 F3d 410.

Decisions made by each U.S. Circuit Court of Appeals are reported on each court's website. Those sites are:

1st Circuit: *www.ca1.uscourts.gov*

2nd Circuit: *www.ca2.uscourts.gov*

3rd Circuit: *www.ca3.uscourts.gov*

4th Circuit: *www.ca4.uscourts.gov*

5th Circuit: *www.ca5.uscourts.gov*

6th Circuit: *www.ca6.uscourts.gov/internet/default.html*

7th Circuit: *www.ca7.uscourts.gov*

8th Circuit: *www.ca8.uscourts.gov*

9th Circuit: *www.ca9.uscourts.gov*

10th Circuit: *www.ca10.uscourts.gov*

11th Circuit: *www.ca11.uscourts.gov*

D.C. Circuit: *www.dccourts.gov/internet/appellate/main.jsf*

Federal Circuit: *www.cafc.uscourts.gov*

Decisions also are published in a series of volumes titled *Federal Reporter* (Thomson Reuters/ West). Tax decisions made by the U.S. Courts of Appeals are reported by CCH in its *United States Tax Cases* (cited as "USTC") and by Thomson Reuters/RIA in its *American Federal Tax Reports* (cited as "AFTR").

Citing an appellate court decision. The citation for the 2001 decision by the Eighth Circuit Court of Appeals in *M. McNamara* is:

M. McNamara, CA-8, 2001-1 USTC ¶ 50,188, 236 F3d 410, 87 AFTR2d 2001-310.

The "CA-8" signifies that the case was decided by the Eighth Circuit Court of Appeals. The "2001-1 USTC ¶ 50,188" signifies that the case is published in paragraph 50,188 of the first volume of the *United States Tax Cases* for the year 2001. The "236 F3d 410" signifies that the first page of the case is published on page 410 of volume 236 of the *Federal Reporter, Third Series.* The "87 AFTR2d 2001-310" signifies that the case has been published at 2001-310 in volume 87 of the *American Federal Tax Reports 2nd Series.*

 Planning Pointer: The appellate court having jurisdiction over the trial court's decision is the court to which the case will be appealed. Accordingly, when selecting a trial court to settle a dispute, taxpayers need to consider decisions made by the appellate court to which the decision will be appealed.

.02 The Supreme Court

The losing party of an appellate court decision may request that the **U.S. Supreme Court** hear an appeal of that decision. However, the U.S. Supreme Court grants very few of such requests. The U.S. Supreme Court will usually review a decision made by a U.S. Court of Appeals only if the decision conflicts with a decision made by another U.S. Court of Appeals or the U.S. Supreme Court itself or the Supreme Court justices decide that the issue warrants their attention.

Example 8: Code Sec. 1221 defines a "capital asset" as property held by a taxpayer (whether or not connected with the taxpayer's trade or business) other than property that falls within one of the enumerated exceptions (e.g., for inventory). Arkansas Best Corporation, a diversified holding company, purchased shares of stock in the National Bank of Commerce to protect its reputation by giving the bank additional capital it needed to prevent its failure. It later sold the stock at a loss. Arkansas Best treated the loss as an ordinary loss rather than as a capital loss and deducted the loss in full on its tax return.

(Capital losses would have been deductible only to the extent of Arkansas Best's capital gains.) The IRS disallowed the deduction.

The U.S. Tax Court agreed with the taxpayer that the company's loss on the sale of the stock was an ordinary loss and decided that stock acquired for a business purpose was not a capital asset. The Eighth Circuit reversed the Tax Court's decision on the ground that the company's motivation for acquiring the stock was irrelevant to the determination whether the stock was a capital asset.[30] The U.S. Supreme Court agreed with the Eighth Circuit and ruled that the exceptions to the general rule regarding what constitutes a capital asset are exclusive, not just illustrative.[31] This standard now provides the final say on how capital assets are defined.

A decision by the U.S. Supreme Court is the final authority as to the interpretation of the language in the Code. Both taxpayers and the IRS must follow decisions rendered by the Supreme Court until Congress enacts legislation that overrules the decision. For example, in *D.A. Gitlitz,* the U.S. Supreme Court held that discharge of indebtedness income excluded from an S corporation's gross income passes through to S corporation shareholders and increases their basis in their stock.[32] When Congress enacted the Job Creation and Worker Assistance Act of 2002 (P.L. 107-147), it amended Code Sec. 108 to overrule the Supreme Court's decision.

U.S. Supreme Court decisions are reported on the court's website at *http://www.supremecourt.gov.* They are also published in bound volumes. The official reporter of U.S. Supreme Court decisions is *U.S. Reports* (cited as "US"). Decisions are also reported in the *Supreme Court Reporter* (cited as "SCt") and *Lawyers' Edition* (cited as "LEd"). Supreme Court tax cases are also reported in the *United States Tax Cases* (CCH) (cited as " USTC ") and the *American Federal Tax Reports* (Thomson Reuters/RIA) (cited as "AFTR").

Citing a Supreme Court decision. An example of a citation for the Supreme Court case of *D.A. Gitlitz* is:

D.A. Gitlitz, SCt, 2001-1 USTC ¶ 50,147, 531 US 206, 121 SCt 701, 148 LE2d 613, 87 AFTR2d 2001-417.

The "SCt" signifies that this is a Supreme Court decision. The "2001-1 USTC ¶ 50,147" signifies that this case is reported in the first volume of the *United States Tax Cases* for the year 2001 beginning at paragraph 50,147. The "531 US 206" signifies that this case is reported in Volume 531 of the *U.S. Reports* beginning on page 206. The "121 SCt 701" signifies that this case can be found in Volume 121 of the *Supreme Court Reporter* beginning on page 701. The "148 LEd2d 613" signifies that this case can be found beginning on page 613 in Volume 148 of the *Lawyers' Edition, Second Series.* The "87 AFTR2d 2001-417" is reported at 2001-417 in volume 87 of the *American Federal Tax Reports 2nd Series.*

RESEARCHING THE TAX LAW

Structuring a transaction to minimize the amount of taxes that a taxpayer has to pay is the goal of tax planning. Eliminating taxes permanently is always a top priority, but being able to defer the tax also is valuable because deferral can provide taxpayers with temporary use of the tax dollars saved to spend or invest. Depending on the circumstances surrounding the taxpayer's situation, expenditures can either be currently deducted, deducted over a number of years, deducted at some later point in time, or never deducted.

---

[30] *Arkansas Best Corp.*, CA-8, 86-2 USTC ¶ 9671, 800 F2d 215, rev'g, *Arkansas Best Corp.*, 83 TC 640, Dec. 41,581 (1984).

[31] *Arkansas Best Corp.*, SCt, 88-1 USTC ¶ 9210, 485 US 212, 108 SCt 971.

[32] *D.A. Gitlitz*, SCt, 2001-1 USTC ¶ 50,147, 531 US 206, 121 SCt 701.

¶ 212 Tax Planning vs. Compliance Research

Business decisions should be made only after thoroughly considering the tax consequences of the transaction. When tax research is conducted on a proposed transaction, it is known as tax planning. **Tax planning research** involves researching an "open fact" situation (i.e., a transaction that has not yet occurred and can be modified to achieve optimal tax savings). **Tax compliance research**, on the other hand, involves researching a "closed fact" situation (i.e., a transaction that already has taken place and needs to be reported properly for tax purposes). Whenever possible, businesses should strive to conduct tax planning research because it gives them flexibility to make changes. However, understanding how to conduct tax research, whether it is in a planning or compliance setting, is necessary in order to make the best decisions.

¶ 213 Tax Evasion vs. Tax Avoidance

A legitimate goal of tax planning is **tax avoidance** (i.e., taking advantage of legal opportunities to reduce tax liability). Sometimes these legal opportunities to reduce tax liability are referred to as "tax loopholes," but that term more often has the negative connotation of an unintentional omission or ambiguity in the tax law that permits a reduction in tax liability not intended by Congress. Tax avoidance should be distinguished from **tax evasion**, which involves illegally paying less federal income tax than one should.

Example 9: Water Colors, Inc. had its manufacturing plant destroyed by a hurricane. It receives $500,000 of insurance proceeds. The company knows that if it does nothing it will have to report $400,000 of gain on the involuntary conversion in its taxable income. However, because of special tax rules governing involuntary conversions, the company can legally avoid having to recognize any of that gain by timely reinvesting the $500,000 in another manufacturing plant.

Example 10: Howden Wired Music reduces its tax liability by taking deductions for expenditures it never made and by not reporting income that it received during the year. Howden is guilty of tax evasion and may be subject to civil and criminal penalties.

¶ 214 Tax Planning Strategies

Typical tax planning strategies involve deferring receipt of income, accelerating deductions, and obtaining credits. However, sometimes businesses can benefit by accelerating the receipt of income and deferring deductions.

Example 11: Ferucci Trailers, Inc. is in the 34-percent tax bracket. If it can defer $10,000 of income, it can save $3,400 ($10,000 × 34%) in federal income tax for the year. If it can take an additional $10,000 in deductions for the year, it also can save $3,400 in federal income taxes.

Example 12: Sopko Tube Fittings, Inc. expects to be in the 25-percent tax bracket for its current tax year but in the 39-percent tax bracket for its next tax year. If the company can accelerate $10,000 of income into the current year, it will pay $2,500 ($10,000 × 25%) of taxes on its income instead of $3,900 ($10,000 × 39%) if it waits to pay tax on the income until next year. The tax savings to Sopko would be $1,400 ($3,900 – $2,500).

Example 13: Assume the same facts as in Example 12, except that Sopko has a choice between spending $20,000 on business expenses during its current tax year or delaying its expenditures until its next tax year. If it makes those expenditures during its current tax year, it will save $5,000 ($20,000 × 25%) in federal income taxes. If it delays making those expenditures until its next tax year, it will save $7,800 ($20,000 × 39%). By delaying those expenditures, the company will save $2,800 ($7,800 – $5,000) in federal income taxes. However, it will have to wait an entire year to realize the $7,800 in tax savings.

Example 14: Geffers Venetian Blinds, Inc. had a $10,000 passive activity loss for its tax year. Pursuant to Code Sec. 469, such losses can be deducted only against income from passive activities. If the company can plan to recognize up to $10,000 in passive activity income (e.g., by selling its interest in a passive activity), the company can take advantage of the loss and not be taxed on any of the passive activity income that it recognizes.

¶ 215 Ethical and Professional Standards

Taxpayers and tax professionals must adhere to specific standards imposed by the federal government and other taxing authorities when they personally take, or advise someone to take, a tax position. If these standards are not met, significant penalties can be imposed on the taxpayer, the tax professional, or both. In addition, professional organizations, such as the American Institute of Certified Public Accountants, impose their own set of professional standards to which tax professionals must adhere.

.01 Professional Standards for Tax Research

The American Institute of Certified Public Accountants (AICPA) has adopted Statements on Standards for Tax Services that are enforceable against members of the AICPA. The AICPA's Statement on Standards for Tax Services No. 1, Tax Return Positions, sets forth reporting and disclosure standards to be followed when recommending a tax return position or preparing or signing a tax return. These standards apply if the applicable taxing authority has no written standards with respect to recommending a tax return position or preparing or signing a tax return or has standards but its standards are lower.[33] Among those standards are:

- As a general rule, a CPA should not recommend a tax return position or prepare or sign a tax return taking a position unless the CPA has a good-faith belief that the position has at least a realistic possibility of being sustained administratively or judicially on its merits if challenged (the "realistic possibility of success standard").[34]

- A CPA may recommend a tax return position that does not satisfy the realistic possibility of success standard if the CPA concludes that there is a reasonable basis for the position (the "reasonable basis standard") and advises the taxpayer to appropriately disclose the position.[35]

- A CPA may prepare or sign a tax return reflecting a position that does not satisfy the realistic possibility of success standard if the CPA concludes that there is a reasonable basis for the position and appropriately discloses the position.[36]

- A CPA should not recommend a tax return position or prepare or sign a tax return reflecting a tax return position if the CPA knows that the position exploits the audit selection process of a taxing authority or serves as a mere arguing position advanced solely to obtain leverage in negotiations with a taxing authority.[37]

- When recommending a tax return position or when preparing or signing a tax return taking a tax position, a CPA should advise the taxpayer regarding potential penalties for taking the position and any opportunity to avoid such penalties by disclosing the position.[38]

To satisfy the realistic possibility of success standard, there must be approximately a 33 percent likelihood that the position will be upheld on its merits if challenged.[39] The realistic possibility of

---

[33] Statement on Standards for Tax Services No. 1, Tax Return Positions, paragraph 5.

[34] Statement on Standards for Tax Services No. 1, Tax Return Positions, paragraph 5.

[35] Statement on Standards for Tax Services No. 1, Tax Return Positions, paragraph 5.

[36] Statement on Standards for Tax Services No. 1, Tax Return Positions, paragraph 5.

[37] Statement on Standards for Tax Services No. 1, Tax Return Positions, paragraph 7.

[38] Statement on Standards for Tax Services No. 1, Tax Return Positions, paragraph 6.

[39] Interpretation No. 1-1, "Reporting and Disclosure Standards" of Statement on Standards for Tax Services No. 1, Tax Return Positions, preface.

success standard is lower than the substantial authority and more-likely-than-not standards (each discussed in ¶ 215.02) but higher than the reasonable basis standard.[40]

Example 15: Teasdale Products, Inc. engaged in a transaction that has been adversely affected by a new Code provision that is clearly drafted, unambiguous, and constitutional. However, the legislative history for the Code provision specifically addresses the company's situation and supports a position favorable to the company. Because the legislative history specifically addresses the company's situation, taking a position based on that legislative history can satisfy the realistic possibility of success standard.[41]

Example 16: Assume that the facts are the same as in Example 15 except that the legislative history for the new Code provision can be interpreted as providing some authority or evidence supporting the company's position but does not specifically address the company's situation. Because the legislative history does not specifically address the company's situation, a position based on that legislative history cannot satisfy the realistic possibility of success standard (but may be able to satisfy the reasonable basis standard).[42]

Example 17: Disanto Electronics, Inc. is affected by a new Code provision that is widely believed to contain a drafting error. Legislation correcting the Code provision has been introduced, and the IRS has issued a pronouncement interpreting the Code provision in accordance with the proposed legislation. Taking a position based on either the new Code provision or the IRS pronouncement can satisfy the realistic possibility of success standard.[43]

Example 18: Assume that the facts are the same as in Example 17 but that the IRS has not issued a pronouncement interpreting the Code provision in accordance with the legislation proposing a correction. Under such circumstances, only a position based on the existing Code language can satisfy the realistic possibility of success standard.[44]

Example 19: Brutger Machines, Inc. asked its adviser whether it can currently deduct an expenditure or whether it has to capitalize the expenditure and expense it over a number of years. The adviser found a revenue ruling requiring taxpayers to capitalize that type of expenditure but also found a U.S. Tax Court decision permitting taxpayers to currently deduct that type of expenditure. The realistic possibility of success standard can be met by either tax return position.[45]

To satisfy the reasonable basis standard, a CPA must reasonably base a position on one or more authorities (taking the relevance and persuasiveness of those authorities into account).[46] This standard, which is lower than the realistic possibility of success standard but significantly higher than the not frivolous or not patently improper standard, generally is considered satisfied if there is approximately a 20 percent likelihood that the position will be upheld on its merits if challenged.[47] The standard is not satisfied by a position that is merely arguable or merely a colorable claim.[48]

---

[40] Interpretation No. 1-1, "Reporting and Disclosure Standards" of Statement on Standards for Tax Services No. 1, Tax Return Positions, paragraph 8.

[41] Interpretation No. 1-1, "Reporting and Disclosure Standards" of Statement on Standards for Tax Services No. 1, Tax Return Positions, paragraphs 32 and 33.

[42] Interpretation No. 1-1, "Reporting and Disclosure Standards" of Statement on Standards for Tax Services No. 1, Tax Return Positions, paragraphs 30 and 31.

[43] Interpretation No. 1-1, "Reporting and Disclosure Standards" of Statement on Standards for Tax Services No. 1, Tax Return Positions, paragraphs 34 and 35.

[44] Interpretation No. 1-1, "Reporting and Disclosure Standards" of Statement on Standards for Tax Services No. 1, Tax Return Positions, paragraphs 36 and 37.

[45] Interpretation No. 1-1, "Reporting and Disclosure Standards" of Statement on Standards for Tax Services No. 1, Tax Return Positions, paragraphs 46 and 47.

[46] Interpretation No. 1-1, "Reporting and Disclosure Standards" of Statement on Standards for Tax Services No. 1, Tax Return Positions, preface.

[47] Interpretation No. 1-1, "Reporting and Disclosure Standards" of Statement on Standards for Tax Services No. 1, Tax Return Positions, preface.

[48] Interpretation No. 1-1, "Reporting and Disclosure Standards" of Statement on Standards for Tax Services No. 1, Tax Return Positions, preface.

Example 20: Perrella Notions, Inc. engaged in a transaction adversely affected by a new Code provision. Prior law was favorable to the company. The company and its adviser both believe that the new Code provision is unfair to taxpayers in the company's situation. However, the Code provision is clearly drafted, unambiguous, and constitutional. Because the Code provision is clear, unambiguous, and constitutional, a position contrary to the Code provision would ordinarily be considered frivolous and not satisfy the reasonable basis standard.[49]

A CPA has no obligation to communicate with a taxpayer when subsequent developments affect advice previously provided with respect to significant matters unless the CPA is assisting the taxpayer in implementing procedures or plans associated with the advice or the CPA has undertaken such an obligation by specific agreement.[50]

.02 Federal Standards for Tax Research

Taxpayers who underpay their income tax will be subject to the accuracy-related penalty if they have a substantial understatement of income tax attributable to an undisclosed item and they do not have substantial authority for their tax treatment of the item.[51] If the substantial understatement is attributable to a disclosed item, taxpayers will be subject to the penalty if they do not have a reasonable basis for their tax treatment of the item.

Reasonable cause exception. No penalty will be imposed if there was reasonable cause for the underpayment and the taxpayer acted in good faith.[52]

Adequate disclosure. Each year the IRS issues a revenue procedure prescribing how to adequately disclose an item on an income tax return. If the revenue procedure does not include an item, disclosure is adequate with respect to the item only if made on a properly completed IRS Form 8275 (Disclosure Statement) or IRS Form 8275-R (Regulation Disclosure Statement).[53]

Substantial authority is an objective standard that is less stringent than the "more-likely-than-not" standard, but more rigorous than the "reasonable basis" standard.[54] Whether substantial authority exists for a position taken on a tax return is made based on all relevant sources of primary authority. The probability that the taxpayer's return will be audited is irrelevant for purposes of determining whether substantial authority exists.

As part of its standards of practice for tax professionals,[55] the IRS has provided standards applicable to those conducting tax research. Best practices require the following:[56]

- Establishing the facts, determining which facts are relevant, evaluating the reasonableness of any assumptions or representations, relating the applicable law (including potentially applicable judicial doctrines) to the relevant facts, and arriving at a conclusion supported by the law and the facts.

- Advising the client regarding the import of the conclusions reached (including, for example, whether a taxpayer may avoid accuracy-related penalties under the Code if the taxpayer acts in reliance on the advice).

A tax return preparer can be penalized for preparing a return or claim of refund that understates tax liability if the understatement is due to an **unreasonable position** that the tax return preparer knew (or reasonably should have known) about.[57]

---

[49] Interpretation No. 1-1, "Reporting and Disclosure Standards" of Statement on Standards for Tax Services No. 1, Tax Return Positions, paragraphs 28 and 29.

[50] Statement on Standards for Tax Services No. 7, Form and Content of Advice to Taxpayers, paragraph 4.

[51] Code Sec. 6662.

[52] Code Sec. 6664(c)(1).

[53] Reg. § 1.6662-4(f)(2).

[54] Reg. § 1.6662-4(d).

[55] Treasury Department Circular No. 230 (31 CFR pt. 10).

[56] 31 CFR § 10.33(a).

[57] Code Sec. 6694(a).

Reasonable cause exception. No penalty will be imposed if there was reasonable cause for the underpayment and the preparer acted in good faith.

What constitutes an "unreasonable position". Three different standards are used to determine whether a position is "unreasonable." Which standard applies varies depending on whether or not the position has been adequately disclosed and whether or not the position is with respect to a tax shelter or reportable transaction to which Code Sec. 6662A applies:

- If a position is adequately disclosed and is not with respect to a tax shelter or reportable transaction to which Code Sec. 6662A applies, it will be considered unreasonable unless the preparer had a reasonable basis for it (*reasonable basis standard*).

- If the position is with respect to a tax shelter or reportable transaction to which Code Sec. 6662A applies, it will be considered unreasonable unless it was reasonable for the preparer to believe that it would more likely than not be sustained on its merits (*more-likely-than-not standard*).

- If the position is not adequately disclosed and is not with respect to a tax shelter or reportable transaction to which Code Sec. 6662A applies, the position will be considered unreasonable unless there is or was substantial authority for it (*substantial authority standard*).

How to satisfy each of the standards used to determine whether a position is "unreasonable". The most difficult to satisfy of the three standards used to determine whether a position is "unreasonable" is the more-likely-than-not standard. The least difficult to satisfy is the reasonable basis standard.

- **Reasonable Basis Standard.** The reasonable basis standard is less stringent than the substantial authority standard and the more-likely-than-not standard but is significantly higher than not frivolous or not patently improper.[58] The reasonable basis standard generally is considered satisfied if there is a 20 percent or greater likelihood that a position will be upheld on its merits if challenged.[59] It is not satisfied by a position that is merely arguable or colorable. If a position is reasonably based on one or more of the authorities set forth in Reg. § 1.6662-4(d)(3)(iii), the position generally will satisfy the reasonable basis standard.

- **Substantial Authority Standard.** The substantial authority standard is an objective standard involving an analysis of the law and application of the law to the relevant facts.[60] It is less stringent than the more-likely-than-not standard but more stringent that the reasonable basis standard. There is substantial authority for the tax treatment of an item only if the weight of authorities supporting the treatment is substantial in relation to the weight of authorities supporting contrary treatment. The substantial authority standard generally is considered satisfied if there is a 40 percent or greater likelihood that a position will be upheld on its merits if challenged.[61] Conclusions reached in treatises, legal periodicals, or opinions rendered by tax professionals are not authority, but authorities used to form those conclusions may be. The possibility that a return will not be audited or, if audited, that an item will not be raised on audit, is not relevant in determining whether the substantial authority standard has been met.

- **More-Likely-Than-Not Standard.** The more-likely-than-not standard is satisfied if the tax return preparer analyzes the pertinent facts and authorities and reasonably concludes in good faith that a position has a greater than 50 percent likelihood of being sustained on its merits.[62] The authorities that can be considered are listed in Reg. § 1.6662-4(d)(3). The

---

[58] Reg. § 1.6694-2(d)(2); Notice 2009-5, 2009-3 IRB 309.

[59] Joint Committee on Taxation, Study of Present-Law Penalty and Interest Provisions as Required by Section 3801 of the Internal Revenue Service Restructuring and Reform Act of 1998 (Including Provisions Relating to Corporate Tax Shelters) (JCS-3-99) (July 22, 1999), Vol. 1, p. 160.

[60] Notice 2009-5, 2009-3 IRB 309.

[61] Joint Committee on Taxation, Study of Present-Law Penalty and Interest Provisions as Required by Section 3801 of the Internal Revenue Service Restructuring and Reform Act of 1998 (Including Provisions Relating to Corporate Tax Shelters) (JCS-3-99) (July 22, 1999), Vol. 1, p. 160.

[62] Reg. § 1.6694-2(b)(1), (2).

possibility that the position will not be challenged by the IRS (e.g., because the return may not be audited or because the issue may not be raised on audit) cannot be taken into account.

Determining whether a position has been "adequately disclosed". Which standard is used to determine whether a position is "unreasonable" depends on whether or not the position has been adequately disclosed. Disclosure is *adequate* if:[63]

- The position is disclosed on a properly completed and filed IRS Form 8275, Disclosure Statement, or IRS Form 8275-R, Regulation Disclosure Statement, as appropriate, or on the tax return in accordance with the annual revenue procedure prescribing disclosure on a tax return.

- The tax return preparer provides the taxpayer with a prepared tax return that includes the disclosure.

- For returns or claims for refund subject to an accuracy-related penalty other than a penalty attributable to a substantial understatement of income tax, the preparer advises the taxpayer of the penalty standards applicable and contemporaneously documents the advice in the preparer's files.

A practitioner advising a client to take a position on a tax return, document, affidavit, or other paper submitted to the IRS or preparing or signing a tax return as a preparer generally may rely in good faith without verification upon information furnished by the taxpayer and upon information and advice furnished by another adviser, another tax return preparer, or other party (including another adviser or tax return preparer at the tax return preparer's firm).[64] A tax return preparer is not required to audit, examine, or review books and records, business operations, documents, or other evidence to verify independently information provided by the taxpayer, adviser, other tax return preparer, or other party. However, a practitioner may not ignore the implications of information furnished to, or actually known by, the practitioner and must make reasonable inquiries if the information furnished appears to be incorrect, inconsistent with an important fact or another factual assumption, or incomplete.

¶ 216 Secondary Sources of Tax Authority

Given the professional and ethical standards taxpayers and tax professionals must abide by when preparing an income tax return, it is essential that they thoroughly research a tax issue prior to taking a position on the tax return. However, the sheer volume and complexity of the federal tax law make it difficult to efficiently research the tax implications of a proposed or completed transaction. Fortunately, secondary sources provide a needed guide through the complexity of federal tax law. There are various types of secondary sources that can be helpful to researchers. These include professional tax services, citators, and other publications, such as legal periodicals and newsletters.

.01 Tax Services

A variety of tax services are available in print, online, and on CD-ROMs. A number of large publishing companies, including CCH, Thomson Reuters/RIA, and BNA, publish a variety of tax services. The distinguishing feature among tax services is how the information is arranged.

Some tax services are organized by Code section. For each Code section, the tax service provides the user with the full-text of the Code provision, committee reports and related regulations, a brief summary of cases and rulings relevant to the Code section, and the publisher's commentary about the Code section. The brief summaries of cases and rulings are called "annotations," which is why tax services organized by Code section are often referred to as **annotated tax services**. Annotated tax services typically provide the following information about each Code provision:

---

[63] Reg. § 1.6694-2(d)(3).

[64] Reg. § 1.6694-1(e); 31 C.F.R. § 10.34(d).

1. The full text of the Code provision;

2. Portions of the various committee reports where the Code provision was discussed;

3. The full text of any final, temporary, and proposed regulations issued for the Code section;

4. The publisher's explanation of the Code provision;

5. Annotations of IRS rulings and judicial decisions interpreting the Code provision and regulations; and

6. Any current developments pertaining to the tax law surrounding the Code section.

CCH's *Standard Federal Tax Reporter* and Thomson Reuters/RIA's *United States Tax Reporter: Income Taxes* are two annotated tax services that provide tax researchers with information relevant to federal income tax laws. CCH's *Federal Estate and Gift Tax Reporter* is an annotated tax service that focuses on the tax laws surrounding federal gift, estate, and generation-skipping transfer taxes.

Topical tax services are arranged by topic. In these services, all tax laws pertaining to a particular topic are grouped together, regardless of in which Code section the information appears. For example, all of the tax laws governing education deductions, exclusions, and credits are all discussed together, despite the fact that the tax implications of incurring education expenses are covered in Code Secs. 25A, 117, 127, 132, 135, 162, 221, 222, 529, and 530. CCH's *Tax Research Consultant,* Thomson Reuters/West's *Mertens Law of Federal Income Taxation*, and Thomson Reuters/RIA's *Federal Tax Coordinator 2d* discuss tax law by topic.

.02 Citators

Before relying on relevant case law or rulings, it is necessary to establish that the tax law is still valid and remains authoritative. Citators can be used not only to determine whether a case or ruling has been modified or supplemented but also whether other cases and rulings have mentioned the case or ruling. Some citators list secondary sources that have commented about a particular primary source. CCH and Thomson Reuters/RIA both publish citators as part of their professional tax services. Lexis-Nexis publishes *Shepard's Citations* and *Auto-Cite*. Thomson Reuters' Westlaw offers *KeyCite*. In WestlawNext, citing references are presented alongside court opinions and rulings.

Example 21: In *Dow Chemical Company*,[65] the U.S. district court for the Eastern District of Michigan allowed Dow Chemical to deduct interest on loans obtained to purchase corporate-owned life insurance (COLI) policies on the lives of thousands of its upper management employees. It rejected the IRS's argument that the deductions should be disallowed because the COLI policies were economic shams with no practical economic purpose apart from generating tax deductions for interest payments. By consulting a case citator, a researcher would find that the district court's decision was reversed by the Sixth Circuit Court of Appeals because the Sixth Circuit decided that the COLI policies were, in fact, economic shams.[66]

Example 22: In Rev. Rul. 74-503,[67] a corporation transferred some of its own shares of stock to another corporation in exchange for stock in that other corporation. In that ruling, the IRS concluded that stock received had a zero basis. By consulting a citator, a researcher would find that the IRS revoked Rev. Rul. 74-503 in Rev. Rul. 2006-2.[68]

.03 Periodicals and Other Publications

Many law reviews and professional journals publish articles on tax law. Some cover a broad range of tax topics; others specialize in particular tax areas. Popular legal periodicals include CCH's *Taxes—The Tax Magazine*, Warren Gorman & Lamont's (WG&L) *Journal of Taxation*, the AICPA's *Tax Adviser*, and the American Bar Association's *Tax Lawyer*. CCH's *Federal Tax Articles* and

---

[65] *Dow Chemical Company*, DC Mich., 2003-1 USTC ¶ 50,346.

[66] *Dow Chemical Company*, CA-6, 2006-1 USTC ¶ 50,126, 435 F3d 594.

[67] Rev. Rul. 74-503, 1974-2 CB 117.

[68] Rev. Rul. 2006-2, 2006-1 CB 261.

WG&L's *Index to Federal Tax Articles* can be used to help locate pertinent articles in legal periodicals. So may H.W. Wilson's *Index to Legal Periodicals*.

Many universities hold tax institutes during the year and then publish papers presented at their sessions. For example, the University of Chicago and New York University hold popular tax institutes and publish their annual proceedings. These papers are often used by tax professionals to help understand particularly difficult areas of tax law.

Tax law publishers send out newsletters to their subscribers to keep them abreast on current developments in tax law. These newsletters may be available online or may be delivered through the mail. CCH's *Federal Tax Day*, Tax Analysts' *Tax Notes Today*, and BNA's *Daily Tax Report* are examples of newsletters.

¶ 217 The Tax Research Process

Although there is no one "right way" to research tax law, the following guidelines can be used to ensure that research is as complete as possible. The basic steps in researching a tax issue should include:

1. Gathering pertinent facts,

2. Identifying the tax issues,

3. Locating primary sources relevant to the tax issues,

4. Analyzing and evaluating authorities,

5. Gathering any additional facts needed and applying the relevant authorities to the additional facts, and

6. Developing conclusions and recommendations.

At any stage in the research process, it may become necessary to gather additional facts. Sometimes while researching a tax issue other issues arise, making it necessary to repeat the steps in the research process. Once conclusions and recommendations have been developed (Step 6), they may have to be communicated to a colleague for review and eventually must be communicated to the taxpayer.

.01 Gathering Facts

The first step in the tax research process is to gather the pertinent facts. Some preliminary facts that need to be established when conducting tax research for a business include:

- What type of legal entity is the business (i.e., a C corporation, S corporation, partnership, limited liability company taxed as a partnership, or limited liability company taxed as a corporation)?

- Is the business a U.S. or foreign business? Are the owners U.S. citizens and residents or foreign citizens and residents?

- What is the business's tax year and method of accounting?

- What is the transaction that the business has completed or is proposing to complete?

- Is the business related to any of the parties involved in the transaction being researched?

- What is the business's marginal income tax rate expected to be for its current tax year and subsequent tax years?

Pertinent facts are not limited to the tax question being researched. They also include constraints on what tax strategies a tax researcher can recommend for a client. For example, although an exchange of property may produce the best tax consequences, a client may need the cash that a sale would realize.

.02 Identifying Issues

Once a tax researcher has gathered the pertinent facts, the adviser needs to identify which tax issues need to be researched. Being able to identify those issues is often the most difficult step in the legal research process. As a preliminary matter, tax researchers should determine whether they have been asked to determine whether income has to be recognized, whether a deduction or credit is available for an expenditure, or whether there has been or will be a sale or exchange triggering the realization of gain or loss.

If a tax researcher determines that there is a question about an item of income, the researcher must determine what type of income is involved, whether it is includible in gross income, and, if so, when it has to be recognized under the taxpayer's method of accounting. If a tax researcher determines that there is a question about an expenditure, the researcher must determine whether a deduction or credit is available for the expenditure and when it can be taken into account under the taxpayer's method of accounting.

Example 23: Genson Calculators, Inc. received interest on a bond and wants to know whether the interest has to be included in the company's gross income. The tax questions are whether the interest is the type of interest that can be excluded from gross income and, if not, when it has to be taken into account under the company's method of accounting.

Example 24: Milbrett Alabaster Products, Inc., a calendar year taxpayer, purchased some machinery in 2015 but did not pay for the machinery until 2016. The tax questions include whether the company is entitled to a deduction or credit for its purchase and, if so, for what year the deduction or credit is available.

If a tax researcher determines that there is a question about a sale or exchange, the researcher must determine the amount of gain or loss realized, whether the sale or exchange is such that gain or loss may or must be deferred, when any gain or loss that must be recognized is taken into account, and how any gain or loss is characterized (i.e., as capital gain or ordinary income) for federal income tax purposes.

Example 25: Automatic Clocks, Inc. exchanged one piece of equipment for another. The tax questions are whether gain or loss must be recognized on the exchange and, if so, how much gain or loss must be recognized and whether the gain or loss is capital or ordinary in nature.

.03 Locating Relevant Sources of Authority

After a tax researcher has gathered pertinent facts and identified which tax issues need to be researched, the researcher needs to locate the primary sources relevant to the tax issues being researched. Usually it is best to start by referring to a secondary source covering the tax issues being researched. Both annotated and topical secondary sources have a place in the research process. Topical secondary sources are a good place to start for those who do not know which Code provisions apply to the tax issue. Those who know which Code provisions apply to a tax issue may save time by using an annotated tax service to determine whether any particular Treasury regulation, IRS ruling, or judicial decision answers the research question.

Conclusions reached in legal treatises, periodicals, or opinions rendered by tax professionals cannot be used as authority for a tax return position. However, the authorities underlying such expressions of opinion can be treated as authority for a tax return position if they are applicable to the facts of the particular case.

Before relying on IRS rulings and judicial decisions identified as relevant, a citator should be used to determine whether the case or ruling is still current law. An authority cannot be relied on to the extent that it has been implicitly or explicitly overruled or modified. For example, a district court opinion is not an authority if overruled or reversed by the U.S. Court of Appeals for that district. However, a U.S. Tax Court opinion is not considered overruled or modified by a court of appeals to which the taxpayer does not have a right of appeal unless the Tax Court adopts the holding of that court of appeals.

.04 Analyzing and Evaluating Relevant Authorities

Once the primary sources relevant to a tax issue have been identified and reviewed, a researcher needs to assess what those authorities have to say about the tax questions that the researcher has identified. Sometimes the primary sources provide a clear answer. Other times there is no clear-cut answer. When there is no clear-cut answer, researchers need to assess the relative importance of those sources.

Primary sources are not given the same weight in answering a tax question. The U.S. Supreme Court is the final authority as to the meaning of a Code provision. All other things being equal, decisions by U.S. Courts of Appeals are given more weight than decisions by trial courts. Decisions by the U.S. Tax Court are often given greater weight than decisions by U.S. district courts and the U.S. Court of Federal Claims because Tax Court judges are considered to have special expertise in tax law. Private letter rulings and TAMs have no precedential value except for the taxpayer to whom they were issued.

.05 Developing Conclusions and Recommendations

The final step in the research process is for a tax researcher to draw a conclusion and make recommendations. Often there is a clear conclusion. Other times it may be unclear how the tax law applies. Under such circumstances, researchers must use their professional judgment to determine how the tax law will be applied.

Before making a recommendation, tax researchers must consider the preferences of their client and what it would cost their client to defend against a challenge by the IRS. The strategy that saves the most in taxes may not necessarily be acceptable to the client or save the taxpayer the most money over the long term.

Example 26: The IRS assessed a $500 deficiency against Schlaq Washing Machine Belts, Inc. Emmett Grassia, whom Schlaq hires for professional tax advice, believes that the IRS's interpretation of the Code provision was incorrect, and some commentators agree with Emmett, but there are no judicial decisions either supporting or opposing the IRS's interpretation. Emmett estimates that it would cost the company $10,000 to challenge the IRS before the U.S. Tax Court and tens of thousands more if the case were appealed to a Court of Appeals. Although Emmett is confident that Schlaq would prevail, he cannot recommend a strategy guaranteed to cost the company at least $10,000 but saving the company no more than $500.

While analyzing and evaluating primary sources of tax authority, a researcher may discover the need to obtain additional facts. If so, those additional facts will have to be obtained, and the relevant authorities will have to be analyzed and evaluated in light of those additional facts.

Example 27: While researching whether Davino Pens, Inc. qualifies for the work opportunity credit, Melanie Skahan noticed that an increased credit is available for hiring long-term family assistance recipients. Melanie went back to the taxpayer and made inquiries to determine whether any of the taxpayer's recent hires qualified as long-term family assistance recipients.

.06 Communicating Research Findings

Once a tax researcher has developed conclusions and recommendations regarding a tax issue, the researcher must communicate those conclusions and recommendations to the researcher's client or to a colleague (typically the partner or supervisor who assigned the research project).

Properly communicating an answer to a tax question is as important as finding the correct answer to the question. If an answer is not properly communicated and it is misunderstood by the client or colleague, an item of income or expense may be improperly reported or a transaction may be improperly structured to achieve the best tax results. A typical memorandum communicating research results is divided into five parts:

1. *Facts.* This portion of a memorandum states the pertinent facts.

2. *Issue.* This portion of a memorandum states the assigned tax question and any ancillary questions that have arisen.

3. *Rule.* This portion of a memorandum sets forth the tax laws that affect the issue.

4. *Analysis.* This portion of a memorandum applies the tax laws to the pertinent facts.

5. *Conclusion.* If the tax issue is a matter of compliance, this portion of a memorandum concludes how an item of income or expense or transaction should be reported. If the tax issue involves tax planning, this portion of a memorandum concludes how best to plan for income not yet received, expenses not yet incurred, and transactions that have not yet occurred to achieve the most favorable tax consequences. Recommendations should include advice as to benefits, as well as risks.

Although a memorandum typically is structured as previously described, that is not the only form that a memorandum can take. If an issue is straightforward, the researcher may wish to start the memorandum by stating the conclusion and then explaining how that conclusion was derived.

¶ 218 Summary

Federal tax law includes not only the Code but also Treasury regulations, IRS rulings and other pronouncements, and judicial decisions. These are referred to as primary sources of tax law. Taxpayers need to know not only what primary sources of tax law are but where they can be found and what weight they should be given. Although secondary sources of tax law cannot be used as authority, they can help tax researchers locate and understand primary sources of tax law.

The goal of a tax researcher is to locate and evaluate all relevant sources of tax law to determine how a transaction will be taxed. If research involves an item of income that has been received, an expense that has been incurred, or a transaction that has been completed, tax research can help a business comply with tax reporting requirements. If the tax question involves income yet to be received, an expense yet to be incurred, or a transaction that has not yet occurred, tax researchers can help businesses time receipt of the income or expenditure or structure the transaction to achieve the most desirable tax consequences.

GLOSSARY OF TERMS INTRODUCED IN THE CHAPTER

Action on decision. An IRS pronouncement that informs the public as to whether the IRS acquiesced to a court decision.

Annotated tax service. A tax service that is organized by Code section rather than by topic. CCH's *Standard Federal Tax Reporter* is an example of an annotated tax service.

Announcements. IRS pronouncements that inform the public as to matters of general interest. They may provide guidance as to both substantive and procedural matters.

Blue book. An explanation of a tax act prepared by the staff of the Joint Committee on Taxation.

Chief Counsel Advice (CCA). Written advice or instructions issued by the Office of Chief Counsel to field or service center employees of the IRS or Office of Chief Counsel.

Court of appeals. The court to which decisions made by the U.S. Tax Court, a U.S. district court, or the U.S. Court of Federal Claims may be appealed. There are 13 Courts of Appeals: 12 geographical (11 numbered and one named) plus the Federal Court of Appeals.

Determination letter. A written determination issued by an IRS Director in response to a written request from a taxpayer or the taxpayer's authorized representative. A determination letter will be issued only when the question presented is specifically answered by a statute, a tax treaty, the regulations, a conclusion stated in a revenue ruling, or an opinion or court decision that represents the IRS's position.

District court. One of the trial courts to which taxpayers may appeal an IRS determination.

Final regulation. A proposed regulation that has been adopted as a regulation having the full force and effect of law.

***Golsen* rule.** This rule provides that the U.S. Tax Court will follow a Court of Appeals decision that is squarely on point when appeal of the Tax Court's decision lies to that Court of Appeals.

Internal Revenue Code. The primary statutory source of federal tax law. It is set forth in Title 26 of the United States Code.

Interpretive regulation. A regulation that interprets the Code. It is promulgated pursuant to the Secretary of the Treasury's general authority to issue regulations.

Legislative regulation. A regulation that defines a statutory term or prescribes a method for implementing a Code provision. It carries more weight than other types of regulations because it is promulgated pursuant to a specific grant of authority by Congress.

News release. An IRS pronouncement issued to the media to announce items of general interest. They often are used to announce that an important new revenue ruling or revenue procedure is going to be released and set forth the text of that ruling or procedure.

Notices. IRS pronouncements issued to the public to provide guidance involving substantive interpretations of the Code. They often are issued to provide taxpayers with guidance about recently enacted legislation or to alert taxpayers about pending regulations.

Precedent. Refers to the principle in law of using past decisions to assist in making current decisions.

Primary source of authority. Part of the tax law. Examples of primary sources include legislative authority (e.g., the Code, tax treaties, and Congressional reports), administrative authority (e.g., Treasury regulations and IRS rulings), and judicial decisions.

Private letter ruling. A written statement issued by the IRS's Office of Associate Chief Counsel that interprets and applies the tax laws to a specific set of facts presented by a taxpayer. A letter ruling is issued at the request of a taxpayer and upon payment of a fee.

Procedural regulation. A regulation that establishes procedure or practice requirements (such as prescribing how an election is made).

Proposed regulation. A Treasury regulation that the Secretary of the Treasury proposes to issue.

Revenue ruling. An official interpretation by the IRS as to the application of the tax laws to a specific set of facts.

Revenue procedure. A ruling issued by the IRS that involves a procedural issue.

Secondary source of authority. A reference that explains, comments on, or updates primary sources of tax authority. Examples include topical and annotated tax services, treatises, journals, papers from tax institutes, newsletters, and citators.

Substantial authority. An objective standard that is less stringent than the "more-likely-than-not" standard, but more rigorous than the "reasonable basis" standard.

Tax authority. Established tax law that can be used to help in reaching a conclusion about a tax issue.

Tax avoidance. The art of reducing tax liability through legitimate means.

Tax compliance research. The process of determining how an item of income already received, an expense already incurred, or a transaction already completed should be reported for tax purposes.

Tax evasion. Understating taxes due the government through unlawful means.

Tax planning research. The process of determining how best to plan for income not yet received, expenses not yet incurred, and transactions that have not yet occurred to achieve the most favorable tax consequences.

Technical advice memorandum (TAM). Written advice from the IRS on the interpretation and proper application of the Code, tax treaties, regulations, revenue rulings, notices, or other precedents to a specific set of facts. A TAM is requested by IRS personnel, not taxpayers. No fee is charged a taxpayer for a TAM.

Temporary regulation. A Treasury regulation issued to provide interim guidance to tax practitioners and the public until final regulations are issued. The rules contained in temporary regulations can be used as authority pending issuance of final regulations.

Topical tax service. A tax service that is arranged by topic rather than by Code section. CCH's *Tax Research Consultant* is an example of a topical tax service.

Treasury regulations. The official interpretation of the Code by the Secretary of the Treasury.

U.S. Court of Federal Claims. One of the trial courts to which taxpayers may appeal an IRS determination.

U.S. Supreme Court. The last resort for those appealing a decision of a Court of Appeals and final authority as to what the Code means.

U.S. Tax Court. One of the trial courts to which taxpayers may appeal an IRS determination. Unlike the U.S. district court or U.S. Court of Federal Claims, there is no requirement that the taxpayer pay any alleged deficiency before the court will hear the taxpayer's appeal.

Unreasonable position. A tax return preparer can be penalized for preparing a return or claim of refund that understates tax liability if the understatement is due to an unreasonable position. If a position (other than a position with respect to a tax shelter or reportable transaction to which Code Sec. 6662A applies) is adequately disclosed, it will be considered unreasonable unless the preparer had a reasonable basis for it (*reasonable basis standard*). If a position (other than a position with respect to a tax shelter or reportable transaction to which Code Sec. 6662A applies) is not adequately disclosed, it will be considered unreasonable unless there is or was substantial authority for it (*substantial authority standard*). If a position is with respect to a tax shelter or reportable transaction to which Code Sec. 6662A applies, it will be considered unreasonable unless it was reasonable for the preparer to believe that it would more likely than not be sustained on its merits (*more-likely-than-not standard*).

Written determinations. A private letter ruling issued by the IRS's Office of Associate Chief Counsel in response to a taxpayer's request, a determination letter issued by an IRS Director in response to a taxpayer's request, a technical advice memorandum issued by the IRS's Office of Associate Chief Counsel at the request of an IRS field office, or a Chief Counsel Advice issued by the Office of Chief Counsel to field and service center employees of the IRS or Office of Chief Counsel.

CHAPTER PROBLEMS

Chapter 2 Discussion Questions

1. What gives Congress the right to impose income taxes?
2. What is a primary source of federal tax law?
3. What is a secondary source of federal tax law?
4. What is the Internal Revenue Code?
5. How can a committee report be helpful in the tax research process?
6. What is a temporary regulation, and what reliance can taxpayers place on it?
7. What is the difference between an interpretive and legislative regulation?
8. What is a revenue ruling?
9. What is the difference between a revenue ruling and a letter ruling?
10. What is the difference between a Technical Advice Memorandum (TAM) and a private letter ruling (PLR)?
11. What is an IRS notice of acquiescence or nonacquiescence?
12. If a taxpayer disagrees with the IRS's assessment of a deficiency, to which court can the taxpayer appeal?
13. What is the main advantage for a taxpayer in appealing an IRS's assessment of a deficiency to the U.S. Tax Court?
14. If a taxpayer doing business in Arkansas finds a decision of the Eighth Circuit Court of Appeals that supports the taxpayer's tax return position but a decision by the Fifth Circuit Court of Appeals that opposes the taxpayer's tax return position, which decision should the taxpayer follow?
15. If the U.S. Supreme Court interprets a Code provision differently than nine of the Circuit Courts of Appeal that have ruled on the same issue, which interpretation can a taxpayer follow?
16. What is the significance of the substantial authority standard in the tax research process?
17. Why is it not advisable for a researcher to rely solely on a secondary source to answer a research question?
18. What are the basic steps in researching a tax issue?
19. What are the similarities and differences between tax avoidance and tax evasion?
20. What obligation does the IRS impose on a tax researcher to question information furnished by a client?

Chapter 2 Problems

1. What types of tax provisions are included in Part VI of Subchapter B of Chapter 1 of Subtitle A of the Internal Revenue Code?
2. What types of expenses does Code Sec. 162(a) permit a business to deduct?
3. What does Reg. § 1.162-2 discuss?
4. What limit, if any, is imposed on the amount of charitable contributions that a corporation can deduct for a tax year? See Code Sec. 170.

5. Why did the Senate Finance Committee say that it proposed Code Sec. 199, the deduction for income attributable to U.S. production activities? See S. Rep. No. 108-192 (November 12, 2003).

6. If a taxpayer receives money for property that is compulsorily or involuntarily converted, how can the taxpayer avoid having to recognize gain on the conversion? See Code Sec. 1033(a)(2).

7. Is improved real estate similar or related in service or use to unimproved real estate? See Reg. § 1.1033(a)-2.

8. What is the issue in Rev. Rul. 2003-20, 2003-1 CB 465, and how was it resolved?

9. What is the status of Rev. Rul. 64-328, 1964-2 CB 11?

10. When is a work location temporary for purposes of determining the deductibility of transportation expenses? See Rev. Rul. 99-7, 1999-1 CB 361.

11. What is the maximum amount of depreciation that a business can deduct for the second tax year that it owns a passenger vehicle if the passenger automobile was first placed in service during calendar year 2014? See Rev. Proc. 2014-21, 2014-11 IRB 641.

12. What did the IRS conclude in IRS Letter Ruling 200607003 (November 10, 2005)?

13. In TAM 200437030 (April 30, 2004), what was the issue and what did the IRS conclude?

14. In *W.J. Heitz*, 75 TCM 2522, Dec. 52,750(M), TC Memo. 1998-220, what factors did the court consider in determining whether the amount of compensation paid a shareholder-employee was reasonable?

15. What is the status of *W.J. Heitz*, 75 TCM 2522, Dec. 52,750(M), TC Memo. 1998-220?

16. What did the court decide in *S.B. Bufferd*, SCt, 93-1 USTC ¶ 50,038, 506 US 523, 113 SCt 927?

17. Zeches Box Partitions, Inc. owns a $1,000 bond that pays 4.4 percent interest. It sells the bond for a $100 loss. That same day, it purchases a $1,000 bond from the same issuer and with the same maturity date but a 5.5-percent interest rate. Can Zeches deduct its $100 loss? See Code Sec. 1091 and Rev. Rul. 60-195, 1960-1 CB 300.

18. After reading in the newspaper that the local government had decided to condemn its storage facility, Chambley Butter Cartons, Inc. sold the facility to obtain what it believed would be a better price. The sales price was $200,000, and the company's adjusted basis in the facility was $50,000. A month later, the company reinvested all of the proceeds received in a new storage facility. Does it have to recognize any of the gain that it realized from its sale of the storage facility? See Code Sec. 1033 and Rev. Rul. 63-221, 1963-2 CB 332.

19. Huesman Farming, Inc. exchanged a farm for an apartment building. Does it have to recognize any gain or loss on the exchange? See Code Sec. 1031 and Reg. § 1.1031(a)-1.

20. Manzueta Magnetic Tapes, Inc. wants to know whether it is entitled to a work opportunity credit for any of its employees. What factual information do you need to obtain from the company? See Code Sec. 51.

21. What changes did the Tax Relief and Health Care Act of 2006 make to the research credit? See Joint Committee on Taxation, Technical Explanation of H.R. 6408, The "Tax Relief and Health Care Act of 2006," pp. 9, 10.

22. Which credits are included in the general business credit? See Code Sec. 38.

23. For purposes of the corporate alternative minimum tax, what is the exemption amount, and how much alternative minimum taxable income does a corporation have to have before the phase-out of the exemption amount is triggered? See Code Sec. 55.

24. Must legal action be taken to enforce payment before a debt can be considered worthless? See Reg. § 1.166-2.

25. Which businesses are eligible to take a credit for expenditures to provide access to individuals with a disability? See Code Sec. 44.

Chapter 2 Review Problems

1. Why did Congress increase the annual dollar limitation under Code Sec. 179 as part of the Jobs and Growth Tax Relief Reconciliation Act of 2003 (P.L. 108-27)? See House Ways and Means Committee Report No. 108-94 (May 8, 2003), p. 25.

2. Why did Congress repeal the Code Sec. 108 stock-for-debt exception to the general rule that income is recognized when debt is cancelled as part of the Revenue Reconciliation Act of 1993 (P.L. 103-66)? See Senate Finance Committee Report No. 103-36 (June 23, 1993), pp. 292-293.

Chapter 2 Research Question

Lempera Chutney, Inc. plans to sell real property but would prefer not to have to recognize any income from the sale until after the year of the sale. How could it structure its sale to achieve that goal? Refer to Code Sec. 453 when answering this question.

CHAPTER 3

Tax Accounting

LEARNING OBJECTIVES

1. Understand the differences between tax accounting and financial accounting and be able to explain how the rules for each are determined.

2. Learn what a tax year is and what choices businesses have in selecting and changing a tax year.

3. Learn what an accounting method is and what choices businesses have in selecting which type of accounting method to use.

4. Understand the different types of accounting methods.

5. Explain the claim of right doctrine and the tax benefit rule.

¶ 300 Introduction

Income tax accounting, or **tax accounting**, is used to report income and expenses so that a taxpayer's taxable income for a particular period can be accurately determined. Congress enacts tax laws that, along with the administrative, judicial, and other legislative authorities introduced in Chapter 2, form the basis for the tax accounting rules. Tax accounting rules, the focus of this chapter; apply to all forms of businesses. Tax accounting differs from financial accounting, which encompasses the rules corporations must abide by when preparing their financial statements.

Before businesses can report their taxable income to the Internal Revenue Service (IRS), they first must determine the period of time over which those taxable amounts are calculated and the rules for determining when income is taxed and when expenses can be deducted. The period over which a business's taxable income is reported is referred to as the taxpayer's "tax year." The rules for determining when a business must recognize income and when it may deduct expenses are referred to as the taxpayer's "method of accounting." This chapter discusses how businesses determine their tax year, what methods of accounting a business may use, and how those methods of accounting are applied.

¶ 301 Tax Accounting Distinguished from Financial Accounting

Businesses often keep two sets of books and records. They prepare a set of financial accounting records for financial statement purposes and keep a separate set of tax accounting records to use in preparing their income tax returns. Two sets of books and records are necessary because the financial accounting rules and the tax accounting rules are written by two different governing bodies that have differing, and sometimes contrary, objectives.

Financial accounting records are intended to provide useful information about a business so that management, owners, potential investors, creditors, and other interested parties can make well-informed investment, credit, and other decisions. The objective of financial accounting is to ensure that the activities and profits of the business are accurately reflected in a company's financial statements.

Corporations are required to prepare financial records in accordance with generally accepted accounting principles (GAAP), which require businesses to use the accrual method of accounting to report their annual net income. Under the accrual method, events affecting a company are reported in the accounting periods in which they are earned (in the case of income) or incurred (in the case of expenses), rather than when the cash is received or paid.

Tax accounting records are kept to record the information necessary to prepare a taxpayer's income tax return. Tax accounting focuses on those items of income and expense that are important for determining taxable income, which is the final amount of income the government taxes after allowed exclusions and deductions have been subtracted. The legislative, administrative, and judicial tax authorities discussed in Chapter 2 form the basis for the tax accounting rules that businesses must follow when preparing their federal income tax returns. As discussed in Chapter 1, Congress often enacts tax laws for any number of reasons, the most important being to raise revenue for the federal government. However, many tax laws are enacted for various economic, social, and political reasons (see ¶ 106).

Not only are the rules governing the two sets of accounting records different, but a business's objectives when applying the two sets of rules are very different as well. For the most part, GAAP rules are intended to fairly present a business's income. GAAP, however, does provide some flexibility and sometimes allows businesses to choose among various acceptable accounting methods. For external (financial) reporting, management is interested in making sure the business is seen by investors and creditors as a successful and thriving business. When given a choice among acceptable accounting methods, management will often select the one that results in the greatest net income. This can involve accelerating accounting income into the current year or slowing down the rate at which expenses are taken on the income statement. For example, a business may choose to use the straight-line (SL) method of depreciation for financial reporting purposes in lieu of the various accelerated depreciation methods that GAAP allows.

In contrast, the goal of tax accounting is to legally pay the least amount of taxes possible. Most often this involves using the tax laws to postpone income to future tax periods or to elect acceptable methods that will accelerate tax deductions into the current tax year. Thus, for tax purposes, businesses usually elect to use the most accelerated depreciation method possible. However, when a business uses the straight-line method for financial accounting purposes and an accelerated depreciation method on its tax return, differences between net income and taxable income will arise.

Most students studying tax for the first time have previously been exposed to the financial accounting rules in an introductory or intermediate accounting course. As the federal income tax laws are presented in Chapters 4 through 9, significant differences in how an item of income or expense is treated for tax accounting versus financial accounting purposes will be discussed in a shaded box entitled "GAAP vs. Code," as illustrated below.

 GAAP vs. Code: Large corporations are required to reconcile the differences between the amounts they report as net income on their income statement with the taxable income they report on their tax return. This reconciliation is done on the corporate income tax return. The reconciliation of net income with taxable income is discussed in Chapter 12.

ACCOUNTING PERIODS

A **tax year** is the period of time taxpayers use to calculate their taxable income. A business's tax year may or may not be the same as the annual accounting period it uses for financial reporting purposes.[1]

Businesses, as well as all other taxpayers, have become accustomed to computing their taxable income over a 12-month period. However, that is not the only acceptable method for computing taxable income. There is no constitutional requirement that income be calculated on an annual basis. Businesses could be required to report their taxable income for shorter periods (such as monthly) or longer periods (such as every two years). Alternatively, they could wait to complete a transaction before having to determine their profits.

Example 1: Voice Communications signs a contract in December 2015 to install equipment. Voice incurs $16,000 of expenses but has no revenue during the 2015 calendar year. In 2016, it incurs an additional $4,000 of expenses and receives $20,000 for its work. If Voice were to report its taxable income using the calendar year, it would report a $16,000 tax loss in 2015 and $16,000 of taxable income ($20,000 – $4,000) in 2016. However, if Voice had been permitted to wait until it had completed its work on the contract, it would have reported no taxable income.

In 1931, the U.S. Supreme Court was asked to decide whether federal income tax could be assessed on the basis of fixed accounting periods or whether it must be assessed based on completed transactions. In upholding the government's right to assess federal income tax based on a fixed annual accounting period, the court ruled:

> It is the essence of any system of taxation that it should produce revenue ascertainable, and payable to the government, at regular intervals. Only by such a system is it practicable to produce a regular flow of income and apply methods of accounting, assessment, and collection capable of practical operation.[2]

---

[1] Code Sec. 441.

[2] *Burnet v. Sanford & Brooks Company*, SCt, 2 USTC ¶ 636, 282 US 359, 51 SCt 150 (1931).

It is possible that taxpayers may be aided or adversely affected by timing differences when income and deductions are reported on an annual basis. However, the Internal Revenue Code (the "Code") includes certain provisions to mitigate problems caused by assessing tax based on an annual accounting period.

Example 2: Referring back to Example 1, the $16,000 of expenses in 2015 did not reduce the amount of tax paid by Voice Communications that year because it was already operating at a loss for the year. However, in 2016 it reports $16,000 of taxable income, even though the entire transaction (when viewed over two years) produced no profits for the company. To mitigate this problem, the Code permits taxpayers to carry over net operating losses from one tax year to offset profits in other (profitable) tax years.[3] (See ¶ 1001.01.)

Example 3: In 2015, Hobbit Tool Bits received $200,000 from a defense contract. In 2015, Hobbit's marginal tax rate was 39 percent. In 2016, it is determined that Hobbit had been overpaid by $25,000. The company repays the $25,000 and deducts that amount when calculating its 2016 taxable income. In 2016, Hobbit's marginal tax rate is 25 percent, so when it deducts the $25,000, its tax liability decreases by $6,250 ($25,000 × 25%). However, in the year it reported the $25,000 overpayment in income, its tax liability increased by $9,750 ($25,000 × 39%). Absent any mitigating provision in the tax law, the company would pay an additional $3,500 ($9,750 – $6,250) in taxes because of the error. However, a provision in the Code protects the taxpayer in situations in which previously deducted amounts must be repaid (see the claim of right doctrine at ¶ 312).[4]

¶ 302 Permitted Tax Years

Most businesses use either a **calendar year,** which is a tax year that begins on January 1 and ends on December 31, or a **fiscal year,** which is a 12-month period that ends on the last day of any month other than December. Businesses that do not keep adequate books and records must report their taxable income using a calendar year.[5]

Once a tax year has been selected, it generally must be used for all subsequent tax years unless permission is requested and granted by the IRS to change to a different year-end. In the first year of a business's existence or in a year in which a business changes its tax year, a tax return must be filed for a period of fewer than 12 months. This is referred to as a "short tax year" (see ¶ 304.02).

C corporations (defined as corporations other than S corporations) are generally allowed to use either a calendar or a fiscal year as long as they maintain their books and records using the annual accounting period they have selected. Other businesses, however, may be restricted in their tax year choice and, in some cases, may be required to use a particular tax year. For example, partnerships and S corporations cannot select a tax year without following a strict set of rules that take into consideration the year-end of their owners[6] (see ¶ 302.01).

Example 4: A business reports its income and expenses based on a year beginning January 1 and ending December 31. The business's tax year is a calendar year.

Example 5: A corporation uses as its tax year the 12-month period beginning on December 1 and ending on November 30. The corporation's tax year is a November 30 fiscal year.

Example 6: A business keeps its books based on a calendar year. Although the business might prefer to use a fiscal year, it cannot do so because it has not kept its books in accordance with a fiscal year.

---

[3] Code Sec. 172.
[4] Code Sec. 1341.

[5] Code Sec. 441(b).
[6] Reg. § 1.441-1(b)(2).

Although a tax year generally may not include a period of more than 12 calendar months, taxpayers may elect to compute their taxable income on the basis of a fiscal year that varies from 52 to 53 weeks. Such a tax year must always end on the same day of the week and must always end on whatever date that day of the week occurs at the end of the calendar month.[7] For example, if a business uses as its tax year a year that always ends on the last Sunday of October, then its tax year is a fiscal year that varies from 52 to 53 weeks.

 Planning Pointer: Taxpayers may wish to use a fiscal year that varies from 52 to 53 weeks rather than a 52-week year if doing so would permit them to more reliably report their business activities. For example, a retailer that does most of its weekly business on the weekend might want to use a 52-to 53-week year ending on a Sunday to make sure that each year includes the same number of weekends.

.01 Required Tax Years

Although C corporations and individuals are allowed to select a fiscal tax year, certain types of businesses are required to use a particular tax year. Businesses that have restrictive year-ends include:

- Partnerships (including limited liability companies taxed as partnerships),

- S corporations, and

- Personal service corporations.

Partnerships, limited liability companies taxed as partnerships, and S corporations are referred to as "flow-through entities." The primary advantage of operating an activity as a flow-through entity is that the profits of the business flow through and are taxed directly to its owners. Owners are considered to have recognized all profits or losses from a flow-through entity on the day of the flow-through entity's year-end. When the flow-through entity and its owners use the same year-end, all income earned by the entity during the year is taxed to its owners in the same tax year. However, when a flow-through entity uses a year-end that is different from the year-end of its owners, a deferral of income results.

For example, if a partnership were to use a January 31 fiscal year-end and its owners a calendar year, partnership profits for the fiscal year that ends on January 31, 2016, would be reported on the calendar year partner's 2016 income tax return (the year that contains January 31, 2016). Thus, even though the entity's profits from February 1, 2015, through December 31, 2015, were actually earned during the 2015 calendar year, those profits would not be taxed to the partners until they filed their 2016 tax return. This potential delay (deferral) in the government receiving the taxes owed on this income prompted Congress to enact rules regarding permitted year-ends for flow-through entities. Congress wanted to limit the amount of time that owners can defer recognition of income received by their businesses.[8]

Required tax year for a partnership. A partnership's tax year must ordinarily be the same tax year used by partners who own more than 50 percent of the partnership's capital and profits.[9] Thus, if partners that collectively own *more than* a 50-percent interest in the partnership's capital and profits have the same year-end, the partnership normally is required to use that same year-end ("majority partners rule").[10] If there is a not a majority of partners that have the same year-end, the partnership usually must use the same year-end of *all* of its principal partners ("principal partners rule").[11] "Principal partners" are partners who own at least five percent of the partnership's capital or

---

[7] Reg. § 1.441-2(a)(1).

[8] Joint Committee on Taxation, *General Explanation of the Tax Reform Act of 1986,* at 534.

[9] Code Sec. 706(b)(1)(B).

[10] Code Sec. 706(b)(4).

[11] Code Sec. 706(b)(1)(B).

profits.[12] If the year-end of *all* of the principal partners is not the same, the tax year that produces the least aggregate deferral is the partnership's required tax year.[13]

Example 7: Ryan Corporation owns a 45-percent profits and capital interest in a partnership. Ryan uses an October 31 fiscal year-end. Rachel Roth owns a 40-percent profits and capital interest in the partnership, and Alan Pascel owns 15 percent. Both Rachel and Alan use a calendar year-end. Because Rachel and Alan use the same year-end and together own more than 50 percent of the partnership's profits and capital, the partnership's required tax year is the calendar year-end used by its majority partners.

Example 8: Birdland Partnership does not have a group of partners that own a majority interest in capital and profits and have the same year-end. Thus, the majority partner rule does not apply, and Birdland must determine whether the principal partners rule is applicable. Ralph, Lane, and Dan are the only partners who own at least a five-percent capital or profits interest in Birdland. The three partners are the only principal partners. If each of them uses the same year-end, then the partnership must use that same year-end. Thus, if Ralph, Lane, and Dan all use the calendar year, the partnership's required tax year is the calendar year.

Example 9: Assume the same facts as in Example 8, except Creski Oil, which uses a fiscal year, purchases a five-percent interest in Birdland. Because all principal partners (which now includes Creski) no longer have the same tax year, Birdland's required tax year is the one that produces the least aggregate deferral of income.

The rules regarding the determination of a tax year that produces the least aggregate deferral of income are beyond the scope of this chapter. Those rules are discussed in detail in Chapter 13 (see ¶ 1304.01).

A partnership may use a tax year other than its required tax year if it (1) establishes to the IRS's satisfaction a business purpose for that requested tax year (see ¶ 304.01), (2) elects a particular tax year permitted by Code Sec. 444 (see ¶ 302.02), or (3) elects to use a 52-53-week tax year that ends with reference to its required tax year or a tax year elected under Code Sec. 444.[14]

Required tax year for an S corporation. An S corporation's tax year must be a permitted year.[15] An S corporation's permitted year is its required tax year (i.e., the calendar year) or any of the following:[16]

- A tax year elected under Code Sec. 444 (see ¶ 302.02),
- A 52- to 53-week tax year ending with reference to the calendar year or a tax year elected under Code Sec. 444, or
- Any other tax year for which the corporation establishes a business purpose to the IRS's satisfaction (see ¶ 304.01).

Required tax year for a personal service corporation. A personal service corporation must use the calendar year as its tax year unless it establishes to the IRS's satisfaction a business purpose for using a different period as its tax year.[17] A corporation is a "personal service corporation" if its principal activity is the performance of personal services and such services are substantially performed by employee-owners. An employee is an "employee-owner" if the employee owns, on any day during the tax year, any of the outstanding stock of the personal service corporation.

.02 Section 444 Election

Partnerships, S corporations, and personal service corporations may make an election under Code Sec. 444 to have a tax year other than their required tax year. However, the deferral period of

---

[12] Code Sec. 706(b)(3).
[13] Reg § 1.706-1(b)(2)(i)(C).
[14] Reg. § 1.706-1(b)(2)(ii).

[15] Code Sec. 1378(a); Reg. § 1.1378-1(a).
[16] Reg. § 1.1378-1(a).
[17] Code Sec. 441(i).

the tax year they select cannot exceed three months. The "deferral period" is the length of time between an entity's elected year-end and its required year-end.

Example 10: A newly formed partnership uses the calendar year as its required tax year. Instead of using the calendar year, the partnership may elect a tax year ending September 30 because the number of months between the end of that year (September 30) and the close of the required tax year (December 31) does not exceed three months. It may also elect a tax year ending October 31 or November 30 because the deferral period of those tax years is fewer than three months (two months in the case of a tax year ending October 31; one month in the case of a tax year ending November 30).

When a flow-through entity uses a tax year other than its required tax year, the government must wait to collect the tax owed on a portion of the income earned by the entity. In Example 10, the partnership would file a tax return reporting profits for the period from October 1, 2015, to September 30, 2016. The profits would not be taxed until reported by the owners in their tax years that contain September 30, 2016. For a calendar year partner, this would be the tax return for the 2016 calendar year. Consequently, income that the partnership earned for the period from October 1, 2015, to December 31, 2015, would not be taxed until the partner files its 2016 tax return. Thus, for the privilege of electing a tax year other than its required tax year, the entity must pay the IRS an amount representing the tax on the deferred income that its owners will not report until the next tax year.[18] The actual amount the entity must pay is calculated using Form 8752, *Required Payment or Refund Under Section 7519.*

Example 11: Continuing with Example 10, if the partnership elects to use a September 30 tax year, it must agree to prepay (i.e., keep on reserve with the IRS) any taxes associated with the profits generated during the first three months of its tax year. Thus, the partnership must pay the IRS the taxes its owners would owe on profits generated from October 1 to December 31. Each year the partnership must compute its estimated tax liability for the first three months of its tax year. If the estimate for the year is higher than the amount currently on reserve with the IRS, it must file Form 8752 and pay the additional taxes owed. If the estimate for the year is less than the taxes on reserve with the IRS, it can request a refund by filing Form 8752.

¶ 303 Adopting a Tax Year

New businesses may adopt any permitted tax year by filing their first income tax return using that tax year. Businesses *do not* adopt a tax year merely by filing an application for an employer identification number, by paying estimated income taxes for a tax year, or by filing an application for an extension of time to file an income tax return.

Example 12: A corporation began operations on April 1. If the corporation files its first income tax return using December 31 as the last day of its tax year, it has adopted the calendar year as its tax year.

Example 13: A corporation files its first income tax return using September 30 as the end of its tax year. It has adopted a fiscal year beginning on October 1 and ending on September 30 as its tax year.

¶ 304 Changing a Tax Year

Once a business adopts a tax year, it must use that tax year to compute its taxable income and file its income tax returns unless it obtains the IRS's approval to change to a different tax year. The IRS ordinarily will approve a business's request to change to a different tax year if the taxpayer establishes a *business purpose* for the requested tax year and agrees to any terms, conditions, and

---

[18] Code Secs. 444(c)(1) and 7519.

adjustments required by the IRS to prevent any substantial distortion of income that otherwise would result from the change.

.01 Business Purpose Tax Year

If a partnership, S corporation, or personal service corporation can establish that it has an acceptable business purpose for using a tax year other than its required tax year, it may use that other tax year.[19] These entities can establish a business purpose to the IRS's satisfaction by showing that the requested tax year is their natural business year or by satisfying a facts and circumstances test.[20] Demonstrating that a tax year other than the taxpayer's required tax year is more of a natural business year for these particular entities generally requires an entity to have been in business for several years to establish a track record that supports a natural business year.

Natural business year. A natural business year can be demonstrated by satisfying the "25-percent gross receipts test." This test requires a calculation of the percentage of gross receipts that comes from the last two months of the requested tax year. A partnership that meets the 25-percent gross receipts test will be granted automatic consent to change to its natural business year regardless of whether the use of the natural business year results in more deferral of income than the tax year the partnership is currently using.[21]

To satisfy the 25-percent gross receipts test, a business computes its gross receipts for the three previous 12-month periods ending on the last day of the requested year-end. For example, if a taxpayer that currently uses the calendar year as its tax year wants to convince the IRS that a fiscal year ending May 31 is a more natural business year, it must calculate its gross receipts for the three previous 12-month periods ending on May 31. If at least 25 percent of the year's gross receipts comes from the last two months in each of those three years, then the 25-percent gross receipts test is satisfied. However, if another tax year also satisfies the 25-percent gross receipts test for the previous three years, then the tax year that produces a higher percentage of gross sales during the last two months will be deemed the business's natural business year.

Example 14: JKL Partnership currently uses the calendar year as its tax year. JKL wants to change to a May 31 fiscal year. JKL would like the change to become effective after the short tax year of January 1 through May 31, 2016. The partnership's gross receipts for the period from June 1, 2014, through May 31, 2015, are $300,000, and its gross receipts for April 2015 and May 2015 total $90,000. Thus, gross receipts for the last two months are 30 percent of total gross receipts for the desired May 31 fiscal year ($90,000/$300,000). When JKL performs this same calculation for the 12-month periods ending May 31, 2014, and May 31, 2013, its percentages of gross receipts in the last two months are 26 and 28 percent, respectively. Because the percentages each exceed 25 percent, JKL has established a May 31 natural business year. However, JKL cannot adopt a May 31 year-end unless it can show that no other tax year would produce a greater percentage of gross receipts in the last two months.

A partnership, S corporation, or personal service corporation may also request a different year-end than its required year-end by showing a natural business year that ends soon after its annual peak period of business. Generally, one month is considered to be "soon after" the peak business period; however, a business that has been in existence fewer than three years typically will have difficulty demonstrating its peak and nonpeak periods. A business whose income is steady from month to month will not be able to establish a natural business year using this special rule.[22]

A partnership, S corporation, or personal service corporation may also be able to establish a natural business year if it can show through its gross receipts for the previous three years that it is open only part of the year.[23] The natural business year of a taxpayer with a seasonal business ends at

---

[19] Code Secs. 706(b)(1)(C) and 1378(b)(2).
[20] Rev. Proc. 2002-39, 2002-1 CB 1046.
[21] Rev. Proc. 2006-46, 2006-2 CB 859.

[22] Rev. Proc. 2002-39, 2002-1 CB 1046, § 5.03(1).
[23] Rev. Proc. 2002-39, 2002-1 CB 1046, § 5.03(2).

or within a month after the business operations end for the season. A seasonal business must have only insignificant receipts (less than 10 percent of the year's receipts) during the portion of the year it is not operational. Certain outdoor businesses that are seasonal due to weather conditions are likely to satisfy this requirement.

Facts and circumstances test. Partnerships, S corporations, and personal service corporations that have difficulty establishing a natural business year may establish a business purpose for a requested tax year that is different from their required tax year based on all the relevant facts and circumstances. The IRS, however, has stated that these entities will be granted permission to adopt, change, or retain a tax year under the "facts and circumstances test" only in rare and unusual circumstances. The following reasons *are not* sufficient to establish a business purpose for a requested tax year:[24]

- Deferral of income to owners;
- Use of a particular year for regulatory or financial accounting purposes;
- Hiring patterns of a particular business;
- Use of a particular year for administrative purposes;
- Partnership's business involves the use of price lists, model years, or other items that change on an annual basis;
- Use of a particular year by a related entity;
- Use of a particular year by competitors;
- Gaining an accountant's reduced rate;
- Record-keeping consistency; and
- Issuance of timely tax information forms to partners.

The IRS has found that a taxpayer's requested tax year can satisfy the facts and circumstances test when (1) another year produced a higher percentage under the 25-percent gross receipts test but the requested year would result in less deferral of income and (2) the requested tax year would have been a natural business year under the 25-percent gross receipts test except for unusual circumstances occurring during the test period that were beyond the taxpayer's control (e.g., a labor strike).[25]

Businesses other than partnerships, S corporations, and personal service corporations that do not otherwise establish a business purpose for their requested tax year generally will be deemed to have established a business purpose if they provide a nontax reason for the requested tax year and agree to certain additional terms, conditions, and adjustments intended to neutralize the tax effects of any resulting substantial distortion of income.

 Planning Pointer: Selecting a tax year that coincides with a business's natural business year can be desirable for several reasons. First, income and expenses are matched. Second, because inventories usually are at their lowest level, it is easier to count and value them. Third, loans usually are at their lowest amounts, which means the business will have a more favorable balance sheet for credit purposes.

.02 Requesting a Change in Tax Year

Unless automatic consent to a change in tax years has been provided, businesses are required to file Form 1128, *Application To Adopt, Change, or Retain a Tax Year,* no earlier than the day after the end of the first year for which the change is to be effective and no later than the original due date (not including extensions) for filing a return for the first effective year. The first effective year is the short period required to effect the change.

---

[24] Rev. Proc. 2002-39, 2002-1 CB 1046.   [25] Rev. Rul. 87-57, 1987-2 CB 117.

A change in tax years is automatically approved for certain businesses. For example, C corporations that comply with Rev. Proc. 2006-45[26] may change their tax years. Partnerships, S corporations, and personal service corporations that comply with Rev. Proc. 2006-46[27] may change their tax years. A request for automatic approval of a change under Rev. Proc. 2006-45 or Rev. Proc. 2006-46 must be filed by the due date (including extensions) of the return for the short period required to effect the change.

Unless the IRS has announced that it will automatically approve a change in tax year, the IRS charges a user fee for requests to change a tax year.

When a business changes from one tax year to another, it is required to file a tax return for the short tax year created by the change. A **short tax year** is a tax year of fewer than 12 months. If a short tax year return were not filed, the taxable income generated during the short period would never be taxed. When a short tax year return is filed, the taxpayer must compute its tax liability using its annualized taxable income. The taxpayer is only responsible for the tax liability for the portion of the year that represents the short tax year.

Example 15: A.G. Generators changes from a tax year ending October 31 to a tax year ending November 30. A.G. must file a tax return for the period beginning November 1 and ending November 30. In doing so, it annualizes taxable income on the short tax year return by taking taxable income for the one-month period of November 1 to November 30 and then multiplying it by 12 to represent a full year of taxable income. A.G. then calculates the tax liability on its annualized taxable income. It then divides the tax liability by 12 to determine the amount of taxes it owes on one month of taxable income.

ACCOUNTING METHODS

As previously discussed, businesses must follow certain rules governing when they must recognize income and when they can deduct expenses. These rules are referred to as a business's **method of accounting**. The term includes not only the overall method of accounting used by a taxpayer but also the accounting treatment of any particular item.[28] For example, the cash method of accounting is a permissible accounting method. Under this method, cash is recognized as income in the year it is received, and expenses are deducted in the year they are paid. However, when a business enters into a long-term construction contract, it may be required to report its income in a tax year other than the year in which the cash is received. Although this method is inconsistent with the cash method of accounting, it nonetheless is the required method that must be used for this particular item of income.

Businesses must keep in mind that the method of accounting they use for financial accounting purposes is not necessarily the one they should use for tax accounting purposes. For financial accounting, businesses need to follow the rules provided under GAAP and to make choices that will maximize their net income and make the company look as profitable and successful as possible. For tax purposes, businesses want to select a method of accounting that will allow them to minimize their income tax liability. Because of the progressive nature of the U.S. income tax system, businesses often can reduce their overall tax liability by keeping their taxable income constant from year to year. They can take advantage of the time value of money by selecting a method of accounting that allows them to defer income until a subsequent tax year or to accelerate expenses into the current tax year.

Example 16: S.W. Belts has a big order at the end of its tax year that will generate $25,000 in taxable income. The company anticipates its taxable income for the year will be

---

[26] 2006-2 CB 851.
[27] 2006-2 CB 859.

[28] Reg. § 1.446-1(a)(1).

$75,000 from other sources. It anticipates its taxable income for the following tax year will be $50,000. If its method of accounting permits it to delay recognizing the $25,000 in taxable income until its next tax year, it will report $75,000 of taxable income in each year and owe $13,750 in taxes each year (or a total of $27,500).

If its method of accounting does not allow S.W. Belts to delay recognition of the $25,000 in taxable income, its taxable income for the current tax year will be $100,000, and its taxable income for its next tax year will be $50,000. Due to the progressive nature of the corporate income tax rates, the company's total federal income tax for the two years will be $29,750 ($22,250 and $7,500, respectively). Although total taxable income for the two years is the same ($150,000 total), the timing of that income can cost S.W. Belts an additional $2,250 ($29,750 – $27,500) in federal income taxes.

Example 17: Mixon Signs purchases equipment for $50,000. Mixon is in the 34-percent tax bracket. For financial accounting purposes, Mixon uses a depreciation method that allows it to deduct $5,000 each year over the 10-year life of the equipment. If Mixon accounts for depreciation the same way for tax purposes, it will save $1,700 in federal income taxes each year ($5,000 × 34%). However, if for tax purposes it can elect to expense the entire $50,000 in the first year, it can reduce its tax liability by $17,000 ($50,000 × 34%) for the year the equipment is placed in service. Although Mixon will not be entitled to any tax depreciation deductions for the equipment in any subsequent years, it will generate an additional $15,300 in tax savings in the first year ($17,000 – $1,700) that it can immediately invest or otherwise use to its advantage.

¶ 305 Permissible Methods of Accounting

No uniform method of accounting for tax purposes is prescribed for all taxpayers.[29] A business usually can adopt any method of accounting, if the method clearly reflects its income and the business regularly uses the method in keeping its books. If the method of accounting used by a business does not clearly reflect its income, its taxable income must be computed under a method that in the IRS's opinion does clearly reflect its income.[30]

The two most common methods of accounting used by businesses are the cash receipts and disbursements method of accounting and the accrual method of accounting.[31] Under the **cash receipts and disbursements method**, a business includes in its gross income an item of income when it actually or constructively receives the cash or a cash equivalent, and it can deduct an expense when it is actually paid. Under the **accrual method**, an item of income must be included in gross income when all events have occurred that fix the right to receive the item and its amount can be determined with reasonable accuracy. An expense can be deducted when (1) all events have occurred that determine the liability, (2) the amount of the liability can be determined with reasonable accuracy, and (3) economic performance has occurred with respect to the liability. The accrual method should be familiar to students who have studied financial accounting because publicly traded companies must use the accrual method to prepare their financial statements.

 GAAP vs. Code: GAAP requires taxpayers to use the accrual method of accounting instead of the cash method because reporting a company's financial transactions based on the cash method can give an incorrect view of the company's financial health and cause those relying on the company's financial reports to make bad decisions.

---

[29] Reg. § 1.446-1(a)(2).
[30] Code Sec. 446(a), (b).

[31] Code Sec. 446(c).

Businesses are also permitted to use a **hybrid method** of accounting, which combines elements of the cash and the accrual accounting methods. For example, the accrual method of accounting for purchases and sales of inventory may be combined with the cash method for other types of income and expenses. The cash method (see ¶ 306), accrual method (see ¶ 307), and hybrid method (see ¶ 308) are referred to as "overall methods of accounting" to distinguish them from methods of accounting required for particular items of income or expense (¶ 309).

A taxpayer that engages in more than one trade or business may use a different method of accounting for each trade or business.[32] A taxpayer can use one method of accounting for the taxpayer's business and a different method of accounting to compute income and deductions not connected with the business.

Example 18:   Kim Striker is engaged in two businesses. Kim sells kaleidoscopes on eBay, and she sells antiques in her store. Kim uses the cash method for her eBay business and the accrual method for her antiques store. She is permitted to use a different method of accounting for each of her businesses.

Example 19:   Nina Zorman owns a card and party shop. She uses the accrual method for that business. Her use of an accrual method for her business does not prevent her from using the cash method for her personal income and expenses.

.01 Limitations on the Use of the Cash Method

Although the cash method is simple to use and less costly to administer than the accrual method, it does have its shortcomings, and Congress has increasingly been restricting its use. A major shortcoming of the cash method is that it can result in a mismatching of income with related expenses.[33] Use of the cash method can also produce a mismatching of income and deductions when one party to a transaction uses the cash method but another party uses the accrual method, as illustrated in Examples 20 and 21.

Example 20:   Creative Designs uses the calendar year as its tax year and the cash method of accounting. During 2015, Creative Designs developed an advertising campaign for one of its clients. It finished the campaign in 2015 and billed the client $22,000 for its services; however, the client did not pay the bill until early in 2016. Under the cash method, the $22,000 is not taxed to Creative Designs until 2016. If the client uses the calendar year but uses the accrual method of accounting, the client would deduct the $22,000 in 2015—the year it incurred the advertising expense.

Example 21:   Rob Guzi, who uses the calendar year as his tax year and the cash method of accounting, performs services in 2015 for Rossa, Inc., which uses an accrual method of accounting. Rob collects his $20,000 fee from Rossa in 2016 and properly reports it as taxable income on his 2016 tax return. However, because the services were performed in 2015, using the accrual method Rossa deducts the $20,000 in 2015 even though payment was not actually made until 2016.

Businesses required to maintain inventory. When a taxpayer is required to maintain inventory, it usually must use an accrual method of accounting with regard to its purchases and sales of such inventory.[34] A taxpayer is required to account for inventories when the production, purchase, or sale of merchandise is an income-producing factor in the taxpayer's business.[35] A business that must use the accrual method to account for purchases and sales of inventory can use the cash method for its other items of income and expense, provided the business is not required to use the accrual method of accounting as its overall accounting method (see the discussion that follows).

---

[32] Code Sec. 446(d).

[33] Joint Committee on Taxation, *General Explanation of the Tax Reform Act of 1986*, at 474-475.

[34] Reg. § 1.446-1(c)(2)(i).

[35] Reg. § 1.471-1.

Reason for the Rule: Because a business usually purchases and pays for inventory before selling it and collecting cash, allowing use of the cash method to account for inventory would result in a distortion of the business's true operating profits. A business that is required to maintain an inventory usually must use the accrual method to account for its purchases and sales because that method requires a business to match the proceeds from sales of goods with the costs associated with those goods.

The IRS exempts certain "qualifying small businesses" from the requirement to account for inventories using the accrual method of accounting. This exemption applies to businesses whose *average annual gross receipts* over the previous three years do not exceed $10 million (and of course, only to businesses that are not otherwise required to use the accrual method). A qualifying small business may use the cash method for all of its trades or businesses if it satisfies one of the following three conditions:[36]

1. The taxpayer reasonably determines that its principal business activity is described in a North American Industry Classification System (NAICS) code other than an ineligible code (relating to manufacturing, retail trade, wholesale trade, information industries, and mining activities).

2. The taxpayer's principal business activity is described in one of the ineligible NAICS codes, but the taxpayer reasonably determines that its principal business activity is the provision of services, including the provision of property incident to those services.

3. The taxpayer's principal business activity is described in one of the ineligible NAICS codes, but the taxpayer reasonably determines that its principal business activity is the fabrication or modification of tangible personal property upon demand in accordance with customer design or specifications.

 Reason for the Rule: The IRS adopted this rule to reduce administrative and tax compliance burdens on certain small businesses and to minimize disputes between the IRS and small businesses as to whether they are required to maintain inventories.[37]

C corporations and partnerships with a C corporation partner. Most C corporations and partnerships that have a C corporation as a partner cannot use the cash method of accounting if their average annual gross receipts for the three previous tax years exceed $5 million. Qualified personal service corporations are exempt from this rule,[38] and special rules apply to corporations and partnerships that engage in farming activities. This restriction on the use of the cash method applies regardless of whether inventory is material to the business.

 Reason for the Rule: In 1986 Congress limited the use of the cash method of accounting by C corporations and partnerships that have a C corporation as a partner because it concluded that the cash method of accounting frequently fails to reflect accurately the economic results of a taxpayer's trade or business over a tax year.[39] Congress continued to allow smaller businesses to use the cash method to avoid the higher compliance costs associated with changing to another method of accounting. It denied use of the cash method of accounting by a partnership that has a C corporation as a partner to prevent an entity that was prohibited from using the cash method from circumventing the rules by operating its business in partnership form.

---

[36] Rev. Proc. 2002-28, 2002-1 CB 815.
[37] Rev. Proc. 2002-28, 2001-1 CB 815.

[38] Code Sec. 448(a), (b).
[39] Joint Committee on Taxation, *General Explanation of the Tax Reform Act of 1986*, at 474-476.

Partnerships engaged in farming that have a C corporation as a partner must use the accrual method. Any C corporation engaged in farming must use an accrual method of accounting if its gross receipts for any tax year since 1975 exceeded $1 million. However, family corporations involved in farming must use the accrual method only if their gross receipts exceeded $25 million in any year after 1985. A "family corporation" is one in which at least 50 percent of the total combined voting power of all classes of stock to vote and at least 50 percent of all other classes of stock are owned by members of the same family.[40]

 Reason for the Rule: Congress enacted this provision as part of the Tax Reform Act of 1976. Congress denied large corporations entering into the farming business the benefit of the cash method of accounting because such corporations have ready access to skilled accounting assistance.[41] The primary justification for permitting farm operations to use the cash method of accounting is its relative simplicity. For example, it does not require taxpayers to identify specific costs incurred in raising particular crops or animals.

As previously mentioned, a qualified personal service corporation is exempt from the rules restricting C corporations from using the cash method. A "qualified personal service corporation" is a C corporation in which 95 percent or more of its employees' time is devoted to the performance of services in the fields of health, law, engineering, architecture, accounting, actuarial science, performance arts, or consulting. In addition, 95 percent or more of the value of its stock must be held *directly or indirectly* by (1) employees performing services in a qualifying field, (2) retired employees who had performed such services for the corporation or the estate of any such employee or retired employee, or (3) any person who acquired stock by reason of the death of such an employee or retired employee (but only for the two-year period beginning on the date of the individual's death).[42]

.02 Special Methods of Accounting

Despite selecting an overall method of accounting in accordance with the rules previously discussed in this chapter, taxpayers may have to use special methods of accounting for certain items of income and expenses. For example, there are special methods of accounting for installment sales, long-term contracts, research and experimental expenditures, crops, and soil and water conservation expenditures. Regardless of which overall method (cash, accrual, or hybrid) the taxpayer uses on its tax return, special rules apply to these specific items. These special rules are discussed in ¶ 309.

¶ 306 Cash Receipts and Disbursements Method

Most individuals and many small businesses use the cash receipts and disbursements method of accounting because it requires a minimum of recordkeeping and gives the taxpayer flexibility in reporting income and deducting expenses. Sole proprietors especially are inclined to use the cash method of accounting because they usually use it for items reported on their personal income tax returns.

 Planning Pointer: Subject to the constructive receipt of income doctrine (see ¶ 306.01), businesses that use the cash method of accounting can control the timing of when income (cash) is received. If toward the end of a tax year a business wishes to delay receipt of income until the next year, the business can delay sending invoices to customers. A business can accelerate or postpone deductions by accelerating or delaying purchases or payments for purchases.

---

[40] Code Sec. 447.

[41] House Ways and Means Committee Report No. 94-658 (November 12, 1975), at 94.

[42] Temp. Reg. § 1.448-1T(e).

.01 Accounting for Income

Under the cash method of accounting, taxpayers generally report income in the year during which they actually or constructively receive the cash or a cash equivalent.[43] Thus, amounts that cash method taxpayers receive as advance payments for goods or services must be included in gross income in the year they are received. If taxpayers receive property or services, they must include the fair market value (FMV) of the property or services in income. A credit sale is not included in income by a cash method taxpayer until the customer pays off the receivable. A customer's promise to pay is not considered income by a cash method taxpayer. A payment by credit card is treated as received in the year the credit card charge is made, regardless when the credit card sponsor is repaid.[44]

Example 22: Mannox Confetti is a cash method taxpayer that uses the calendar year as its tax year. Mannox receives a promissory note in payment for some confetti it sold to a customer. The promissory note has no value and is not readily converted into cash. Receipt of the promissory note is not treated as income. As Mannox receives payments pursuant to the promissory note, it will include the payments in its calculation of gross income.

Example 23: Wax Aquariums is a cash method taxpayer that uses the calendar year as its tax year. In December 2015, Wax agrees to install and stock a custom aquarium in a dentist's office. Under the terms of the sale, $1,000 is payable up front on December 15 when the contract is signed. The remainder is due when the aquarium is installed. Wax finishes installing the aquarium on January 5, 2016. Wax includes the $1,000 advance in gross income in 2015.

Example 24: Morelli Shoes is a cash method taxpayer that uses the calendar year as its tax year. On November 30, 2015, Morelli sells $10,000 of shoes to a customer. Payment is due in 30 days, but payment is not actually received until January 2, 2016. Because the company uses the cash method, it does not include the $10,000 in its gross income until the year it receives the payment (2016).

Example 25: Pointe Carpet Cleaners accepts plumbing services from a customer in lieu of cash payment. The value of those plumbing services must be included in the company's gross income for the year.

Constructive receipt of income doctrine. Under the **constructive receipt of income doctrine**, a business constructively receives income in the tax year during which the income is credited to the business's account, set apart for the business, or otherwise made available without any substantial limitation or restriction. A business may be treated as having constructively received income even though it does not have actual possession of the income until after the end of the year. If a business authorizes someone to receive income on its behalf as its agent, the business will be considered to have received income when its agent receives income on its behalf.[45]

A check is considered received when it is delivered into the hands of the payee, unless the check is later dishonored. However, if a check could have been delivered in one year but the payee requests that delivery be delayed, the payee will be considered to have constructively received the check in the year it could have been delivered.

Example 26: Pettway Check Printing is a cash method taxpayer that uses the calendar year as its tax year. Pettway has a bank account that pays interest on the last day of the month. It must include the interest in its gross income when the interest is credited to its account, even if Pettway does not attempt to withdraw the interest from the bank account.

---

[43] Code Sec. 446(b).
[44] Rev. Rul. 78-39, 1978-1 CB 73.

[45] Rev. Rul. 79-379, 1979-2 CB 204.

Example 27: Sealy Rentals authorizes Ming Sealy to act as its agent and to receive rental payments from tenants. The company is considered to have received rental payments when they are delivered to Ming.

Example 28: Sandy Fuller was out of town during the last two weeks of 2015 and did not return home until January 1, 2016. While she was away, Sandy received a check for $10,000 from a client for services previously rendered and billed. Sandy must report the $10,000 in income for 2015, even though she was unable to cash the check until the next year. The fact that the amount was made available to Sandy without substantial limitation or restriction during 2015 is sufficient for her to be required to pay tax on that amount during 2015.

Example 29: Assume the same facts as in Example 28, except the customer encloses a note along with the check and asks Sandy not to cash the check until after the first of the year because until then the bank account will not have sufficient funds to cover the check. Because there are substantial limitations placed on the check, Sandy does not take constructive receipt of the $10,000 until 2016.

Example 30: Matava Coffees received payment for an order of its products on December 31 but could not get to the bank to cash the check until January 2. The company is considered to have received the payment on December 31.

Example 31: Hendrix Extracts is a cash method taxpayer that uses the calendar year as its tax year. On December 10, 2015, Hendrix sells $2,000 of its products to Brian Hudnell. Payment is not due until January 9, 2016, but the invoice states that Brian can receive a one-percent discount if he pays by December 20. Brian tells Hendrix he will send a check by December 20; however, the company tells him it will honor the one-percent discount if he delays payment until January 1. Brian agrees to the new terms. Hendrix must include the $2,000 in its gross income for 2015 because it could have received the cash in 2015. Hendrix cannot avoid paying tax on the $2,000 that Brian had intended to pay to it in 2015 by refusing or altering the terms to accept the payment in another tax year.

Reason for the Rule: The constructive receipt doctrine for income was developed to prevent taxpayers from refusing to accept income that was available to them. If taxpayers could refuse to accept income made available to them, they could indefinitely delay having to pay tax on that income or could time receipt to take advantage of lower marginal income tax rates. It is important to note that the constructive receipt doctrine does not prevent taxpayers from delaying billing for their goods or services.

Original issue discount. Because cash method taxpayers recognize income upon the receipt of cash, taxpayers using the cash method could avoid being taxed on interest income by structuring loans so that no payments for interest are received until the note matures. These types of loans are issued at a discount (below the amount due at maturity), and the difference between the loan proceeds and the amount due at maturity is interest that is called "original issue discount" (OID). If the borrower uses the accrual method, this type of loan arrangement could result in the accrual method borrower deducting interest expense over the life of the loan and the cash method lender delaying recognition of income until the interest is paid at the end of the loan. To prevent such situations from occurring, the tax laws require that cash method taxpayers use the accrual method for recording interest income from loans involving OID.[46]

---

[46] Code Secs. 1272(a)(3) and 1273(a).

.02 Accounting for Expenses

Under the cash method of accounting, businesses ordinarily may not deduct (or capitalize) an expense until the year that the expense is actually paid. Although one might expect that there would be a tax law comparable to the constructive receipt doctrine for payments, no such rule exists. A taxpayer's mere promise to make a payment is not considered an actual payment, even though the promise is secured by collateral or a letter of credit. However, an expense may be deducted the year payment is made, even though payment is made with borrowed funds.

Amounts paid by check are considered paid when the check is mailed or delivered, provided that the bank honors the check. Amounts paid by credit card are considered paid when the amount is charged, regardless of when the taxpayer pays the credit card bill. If a taxpayer authorizes an agent to make a payment, payment is considered made by the taxpayer when made by the agent (e.g., when the agent mails a check).

Reason for the Rule: Because of differences between the Code's treatment of income and deductions, the courts have rejected the notion of a constructive payment doctrine as a corollary to the constructive receipt of income doctrine.[47] "Gross income" is broadly construed because the Code is presumed to tax all income unless specifically excluded from gross income by the tax laws. In contrast, deductions are narrowly construed and considered a matter of legislative grace. The constructive receipt of income doctrine helps prevent taxpayers from evading the intent of the Code to tax all income. A constructive payment doctrine would hinder Congress's intent to limit deductions to amounts actually paid.

Example 32: A cash method taxpayer uses the calendar year as its tax year. On December 10, 2015, the company purchases office supplies for $500 and pays for them on January 8, 2016. Because the company uses the cash method, it may not deduct its payment as a trade or business expense until 2016, the year it makes the payment.

Example 33: Harbor Motors is a cash method taxpayer that uses the calendar year as its tax year. On November 10, 2015, Harbor hires an advertising agency and agrees to pay $2 million for its services. The amount was billed and was due in 2015, but Harbor waited until 2016 to pay the bill. Because there is no rule comparable to the constructive receipt of income doctrine for payments, Harbor deducts the $2 million in 2016.

Example 34: Johnson Industrial Clothing is a cash method taxpayer that uses the calendar year as its tax year. On November 10, 2015, Johnson purchases exterminating services and gives the exterminator a $250 merchandise credit as payment for the services. Although the exterminator must include the $250 in its gross income for 2015, Johnson cannot deduct the $250 until the exterminator actually uses the credit to purchase merchandise from Johnson.

Example 35: Westly Moccasins is a cash method taxpayer that uses the calendar year as its tax year. On December 28, 2015, one of Westly's employees charges an airline ticket on the company's credit card. The company receives the credit card statement containing the airline ticket charge in January and pays the bill on February 2, 2016. Because amounts paid by credit card are considered paid when the amount is charged, regardless of when the bill is paid, the company deducts the travel expense in 2015.

---

[47] *Vander Poel, Francis & Co., Inc.*, 8 TC 407, Dec. 15,628 (1947).

Example 36: Ramone, Inc. is a cash method taxpayer that uses the calendar year as its tax year. On December 31, 2015, the company mails a check for $150 in payment for supplies that were delivered earlier in the month. Assuming there are sufficient funds in the bank, Ramone is considered to have paid for the supplies in 2015.

Example 37: Photographic Silk Screens is a cash method taxpayer that uses the calendar year as its tax year. On December 14, 2015, the company borrows $35,000 to purchase a minivan. On December 15, 2015, it uses the borrowed funds to purchase the minivan. It does not start repaying the loan until January 2016. The company will be treated as having paid for the minivan in 2015.

Example 38: Tes Realtors hires a real estate management firm to act as its agent in managing one of its apartment buildings. On June 14, 2015, the management firm pays $1,000 to a pesticide firm. The payment will be considered to be made by Tes Realtors on June 14, 2015.

Prepaid expenses. Prepaid expenses are treated the same way for cash method and accrual method taxpayers. As a general rule, prepaid expenses must be capitalized and amortized over the period to which the amounts paid apply.

Example 39: Goodwater Packaging is a cash method taxpayer that uses the calendar year as its tax year. On December 1, 2015, Goodwater pays $96,000 for a two-year lease of office space. Goodwater cannot deduct the $96,000 in 2015 but instead must amortize the $96,000 over the two-year term of the lease. For each month during the year that Goodwater occupies the office space, it may deduct $4,000 ($96,000/24). Thus, it deducts $4,000 in 2015, $48,000 in 2016 ($4,000 × 12), and $44,000 in 2017 ($4,000 × 11).

If the prepaid amount covers services that will be completed in accordance with the **12-month rule**, a cash method taxpayer can deduct the full amount paid in the current year. The 12-month rule applies if the amount paid creates (or facilitates the creation of) any right or benefit for the taxpayer that does not extend beyond the *earlier* of (1) 12 months after the first date on which the taxpayer realizes the right or benefit or (2) the end of the tax year following the tax year in which the payment is made.[48]

Example 40: Plastics Recycling is a cash method taxpayer that uses the calendar year as its tax year. On December 10, 2015, Plastics pays $5,000 for its annual premium on a property insurance policy effective from December 16, 2015, to December 15, 2016. Because the benefit (insurance coverage) attributable to the $5,000 payment does not extend more than a year beyond the *earlier* of December 16, 2016 (12 months from the date the first benefit was received) or the end of 2016 (the next tax year), Plastics Recycling may deduct the entire $5,000 in 2015 under the 12-month rule.

Example 41: Sacred Files is a cash method taxpayer that uses the calendar year as its tax year. On December 27, 2015, Sacred Files pays $1,825 for its annual premium for a property insurance policy effective January 2, 2016, to January 1, 2017. Because the benefit (insurance coverage) attributable to the $1,825 payment extends beyond the *earlier* of January 2, 2017 (12 months from the date the first benefit was received) or the end of 2016 (the end of the next tax year), it cannot deduct the payment in 2015 but instead must capitalize the payment. For each day of coverage during the year, it may deduct $5 ($1,825/365). Although it cannot deduct anything in 2015, it can deduct $1,820 ($5 × 364) in 2016, and $5 in 2017.

Interest. The special 12-month rule does not apply to interest expense. A cash method taxpayer can deduct interest only in the year it was paid. If interest is withheld from the proceeds of

---

[48] Reg. § 1.263(a)-4(f).

¶ 306.02

a loan or paid by means of an additional loan extended by the same lender, it cannot be deducted by the borrower for the year it was withheld or paid by means of an additional loan. Similarly, a cash method taxpayer can deduct prepaid interest only in the tax year to which the interest relates.[49]

Example 42: In 2016, Rick's Soft Pretzels borrows $1 million to help pay for a new office building. During 2017, the company falls behind on its payments, but the lender agrees to let the company pay the overdue amount (which includes $10,000 of interest) over a five-year period at a higher interest rate. Rick's cannot deduct the $10,000 of interest in 2017 because it was paid with the new loan.

Example 43: Assume the same facts as in Example 42, except Rick's borrows money from a different lender and uses the proceeds from that loan to pay the overdue amount. In this situation, Rick's may take a deduction in 2017 for the $10,000 of interest that it paid to the original lender.

Special rule for points paid by individuals. Individual taxpayers are allowed an itemized deduction for interest they pay in connection with loans associated with their personal residences. Individual taxpayers who use the cash method of accounting may deduct as an itemized deduction the full amount of points paid for a mortgage loan in the year paid under certain conditions. Businesses are required to amortize any points paid over the life of the loan.

> "Points" defined. **Points** represent prepaid interest a lender charges in exchange for a lower interest rate over the life of the loan. These amounts, sometimes called "loan origination fees," are expressed as a percentage of the loan amount and result in a lower interest rate to the borrower.

When points are paid on the purchase or improvement of a principal residence, individuals can deduct the points as interest expense in the year paid. Points paid for any other reason, including the refinancing of a residence or the purchase of a residence other than the taxpayer's principal residence must be amortized over the life of the loan.[50]

Example 44: Janice Copper purchases a home for $500,000 in 2015 by paying $100,000 down and taking out a $400,000 mortgage. At the closing, Janice pays a two-percent loan origination fee. During 2015, Janice also pays $10,000 in interest on the loan. On her 2015 tax return, Janice can deduct the $10,000 as home mortgage interest plus the $8,000 ($400,000 × 2%) of points paid in connection with the loan used to purchase her principal residence.

Example 45: A business borrows $1 million to help pay for a new office building. In order to obtain a lower interest rate over the term of the loan, the business pays $10,000, which is equal to one percentage point ($1,000,000 × 1%). The business cannot take a deduction for the $10,000 for the year it borrowed the money, but it may deduct the $10,000 ratably over the term of the loan.

.03 Other Special Rules for Cash Method Taxpayers

Other provisions of the Code and regulations applicable to cash method taxpayers may supersede these general rules. For example, some expenses cash method taxpayers pay in the current year must be capitalized and deducted over several tax years.[51] Cash method taxpayers may be required to capitalize certain costs associated with real or tangible personal property they produce or acquire for resale.[52] They also may be required to use the percentage of completion method to account for certain long-term contracts. Each of these special rules is discussed at ¶ 309. When these special rules apply, the taxpayer will receive a deduction in years in which no cash is paid.

---

[49] Code Sec. 461(g)(1).
[50] Code Sec. 461(g)(2); Rev. Rul. 87-22, 1987-1 CB 146.
[51] Code Secs. 263 and 168.
[52] Code Sec. 263A.

Example 46: Divine Stoves purchases a new office building in 2015 for $1,950,000. Divine cannot deduct the entire cost of the building in 2015, even though it paid cash for the building. Instead, the tax laws allow Divine to begin taking depreciation deductions for the building starting in 2015. Thus, in 2016 Divine will be entitled to a depreciation deduction against gross income, even though it will make no actual payment with respect to the building in 2016.

¶ 307 Accrual Method of Accounting

Under the accrual method of accounting, businesses generally report income in the tax year during which they earn the income, regardless of when they receive payment for it. They also deduct expenses in the tax year during which they incur expenses, regardless of when the expenses are paid. Although the accrual method of accounting does not give businesses as much control over the year in which income and expenses must be taken into account, it still provides some flexibility. For example, a business using the accrual method of accounting can defer receipt of income to a subsequent tax year by delaying the shipment of goods to its customers.

.01 Accounting for Income

Under the accrual method, taxpayers include income on their tax returns for the tax year during which all events have occurred to fix their right to receive the income and the amount of the income becomes determinable with reasonable accuracy. This is referred to as the **all-events test.** Under the accrual method, it is not the actual or constructive receipt of income, but the right to receive income, that governs the timing of when income must be included in gross income. Taxpayers have a fixed right to receive income when *any* one of the following events occurs:

1. Required performance is completed,

2. Payment of the income becomes due, or

3. Payment is received.

Example 47: Capelli Architects is an accrual method taxpayer that uses the calendar year as its tax year. Capelli performs architectural services for a customer and bills the customer $3,000 on December 20, 2015. It receives payment from the customer on January 19, 2016. Although the company did not receive actual payment from the customer during 2015, it must include the $3,000 in its gross income for that year because all events occurred to fix the company's right to receive the income and the amount of the income became determinable with reasonable accuracy during 2015.

Example 48: Sluman Steel, Inc. is an accrual method taxpayer that uses the calendar year as its tax year. On December 23, 2015, Sluman sells steel to a customer for $100,000, but it does not bill the customer for the purchase until January 2, 2016. The customer pays the company's invoice on February 1, 2016. Sluman must include the $100,000 in its gross income for 2015, the year it sold the steel, because that is when it had a fixed right to receive the income.

Although a taxpayer has a fixed right to receive income, the income need not be included in the taxpayer's gross income if there is a reasonable expectancy that the claim will not be paid.[53]

Advance receipt of payments for services. As a general rule, advance payments received for services to be performed in a future tax year (or tax years) are included in the accrual method taxpayer's gross income in the year the payments are received, regardless whether the taxpayer recognizes the full amount of the advance payments for that tax year for financial reporting purposes and regardless whether the taxpayer earned the full amount of the advance payments in that tax year.

---

[53] *The Corn Exchange Bank*, CA-2, 2 USTC ¶ 455, 37 F2d 34; *M. Suffolk*, 40 BTA 1121, Dec. 10,925.

Taxpayers can elect to include an advance payment in their gross income for the tax year it is received to the extent that they include the payment in their income in their applicable financial statement for that tax year and include the remaining amount of the advance payment in their gross income for the next tax year.[54] This special rule (referred to as the "deferral method") does not apply to advance payments of interest because interest must be included in gross income in the year it is received, regardless of the taxpayer's method of accounting. This special rule also applies to sales of goods and to sales of gift cards.

Example 49: DeSanto Musical Instruments is an accrual method taxpayer that uses the calendar year as its tax year. DeSanto offers lessons and has chosen to use the deferral method to report advance payments for its lessons. On November 1, 2015, the company received an advance payment of $1,200 for 48 music lessons. It provided eight lessons in 2015 and 40 lessons in 2016. In its applicable financial statement, it includes $200 ($1,200/48 × 8) of the advance payment in its revenues for 2015. It includes $1,000 ($1,200/48 × 40) of the advance payment in its revenues for 2016. For federal income tax purposes, it must include $200 of the advance payment in its gross income for 2015 and the remaining $1,000 of the advance payment in its gross income for 2016.

Example 50: Zedd Appliance Repairs is an accrual method taxpayer that uses the calendar year as its tax year. Zedd has chosen to use the deferral method to report advance payments for services. In 2015, Zedd receives $200 for a two-year contract under which it agrees to repair a customer's television set should any problems arise. In its applicable financial statement, it recognizes one-fourth of the payment in its revenues for 2015, one-half of the payment in its revenues for 2016, and the remaining one-fourth in its revenues for 2017. For federal income tax purposes, it must include $50 ($200 × ¼) in gross income for 2015 and the remaining $150 ($200 × ¾) in gross income for 2016. Although it actually will earn $50 ($200 × ¼) of the advance payment in 2017, it cannot delay paying taxes on the advanced payment beyond 2016 (the next tax year).

GAAP vs. Code: For financial reporting purposes, Zedd from Example 50 would recognize the $200 over three years as it earned the income. For tax purposes, the income is recognized over two years. This difference in the treatment of prepaid income for financial accounting and tax accounting purposes will result in a difference between Zedd's net income and taxable income in both 2016 and 2017.

Advance receipt of payments for sales of goods. As a general rule, advance payments are included in gross income in the year they are received. However, an accrual method taxpayer can elect to use the same deferral method used for advance payments for services and in addition can wait to recognize income from advance payments from the sale of goods if the taxpayer accounts for the sale using the same method for financial and tax accounting purposes.[55] Under this alternative method of reporting, an advance payment is included in a taxpayer's gross receipts on the *earlier* of:

1. The tax year in which the payments are included in gross income under the accrual method of accounting, or

2. The tax year in which the taxpayer includes any portion of the advance payments in income for financial reporting purposes.

Example 51: Mahl Shoes, Inc. is a retailer that uses the accrual method of accounting and the calendar year as its tax year. On December 15, 2015, the company sells some shoes and receives an advance payment of $200. The shoes are shipped on January 2, 2016.

---

[54] Rev. Proc. 2004-34, 2004-1 CB 991, modified and clarified by Rev. Proc. 2011-18, 2011-5 IRB 443.

[55] Reg. § 1.451-5.

Normally Mahl would include the $200 in gross income for 2015. However, if the company accounts for sales of goods when they are shipped for both tax and financial reporting purposes, under the alternative method Mahl may include the $200 in gross receipts for 2016 (the year during which the goods were shipped).

 Planning Pointer: If it would benefit the business to delay receipt of income to the subsequent tax year, the business should consider taking advantage of the rules regarding when its right to income becomes fixed. For example, if income is accrued at the time goods are shipped, the business should consider delaying shipments to the next tax year. If income is accrued when title to goods changes, the business should consider shipping F.O.B. (free on board) destination.

Contested amounts. An accrual method business is not required to include in gross receipts amounts accrued but being contested. In such situations, the taxpayer recognizes gross income when the contested amounts are received.[56]

.02 Accounting for Expenses

Taxpayers using the accrual method of accounting may deduct or capitalize a business expense when the all-events test has been satisfied and economic performance has occurred with respect to the liability. The all-events test is satisfied when all events have occurred to establish the existence of the liability and the amount of the liability can be determined with reasonable accuracy.

Example 52: Berdin Tape, which uses as its tax year a fiscal year ending on September 30, purchases equipment on September 30 but does not pay for the equipment until December 1. Because the company uses the accrual method of accounting, it may capitalize the equipment and begin depreciating it in the tax year of the purchase. It need not wait until the year it pays for the equipment.

Economic performance. The tax laws provide various principles to be used to determine when economic performance occurs.[57] In the case of interest, economic performance occurs as the interest economically accrues daily (as the borrower uses the borrowed funds), not as payments are made. When the taxpayer's liability arises from another party providing services or property to the taxpayer, economic performance occurs as the property or services are provided. If a taxpayer's liability arises out of the use of property by the taxpayer, economic performance occurs ratably over the period of time the taxpayer is entitled to the use of the property. When the taxpayer's liability requires the taxpayer to provide services or the use of property to another person, economic performance occurs as the taxpayer provides the services or the use of property.

 Reason for the Rule: The requirement that economic performance must occur before all events establishing the existence of a liability will be considered to have occurred was added by the Tax Reform Act of 1984 to take into account the time value of money.[58] As Congress noted, permitting accrual method taxpayers to currently deduct expenses that are attributable to activities to be performed or amounts to be paid in the future overstates the true cost of the expense and causes revenue loss to the government (particularly in high inflationary times).

---

[56] *Burnet v. Sanford & Brooks Company*, SCt, 2 USTC ¶ 636, 282 US 359, 51 SCt 150 (1931).

[57] Code Sec. 461(h).

[58] House Ways and Means Committee Report No. 98-432 (October 21, 1983, and March 5, 1984), at 917.

Recurring item exception. Under the "recurring item exception" to the economic performance requirement, a business can treat a liability as incurred for a tax year if the all-events test is met *and* the following requirements are satisfied:

1. Economic performance with respect to the liability occurs on or before the date the taxpayer files a timely (including extensions) return for that tax year or, if sooner, 8½ months after the close of the tax year.

2. The liability is recurring in nature and the taxpayer consistently treats similar liabilities as incurred in the tax year during which the all-events test is satisfied. A liability is recurring if it can generally be expected to be incurred from one tax year to the next. However, it need not actually be incurred by the taxpayer each year. A liability never previously incurred by a taxpayer may be treated as recurring if it is reasonable to expect that the liability will be incurred on a recurring basis in the future.

3. Either the amount of the liability is not material or accruing the liability for that tax year would result in a better matching of the liability with the income to which it relates than would result from accruing the liability for the tax year in which economic performance occurs.

To determine whether a liability is "material," the amount of the liability in absolute terms and in relation to the amount of other items of income and expense attributable to the same activity must be considered. A liability is material if it is material for financial statement purposes under GAAP. However, a liability that is immaterial for financial statement purposes under GAAP nevertheless may be material for tax purposes.[59]

Certain liabilities cannot qualify for the recurring item exception:[60]

- A liability to pay interest;

- Liabilities arising under a workers' compensation act or out of any tort, breach of contract, or violation of law;

- A liability for which economic performance rules are not provided; and

- A liability incurred by a tax shelter.

Example 53: Digital Video Recorders is an accrual method taxpayer that uses the calendar year as its tax year. Digital offers customers a refund if they are not satisfied with their products. During 2015, 100 customers request a refund of the $500 purchase price. Digital refunds $30,000 on or before September 15, 2016, the extended due date for its 2015 tax return. It refunds the remaining $20,000 after September 15, 2016. If Digital adopts the recurring item exception with respect to these refunds, economic performance will be treated as having occurred in 2015 with respect to the $30,000 refunded on or before September 15, 2016. Economic performance will not be treated as having occurred with respect to the $20,000 refunded after September 15. That amount is not eligible for recurring item treatment because the refund occurred more than 8½ months after the end of the 2015 tax year.

Prepaid expenses. Unless the 12-month rule applies, prepaid expenses must be capitalized and amortized over the period covered by the payment. If the 12-month rule applies, a business deducts the amount of prepaid expenses in the year paid. The 12-month rule applies if the amount paid creates (or facilitates the creation of) any right or benefit for the taxpayer that does not extend beyond the *earlier* of (1) 12 months after the first date on which the taxpayer realizes the right or benefit or (2) the end of the tax year following the tax year in which the payment is made. This is the same 12-month rule that applies to taxpayers using the cash method of accounting (see ¶ 306.02).

Example 54: On November 1, 2015 Shatran Ticket Brokers, an accrual method taxpayer using the calendar year as its tax year, pays $72,000 for a two-year lease of office space. Shatran

---

[59] Reg. § 1.461-5(b).   [60] Reg. § § 1.461-4(g)(2)-(6) and 1.461-5(c).

cannot deduct the entire $72,000 in 2015 but instead must amortize the $72,000 over the two-year lease term. For each month during the year that it occupies the office space, the company may deduct $3,000 ($72,000/24). Therefore, it can deduct $6,000 for 2015 ($3,000 × 2 months), $36,000 for 2016 ($3,000 × 12), and $30,000 for 2017 ($3,000 × 10).

Example 55: Babjeck Traders is an accrual method, calendar year taxpayer. On November 1, 2015, Babjeck pays the $2,000 annual premium for a property insurance policy effective November 15, 2015, to November 14, 2016. Because the benefit (the insurance coverage) attributable to the $2,000 does not extend beyond the *earlier* of November 15, 2016, or the end of 2016, Babjeck deducts the entire $2,000 in 2015.

Example 56: Danville Tubing is an accrual method, calendar year taxpayer. On December 27, 2015, Danville pays its $2,190 annual premium for a property insurance policy effective January 5, 2016, to January 4, 2017. Because the benefit (insurance coverage) attributable to the $2,190 payment extends beyond December 31, 2016 (the end of the tax year following the tax year in which the payment was made), the company cannot deduct the payment in 2015 but instead must capitalize the payment. For each day of coverage during the year, it may deduct $6 ($2,190/365). Therefore, it deducts $0 for 2015, but it can deduct $2,166 in 2016 ($6 × 361) and $24 ($6 × 4) in 2017.

Expenses owed to a related party. When amounts are accrued to a related party, the tax laws require that the accrual method taxpayer postpone the timing of the deduction until the cash method recipient includes the amount in income.[61] This rule continues to apply even after a taxpayer's relationship with a person has ended. It ensures that the amount reported in income by the recipient and the deduction taken by the payer are accounted for at the same time.

Example 57: The employee of a corporation (who is also a shareholder) uses the calendar year as its tax year and the cash method of accounting. The corporation also uses a calendar year-end, but it uses the accrual method of accounting. If, in December 2015, the corporation declares a $50,000 bonus to be paid to the employee in January 2016, the corporation normally would deduct the compensation incurred in December on its 2015 income tax return, and that would reduce the corporation's 2015 income tax liability. The cash method shareholder, however, will not include the $50,000 in income until 2016. Therefore, the government will not receive the taxes due on that amount for an entire year. However, if the employee/shareholder and the corporation are related parties, then the corporation must wait until 2016 to take the deduction.

Whether the two parties are related is determined as of the close of the tax year for which the expense otherwise could be deducted. Figure 3-1 summarizes the relationships involving business entities that are considered related parties for purposes of this special rule. The rules regarding what relationships constitute a "related party" are discussed in Chapter 8 (see ¶ 804).

Figure 3-1 Related Parties

1. An individual and the individual's spouse, siblings, ancestors (parents, grandparents, etc.), or descendants (children, grandchildren, etc.);

2. An individual and a corporation in which the individual *directly or indirectly* owns more than 50 percent of the value of its outstanding stock;

3. An individual and a partnership in which the individual *directly or indirectly* owns more than 50 percent of the capital or profits interest;

---

[61] Code Sec. 267(a)(2).

4. Two corporations that are members of the same controlled group (in which one corporation owns at least 80 percent of both the voting shares and the value of the other corporation's stock);

5. A corporation and a partnership if the same person(s) own more than 50 percent of the value of the corporation's outstanding stock and more than 50 percent of the capital or profits interests in the partnership;

6. An S corporation and another S corporation if the same person(s) own more than 50 percent of the value in the outstanding stock of each corporation;

7. An S corporation and a C corporation if the same person(s) own more than 50 percent of the value in the outstanding stock of each corporation; and

8. Two partnerships in which the same persons *directly or indirectly* own more than 50 percent of the capital or profits interest.

Reason for the Rule: This rule prevents an accrual method business from claiming a deduction for an accrued expense that the related cash method taxpayer is not required to include in gross income until some subsequent time, if at all.[62] If in Example 57, the employee were also the sole shareholder of the corporation, the corporation and the shareholder would be related parties. The tax laws would delay the corporation's deduction of the bonus until 2016—the year the shareholder includes it in gross income. This allows the government to receive the tax revenues from the employee's income in the same year that it provides a tax benefit to the corporation.

Contested liabilities. A business that transfers money or other property in satisfaction of a liability that it is contesting is allowed to take a deduction for the tax year in which the amount is paid.[63] To take the deduction, the money or other property used to satisfy the asserted liability must be transferred beyond the taxpayer's control. It is not sufficient that the taxpayer transfer money or other property to an escrow agent or purchase a bond to guarantee payment.

If a business takes a deduction for a contested liability in the year that money or other property is transferred in satisfaction of the liability and a portion of the contested liability is recovered after the contest is settled, the business must include the recovered amount in gross income for the year of the settlement. See ¶ 313 for further discussion of the tax benefit rule.

Example 58: Medlock Vending is an accrual method taxpayer that uses the calendar year as its tax year. In 2015 Medlock pays a $10,000 real property tax bill that it receives but contests $500 of the amount owed. In 2017, the contest is settled and Medlock receives a $100 refund. Medlock deducts the $10,000 it paid in 2015 but must include the $100 refund in its gross income for 2017.

Reason for the Rule: This provision was added to the Code by the Revenue Act of 1964 to reverse a 1961 U.S. Supreme Court decision holding that a contested amount could not be deducted until the contest terminated because all of the events that would determine whether the amount ultimately would have to be paid could not be determined until that time.[64] Congress believed that taxpayers should not be denied a deduction with respect to an item when payment actually has been made, even though the liability is being contested.

---

[62] House Ways and Means Committee Report 98-432 (October 21, 1983, and March 5, 1984), at 1578.

[63] Code Sec. 461(f).

[64] Senate Finance Committee Report No. 88-830 (January 28, 1964), 1964 U.S. Code Congressional & Administrative News, at 1773.

¶ 308 Hybrid Method of Accounting

A business is not limited to either the cash or the accrual method of accounting. Instead, a business can use a combination of accounting methods if the combination clearly reflects its income and is consistently used.[65] For example, a taxpayer can use the accrual method to account for its purchases and sales of goods and the cash method to report all other items. This, of course, assumes that the tax law does not require the taxpayer to use the accrual method as its overall method of accounting (see ¶ 305.01).

Although a business is not limited to either the cash or the accrual method of accounting, there are limitations on the combinations that a business may use. For example, if a business is required to maintain an inventory to account for its income, it must use the accrual method to account for its purchases and sales. The business may, however, be allowed to use the cash method of accounting for all other items of income and expenses. A business that uses the cash method of accounting for reporting its income must use the cash method of accounting for reporting its expenses. Similarly, a business that uses the accrual method of accounting for reporting its expenses must use the accrual method for reporting its income. Finally, if a combination of accounting methods includes any special methods of accounting, the business must comply with the requirements relating to such special methods. (See ¶ 309.)

¶ 309 Special Accounting Methods

As previously mentioned in this chapter, special methods of accounting may apply to certain items of income and expense. For example, special methods of accounting are required when there are installment sales, long-term contracts, research and experimental expenditures, crops, and soil and water conservation expenditures. Each of these special methods is discussed in the sections that follow. When applicable, taxpayers must abide by these special rules, regardless of the overall method of accounting (cash, accrual, hybrid) that they use.

.01 Installment Method of Accounting

If a business disposes of property and at least one payment is received after the close of the tax year during which the disposition occurred, the business must report the gain from the sale using the **installment method** of accounting.[66] Under the installment method, gain is recognized as the payments are received rather than at the time that the sale occurs. This is consistent with the "wherewithal-to-pay concept," introduced in Chapter 1 (see ¶ 104.07), that taxpayers should recognize income when they are best able to pay tax on that income.

The installment method resembles the cash method of accounting because income is recognized as the cash is received. Unless the taxpayer elects out of the installment method, this method must be used to recognize income from installment sales, regardless of the taxpayer's overall accounting method. When a taxpayer elects out of using the installment method, the entire gain is recognized in the year of the sale.

Under the installment method, the amount of gain recognized for a tax year is computed by multiplying the amount of payments received during the year by a fraction whose numerator is the seller's gross profit from the sale and whose denominator is the total contract price. Further details regarding the installment method are provided in Chapter 8 (see ¶ 810).

Example 59: Racket Accessories sells land on October 10, 2015. The terms of the sale require that equal payments are to be received over five years. The total contract price is $50,000, and the company's gross profit from the sale is $40,000. Thus, under the installment method, for every dollar of proceeds that Racket receives, 80 percent ($40,000/$50,000) represents gross profit from the sale. If Racket's payments during 2015 total $3,000, then, under the installment method, Racket includes $2,400 of the

---

[65] Reg. § 1.446-1(c)(1)(iv).   [66] Code Sec. 453.

gain in gross income in 2015 ($3,000 × 80%). If it receives $10,000 in 2016, it includes $8,000 in gross income in 2016 ($10,000 × 80%). If Racket elects out of using the installment method, it will report the entire $10,000 of gain on its 2015 tax return. Electing out of the installment method is consistent with the accrual method of accounting because all profits are recognized in 2015 at the time of the sale.

 GAAP vs. Code: The installment method applies the wherewithal-to-pay concept, which says that income should be recognized when taxpayers have the means to pay tax on that income. Under the accrual method of accounting, the entire gain is recorded in the year of the sale because that is when the earnings process is complete. Accordingly, the installment method is not an acceptable method for financial accounting purposes. Businesses that do not elect out of the installment method will include different amounts of income from the sale in net income versus taxable income, not only in the year of the sale, but for all subsequent periods in which the cash is received.

.02 Long-Term Contracts

Businesses are required to use a special method of accounting to report income from long-term contracts, regardless of the overall method of accounting that they have chosen.[67] Usually the method that businesses are required to use is the percentage of completion method. However, under limited circumstances a business may use the completed contract method.

For tax purposes, a contract is a "long-term contract" if it satisfies each of the following three requirements:

1. It is a contract for the manufacture, building, installation, or construction of property;

2. It will not be completed within the contracting year; and

3. If it is a contract for the manufacture of property, it involves personal property that is a unique item not normally carried in the taxpayer's inventory or an item that normally requires more than 12 calendar months to complete.

Percentage of completion method. Under the **percentage of completion method (PCM),** taxpayers include in gross income each year the portion of the total contract price that corresponds to the percentage of the contract that they completed during the year. That amount is determined by multiplying the total contract price by the percentage of the total *estimated* contract costs that the taxpayer incurred during the tax year.

Example 60: Page Contracting is in the process of constructing an office building. The total contract price is $5 million, and Page estimates its total contract costs will be $3 million. During the first tax year, Page incurs $750,000 of contract costs. Because this amount represents 25 percent of the total estimated contract costs ($750,000/$3,000,000), it must include 25 percent of the contract price in its gross income. Thus, Page includes $1.25 million ($5,000,000 × 25%) in its gross income for the first year. From this amount, Page deducts the $750,000 of costs it incurs during the year. Thus, $500,000 ($1,250,000 – $750,000) will be included in Page's taxable income in the first year.

For tax purposes, businesses may elect not to include in their gross income any amount from a long-term contract until they have incurred at least 10 percent of the estimated total contract costs. An election is made on a business's original federal income tax return for the year of the election. An election applies to all long-term contracts entered into during and after the election year.[68]

---

[67] Code Sec. 460.

[68] Code Sec. 460(b)(5) and Reg. § 1.460-4(b)(6).

Example 61: Steele Contracting is constructing a retail store. The total contract price is $3 million, and Steele estimates its total contract costs will be $1.5 million. During 20X0, its first year working on the contract, Steele incurs $125,000 of contract costs. Because the amount of costs incurred is less than 10 percent of the estimated total contract costs ($1,500,000 × 10% = $150,000), the company may elect not to include any amount from the contract in its gross income for 20X0. If Steele makes such an election and incurs an additional $375,000 of contract costs during 20X1, the amount it includes in its gross income for 20X1 must be based on the percentage of total contract costs incurred not only for the current year, but for 20X0 as well. Thus, in 20X1, Steele is considered to have incurred $500,000 of contract costs ($125,000 + $375,000). Because this amount represents one-third of the total contract costs ($500,000/$1,500,000), Steele must report one-third of the $3 million, or $1 million, of the contract price in gross income for 20X1. From this amount, Steele can deduct the $500,000 of contract costs incurred thus far on the contract.

 GAAP vs. Code: Unlike the Code, which permits businesses to use the completed contract method of accounting only in limited circumstances, GAAP permits businesses to use the PCM only if certain conditions are met. Consequently, there likely will be a difference between net income and taxable income when a corporation enters into a long-term contract. This difference will occur for all years during the contract period.

After a business completes a long-term contract using the PCM, it is required to go back to all prior tax years and reapply the PCM using its *actual total contract price* and its *actual contract costs*. This process is referred to as the "look-back method." The taxpayer must then pay interest on any amount of tax that was deferred because it underestimated the total contract price or overestimated total contract costs. It is entitled to receive interest on any extra tax that it paid because it overestimated the total contract price or underestimated total contract costs. The rate of interest for both underpayments and overpayments is the same interest rate the IRS pays taxpayers for overpayments of federal income tax. However, the look-back method does not correct for differences in tax liability resulting from tax rates changing during the term of the contract.[69]

Example 62: Destine Contractors is a cash method taxpayer that uses the calendar year as its tax year. In 2015, the company enters into a contract to construct an apartment building. The total contract price is $2 million. Destine estimates that its total contract costs will be $1 million. During 2015, it incurs $300,000 of contract costs. This represents 30 percent of its estimated contract costs; therefore, the amount that Destine includes in gross income for 2015 is $600,000 ($2,000,000 × 30%). Destine offsets its gross income by the $300,000 of contract costs incurred during the year.

During 2016, Destine incurs $450,000 of contract costs, which represents another 45 percent of its estimated total costs. Thus, in 2016 Destine will report $900,000 in gross income ($2,000,000 × 45%). It will offset its gross income by the $450,000 of contract costs incurred during 2016. During 2017, the company incurs $750,000 of contract costs to complete its construction of the apartment building. For 2017, it must include all amounts not previously included in gross income, or $500,000 ($2,000,000 – $600,000 – $900,000). It then must apply the look-back method to determine how much tax it over- or underpaid in 2015 and 2016.

Using its actual costs ($1.5 million), the company calculates that in 2015 it should have included 20 percent of the contract price in gross income ($300,000/$1,500,000). Thus, its 2015 gross income should have been $400,000 ($2,000,000 × 20%). In 2016, Destine should have included 30 percent

---

[69] Reg. § 1.460-6.

($450,000/$1,500,000) of the $2 million in gross income. Net income (gross income – contract costs) reported using the estimated contract price and costs, and net income reported using the actual price and costs are summarized below.

Year	Using Estimates	Using Actual Amounts	Overpayment
2015	$300,000	$100,000	$200,000
2016	450,000	150,000	300,000

Because of these overpayments, Destine overpaid taxes on $200,000 of income in 2015 and on $300,000 of income in 2016. If Destine's marginal tax rate is 34 percent in each of those years, it would have overpaid $170,000 in taxes ($500,000 × 34%). Destine is owed back interest on the overpayment of the taxes.

The look-back method is not required for any long-term contract completed within two years of the contract commencement date if the actual gross contract price does not exceed the *lesser* of $1 million or one percent of the taxpayer's average annual gross receipts for the three tax years preceding the tax year in which the contract was completed. In addition, taxpayers may elect not to apply the look-back method if their cumulative taxable income (or loss) under a contract as of the close of each prior contract year is within 10 percent of the cumulative look-back income (or loss) under the contract as of the close of that prior contract year.[70]

 Reason for the Rule: Congress requires that variances between the estimated and actual completion during each year of the contract be accounted for at the end of the contract through an interest charge or credit to the taxpayer. Congress does this because it recognizes that the use of the PCM may produce harsh results for taxpayers in some cases. For example, this can occur when the taxpayer has an overall loss on the contract or actual profits are significantly less than projected.[71]

Completed contract method. The PCM is not required for certain types of contracts. Instead, the income from these contrasts can be recognized either under the PCM or under the completed contract method. Under the **completed contract method**, no income or expenses related to the contract are recognized until the contract is completed. The types of contracts for which a taxpayer can use the completed contract method include exempt construction contracts and residential construction contracts.

A contract is an "exempt construction contract" if it is a home construction contract or another type of construction contract that the taxpayer estimates will be completed within two years, but only if the taxpayer's average annual gross receipts for the three tax years preceding the contracting year do not exceed $10 million. A long-term construction contract is a "home construction contract" if a taxpayer reasonably expects to attribute 80 percent or more of the estimated total allocable contract costs to (1) the construction of dwelling units in buildings containing four or fewer dwelling units and (2) improvements to real property directly related to, and located at the site of, the dwelling units. A "residential construction contract" is a home construction contract, except that the building or buildings constructed contain more than four dwelling units.[72] A "dwelling unit" is a home or apartment to provide living accommodations. It does not include a unit in a hotel, motel, or other establishment when more than half of the units are used on a transient basis.[73] "Allocable contract costs" include the cost of land, materials, and services as determined as of the close of the contracting year.

Example 63: On June 1, 20X1, Davidson Construction enters into a contract with Gina Kelsey to build a restaurant for $500,000. The estimated total costs for the contract are

---

[70] Code Sec. 460(b)(3)(B).
[71] Joint Committee on Taxation, *General Explanation of the Tax Reform Act of 1986*, at 527.
[72] Code Sec. 460(e)(1) and (6).
[73] Code Sec. 168(e)(2)(A)(ii).

$400,000. On March 31, 20X2, the contract is completed, and Gina accepts the building. As of December 31, 20X1, Davidson incurred $370,000 of job costs tied to the contract. From January 1 to March 31, 20X2, another $30,000 of job costs were incurred. Using the completed contract method, Davidson must capitalize all the job costs related to the restaurant contract and wait to deduct them until the job is completed, which is the same time the income is reported in 20X2. As a result, Davidson's 20X2 taxable income will increase by $100,000 ($500,000 – $400,000 total contract costs).

Reason for the Rule: Prior to the Tax Reform Act of 1986, taxpayers could elect to account for income from long-term contracts under either the PCM or the completed contract method. Congress decided to restrict use of the completed contract method of accounting for long-term contracts because it believed that use of that method of accounting permitted an unwarranted deferral of the income from long-term contracts.[74]

.03 Research and Experimental Expenditures

When taxpayers incur research and experimental expenditures, they have three options: (1) capitalize the expenditures (and do nothing else), (2) capitalize and amortize (expense) the expenditures over 60 months, or (3) deduct them entirely in the current year.[75] The second option (to capitalize and amortize) most closely reflects how the expenses are treated under the accrual method of accounting. The third option most closely resembles how expenses are treated under the cash method. However, any of the three options is available to all taxpayers, regardless of whether the taxpayer uses the cash, accrual, or hybrid method as its overall method of accounting. Thus, even when a corporation is required to use the accrual method of accounting, it has the option of expensing its research and experimental expenditures in the year in which the costs are incurred. The tax treatment of research and experimental expenditures is discussed in detail in Chapter 5 (see ¶ 507).

Example 64: Miller Presses incurs $60,000 of research and experimental expenditures during the year. The company has the option of capitalizing the expenditures (and not deducting them), capitalizing and then amortizing the expenditures ratably over 60 months, or expensing the entire $60,000 in the current tax year. It is irrelevant which method Miller uses as its overall accounting method.

.04 Crop Method of Accounting

Under the crop method of accounting, if crops are not harvested and sold in the same year during which they were planted, the cost of producing the crop cannot be deducted until the year in which the farmer realizes the gross income from the crop.[76] The use of the crop method is elective and requires the IRS's consent. The advantage of using the crop method is that it permits a farmer to deduct expenses attributable to the planting and growing of the crops in the year income is realized from the crops, thereby reducing taxable income for that year. If elected, the crop method applies to inventories of crops, regardless of which accounting method the taxpayer uses as its overall accounting method.

Example 65: Duett Farms incurs $30,000 in costs to plant wheat during 2015. It harvests the wheat in 2015 but delays selling the wheat until 2016. If Duett elects (with the IRS's consent) to use the crop method of accounting, it deducts its $30,000 in costs in 2016, the year it sells the wheat.

---

[74] Joint Committee on Taxation, *General Explanation of the Tax Reform Act of 1986*, at 527.

[75] Code Sec. 174.
[76] Reg. § 1.162-12(a).

.05 Soil and Water Conservation or Endangered Species Recovery Expenditures

Taxpayers engaged in the business of farming may treat as capital expenditures any expenses they pay or incur during the year for soil or water conservation of farmland, to prevent farmland erosion, or for endangered species recovery, or they may elect to take a current deduction for such expenditures.[77] However, the amount currently deducted cannot exceed 25 percent of a farmer's gross income from farming.

Example 66: Shadow Farms pays $15,000 to construct a terrace to stop soil erosion. Shadow can treat the $15,000 as a capital expenditure, or it can elect to currently deduct the $15,000 as a soil and water conservation expenditure. These two options are the only options available to Shadow, regardless of which accounting method it uses as its overall accounting method.

¶ 310 Adopting an Accounting Method

Businesses may choose any permissible method of accounting when they file their first tax return. Business owners are not required to use the same method of accounting to determine how to report their personal income and expenses and their business income and expenses. Taxpayers with separate and distinct businesses may use a different method of accounting for each business, provided that they keep separate books and records for each business.

If the IRS decides that a taxpayer's method of accounting does not clearly reflect the taxpayer's income and expenses, the IRS may compute the taxpayer's taxable income under a method of accounting that the IRS believes does clearly reflect the taxpayer's income and expenses. The IRS's exercise of its discretion will be upheld unless its decision clearly was unlawful or an abuse of its discretion.[78] The IRS may not require a taxpayer to change from a method of accounting that clearly reflects the taxpayer's taxable income merely because a different method more clearly reflects the taxpayer's taxable income.[79]

¶ 311 Changing an Accounting Method

Once a business has selected a method of accounting, it may change that method of accounting only with the IRS's consent,[80] even if the business is changing from an impermissible to a permissible method of accounting. Consent from the IRS must be obtained before a taxpayer can change from an impermissible to a permissible method of accounting. Taxpayers file Form 3115, *Application for Change in Accounting Method*, to request the IRS's consent to a change in method of accounting. Before the IRS will consent to a change, it will require the business to agree to terms and conditions intended to prevent any substantial distortion of income that otherwise would result from the change.

 Planning Pointer: Form 3115 must be filed during the year for which a change is desired and should be filed as early during the year as possible to give the IRS time to consider the request before the taxpayer's tax return for the year of the change is due. Unless the taxpayer is eligible to receive an automatic change (see ¶ 311.01 below), the IRS will charge the taxpayer a user fee.

---

[77] Code Sec. 175.
[78] *Thor Power Tool Co.*, SCt, 79-1 USTC ¶ 9139, 439 US 522, 99 SCt 773.

[79] *Wolf Bakery & Cafeteria Co.*, 5 TCM 389, Dec. 15,186(M); *H.L. Russell*, CA-1, 2 USTC ¶ 617, 45 F2d 100.
[80] Code Sec. 446(e).

.01 Automatic Changes

A business that complies with the applicable provisions of Rev. Proc. 2015-13,[81] which has been modified, clarified, and amplified by a number of other revenue procedures, will be deemed to have obtained the IRS's consent to change its method of accounting and will not be required to pay a user fee for requesting a change. Rev. Proc. 2015-14[82] lists the accounting method changes that may be made using the automatic change request procedures. Form 3115 usually must be filed with a taxpayer's income tax return to request an automatic change. A list of the automatic changes for which Form 3115 must be filed is included in the instructions for that form. Approval of the change will be granted for the tax year for which a change is requested.

¶ 312 Claim of Right Doctrine

Under the **claim of right doctrine**, a business that receives money or other property under a "claim of right" (i.e., the business treats the property as its own) without restriction as to the disposition of the property must include the amount of money or the fair market value of the property received in its gross income for the year of receipt, regardless of the taxpayer's overall method of accounting. The amount of money or FMV of the property received must be included in gross income even though the business may not be entitled to keep the money or property and will be required to refund the money or property in a subsequent tax year. For the claim of right doctrine to apply, each of the following requirements must be satisfied:

1. The business must receive cash or other property,

2. The cash or other property must constitute income for the business under its method of accounting,

3. The business must have unrestricted control over the use and disposition of the cash or other property received, and

4. The business must possess the cash or other property under a claim of right.

Example 67: Scoundrels, Inc. creates a Web page that duplicates the Web page of a bank and encourages visitors to the site to provide the company with financial and personal information. Scoundrels illegally obtains $500,000 from unsuspecting persons. Although the $500,000 was obtained through illegal actions, Scoundrels must include that amount in its gross income for the year under the claim of right doctrine.

 Reason for the Rule: The rule was adopted because the federal government did not want to wait to tax income until all disputes regarding the recipient's right to the income have been resolved.

A business that is required to refund an amount previously included in its gross income is entitled to a deduction for the amount refunded. However, because of the progressive nature of the federal income tax rates, the tax benefit of the deduction may not be as great as the tax cost of the income initially received. To mitigate this problem, taxpayers are entitled to reduce their tax liability for the year of repayment by the amount of the tax attributable to the inclusion of the item in gross income.[83] However, this mitigation rule applies only to deductions that exceed $3,000.

Example 68: Farmington Water Filtration is an accrual method taxpayer that uses the calendar year as its tax year. In 2015 Farmington's natural gas supplier gave Farmington a $5,000 refund. Because the claim of right doctrine applies, Farmington includes the refund in its gross income for 2015. However, in 2017 the natural gas supplier discovers that it made a mistake in making the refund and demands that the money

---

[81] 2015-5 IRB 419.
[82] 2015-5 IRB 450.

[83] Code Sec. 1341.

be returned. Farmington deducts the $5,000 it returns to its natural gas supplier in 2017.

Example 69: Continuing with Example 68, in 2015 when Farmington includes the $5,000 in its gross income, its marginal income tax rate is 39 percent. This results in an additional payment of taxes of $1,950 ($5,000 × 39%) in that year. When it deducts the $5,000 in 2017, Farmington's marginal income tax rate is 25 percent, which results in a tax savings equal to $1,250 ($5,000 × 25%). The difference between the tax increase in 2015 and the taxes saved in 2017 is $700 ($1,950 − $1,250). However, because the amount of the deduction exceeds $3,000, Farmington can reduce its 2017 tax liability by the same $1,950 that it paid on the $5,000 in 2015. If its deduction did not exceed $3,000, the company would not have been able to recoup the full amount of taxes the refund cost it in 2015.

¶ 313 Tax Benefit Rule

Under the **tax benefit rule**, if a taxpayer deducts an expense for one tax year and later recovers all or a portion of the amount deducted, it may have to include the amount recovered in its gross income for the year the amount is recovered. For this rule to apply, the taxpayer must have deducted an amount in a prior tax year that resulted in a tax benefit to the taxpayer.[84] Thus, none of the amount recovered is included in a taxpayer's gross income to the extent that the amount did not reduce the taxpayer's income tax liability in a prior tax year.[85]

Example 70: Kara Adhesives deducts $10,000 for real property tax that it paid in 2015. In 2017, the company receives a $500 refund of the real property tax that it paid in 2015. Under the tax benefit rule, the company includes that $500 in its gross income for 2017.

Example 71: Knipper Alarms deducts $1,000 as a bad debt expense in 2015. In 2016, it recovers $250 of the $1,000 it had been owed by the customer. Under the tax benefit rule, the company includes the $250 in its gross income for 2016.

Example 72: Assume the same facts as in Example 71, except in 2015 Knipper Alarms reported a net operating loss and therefore reported no income tax liability in that year. Because Knipper did not benefit from the deduction in 2015, it does not include the $250 in its 2016 gross income. Instead it reduces its net operating loss carryover from 2015 by $250 (see ¶ 1001).

 Reason for the Rule: The purpose of the tax benefit rule is to approximate the results produced by a tax system based on transactional rather than annual accounting and to protect the government and the taxpayer from the adverse effects of reporting a transaction on the basis of assumptions that prove to have been erroneous.[86]

¶ 314 Summary

Tax accounting rules should be distinguished from financial accounting rules. Both sets of rules are used to determine when income and expenses must be recognized; however, they differ in their derivation and objectives. The goal of financial accounting rules that govern financial reporting is to require a business to provide useful information for its management, owners, creditors, potential investors, and other interested parties. By contrast, the goal of Congress when enacting federal income tax legislation is to raise revenues for the federal government in an equitable manner, along with a variety of other secondary reasons discussed in Chapter 1 (see ¶ 106).

---

[84] Code Sec. 111.
[85] Code Sec. 111.

[86] *Hillsboro National Bank*, SCt, 83-1 USTC ¶ 9229, 460 US 370, 103 SCt 1134.

For businesses to be able to determine their taxable income, they need to know their tax year and method of accounting. C corporations have the flexibility of using a calendar year or a fiscal year. Personal service corporations and flow-through entities, such as S corporations, partnerships, and limited liability companies taxed as partnerships, generally are required to have the same tax year as their owners to prevent undue deferral of tax. However, some flexibility exists in cases in which the entity is willing to pay the tax effects of the deferral in advance or in cases in which a valid business purpose exists for using a different tax year.

Small businesses generally use the cash method of accounting (or a combination of the cash and accrual methods) to determine when and how they should report their income and expenses. Large businesses usually use the accrual method of accounting. These methods of accounting are referred to as "overall methods of accounting." "Special" methods of accounting are used to report particular types of income and expenses.

GLOSSARY OF TERMS INTRODUCED IN THIS CHAPTER

Accrual method. Income is included in gross income when all events have occurred that fix the right to receive the item and its amount can be determined with reasonable accuracy. Expenses are deducted when all events have occurred that determine the liability exists, the amount of the liability can be determined with reasonable accuracy, and economic performance has occurred with respect to the liability.

All-events test. A test used to determine when an accrual method taxpayer has to report income and can deduct or capitalize an expense.

Calendar year. A tax year that begins January 1 and ends December 31.

Cash receipts and disbursements method. A method of accounting under which a business is required to recognize income when it is received and may deduct expenses when they are paid.

Claim of right doctrine. A rule that requires taxpayers that receive money or other property under a claim of right without restriction to include the amount received in gross income for the year of receipt, regardless of the taxpayer's method of accounting.

Completed contract method. A special method of accounting for long-term contracts. No income or expenses related to the contract are recognized until the contract is completed.

Constructive receipt of income doctrine. A rule that requires cash method taxpayers to report gross income in the tax year during which amounts are credited to the business's account, set apart for the business, or otherwise made available without any substantial limitation or restriction. A business may be treated as having constructively received income even though it does not have actual possession of the income until after the end of the year.

Financial accounting. Rules used to determine how information, including income and expenses, should be reported on a business's financial statements.

Fiscal year. A tax year that ends on the last day of any month other than December.

Hybrid method. A method of accounting that combines elements of the cash and accrual methods of accounting.

Installment method. A special method of accounting requiring taxpayers to recognize gain from an installment sale as payments are received rather than at the time the sale occurs.

Method of accounting. The rules that govern when a business must recognize income and when it may deduct expenses. It refers not only to the overall method of accounting that a taxpayer uses but also to a taxpayer's accounting treatment of any particular item.

Percentage of completion method (PCM). A special method of accounting that applies to long-term contracts. Taxpayers include in their gross income each year a portion of the total contract price that corresponds to the portion of the total estimated contract costs actually incurred during the year.

Points. Term used to describe the prepaid interest that a lender charges in exchange for a lower interest rate to the borrower over the term of the loan.

Short tax year. A tax year lasting fewer than 12 months.

Tax accounting. Rules used to determine when income and expenses are recognized for tax purposes.

Tax benefit rule. A tax rule under which an amount recovered must be included in gross income for the year of the recovery if all or a portion of the expense deducted in a prior tax year is recovered in a subsequent tax year and if the deduction resulted in a tax benefit for the taxpayer.

Tax year. The period of time over which taxable income is computed.

12-month rule. A tax law that allows taxpayers to deduct a prepaid expense in full in the year it is paid provided that it creates (or facilitates the creation of) any right or benefit that does not extend beyond the earlier of (1) 12 months after the first date any right or benefit is realized or (2) the end of the tax year that follows the tax year in which the payment was made.

CHAPTER PROBLEMS

Chapter 3 Discussion Questions

1. How does tax accounting differ from financial accounting?
2. What is a fiscal year?
3. What is a tax year?
4. What is a required tax year, and to whom does it apply?
5. Can businesses that have a required tax year use any other tax year?
6. Can a business change its tax year? If so, how?
7. Which types of C corporations are prohibited from using the cash method of accounting?
8. What is the general rule for accounting for income under the cash method of accounting?
9. What is the general rule for accounting for expenses under the cash method of accounting?
10. What is the constructive receipt of income doctrine?
11. Is there a constructive payment of income doctrine?
12. How does a cash method taxpayer treat the advance payment of expenses?
13. When must a business using an accrual method of accounting include an item of income in its gross income?
14. When may a business using an accrual method of accounting take an expense into account?
15. If an accrual method business receives an advance payment for the sale of goods, how can it account for the payment?
16. What is a hybrid method of accounting and what restrictions are placed on its use?
17. What is the claim of right doctrine?

18. What is the tax benefit doctrine?

19. How are businesses supposed to account for income from most types of long-term contracts for tax accounting purposes?

20. How can a business change its method of accounting?

Chapter 3 Problems

1. Eader Jewelry is a partnership with six partners. Carey Sirin, which uses the calendar year as its tax year, owns a 10-percent interest in the profits and capital of the partnership. Delsie Ayudan, a calendar year taxpayer, owns a 20-percent interest in the profits and capital of the partnership. Ronin Pens, Inc., which has a fiscal year ending on January 31, owns a 30-percent interest in the profits and capital of the partnership. Goggles, Inc., which has a fiscal year ending February 28, owns a 25-percent interest in the profits and capital of the partnership. Three other partners, each using the calendar year as its tax year, each owns a five-percent interest in the profits and capital of the partnership. What is the partnership's majority interest tax year?

2. Yero is a calendar year taxpayer that uses the cash method of accounting. On December 25, 20X1, it receives a check for $1,000; the company deposits the check in its bank account on December 28. On December 31, it receives a check for $1,500 too late in the day to be able to deposit the check in its bank account. It deposits the check on January 2, 20X2. Based on these facts, how much must Yero include in its gross income for 20X1?

3. A calendar year taxpayer uses the cash method of accounting. The company sold display boxes to two customers on December 20, 2015. It billed one customer $100 on December 21, received payment on December 31, and cashed the check on January 2. It waited until January 2 to bill the second customer $3,000 because it wanted to include the $3,000 in its gross income for 2016. The company received a check for $3,000 on January 20 and cashed it on January 21. Based on these facts, how much does the company include in its gross income for 2015?

4. Stolberg Dyes is a calendar year taxpayer that uses the cash method of accounting. The company sells merchandise to Emily Kezar on November 1, 2015. Emily mails a check for $1,500 to Stolberg on November 30, and the company cashes it on December 4. Instead of mailing a check for the remaining amount due by January 1, Emily delivers a $1,000 check to her neighbor, Benita Stolberg, who is the daughter of the owner of Stolberg. Benita does not work for her mother's company. Benita gives the check to her mother on January 1, the next time they see each other. Based on these facts, how much does Stolberg include in its gross income for 2015?

5. Beaushaw Services is a cash method taxpayer that uses the calendar year as its tax year. Beaushaw pays $10,000 for an advertisement by mailing a check to the advertising firm on December 28, 2015. The firm receives the check on January 4 and cashes it on January 5. Beaushaw pays $2,000 for shipping supplies on December 31 by using its credit card. It pays its credit card charge on February 8 when its next statement is due. Based on these facts, what amount does the company deduct as expenses for 2015?

6. Blackhurst Cribs is a cash method taxpayer that uses the calendar year as its tax year. In 2015 the company receives a $200 advance for a crib to be delivered in 2016. It also receives a $1,000 promissory note for five cribs that it delivers in 2015. Based on these facts, how much income must the company include in its gross income for 2015?

7. Assume the same facts as in Problem 6, except Blackhurst receives payments totaling $800 with respect to the promissory note in 2016. Based on these facts, how much income must the company include in its gross income for 2016?

8. Trana Transmission is a cash method taxpayer that uses the calendar year as its tax year. During 2015 Trana borrows $10,000 to pay for an advertisement to be run in 2016. It also executes a $5,000 promissory note to pay for repairs to its manufacturing plant that were

made in 2015. Based on these facts, how much of these expenses can the company take into account for 2015?

9. Assume the same facts as in Problem 8, except Trana makes $4,000 of payments with respect to the promissory note and repays $5,000 of the amount borrowed in 2016. Based on these facts, how much of these expenses can the company take into account for 2016?

10. Shimko Kitchens and Baths, Inc. is an accrual method taxpayer that uses the calendar year as its tax year. In 2015 it agrees to refurbish a homeowner's kitchen for $100,000. It receives $50,000 in 2015, $40,000 in 2016, and $10,000 in 2017. It has no applicable financial statement for any of those years, but its records show that it completed 25 percent of its work in 2015, another 50 percent of its work in 2016, and the remaining 25 percent of its work in 2017. How much does Shimko include in its gross income for 2016 if it uses the deferral method to account for advance payments for services?

11. A cash method taxpayer uses the calendar tax year. On December 28, 2015, the company makes a $24,000 advance payment for a lease commencing January 12, 2016, and ending January 11, 2017. How much of the advance payment may the company deduct as an expense in 2015?

12. An accrual method taxpayer uses the calendar year as its tax year. On September 1, 2015, the company prepays $2,400 for its premium for a property insurance policy covering the period beginning September 1, 2015, and ending August 31, 2016. How much of this expense may the company deduct in 2015?

13. An accrual method taxpayer uses the calendar year as its tax year. On July 1, 2015, the company borrows $4.8 million to construct a new manufacturing plant. To obtain the loan, which was repayable over 12 years, it paid one point, which amounted to $48,000 ($4,800,000 × 1%). How much of the $48,000 can the company deduct for 2015?

14. Assume the same facts as in Problem 13, except the company is a cash method taxpayer and uses the calendar year as its tax year. How much of the $48,000 can it deduct in 2015?

15. Marran Caskets is an accrual method taxpayer that uses the calendar year as its tax year. On December 1, 2015, the company agrees to refund $2,000 of the price of a casket. It pays the refund on January 5, 2016. On December 15, 2015, it has its roof repaired but does not pay the $1,000 invoice until January 4, 2016. Based on these facts, how much can Marran deduct for 2015?

16. Hyrkas Checks, Inc. is an accrual method taxpayer that uses the calendar year as its tax year. On November 1, 2015, it became liable for a $20,000 workers' compensation award, but it did not pay the award until 2016. On August 1, 2015, it rented printing equipment for one year at an annual rental of $2,000 per month. How much of these expenses can it deduct in 2015?

17. Wunderlin Color Prints is an accrual method taxpayer that uses the calendar year as its tax year. On December 1, 2015, Wunderlin hires Raphael Bacot for one day to consult on a project. Raphael owns 60 percent of the common stock of Wunderlin and is a cash method taxpayer using the calendar year. Raphael bills Wunderlin $1,000 in December 2015 but is not paid until 2016. On November 25, 2015, Wunderlin hires a partnership owned by the same persons who own Wunderlin to repair its printing equipment. The partnership, which uses the accrual method and a calendar year-end, bills Wunderlin $2,000 for its services but does not receive payment until 2016. How much of its expenses may Wunderlin deduct in 2015?

18. Copper Castings is a cash method taxpayer that uses the calendar year as its tax year. On December 20, 2015, Copper was overpaid $100 by one of its customers for one of its invoices. Copper did not discover the error until 2016. On December 21, 2015, one of its employees discovered that a wallet containing $200 had been left on the company's premises and turned it over to a person in charge of "lost and found." Consequently, Copper never treated the money as its own. How much of these amounts does the company have to include in its gross income for 2015?

19. Jakobson Processing, Inc. is an accrual method taxpayer that uses the calendar year as its tax year. In 2015, it included $15,000 in its gross income under the claim of right doctrine. In 2016, it refunded the $15,000. In 2015, its marginal income tax rate was 25 percent. In 2016, its marginal income tax rate was 15 percent. How much does the $15,000 reduce its tax liability for 2016?

20. Diwan Remodeling, Inc., which is an accrual method taxpayer using the calendar year as its tax year, is remodeling a suite of offices. The total contract price is $2 million. It estimates that its total contract costs will be $1.2 million. During 2015, Diwan incurs $300,000 of contract costs. During 2016, Diwan incurs $600,000 of contract costs. During 2017, Diwan Remodeling completes the project and incurs $100,000 of contract costs. How much income from the contract must it include in its gross income for 2015, 2016, and 2017?

21. Malloy Partnership has 15 partners who each own four percent of the partnership's capital and profits, one partner who owns 25 percent of the partnership's capital and profits, and one partner who owns 15 percent of the partnership's capital and profits. Twelve of the 15 partners who each own four percent of the partnership's capital and profits use the calendar year as their tax year; the other three use as their tax year a fiscal year ending August 31. The other two partners each use a fiscal year ending January 31. What is the required tax year for Malloy Partnership?

22. Lair Laquers, Inc., an S corporation, wants to establish May 1 through April 30 as its tax year. It had $200,000 in gross receipts from sales for the 12-month period ending April 30, 2015. Its gross receipts from sales during March and April 2015 totaled $60,000. It had $180,000 in gross receipts from sales for the 12-month period ending April 30, 2014. Its gross receipts from sales during March and April 2014 totaled $45,000. It had $150,000 in gross receipts from sales during the 12-month period ending April 30, 2013. Its gross receipts from sales during March and April 2013 totaled $42,000. Does an April 30 year-end qualify as Lair Laquers' natural business year?

23. Williamson Plumbing, Inc. is a cash method taxpayer that uses the calendar year as its tax year. On December 28, 2015, it accepted a $200 payment by credit card for plumbing services it had performed. The payment was credited to Williamson on January 5, 2016. On December 15, 2015, Williamson also received free accounting services (worth $1,000) in exchange for plumbing work it did for an accountant on November 20, 2015. How much of these amounts does it have to include in its gross income for 2015?

24. Same facts as Problem 23 except that Williamson Plumbing is an accrual method taxpayer that uses the calendar year as its tax year. How much does it have to include in its gross income for 2015?

25. Oday Ornamental Shrubs, Inc. is a cash method taxpayer that uses the calendar year as its tax year. On December 20, 2015, Oday charged to its credit card $2,000 for an advertisement in a local newspaper that ran the first week of January 2016. Oday did not pay the credit card bill until January 16, 2016. On December 1, 2015, Oday obtained a 15-year mortgage loan for its new store and paid $3,600 in point for the loan. What amount of these expenses can Oday deduct from its gross income in 2015?

Chapter 3 Review Problem

How does the 12-month tax year fit in with notions of what makes for a good tax?

Chapter 3 Research Question

Does an amount paid or incurred to remediate environmental contamination that occurred in prior tax years qualify for special treatment under Code Sec. 1341 as an amount held under a claim of right that was restored? See Rev. Rul. 2004-17, 2004-1 CB 516. What argument did the taxpayer use, and how did the IRS respond?

PART II:
Federal Taxation of Business Income and Deductions

CHAPTER 4

Federal Income Taxes and Gross Income

CHAPTER CONTENTS

LEARNING OBJECTIVES

1. Understand the formula for calculating taxable income.

2. Learn which items have to be included in gross income and which items can be excluded from gross income.

3. Learn what amounts may be deducted when calculating taxable income.

4. Be able to calculate the federal income tax on a taxpayer's taxable income.

5. Learn what types of credits can be applied against a taxpayer's income tax liability.

6. Learn what estimated tax payments are and how they are calculated.

¶ 400 Introduction

One of the consequences having a successful business is that profits have to be shared with the federal government in the form of federal income taxes. Depending upon which form of business entity is used to operate the business, the income taxes on profits can be taxed to the business entity itself, to the owners of the business, or sometimes to both.

The profits of a business operated as a sole proprietorship are included on the owner's personal income tax return, along with any nonbusiness gross income and deductions the owner generates during the year. The profits of a business operated as a C corporation are taxed to the corporation when the profits are earned and again when the after-tax profits are distributed to the shareholders in the form of dividends. Businesses that operate as a partnership, an S corporation, or a limited liability company are separate entities, but the entity itself generally does not pay income taxes. Instead, the business passes through to its owners its items of gross income, gain, deductions, losses, and credits. That's why such entities are referred to as "flow-through" or "pass-through" entities. The owners are responsible for reporting on their own income tax return the items passed through to them.

For the most part, the rules regarding what types of income are taxed and what expenses can be deducted are the same for all types of taxpayers. However, because the individual income tax return includes not only business activities but also the taxpayer's personal activities, a number of exclusions and deductions are available only to individual taxpayers. For example, individuals are entitled to deduct various personal expenses when computing their taxable income.

This chapter sets the stage for the upcoming chapters in the textbook. It begins with an overview of the basic taxable income formula, which is the focus of the next five chapters. It then discusses how taxes are calculated and how taxpayers can use tax credits to reduce the taxes they owe. The rules regarding the required prepayment of taxes are also presented in this chapter. The chapter concludes with a discussion of the types of income the federal government taxes and the types of income it does not tax.

CALCULATING TAXABLE INCOME

The true success of a business can be measured only over a long period of time. However, when a business generates profits during its existence, the government requires that those profits be taxed. As discussed in Chapter 3, the typical accounting period is one year in length.

¶ 401 Taxable Income Formula

Before taxes owed can be calculated, it is first necessary to determine who is responsible for paying the taxes owed and what tax base is used to calculate those taxes. Only individuals and C corporations actually pay income taxes to the federal government. These taxpayers calculate their income tax by applying a progressive income tax rate to a tax base known as **taxable income**. Gross income and deductions are the major components in the calculation of taxable income. Taxable gains are included in gross income, and deductible losses are included in deductions. The amount of a business's taxable income is the difference between its gross income and the sum of the deductions that the tax laws allow the business to deduct.[1] Simply put, a taxable income can be expressed by the following formula:

---

[1] Code Sec. 63(a).

Income (broadly defined)	$ xx,xxx
Less: Exclusions	(xx,xxx)
Gross income	$ xx,xxx
Less: Deductions	(xx,xxx)
Taxable income	$ xx,xxx

Example 1: Ambrack, a C corporation, has a gross income of $300,000 for 2015 and deductions totaling $240,000. Its taxable income equals $60,000 ($300,000 – $240,000).

The federal government actually has two income tax systems that it uses to determine a taxpayer's taxes. The first income tax system is the "regular income tax system," which is the tax system introduced in Chapter 1 (see ¶ 104.07). The regular income tax system uses taxable income as its tax base and progressive tax rates. The second income tax system is called the "alternative minimum tax system," which is introduced later in this chapter (see ¶ 406). Taxpayers are required to pay the tax associated with the *greater* of the amounts computed under the two income tax systems.

From income tax liability, taxpayers subtract tax credits, which can be refundable or nonrefundable. Nonrefundable tax credits can reduce a taxpayer's tax liability to zero, but they cannot create a refund. Refundable tax credits can reduce any remaining income tax liability. Any excess is refunded to the taxpayer. The formula for calculating taxes owed at the end of each accounting period is shown below:

Total income tax liability	$ xx,xxx
Less: Nonrefundable tax credits	(xx,xxx)
Remaining tax liability (not less than $0)	$ xx,xxx
Less: Refundable tax credits, including prepayment of taxes	(xx,xxx)
Tax owed (refund due)	$ xx,xxx

Understanding how taxpayers compute their tax liability is important because proper tax planning involves understanding the tax benefits associated with a deduction or an exclusion, as well as the costs associated with additional amounts of gross income. As introduced in Chapter 1, the taxpayer's "marginal tax rate" is the rate of tax the taxpayer pays on its last dollar of income. It also represents the tax savings that a taxpayer derives by reducing taxable income by $1.

The tax rates used in the regular income tax system are progressive. The regular income tax rates that apply to corporations range from 15 percent to 35 percent. However, surtaxes (additional taxes) applied to certain levels of corporate taxable income can make the actual federal marginal tax rate as high as 39 percent (see ¶ 405.01). Under the alternative minimum tax (AMT) system, the corporate tax rate is a flat 20 percent, but the tax base used to compute AMT (called alternative minimum taxable income (AMTI)) is much broader, due to its more restrictive exclusions and deductions. For individuals, the income tax rates range from 10 percent to 39.6 percent. A two-tiered tax rate structure is used in the individual AMT system (26- and 28-percent). Again, the tax base used in the AMT system (AMTI) is much broader than that used in the regular income tax system.

If a taxpayer is subject to the AMT, the marginal tax rate used in determining the tax consequences of a proposed transaction is the taxpayer's marginal tax rate under the AMT system. For example, if a corporation is subject to the AMT and has the opportunity to generate an additional $10,000 of income for the year that will be included in the corporation's AMTI, then the tax on that income would be $2,000 ($10,000 × 20% corporate AMT rate). However, if the taxpayer is not subject to the AMT, the marginal tax rate from the progressive income tax schedules should be used to determine the tax consequences of a transaction. Of course, all other relevant taxes, including state, local, and foreign income taxes, as well as employment and other taxes, should be taken into consideration when computing the tax effects of any proposed transaction.

Example 2: Ambrack from Example 1 calculates its regular tax liability on its $60,000 taxable income using the progressive corporate income tax rates provided in Table 4-1 at ¶ 405.01. Taxable income of $60,000 falls between $50,000 and $75,000, which means that Ambrack's last dollar of income is taxed at 25 percent. Thus, assuming that Ambrack's AMT does not exceed its regular income tax liability, its marginal tax rate is 25 percent. If Ambrack were to earn an additional $10,000 of income during the year, the additional taxes owed would increase by $2,500 ($10,000 × 25%).

Flow-through entities generally do not pay income taxes, but instead keep track of their gross income (including gains), deductions (including losses), and tax credits using the same methods that other taxpayers use. At the end of each accounting period, the entity passes along the information to its owners, who are then responsible for reporting their respective shares of the amounts on their own income tax returns. Because ultimately the owners of all businesses are individuals, whether they are partners in a partnership, shareholders in a corporation, or owners of a sole proprietorship, it is important to understand not only how the profits of a C corporation are taxed, but also how the tax laws impact an individual taxpayer.

Example 3: Assume the same facts as in Example 1, except Ambrack is operated as an S corporation that has two equal shareholders. The shareholders would each include $30,000 ($60,000 × 50%) of the profits reported by Ambrack on their respective income tax returns.

 GAAP vs. Code: Because of differences between the rules for determining income and expenses for financial accounting versus the rules for computing gross income and deductions on the tax return, a business's taxable income typically is different from the net income it reports on its income statement. Larger corporations are required to reconcile these differences when they file their corporate income tax returns. In Chapter 12, when the special tax rules that pertain to C corporations are discussed, the various differences between the financial accounting and tax accounting rules are summarized.

¶ 402 Overview of Gross Income

Gross income is the starting point for determining the income tax liability for both corporate and individual taxpayers. Although flow-through entities do not pay tax on their taxable income, they still must be able to compute their gross income for the year so that they can pass the amounts on to their owners, who then report the gross income on their own income tax returns. **Gross income** is a tax term that represents the amount of income the government has decided to tax. It is similar to the concept of gross profit reported on the income statement. However, as discussed in Chapter 3, the accounting rules and tax rules often differ both in their objectives and rules.

As discussed in Chapter 3, the tax laws take an all-inclusive approach to defining gross income. Specifically, if an event or transaction causes a taxpayer's wealth or net worth to increase, then income is realized. Taking out a loan does not generate gross income because the increase in wealth from the cash received from the loan is offset by the increase in the taxpayer's debt. However, if the taxpayer's debt is forgiven, income is realized because the reduction in liabilities causes the taxpayer's wealth to increase. Thus, the amount of the forgiveness is included in the taxpayer's gross income, unless one of the provisions in the tax law allowing taxpayers to exclude certain forgiven debts applies.

.01 Gains from Sales or Exchanges of Property

The tax accounting rules do not require that the mere appreciation in value of an asset be included in income. Although such appreciation causes a taxpayer's net worth to increase, it is difficult to ascertain what the true appreciation in the asset's value is prior to selling it to an unrelated party. Thus, the tax laws omit appreciation in value from income and instead operate under the "realization principle." Under this principle, income is realized when property is disposed. The realization principle follows the "wherewithal-to-pay concept," which recognizes that mere appreciation in value does not necessarily mean the owner has the resources (wherewithal) to pay the tax associated with the appreciation. The wherewithal-to-pay is assured when the property is disposed of and the proceeds can be used to pay the necessary taxes.

The "capital recovery doctrine" ensures that, when taxpayers dispose of property, the portion of the proceeds representing a recovery of their investment in the property will not be taxed. Thus, only the excess of the proceeds over a taxpayer's investment is included in income. The tax term used to describe a taxpayer's investment in property is "adjusted basis," which is comparable to the term "net book value" used in financial accounting. The details regarding the calculation of adjusted basis are presented in Chapters 7 and 8. The capital recovery doctrine applies to sales of all types of property, including inventory. Therefore, only **gross profit** (computed as the excess of sales price over cost of goods sold) is included in a taxpayer's gross income.

Example 4: A corporation sells inventory for $10,000. Its adjusted basis in the inventory is $2,500. The corporation's income from the sale is $7,500 ($10,000 – $2,500). The $2,500 adjusted basis represents a return of its investment in the property sold.

Most types of property are characterized as capital assets.[2] Excluded from the definition of "capital asset" are such items as inventory, property held primarily for sale to customers in the ordinary course of a taxpayer's trade or business, depreciable property, and real property used in a taxpayer's trade or business.

When a taxpayer sells a capital asset for more than its adjusted basis, a "capital gain" results. When a taxpayer sells a capital asset for less than its adjusted basis, a "capital loss" results. Gain from the sale or exchange of a capital asset held for more than one year is long-term capital gain. Gain from the sale or exchange of a capital asset held for one year or less is short-term capital gain.

A taxpayer's deduction for losses from sales or exchanges of capital assets is limited.[3] Corporations can deduct capital losses only to the extent of their gains from such sales or exchanges. Individuals can offset their capital losses against their capital gains and deduct up to $3,000 of any excess as an ordinary loss.

There are special rules for "Section 1231 property," which is defined by Code Sec. 1231 to include depreciable property and real property if the property (1) is used in a taxpayer's trade or business and (2) has been held for more than one year. If Section 1231 gains for a tax year exceed Section 1231 losses for the tax year, the gains and losses are treated as long-term capital gains or losses. However, if Section 1231 gains for a tax year do not exceed Section 1231 losses for the tax year, the gains and losses will be treated as ordinary gain and losses. Ordinary gains are included in gross income; ordinary losses are deducted from gross income. There is no limit on the amount of Section 1231 losses that can be deducted.

Example 5: Waterman Enterprises sells land used in its business for a $10,000 gain. Waterman includes the $10,000 gain in its income for the year. Because the land was used in the taxpayer's business, the $10,000 gain will be classified as a Section 1231 gain if Waterman held the land for more than one year. Otherwise, the $10,000 gain will be taxed as ordinary income.

Example 6: Assume the same facts as in Example 5, except the land was not used in Waterman's business but instead was held as an investment. Because the land is not inventory or property used in the taxpayer's business, by default the land is classified as a capital asset, and the $10,000 gain will be considered capital gain. If Waterman held the land for more than a year, the gain will be classified as a long-term capital gain. Otherwise,

---

[2] Code Sec. 1221.   [3] Code Sec. 1211.

it will be classified as a short-term capital gain. Waterman can deduct capital losses against the gain. (See ¶ 403.02.)

.02 Items of Gross Income Unique to Individual Taxpayers

The definition of "gross income" is the same for individual taxpayers as it is for all other taxpayers, including C corporations, partnerships, and S corporations. However, individuals receive certain types of income that businesses do not receive. Although the discussion of these types of income items is beyond the scope of this chapter, gross income from these items increases the taxpayer's taxable income and may impact a sole proprietor's marginal tax rate. Hence, it is important to understand that the nonbusiness activities of a sole proprietor may affect the amount of additional tax the business owner will pay on additional business profits as well as the tax savings derived from additional business deductions. Because married couples have the option of filing a joint return, the personal activities of a taxpayer's spouse will also impact the couple's taxable income and may affect the taxpayer's marginal tax rate. The following is a list of some of the types of nonbusiness income that may be included on an individual income tax return:

- Wages, bonuses, and other compensation;

- Pension and other retirement income;

- Annuities;

- Alimony and separate maintenance payments;

- Prizes and awards;

- Gambling winnings (to the extent that they exceed gambling losses);

- Up to 85 percent of Social Security benefits;

- Income from an interest in an estate or trust; and

- Damage awards for back pay or replacing lost earnings.

.03 Exclusions

Despite the fact that the tax laws define income broadly, some types of income are exempt from federal income tax. Income the government does not tax is called an **exclusion**. For example, when a bondholder receives a semiannual interest payment from a corporation, the interest is included in income under the all-inclusive approach to defining gross income taken by the Internal Revenue Code (the "Code"). However, when the bond is issued by a state or local government, the interest received is excluded from gross income for federal income tax purposes. This type of interest is known as "municipal interest" (or "muni interest" for short) because the bond was issued by a municipality rather than a private corporation. A more detailed discussion of the concepts of income and exclusions is included later in this chapter (see ¶ 412).

Example 7: During the year, a corporation receives $14,000 of interest from a bond issued by Alman, Inc., a private corporation. It also receives $41,000 of interest from State of Iowa municipal bonds it owns. The corporation computes its gross income from these bonds as follows:

Interest from the corporate bond	$14,000
Interest from the municipal bond	41,000
Total income	$55,000
Less: Exclusion for municipal interest	(41,000)
Gross income from interest	$14,000

¶ 403 Overview of Deductions

Deductions are amounts that reduce a taxpayer's taxable income. Typically, a deduction arises from an expenditure paid or incurred by a taxpayer. Because businesses are required to include in gross income the gross profits from sales of their products or services, it is only fair that they be allowed to deduct from their gross income the costs they pay or incur in the normal course of generating the gross profits. Thus, only the excess of gross income over allowable deductions is subject to tax.

Unlike the all-inclusive approach used to define "gross income," a deduction is allowed only if a specific provision in the tax laws allows the expenditure to be deducted. Many business deductions are allowed by Code Sec. 162(a), which allows businesses to deduct all "ordinary and necessary expenses incurred in the operation of their trade or business." Some of the more common types of deductible expenses include compensation paid to employees, rental expenses, repairs, maintenance, insurance, interest, and taxes. The year in which expenses can be deducted depends on the taxpayer's method of accounting and tax year (both discussed in Chapter 3). A detailed discussion of business deductions is the focus of Chapters 5 to 7. The discussion that follows provides an overview of the deductions that businesses can subtract from gross income.

Example 8: A corporation spends $2,000 to repaint its office, $150 to repair a leaky faucet, and $500 to replace some shingles on the roof of its office building. The corporation deducts each of these expenses as ordinary and necessary business expenses.

The rules for determining what amounts can be deducted apply to all types of business entities. The only difference is that C corporations and sole proprietors use the deductions to reduce their taxable income and, thus, the amount of tax they must pay to the federal government. Flow-through entities offset ordinary deductions against ordinary gross income and pass through the net amount to their owners. Some deductions are passed through separately to the owners to be deducted on the owners' own income tax returns (see ¶ 1406.01).

Example 9: Mineral Investments, Inc. receives $30,000 in royalties from the sale of minerals. The tax laws allow Mineral to take a $20,000 depletion deduction with respect to those royalties. Mineral must include the $30,000 in its gross income, but the company will be allowed to deduct its depletion expense.

Example 10: Industrial Equipment receives $20,000 in royalties from a patent it owns. The tax laws allow Industrial to deduct (amortize) the cost of the patent over 15 years. Industrial must include the $20,000 in its gross income, but it may deduct the amortization expense associated with the cost of the patent.

Example 11: A corporation has $100,000 in gross income from its business operations and $110,000 in business expenses. It also has interest income of $5,000. The corporation can offset its $110,000 of business expenses against both its income from business operations and its interest income.

.01 Capital Expenditures

Not all ordinary, necessary, and reasonable amounts paid or incurred by a business as part of its operations can be deducted as business expenses. If an expenditure creates an asset that can be expected to benefit the business for a period of time that extends beyond the current year, the expenditure is a **capital expenditure** that must be reported as a business asset. Some capital expenditures can be expensed over a specified period. Others can never be deducted.

Example 12: Home Remodelers purchases equipment for $50,000. The company expects to be able to use the equipment for 10 years. Because the $50,000 was expended for an asset with a useful life in excess of one year, Home Remodelers capitalizes the $50,000 to an asset account and uses the tax depreciation rules presented in Chapter 7 to determine how quickly it can expense (depreciate) the equipment.

Example 13: Ultrasonic Research pays $5,000 for a new roof. This expense is a capital expenditure because the benefits from the new roof will extend beyond the current tax year. Thus, Ultrasonic cannot deduct the $5,000 as a business expense; however, it may depreciate the roof using the depreciation rules discussed in Chapter 7.

 Reason for the Rule: If a business were allowed to reduce its taxable income for a year by the entire cost of an asset that has a useful life of more than one year, it would understate both its net income and taxable income for the year that the asset was purchased. In addition, the business would overstate its net income and taxable income for the remaining years that the asset was used. The depreciation deduction is intended to more closely match a business's income with its expenses.

.02 Losses from Disposing Business or Investment Property

Losses from the sale of business and investment property are, subject to certain limitations, deducted from gross income. When the property sold is a capital asset (see ¶ 402.01), the recognized loss is a capital loss. The tax laws limit the amount of capital losses that can be deducted in any one year. For corporate taxpayers, capital losses are deductible to the extent of the capital gains included in their gross income. Any excess capital losses over capital gains can be carried back three years to offset excess capital gains reported in gross income in those years. Excess losses can be carried forward five years to offset future capital gains.[4] (See ¶ 901)

Example 14: Insulated Containers receives $6,000 on the sale of 100 shares of ABC stock. Insulated's adjusted basis in the stock is $4,000. Insulated also sells 100 shares of XYZ stock with an adjusted basis of $4,000 for $1,000. Because stock is not inventory, accounts receivable, or other business property, the gains and losses on the sale of these assets are capital gains and losses. Insulated recognizes a $2,000 gain on the sale of the ABC stock ($6,000 – $4,000) and a $3,000 loss on the sale of XYZ stock ($1,000 – $4,000). As a C corporation, Insulated can only deduct the loss on the sale of XYZ stock to the extent of the capital gains it includes in its gross income. Its loss for the tax year is limited to $2,000. However, it can carry back the $1,000 excess for up to three years and can carry forward any remaining loss for up to five years.[5]

Capital gain from the sale of ABC stock	$2,000
Less: Capital loss deduction	(2,000)
Amount included in taxable income	$ 0

The tax laws regarding the deduction of capital losses for individual taxpayers are different. When an individual taxpayer incurs capital losses, such losses are deductible to the extent of the capital gains included in gross income plus $3,000. Any excess capital losses can be carried forward indefinitely to offset capital gains plus up to $3,000 of ordinary income in future tax years.[6]

Example 15: Pete Tallon operates a kitchen accessories business as a sole proprietor. During the year, Pete receives $4,000 when he sells 100 shares of ABC stock. His adjusted basis in those shares is $2,000. He also realizes $2,000 on the sale of 200 shares of XYZ stock that has an adjusted basis of $8,000. Pete's realized gain on the sale of the ABC stock is $2,000 ($4,000 – $2,000), and his realized loss on the sale of the XYZ stock is $6,000 ($2,000 – $8,000). Although Pete's capital losses exceed his capital gains by more than $3,000, he is allowed to deduct up to $5,000 of the capital loss against his

---

[4] Code Sec. 1211(a).
[5] Code Sec. 1212(a).
[6] Code Sec. 1211(b).

gross income ($2,000 capital gain + $3,000). He carries forward the excess $1,000 loss indefinitely to future tax years.

Capital gain from the sale of ABC stock	$2,000
Less: Capital loss deduction	(5,000)
Amount that reduces Pete's AGI	($3,000)

As previously mentioned, when a taxpayer sells depreciable property or land used in business and that property has been held for more than a year ("Section 1231 property"), the gain or loss is a Section 1231 gain or loss. Section 1231 gains are included in gross income, and Section 1231 losses are deducted from gross income. Section 1231 gains and losses are summed up at the end of the year. If the taxpayer's Section 1231 gains exceed its amount of Section 1231 losses, the excess gain ("net Section 1231 gain") is treated as a long-term capital gain. If a taxpayer's Section 1231 losses exceed the taxpayer's Section 1231 gains, the excess loss ("net Section 1231 loss") is treated as an ordinary loss.

Section 1231 favors taxpayers because it allows them to treat gains as capital gains subject to the favorable capital gains tax rate and losses as ordinary losses that are entirely deductible from ordinary income (instead of being treated as capital losses that can be deducted only to a limited extent).

Example 16: Amadia Golf Supplies, Inc. sells the following property during the year:

Gain on the sale of inventory	$50,000
Section 1231 gain	60,000
Section 1231 loss	(20,000)
Capital loss	(25,000)

Both the $50,000 gain on the sale of inventory and the $60,000 Section 1231 gain are included in the taxpayer's gross income. The $20,000 Section 1231 loss is deducted from Amadia's gross income. Normally the $25,000 capital loss would not be deductible because there are no capital gains in gross income for the capital loss to offset. However, the tax laws allow Amadia to treat the $40,000 net Section 1231 gain ($60,000 – $20,000) as long-term capital gain. Therefore, the entire $25,000 of capital loss can be deducted from gross income to offset the long-term capital gain.

Gain from the sale of inventory	$ 50,000
Section 1231 gain	60,000
Gross income	$110,000
Less: Section 1231 loss	(20,000)
Less: Capital loss deduction	(25,000)
Net increase in taxable income	$ 65,000

Example 17: Assume the same facts as in Example 16, except Amadia's Section 1231 loss is $40,000.

Gain on the sale of inventory	$50,000
Section 1231 gain	60,000
Section 1231 loss	(40,000)
Capital loss	(25,000)

Because Amadia's net Section 1231 gain is $20,000 ($60,000 – $40,000), the company can only use $20,000 of the capital loss to offset its $20,000 capital gain (from the net Section 1231 gain). The remaining $5,000 capital loss ($25,000 – $20,000) is carried over to another tax year.

Gain from the sale of inventory	$ 50,000
Section 1231 gain	60,000
Gross income	$110,000
Less: Section 1231 loss	(40,000)
Less: Capital loss deduction	(20,000)
Net increase in taxable income	$ 50,000

¶ 404 Expanded Taxable Income Formula for Individual Taxpayers

The steps in determining the taxable income of an individual are similar to those used to determine the taxable income of a corporation. Both must determine their total income, and both must exclude certain items of income from gross income. Both are entitled to deduct certain amounts from their gross income when calculating their taxable income.

The major difference between the steps in determining the taxable income of a C corporation and the steps in determining the taxable income of an individual taxpayer is that individuals have two types of deductions. The first type of deduction is referred to as a deduction for **adjusted gross income** (AGI), sometimes called an "above-the-line" deduction. The second type of deduction is called a deduction from AGI (sometimes referred to as a "below-the-line deduction"). The taxable income formula for individual taxpayers is expanded to include these two types of deductions and the intermediary calculation of AGI.

Income	$ xx,xxx
Less: Exclusions	(xx,xxx)
Gross income	$ xx,xxx
Less: Deductions for AGI	(xx,xxx)
Adjusted gross income (AGI)	$ xx,xxx
Less: Deductions from AGI	(xx,xxx)
Taxable income	$ xx,xxx

Individuals are allowed to deduct *for* AGI many of the deductions corporations subtract from gross income. Individual taxpayers also are allowed to deduct certain personal expenses *from* AGI when computing their taxable income. Figure 4-1 lists the various deductions that individuals are allowed. Although most business expenses for a sole proprietorship are deducted for AGI on an individual's income tax return, some deductions are available only as itemized deductions to individual taxpayers.

Figure 4-1 Deductions Allowed in Computing Individual Taxable Income

Deductions for AGI

- Trade or business expenses*
- Reimbursed expenses of employees*
- Losses from the sale or exchange of property*
- Deductions attributable to rents and royalties*

- Health savings account deduction
- Moving expenses*
- One-half of the self-employment tax (not including the additional 0.9 percent tax imposed on individuals with high self-employment income or the additional 3.8 percent tax imposed on the net investment income of individuals with high adjusted gross income)*
- Self-employed contributions to employer-sponsored qualified retirement plans*
- Self-employed health insurance deduction*
- Contributions to traditional IRAs
- Penalty on early withdrawals of savings
- Alimony paid
- Student loan interest
- Qualified tuition and related expenses
- Required repayments of supplemental unemployment compensation benefits
- Jury duty pay remitted to employer
- Costs relating to claims of unlawful discrimination
- Attorney fees and court costs relating to awards to whistleblowers
- Domestic production activities deduction*
- Reforestation expenses*
- Depreciation and depletion deductions allowed life tenants of property and income beneficiaries of trusts

Itemized Deductions
- Medical expenses
- State and local income taxes*
- State and local general sales taxes*
- Real estate taxes*
- Personal property taxes*
- Home mortgage interest
- Qualified mortgage insurance premiums
- Investment interest*
- Charitable contributions*
- Casualty and theft losses*
- Unreimbursed employee expenses
- Impairment-related work expenses of an individual with a disability
- Tax preparation fees*
- Investment fees and expenses*
- Gambling losses (but only to the extent of gambling winnings)
- Federal estate tax on income in respect of a decedent
- Repayment of amounts under a claim of right

---

* Designates business expenses that may be deducted on the individual tax return.

Example 18: Ray Alton operates a business as a sole proprietorship. The gross income, deductions, and tax credits generated by his business are reported on his individual income tax return. These amounts are added to his other items of gross income, deduction, and tax credit when computing his taxable income and taxes owed at the end of the year. Ray uses the taxable income formula for individuals to compute his taxable income.

Example 19: Assume the same facts as in Example 18, except the business is operated as a partnership in which Ray owns a 75-percent interest. At the end of the partnership's accounting period, the partnership's gross income, deductions, and tax credits for the year are computed. Ray will include 75 percent of each item on his personal income tax return. He will add the amounts to his other items of gross income, deductions, and tax credit. Ray will then compute his taxable income using the taxable income formula for individual taxpayers.

CALCULATING TAXES OWED

Once taxable income has been calculated, corporate and individual taxpayers compute their regular income tax liability using their respective progressive income tax rates. In addition to income taxes based on taxable income, some taxpayers are also subject to the alternative minimum tax (AMT). The two taxes comprise a taxpayer's total income tax liability. Sole proprietors are subject to self-employment taxes on profits from their sole proprietorship. Although self-employment taxes are an employment tax rather than an income tax, they are included as part of an individual taxpayer's total tax liability.

Once a taxpayer's total tax liability is computed, the taxpayer reduces the tax liability by allowable tax credits. The taxpayer then offsets any remaining tax liability by amounts previously paid to the IRS for federal taxes owed, either through withholdings (as in the case of individual taxpayers), or prepayments (in the case of both individual and corporate taxpayers).

Example 20: Briss & Company determines that its regular tax for the year is $115,000 and that it owes an additional $10,000 under the AMT system. Briss's allowable tax credits for the year are $20,000, and it made estimated tax payments totaling $100,000 during the year. When it files its income tax return, Briss will owe an additional $5,000 in taxes.

Regular tax	$115,000
Plus: AMT	10,000
Total income tax liability	$125,000
Less: Tax credits	(20,000)
Less: Prepayments	(100,000)
Tax (refund) due	$ 5,000

Example 21: Rumill & Company determines that its regular tax for the year is $155,000 and that it is not subject to AMT. Rumill is entitled to $30,000 in tax credits, and it made a total of $135,000 in estimated tax payments during the year. When it files its income tax return, Rumill will request that a $10,000 overpayment be refunded.

Regular tax:	$155,000
Plus: AMT	0
Total income tax liability	$155,000
Less: Tax credits	(30,000)
Less: Prepayments	(135,000)
Tax (refund) due	($ 10,000)

¶ 405 Regular Income Tax Liability

The income tax system uses progressive tax rates. Lower tax rates are imposed on taxpayers with lower amounts of taxable income, and higher tax rates are imposed on taxpayers with higher amounts of taxable income. Although both an individual's taxable income and a corporation's taxable income are subject to progressive tax rates, different rates apply to each type of taxpayer.

.01 Tax Rates for Corporations

Corporations use the progressive tax rates listed in Table 4-1 to compute their regular income tax liability on their taxable income.[7] Unlike the tax brackets for individuals, the corporate tax brackets are not indexed for inflation. Thus, the first $50,000 of corporate taxable income is taxed at 15 percent each year.

Table 4-1 Corporate Income Tax Rates

If taxable income is over	But not over	The tax is:
$0	$50,000	15% of the amount over $0
$50,000	$75,000	$7,500 plus 25% of the amount over $50,000
$75,000	$100,000	$13,750 plus 34% of the amount over $75,000
$100,000	$335,000	$22,250 plus 39% of the amount over $100,000
$335,000	$10,000,000	$113,900 plus 34% of the amount over $335,000
$10,000,000	$15,000,000	$3,400,000 plus 35% of the amount over $10,000,000
$15,000,000	$18,333,333	$5,150,000 plus 38% of the amount over $15,000,000
$18,333,333		35% of the amount over $0

Example 22: A corporation reports taxable income of $40,000. It calculates its $6,000 regular income tax liability for the year as follows:

Taxable income	$40,000
Times: Marginal tax rate	× 15%
Regular income tax liability	$ 6,000

Example 23: A corporation has $90,000 of taxable income. It calculates its regular income tax liability for the year to be $18,850, as shown below:

Taxable income	$90,000
Less: Threshold amount	(75,000)
Excess over $75,000	$15,000
Times: Marginal tax rate	× 34%
Tax on excess	$ 5,100
Plus: Tax on first $75,000 of taxable income	13,750
Regular income tax liability	$18,850

[7] Code Sec. 11.

Example 24: A corporation has a taxable income of $140,000. It computes its regular income tax liability as follows:

Taxable income	$140,000
Less: Threshold amount	(100,000)
Excess over $100,000	$ 40,000
Times: Marginal tax rate	× 39%
Tax on excess	$ 15,600
Plus: Tax on first $100,000 of taxable income	22,250
Regular income tax liability	$ 37,850

Example 25: A corporation has a taxable income of $12 million. Its $4.1 million regular income tax liability for the year is calculated as follows:

Taxable income	$12,000,000
Less: Threshold amount	(10,000,000)
Excess over $10,000,000	$ 2,000,000
Times: Marginal tax rate	× 35%
Tax on excess	$ 700,000
Plus: Tax on first $10,000,000 of taxable income	3,400,000
Tax liability	$ 4,100,000

The highest corporate tax rate is 35 percent. However, a 39 percent rate is imposed on taxable income between $100,000 and $335,000. This rate includes the 34-percent marginal tax rate plus a five percent surcharge intended to eliminate the tax benefits from the lower 15- and 25-percent tax rates for taxable income less than $75,000. Therefore, by the time taxable income reaches $335,000, corporations will have paid a flat tax rate of 34 percent on its taxable income, as shown below:

Tax on $335,000 of taxable income using Table 4-1:

Taxable income	$335,000
Less: Threshold amount	(100,000)
Excess taxed at marginal tax rate	$235,000
Times: Marginal tax rate	× 39%
Tax on excess	$ 91,650
Plus: Tax on first $100,000 of taxable income	22,250
Tax liability	$113,900

Tax on $335,000 using a flat 34-percent tax rate:

$335,000 × 34%	$113,900

The flat 34-percent tax rate continues for corporations with taxable income between $335,000 and $10 million. Once taxable income reaches $10 million, the rate increases to 35 percent until it reaches $15 million. At taxable income of $15 million, a three-percent surcharge is assessed until all taxable income that was taxed at 34 percent is taxed at 35 percent. This requires that the 38 percent tax rate (35% + 3% surcharge) remain in effect until taxable income reaches $18,333,333.

Tax on $18,333,333 taxable income using Table 4-1:

Taxable income	$18,333,333
Less: Threshold amount	(15,000,000)
Excess taxed at marginal tax rate	$ 3,333,333
Times: Marginal tax rate	× 38%
Tax on excess	$ 1,266,667
Plus: Tax on first $15,000,000 of taxable income	5,150,000
Tax liability	$ 6,416,667

Tax on $18,333,333 using a flat 35-percent tax rate:

$18,333,333 × 35%	$ 6,416,667

Reason for the Rule: Congress believed that graduated income tax rates should be retained for smaller corporations to encourage their growth. However, it believed that larger corporations should not benefit from the lower rates and instead should pay a flat tax rate on their taxable income.[8]

Planning Pointer: Although the highest corporate tax rate is 35 percent, for tax planning purposes the marginal tax rate when making decisions must include any surcharge in effect for the corporation's taxable income.

.02 Tax Rates for Individuals

The income tax rates for individuals are graduated, ranging from 10 to 39.6 percent. However, unlike C corporations, individuals do not lose the benefit of the graduated rates as their taxable income increases. The amount of taxable income to which a particular tax rate applies varies depending on an individual's filing status. There are five filing statuses: married filing jointly (MFJ), surviving spouse, head of household, married filing separately (MFS), and single. A different tax rate schedule applies to each filing status, with the exception of surviving spouse, which shares the MFJ tax rates. The 2015 tax rate schedules for individual taxpayers are reproduced in the Appendix at the back of this textbook.

Table 4-2 2015 Tax Rates for Married Individuals Filing Jointly and Surviving Spouses

If taxable income is:	*The tax is:*
Not over $18,450	10% of taxable income
Over $18,450 but not over $74,900	$1,845 plus 15% of the excess over $18,450

---

[8] Joint Committee on Taxation, *General Explanation of the Tax Reform Act of* 1986, at 272.

If taxable income is:	*The tax is:*
Over $74,900 but not over $151,200	$10,312.50 plus 25% of the excess over $74,900
Over $151,200 but not over $230,450	$29,387.50 plus 28% of the excess over $151,200
Over $230,450 but not over $411,500	$51,577.50 plus 33% of the excess over $230,450
Over $411,500 but not over $464,850	$111,324 plus 35% of the excess over $411.500
Over $464,850	$129,996.50 plus 39.6% of the excess over $464,850

Example 26: John Jacobs operates a sole proprietorship. John is married and files a joint return with his wife. During 2015, the couple's taxable income is $96,500. Using the income tax rates in Table 4-2, the Jacobs' tax liability can be calculated as $15,712.50 [$10,312.50 + $5,400 (($96,500 – $74,900) × 25%)].

Special tax rates on qualified dividend income and net capital gain. An individual taxpayer's qualified dividend income and net capital gain are taxed at a lower income tax rate than other types of income.

- **Qualified dividend income** means dividends received during the year from U.S. corporations and qualified foreign corporations with respect to stock that the individual held for at least 60 days during the 121-day period beginning 60 days before the ex-dividend date.[9]

- **Net capital gain** (discussed in Chapter 9) is the difference between a taxpayer's net long-term capital gain (i.e., the difference between a taxpayer's gains and losses from the sale or exchange of capital assets held for more than one year) for a tax year and the taxpayer's net short-term capital loss (i.e., the difference between a taxpayer's losses and gains from the sale or exchange of capital assets held for one year or less) for the tax year.

Qualified dividend income and net capital gain are taxed at the same income tax rate. Taxpayers in the 10- and 15-percent tax brackets are not taxed on their qualified dividend income and net capital gain. Taxpayers in the 25-, 28-, 33-, or 35-percent income tax bracket have to pay a 15 percent income tax on their qualified dividend income and net capital gain. Taxpayers in the 39.6 percent income tax bracket have to pay a 20 percent tax on their qualified dividend income and net capital gain.

Collectible gain (i.e., gain from the sale or loss of a collectible, such as a work of art, metal, gem, stamp, or coin, that is a capital asset held for more than one year) and Section 1202 gain (i.e., gain from the sale or exchange of qualified small business stock held for more than five years that is not excluded from gross income by Code Sec. 1202) may be taxed at up to a 28-percent rate. Unrecaptured Code Sec. 1250 gain (i.e., depreciation recaptured when depreciable real property is sold or exchanged) may be taxed at up to a 25-percent rate.

Example 27: Gina Lopez's taxable income for 2015 falls in the 28-percent tax bracket. Gina's taxable income includes $45,000 of net capital gain. When Gina calculates her taxable income, she will back out $45,000 and calculate its tax at 15 percent. The remainder of her taxable income will be taxed using the progressive individual tax rates for her filing status. Gina's total tax liability will be the sum of the two amounts.

Example 28: Claude Van Dyke's taxable income falls in the 15-percent tax bracket. Included in his taxable income for 2015 is $5,000 of qualified dividend income. When Claude calculates his tax liability, his qualified dividends will not be taxed. The rest of his taxable income will be taxed using the progressive tax rates for his filing status. The sum of these two amounts will be Claude's total regular income tax liability.

[9] Code Sec. 1(h)(1) and (11).

.03 Tax Rate for Personal Service Corporations

"Qualified personal service corporations" are C corporations that are not entitled to use the graduated tax rates that apply to other C corporations. Instead they must pay a flat 35 percent tax on all taxable income.[10] A corporation is a **qualified personal service corporation** if its employees spend at least 95 percent of their time performing services in a qualifying field (i.e., health, law, engineering, architecture, accounting, actuarial science, performing arts, or consulting) and at least 95 percent of the value of its stock is held directly or indirectly by employees performing services in a qualifying field, retired employees who performed such services for the corporation, the estate of such an employee or retired employee, or any other person who acquired stock in the corporation by reason of the death of such an employee or retired employee (but only for the two-year period beginning on the date of that individual's death).[11]

Example 29: Cocco Engineering provides engineering consulting services. Its taxable income for the year is $100,000. Its employees devote 100 percent of their time providing consulting services, and all of Cocco's stock is owned by its employees. Cocco is a qualified personal service corporation. Therefore, its regular income tax liability equals $35,000 ($100,000 × 35%). If Cocco were not a qualified personal service corporation, its regular income tax liability would be $22,250 (using Table 4-1).

> **Reason for the Rule:** Qualified personal service corporations were denied the benefit of graduated income tax rates by the Revenue Act of 1987. Congress noted that the income from these corporations is taxed to employee-owners at the individual graduated income tax rates because it is paid out as salary. Congress believed that it was inappropriate to allow retained earnings to be taxed at lower corporate graduated rates.[12]

¶ 406 Alternative Minimum Tax

Individual taxpayers and larger C corporations may be subject to the alternative minimum tax (AMT), which is a tax enacted to ensure that taxpayers pay their fair share of income taxes. The AMT is imposed in addition to the regular income tax. The corporate and individual AMT are described in greater detail in Chapter 10. Because the marginal tax rate for taxpayers subject to AMT will be affected, a brief overview of the tax is presented in this chapter.

> **Reason for the Rule:** Congress imposes the AMT on corporations because it concluded that both the perception and the reality of fairness had been harmed by instances in which corporations paid little or no tax in years when they reported substantial earnings and may even have paid substantial dividends to shareholders. The AMT is designed to attempt to ensure that companies with significant earnings pay at least some tax for the year.[13]

The AMT is a tax system that is parallel to the regular tax system. The AMT system has its own set of rules regarding exclusions and deductions (see ¶ 1008.05). Under the AMT system, a taxpayer's tentative minimum tax is computed. If this amount exceeds the taxpayer's regular income tax liability, the excess represents the taxpayer's AMT owed for the year.[14]

---

[10] Code Sec. 11(b)(2).

[11] Temp. Reg. § 1.448-1T(e).

[12] House Ways and Means Committee Report No. 100-391 (October 26, 1987), at 1097.

[13] Joint Committee on Taxation, General Explanation of the Tax Reform Act of 1986, at 433-434.

[14] Code Sec. 55(a).

Example 30: A taxpayer's regular income tax liability is $30,000, and its tentative minimum tax is computed to be $35,000. The taxpayer's AMT equals $5,000 ($35,000 – $30,000).

Example 31: A taxpayer's regular tax liability for the year is $40,000, and its tentative minimum tax is $35,000. Because the amount of regular tax liability exceeds the tentative minimum tax, the taxpayer reports no AMT on its income tax return.

Although the AMT system is separate from the regular income tax system, many of the items of income and deduction that are used in computing taxable income are used in computing alternative minimum taxable income (AMTI). Accordingly, the taxpayer starts the calculation of the tentative minimum tax by adjusting its taxable income to compute AMTI. The AMT system allows taxpayers to deduct an exemption from AMTI in arriving at the AMT tax base (the AMT equivalent to taxable income). The AMT tax rates are then applied to the AMT base to determine the minimum income tax the taxpayer will owe for the year. If the amount exceeds the amount of income tax computed under the regular income tax system, the excess represents the taxpayer's AMT liability for the year.

.01 Corporate AMT

Corporations calculate their tentative minimum tax using the following formula:[15]

Taxable income	$ xx,xxx
Plus or minus necessary adjustments	xx,xxx
AMTI	$ xx,xxx
Less: AMT exemption	(xx,xxx)
AMT base	$ xx,xxx
AMT tax rate	20%
Tentative minimum tax	$ xx,xxx

Example 32: Strole Industrial Paints has a regular tax liability for the year of $20,000. Its AMTI is calculated to be $150,000, and its AMT exemption amount is $40,000. Because Strole's $22,000 tentative minimum tax exceeds its $20,000 regular income tax liability, Strole is required to pay a minimum of $22,000 in income taxes for the year. Accordingly, Strole's AMT equals $2,000 ($22,000 – $20,000). When Strole files its tax return, it will report a regular income tax liability of $20,000 and an AMT of $2,000.

AMTI	$150,000
AMT exemption	(40,000)
AMT base	$110,000
AMT tax rate	× 20%
Tentative minimum tax	$ 22,000

.02 Individual AMT

Like corporations, individuals compute their AMT by starting with their taxable income and making the necessary adjustments to compute AMTI. Because of the differences in how taxable income is calculated for individuals and corporations, the adjustments made to taxable income differ. Like corporations, individuals are allowed an exemption against AMTI, but the amount varies, depending on the individual's filing status. Unlike the corporate AMT rate, which is a flat 20 percent,

---

[15] Code Sec. 55(b).

a two-tier system of tax rates applies to individuals when computing tentative minimum tax. For a tax year beginning in 2015, individuals are taxed at a 26-percent tax rate on the first $185,400 ($92,700 for a married individual filing a separate return) of their AMT base and at a 28-percent tax rate on any excess. In the AMT system, net capital gains and qualified dividends are subject to the same lower tax rates to which they are subject under the regular income tax system. The individual AMT is described in greater detail in Chapter 10.

Example 33: Shirley Augustine, who is unmarried, has a regular tax liability for 2015 of $15,000. Her AMTI is $137,900, her AMT exemption amount is $48,925, and her AMT base is $88,975. Her tentative minimum tax is $23,133.50. Because her tentative minimum tax exceeds her regular tax liability ($15,000), she has to pay $8,133.50 in AMT in addition to her regular tax liability of $15,000.

AMTI	$137,900
AMT exemption	($ 48,925)
AMT base	$ 88,975
AMT tax rate	× 26%
Tentative minimum tax	$ 23,133.50

Example 34: Assume the same facts as in Example 33, except Shirley's regular income tax liability is $28,000. Because through the regular income tax system Shirley is paying at least the $23,133.50 minimum tax calculated under the AMT income tax system, she will not be subject to AMT in 2015.

¶ 407 Self-Employment Tax

In Chapter 1, the concept of employment taxes was introduced. Compensation is subject to Federal Insurance Contributions Act (FICA) taxes, which consist of Social Security and Medicare taxes. The responsibility for paying FICA taxes is shared equally by the employer and employee (see ¶ 104.06).

An individual who is self-employed acts both as an employee and as an employer of the business. Therefore, sole proprietors are required to contribute both the employer and employee portions of Social Security (OASDI) and Medicare taxes. When those taxes are paid on the profits of a sole proprietorship, they are called the "self-employment tax."

The self-employment tax is 15.3 percent of *net earnings from self-employment* (up to $118,500 for a tax year beginning in 2015). After that dollar threshold, the self-employment tax rate drops to 2.9 percent for most taxpayers. Individuals with self-employment income exceeding $200,000 ($250,000 if married and filing a joint return; $125,000 if married and filing a separate return) have to pay an additional 0.9% tax on that excess self-employment income.

Sole proprietors add the amount of their self-employment taxes for the year to their income tax liability (regular income tax plus AMT). They are expected to make quarterly estimated tax payments during the year to cover any amounts of self-employment taxes that are not otherwise prepaid through other means (withholding). Failure to prepay these taxes during the year may result in substantial understatement penalties (see ¶ 410.02).

¶ 408 Medicare Contribution Tax on Net Investment Income

Individuals (excluding nonresident aliens) whose modified adjusted gross income exceeds $200,000 ($250,000 if married and filing a joint return or a surviving spouse; $125,000 if married and filing a separate return) have to pay an additional 3.8 percent Medicare contribution tax on the lesser of their net investment income or the difference between their modified adjusted gross income and the threshold amount.[16]

"Net investment income" is calculated by taking the sum of the following amounts (minus any deductions properly allocable to such income):

- Interest, dividends, annuities, royalties, and rents (other than income derived in the ordinary course of a trade or business not subject to the Medicare contribution tax).

- Other gross income derived from a trade or business that is a passive activity with respect to the taxpayer or a trade or business of trading in financial instruments or commodities.

- Net gain (to the extent taken into account in computing taxable income) attributable to the disposition of property (other than property held in a trade or business not subject to the Medicare contribution tax).

"Net investment income" does not include distributions from qualified retirement plans or any amounts subject to the self-employment tax.

¶ 409 Tax Credits

The tax laws allow taxpayers to subtract from their total tax liability certain amounts known as "tax credits." In the case of flow-through entities, tax credits flow through to the owners of the business and are taken as tax credits on the owners' income tax returns. Tax credits are discussed in detail in Chapter 11, but a brief introduction is included in this chapter.

Tax credits need to be distinguished from deductions. A *tax credit* reduces a taxpayer's tax liability dollar for dollar. By contrast, a *deduction* reduces a taxpayer's tax liability by the amount of the deduction multiplied by the taxpayer's marginal income tax rate. If the deduction is one that reduces a sole proprietor's self-employment taxes, the reduction in both income and self-employment taxes must be considered.

Example 35: Shetlar Hair Dyes, Inc. had $100,000 of taxable income for its tax year and owed $22,250 on its taxable income. Its tax credits for the year are $2,500. That credit reduces its tax liability dollar for dollar to $19,750 ($22,250 – $2,500).

Example 36: Assume the same facts as in Example 35, except Shetlar incurs $2,500 in deductible expenses for the year instead of a $2,500 tax credit. An additional $2,500 of expenses reduces the company's taxable income to $97,500 ($100,000 – $2,500). Without the deduction, the company's tax liability for the year on $100,000 of taxable income would have been $22,250 (see Example 35). When the deduction is taken, its tax liability on $97,500 of taxable income is $21,400 (using Table 4-1). The result is a reduction in taxes equal to $850 ($22,250 – $21,400). This amount is equivalent to the deduction multiplied by the taxpayer's marginal income tax rate ($2,500 × 34% = $850). In contrast, the $2,500 tax credit reduces the company's tax liability by $2,500.

Example 37: Mai Trammell operates a sole proprietorship. Mai is not subject to AMT, and her taxable income falls in the 28-percent tax bracket. If Mai incurs an additional $1,000 of business expenses that reduce both her sole proprietorship profits and her taxable income, her tax savings from this deduction equals approximately $433 ($1,000 × (28% income tax rate + a 15.3% self-employment tax rate)). Thus, the total cost of the expenditure to Mai is only $567 ($1,000 – $433).

Example 38: Assume the same facts as in Example 37, except the deduction reduces Mai's taxable income but is not deductible in computing her business profits subject to self-employment taxes. Mai's tax savings from the deduction is $280 ($1,000 × 28%), and

---

[16] Code Sec. 1411.

her out-of-pocket costs after considering the federal income tax savings is $720 ($1,000 – $280).

Three primary tax credits are available to businesses: the general business credit, foreign tax credit, and minimum tax credit. Businesses are also allowed a tax credit for any amounts they have prepaid toward the current year's tax liability. In addition to the various business tax credits, individual taxpayers also have a variety of personal tax credits that they can use to reduce their tax liabilities. These credits are discussed in Chapter 11.

.01 General Business Credit

The "general business credit" is a combination of a variety of business credits, each of which is computed under its own set of rules.[17] The various credits are combined into one general business credit to limit the amount of the combined credits that can offset a taxpayer's income tax liability and to prevent businesses from completely offsetting their income tax liability for any one tax year. Any unused general business credit can be carried back one year and then carried forward 20 years.[18] Both this limitation and the credits that comprise the general business credit are discussed in Chapter 11. A partial list of credits that comprise the general business credit is shown in Figure 4-2.

Figure 4-2 Partial List of Tax Credits That Comprise the General Business Credit

Tax Credits Aimed at Encouraging Employers to Hire Certain Workers
- Work opportunity credit,
- Empowerment zone employment credit,
- Indian employment credit, and

Tax Credits Aimed at Encouraging Conservation of Energy
- Alternative motor vehicle (hybrid car) credit,
- Plug-in electric drive motor vehicle credit,
- Alternative fuel vehicle refueling property credit,
- Home builder's credit for new energy efficient homes,
- Investment credit,
- Alcohol fuels credit,
- Biodiesel fuels credit,
- Renewable electricity production credit,
- Marginal oil and gas well production credit,
- Nonconventional source production credit,
- Low sulfur diesel fuel production credit, and
- Carbon dioxide sequestration credit.

Tax Credits Aimed at Rewarding Research in Certain Areas
- Research credit and
- Orphan drug credit.

Tax Credits to Encourage Economic Development
- Empowerment zone and renewal community employment credit and
- New markets tax credit.

---

[17] Code Sec. 38.   [18] Code Sec. 39.

Tax Credits Used to Subsidize Businesses for Certain Expenditures Made During the Year

- Employer social security tax credit,
- Rehabilitation credit,
- Low-income housing credit,
- Disabled access credit,
- Employer-provided child care credit,
- Small employer pension plan start-up cost credit,
- Small employer health insurance credit,
- Employer wage credit for employees who are active duty members of the Uniformed Services,
- Agricultural chemicals security credit, and
- Mine rescue team training credit.

The work opportunity credit, empowerment zone employment credit, Indian employment credit, home builder's credit for new energy efficient homes, alcohol fuels credit, biodiesel fuels credit, research credit, new markets tax credit, and mine rescue team training credit terminated December 31, 2014, but Congress has been renewing them from year to year. The alternative motor vehicle credit is available only with respect to new qualified fuel cell motor vehicles purchased no later than December 31, 2014. The alternative fuel vehicle refueling property credit is available with respect to placed in service (i.e., ready for use) before 2015.

.02 Foreign Tax Credit

When U.S. businesses receive income from a foreign country, the foreign-source income may be subject to income tax imposed by both the foreign country and by the U.S. To reduce the possibility of double taxation on the same income, U.S. citizens and residents as well as certain nonresident taxpayers are permitted to take an income tax credit for income taxes paid or accrued during the tax year to a foreign country or to a U.S. possession.[19] The availability and calculation of this credit are discussed in Chapter 11 (see ¶ 1116).

.03 Minimum Tax Credit

The "minimum tax credit" is a tax credit allowed in certain situations when the taxpayer has previously been subject to the AMT.[20] It is discussed in Chapter 10 (see ¶ 1010).

.04 Prepayments of Federal Income Taxes

In addition to the various tax credits taxpayers are allowed to use to reduce their income tax liability, any amounts that a taxpayer has prepaid the government toward its tax liability are treated as a refundable credit when it files its income tax return. Thus, if the taxpayer has overpaid its tax liability for the year, it can request a refund of the excess when it files its income tax return. Alternatively, the taxpayer can apply the overpayment to the next year's income tax liability and treat it as a refundable tax credit in the subsequent tax year.

Example 39: Ariel Industries determines that its regular tax for the year is $160,000 and that it is not subject to the AMT. Ariel is entitled to $20,000 of tax credits, and it made a total of $155,000 in estimated tax payments during the year. When it files its income tax return, Ariel can either request that its $15,000 overpayment be refunded or that the overpayment be applied toward its next year's taxes.

---

[19] Code Sec. 901(a).   [20] Code Sec. 53.

Regular tax	$160,000
Plus: AMT	0
Total tax liability	$160,000
Less: Tax credits	(20,000)
Less: Prepayments	(155,000)
Tax (refund) due	($ 15,000)

¶410 Estimated Tax Payments

Because the federal government requires a steady source of revenue to pay its expenses, it requires taxpayers to periodically make payments toward their current year's tax liability. This includes amounts owed for regular income tax, AMT, and self-employment tax plus any other taxes owed with the taxpayer's income tax return in excess of any allowable tax credits.

Employees are required to have taxes withheld from their paychecks. Taxpayers can arrange to have amounts withheld from interest and dividend income and pensions that they receive during the year. When taxes are prepaid through withholdings, the amounts are withheld by the payer and remitted periodically to the government. For all other types of income, the government requires that taxpayers make **estimated tax payments** to cover their taxes owed for the year. The government imposes penalties if required amounts are not timely prepaid.

C corporations are required to make estimated tax payments during the year unless their total tax liability for the year, reduced by tax credits, is less than $500.[21] Individuals must make estimated tax payments on income not subject to withholding unless their total tax liability for the year, reduced by tax credits and amounts withheld from wages, etc., is less than $1,000.[22] A taxpayer that fails to make the appropriate amounts of estimated payments may be subject to an underpayment penalty when filing its tax return. The penalty is equivalent to the amount of interest that would have accrued on the tax underpayment during the period of the underpayment. In such situations, the interest rate charged is the government's applicable federal rate.

 Reason for the Rule: The government requires taxpayers to make payments periodically during the year because the government needs a steady stream of revenue to pay its expenses and because it is easier for taxpayers to pay their tax in installments. The requirement helps the government avoid losing tax revenues because the taxpayer becomes insolvent or is otherwise is unable to pay required taxes.

.01 Avoiding the Underpayment Penalty—Corporate Taxpayers

C corporations are required to pay the estimated tax in four installments during the year. These installments are due on the 15th day of the fourth, sixth, ninth, and twelfth months of the corporation's tax year. If the 15th of a month falls on a weekend or a federal holiday, the payment is due the next business day.

Example 40: Lyber Books uses the calendar year as its tax year. Lyber's estimated tax payments each year are due no later than April 15, June 15, September 15, and December 15. If any of these dates falls on a weekend or a federal holiday, the payment is due the next business day.

---

[21] Code Sec. 6655.   [22] Code Sec. 6654.

Example 41:   Rhynard Stamps uses a January 31 fiscal year-end. Rhynard's estimated tax payments are due no later than May 15, July 15, October 15, and January 15. If any of these dates falls on a weekend or a federal holiday, the payment is due the next business day.

Large corporations are required to pay as estimated tax 100 percent of the tax shown on their return for the current tax year. A "large corporation" is one whose taxable income is at least $1 million for any of the previous three tax years. The corporation's taxable income is computed without regard to any net operating loss (NOL) deduction (see ¶ 1002) or capital loss carryforward (see ¶ 901.01).

Example 42:   Radiant Heating, which qualifies as a large corporation, owed $400,000 in taxes for its 2015 tax year and expects to owe $100,000 in taxes for 2016. For 2016, Radiant must make equal estimated tax payments that total at least $100,000 (100 percent of its 2016 income tax liability).

Example 43:   Assume the same facts as in Example 42, except Radiant's tax liability in 2016 was $300,000. Because Radiant is a large corporation, its 2016 estimated tax payments must have totaled $300,000 (100 percent of its 2016 income tax liability).

To avoid an underpayment penalty, corporations that are not large corporations must make estimated payments equal to the *lesser* of (1) 100 percent of the tax shown on their return for the current tax year or (2) 100 percent of the tax shown on their return for the preceding tax year.

Example 44:   Hawthorn is not a large corporation. Its federal tax liability for 2015 was $20,000. To avoid a penalty for underpayment of taxes, Hawthorn must make estimated payments totaling the *lesser* of $20,000 or its 2016 tax liability.

 Planning Pointer: If a corporation that is not considered a large corporation is uncertain as to its current year's tax liability, it should consider making estimated payments using 100 percent of its prior year's tax liability. This will ensure that the corporation is not subject to any underpayment penalty in case its actual tax liability for the year unexpectedly increases. For example, in Example 44, Hawthorn can make estimated payments based on the last year's actual tax liability of $20,000 and be guaranteed not to be subject to any underpayment penalty. The downside to using this "safe harbor" approach to paying estimated taxes is that if the taxpayer's actual tax liability in the current year is significantly less than in the prior year the corporation will have allowed the federal government interest-free use of its overpayment.

The amount of each required installment generally is one-fourth of the amount of estimated tax due for the year. Corporations that receive most of their taxable income toward the end of the year may benefit by annualizing their income and using the tax liability calculated based on that annualized income to determine the required amount of each installment.

 Planning Pointer: Businesses that receive most of their taxable income at the end of the year should consider using the annualized method to compute each required installment of estimated tax even though it results in a large payment at the end of the year. When businesses overpay their estimated tax during the year, they make an interest-free loan to the government. It is better for a business to retain that money for as long as possible and to let it earn money for the business.

.02 Avoiding the Underpayment Penalty—Individual Taxpayers

Sole proprietors and other individuals are required to make estimated tax payments when the amounts withheld from other sources are not sufficient to cover the amounts the government expects them to prepay during the year. Individual taxpayers (other than farmers and fishermen) must make total payments during the year equal to the *lesser* of (1) 90 percent of the tax shown on their tax return for the current tax year or (2) 100 percent of their tax liability for the preceding tax year. The percentage increases to 110 percent of the prior year's tax liability for taxpayers whose AGI exceeded $150,000 in the previous tax year ($75,000 if married filing separately). Farmers and fishermen are required to pay 66.67 percent of the *lesser* of (1) the tax reported on their current year's tax return for the year or (2) their tax liability for the preceding tax year.

Individuals are required to pay their estimated taxes in four installments. For individuals using a calendar year-end, their estimated payments are due on April 15, June 15, September 15, and January 15 of the following year. If the 15th of the month falls on the weekend or a holiday, the taxes are due the following business day. The amount of each required installment generally is one-fourth of the amount of the estimated tax due for the year. Individuals who receive most of their taxable income toward the end of the year may benefit by annualizing their income and using the tax liability calculated based on that annualized income to determine the required amount of each installment.

Example 45: Jay Keith is a sole proprietor who uses the calendar year as his tax year. His estimated tax payments for 2015 are due by April 15, 2015, June 16, 2015 (because June 15 is a Sunday), September 15, 2015, and January 15, 2016.

 Planning Pointer: If an individual taxpayer is uncertain about its current year's tax liability, the taxpayer should consider making estimated payments using 100 percent of the prior year's tax liability (110 percent if the individual's AGI for the prior year was more than $150,000). This will protect the taxpayer if the taxpayer's actual tax liability for the year unexpectedly increases.

GROSS INCOME

Up to this point, this textbook has presented an overview of the entire federal income tax system. It is now time to begin taking a more in-depth look at some of the components of the taxable income formula.

¶ 411 Identifying Income

The Code defines "gross income" as follows:[23]

General Definition—Except as otherwise provided in this subtitle, gross income means all income from whatever source derived, including (but not limited to) the following items:

1. Compensation for services, including fees, commissions, fringe benefits, and similar items;
2. Gross income derived from business;
3. Gains derived from dealings in property;
4. Interest;
5. Rents;
6. Royalties;
7. Dividends;
8. Alimony and separate maintenance payments;
9. Annuities;
10. Income from life insurance and endowment contracts;
11. Pensions;
12. Income from discharge of indebtedness;

---

[23] Code Sec. 61.

13. Distributive share of partnership gross income;

14. Income in respect of a decedent; and

15. Income from an interest in an estate or trust.

The Code takes an all-inclusive approach to determining what is included in gross income. As specifically provided in Code Sec. 61, all income is gross income, "[e]xcept as otherwise provided." The more common types of gross income are listed in the Code provision, but this list is not intended to be comprehensive.

The presumption is that all receipts by a taxpayer are included in gross income unless a specific statutory provision excluding them can be identified. This means that unless a provision in the tax law exists to not tax an item of income, the income is taxed.[24]

The statutory definition of "gross income" has been interpreted as including all accessions to wealth, clearly realized, over which a taxpayer has complete dominion.[25] Accordingly, income includes only items that increase a taxpayer's wealth, and then only those items that are realized during the tax year. Any items that reduce a taxpayer's wealth are considered deductions, if anything at all. Wealth is considered realized when it is reduced to cash or property other than cash.

Example 46: Cratten Sealers borrows $1 million to purchase a new office building. The loan proceeds do not have to be included in the company's gross income because they do not increase the company's net wealth. Although the company receives an additional $1 million, its debt increased by $1 million, and, consequently, no wealth has been created.

Example 47: Sidewalk Lighting has its manufacturing plant appraised and discovers it has increased in value by $50,000 since the beginning of the year. Although the company's wealth technically has increased by $50,000, it does not have to include that amount in its gross income for the year because it did not realize any of the $50,000.

Reason for the Rule: The realization principle was adopted for several reasons. First, it would be costly to require taxpayers to have all of their property appraised each year to determine the change in their net wealth during the year. Second, it would be costly and difficult for the government to determine whether taxpayers properly appraised their property. Third, taxpayers might find it necessary to sell their property (perhaps in a forced sale at a loss) to pay tax owed on unrealized appreciation. Fourth, taxpayers might be able to save taxes by deducting a loss they might never actually incur.

Spotlight: Due to the all-inclusive approach to defining gross income, the IRS often uses a technique called the "bank deposits test" to search for unreported or under-reported income. The IRS will require a taxpayer to bring in 12 months of bank statements. The IRS agent then totals all deposits into the taxpayer's bank accounts and compares that total to the gross income reported on the tax return. Any difference (if deposits exceed reported income) is presumed to be an underreporting, and the taxpayer must specifically provide evidence to rebut this presumption.

Income is not limited to cash received; it also includes the fair market value (FMV) of property and services received.[26] This is true even though the business uses the cash method of accounting. Income usually is not realized when property is purchased, even though the property is purchased

---

[24] Code Sec. 61.
[25] *Glenshaw Glass Co.*, SCt, 55-1 USTC ¶ 9308, 348 US 426, 75 SCt 473.

[26] Reg. § 1.446-1(a)(3).

at a discount. However, gross income can be realized from the purchase of property at less than its FMV if the bargain element is a disguised dividend or disguised compensation.

Example 48: Bigsby Management performs consulting services in exchange for a computer worth $2,000. Bigsby must include the $2,000 value of the computer in its income.

Example 49: McKenzie Chemical Engineers went shopping for a computer and found one with a retail price of $2,000 that was on sale for $1,750. The company does not have to include the difference between the computer's retail price and the sale price in its income.

Example 50: Adu Boxes has its eye on some land with an estimated FMV of $300,000. When the owner of the land suffers a financial reversal and needs to sell the land in a hurry, the owner offers the land to Adu for $250,000. Although Adu purchases the property for $50,000 less than its estimated FMV, it does not realize any income from the purchase.

Example 51: Taurus Industries performs consulting services for Wollmuth Flooring and charges Wollmuth $15,000 (half its going rate) for the services. A week later, Wollmuth sells Taurus a vehicle worth $25,000 but charges Taurus only $10,000. If the IRS can establish that the $15,000 reduction in the vehicle's price was disguised compensation to Taurus, Taurus will be required to include the $15,000 in its income.

Income is not necessarily the same as **gross receipts**, which is the total FMV of property received in exchange for selling property or performing services. The concept of gross receipts is an even broader term than income and includes nontaxable returns of capital (such as the cost of goods sold) as well as income. The cost of goods sold must be subtracted from gross receipts when determining the amount to include in income. Income must also be distinguished from **gross sales**, which is the total amount of sales at invoice prices, not reduced by any discounts, returns, or allowances. The amount of any discounts, returns, and allowances is subtracted from gross sales to determine how much has to be included in income.

Example 52: Solt Telephones had gross sales of $100,000 during its tax year. Its cost of goods sold was $30,000. The value of returned goods was $5,000, and the amount of discounts and allowances was $8,000. The amount that Solt includes in income is $57,000.

Gross sales	$100,000
Less: Sales returns	(5,000)
Less: Sales discounts	(8,000)
Net sales	$ 87,000
Less: Cost of goods sold	(30,000)
Gross income from sales	$ 57,000

.01 Gross Profit

In accordance with the capital recovery doctrine, if a merchant purchases inventory costing $4,000 and later sells it for $10,000, the taxpayer's gross income from the transaction is $6,000 ($10,000 – $4,000). In this way, the tax concept of "gross income" is similar to the accounting term "gross profit."

Inventories. Gross profit from business operations is computed by deducting the cost of goods sold (COGS) from gross receipts. If inventories are material, then the accrual method must be used to compute gross profit from inventories (see ¶ 305.01). As is done in financial accounting, COGS is determined either (1) by aggregating the cost of each specific item sold or (2) by adding the cost of inventory from the beginning of the year to the cost of goods purchased or produced during the year and then subtracting the cost of inventory remaining at the end of the year.

Example 53: Pink Co. is a small corporation that buys auto parts at wholesale and resells them to the general public. At the beginning of its tax year, the costs associated with its inventories were $60,000; at the end of the year they were $50,000. During the tax year Pink paid $30,000 for carburetors, $18,000 for mufflers, and $10,000 for air filters. Its gross receipts for the year were $110,000. Pink computes its gross profit as follows:

Gross receipts		$110,000
Less: Cost of goods sold		
Beginning inventory	$ 60,000	
Plus: Purchases	58,000	
Goods available for sale	$118,000	
Less: Ending inventory	(50,000)	(68,000)
Gross profit		$ 42,000

Uniform capitalization rules. Businesses that manufacture their own goods or acquire property for resale must abide by the uniform capitalization (UNICAP) rules and capitalize direct costs and an allocable portion of most indirect costs that are incurred because of production or resale activities.[27] Thus, certain expenses incurred during the year are included in the cost basis of property produced or in inventory costs, rather than being expensed immediately. These costs are recovered through COGS when the property is sold. This method is very similar to full absorption costing used to report inventories and COGS on financial statements.

Under the UNICAP rules, direct material costs and direct labor costs incurred for production or resale of property must be capitalized. "Direct material costs" include the cost of those materials that become an integral part of the asset plus the cost of materials that are used in the ordinary course of the production of the asset. "Direct labor costs" include the cost of labor that can be identified or associated with a particular activity. This includes all types of compensation (basic, overtime, sick, vacation, etc.) plus payroll taxes and payments to a supplemental unemployment benefit plan. All costs other than direct material or direct labor are treated as "indirect costs." Certain types of costs may directly benefit a particular activity or be incurred because of a particular activity even though the same costs also benefit other activities. Therefore, costs that benefit more than one activity must be reasonably allocated to determine the portion that is attributable to each activity.

Inventory costing. Whether a business manufactures its own inventory or whether it purchases inventory from a supplier and resells it to customers, a method is needed to assign a cost to the units sold during the year. Two common costing methods are the last-in, first-out (LIFO) and the first-in, first-out (FIFO) methods. Under LIFO, the last units produced/purchased are deemed to be the first units sold (and therefore the ones included in COGS). Under FIFO, the first units produced/purchased are the ones that are deemed to have been sold (and therefore the ones included in COGS). In inflationary times, the LIFO method produces the highest COGS (and thus, the lowest gross profit), whereas FIFO produces lower COGS (and higher profits). Accordingly, many businesses prefer to use the LIFO costing method for tax purposes and to use FIFO to calculate COGS on their income statement. Although this strategy is in the best interest of the business, the tax laws generally permit a business to use LIFO for tax purposes only if the business also uses LIFO for financial accounting purposes.[28]

 Spotlight: In inflationary times the use of LIFO results in lower gross profit. Therefore, under such conditions, businesses that want to use LIFO for tax purposes will be

---

[27] Code Sec. 263A.

[28] Reg. § 1.472-2.

selecting a method that results in higher cash flows (through paying less taxes) but lower profitability reported on their financial statements.

 GAAP vs. Code: A corporation that wants to use LIFO for tax purposes must also use LIFO for financial reporting purposes. If a corporation does not want to use LIFO for financial reporting purposes, it will use FIFO for both financial and tax purposes. Consequently, no differences between net income and taxable income should arise in the corporation's reports. However, any differences in the amounts required to be capitalized to cost of goods sold during the year need to be accounted for when reconciling net income to taxable income on the corporation's income tax return.

Installment sales. As discussed in Chapter 3, regardless of a taxpayer's method of accounting gross profit from installment sales is taxed when cash flows are received, rather than when income is realized. This rule controls when gain has to be recognized unless the taxpayer elects to recognize the entire gain in the year of the sale. (See ¶ 309.01.)

 GAAP vs. Code: The installment sale method is not an acceptable method for reporting gross profit on the income statement. Therefore, corporations that use the installment method for tax purposes will report different amounts of gain on their tax return than on the income statement. For large corporations, this difference will need to be reconciled on the corporate income tax return. The details behind the calculation of gross profit reported each year from an installment sale are discussed in Chapter 8 (see ¶ 810).

.02 Gains from Sales of Property

When property is sold or exchanged, the amount included in income is the difference between the amount realized and the taxpayer's adjusted basis in the property.[29] A taxpayer's "adjusted basis in property" is the amount invested in the property reduced by certain amounts (such as deductions for depreciation, depletion, and amortization) and increased by other amounts (such as amounts expensed for capital improvements).[30] If the amount realized from a disposition of property is less than the adjusted basis of the property, the difference is a loss, which can be deducted from gross income. (See ¶ 403.02.) The tax laws surrounding the calculation of the amount realized and the adjusted basis are the focus of Chapter 8. Also discussed in Chapter 8 are the situations in which gains realized from the sale or exchange of property are not recognized on the tax return and, therefore, are not included in a taxpayer's gross income. This occurs because a tax law either excludes the gain from gross income or postpones recognition of the gain to another tax year.

Example 54:   Fire Gemstone invests $100,000 in a parcel of land and later sells it for $250,000. Only $150,000 ($250,000 – $100,000) is included in gross income because that is the amount by which Fire Gemstone's net worth was increased. The remaining $100,000 represents a return of the company's investment in the land.

.03 Rental Income

Amounts received by property owners for the right to use their property are taxed as rental income. As discussed in Chapter 3, regardless of the taxpayer's method of accounting receipt of rents in advance of providing the rental services generally must be included in gross income in the tax year in which the advance rent is received. Expenses for items (such as repairs, interest, taxes,

---

[29] Code Sec. 1001(a).   [30] Code Sec. 1016.

and depreciation) that relate to the rental property are deductions and do not reduce gross rental receipts.

Example 55: Syddel Realty receives $20,000 in rental income from an apartment building that it leases out to tenants. During the year, Syddel pays $1,000 for repairs made to the building. It also pays $5,000 in property taxes and $4,000 in interest on the mortgage loan it obtained to purchase the building. Syddel also deducts a depreciation expense of $12,500. Although Syddel realized a $2,500 loss from its rental of the apartment building during the year ($20,000 – $1,000 – $5,000 – $4,000 – $12,500), it must include $20,000 in its gross income. It can separately deduct the various rental expenses from its gross income.

Example 56: Redd Tooth, Inc. enters into a 10-year lease to rent a building that it owns. In addition to $7,000 for the first year's rent, that same year it also receives a $7,000 advance as rent for the tenth and last year of the lease. Redd Tooth must include $14,000 in its gross income in the first year.

 GAAP vs. Code: On the income statement, a corporate landlord "matches" rental income to the period to which the rental services are provided (when the revenue is earned). On the tax return, rents are included in gross income in the period in which they are received. This is particularly important in the case of advance lease payments, which are recorded on the books as unearned rent revenue but included in gross income for tax purposes. This difference will be reversed in the year in which the rental services are finally provided. In Example 56, during the first year of the lease Redd Tooth includes $7,000 in net income and $14,000 in taxable income. Therefore, when reconciling net income with taxable income on that year's tax return, Redd Tooth will need to add $7,000 to its net income. In the tenth year of the lease, Redd Tooth will report $7,000 of rental income in net income, but nothing on the tax return. Thus, it will need to subtract the $7,000 from its net income when reconciling its net income with its taxable income on that year's tax return.

Taxes and other expenses paid by a tenant. When a tenant pays a property owner's expenses, the amounts paid on the property owner's behalf are treated as additional rent[31] and are includible in the property owner's gross income. A common business lease type is a "triple net lease" in which the lessee pays taxes, insurance, and maintenance costs of property. Under this arrangement, payments for taxes and insurance by the lessee are regarded as income for the lessor. These payments may be deductible rental expenses, although the timing of the expenses may differ from the recognition of income.

Example 57: Leonard Enterprises insures its factory building against fire. The premiums, payable every three years, are $3,500. As part of the terms of the lease, a new tenant agrees to pay the premiums on the policy by forwarding the money directly to the insurance company. The tenant's $3,500 payment is treated by the tenant as additional rent, and the entire sum has to be included in Leonard's gross income. Leonard will be entitled to a deduction for the insurance expense.

.04 Dividend Income

When a C corporation generates taxable income, it pays taxes on that income. When the board of directors of a C corporation decides to distribute the corporation's after-tax profits to the corporation's shareholders, the distribution is treated as a dividend to the extent of the corporation's current and accumulated earnings and profits.[32] Earnings and profits (E&P) is an account that keeps track of a corporation's ability to make distributions to shareholders from the corporation's current

---

[31] Reg. § 1.61-8(c).

[32] Code Secs. 301 and 316(a).

and accumulated profits. This account is increased by the after-tax amounts the corporation earns that enhance its ability to pay dividends and is decreased when the corporation incurs expenses or makes distributions to shareholders. The calculation of a C corporation's E&P is described in detail in Chapter 12 (see ¶ 1207).

When a shareholder of a C corporation receives dividend income, the amount received causes the shareholder's wealth to increase and, accordingly, represents income to the shareholder. When the shareholder is another C corporation, some or all of the income may not be taxed (see discussion at ¶ 412.02 later in the chapter). When a shareholder of a C corporation is an individual and the individual receives dividend income, the full amount represents income to the shareholder.

Gross income from flow-through entities is taxed to its owners. Because the owners have already paid tax on the income, distributions from these entities are not dividends and are not included in gross income. The rules governing distributions received from various entities are summarized in Table 4-3. How flow-through entities are taxed is discussed in greater detail in Chapters 13 and 14.

Table 4-3 Summary of Distributions from Business Entities

Distributor	Recipient	Tax Consequences
Sole proprietorship	Proprietor	Tax-free distribution because the earnings have been taxed on the sole proprietor's individual income tax return.
Partnership	Partner	Tax-free distribution because the earnings have been taxed on the partner's income tax return.
Limited liability company taxed as a partnership	Member	Tax-free distribution because the earnings have been taxed on the member's income tax return.
S corporation	Shareholder	Tax-free distribution because the earnings have been taxed on the shareholder's income tax return.
C corporation	Individual	Taxed as dividend income.
	Partnership	Flows through to the partners as dividend income.
	S corporation	Flows through to the shareholders as dividend income.
	C corporation	Taxable after taking the dividends received deduction into consideration. (See ¶ 412.02.)

.05 Interest Income

Interest is the compensation allowed by law for the use, forbearance, or detention of money or its equivalent. This includes interest earned from certificates of deposit and money market accounts as well as interest earned from notes and bonds. Although most interest is taxable, the tax laws exempt municipal interest from gross income. (See ¶ 412.01.)

Imputed interest on original issue discount bonds. When a corporation attempts to issue bonds that promise to pay a face rate of interest below the current market interest rate, the bonds cannot be sold at face value (the amount due at maturity) because investors expect to receive the market rate of interest. Because the interest rate associated with the bonds is inadequate compared to the market rate investors can get elsewhere, the issuing corporation will find it necessary to issue the bonds at a discount (less than face value). The amount of the required discount (known as original issue discount (OID)) is an amount sufficient to give the bondholder the amount of interest the bondholder would have earned if the bond had paid the market rate of interest when it was first issued. Some corporations issue bonds that make no periodic interest payments (that is, with a zero percent face rate of interest). These bonds, which are issued at the deepest of discounts, are called "zero-coupon bonds." Because the full face value of such bonds is repaid when the bond matures, the amount of the OID represents additional interest that the investor earns over the life of the bond.[33] The tax laws require that bondholders include in gross income a portion of the OID.

The amount of each period's OID included in gross income is the carrying value of the bonds multiplied by the market rate of interest for the period (as determined at the time the bonds were issued). The carrying value of the bonds is then increased by the amount of the OID included in income. By increasing the carrying value of the bond by the taxable OID, the carrying value of the bonds will approach face value by the time the bonds mature. Therefore, when the bondholders receive full face value at maturity, no gain or loss will be realized by the bondholders.

Example 58: On July 1, 2015, a 10-year zero-coupon bond with a face value of $10 million is issued by a corporation for $4,788,923. The bonds are issued to yield the equivalent of a 7.5-percent annual interest market interest rate, with interest compounded semiannually (therefore, a 3.75-percent semiannual interest rate). The OID associated with the bond is $5,211,077 ($10,000,000 – $4,788,923). Because the bonds pay a zero rate of interest, the owner of the bonds will receive nothing until maturity. However, over the next 10 years (20 semiannual periods), the bondholders will collectively earn income equal to $5,211,077. To determine the taxable OID for 2015 (the six months from July 1, 2015, to December 31, 2015), the carrying value of the bonds ($4,788,923) is multiplied by the semiannual market rate of interest at the time the bonds were issued (3.75%). Thus, the total taxable OID for the first six months is $179,585 ($4,788,923 × 3.75%). The carrying value of the bond is increased by this amount to $4,968,508 ($4,788,923 + $179,585).

To determine the taxable OID for each of the later periods, the periodic market rate is applied to the (adjusted) carrying value at the beginning of the accrual period. The carrying value of the bond is the sum of the original issue price plus all taxable OID over the prior accrual periods.

Example 59: The taxable original issue discount amount for the second accrual period of the bond (first half of 2016) in Example 58 is $186,319 ($4,968,508 × 3.75%). The amortization of OID for the first 2½ years of the bond's life is shown in the table below:

Payment	Taxable OID*	Carrying Value**
		$4,788,923
12/31/2015	$179,585	4,968,508
6/30/2016	186,319	5,154,827
12/31/2016	193,306	5,348,133
6/30/2017	200,555	5,548,688
12/31/2017	208,076	5,756,764

*Determined by multiplying the carrying value at the beginning of the period by the 3.75% market rate per period.

**Determined by adding the taxable OID to the carrying value of the bond.

 Spotlight: Amortizing OID accomplishes two results. First, the interest accrues to the owner as it is earned, not when it is received. Although this is consistent with the accrual method of accounting, both cash and accrual method taxpayers are required to

[33] Code Secs. 163(e) and 1272(a).

¶ 411.05

report this imputed interest in income as it is earned. Second, because the basis of the bond to the bondholder is increased on a regular basis, when the bonds are sold or redeemed at maturity the bondholder is not taxed a second time on the OID. Amortizing OID prevents bondholders from reporting the difference between the amount of cash received at maturity and the cash paid for the bond as a capital gain, rather than as interest income.

De minimis **OID.** The tax laws treat OID as $0 if the total OID on a debt instrument is less than one-fourth of 1 percent (.0025) of the redemption price at maturity multiplied by the number of full years from the date of original issue to maturity.[34]

Example 60: A corporation purchases a 10-year bond with a redemption price at maturity of $1,000. The bond is issued at $980 with OID of $20 ($1,000 – $980). One-fourth of 1 percent of $1,000 times 10 full years from the issue date to maturity is $25 ($1,000 × .0025 × 10). Under the *de minimis* rule, the taxpayer can disregard the OID because the $20 discount for the bond is less than $25.

Example 61: Assume the same facts as in Example 60, except that the bond was issued at $950. Because the $50 of OID is greater than the $25 *de minimis* threshold amount for the bond, the taxpayer must include part of the $50 OID in gross income each year. The amortized OID will be added to the carrying value of the bond so that at maturity the bond's carrying value will equal its redemption price.

 Spotlight: The amount of interest required to be included in gross income by the recipient of the OID (bondholder) is the same as the amount of interest expense that is deducted by the payer (the corporation issuing the bonds).

Imputed interest on below market loans. When a business loans money, it normally charges the borrower interest at the current market rate. Likewise, when a business borrows money, it expects to pay interest to the lender at the market rate. Thus, when a loan is made for which the interest charged is less than the market rate, it is usually because a special relationship exists between the lender and the borrower. For example, a corporation may loan money to an employee or to one of its shareholders. When the terms of a loan do not include an "adequate rate of interest," the IRS will consider that adequate interest was charged by the lender and paid by the borrower, even though it is not the same amount as the actual cash interest paid by the borrower. The term used to describe such loans is **below market loans**, and the amount of "deemed" interest paid by the borrower is called **imputed interest**.[35]

Adequate interest. The amount of interest deemed "adequate" depends on the type of loan arrangement the parties enter into. If the terms of the loan call for a scheduled date or dates at which the principal must be repaid, the loan is a "term loan." If the loan proceeds must be repaid immediately upon request of the lender, or if the terms of the loan do not specify a maturity date, the loan is a "demand loan."

In the case of a term loan, adequate interest is based on the applicable federal rate (AFR) in effect as of the day on which the loan was made, compounded semiannually. The AFR is a statutory federal rate of interest that is adjusted monthly and is published by the IRS. The rates are based on the average market yield on outstanding marketable obligations of the United States during the one-month period ending on the 14th day of the preceding month.[36] There are three categories of AFRs, referenced by the term of the loan, as shown below. In the case of a demand loan, the loan amount is

---

[34] Code Sec. 1273(a)(3).
[35] Code Sec. 7872.
[36] Code Sec. 1274(d).

considered as a series of one-day term loans. Thus, adequate interest on such a loan is the amount of interest that is computed on a daily basis using the federal short-term rate.

Term of the Loan	Applicable Federal Rate
Not more than three years	The federal short-term rate
More than three years but not more than nine years	The federal mid-term rate
More than nine years	The federal long-term rate

When a corporation makes a below market loan to a shareholder, the IRS treats the shareholder as having paid adequate interest to the corporation. To the extent that the amount considered adequate interest is less than the actual amount of interest paid, the difference represents a "deemed" interest payment that the shareholder makes to the corporation. The corporation is then deemed to distribute back to the shareholder the same amount. Because the deemed payment by the shareholder to the corporation and the deemed distribution by the corporation to the shareholder are for the same amount, these amounts offset one another and no cash is actually ever exchanged. These deemed payments are depicted in Figure 4-3.

Figure 4-3 Corporation-Shareholder Below Market Loan

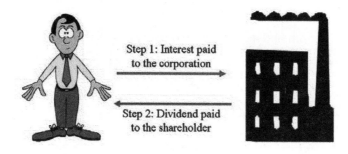

In a corporation-shareholder below market loan, the borrower (shareholder) is deemed to pay interest to the lender (corporation) in an amount equal to the amount of imputed interest charged on the loan. The corporation includes the imputed interest in gross income, and the shareholder may or may not be able to deduct the interest (depending on the nature of the loan). The corporation is then deemed to have made a distribution the shareholder equal to the amount of the imputed interest. The distribution is treated as a dividend to the extent of the corporation's current and accumulated profits and is taxed as such to the shareholder. The corporation gets no deduction for the corresponding dividend distribution. Consequently, neither party has escaped taxation by using this arrangement.

Example 62: Greene & Company loans its sole shareholder, Margaret Greene, $200,000 for five years with no stated interest rate. At the time the loan was made, the current annual AFR mid-term rate (for loans between three and nine years) was nine percent, which when compounded semiannually yields 9.2025 percent. Because no interest is paid in cash on the note, each year Margaret is deemed to have paid $18,405 of interest to the corporation ($200,000 × 9.2025%), which the corporation includes in gross income. Greene & Company is then deemed to pay an $18,405 dividend to Margaret. Margaret reports the dividend income of $18,405 in her gross income. She also has $18,405 of interest expense that she may or may not be able to deduct.

Reason for the Rule: Because corporations cannot deduct dividends paid from their gross income, corporations (particularly closely held corporations) have an incentive to attempt to characterize transfers of cash to their owners as something other than a dividend. One way they attempt to do this is to call the payments a loan to the shareholder. In this case, the shareholder receives free use of cash from the corporation. As can be seen in Figure 4-3 and Example 62, the tax laws address this problem by treating the arrangement as dividend income to the shareholder and interest income to the corporation. Thus, both parties pay tax on income that was never actually exchanged.

The imputed interest rules also apply to any below market loan that involves a compensation-related loan between an employer and an employee or between an independent contractor and a person for whom the independent contractor provides services. The imputed interest rules also apply to any loan that has tax avoidance as one of its principal purposes. Figure 4-4 depicts the tax consequences of a compensation-related below market loan.

Figure 4-4 Employer-Employee Below Market Loan

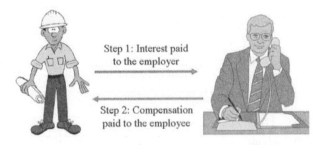

In a compensation-related loan between an employer and an employee, the employee is deemed to pay to the employer the amount of imputed interest charged on the loan. The employer is then deemed to pay the employee compensation equal to the same amount. The employer includes the interest in gross income, and, depending on the use of the funds, the employee may or may not be able to deduct the interest expense. The employer deducts the deemed amount paid as wage expense, and the employee includes the deemed amount in gross income as compensation.

Example 63: Assume the same facts as in Example 62, except Margaret is not a shareholder but, instead, is an officer and employee of the corporation. Each year, Margaret is deemed to pay $18,405 of interest to the corporation. The corporation is deemed to pay $18,405 in compensation to Margaret. The corporation deducts the $18,405 as compensation paid, and Margaret includes the amount in gross income as compensation. The corporation includes the imputed interest in gross income, and, depending on the use of the funds, Margaret may or may not be able to deduct the interest expense.

Example 64: Assume the same facts as in Example 63, except that the terms of the loan require Margaret to pay interest equal to an annual rate of five percent (5.0625 percent when compounded semiannually). Each year, the deemed payment is reduced by the $10,125 of actual interest paid by Margaret ($200,000 × 5.0625%). Thus, the imputed interest deemed paid equals $8,280 ($18,405 – $10,125).

De minimis loans. A *de minimis* exception to the below market loan rules exists. In the case of any compensation-related or corporation-shareholder below market loan, no interest is imputed to either the borrower or the lender for any day on which the aggregate amount of all outstanding loans between the borrower and the lender does not exceed $10,000. This exception does not apply to loans for which tax avoidance is a principal purpose.[37]

.06 Distributive Shares from Flow-Through Entities

If a taxpayer is an owner of a flow-through entity, the taxpayer includes in its gross income its distributive share of the entity's items of gross income, regardless of whether the share is distributed to the taxpayer. The calculation of the taxpayer's distributive share of a flow-through entity's gross income is discussed in Chapters 13 and 14.

Example 65: Luffman Supplies is a partner in ABC Partnership. Luffman's share of the partnership's income for the year is $5,000. However, none of that amount was distributed to Luffman. Even though none of that $5,000 was distributed to Luffman, it includes the entire $5,000 in its gross income for the year. When the $5,000 is eventually distributed, Luffman will not pay tax on the $5,000 a second time.

Example 66: Donaldson Company is a partner in ABC Partnership. During the year, ABC receives $10,000 of interest income from corporate bonds. Donaldson's share of the interest is $3,000. The $3,000 represents taxable interest income to Donaldson.

.07 Other Items of Income

Common forms of other income include damages and insurance, tax benefits, and income from the discharge of indebtedness.

Damages and insurance. Damage awards businesses receive for replacement of lost business profits and punitive damages must be included in income. Recoveries representing a replacement for lost income are taxed in the same manner as the lost income would have been taxed had it not been lost. Similarly, if the taxpayer is insured against a loss of net profits, the proceeds are taxable income. On the other hand, a recovery for property or property rights that were diminished in value is a nontaxable recovery of capital to the extent the recovery does not exceed the taxpayer's adjusted basis in the property or the property right. Any excess is taxed. If the amount of the recovery is less than the adjusted basis of the property or the property right, the adjusted basis is reduced by the amount of the recovery.

Example 67: Erne Compactors sues a competitor for antitrust violations and is awarded $150,000 in damages for its lost profits. Erne includes the $150,000 in its income.

Example 68: Lentine Gaskets successfully sues a company for illegally interfering with its suppliers and is awarded $50,000 in punitive damages. Lentine includes the damages in its income.

Tax benefit rule. If a taxpayer deducts an item in one tax year and that item is refunded to the taxpayer in a subsequent tax year, the tax benefit rule (see ¶ 313) applies to the recovered amount.

Example 69: In 2015, Bellomo (a calendar year corporation) deducts as a bad debt expense a $3,000 loan it made to an employee when the loan becomes uncollectible. In 2016, Bellomo receives $1,000 from the employee as partial repayment of the loan. The company includes the $1,000 in its gross income for 2016.

Income from discharge of indebtedness. The cancellation of a taxpayer's debt results in income to the taxpayer. Because the debt no longer has to be repaid, the taxpayer's net worth increases. However, see ¶ 412.04 for situations in which discharge from indebtedness may be excluded from gross income. If a corporation satisfies a debt by transferring shares of its own corporate stock or the corporate stock of its parent company to the creditor, the corporation is treated as if it had paid the creditor with money equal to the FMV of the stock.[38] Thus, the

---

[37] Code Sec. 7872(c)(3).   [38] Code Sec. 108.

corporation has income from the discharge of indebtedness to the extent that the principal of the debt exceeds the value of the stock (and any other property transferred).

Example 70: Finnigan Brass owes its creditors $10,000. The creditors reduce the debt owed to $8,000. The $2,000 reduction in indebtedness increases Finnigan's net worth and must be included in its gross income unless an exception applies (see ¶ 412.04).

Example 71: Olin Services owes $5,000 to one of its shareholders, James Olin. When James cancels the debt, that cancellation is likely to be viewed as a contribution to the capital of the corporation. Thus, none of the $5,000 represents income to Olin Services.

Example 72: Big Foot, Inc. owes a creditor $20,000. The creditor agrees to cancel the debt in exchange for $1,000 in cash and stock in Big Foot that has a FMV of $14,000. Big Foot recognizes income from the discharge of indebtedness in the amount of $5,000 ($20,000 – ($1,000 cash + $14,000 stock)) unless one of the exceptions applies.

¶ 412 Exclusions

Not all items of income are taxed by the federal government. The Code includes numerous provisions that specifically exclude certain items from gross income. These exclusions are considered matters of legislative grace that must be narrowly construed. Taxpayers have the burden of proving that they qualify for an exclusion.[39] Exclusions should be distinguished from deductions. Deductions are amounts that are subtracted from gross income in order to arrive at a business's taxable income. By contrast, exclusions are items of income that are never included in gross income.

.01 Municipal Interest

Interest income is specifically included in the list of broadly defined income in Code Sec. 61. However, Code Sec. 103 excludes from gross income interest received from state and local government bonds ("municipal bonds"). This exclusion does not extend to bonds issued by corporations or by the federal government. Furthermore, the exclusion only applies to the interest generated from the bonds. It does not extend to the gain realized on the sale of municipal bonds.

 Spotlight: In 1895, the Supreme Court set forth the doctrine of intergovernmental tax immunity, which says that interest from state and local government bonds is not subject to federal income tax.[40] However, in 1998 the Supreme Court set aside the doctrine and ruled that such interest is no longer immune from federal income taxes.[41] But by enacting Code Sec. 103, Congress has chosen as a matter of public policy to confer these benefits on the holders of state and local government bonds (thus benefiting the issuing state and local governments by allowing them to offer lower interest rates than those who issue taxable bonds).

.02 Dividends Received Deduction

A C corporation is the only type of business whose profits are taxed twice—once when earned by the corporation and a second time when distributed to shareholders as dividends. When the shareholder is a C corporation, the potential for triple taxation exists. To combat this, the tax laws allow corporations to reduce the amount of taxable dividends by granting them a **dividends received deduction (DRD)** of from 70 to 100 percent of the amount of dividends received.

---

[39] *See,* e.g., *A.J. Hackl Sr.,* CA-7, 2003-2 USTC ¶ 60,465, 335 F3d 664.

[40] *Pollock v. Farmers' Loan & Trust Co.,* SCt, 157 US 429, 15 SCt 673 (1895).

[41] *South Carolina v. Baker,* SCt, 88-1 USTC ¶ 9284, 485 US 505, 108 SCt 1355.

Although called a "deduction," the DRD does not result from an expenditure but instead is computed as a percentage of the dividends received during the year.

A C corporation may take a DRD for dividends received from either (1) a domestic (U.S.) corporation that is subject to income tax or (2) a foreign corporation that was once a domestic corporation if the distribution is made from earnings and profits accumulated when the corporation was a domestic corporation and subject to federal income taxation.

The DRD is 70 percent of dividends received if the corporation owns less than 20 percent of the stock of the distributing corporation. The deduction is increased to 80 percent if the corporation receiving the dividends owns at least 20 percent but less than 80 percent of the distributing corporation's stock. If the corporation receiving the dividends owns at least 80 percent of the distributing corporation's stock, the two companies are affiliated companies, and 100 percent of the dividend received can be excluded from gross income.[42]

For DRD purposes, stock ownership in another corporation is determined by the amount of voting stock as well as the value of the corporation's stock that the corporation receiving the dividend income owns in the distributing corporation. Shares of preferred stock owned in the distributing corporation are not taken into account when determining the ownership percentage for the DRD.

Example 73: During the year, Silk Finishers receives dividends from Folwell Publications. If Silk owns one percent of the outstanding common stock in Folwell, it is entitled to a 70-percent DRD.

Example 74: During the year, Isher Steel receives dividends from Razar Equipment. Isher owns 24 percent of the outstanding common stock of Razar. Isher's DRD is 80 percent.

Example 75: Assume the same facts as in Example 74, except Isher owns 80 percent of the outstanding common stock of Razar. Isher's DRD is 100 percent.

Reason for the Rule: When a corporation earns income, that income is taxed, and when the corporation distributes that income to its shareholders the income is taxed a second time to the shareholders. Without the DRD deduction, a corporation's income could be taxed at least three times: once when earned by the corporation, a second time when distributed to corporate shareholders, and a third time when those corporate shareholders distribute the income to their shareholders.

Taxable income limitation. For corporations owning less than 20 percent of the stock in the distributing corporation, the DRD is limited to the *lesser* of (1) 70 percent of the dividends received or (2) 70 percent of the corporation's taxable income (with modifications). For corporations owning at least 20 percent but less than 80 percent of the stock in the distributing corporation, the DRD is limited to the *lesser* of (1) 80 percent of the dividends received or (2) 80 percent of the corporation's taxable income (with modifications).

In neither instance does the taxable income limitation apply if, after subtracting the full DRD, the taxpayer has a net operating loss for the year. The taxable income limitation also does not apply to dividends received from corporations that are part of an affiliated group.[43] For purposes of the taxable income limitation, taxable income is computed without deductions allowed for dividends received, net operating losses, income attributable to domestic production activities, any adjustment required when an extraordinary dividend is received, or any capital loss carryback to the year.

---

[42] Code Sec. 243.   [43] Code Sec. 246(b).

Example 76: Fulton Incorporated owns less than 20 percent of the stock in Dreamcasters, Inc. During the year, Dreamcasters pays Fulton a $100,000 dividend. Fulton's taxable income is computed as follows:

Dividend income	$100,000
Sales revenue	40,000
Less: Business expenses	(80,000)
Taxable income before DRD	$ 60,000
Less: DRD ($100,000 × 70%)	(70,000)
Taxable loss	($ 10,000)

Because deducting 70 percent of dividends received produces a taxable loss, the taxable income limit does not apply, and Fulton's DRD equals $70,000 (70% × $100,000).

Example 77: Napier owns 20 percent of the stock in Rockpoint. During the year, Napier receives $100,000 of dividends from Rockpoint. Napier computes its taxable income as follows:

Dividends received	$100,000
Ordinary income	40,000
Less: Business expenses	(50,000)
Taxable income before DRD	$ 90,000
Less: DRD (limited to 80% of $90,000)	(72,000)
Taxable income	$ 18,000

Because Napier owns at least 20 percent but less than 80 percent of the stock in Rockpoint, its DRD cannot exceed 80 percent of the $100,000 of dividends it receives from Rockpoint during the year. However, if Napier were to deduct the full $80,000 ($100,000 × 80%) against its taxable income, the result does not create a tax loss, and therefore, the DRD is computed as the *lesser* of 80 percent of (1) the dividends received or (2) the taxable income before the DRD. Napier reduces its taxable income by $72,000 ($90,000 × 80%).

Example 78: Frampton, Inc. receives $150,000 of dividends from Ranmark Corporation, in which Frampton owns 80 percent of the stock. Because Frampton owns at least 80 percent of the stock in Ranmark, its DRD is 100 percent of the dividends received. The taxable income limitation does not apply to dividends between members of an affiliated group.

Example 79: Black, Inc. owns 75 percent of Yellow Co. The remaining 25 percent is held by unrelated parties. If Yellow declares and pays $4 million of dividends during the year, Black's dividend income is $3 million ($4,000,000 × 75%). Assuming that the taxable income limitation does not apply, Black's DRD equals $2.4 million ($3,000,000 × 80%), which effectively reduces Black's taxable dividends to $600,000 ($3,000,000 – $2,400,000). If Black's marginal tax rate is 35 percent, its tax on the taxable portion of the dividend income is $210,000 ($600,000 × 35%). Thus, it effectively pays a seven-percent tax rate on the total dividends it receives during the year ($210,000 ÷ $3,000,000).

Example 80: White, Inc. receives $50,000 of dividends from short-term corporate investments in which it holds less than 10-percent ownership. Assuming the taxable income limitation does not apply, White recognizes $50,000 of dividend income but will pay tax only on $15,000 after it reduces its dividend income by the $35,000 DRD ($50,000 × 70%). If White is in the 35-percent tax bracket, then the tax on its taxable dividends equals $5,250 ($15,000 × 35%). Thus, White effectively pays a 10.5-percent tax on the $50,000 of dividend income ($5,250 ÷ $50,000).

 GAAP vs. Code: The DRD is a tax concept. It has no equivalent in the financial accounting rules. Because the DRD may be subject to the taxable income limitation on the federal income tax, the DRD is one of the last items reported as a reduction in taxable income. When large corporations are required to reconcile their net (book) income with their taxable income on the corporate tax return, they are required to reconcile net income with taxable income before the DRD or NOL deduction (see ¶ 1004). Consequently, there is no need to show the difference between these two methods in the reconciliation of net income and taxable income.

.03 Improvements Made by a Tenant

Ordinarily, a property owner reports no gross income in the year a tenant makes repairs or improvements on property that will revert to the property owner at the end of the lease term. However, if the parties intend the improvements to be, in whole or in part, a substitute for rental payments, then the property owner realizes rental income.[44] When such improvements that are not a substitute for rental payments revert to the property owner at the end of the lease, the property owner takes a zero basis in the improvements.[45] Thus, when the property owner eventually disposes of the property, any remaining value from the improvements will be recognized as taxable gain. To the extent that improvements are a substitute for rental payments, that amount becomes part of the lessor's basis in the improvements.

Example 81: Ponson Realty, Inc. leases land to Girard, Inc. for 20 years. Girard builds a manufacturing plant on the land. After 10 years, the tenant defaults on the lease, and Ponson repossesses the property. At that time, the manufacturing plant is worth $500,000. Ponson is not taxed on the $500,000. However, Ponson's adjusted basis in the plant is $0. Therefore, when it sells the plant the $500,000 previously untaxed income will be recognized.

.04 Cancellation of Indebtedness

Normally when a taxpayer's debt is forgiven, that constitutes income because the decrease in liabilities increases the taxpayer's wealth. However, when the forgiveness of debt results when a business is insolvent,[46] the taxpayer excludes from gross income the cancellation of debt to the extent of the insolvency.[47] A taxpayer is insolvent if its liabilities exceed the FMV of its assets. Thus, the extent of the insolvency is the amount by which the taxpayer's liabilities exceed the FMV of its assets. Accordingly, the taxable amount realized by an insolvent debtor from the cancellation of indebtedness is the *lesser* of (1) the amount of the indebtedness cancelled or (2) the excess of its assets over liabilities after the cancellation of the debt. Cancellation of indebtedness while the taxpayer is going through bankruptcy proceedings is entirely excluded from gross income, regardless of the extent of the taxpayer's insolvency at the time the debt is forgiven.[48]

Example 82: Furber Fabrics' liabilities total $1 million, and the FMV of its assets is $300,000. Because its liabilities exceed its assets, Furber is insolvent, and the extent of its insolvency is $700,000 ($1,000,000 – $300,000). In settlement of its debts to its creditors, Furber transfers all of its assets to its creditors. Because of that transfer,

---

[44] Code Sec. 109.
[45] Code Sec. 1019.
[46] Code Sec. 108(a)(1)(B).

[47] Code Sec. 108(a)(3).
[48] Code Sec.108(a)(1)(A).

Furber is discharged of its $700,000 of liabilities. The $700,000 discharge of indebtedness constitutes income to Furber because it increases its wealth by that amount. However, because the amount discharged does not exceed the extent to which Furber is insolvent, the entire $700,000 is excluded from Furber's gross income.

Example 83: Helstrom Mailing's liabilities total $500,000, and the FMV of its assets total $450,000. Helstrom settles a $75,000 debt it owes one of its suppliers for $20,000. Accordingly, its income from discharge of indebtedness equals $55,000 ($75,000 – $20,000). Because the amount excluded under the insolvency exception cannot exceed $50,000 (the amount by which the company is insolvent ($500,000 – $450,000)), Helstrom can only exclude $50,000 from its gross income. Helstrom's gross income will increase by $5,000 ($55,000 – $50,000).

Example 84: Leander owes $10,000 to its supplier. Leander files for bankruptcy, and the debt is discharged. Because the debt was discharged in bankruptcy, Leander excludes the entire amount from gross income, regardless of the extent of its insolvency. None of the $10,000 will be included in Leander's gross income.

 Reason for the Rule: To the extent that a discharge of indebtedness does not make a taxpayer solvent, no additional income is considered made available to the taxpayer.

.05 Life Insurance Proceeds

The proceeds from a life insurance policy paid by reason of the death of the insured increase the beneficiary's wealth and therefore represent income to the beneficiary. However, the tax law generally excludes these amounts from the beneficiary's gross income.[49] In the case of an employer-owned life insurance contract issued after August 17, 2006, the amount of death benefits received by the employer that the employer can exclude from gross income is limited to the amount of premiums and other amounts paid for the policy unless the insured was employed by the policyholder during the 12-month period before the insured's death or was a director or highly compensated employee of the employer at the time that the policy was issued.[50] This exception to the general rule also does not apply to death benefits received by an employer that are paid to the insured's heirs. These are called "key-person life insurance" policies. To maintain equity, the premiums paid on these policies are not deductible by the company.[51]

¶ 413 Summary

C corporations and sole proprietorships pay federal income tax on their taxable income from business operations. Flow-through entities do not pay federal income taxes because they are not considered separate tax-paying entities. However, they still must compute the various components of the taxable income formula in order to properly pass along income, deductions, and credits to their owners.

The starting point for computing taxable income is gross income, which is defined by the Code as all income unless specifically excluded from gross income by a Code provision.

Taxable income is calculated by first determining gross income and then subtracting allowable deductions. Taxable income is the tax base against which the regular income tax rates are applied to determine a business's regular income tax liability. Some individuals and larger corporations may be subject to AMT, which is an additional income tax that is added to the taxpayer's regular income tax liability. Sole proprietors also must pay self-employment taxes on their net earnings from self-employment.

---

[49] Code Sec. 101(a).

[50] Code Sec. 101(j).

[51] Code Sec. 264(a).

Once a business calculates its total tax liability for the year, it determines the amount of tax it owes by subtracting tax credits, which include any prepayments of income taxes that it made toward that year's tax liability. In order to avoid paying a penalty on amounts owed with the taxpayer's income tax return, individual and corporate taxpayers need to ensure that each year they properly prepay the minimum amounts required under the tax laws.

GLOSSARY OF TERMS INTRODUCED IN THIS CHAPTER

Adjusted gross income (AGI). An intermediate step between gross income and taxable income that only individuals calculate. Only certain types of deductions are subtracted from gross income when computing AGI.

Applicable federal rate (AFR). A statutory federal rate of interest that is adjusted monthly and is published by the IRS. The rates are based on the average market yield on outstanding marketable obligations of the United States during the one-month period ending on the 14th day of the preceding month.

Below market loan. A loan charging an interest rate below the market rate.

Capital expenditure. An expenditure that creates an asset expected to benefit a business for more than one year.

Deduction. An expenditure made by a taxpayer that the government allows the taxpayer to use to reduce taxable income.

Dividends received deduction. The amount of dividend income received by a C corporation that is not subject to taxation. It can be 70, 80, or 100 percent of the dividend income.

Estimated tax payments. Amounts that C corporations and individuals with taxable income not subject to withholding must pay during the year in order to avoid an underpayment of tax penalty.

Exclusion. An item of income that is not subject to taxation.

Gross income. All income from whatever source derived, except as specifically excluded by a provision in the Internal Revenue Code or other tax law. Represents the income the government has chosen to tax.

Gross receipts. The total amount of money and the fair market value of any other property received for selling property or performing services.

Gross sales. The total amount of sales at invoice prices, not reduced by any discounts, returns, or allowances.

Imputed interest. The "deemed" interest payments a borrower makes to a lender on a below market loan, including a loan involving original issue discount. *See also* Below market loan *and* Original issue discount.

Municipal interest. Interest from state and local government bonds (municipal bonds, or "muni" bonds for short).

Original issue discount (OID). Additional interest income representing the difference between the amount due at maturity (i.e., the face value of an obligation) and the obligation's issue price. It is a function of the difference between the face rate associated with the bond and the current market interest rate.

Qualified dividend income. Dividends received during the year from U.S. corporations and qualified foreign corporations with respect to stock that the individual held for at least 60 days during the 121-day period beginning 60 days before the ex-dividend date.

Qualified personal service corporation (QPSC). A corporation is a "qualified personal service corporation" if its employees spend at least 95 percent of their time performing services in a qualifying field (i.e., health, law, engineering, architecture, accounting, actuarial science, performing arts, or consulting) and at least 95 percent of the value of its stock is held directly or indirectly by employees performing services in a qualifying field, retired employees who performed such services for the corporation, the estate of such an employee or retired employee, or any other person who acquired stock in the corporation by reason of the death of such an employee or retired employee (but only for the two-year period beginning on the date of that individual's death).

Taxable income. The difference between a taxpayer's gross income and the total deductions a taxpayer is allowed. The tax base used in the regular income tax system.

CHAPTER PROBLEMS

Chapter 4 Discussion Questions

1. What types of businesses pay federal income taxes? If a business does not have to pay federal income tax on its earnings, who, if anyone, does?

2. How is a taxpayer's taxable income computed?

3. What is adjusted gross income (AGI), and how is it different from gross income and taxable income?

4. How does the Code define "gross income"?

5. What is an exclusion, and how does it differ from a deduction?

6. What is a capital expenditure?

7. What steps are required to determine how much tax a corporation owes for the year? How does this differ from how a sole proprietor determines the amount of taxes it owes for the year?

8. Are C corporations taxed at progressive tax rates as individuals are?

9. What is a taxpayer's marginal tax rate?

10. How are personal service corporations taxed on their income?

11. What businesses may be subject to alternative minimum tax (AMT)?

12. What is the relationship between the alternative minimum tax and the regular income tax?

13. What steps are required to calculate a corporation's alternative minimum tax?

14. Under what circumstances does a C corporation have to make estimated tax payments?

15. When during a tax year must a calendar year C corporation make estimated tax payments? When must corporations using a fiscal tax year make estimated payments?

16. Are improvements made by a tenant taxable to the landlord?

17. A corporation loans an employee $100,000 for two years with no stated interest rate. At the time the loan is made, the current applicable federal rate (AFR) short-term, mid-term, and long-term rates are 4.5 percent, 5.6 percent rate, and 7.4 percent, respectively. Discuss how the tax laws treat this type of loan arrangement.

18. Assume the same facts as in Question 17, except the term of the loan is six years. Discuss how the tax laws treat this type of loan arrangement. Would your answer change if the terms of the loan required that the employee pay four-percent interest, compounded semiannually?

19. The X Corporation was engaged in the business of selling electrical appliances. Due to the discriminatory acts of certain distributors of electrical appliances, the corporation sustained damages and loss of profits. In a suit instituted under the Clayton Act, the court that tried the antitrust suit found that the corporation, but for the wrongful acts of the distributors, could have earned profits amounting to $150,000. The court awarded the X Corporation triple the amount of damages, as was required under the Clayton Act (i.e., treble damages). Judgment in the amount of $450,000 was recovered. How much of the award is the taxpayer required to include in income?

20. How do the tax laws differ on the amount included in gross income from discharge of indebtedness when the taxpayer is insolvent versus going through bankruptcy procedures?

Chapter 4 Problems

1. Interior Decorators has a gross income of $200,000, deductions totaling $80,000, and tax credits totaling $25,000. What is its taxable income?

2. During its tax year, Kantz, Inc. receives a loan for $100,000 and sells for $70,000 equipment with an adjusted basis of $60,000. Based on these facts, what is the company's gross income for the year?

3. A corporation manufacturing luggage receives legal services with an FMV of $200 in exchange for a piece of luggage, and it receives a cabinet with an FMV of $50 in exchange for repairs on a piece of luggage. It also receives a 10-percent discount on a computer normally retailing for $2,000. Based on these facts, what amount must the company include in its gross income?

4. A corporation has gross receipts of $250,000 from sales of meat choppers during its tax year. The cost of the goods sold was $60,000, and the returns totaled $10,000. Based on these facts, what amount has to be included in the company's gross income for the year?

5. A corporation receives $20,000 in dividends from a U.S. company, $2,000 in interest from a Treasury bond, and $1,000 in interest from a state bond. The corporation owns five percent of the stock of the company paying the dividends. Based on these facts, how much of these amounts is taxable?

6. Real Property Development, Inc. receives $100,000 in rentals from one of its apartment buildings. During the same year, it pays $10,000 in real property taxes, $1,000 for repairs, and $20,000 in interest on a mortgage loan for the apartment building. Based on these facts, what amount must the company include in its gross income?

7. A corporation sells equipment with an adjusted basis of $30,000 for $50,000. It also sells stock with an adjusted basis of $25,000 for $15,000. Based on these facts, what amount must the company include in its gross income?

8. A corporation computes its regular tax to be $30,000 and its tentative minimum tax to be $40,000. The corporation's credits for the year totaled $20,000, and its estimated tax payments for the year totaled $35,000. Based on these facts, what amount of refund, if any, is the company owed for the tax year?

9. A corporation has a taxable income of $400,000. What is the amount of its regular income tax?

10. A corporation has $400,000 of gross income, $200,000 of deductions, and $30,000 of credits. How much regular income tax does it owe?

11. A corporation (not qualifying as a large corporation) paid $30,000 in federal income tax for 2015 and anticipates that it will owe $35,000 in tax for 2016. The most taxable income the corporation has had in the last three years is $400,000. What is the amount of estimated tax payments that the company should make for 2016?

12. A corporation pays $170,000 in federal income tax for 2015. It anticipates that it will owe $300,000 in federal income tax for 2016. Its taxable income for 2013 was $1 million, but its

taxable income for 2014 was $700,000, and its taxable income for 2015 was $500,000. What amount of estimated tax payments should it make for 2016?

13. Annett Kaizer, who is unmarried, works full time for a library but also publishes books. Her tax for 2015 was $18,500. She anticipates that her tax for 2016 will be $38,250. Her full-time employer is withholding $9,165 from her wages. What amount of estimated tax payments must she make for 2016?

14. Stenson & Company loans its sole shareholder, Ralph Stenson, $100,000 for 10 years with no stated interest rate. At the time the loan is made, the current AFR short-term, mid-term, and long-term rates are 6.75 percent, 7.6 percent, and 8.4 percent, respectively.

   a. Compute the deemed payment if the terms of the loan require that Ralph pay a three percent annual rate of interest, compounded semiannually.

   b. How does the deemed payment affect Stenson's taxable income?

   c. How does the deemed payment affect Ralph's taxable income?

15. Babson Enterprises owns 15 percent of the stock in a corporation. During the year, Babson receives dividends totaling $50,000 from the corporation. Babson's only other items of gross income and deduction are sales revenue of $80,000, cost of goods sold of $45,000, and business expenses of $20,000.

   a. What is its dividends received deduction and taxable income for the year?

   b. How would your answer differ if Babson's business expenses were $40,000?

16. Gonzolas, Inc. owns 35 percent of the stock in a corporation. During the year, Gonzolas receives dividends totaling $85,000 from the corporation. Its only other items of gross income and deductions are sales revenue of $120,000 and business expenses of $95,000.

   a. What are its dividends received deduction and its taxable income for the year?

   b. How would your answer differ if Gonzolas owned 80 percent of the corporation's stock?

17. A lessor rented property to a tenant for one year. The lessor buys an insurance policy to cover the property, and the tenant agrees to pay the premium of $3,000. What is the tax effect of this transaction on the lessor and the tenant?

18. A landlord receives the first year and last year lease payments of $10,000 each. In addition, the landlord receives a security deposit of $10,000. In addition, the landlord takes out a fire policy on the rental and the tenant agrees to pay the three-year premium of $3,000 in the first year. Also, in the first year of the lease the tenant spends $5,000 on improvements to the rental property for which no credit is given against rent. What is the effect of these transactions on the landlord's tax return in the first year of the lease?

19. A 30-year zero-coupon original issue discount bond was issued for $200,000. There is no provision for recalling the bond. The semiannual yield to maturity of the obligation is 6 percent. Compute the original issue discount for the first and second accrual periods.

20. A corporation receives $200,000 from a life insurance policy that it owned on a director's life. It also had a seller reduce the amount it owed on a purchase by $1,000. Based on these facts, what amount must the company include in its gross income?

21. For 2015, Rita Picard, who was self-employed, had $50,000 of net earnings from self-employment, $10,000 in dividends, and $5,000 in taxable interest. She deducts $3,000 for self-employed health insurance and $3,825 for her deduction for self-employment taxes. She also deducts $8,000 for home mortgage interest, $2,000 for state income taxes, and $4,000 for real estate taxes. Rita is single with no dependents. Based on these facts, what is Rita's adjusted gross income?

22. Same facts as in Problem 21. Based on these facts, what is Rita's taxable income for 2015?

23. Mike Hyman had $40,000 net earnings from self-employment for 2015. How much does he owe in self-employment taxes?

24. Rhonda Dow had $120,000 net earnings from self-employment for 2015. How much does she owe in self-employment taxes?

25. Curtis Bergin, who is self-employed, had a regular tax of $5,000, a tentative minimum tax of $6,000, and an alternative minimum tax of $1,000. Based on these facts, how much does he owe in taxes?

Chapter 4 Review Problems

1. Downum Taffetas, Inc. is an accrual method taxpayer that uses the calendar year as its tax year. The company sold and delivered $1,000 of taffeta sheets to a customer on December 20, 2015, but was not paid for the sale until January 18, 2016. The cost of the goods sold was $250. The delivery of the sheets cost $50, but the company did not pay the delivery charge until January 12, 2016. Based on these facts, what is the company's taxable income for 2015?

2. Badasci Fishing Tours, Inc. is a cash method taxpayer using the calendar year as its tax year. On December 20, 2015, a customer chartered a fishing boat from Badasci for $2,000 but did not pay Badasci until January 3, 2016. Another customer chartered a boat on December 21, 2015. That customer gave the company a check for $1,500 on December 31, 2015, but Badasci could not deposit the check until January 2, 2016. The company hired someone to do repairs on the boats for $1,000 and paid for the repairs by credit card on December 30, 2015. It did not pay the credit card statement until 2016. Based on these facts, what is Badasci's taxable income for 2015?

Chapter 4 Research Question

Does the IRS have discretion to waive or disregard the statutory formula in Code Sec. 63 for determining taxable income? See the *CCH Standard Federal Tax Reporter*.

CHAPTER 5

Business Deductions: Ordinary and Necessary Business Expenses

LEARNING OBJECTIVES

1. Explain the deductibility requirements for a business expense.

2. Distinguish between a current expense and a capital expenditure, and describe which capital expenditures can be depreciated, amortized, or depleted and which cannot.

3. Describe the deductions available for research and experimentation expenditures.

4. Explain the deductions available to manufacturers of domestic products.

5. Describe how businesses handle bad debts.

6. Describe what qualifies as a charitable contribution and the limits that apply to corporate taxpayers that make charitable donations.

¶ 500 Introduction

The focus of the previous chapter was the government's all-inclusive approach to defining income and the tax laws governing the various types of income and exclusions that businesses might encounter. In the next three chapters, the deductibility of the various expenditures businesses incur during the process of generating taxable income is discussed. As a rule, businesses are allowed to offset their business revenues by the expenses they incurred during the tax year that enable them to generate taxable revenues. If the tax laws did not permit these expenditures to be deducted against gross income, businesses would be taxed on their gross receipts from a trade or business and not on their net profit. However, special rules and limitations apply to certain expenditures.

This chapter provides an introduction to the general deductibility rules and provides a detailed discussion of some of the more common expenditures businesses must make in their pursuit of generating revenues. Chapter 6 continues with a discussion of the rules surrounding a business's employment-related expenses. In Chapter 7, the rules governing the depreciation, amortization, and depletion of long-term assets are introduced.

¶ 501 General Requirements for Deductibility

Unlike the government's all-inclusive approach to defining income, expenses are only deductible if the tax laws specifically state that they are. Many expenses are deductible under a general provision in the Internal Revenue Code (the "Code") that allows a deduction for all *ordinary and necessary* expenses paid or incurred in carrying on a trade or business. This provision allows businesses to reduce their gross income by various expenditures, including wages they pay to employees, as well as rent, insurance, interest, and taxes, to name a few. In addition to the ordinary and necessary test, expenditures must also be reasonable in amount and not items that are capital in nature. Finally, expenditures the tax law specifically identifies as nondeductible do not qualify as deductions, even if they have met all of the other general requirements for deductibility.

.01 Ordinary and Necessary

Under Code Sec. 162(a), taxpayers can deduct against gross income ordinary and necessary expenses paid or incurred in the conduct of a trade or business. Therefore, to deduct an expense currently under Code Sec. 162(a), the taxpayer must already be carrying on in a trade or business at the time the expenditure is paid or incurred. The Code does not define the terms ordinary and necessary, but when asked to interpret terms not specifically defined in the Code, the courts typically interpret them using their commonly accepted meanings. Accordingly, a **necessary expense** is one that is appropriate or helpful to the continuation of the taxpayer's business, and an **ordinary expense** refers to an expense that is customary and acceptable in the taxpayer's type of business.[1] An expense may be ordinary even though the particular taxpayer has only incurred the expense one time.[2]

To illustrate how the terms "ordinary" and "necessary" have been interpreted by the courts, the Tax Court ruled that the cost of gold coins purchased and melted down for use in dental castings was an ordinary and necessary business expense of a dental practice,[3] and payments by a cotton factory to a fund that was used to eradicate the boll weevil were considered ordinary and necessary business expenses.[4] However, the Tax Court also determined that amounts an attorney paid for a framed picture and a plant for an office furnished by her employer were not deemed necessary or helpful in the performance of her required services,[5] and amounts a sole proprietor paid to an

---

[1] *T.H. Welch*, SCt, 3 USTC ¶ 1164, 290 US 111, 54 SCt 8 (1933).

[2] *S.B. Heininger*, SCt, 44-1 USTC ¶ 9109, 320 US 467, 64 SCt 249.

[3] *M.L. Cochran*, 56 TCM 1433, Dec. 45,529(M), TC Memo. 1989-102.

[4] *Alexander Sprunt & Son, Inc.*, 24 BTA 599, Dec. 7250 (Acq.).

[5] *H.F. Henderson, Jr.*, 46 TCM 566, Dec. 40,233(M), TC Memo. 1983-372.

ordained minister for spiritual advice provided to him and his employees were not "ordinary" in the taxpayer's industry.[6]

.02 Reasonable in Amount

The requirement that expenses be reasonable in amount is to prevent businesses from deducting lavish or extravagant expenditures. Although the Code specifically applies a reasonableness test only to compensation,[7] the courts have been known to apply this standard to all business expenses.[8]

The determination of whether an expense is reasonable depends upon the facts and circumstances of the particular situation. For example, the Tax Court held that the costs associated with providing a chauffeured luxury car to an employee who was a securities investment advisor were not extravagant given the "obnoxious traffic" the employee faced coupled with the fact that many of the employee's clients were wealthy Europeans. The costs were not only ordinary and necessary in the taxpayer's line of business, but also reasonable in amount.[9]

.03 Not Capital in Nature

The tax laws require that an expenditure be capitalized to an asset account if it creates an asset with a useful life extending substantially beyond the current tax year.[10] Since capital expenditures provide benefits to a business for a number of years, it is appropriate that their costs be spread out to offset gross income generated in those years. Often these expenditures are deducted over a period of years, but occasionally they remain as assets on the company's books and are never written off.

Prepaid expenses. When taxpayers pay expenses that relate to a future tax year, such amounts must be capitalized to an asset account and expensed in the period to which they relate. This rule applies to both cash and accrual method taxpayers. However, see ¶ 306.02 and ¶ 307.02 for a discussion of the *12-month rule* that applies to prepaid expenses that will be incurred within the next 12 months.

Example 1: During 2015, Triebina Corporation signs a lease for office space and pays $36,000 for three years' rent. The $36,000 represents a prepaid expense that must be capitalized and deducted over the next 36 months.

Depreciation, depletion, and amortization. The purchase of a machine used in a manufacturing business is another example of a capital expenditure. Since the machine will help generate revenues over several years, both cash and accrual method taxpayers must write off its costs over a specified number of years. **Depreciation** is the annual deduction taken to recover the capitalized cost of business or income-producing property that is either tangible personal property or real property (other than land).

In Chapter 1, real property was defined as all real estate, which includes land and buildings. Apartment complexes, office buildings, warehouses, and parking lots are examples of real property. Personal property was defined as all property other than real property, and it could be tangible or intangible. Examples of tangible personal property that might be used in a trade or business include automobiles, machinery, and equipment. The furnishings in rental property are an example of tangible personal property that is also income-producing property. The rules that govern how quickly taxpayers can deduct the cost of depreciable property are a focus of Chapter 7.

Personal property that does not have physical characteristics is intangible property. The costs associated with the creation of an intangible asset that will benefit the business beyond the current

---

[6] *L.F. Trebilcock*, 64 TC 852, aff'd, CA-6, 77-2 USTC ¶ 9530, 557 F2d 1226.

[7] Code Sec. 162(a)(1).

[8] *Lincoln Electric Co.*, CA-6, 47-1 USTC ¶ 9282, 162 F2d 379.

[9] *R.J. Denison*, 36 TCM 1759, Dec. 34,799(M), TC Memo. 1977-430.

[10] Reg. § 1.263(a)-2.

tax year must be capitalized. Typically, the tax laws allow these costs to be expensed over a period of years; however, some intangible assets cannot be expensed and will remain as assets on the company's books. **Amortization** is the systematic recovery (expensing) of intangible assets. In financial accounting, goodwill, copyrights, patents, and trademarks are often given as examples of intangible assets. The rules for amortizing these types of intangible property are discussed in Chapter 7. In this chapter, the amortization of organizational costs and business start-up costs is discussed.

Costs incurred in the acquisition of natural resources, such as mines, oil and gas wells, and timber fields are another type of capital expenditure that taxpayers can deduct over the periods in which the asset provides usefulness to them.[11] The deduction for **depletion** is similar to depreciation, except that depletion allows owners to recover their investment in productive natural resources. As the natural resources are used up through the processes of mining (in the case of coal, metals and other minerals), quarrying (in the case of stone), drilling (in the case of oil and gas), and felling (in the case of timber), the taxpayer is allowed to expense (deplete) the costs associated with the extracted resources. Thus, depletion represents the reduction in the contents of the reserves from which the resource is taken.[12] The rules governing the two methods allowed for computing the depletion deduction are discussed in Chapter 7.

Operators of a domestic oil, gas, or geothermal wells may elect to currently deduct intangible drilling and development costs (IDC) rather than capitalize and recover them through depletion or depreciation. IDC generally includes all expenditures by the operator incident to and necessary for the drilling of wells and the preparation of wells for the production of oil, gas, or geothermal energy that are neither for the purchase of tangible property nor part of the acquisition price of an interest in the property. This includes the cost of labor, fuel and power, materials and supplies, tool rental, truck and auto hire, repairs to drilling equipment, and depreciation on drilling equipment.[13]

Uniform capitalization (UNICAP) rules. When real or tangible personal property is produced by a taxpayer, the **uniform capitalization (UNICAP) rules** require that certain costs be capitalized to the cost of the property. If the property produced is later placed in service in the taxpayer's business, the taxpayer can recover (expense) these capitalized costs over a number of years by taking annual depreciation deductions. If the property produced is subsequently sold, the taxpayer can use the capitalized costs to reduce the taxable amount realized from the sale.[14]

Under the UNICAP rules, the wages paid to employees engaged in the manufacture of a machine that will be used in the taxpayer's business must be capitalized to the cost of the machine and must later be recovered through depreciation expense. Since the machine is expected to help generate revenues for the taxpayer's business over many years, any expenses that are incurred in the production of the machine must be capitalized and depreciated. Thus, the UNICAP rules seek to match income and expenses, which is consistent with how prepaid expenses are treated under both the cash and accrual methods of accounting.

 Reason for the Rule: If given a choice between capitalizing and depreciating costs associated with an asset versus expensing the costs immediately, most taxpayers would choose immediate expensing since it normally would produce the greatest tax savings in the current year. When a taxpayer purchases depreciable property from the manufacturer, the costs the manufacturer incurred during production of the asset are included in the cost of the property. These costs are then recovered by the taxpayer over a number of years through annual depreciation deductions. When the taxpayer produces its own property, all of the same costs that a manufacturer incurs (materials, labor costs, etc.) are capitalized to the cost of the property under the UNICAP rules, and depreci-

---

[11] Code Sec. 611.

[12] *C.A. Ludey*, SCt, 1 USTC ¶ 234, 274 US 295, 47 SCt 608.

[13] Code Sec. 263(c); Reg. § 1.612-4.

[14] Code Sec. 263A.

ated over several years. Without the UNICAP rules, taxpayers that produce their own property might be allowed to immediately expense certain costs that are part of the costs associated with long-lived assets. Thus, the UNICAP rules attempt to provide parity between taxpayers that purchase property directly from the manufacturer and those that manufacture their own property.

The UNICAP rules do not apply to property that is used for personal purposes or to any property that the taxpayer produces under a long-term contract (¶ 309.02 described how these costs are handled).[15] The rules also do not apply to certain types of expenses, including research and experimental costs, intangible drilling costs, mining exploration, and development costs,[16] or to the qualified creative costs of freelance artists, authors, and photographers.[17] Also, these rules only require that interest paid or incurred in the construction of certain types of property be capitalized to the asset. These special rules regarding the capitalization of interest are discussed later in the chapter (see ¶ 505.03).

 GAAP vs. Code: For financial reporting purposes, all costs incurred to prepare an asset for its intended use are capitalized, regardless of whether the asset is to be held for sale or used within the business. Depending on the business's materiality thresholds, certain amounts may not be capitalized for financial reporting purposes but would have to be capitalized for tax purposes. Any differences in amounts capitalized would result in a difference between the calculation of net income on the financial statements and taxable income on the tax return. Such differences would need to be reflected when reconciling net income to taxable income on the corporate tax return.

Special rule for certain barrier removal costs. Despite the rule that denies a current deduction for expenditures that are capital in nature, the tax laws allow taxpayers to elect to currently deduct up to $15,000 of qualified architectural and transportational barrier removal expenses. To be expensed currently, the costs must be incurred to remove an existing barrier so that a business facility or public transportation vehicle owned or leased by the taxpayer for business use is made more accessible to and usable by handicapped or elderly persons.[18]

 Spotlight: Normally, capitalized costs such as these would be depreciated over the life of the asset to which they relate. For a building, this could be as long as 39 years. By allowing businesses to deduct up to $15,000 of these costs immediately, taxpayers can accelerate the timing of their tax savings. The amount of tax savings generated from the immediate expensing equals the amount expensed times the taxpayer's marginal tax rate. Therefore, a taxpayer in the 35-percent tax bracket who is allowed to write off $15,000 of these costs in the year in which they are paid will recuperate $5,250 ($15,000 × 35%) of the costs in the first year.

.04 Not Otherwise Disallowed

Sometimes an expenditure may appear to meet the general requirements for deductibility, but due to any number of policy considerations, tax law specifically states that it cannot be deducted. For example, the Code is clear that amounts paid to satisfy government-imposed fines and penalties cannot be deducted as business expenses.[19] The courts have denied a deduction for fines and penalties on the grounds that allowing them to be deducted would frustrate public policy by

---

[15] Code Sec. 263A(c)(4).

[16] Code Secs. 59(e) and 263A(c)(6).

[17] Code Sec. 263A(h).

[18] Code Sec. 190.

[19] Code Sec. 162(f).

reducing the taxpayer's cost of the penalty by the amount of the tax benefit resulting from the deduction.[20] The Code also specifically disallows or limits the deductibility of lobbying costs and political contributions.

Violation of public policy.   Under Code Sec. 162(a), ordinary and necessary business expenses are deductible against gross income. Thus, professional truck drivers might argue that traffic tickets are not only normal and customary in the trucking industry, but since drivers are often compensated by the haul and not by the hour, speeding tickets are also helpful in generating revenues. Although these arguments may seem valid given the environment of the trucking industry, the Supreme Court has ruled that any expenditure incurred while violating public policy is not a necessary expense[21] and, accordingly, is not deductible. Thus, fines and penalties paid to a government for the violation of any law are not deductible business expenses,[22] including settlement payments made to other persons or businesses. However, the tax laws do allow taxpayers to deduct legal fees and related expenses paid or incurred in the defense of an action that culminates in a fine or penalty, as well as any court costs imposed against the taxpayer.[23]

It is interesting to note that expenses that normally would constitute ordinary and necessary business expenses are only disallowed on account of illegality if the expenditure itself constitutes an illegal payment under U.S. federal or state laws.[24] This rule allows taxpayers to deduct normal operating expenses incurred while carrying on an illegal business activity.[25] For example, wages and rents paid in connection with operating an illegal gambling business would be deductible against the gross income generated by the illegal activity.[26] Furthermore, an expenditure is deemed to be illegal under state law only when the state law is generally enforced.[27] Payments that violate an unenforced state law do not frustrate public policy and, accordingly, can be deducted against gross income.

Illegal bribes and kickbacks paid to public officials or government employees are never deductible because the kickbacks themselves are illegal under U.S federal laws. Similar rules apply to payments made to foreign officials that are unlawful under the Foreign Corrupt Practices Act of 1977.

Kickbacks include a payment in consideration of the referral of a client, patient or customer. Kickbacks paid to individuals who are not public officials may be legal or illegal, depending on local law. The Supreme Court has ruled that kickbacks that do not violate government laws are deductible as an ordinary and necessary business expense if they reflect an established and widespread practice in the taxpayer's industry.[28]

Example 2:   A subcontractor at a mall construction site paid kickbacks to the supervisor of the site's primary contractor as a condition of continued employment and timely payment. There was a logical connection between the kickbacks, which were legal under local law (and deemed necessary), and the ability to continue work on the construction project. Thus, the kickbacks—a cost of doing business—were ordinary and were currently deductible by the subcontractor.[29]

However, the deduction for kickbacks was denied to a paving subcontractor who obtained contracts for the construction of a mall by paying for services and materials used in the construction of the personal residence of the person in charge of awarding

---

[20] *B.T. Smith*, 34 TC 1100, Dec. 24,365 (1960), aff'd, *per curiam*, CA-5, 61-2 USTC ¶ 9686, 294 F2d 957; *W.L. Kolberg*, 24 TCM 913, Dec. 27,450(M), TC Memo. 1965-171.

[21] *Tank Truck Rentals, Inc.*, SCt, 58-1 USTC ¶ 9366, 356 US 30, 78 SCt 507.

[22] Code Sec. 162(f).

[23] Reg. § 1.162-21(b)(2).

[24] Code Sec. 162(c)(2); Reg. § 1.162-18(b).

[25] No deduction is allowed for any expenses paid or incurred in the trade or business of trafficking of controlled substances prohibited by Federal or State law. Code Sec. 280E.

[26] *N. Sullivan*, SCt, 58-1 USTC ¶ 9368, 356 US 27, 78 SCt 512.

[27] Code Sec. 162(c)(2); Reg. § 1.162-18(b)(3); *Greater Display & Wire Forming, Inc.*, 55 TCM 922, Dec. 44,802(M), TC Memo. 1988-231.

[28] *T.B. Lilly*, SCt, 52-1 USTC ¶ 9231, 343 US 90, 72 SCt 497.

[29] *Raymond Bertolini Trucking Co.*, CA-6, 84-2 USTC ¶ 9591, 736 F2d 1120, rev'g TC, 45 TCM 44, Dec. 39,474(M), TC Memo. 1982-643.

subcontracts. The kickbacks were found to be unnecessary, since the subcontractor had obtained nearly all of its other contracts, including 20 from the same contractor, without paying kickbacks.[30]

Lobbying expenditures and political contributions. Amounts paid or incurred in connection with influencing legislation, including amounts paid to lobbyists and campaign contributions to a candidate for public office, are specifically not deductible.[31] Similarly, amounts paid to advertise in political convention programs and for tickets to political dinners, inaugural balls, and the like are not deductible.[32] This rule does not apply to professional lobbyists. It does, however, apply to amounts other businesses pay lobbyists.

Example 3: John Trippleton operates his consulting practice as a sole proprietorship. During 2015, John pays $475 in dues to the American Institute of Certified Public Accountants (AICPA). Included in the dues is $75 for a political action committee fee that enables the AICPA to lobby before Congress regarding legislation relevant to the accounting profession and its clients. In preparing his tax return for 2015, John is not permitted to deduct $75 of the dues paid to the AICPA. He can deduct the $400 of professional fees ($475 – $75) as an ordinary and necessary business expense.

 Reason for the Rule: Congress feared that allowing a deduction for lobbying expenditures and political contributions might enable taxpayers to exercise undue influence on the political process. Although taxpayers are entitled to make political contributions and hire professional lobbyists in an attempt to influence legislation that could affect the taxpayer's business, the federal government will not subsidize the taxpayer's efforts, which would be the result if it allowed taxpayers to use political and lobbying expenditures to reduce their taxable income (and corresponding tax liability).

Taxpayers are allowed to deduct in-house expenditures paid or incurred during the tax year for lobbying activities, provided the expenditures do not exceed $2,000. In-house expenditures do not include amounts paid to lobbyists or amounts paid for dues to organizations to the extent that such dues are allocable to these types of activities.[33] Should the taxpayer exceed the $2,000 threshold, all in-house expenditures are nondeductible.[34]

Example 4: In 2015, Pradyolin Corporation approached members of Congress to gain their support for a pending bill. Pradyolin spent $1,200 to draft and print a position letter on the bill and $200 to distribute the letter to members of Congress. These were the only costs Pradyolin incurred for in-house lobbying activities in 2015. Pradyolin can deduct the entire amount of $1,400 incurred for in-house lobbying activities on its 2015 tax return.

Example 5: Assume the same facts as in Example 4, except that Pradyolin spent $3,200 to draft and print its position letter and $300 to distribute the letter to members of Congress. Since the amount spent exceeds the $2,000 *de minimis* threshold, none of the $3,500 can be deducted.

Taxpayers can deduct ordinary and necessary expenses directly attributable to appearances before local legislative councils in connection with existing or proposed legislation that will, or may reasonably be expected to, affect the taxpayer's trade or business. A deduction is also allowed for amounts spent to communicate information on local legislative matters to businesses or trade organizations of which the taxpayer is a member, provided that the legislative matter is of direct interest to both the taxpayer and the organization.[35]

---

[30] *Car-Ron Asphalt Paving Co., Inc.,* CA-6, 85-1 USTC ¶ 9298, 758 F2d 1132, aff'g TC, 46 TCM 1314, Dec. 40,434(M), TC Memo. 1983-548.

[31] Code Sec. 162(e).

[32] Code Sec. 276.

[33] Code Sec. 162(e)(5)(B).

[34] Conference Committee Report to P.L. 103-66 (1993), H.R. Conf. Rep. No. 103-213.

[35] Code Sec. 162(e)(2).

Example 6: John Smith, the President of Newbury Corporation, is invited to provide testimony at a county board hearing concerning a bill that will significantly affect Newbury's business. The expenses Newbury incurs for John's travel expenses are deductible.

 GAAP vs. Code: For financial reporting purposes, the payment of a governmental fine or penalty or payments for lobbying expenses and political campaign contributions are expensed in the period incurred. For tax purposes, these costs are generally not deductible. The difference in treatment creates a permanent difference between how net income and taxable income are calculated. For example, if a paint manufacturer is fined by the Environment Protection Agency for violating a federal toxic waste provision, the company will not be able to deduct the fine on its tax return. However, it will be required to expense this amount on the income statement in arriving at net income. Accordingly, when reconciling net income to taxable income on the corporate tax return, the corporation will need to add the amount paid for the fine back to its net income.

¶ 502 Timing of the Deduction

The year in which a tax deduction can be taken depends upon whether the taxpayer uses the accrual or cash method of accounting. As discussed in Chapter 3, under the accrual method, the taxpayer takes a deduction when all events have occurred to establish the existence of the liability and the amount of the liability can be determined with reasonable accuracy. Under the cash method, the taxpayer takes a deduction in the year in which the expense is paid, regardless of when it was incurred. However, in the case of prepaid expenses, cash method taxpayers must always wait until the year in which the expense is incurred before taking the deduction (however, see ¶ 306.02 and ¶ 307.02 for an exception under the *12-month rule*). Hence, cash and accrual method taxpayers use the accrual method to handle prepaid expenses.

Example 7: Sand Co. (a calendar year, accrual method corporation) pays its employees every Friday. During 20X1, December 31 ends on a Wednesday. On its 20X1 tax return, Sand will deduct the $26,240 of wages it accrued for work its employees performed from the previous Saturday through Wednesday, December 31.

Example 8: Assume the same facts as in Example 7, except that Sand uses the cash method. The deduction for the wages accrued in 20X1 will not be paid until Friday, January 2, 20X2. Accordingly, the $26,240 of wages cannot be deducted until 20X2, the year in which it is paid.

Example 9: On October 1, 2015, Triebina Corporation signs a lease for office space and pays $36,000 for three years' rent. The $36,000 represents a prepaid expense, which must be capitalized and deducted over the next 36 months, beginning on October 1, 2015. Thus, if Triebina uses a calendar year-end, it will be able to deduct $3,000 ($36,000/36 × 3 months) on its 2015 tax return, regardless of whether it uses the cash or accrual method of accounting. In 2016 and 2017, Triebina will deduct $12,000 for rent expense ($36,000/36 × 12 months), and in 2018 it will deduct $9,000 ($36,000/36 × 9 months).

¶ 503 Organizational Expenditures

Expenditures paid or incurred that are incidental to the formation of a corporation, including C corporations and S corporations, are known as **organizational costs**. Organizational costs include expenses for legal services to obtain the corporate charter, fees paid to the state of incorporation, and the expenses of temporary directors, such as costs of travel and office rent.[36] Only expenditures

---

[36] Reg. § 1.248-1(b)(2).

incurred before the end of the taxable year in which the corporation begins business qualify as organizational expenditures.[37]

Costs associated with the issuing and selling of stock, such as commissions, professional fees, and printing costs are not organizational costs.[38] Instead, these costs offset the proceeds from the stock issue and reduce the corporation's paid-in capital account.[39] The costs associated with reorganizing or merging activities are not organizational costs, but instead are costs that are capitalized and recovered upon liquidation of the corporation. Code Sec. 248 allows corporations to elect to deduct up to $5,000 of organizational expenditures for the tax year in which the corporation begins its business operations. The $5,000 amount is reduced dollar for dollar when the total organizational costs exceed $50,000. Thus, no current deduction is allowed to corporations that incur over $55,000 in organizational costs. At the taxpayer's election, any costs not currently expensed may be amortized ratably over a 180-month period, starting in the month in which the business begins.[40]

Example 10: Baker Industries incurred $52,000 of organizational costs prior to the end of 2015, the tax year in which it began operations. Since the organizational costs exceed $50,000, Baker can elect to expense only $3,000 ($5,000 – $2,000) in 2015; it can elect to amortize the remaining $49,000 ($52,000 – $3,000) over 180 months beginning with the month on which its business began.

Example 11: Shaw Company began its business operations on June 1, 2015. Shaw elected to use a calendar year to file its corporate tax return. Prior to December 31, 2015, Shaw incurred the following expenditures:

Date	Description of Expenditure	Amount
2/5/15	State incorporation fee	$ 150
4/7/15	Legal fees in the drafting of the Articles of Incorporation	5,000
5/15/15	Board of directors meeting	5,250
6/20/15	Other legal and accounting fees incident to organization	5,400
7/15/15	Stock printing costs	15,500
		$31,300

The stock printing costs are not organizational costs; therefore, Shaw's organizational expenditures total $15,800 ($150 + $5,000 + $5,250 + $5,400). Since the total organizational costs do not exceed $50,000, Shaw can elect to deduct $5,000 of these expenses in 2015, and it can elect to amortize the remaining $10,800 ($15,800 – $5,000) over a period of 180 months beginning in June 2015. If Shaw elects to amortize these remaining costs, it will deduct $420 against its 2015 gross income ($10,800/180 × 7 months) and $720 ($10,800/180 × 12 months) each year from 2016–2029. In 2030, Shaw will deduct the last $300 of organizational costs ($10,800/180 × 5 months).

 Reason for the Rule: The rules regarding the deductibility of organizational costs apply to both C and S corporations. Similar rules regarding organizational costs apply to partnerships.[41] Prior law allowed these businesses to amortize their organizational costs

---

[37] Code Sec. 248(b); Reg. § 1.248-1(a)(2).

[38] Reg. § 1.248-1(b)(3).

[39] *Surety Finance Co. of Tacoma*, CA-9, 35-1 USTC ¶ 9354, 77 F2d 221.

[40] Code Sec. 248(a)(1), as amended by the American Jobs Creation Act of 2004 (P.L. 108-357).

[41] Code Secs. 1363(b)(3) and 709.

over a period of not less than 60 months. With the passage of the American Jobs Creation Act of 2004, the Code now allows smaller businesses (those that incur no more than $50,000 of such costs) to immediately expense up to $5,000 of their costs, while extending the amortization period to 15-years for costs that do not qualify for immediate expensing. Congress felt that allowing a fixed amount of these costs to be deducted immediately might help encourage the formation of new businesses that do not require significant organizational costs to be incurred. Extending the amortization to a 15-year period was consistent with the period over which most intangible assets are currently required to be amortized.[42]

.01 Beginning of Business Operations

The date on which a corporation begins business operations and is engaged in a "trade or business" for the purpose of taking current tax deductions is not the same date on which it enters into existence. A corporation comes into existence on the date of its incorporation, which is usually well before it is ready to begin operations. Thus, a mere organizational activity, such as obtaining a corporate charter, is not sufficient to establish the beginning of business operations. The actual date on which a corporation begins business operations can only be answered after taking into consideration all of the circumstances surrounding the activities of the corporation. For example, the acquisition of the operating assets necessary to the type of business being considered may indicate that business has begun.[43]

.02 Election to Amortize

A corporation is deemed to have made an election to deduct/amortize organizational expenses for the tax year in which the corporation begins business. A corporation can elect to forego the deemed election by affirmatively electing to capitalize its organizational expenses on a timely filed federal income tax return (including extensions) for the taxable year the corporation begins business. If the corporation elects to forego the deemed election and capitalizes its organizational expenses, the expenses will be recovered in the year the corporation is liquidated. The election to either deduct/amortize or capitalize organizational expenses is irrevocable and applies to all organizational expenses of the corporation.[44]

 GAAP vs. Code: For financial reporting purposes, organizational costs are expensed in the period in which they are incurred. For tax purposes, the expenses are capitalized or expensed (either immediately or amortized over 15 years). If an election is made to capitalize these amounts, then the amount expensed on the income statement must be added back to net income when reconciling net income to taxable income on the tax return. To the extent the election to immediately expense organizational costs is made, there will not be a difference between the amounts expensed on the income statement and on the tax return. However, to the extent the corporation amortizes any of the organizational costs, there will be a difference between net income and the amortization expense on the tax return for 16 tax years. In the first year, any excess amount deducted from net income would be added back in the reconciliation of net income and taxable income. In all subsequent years, the amortized costs deducted on the tax return would be subtracted from net income in reconciling net income to taxable income.

For example, Shaw Company from Example 11 would be required to expense the entire $15,800 against net income on its 2015 financial statements. However, for tax purposes, the best it can do is to deduct $5,420 on its 2015 tax return ($5,000 expensed

---

[42] Senate Committee Report (S. Rep. No. 108-192).

[43] Reg. § 1.248-1(a)(3).

[44] Reg. § 1.248-1(c).

immediately + $420 amortized in 2015). Consequently, in reconciling its net income and taxable income in 2015, Shaw would need to add back the $10,380 difference ($15,800 – $5,420) to net income to arrive at the amount reflected in taxable income. Each year from 2016–2030, Shaw would need to reduce its net income by the amortization expense taken on the tax return when it reconciled net income to taxable income on its tax returns for those years.

¶ 504 Start-Up Costs

Code Sec. 162 allows a deduction for ordinary and necessary costs paid or incurred in *carrying on a trade or business*. However, costs incurred prior to the start of business operations (see the discussion in ¶ 501.01) are not deductible under Code Sec. 162. Such expenditures may be start-up costs deductible in accordance with the rules of Code Sec. 195.

Start-up costs are costs that normally would be currently deductible if they were incurred in connection with the operation of an existing trade or business; they can include expenditures incurred to investigate entering into or acquiring a *new* active trade or business. The process of investigating the creation or acquisition of a *new* business might involve reviewing the prospective business prior to reaching a final decision on whether to acquire or enter into it. The costs associated with the analysis or survey of potential markets, products, labor supply, and transportation facilities generally qualify as start-up costs. Normally, any amounts paid or incurred in order to determine whether to enter a new business and which new business to enter are start-up expenditures, provided the costs themselves are not capital in nature (see ¶ 501.03).

The tax treatment of start-up costs is similar to that of organizational costs in that taxpayers may elect to deduct up to $5,000 of start-up expenditures, but the $5,000 is reduced by the amount by which the start-up expenditures exceed $50,000. The remainder may be ratably amortized over 180 months beginning with the month in which the active trade or business begins.[45] The rules that apply to start-up costs are available to all types of businesses, including sole proprietorships, C corporations, and the various flow-through entities.[46]

.01 Start-Up Costs Distinguished from Other Types of Expenses

Organizational expenditures, acquisition costs, and expansion costs are sometimes mistaken for start-up costs, but their purposes and/or their tax treatments are different. Therefore, start-up costs must be distinguished from those other types of expenses.

Organizational expenditures. Although their tax treatment is similar, organizational expenditures and start-up costs are different types of expenses. Organizational expenditures are expenses incurred in forming a separate legal entity, while start-up costs are incurred in investigating the creation or acquisition of a new active trade or business.[47] Entities are allowed separate deductions for organizational and start-up expenditures. For example, when a corporation is formed and enters into a trade or business, it could conceivably expense up to $10,000 in costs associated with its formation and the start of its business: $5,000 of organizational expenses under Code Sec. 248 and $5,000 of start-up costs under Code Sec. 195.

Acquisition costs. Costs incurred in the attempt to acquire a specific business are not start-up expenditures but instead are acquisition costs that must be capitalized under Code Sec. 263. To distinguish between a start-up cost and an acquisition cost, the taxpayer must analyze the nature of the cost based on all the facts and circumstances of the transaction. The taxpayer must determine whether it is (1) an investigatory cost incurred to facilitate the taxpayer's decision regarding whether to enter into a new line of business or which new line of business to enter into or (2) a cost

---

[45] Code Sec. 195(b).

[46] Code Sec. 195(b); Reg. § 1.195-1.

[47] Code Sec. 195(c)(1).

incurred to acquire or enter into a specific business. The former are start-up costs; the latter are acquisition costs. The label the taxpayer uses to describe the cost is not indicative of the true nature of the cost.[48]

Expansion costs. The expansion of an existing trade or business of a taxpayer is currently deductible as an ordinary and necessary business expense under Code Sec. 162. The distinction between the expansion of an existing business (for which the expenses are deductible under Code Sec. 162) and the creation or acquisition of a *new line of business* (for which the costs must be amortized over 180 months) is not always easily drawn.[49]

.02 Start-Up and Acquisition Costs for Abortive Business Ventures

Acquisition costs a taxpayer incurs in the unsuccessful attempt to acquire a specific business, such as legal expenses incurred in drafting purchase documents, are deductible as losses under Code Sec. 165.[50] The rules applicable to start-up costs for businesses the taxpayer does not acquire or enter into are more complicated and less certain. The IRS and courts generally regard expenses incurred by an individual in the course of a preliminary investigation, that is, not connected with any specific line of business, to be nondeductible personal costs.[51] However, if an individual taxpayer's investigation advances beyond the preliminary stages, costs incurred may be deductible under Code Sec. 165 as losses incurred in a trade or business or for the production of income.[52] A corporation's losses are generally presumed not to be personal.[53] Accordingly, a corporation should be able to deduct start-up costs for businesses it does not acquire, including those incurred in the preliminary investigation of new trades or businesses, as losses under Code Sec. 165.

 Spotlight: As should be apparent from the above discussion, whether any particular expense is a start-up cost, an acquisition cost, an expansion cost, a loss, or a nondeductible personal expenditure is often a matter of interpretation. Taxpayers would generally prefer to deduct such expenditures as ordinary and necessary business expenses under Code Sec. 162 or losses under Code Sec. 165. However, the IRS can (and frequently does) challenge the treatment of such costs when they are deducted currently.

Example 12: Maxis Corporation designs and manufactures clothing for teens. Maxis spent $25,000 to investigate expanding its existing line of teen clothing. Since the costs incurred are in the same line as Maxis' existing business, Maxis deducts the entire $25,000 in the current year.

Example 13: Marvin Garden incurred $6,080 in qualified start-up expenses in connection with his landscaping business, which began operations on September 1, 2015. Marvin deducts $5,000 of the costs in 2015 and amortizes the rest over 180 months. His total deduction for 2015 equals $5,024 [$5,000 + (($6,080 – $5,000)/180 × 4 months)].

Example 14: Gatewell Industries incurred $68,400 in qualified start-up costs in connection with investigating the acquisition of a new business. Gatewell acquired the business on November 2, 2015. Since the start-up costs exceed $55,000, Gatewell capitalizes and elects to amortize this amount over 180 months beginning in November 2015. Gatewell deducts $760 ($68,400/180 × 2 months) in 2015 and will deduct $4,560 ($68,400/180 × 12 months) each year from 2016–2029. In 2030, Gatewell will deduct the final $3,800 ($68,400/180 × 10 months) of amortization expense.

---

[48] Rev. Rul. 99-23, 1991-1 CB 998, as corrected by Announcement 99-89, 1999-2 CB 408.

[49] *Briarcliff Candy Corp.*, CA-2, 73-1 USTC ¶ 9288, 475 F2d 775.

[50] Rev. Rul. 77-254, 1977-2 CB 63.

[51] *Id.*; *R.C. Honodel*, CA-9, 84-1 USTC ¶ 9133, 722 F2d 1462.

[52] Code Sec. 165(c); *H.W. Seed*, 52 TC 880, Dec. 29,719 (1969) (Acq.).

[53] *International Trading Co.*, CA-7, 73-2 USTC ¶ 9582, 484 F2d 707.

GAAP vs. Code: For financial reporting purposes, start-up costs are expensed in the period in which they are incurred. For tax purposes, the expenses are capitalized and then expensed (either immediately or amortized over 15 years). To the extent that the election to immediately expense the costs is made, there will not be a difference between the amounts expensed on the income statement and on the tax return. However, if the taxpayer elects to amortize its start-up costs, there will be a difference between net income and the amortization expense on the tax return for 16 tax years. In the first year, any excess amount deducted from net income would be added back in the reconciliation of net income and taxable income. In all subsequent years, the amortized costs deducted on the tax return would be subtracted from net income in reconciling net income to taxable income.

For example, Gatewell Industries from Example 14 would be required to expense the entire $68,400 against net income on its 2015 income statement. However, for tax purposes, Gateway amortizes $760 of these costs on its 2015 tax return. Consequently, in reconciling its net income and taxable income in 2015, Gatewell will need to add back the $67,640 difference ($68,400 – $760) to net income to arrive at the amount reflected in taxable income. Each year from 2016–2030, Gatewell will reduce its net income by the amortization expense taken on the tax return when reconciling net income to taxable income on its tax returns for those years.

.03 Election to Amortize

A taxpayer is deemed to have made an election to deduct/amortize start up expenses for the taxable year in which the active trade or business to which the expenses relate begins. A taxpayer may choose to forego the deemed election by affirmatively electing to capitalize its start up expenses on a timely filed income tax return (including extensions) for the taxable year in which the active trade or business to which the expenses relate begins. The election to deduct/amortize or capitalize start up expenses is irrevocable and applies to all start up expenses that are related to the active trade or business.[54]

¶ 505 Interest Expense

Because borrowing to finance business operations is normal and appropriate in any business, the Code allows a deduction for interest expense paid and incurred (in the case of a cash method taxpayer) or incurred (in the case of an accrual method taxpayer) during the year.[55] The rationale behind allowing the deduction for interest expense is that the proceeds from the indebtedness will be used to help generate taxable revenues for the business. In situations in which the taxpayer uses the proceeds to purchase assets that do not produce taxable income, the tax laws do not allow the related interest expense to be deducted. For example, if a taxpayer were to borrow $100,000 to purchase tax-exempt municipal bonds, the interest paid or incurred with respect to the loan would not be deductible.[56] Other examples in which the tax laws may limit the deductibility of interest paid or incurred during the year involve interest associated with the construction of certain long-lived assets and interest individual taxpayers pay on income tax deficiencies. Noncorporate taxpayers may also be limited on the amount of investment interest expense paid or incurred during the tax year.

.01 Deficiency Interest

When taxpayers fail to pay the proper amount of taxes on their income tax returns, the taxpayers must not only pay the taxes owed but also interest and penalties the government imposes on tax deficiencies. The interest charged on these tax deficiencies is called **deficiency interest**.

---

[54] Reg. § 1.195-1(b).
[55] Code Sec. 163(a).

[56] Code Sec. 265(a)(2).

Normally, if the deficiency interest paid or incurred during the year related to a deficiency in paying taxes owed on business profits, such interest would be deductible under the normal rules for deducting interest expense. However, the tax deficiency of an individual taxpayer is automatically considered to be personal in nature, and consequently, any interest on the deficiency constitutes nondeductible personal interest.[57] Thus, when individual taxpayers fail to pay the correct amount of taxes on income from their sole proprietorship activities (or on their distributive shares of partnership or S corporation income), any resulting interest is a nondeductible expense. This is one example in which operating a business as an entity other than a C corporation may result in greater taxes owed.

.02 Investment Interest Expense

Individual taxpayers can deduct investment interest expense only as an itemized deduction (a deduction from adjusted gross income (AGI)) in computing their taxable income. Investment interest expense is interest paid or incurred on amounts borrowed to purchase taxable investments such as stock, corporate bonds, and mutual funds. This deduction is allowed because it relates to investments that generate taxable income. Accordingly, the tax laws limit the amount of investment interest expense individuals can deduct in any one tax year to the amount of taxable *net investment income* reported on their tax returns. As previously mentioned, interest on amounts borrowed to buy tax-exempt bonds is nondeductible. The rules governing the investment interest expense deduction are discussed further in Chapter 13.

Corporations are not subject to the investment interest expense limitation rules. Therefore, when corporations borrow money to purchase investments that produce taxable investment income, the interest associated with the loans is fully deductible. However, businesses that operate as flow-through entities often have individuals as their owners; consequently, any investment interest expense paid or incurred by flow-through entities must be tracked separately because the amounts flow through to the owners and are reported on the owners' tax returns. The separate reporting of these types of expenditures is discussed in greater detail in Chapters 13 and 14. As in the case of individuals, interest paid on amounts borrowed by corporations and flow-through entities to purchase investments that generate tax-exempt income is not deductible, regardless of the amount of the entity's taxable investment income.

.03 Required Capitalization of Interest

When interest is paid or incurred in conjunction with a loan associated with property produced by a taxpayer, special capitalization rules may apply. Specifically, interest on a debt must be capitalized if the debt is incurred or continues to exist in order to finance the construction, building, installation, manufacture, development, or improvement of real or tangible personal property produced by the taxpayer if any one of the following conditions is met:

1. The property being produced has a "long useful life,"
2. The estimated production period exceeds two years, or
3. The estimated production period exceeds one year and the property will cost more than $1 million to produce.[58]

Property with a long useful life is real property (such as land and buildings) or property with a class life of 20 years or more. For purposes of estimating the production period, the production period ends on the date the property is ready to be held for resale to customers or to be placed in service in the taxpayer's business.[59]

Example 15: In 2015, Py Co. begins building its own warehouse, which will replace its current storage facility. The cost of the building will be $2 million and it will take the

---

[57] Code Sec. 163(h)(1); Temp. Reg. § 1.163-9T(b)(2)(i)(A).   [59] Code Sec. 263A(f)(4)(B).

[58] Code Sec. 263A(f).

company three years to complete. Py finances the cost of the building and incurs interest each year from 2015–2018 as it constructs the building. Since the building has a long useful life, Py must capitalize the interest costs to the cost of the building. Once the warehouse is placed in service, Py will depreciate the total cost of the building using the depreciation rules discussed in Chapter 7.

Example 16: Braylin Corporation, a furniture manufacturer, constructs its own machinery that it uses in the construction of sofa sleepers that it sells. It was estimated that the production period will last 18 months and the total costs to construct the machinery are $65,000. Braylin obtained financing for the project and paid interest on the loan balance in 2015 and in 2016. The machinery was placed in service in December 2016. Even though the production process took longer than a year, the costs did not exceed $1 million. Therefore, since the property does not have a "long useful life" and the machine took less than two years to complete, the interest on financing the project does not need to be capitalized and it can be deducted in the period in which it was paid or incurred.

Example 17: Assume the same facts as in Example 16, except that it cost Braylin $1,500,000 to produce the machine. Because the costs exceed $1 million and the estimated production period extends beyond one year, the interest incurred in financing the production of the machinery must be capitalized and added to the cost of the machinery. Once the machine is placed in service, Braylin will depreciate the total cost of the machine using the methods discussed in Chapter 7.

 GAAP vs. Code: For tax purposes, the interest associated with the production of certain assets must be capitalized in accordance with the rules of Code Sec. 263A(f). For financial reporting purposes, interest expense must be capitalized only for the acquisition of "qualifying assets," since in some instances the benefits of capitalizing the interest may not justify the additional accounting and administrative costs involved in providing this information.[60] Due to the different standards used to determine whether interest must be capitalized or currently deducted, any differences between the two methods must be taken into consideration when reconciling net income to taxable income on the corporate tax return in the tax years when interest on construction of an asset is incurred.

¶ 506 Taxes

Businesses pay various taxes in the normal course of business. For example, property taxes are often levied annually on the owners of property. Businesses also regularly pay federal and state unemployment taxes on behalf of their employees[61] as well as the employer's share of social security and Medicare ("FICA") taxes. Sole proprietorships and partners pay self-employment taxes on their self-employment income.[62] Many of these taxes are currently deductible; however, some are nondeductible. Table 5-1 lists the various taxes the taxpayer may incur while engaging in a trade or business and the circumstances under which the taxes are currently deductible or must be capitalized.

---

[60] "Capitalization of Interest Cost," *Statement of Financial Accounting Standards No. 34* (Stamford, Conn: FASB 1979). "Determining Materiality for Capitalization of Interest Cost," *Statement*

of Financial Accounting Standards No. 42 (Norwalk, Conn: FASB 1980).

[61] Reg. § 1.162-10(a).

[62] Code Secs. 164(a) and (f).

Table 5-1 Tax Treatment of Taxes

Type of Tax	Deductible	Capitalized
Property	Yes.	No.
Income (state and local)	Yes, but always a deduction from AGI on an individual's income tax return.	No.
Sales (state and local)[a]	No. But where paid in the acquisition of a nondepreciable item, the tax is added to the cost of the item and deducted as a business expense.	Yes. May be added to cost basis of property.
Gasoline[b]	Yes.	No.
Foreign[c]	Yes. But only to the extent not claimed as a tax credit.	No.
Excise	Yes.	No.
State Stamp[d]	Yes. Security dealers or investors in real property may deduct state stock transfer or real estate transfer taxes as a business expense.	No.
Unemployment[e]	Yes.	No.
Paid on shareholder's behalf[f]	Yes, if shareholders do not reimburse corporation for taxes paid on account of their ownership in the payor.	No.
Employment (FICA, FUTA)	Yes.	No.
Self-Employment[g]	Yes. Individuals may deduct one-half of the amount of their self-employment tax when computing AGI.	No.
Federal Income[h]	No.	No.
Estate and Gift[i]	No.	No.

[a] Code Sec. 164(a) and (b)(5). For tax years beginning in 2004–2014, individual taxpayers may elect to deduct state and local general sales taxes in lieu of state and local income taxes as an itemized deduction on their federal income tax return. Although this deduction expired on December 31, 2014, Congress has been extending this deduction.

[b] Reg. § 1.164-5.

[c] Code Secs. 164(a) and 275(a)(4); Reg. § 1.164-2.

[d] Reg. § 1.164-1; Rev. Rul. 65-313, 1965-2 CB 47.

[e] *J.R. McGowan*, 67 TC 599, Dec. 34,200 (1976); *A. Trujillo*, 68 TC 670, Dec. 34,554 (1977); Rev. Rul. 75-156, 1975-1 CB 66; Rev. Rul. 75-444, 1975-2 CB 66.

[f] Code Sec. 164(e); Reg. § 1.164-7.

[g] Code Sec. 164(f).

[h] Code Sec. 275(a)(1).

[i] Code Sec. 275(a)(3).

Sales tax paid in connection with the purchase of property used in a business must be treated as part of the cost of the property.[63] If the property acquired is depreciable property, the capitalized sales tax will be depreciated along with the cost of the property. If the property acquired is currently deductible (for example, supplies), the sales tax is currently deductible as a business expense. Similar rules apply to use taxes and excise taxes paid or incurred during the year.[64]

State, local, and foreign income taxes businesses pay during the tax year are deductible,[65] but federal income taxes are not.[66] Foreign income taxes that taxpayers elect to take as a tax credit cannot be deducted. (See ¶ 1116 for a discussion of the option to claim a foreign tax credit in lieu of a deduction.) In addition, any state and local income taxes paid by an individual are automatically considered personal expenditures, and while still deductible, they are allowed only as itemized deductions and therefore cannot be used to reduce profits from a sole proprietorship.[67] As with the interest deduction for deficiency interest charged to a sole proprietor's business, the tax laws surrounding the deduction for state and local income taxes is another disadvantage to operating a business as a sole proprietorship.

 GAAP vs. Code: Most taxes deducted on the income statement are also deductible on the tax return. However, a difference does exist in the treatment of federal income taxes. On the income statement, federal income taxes are reported as an expense deducted in arriving at net income. For tax purposes, no such deduction is allowed. This permanent difference in the treatment of this expenditure will result in less net income than taxable income for the year. Consequently, the amount of federal income taxes reported on the income statement must be added back to net income when the corporation reconciles its net income to taxable income. For example, if a corporation reports a deduction for federal income taxes of $640,000 on its income statement in arriving at net income, the amount must be added back when net income and taxable income are reconciled on the corporate tax return. Similar adjustments must be made for any taxes deducted in computing net income that are not deductible in the calculation of taxable income.

¶ 507 Research and Experimentation Expenditures

For businesses that regularly carry on research activities, research expenditures constitute ordinary and necessary business expenses. However, when a research project could provide benefits to a company for years to come, one might argue that the costs should be capitalized. However, once capitalized, it may be difficult to ascertain the project's useful life for purposes of amortizing the costs. To eliminate the need to make subjective determinations regarding such issues, the tax laws allow taxpayers to choose one of the following three methods for accounting for research and experimentation (R&E) costs paid or incurred in connection with a trade or business:[68]

1. Deduct the expenditures in the year in which they are paid or incurred,

2. Capitalize the expenditures and amortize them ratably over a period of at least 60 months beginning in the month that the benefits are first realized,[69] or

3. Capitalize the expenditures, but do not amortize them.

If the taxpayer chooses to currently deduct its R&E costs or to capitalize and amortize its costs, it must make an election. Generally the election must be made on the original tax return for the year in which the costs are paid or incurred. Once the election to use a method is made for a specific research project, it must be used in all subsequent tax years. If the taxpayer fails to make an election

---

[63] Code Sec. 164(a).
[64] Reg. § 1.164-2(f).
[65] Code Sec. 164(a).
[66] Code Sec. 275(a)(1); Reg. § 1.164-2(a).

[67] *D.H. Tanner*, CA-4, 66-2 USTC ¶ 9537, 363 F2d 36, aff'g, 45 TC 145.
[68] Code Sec. 174(a).
[69] Code Sec. 174(b); Reg. § 1.174-4.

on the original tax return or would like to change to a different method, it must obtain the consent of the IRS.[70] If the taxpayer chooses to capitalize and not currently deduct or amortize its R&E costs, the capitalized amounts cannot be deducted until the research project is abandoned or deemed worthless.[71]

The choice of whether to deduct, defer and amortize, or capitalize R&E costs depends upon when it is best for the taxpayer to recover these costs. Generally, it will be preferable for the taxpayer to currently deduct its R&E costs. However, a business may elect to amortize its R&E costs if it believes it does not have sufficient income in the current year and has such significant net losses in prior years that it is worried that the losses generated by immediate expensing its R&E costs might not be fully utilized. In other instances in which the taxpayer anticipates a higher tax rate in future tax years, it may decide to amortize its R&E costs rather than take a current deduction.

Example 18:   During 2015, Nycorm (a calendar year taxpayer), incurred $36,000 of R&E expenditures. Nycorm anticipates that it will have taxable income (before R&E costs) of $50,000 for both 2015 and 2016. Nycorm can select among the following three options for treating the R&E expenditures:

1. Elect to deduct the full amount in 2015 and reduce its 2015 taxable income to $14,000 ($50,000 – $36,000). Its 2016 taxable income will be $50,000.

2. Elect to capitalize and amortize the R&E expenditures over a period of not less than 60 months. Assuming that Nycorm first realizes benefits on July 1, 2015, it could amortize $3,600 ($36,000/60 × 6 months) of R&E expenditures in 2015 and $7,200 ($36,000/60 × 12 months) in 2016. The amortization would reduce its 2015 taxable income to $46,400 ($50,000 – $3,600) and its 2016 taxable income to $42,800 ($50,000 – $7,200). Nycorm would amortize the rest of the R&E costs from 2017 to 2020.

3. Capitalize the $36,000 of R&E expenditures. Assuming that the research project is not abandoned or deemed worthless in 2015 or 2016, no deduction can be taken in either year. Thus, its taxable income will remain at $50,000 for both years.

.01 Activities That Constitute Research and Experimentation

To qualify as an R&E cost, the expenditure must be incurred in connection with the taxpayer's trade or business that represent research costs in the experimental or laboratory sense. It includes all such costs incident to the development or improvement of a product. This would include the development of any pilot model, process, formula, invention, technique or patent. Expenditures represent research costs in the experimental or laboratory sense if they are for activities intended to discover information that would eliminate uncertainty concerning the development or improvement of a product.[72] Whether costs qualify as R&E expenditures depends on the nature of the activity to which the expenditures relate, not the nature of the product or improvement being developed.[73] R&E costs do not include expenditures for efficiency surveys, management studies, market research, advertising or promotions, normal product testing costs, the acquisition of another's patent, model, production or process, or research in connection with literary, historical or similar projects.[74] R&E costs are eligible for current deduction or deferral and amortization only to the extent the amount of the expense is reasonable under the circumstances.[75]

Example 19:   On January 1, 2013, AXY Company began work on a special research project. During 2013, AXY purchased a building for $113,400 and used 50 percent of its facilities in connection with the special research project. AXY has not been profitable for the past

---

[70] Reg. § 1.174-3.

[71] Code Sec. 165.

[72] The costs of producing a product after uncertainty concerning the development or improvement of a product is eliminated are not R&E costs. Proposed Reg. § 1.174-2.

[73] Reg. § 1.174-2(a)(1).

[74] Reg. § 1.174-2(a)(3).

[75] Code Sec. 174(e); Reg. § 1.174-2(a)(6).

several years, and it does not anticipate it will report taxable income until at least 2017. Thus, AXY elects to capitalize its R&E costs related to this project and amortize them over 60 months. In 2013, AXY incurred the following R&E expenditures:

Salaries	$40,000
Heat and light	1,200
Laboratory material	7,500
Attorney's fees	1,500
Depreciation on building attributable to the project (50% × $3,600 allowable depreciation)	1,800
Total R&E expenditures	$52,000

The $52,000 of expenditures resulted in a process that is marketable but not patentable and has no determinable useful life. If AXY first realizes benefits from the special research project in January 2015, on its 2015 tax return, AXY is entitled to deduct amortization of $10,400 ($52,000/60 × 12 months).

The options to deduct, amortize, or capitalize R&E costs do not extend to amounts spent for land or for depreciable property used in experimentation.[76] For example, a taxpayer cannot expense the cost of acquiring a site for a laboratory or the costs of constructing a laboratory. However, depreciation taken on property used in connection with a research project is considered an R&E expenditure. If the taxpayer elects to capitalize or amortize R&E expenditures that later result in the creation of depreciable property, any unamortized costs are added to the basis of the depreciable property and recovered through annual depreciation deductions.[77]

Example 20: In 2015, LED Corporation (a calendar year taxpayer) incurred R&E costs totaling $48,000 for a research project that did not relate to the creation of depreciable property. LED elected to capitalize and amortize the R&E costs over 60 months. The benefits were first realized on December 1, 2015. For 2015, LED can amortize $800 of its R&E expenditures ($48,000/60 × 1 month). For 2016, it can amortize $9,600 ($48,000/60 × 12 months).

On January 3, 2017, using the research from this project, machinery was produced that will be used in the company's manufacturing plant. In 2016, the $37,600 ($48,000 – $800 – $9,600) unamortized costs of R&E expenditures must be added to the basis of the machinery. Using the depreciation rules described in Chapter 7, LED will be able to recover these remaining costs through annual depreciation deductions.

.02 Research Credit in Lieu of a Deduction

The cost of certain research expenditures may be claimed as a tax credit, including a nonrefundable credit for the expenses paid or incurred for the clinical testing of a drug used for a rare disease or condition and amounts that represent an increase in the taxpayer's research activities. These credits are discussed in Chapter 11. If the taxpayer elects to take a tax credit for any R&E costs, it must reduce the amount of the tax deduction by the amount of the credit taken.

.03 Special Rule for Patents

A **patent** is an intangible asset that gives its owner the exclusive right to commercially profit from a specified product or process for a limited number of years. By filing for a patent, a business discloses its trade secrets regarding the product, but during the legal life of a patent (generally 20 years), others are specifically prohibited from profiting from the patented invention. The Code has

---

[76] Reg. § 1.174-2.   [77] Reg. § 1.174-4(a)(4).

established several alternatives regarding expensing the R&E costs associated with obtaining a patent.

First, R&E costs associated with the development of a patent can be deducted currently, regardless of whether the patent is eventually granted. These expenses may include the costs of obtaining a patent, such as the legal fees incurred in making and perfecting a patent application.[78] Second, the taxpayer can choose to capitalize the costs; however, if the patent is never obtained, the taxpayer must wait until the year the project is abandoned to deduct the costs.[79] Third, the taxpayer can elect to amortize the R&E costs over a period of no less than 60 months; however, if the patent is eventually issued, any unrecovered expenditures must be recovered through amortization deductions over the life of the patent (see ¶ 708).[80]

Example 21: Zyluss, Inc. reports its taxable income using a calendar year-end. In 2015, Zyluss elects to capitalize and amortize over a period of 60 months $60,000 of R&E expenditures made in connection with a particular project. During 2015, Zyluss developed a process that it seeks to patent. On July 1, 2015, Zyluss first realized benefits from the marketing of products resulting from the process. Therefore, the expenditures are deductible ratably over the 60-month period beginning July 1, 2015. On its 2015 tax return, Zyluss deducts $6,000 ($60,000/60 × 6 months), and on its 2016 tax return, Zyluss deducts $12,000 ($60,000/60 × 12 months). On October 1, 2017, a patent protecting the process is obtained. In its 2017 tax return, Zyluss is entitled to a deduction of $9,000, representing the amortizable portion of the R&E costs attributable to the period prior to October 1, 2017 ($60,000/60 × 9 months). The balance of the $33,000 of unamortized costs ($60,000 – $6,000 – $12,000 – $9,000) is recovered over the patent's useful life beginning October 1, 2017.

 GAAP vs. Code: For financial reporting purposes, R&E costs are expensed in the period incurred unless the cost has an alternative future use (such as an intangible asset or property, plant, or equipment).[81] Depending on the tax treatment selected, there may or may not be a difference as to how these amounts are treated for financial reporting versus tax purposes. If the R&E costs are expensed immediately on the tax return, usually there will be no adjustment necessary between net income and taxable income. However, if the corporation chooses to amortize the R&E costs, then in the year the expenses are incurred, the corporation will need to add back to net income the difference between the amounts deducted in arriving at net income and the amortized expense deducted on the tax return. In all subsequent tax years, the amortization of the costs would need to be subtracted from net income in arriving at taxable income. Finally, if the R&E expenditures are capitalized and not amortized for tax purposes, then the amount expensed on the income statement in the first year would be added back to net income to arrive at taxable income.

For example, Zyluss, Inc. from Example 21 capitalizes the $60,000 of R&E costs for tax purposes and deducts (amortizes) $6,000 of the costs in 2015. On its financial statements, Zyluss expenses the entire $60,000 of R&E expenses. Consequently, when reconciling net income to taxable income on its 2015 corporate tax return, Zyluss needs to add back the $54,000 ($60,000 – $6,000) difference between the amount deducted on the income statement and the deduction taken on the tax return. Adjustments will also need to be made in 2016 and 2017 when Zyluss continues to amortize the R&E costs on its tax return, with no such expense being deducted against net income.

---

[78] Rev. Rul. 68-471, 1968-2 CB 109.
[79] Code Sec. 165.
[80] Reg. § 1.174-4(a)(4).

[81] "Accounting for Research and Development Costs," *Statement of Financial Accounting Standards No. 2* (Stamford, Conn.: FASB, 1974), Para. 12.

> Similarly, the amount a corporation is required to expense on the income statement for the costs associated with patents may not be the same as the amount a corporation is allowed to deduct on the tax return. An analysis similar to the one illustrated above with respect to R&E expenses would also apply to any amortization expense of a patent.

¶ 508 Dividends Received Deduction

Corporations are the one form of business entity for which the profits of the business are taxed twice—once by the corporation and a second time when the shareholders are paid a dividend from the corporation's earnings and profits. In the case of a corporate shareholder, the potential for triple taxation exists. Chapter 4 discussed the rules that allow corporations to reduce the amount of dividends they must report in their gross income to circumvent this potential problem. The percentage by which corporations can reduce their taxable dividends ranges from 70 percent to 100 percent, depending on the percentage of stock owned by the corporate shareholder. Although this amount is referred to as the "dividends received deduction," the deduction is not the result of an expenditure; it is computed as a percentage of dividends received during the year. See ¶ 412.02 for more details on the calculation of this deduction.

¶ 509 Domestic Production Activities Deduction

Businesses that produce goods in the United States can claim a deduction, referred to as the manufacturers' deduction or domestic production activities (DPA) deduction.[82] The DPA deduction is available to all businesses engaged in domestic production activities, regardless of the type of entity under which the business is operated. Thus, sole proprietorships, partnerships, limited liability companies, limited liability partnerships, and corporations are all entitled to the DPA deduction if they meet the applicable requirements.

The DPA deduction is determined in accordance with the rules of Code Sec. 199, which contains a number of defined terms and is (perhaps needlessly) complex. However, the basic rule is simple enough: the DPA deduction is essentially a percentage of net income (gross receipts minus costs) derived from domestic production activities.

.01 Domestic Production Activities

Domestic production activities include not only traditional manufacturing but also such activities as construction, engineering, architectural services, and motion picture or video production. Taxpayers producing agricultural products can qualify for the deduction if they perform storage, handling, or other processing activities (other than transportation activities) within the United States.[83] Generally, the DPA deduction is for businesses that produce goods, not those that provide services (other than construction, engineering, or architectural services). The deduction is also unavailable for activities involving the sale of food and beverages prepared by the taxpayer at a retail establishment; the leasing, rental, licensing, sale, exchange or other disposition of land; or the leasing, licensing, or rental of property by the taxpayer for use by any related person.[84]

If a taxpayer is engaged both in producing goods and in providing services related to those goods, a distinction must be made between those activities related to producing the goods and those activities related to providing services. For example, producing electricity, natural gas, or potable water is considered a domestic production activity, but transmitting or distributing those products is not.[85] Therefore, in calculating its DPA deduction, a utility that both produces and transmits or distributes electricity, natural gas, or potable water must determine which of its activities relate to production and which relate to transmission or distribution.

---

[82] Code Sec. 199.
[83] Code Sec. 199(c).

[84] Code Sec. 199(c)(4)(B).
[85] Code Sec. 199(c)(4).

.02 Calculating the Amount of the Deduction

Taxpayers are eligible for the DPA deduction if they derive income from domestic production activities. The DPA deduction rate is nine percent.[86] The amount of the deduction is nine percent of the *lesser of* a taxpayer's (1) qualified production activities income (QPAI) or (2) taxable income.[87] In no case can this deduction exceed 50 percent of employer's Form W-2 wages for the year that are used in computing QPAI.[88] Wages taken into account in applying the 50 percent wage limitation only include wages that are allocable to domestic production gross receipts.[89]

For the purposes of computing the DPA deduction, QPAI equals the taxpayer's receipts from domestic production activities (domestic production gross receipts) reduced by:

1. Cost of goods sold (COGS) that is allocable to domestic production gross receipts;

2. Other deductions, expenses, or losses directly allocable to domestic production gross receipts, such as selling and marketing expense; and

3. Proper share of other deductions, expenses, and losses not directly allocable to domestic production gross receipts or another class of income, such as general and administrative expense properly allocable to sales and marketing activities.[90]

For the purposes of reducing QPAI by COGS, an item or service brought into the United States is treated as acquired by purchase, and its cost cannot be less than its value immediately after it entered the United States.[91]

Example 22: Pentwater Manufacturing has domestic production gross receipts in the amount of $1 million derived from the sale of auto parts manufactured in the United States. The COGS for those auto parts is $500,000. Its sales and marketing expenses directly allocable to receipts from auto parts manufactured in the United States are $100,000, and it is proper to allocate $200,000 of indirect expenses to its receipts from the auto parts. Pentwater's QPAI is $200,000 ($1 million – ($500,000 + $100,000 + $200,000)).

Example 23: Burns Electric has as its sole business the production of electricity in its nuclear power plant. The electricity is transmitted to the town of Springfield by an unrelated company. For 2015, Burns has gross receipts of $1.5 million and expenses of $1 million, of which $500,000 is W-2 wages and $500,000 is other expenses. Because its sole activity (generating electricity) is a domestic production activity, all of its receipts and expenses are used in calculating its QPAI. Burns' QPAI equals $500,000 ($1.5 million – $1 million), and its DPA deduction equals $45,000 ($500,000 × 9%). Thus, for 2015 Burns' taxable income equals $455,000 ($500,000 – $45,000).

Example 24: Assume the same facts as in Example 23, except that the power plant is largely automated and Burns's W-2 wages are only $80,000. Its other expenses total $920,000. Burns' DPA deduction is limited to 50 percent of its W-2 wages, or $40,000. Thus, in 2015, Burns' taxable income will be $460,000 ($500,000 – $40,000).

Example 25: Moe's Taverns, Inc., a chain of bar-and-grill style restaurants, has gross receipts of $1.5 million and expenses of $1 million. Because Moe's does not engage in domestic production activities, it is not eligible for the DPA deduction. Therefore, its taxable income is $500,000 ($1.5 million – $1 million).

---

[86] Code Sec. 199(a). The DPA deduction rate was phased in from 2005 through 2009. The phased-in rates for tax years 2005 and 2006 are three percent. For 2007, 2008, and 2009, the phased-in rates are six percent.

[87] Taxpayers having oil-related production activities income must reduce their DPA deduction by three percent of the least of (1) taxpayer's oil-related QPAI, (2) taxpayer's QPAI, or (3) taxpayer's taxable income (determined without regard to the DPA deduction). Code Sec. 199(d)(9).

[88] Code Sec. 199(b).

[89] Code Sec. 199(b)(2).

[90] Code Sec. 199(c); Prop. Reg. §1.199-4(a). The "proper share" of indirect costs can be determined in several ways. The interested reader can consult Prop. Reg. §1.199-4 or James M. Kehl, *Practical Guide to the Sec. 199 Deduction* (Chicago: CCH, 2007).

[91] Code Sec. 199(c)(3)(A).

Domestic production gross receipts are the gross receipts the taxpayer derives from any lease, rental, license, sale, exchange, or other disposition of:

- Qualifying production property, a significant part of which was manufactured, produced, grown, or extracted by the taxpayer within the United States;

- Any qualified film produced by the taxpayer; or

- Electricity, natural gas, or potable water produced by the taxpayer in the United States.[92]

"Qualified production property" includes all tangible personal property, computer software, and sound recordings (discs, tapes, etc.).[93] Gross receipts from the sale of real property are not eligible for the DPA deduction unless the taxpayer is in the construction business or provides architectural or engineering services in the construction of a building within the United States.[94] A "qualified film" is any motion picture film, video tape, or television program for which at least 50 percent of the total compensation relating to the film's production is compensation for services performed in the United States by actors, production personnel, directors, and producers. However, the term "qualified film" does not include pornography, and consequently, taxpayers cannot take a DPA deduction for income from pornographic films.[95]

Example 26: Mortiendi Corporation has the following gross receipts totaling $224.5 million and $102 million in direct costs for the current tax year for the following activities. Mortiendi also incurred $10 million of indirect costs during the year.

Item	Gross Receipts	Direct Costs (including COGS)
Electricity (produced in the United States)		
Consumed in the United States	$ 52,000,000	$ 25,000,000
Exported to Canada	1,500,000	1,000,000
Natural gas (produced in Canada)		
Consumed in Canada.	2,000,000	1,000,000
Exported to the United States	15,000,000	11,000,000
Corn syrup (produced in the United States)	5,000,000	4,000,000
Films		
Film 1 (shot overseas)	124,000,000	50,000,000
Film 2 (shot in the United States)	25,000,000	10,000,000
	$224,500,000	$102,000,000

Mortiendi's domestic production gross receipts include all receipts from electricity (because that is produced in the United States) but none of the receipts from natural gas (because that is produced in Canada). The gross receipts from corn syrup are included because the corn syrup is tangible personal property (and, thus, qualified production property) produced in the United States. The gross receipts from Film 1 are not included because the film was shot outside the United States. However, the gross receipts from Film 2 are included as domestic production gross receipts because the film was shot in the United States. Thus, Mortiendi's domestic production gross receipts equal $83.5 million ($52 million + $1.5 million + $5 million + $25 million).

Calculating domestic production gross receipts is the first step in determining a taxpayer's DPA deduction. Next, the taxpayer must deduct costs allocable to its domestic production gross receipts

---

[92] Code Sec. 199(c)(4)(A)(i).
[93] Code Sec. 199(c)(5).
[94] Code Sec. 199(c)(4)(A).
[95] Code Sec. 199(c)(6).

to determine its QPAI. The taxpayer's DPA deduction will be equal to a percentage of QPAI, but it cannot exceed 50 percent of its W-2 wages from its domestic manufacturing activities.

Example 27: Assume the same facts as in Example 26. To arrive at its QPAI, Mortiendi must reduce its domestic production gross receipts by costs directly allocable to domestic production gross receipts and an allocable portion of indirect costs. Directly allocable costs associated with the activities that are included in the calculation of domestic production gross receipts total $40 million ($25 million + $1 million + $4 million + $10 million). Indirect costs must be allocated between domestic production gross receipts and Mortiendi's other receipts. One way to allocate these costs is on the basis of percentage of total gross revenues. Mortiendi's total gross revenues are $224.5 million. Its domestic production gross receipts total $83.5 million. Thus, its domestic production gross receipts are 37.2 percent of its total gross revenues ($83.5 ÷ $224.5). Accordingly, $3.72 million ($10 million × 37.2%) of its indirect costs are allocable to its domestic production gross receipts. Mortiendi's QPAI equals $39.78 million ($83.5 million – ($40 million + $3.72 million)). Mortiendi's DPA deduction will be a percentage of its QPAI.

Reason for the Rule: Congress chose to define broadly what constitutes qualified production activities so the deduction would be available to more businesses than just those that engage solely in traditional manufacturing activities. This is an example of Congress's use of the tax laws to encourage (and reward) certain activities (here, domestic production). However, it is important to note that in doing so, Congress introduces substantial additional complexity into the tax laws.

For the purposes of computing the DPA deduction, "W-2 wages" are defined as the taxable wages plus any elective deferral amounts reported on an employee's Form W-2. Taxable wages are those wages employees include in gross income when filing their personal income tax returns (typically the amount in box 1 on the employee's Form W-2). Elective deferrals are amounts an employee chooses to contribute to certain retirement plans and to exclude from the employee's current wages.[96] The most common example of an elective deferral is a contribution by an employee to a Code Sec. 401(k) plan (see discussion at ¶ 603.04).

Example 28: Bad Axe Manufacturing Corporation pays taxable wages allocable to domestic production activities reported in box 1 of its workers' Forms W-2 of $2 million. In addition, its employees make elective deferrals to their Code Sec. 401(k) accounts equal to $500,000. Bad Axe's W-2 wages are $2.5 million and its DPA deduction will be limited to $1.25 million ($2.5 million × 50%).

GAAP vs. Code: The DPA deduction is a tax incentive, not an expense, for financial reporting purposes. Accordingly, any amounts deducted on the tax return for the DPA deduction must be subtracted from net income when reconciling net income to taxable income on the corporate tax return. For example, assume that a corporation's taxable income for 2015 equals $523,000, but included in this amount is $34,000 for the DPA deduction. When preparing the reconciliation of net income to taxable income on the corporate tax return, net income must be reduced by $34,000.

¶ 510 Bad Debts

A bad debt occurs when money owed to a taxpayer becomes uncollectible. The tax laws allow a deduction for both business and nonbusiness bad debts, but the timing and character of the

---

[96] Code Sec. 199(b).

deductions differ. Business bad debts are deductible in full against business gross income. Nonbusiness bad debts are deductible as short-term capital losses. Taxpayers that incur a business bad debt can begin writing off the bad debt in the year it starts to become worthless. Nonbusiness bad debts must be fully worthless before they can be written off.[97]

All bad debts of a corporation are business bad debts. Individuals (including sole proprietors), partnerships, and S Corporations can have both business and nonbusiness bad debts. A **business bad debt** is one that is closely related to a taxpayer's trade or business.[98] There must have been a business reason for entering into the debt arrangement. Business bad debts are usually the result of credit sales of goods or services to customers and loans to suppliers, clients, employees, or distributors. A nonbusiness bad debt is any bad debt other than a business bad debt.

In order to claim a bad debt deduction, the taxpayer must have included the amount in gross income in the year the deduction is claimed or in a prior year. Thus, for businesses using the cash method of accounting, a bad debt deduction usually cannot be claimed from a receivable that is never paid because the defaulted payment would not have been included in gross income.

Furthermore, only a *bona fide* debt qualifies for a bad debt deduction. A *bona fide* debt arises from a debtor-creditor relationship based upon a valid and enforceable obligation to pay a fixed or determinable sum of money. A debt arising out of an accrual method taxpayer's receivables is considered a legally enforceable obligation, deductible as a bad debt at the time of worthlessness, provided the amount of the debt is included in income of the current or a prior tax year. A gift or contribution to capital is not considered a debt for purposes of a bad debt deduction. Similarly, an advance by a taxpayer may not be taken as a bad debt deduction if it is clear from the circumstances that repayment was not intended or expected.[99]

Example 29: Sol Winters owns all of the stock of a corporation. Sol advances $20,000 to the corporation so it could pay off its creditors. No payment of principal or interest was ever made by the corporation to Sol, and none was expected. The advance is a capital contribution or a gift, but it is not a loan. No bad debt deduction for the advance would be allowed.[100]

Example 30: Frank Wilson advanced $12,000 to his son-in-law to use in a new business venture. The son-in-law had no other income. Frank did not investigate the soundness or practicality of the venture. The $12,000 advance was not a loan, since the parties obviously did not intend a debtor-creditor relationship. Therefore, if the business failed, no bad debt deduction would be allowed.[101]

Normally, losses from the sale or exchange of property between related persons (e.g., relatives or between a majority stockholder and the corporation) are disallowed under Code Sec. 267 (see ¶ 804). A bad debt loss, however, does not involve a sale or exchange, and therefore a bad debt between related parties may be deductible if the debt is legally enforceable and otherwise *bona fide*.

Example 31: Assume the same facts as in Example 30, except Frank has his son-in-law sign a note, and the terms of the note include terms for repayment of the loan, along with an interest rate comparable to the current market rate of interest. Under these conditions, if the son-in-law's business goes bankrupt, Frank will be able to deduct the amounts he cannot recover from the loan as a nonbusiness bad debt. Because the loan made to the son-in-law was personal in nature to Frank (the taxpayer), it does not qualify as a business loan.

An individual who operates a business as a sole proprietorship can have a business bad debt if the nature of the loan is related to the taxpayer's business. If the bad debt results from a loan to a

---

[97] Code Sec. 166.

[98] Code Sec. 166; Reg. § 1.166-5(b).

[99] *E.J. Cornish,* 22 BTA 474, Dec. 6750.

[100] *L. Rosenberg,* 5 TCM 138, Dec. 15,042(M).

[101] *J. Griffiths,* CA-7, 1934 CCH ¶ 9195, 70 F2d 946.

relative, friend, or some other nonbusiness connection, the bad debt is a nonbusiness bad debt. Although a sole proprietor can deduct a nonbusiness bad debt as a short-term capital loss, such a loss is not deducted against the profits of the business but instead is used to reduce other capital gains the individual taxpayer generated during the year. The tax consequences of nonbusiness bad debts and ways to distinguish business bad debts from nonbusiness bad debts are discussed further in Chapter 13. The tax treatment of capital gains and losses is discussed in Chapter 9.

.01 Computing the Amount of the Deduction

If a debt becomes worthless, the amount allowed as a bad debt deduction is the adjusted basis of the debt.[102] The adjusted basis of the debt is the same as the amount that would be used to determine gain or loss from the sale of the debt.[103]

Example 32: A collection agency purchases a company's accounts receivable for $3,000. The face value of the receivables is $4,000. The accounts receivable became worthless in its entirety in the following year. For that year, the purchaser will report a bad debt of $3,000 because that amount would be used to compute the loss if the purchaser had sold the accounts receivable before it became totally worthless. If the agency had instead collected $3,500 from the receivables, it would recognize $500 of income ($3,500 – $3,000 adjusted basis).

The taxpayer's method of accounting must also be considered when computing the amount of the deduction. A taxpayer using the accrual method includes fees and rents in income when they are earned or become due and takes bad debt deductions when the debtor is unable to pay. A taxpayer using the cash method can take a bad debt deduction only if an actual cash loss has been sustained or if the amount deducted was previously included in income. Since fees and rents are not included in income on the cash method until they are received, they cannot be deducted as bad debts upon the default of the debtor. If notes are received by the cash method taxpayer in payment of these debts and are included in income at their fair market value when received, that value can be deducted if the notes become worthless.

Example 33: An accountant using the cash method submitted a $400 bill to one of his clients. No part of the $400 was ever paid. The accountant will not include the unpaid bill in his gross income; therefore, he cannot take a bad debt deduction.

Example 34: Assume the same facts as in Example 33, except that the accountant uses the accrual method of accounting. The accountant reports the $400 in gross income at the time the services are performed. Assuming that the debt becomes worthless in a later year with the whole sum unpaid, the accountant can take a bad debt deduction for $400 in that year.

If a business debt becomes partially worthless, the part that has become worthless may be deducted on that year's tax return. In order to deduct a partially worthless business bad debt, the taxpayer must have evidence to support the probable amount that will be recovered at some point in the future.[104]

Example 35: A customer owes XYZ Company $12,000. XYZ uses the accrual method. In 2015, the customer files for bankruptcy, and an appraisal of the assets shows that only 25 percent of the amount due XYZ is recoverable. In 2015, XYZ can deduct $9,000 ($12,000 × 75%) as a partial bad debt.[105] If in 2016 the assets of the bankrupt company are disposed of and XYZ receives a final payment for $2,400, it can deduct the remaining $600 loss ($12,000 – $9,000 – $2,400) in 2016.

Example 36: Assume the same facts as in Example 35, except in 2016 XYZ receives $3,600 instead of $2,400. Since XYZ deducted $9,000 as a partial bad debt in 2015, the amount it

---

[102] Code Sec. 166(b); Code Sec. 1011.
[103] Reg. § 1.166-1(d).

[104] Code Sec. 166(a)(2); Reg. § 1.166-3.
[105] *S.S. Denton Est.*, 11 TCM 802, Dec. 19,134(M).

deducted exceeds its actual loss of $8,400 ($12,000 – $3,600). Therefore, XYZ would report the $600 excess in gross income in 2016 under the tax benefit rule (see ¶ 313).

.02 Proof of Worthlessness

Except for a business bad debt that becomes partially uncollectible, a deduction is usually allowed only in the year a debt becomes worthless. A worthless debt is deductible in the year of worthlessness even when the debt is not due until a later year. The deduction is allowed in the year the surrounding circumstances show that the debt is worthless and uncollectible, not when the taxpayer finally gives up attempting to collect the debt and decides to write it off.[106]

All the circumstances surrounding the situation are used to determine whether the debt is actually worthless. The running of the statute of limitations barring the creditor from bringing suit on the debt, the debtor's bankruptcy, or the death of the debtor leaving no assets are general indications, but not necessarily proof, of when a debt becomes worthless.

Example 37: Carl Dickenson loans Dan Hughes $180,000. In the following year, Dan is severely injured in an auto accident. It is unlikely that he will be able to work again and repay the loan. Carl can take a bad debt deduction for the year in which Dan was injured.[107]

Example 38: Jess Jones made a *bona fide* loan of $10,000 to Zeke Smith. Three years later, with the entire amount still unpaid, Zeke has left the state to places unknown, taking all of his property with him. On these facts, the $10,000 loan became worthless in the year of Zeke's departure. Therefore, Jess may deduct the bad debt in that year.[108]

 GAAP vs. Code: For financial reporting purposes, bad debt expense is an estimate taken in the year of sale in accordance with the matching principle. For tax purposes, the specific charge-off method is used. Therefore, the difference between the bad debt expense reported on the income statement and that which is deducted on the tax return would need to be taken into consideration when reconciling net income to taxable income on the corporate tax return.

¶ 511 Charitable Contributions

Contributions a taxpayer makes to a qualified charitable organization are usually deductible in computing taxable income. However, the amount of the deduction depends not only on the type of property contributed but also on the type of charitable organization to which the property was contributed. Different rules apply to contributions made to public versus private foundations as well as to contributions of ordinary income versus capital gain property. Finally, limitations on the amount that can be deducted in any one tax year differ depending on the type of taxpayer making the contribution.

.01 Qualified Charitable Organizations

Taxpayers can only deduct contributions they make to qualified charitable organizations. A **qualified charitable organization** is a tax-exempt, nonprofit organization formed and operated exclusively for the purposes specified in Code Sec. 501(c)(3).[109] Qualified charitable organizations can be classified as public charities or private foundations, depending upon whether they receive funding from the general public or from private sources. Churches, public universities, and many other organizations like the Red Cross, the United Way, and Goodwill receive their funding from the general public and are examples of **public charities**.

---

[106] Reg. § 1.166-5.
[107] *A.M. Smyth*, CA-10, 35-2 USTC ¶ 9405, 77 F2d 77.
[108] *E.K. Johnstone*, 17 BTA 366, Dec. 5417 (Acq.).
[109] Code Sec. 170(c).

Private foundations, on the other hand, are entities formed with the express purpose of making grants to unrelated organizations or institutions or to individuals for scientific, educational, cultural, religious, or other charitable purposes. Private foundations typically receive most of their funding from one source, whether it be a family, a group of individuals, or a corporation.[110] **Private operating foundations** directly carry out their own activities; they are required to spend at least 85 percent of their earnings on carrying out these activities as well as to pass certain other tests. For example, a private operating foundation might conduct scientific research or operate a museum.[111] A **private nonoperating foundation** is a privately funded, tax-exempt, nonprofit organization that does not meet the definition of a private operating foundation. Most private foundations make contributions to other qualifying charities in carrying out their role as qualified charitable organizations.

.02 Calculating the Amount of the Contributions

When taxpayers donate money to a qualified charitable organization, the deduction is the amount of money donated. When property is contributed, taxpayers usually are allowed to deduct the fair market value (FMV) of the contributed property, which is the price for which the property would sell on the open market on the date of contribution.[112] However, exceptions to this general rule exist, including exceptions for contributions of ordinary income and tangible personal property.

Contributions of ordinary income property. Ordinary income property is appreciated property that, if sold at its FMV on the date of contribution, would generate ordinary income or short-term capital gain. Appreciated property is property whose FMV exceeds its basis. Examples of ordinary income property include inventory, assets held for one year or less, and depreciable property used in a trade or business subject to depreciation recapture. When ordinary income property is contributed to a qualified charitable organization, the amount of the deduction is limited to the taxpayer's basis in the property.[113]

Example 39: BT Company donated to the United Way corporate stock it purchased six months earlier for $20,000. At the time of the donation to the United Way, the FMV of the stock was $28,000. Because BT donated stock it had held for one year or less (short-term property), its charitable contribution is limited to $20,000—its basis in the stock.

There are two exceptions to the ordinary income property rule that applies to corporations. Under the exceptions, the corporation is allowed to deduct its basis in the property plus half of the amount of the appreciation (FMV in excess of basis). However, the deduction is limited to twice the corporation's basis in the contributed property.[114]

One exception to the ordinary income property rule applies to corporations (other than S corporations) that contribute inventory and other ordinary income property to a qualified public charity or private operating foundation for use in the care of the ill, the needy, or infants. To qualify, the donee's use of the property must be related to its tax-exempt purpose or function; the organization cannot transfer the contributed property for money, property, or services; and the organization must provide the corporation with a written statement to this effect.[115]

Example 40: Mathis Corporation contributes men's overcoats with an FMV of $2,000 to a public charity. The charity will use the overcoats for the care of the ill and needy, which is consistent with its tax-exempt purpose. Mathis's basis in the overcoats is $600. Mathis initially computes its deduction as its $600 basis in the overcoats plus $700, which represents half of the appreciation (($2,000 – $600)/2). However, since this amount ($600 + $700 = $1,300) exceeds twice its basis in the overcoats of ($600 × 2 = $1,200), Mathis's charitable deduction is limited to $1,200.

---

[110] Code Sec. 509(a).
[111] Reg. §53.4942(b)-1(b).
[112] Reg. §1.170A-1(c)(2).

[113] Code Sec. 170(e)(1).
[114] Code Sec. 170(e)(3)(B), (e)(4)(A), and (e)(6)(A).
[115] Code Sec. 170(e)(3)(A).

The second exception to the ordinary income rules that applies to corporations (other than S corporations, personal holding companies, or service organizations) involves contributions of ordinary income property to colleges, universities, or scientific tax-exempt organizations for use in research. To qualify for this special rule:

1. The contributed property must be constructed or assembled by the donor and contributed within two years of its construction or assembly;

2. The original use of the property must be by the donee;

3. The charitable organization must use the property at least 80 percent of the time for research or experimentation in the physical or biological sciences;

4. The charitable organization cannot exchange the property for money, other property, or services; and

5. The corporation must receive a written statement from the organization verifying that the previous two requirements have been met.[116]

Example 41: Gentran Corporation, a computer manufacturer, donates computers to Southern College; Gentran's basis in the computers is $100,000. The computers (FMV $140,000) will be used to assist in research projects conducted by Southern College's biology department. Gentran's charitable contribution deduction equals $120,000, which is the $100,000 basis in the computers plus $20,000 (50 percent of the $40,000 appreciation).

Contributions of capital gain property. Usually, taxpayers can deduct the FMV of property they contribute to a qualified charitable organization when they have held the property for more than a year (i.e., when it is long-term property). However, if capital gain property is donated to a private nonoperating foundation, then the amount of the deduction is limited to the taxpayer's adjusted basis in the property, except when the property is publicly traded stock, in which case FMV can still be deducted. Capital gain property is property that, if sold, would produce long-term capital gain or Section 1231 gain. This generally involves business property held long-term or property held long-term as an investment or as a personal belonging (in the case of an individual). Also, if tangible personal property is donated to a public charity where it is put to an unrelated use by the charitable organization, then the deduction again is limited to the taxpayer's adjusted basis in the property. Unrelated use is determined by reference to the purpose or function upon which the organization's tax-exempt status was based.[117] Unrelated use can also be determined by the sale, exchange, or disposal of property by the donee before the last day of the taxable year in which the contribution was made to which the donee has not made a certification as to the use, or intended use, of the donated property to the donee's exempt purpose.[118]

Example 42: TR Corporation donates a painting to a public university. The painting was purchased five years earlier for $10,000. At the time of the donation, the painting is worth $50,000. The university immediately sells the painting and uses the proceeds for educational purposes. TR's charitable contribution is limited to $10,000.

Example 43: Assume the same facts as in Example 42, except TR donates the painting to an art museum which displays the painting. TR's charitable contribution equals $50,000 because the tangible personal property donated to a charity is put to a use that is related to the organization's tax-exempt function.

Example 44: Angrella, Inc. donates land worth $100,000 to a public charitable organization. Angrella purchased the land for $20,000 several years earlier. Since land is not tangible personal property, no special limits apply and Angrella's charitable contribution equals $100,000.

---

[116] Code Sec. 170(e)(4)(B).

[117] Code Sec. 170(e)(1)(B)(i).

[118] Id.

Example 45: Deckright & Sons donates stock to a public charitable organization. Deckright paid $5,000 for the stock several years earlier, and it is currently worth $50,000. The charitable organization sells the stock immediately after it had been donated. Although stock is considered personal property, it is intangible property, and therefore, the special limitations would not apply. Deckright's charitable contribution equals $50,000.

Recapture of charitable contribution deduction. If a charitable organization receives appreciated tangible personal property as a charitable contribution in which the claimed value of the property exceeds $5,000 and later disposes of the property within three years of receiving it, the donor's charitable contribution deduction is limited to the amount of the property's basis. This recapture rule will not apply if the donee provides a certification that the property was intended to be used or was put to a use related to the donee's exempt purpose.[119]

 Planning Pointer: Taxpayers need to be aware of the rules for donating appreciated property to a charitable organization. In certain situations, the amount of the contribution may be limited to the taxpayer's basis in the property. In such situations, the taxpayer may be better off selling the property, paying any tax on the gain, and then making a cash donation to the charitable organization. For example, if tangible personal property worth $20,000 is donated to a charitable organization that puts the property to a use that is unrelated to its charitable purpose, the taxpayer's charitable contribution will be limited to the taxpayer's basis in the property. If the taxpayer paid $5,000 for the property several years ago, it may be more advantageous to the taxpayer to sell the property for $20,000 and pay taxes on the $15,000 gain. The taxpayer can contribute some of the proceeds from the sale to the charitable organization. However, since this special rule only applies to appreciated tangible personal property, taxpayers can deduct the full FMV of donations of intangible assets (such as stock and bonds) or real property (land and buildings), provided the taxpayer has owned the property for more than one year.

.03 Timing of the Contributions

Contributions are typically deducted in the year in which they are paid, regardless of the taxpayer's method of accounting.[120] Payments made by credit card are deductible in the year in which the credit card is charged, regardless of when the taxpayer actually pays the credit card bill.[121] Since most corporations must use the accrual method, the tax laws allow accrual method corporations to elect to accrue a contribution authorized by the board of directors by the end of the corporation's tax year, provided the contribution is paid within 2½ months after the close of the tax year.[122] An election to treat such a contribution as having been paid during the tax year must be made at the time of filing the tax return for such year.[123]

Example 46: In December 2015, the board of directors of a corporation passes a resolution to contribute $500,000 to the local university. The corporation uses the accrual method of accounting and a calendar tax year. The check is mailed on March 1, 2016. At the time it files its 2015 tax return, the corporation may elect to deduct the contribution in 2015. If it fails to make the election, the deduction will be taken on the corporation's 2016 tax return.

---

[119] Code Sec. 170(e)(7).

[120] Code Sec. 170(a)(1).

[121] Rev. Rul. 78-38, 1978-1 CB 67, distinguishing Rev. Rul. 68-174, 1968-1 CB 81.

[122] In TAM 200004001, the IRS has stated this election does not apply to S Corporations.

[123] Code Sec. 170(a)(2); Reg. § 1.170A-11(b).

.04 Limitations

The amount of the deduction that can be taken for charitable contributions in any given tax year is limited for both individuals and corporations. There is no overall limit imposed on businesses operated as flow-through entities, but the amounts of the contributions those entities make during the year are allocated separately to their respective owners, who then apply the limits on their own income tax returns. Although the details for the limitation imposed on individuals is discussed in detail in Chapter 13, it should be noted here that all contributions made by an individual are treated as itemized deductions, even if the contribution is paid from a business operated as a sole proprietorship or a flow-through entity. As mentioned in Chapter 1, only individuals whose total itemized deductions exceed their standard deduction benefit from itemized deductions; therefore, this rule is yet another disadvantage to operating an unincorporated business.

Reason for the Rule: Charitable contributions made by a sole proprietor are always considered personal expenditures. A business operated as a sole proprietorship is not allowed to reduce taxable business profits by any charitable contributions made by the sole proprietor. To better understand why this rule exists, take as an example Sarah Conrad, who operates her greeting card business as a sole proprietorship. For 2015, Sarah's net profit from her business totals $50,000. Sarah is very active in her community and donates her time and money to a homeless shelter, which is a qualified charitable organization. Several times during the year, Sarah writes checks from her business account as a donation to the homeless shelter. In 2015, Sarah's contribution to the homeless shelter totals $4,000. If Sarah were allowed to deduct her contributions of $4,000 to the homeless shelter as a business expense on Schedule C, *Profit or Loss From Business*, her federal income tax liability would be reduced due to the $4,000 reduction in her business profits. She would also pay less self-employment taxes as a result of having less profits subject to self-employment taxes. However, because Sarah is only able to deduct the $4,000 charitable contribution as an itemized deduction, it will only reduce her income taxes if her total itemized deductions exceed her standard deduction in 2015. The reason Congress only allows individual taxpayers to claim charitable contributions as itemized deductions is because anyone with a sole proprietorship would claim that his or her charitable contributions came from the business and were not made for personal reasons.

For corporate taxpayers, the allowable deduction for charitable contributions may not exceed 10 percent of the corporation's taxable income, computed before taking into consideration any of the following items:

- Charitable contribution deduction,
- Dividends received deduction (see ¶ 508),
- Deduction relating to the limitation of bond-premium deduction on repurchase,[124]
- Any capital loss carryback (see ¶ 901.01),
- Any net operating loss carryback (see ¶ 1004.02), and
- Domestic production activities deduction (see ¶ 509).

Any contributions in excess of the annual limit can be carried forward by the corporation to the next five tax years. At the end of five years, any excess contributions that could not be deducted are lost. The total deduction for the year to which an unused contributions deduction is carried over is also subject to the 10-percent limit. In years in which charitable contributions are being carried over, the current year's contributions are applied first against the limit, followed by the carryover contributions using a first-in, first-out method.[125]

---

[124] Code Sec. 249.

[125] Code Sec. 170(d)(2)(A); Reg. § 1.170A-11(c).

Example 47: A corporation makes a $25,000 charitable contribution during the year. The corporation's taxable income before deducting the charitable contribution is $180,000; however, included in this calculation is a $12,000 deduction for domestic production activities and a $20,000 dividends received deduction. The corporation's charitable contribution deduction for the year is limited to $21,200. It carries over the remaining $3,800 ($25,000 – $21,200) of charitable contributions to the next five years. The corporation's taxable income for the year is $158,800 ($180,000 – $21,200).

Taxable income before the charitable contribution		$180,000
Plus:	Dividends received deduction (DRD)	20,000
	Domestic production activities (DPA) deduction	12,000
		$212,000
		× 10%
Charitable contribution limit		$ 21,200

Example 48: A calendar year corporation makes a charitable contribution of $30,000 in 2015. Its taxable income in 2015 determined without regard to the charitable deduction is $100,000. Therefore, the corporation's charitable contribution deduction for 2015 is limited to $10,000 ($100,000 × 10%). The $20,000 excess charitable contribution ($30,000 – $10,000) that could not be deducted in 2015 is carried forward to 2016. In 2016, the corporation has $125,000 of taxable income determined without regard to the charitable deduction. During 2016, it makes a $5,000 charitable contribution. For 2016, the corporation may deduct $12,500 as a charitable contribution ($125,000 × 10%). The corporation's $12,500 deduction consists of the $5,000 contribution made in 2016 and $7,500 carried over from 2015. The remaining $12,500 carryover from 2015 ($20,000 – $7,500) is carried forward to 2017.

.05 Sequencing of Deductions

In calculating taxable income, special consideration must be made for the order in which specific deductions, such as the charitable contribution deduction, dividends received deduction, capital loss carrybacks, NOL deduction and the domestic production activities deduction are taken. In calculating taxable income the sequence in taking the following five deductions must be followed:

1. Charitable contribution (CC) deduction,
2. Dividends received deduction (DRD),
3. Capital loss (CL) carryback,
4. NOL deduction, and
5. Domestic production activities (DPA) deduction.

The following example illustrates the sequencing of these deductions in calculating taxable income.

Example 49: The following is the 2015 tax information for Xtra, Inc.:

Sales revenue	$100,000
Dividend income from Rockpoint (Xtra, Inc. owns 15% of Rockpoint's stock)	50,000
Capital gains	15,000
Business expenses	25,000
Charitable contributions	20,000
Capital loss carryback	5,000
NOL carryback	40,000

For corporations, the charitable contribution (CC) deduction cannot exceed 10 percent of taxable income before taking any of the five deductions as listed. In determining the CC deduction, NOL carryforwards are reflected in computing taxable income for purposes of the 10-percent limitation.

Sales revenue	$100,000
Dividend income	50,000
Capital gain	15,000
Total income	$165,000
Less: Business expenses	(25,000)
Taxable income before CC, DRD, CL carryback, NOL and DPA	140,000
	× 10%
Charitable contribution (CC) deduction	$ 14,000

The amount of the CC deduction for 2015 is $14,000. The remaining amount of the charitable contributions of $6,000 ($20,000 – $14,000) will be carried over to 2016. In determining the CC deduction, a capital loss **carryforward** (but not carryback—item #3) would be subtracted by the company to the extent it has capital gains. If Xtra, Inc. had a $5,000 capital loss carryforward, instead of a carryback, the CC deduction would have been limited to $13,500 ((($165,000 total income – $5,000 capital loss carryforward) – $25,000 business expenses) × 10%)).

After computing the CC deduction, the dividends received deduction (DRD) is calculated (see ¶ 411.02). When applying the taxable income limitation to the DRD, taxable income is computed before subtracting items 2–5 as listed. The CC deduction (item #1) is subtracted before computing the DRD.

Sales revenue		$100,000
Dividend income		50,000
Capital gain		15,000
Total income		$165,000
Less: Business expenses	$25,000	
Charitable contribution (CC) deduction	14,000	(39,000)
Taxable income before DRD, CL carryback, NOL and DPA		$126,000
Less: DRD ($50,000 × 70%)		(35,000)
Taxable income before CL carryback, NOL, and DPA		$ 91,000

The DRD is $35,000 calculated by taking the *lesser* of (1) 70 percent of the dividends received or (2) 70 percent of the corporation's taxable income before the DRD. If the corporation also received dividends subject to the 100 percent or 80 percent DRD, taxable income is first reduced by the 100 percent DRD then the aggregate amount of dividends subject to the 80 percent DRD before taking the 70 percent deduction.

After calculating the DRD, any capital loss carrybacks and/or NOL deduction are subtracted from taxable income.

¶ 511.05

Taxable income before CL carryback, NOL, and DPA		$ 91,000
Less: Capital loss carryback	$ 5,000	
NOL carryback	40,000	(45,000)
Taxable income before the DPA deduction		$ 46,000

The DPA deduction is calculated after all the items listed from 1–4 have been subtracted. In this example, Xtra, Inc. has determined its DPA deduction to be $1,380 after considering items 1–4. Xtra Inc.'s taxable income:

Taxable income before the DPA deduction	$ 46,000
Less: Domestic production activities (DPA) deduction	(1,380)
Taxable income	$ 44,620

.06 Substantiation

Taxpayers making charitable contributions of cash, checks, or other monetary gifts must retain certain records of the gift, *regardless of the amount.* Taxpayers must maintain either: a bank record; *or* a receipt from the charity indicating the name of the charitable organization, the date the contribution was made, and the amount of the contribution. If these records are not kept for each donation made, no deduction is allowed for the charitable contribution.[126]

Taxpayers making noncash charitable contributions should file Form 8283, *Noncash Charitable Contributions,* to report information about the donated property. For noncash donations of property valued at more than $500, individuals, closely held corporations, personal service corporations, partnerships, and S corporations must file Form 8283 to report information about the donated property. When noncash donations exceed $500, the taxpayer must maintain a written record as to (1) the approximate date and manner of the acquisition of the property or the approximate date of completion if the taxpayer created the property and (2) the adjusted basis of the property.[127] For contributions valued over $5,000, a qualified appraisal must be attached to the tax return when filed.

A deduction for the charitable contribution of a clothing or household item by a corporation, an individual, or partnership will only be permitted if the item is in good used condition or better.[128] The IRS will not deny a deduction for a charitable contribution of a clothing or household item if:

1. A deduction of more than $500 is claimed for the single clothing or household item, and
2. The taxpayer includes a qualified appraisal with respect to the item with the tax return on which the deduction is claimed.

"Household items" include furniture, furnishings, electronics, appliances, linens, and other similar items. The term does not include food, paintings, antiques, other objects of art, jewelry, gems, or collections.

Corporations, other than S corporations, personal service corporations, and closely held corporations, file Form 8283 only if the amount claimed as a deduction exceeds $5,000. For C corporations, the substantiation requirements for property exceeding the $5,000 level do not apply to donations of:

1. Cash,
2. Publicly traded securities,
3. Inventory, and
4. Any qualified vehicles sold by a donee organization without any significant intervening use or material improvement and for which an acknowledgement is provided.

---

[126] Code Sec. 170(f)(17).
[127] Reg. § 1.170A-13(b)(3).

[128] Code Sec. 170(f)(16)(A).

GAAP vs. Code: For financial reporting purposes, the amount of charitable contributions paid or accrued is expensed in the period incurred. For tax purposes, charitable contributions, made by a C corporation, are subject to a 10-percent limitation. Thus, in any year in which a corporation's charitable contribution deduction is limited, the disallowed amount must be added back to net income when reconciling net income to taxable income. Likewise, in the years in which the carryover amounts are deducted on the corporation's tax return, such amounts must be subtracted from net income in arriving at taxable income.

For example, the corporation from Example 48 makes a $30,000 qualified charitable contribution during 2015. When computing its taxable income after applying the annual limit, only $10,000 of the contribution is allowed. When computing net income, the corporation deducts the $30,000 as a charitable contribution expense. When reconciling its net income to its taxable income in 2015, the corporation must add back the $20,000 difference to net income to compute taxable income. In 2016, the corporation deducts the $5,000 contribution it makes during the year in arriving at net income. However, due to the carryover, after applying the annual limit, the corporation deducts $12,500 on its 2016 tax return. The excess $7,500 of deductions taken on the tax return due to the charitable contribution carryover from 2015 must be subtracted from net income when reconciling net income to taxable income on the 2016 corporate tax return.

¶ 512 Business Gifts and Achievement Awards

Deductions for business gifts are limited to $25 per individual each year.[129] Items distributed by the taxpayer that do not cost more than $4 and on which the taxpayer's name is permanently imprinted (such as pens, key chains, etc.) are not subject to the $25 limit. Also, signs, display racks, or other promotional materials to be used by the recipient at the recipient's place of business are not subject to the $25 limit. Generally, there is no $25 limitation on the deductibility of a business gift (which is not entertainment, see ¶ 605.02) if it is to a corporation, partnership, or other business entity and not intended for the eventual personal use or benefit of an individual who is an employee, stockholder, or owner of the business.[130]

Achievement awards are not considered business gifts, but may be deductible by the employer as a business expense.[131] The employer's deduction depends on whether the award is a qualified or nonqualified plan award. The deduction to the employer for the cost of qualified plan awards made to any employee is limited to $1,600 per year, taking into account all other qualified and nonqualified awards made to that employee during a tax year. The employer's deduction for the cost of nonqualified plan awards made to any one employee during the tax year is limited to $400. A qualified plan award is one that is part of an established written plan or program set up by the employer that does not discriminate in favor of highly compensated employees as to eligibility for award benefits.[132]

 GAAP vs. Code: Because of the tax limitation on the amount paid for business gifts, there generally will be a difference between the amount expensed in arriving at net income versus that deducted on the tax return. For example, if a corporation sends out to 100 of its regular customers gifts costing $75 each, then the corporation will deduct

---

[129] Code Sec. 274(b)(1).
[130] Reg. § 1.274-3(e)(2).
[131] Code Sec. 274(j)(2).
[132] Code Sec. 274(j)(3)(B).

$7,500 ($75 × 100) as gifts in arriving at its net income. On the tax return, the corporation will be able to deduct $2,500 ($100 × $25). The $5,000 difference would be added to net income when the corporation reconciles net income to taxable income on the corporate tax return.

¶ 513 Summary

Although most expenses taxpayers incur in the normal course of business meet the ordinary, necessary, and reasonable requirements, Congress has sought to deny or limit certain business expenses for a variety of reasons. Since every dollar taken as a deduction results in tax savings equal to the taxpayer's marginal tax rate, it is important that businesses understand all of their options with respect to the amount and timing of deductions available to them. This chapter focused on some of the more common expenses that businesses encounter during the normal course of business. This discussion continues in Chapter 6 with a discussion of employment-related expenses.

GLOSSARY OF TERMS INTRODUCED IN THE CHAPTER

Amortization. The annual deduction taken to recover the cost of intangible assets over time.

Business bad debt. A *bona fide* debt that is closely related to a taxpayer's trade or business. There must have been a business reason for entering into the debt arrangement.

Deficiency interest. The interest charged on tax deficiencies when taxpayers fail to pay the proper amount of taxes on their income tax returns.

Depreciation. An annual deduction taken to recover the capitalized cost of business or income-producing property that is either tangible personal property or real property (other than land).

Depletion. The annual deduction taken to recover an investment in productive natural resources.

Domestic production gross receipts. The gross receipts the taxpayer derives from any lease, rental, license, sale, exchange, or other disposition of (1) qualifying production property, a significant part of which was manufactured, produced, grown, or extracted by the taxpayer within the United States; (2) any qualified film produced by the taxpayer; or (3) electricity, natural gas, or potable water produced by the taxpayer in the United States.

Necessary expense. An expense that is appropriate or helpful to the continuation of the taxpayer's business.

Nonbusiness bad debt. A *bona fide* debt that is not a business bad debt. *See also* Business bad debt.

Ordinary expense. An expense that is customary and acceptable in the taxpayer's type of business.

Organizational costs. Certain costs incurred in the process of incorporating a business.

Patent. An intangible asset that gives its owner the exclusive right to commercially profit from a specified product or process for a limited number of years.

Private nonoperating foundation. A privately funded, tax-exempt, nonprofit organization that does not meet the requirements of a private operating foundation.

Private operating foundation. A privately funded organization that directly carries out its own activities and is required to spend at least 85 percent of its earnings carrying out its activities and to pass certain other tests.

Public charities. Charitable organizations such as churches, public universities, the Red Cross, and the United Way that receive their funding from the general public.

Qualified charitable organization. A tax-exempt, nonprofit organization formed and operated exclusively for the purposes specified in Code Sec. 501(c)(3).

Start-up costs. Costs that normally would be currently deductible if they were incurred in connection with the operation of an existing trade or business and that are not organizational costs.

Uniform capitalization (UNICAP) rules. The rules that require a taxpayer to capitalize certain costs as part of the cost of real or tangible personal property the taxpayer produces.

CHAPTER PROBLEMS

The following questions and problems relate to the discussion in Chapter 5, Business Deductions: Ordinary and Necessary Business Expenses, which begins at ¶ 500 in *Part II: Federal Taxation of Business Income and Deductions*.

Chapter 5 Discussion Questions

1. Match the terms listed with the appropriate definition. A term can only be used once.

   (a) bad debt
   (b) domestic production activities deduction
   (c) charitable contribution deduction
   (d) illegal bribe paid to a public official
   (e) research and experimentation expenditure
   (f) ordinary, necessary, and reasonable
   (g) business creation and preopening costs
   (h) uniform capitalization rules
   (i) state incorporation fee

       f 1. Conditions for a business expense to be deducted.

       i 2. Organizational expenditure.

       d 3. Nondeductible business expense that violates public policy.

       h 4. Business taxpayers must capitalize and then depreciate costs that are incurred because of production or resale activities.

       g 5. Start-up expenditures.

       b 6. Business deduction that encourages businesses to engage in manufacturing activities within the United States.

       a 7. Money that is uncollectible that is owed to a taxpayer.

       c 8. Corporate deduction limited to 10 percent of the corporation's taxable income, computed with adjustments.

       e 9. Expenditure that includes all costs incident to developing or improving a plant process, product, formula, invention, or similar property.

2. Of the following, which are deductible as business expenses?

   a. Penalty for not filing an income tax return.

   b. Penalty for nonperformance of a contract.

   c. Fine for violation of a city housing code.

   d. Fine for truckers in violation of air quality laws.

   e. Fine for driving in excess of the speed limit.

   f. Kickbacks paid by tennis instructor to sporting goods dealer that violate state law (which is never enforced), but not federal law.

3. Smith & Wesson Investment Co. employed Wheeler Dealer, a securities broker with significant connections to the board rooms of several large, publicly traded corporations. During the course of a business lunch, Wheeler received some insider information that he promptly put to use in his trading activities, thereby turning a handsome profit for himself and Smith & Wesson. With almost equal promptness, Wheeler's activities were detected by the SEC and he was tried and found guilty on several criminal counts of securities law violations. Smith & Wesson incurs considerable legal expenses in Wheeler's defense. Nevertheless, Wheeler is found guilty on all counts. Are Wheeler's legal fees deductible by Smith & Wesson as an ordinary and necessary business expense?

4. A business pays a lobbyist to try to influence elected representatives concerning impending legislation. In addition, the business incurs expenses in communicating its concerns regarding the legislation to a trade organization in which the business is a member. Are these expenses deductible?

5. Which of the following are capital expenditures?

   a. Cost of partitions to convert a warehouse to an office building.

   b. Interest on a debt incurred to finance construction of a building.

   c. Cost of mending leaks in a roof.

   d. Cost of a building project to comply with the city building code.

6. At formation, WPJ Corporation incurred the following expenses: legal services to obtain corporate charter—$500, state incorporation fees—$400, and stock issue costs—$300. How quickly will the corporation be allowed to deduct these costs?

7. Eleco and Ampco are public utilities that enter into an agreement to share the costs of constructing and operating a power plant. Eleco incurs costs in providing training to individuals on the operation of the plant prior to the start of its operation. Under the agreement Ampco reimburses Eleco for its share of the costs. May Ampco take a current deduction for the amounts?

8. Which of the following amounts must be capitalized and which may be deducted at the election of the taxpayer?

   a. Interest paid by a manufacturer to construct machinery to be used in its factory. It will take 1½ years to construct the machinery and cost $1.5 million.

   b. Interest and taxes on unimproved real property.

   c. Interest paid by a contractor during the two-year construction period of an office building.

9. CYG Company purchases a number of computers. The total price of the computers purchased is $18,000, of which $1,200 is sales tax. Can CYG Company deduct the $1,200 on its current tax return?

10. A business pays property tax of $500, sales tax of $600 paid on the purchase of office equipment, gas tax of $200, and employment taxes of $500. Which taxes may be deducted in the current year?

11. In the current year, a taxpayer incurs $1,200 of research and experimentation costs. The taxpayer elects to amortize the research and experimentation cost, over 60 months, in the first year. Benefits from the cost of the project are realized in the first year only. At the end of the second year, the project is abandoned. What are the effects on the taxpayer's returns for both years?

12. What is the domestic production activities deduction, and what is the amount of the deduction?

13. What types of business entities can claim a domestic production activities deduction?

14. A taxpayer makes a personal loan to a friend, saying, "You need not pay it back unless you feel like it." Five years later the friend has not repaid the loan, and the taxpayer claims a bad debt deduction. Is this proper?

15. Determine the bad debt deduction that may be claimed for the current tax year by the taxpayers described below:

    a. A taxpayer charges off a $1,000 business debt in the current tax year. The debt became totally worthless during the preceding tax year.

    b. A $1,000 business debt becomes totally worthless during the current tax year. The debt is due in the following tax year.

16. The taxpayer, a merchandising corporation, ascertains in the current year that a debt owed to it is worthless. Had the corporation attempted to enforce the debt in the preceding year, it would have found then that it could not be collected. However, there was no way in the ordinary course of business of determining the condition of the debt until this year, and therefore it charges the amount off this year. Can the debt be deducted as a bad debt for the current year?

17. For each situation described below, determine the allowable bad debt deduction.

    a. Star Painting Company, a cash method taxpayer, agrees to paint Fred Blum's apartment building for $5,000. After completing the job, the company learns that Fred has sold the building and moved to Mexico. There is no reasonable prospect that Star will ever be paid.

    b. A collection agency purchases accounts receivable with a face value of $1,000 for $500. It collects $750 of the debt. The remainder becomes worthless.

18. A corporation wants to make a charitable contribution for the current tax year; however, the corporation wants to wait as long as possible to make the donation. If the corporation is a calendar-year corporation that uses the accrual method, how long can the corporation wait to make the contribution, and what process is necessary?

19. If a corporation contributes its inventory to a qualified charitable organization, what amount can it generally deduct?

20. What deduction is allowed to a company for a gift to an individual customer of a digital recorder costing $50?

Chapter 5 Problems

1. PAZ Corporation incurred the following expenses during the year:

Federal (EPA) fine paid for violation of air quality laws	$ 50,000
Bribes paid to foreign officials to approve foreign construction project	200,000
Kickbacks paid to local police officers	25,000
Legal fees incurred in contesting EPA fine	250,000
Court costs incurred in contesting EPA fine	1,000

   What is the amount of expenses that PAZ Corporation can deduct for the year?

2. QT Corporation incurred the following politically related expenses:

Payments to state lobbyists to secure passage of favorable legislation	$550,000
Political contributions	250,000
Political dinner (table purchased)	10,000
Expenses incurred by QT President to appear before local county board to discuss proposed legislation that will affect QT	2,000

   What is the amount of expenses that QT Corporation can deduct?

3. John Porter, sole shareholder of Canit Inc., incurred the following expenses for the year that were reimbursed by the company:

Parking tickets incurred while on business	$550
Traffic ticket for running a stop sign when going to a business meeting	150
Political contributions on behalf of the company	750

What is the amount of expenses that Canit Inc. can deduct?

4. Kip Sims, a yacht broker, paid $15,000 to AB Marina and $35,000 to CU Marina as kickbacks for customer referrals. There is a state law against these payments, but the law is never enforced. There is no federal law against these payments. How much of the kickback payments can Kip Sims deduct, if any?

5. James Jacobs and Sons was a partnership operating a printing business. The partners decided to incorporate their business and consulted an attorney to file the Articles of Incorporation. They also hired an accountant for audit work incidental to the incorporation. The following expenditures were made as a result of forming the corporation:

Attorney's fees relating to drawing up the corporate charter	$6,000
Accountant's fees incident to organization	3,000
State fee for incorporating	300
Expense of issuing stock	120
Transfer fees for transferring assets to the corporation	60

The corporation was formed on June 28, 2015, and began business in July of 2015. It elected to file its tax return using a calendar year. The officers of the corporation requested the bookkeeper to currently deduct expenses where possible and to amortize the remaining expenses over the shortest possible period for federal income tax purposes. What is the amount deductible on the corporation's tax return in 2015?

6. Zig Corporation incurs advertising and training costs of $52,500 before its business actually begins. Zig Corporation began business on May 1, 2015. Compute the maximum amount of Zig Corporation's deduction for start-up costs for 2015.

7. A trucking company had the following expenses for the tax year:

Stamps, stationery, and office supplies	$ 3,500
Office expense and salaries	150,000
Heat and light	10,000
Miscellaneous repairs to trucks	3,000
Tire replacements (consumed within one year)	4,000
Oil and gas for machines and trucks	30,000
Two new fax machines	980

The company also built an addition to its building to be used as a shipping room at a cost of $3,000. How are these items treated on the tax return for the year?

8. In 2015, MYB Co. purchased $160,000 of equipment to be used in its manufacturing plant. What is the correct tax treatment of this expenditure?

9. C&J Corporation incurred the following expenses at formation: legal services to obtain corporate charter—$600, investigation costs leading to the decision to incorporate—$1,000, state incorporation fees—$500, and stock issue costs—$100. How quickly will the corporation be allowed to deduct these costs?

10. W&Z Corporation, a calendar year taxpayer, begins work on a project in 2013 and elects to amortize related research and experimental costs over a 60-month period. On September 1, 2015, W & Z Corporation begins to market products produced from a process resulting

Qualified Production activities Income

from the project. As of September 1, 2015, W & Z has deferred a total of $259,200 of research expenses. What is the amount of research and experimental costs that can be deducted by W & Z in 2015?

11. ABC Company incurs $15,200 in R&E costs in conjunction with developing a patent. How much can ABC Company deduct in the first year for the patent?

12. In 2015, a company hires a contractor to construct a building for its operations. The building cost $10 million. During construction, the company incurs interest costs of $100,000 in 2015 and $150,000 in 2016 related to construction financing. In 2017, during the first year following construction, the company uses the building and incurs an additional $75,000 of interest expense due to a mortgage on the building. How much interest should be capitalized?

13. The corporation's books, which are maintained on the accrual method, show the following income and expense items for the 2015 tax year:

Net sales	$600,000
Cost of goods sold	250,000
Salary and wage expenses (not included in cost of goods sold)	120,000
Selling and marketing expenses	100,000
General and administrative expenses	75,000

(W-2 wages for the year used in computing QPAI are $150,000)

If the corporation's QPAI for the year is $70,000, determine its 2015 taxable income.

14. Determine the allowable bad debt deduction for the current tax year in the situations described below:

a. A business debt becomes partially worthless during the current tax year. The debt is for $1,000. However, only $600 of the debt is worthless.

b. A $1,000 business debt becomes totally worthless during the current tax year.

c. Tom makes a $1,000 *bona fide* loan to his friend. It is determined during the current tax year that the debt is worth only $500.

15. In 2013, the Jones Corporation sells merchandise to Doake for $5,000. In 2015, there was still a balance due of $3,000. Doake is adjudicated bankrupt. Although there are some substantial assets in the bankrupt estate, the Jones Corporation charges the entire balance off on December 31, 2015, for financial accounting purposes, while bankruptcy proceedings are still pending. An examination of the bankruptcy file would indicate a probable recovery of 20 percent. In 2016, the bankrupt's assets are liquidated, 16 percent of the debt is paid, and the bankruptcy debt is discharged.

a. How much can the Jones Corporation deduct of the Doake debt in 2015?

b. For 2016? Why?

c. Can the Jones Corporation instead deduct the entire amount of $3,000 in 2016?

16. D Corporation, a computer manufacturer, donated some of its computers with a basis of $50,000 to LV University. The computers will be used in LV's biological sciences research lab. The fair market value of the computers is $160,000. Assume the donation requirements are met. What is the amount of D Corporation's charitable contribution?

17. Comment on the deductibility of the following business expenses:

a. Amounts paid to a lobbyist to secure the passage of favorable legislation.

b. Fines paid by a trucker for inadvertently exceeding the state's maximum weight laws.

c. Advertising by a public utility company to defeat public power legislation.

d. Current research and development expenses incurred for the first time, assuming that the taxpayer desires to deduct the expenses.

18. M Company manufactures blankets. M Company donated its inventory of blankets with a fair market value of $15,000 to a public charity. The blankets will be used by the charity for the care of the ill and needy. M Company's basis in the blankets is $10,000. What is the amount of M Company's charitable contribution?

19. G Corporation uses the accrual method and reports on the calendar year. During the December meeting of the board of directors in 2015, the board authorized the corporation to make a $20,000 charitable contribution to the Community Chest, a public charity, and the check was mailed in January 2016. The corporation's taxable income, before the charitable contribution deduction, for 2015 was $180,000, and for 2016 it was $250,000. What is the earliest year or years in which the contribution is deductible?

20. A C corporation has taxable income of $100,000 after all deductions except the charitable contribution deduction, but including a $7,000 dividends received deduction. The corporation made a $20,000 charitable contribution for the year. There are no charitable contribution carryforwards.

   a. Compute the charitable contribution deduction.

   b. Compute the charitable contribution carryforward (if any).

21. Outerwear, Inc., a clothing manufacturer, donated the following items to a local homeless shelter during the year. The shelter is a qualified public charity.

   a. Stock in ABC Corporation which was purchased nine months ago for $25,000, FMV $35,000;

   b. A painting which was purchased three years ago for $5,000, FMV $55,000;

   c. Stock in LMN Corporation which was purchased two years ago for $60,000, FMV $100,000;

   d. Coats, scarves, and sweaters from its inventory that cost $3,000 to manufacture, with an FMV of $10,000; and

   e. Unimproved land which was purchased five years ago for $5,000, FMV $20,000.

   The shelter provided Outerwear with a certification that it will sell the stock, land, and painting immediately, and use the donated clothing in its care of the needy. Compute the value of Outerwear's charitable contribution deduction for the year (prior to taking into consideration the 10 percent taxable income limitation).

22. A corporation donated stock in another company, which it had held for five months, to a qualified public charity. The corporation had purchased the stock for $30,000 and at the time of its donation the stock was worth $45,000. The corporation's taxable income for the year, excluding its charitable contribution deduction, is $75,000. Included in taxable income is a $3,000 dividends received deduction and a $2,000 domestic production activities deduction. The corporation did not make any other charitable contributions for the year.

   a. What is the amount of the corporation's charitable contribution deduction for the year?

   b. What is the amount of the charitable contribution carryover?

23. Reflex, Inc., a calendar year company, prepaid three years' rent of $54,000 on August 1, 2015. If Reflex uses the cash method of accounting, how much rent can it deduct on its 2015 income tax return?

24. In 2015, Palmera Corporation, a cold cereal manufacturer, determined based on market conditions that it should expand its business. The corporation, which is on a calendar year, spent the following amounts in 2015 toward investigating the expansion of its business:

Marketing and cost analysis study in producing and selling frozen foods	$50,000
Legal and accounting fees incurred in locating a frozen foods manufacturing business	150,000
Feasibility study on producing a new organic cereal line	30,000

| Marketing and cost analysis study in manufacturing specialty chocolates | 45,000 |
| Legal and accounting fees incurred in locating a chocolate manufacturing business | 100,000 |

Palmera made an offer to purchase a frozen foods manufacturing plant, but at the last minute the deal fell through. The corporation decided not to start a new line of organic cereals because of the cost. On December 1, 2015, Palmera purchased a specialty chocolates manufacturing business. How should Palmera treat its business expansion costs incurred in 2015?

25. Bliss Inc.'s books, which use the accrual method, had the following income and expense items for the 2015 tax year:

Net sales	$450,000
Cost of goods sold	200,000
Operating expenses (100% allocable to production activities)	100,000
Charitable contributions	35,000

(W-2 wages for the year, included in cost of goods sold and operating expenses, are $40,000)

Determine Bliss Inc.'s taxable income for 2015.

Chapter 5 Review Problems

1. A corporation's books, which are maintained using the accrual method, show the following income and expense items for the 2015 tax year:

Gross sales and receipts	$800,000
Returns and allowances	2,000
Cost of goods sold	200,000
Taxable interest income	20,000
Office rent expense	50,000
Salaries and wages expense	300,000
Charitable contributions	25,000
Miscellaneous business expenses	75,000
School tuition paid for major shareholder's son's education	10,000
New truck purchased	25,000
Depreciation for new truck	5,000

   a. Determine the corporation's taxable income for the 2015 tax year. (*The company does not qualify to take the domestic production activities deduction.*)

   b. What is the amount of the corporation's charitable contribution carryover (if any)?

2. The corporation's books, which are maintained using the accrual method, show the following income and expense items for the 2015 tax year:

Gross sales	$950,000
Returns and allowances	5,000
Cost of goods sold	350,000
Taxable interest income	20,000
Office rent expense	60,000
Salaries and wages expense	150,000
Charitable contributions	55,000
Kickbacks paid to foreign government officials	65,000

Miscellaneous business expenses	75,000
New machines purchased	600,000
Depreciation on new machines	120,000
Research and experimentation expenses (corporation elected to currently deduct)	50,000

   a. Determine the corporation's taxable income for 2015. *(The company does not qualify to take the domestic production activities deduction.)*

   b. What is the amount of the corporation's charitable contribution carryover (if any)?

Chapter 5 Research Question

ABC Corporation manufactures chemicals. The Environmental Protection Agency (EPA) brought a 10-count criminal indictment against ABC Corporation and two of its employees for misrepresenting to the EPA the amount of toxins discharged from ABC's manufacturing plant. The corporation was found guilty on all 10 counts and could have been fined $5 million and the two employees could have been sentenced to 10 years in prison.

ABC entered into a plea agreement with the government's attorney to pay the maximum fines and to pay $1 million to a trust fund designated by the government's attorney for the purpose of study and research in the field of toxic chemical cleanup. As part of the plea agreement, the government agreed to dismiss nine counts against ABC Corporation and to dismiss all counts against the two employees. The government also agreed not to institute further criminal or civil actions against ABC and the two employees. ABC paid the maximum fine and made a payment of $1 million to the trust fund.

You have been requested by the corporation to determine whether the $1 million payment made to the trust fund or a portion thereof can be deducted as a business expense. Give your opinion. Show authorities, citing laws, regulations, interpretations, and decisions applicable, and cite the *CCH Standard Federal Tax Reporter* paragraphs where they may be found.

CHAPTER 6
Business Deductions: Employment-Related Expenses

CHAPTER CONTENTS

LEARNING OBJECTIVES

1. Gain a better understanding of a business's total employment costs, including the difference in costs associated with hiring employees versus independent contractors.

2. Identify the costs involved when employers offer various employee benefit plans to their employees, including health care, flexible spending accounts, and educational assistance.

3. Explain the various retirement plans employers may offer their employees and the costs associated with each of these plans.

4. Explain the various ordinary and necessary business expenses that employers might reimburse their employees for and the tax consequences of the amounts businesses pay to reimburse their employees under an accountable versus a nonaccountable reimbursement plan.

5. Describe how the tax laws treat employment-related expenses incurred by sole proprietors, including amounts paid on behalf of their employees as well as amounts paid on behalf of themselves.

¶ 600 Introduction

Most businesses hire employees as part of the process of generating revenues and profits. Employment-related expenses are generally considered ordinary and necessary business expenses that are deductible against gross income. These expenses include not only the amounts that businesses pay to workers, but also business expenses they reimburse employees for travel, transportation, and relocation costs. It also includes amounts businesses pay for health insurance and educational assistance they provide to their employees, as well as contributions they make to their employees' retirement plans. This chapter introduces the tax laws regarding the deductibility of employment-related expenses.

For businesses operated as sole proprietorships, the owner generally performs the services for the business and, accordingly, incurs employment-related expenditures in conjunction with those services. Since the profits from the sole proprietorship are included on the owner's personal income tax return, different rules govern how employment-related costs are treated when incurred on behalf of the owner versus those paid by the business on behalf of an employee of the sole proprietor. The tax laws surrounding the deductibility of employment-related costs incurred by sole proprietors in connection with their own businesses are also discussed in the chapter.

¶ 601 Compensation Paid to Workers

When a business hires workers, it must compensate them for the services they perform for the company. Compensation paid to workers not only includes wages and bonuses paid to employees but also amounts paid to independent contractors. Although both amounts are deductible against business income,[1] the distinction between these two types of workers is significant, as the costs associated with hiring workers as employees is greater than those associated with hiring workers as independent contractors. The classification of a worker as either an employee or independent contractor is made based on the facts and circumstances surrounding the employment arrangement between the business entity and the worker.

.01 Employee vs. Independent Contractor

Independent contractors are self-employed individuals who perform services for another individual or business entity but are not employees of the persons or businesses that hire them. Although businesses can deduct the compensation they pay to workers, whether those workers are classified as employees or independent contractors will determine the employers' total out-of-pocket employment costs.

As a general rule, employers are responsible for withholding amounts from an employee's wages to cover any federal, state, and local income taxes the employee owes on the taxable wages. Employers also must withhold the employee's share of FICA taxes (social security and Medicare). Although the amounts withheld from an employee's wages are costs borne by the employee, the employer incurs administrative costs associated with making sure the proper amounts are withheld and remitted to the appropriate government agencies. In addition, employers are required to make matching contributions for their employees' FICA taxes and are responsible for paying unemployment taxes on those wages. The costs for these taxes are borne by the employer.

In contrast, amounts paid to independent contractors are not subject to withholdings or unemployment taxes. Workers hired as independent contractors are self-employed individuals who operate their own businesses as sole proprietorships. Sole proprietors report the amounts they receive as an independent contractor as earnings from self-employment, and are allowed to offset these amounts by any business expenses paid or incurred in generating those earnings. Sole proprietors are subject to self-employment taxes on the net earnings from self-employment, which reflect their share of the employer and employee portions of FICA taxes. Furthermore, since no

---

[1] Code Secs. 61(a)(1) and 162(a).

amounts are withheld from the compensation sole proprietors receive, sole proprietors are responsible for making quarterly estimated payments to cover both the income and self-employment taxes owed on any taxable amounts their businesses generate (see ¶ 407).

Table 6-1 summarizes some of the differences for the tax treatment of employees and independent contractors. It illustrates the difference in costs to the employer associated with hiring a worker as an employee versus hiring an independent contractor.

Table 6-1 Tax Implications of Classifying Workers as Employees vs. Independent Contractors

Issue	*Workers Classified as Employees*	*Workers Classified as Independent Contractors*
Party responsible for remitting income taxes on the compensation paid to the worker.	The employer withholds amounts from the employee's pay and remits these amounts to the appropriate government agencies. Therefore, the administrative costs are borne by the employer.	The worker is responsible for paying these amounts to the government by making quarterly estimated payments to cover the amounts owed.
Party responsible for the employee's share of FICA taxes.	The employer withholds amounts from the employee's pay and remits these amounts to the government.	The worker is responsible for paying these amounts to the government by making quarterly estimated payments to cover the amounts owed.
Party responsible for the employer's share of FICA taxes.	The employer matches the amounts it withholds from the employee's pay and remits the matching amount to the government.	The worker is responsible for paying these amounts to the government by making quarterly estimated payments to cover the amounts owed.
Party responsible for paying state and federal unemployment taxes.	The employer is required to contribute to these funds for each of its employees.	Sole proprietors are not required to pay unemployment taxes on self-employment income.
Eligibility for employer-provided benefits, like health care and participation in employer-sponsored retirement programs.	Yes, but usually only for full-time employees. Amounts paid by the employer are generally excluded from employees' wages, but can be deducted as business expenses on the employer's tax return.	No. These items must be paid for and provided by sole proprietors themselves, who then deduct these costs from gross income on their personal income tax returns.

Most employers prefer to classify their workers as independent contractors since employers must pay unemployment taxes and the employer's share of FICA taxes on employees' wages. These additional taxes incurred plus the administrative costs associated with the withholding of employees' income and FICA taxes contribute to the higher costs associated with hiring workers as employees versus independent contractors. Employers are also finding that to stay competitive in the marketplace and to continue to be able to attract the best workers, they often must offer a variety of benefit programs to their employees, the most common of which are participation in company's health care and retirement programs. Because employers that offer these programs are typically required to make them available to all full-time employees, not only does the employer incur the administrative costs associated with offering these programs, but usually a large portion of the funding for these programs comes from the employer. Since workers classified as independent contractors are not allowed to participate in these programs and they are responsible for all income and payroll taxes associated with their self-employment earnings, the employer's costs can be significantly reduced by hiring workers that can be classified as independent contractors.

Example 1: Becktel Company pays its employee, Susan Cross, an annual salary of $50,000. In addition to Susan's salary, Becktel pays $3,825 in FICA taxes, $378 in state unemployment taxes, and $42 in federal unemployment taxes. Becktel provides health insurance coverage for its full-time employees, and during the year, it paid health insurance premiums on behalf of Susan totaling $6,200. During the year, Becktel hires Bob Knight as an independent contractor and pays him a contractual fee of $50,000. As shown below, Becktel incurs significantly more employment-related costs by hiring Susan as an employee over Bob as an independent contractor. To accurately determine the company's true additional costs, the tax savings from being able to deduct these employment-related costs must be considered. For example, if Becktel's marginal tax rate is 35 percent, its total out-of-pocket costs of hiring Susan as an employee versus Bob as an independent contractor increase by $6,789 ($39,289 – $32,500).

	Susan Cross	*Bob Knight*
Compensation	$50,000	$50,000
Employee benefits	6,200	
Payroll Taxes:		
FICA	3,825	
State unemployment	378	
Federal unemployment	42	
Total employment-related costs	$60,445	$50,000
Less: Tax savings at 35%	(21,156)	(17,500)
Total out-of-pocket costs to Becktel	$39,289	$32,500

To prevent employers from inappropriately classifying workers as independent contractors to avoid these higher costs, the tax laws provide guidance on how to correctly classify workers. In some instances, the Code specifically categorizes workers as independent contractors. For example, real estate agents are self-employed workers for income tax purposes.[2] However, in most instances, the distinction hinges primarily on whether the worker is subject to the control and direction of the person who hires them, not only as to the results to be accomplished but also to the method of accomplishing them. If such control and direction exists, then the relationship is deemed to be one between an employer and employee. It is important to note that it is not necessary that the employer ever exercise control or direction over the worker; just having the right to do so is sufficient to classify a worker as an employee.[3] The IRS considers three aspects of control when determining whether a business employs a worker as an employee or an independent contractor: behavioral controls, financial controls, and the relationship of the parties.[4]

Example 2: Abe Gable is the West Coast distributor for a movie company, Motion Pictures, Inc. The company is interested only in Abe's sales results, and accordingly, Abe is paid a commission for each movie he sells. Abe is required to furnish his own office and to find his own prospects. Motion Pictures properly classifies Abe as an independent

---

[2] Code Sec. 3508.
[3] Reg. §31.3401(c)-1(a) and (b).

[4] IRS Publication 1779 (Revised 3-2012); IRS Publication 15A (2015).

contractor. Thus, the commissions it pays to Abe are deductible against business income and the company is not required to withhold amounts for income or FICA taxes. Likewise, Motion Pictures is not required to pay FICA or unemployment taxes on any commissions it pays to Abe, and Abe cannot participate in any benefit programs Motion Pictures offers its employees.

.02 Employee Compensation

Amounts paid to employees are included in the employee's gross income[5] and are deducted as wage expense by the employer.[6] Taxable wages include regular salary and wages, overtime pay, bonuses, vacation pay, commissions and tips, as well as reimbursements for business expenses not covered under an accountable plan (see ¶ 601.03).

Reasonable compensation. The deduction for wages paid to employees is subject to the general deductibility requirements outlined in Chapter 5; therefore, only amounts paid to employees that are reasonable in amount can be deducted by the employer.[7] Because the profits of a corporation are subject to tax not only at the corporate level but also at the shareholder level when the profits are distributed to shareholders as dividends, the potential for abuse exists when a corporation has employees who are also shareholders in the corporation. Since wages are deductible, whereas dividends are not, the corporation pays less taxes by classifying a payment to an employee/shareholder as compensation rather than as a dividend distribution.

Although a corporation is liable for unemployment taxes and its share of FICA taxes (social security and Medicare taxes) on employees' wages, federal unemployment (FUTA) taxes are only assessed on the first $7,000 of employee wages, and in 2015, employers are required to pay the (matching) 6.2 percent social security taxes on the first $118,500 of employee wages and 1.45 percent Medicare taxes on employee wages. Likewise, the employee is responsible for paying social security taxes of 6.2 percent on the first $118,500 of wages received in 2015 and 1.45 percent Medicare taxes on wages (see ¶ 604.01). Thus, when the tax consequences to both the employer and employee are considered together, there may be advantages to classifying a distribution to an employee-shareholder as wages rather than as a dividend.

The reasonableness test is more likely an issue with **closely-held corporations,** which are corporations whose stock is held by a small number of shareholders, possibly from the same family or a related group of individuals. Often employee-shareholders of closely-held corporations are officers of the corporation, and their total compensation already exceeds the maximum wages subject to social security taxes. Accordingly, when distributions to these officer-shareholders are treated as salaries, the corporation's tax liability is reduced significantly. The reasonableness requirement prevents the corporation from deducting as salaries what are actually distributions of corporate profits (dividends). The reasonableness requirement also might come up in situations where the salary is paid to a family member that is significantly higher than the value of the services the person is providing. In this case, the business may be attempting to shift the tax burden to a family member in a lower tax bracket, for example, a child.

Example 3: Heather Hill is the sole owner of HH Corporation. The marginal tax rate for both Heather and HH is 35 percent. During the year, HH pays Heather a salary totaling $120,000. In December, HH pays Heather a $50,000 bonus. Assuming the bonus is taxed as additional compensation to Heather, Heather's income tax liability will increase, and HH's income tax liability will decrease by the same $17,500 ($50,000 × 35%). Since Heather and HH have already paid in the maximum amounts for social security taxes for the year, both will be liable for an additional $725 in FICA taxes ($50,000 × 1.45%) on Heather's taxable wages. HH's tax savings on its $725 deduction of FICA taxes is $254 ($725 × 35%). In the end, Heather will net $31,775 after taxes

---

[5] Code Sec. 61(a)(1).
[6] Code Sec. 162(a).

[7] Code Sec. 162(a)(1); Reg. §1.162-7.

from the $50,000 bonus ($50,000 – $17,500 additional income taxes – $725 additional payroll taxes), and the total costs of HH for paying the bonus will be $32,971 ($50,000 + $725 payroll taxes – $17,500 tax savings – $254 tax savings).

Example 4: Assume the same facts as in Example 3, except that the $50,000 is treated as a dividend distribution. Since corporations do not deduct amounts paid as dividends to their shareholders, HH does not derive any tax savings by making this distribution. Thus, the out-of-pocket costs to HH would be $50,000. The $50,000 of dividend income will be included in Heather's gross income. Her tax liability would increase by $7,500 ($50,000 × 15% tax rate on qualified dividends) (see ¶ 405.02). Heather would benefit from having the $50,000 payment treated as a dividend distribution (she would net $50,000 – $7,500 = $42,500 vs. $31,775), HH's out-of-pocket costs would be significantly higher ($50,000 vs. $32,971).

A corporation will be unable to deduct compensation to the extent it is determined to be unreasonable. The portion of the employee-shareholder's salary determined to be unreasonable is treated as a dividend distribution from the corporation to the employee-shareholder.

The factors the Tax Courts use to determine whether salary and wages paid to employees are reasonable in amount include the following:

1. The employee's role in the company, responsibilities shouldered, and duties performed,
2. The ability and achievements of the employee,
3. How the employee's salary compares with similarly situated employees,
4. The character and condition of the company,
5. Whether the business is earning a satisfactory return on equity,
6. The cost of living in the locality, and
7. The internal consistency of salaries paid to all employees in the company.[8]

Other courts have used a hypothetical independent investor approach. The court determines whether a hypothetical independent investor would be willing to compensate the employee at his or her compensation level.[9]

When no personal relationship exists between the employee and the employer or in situations where the employee has no real influence over the employer (for example, as a controlling shareholder), there is little need to question the amount deducted for salary and wages. However, when such influence or personal relationship exists, the IRS can reclassify the payment as a dividend distribution for any amounts it deems unreasonable in light of the facts and circumstances surrounding the business. The taxpayer may contest the IRS's decision to reclassify the payment, but the burden rests with the taxpayer to prove that the amount originally claimed is reasonable.[10]

Publicly-held corporations typically cannot deduct compensation paid to covered employees to the extent that the compensation exceeds $1 million per year.[11] **Publicly-held corporations** are corporations whose stock is traded on one of the U.S. stock exchanges, such as the American Stock Exchange, New York Stock Exchange, or NASDAQ. "Covered employees" are those who on the last day of the tax year are either the chief executive officer (CEO) of the corporation (or someone who acts in that capacity) or among the four highest paid officers of the corporation, other than the CEO.

There are a number of ways by which corporations can get around the $1 million limit. Exceptions to this limit include specified commissions, compensation based on performance goals, income payable under a written binding contract that was in effect on February 17, 1993, and

---

[8] *Elliots, Inc.* CA-9, 83-2 USTC ¶ 9610, 716 F2d 1241; *Mayson Manufacturing Co.,* CA-6, 49-2 USTC ¶ 9467, 178 F2d 115.

[9] *Exacto Spring Corporation*, CA-7, 99-2 USTC ¶ 50,964, 196 F3d 833, reversing the Tax Court which used the seven factor test.

[10] *Long Island Drug Co.*, CA-2, 40-1 USTC ¶ 9446, 111 F2d 593, cert. denied, 311 US 680.

[11] Code Sec. 162(m).

compensation paid prior to the corporation becoming a publicly-held company.[12] Accordingly, businesses that pay their top executives more than $1 million annually will want to structure their employment arrangements to fall under one of these exceptions.

Example 5: Beta Corporation pays its CEO $1.35 million in 2015. Unfortunately, Beta cannot justify why the $1 million limit should not be imposed. Consequently, Beta can pay its CEO $1.35 million but only deduct $1 million on its 2015 tax return.

Example 6: In 2015, YUL Corporation, a calendar year, publicly-held corporation, establishes a bonus plan under which its CEO, Carl Smith, will receive a $500,000 cash bonus if year-end corporate sales increase by at least five percent. The bonus plan was established at the start of the year, and Carl's annual salary is $950,000 prior to any bonuses. YUL retains the right, if the performance goal is met, to reduce the bonus payment to Carl if, in its judgment, other subjective factors warrant a reduction.

At the end of the year, YUL's sales had increased by eight percent and the corporation agrees to pay Carl the $500,000 bonus. Because the bonus is based on acceptable performance goals, the bonus paid to Carl is not subject to the $1 million compensation limitation. For 2015, YUL will be able to deduct Carl's salary of $950,000 plus his year-end accrued bonus of $500,000.

 GAAP vs. Code: Since the $1 million limit on executive compensation is imposed by the Code, it does affect the amounts that corporations actually pay to their executives or the amount they expense on the income statement. Any amounts that are paid but cannot be deducted in arriving at taxable income must be added back to net income when the net income and taxable income are reconciled on the corporate tax return. In Example 5, Beta would need to add $350,000 to its net income as a result of the limitation imposed on the deduction for the compensation paid to its CEO.

Timing of the deduction. The timing of the deduction for compensation is largely governed by the employer's methods of accounting. If the employee uses the cash method (which most individual taxpayers use), then the amounts are taxed in the year in which they are received, regardless of when they are incurred by the accrual method employer. Consequently, when an accrual method business accrues compensation expense at the end of the tax year that is not paid until the next tax year, the tax benefits from taking the deduction are realized by the business one year in advance of when the income is taxed to the employee.

Example 7: On December 14, 2015, the Board of Directors of an accrual method calendar year corporation votes to pay each of its 10 managers a $10,000 year-end bonus and an additional $2,500 bonus in recognition of valuable services rendered in prior years. These amounts represent reasonable compensation. The corporation pays these amounts to the managers on January 5, 2016. These amounts are deducted by the corporation in 2015, the year in which they are incurred, and would be taxed to the managers in 2016.[13] The corporation would take a deduction for $125,000 ($12,500 × 10) on its 2015 tax return, and assuming the corporation's marginal tax rate is 35 percent, this deduction will reduce its taxes by $43,750 ($125,000 × 35%). Although the government will generate tax revenues by requiring that these amounts be included in the managers' gross income, these amounts will not be taxed until 2016, and consequently, the government loses out on the use of those revenues for an entire year.

In situations where the employee has significant influence over the company, the potential for abuse exists. For example, when a majority shareholder is also an employee of the corporation, the

---

[12] Code Sec. 162(m)(4)(C).

[13] *Lucas v. Ox Fibre Brush Co.*, SCt, 2 USTC ¶ 522, 281 US 115, 50 SCt 273.

shareholder can influence when certain payments are accrued by the corporation and when such amounts are paid to employees. Although taxes on these amounts will eventually be paid, as illustrated in Example 7, the revenues the government generates from these amounts is delayed an entire year. Thus, when amounts are accrued to *related parties*, the tax laws require that the accrual method taxpayer postpone the timing of the deduction until the employee includes the amount in income.[14] For purposes of this rule, a corporation and an employee are related if the employee directly or indirectly owns more than 50 percent of the value of the outstanding stock in the corporation.[15] (See ¶ 804 for more on the related party rules.) This rule ensures that the amount reported in income by the employee and the deduction taken by the employer is accounted for at the same time.

Example 8:   John Starks is an employee and sole shareholder of Markel Corporation. John uses the cash method; Markel uses the accrual method of accounting. Both use a calendar year end. In December 2015, John has Markel declare a $50,000 bonus to him to be paid in January 2016. Without the required "matching" rule for related parties, Markel could deduct this amount in 2015, and John would be able to defer the recognition of income in his tax return until 2016. However, the matching rule requires that Markel wait until 2016 to deduct the bonus it pays to John in that year.

Businesses can deduct wages and salaries for services rendered in prior years; however, payments for services to be provided in future tax years must be capitalized and deducted in the year in which the services are rendered.[16] Pursuant to the all-events tests introduced in Chapter 3, accrual method taxpayers may deduct an item if all the events have occurred that establish that a liability exists, the amount of the liability can be determined with reasonable accuracy, and economic performance has occurred with respect to the liability.[17] Accordingly, it is not required that the exact amount of compensation to be paid be known with absolute certainty by the end of the year in order for an accrual method taxpayer to deduct it in that year.[18] For example, when compensation is based on a percentage of sales, the amount of accrued sales revenue may not be known with certainty by the close of business on the last day of the tax year. As long as the percentage is known and the liability is fixed, accrual method taxpayers can accrue (deduct) these amounts as compensation in the year in which they are incurred.

 GAAP vs. Code: Generally the timing of the deduction for compensation will be the same for book and tax purposes. However, this is not the case where an employee/shareholder has significant influence over when compensation is paid. In that instance, the corporation will accrue an expense on its books but will be unable to deduct the expense for tax purposes until the compensation is paid. In Example 8, Markel Corporation was unable to deduct the bonus to its employee and sole shareholder until 2016 when the amount was paid. On its 2015 financial statements, Markel reduces its net income by the $50,000 bonus. Accordingly, on its 2015 corporate tax return, Markel adds back the $50,000 bonus to its net income when reconciling net income to taxable income. Markel will then need to subtract the $50,000 bonus from its net income when reconciling net income to taxable income on its 2016 corporate tax return.

.03 Reimbursements from Nonaccountable Plans

When an employer reimburses employees for business expenses under an accountable plan, the reimbursements are excluded from the employee's gross income[19] and are deducted by the employer as the tax laws permit. Since these reimbursements are not taxable wages to the

---

[14] Code Sec. 267(a)(2).

[15] Code Sec. 267(b)(2).

[16] Reg. § 1.162-7(b)(1).

[17] Code Sec. 461(h)(4); Reg. § 1.461-1(a)(2).

[18] Reg. § 1.162-7(b)(2); Rev. Rul. 61-127, 1961-2 CB 36, modifying Rev. Rul. 55-446, 1955 CB 531; Rev. Rul. 2011-29, IRB 2011-49, 824, November 9, 2011.

[19] Code Sec. 62(a)(2).

employee, they are not subject to income tax withholding, nor are they subject to FICA or unemployment taxes. An **accountable plan** requires that employees submit adequate documentation or receipts for any reimbursed expenses and requires that they return to their employers any advances they receive in excess of the substantiated expenses.[20]

Reimbursements paid through a system that does not meet the requirements for an accountable plan are considered reimbursements from a **nonaccountable plan**. Amounts paid to an employee under a nonaccountable plan are treated as taxable compensation to the employee and as wage expense to the employer. Thus, the employee is subject to income and FICA tax withholdings on these amounts, and the employer is responsible for the employer's share of FICA plus unemployment taxes on the additional wages. Although the employee is allowed to deduct amounts reimbursed from a nonaccountable plan as employee business expenses, such expenses are miscellaneous itemized deductions and can only be deducted if the employee's total miscellaneous expenses exceed two percent of the employee's adjusted gross income (AGI) and the employee's itemized deductions exceed his or her standard deduction.[21]

Example 9: An employee of Macintye, Inc. is reimbursed $1,000 for travel expenses incurred while away on business. The amounts are reimbursed under a nonaccountable plan. Macintye is required to include the $1,000 in the employee's wages and accordingly, it deducts this amount as wage expense. Macintye also must pay its share of FICA and unemployment taxes on the $1,000, as well as withhold from the employee's pay income taxes and the employee's share of FICA taxes. The employee is allowed to deduct the $1,000 as an unreimbursed employee business expense, which is a miscellaneous itemized deduction subject to the two-percent AGI floor.

Example 10: Assume the same facts as in Example 9, except that the $1,000 was reimbursed from an accountable plan. Here, the $1,000 is excluded from the employee's gross income, and the full $1,000 is deducted as travel expense on Macintye's tax return.

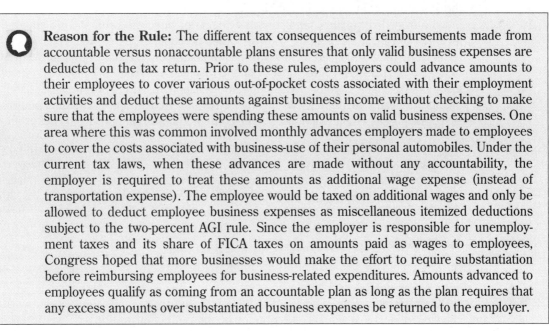

Reason for the Rule: The different tax consequences of reimbursements made from accountable versus nonaccountable plans ensures that only valid business expenses are deducted on the tax return. Prior to these rules, employers could advance amounts to their employees to cover various out-of-pocket costs associated with their employment activities and deduct these amounts against business income without checking to make sure that the employees were spending these amounts on valid business expenses. One area where this was common involved monthly advances employers made to employees to cover the costs associated with business-use of their personal automobiles. Under the current tax laws, when these advances are made without any accountability, the employer is required to treat these amounts as additional wage expense (instead of transportation expense). The employee would be taxed on additional wages and only be allowed to deduct employee business expenses as miscellaneous itemized deductions subject to the two-percent AGI rule. Since the employer is responsible for unemployment taxes and its share of FICA taxes on amounts paid as wages to employees, Congress hoped that more businesses would make the effort to require substantiation before reimbursing employees for business-related expenditures. Amounts advanced to employees qualify as coming from an accountable plan as long as the plan requires that any excess amounts over substantiated business expenses be returned to the employer.

¶ 602 Employee Benefits

To attract and retain the best employees, employers often offer a variety of benefits to their employees, including health care coverage, educational assistance, and participation in employer-

---

[20] Reg. § 31.3401(a)-4(a).   [21] Code Sec. 67; Temp. Reg. § 1.67-1T(a).

sponsored retirement programs. Since "income" generally includes all increases in net worth, from whatever source derived, fringe benefits provided to an employee in connection with the performance of services would be considered additional compensation and normally would be taxable to the employee.[22] However, certain provisions in the Code allow the costs associated with a variety of fringe benefits employers provide to their employees to be excluded from the employees' gross income but still be deducted by the employer.

.01 Contributions to Accident and Health Plans

Premiums employers pay to provide their employees with accident or health insurance (including coverage to the employee's spouse, dependents, and adult children under the age of 27) are deductible by the employer and not taxed to the employee.[23] These rules apply regardless of the type of business entity the business is operated under. Thus, amounts corporations as well as amounts sole proprietors and partnerships pay for health and disability (accident) insurance for their employees are deducted from the gross income generated by their respective businesses. However, when sole proprietors pay the premiums for their own health insurance, these amounts are deducted in arriving at AGI on the proprietor's individual income tax return but not as a deduction against the profits of the sole proprietorship. Since a sole proprietor's self-employment tax is assessed on profits from the business, amounts paid for the proprietor's own health insurance reduce the amount of income taxes owed by the sole proprietor, but not their self-employment taxes. Generally, the sole proprietor is not allowed a deduction for the proprietor's payments for disability insurance coverage. In contrast, amounts sole proprietors pay for their employees' health or disability insurance reduce both their income and self-employment tax liabilities.

Example 11: Dr. Allen Bell operates a medical practice as a sole proprietorship. In 2015, Allen paid $4,000 for his employees' health insurance and $6,000 for his own health insurance. Allen's profits from his sole proprietorship are $84,000 before taking into consideration the health insurance paid during the year. On his 2015 tax return, Allen deducts the $4,000 of premiums paid for his employee's health insurance against the gross income from his business and reports $80,000 of business profits. This amount is included in Allen's AGI, along with his other personal items of AGI. Allen's AGI is reduced by the $6,000 paid for his own health insurance. If Allen's other items of AGI total $50,000, his AGI would equal $124,000 ($50,000 + $80,000 – $6,000). His regular income tax liability would be computed by applying the appropriate individual income tax rates to his taxable income ($124,000 AGI minus his deductions from AGI). Allen's self-employment tax will be computed based on his $80,000 net profit.

Example 12: Assume the same facts as in Example 11, except that Dr. Bell operates his medical practice as a personal service corporation, AB Medical. Allen Bell is an employee of the corporation and is included in the employees' group health insurance plan. In 2015, AB pays $10,000 for its employees' group health insurance. On its 2015 corporate income tax return, AB deducts the $10,000 paid for employees' health insurance. The FICA taxes owed on the salary paid to Allen will be shared by Allen and AB Medical.

 Spotlight: When employers deduct wage expense, it reduces their taxable income. The resulting tax savings to employers (and reduction in tax revenues by the government) from allowing deductions equals the amount of the deduction multiplied by the taxpayer's marginal tax rate. However, since these amounts are included in employees' gross income, the taxes generated from these wages equals the amount of taxable wages times the employee's marginal tax rate. Thus, while the government loses out on

---

[22] Code Sec. 61(a)(1).

[23] Code Sec. 106; Reg. § 1.106-1; Code Sec. 105, as amended by the Health Care and Education Reconciliation Act of 2010 (P.L. 111-152).

revenues when it allows a deduction for wage expense, it generates revenues by taxing the workers who ultimately use and control the amounts paid to them as compensation.

When employers pay health insurance premiums on behalf of their employees, the tax laws allow employers to deduct these costs against profits generated by the business and allow employees to exclude these benefits from gross income. The tax savings to businesses from the deduction represents the portion of the costs of providing health care to employees that is being subsidized by the government. To illustrate, take as an example a corporation with a 35-percent marginal tax rate that pays $10,000 in health insurance premiums for one of its employees during the year. The corporation's tax liability is reduced by $3,500 ($10,000 × 35%), and therefore, of the $10,000 of premiums paid, $6,500 of the costs are paid by the employer ($10,000 minus $3,500 reduction in tax liability) and $3,500 is paid by the federal government (via lost revenues). Because any medical expenses paid from this employer-provided health care plan are not taxable to the employee, the overall result is a net loss of revenues to the federal government.

The government's subsidizing of employee-provided benefits does not extend to all employee benefits. For example, the employer can deduct premiums it pays for disability insurance for its employees. Although the premiums paid by the employer are tax free to the employee, any benefits the employee receives from the disability policy are taxable. Thus, if an employer pays the entire premiums on a disability insurance policy, each year the employer deducts the cost of the premiums from its gross income, and there are no tax consequences to the employees. However, if in a given year an employee is injured and receives $20,000 in disability benefits, the entire $20,000 is taxable to the employee since the entire premiums were paid for by the employer.[24]

The Patient Protection and Affordable Care Act (PPACA). The Patient Protection and Affordable Care Act (PPACA) fundamentally alters the health care landscape for individuals and employers. Beginning in 2014 many individuals will be required to have minimum essential health insurance coverage for themselves and their dependents or otherwise pay a shared responsibility penalty each month for noncompliance.[25] The requirement to maintain minimum essential health coverage is known as the "individual mandate." Minimum essential health insurance coverage includes coverage under any of the following: an eligible employer-sponsored plan, an individual market plan (health insurance coverage offered to individuals other than in connection with a group health plan), self-funded coverage offered to students by universities, an employer's grandfathered health plan, coverage under Medicaid or Medicare, or other government sponsored coverage.

Small businesses, self-employed individuals, and qualified individuals can purchase health insurance coverage through the health insurance Marketplace (also known as the Affordable Insurance Exchange) which opened on October 1, 2013 in all 50 states and the District of Columbia. Some states operate their own Marketplace while in other states the Marketplace is run by the federal government. The Marketplace has five levels of coverage: bronze, silver, gold, platinum, and catastrophic. Eligible middle- and lower-income individuals who obtain coverage through the Marketplace may qualify for a premium assistance tax credit, which is a refundable tax credit.

A large employer (an employer with 50 or more full time employees) must offer its full-time employees (and their dependents) the opportunity to enroll in minimum essential health coverage under an eligible employer-sponsored plan. Starting in 2015 if a large employer does not offer minimum essential coverage to its full-time employees (and their dependents), the employer may be subject to penalties if any of its full-time employees enroll in an Exchange and receives a premium assistance tax credit.[26] This is known as the "employer mandate."

---

[24] Code Secs. 104 and 105(a).
[25] Code Sec. 5000A.

[26] Code Sec. 4980H.

Small employers that provide health care coverage to its employees may claim a tax credit to help offset the cost of employer-provided health coverage. An eligible small employer may claim a 50-percent tax credit (35-percent in the case of a tax-exempt eligible small employer) for premiums it pays toward health coverage for its employees. Generally, an eligible small employer is an employer that has no more than 25 full-time employees and the average annual wages of these employees is not greater than $50,000.[27] (For a discussion of the credit, see ¶ 1115.)

.02 Flexible Spending Accounts (FSAs)

As a way of helping subsidize health care costs, the federal government allows employers to provide their employees with the opportunity to contribute to accounts from which unreimbursed health care costs (not including health insurance premiums) can be made. This type of account, called a **flexible spending account (FSA)**, can also be offered to employees to cover their dependent care costs. An FSA allows employees to elect to set aside each year pre-tax wages from which they can pay up to $2,500 of their qualified health care costs (in the case of health FSAs) or up to $5,000 of their qualified child care costs (in the case of dependent care FSAs).[28] For health FSAs, the amount of the limitation is indexed for inflation.[29] The cap is $2,550 for 2015.[30] Amounts employees contribute to these accounts are done automatically through employer withholdings. FSAs benefit employees because amounts from their salaries that are contributed to FSAs do not show up as taxable wages on their W-2s, thus making them paid with pre-tax dollars. Accordingly, employees who contribute to FSAs pay less tax than they would if they did not participate.

Employees can contribute annually to each type of FSA their employer offers. Therefore, when an employer offers both types of FSAs and for health FSAs allows its employees to contribute a maximum of $2,500, adjusted for inflation, employees can elect to contribute up to $7,500 annually to their two FSA accounts. However, these two accounts are kept separate from one another, so only amounts spent on qualified health care can be reimbursed from the employee's health FSA. Likewise, only amounts the employee spends on qualified dependent care can be reimbursed from the employee's dependent care FSA.

Example 13: Julie Adams' employer offers both health and dependent care FSAs for its employees. Julie's employer allows its employees to contribute a maximum of $2,500 to their health FSA. Julie has the option of participating in one, both, or neither FSA plan. Assuming that Julie elects to participate in both FSAs, she can contribute up to $2,500 to her health FSA and $5,000 to her dependent care FSA. If she contributes the maximum possible amount, Julie's taxable wages will be reduced by $7,500.

As employees pay for unreimbursed qualified medical costs, they submit their receipts for reimbursement from their health FSA accounts.[31] Likewise, as employees who contribute to dependent care FSAs pay qualified child care costs, they submit their receipts for reimbursement. Because these amounts are paid for with pre-tax dollars, each expenditure that is reimbursed through an FSA account reduces the employee's out-of-pocket costs for the expenditure. In conformity with IRS regulations an employer may allow its employees with a health FSA to pay their medical costs with an employer-provided debit, credit or stored value card.[32] A similar rule applies to dependent care FSAs.

Example 14: Todd Smalls works for a company that offers its employees a cafeteria plan that includes a health FSA. Todd participates in the company's health FSA by contributing $1,300 during the year. Todd does not participate in any other FSA or tax deferred compensation plan. In 2015, Todd earns $30,000, which includes his contributions to his health FSA. By participating in his employer's health FSA, Todd's

---

[27] Code Sec. 45R, as added by the Patient Protection and Affordable Care Act (P.L. 111-148).

[28] Code Secs. 125(d)(2)(D) and 129; Prop. Reg. § 1.125-5.

[29] Code Sec. 125(i)(1) as amended by the Patient Protection and Affordable Care Act (P.L. 111-148).

[30] Rev. Proc. 2014-61, IRB 2014-47, October 30, 2014.

[31] Qualified medical costs conform to the definition used for the medical expense itemized deduction. The cost of over-the-counter medication will be reimbursed through a health FSA if it is a prescribed drug or insulin. Code Sec. 106(f).

[32] Prop. Reg. § 1.125-6.

taxable wages are reduced by amounts he contributes to his FSA, and accordingly, his taxable wages for the year are $28,700 ($30,000 – $1,300). Had Todd not participated in the FSA, his taxable wages would have been $30,000. If Todd's marginal tax rate is 15 percent, he saves $195 ($1,300 × 15%) in federal income taxes by participating in the FSA.

Although his take-home pay is reduced by the $1,300 that the company with-holds from his paychecks and contributes to the health FSA plan, the first $1,300 of his out-of-pocket medical expenses are paid from the FSA plan. Accordingly, Todd's total out-of-pocket costs for the first $1,300 of unreimbursed medical expenses equal $1,105 ($1,300 – $195 taxes saved). In contrast, if Todd had not participated in the company's health FSA plan, the $1,300 of unreimbursed medical costs would have cost him $1,300 and he likely would not receive any tax benefit for his medical expenses because only amounts in excess of 10 percent of AGI are deductible as itemized deductions.[33] Thus, by participating in the health FSA plan, Todd is able to pay for the first $1,300 of unreimbursed medical costs with pre-tax dollars.

The downside to FSAs is their "use it or lose it" feature. If the employee does not spend the amounts they contribute during the year on qualified expenses, then the amounts not used are forfeited back to the employer.[34] To be reimbursed for these amounts, employees must submit their documentation to their employer no later than March 31 of the subsequent year for calendar year plans. Amounts normally must be spent by the end of the plan year in which they were contributed in order to avoid being forfeited; however, the IRS allows employers to change their plans to allow employees a grace period of up to 2½ months after the end of the plan year (March 15 of the following year for calendar year plans) to spend amounts they contributed during the prior year.[35]

Example 15: In 2015, Julie Adams contributes $2,500 to her employer's health FSA and $5,000 to her employer's dependent care FSA. Before the end of 2015, Julie's employer changes its FSA plans and allows employees until March 15, 2016, to spend amounts they contributed during 2015. During 2015, Julie submits receipts totaling $2,000 for her medical expenses and $4,000 for her dependent care expenses. This leaves Julie with unspent amounts in her health and dependent care FSAs of $500 ($2,500 – $2,000) and $1,000 ($5,000 – $4,000), respectively. On March 15, 2016, Julie submits receipts for $500 in medical costs and $1,000 of dependent care costs paid between January 1, 2016, and March 15, 2016. Because Julie incurred these expenses during the grace period allowed under the plan, she will be reimbursed for these amounts and will not lose any of the $7,500 that she contributed to her FSA plans during 2015. As a result of contributing a total of $7,500 to her employer's FSA plans, Julie's taxable wages are reduced by $7,500. Assuming Julie's marginal tax rate is 25 percent, her tax liability will be reduced by $1,875 ($7,500 × 25%). Thus, Julie's total out-of-pocket costs for the $7,500 of receipts she submits for health and dependent care costs is actually $5,625 ($7,500 – $1,875).

Example 16: Assume the same facts as in Example 15, except that Julie's employer did not change its plans to allow reimbursement for expenses incurred after the end of the year. In this scenario, Julie would only have been reimbursed for expenses paid during 2015 that she submitted by the March 31, 2016, deadline. Consequently, she would have lost $500 of her health FSA and $1,000 of her dependent care FSA. Julie's taxable wages for 2015 are still reduced by $7,500, and her 2015 tax liability is lower by $1,875. However, the $1,500 withheld from her pay that she could not utilize from her FSAs is lost and effectively reduces her overall benefit to participating in the FSA plans to $375 ($1,875 taxes saved – $1,500 forfeited).

---

[33] For individuals (or their spouses) age 65 and older the medical expense threshold will continue to be 7.5 percent until 2017.

[34] Prop. Reg. § 1.125-5(c).

[35] Prop. Reg. § 1.125-1(e).

To reduce the sting of the "use it or lose it" feature of health FSAs, the IRS has announced relief for health FSAs by allowing a new up-to-$500 carryover option for year-end balances.[36] The carryover amount will not count toward the following year's $2,500 inflation-adjusted salary reduction limit. Any unused health FSA year-end balance above $500 will be forfeited. This carryover option is effective for plan years starting in 2013. To provide for this new option employers must amend their plan. A health FSA cannot have both a carryover and a grace period: it can have one or the other or neither. Employers that have a grace period and want to adopt this new carryover option must eliminate their grace period. To be effective for 2013, the IRS will allow employers until the end of their 2014 plan year to amend their plans.

A health FSA should not be confused with a health reimbursement arrangement (HRA). Some of the rules regarding health FSAs and HRAs are similar such as amounts are used to reimburse medical expenses. However, HRAs are funded solely by the employer, not on a salary reduction basis. The use-it-or-lose-it rule does not apply to HRAs and any amounts remaining in an HRA can be carried forward.[37]

.03 Cafeteria Plans

A cafeteria plan is a written, employer-sponsored plan under which the participants have the opportunity to choose from a variety of benefits they want to receive and/or participate in. Only workers properly designated as employees can participate in a cafeteria plan.[38] A cafeteria plan gets its name because participants may choose among two or more benefits consisting of cash and qualified nontaxable benefits. If the participant chooses to receive cash from the plan, the amount received is included in the employee's gross income as compensation and is deductible as a wage expense by the employer. Because these amounts represent taxable wages, they are subject to withholding, as well as FICA and unemployment taxes. If the employee chooses to receive qualified benefits, these amounts are generally excluded from the employee's gross income. These types of benefits are often referred to as **perquisites,** as they represent a privilege employees are entitled to receive. Workers classified as independent contractors are not eligible for these benefits.

Qualified benefits include FSAs (previously discussed), up to $50,000 of group-term life insurance coverage, adoption assistance, disability benefits, and accident and health benefits. Although participation in a cafeteria plan is restricted to employees, employers can require a minimum of three years of employment before an employee is eligible to participate in the plan.[39] The three-year minimum employment requirement is optional, thus employers have the option of allowing employees with less than three years of employment to participate. However, whatever minimum employment requirement is chosen by the employer, it must apply equally to all eligible employees. Once the employment requirement is satisfied, the employee must be allowed to participate in the plan. Cafeteria plans are also subject to other discrimination rules that are beyond the scope of this discussion.[40] Employers deduct the costs they pay or incur in offering these benefits to their employees as employee benefits.

.04 Other Employee Fringe Benefits

Employers may provide their employees with several noncash fringe benefits that are not taxable to the employee but are deductible by the employer. These include reimbursing employees for qualified transportation and relocation costs, as well as providing qualified retirement planning services and educational assistance to employees.[41] These benefits are excluded from the employee's wages for purposes of income and FICA tax withholding. In addition, the employer is not responsible for FICA or unemployment taxes on these amounts.[42] A fringe benefit program may not discriminate in favor of officers, owners, and highly compensated employees. If the benefits are

---

[36] Notice 2013-71, IRB 2013-47, 532, November 18, 2013.

[37] Notice 2002-45, 2002-2 CB 93, June 26, 2002.

[38] Code Sec. 125(d); Prop. Reg. § 1.125-1.

[39] Code Sec. 125(g)(3); Prop. Reg. § 1.125-7(b)(2).

[40] For more on these restrictions, *see* Code Sec. 125(b)(2); Prop. Reg. § 1.125-7; and Notice 2010-78, IRB 2010-49, 808, December 6, 2010.

[41] Code Sec. 132 and Code Sec. 127.

[42] IRS Publication 15-B (For use in 2015).

discriminatory, then only employees receiving benefits who are not members of the favored group can exclude the benefits from gross income. Those in the favored group who receive benefits must include the value of the benefits received in gross income as compensation.[43] Consequently, these taxable benefits would be subject to income and FICA tax withholdings, as well as FICA and unemployment taxes that must be paid by the employer.

Example 17: A department store offers a 15-percent discount as a noncash fringe benefit to its regular employees and a 25-percent discount to a favored group (officers, owners, and highly compensated employees). Because the fringe benefit program is discriminatory, the entire discount members of the favored group receive is includible in their gross income, while the nonfavored employees may continue to exclude the 15-percent discount they receive.

The personal use of an employer provided cell phone which is provided to an employee primarily for noncompensatory business reasons, is treated as a fringe benefit.[44]

Qualified transportation. In general, expenses employees pay in commuting to and from home and work are not deductible.[45] However, when an employer offers transportation fringe benefits to its employees, some of the employee's transportation and parking costs can be reduced by having them pay for these costs with pre-tax dollars. This is accomplished by having amounts withheld from the employees' pay (subject to monthly limits, see below) and then having the employee submit documentation to be reimbursed for qualified transportation and parking costs. In many ways, this is similar to how FSAs work.

Alternatively, an employer may provide their employees with parking benefits, transit passes, transportation to and from work in a commuter vehicle (such as a van), or may reimburse employees for the cost of such benefits on a tax-free basis, as long as the benefits are provided in addition to, and not in lieu of, other compensation. In the case of qualified parking, the excludable benefit in 2015 is limited to $250 per month. In the case of the aggregate value of transit passes and commuter highway vehicle transportation, the excludable benefit is $130 per month. Congress may increase the amount of this benefit so that it has parity with the amount of the excludable benefit for qualified parking. Qualified transportation fringes also includes qualified bicycle commuting reimbursements in which the employer provides benefit to employees who commute to/from work using a bike.[46] The excludable benefit is $20 per month in which (1) the employee uses a bike for a substantial portion of travel between the employee's home and the place of employment, and (2) the employee does not receive any other transportation fringe benefits. The limits for these benefits are adjusted annually for inflation (with the exception of the bicycle commuting fringe benefit).[47]

Example 18: In 2015, Warren Smith receives from his employer qualified parking valued at $260 per month. Because the value of the parking exceeds the amount allowed by $10 a month ($260 – $250), Warren's employer must include $120 ($10 × 12 months) in his 2015 taxable wages on his Form W-2. Warren's gross income increases by the $120 of additional wages; and the employer's wage expense increases by $120.

Relocation costs. Amounts employers pay or reimburse employees for qualified moving expenses are not taxable to employees, but are deducted by the employer.[48] Qualified moving expenses include costs incurred in relocating an employee and the employee's family so that the employer can begin work in a new location. These costs include the cost of hiring a moving company to pack and move the family's personal belongings as well as reimburse the employee to get to the new location (including $.23 per mile in 2015 if the employee's own automobile is used; however, no reimbursement is allowed for meals en route).[49]

---

[43] Reg. § 1.132-8.

[44] Notice 2011-72, IRB 2011-38, 407, September 14, 2011.

[45] Reg. § 1.162-2(e).

[46] Code Sec. 132(f)(1)(D).

[47] Code Sec. 132(f); Rev. Proc. 2014-61, IRB 2014-47, October 30, 2014.

[48] Code Sec. 132(a).

[49] Notice 2014-79, IRB 2014-53, December 10, 2014.

Only reimbursement of qualified moving expenses for moves deemed necessary can be excluded from an employee's gross income (and therefore deductible as qualified moving expenses by the employer). A move is considered justified if it passes both the time and mileage tests. The *mileage test* is met if the employee's commute to the new job would increase by at least 50 miles. Thus, the distance between the employee's current residence and the location of the new job must be 50 miles further than the distance between the employee's current residence and the location of the old job. The *employment test* is met if the employee is employed full-time in the new location for at least 39 of the first 52 weeks after the move. It is not necessary that the 39 weeks be consecutive or with the same employer.[50]

Any amounts an employer reimburses its employees for moving expenses that do not qualify as deductible moving costs are taxable as additional wages to the employee and are deductible as wage expense by the employer. Hence, these amounts would be subject to withholding from the employee's wages as well as FICA and unemployment taxes by the employer.[51]

Example 19: Luisa Landrey receives a promotion from her employer and must relocate to New York City where the company's corporate headquarters are located. Her employer pays her relocation costs, which include $3,000 to professional movers for packing and relocating her personal belongings and $220 for actual hotel and transportation costs en route to New York City. Her employer also reimbursed Luisa $600 that she had to pay to her landlord in Chicago to cancel her lease agreement.

Luisa's qualified moving expenses total $3,220 ($3,000 + $220). The lease cancellation costs are not qualified moving expenses. The $600 is added to Luisa's taxable wages and therefore is subject to income and FICA withholding. Her employer deducts the amounts it reimburses for qualified moving expenses against its taxable income. The nonqualified moving expenses are deductible as wage expense, as are the payroll taxes paid by her employer on the additional taxable wages.

Sole proprietors can deduct amounts they reimburse to their employees for relocation expenses provided that the amounts reimbursed are for qualified moving expenses. Sole proprietors can also deduct as moving expense amounts they pay to move themselves and their families to a new location, provided they pass the mileage test and a more stringent time test. In order for a sole proprietor to deduct moving expenses, the proprietor must also work full-time during 78 of the first 104 weeks after relocating to the new location. As with employees, these weeks need not be consecutive.[52] Although these qualified moving expenses are deducted in arriving at the proprietor's AGI, they cannot be used to reduce business profits.[53] Hence, these amounts reduce the proprietors' income tax liability but not their self-employment taxes. Self-employment taxes are discussed in greater detail in Chapter 13.

Educational assistance. Employers can provide their employees with and deduct amounts paid to further their employees' education. In return, employees can exclude up to $5,250 per year of employer-provided educational assistance.[54] If an employee works for more than one employer, then the $5,250 cap applies to the aggregate amount of educational assistance benefits received from all employers.[55] Any excess of benefits over $5,250 that cannot be excluded as job-related education (see ¶ 608) are included in the employee's wages, and therefore subject to withholding and employment taxes. The amounts included in the employees' gross income as wages would be deducted by the employer as wage expense.

Example 20: In 2015, the PG Law Firm, LLC establishes an educational assistance program for its employees that reimburses up to $5,250 per year for undergraduate and graduate level course work. Samuel Johnson, a paralegal who works for PG, is working on his

---

[50] Code Sec. 217(c)(2).
[51] Code Sec. 82.
[52] Code Sec. 217(c)(2)(B); Reg. § 1.217-2(c)(4)(i)(b).

[53] Code Sec. 1402(a).
[54] Code Sec. 127; Notice 96-68, 1996-2 CB 236.
[55] Code Sec. 127(a)(2).

law degree and incurs $5,000 of qualified educational expenses during the year. When PG reimburses Samuel $5,000 for his educational expenses, he is not required to include these amounts in his gross income. However, PG is allowed to deduct the $5,000 as an employee benefit on its tax return.

Adoption assistance. Employers can also provide their employees with financial assistance in the adoption of a child. Employees may exclude from gross income amounts paid or expenses incurred by an employer for the employee's qualified adoption expenses pursuant to a qualified adoption assistance program.[56] The exclusion is for each effort to adopt an eligible child and is cumulative over all tax years, rather than being an annual limitation. However, amounts excluded are subject to FICA and unemployment taxes. For 2015, the total amount excludable for the adoption of a child cannot exceed $13,400.[57] The exclusion is reduced starting when the employee's modified AGI exceeds $201,100 and is fully phased-out when modified AGI is $241,010 or more. The amount of the exclusion and the phase out range are adjusted annually for inflation.[58]

Qualified adoption expenses include reasonable and necessary adoption fees, court costs, attorney's fees, and other expenses that are directly related to, and the principal purpose of which is, the legal adoption of an eligible child. An eligible child is an individual who has not attained the age of 18 as of the time of adoption, or who is physically or mentally incapable of caring for him or herself.[59]

Example 21: In 2015, under its adoption assistance program, Universal Corporation pays $16,000 of qualified adoption expenses on behalf of its employee, Sarah Knight, in connection with her efforts to adopt an eligible child. The $16,000 includes $6,000 of qualified adoption expenses to an agency for an unsuccessful attempt to adopt a child plus $10,000 of qualified adoption expenses to another agency for the successful final adoption of a different child. In 2015, Sarah's modified AGI is $80,000. Of the $16,000 that Sarah receives from Universal, $13,400 is excluded from her gross income. The remaining $2,600 ($16,000 – $13,400) is taxed to her as additional wages in 2015. Universal deducts the entire $16,000 on its tax return—$13,400 as a qualified employee benefit and $2,600 as wage expense.

¶ 603 Contributions Made to Employees' Retirement Plans

Contributions made by the employer to an employee's qualified retirement plan plus any subsequent amounts those contributions earn are not taxed to the employee until withdrawn. Some employer's plans allow employees to contribute to the retirement plans. In most cases the amounts are contributed with pre-tax dollars, meaning that the employee's taxable wages are reduced by any contributions they make during the year. Since the contributions both the employer and employee make plus any earnings that accumulate over the years are eventually taxed when withdrawn (presumably after retirement), these amounts are not tax-free, but instead grow tax deferred.[60] Income that is never taxed is known as an exclusion. When income or gain is postponed to some future point in time but is eventually taxed, the term used to describe this is **tax deferred**.

The annual contributions employers make to retirement plans for their employees are deductible and therefore reduce business profits. Self-employed individuals can establish a variety of retirement plans and make contributions to those plans for both themselves and their employees. Although amounts sole proprietors contribute to such plans are also deductible, only contributions made on behalf of the employees reduce business profits. Hence, contributions sole proprietors make to their own retirement plans reduce their income tax liability reported on their individual income tax returns, but they do not reduce net earnings from the business and, consequently, do not reduce a sole proprietor's self-employment taxes. The specific rules regarding retirement plans

[56] Code Sec. 137.
[57] Rev. Proc. 2014-61, IRB 2014-47, October 30, 2014.
[58] Code Sec. 137(f).
[59] Code Sec. 23(d)(2).
[60] Code Sec. 401.

offered by self-employed businesses are discussed in Chapter 13. The following discussion focuses on the types of retirement plans businesses can offer their employees and the employer's costs associated with each type of plan. As you will see, some retirement plans are funded entirely by employer's contributions, whereas other plans are funded with contributions from employers and employees, or from employee contributions only.

.01 Qualified Retirement Plans

Only contributions to qualified retirement plans can receive tax deferred treatment. A qualified plan cannot be offered only to key employees, and consequently, most qualified retirement plans must be made available to all full-time employees after a specified length of service.[61] Although further discussion as to what constitutes a qualified retirement plan is beyond the scope of this textbook, employers only can deduct contributions they make to qualified plans.[62] Contributions to nonqualified plans are taxed to employees as additional compensation and accordingly would be deducted as wages expense (and be subject to income, employment, and unemployment taxes).

There are two basic types of qualified retirement plans: defined benefit plans and defined contribution plans. A **defined benefit plan** promises participants specified benefits during retirement years and continuing until the death of the participant, and often until the death of the spouse of the participant.[63] The amounts that can be expected upon retirement are often a function of the employee's length of service to the company as well as the level of compensation earned during those years. Typically the benefits are indexed annually to cover inflation.

Example 22: An employee's defined benefit plan specifies that for each year of service, the employee will receive benefits equal to two percent of the average pay during his last three years of service. Annual benefits are increased three percent annually for inflation, and payments to the participant's spouse are reduced by 50 percent upon the participant's death. Jake Winters retires after working for the company for 35 years. His salary averaged $80,000 during his last three years. Jake can expect to receive pension benefits of $56,000 during his first retirement year ($80,000 × 2% × 35 years) and $57,680 during the second year ($56,000 plus 3% of $56,000).

Under a defined benefit plan, benefits paid to employees are based on the employee's length of service and compensation earned over the years of employment. At the time contributions are made to these plans, these amounts are not known with any degree of certainty and therefore must be estimated. In addition, once benefits begin, they generally continue for the life of the participant (and of the spouse in many cases), and since this length of time is unknown, additional factors must be estimated adding to the uncertainty regarding the contributions necessary each year to adequately fund these types of retirement plans. The calculation of contributions to a defined benefit plan is extremely complex and generally must be performed by an actuary, who is a professional trained in this area. Amounts contributed to a defined benefit plan are contributed to one account and not designated to any of the plan participants.[64] Typically, the employer is responsible for a large portion of the contributions made to defined benefit plans. This reason, plus the costly administrative costs incurred in offering these plans, may explain why the number of employers offering defined benefit plans to their employees has declined significantly over the past couple of decades.

Under a **defined contribution plan**, the employer can make specific contributions on behalf of each employee covered under the plan. The amount of the contribution is usually a percentage of the employee's compensation. Unlike contributions to defined benefit plans, contributions to defined contributions plans must be allocated among individual accounts maintained for each participant. Thus, these accounts resemble individual retirement savings accounts. At retirement, employees are

---

[61] Code Sec. 416.
[62] Code Sec. 404.

[63] Code Sec. 414(j).
[64] Reg. § 1.401-1(b)(1)(i).

entitled to whatever the balance has accumulated in their own accounts.[65] A 401(k) plan is a popular defined contribution plan.

.02 Employer Contributions

Contributions to qualified plans are generally deductible by the employer in the year in which they are paid, regardless of whether the employer uses the cash or accrual method. However, in certain instances a payment will be considered as paid by the end of the preceding tax year.[66] Due to the attractiveness of the tax deferral feature of retirement accounts, the Code limits the amounts that can be contributed to retirement plans each year. Different limits apply depending on the type of retirement plan offered by the employer and the limits are indexed annually for inflation. The Code limits the maximum amount that employers can contribute on behalf of an employee to a defined contribution plan to the *lesser of* (1) 100 percent of a participant's compensation or (2) a specified amount ($53,000 for 2015), which is adjusted annually for inflation.[67] The calculation of the amounts that need to be contributed to a defined benefit plan each year to provide adequate benefits to participants upon retirement is extremely complex and requires the assistance of an actuary.[68] However, the Code limits the amounts of an employee's compensation that may be taken into account in the calculation to the *lesser of* (1) a dollar amount ($210,000 for 2015), or (2) 100 percent of the participant's average compensation for the three highest consecutive years.[69]

To discourage taxpayers from using qualified retirement plans as tax deferred savings accounts for purposes other than retirement, Congress imposed a special 10-percent tax on early distributions.[70] The 10-percent tax on early distributions is assessed against the employee on their individual income tax return. The 10-percent tax will not apply if the distribution from the plan qualifies for one of the exceptions to the penalty (e.g., the employee is at least 59½).

 GAAP vs. Code: For tax purposes, accrual method taxpayers deduct contributions to qualified plans in the year in which they are paid. For financial statement purposes, corporations expense contributions in the year to which they are accrued, regardless of when they are paid. Thus, should a corporation accrue amounts that are not paid until the following tax year, this temporary difference will result in a difference between net income and taxable income in both the year accrued and in the year paid. The difference would require an adjustment to net income (that is, an increase to net income in the year accrued, followed by a decrease in the year paid) when reconciling net income to taxable income on the corporate tax return.

.03 Simplified Employee Pension (SEP) Plans

Simplified employee pension (SEP) plans are geared toward smaller employers who may be discouraged by the complexities of establishing a regular qualified plan.[71] Under a SEP, the employer agrees to make contributions to an individual retirement account (IRA) for each eligible employee. To establish a SEP plan, the following three conditions must be met.

1. The employer must execute a formal written agreement to provide benefits to all eligible employees,

2. The employer must provide certain information about the plan to each eligible employee, and

---

[65] Code Sec. 414(i).

[66] Code Sec. 404(a)(6); Rev. Rul. 76-28, 1976-1 CB 106, modified by Rev. Rul. 76-77, 1976-1 CB 107.

[67] Code Sec. 415(c)(1)(A). Notice 2014-70, IRB 2014-48, 905, November 21, 2014.

[68] See Code Secs. 412, 430, and 404(a)(1)(A)(ii) and (iii).

[69] Code Sec. 415(b); Notice 2014-70, IRB 2014-48, 905, November 21, 2014.

[70] Code Sec. 72(t)(1).

[71] Code Sec. 408(k).

3. The employer must establish a SEP-IRA for each employee over the age of 20 whose compensation is at least $550 and who has performed services for the employer during at least three out of the preceding five calendar years.

For 2015, annual contributions by an employer to a SEP are excluded from the employee's gross income to the extent that the contributions do not exceed the *lesser of* (1) $53,000 or (2) 25 percent of the participant's compensation. If the employer exceeds the annual limit on contributions, the employee is generally taxed on the amount of the excess contributions as additional wages.[72]

The employer deposits its contributions in a SEP-IRA account set up for the individual employee. An employer is not required to make contributions every year, but in years the employer does make contributions, it must contribute amounts for each participant. Thus, if a sole proprietor establishes a SEP-IRA for himself and his employees, in order to contribute to his own retirement account, the sole proprietor must contribute to each eligible employee's respective accounts. The contributions that are made must be allocated among employees according to a written formula and must not discriminate in favor of highly compensated employees. A SEP can be established as late as the due date (including extensions) of the employer's tax return for the year.[73] Employers' SEP-IRA contributions for their employees are deductible as employee benefits and reduce business profits. Any contributions sole proprietors made to their own SEP-IRAs are deducted in computing AGI, but do not reduce business profits. Consequently, these contributions lower sole proprietors' income tax liabilities, but not their self-employment taxes.

Example 23: Paul Vargas is self-employed and has one employee, Cynthia Smith. Paul has adopted a SEP-IRA for his business and for 2015 decides to contribute the maximum 25 percent to the retirement plan. Cynthia's salary in 2015 is $30,000, and accordingly, Paul must contribute $7,500 ($30,000 × 25%) to her SEP-IRA. Paul will deduct the $7,500 contribution as a pension and profit-sharing expense against his business profits. The contribution he makes to his own SEP-IRA does not reduce business profits but is deducted in computing his AGI. Accordingly, the contribution Paul makes to his own retirement account reduces his income tax liability, but not his self-employment tax. The contribution he makes on behalf of his employee reduces both his income and self-employment taxes. Thus, Paul's out-of-pocket cost of contributing to his employee's retirement plan is less than his costs of contributing to his own retirement plan.

.04 401(k) and 403(b) Plans

401(k) plans are a very popular type of employer-sponsored defined contribution retirement plan. These plans, which are sometimes called cash or deferred arrangements (CODAs), allow employees to either elect to defer a portion of their salary or receive it in cash. Benefits paid in cash are taxable to the employee as wages and deducted as wage expense by the employer. Noncash benefits are not taxable to the employee, but are deducted by the employer as employee benefits. Most businesses can adopt 401(k) plans for their employees.[74] A 403(b) plan is very similar to a 401(k), except that a 403(b) plan is available to certain types of employees, including government workers. Unless otherwise stated in the discussion that follows, the rules that apply to 401(k) plans apply to 403(b) plans as well.

Limit on employee contributions. For 2015, the maximum amount of wages that employees can contribute to their 401(k) plans is $18,000. However, employees who will be at least 50 years old by the end of the year are able to make "catch up" contributions, which would allow them to contribute up to $6,000 more to their accounts.[75]

An employee's contributions to a 401(k) plan are not subject to income tax withholding to the extent that they do not exceed the maximum annual limit. However, these contributions are treated

---

[72] Code Sec. 402(h)(2) and 4973(a).
[73] Prop. Reg. § 1.408-7(b); Code Sec. 404(h).

[74] Code Sec. 401(k)(4)(B).
[75] Code Sec. 414(v).

as taxable wages for purposes of FICA and unemployment taxes.[76] As a general rule, extra amounts contributed to an employee's 401(k) plan by the employer (matching contributions) are not subject to income tax withholding and are exempt from FICA and unemployment taxes. Furthermore, employers' contributions to employees' 401(k) plans do not count towards the maximum annual limit.[77]

Qualification requirements. To be a qualified 401(k) plan, the plan must satisfy the following requirements.[78]

1. The plan must give the participant the option of having the employer contribute amounts to the plan or receiving those amounts in cash.

2. The plan must prohibit distributions except in certain situations, such as the participant reaching age 59½, the participant being severed from employment, the participant being severed from employment due to death or disability, the participant enduring a financial hardship, or the employer terminating the plan without establishing a successor plan.

3. The plan must provide that the amounts in the participant's account attributable to elective contributions are fully vested (nonforfeitable) at all times.

4. The plan can require as a condition of participation that an employee complete one year of service with the employer, but it cannot require any longer periods of employment to be completed.

5. The plan cannot place conditions on the benefits under the 401(k) plan or any other plan upon an employee's elective contributions. However, this rule does not prevent an employer from basing its contributions on the elective contributions of employees.

A hardship distribution is a distribution made because of the participant's immediate and heavy financial need, and is limited to the amount necessary to satisfy that financial need.[79] Amounts distributed to pay medical expenses; costs of post-secondary education for the participant, spouse, children or dependents; and expenditures to purchase, or to stave off eviction or foreclosure with respect to the participant's principal residence, all qualify as financial hardship distributions.[80] A hardship distribution is subject to the 10-percent tax on early distributions unless it qualifies for one of the exceptions to the tax penalty.[81]

In addition to the five special requirements listed above, a 401(k) plan must meet an annual nondiscrimination test. This test is used to determine if the contributions of highly-compensated employees exceed the contributions of rank and file employees by a specified ratio.[82] A safe harbor has been added for 401(k) plans that contain an automatic employee enrollment feature in which the employer makes elective contributions in an amount equal to a qualified percentage (not to exceed 10 percent) of the employee's compensation.[83] The employer is required to make matching contributions or a nonelective contribution of three percent of compensation to all participants.[84] Plans that satisfy the safe harbor requirements will be treated as satisfying the nondiscrimination rules. If a plan adopts the safe harbor rules, an employee must affirmatively elect not to have elective contributions made or can elect to change the level of the elective contributions.

.05 Roth 401(k) Plans

Employers can offer Roth 401(k) plans to their employees. Employees' contributions to a Roth 401(k) are made with after-tax funds, meaning that the wages used to contribute to a Roth 401(k) are reported in their taxable wages on their Form W-2s. Only the participant can contribute to a Roth

---

[76] Code Secs. 3121(v)(1) and 3306(r)(1). Notice 2014-70, IRB 2014-48, 905, November 21, 2014.

[77] Code Sec. 401(k)(3)(D).

[78] Code Sec. 401(k)(2) and (4).

[79] Reg. § 1.401(k)-1(d)(3)(i).

[80] Reg. § 1.401(k)-1(d)(2)(iv)(A).

[81] Code Sec. 72(t)(2). A hardship distribution to pay medical expenses to the extent the employee has deductible medical expenses for the year (whether the employee itemizes or not) is exempt from the 10-percent tax on early distributions.

[82] Code Sec. 401(k)(3)(A).

[83] Code Sec. 401(k)(13); Prop. Reg. § 1.401(k)-3.

[84] Code Sec. 401(k)(12).

401(k); employer contributions are not permitted.[85] Although contributions to Roth 401(k) plans are made with post-tax dollars, all amounts in a Roth 401(k) plan grow tax-free. Thus, when qualified distributions are eventually made from a Roth 401(k), both employee contributions and the accumulated earnings are exempt from tax. Roth 401(k) plans are subject to the same contribution limits that apply to 401(k) plans, including catch up provisions for participants age 50 or older.[86]

The amount of an individual's designated Roth contributions will be subject to the annual limit on elective deferrals, reduced by the amount of the participant's other elective deferrals under a 401(k) or 403(b) plan.[87] The applicable limit applies to the total of all of the employee's pre-tax elective deferrals (including contributions to a SEP and elective employer contributions to a SIMPLE plan) and after-tax Roth contributions.[88]

Example 24:   Earl Jones (age 46) participates in a 401(k) plan maintained by his employer. In 2015, he may designate up to $18,000 of his authorized elective deferrals as an after-tax Roth contribution if he makes no pre-tax contributions to his 401(k) plan. By contrast, if he makes pre-tax elective deferrals of $10,000 to his 401(k) plan, he may designate only $8,000 as a Roth contribution.

Unlike Roth IRAs, which are available only to taxpayers with an AGI below a certain level, qualified Roth contribution programs are available to any employee, regardless of income level, who is a participant in a 401(k) or 403(b) plan that allows Roth deferrals.

Qualified distributions from a Roth IRA are not included in the individual's gross income and are not subject to the 10-percent penalty for early withdrawals. To be treated as a *qualified distribution*, the Roth 401(k) must have been around for at least five years and distributions must be made for one of the following events:

1. The distribution is made on or after the date the participant reaches age 59½,
2. The distribution is made to a beneficiary (or the estate) after the participant's death, or
3. The distribution is made because the participant is disabled.[89]

.06 SIMPLE Plans

Employers with 100 or fewer employees that are paid at least $5,000 in compensation from the employer in the preceding year may adopt a retirement plan known as a Savings Incentive Match Plan for Employees (SIMPLE) plan.[90] Generally, the SIMPLE plan must be the employer's only qualified retirement plan. A SIMPLE plan allows employees to make elective contributions of up to $12,500 per year for 2015 and requires that employers make matching contributions.[91] Employees who are at least age 50 may make an additional catch-up contribution of $3,000 during 2015.

As with most other types of qualified plans, amounts contributed to the participant's account grow tax-deferred and are not taxed to the participant until withdrawn. Contributions employers make to their employee's SIMPLE accounts are deductible in the year the contributions are made. Unlike most qualified plans, SIMPLE plans are not subject to the nondiscrimination rules, top-heavy provisions, and other complex requirements that qualified plans must generally satisfy. Employers may set up a SIMPLE plan as a SIMPLE-IRA or as a SIMPLE-401(k).[92] Contributions employers make to their employees' SIMPLE-IRAs or SIMPLE-401(k)s are deducted as employee benefits and reduce business profits. However, contributions sole proprietors make to their own SIMPLE plans cannot reduce business profits, but are deducted in arriving at their AGI.

---

[85] Code Sec. 402A.

[86] Code Sec. 402A(c)(2); Code Sec. 402(g).

[87] Code Sec. 402A(c)(2); Code Sec. 402(g)(1).

[88] Code Sec. 402(g).

[89] Code Sec. 402A(d)(2)(A); Reg. §1.402A-1, Q&A 2.

[90] Code Sec. 408(p).

[91] Code Sec. 401(k)(11)(B)(i); Notice 2014-70, IRB 2014-48, 905, November 21, 2014.

[92] Code Secs. 408(p) and 401(k)(11); Prop. Reg. §1.401(k)-4.

Table 6-2 Summary of Retirement Plans Employers May Offer Their Employees

Retirement Plan	Requirements	Contribution Limits
Defined Benefit Plans		
Pension Plan	Contributions are calculated by an actuary.	The amount that would be projected to yield a benefit not to exceed the *lesser of* (1) a dollar limit ($210,000 in 2015) or (2) 100% of the employee's average compensation over the three highest consecutive years
Defined Contribution Plans		
401(k) Plan	Employees contribute using either pre-tax or after-tax wages. Employer matching permitted, but not required.	$18,000 $6,000 catch-up contribution for employees age 50 and older
Roth 401(k)	Employees contribute with after-tax dollars. Employer matching is not allowed.	$18,000 $6,000 catch-up contribution for employees age 50 and older
SIMPLE Plan	Available to employers with 100 or fewer employees who received at least $5,000 of compensation in the previous year. Employer matching required.	$12,500 $3,000 catch-up contribution for employees age 50 and older
Simplified Employee Pension (SEP) Plan	Employers must contribute to a 401(k) or IRA for each eligible employee. Contributions made entirely by employers.	The *lesser* of (1) $53,000 or (2) 25% of the participant's compensation

 GAAP vs. Code: The amount of the employer's contribution accrued on the company's financial statements may be different from the actual amount contributed to the employees' retirement plan. For tax purposes, the employer is only able to deduct the actual amount contributed to the employees' retirement plan. Generally, the contribution must be paid before the due date of the tax return (including extensions), thereby allowing the employer some flexibility in determining the amount of the contribution in order to reduce the company's taxable income. Any difference between the amount deducted in arriving at net income and the deduction taken on the corporate tax return would be reported as an adjustment to net income when reconciling it with taxable income on the corporate tax return.

¶ 604 Employment Taxes

Employers are responsible for payroll taxes imposed on wages they pay to their employees. Employers must match the amounts of social security and Medicare taxes that their employees pay and must also pay unemployment taxes on employees' wages. Businesses are not subject to payroll taxes on amounts they pay to independent contractors.

In 1935, Congress enacted the Federal Social Security Act, which established a federal unemployment insurance program and a program to provide old-age, survivors, and disability benefits to employees. Financing for the two programs is achieved through taxes imposed on both employers and employees under the **Federal Insurance Contributions Act (FICA)** and on employers under the **Federal Unemployment Tax Act (FUTA).** In 1950, the tax laws were amended to include FICA coverage for self-employed individuals. Financing for FICA for self-employed taxpayers is accomplished through the self-employment tax.

.01 Federal Insurance Contributions Act (FICA)

The old-age, survivors, and disability insurance (OASDI) portion of the FICA tax, commonly referred to as **social security taxes**, provides benefits to the elderly and their survivors as well as disabled individuals. In 1965, FICA was expanded to add a separate tax for hospital insurance (HI) for the elderly. This tax is commonly referred to as **Medicare taxes**. The FICA tax rate of 7.65 percent is comprised of 6.2 percent for social security taxes and 1.45 percent for Medicare taxes.

The rate is imposed on both the employer and employee for a combined rate of 15.3 percent. For employees and employers, the maximum amount of wages subject to social security taxes in 2015 is $118,500; whereas all wages are subject to the Medicare tax.[93] The wage ceiling for social security taxes is adjusted annually for inflation.

The maximum amount of social security tax that an employee is required to pay in 2015 is $7,347 ($118,500 × 6.2%). Employers are required to withhold social security taxes on all wages up to the maximum limit. Therefore, employees who receive wages from more than one employer during 2015 may have more than $7,347 of social security tax withheld during the year. This excess is claimed as a tax credit on the employee's individual tax return.

FICA wages. For purposes of FICA, the term wages means all remuneration for employment, including both cash and noncash compensation.[94] FICA wages include, but are not limited to, employees' wages, tips, bonuses, commissions, most employer-provided prizes and awards, and reimbursements of employees' business expenses under a nonaccountable plan. FICA wages also include employee contributions to an employer-provided retirement plan. Excluded from FICA wages are certain nontaxable fringe benefits and reimbursements to employees under an accountable plan. Also excluded from FICA wages are wages paid to the taxpayer's children who are under age 18 and who work for their parents in a trade or business operated as a sole proprietorship or a partnership (provided that each partner is the child's parent).

Example 25: In 2015, Karen Hodges earns $150,000 working at Quentin Development Company. At the end of the year Quentin pays Karen a $20,000 bonus. Karen's FICA wages equal $170,000 ($150,000 + $20,000), and the amount of FICA withheld from Karen's earnings for the year include the maximum amount withheld for social security taxes of $7,347 ($118,500 × 6.2%) plus $2,465 for Medicare taxes ($170,000 × 1.45%), which totals $9,812 ($7,347 + $2,465). Quentin matches these amounts and pays FICA taxes totaling $9,812. Quentin remits to the federal government $19,624 ($9,812 withheld from Karen's earnings plus $9,812 it pays in payroll taxes).

---

[93] Code Secs. 3101, 3111, and 3121.   [94] Code Sec. 3121(a).

For tax years beginning after 2012, employees with wages in excess of $200,000 ($250,000 married filing joint tax returns and $125,000 married filing separate tax returns), the employee share of Medicare taxes are increased by an additional .9 percent (to 2.35 percent).

Sole proprietors pay a combined rate of tax on self-employment income of 15.3 percent: a 12.4-percent component for social security (OASDI) and a 2.9-percent component for Medicare. For tax years beginning after 2012, sole proprietors are subject to an additional .9 percent Medicare tax on self-employment income in excess of $200,000 ($250,000 married filing joint tax returns and $125,000 married filing separate tax returns).

Tips an employee receives in the course of employment are subject to both federal income tax and FICA tax. Every employee who receives cash tips of $20 or more per month with one employer must report to their employer the total amount of tips they received during the period.[95] These taxable tips are then included as taxable wages on the employee's Form W-2 and therefore are subject to FICA taxes as well as income tax withholding.[96]

Large food or beverage establishments are required to allocate the amount of tips their employees earn in certain circumstances. These allocated tips are not subject to income tax withholding or FICA taxes. The employer reports the amount of the allocated tips on the employee's Form W-2. The employee includes the amount of the allocated tips in his or her taxable income and must also pay FICA taxes on the amount, unless the employee has adequate records to show he or she received less tips in the year than the allocated amount.

Normally, employers deduct their FICA contributions as an ordinary and necessary business expense. However, to encourage businesses to comply with the tax laws requiring them to impute tips on behalf of their employees, the federal government allows employers to take a tax credit equal to 100 percent of their contribution that result from amounts paid with respect to tips for food or beverages received by their employees, provided that the employee tips are not needed to allow the employee to earn a minimum wage.[97]

 Reason for the Rule: As you may recall from Chapter 1, all other things being equal, a tax credit is preferred over a tax deduction. By allowing employers to take a tax credit for 100 percent of the amounts they pay towards FICA on employees' tip income, the federal government is encouraging employers to report their employees' tips as taxable wages by rewarding them with tax incentives.

.02 Federal Unemployment Tax Act (FUTA) Taxes

FUTA was enacted by Congress to finance the federal unemployment program. Under FUTA, a tax is imposed on an employer at a specified rate on the first $7,000 in wages paid to each employee during a calendar year, regardless of the year used for accounting purposes. The FUTA tax rate is 6 percent.[98] The tax applies to the wages that are actually paid by the employer, regardless of the accounting method used.

FUTA wages. An employer is subject to FUTA taxes if the employer employs at least one person on one day in each of 20 weeks during the current or preceding calendar year or the employer pays at least $1,500 in wages during any calendar quarter in the current or prior year. Amounts paid for nontaxable fringe benefits, employer reimbursements under an accountable plan, and wages paid to children who are under age 21 who work for their parents (regardless of whether such work is in the taxpayer's trade or business) are not subject to FUTA tax. Also excluded from FUTA tax are wages paid to a spouse who works for the taxpayer's trade or business.

---

[95] Code Sec. 6053.
[96] Code Sec. 3102.

[97] Code Sec. 45B(b).
[98] Code Sec. 3301(2).

State unemployment taxes. Although the federal government provides funding for unemployment benefits, the responsibility for distributing those amounts to unemployed persons rests with the state governments. Accordingly, most states also impose unemployment taxes on employee wages. State tax rates range anywhere from zero percent to just over 10 percent, and the amount of wages subject to state unemployment taxes often exceeds the $7,000 maximum imposed by the federal government.

Employers are required to pay both the federal and state unemployment taxes. However, they are allowed to subtract from the amounts owed to the federal government contributions they make to the state, up to 5.4 percent of the first $7,000 of an employee's wages.[99] Thus, in a state that imposes a 5.4-percent tax rate or higher, the FUTA tax rate is reduced to .6 percent (6% minus 5.4%).

Example 26: In 2015, the M&R Manufacturing Company has taxable FUTA wages of $300,000. M&R's federal unemployment tax liability equals $18,000 ($300,000 × 6%); its state unemployment tax liability is $25,000. The state's tax rate exceeds 5.4 percent. M&R pays $25,000 to the state and reduces its obligation to the federal government by $16,200 ($300,000 × 5.4%). Thus, M&R's payment to the federal government for unemployment taxes equals $1,800 ($18,000 – $16,200). M&R's total unemployment taxes for the year are $26,800 ($25,000 + $1,800). It deducts this amount from its gross income on its income tax return.

Table 6-3 summarizes the requirements for paying FICA and FUTA taxes on employee compensation. Any amounts subject to FICA tax are subject to both social security and medicare taxes (with social security taxes limited to the first $118,500 of compensation during 2015). FICA taxes are paid by both the employer and employee. Only employers are subject to FUTA taxes.

Table 6-3 Amounts Subject to FICA and FUTA Taxes

Type of Payment	Subject to FICA Taxes?	Subject to FUTA Taxes?
Compensation for services performed in the United States, including taxable tips	Yes	Yes
Amounts contributed to dependent care assistance programs	Only to the extent the annual limits are exceeded ($5,000 in 2015)	Only to the extent the annual limits are exceeded ($5,000 in 2015)
Reimbursements for qualified educational assistance	Only to the extent the annual limits are exceeded ($5,250 in 2015)	Only to the extent the annual limits are exceeded ($5,250 in 2015)
Reimbursements for parking, transportation, and bicycle commuting	Only to the extent the monthly limits are exceeded (Qualified Parking $250, Transportation $130, and Bicycle commuting $20 in 2015)	Only to the extent the monthly limits are exceeded (Qualified Parking $250, Transportation $130, and Bicycle commuting $20 in 2015)
Reimbursements from an accountable plan	No	No

[99] Code Sec. 3302.

Type of Payment	Subject to FICA Taxes?	Subject to FUTA Taxes?
Reimbursements from an nonaccountable plan	Yes	Yes
Payments to a child employed by a parent (or partnership where each partner is a child's parent)	Not until the child reaches the age of 18	Not until the child reaches the age of 21
Payments to a spouse employed in the taxpayer's business	Yes	No
Payments to parents employed in their child's business	Yes	No
Payments for accident and health insurance premiums and group life insurance premiums	No, except for costs associated with group term life insurance coverage in excess of $50,000	No
Employer contributions to a qualified retirement plan, including 401(k) or SEP-IRA plans	No	No
Employees' elective contributions to an employer's 401(k) or SIMPLE plan	Yes	Yes

¶ 605 Meals and Entertainment Expenses

Taxpayers generally can deduct meal and entertainment expenses provided that the expenses are directly related to or associated with the taxpayer's trade or business. The taxpayer must substantiate the amounts spent and the business nature of the expense. Even if the taxpayer meets these requirements, typically only 50 percent of the meals and entertainment can be used to reduce business profits.

.01 Meals

The costs associated with meals are not deductible if neither the taxpayer nor an employee of the taxpayer is present at the meal. Also, no deduction is allowed for food and beverages to the extent that they are lavish or extravagant under the circumstances.

Example 27: Lucia Jones spent $100 for a business-related meal. If $40 of that amount is considered lavish and extravagant, it is not deductible and the remaining $60 is subject to the 50-percent deduction limit. Therefore, Lucia may deduct only $30 ($60 × 50%) for the meal in arriving at business profits.

Transportation workers. A greater percentage of the cost of meals consumed by certain transportation workers is allowed.[100] Eighty percent of the cost of meals are allowed as a deduction. The increased meal deduction is available for food or beverages consumed while away from home by an individual during, or incident to, a period of duty subject to the Department of Transportation's hours of service limitations. Individuals subject to the hours of service limitations include:

- Certain air transportation employees, such as pilots, crew, dispatchers, mechanics, and control tower operators;

- Interstate truck operators and interstate bus drivers;

- Certain railroad employees, such as engineers, conductors, train crews; and

- Certain merchant mariners.

 Reason for the Rule: This increase in the amount allowed to be deducted by transportation workers is intended to restore meal deductions to certain workers who are forced to eat away from home and are unlikely to abuse the deduction.

 GAAP vs. Code: For financial reporting purposes, all meals and entertainment expenses incurred are deducted in arriving at net income. For tax purposes, only a portion of deductible meals reduce taxable income. This differential treatment creates a permanent difference which must be added back to net income when reconciling net income to taxable income on the corporate tax return. For example, if a corporation incurs costs totaling $20,000 during the year for business meals, the entire $20,000 would be deducted in arriving at net income, but only $10,000 ($20,000 × 50%) would be deducted on the tax return. Therefore, when reconciling net income to taxable income, the $10,000 of disallowed business meal expense would be added back to net income.

.02 Entertainment

No deduction is allowed for any expense of an activity considered to be entertainment, amusement, or recreation, except to the extent that it is established that the expense was *directly related to* the active conduct of a trade or business. However, entertainment expenses incurred directly before or after bona fide business discussions that are *associated with* the active conduct of the business are allowed even though they are not directly related to the business.[101] The Tax Court ruled that expenses incurred in entertaining 200 people at a cocktail party were not directly related to the active conduct of a taxpayer's dental practice, even though the expenditures were motivated by business considerations and generated referral patients for the taxpayer.[102] The Tax Court also held that an attorney could not deduct the costs of hosting a birthday party as promotion and public relations business expenses.[103] Entertainment costs that meet the directly related to or associated with conditions are subject to the 50-percent limitation. Costs that do not qualify as entertainment expenses or any other deductible expense under the tax laws would be nondeductible expenditures.

Entertainment facilities. The deduction for tickets to any entertainment activity or facility is limited to the face value of the tickets.[104] This limitation does not apply to a ticket for a sports event that is organized for the primary purpose of benefiting a tax-exempt charitable organization, provided that all of the proceeds are contributed to the organization and the organization utilizes volunteers for substantially all of the work performed in carrying out the event. When a taxpayer leases a luxury skybox at a sports arena for more than one event, the deduction is limited to the cost

---

[100] Code Sec. 274(n)(3).

[101] Code Sec. 274(a)(1)(A); Reg. § 1.274-2(a).

[102] *J.E. Gardner*, 45 TCM 1116, Dec. 40,000(M), TC Memo. 1983-171.

[103] *J.L. Flaig*, 47 TCM 1361, Dec. 41,091(M), TC Memo. 1984-150.

[104] Code Sec. 274(l)(1).

of the highest-priced nonluxury box seat tickets generally held for sale to the public for the same event, multiplied by the number of seats in the skybox.[105]

Example 28: Playright Company paid $10,000 to rent a 10-seat skybox at Wrigley Field for three baseball games during the season. The cost of the highest-priced nonluxury box seat is $25. The deduction for the purchase of skybox seats is limited to 50 percent of the value of the highest-priced nonluxury skybox seats. Thus, Playright's tax deduction of the skybox will be limited to $375 (($25 × 10) × 3 games × 50%).

Example 29: Tiana Smith, an employee of Warner Enterprises, purchased four concert tickets on behalf of her employer and gave them to a client. Tiana was reimbursed by her employer under an accountable plan. Tiana paid a ticket agency $300 for the four tickets, which had a face value of $240. Warner can deduct $120 as entertainment expense ($240 × 50%) on its corporate tax return.

 GAAP vs. Code: For financial accounting purposes, the entire amount of entertainment expenses incurred during the year is deducted in arriving at net income. When calculating taxable income, only 50 percent of deductible entertainment expenses are allowed. The difference in these rules creates a permanent difference between net income and taxable income. When reconciling net income to taxable income on the corporate tax return, any disallowed amounts would need to be added back to net income. Thus, in Example 29, Warner Enterprises would add to net income the $180 ($300 − $120) disallowed entertainment expenses to arrive at the amount reflected in taxable income.

No deduction is allowed for amounts paid or incurred for dues and fees paid to social, athletic, sporting, or country clubs. Also, no deduction is allowed for any expense paid or incurred with respect to an entertainment, recreation, or amusement facility,[106] which includes any property that is owned, rented, or used by the taxpayer for entertainment. Entertainment facilities for which a taxpayer generally may not deduct any expenses include yachts, hunting lodges, fishing camps, swimming pools, tennis courts, bowling alleys, cars, airplanes, apartments, hotel suites, and homes located in a vacation resort. A taxpayer may, however, deduct out-of-pocket expenses for the business use of those facilities that are directly related to and associated with entertainment of customers at the facilities.

Example 30: Asten, Inc. owns a hunting lodge which is used by its executives for both business and personal purposes. During the year Asten incurs $10,200 of expenses to operate the lodge. The lodge was used by the company's executives 55 percent for business, which includes 35 percent for directly-related entertainment and 20 percent associated with entertainment. In addition, the corporation pays $2,000 for food and beverages in entertainment that was directly related to the active conduct of business and $1,200 for food and beverages in relation to entertainment that was associated with the active conduct of Asten's trade or business. When preparing its tax return for the year, Asten will be allowed to deduct 50 percent of the $3,200 ($2,000 + $1,200) of meal and entertainment expenses directly related to or associated with the active conduct of its business. It will not be allowed to deduct the lodge's operating expenses of $10,200.

 GAAP vs. Code: For financial reporting purposes, all entertainment expenses reduce net income. However for tax purposes, the deduction for entertainment is limited or sometimes disallowed, depending on the circumstances. For example, in Example 30,

---

[105] Code Sec. 274(l)(2).   [106] Code Sec. 274(a)(1)(B).

the $10,200 of operating expenses for the lodge plus all $3,200 of meal and entertainment expenses would be deducted on the income statement in arriving at net income. However, it can only deduct $1,600 ($3,200 × 50%) on its tax return. Accordingly, when reconciling net income to taxable income, Asten will add back the $11,800 difference ($13,400 total costs – $1,600) to net income.

Example 31: Zander Company is a member of the Golf Duffs Country Club so that its executives can use the facilities to entertain clients. Zander pays annual dues of $1,200 to Golf Duffs. Meal and entertainment expenses incurred at the club meet the *directly related to* or *associated with* tests and therefore, 50 percent are deductible. During the year, Zander incurs meal and entertainment expenses totaling $2,500. On its tax return, Zander is allowed to deduct $1,250 of the meals and entertainment costs ($2,500 × 50%). It cannot deduct the $1,200 of club dues.

Planning Pointer: Detailed records showing dates, amounts, places, the business relationship to the persons involved, and the business purpose are the best proof to assure deductibility of entertainment expense. There is adequate substantiation if the taxpayer maintains a notebook or similar record in which the information as to each element of an expense is recorded in a contemporaneous and consistent manner throughout the tax year. In addition, documentary evidence (such as itemized receipts or paid bills) is required for each expenditure of $75 or more.

Spotlight: Since only 50 percent of entertainment expenses can be deducted, businesses are better off classifying expenditures as something other than entertainment. For example, it would be to the taxpayer's advantage to classify an expenditure that could be viewed as either an entertainment or advertising expense as advertising. The furnishing of food and beverages, a hotel suite, a vacation cottage, or an automobile to a customer or member of his family is considered entertainment. Other activities generally considered to be entertainment include the entertaining of guests at nightclubs, football games, theaters, or prizefights, as well as the costs of hunting, fishing, vacation, and similar trips. However, the particular trade or business activity of the taxpayer claiming the deduction determines whether an activity is entertainment.[107] For example, a hunting trip is not entertainment to a professional big game hunter, but it would be considered entertainment to a clothing sales representative.

¶ 606 Travel Expenses

Travel and transportation are two types of expenses that employers may incur on behalf of their employees during the normal conduct of business. Accordingly, these amounts, whether paid directly by the employer or reimbursed to the employee under an accountable plan, are usually deductible under the general deductibility provisions of Code Sec. 162(a). Travel and transportation can also be deducted by a sole proprietor under this same Code provision. Travel expenses are those costs paid or incurred while traveling away from home overnight for business. Transportation expenses are costs paid or incurred while traveling around town on business.

Ordinary and necessary expenses incurred in the pursuit of business while away from home are deductible as business expenses.[108] Generally, business away from home expenses are travel costs incurred while temporarily away from home. Although the rules generally require an overnight stay, an individual does not have to be away from the tax home for an entire 24-hour day or from dusk to

---

[107] Reg. § 1.274-2(b)(1)(ii).

[108] Code Sec. 162(a)(2).

dawn, so long as the period of absence is substantially longer than a normal working day and, during the time away, it is reasonable for the traveler to need sleep or rest for the requirements of the job.[109]

The purpose of the travel may be to contact customers, to attend business and professional meetings, or to attend business and professional conventions and seminars. The types of expenses that may be incurred while traveling away from home include transportation costs (airplane, train or bus fares, and automobile expenses), meals and lodging to the extent that they are not lavish or extravagant and do not relate to purely personal activities, laundry and dry cleaning charges, taxicab fares, and tips.

.01 Away from Home

The location of a taxpayer's tax home for purposes of the "away from home" requirement is generally based on the facts surrounding the traveler's situation.[110] For years, the IRS insisted that for the purposes of deducting travel expenses, the tax home was the principal place of business or employment, regardless of where a residence is maintained.[111] Although the courts generally agreed with this assessment, some support exists for the position that a taxpayer's home is where his residence is located.[112] However, even if it is accepted that the tax home is where the principal place of business is located, the taxpayer may have two places of business. Thus, to determine which one is the taxpayer's *principal place of business*, the IRS employs a three-prong test which examines (1) the length of time spent in each location performing duties, (2) the degree of business activity in each location, and (3) the relative amount of income derived from each location.[113]

Temporary vs. indefinite. Only costs incurred while temporarily traveling away from home overnight are deductible. If the assignment is temporary in nature, the individual is considered away from home, and a travel expense deduction is allowed. If the assignment is for an indefinite period of time, the location of the assignment becomes the individual's new tax home, and the taxpayer may not claim traveling expenses while there.

In determining whether an assignment is temporary or indefinite, the Code applies fixed time frames based on the expected and actual duration of the assignment or employment.[114] Employment in a single location away from home that is expected to and, in fact, does last one year or less will be considered temporary. Employment expected to last more than one year will be treated as indefinite, regardless of whether the employment exceeds one year. Employment initially expected to last one year or less which is later expected to last longer than a year will be treated as temporary until the date the expectation changes.[115]

Example 32: Leo Strauss lives in Atlanta, where he works as an employee at Sealproof, Inc. During the year, Sealproof sends Leo to the company's headquarters in Los Angeles for a temporary assignment of 10 months. After nine months in Los Angeles, the company asked Leo to stay an additional five months. The company reimburses Leo for his travel expenses. Since during the first nine months Sealproof believed that Leo's assignment would last for one year or less, the travel expenses are deductible against gross income from the business. However, once the assignment was extended by five months and it became clear that Leo's assignment no longer met the definition of "temporary," all costs incurred after that point are no longer deductible travel expenses. If Sealproof continues to pay Leo's living expenses, those amounts will be taxable as additional wages to Leo (as deductible wage expense to Sealproof).

---

[109] Rev. Rul. 75-168, 1975-1 CB 58 and Rev. Rul. 75-170, 1975-1 CB 60.

[110] Rev. Rul. 75-432, 1975-2 CB 60.

[111] IRS Pub. 463, *Travel, Entertainment, Gift, and Car Expenses.*

[112] *W.R. Wallace*, CA-9, 44-2 USTC ¶ 9437, 144 F2d 407; *Burns v. Gray*, CA-6, 61-1 USTC ¶ 9294, 287 F2d 698; *R. Rosenspan*, CA-2, 71-1 USTC ¶ 9241, 438 F2d 905.

[113] *N.E. Soliman*, SCt, 93-1 USTC ¶ 50,014, 506 US 168, 113 SCt 701.

[114] Code Sec. 162(a).

[115] Rev. Rul. 93-86, 1993-2 CB 71.

Reason for the Rule: Commuting expenses are not deductible. When a stay away from home is expected to last more than a year, then the trip between work and home begins to resemble a commute rather than travel while away from home.

The IRS provides a safe harbor for the deduction of employee expenses paid or incurred for lodging while not traveling away from home (local lodging) if:

1. the lodging is necessary for the employee to participate fully in or be available for a bona fide business meeting, conference, training activity, or other business function,

2. the period of lodging does not exceed five calendar days and does not recur more frequently than once per calendar quarter;

3. the employer requires the employee to remain at the activity or function overnight; and

4. the lodging is not lavish or extravagant and does not provide significant personal pleasure, recreation or benefit.[116]

.02 Combined Business and Personal Travel

Sometimes when business owners or their employees travel out of town for business, they stay a few extra days to sightsee or to visit with friends and family. Although the expenses incurred during these personal days are not deductible, it does not prevent the business owner from deducting the expenses that are properly allocable to business. Travel expenses of a spouse, dependent, or other person accompanying the traveler are disallowed unless the companion is also an employee of the person paying for or reimbursing the expenses, the travel serves a bona fide business purpose, and the expenses are otherwise deductible.[117]

Example 33: Susan Harris, a self-employed attorney, makes a trip to Washington, D.C. to attend a conference sponsored by the American Bar Association. The trip lasted seven days, but she spent three days sightseeing. Susan will be able to deduct the costs associated with the business portion of her trip against her business profits on her tax return.

Domestic travel. When business owners or their employees travel within the United States on business, the costs of traveling to and from the business destination are fully deductible, assuming that the purpose of the trip is primarily for business. Generally the number of days spent on business versus for personal travel is indicative of whether the trip is primarily for business or personal in nature. Days spent en route to the business destination are usually considered business days. Even if the nature of the trip is primarily for business, and thus all expenses of traveling to and from the destination are fully deductible, only the business portion of the other costs of the trip are deductible.[118]

Example 34: Continuing with Example 33, assume that Susan's costs for the trip were $415 for airfare, $150 a night for a hotel room, $95 per day for meals, and $300 for sightseeing tours. Because over half of the days Susan was gone were spent conducting business, her trip was primarily for business purposes, and therefore, she can deduct the entire costs of the airfare against business profits. She also can deduct the hotel costs for the four days that were spent conducting business as well as 50 percent of the meals for those four days. She cannot deduct the costs associated with sightseeing (personal)—the three days of meals and lodging or the costs of the sightseeing tours.

Example 35: Mary Bright is employed by a CPA firm located in Long Island, New York. The firm sends Mary to a five-day conference in Miami on estate planning. After the conference, Mary spends four days visiting with her sister, who lives in Miami. The cost of

---

[116] Prop. Reg. § 1.162-31.

[117] Code Sec. 274(m)(3).

[118] Reg. § 1.162-2(b)(1).

Mary's round trip airfare to Miami is $300. The cost of lodging is $750, and meals during the conference are $250. After the conference, while visiting her sister, Mary incurs meal and entertainment expenses of $300. Because over half of the days were spent conducting business, Mary's trip is primarily for business purposes. If the firm reimburses Mary for the business portion of her trip under an accountable plan, she will be reimbursed $1,300 ($300 total costs of domestic airfare + $750 + $250). This amount will be excluded from Mary's gross income because the company reimburses her from an accountable plan. However, the CPA firm can only deduct $1,175 since only 50 percent of the business meals and entertainment are deductible ($300 airfare + $750 lodging + ($250 × 50% for meals)).

Foreign travel. When business owners or their employees travel away from home outside of the United States for business, generally all costs, including the costs of traveling to and from the destination, must be allocated between business and personal. This rule applies to expenses of foreign travel away from home that lasts more than seven consecutive days or if the number of personal days during the trip represents at least 25 percent of the days away from home.[119] No allocation of the costs of traveling to and from the destination is required on a foreign trip if the individual had no substantial control over arranging the business trip or if the person's taking of a personal vacation was not a major consideration in making the trip.[120] However, only the business portion of all other costs (lodging, 50 percent of meals and entertainment, etc.) is deductible.

Example 36: The president and controlling stockholder of Appleview Corporation takes a 15-day European trip, spending two days flying, eight days on business, and five days sightseeing. Since the trip lasted longer than seven days and the five personal days exceeded 3.75 days (25% of the 15 days away from home), only the business portion of all expenses is deductible. Thus, under an accountable plan, Appleview can only reimburse the president for two-thirds (10 business days ÷ 15 total days) of the cost of the trip. It can deduct the amounts reimbursed (minus 50 percent of meals and entertainment) on its tax return.

Example 37: Assume the same facts as in Example 36, except that later in the year the president takes a seven-day trip to Asia, spending two days flying, three days on business, and two days visiting relatives. Since the business trip outside the United States did not last longer than seven days, the entire cost of the airfare can be reimbursed (and deducted) by Appleview, along with 5/7ths of the other business-related travel costs.

.03 Attendance at Conventions

The deduction of convention expenses depends on whether attendance at the convention or other meeting benefits or advances the interests of the taxpayer's trade or business. If the convention is for political, social, or other purposes unrelated to the taxpayer's trade or business, the expenses are not deductible.[121] Furthermore, no deduction is allowed for travel or other costs incurred in connection with attending a convention, seminar, or other similar meeting relating to investments, financial planning, or other income-producing activities.[122]

Under certain circumstances, a limited business expense deduction is allowed for the cost of attending conventions, seminars, and similar meetings held on a U.S. cruise ship. However, no deduction is allowed for conventions held outside North America unless it is as reasonable for the convention to be held outside the North American area as within it.[123] A business deduction is allowed for attending conventions in certain Caribbean countries provided the country is a designated beneficiary country with which the United States maintains a bilateral or multilateral tax information exchange agreement.[124]

---

[119] Code Sec. 274(c); Reg. § 1.274-4.
[120] Reg. § 1.274-4(f)(5).
[121] Reg. § 1.162-2(d).

[122] Code Sec. 274(h)(7).
[123] Code Sec. 274(h).
[124] Code Sec. 274(h)(6); Act Sec. 212 of the Caribbean Basin Economic Recovery Act (P.L. 98-67).

Example 38: Dr. Henry Stark is a self-employed doctor. Henry attends a five-day medical convention in San Juan, Puerto Rico. His wife, who is a nurse and a medical assistant for his medical practice, also attends the convention. Since the convention is held in Puerto Rico, it is considered as held in the "North American area," and accordingly, Henry's travel costs will be deductible. Because his wife works for him, her travel is for a bona fide business purpose and therefore also will be deductible.

 GAAP vs. Code: Because there are limitations on the amount that can be deducted for travel expenses, there usually is a difference between the amount reported as travel expenses for financial reporting purposes and the amount deducted on the tax return. For example, if a corporation reimbursed its employee $1,300 for deductible travel expenses but can only deduct $1,100 due to the 50-percent limitation on meals and entertainment, the $200 difference must be added to net income when reconciling it with taxable income.

.04 Substantiation

As with entertainment expenses, the taxpayer must obtain documentary evidence (like receipts or paid bills) for any lodging expense or any other expenditure of $75 or more.[125] In general, an employee who is required to account to the employer for reimbursed travel expenses connected with the employer's business is not required to furnish additional travel expense information.

Employers that have an accountable plan can use a per diem allowance for employees' away-from-home travel expenses. The **per diem** method covers three types of employer reimbursement arrangements: (1) an allowance for an employee's lodging, meals, and incidental expenses; (2) an allowance for an employee's meals and incidental expenses only (M&IE rate); or (3) an allowance for an employee's incidental expenses only. The per diem method can be used in lieu of actual receipts for employees' meals and lodging. Where the employee does not use the full per diem amount given by the employer, the excess does not have to be refunded to the employer. Any amount the employee generally spends over the per diem amount is not reimbursed by the employer, and any amount over the per diem rate that is advanced by the employer but is not accounted for by the employee or refunded to the employer must be included in the employee's wages. When travel costs are incurred by a sole proprietor in the pursuit of business, per diems for meals are allowed but the deduction for lodging must be based on the actual amount paid.

Example 39: Priscilla Thomas lives and works in San Diego, California. Her employer sends her to Little Rock, Arkansas on a three-day business trip in January 2015. Priscilla's employer reimburses her using the federal per diem rate for Little Rock, Arkansas of $148 per day ($87 lodging plus $61 M&IE). Priscilla's actual expenses were $126 per day.

Because Priscilla did not spend more than the federal per diem rate, she does not have to refund the $66 excess to her employer (($148 – $126) × 3 days) and it is not included in her gross income. The employer is allowed to deduct $352.50 ($87 × 3 + 50% of the $61 × 3 for M&IE) as travel expenses on its tax return.

Example 40: In February 2015, Morris Daley, a self-employed architect, took a two-day business trip to Boston to meet with clients. The federal per diem rate for lodging is $170 and M&IE is $71. Morris's actual lodging cost was $115 per day. Morris uses the per diem rates. Because Morris is self-employed, he cannot use the per diem rate for his

---

[125] Code Sec. 274(d); Notice 95-50, 1995-2 CB 333.

lodging costs. However, he can use the per diem rate for his meals and incidental expenses. Thus, Morris will be able to deduct against his business profit his actual lodging costs of $230 ($115 × 2 days) plus 50 percent of the per diem M&IE ($71 × 2 days × 50% = $71).

 Reason for the Rule: The U.S. General Services Administration annually publishes per diem rates for U.S. governmental travel within the Continental United States (CONUS). Businesses use these rates when setting their own per diem rates for travel. The rates help businesses reduce the administrative expenses associated with the substantiation requirements governing travel expenses. The per diem rates can be found on the U.S. General Services Administration (GSA) website: *http://www.gsa.gov.*

¶ 607 Transportation Expenses

Local transportation costs that are deductible as business expenses are the actual costs of transportation while the taxpayer or the taxpayer's employees are not away from the tax home. As such, these expenses include the costs of traveling from one work location or assignment to another during a day in the general geographical area where the taxpayer usually works. Costs of commuting between the individual's tax home and the place of employment are not deductible. When transportation costs are paid or incurred by sole proprietors, these costs can be used to offset their business profits, and therefore not only reduce their income taxes, but also their self-employment taxes.

Local transportation costs do not include meals and lodging. They do include transportation costs, whether the transportation is furnished by the employer, employee, or by others. Business transportation expenses include taxi fares, car rental, and other payments for transportation reimbursed to employees, as well as reimbursements to employees for expenses incurred in conjunction with the use of their cars for business purposes.

.01 Automobile Expenses

Expenses paid or incurred for automobiles used for business, such as gasoline, oil, tires, repairs, insurance, depreciation, parking fees and tolls, licenses, interest on a car loan, and garage rent are deductible against business profits. Expenses incurred by employees who are not reimbursed or who are reimbursed under a nonaccountable plan can be deducted only as itemized deductions, subject to the two-percent AGI floor. Furthermore, employees who are not reimbursed for their automobile expenses cannot deduct the business portion of any interest from their car loans.

Self-employed individuals and employees can compute their deductible expenses for operating an automobile for business purposes using one of two methods: by using the standard mileage rate or by using the actual expense method. When an employee is reimbursed for transportation expenses under an accountable plan (see ¶ 601.03), the employer deducts the amounts reimbursed as transportation expense.

Actual expense method. Taxpayers can deduct the business portion of actual expenses paid or incurred in operating an automobile. Actual expenses include such items as gas and oil, insurance, interest on car loans, repairs, licenses, tires, and depreciation. Generally, the deduction for actual expenses is based on a percentage that is computed by dividing the business miles driven in a tax year by the total miles driven in the tax year. The use of the actual expense method is required for automobiles owned by a corporation.

Example 41: Sharon Schmitt, a self-employed doctor, incurs the following automobile expenses during 2015.

Gas and oil changes	$2,755
Parking (100% for business)	100
Auto insurance	1,200
License renewal fees	80
Automobile repairs	750
Depreciation	3,000
Total costs	$7,885

Sharon drove her car a total of 21,150 miles during the year. Her business miles totaled 14,805. Since Sharon used her automobile 70 percent (14,805 ÷ 21,150) for business during the year, using the actual expense method, she can deduct $5,550 as automobile expenses against her business profits. The $100 of parking is entirely business-related and therefore not allocated with the other automobile expenses.

Gas and oil changes	$2,755
Auto insurance	1,200
License renewal fee	80
Automobile repairs	750
Depreciation	3,000
Total automobile expenses	$7,785
Business percentage	× 70%
	$5,450
Plus: Business parking	100
Deductible automobile expenses	$5,550

Standard mileage rate. Employers can deduct amounts they reimburse to employees for the business use of their vehicles up to the amount computed using the standard mileage rates. The standard mileage rate for business use of an automobile for 2015 is 57.5 cents a mile.[126] Sole proprietors can use the standard mileage rate to reimburse their employees. They also can deduct amounts as transportation expenses for the business use of their own automobiles.

Example 42: Mary Smith works for a consulting company and is reimbursed for her transportation costs based on business miles she accumulates meeting with clients and potential clients. Mary substantiates her business miles to her employer who reimburses her at the standard mileage rate. During 2015, Mary drove her automobile 20,000 business miles and is reimbursed $11,500 (20,000 × $.575) by her employer under an accountable plan. The $11,500 is not taxed to Mary and is deductible by her employer as transportation expense.

Example 43: Assume the same facts as in Example 42, except that the reimbursement is made from a nonaccountable plan. The $11,500 is included in Mary's taxable wages and deducted as a wage expense by her employer. Furthermore, this amount is subject to withholding and the employer is responsible for FICA and unemployment taxes on this amount. Mary will be able to deduct the $11,500 as a miscellaneous itemized deduction subject to the two-percent AGI floor.

The standard mileage rate replaces all actual operating and fixed expenses and depreciation in determining the deductible business costs of operating a passenger car, including vans and pickup trucks. However, parking and tolls and interest on loans attributable to business use of the vehicle

---

[126] Notice 2014-79, IRB 2014-53, December 10, 2014.

are deductible in addition to the standard mileage deduction. Employees may not claim an interest deduction on car loans if they are not reimbursed for their transportation expense.[127]

The standard mileage rate deduction does away with the requirement that the taxpayer keep detailed records of expenditures associated with operating the automobile. Taxpayers can use the standard mileage rate to compute deductible costs of vehicles used for hire (such as taxicabs and limousines).[128]

Use of the standard mileage rate is restricted to individual taxpayers; therefore, corporations must use the actual expense method to compute their deductions for automobile expenses. However, if a corporation reimburses its employees for business use of their employees' own automobiles, the amounts reimbursed are deductible by the corporations, provided it does not exceed the standard mileage rate in effect at the time. Some corporate employers opt to reimburse their employees for the costs of operating their cars so that the standard mileage rate can be used.

 Reason for the Rule: Like per diems for travel expenses, the standard mileage method eliminates much of the paperwork and substantiation required under the actual method. The mileage rates vary. The rates are published by the IRS as a Notice in the Internal Revenue Bulletin.

¶ 608 Education

Employers can deduct amounts they pay for educating their employees, provided that the education maintains or improves the employee's skills required in the employer's trade or business or allows the employee to meet the employer's educational requirements or legal requirements which are imposed as a condition for retention of employment relationship, status, or rate of pay. However, if the education allows the employee to meet the minimum education requirements for the position or allows the employee to enter into a new trade or business, the education costs are never deductible.[129]

Deductible educational expenses include tuition, books, supplies, lab fees, certain transportation and travel costs, and other educational expenses, such as costs of researching and typing a paper for a class. If the employer reimburses its employee for educational expense that qualifies for deduction, the tax treatment of the reimbursement depends upon whether the employer's reimbursement arrangement is an accountable plan or nonaccountable plan. Where the reimbursement is from an accountable plan, the educational reimbursement will not be included in the employee's income. Where the reimbursement is from a nonaccountable plan, the amount of the reimbursement is included in the employee's income and is subject to employment taxes.

Example 44: Lauren Smith has completed two years of a three-year course leading to a law degree. Lauren is hired by a law firm as a full-time paralegal. As a condition to continued employment, Lauren is required to obtain a law degree and pass the state bar examination. She completes her law school education by attending night school and takes a bar review course in order to prepare her for the state bar examination. The law courses and the bar review course constitute education that meet the minimum educational requirements in her intended business. Therefore, if these costs are reimbursed by her employer, these amounts will not be deductible as education expenses by her employer. The amounts paid would be taxable wages to Lauren and deducted as wage expense by the law firm.

However, if these amounts were paid from the employer's established, written educational assistance program, Lauren would be able to exclude up to $5,250 of the

---

[127] Code Sec. 163(h)(2)(A).

[128] Rev. Proc. 2010-51, IRB 2010-51, 883, December 20, 2010.

[129] Reg. § 1.162-5.

benefits paid by her employer each year. The law firm would then deduct these amounts as an employee benefit (see ¶ 602.04).

¶ 609 Summary

In addition to the various ordinary and necessary business expenses that were discussed in Chapter 5, businesses can also deduct a number of employment-related expenditures they incur during the year. An understanding of the various tax laws surrounding the deductibility of employment-related expenses is essential in order to help businesses reduce the amount of income and payroll taxes they must pay each year.

GLOSSARY OF TERMS INTRODUCED IN THE CHAPTER

Accountable plan. Requires employees to submit adequate documentation or receipts for any reimbursed expenses and any advances in excess of substantiated expenses must be returned to the employer.

Closely-held corporations. Corporations whose stock is held by a small number of shareholders, typically from the same family or a related group of individuals.

Defined benefit plan. A type of retirement plan that promises participants specified benefits during retirement years and continuing until the death of the participant, and often until the death of the spouse of the participant.

Defined contribution plan. A type of retirement plan where the amounts are contributed to an employee's own account, and the amount available upon retirement depends on the performance of the investments in the account.

Federal Insurance Contributions Act (FICA). A program enacted under the Federal Social Security Act that established a federal unemployment insurance program (Medicare) and a program to provide old-age, survivors, and disability benefits to employees (social security). Contributions to this plan are shared by employers and employees through FICA withholding and self-employment taxes.

Federal Unemployment Tax Act (FUTA). FUTA was enacted by Congress to finance the federal unemployment program. Contributions to this plan are funded entirely by employers.

Flexible spending account (FSA). This type of account is offered to employees to cover their dependent care costs and/or medical costs. Employees can set aside each year pre-tax wages from which they can pay up to $2,500 of qualified health costs (in the case of Health FSAs) or up to $5,000 qualified child care costs (in the case of Dependent Care FSAs).

Medicare taxes. The hospital insurance (HI) portion of the FICA tax.

Nonaccountable plan. Reimbursements paid through a system that does not meet the requirements for an accountable plan.

Per diem. Established amounts allowed by the IRS to be deducted in lieu of substantiation for an employee's lodging, meals, and incidental expenses or a sole proprietor's for meals and incidental expenses.

Perquisites. Fringe benefits that represent privileges that businesses make available to their employees.

Publicly-held corporations. Corporations whose stock is traded on one of the U.S. stock exchanges, such as the American Stock Exchange, New York Stock Exchange, or NASDAQ.

Social security taxes. The old-age, survivors, and disability insurance (OASDI) portion of the FICA tax.

Tax deferred. When income or gain is postponed to some future point in time but is eventually taxed.

CHAPTER PROBLEMS

The following questions and problems relate to the discussion in Chapter 6, Business Deductions: Employment-Related Expenses, which begins at ¶ 600 in *Part II: Federal Taxation of Business Income and Deductions.*

Chapter 6 Discussion Questions

1. Edgar Berger is the VP of Marketing for Sandsun Corporation. Edgar is the fifth highest paid officer of Sandsun, other than its CEO. In 2015, Edgar's salary was $1.2 million dollars. How much can Sandsun Corporation deduct on its 2015 income tax return for Edgar's salary?

2. Cynthia Moss is an employee and sole shareholder of GO Corporation. Cynthia uses the cash method; GO Corporation uses the accrual method of accounting. Both Cynthia and GO use a calendar year end. In July 2015, Cynthia has the corporation declare a $30,000 bonus to her, which will be paid to her in February 2016. GO accrued the bonus on its books in 2015. In what tax year can GO deduct the bonus paid to Cynthia?

3. Herbert Cohn, who works for the RT Manufacturing Company, received a $1,200 reimbursement from RT for a business trip he took on behalf of the company. Herbert attached the receipts to his expense report to substantiate the expenses he incurred on his business trip. What is the tax treatment to RT and to Herbert if the company has an accountable plan? What would be the tax treatment to RT and Herbert if the company has a nonaccountable plan?

4. What is the maximum amount that employees can elect to contribute to a flexible spending account (FSA)? What is the benefit to an employee in contributing to an FSA?

5. Under an employer-provided educational assistance plan, an employee receives reimbursement for tuition for an undergraduate course. Must the employee include the employer's tuition reimbursement in gross income? Can the employer deduct the amounts it reimburses its employees?

6. In 2015, the LB Advertising Company established a qualified adoption assistance program for its employees. What is the maximum amount an employee of the LB Advertising Company can exclude from his or her gross income for amounts paid or expenses incurred by LB for its employees' qualified adoption expenses? What costs are included as qualified adoption expenses? Are there any income limits the employee must meet to exclude the amount from his or her income? How does LB treat these amounts paid on its tax return?

7. What is the mileage test for purposes of being able to deduct moving expenses paid on behalf of an employee?

8. Ike entertains one of his employer's customers by taking him to a cocktail party at the yacht club and afterwards to the opera. No business discussions took place during the party or at the opera. However, earlier in the day, Ike and his customer had discussed business for several hours. Ike's employer fully reimbursed him under an accountable plan. Can Ike's employer deduct as an entertainment expense the cost of entertaining the customer?

9. DFG Company adopted a Roth 401(k) plan for its employees. The plan is not discriminatory. DFG's CEO, who is 55 years old, wants to participate in the Roth 401(k) plan. The CEO earns an annual salary of $350,000. What is the maximum contribution the CEO can

make to the company's Roth 401(k) for 2015? How much can DFG make and deduct for contributions to its employees' Roth 401(k) plans?

10. A president and controlling shareholder of a corporation takes a seven-day trip to Europe. The corporation reimburses the president for his deductible travel expenses. The president spends half of the time during the trip on business and half on vacation. What amounts represent deductible travel expenses by the corporation?

11. Can independent contractors participate in an employer's cafeteria plan?

12. Paul Goddard is an accountant who works for a growing manufacturing company in Dallas, Texas, where he resides. Paul's company purchases another manufacturing plant in La Porte, Indiana, and the company sends Paul to the La Porte plant on a temporary nine month assignment to update its accounting system. After seven months in La Porte, the company asks Paul to stay an additional four months. Paul works the additional four months and then returns home to Dallas. During his stay in LaPorte, the company reimburses Paul for his travel expenses for each of the 11 months. Can Paul's employer deduct the 11 months of travel expenses?

13. Sarah Croft, age 46, has been employed by Kybar Corporation for a number of years. Kybar has never offered any type of pension or retirement plan to its employees. Concerned with planning for her retirement, Sarah recently heard of a SIMPLE-IRA that allows employees to contribute $12,500 to an IRA for 2015. She has asked your advice how she should go about opening a SIMPLE-IRA. How would you advise Sarah?

14. Bruce Zen, age 55, is employed by Lee Corporation at a salary of $250,000. His employer allows him to contribute 10 percent of his salary to a 401(k) plan. For 2015, what is the maximum contribution that Bruce may make to his 401(k) plan?

15. Which of the following are characteristics of a SIMPLE plan?

   a. The maximum annual contribution that an employee may make is $5,500.

   b. The plan may be structured as an IRA or 401(k) arrangement.

   c. The plan must follow strict nondiscrimination rules.

   d. Self-employed individuals may participate.

16. The 10-percent penalty on early distributions from a Roth 401(k) will apply to which of the following distributions from a qualified retirement plan during 2015?

   a. A distribution to a former employee who is age 61.

   b. A distribution to a disabled employee.

   c. A distribution made because of the death of the employee.

17. The FICA tax is made up of two component taxes. Discuss each tax.

18. Compare and contrast FICA and FUTA taxes as to their imposition and rate requirements.

19. What is the FUTA tax rate and its wage base limit for 2015?

20. Thomas Andrews, age 48, is employed as a designer by the Harlan and Wolff Corporation. The corporation permits its employees to contribute a maximum of 10 percent of their wages to a 401(k) plan. Depending on its profits for the year, the corporation has the option of making additional contributions to each employee's 401(k) plan account. During 2015, Thomas will earn a salary of $100,000, and he will contribute $10,000 to his 401(k) plan account. In December 2015, the corporation informs its employees that it will make an extra contribution to each employee's 401(k) plan account by the end of the year. Thomas is informed that the extra contribution to his 401(k) for 2015 will be $9,000. Late in 2015, while meeting with his accountant to discuss some year-end tax planning possibilities, the accountant mentions that because the maximum tax-deferred contribution that can be made to a 401(k) plan for 2015, by an employee under age 50, is $18,000, Thomas will be required to include the excess contribution of $1,000 ($19,000 total amount contributed to his 401(k) minus $18,000 maximum contribution allowable) in his gross income for 2015. Is

the accountant correct? How will the company treat its $9,000 contribution to Thomas's plan on its tax return?

Chapter 6 Problems

1. In 2015, Katy Jones received qualified parking valued at $275 per month from her employer for the year.

   a. Is any portion of the parking Katy received includable in her income for 2015?

   b. How does Katy's employer treat the amounts paid to Katy?

2. In 2015, under its adoption assistance program, RAY Corporation pays $15,000 of qualified adoption expenses on behalf of its employee Hugh Grand in connection with Hugh's effort to adopt an eligible child. The $15,000 included qualified adoption expenses from an adoption agency for a successful adoption of a baby. Hugh's modified AGI in 2015 is $100,000.

   a. What is the total amount that will be included in Hugh's income (if any) for qualified adoption expenses?

   b. How is the $15,000 treated by RAY?

3. Y Company paid $12,000 to rent a 15-seat skybox at Chicago's U.S Cellular Field for two baseball games. The cost of the highest-priced, nonluxury box seats is $100 a seat. How much can Y deduct for the cost of the luxury skybox?

4. To celebrate closing a profitable contract, Lester Briggs took his client and his client's wife out for dinner at an expensive French restaurant immediately after the contract had been signed. The bill for the meal was $550. Of the amount spent, $150 of the bill is considered lavish and extravagant. Lester's employer reimbursed him the amount he had spent under its accountable plan. How much can Lester's employer deduct for meals and entertainment expense?

5. In 2015, Sam Wilson took several graduate-level courses in business from a local university. Sam's employer has an educational assistance program. The cost of the tuition, books, and fees, which were reimbursed by Sam's employer, totaled $8,000.

   a. How much is Sam's employer allowed to exclude from Sam's income?

   b. How much can the employer deduct?

6. A corporation, of which John Stevens is the sole owner, employs John's wife as secretary and treasurer at a salary of $58,000 per year. She performs certain work regularly, but efficient and bonded help for the same work can easily be obtained for $18,000 per year. How much may the corporation deduct regarding her salary, in arriving at its taxable income?

7. David Parks is president and the sole shareholder of the DP Retail Company. DP owns a yacht which David uses during the tax year for both personal and business purposes. The operating expenses of the yacht, including depreciation, totaled $16,200 during the tax year. David used the yacht 55 percent for business (35 percent for directly related entertainment and 20 percent for associated entertainment). In addition to these expenses, David incurred the following expenses in connection with entertaining customers on the yacht which were 100 percent reimbursed by DP:

   - $3,500 for food and beverages in entertainment that was directly related to the active conduct of DP's business.

   - $4,600 for food and beverages in entertainment that was associated with the active conduct of DP's business.

   - $2,000 for personal and family consumption of food and beverages.

   What is the amount of expenses that can be deducted by the DP Retail Company?

8. Peter Smalts is employed by Major Foods and works at the company's Los Angeles location. In 2015, Peter is transferred by his employer to Omaha, Nebraska. Major Foods

pays $5,000 for Peter's moving, which includes $3,600 to professional movers; $1,000 to fly Peter and his family to Omaha; and $400 to cover temporary living expenses until their furnishings arrive. How is the $5,000 reimbursement under the company's accountable plan treated by Peter and Major Foods?

9. Humphrey Long, an employee of XYZ Company, uses his car for business. He drove his car a total of 30,000 miles in 2015, 25,000 of which were for business. Humphrey's employer has an accountable plan and reimburses its employees based upon the standard mileage rate. Humphrey submitted his business miles to his employer. How much was Humphrey reimbursed by his employer for 2015, and how is this amount handled on XYZ's tax return?

10. Jane Croft, an employee, uses her car 100 percent for business reasons. During 2015, she paid $2,000 in interest on her business car loan. May she deduct any of the interest expense? How would your answer change if Jane were self-employed?

11. Mr. Sands, an account executive at an advertising agency in San Francisco, incurs the following expenses in Los Angeles with respect to a client:

   • $200 for airfare to and from Los Angeles,

   • $250 for one overnight stay in a hotel in Los Angeles,

   • $600 for dinner for himself and five persons during which business was discussed, and

   • $600 for six tickets to a sports event directly following the dinner. The face value of the tickets is $270.

   Mr. Sands is reimbursed $1,650 by his company under a plan that requires an employee to substantiate the expenses and to return amounts in excess of the substantiated expenses. Will any portion of these expenditures be deductible on Mr. Sands's income tax return? Will any portion of these expenditures be deductible on the employer's tax return?

12. A.B. Call is employed as sales manager by the C-D Manufacturing Company. He incurs the following expenses for days away from home on business during 2015:

   • $1,000 for meals,

   • $2,000 for lodging,

   • $1,000 for airfare, and

   • $3,000 for entertainment of business customers.

   A.B. was reimbursed by his company to cover his business expenses under an accountable plan. What amounts may be deducted by A.B. or C-D Manufacturing?

13. Alfredo, who operates a small manufacturing company, spent $1,500 for entertainment in a hospitality room at a business convention where he displayed and discussed his products. He also entertained his customers by taking them to a cocktail party at a country club and afterwards to the theater. No business discussions took place during the party or at the theater. However, they had spent several hours earlier discussing new product lines. The cost of entertaining the customers at the country club and theatre totaled $15,000. Alfredo's company has an accountable plan and reimbursed him for the amounts incurred. How much can the company deduct for entertainment expenses?

14. A corporation is on a calendar-year basis and uses the accrual method of accounting. The Board of Directors meets on December 4, 2015, and determines that the corporate officers, who are not related parties to the corporation, will be paid a bonus equal to one percent of profits. In February 2016, the profits are determined and the officers are paid. When can the corporation deduct the bonus?

15. Julie is employed as a waitress at two restaurants. In July, she received $18 in tips from one restaurant and $82 from the other. What amount of tips for the month of July must be reported and is subject to FICA withholding?

16. Michael's Mirror & Glass has three employees. The employees were paid $5,000, $6,000, and $10,000, respectively in 2015. What is the amount of wages subject to FUTA?

17. Bob made $120,000 while working at Williamston, Inc. during 2015.

    a. Compute the amount Williamston will pay (and deduct) for FICA taxes on Bob's wages.

    b. Compute the amount Williamston will withhold for FICA taxes from Bob's wages.

18. For the calendar year 2015, a company paid its eight employees a total of $118,000. All of the employees earned over $7,000. The company's wage base for state unemployment insurance purposes amounts to $64,000, which is subject to a six-percent state unemployment rate. Compute the FUTA tax that is payable.

19. In 2015, Joseph Sears earned $50,000 while working at JL Putz, Inc.

    a. Compute JL's FICA taxes on Joseph's wages.

    b. Compute the amount of FICA taxes JL will withhold from Joseph's wages.

20. Thomas Rigney has contributed six percent of his salary to his employer's 401(k) plan for a number of years. His total elective contributions in the plan now total $80,000. Rigney incurred $20,000 of medical expenses in the current year. Rigney wants to withdraw $20,000 from his 401(k) plan to pay his medical expenses. Based upon these facts, has Rigney satisfied the tests for a hardship withdrawal from the 401(k) plan?

21. Sam Stone is an employee and the sole shareholder of PPD Company. PPD paid Sam $950,000 as salary for its 2015 tax year. PPD did not pay any dividends for the year. A reasonable salary for Sam's job is $500,000. If the IRS selects PPD's tax return for audit, what may be their determination of Sam's salary of $950,000?

22. Tom Hughes, a corporate executive at MYH Co., went to China to investigate MYH's expansion into China. Tom's trip to China, which he scheduled, lasted 20 days. Two days were spent flying to and from China; ten days were spent attending meetings; and eight days were spent sightseeing. Tom's expenses were $1,500 airfare, $250 per day for lodging, $100 per day for meals. Tom also spent $300 on sightseeing tours. MYH reimbursed Tom for his expenses, except for the sightseeing tours, under its accountable plan. How much can MYH deduct for Tom's trip?

23. In 2015, Sam Jones, who is 16, worked part-time as an employee in his father's dry-cleaning business. Sam's gross salary was $10,000. In 2015, how much FICA and federal unemployment taxes should be paid regarding Sam's salary?

24. SQL Trucking Co. employs eight interstate truck drivers who are out on the road a continuous five days a week, 40 weeks per year. In 2015, SQL reimburses its truck drivers $59 per day (federal per diem rate) for meals while away from home. How much can SQL deduct on its 2015 tax return of the truck driver's meals?

25. Payout Co. hired Sally Smith as an employee in its payroll department. Employees that work in the payroll department must have at least two semesters of college accounting to work in the department. When Sally was hired she did not have two semesters of college accounting. Sally spent a total of $1,200 for tuition and books for two accounting classes. This amount was reimbursed by Payout under its accountable plan. How much can Payout deduct of Sally's educational expenses? Would your answer be different if Payout had an educational assistance program?

Chapter 6 Review Problems

1. Tim Davis is president of a small manufacturing company. During the year, Tim incurred the following entertainment expenses that were reimbursed by the company:

   • $200 for dues to a social club. Tim took his customers to the social club for business conferences and did not use it in any other way.

   • $1,200 for the cost of the meals provided Tim's customers at the club in which business was discussed.

   • $200 for Tim's meals with customers.

   • $400 for gifts Tim gave to four customers (individuals) costing $100 each.

- $500 for watches (costing $100 each) given to five foremen in Tim's manufacturing plant as part of a plant safety achievement (non-qualified plan) award.

What amount of the reimbursed expenses is deductible by the company?

2. On the draft of the tax return for XYZ Corporation, taxable income for the calendar year was $29,182. An examination developed the following questionable items:

   a. Salary paid to the sole shareholder was $800,000. A reasonable salary would be $250,000.

   b. 100-percent deduction taken on $25,500 of business meal expenses (which is subject to the 50-percent limitation).

   c. $2,500 deduction taken on country club dues.

   d. Mortgage interest of $12,500 paid on a hunting lodge used exclusively by the sole shareholder.

   What is the correct amount of taxable income that should be reported for XYZ Corporation?

Chapter 6 Research Question

Mr. Jones is the president of a corporation that is owned by him and members of his family. During a tax year under audit, Mr. Jones was paid a salary of $48,000 by the corporation. The corporation also contributed $12,000 to a pension plan on Mr. Jones's behalf in that year. A dispute has arisen over the compensation paid to Mr. Jones in that tax year. The IRS agent claims that both the salary paid to Mr. Jones and pension plan contribution made on his behalf must be taken into account in determining whether the total compensation is reasonable in amount. The agent is about to disallow a portion of the deduction for the compensation.

You have been requested by the corporation to determine whether the pension plan contributions must be taken into account in determining whether the compensation is reasonable. Give your opinion. In it show authorities, citing laws, regulations, interpretations and decisions applicable, and the *CCH Standard Federal Tax Reporter* paragraphs where they may be found.

CHAPTER 7

Depreciation, Depletion, and Amortization

CHAPTER CONTENTS

LEARNING OBJECTIVES

1. Understand what depreciation is and how it is calculated.

2. Be able to describe how Code Sec. 179 immediate expensing can be used to write off the costs of tangible personal property and how Code Sec. 179 can be elected.

3. Understand what depletion is and how it is calculated.

4. Understand what amortization is and how it is calculated.

¶ 700 Introduction

The cost of business property and property held for the production of income must be spread over the tax years in which the property is utilized. "Depreciation" is the annual deduction taken to recover the capitalized costs of tangible personal and real property (other than land). "Amortization" is a deduction allowed to recover the cost of intangible assets over time. "Depletion" is a deduction allowed to recover the cost of natural resources, so-called wasting assets.

The concepts of depreciation, depletion, and amortization for tax purposes are similar to those used in financial accounting. However, the financial accounting and tax accounting rules are written by different governing bodies, each having its own agenda. In financial accounting, the cost recovery rules are intended to match the expensing of assets to the accounting periods in which the assets help generate revenues. Congress, on the other hand, is not as concerned with the proper matching of revenues and expenses but instead often chooses to use the cost recovery rules to influence capital investment and economic growth.

This chapter introduces the methods taxpayers can use to depreciate business property and property used in the production of income. Unless otherwise indicated, the rules discussed in this chapter apply to all businesses, regardless of whether they are operated as a corporation, partnership, or sole proprietorship. This chapter also discusses the amortization rules that apply to the costs of acquiring intangible assets and the depletion rules that govern the expensing of the costs associated with the acquisition of productive natural resources.

In many instances, the tax laws provide some flexibility in selecting how quickly taxpayers can expense the costs associated with productive assets. Proper tax planning requires a general understanding of the various alternatives available because every dollar expensed on the tax return generates cash flows in the form of reduced tax liability. All other things being equal, the ability to accelerate the timing of these cash flows can benefit a company because the amounts can be invested or used to pay business expenses. However, before deciding whether to select a cost recovery method that accelerates deductions into earlier tax years, it is important to keep in mind that a taxpayer's marginal tax rate often varies from year to year.

DEPRECIATION

¶ 701 The Concept of Depreciation

Because capital expenditures benefit a business for a number of years, it is appropriate that their cost be spread out (deducted) to offset business income generated in the years that the asset is productive. In financial accounting, depreciation matches the costs associated with the acquisition of a productive asset over the years in which the asset helps generate revenues for the business. If a business were to expense the entire cost in the year the asset was acquired, net income in the year the asset was purchased would be understated, and net income in all subsequent years the asset was used would be overstated. Thus, in order to accurately determine the net income of a business on a year-to-year basis, the cost needs to be allocated (depreciated) over the number of years that the asset is used in the business. Depreciation represents the periodic expensing of a productive tangible asset whose useful life extends over more than one year.

The tax laws regarding depreciation, on the other hand, are intended solely to write off the cost of tangible property in a systematic manner that is not necessarily intended to correspond to the expected usefulness of the asset in the taxpayer's business. As with all expenses deducted in arriving at taxable income, the amount a taxpayer deducts for depreciation expense produces tax savings equal to the amount of the deduction multiplied by the taxpayer's marginal tax rate. Because depreciation expense helps a taxpayer recoup some of the initial costs associated with the acquisition of an asset, the quicker the asset is depreciated, the faster the taxpayer realizes the tax savings.

Thus, the taxpayer can either invest the extra cash or use it to pay expenses. The depreciation rules have often been used by Congress to stimulate economic growth by temporarily accelerating the rate at which productive, long-lived assets can be expensed.

In 1981, Congress enacted the Accelerated Cost Recovery System (ACRS) to allow taxpayers to recover capital costs using accelerated methods over predetermined recovery periods that were much shorter than the properties' useful lives. One of the principal reasons for enacting ACRS was to provide faster tax savings to businesses in an attempt to stimulate capital formation and the growth of the economy.[1] By allowing these assets to be written off over shorter periods, the tax savings from the depreciation deduction could be realized earlier, thereby accelerating cash flows into the earlier years of the assets' useful lives. In 1986, Congress enacted the Modified Accelerated Cost Recovery System (MACRS), which slowed down the pace at which assets were expensed but still allowed cost recovery periods much shorter than the assets' actual useful lives. MACRS is the depreciation system in effect today.

¶ 702 Financial Accounting Depreciation Rules

In financial accounting, the depreciable cost of an asset is written off over the accounting periods (the asset's "estimated useful life") in which the company expects to use the asset in its operations. The **depreciable cost** equals the costs associated with the acquisition of the asset minus the estimated salvage value. **Salvage value** of a depreciable asset is the amount the company estimates the asset's sales, trade-in, or scrap value will be at the end of its useful life. The difference between the amount the company pays for the asset and the amount it expects to receive when it sells it in the future is the company's out-of-pocket costs with respect to its investment in the asset. It is this amount that the financial depreciation rules attempt to allocate to expense over the asset's useful life.

As depreciation expense is deducted each year in arriving at net income, the book value of the asset reported on the balance sheet decreases accordingly. **Book value** is the asset's cost plus any improvements made to the asset minus the accumulated depreciation taken on the asset over the years. Book value is deducted from the net sales price to determine the gain or loss reported on the income statement when the company eventually disposes of the asset.

.01 Methods for Depreciating Property

The financial accounting rules allow businesses to use several methods to allocate the depreciable cost of a productive asset over its estimated useful life. Four common methods are the:

1. Straight-line method (the method that achieves the slowest write-off of costs);
2. Declining-balance method (an accelerated method that achieves a fast write-off of costs);
3. Sum-of-the-years' digits method (also an accelerated method); and
4. Units-of-production method (a method that relates depreciation to the usage of the asset). The calculation of depreciation expense for each method is discussed below.

Straight-line method. As the name suggests, the straight-line (SL) method allows for an even amount of depreciation expense each year. Under the straight-line method, annual depreciation equals the depreciable cost of an asset divided by the asset's estimated useful life.

Example 1: An asset costing $12,000 has an estimated useful life of five years and a salvage value of $2,000. The depreciable cost equals $10,000 ($12,000 – $2,000 salvage value). Under the SL method, this amount is expensed evenly over the asset's five-year useful life ($10,000 ÷ 5 = $2,000 annual depreciation). At the end of five years, a total of $10,000 of

---

[1] Staff of the Joint Committee on Taxation, 97th Cong., General Explanation of the Economic Recovery Tax Act of 1981, pages 75–76 (Comm. Print 1981).

accumulated depreciation will have been taken on the asset, thereby reducing its book value to $2,000 ($12,000 – $10,000).

Year	Beginning Book Value	Depreciation Expense	Ending Book Value
1	$12,000	$ 2,000	$10,000
2	10,000	2,000	8,000
3	8,000	2,000	6,000
4	6,000	2,000	4,000
5	4,000	2,000	2,000
Accumulated Depreciation		$10,000	

Declining-balance method. The "declining-balance method" expenses a portion of an asset's book value each year. The amount expensed under this method is the asset's book value at the beginning of the year times a multiple of the straight-line rate. For example, under the "double declining-balance (DDB) method," annual depreciation equals the asset's book value at the beginning of the year times twice (double) the straight-line rate. Under the "150-percent declining-balance method," annual depreciation equals the book value at the beginning of the year times 150 percent of the straight-line rate. Because the beginning book value is used in computing the amount of annual depreciation expense, the amount of depreciation deducted for the year cannot cause the asset's book value to fall below its salvage value.

Example 2: Assume the same facts as in Example 1, except that the asset is depreciated using the DDB method. At the beginning of the first year, the book value of the asset equals $12,000 because there is no accumulated depreciation. Twice (double) the straight-line rate for an asset with a five-year life is 40 percent (1/5 × 2). Therefore, depreciation for the first year equals $4,800 ($12,000 × 40%). Book value of the asset at the beginning of year 2 equals $7,200 ($12,000 – $4,800).

Depreciation expense for the second year equals $2,880 ($7,200 × 40%), which further reduces the book value of the asset to $4,320 ($7,200 – $2,880). In the third year, depreciation expense equals $1,728 ($4,320 × 40%), and book value is reduced to $2,592 ($4,320 – $1,728). In the fourth year, the amount of depreciation expense is limited to $592 because depreciation equal to 40 percent of book value ($2,592 × 40% = $1,037) would cause the book value of the asset to fall below its estimated salvage value.

Year	Beginning Book Value	Depreciation Expense	Ending Book Value
1	$12,000	$ 4,800	$7,200
2	7,200	2,880	4,320
3	4,320	1,728	2,592
4	2,592	592	2,000
5	2,000	0	2,000
Accumulated Depreciation		$10,000	

As with the straight-line method, total depreciation expense over the asset's five-year assigned life using the DDB method equals $10,000. However, the amount deducted each year differs between these two methods. The declining-balance method is known as an "accelerated depreciation method" because depreciation expense is highest in the earliest years of the asset's useful life. In the later years, depreciation expense decelerates. This can be seen by comparing the annual depreciation expenses in Examples 1 and 2.

Example 3: Assume the same facts as in Example 2, except the asset is depreciated using the 150-percent declining-balance method. Since 150 percent of the straight-line rate for a five-year property life equals 30 percent (1/5 × 150%), first-year depreciation equals $3,600 ($12,000 × 30%) and book value is reduced to $8,400 ($12,000 – $3,600).

Depreciation for the second year would then equal $2,520 ($8,400 × 30%), which reduces the asset's book value. This process continues for years 3 to 5, while ensuring that the amount of depreciation expense does not cause book value to fall below the $2,000 salvage value.

Year	Beginning Book Value	Depreciation Expense	Ending Book Value
1	$12,000	$ 3,600	$8,400
2	8,400	2,520	5,880
3	5,880	1,764	4,116
4	4,116	1,235	2,881
5	2,881	881	2,000
Accumulated Depreciation		$10,000	

Sum-of-the-years' digits method. Under the "sum-of-years' digits depreciation method," each year the depreciable cost is multiplied by a fraction whose numerator is the number of years of the asset's useful life left at the beginning of the year and whose denominator is the sum of the years in the asset's estimated useful life. For example, the denominator for an asset with a five-year estimated useful life is 15 (5 + 4 + 3 + 2 + 1). For the first full year, the depreciable cost of the asset is multiplied by 5/15 because there are 5 years of useful life remaining at the beginning of the first year.

Example 4: Assume the same facts as in Example 1, except that the asset is depreciated using the sum-of-the-years' digits method. In the first year, depreciation expense equals $3,333 ($10,000 × 5/15). In the second year, the depreciable cost would be multiplied by 4/15 to yield depreciation expense of $2,667 ($10,000 × 4/15). In the third year, the $10,000 would be multiplied by 3/15, etc.

Year	Beginning Book Value	Depreciation Expense	Ending Book Value
1	$12,000	$ 3,333	$8,667
2	8,667	2,667	6,000
3	6,000	2,000	4,000
4	4,000	1,333	2,667
5	2,667	667	2,000
Accumulated Depreciation		$10,000	

Units-of-production method. The "units-of-production depreciation method" expenses the depreciable cost of an asset based on the usage of the asset. Each year the portion of the depreciable cost is multiplied by a fraction whose numerator is the units produced during the year and whose denominator is the total estimated units the asset is expected to produce during its useful life. Units can be measured in number of hours (in the case of a machine) or miles (in the case of an automobile). When this method is used, depreciation expense varies directly with production. Thus, among all of the depreciation methods that are acceptable methods for the purposes of financial accounting, this method does the best job at matching the costs of an asset with the periods in which the asset is utilized.

.02 Partial-Year Depreciation

Because depreciable assets are rarely placed in service on the first day of the fiscal year, or disposed of on the last day of the fiscal year for financial reporting purposes each year's depreciation expense must be allocated between two fiscal years, which involves "partial-year depreciation." Although any reasonable, consistently applied method for selecting a day to begin and end depreciating an asset is allowed, the most common approach is starting and ending depreciation of an asset based on the nearest full month. Accordingly, assets placed in service during the first half of the month are assumed to have been placed in service on the first day of the month, and assets placed in service during the last half of the month are assumed to have been placed in service on the first day of the following month. The same rules apply to the disposition of assets. Assets disposed of in the first half of the month are deemed disposed of on the first day of that month, and those disposed of during the last half of the month are deemed disposed of on the first day of the following month.

To illustrate the "nearest month rules," assume that a calendar year corporation places an asset into service on May 12, 2015. Because the asset is deemed to have been placed in service on May 1, 2015, 8/12ths of the first year of depreciation is deducted in calculating 2015 net income. The remaining 4/12ths of the first-year depreciation plus 8/12ths of the second year depreciation would be deducted in 2016, and so forth. If the asset is later sold on October 25, the depreciation on that asset would be taken until November 1 of that year.

¶ 703 Tax Depreciation Rules in General

The tax laws regarding depreciation are intended solely to write off the cost of tangible property in a systematic manner that is not necessarily intended to correspond to the expected usefulness of the asset in the taxpayer's business. The depreciation rules have often been used by Congress to stimulate economic growth by temporarily accelerating the rate at which productive, long-lived assets can be expensed.

Tax law generally allows property to be depreciated if it (1) is used in a trade or business or held for the production of income; (2) has a useful life that is longer than one year; and (3) wears out, decays, gets used up, becomes obsolete, or loses value from natural causes.[2] Consequently, land and artwork are not depreciable assets because they do not wear out, get used up, or become obsolete.[3] However, an asset does not necessarily need to decline in value to be a depreciable asset. For example, professional musicians are allowed to depreciate the cost of antique musical instruments that continue to appreciate in value because the instruments are used in their business and are subject to wear and tear.[4] Similarly, individuals in the business of displaying exotic cars are entitled to depreciate the cars because the cars are subject to obsolescence.[5]

Because only property used in a trade or business or held for the production of income can be depreciated, no deduction for depreciation is allowed for "personal-use" assets.[6] It is important to distinguish between the terms "personal-use" and "personal property." Personal-use assets are those such as a taxpayer's residence or an automobile used for personal purposes only. "Personal property" is property that is not realty (e.g., equipment and machinery). Many assets are "mixed-use assets" (i.e., used partly for personal purposes and partly for business or investment purposes). Only the portion of the cost of the asset allocable to business or investment use of mixed-use assets is depreciable. Mixed-use assets are often found in businesses operated as sole proprietorships (see ¶ 1303).

---

[2] Reg. § 1.167(a)-2.

[3] See, e.g., Rev. Rul. 68-232, 1968-1 CB 79.

[4] B.P. Liddle, CA-3, 95-2 USTC ¶ 50,488, 65 F3d 329; R.L. Simon, CA-2, 95-2 USTC ¶ 50,552, 68 F3d 41.

[5] B. Selig, 70 TCM 1125, Dec. 50,975(M), TC Memo. 1995-519.

[6] Code Sec. 167(a).

Property used by a business to construct a capital asset is generally not expensed; instead it is capitalized as part of the cost of the asset. The entire capitalized cost of the constructed asset may be depreciated once construction is completed and the asset is placed in service.

Example 5: Pretty Good Construction, Inc. uses a payloader to construct a building in year 20X0. The payloader's sole use in 20X0 is to construct the building, and $20,000 of depreciation on the payloader is allowable to Pretty Good in that year. Pretty Good may not take a deduction for the $20,000 of depreciation on its 20X0 tax return. Instead, it must add the $20,000 to the basis of the building. Thus, Pretty Good will recover the depreciation expense on the payloader over the depreciation period of the building, not the payloader.

Although the concept of depreciation for tax purposes is similar to that used for financial reporting purposes, the tax laws surrounding the rules for deducting tax depreciation are somewhat different. Current tax depreciation rules allow taxpayers to recover the entire basis of depreciable assets over a specified recovery period (as if the salvage value were zero). The specified recovery periods for depreciable real property (such as apartment buildings and warehouses) are considerably longer than those assigned to personal property (like machinery and automobiles). However, the recovery periods used to determine depreciation are only indirectly related to, and are usually shorter than, the estimated useful lives of the properties depreciated. Assigning a specific recovery period to each type of property eliminates most controversies regarding the recovery periods that should be used to depreciate assets. Furthermore, unlike for financial accounting, in which salvage value is considered when computing annual depreciation deductions, for tax purposes, the entire cost basis of depreciable property is expensed over the assigned recovery periods.

 Reason for the Rule: Prior to 1981, taxpayers could choose from a number of acceptable depreciation methods and write off the cost of assets over a variety of estimated useful lives. These depreciation rules were similar to those used in financial reporting, but they unfortunately required decisions to be made regarding the depreciation method to use, the asset's useful life, and its estimated salvage value. These rules resulted in a greater administrative burden on the IRS. In 1981, Congress enacted the Accelerated Cost Recovery System (ACRS). A hallmark of ACRS was that it specified rates and methods for all classes of assets. This had the effect of lowering compliance and administrative costs by simplifying the methods that were acceptable for depreciating property and by assigning specific class lives to various categories of real and tangible personal property. The depreciation system in effect today is a modified version of ACRS, known as the Modified Accelerated Cost Recovery System (MACRS).

Adjusted basis is the tax equivalent to book value for financial accounting purposes. Adjusted basis equals the initial basis of the asset (typically its cost in the case of an acquired asset) plus any capitalized improvements made to the property minus accumulated depreciation taken on the property. When property is disposed of, adjusted basis is used to determine the amount of gain or loss realized from the disposition. The tax laws require that the adjusted basis of property be reduced by the depreciation allowed or allowable, even if the taxpayer failed to deduct some or all of it.[7] Where no depreciation deductions have been taken on an asset, "allowable depreciation" refers to depreciation that would have been allowed using the straight-line method.

Example 6: Bradley Jones, a sole proprietor, purchased an item of machinery costing $12,000 for his business in 2013. He neglected to take depreciation on the machinery in 2013 through 2015 amounting to $3,500. Bradley sold the machine in 2016. The adjusted basis must be reduced by the $3,500 of depreciation deductions down to $8,500 so that the proper amount of gain or loss realized from the sale can be calculated.

---

[7] Code Sec. 1016(a)(2).

Tax depreciation rules are currently governed by the **Modified Accelerated Cost Recovery System (MACRS).** MACRS allows taxpayers two options for depreciating real and tangible personal property: the general depreciation system (GDS) and the alternative depreciation system (ADS). The main distinction between the GDS (hereafter referred to as MACRS because MACRS incorporates the GDS) and ADS is how quickly the cost of depreciable property can be expensed. Unless a taxpayer elects to use ADS or the tax laws specially require that it be used, MACRS is used to compute tax depreciation. Under both MACRS and ADS, the cost of depreciable property (both new and used property) must be recovered using the applicable depreciation method, recovery period, and convention.[8]

GAAP vs. Code: Due to the different rules that govern the calculation of depreciation expenses for financial accounting versus tax reporting purposes, differences inevitably occur between the amount of depreciation deducted in arriving at net income and the amount deducted in computing taxable income. The difference must be taken into consideration when reconciling net income to taxable income on the corporate tax return. If the amount of depreciation taken on the tax return is greater, the excess must be subtracted from net income when reconciling net income with taxable income, and vice versa.

The differences due to the different methods used to depreciate property are merely timing differences that eventually will reverse themselves. However, this may not occur until the property is sold in a taxable transaction. To illustrate, take an asset that costs $12,000 and has an estimated $2,000 salvage value. Because salvage value is used to compute depreciation for financial statement purposes, over several years a total of $10,000 will be deducted on the income statement with respect to this asset. However, on the tax return, a total of $12,000 (full cost basis) will be deducted. This $2,000 timing difference will be reflected in the adjustments made over the years when reconciling net income with taxable income on the corporate tax returns.

Once the asset is fully depreciated, its book value for financial statement purposes will be $2,000 ($12,000 – $10,000), but its adjusted basis for tax purposes will be $0. This last $2,000 difference in the treatment of depreciation expense will be reversed when the asset is disposed of in a taxable transaction. For example, if this fully depreciated asset is sold for $3,000, the $1,000 gain reported on the income statement ($3,000 – $2,000) will be less than the $3,000 gain reported on the tax return. Consequently, the extra $2,000 of depreciation deducted over the years on the tax return will be offset by the additional $2,000 gain recognized as taxable income in the year the property is sold. This $2,000 difference will result in an additional amount added to net income to reconcile it with taxable income on the corporate tax return in the year the corporation sells the asset.

¶ 704 Depreciating Personal Property

This section discusses the tax rules for depreciating personal property. To calculate their depreciation deduction for property, taxpayers need to know the property's basis for depreciation, the property's recovery period, the depreciation method for the property, and the applicable convention.

.01 Basis for Depreciation

To determine a property's basis for depreciation, the taxpayer's basis in the property has to be multiplied by the percentage of business/investment use. For example, if a taxpayer purchased

---

[8] Code Sec. 168.

equipment for $1,000 and its business use was 100 percent, all of the cost is part of the basis for depreciation.

Deductions and credits allocable to the property have to be subtracted when calculating the property's basis for depreciation. For example, the following are examples of deductions and credits that reduce the basis for depreciation:

- Section 179 expense deduction.

- Deduction for removal of barriers to the disabled and the elderly.

- Disabled access credit.

- Credit for employer-provided child care facilities and services.

- Any basis for investment credit property.

.02 Recovery Period

Tax law categorizes property into *property classes*, which establish the recovery periods under MACRS.[9] Rev. Proc. 87-56 lists the MACRS (general MACRS) and ADS (alternative MACRS) recovery periods for most assets.[10] The class life (MACRS recovery period) for many of the more common types of depreciable personal property is shown in Table 7-1.

Table 7-1 General MACRS Recovery Periods for Personal Property

Property Class (MACRS recovery period)	Examples
3-year property	Race horses that are over two years old, or any breeding or work horse over 12 years old at the time it is placed in service
	All race horses placed in service after 2008 and before 2015
	Qualified rent-to-own property (e.g., televisions and furniture) that a dealer leases to its customers
5-year property	Automobiles, taxis, limousines, buses, light general-purpose trucks, and noncommercial aircraft
	Computers and peripheral equipment (such as printers)
	Personal property used for research and experimentation
	Appliances, carpet, furniture, etc., used in residential rental property
	Office equipment, such as fax machines, phones, and copiers
7-year property	Office furniture
	Most machinery and equipment
	Commercial airplanes
10-year property	Water transportation assets (vessels, barges, tugs)
15-year property	Any qualified leasehold improvement property, qualified restaurant property, or qualified retail improvement property placed in service before 2015
20-year property	Farming structures

---

[9] Code Sec. 168(e).

[10] 1987-2 CB 674, clarified and modified by Rev. Proc. 88-22, 1988-1 CB 785.

Although cars, light general-purpose trucks, and computer equipment have five-year ADS recovery periods, office furniture has a recovery period of 10 years under ADS. Table 7-2 shows the differences in the recovery periods for several types of depreciable personal property. A full list can be found in Rev. Proc. 87-56.[11]

Table 7-2 General vs. ADS Recovery Periods for Personal Property

Examples	General Recovery Period	ADS Recovery Period
Race horses that are over two years old, or any breeding or work horse over 12 years old at the time it is placed in service (but see exception in Table 7-1 for certain race horses placed in service after 2008 and before 2015)	3 years	12 years
Qualified rent-to-own property (e.g., televisions and furniture) that a dealer leases to its customers	3 years	12 years
Automobiles, taxis, limousines, buses, light general-purpose trucks, and noncommercial aircraft	5 years	5 years
Computers and peripheral equipment (such as printers)	5 years	5 years
Personal property used for research and experimentation	5 years	6 years
Office equipment, such as fax machines, phones, and copiers	5 years	6 years
Office furniture	7 years	10 years
Most machinery and equipment	7 years	12 years
Water transportation assets (vessels, barges, tugs)	10 years	18 years
Land improvements (sidewalks, roads, canals, drainage facilities, sewers, but *not* municipal sewers), wharves and docks, bridges, landscaping and shrubbery	15 years	20 years
Farming structures	20 years	25 years

ADS must be used to recover the cost of tangible personal property used predominantly outside the United States, tax-exempt personal use property, and personal property financed through the issuance of tax-exempt bonds. ADS must also be used to depreciate certain types of property (called "listed property) that are used 50 percent or less for business.[12] Listed property becomes an issue for businesses operated as sole proprietorships, which are discussed in Chapter 13. ADS is also sometimes required in the calculation of alternative minimum tax (AMT). This is discussed in Chapter 10.

In addition to the situations in which the use of ADS is required, taxpayers may irrevocably elect to use ADS to depreciate personal property placed in service during the year.[13] Such an election is made on a *class-by-class* basis. For example, if taxpayers want to elect ADS for a light, general-purpose truck placed in service during the year, they must also use ADS to depreciate all other five-year property placed in service during the year.[14] However, taxpayers may elect to use MACRS for all other classes of personal property placed in service during the year. They may also then use MACRS to depreciate five-year property placed in service in a subsequent year if they so choose.

---

[11] 1987-2 CB 674, clarified and modified by Rev. Proc. 88-22, 1988-1 CB 785.

[12] Code Sec. 280F(b)(2).

[13] Code Sec. 168(g)(7).

[14] *Id.*

.03 Depreciation Methods

MACRS allows personal property to be depreciated over the assigned recovery period using either the declining-balance or straight-line method. Most personal property is depreciated using the 200-percent declining-balance method, switching to the straight-line method in the first tax year that the straight-line rate exceeds the declining-balance rate. However, the 150-percent declining-balance method, switching to the straight-line method in the first tax year that the straight-line method exceeds the declining-balance rate, is used to depreciate most types of 15- and 20-year property and property used in a farming business. By contrast, the applicable depreciation method under ADS is the straight-line method.[15]

Taxpayers permitted to use the 200-percent declining-balance method can instead elect to use either the 150-percent declining-balance method or the straight-line method. Taxpayers permitted to use the 150-percent declining-balance method can elect to use the straight-line method. An election is made on IRS Form 4562, *Depreciation and Amortization.*

 Planning Pointer: Even though the tax deductions are higher in the earlier years when the declining-balance method is used, taxpayers should look at the overall picture before automatically assuming that MACRS will yield the greatest overall tax savings. Lower depreciation deductions in the earlier years may be preferred when taxpayers are in a relatively low tax bracket and expect to be in a higher tax bracket in future years. In such situations, using ADS will allow the taxpayer to delay some of the depreciation to those tax years in which they can obtain greater tax savings. In making these decisions, taxpayers should consider the time value of money (i.e., whether the present value of the tax savings in future years exceeds the present value of the tax saved with the earlier deductions).

.04 Applicable Convention

The applicable convention is used to determine when property was placed in service or disposed of during a tax year. The applicabale convention determines the portion of a tax year for which depreciation in allowable during the year that the property was placed in service or disposed.[16]

There are two applicable conventions for personal property: the half-year convention and the mid-quarter convention.[17] The mid-quarter convention applies when more than 40 percent of the cost of personal property placed in service during a tax year is placed in service during the last three months of the tax year.[18]

The **half-year convention** deems that personal property is purchased and sold halfway through the taxpayer's tax year, regardless of the actual dates on which the events occur. Consequently, depreciation in the first and final years is always half of a full year's depreciation under the half-year convention.[19]

Under the **mid-quarter convention**, property is deemed to have been placed in service (or disposed) in the middle of the quarter in which it was actually placed in service (or disposed).[20] For example, if a calendar year taxpayer acquires and places in service property on July 5, 20X1 (the third quarter), the taxpayer is deemed to have placed the property in service on August 15, 20X1 (the middle of the third quarter) and can deduct 4.5/12 of the first year's depreciation in 20X1 (from August 15, 20X1, to December 31, 20X1). In each subsequent year (until the final year), a full year's depreciation is allowed, assuming that the property is kept in service the entire year. If the same

---

[15] Code Sec. 168(g)(2)(A).
[16] Code Sec. 168(i)(4).
[17] Code Sec. 168(d)(1).

[18] Code Sec. 168(d)(3).
[19] *Id.*
[20] *Id.*

corporation were to sell the property on January 25, 20X5, under the mid-quarter convention it would be deemed to have disposed of the property on February 15, 20X5 (halfway through the first quarter). Consequently, the corporation would be entitled to 1.5/12 of a full year's depreciation in the final year (from January 1, 20X5, to February 15, 20X5).

The **mid-quarter convention** applies to all depreciable personal property placed in service during a tax year if more than 40 percent of the aggregate cost of all depreciable personal property placed in service during such tax year is placed in service during the last three months of the tax year.[21] In determining if the mid-quarter convention applies, only the basis of personal property placed in service during the year is used.[22] Therefore, the depreciable basis of property not subject to MACRS is disregarded, as is the cost of depreciable real property or any portion of the property that is expensed under Code Sec. 179.[23] If the 40-percent test is not met, the half-year convention applies to all personal property placed in service during the year.

Reason for the Rule: When ACRS was first enacted in 1981, Congress simplified the timing of when depreciation would begin and end by assuming that all personal property was placed in service halfway through the tax year. Although only a half-year's depreciation was allowed on property placed in service during the first half of the tax year, such loss of depreciation was offset by allowing a half year of depreciation on property placed in service toward the end of the year. This simplified method was based on the assumption that property would be placed in service evenly throughout the tax year. Over the next several years, taxpayers began acquiring and placing in service personal property toward the end of the tax year to take advantage of the half-year convention. Taxpayers were able to deduct a half year of depreciation for property placed in service a few days before the end of the year. In 1986, Congress attempted to curb any potential abuses by enacting the mid-quarter convention. If property is placed in service evenly throughout the year, then only 25 percent of all personal property should be placed in service during the last quarter of the year. Accordingly, Congress decided that placing in service more than 40 percent of all personal property during the fourth quarter constitutes abuse of the leniency of the half-year convention.

Under the mid-quarter convention, the percentages allowed in the first year for property placed in service during the first two quarters are greater than under the half-year convention. For example, 35 percent of five-year property placed in service during the first quarter is allowed in the first year under the mid-quarter convention (see Table 7-4), whereas only 20 percent is allowed under the half-year convention (see Table 7-3). However, with respect to five-year property placed in service in the fourth quarter, only five percent of the cost is depreciated in the first year. In order for the mid-quarter convention to apply, more than 40 percent of the cost of all personal property placed in service during the year is subject to the lower depreciation rates in the first year. Accordingly, overall depreciation expense is generally much lower in the first year when the mid-quarter convention applies, as evidenced by comparing the first years' total depreciation in Examples 12 and 13 ($880 versus $270).

Planning Pointer: For purposes of determining whether the half-year or mid-quarter convention applies to personal property placed in service during the year, any amount expensed under Code Sec. 179 is not considered when applying the 40-percent test. Therefore, when deciding which properties to elect to expense under Code Sec. 179, taxpayers should consider expensing property placed in service during the fourth

---

[21] Code Sec. 168(d)(3)(A).
[22] Code Sec. 168(d)(3)(A).

[23] Ltr. Rul. 9126014, 3-29-91.

quarter, if doing so will prevent the taxpayer from being subject to the mid-quarter convention.

.05 Calculating the Depreciation Allowance

Once a taxpayer has determined a property's basis for depreciation, the property's recovery period, the depreciation method for the property, and the applicable convention, the taxpayer can determine the amount of depreciation allowable for the property.

Example 7: On November 5, 20X1, a calendar year business places in service an asset that costs $10,000. The asset is five-year property for the purposes of MACRS. Under the straight-line method, the entire $10,000 cost would be expensed evenly over the asset's five-year life. Assuming the half-year convention applies, only half of a full year's depreciation is allowed in the first year, and the depreciation expense for 20X1 equals $1,000 ($10,000/5 × ½). Assuming the asset is not sold, for each year from 20X2 to 20X5, depreciation of $2,000 ($10,000/5) is deducted against business income. In the sixth year (20X6), the remaining $1,000 of depreciation expense is deducted.

Year	Beginning Adjusted Basis	Depreciation Expense	Ending Adjusted Basis
20X1	$10,000	$1,000	$9,000
20X2	9,000	2,000	7,000
20X3	7,000	2,000	5,000
20X4	5,000	2,000	3,000
20X5	3,000	2,000	1,000
20X6	1,000	1,000	0
Accumulated Depreciation		$10,000	

The adjusted basis of the property is reduced by the amount of depreciation taken on the property each year. Because salvage value is ignored, the adjusted basis of the property will equal $0 when the property is fully depreciated, if the taxpayer does not dispose of the property during the recovery period.

Example 8: Assume the same facts as in Example 7, except the DDB method is used to depreciate the property. Depreciation expense is now calculated using twice the straight-line rate, or 40% (1/5 years × 2), and the first year's depreciation equals $2,000 ($10,000 × 40% × ½). This amount reduces the adjusted basis of the property at the end of 20X1 to $8,000 ($10,000 – $2,000), and is the starting point for calculating the depreciation expense for 20X2.

The depreciation expense for 20X2 equals $3,200 ($8,000 × 40%), and the property's adjusted basis is reduced to $4,800 at the end of 20X2 ($8,000 – $3,200). The depreciation expense for 20X3 equals $1,920 ($4,800 × 40%). At the end of 20X3, the adjusted basis of the property equals $2,880 ($4,800 – $1,920) and 2½ years of depreciation remain. If the adjusted basis of $2,880 were expensed using the straight-line method, annual depreciation would be $1,152 ($2,880/2.5). Under the DDB method, depreciation expense for 20X4 also equals $1,152 ($2,880 × 40%). Therefore, at the end of the third tax year, depreciation expense under the straight-line method has caught up with the depreciation expense under the DDB method. Accordingly, starting with 20X4, the switch is made to the straight-line method. The depreciation expense for 20X4 and 20X5 equals $1,152, and in 20X6 it equals $576 ($1,152 × ½).

Year	Beginning Adjusted Basis	Depreciation Expense	Ending Adjusted Basis
20X1	$10,000	$ 2,000	$8,000
20X2	8,000	3,200	4,800
20X3	4,800	1,920	2,880
20X4	2,880	1,152	1,728
20X5	1,728	1,152	576
20X6	576	576	0
Accumulated Depreciation		$10,000	

Example 9: Assume the same facts as in Example 8, except the mid-quarter convention applies and the property is sold on April 10, 20X3. Because the property was placed in service during the fourth quarter of 20X1, for purposes of computing depreciation for 20X1, the property is deemed to have been placed in service on November 15, 20X1—halfway through the fourth quarter. Thus, the depreciation expense for the first year equals $500 ($10,000 × 40% × 1.5 months/12). This amount reduces the adjusted basis of the property to $9,500 ($10,000 – $500) at the end of 20X1.

For 20X2, a full year's depreciation is allowed ($9,500 × 40% = $3,800). This amount reduces the property's adjusted basis to $5,700 ($9,500 – $3,800) at the end of 20X2. In 20X3, the property was actually disposed of in the second quarter; therefore, it is deemed to have been disposed of on May 15, 20X3. Consequently, the property is depreciated from January 1, 20X3, through May 15, 20X3, and the depreciation expense for that year equals $855 ($5,700 × 40% × 4.5/12). The $4,845 adjusted basis of the property on the day it is sold is used in determining the gain or loss resulting from the sale (see ¶ 801).

Year	Beginning Adjusted Basis	Depreciation Expense	Ending Adjusted Basis
20X1	$10,000	$ 500	$9,500
20X2	9,500	3,800	5,700
20X3	5,700	855	4,845
Accumulated Depreciation		$5,155	

The previous examples show how the depreciation calculations can be made manually. However, an easier way to calculate MACRS on personal property is to use depreciation tables provided by the IRS.[24] These tables are reproduced in Tables 7-3 and 7-4 below for both five-and seven-year property.

Table 7-3 MACRS 5-Year and 7-Year Recovery Rates (Double Declining-Balance Method; Half-Year Convention)

Recovery Year	5-Year Property	7-Year Property
1	20.00%	14.29%
2	32.00	24.49
3	19.20	17.49
4	11.52	12.49

[24] Rev. Proc. 87-57, 1987-2 CB 687.

Recovery Year	5-Year Property	7-Year Property
5	11.52	8.93
6	5.76	8.92
7		8.93
8		4.46

Under the half-year convention, a full year's depreciation under the DDB method equals 40 percent of the straight-line rate for five-year property (1/5 × 2) and 28.57 percent for seven-year property (1/7 × 2). The first-year recovery rates from Table 7-3 are half of these rates (40% × ½ = 20%; 28.57% × ½ = 14.29%), which properly reflect the fact that the property was deemed to have been placed in service halfway through the year. Each subsequent year's recovery rate reflects a full year's depreciation.

For example, at the beginning of year 2, 80 percent of the asset's cost of five-year property has not been depreciated (100% – 0% expensed in year 1). In year 2, 40 percent of the remaining 80 percent adjusted basis equals 32 percent—the amount shown in Table 7-3. At the beginning of year 3, 52 percent of the asset has been depreciated (20% + 32%), leaving 48 percent yet to be depreciated. Forty percent of that amount equals 19.2 percent, which is the percentage shown for year 3 in the table. In the final year, the remaining half-year's depreciation is allowed. If an asset subject to the half-year convention is sold in the last recovery year, no adjustment is made to the table percentage because the percentage already reflects six months' depreciation.

To calculate the amount of MACRS depreciation each year, the unadjusted cost of the property is multiplied by the applicable recovery rate from the table. However, if the property is disposed of prior to being fully depreciated (before the sixth year for five-year property; before the eighth year for seven-year property), the percentages from Table 7-3 must be reduced by half to reflect the deemed disposal of the property halfway through the year.

Example 10: Seven-year property costing $10,000 is placed in service during 20X6 and is sold during 20X9. The half-year convention applies to all seven-year property placed in service during 20X6.

Year	Cost Basis		Recovery Rate		Depreciation Expense
20X6	$10,000	×	14.29%	=	$1,429
20X7	10,000	×	24.49%	=	2,449
20X8	10,000	×	17.49%	=	1,749
20X9	10,000	×	12.49% × ½	=	625

Table 7-4 MACRS 5- and 7-Year Recovery Rates (Double Declining-Balance Method; Mid-Quarter Convention)

Placed in Service During:

Year	1st Quarter		2nd Quarter		3rd Quarter		4th Quarter	
	5-year	7-year	5-year	7-year	5-year	7-year	5-year	7-year
1	35.00%	25.00%	25.00%	17.85%	15.00%	10.71%	5.00%	3.57%
2	26.00	21.43	30.00	23.47	34.00	25.51	38.00	27.55
3	15.60	15.31	18.00	16.76	20.40	18.22	22.80	19.68
4	11.01	10.93	11.37	11.97	12.24	13.02	13.68	14.06

	Placed in Service During:							
	1st Quarter		2nd Quarter		3rd Quarter		4th Quarter	
Year	5-year	7-year	5-year	7-year	5-year	7-year	5-year	7-year
5	11.01	8.75	11.37	8.87	11.30	9.30	10.94	10.04
6	1.38	8.74	4.26	8.87	7.06	8.85	9.58	8.73
7		8.75		8.87		8.86		8.73
8		1.09		3.34		5.53		7.64

Under the mid-quarter year convention, the first full year's depreciation under the DDB method must be reduced to reflect the portion of the year that the property was deemed placed in service. For example, a calendar year taxpayer that places property in service during the third quarter will be deemed to have placed it in service on August 15. Consequently, depreciation is allowed from August 15 to December 31, or for $4\frac{1}{2}$ months. Depreciation for the first year is 15 percent for five-year property ($1/5 \times 2 \times 4.5/12$) and 10.71 percent for seven-year property ($1/7 \times 2 \times 4.5/12$)—the percentages shown in the 3rd Quarter columns for year 1 in Table 7-4. Each subsequent year's recovery rate reflects a full year's depreciation. Therefore, if the property is disposed of prior to being fully depreciated, the percentages from Table 7-4 must be reduced to reflect only the portion of the year up until the middle of the quarter in which the property is disposed of.

Example 11: A calendar year corporation places in service seven-year property costing $10,000 on April 29, 20X1. The corporation sells the property on September 5, 20X5. The mid-quarter convention applies to all seven-year property placed in service during 20X1.

Year	Cost Basis		Recovery Rate		Depreciation Expense
20X1	$10,000	×	17.85%	=	$1,785
20X2	10,000	×	23.47%	=	2,347
20X3	10,000	×	16.76%	=	1,676
20X4	10,000	×	11.97%	=	1,197
20X5	10,000	×	8.87% × 7.5/12	=	554

Because the property was placed in service during the second quarter (April to June for calendar-year taxpayers), the column that corresponds to the second quarter for seven-year property is used to depreciate the property each year. In 20X5 the property is sold in the third quarter (July to September). Therefore, the property is deemed sold on August 15, 20X5—the middle of the third quarter. MACRS on the property during 20X5 is reduced to reflect the $7\frac{1}{2}$ months during 20X5 that the property was deemed to have been in service.

Example 12: During 20X0, John Frank purchases and places in service in his business a computer costing $3,000, a desk costing $700, and a copier costing $900. The computer is placed in service in January, the desk in August, and the copier in November. The aggregate basis of the personal property placed in service during the year equals $4,600. For the mid-quarter convention to apply to John's personal property placed in service during 20X0, more than $1,840 ($4,600 × 40%) must have been placed in service during the fourth quarter. Because the $900 copier is the only property placed in service during the fourth quarter, the mid-quarter convention does not apply and John uses the half-year convention (Table 7-3) to depreciate the personal property placed in service during 20X0.

The depreciation expense for the first two years for each of these assets is shown below. The rates used to compute the depreciation expense are from the applicable columns in Table 7-3.

Depreciation expense for 20X0

Item	Unadjusted Basis		Depreciation Rate		Depreciation Expense
Computer (5-year)	$3,000	×	20.00%	=	$ 600
Desk (7-year property)	700	×	14.29%	=	100
Copier (5-year property)	900	×	20.00%	=	180
Total depreciation expense					$ 880

Depreciation expense for 20X1

Item	Unadjusted Basis		Depreciation Rate		Depreciation Expense
Computer (5-year)	$3,000	×	32.00%	=	$ 960
Desk (7-year property)	700	×	24.49%	=	171
Copier (5-year property)	900	×	32.00%	=	288
Total depreciation expense					$1,419

Example 13: The facts are the same as in Example 12, except both the $900 copier and the $3,000 computer are placed in service in November. Because John placed more than 40 percent of the cost of the personal property in service during the fourth quarter, the mid-quarter convention (Table 7-4) must be used to compute depreciation for each of the three assets placed in service during 20X0.

Depreciation expense for the first two years for each of these assets is shown below. The rates used to compute depreciation expense are from the applicable columns in Table 7-4 (third quarter for the desk and fourth quarter for the computer and copier).

Depreciation expense for 20X0

Item	Unadjusted Basis		Depreciation Rate		Depreciation Expense
Computer (5-year)	$3,000	×	5.00%	=	$ 150
Desk (7-year property)	700	×	10.71%	=	75
Copier (5-year property)	900	×	5.00%	=	45
Total depreciation expense					$ 270

Depreciation expense for 20X1

Item	Unadjusted Basis		Depreciation Rate		Depreciation Expense
Computer (5-year)	$3,000	×	38.00%	=	$1,140
Desk (7-year property)	700	×	25.51%	=	179
Copier (5-year property)	900	×	38.00%	=	342
Total depreciation expense					$1,661

MACRS optional tables. The IRS provides[25] depreciation tables for each of the acceptable methods under MACRS, which include both 200-percent and 150-percent declining-balance methods as well as the straight-line method. As with the tables reproduced in Tables 7-3 and 7-4, the percentages listed for the first year already reflect the portion of the first year that the property was deemed to be in service under the applicable averaging convention. All subsequent years (except the last one) reflect a full year's depreciation. These IRS tables are reproduced in the Appendix at ¶ 725. The following expenses show how depreciation is calculated using these optional tables.

Example 14: In August of 20X1, Glass On Demand, a wholesaler of automotive glass, pays $50,000 for new steel racks for transporting the glass to its customers. According to Rev. Proc. 87-56, the racks qualify as three-year property. Assuming Glass uses a calendar year and the half-year convention applies, its depreciation deduction for 20X1 equals $16,665 ($50,000 × 33.33%), and its deduction for 20X2 equals $22,225 ($50,000 × 44.45%). These percentages are from the 3-year recovery period column of Table 7A in the Appendix to this chapter (see ¶ 725).

Example 15: The facts are the same as in Example 14, except Glass elects to use straight-line depreciation for all three-year property placed in service in 20X1. The depreciation expense for the racks in 20X1 equals $8,335 ($50,000 × 16.67%), and depreciation for 20X2 equals $16,665 ($50,000 × 33.33%). These percentages are from the 3-year recovery period column of Table 7F in the Appendix to this chapter (see ¶ 725).

Example 16: The facts are the same as in Example 14, except the racks were placed in service in November and were the only property placed in service during the year. Because the 40-percent test has been met, the mid-quarter convention applies to all personal property placed in service during 20X1. Depreciation expense for 20X1 now equals $4,165 ($50,000 × 8.33%), and depreciation expense for 20X2 equals $30,555 ($50,000 × 61.11%). These percentages are taken from the 3-year recovery period column of the Table 7E in the Appendix to this chapter (see ¶ 725).

Example 17: In February of 20X1, John Smith purchases a machine for $20,000. The machine is used exclusively for business, and the half-year convention applies. The machine is seven-year property for the purposes of MACRS, but its recovery period for the purposes of ADS is 10 years. If John elects ADS to depreciate all seven-year property placed in service in 20X1, his depreciation deduction for 20X1 under the half-year convention equals $1,000 ($20,000 × 5%), and his depreciation deduction in 20X2 and 20X3 equals $2,000 ($20,000 × 10%). These percentages are from the 10-year recovery period column of Table 7F in the Appendix to this chapter (see ¶ 725). If John sells the machine in 20X4, his depreciation expense that year will equal $1,000 ($20,000 × 10% × ½ year).

Example 18: In July of 20X2, J.W. Smith & Co., a calendar-year taxpayer, places in service a $700 desk in July and a $3,000 computer in November. The desk is seven-year property, and the computer is five-year property. Assuming no other property is placed in service during the tax year, the mid-quarter convention applies because more than 40 percent of all personal property ($3,700 × 40% = $1,480) was placed in service in the last quarter. Depreciation for 20X1 and 20X2 for the desk equals $75 ($700 × 10.71%) and $179 ($700 × 25.51%), respectively. These percentages come from the column for 7-year property placed in service in the third quarter in Table 7-4 (and in Table 7D in the Appendix to this chapter (see ¶ 725)). Depreciation for 20X1 and 20X2 for the computer equals $150 ($3,000 × 5%) and $1,140 ($3,000 × 38%), respectively. These percentages also come from Table 7-4 (and Table 7E in the Appendix to this chapter (see ¶ 725)).

---

[25] Rev. Proc. 87-57, 1987-2 CB 687.

¶ 704.05

Example 19: Continuing with Example 18, Smith sells the desk in January 20X3. Because the desk is deemed to have been sold on February 15, 20X3, depreciation on the desk for 2003 under the mid-quarter convention is $16 ($700 × 18.22% × 1.5/12). Depreciation for the computer in 20X3 equals $684 ($3,000 × 22.8%). Smith continues to depreciate the computer using the same column from the same depreciation table for as long as the property is used in its business.

.06 Additional Depreciation for the Year Placed Into Service

The events of September 11, 2001, led Congress to liberalize the amount of depreciation that can be taken in the year that the asset is first placed into service. Congress wanted to encourage businesses to acquire new machinery, equipment, and other depreciable personal property and boost the economy. The liberalization of depreciation rules took two forms:

1. Additional first-year depreciation (called bonus depreciation); and

2. Enhanced Code Sec. 179 expensing

Several tax acts since then have further liberalized and extended these favorable provisions. Code Sec. 179 is discussed at ¶ 707. The effect of the various acts on the bonus depreciation is as follows:

Year(s) of Acquisition	Maximum Bonus Depreciation Rate
January 1, 2008 through September 8, 2010	50 percent
September 8, 2010 through December 31, 2011	100 percent
January 1, 2012 through December 31, 2014 (December 31, 2015 in the case of property with a long production period and certain noncommercial aircraft)	50 percent

Eligible property. Bonus depreciation for property acquired after December 31, 2007 and before January 1, 2015 is allowed for MACRS property with a recovery period of 20 years or less, as well as computer software, certain water utility property, and certain qualified leasehold improvement property. The taxpayer reduces the adjusted basis of the property by the amount of bonus depreciation taken.

 Spotlight: Taxpayers that do not want to deduct bonus depreciation may elect out of this provision. The taxpayer then depreciates the full basis of the property under the MACRS rules. Note that bonus depreciation is *not* allowed on used property.

¶ 705 Depreciating Real Property

The tax laws allow taxpayers to depreciate the costs associated with the acquisition of real property using the straight-line method. Because land does not wear out, decay, get used up, become obsolete, or lose its value from natural causes, it is not depreciable. Only improvements on the land are depreciable.

The recovery period for depreciable realty is long—27.5 years or 39 years, depending on its use. Fortunately however, a not insignificant portion of the "cost" of a typical business or rental building is actually personal property, not realty. Once segregated for depreciation purposes (taxpayers often hire experts to do costs segregation), these separate personal property components may be depreciated over the shorter prescribed period for personal property.

Generally, the cost of grading, clearing, planting, and landscaping are considered part of the cost of the land. However, land preparation costs may be depreciable if they are so closely associated with a depreciable asset that it is not possible to ascertain a life for the preparation costs that is separate from the life of the asset with which they are associated. Certain other land improvements that may be depreciated include sidewalks, roads, canals, drainage facilities, waterways, sewers, wharves, docks, bridges, and fences. These depreciable land improvements are treated as personal property and can be depreciated over a 15-year recovery period.

Example 20: Jones & Sons is in the process of constructing a new building for its business. Jones incurs costs for grading, clearing, seeding, and planting trees. Some of the bushes and trees are planted in the immediate vicinity of the building, while others are planted around the outer perimeter of the lot on which the new building is placed. If Jones were to replace the building, it would have to destroy the bushes and trees immediately adjacent to it. Therefore, Jones can depreciate the cost of landscaping right next to the building. It also can treat the cost of grading land directly under the building, including trenches for concrete footers, as part of the cost of the building. It cannot, however, depreciate the cost of the rest of the landscaping, which must be added to the basis of the land.

Under MACRS, the recovery period is 27.5 years for residential rental property and 39 years for nonresidential real property.[26] Under ADS, all real property is depreciated over 40 years.[27]

The **mid-month convention** is used to determine the dates that real property is deemed to be placed in service and disposed of, regardless of whether MACRS or ADS is used.[28] Under the **mid-month convention**, property is deemed placed in service in the middle of the month in which it is actually placed in service and disposed of in the middle of the month in which it is actually disposed.

Example 21: Depreciable real property is placed in service on February 3, 2015, by a calendar-year taxpayer. For 2015, depreciation may be claimed for 10.5 months (February 15, 2015, to December 31, 2015).

Example 22: Assume that the property in Example 21 was sold in March 2016. The property is considered in service in 2016 until March 15, 2016. Therefore, 2½ months of depreciation may be deducted on the taxpayer's 2016 tax return with respect to the property.

A building or structure is **residential rental property** if 80 percent or more of the gross rental income from the building or structure is rental income from dwelling units.[29] A **dwelling unit** is a house or apartment used to provide living accommodations. It does not include a unit in a hotel, motel, inn, or other establishment if more than 50 percent of the units in the motel, inn, or other establishment are used on a transient basis. Dwelling units include mobile homes and manufactured homes. Apartment buildings are an example of residential real property. Depreciable real property that does not meet the definition of residential rental property is "nonresidential real property." Examples of nonresidential real property include warehouses, office buildings, and certain manufacturing facilities.

Example 23: On May 1, 2015, John Jones pays $240,000 for real property. $40,000 of the cost is allocable to land. The building consists of a single storefront and six similar upper story apartments. Jones receives $400 per month for each of the six apartments and $700 per month for the store. Because the $2,400 gross rental income from the apartments ($400 × 6 units) is less than 80 percent of the gross rental income from the building ($2,400 + $700 = $3,100 × 80% = $2,480), the building is not residential rental property and must be depreciated over a 39-year recovery period under MACRS.

---

[26] Code Sec. 168(c).

[27] Code Sec. 168(g)(2)(C).

[28] Code Sec. 168(d)(2), (g)(2)(B).

[29] Code Sec. 168(e)(2)(A).

Example 24: The facts are the same as in Example 23, except that each apartment rents for $500 per month. Gross rental income from the building is then equal to $3,700 ($500 × 6 = $3,000 + $700). Because at least 80 percent of the gross rental income ($3,700 × 80% = $2,960) from the building comes from renting the apartments ($500 × 6 = $3,000), the building is residential rental property and can be depreciated over 27.5 years under MACRS.

The IRS provides depreciation tables for real property.

Example 25: Continuing with Example 24, assume that the depreciable basis of the rental portion of the building is $172,973. The building is deemed placed in service on May 15, 2015. Therefore, depreciation for 2015 equals $3,931 ($172,973/27.5 × 7.5/12). Depreciation for 2016 is $6,290 ($172,973/27.5).

Example 26: In December of 2015, Primex, Inc. (a calendar year taxpayer) purchases an office building for $450,000, of which $50,000 is allocable to the cost of the land. Depreciation expense for the building in 2015 equals $427 ($400,000/39 × .5/12).

Example 27: Continuing with Example 26, Primex sells the office building on November 10, 2019. Primex continues to depreciate the building until November 15, 2019. Therefore, in 2016, 2017, and 2018, Primex deducts $10,256 ($400,000/39), and on its 2019 tax return, it deducts $8,974 ($400,000/39 × 10.5/12). Primex's adjusted basis in the building at the time it is sold equals $359,831 ($400,000 − $427 − ($10,256 × 3) − $8,974).

Example 28: Assume the same facts as in Examples 26 and 27, except that Primex elects to depreciate the building using ADS. Under ADS, all real property is depreciated over 40 years. Therefore, 2015 depreciation equals $417 ($400,000/40 × .5/12), and the amount of depreciation that can be deducted in 2016, 2017, and 2018 is $10,000 ($400,000/40). In 2019, Primex's depreciation deduction is $8,750 ($400,000/40 × 10.5/12). Its adjusted basis in the building at the time of the sale equals $360,833 ($400,000 − $417 − ($10,000 × 3) − $8,750).

An irrevocable election may be made to use ADS for any class of property placed in service during a tax year.[30] Unlike the election to use ADS for personal property, which is done on a class-by-class basis, the ADS election for real property is made on a property-by-property basis.[31] Accordingly, taxpayers can elect to use ADS for one real property placed in service during the year but still use MACRS to depreciate another piece of real property placed in service during the year.

¶ 706 Depreciating Improvements

Any depreciation deduction for any addition or improvement to property (including structural components that are added to a building after its construction) is computed in the same manner as the deduction for the underlying property would be computed if the property were placed in service at the same time as the addition or improvement.[32] For example, a roof replaced on a commercial building is separately depreciated as 39-year nonresidential real property beginning in the year the new roof is placed in service. The cost of an addition to or improvement of property, which must be depreciated, should be distinguished from a repair or maintenance expense, which can be deducted currently.

Example 29: In June 2015, the American Furniture Company purchases a new transmission for its delivery truck (five-year property). The truck is four years old and has been driven 300,000 miles. The transmission costs $2,000. The depreciation period for the transmission begins during 2015 following its installation in the truck. Assuming the

---

[30] Code Sec. 168(g)(7).
[31] Code Sec. 168(g)(7)(A).

[32] Code Sec. 168(i)(6).

half-year convention applies to personal property placed in service during 2015, the depreciation expense of $400 ($2,000 × 20%) would be calculated using the 5-year column in Table 7-3.

Additions or improvements made to real property that is leased are also treated as separate property items for depreciation purposes. MACRS depreciation on such additions or improvements is computed in the same way depreciation generally would be computed on the property added to or improved if such property had been placed in service at the same time as the addition or improvement.[33]

Any unrecovered basis in property owned by the lessee and abandoned without compensation upon termination of the lease may be deducted as a loss. A lessor that disposes of or abandons a leasehold improvement made by the lessor upon termination of a lease may also claim a loss.[34]

¶ 707 Section 179 Expensing

Code Sec. 179 allows taxpayers to elect to immediately expense (i.e., currently deduct) certain depreciable personal property (known as "Section 179 property"[35]) placed in service during the year rather than depreciate it over several tax years. When a taxpayer elects to expense all or a portion of the depreciable property under Code Sec. 179, the adjusted basis of the property is reduced by the amount expensed for purposes of depreciating the remainder of the cost basis under MACRS or ADS.[36]

Reason for the Rule: If the tax laws did not require taxpayers to reduce the property's basis by the full amount it elects to expense under Code Sec. 179, taxpayers could expense more than the total cost of the property.

Planning Pointer: When deciding which property to expense under Code Sec. 179, taxpayers should consider expensing seven-year property in preference to five-year property placed in service in the same tax year. Because the cost of five-year property will be expensed over six years under MACRS (versus eight years for seven-year property), electing to first expense seven-year property will accelerate the deductions allowed to the taxpayer.

.01 Section 179 Property

Section 179 property is depreciable tangible personal property or computer software (if placed in service in a tax year beginning before 2015) that is acquired *by purchase* for use in the *active conduct of a trade or business*. Code Sec. 179 expensing is not allowed for property used outside the United States or for the most real property,[37] other than "qualified real property" (for a tax year beginning in 2010, 2011, 2012, 2013, or 2014).[38] The term "qualified real property" includes qualified leasehold improvement property, qualified restaurant property, and qualified retail improvement property.[39]

Property is not considered acquired by "purchase" if it is acquired from a related party or if it is acquired in a transaction on which recognition of gain or loss is deferred under the tax laws, such as a like-kind exchange or involuntary conversion.

---

[33] Code Sec. 168(i)(8).

[34] Code Sec. 168(i)(8)(B).

[35] Code Sec. 179(d)(1).

[36] Reg. § 1.179-1(f)(1).

[37] Code Sec. 179(d).

[38] Code Sec. 179(f)(1).

[39] Code Sec. 179(f)(2). Code Sec. 168(e) defines these three items.

Property acquired by trade-in. The cost of property for purposes of the expense election does not include the basis of other property held at any time by the person acquiring the property.[40] In other words, when used property is traded in for other property, only the boot paid is eligible for the expense election.

Example 30: Fred Farmer traded in his old combine, which had an adjusted basis of $40,000, for a new combine. He paid $60,000 in cash. Although the initial basis of his new combine is $100,000 ($40,000 + $60,000), only the $60,000 boot paid is eligible for the expense election.

.02 Dollar Limitation

The maximum Code Sec. 179 deduction cannot exceed the dollar limitation. Starting with tax years beginning in 2011, the dollar limitation has been $500,000. The dollar limitation will fall to $25,000 for tax years beginning after 2014 unless Congress once again increases the limit.

Example 31: Onandaga, Inc. purchases $572,000 of Section 179 property in 2014. It may elect to expense up to $500,000 of the property in 2014. It will have $72,000 ($572,000 – $500,000) of remaining basis that it may depreciate beginning in 2014.

Reduction in dollar limitation. To the extent that the taxpayer's total Section 179 property placed in service during the year exceeds a certain threshold, the dollar limitation is reduced dollar for dollar.[41]

Beginning with tax years starting in 2010, the investment limitation has been $2,000,000.[42] The investment limitation will fall to $200,000 in tax years beginning after 2014 unless Congress once again increases the limit.

Thus, for a tax year that begins in 2014, the investment limitation prevents taxpayers that place $2,500,000 ($2,000,000 + $500,000) or more of Section 179 property in service during the year from benefiting from Code Sec. 179. Amounts disallowed may not be expensed in later tax years.

Example 32: During 2014, Amcast, Inc., a calendar year manufacturing company, places in service $2,100,000 of Section 179 property. Amcast can elect to immediately expense up to $400,000 of the property in 2014 ($500,000 – ($2,100,000 – $2,000,000)) and recover the remainder of the cost under the normal cost-recovery rules.

 Reason for the Rule: In enacting Code Sec. 179, Congress wanted to give small businesses an incentive to purchase equipment and other depreciable personal property. For purposes of this rule, "small business" is defined by how much tangible personal property is placed in service during the year.

Spouses. Spouses are treated as one taxpayer, regardless of which spouse purchased the property or placed it in service and regardless whether the spouses filed a joint return or separate returns. Taxpayers who are married and filing separate returns must allocate the dollar limitation (as reduced) for the year. Unless the spouses elect otherwise, 50 percent of the dollar limitation will be allocated to each of them.[43]

---

[40] Code Sec. 179(d)(3).
[41] Code Sec. 179(b)(2), (5).

[42] Economic Stimulus Package Act of 2008, Sec. 201. Rev. Proc. 2009-50, 2009-45 IRB, American Tax Payer Relief Act of 2012.
[43] Code Sec. 179(b)(4).

.03 Taxable Income Limitation

Taxpayers cannot elect to expense an amount exceeding the taxable income that they derive from the active conduct of any trade or business.[44] This taxable income limitation is applied after the dollar limitation.

Taxable income attributable to services performed as an employee is considered taxable income from the active conduct of a trade or business. Taxable income from the active conduct of a trade or business is computed without regard to any Code Sec. 179 expense, but after all other business expenses, including depreciation.[45]

Any amounts disallowed because of the taxable income limitation are carried forward to the next tax year and are added to the amount allowable as a Code Sec. 179 deduction for that year, subject to the dollar and taxable income limitations for the year.[46] Generally, disallowed Code Sec. 179 deductions may be carried forward indefinitely. Furthermore, any amounts the taxpayer elects to expense under Code Sec. 179 (regardless of whether there is sufficient taxable income to deduct the full amount in the current year) reduces the basis of the property for purposes of depreciating it under MACRS or ADS.[47]

Example 33: Hagerton Company places in service $1,200,000 of Section 179 property during 2014. Hagerton elects to expense the full $500,000 that it is allowed under the dollar limit. It can then take depreciation deductions for the remaining $700,000 basis ($1,200,000 – $500,000) using MACRS. If Hagerton's taxable income derived from its trade or business is $270,000 in 2014, it may still elect to expense the full $500,000 in 2014. However, it will only be able to use $270,000 to reduce its taxable income in 2014. The remaining $230,000 ($500,000 – $270,000) will be carried over to 2015.

Example 34: If, in Example 33, Hagerton is concerned that it may not be able to utilize the $230,000 of Code Sec. 179 expense carried over due to the taxable income limitation in the near future, it can elect to expense a smaller amount in 2014. For example, if Hagerton were to elect $270,000 of Code Sec. 179 expense in 2014, it would reduce its basis in the personal property to $930,000 ($1,270,000 – $270,000), and its MACRS deduction over the next several years would be higher than if it elected the full $500,000.

Spouses. If spouses files separate returns, the taxable income limitation is applied separately on each spouse's separate return.

Example 35: Marvin and Loretta English filed separate returns in 2014. They placed $1,700,000 and $500,000 of Section 179 property in service, respectively, for a combined total of $2,200,000. Marvin has $600,000 of taxable income from the active conduct of a trade or business; Loretta has $3,000. If they file a joint return, they can elect to expense up to $300,000 ($500,000 – ($2,200,000 – $2,000,000)), and they can deduct the entire amount in 2014 because their combined taxable business income exceeds this amount. If Marvin and Loretta decide to file separate returns, absent a contrary election, each spouse is allocated 50 percent of the $300,000, or $150,000. Loretta's deduction would be limited to $3,000, her taxable business income. She could carry the $147,000 excess over to future tax years. Amounts carried over would be subject to the applicable dollar and taxable income limitations each year.

.04 Partnerships and S Corporations

In the case of partnerships and S corporations, both the entity and each of its respective owners are subject to the annual dollar and taxable income limitations. However, in determining whether more than the dollar limitation on Section 179 property has been placed in service during the tax

---

[44] Code Sec. 179(b)(3).
[45] Code Sec. 179(b)(3).

[46] Code Sec. 179(b)(3)(B).
[47] Reg. § 1.179-1(f)(1).

year by the owner, the cost of Section 179 property placed in service by the *entity* is not taken into consideration by the owner.[48]

Example 36: In 2014, Christina Campbell and Colleen Collins form a partnership to operate a bakery. The partnership purchases an oven and a refrigerator for a total cost of $334,000. Both Christina and Colleen are active in the conduct of the business. In the same year, Colleen enters into a separate business venture, a flower shop operated as a sole proprietorship, for which she purchases $3,000 worth of equipment.

Assuming the partnership has sufficient taxable income, it can elect to expense all $334,000 of the cost of the oven and refrigerator. Each partner's share of the expense deduction is $167,000. Colleen can elect to expense up to $170,000 ($167,000 + $3,000) if she has in aggregate at least $170,000 of taxable income from the partnership, flower shop, and/or other trade or business in which she actively participates. Christina may expense $167,000 if she satisfies the taxable income limitation.

.05 Disposition of Section 179 Property

A Code Sec. 179 expense deduction is treated as a depreciation deduction for purposes of computing the adjusted basis of property. However, when a Section 179 expense is elected, but the deduction is disallowed due to the taxable income limitations, any amount of Section 179 expense carried over and not deducted before disposition of the asset does not reduce the adjusted basis of the asset for the purpose of determining the gain or loss recognized on the disposition of the property.[49]

¶ 708 Special Rules for Motor Vehicles

The tax laws limit the amount of depreciation deductions that may be claimed each year on passenger automobiles.[50] These rules are often referred to as the "luxury automobile limitations," even though they limit the amount of depreciation that may be claimed on all but the most inexpensive vehicles.

.01 Annual Depreciation Limits for Motor Vehicles

For a passenger automobile first placed in service in 2015, the limit on depreciation deductions is $3,160 for the first year ($11,160 if the additional first-year depreciation deduction applies), $5,100 for the second tax year, $3,050 for the third tax year, and $1,875 for the fourth and subsequent tax years. For trucks and vans first placed in service in 2015, the limit on depreciation deductions is $3,460 for the first tax year ($11,460 if the additional first-year depreciation deduction applies), $5,600 for the second tax year, $3,350 for the third tax year, and $1,975 for the fourth and subsequent tax years. The limits for other years are listed in ¶ 726.

A car is classified as a "passenger automobile" if its unloaded gross vehicle weight (curb weight) is 6,000 pounds or less.[51] Trucks and vans, including sports utility vehicles (SUVs) built on a truck chassis, are classified as passenger automobiles if their gross vehicle weight rating (GVWR) is 6,000 pounds or less. GVWR is the curb weight of the vehicle plus its maximum allowable payload. Ambulances, hearses, taxis, and limousines are not considered passenger automobiles for the purposes of the limits imposed on such vehicles.

Code Sec. 179 expense and any bonus depreciation are treated as depreciation deductions for purposes of the depreciation caps.[52] Consequently, the sum of any bonus depreciation, Code Sec.

---

[48] Code Sec. 179(d)(8); Reg. § 1.179-2(b)(3).
[49] Reg. § 1.179-3(f)(1).
[50] Code Sec. 280F.

[51] Code Sec. 280F(d)(5).
[52] Code Sec. 280F(d)(1); Temp. Reg. § 1.280F-2T(b)(4).

179 expense, and MACRS or ADS depreciation in the first year may not exceed the applicable first-year depreciation cap.

 Planning Pointer: Generally, there is no benefit in claiming a Code Sec. 179 expense allowance for a passenger automobile because the depreciation deductions without regard to Code Sec. 179 will almost always exceed the depreciation caps.

If a truck, SUV, or van has a GVWR in excess of 6,000 pounds, it is not subject to the annual depreciation limitations that apply to lighter vehicles. However, the maximum amount of the cost of SUVs weighing between 6,000 and 14,000 pounds that may be expensed under Code Sec. 179 is $25,000.[53]

Example 37: A taxpayer places a passenger car with a GVWR of 2,500 pounds in service in the taxpayer's trade or business. The vehicle is subject to the luxury automobile limitations, and none of its cost can be expensed under Code Sec. 179.

Example 38: A taxpayer places an SUV with a GVWR of 7,500 pounds in service in the taxpayer's trade or business. The vehicle is not subject to the luxury automobile limitations, but no more than $25,000 of the vehicle's purchase price can be expensed under Code Sec. 179.

 Reason for the Rule: When the luxury automobile rules were first enacted, most automobiles weighed fewer than 6,000 pounds. Later, taxpayers found that they could purchase a HUMMER or other SUV weighing more than 6,000 pounds and expense its entire cost in one year. Code Sec. 179 now limits the cost of these heavier vehicles that can be expensed to $25,000. Only vehicles weighing over 14,000 pounds are exempt from the limits imposed on expensing.

If the basis of a vehicle is not fully deducted during its recovery period because of the annual luxury automobile limitations on the depreciation deductions, any unrecovered basis attributable to the depreciation limits is recovered beginning with the first tax year after the regular depreciation recovery period.[54] The deduction for each year in the post-recovery period, however, is limited to the maximum annual cap allowed as a deduction for the final year of the recovery period (or the remaining unrecovered basis, if less). This assumes, of course, that the vehicle is still being used for business purposes.

Example 39: A new automobile used exclusively for business purposes is purchased in January 2015 for $40,000. The automobile is depreciated under MACRS. Assume the half-year convention applies, no Code Sec. 179 expense allowance is claimed, and that the taxpayer elects out of bonus depreciation. For each year of the recovery period, the taxpayer must compare the applicable depreciation limit with the depreciation computed under MACRS. The $3,160 first-year limit is compared to the sum of the regular first-year MACRS depreciation ($40,000 × 20% = $8,000) plus any Code Sec. 179 depreciation ($0). The allowable first-year deduction is $3,160 because that is less than $8,000. The taxpayer may deduct the lower of the limit or the depreciation allowed without regard to the limit as shown below.

---

[53] Code Sec. 179(b)(5).

[54] Code Sec. 280F(a)(1)(B).

Year	Limit	MACRS	Allowable Deduction
2015	$ 3,160	$ 8,000	$ 3,160
2016	5,100	12,800	5,100
2017	3,050	7,680	3,050
2018	1,875	4,608	1,875
2019	1,875	4,608	1,875
2020	1,875	2,304	1,875
	Total depreciation taken after six years		$16,935

The unrecovered basis of $23,065 ($40,000 – $16,935) may be claimed at the rate of $1,875 per year beginning in 2021, assuming the vehicle continues to be used exclusively for business purposes.

.02 Partial Business Use Limitations

If a passenger automobile is used less than 100 percent in a trade or business or for the production of income, the depreciation deduction limits are determined by multiplying the limitation amount by the percentage of business and investment use. In addition, if the business use percentage for any year is less than 50 percent, depreciation must be computed using ADS and the applicable convention.

.03 Leased Motor Vehicles

In order to prevent lessees of automobiles from bypassing the depreciation limits, lessees may be required to reduce their allowable lease expense deduction by what is termed the "inclusion amount."[55]

The inclusion amount is a percentage of part of the fair market value (FMV) of the leased automobile multiplied by the percentage of business use of the vehicle for the tax year. The inclusion amount is prorated for the number of days of the lease term included in the tax year. Although the restrictions are not as severe as the luxury limits, these inclusion amounts tend to partially offset the benefits from leasing expensive autos to circumvent the luxury auto limits. In determining the proper inclusion amount, the taxpayer should use the tables that have been prepared by the IRS.[56] (See Table 7I in the Appendix at ¶ 727.)

Example 40: Meisenheimer Corporation leases a passenger automobile with an FMV of $46,800 for use in its trade or business. Meisenheimer pays $700 per month for the automobile. The five-year lease term begins on February 1, 2014. Meisenheimer must reduce its deduction for each year of the lease by the appropriate amount from Table 7I in the Appendix at ¶ 727. The first-year inclusion for an automobile placed in service during 2014 with an FMV between $46,000 and $47,000 is $27. However, Meisenheimer's lease began on February 1, so this amount must be apportioned to reflect the 335 days the corporation leased the automobile during the year. Thus, for 2014, Meisenheimer must reduce its $7,700 lease expense ($700 × 11) by $25 ($27 × 335/365), so it only deducts $7,675 ($7,700 – $25).

---

[55] Code Sec. 280F(c).

[56] Reg. § 1.280F-7. The IRS issues an annual Revenue Procedure containing such tables.

In each subsequent year from 2015 to 2019, Meisenheimer pays $8,400 to lease the automobile ($700 × 12); however, it must reduce its deduction by the amounts from the lease inclusion table reproduced in Table 7I in the Appendix at ¶ 727 as shown below:

Year	Inclusion Amount	Allowable Deduction
2014 (year 1)	$ 25	$ 7,675
2015 (year 2)	58	8,342
2016 (year 3)	87	8,313
2017 (year 4)	104	8,296
2018 (year 5)	120	8,280
2019 (year 6)	10	690

In 2019, Meisenheimer pays the final lease payment of $700 in January. It must reduce its deduction by the portion of the $120 inclusion amount to reflect the 31 days that it leased the automobile during the year ($120 × 31/365 = $10).

DEPLETION

The costs associated with the acquisition of natural resources (often called wasting assets) are recovered through an annual depletion expense. Examples of assets subject to depletion include, but are not limited to, coal, oil, gas, iron ore, sand, and timber. The tax laws allow two depletion methods: cost depletion and percentage depletion. Taxpayers are usually required to use whichever method produces the greatest deduction.[57] However, in the case of timber, cost depletion is the only method allowed.[58] The amount of depletion allowable reduces the adjusted basis of the property (but never below zero).[59]

 Planning Pointer: A depletion deduction cannot be increased in a later year because no allowance, or an inadequate one, was taken in a prior year. The remedy for deducting less than the allowable depletion is to file an amended return for the year(s) involved.

¶ 709 Cost Depletion

The allowable **cost depletion** is calculated by dividing the adjusted basis of the depletable asset by the estimated recoverable reserves and then multiplying the result by the number of units sold during the tax year.[60] Recoverable reserves can be measured in tons (in the case of ore, gold, or other similar resources) or barrels (in the case of oil). The cost depletion method resembles the units-of-production depreciation method that is used for financial statement purposes.

Example 41: Smith & Sons bought a mine for $12,000. An engineer estimated that 60,000 tons of iron ore could be extracted from the mine. During 20X1, the first year, 6,500 tons were extracted and 6,000 sold. Cost depletion for 20X1 is computed as follows:

$12,000 (cost) ÷ 60,000 (tons available) = $.20 per ton (depletion rate)

6,000 (tons sold) × $.20 = $1,200 depletion expense for 20X1

$12,000 – $1,200 = $10,800 adjusted basis at the end of 20X1

Cost depletion can be deducted each year based on the estimated remaining recoverable units. If the estimate changes, the formula for computing cost depletion in future periods is adjusted to reflect the new estimate. It is important to note that cost depletion is computed based on the number of units sold during the year, regardless of the number of units extracted.

---

[57] Reg. § 1.611-1(a)(1).
[58] Reg. § 1.611-1(a)(1).
[59] Code Sec. 1016(a)(2).
[60] Reg. § 1.611-2(a).

Example 42: Assume the same facts as in Example 41, except that at the end of 20X1 it is estimated that another 90,000 recoverable tons remain. Another 6,000 tons are sold in 20X2. Cost depletion for 20X2 would then be calculated as follows:

$10,800 (adjusted basis) ÷ 90,000 (tons available) = $.12 per ton (depletion rate)

6,000 (tons sold) × $.12 cents (depletion rate) = $720 depletion expense for 20X2

$10,800 – $720 = $10,080 adjusted basis at the end of 20X2

The cost depletion method must be used to calculate depletion of timber. Any costs associated with the land purchased in conjunction with the timber must be separated out and cannot be depleted.[61]

Example 43: A taxpayer bought a 500-acre timber tract for $20,000. $5,000 was for land, and $15,000 was for timber. It was estimated that there were 150,000 board feet on the tract. During the first year, the taxpayer felled and sold 50,000 board feet. The depletion deduction is computed as follows:

$15,000 (adjusted basis) ÷ 150,000 = $.10 per board foot (depletion rate)

50,000 (board feet felled) × $.10 = $5,000 depletion expense

$15,000 – $5,000 = $10,000 adjusted basis at the end of the first year

¶710 Percentage Depletion

In general, **percentage depletion** is determined by multiplying the applicable percentage (as specified for the particular natural resource) by the gross income from the property. However, the deduction for percentage depletion is generally limited to 50 percent of the taxable income from the property before the depletion deduction. Exceptions to the general rule are provided for oil and gas properties. The limitation is 100 percent of taxable income for oil and gas properties (65 percent of taxable income for independent producers and royalty owners).[62] All expenses related to the property other than depletion and the domestic production activities deduction are subtracted from gross income from the property when applying the taxable income limit.

The applicable percentage varies depending on the type of resource being extracted. Table 7-5 lists the applicable percentages for some of the more common types of natural resources.

Table 7-5 Percentage Depletion Rates

Natural Resource	Depletion Rate
Sulfur, lead, nickel, tin, and uranium	22%
Gold, silver, copper, and iron ore	15%
Coal and perlite	10%
Gravel, peat, and sand	5%

Example 44: Refer back to Example 41, in which Smith & Sons purchased a mine for $12,000. If gross income from the mine is $15,000 and expenses connected with operating the mine are $12,000, the taxable income from the mine before depletion expense is $3,000 ($15,000 – $12,000). Applying the 15-percent depletion percentage to gross

---

[61] Reg. § 1.611-3(d)(2).   [62] Code Secs. 613(a), 613A(d)(1).

income yields preliminary depletion of $2,250 ($15,000 × 15%). However, allowable percentage depletion is limited to 50 percent of taxable income from the property, or $1,500 ($3,000 × 50%). Because the percentage depletion ($1,500) is greater than the $1,200 of cost depletion that would be allowed, the allowable depletion deduction is $1,500. The adjusted basis of the mine is reduced to $10,500 ($12,000 – $1,500). This adjusted basis is then used to compute cost depletion in 20X2.

 Spotlight: Percentage depletion is computed without regard to the adjusted basis of the property being depleted. Percentage depletion is a function of the applicable depletion rate and the gross income from the property. Therefore, the percentage depletion amount typically is greater than the depletion expense using cost depletion. However, because of the taxable income limit, when expenses (other than depletion) related to the property are very high the amount of percentage depletion may be limited.

.01 Percentage Depletion for Oil and Gas

Most large oil and gas producers are not allowed to use percentage depletion.[63] However, a 22-percent allowance is allowed for production for certain domestic gas wells, and a 10-percent rate is allowed for certain natural gas from geo-pressured brine.[64] Independent producers and royalty owners are allowed a 15-percent rate for oil and gas, and certain marginal oil and gas wells are allowed a higher percentage depletion rate.[65] For oil and gas properties, the depletion deduction may not exceed the taxable income for the property, computed without regard to the depletion allowance and any domestic production activities deduction.[66]

Example 45: Magic Gas Inc. purchases for $15,000 gas-producing wells that are eligible for the 22-percent depletion rate. In its first year of production, its gross income from the property is $20,000, and its expenses are $5,000, generating $15,000 of taxable income from the property prior to depletion and the domestic activities production deduction. Magic Gas computes percentage depletion, yielding a preliminary depletion deduction equal to $4,400 ($20,000 × 22%). Because this amount is less than its taxable income from the property, Magic Gas's percentage depletion deduction is $4,400. Assuming the cost depletion method yields a smaller deduction, Magic Gas' depletion deduction for the year would be $4,400, and Magic Gas would reduce its adjusted basis in the land to $145,600 ($150,000 – $4,400).

.02 Small Independent Producers and Royalty Owners

Percentage depletion for a small independent producer or a royalty owner for domestic production is calculated based on a 15-percent depletion rate.[67] The allowable percentage depletion is limited to the *lesser of* (1) 65 percent of the *taxpayer's taxable income* as computed without taking into account the depletion allowance, the domestic production activities deduction (¶ 509), NOL carrybacks (¶ 1001), or capital loss carrybacks (¶ 901.01) or (2) 100 percent of *taxable income from the property* before the depletion allowance and any domestic production activities deduction.[68] The maximum depletable quantity is 1,000 barrels of domestic crude a day or six million cubic feet of gas.[69] Any depletion deduction disallowed under the 65-percent limit may be carried over to subsequent tax years.[70]

Example 46: Samuel Chavez, a taxpayer who owns royalty interests in various oil-producing properties, has taxable income (before depletion deductions) for the current year of $100,000. Samuel does not qualify for the domestic production activities deduction

---

[63] Code Sec. 613(d).
[64] Code Sec. 613A(b)(1) and (2).
[65] Code Sec. 613A(c)(1) and (6).
[66] Code Sec. 613(a).

[67] Code Sec. 613A(c).
[68] Code Sec. 613A(d)(1).
[69] Code Sec. 613A(c)(3) and (4).
[70] Code Sec. 613A(d)(1).

and does not have an NOL or capital loss carrybacks. He is allowed a depletion deduction of $70,000 with respect to his royalty interests. Because the amount exceeds 65 percent of his taxable income ($100,000 × 65% = $65,000), $5,000 of depletion allowances are disallowed for the current tax year and must be carried over and deducted in the next year.

Spotlight: Each year taxpayers use the depletion method that produces the greatest expense deduction. The amount reduces the adjusted basis of the property, which becomes the starting point for calculating the cost depletion for the subsequent tax year. Because percentage depletion is often much greater than cost depletion, it is possible that the adjusted basis of the property will be reduced to $0 before all of the resources have been extracted. The tax laws allow the taxpayer to continue to use the percentage depletion method for all subsequent tax years in which there is gross income from the property. Because the adjusted basis of the property cannot be reduced below $0, it will remain at $0 during each of those years.

GAAP vs. Code: The cost method is the only acceptable method for financial statement purposes. The cost method used in financial reporting closely resembles the unit-of-production depreciation method, in that the depletable cost is allocated based on the estimated number of units the resource is expected to produce. Because the greater of cost depletion or percentage depletion is used for tax purposes, significant annual differences between the amount of depletion deducted on the income statement and that deducted on the tax return are likely to exist. Even when cost depletion is used for tax purposes, differences in amounts will likely occur. For example, the income tax basis of the property may differ from the book value for financial purposes. In addition, tax depletion is based on the units sold, whereas depletion for financial purposes is based on units produced. Accordingly, the difference between the two depletion amounts needs to be considered when reconciling net income to taxable income on the corporate tax return.

¶711 Intangible Drilling and Development Costs

As discussed in Chapter 5, operators of a domestic oil, gas, or geothermal well may elect to currently deduct intangible drilling and development costs (IDC) rather than capitalize and recover the costs through depletion or depreciation. IDC generally includes all expenditures by the operator incident to and necessary for the drilling of wells and the preparation of wells for the production of oil, gas, or geothermal energy, including expenditures for wages, fuel, repairs, hauling, and supplies.[71] However, IDC does not include the cost of tangible property or any portion of the acquisition price of an interest in the property.[72]

Preliminary exploration costs are not considered IDC, but instead are considered capital expenditures in nature[73] and generally are recoverable through depletion. However, geological and geophysical (G&G) expenses paid or incurred in connection with the exploration for, or development of, oil or gas within the United States can be deducted ratably over the 24-month period beginning on the date that the expense was paid or incurred.[74] The exploration phase stops and the development stage begins at the point at which the preparation for exploratory drilling begins. The operator's decision to drill normally triggers the beginning of the development phase.[75]

---

[71] Reg. §§ 1.612-4(a), 1.612-5(a).

[72] Reg. §§ 1.612-4(c), 1.612-5(c).

[73] Rev. Rul. 77-188, 1977-1 CB 76.

[74] Code Sec. 167(h).

[75] *Gates Rubber Co.*, 74 TC 1456, Dec. 37,292, aff'd, CA-10, 82-2 USTC ¶ 9702, 694 F2d 648.

An election to deduct these costs must be made in the first year in which the costs are paid or incurred.[76] A failure to deduct the costs as expenses in the year they are incurred is deemed to be an election to capitalize them (i.e., add them to the basis of the property). The election, once made, is binding for all future years. If the operator has elected to capitalize IDCs, and the well proves to be nonproductive (a dry hole), the operator may elect to deduct the costs as an ordinary loss.

Example 47: End Run Oil company spends $50,000 investigating the oil producing capabilities of a piece of land: $25,000 in G&G costs and $25,000 in other exploratory costs. In the same year, the company buys the land for $250,000 and spends $100,000 sinking wells on the property. End Run may deduct the $100,000 as IDC and may amortize the $25,000 of G&G costs over 24 months. The remaining $25,000 in exploratory costs is added to the purchase price of the land, yielding an adjusted basis of $275,000. If End Run does not elect to deduct its IDC, they will be added to the adjusted basis of the land and recovered through depletion deductions.

AMORTIZATION

Depreciation and amortization are similar concepts, but they apply to two different types of assets: tangible assets are "depreciated"; intangible assets are "amortized." Intangible property is personal property that does not have physical characteristics, such as copyrights, franchises, patents, trademarks, and trade names. The cost of intangibles used in a trade or business or for the production of income can often be recovered over time through amortization, much as the cost of depreciable business assets can often be recovered over time through depreciation. Amortizable intangible assets can be grouped into two broad categories: (1) intangibles that are amortized under Code Sec. 197 ("Section 197 intangibles") and (2) other amortizable intangibles.

¶ 712 Amortization of Section 197 Intangibles

Most types of intangible property qualify as Section 197 intangibles. **Section 197 intangibles** are intangibles listed in Code Sec. 197 that are *acquired by the taxpayer* and held in connection with the conduct of a trade or business or for the production of income.[77] Intangibles that are not acquired by the taxpayer but are created by the taxpayer's own efforts are not Section 197 intangibles and are amortizable only if such treatment is allowed by some other provision in the tax law. Amortization under Code Sec. 197 is claimed ratably over 180 months (15 years) beginning on the first day of the month that the intangible is placed in service. Accordingly, a Section 197 intangible is amortized without respect to its actual or estimated useful life.

Figure 7-1 Section 197 Intangibles
- Goodwill and going concern value;
- Workforce in place;
- Business books and records, operating systems, or any other information base (including lists or other information with respect to current or future customers);
- Patents, copyrights, formulas, processes, designs, patterns, know-how, formats, or similar items;
- Customer-based intangibles, such as a business's market composition or market share;
- Supplier-based intangibles, such as a business's favorable relationships with distributors;
- Licenses, permits, or other rights granted by a governmental unit or agency, such as a liquor license, a taxi-cab medallion or license, or a television or radio broadcasting license (including issuance and renewal costs);

---

[76] Reg. § § 1.612-4(d) and 1.612-5(d).   [77] Code Sec. 197(c).

- Franchises, trademarks, or trade names; and

- Covenants not to compete entered into in connection with the acquisition of a business.

Example 48: Kumquat Computer Corporation pays a departing executive, Stephanie Works, $10,000 not to compete with it for a period of three years. The covenant not to compete is not a Section 197 intangible because it was not entered into in connection with the acquisition of a trade or business.

Example 49: Specific Engines Corporation, acquires substantially all of the assets of Parrot Software on July 15, 2015. Of the purchase price, $18 million is allocated to goodwill. Because goodwill is a Section 197 intangible, the $18 million cost basis for the goodwill must be amortized using the straight-line method over 180 months beginning on July 1, 2015. If Specific Engines uses the calendar year, it can deduct $600,000 ($18,000,000/180 × 6 months) against gross income on its 2015 tax return. From 2016 through 2029, Specific Engines will deduct $1,200,000 ($18,000,000/180 × 12) of amortization each year. In 2030, Specific Engines can claim the final six months of amortization ($18,000,000/180 × 6 = $600,000).

When more than one amortizable Section 197 intangible is acquired in a single transaction, no loss may be claimed on any Section 197 intangible that is later separately disposed of.[78] Instead, the amount of the loss is allocated proportionately among the remaining Section 197 intangibles acquired in the transaction as an increase in basis. As a result, the loss will be recovered through amortization deductions over the remainder of the 15-year amortization period.

Example 50: Assume the same facts as in Example 49, except that Parrot has three separate businesses, to which $6 million of goodwill is allocated. After taking $3 million of amortization ($1 million for the goodwill of each business), Specific Engines sells one of the businesses for a loss in an asset sale. It allocates $2 million of the loss to the business's goodwill. Specific Engines may not take an immediate loss deduction for this amount; instead it must add $1 million to the basis of the goodwill of each of the two remaining businesses and recover the loss through amortization deductions.

 Reason for the Rule: The treatment of costs incurred to acquire intangible property has been a source of considerable controversy between taxpayers and the IRS. In an attempt to minimize the controversy surrounding the identification, valuation, and establishment of useful lives of intangible property, Congress added Section 197 to the Code in the Omnibus Budget Reconciliation Act of 1993 to provide a single method and recovery period for most acquired intangibles.[79]

¶ 713 Amortization of Non-Section 197 Intangibles

In Chapter 5, organizational costs, start-up costs, and research and experimental costs are discussed. These costs are all intangible costs that are capitalized and either expensed in the current period or amortized over 180 months (in the case of organizational costs and start-up costs) or 60 months (in the case of research and experimental costs) (see ¶ 503, ¶ 504, and ¶ 507). Certain other intangible property not specifically listed in Code Sec. 197, including leaseholds and computer software, may be amortized.

---

[78] Code Sec. 197(f)(1).

[79] House Committee Report, Omnibus Budget Reconciliation Act of 1993 (P.L. 103-66).

.01 Leaseholds

If a leasehold is acquired for business purposes, the taxpayer may amortize the cost of acquiring the lease over the term of the lease plus all renewal options and any other period for which the parties reasonably expect the lease to be renewed if less than 75 percent of such cost is attributable to the period of the lease term remaining on the date that the lease is acquired.[80] In addition, amounts paid to obtain a lease on property used in a business (such as commissions, bonuses, fees and other amounts) are amortized as part of the cost of the lease.

Example 51: On June 1, 2015, the American Pie Company (a calendar year corporation) purchases the leasehold interest of Don Donaldson in a one-story building from which American Pie operates a bakery. American Pie pays $25,000 for Donaldson's 15-year lease, on which 10 years (120 months) remain. American Pie deducts $1,458 ($25,000/120 × 7 months) as a business expense in 2015. It deducts $2,500 ($25,000/120 × 12) each year from 2016 to 2024, and it will deduct the final $1,042 ($25,000/120 × 5 months) in 2025.

.02 Computer Software

Computer software acquired in connection with a trade or business is amortizable over 15 years as a Section 197 intangible. Computer software that is not amortizable under Code Sec. 197 is depreciable over 36 months using the straight-line method beginning in the month of acquisition provided that it is readily available for purchase by the general public, is subject to a nonexclusive license, and has not been substantially modified.[81] Computer software whose cost is included in the total cost of a computer is not separately depreciated. Instead, it is considered part of the depreciable cost basis of the computer.

Example 52: St. Ignace Corporation purchases the business of Hancock Company in an asset acquisition. It allocates $100,000 of the purchase price to software owned by Hancock. In the same year, St. Ignace buys word processing software readily available for purchase by the public. St. Ignace may depreciate the cost of the word processing software over 36 months. However, it must recover the $100,000 of the purchase price allocated to the Hancock software over 15 years.

 GAAP vs. Code: For financial statement purposes, the costs associated with the acquisition of intangible assets having a finite life are amortized ratably over the asset's remaining useful life. Intangible assets with an infinite life are subject to an annual impairment test and are only written off when impaired. However, the economic downturn that began in late 2007 has resulted in the impairment, and resulting write-down, of a considerable amount of goodwill, as well as other intangible assets. For tax purposes, most intangible assets are amortized ratably over 15 years. Accordingly, the amount of amortization expense reported on the income statement is rarely the same as amortization expense deducted on the tax return. This difference must be taken into consideration when reconciling net income to taxable income on the corporate tax return.

¶ 714 Summary

Generally, a taxpayer may not expense the purchase price of property that will provide benefits beyond the current tax year but instead must depreciate (tangible personal property and depreciable real property), deplete (natural resource property) or amortize (intangible property) such assets. There are two main exceptions to the foregoing rule. First, land is not depreciable. Second, certain taxpayers can elect to expense a certain amount of the purchase price of certain depreciable assets

---

[80] Code Sec. 178.

[81] Code Sec. 167(f)(1); Code Sec. 197(e)(3).

under Code Sec. 179. Tax rules applicable to cost recovery deductions for depreciation, depletion, and amortization differ significantly from financial accounting rules for such deductions.

APPENDIX

¶ 725 MACRS and ADS Depreciation Tables

The following are some of the IRS depreciation tables used for 3-, 5-, 7-, 10-, 15-, and 20-year MACRS property. Table 7A is used if the half-year convention applies. Tables 7B through 7E reflect the mid-quarter convention. If the mid-quarter convention applies, use the table designated for the quarter that the asset was placed in service. Table 7F is used to compute depreciation under the general depreciation system (general MACRS) straight-line method and MACRS alternative depreciation system (ADS) if the half-year convention applies. The straight-line method and ADS mid-quarter convention tables are not reproduced. The 150-percent declining-balance election half-year and mid-quarter convention tables are also not reproduced. These tables can be found in Appendix A in IRS Publication 946 and Rev. Proc. 87-57, 1987-2 CB 687.

Table 7A

General Depreciation System (general MACRS)

Applicable Depreciation Method: 200 or 150 percent

Declining Balance Switching to Straight Line

Applicable Recovery Periods: 3, 5, 7, 10, 15, 20 Years

Applicable Convention: Half-Year

[All amounts in the table reflect percentages; only depreciation percentages for the first 10 recovery years are reproduced.]

If the Recovery Year Is:	and the Recovery Period Is:					
	3-year	5-year	7-year	10-year	15-year	20-year
	the Depreciation Rate Is:					
1	33.33	20.00	14.29	10.00	5.00	3.750
2	44.45	32.00	24.49	18.00	9.50	7.219
3	14.81	19.20	17.49	14.40	8.55	6.677
4	7.41	11.52	12.49	11.52	7.70	6.177
5		11.52	8.93	9.22	6.93	5.713
6		5.76	8.92	7.37	6.23	5.285
7			8.93	6.55	5.90	4.888
8			4.46	6.55	5.90	4.522
9				6.56	5.91	4.462
10				6.55	5.90	4.461
				. . .	. . .	. . .

Table 7B

General Depreciation System (general MACRS)

Applicable Depreciation Method: 200 or 150 percent

Declining Balance Switching to Straight Line

Applicable Recovery Periods: 3, 5, 7, 10, 15, 20 Years

Applicable Convention: Mid-quarter (property placed in service in first quarter)

[All amounts in the table reflect percentages; only depreciation percentages for the first 10 recovery years are reproduced.]

If the Recovery Year Is:	and the Recovery Period Is:					
	3-year	5-year	7-year	10-year	15-year	20-year
	the Depreciation Rate Is:					
1	58.33	35.00	25.00	17.50	8.75	6.563
2	27.78	26.00	21.43	16.50	9.13	7.000
3	12.35	15.60	15.31	13.20	8.21	6.482
4	1.54	11.01	10.93	10.56	7.39	5.996
5		11.01	8.75	8.45	6.65	5.546
6		1.38	8.74	6.76	5.99	5.130
7			8.75	6.55	5.90	4.746
8			1.09	6.55	5.91	4.459
9				6.56	5.90	4.459
10				6.55	5.91	4.459
				. . .	. . .	. . .

Table 7C

General Depreciation System (general MACRS)

Applicable Depreciation Method: 200 or 150 percent

Declining Balance Switching to Straight Line

Applicable Recovery Periods: 3, 5, 7, 10, 15, 20 Years

Applicable Convention: Mid-quarter (property placed in service in second quarter)

[All amounts in the table reflect percentages; only depreciation percentages for the first 10 recovery years are reproduced.]

If the Recovery Year Is:	and the Recovery Period Is:					
	3-year	5-year	7-year	10-year	15-year	20-year
	the Depreciation Rate Is:					
1	41.67	25.00	17.85	12.50	6.25	4.688
2	38.89	30.00	23.47	17.50	9.38	7.148
3	14.14	18.00	16.76	14.00	8.44	6.612
4	5.30	11.37	11.97	11.20	7.59	6.116
5		11.37	8.87	8.96	6.83	5.658
6		4.26	8.87	7.17	6.15	5.233
7			8.87	6.55	5.91	4.841
8			3.33	6.55	5.90	4.478
9				6.56	5.91	4.463
10				6.55	5.90	4.463
				. . .	. . .	. . .

Table 7D

General Depreciation System (general MACRS)

Applicable Depreciation Method: 200 or 150 percent

Declining Balance Switching to Straight Line

Applicable Recovery Periods: 3, 5, 7, 10, 15, 20 Years

Applicable Convention: Mid-quarter (property placed in service in third quarter)

[All amounts in the table reflect percentages; only depreciation percentages for the first 10 recovery years are reproduced.]

If the Recovery Year Is:	and the Recovery Period Is:					
	3-year	5-year	7-year	10-year	15-year	20-year
	the Depreciation Rate Is:					
1	25.00	15.00	10.71	7.50	3.75	2.813
2	50.00	34.00	25.51	18.50	9.63	7.289
3	16.67	20.40	18.22	14.80	8.66	6.742
4	8.33	12.24	13.02	11.84	7.80	6.237
5		11.30	9.30	9.47	7.02	5.769
6		7.06	8.85	7.58	6.31	5.336
7			8.86	6.55	5.90	4.936
8			5.53	6.55	5.90	4.566
9				6.56	5.91	4.460
10				6.55	5.90	4.460
				. . .	. . .	. . .

Table 7E

General Depreciation System (general MACRS)

Applicable Depreciation Method: 200 or 150 percent

Declining Balance Switching to Straight Line

Applicable Recovery Periods: 3, 5, 7, 10, 15, 20 Years

Applicable Convention: Mid-quarter (property placed in service in fourth quarter)

[All amounts in the table reflect percentages; only depreciation percentages for the first 10 recovery years are reproduced.]

If the Recovery Year Is:	and the Recovery Period Is:					
	3-year	5-year	7-year	10-year	15-year	20-year
	the Depreciation Rate Is:					
1	8.33	5.00	3.57	2.50	1.25	0.938
2	61.11	38.00	27.55	19.50	9.88	7.430
3	20.37	22.80	19.68	15.60	8.89	6.872
4	10.19	13.68	14.06	12.48	8.00	6.357
5		10.94	10.04	9.98	7.20	5.880
6		9.58	8.73	7.99	6.48	5.439
7			8.73	6.55	5.90	5.031
8			7.64	6.55	5.90	4.654
9				6.56	5.90	4.458
10				6.55	5.91	4.458
				. . .	. . .	. . .

Table 7F

General Depreciation System (MACRS SL) and Alternative Depreciation System (ADS)

Applicable Depreciation Method: Straight Line

Applicable Recovery Periods: 2.5—17 Years

Applicable Convention: Half-Year

[All amounts in the table reflect percentages; only depreciation percentages for the first 10 recovery years are reproduced.]

[IRS mid-quarter convention tables for depreciation under the general and alternative MACRS methods are not reproduced.]

If the Recovery Year Is:	and the Recovery Period Is:														
	2.5	3.0	3.5	4.0	4.5	5.0	5.5	6.0	6.5	7.0	7.5	8.0	8.5	9.0	9.5
	the Depreciation Rate Is:														
1	20.00	16.67	14.29	12.50	11.11	10.00	9.09	8.33	7.69	7.14	6.67	6.25	5.88	5.56	5.26
2	40.00	33.33	28.57	25.00	22.22	20.00	18.18	16.67	15.39	14.29	13.33	12.50	11.77	11.11	10.53
3	40.00	33.33	28.57	25.00	22.22	20.00	18.18	16.67	15.38	14.29	13.33	12.50	11.76	11.11	10.53
4		16.67	28.57	25.00	22.23	20.00	18.18	16.67	15.39	14.28	13.33	12.50	11.77	11.11	10.53
5				12.50	22.22	20.00	18.19	16.66	15.38	14.29	13.34	12.50	11.76	11.11	10.52
6						10.00	18.18	16.67	15.39	14.28	13.33	12.50	11.77	11.11	10.53
7							8.33	15.38	14.29	13.34	12.50	11.76	11.11	10.52	
8									7.14	13.33	12.50	11.77	11.11	10.53	
9										6.25	11.76	11.11	10.52		
10												5.56	10.53		

If the Recovery Year Is:	and the Recovery Period Is:														
	10.0	10.5	11.0	11.5	12.0	12.5	13.0	13.5	14.0	14.5	15.0	15.5	16.0	16.5	17.0
	the Depreciation Rate Is:														
1	5.00	4.76	4.55	4.35	4.17	4.00	3.85	3.70	3.57	3.45	3.33	3.23	3.13	3.03	2.94
2	10.00	9.52	9.09	8.70	8.33	8.00	7.69	7.41	7.14	6.90	6.67	6.45	6.25	6.06	5.88
3	10.00	9.52	9.09	8.70	8.33	8.00	7.69	7.41	7.14	6.90	6.67	6.45	6.25	6.06	5.88
4	10.00	9.53	9.09	8.69	8.33	8.00	7.69	7.41	7.14	6.90	6.67	6.45	6.25	6.06	5.88
5	10.00	9.52	9.09	8.70	8.33	8.00	7.69	7.41	7.14	6.90	6.67	6.45	6.25	6.06	5.88
6	10.00	9.53	9.09	8.69	8.33	8.00	7.69	7.41	7.14	6.89	6.67	6.45	6.25	6.06	5.88
7	10.00	9.52	9.09	8.70	8.34	8.00	7.69	7.41	7.14	6.90	6.67	6.45	6.25	6.06	5.88
8	10.00	9.53	9.09	8.69	8.33	8.00	7.69	7.41	7.15	6.89	6.66	6.45	6.25	6.06	5.88
9	10.00	9.52	9.09	8.70	8.34	8.00	7.69	7.41	7.14	6.90	6.67	6.45	6.25	6.06	5.88
10	10.00	9.53	9.09	8.69	8.33	8.00	7.70	7.40	7.15	6.89	6.66	6.45	6.25	6.06	5.88

* * *

¶726 Passenger Automobile Limits

The maximum MACRS depreciation amounts for a passenger automobile for the first, second, third, and succeeding tax years in the depreciation period and in post-recovery period years are listed in Table 7G. The limitation amounts in Table 7G do not apply to trucks (including SUVs built on a truck chassis) and vans placed in service after 2002 that are subject to the depreciation caps because they have a gross vehicle weight rating of 6,000 pounds or less. The limits on these vehicles are listed in Table 7H.

Table 7G

		Depreciation Allowable in—			
For Cars Placed in Service After	*Before*	*Year 1*	*Year 2*	*Year 3*	*Year 4, etc.*
12/31/04	1/1/06	2,960	4,700	2,850	1,675
12/31/05	1/1/07	2,960	4,800	2,850	1,775
12/31/06	1/1/08	3,060	4,900	2,850	1,775
12/31/07	1/1/10	2,960/10,960*	4,800	2,850	1,775
12/31/09	1/1/12	3,060/11,060*	4,900	2,950	1,775
12/31/11	1/1/16	3,160/11,160*	5,100	3,050	1,875

* If bonus depreciation applies.

Table 7H

		Depreciation Allowable in—			
For Trucks and Vans Placed in Service After	*Before*	*Year 1*	*Year 2*	*Year 3*	*Year 4, etc.*
12/31/04	1/1/07	$ 3,260	$ 5,200	$ 3,150	$ 1,875
12/31/06	1/1/08	3,260	5,200	3,050	1,875
12/31/07	1/1/09	3,160/11,160*	5,100	3,050	1,875
12/31/08	1/1/10	3,060/11,060*	4,900	2,950	1,775
12/31/09	1/1/11	3,160/11,160*	5,100	3,050	1,875
12/31/10	1/1/12	3,060/11,260*	5,200	3,150	1,875
12/31/11	1/1/13	3,160/11,360*	5,300	3,150	1,875
12/31/12	1/1/15	3,360/11,360*	5,400	3,250	1,975
12/31/14	1/1/16	3,460/11,460*	5,600	3,350	1,975

* If bonus depreciation applies.

¶727 Inclusion Amounts for Leased Automobiles

Table 7I shows the inclusion amounts for leased automobiles placed in service during 2014 that have an FMV between $18,500 and $60,000. For inclusion amounts for leased automobiles placed in service during 2014 with an FMV in excess of $60,000, see Rev. Proc. 2014-21, 2014-11 IRB 641. (The 2015 inclusion amounts were not available at the time this book went to the printer.)

Table 7I Dollar Amounts for Passenger Automobiles (That Are Not Trucks or Vans) with a Lease Term Beginning in Calendar Year 2014

Fair Market Value of Passenger Automobile		Tax Year During Lease				
Over	Not Over	1st	2nd	3rd	4th	5th & later
18,500	19,000	3	5	8	10	11
19,000	19,500	3	6	10	11	13
19,500	20,000	3	8	11	13	14
20,000	20,500	4	8	13	14	17
20,500	21,000	4	9	14	17	18
21,000	21,500	5	10	15	18	21
21,500	22,000	5	11	17	20	22
22,000	23,000	6	13	18	23	25
23,000	24,000	7	14	22	26	29
24,000	25,000	8	16	25	29	33
25,000	26,000	8	19	27	32	38
26,000	27,000	9	20	31	35	42
27,000	28,000	10	22	33	40	45
28,000	29,000	11	24	36	43	49
29,000	30,000	12	26	39	46	53
30,000	31,000	13	28	41	50	57
31,000	32,000	14	30	44	53	61
32,000	33,000	14	32	47	56	65
33,000	34,000	15	34	50	59	69
34,000	35,000	16	36	52	64	72
35,000	36,000	17	38	55	67	76
36,000	37,000	18	39	59	70	80
37,000	38,000	19	41	61	74	84
38,000	39,000	20	43	64	77	88
39,000	40,000	21	45	67	80	92
40,000	41,000	21	47	70	84	96
41,000	42,000	22	49	73	87	100
42,000	43,000	23	51	75	91	104
43,000	44,000	24	53	78	94	108
44,000	45,000	25	55	81	97	112
45,000	46,000	26	56	84	101	116
46,000	47,000	27	58	87	104	120
47,000	48,000	28	60	90	107	124
48,000	49,000	28	62	93	111	127
49,000	50,000	29	64	96	114	131
50,000	51,000	30	66	98	118	135
51,000	52,000	31	68	101	121	139
52,000	53,000	32	70	104	124	143
53,000	54,000	33	72	106	128	147
54,000	55,000	34	74	109	131	151
55,000	56,000	34	76	112	135	155

Fair Market Value of Passenger Automobile		Tax Year During Lease				
Over	Not Over	1st	2nd	3rd	4th	5th & later
56,000	57,000	35	78	115	138	159
57,000	58,000	36	80	118	141	163
58,000	59,000	37	81	121	145	167
59,000	60,000	38	83	124	148	171

GLOSSARY OF TERMS INTRODUCED IN THE CHAPTER

Adjusted basis. The tax equivalent to book value. Adjusted basis equals the initial cost basis of an asset (typically its purchase price) plus the cost of any improvements made to the asset minus the accumulated depreciation taken on the asset.

Alternative Depreciation System (ADS). An alternative to depreciating property under general MACRS. Recovery periods tend to be longer, and use of the straight-line method is required.

Book value. The financial accounting equivalent of adjusted basis (i.e., cost less accumulated depreciation).

Cost depletion. One of two acceptable tax methods for expensing the costs of a natural resource. This method is similar to the units-of-production method of depreciation and is the only acceptable method of depletion for financial reporting.

Depreciable cost. In financial accounting, it represents the portion of the cost of an asset that may be written off over the asset's useful life (i.e., the costs associated with the acquisition of the asset minus the estimated salvage value). *See also* Salvage value.

Dwelling unit. A house or apartment used to provide living accommodations; includes mobile homes and manufactured homes; does not include a unit in a hotel, motel, inn, or other establishment in which more than 50 percent of the units are used on a transient basis. *See also* Residential rental property.

Half-year convention. Averaging convention used for tax depreciation. Property put in service in a trade or business during a tax year is deemed to have been placed in service in the middle of the year.

Mid-month convention. Averaging convention used for tax depreciation. Property put in service in a trade or business during a tax year is deemed to have been placed in service in the middle of the month in which it was actually placed in service.

Mid-quarter convention. Averaging convention used for tax depreciation. Property put in service in a trade or business during a tax year is deemed to have been placed in service in the middle of the quarter in which it was actually placed in service.

Modified Accelerated Cost Recovery System (MACRS). A system for recovering the cost of capital expenditures through periodic depreciation deductions. MACRS applies to depreciable tangible property placed in service after 1986.

Percentage depletion. One of two acceptable tax methods for expensing the costs of a natural resource. Because the expense is calculated as a percentage of gross profits generated by the resource, over time the costs expensed can exceed the income tax basis of the property.

Residential rental property. Rental property for which 80 percent or more of the gross rental income is derived from the rental of dwelling units. *See also* Dwelling unit.

Salvage value. Term used in financial accounting. The amount that the owner of an asset believes an asset could be sold at the end of its useful life.

Section 179 property. Property eligible for immediate expensing under Code Sec. 179. Section 179 property is tangible personal property that is depreciable under MACRS and is acquired by purchase for use in the active conduct of a trade or business.

Section 197 intangibles. Intangible assets for which amortization deductions may be taken under Code Sec. 197. Section 197 intangibles are intangibles listed in Code Sec. 197 that are acquired by the taxpayer and held in connection with the conduct of a trade or business or for the production of income.

Taxable income limitation. A limitation that disallows any Section 179 expense from being deducted in the current year to the extent that it exceeds the aggregate of the taxpayer's taxable income derived from the active conduct of any trade or business.

CHAPTER PROBLEMS

Chapter 7 Discussion Questions

The following questions relate to the discussion in Chapter 7, Business Deductions: Depreciation, Depletion, and Amortization. Unless indicated otherwise in a particular question, assume:

- No amount is expensed under Code Sec. 179 and additional "bonus" depreciation is not claimed (with the taxpayer filing any necessary election).
- With respect to MACRS personal property, the half-year convention applies unless enough information is provided to determine whether more than 40 percent of assets were placed in service in the fourth quarter of the tax year.
- Depreciation deductions are computed using MACRS general depreciation system unless it can be determined from the facts that the alternative depreciation system (ADS) is required.
- No election is made to use the MACRS straight-line, MACRS 150-percent declining balance, or the ADS methods, unless otherwise stated.

1. Explain whether the following assets are eligible for depreciation or amortization:
   a. Car used only for personal reasons,
   b. Lubricating oil purchased for business machinery,
   c. Construction company truck,
   d. Truck used by utility company to construct towers for its power lines,
   e. Farmland used to grow corn,
   f. A new apartment building with construction completed but unoccupied,
   g. Boats held for sale by a marina,
   h. Broadcasting license acquired in connection with the purchase of a television station, and
   i. Leasehold improvements made by a tenant who has five years remaining on a lease.
2. What are the various cost recovery methods available to depreciate office furniture placed in service in 2015?
3. Fred Austin purchases a computer at a cost of $30,000 on January 1 and uses it in his business. Compute his maximum allowable MACRS deduction for the year of purchase. May Fred claim the Code Sec. 179 expense allowance?

4. Which of the following vehicles is subject to the luxury car depreciation limits if used for business purposes?

   a. A farm tractor,

   b. An SUV (sports utility vehicle) with a gross vehicle weight rating of 8,000 pounds that is built on a truck chassis,

   c. A small truck with a gross vehicle weight rating of 5,000 pounds, and

   d. A station wagon with an unloaded gross vehicle weight of 5,000 pounds.

5. Raymond George purchased a building in 20X1 for $100,000 and used it as nonresidential real property in a trade or business. In 20X9, he replaced the roof on the building at a cost of $20,000. How should he compute his depreciation deductions?

6. On January 1, 20X1, Sam Johnson agreed to lease 1,000 acres of pastureland for a period of five years. He uses the land to raise livestock. On March 1, 20X5, he erects a small fabricated storage building, which will be used primarily to store feed, for a total cost of $3,000. Assume that the building is 10-year MACRS property. Compute Sam's 20X5 MACRS depreciation deduction.

7. John Jacob operates a business as a sole proprietorship. In the current tax year, he will have a $5,000 loss before considering any Code Sec. 179 expense deduction. John's spouse, Denise, operates a word processing business as a sole proprietorship; it generates $50,000 in net profits. The couple has no other items of gross income and reports the tax items from their businesses on Schedule C of their joint Form 1040 tax return. If John were to purchase $15,000 in computer equipment and office furniture and fixtures, would he be able to expense them as a Code Sec. 179 deduction on his Schedule C?

8. In Question 7, assume that instead of having her own business, Denise is employed by Veriti Corporation and earns W-2 income of $50,000. How would your answer change regarding John's ability to take the Code Sec. 179 election for the $15,000 in new acquisitions he made for his business?

9. Sherry is a 50-percent partner in three separate partnerships, A, B, and C, in which she actively participates. For one tax year, she received three Form 1065 K-1s, each indicating a $7,000 Code Sec. 179 expense allocation from the partnerships. Assume that each of the partnerships met all the requirements for electing Code Sec. 179 (i.e., the dollar limit, the investment limit, and the aggregate taxable income limit). Sherry is engaged in other business activities that generate losses and her aggregate taxable income from her businesses for the year, including her partnership income allocations, is $9,000. How much may Sherry expense on her Form 1040?

10. A taxpayer depreciates the entire $10,000 cost of an item of MACRS property placed in service in a trade or business. If the taxpayer sells the property in a later year for $1,000, what is the gain from the sale?

11. Onondaga Corporation, a calendar year taxpayer, begins business operations on March 15, 20X1. During 20X1, Onondaga placed in service $10,000 of five-year MACRS property. On what date does the recovery period for the property begin, and on what date does it end under the half-year convention?

12. Chris's Cutlery, Inc. is opening a new retail outlet. The building it purchased has three unfinished walls, an unfinished ceiling, basic plumbing and electrical connections, a concrete slab floor, and no front wall. Chris's plans to have the following improvements made to make the site suitable for its use:

    a. Electrical connections,

    b. Plumbing connections,

    c. Permanent interior walls,

    d. Front wall and window,

    e. Side and rear walls,

    f. Drop ceiling,

    g. Lighting fixtures, and

    h. Heating and cooling system.

In addition, Chris's purchases the following assets for use at the site:

    i. Computers and

    j. Office furniture.

Assume that items (a) through (h) are structural components. What are the MACRS depreciation periods of the items?

13. What method of cost recovery can be used in Question 12 if Chris's goal is to deduct as much depreciation as possible in the first year?

14. What is the ADS depreciation period of the items in Question 12?

15. How is computer software amortized for tax purposes?

16. A taxpayer owned a building that was used in the taxpayer's business. The building cost $100,000 and the depreciation taken was $20,000. The building was idle for two years and the taxpayer took no depreciation. The depreciation that could have been taken during the idle period was $10,000. The taxpayer sold the building for $110,000 without using the building again. Ignoring any recapture considerations, what is the taxpayer's adjusted basis in the building?

17. Which of the following elections is *not* available under MACRS:

    a. 200-percent declining balance election,

    b. 150-percent declining balance election,

    c. Straight-line election, or

    d. Alternative depreciation system (ADS) election.

18. The cost of seven-year MACRS property placed in service by a calendar year taxpayer is depreciated over:

    a. Six tax years,

    b. Seven tax years,

    c. Eight tax years, or

    d. Nine tax years.

19. A taxpayer places property in service that costs $10,000 and expenses it under Code Sec. 179. Three years later, the property is sold for $4,000. How is the adjusted basis of the property determined for purposes of computing the gain or loss on the sale?

20. To which of the following do the luxury automobile limitations apply?

    a. Leased passenger automobile,

    b. 5500-pound four-wheel truck,

    c. 7500-pound SUV, or

    d. Hearse.

Chapter 7 Problems

The following problems relate to the discussion in Chapter 7, Business Deductions: Depreciation, Depletion, and Amortization. Unless indicated otherwise in a particular problem, assume:

- No amount is expensed under Code Sec. 179, and additional "bonus" depreciation is not claimed (with the taxpayer filing any necessary election).

- With respect to MACRS personal property, the half-year convention applies unless the midquarter convention applies because more than 40 percent of assets were placed in service in the fourth quarter of the tax year.

- Depreciation deductions are computed using MACRS unless it can be determined from the facts that the alternative depreciation system (ADS) is required.

- No election is made to use the MACRS straight-line, MACRS 150-percent declining balance method, or the ADS, unless otherwise stated.

1. As part of the purchase price of a business, on January 1, Sam Farrow pays $100,000 for the patent to an industrial gear. In addition, as part of the same purchase, Sam pays $10,000 for the business's goodwill and another $10,000 for the seller's covenant not to compete for the next five years. Compute Sam's amortization deduction for the year of purchase.

2. Seymour Scagnetti bought an apartment building for $180,000 and rented all of the units out to tenants. Land accounted for $30,000 of the purchase price. What is Seymour's depreciable basis for the property?

3. A corporation places in service two properties during the year. The first property is five-year property costing $55,000 that was placed in service on June 6. The second is seven-year property costing $39,000 that was placed in service on December 6. Compute MACRS depreciation on these properties for the current year.

4. A calendar year corporation places in service machinery costing $2,300,000 on April 8, 2014. This is the only property placed in service during the year. Assuming the corporation elects to expense as much of the machine as possible under Code Sec. 179, what is the adjusted basis in the machinery on December 31, 2014, if the corporation's taxable income of the corporation (before Section 179 expense) is $1,000,000.

5. On January 31, 2000, a corporation with a calendar tax year purchased and placed in service land and a commercial building for $125,000, of which $25,000 is properly allocable to the land. The building qualifies as depreciable property under MACRS. It has an expected useful life of 30 years. Compute the corporation's MACRS depreciation deduction for 2015.

6. Assume the same facts as in Problem 5, except compute the corporation's depreciation deduction assuming it uses ADS to depreciate the property.

7. Jackson Corporation purchases a computer on December 31, 2015, for use in its trade or business. The computer cost $20,000. Determine its 2015 MACRS and ADS deductions. Assume this was the only depreciable personal property Jackson purchased in 2015.

8. Assume, in Problem 7, that Jackson also purchases a computer at a cost of $20,000 on November 1, 2015. What are the MACRS and ADS deductions for the computers in 2015 and 2016?

9. Popcorn Inc. purchases a sports sedan on June 1, 2014, for $30,000. The vehicle is used 100 percent for business reasons by the company president, Colonel Popper. Taking the luxury car depreciation limits into consideration, and assuming that the maximum bonus depreciation is taken, compute the company's MACRS depreciation deduction for the years 2014–2018.

10. Kedzie Company places nonresidential real property that cost $200,000 (exclusive of land cost) in service on December 31, 2015. Compute the MACRS deductions on the property for 2015 and 2016.

11. Hargarten Corporation, a calendar year taxpayer, purchases a depreciable two-story build-ing for $120,000 on March 1, 2015. Of the total purchase price, $20,000 was for the land. The corporation rents the upper story to a family for $500 per month. The downstairs is rented to a retailer for $1,000 per month. Compute the MACRS depreciation allowance for 2015 and 2016.

12. James Johnson, a real estate developer, purchased an abandoned warehouse as an invest-ment in 2009 for $70,000, of which $50,000 was attributable to depreciable real property. He converted the warehouse into apartments at a cost of $1 million; he placed the apartments in service in a trade or business on October 1, 2015. The fair market value of the building on October 1, 2015, was $1,150,000. Compute his 2015 MACRS depreciation deduction.

13. Coldwater Properties, Inc. purchases and places an apartment building in service on May 16, 1997. The building cost $80,000. On March 1, 2015, Coldwater replaced the roof at a cost of $3,000. Compute the 2015 depreciation deduction on the roof.

14. Shreve Corporation, a calendar year taxpayer, is planning its 2015 asset acquisitions. All the acquisitions will be five-year property, and Shreve will use MACRS. The company would like to know the difference in the total first- and second-year depreciation deductions resulting from the two cost acquisition patterns outlined below:

Property Acquisition Dates:	Plan A	Plan B
1/28/2015	$200,000	$200,000
5/2/2015	150,000	50,000
11/16/2015	100,000	200,000
Total:	$450,000	$450,000

15. Olga Corporation, a calendar year taxpayer, purchased an item of three-year property costing $10,000 on February 1, 2013. It sells the property on October 21, 2015.

   a. Compute Olga's depreciation expense for 2013–2015 assuming the half-year convention applies to all three-year property placed in service during 2013.

   b. Compute Olga's depreciation expense for 2013–2015 assuming the mid-quarter conven-tion applies to all three-year property placed in service during 2013.

16. A calendar year taxpayer placed in service on June 10, 2015, listed property (computer and peripheral equipment) that cost $100,000. The property was used 10 percent of the time in the taxpayer's trade or business. Compute the 2015 depreciation allowed on the property.

17. A computer costing $5,000 is placed in service on February 3 in a calendar year business and is used 80 percent for business. Compute the first-year depreciation.

18. A taxpayer bought a mine in 20X1 for $80,000 and estimated there were 100,000 tons of ore to be extracted. In 20X1, he mined 7,500 tons and sold 7,000. In 20X2, he mined 6,000 tons and sold the 500 tons remaining from 20X1 and 5,500 tons of the ore mined in 20X2. However, at the end of 20X2, he estimated that 180,000 tons of ore remained, including the ore extracted but unsold. Compute the taxpayer's allowable cost depletion for 20X1 and 20X2.

19. A corporation bought 100 acres of timber for $40,000, of which $30,000 was allocable to the timber and $10,000 was allocable to the land. It was estimated that there were 1.5 million board feet of timber on the land. The first year, the corporation felled 500,000 board feet and sold 300,000 board feet for $18,000. The corporation's deductible expenses from these operations amounted to $8,000. Compute the depletion allowable for the first year.

20. A taxpayer buys a mine for $100,000. The mine is estimated to hold 50,000 tons of ore at the beginning of the tax year. During the first year, 4,000 tons are sold from the 5,000 tons extracted. No change in the original estimate is made for the first year. In the second year, 6,000 tons of ore are extracted and 5,000 tons are sold. The mine is estimated to have 60,000 tons at the end of the second year. Compute the cost depletion for both years.

21. A corporation places in service on May 1, 2014, property that qualifies as seven-year property under MACRS that cost $1,800,000. The corporation has taxable income of $3,000,000 in 2014. There is no other Section 179 property acquired in 2014. What are the allowable Section 179 and other depreciation deductions? How much tax savings will this produce if the corporation is in the 35-percent tax bracket?

22. During 2014, Pitterle, Inc, a calendar year manufacturing company, places in service $2,880,000 of Section 179 property. How much can Pitterle, Inc. elect to immediately expense?

23. A corporation places in service $800,000 of seven-year property in 2014. Before deducting the Section 179 expense election, the corporation has taxable income of $1,240,000. If the corporation elects the maximum Section 179 expense allowed by law, compute its total depreciation deduction for 2014, including bonus depreciation.

24. Schoeberle, Inc. acquired substantially all the assets of Luke, Inc. on July 10, 2015. Luke had four separate businesses. $16 million of the purchase price was allocated to goodwill. After taking $2 million of amortization ($500,000 per business), Schoeberle, Inc. sells one of the businesses in a loss in an asset sale. It allocates $3.5 million of the loss to the business's goodwill. What is the amount of the immediate loss deduction that can be taken for the business's goodwill?

25. On August 1, 2015, Meitner, Inc. (a calendar year corporation) purchases the leasehold interest of Cats R Us in a one-story business from which Meitner, Inc. operates a pet shop. Meitner pays $75,000 for Cats R Us' 10-year lease on which 5 years (60) months remain. How much does Meitner, Inc. deduct as a business expense in 2015 and 2016?

Chapter 7 Review Problems

1. In January 2015, Alder Corporation purchased a coal mine for $800,000. The mine had been producing minerals for several years, but it had an estimated 120,000 tons remaining at the time of purchase. During 2015, 16,800 tons were mined and sold for $386,400. Costs of operating the mine were as follows:

Labor for operating and servicing mining equipment	$120,000
Repairs to equipment	21,000
Real estate taxes on mine	46,000
Costs of gasoline to operate equipment	5,200

   a. Compute Alder's taxable profit from the mine after taking into consideration all expenses incurred in operating the mine.

   b. What is Alder's basis in the mine at the end of 2015?

2. Menominee Corporation, whose books were kept on the accrual method, showed the following cash receipts and disbursements for 2015:

Receipts:

Cash sales	$245,862
Collection of receivables	833,317
Interest on notes receivable	654

Disbursements:

Purchases	$639,034
Bank loan ($794 interest and $12,048 principal)	12,842
Fire and casualty insurance premium	3,870
Other operating expenses	374,377
Payments for returned merchandise	5,629

Receivables collected in 2015 included 2014 receivables totaling $32,561. Interest collected on notes receivable included $78 accrued in 2014. Disbursements included payment for 2014 purchases of $21,725 and other 2014 operating expenses of $7,541. The bank loan payments were on amounts that accrued in 2015.

The following amounts were accrued as of December 31, 2015:

Accounts and notes receivable	$41,578
Interest on notes receivable	27
Accounts payable	27,652
Other operating expenses	6,687

Merchandise inventories were valued at $123,428 on January 1, 2015, and at $135,223 on December 31, 2015.

The fire and casualty insurance premium paid in 2015 was for a two-year period beginning May 1, 2015. The three-year policy that expired on April 30, 2015, had cost $1,785.

Menominee is entitled to depreciation on the following assets:

Description of Property	Date Acq.	Cost
Office building	1/1/2000	$83,000
Copy machine	1/1/2013	8,000
Printer	6/1/2013	4,000
Computer	4/10/2011	700
Furniture	8/1/2014	6,781

Assume that this is the only depreciable property that Menominee has placed in service in a trade or business for the relevant time frame. Of the $83,000 cost of the office building, $5,000 is allocable to land. The corporation did not take the Code Sec. 179 deduction for any of these properties. Assume also that Menominee did not claim any first-year additional "bonus depreciation," making any necessary elections.

Compute Menominee's taxable income in 2015.

Comprehensive Review Question

Webster, Inc. has the following items of income and expense for 2014, its first year of operations. Webster began operations on April 1 and uses a calendar year end.

Gross receipts from sales	$1,391,222
Charitable contributions	15,000
Employment taxes	10,250
Interest expense	30,000
Organizational costs	52,600
Office rent expense	31,000
Real estate taxes	15,600
Utilities expense	11,300
Wage expense	93,540

In addition to these items, Webster purchased machinery and equipment costing $1,430,000 and furniture costing $112,000 on April 9, 2014, and a warehouse costing $190,000 on May 2, 2014.

Webster wants to minimize its 2014 income tax liability, which means electing Section 179 expense for the maximum the tax law allows, as well as taking the 50-percent bonus depreciation. Compute Webster's 2014 taxable income and income tax liability.

Chapter 7 Research Question

Are there any conditions under which a depletion deduction may be taken on water? Use the complete CCH Federal Tax Library in your school or local library to find your answer and provide the following:

1. Give your opinion. In it, show authorities, citing law, regulations, decisions applicable, and the *CCH Standard Federal Tax Reporter* paragraph references where they may be found.

2. Explain carefully every step you take in reaching your result.

PART III:

Transactions Involving Business Property

CHAPTER 8

Property Transactions: Realized and Recognized Gains and Losses

LEARNING OBJECTIVES

1. Calculate the realized gain or loss on the sale or exchange of property and determine which gains and losses are recognized on the tax return.

2. Define the loss disallowance provisions for wash sales and related party transactions and explain what happens to the disallowed loss.

3. List the rules behind the nonrecognition of gain or loss on like-kind exchanges and explain how the gains and losses are eventually recognized on the tax return.

4. Describe what constitutes an involuntary conversion and the circumstances under which realized gains can be postponed.

5. Explain when gains from the sale of certain securities can be excluded or postponed.

6. Describe how the tax laws and financial reporting rules differ with respect to dispositions of property.

¶ 800 Introduction

The accountant's definition of "income" generally rests on the revenue principle, also known as the realization concept. Under the revenue principle, for income to be realized there must be an exchange with an outsider. The realization concept is based on the accountant's desire to have an objective basis for measuring income. Therefore, unrealized gains and losses and imputed income are rejected as being too subjective to allow recognition.

Income tax law generally follows the realization concept. Therefore, increases and decreases in value of assets that are held (often called "paper gains and losses") do not constitute gross income. Income or loss from changes in the value of property is reported only when taxpayers realize gain or loss by disposing property.

Mere appreciation in value is not indicative of the owner's wherewithal to pay taxes on the income generated. Instead, the wherewithal is realized when the owner sells the property and can use the proceeds from the sale to pay the corresponding taxes.

Good tax planning requires an understanding of the tax laws regarding gains and losses on the disposition of property so that businesses can take advantage of opportunities to exclude or postpone gains. Likewise, businesses need to understand how the tax laws operate so that they can avoid situations in which a realized loss is postponed or lost. This chapter introduces the tax laws that govern the sale or exchange of property and discusses the exceptions to the general rule regarding the taxation of gains and the deductibility of losses on the disposal of business and investment property.

¶ 801 Realized vs. Recognized Gains and Losses

Realized gain or loss is the term used to describe taxpayers' gain or loss when they dispose of property. Realized gains and losses result when taxpayers dispose of property in a sale or exchange or abandonment of property. Gains and losses resulting from mere appreciation or decline in value are **unrealized gains and losses**.

Recognized gain or loss is the term used to describe the amount of realized gain or loss that taxpayers report on their tax returns. Only recognized gains and losses affect the taxpayer's tax liability.

As a general rule, all realized gains and losses from the sale or exchange of business and investment property are recognized.[1] In situations in which all of a realized gain or loss is not recognized, often recognition of the gain or loss is merely postponed. However, in a few instances, the gain or loss is never recognized.

When a transaction results in gain that is excluded from gross income, the gain is never taxed. When gain is postponed, the associated taxes are deferred until some point in the future. Until the gain is recognized, the taxpayer has full use of the temporary tax savings either to invest or to spend. When a transaction results in losses that are postponed, the tax savings that would have been generated from deducting the loss are postponed as well. If the transaction results in the permanent disallowance of the loss, the tax savings are forever lost.

 GAAP vs. Code: The objective of financial reporting is to provide users of financial statements the most relevant and reliable information about a company's financial activities. Because the market value of publicly traded stocks and bonds (collectedly called "marketable securities") is a readily available and highly reliable measure of their true value, generally accepted accounting principles (GAAP) require that unrealized

---

[1] Code Sec. 1001(c).

gains and losses from trading securities be reported on the income statement. "Trading securities" are stocks and bonds a corporation buys primarily for the purpose of selling them in the near future.[2]

Because the tax laws operate under the realization principle, unrealized gains and losses on securities are not reported on the tax return. Thus, to the extent unrealized gains and losses are reflected in the calculation of net income, such amounts must be backed out of net income when reconciling net income to taxable income on the corporate tax return. "Backing out" the amounts involves adding back to net income any unrealized losses and subtracting any unrealized gains. The difference in how unrealized gains and losses are treated for financial purposes versus tax purposes is merely a timing difference that will reverse when the securities are eventually sold. In the year trading securities are sold, the difference between the gain or loss reported on the income statement and the amount reported in the calculation of taxable income must be considered in the reconciliation of net income with taxable income.

¶ 802 Realized Gains and Losses

As previously mentioned, realized gains and losses are gains and losses that result from the sale, exchange, or abandonment of property. Realized gains and losses can also result from condemnations and casualties. An **exchange** involves two parties trading property other than cash. Sometimes the properties exchanged are similar; sometimes they are not similar. Exchanges of similar property, known as "like-kind exchanges," are discussed later in the chapter (see ¶ 808). All other transactions between a buyer and a seller that are not exchanges are sales. In a typical sale, the seller receives cash in exchange for the property, but other forms of consideration may be exchanged (see ¶ 802.01).

Under the capital recovery doctrine, taxpayers that dispose of property are allowed a tax-free recovery of their investment in the property. Thus, only the excess of the amount realized over a taxpayer's adjusted basis in the investment is taxed. Adjusted basis is the tax term used to describe the taxpayer's investment in property (see ¶ 802.02). Thus, realized gains and losses are computed as follows:

Amount realized	$ xx,xxx
Less: Adjusted basis	(xx,xxx)
Realized gain (or loss)	$ xx,xxx

Example 1: Swanson Company sold a machine it used in its business for $45,000. The adjusted basis in the machine is $36,000. Swanson's realized gain equals $9,000 ($45,000 – $36,000).

Example 2: Sanders Company sells land it used in its business for $27,000. If Sanders's adjusted basis in the land is $32,000, the realized loss equals $5,000 ($27,000 – $32,000).

 Spotlight: When a company purchases land for $100,000, its cash decreases by $100,000. If the company later makes a cash sale of the land for $150,000, its cash will increase by $150,000. When these two transactions are viewed together, the company's assets increase by $50,000 ($150,000 – $100,000). This amount is the company's realized gain from owning the land. Now consider a company that purchases stock for $60,000

---

[2] "Accounting for Certain Investments in Debt and Equity Securities," *Statement of Financial Accounting Standards No. 115* (Norwalk, Conn.: FASB, 1993).

> and later sells it for $35,000. The company spends $60,000 to purchase the stock but only receives $35,000 from the sale. When viewed together, the company's cost of the transaction is $25,000, which represents its realized loss from owning the stock. Accordingly, realized gains and losses represent the taxpayer's true economic gains and losses from the sale or exchange of property.

.01 Amount Realized

The starting point in the calculation of realized gain or loss is determining the **amount realized**, which is the amount that the seller receives from the buyer minus any expenses related to the sale (selling expenses). The amount realized includes cash received and the fair market value (FMV) of property as well as any services received in the sale or exchange.[3] As previously discussed, FMV is the amount that a willing buyer would pay to a willing seller if neither party were compelled to complete the transaction and if both parties had reasonable access to the same information. The seller often receives cash, but sometimes the seller provides financing to the buyer. Accordingly, the value (generally the face amount) of any notes received from the buyer is included in the seller's amount realized.

Example 3: Stephens Company sold land to Bragg Company. Bragg paid Stephens $90,000 in cash and gave Stephens industrial diamonds worth $50,000. Stephens's amount realized from the sale is $140,000.

Cash received	$ 90,000
FMV of diamonds received	50,000
Amount realized	$140,000

Example 4: Southard Company sold land to Bradshaw Company. Bradshaw paid $50,000 cash and signed a $200,000 interest-bearing note. The note is secured by a mortgage on the land and bears annual interest of 10 percent. Southard's amount realized from the sale is $250,000. Only the face value (principal) of the note is included in the amount realized. Southard will include in gross income the interest income it receives on the note as it is accrued or received, depending on Southard's accounting method.

Cash received	$ 50,000
Face value of the note received	200,000
Amount realized	$250,000

 Reason for the Rule: When property is disposed of, taxpayers must include the FMV of all property they receive from the transaction. If the amount realized included only the cash received from the transaction, taxpayers could avoid paying taxes by exchanging only noncash property.

Release from liability. The amount realized includes any debt from which a seller is relieved as a part of a sale or exchange.[4] The seller of a property can be released from recourse or nonrecourse liabilities.

---

[3] Code Sec. 1001(b).

[4] Reg. § 1.1001-2(a)(1); *B.B. Crane*, SCt, 47-1 USTC ¶ 9217, 331 US 1, 67 SCt 1047.

A **recourse liability** is a liability for which the seller is personally liable. A **nonrecourse liability** is a liability for which the seller is not personally liable, but for which the creditor can only look to property specified in the loan agreement for satisfaction of the debt. Nonrecourse liabilities are discussed in ¶ 802.02.

Example 5: Tom Gonzalez takes out a nonrecourse loan from Franklin Savings and Loan to buy a house. The loan agreement specifies that Franklin can repossess the house if Tom fails to make required payments on the loan. Tom defaults on the loan. Franklin can repossess the house, but it cannot look to Tom's other assets to satisfy the debt.

Example 6: Assume the same facts as in Example 5, except the loan is for an office building and is a recourse loan. Franklin can repossess Tom's office building and, if the proceeds from the sale of the office building do not fully satisfy the amount of the loan, it can pursue Tom individually for the balance.

Release from a liability occurs when the buyer assumes the seller's debt, takes property subject to the seller's debt, or pays off the seller's debt. In these instances, the seller's liabilities decrease, and the seller's wealth increases. Consequently, release from liability release constitutes the equivalent of cash and must be included in the amount realized.

Example 7: Milwood, Inc. sells a building to Jefferson Company for $700,000. Milwood's amount realized from the sale equals the $700,000 cash received. At the time of the sale, Milwood still owes $200,000 on the mortgage it took out when it purchased the property. Milwood can use $200,000 of the cash it receives from Jefferson to pay off the remaining balance of the mortgage. The lender will likely require Milwood to pay off the $200,000 mortgage because many mortgages include a due-on-sale clause.

Example 8: Assume the same facts as in Example 7, except that the terms of the sale stipulate that Jefferson will pay Milwood $500,000 cash and issue a five-year interest-bearing note for $200,000. Milwood's amount realized equals $700,000 ($500,000 + $200,000). Milwood can use the cash it receives from Jefferson to pay off the remaining balance of the mortgage.

Example 9: Assume the same facts as in Example 7, except that the terms of the sale stipulate that Jefferson will pay Milwood $500,000 cash and assume the remainder of Milwood's mortgage with the consent of the lender. The lender thereby discharges Milwood from any liability on the $200,000 balance on the mortgage. Milwood's amount realized on the sale equals $700,000 ($500,000 cash + $200,000 release from debt).

In each of the three examples, the seller (Milwood) received consideration from the buyer (Jefferson) equal to the FMV of the building ($700,000). The difference in the examples is how the transaction was structured.

Example 10: JP Richards & Co. exchanges land for a building owned by Kettlemore, Inc. At the time of the exchange, the land is worth $150,000, and the FMV of the building is $200,000. Kettlemore still owes $50,000 on the building. As part of the exchange, Richards agrees to take over the mortgage payments with the consent of the lender. As depicted in the diagram below, each party receives property worth $200,000 on the exchange. Richards receives a building worth $200,000, and Kettlemore receives land valued at $150,000 plus release from $50,000 of debt.

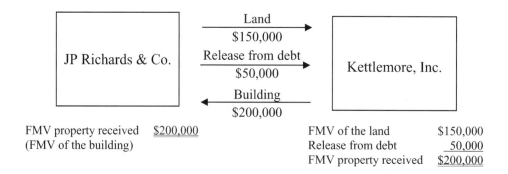

	Land $150,000	
JP Richards & Co.	Release from debt $50,000	Kettlemore, Inc.
	Building $200,000	

FMV property received $200,000
(FMV of the building)

FMV of the land	$150,000
Release from debt	50,000
FMV property received	$200,000

> **Spotlight:** When property is sold, the amount that the buyer is willing to pay and the seller is willing to receive determines the FMV of the property. When property is sold for cash, the amount of cash represents the FMV of the property sold. When property is sold for property other than cash, the FMV of the property received by the seller is the FMV of the property being sold. Therefore, on exchanges of property, the FMV of the property (or properties) given up is considered for income tax purposes to be equal to the FMV of the property (or properties) received.

Example 11: Alpena Company sells a property for $1.5 million cash. The property is subject to a nonrecourse liability of $250,000. Alpena's amount realized on the sale is $1.75 million ($1,500,000 + $250,000).

Real estate taxes. Local governments levy real estate taxes on the owners of real property. When real property is sold during the year, for federal income tax purposes the seller is presumed to be responsible for any real estate taxes accrued for the year up until the day of the sale, and the buyer is presumed to be responsible for any real estate taxes accrued on and after the day of the sale.[5] However, because the owner at the time the taxes are levied is responsible under local law for paying the taxes due as part of the sales agreement the buyer usually requires the seller to pay at the closing the seller's share of the real estate taxes for the year.

Example 12: Dean Enterprises (a calendar year taxpayer) sold land on May 11, 20X6, for $600,000. Real estate taxes on the land for 20X6 are estimated to be $10,000. At the closing, Dean remits to the buyer $3,561.64 ($10,000 × 130/365), which represents its share of the real estate taxes for the 130 days it owned the land during 20X6. Dean deducts this amount on its 20X6 tax return. At the end of the year, the local government will send the $10,000 property tax bill to the (new) owner of the property. However, the buyer's out-of-pocket costs will be $6,438.36: the $10,000 taxes owed minus the $3,561.64 that it received from Dean at the closing. Therefore, the buyer may deduct $6,438.36 on its income tax return for real estate taxes.

If the real estate taxes for the year of the sale are not apportioned between the seller and the buyer at the closing, then one party or the other may be liable for more than its share of real estate taxes owed. If the buyer pays taxes owed by the seller, then the amount paid has to be included in the amount realized by the seller (and added to the basis of the property being purchased).[6]

Example 13: Assume the same facts as in Example 12, except that no amounts are allocated or paid to the buyer at the closing for real estate taxes owed by Dean for the period during 20X6 in which it owned the property. In this case, Dean's amount realized from the sale increases to $603,561.64 ($600,000 + $3,561.64). The purchaser's basis in the property equals $603,561.64 ($600,000 + $3,561.64).

---

[5] Code Secs. 164(d) and 1001(b)(2).   [6] Code Sec. 1001(b)(2).

Selling expenses. Any costs paid in conjunction with a sale or exchange are subtracted when determining the amount realized. Common examples of selling expenses include commissions paid to stockbrokers and real estate agents and advertising expenses.

Example 14: Gibson Properties, LLC sells land for $500,000 and in the process pays a $30,000 commission. Gibson's amount realized equals $470,000 ($500,000 – $30,000).

Example 15: Smith Company sold land to Bennett Company. Bennett paid Smith $20,000 in cash, assumed Smith's mortgage of $80,000 on the land, and issued Smith an interest-bearing note for $10,000. Smith incurred $7,000 in selling expenses. Smith's $103,000 amount realized is calculated as follows:

Cash received	$ 20,000
Plus: Release from liability	80,000
Plus: Face value of the note received	10,000
Total FMV of the property received	$110,000
Less: Selling expenses	(7,000)
Amount realized	$103,000

Condemnations. Although not a sale in the traditional sense, taxpayers realize a gain or loss when their real property is condemned by the government. A **condemnation** occurs when the government takes possession of real property. Amounts paid to a property owner by the government when property is condemned are included in the amount realized by the property owner.

Casualties and thefts. When property is damaged from a casualty or stolen, its owner usually realizes a loss (but sometimes a gain). Insurance proceeds are included in the amount realized. (See ¶ 802.02.)

Worthless securities. Tax law treats worthless securities (stocks and bonds) as sold for $0 on the last day of the tax year in which they become worthless, regardless of the actual date on which the securities lose all of their value.[7] Because no amount is realized from a worthless security, the realized loss is equal to the taxpayer's adjusted basis in the securities.

Example 16: Wineland, Inc. purchased 100 shares of Wentbroke Corporation for $2,500 on October 6, 20X1. On May 8, 20X3, Wineland was notified that Wentbroke filed for bankruptcy and that its stock was worthless. Wineland is deemed to have sold the 100 shares for $0 on December 31, 20X3. Its realized loss from the deemed sale equals $2,500.

 Planning Pointer: If the taxpayer is having difficulty proving that a security is worthless, the taxpayer can sell it to an unrelated party in an arm's-length transaction for a small amount (for example, $1). The taxpayer would then realize a loss on the sale. However, the taxpayer must be careful not to sell the security to a related party because the related-party rules would prohibit the seller from recognizing the loss. (See ¶ 804.)

Call options and put options are not considered securities for purposes of this rule. A call (put) option involves the payment for a right to purchase (sell) stock for a certain price in the future. If the holder of a call option or a put option allows the option to expire, the expiration of the option is treated as a sale or exchange of the option on the expiration date.[8]

Example 17: On January 24, 20X7, Holt Company bought 100 call options on Andrews Company as an investment for $2.20 per option, including commissions and fees. Therefore, Holt

---

[7] Code Sec. 165(g).   [8] Rev. Rul. 78-182, 1978-1 CB 265.

paid $2,200 for the 100 call options ($2.20 × 100). The price of Andrews's stock began to go down rapidly after Holt bought the call options. On May 18, 20X7, the call options expired, worthless. Holt is treated as if it sold the call options for $0 on May 18, 20X7, the date that they expired.

.02 Adjusted Basis

After the amount realized is computed, the next step in determining the realized gain or loss involves calculating the taxpayer's adjusted basis in the property at the time of the sale or exchange.

"Adjusted basis," a tax term, is similar to book value in financial accounting. Adjusted basis represents taxpayers' unrecovered costs in property they own. The unrecovered cost is equivalent to the amounts invested in the property (initial cost plus any improvements) minus any amounts recovered over the years (e.g., from depreciation or casualty loss deductions). Under the capital recovery doctrine, a taxpayer's unrecovered costs are subtracted from the amount realized in determining the taxpayer's true economic gain or loss from owning the property.

As in financial reporting, the "initial cost" of an asset includes all of the costs necessary to get the property in place and ready for use. Thus, the initial cost of equipment includes the purchase price, sales taxes, delivery costs, and insurance while in transit as well as amounts paid for installation and testing. The "initial basis" in real property includes many of the closing costs incurred in acquiring the property. Closing costs included in the initial basis of property include recording fees, taxes on the deed or mortgage, fees charged to obtain credit reports, appraisals, and title insurance plus any legal fees or surveying costs.

Example 18: Weaver Company ordered a specialized machine to use in its business. The invoice price of the equipment was $35,000. Weaver also paid $2,100 in sales taxes, $250 in delivery charges, $50 for insurance while in transit, $150 for installation, and $80 for testing. Each of these amounts is included in Weaver's $37,630 initial cost for the equipment. As the equipment is depreciated under MACRS or expensed under Code Sec. 179, Weaver reduces its adjusted basis in the equipment. (See ¶ 702).

To determine adjusted basis, the taxpayer adds any capital improvements it has made to the initial basis. The taxpayer then subtracts accumulated cost recovery amounts.

Liabilities. As a rule, initial basis includes the amount of any nonrecourse liabilities secured by the property and any recourse liabilities assumed by the purchaser of the property.

Example 19: Petosky Corporation purchases a tract of land from Escanaba, Ltd. Petosky pays $1 million cash and agrees to assume Escanaba's $500,000 recourse liability. In addition, the land is subject to a $100,000 nonrecourse liability. Petosky's basis in the property is $1.6 million ($1,000,000 + $500,000 + $100,000).

Basket purchases. When a taxpayer acquires more than one property in a single transaction, called a "basket purchase," the purchase price is generally allocated to the various items acquired based on each property's relative FMV.[9] "Relative FMV" is the FMV of the individual property divided by the total FMV of all properties acquired in the purchase. A common example of a basket purchase is the purchase of real property with one or more items of personal property. Another example involves the purchase of land (nondepreciable realty) and a building (depreciable realty) for a single, lump sum amount.

Example 20: Brenda Davis operates a sole proprietorship. Brenda pays $480,000 for land, an office building, a refrigerator, and a conference table. The FMV of the land and the office building were $100,000 and $498,000, respectively. The FMV of the refrigerator and

---

[9] Note that this rule does not apply when the basket of assets purchased constitutes a trade or business. In that case, the residual allocation method of Code Sec. 1060 must be used.

conference table were $700 and $1,300, respectively. Brenda must allocate the $480,000 purchase price to the various properties based on their relative FMVs as shown below.

	FMV	Relative FMV	Cost	Basis
Land	$100,000	$100,000/$600,000 × $480,000 =		$ 80,000
Office building	498,000	$498,000/$600,000 × $480,000 =		398,400
Refrigerator	700	$700/$600,000 × $480,000 =		560
Conference table	1,300	$1,300/$600,000 × $480,000 =		1,040
Totals	$600,000			$480,000

Reason for the Rule: Land is not depreciable, and different depreciation rules apply to different types of depreciable property. In addition, the various properties acquired may be sold at different times. Therefore, an initial basis must be assigned to each property acquired. If left to their own discretion, taxpayers typically would assign as much of the cost as possible to depreciable property with the shortest recovery period because that would produce the greatest tax savings in the quickest period of time. Thus, an objective method for allocating the purchase price among the various assets acquired is needed. The relative FMV approach to allocating the initial cost is an objective method. It is also used to allocate costs for financial reporting purposes.

Abandonments. An **abandonment** occurs when the owner walks away from property and receives no consideration. Because no amount is realized upon the disposition, the taxpayer's realized loss equals its adjusted basis in the property.[10]

Example 21: Mark Grooms operates a sole proprietorship. During the year, a truck that Mark used exclusively in his business broke down while he was traveling in a remote location. Mark's adjusted basis in the truck is $950. At the time the truck broke down, it was worth $600. When Mark learned that the cost to repair the truck would be $800, he abandoned it rather than have it repaired. Mark's realized loss on the abandonment equals $950 ($0 amount realized – $950 adjusted basis).

Property involved in a casualty. When the insurance proceeds exceed the taxpayer's adjusted basis in property damaged in a casualty, the excess results in a realized casualty gain. For the purpose of computing a realized loss from a casualty, the amount used to offset the insurance proceeds depends on whether the property was partially or completely destroyed in the casualty. When property is *completely destroyed*, the adjusted basis of the property is offset by the insurance proceeds, and the excess is the taxpayer's realized loss from the casualty. When property is only *partially destroyed* in the casualty, the realized casualty loss is equal to the *lesser of* the decline in FMV of the property or its adjusted basis, offset by the insurance proceeds.[11]

Example 22: Dunlap Company's delivery van was damaged in an accident. The FMV of the van before the accident was $4,000; its FMV after the accident was $3,000. Dunlap Company chose not to repair the van because the damage was only cosmetic. The adjusted basis of the van at the time of the accident was $2,500. Because the van was only partially destroyed, the amount of Dunlap's loss is measured as the *lesser of* the $1,000 decline in FMV ($4,000 – $3,000) of the van or its $2,500 adjusted basis. Thus, Dunlap's realized casualty loss equals $1,000 because there are no insurance proceeds to further reduce the loss.

---

[10] *L&C Springs Associates*, CA-7, 99-2 USTC ¶ 50,777, 188 F3d 866, aff'g, 74 TCM 928, TC Memo. 1997-469.   [11] Reg. § 1.165-7(b)(1).

Property involved in a theft. The term "theft" includes, but is not necessarily limited to, larceny, embezzlement, and robbery.[12] When property is stolen, the taxpayer incurs a loss equal to the adjusted basis of the property.[13] If the property is covered by insurance, the amount of the theft loss is reduced by the amount of the insurance proceeds. When the insurance proceeds exceed the adjusted basis of the stolen property, the taxpayer realizes a theft gain. Taxpayers recognize a theft loss in the year in which they discover the property has been stolen.[14]

Example 23:   On December 30, 20X8 the offices of Midwestern Supply, Inc. were broken into and $800 in petty cash was stolen. The theft was discovered on January 2, 20X9 when the company reopened after the holidays. The theft loss is deductible in the year 20X9.

¶ 803 Recognized Gains and Losses

Recognized gains and losses are realized gains and losses that the taxpayer must include in gross income. Figure 8-1 lists situations in which realized gains and losses are not recognized on the tax return. Sometimes the gains and losses are never taxed. Often, however, recognition of the gain or loss is merely postponed. The remainder of this chapter focuses on the tax laws that govern these special transactions.

Figure 8-1 Summary of Realized Gains and Losses Postponed or Never Taxed

- Losses from the sale, exchange, or abandonment of personal-use property;

- Losses on the sale of property to a related party;

- Losses on the sale of securities that are involved in a wash sale;

- Gains and losses from exchanges of like-kind property;

- Gains from involuntary conversions of business or investment property;

- Gains from the sale of Section 1244 stock; and

- Gains from the sale of SSBIC stock.

 GAAP vs. Code: When corporations dispose of depreciable property, the gain or loss reported on the income statement often is different from that reported on the tax return due to the different methods used to depreciate property. The amount of depreciation expense deducted on the tax return is reflected in the adjusted basis of property and therefore impacts the amount of gain or loss reported on the tax return. Similarly, the amount of depreciation expense deducted on the income statement is reflected in the book value of the asset and impacts the gain or loss reported in the calculation of net income in the year the asset is sold. Thus, just as the differences in depreciation expense taken each year are taken into consideration when reconciling net income and taxable income, in the year a business disposes of property the cumulative differences are reversed when the amount of gain or loss included in net income is reconciled with the amount reported in taxable income.

---

[12] Reg. § 1.165-8(d).
[13] Reg. § 1.165-8(c).

[14] Reg. § 1.165-8(a)(2).

¶ 804 Losses between Related Parties

No deduction is allowed for a loss from the sale or exchange of property directly or indirectly between related persons.[15] The tax laws disallow the loss even when the property is sold at its FMV in an arm's-length transaction.

Related persons include not only family members but also other relationships. Figure 8-2 describes several types of relationships between persons that will result in a disallowed loss on a sale or an exchange of property.[16]

Figure 8-2 Related Persons

1. An individual and the individual's spouse, siblings, ancestors, or lineal descendants;

2. An individual and a corporation in which the individual *directly or indirectly* owns more than 50 percent of the value of the outstanding stock;

3. An individual and a partnership in which the individual *directly or indirectly* owns more than a 50-percent capital or profits interest;

4. Two corporations that are members of the same controlled group;

5. A corporation and a partnership if the same person or persons own more than 50 percent of the outstanding value of the stock in the corporation and more than a 50-percent capital or profits interests in the partnership;

6. An S corporation and another S corporation if the same person or persons own more than 50 percent of the value in the outstanding stock of each corporation;

7. An S corporation and a C corporation if the same person or persons own more than 50 percent of the value in the outstanding stock of each corporation; and

8. Two partnerships in which the same person or persons *directly or indirectly* own more than a 50-percent capital or profits interest.

For the related party rules, "siblings" include an individual's brothers and sisters, as well as half brothers and half sisters. "Descendents" of the individual include the individual's children and grandchildren. "Ancestors" include parents and grandparents. In determining whether a taxpayer directly or indirectly owns more than 50 percent of a corporation's stock, the IRS considers stock the taxpayer actually owns as well as stock the taxpayer constructively owns. Similar rules apply to constructive ownership of partnership interests (see ¶ 804.01).

The term "controlled group" covers two distinct types of ownership arrangements: "brother-sister controlled groups" and "parent-subsidiary controlled groups."[17] Two corporations can be related through a brother-sister controlled group when five or fewer persons own more than 50 percent of either the voting shares or value of the stock in both corporations. Parent-subsidiary controlled groups for purposes of the loss disallowance rules consist of one or more chains of corporations connected through stock ownership with a common parent corporation if two conditions are met:

1. one or more of the corporations own either a minimum of 50 percent of the total *combined voting power* of all stock eligible to vote, or a minimum of 50 percent of the total value of shares of all classes of stock, and

---

[15] Code Sec. 267(a)(1).

[16] Code Secs. 267(b) and 707(b).

[17] Code Sec. 267(f).

2. the common parent corporation owns directly stock (options are counted as stock for this purpose) with at least 50 percent of either the total *combined voting power* of all stock eligible to vote, or at least 50 percent of the total *value* of shares of all classes of stock.[18]

Example 24: Delightful Foods owns 70 percent of the outstanding stock of Baker Supply and 40 percent of Pantry Supply. Baker Supply also owns 60 percent of Pantry Supply. The relationship among these corporations is illustrated below.

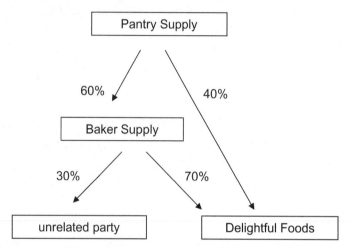

More than 50 percent of Pantry Supply is owned by Baker Supply (60 percent) and Delightful Foods (40 percent). In addition, more than 50 percent of Baker Supply is owned by Delightful Foods (70 percent) and Pantry Supply (zero percent). Thus, for purposes of the loss disallowance rules, Delightful Foods, Baker Supply, and Pantry Supply are members of a parent-subsidiary controlled group with Delightful Foods as the common parent.

Example 25: Sara sold land to her brother Bill for $60,000. Sara purchased the land for $100,000 several years earlier. Sara's realized loss equals $40,000 ($60,000 – $100,000), but she cannot recognize the loss because she sold the land to a related party.

Example 26: Bea sold land to her nephew Andy for its FMV of $16,000. Bea purchased the land for $18,000 two years earlier. Bea's realized loss is $2,000 ($16,000 – $18,000). Even though she and her nephew are relatives, they are not considered related parties for tax purposes. Therefore, Bea can recognize her $2,000 loss on her tax return.

Reason for the Rule: The tax laws allow taxpayers to deduct losses on the disposal of business and investment property based on the assumption that the seller has suffered a true economic loss. When related parties are involved in a sale or an exchange, the seller may be able to formally dispose of the property without truly relinquishing control over it because of the special relationship that exists between the buyer and the seller. Therefore, the taxpayer may be able to influence the (related) buyer to sell the property back to the (related) seller at its lower FMV. This practice would allow taxpayers to turn unrealized losses into recognized losses.

The tax laws do not attempt to determine whether the seller's motive for selling the property is something other than a valid business or investment reason. Instead, an objective test is used to determine whether such a motivation might exist. The tax laws normally assume that certain transactions, such as those between family members or

---

[18] Code Secs. 267(f)(1) and 1563(a)(1).

those between a corporation and a controlling shareholder, are made to generate recognized losses without actually relinquishing control of the property. For the purpose of defining family members, the government applies an objective test and automatically assumes that taxpayers can control the decisions and actions of certain close family members. Accordingly, a taxpayer is allowed to recognize a loss on the sale of property to an aunt, but not to a sister, even when a closer bond exists between the taxpayer and the aunt. A taxpayer may not avoid the application of the rules by showing that the sale was a *bona fide* sale for the FMV of the property.[19] Nor can the tax consequences of the related party rules be avoided by demonstrating that the taxpayer and a related party do not have an amicable relationship.[20]

.01 Constructive Ownership

Under the **constructive ownership** rules, a taxpayer may be treated as owning stock that is actually owned by another person or entity in which the taxpayer has an ownership interest. For example, stock owned by a business entity (corporation or partnership) is treated as owned proportionately by the entities' owners.[21] Thus, if a partnership with two equal partners owns 10 percent of the stock in a corporation, each partner is treated as owning five percent of the stock in that corporation, even though neither partner actually owns any stock in the corporation. Similarly, if ABC Corporation owns 40 percent of the stock in DEF Corporation, a shareholder who owns 30 percent of the stock in ABC is treated as owning 12 percent (30% × 40%) of the stock in DEF.

The constructive ownership rules extend to stock owned by some of an individual's family members. Stock owned by the taxpayer's spouse, lineal descendants, ancestors, or siblings is treated as owned by the taxpayer.[22] Furthermore, the tax laws treat relationships established by legal adoption the same as those established by blood when applying the constructive ownership rules.[23] For example, if a taxpayer and the taxpayer's spouse each own 35 percent of the stock in a corporation, they are treated as owning each other's stock. Therefore, each is treated as owning 70 percent of the corporation, and any transactions between the corporation and either spouse would fall under the related party rules.

The constructive ownership rules involve a series of complex rules regarding individuals and any business entities they own. For example, under the constructive ownership rules, a partner who owns stock in a corporation is treated as owning any stock that his or her partner actually owns in the corporation.[24] However, if the partner does not personally own stock in a corporation, the partner is not considered to constructively own stock that a partner owns. For example, if Anne and Bob (unrelated to one another) are 50-50 partners in Anne & Bob's and each owns 30 percent of the stock in XYZ Corporation, each is treated as owning 60 percent of the stock in XYZ. However, if Bob does not actually own any stock in XYZ, then he is not treated as owning the 30 percent that his partner (Anne) owns.[25]

Stock constructively owned by a person as a shareholder or partner is treated as actually owned by the person for purposes of applying other constructive ownership rules.[26] However, stock attributed to a person because of a family relationship or partnership will not be treated as owned by the person for purposes of making someone else the constructive owner of such stock.

Example 27: Edward Blake and Ralph Davis are 50-50 partners in BD partnership. Edward and Ralph each own stock in General Distributors Corporation, which is owned by the following individuals:

---

[19] *R.C. Camp*, 31 TCM 297, Dec. 31, 316(M), TC Memo. 1972-74.

[20] *D.L. Miller*, 75 TC 182, Dec. 37,376 (1980).

[21] Code Sec. 267(c)(1).

[22] Code Sec. 267(c)(2) and (c)(4).

[23] Reg. § 1.267(c)-1(a)(4).

[24] Code Sec. 267(c)(3).

[25] Code Sec. 267(c)(5).

[26] Code Sec. 267(c)(5).

	Actual Ownership
Edward Blake	35%
Patsy Blake (Edward's wife)	35%
Susan Rogers (the Blakes's daughter)	15%
Ralph Davis (Edward's partner)	15%
	100%

Because Edward owns stock in General Distributors, in addition to the 35 percent that he personally owns he is deemed to own the 15 percent that his partner, Ralph Davis, owns. He is also treated as owning the 35 percent owned by his spouse and the 15 percent owned by his daughter. Therefore, Edward's total ownership (actual + constructive) is 100 percent of General Distributors.

Patsy actually owns 35 percent of the stock in General Distributors; however, through the constructive ownership rules, she is deemed to also own stock owned by her husband (Edward) and her child (Susan). Thus, Patsy's total ownership (actual + constructive) is 85 percent (35% + 35% + 15%). The stock Edward is deemed to own through his partner, Ralph, is not "reattributed" to any of his family members. Susan's total ownership is 85 percent because she is deemed to own the stock that her parents own (15% + 35% + 35%).

Because Ralph is deemed to own the stock actually owned by Edward, his total ownership in General Distributors is 50 percent (15% + 35%). Edward's constructive ownership of the stock owned by his family members is not reattributed to Ralph.

	Actual Ownership	*Constructive Ownership*	*Total Ownership*
Edward Blake	35%	65%	100%
Patsy Blake (Edward's wife)	35%	50%	85%
Susan Rogers (the Blakes's daughter)	15%	70%	85%
Ralph Davis (Edward's partner)	15%	35%	50%

Because Edward, Patsy, and Susan each own (directly or indirectly) own more than 50 percent of General Distributors, any realized loss from the sale of property between any of them and General Distributors would be disallowed under the related party rules. However, any realized loss from a sale between Ralph and General Distributors would be recognized because Ralph's ownership does not exceed 50 percent.

Reason for the Rule: The related party rules exist because Congress believes that taxpayers may be able to influence the decisions and actions of certain persons or entities. The constructive ownership rules go one step further and assume that stock owned by certain (related) parties is stock they can control as well. Without the constructive ownership rules, taxpayers could have family members and certain related entities purchase the property from them and turn an unrecognized loss into a recognized loss without truly relinquishing control over the property.

.02 Subsequent Use of Disallowed Loss by Purchaser

When property is sold to a related person, the seller's realized loss is permanently disallowed with respect to the seller. The related party purchaser, however, may use the disallowed loss to reduce or eliminate any gain realized on the subsequent sale or exchange of the property.[27] But the disallowed loss cannot cause or increase a loss.[28]

The related party purchaser may be unable to use some or all of the disallowed loss if the property acquired does not appreciate enough to produce sufficient realized gain to absorb the disallowed loss. Consequently, before selling or exchanging property that will generate a realized loss, it is important that taxpayers, and especially business entities, understand the related party rules.

Example 28: Fletcher Corporation sells land to Kevin Barnes for $14,000. Fletcher's adjusted basis in the land is $25,000. Because Kevin owns 60 percent of the outstanding stock of Fletcher, Fletcher cannot recognize any of its $11,000 realized loss ($14,000 – $25,000) on the sale. Kevin's basis in the land is what he paid for it ($14,000). If Kevin later sells the land for $31,000, his realized gain equals $17,000 ($31,000 – $14,000). He can use the $11,000 disallowed loss realized by Fletcher to reduce his recognized gain to $6,000 ($17,000 – $11,000).

Example 29: Assume the same facts as in Example 28, except Kevin sells the land for $22,000. Kevin's realized gain equals $8,000 ($22,000 – $14,000). He can use $8,000 of the $11,000 disallowed loss to reduce his recognized gain to $0. He cannot use the remaining $3,000 of the disallowed loss to create a loss from the sale. The $3,000 of disallowed loss is lost, and neither Fletcher Corporation nor Kevin Fletcher will benefit from it on their respective tax returns.

Example 30: Assume the same facts as in Example 28, except Kevin sells the land for $12,000. Kevin realizes and recognizes a $2,000 loss ($12,000 – $14,000). Neither he nor Fletcher will benefit from the $11,000 disallowed loss.

The benefit of the rule is available only to the original transferee, not to any subsequent transferee and not to any original transferee who acquired the property in any manner other than by purchase or exchange (e.g., by gift).[29]

 GAAP vs. Code: When computing net income on the income statement, all losses are deducted from net income, regardless of who buys the property. Thus, when a corporation sells property to a related party, the disallowed loss must be added back to the corporation's net income when reconciling net income to taxable income on the corporation's income tax return. When a corporation purchases property from a related party and is later able to use some or all of the seller's disallowed loss to reduce its recognized gain, the corporation must subtract from net income the difference between the gain reported on the income statement and the (reduced) gain recognized on the tax return when reconciling net income to taxable income on the tax return.

¶ 805 Wash Sales

A **wash sale** occurs when a taxpayer realizes a loss on the sale of securities (stocks and bonds) but acquired (by purchase or by an exchange on which the entire amount of gain or loss is recognized by law), or entered into a contract or option to acquire, substantially identical securities within 30 days before or after the date of the sale. The tax laws do not allow taxpayers to recognize losses that result from wash sales.[30] For purposes of the wash sale rules, call options and put options on stock are treated as securities unless the regulations state otherwise.[31]

---

[27] Code Sec. 267(d); Reg. § 1.267(d)-1(a)(1).
[28] Reg. § 1.267(d)-1(a)(4) (Example 2).
[29] Reg. § 1.267(d)-1(a)(3).
[30] Code Sec. 1091(a).
[31] Code Sec. 1091(a).

Example 31: Rickers Company purchased 1,000 shares of common stock in Appleton, Inc. several years ago for $50,000. As of December 31, 20X1, the stock was selling for $10,000. Because the decline in value represents an unrealized loss, Rickers cannot deduct the loss in computing taxable income on its 20X1 tax return.

Example 32: Assume the same facts as in Example 31, except that on December 31, 20X1, Rickers sells the 1,000 shares in Appleton. Rickers's realized loss on the sale equals $40,000 ($10,000 – $50,000). Rickers can recognize the $40,000 loss when computing its 20X1 taxable income.

Example 33: Assume the same facts as in Example 32, except that on January 2, 20X2, Rickers repurchases 1,000 shares of Appleton common stock for $10,000. Because Rickers repurchased the same stock in the same company within 30 days after the sale that resulted in a realized loss (the December 31 sale), Rickers's realized loss is disallowed on its 20X1 tax return.

Example 34: Deborah Williams bought 1,000 shares of High Hope Corporation on September 21, 20X1, for $30,500. She bought another 1,000 shares of High Hope on April 2, 20X3, for $29,000. On April 23, 20X3, she sold the 1,000 shares that she had bought on September 21, 20X1, for $28,100 and realized a loss of $2,400 ($28,100 – $30,500). Deborah may not recognize the loss because she bought the same or substantially identical stock within 30 days before she sold the shares at a loss.

> **Reason for the Rule:** The wash sale rules were enacted in 1921 to prevent taxpayers from reducing their tax liability by taking losses on the sale of securities and then reacquiring the same securities within a short time, thereby essentially leaving them in the same economic position.[32] In Example 33, Rickers originally owned 1,000 shares of common stock in Appleton and, except for a few days, continued to own 1,000 shares of Appleton common stock. Without the wash sale rules, Rickers would have been able to recognize a loss without changing her economic position. The language applying the wash sale rules to repurchases 30 days before or after the sale was included to make it clear that a window period was intended.

.01 Substantially Identical

The wash sale rules apply if a taxpayer repurchases the *same or substantially identical* securities within 30 days before or 30 days after selling securities at a loss. In determining whether securities are substantially identical, all the facts and circumstances must be considered.[33] With respect to shares of stock sold at a loss, substantially identical securities would be shares of stock in the same company. Normally, common stock of one corporation is not substantially identical to common stock of another corporation,[34] and nonconvertible preferred stock of a corporation is not substantially identical to common stock of the same corporation.[35] Bonds or preferred stock of a corporation are not ordinarily considered substantially identical to the common stock of the same corporation. However, when the bonds or preferred stock are convertible into common stock of the same corporation, the relative values, price changes, and other circumstances may make the bonds or preferred stock and the common stock of the corporation substantially identical.[36]

Bonds are not substantially identical if they are substantially different in any material feature or because of differences in several material features considered together.[37] Maturity date, face rate of interest, call, and convertible features are all features associated with bonds. To determine whether

---

[32] H.R. Rep. No. 350-67, at 11 (1921).

[33] Reg. § 1.1233-1(d)(1); Rev. Rul. 77-201, 1977-1 CB 250.

[34] Reg. § 1.1233-1(d)(1); Rev. Rul. 77-201, 1977-1 CB 250.

[35] Rev. Rul. 77-201, 1977-1 CB 250.

[36] Reg. § 1.1233-1(d)(1); Rev. Rul. 77-201, 1977-1 CB 250; GCM 37004 (Feb. 15, 1977).

[37] Rev. Rul. 58-211, 1958-1 CB 529.

a difference in maturity dates is material, it is necessary to compare the differences in maturity dates in conjunction with the length of time until the bonds mature. Thus, two bonds issued by the same company that have similar features except for maturity dates that are six months apart are substantially identical if the duration of the bond is 20 years but not if the duration of the bond is one year.[38] Differences in interest payment dates are not considered substantial when the bonds have the same number of annual interest payments. For example, the difference in bonds that pay interest every February 1 and August 1 and bonds that pay interest every October 1 and April 1 is not considered a substantial difference because both bonds pay interest semiannually.[39]

 Spotlight: The wash sale rules apply only to losses realized on the sale of securities. Taxpayers who sell securities for a gain and purchase the same or substantially identical securities within 30 days on either side of the sale date recognize the gain under the normal recognition rules.

.02 Eventual Recognition of the Loss from the Wash Sale

Unlike the related party rules, which permanently deny recognition of the loss to the seller, the wash sale rules merely postpone the loss until the taxpayer sells the securities in a nonwash sale transaction.[40]

To ensure that taxpayers eventually benefit from the disallowed loss, the disallowed loss is added to the basis of the newly acquired shares that caused the loss to be disallowed.[41] The holding period of the shares purchased includes the holding period of the shares sold that resulted in a wash sale.[42]

Example 35: In Example 33, Rickers Company's $40,000 disallowed loss will be added to the basis of the shares purchased on January 2, 20X2. Therefore, the basis in the new shares will be $50,000 ($10,000 + $40,000 disallowed loss). If Rickers immediately sells the newly acquired shares for their $10,000 FMV, the realized loss will equal $40,000 ($10,000 – $50,000). If Rickers can avoid repurchasing these shares for the 61 days surrounding the date of the sale, it will recognize the $40,000 loss that was originally disallowed under the wash sale rules.

If a taxpayer purchases fewer shares than those sold, only a portion of the loss is disallowed and the taxpayer is allowed to recognize the loss on the shares of stock that were sold and not repurchased within the 61-day window. The disallowed loss is added ratably to the basis of the shares repurchased within the 61-day window.[43]

Example 36: On August 11, 20X2, Leah Starnes sold 600 shares of stock in Skate Rinks Corporation for $6,000. Leah's purchases of stock in Skate Rinks were as follows:

Date	Number of Shares	Price Per Share	Total Paid
June 14, 20X1	600	$25	$15,000
August 28, 20X2	400	14	5,600
September 13, 20X3	200	13	2,600

Leah's realized loss on the sale of the 600 shares sold on August 11, 20X2, equals $9,000 ($6,000 – $15,000). Because she repurchased 400 shares of the stock within 30 days before or after that date, $6,000 of the loss is disallowed ($9,000 × 400/600) and must be added to the basis in the shares involved in the wash sale (the

---

[38] *M. Hanlin*, 39-2 USTC ¶ 9783, 108 F2d 429.
[39] Rev. Rul. 58-210, 1958-1 CB 523.
[40] Code Sec. 1091(d).

[41] Code Sec. 1091(d).
[42] Code Sec. 1223(3).
[43] Code Sec. 1091(d); Reg. § 1.1091-2(a).

400 shares purchased on August 28, 20X2). Thus, Leah will recognize $3,000 of the loss ($9,000 – $6,000), and her basis in the shares acquired on August 28, 20X2, equals $11,600 ($5,600 + $6,000). Leah's holding period for those shares dates back to June 15, 20X1—the date after the shares involved in the wash sale were originally purchased.

 GAAP vs. Code: For financial reporting purposes, all gains and losses on the sale of securities are reported in the calculation of net income. For tax purposes, the wash sale rules affect the timing of the recognition of loss on the sale of securities involved in a wash sale. Because the disallowed loss from a wash sale is eventually recognized, the difference between net income and taxable income in the year the securities are sold at a loss will later be reversed when the repurchased shares are sold at either a gain or in a nonwash sale transaction. Thus, in the year of the wash sale, the disallowed loss must be added back to net income when reconciling net income to taxable income. In the year in which the disallowed loss is finally recognized on the tax return, the loss must be subtracted from net income when reconciling net income to taxable income on that year's corporate tax return.

¶ 806 Qualified Small Business Stock

When a noncorporate taxpayer sells or exchanges qualified small business stock (sometimes referred to as "Section 1202 stock") that the taxpayer has held for more than five years, 50 percent of the realized gain is excluded from the taxpayer's gross income[44] (75 percent of the realized gain may be excluded if the stock was acquired after February 17, 2009 and before September 28, 2010,[45] and 100 percent of the realized gain may be excluded if the stock was acquired on or after September 28, 2010 and before January 1, 2015[46]).

The amount of gain from the sale of stock in any one corporation that can be excluded cannot exceed the *greater of* (1) $10 million ($5 million for married taxpayers who file separate returns from their spouses) minus all amounts excluded for previous tax years with respect to stock in that particular corporation or (2) 10 times the aggregate bases of qualified small business stock issued by the corporation and sold or exchanged by the taxpayer during the year.[47]

"Qualified small business stock" is stock that satisfies all of the following requirements:[48]

- It is stock in a C corporation.
- It was originally issued after August 10, 1993.
- The corporation was a qualified small business as of the date that the stock was issued.
- The stock was acquired by the taxpayer at its original issue (directly or through an underwriter) in exchange for money or other property (not including stock) or as compensation for services provided to the corporation (other than services performed as an underwriter of such stock). If the stock was acquired solely through the conversion of other stock in the corporation that is qualified small business stock in the hands of the taxpayer, the stock so acquired will be treated as qualified small business stock in the hands of the taxpayer and will be treated as having been held during the period that the converted stock was held.[49] If a taxpayer acquires qualified small business stock by gift, at death, or as a partner from a partnership, the transferee will be treated as having acquired the stock in the same manner as the transferor and as having held the stock during the period held by the transferor.[50]

[44] Code Sec. 1202(a)(1).
[45] Code Sec. 1202(a)(3).
[46] Code Sec. 1202(a)(4).
[47] Code Sec. 1202(b).
[48] Code Sec. 1202(c).
[49] Code Sec. 1202(f).
[50] Code Sec. 1202(h).

- The corporation is an eligible corporation. A domestic corporation is an "eligible corporation" unless it is a DISC or former DISC; a corporation with respect to which an election under Code Sec. 936 (for the Puerto Rico and possessions tax credit) is in effect or which has a direct or indirect subsidiary with respect to which an election is in effect; a regulated investment company, real estate investment trust, or REMIC; or a cooperative.[51]

- During substantially all of the taxpayer's holding period for the stock, the corporation is a C corporation and at least 80 percent (by value) of the corporation's assets are used by the corporation in the active conduct of one or more qualified trades or businesses. A specialized small business investment company is treated as satisfying this active business test. A "qualified trade or business" is any trade or business other than any trade or business involving the performance of services in the fields of health, law, engineering, architecture, accounting, actuarial science, performing arts, consulting, athletics, financial services, brokerage services, or any trade or business where the principal asset of the trade or business is the reputation or skill of one or more of its employees; any banking, insurance, financing, leasing, investing, or similar business; any farming business (including the business of raising or harvesting trees); any business involving the production or extraction of products of a character with respect a deduction is allowable for percentage depletion under Code Sec. 613 or Code Sec. 613A; or any business of operating a hotel, motel, restaurant, or similar business.[52]

- Within the period beginning two years before and ending two years after the stock was issued, the corporation did not purchase more than a de minimis amount of its stock from the taxpayer or a related party.

- Within the period beginning one year before and ending one year after the stock was issued, the corporation did not purchase more than a de minimis amount of its stock from anyone, unless the total value of the stock purchased is five percent or less of the total value of all of its stock.

A "qualified small business" is a domestic C corporation if its gross assets (or any predecessor's gross assets) at all times on or after August 10, 1993 and before issuance of the stock did not exceed $50 million, its aggregate gross assets immediately after issuance of the stock (determined by taking into account amounts received in issuing the stock) did not exceed $50 million, and the corporation agreed to submit such reports to the Secretary of the Treasury and to its shareholders as the Secretary of the Treasury may require.[53]

Example 37: Beth Yarbrough purchased common stock in a qualified small business on January 15, 2009 for $36,000. She sold the stock on September 10, 2015 for $86,000. Her realized gain is $50,000 ($86,000 – $36,000). Beth may exclude $25,000 ($50,000 × 50%) of the gain from her gross income because she held the qualified stock for more than five years.

If a taxpayer other than a corporation sells qualified small business stock held for more than six months, the taxpayer may elect to recognize gain from the sale only to the extent that the amount realized exceeds the cost of any qualified small business stock purchased by the taxpayer during the 60-day period beginning on the date of the sale reduced by any portion of the cost previously taken into account under this provision.[54] The taxpayer's basis in the new qualified small business stock is reduced by the amount of gain not recognized.[55] The taxpayer's holding period for the stock purchased includes the holding period for the stock sold, except for the purpose of applying the six-month holding period requirement for rolling over gain.

---

[51] Code Sec. 1202(e)(4).
[52] Code Sec. 1202(e)(3).
[53] Code Sec. 1202(d)(1).

[54] Code Sec. 1045(a).
[55] Code Sec. 1045(b)(3).

Reason for the Rule: Code Sec. 1202 was enacted as part of the Omnibus Budget Reconciliation Act of 1993 to encourage investment in new ventures, small businesses, and specialized small business investment companies (SSBICs). Due to the higher risk involved in such investments, Congress hoped that offering special tax incentives to noncorporate investors would encourage them to take a chance on these investments. For example, although Beth's realized gain from Example 37 is $50,000, she is taxed on only $25,000 of the gain. If her tax rate on the gain is 15 percent, then Beth will pay a total of $3,750 of tax on the $50,000 gain ($25,000 × 15%), which makes her tax rate on the realized gain 7.5 percent ($3,750 ÷ $50,000).

¶ 807 Rollover of Gain on the Sale of Publicly Traded Securities

Generally, gain realized on the sale of stock must be recognized. A special provision in the tax law allows individuals and C corporations (but not estates, trusts, S corporations, or partnerships) to postpone gain realized from the sale of publicly traded securities by investing the proceeds from the sale in the common stock of or partnership interest in a special small business investment company (SSBIC).[56] Publicly traded securities include stocks and bonds traded on an established securities market[57] such as the New York Stock Exchange or the NASDAQ. If the stock in the SSBIC is qualified small business stock under Code Sec. 1202, then an individual investor may also be able to exclude all or a portion of the gain on the sale of the stock after five years. However. However, the exclusion is available only for appreciation in stock purchased by an individual investor (see ¶ 807.02).

Reason for the Rule: SSBICs are licensed by the Small Business Administration. They are financial institutions that invest in and provide financing to the small business community. Currently more than 100 SSBICs operating in the United States provide financing to small businesses. These small businesses are primarily owned by socially or economically disadvantaged persons. Because such companies are often riskier investments, Congress enacted Code Sec. 1044 as part of the Revenue Reconciliation Act of 1993 to provide tax incentives to individuals and corporations to invest in SSBICs.

.01 Calculating the Postponed Gain

When a taxpayer realizes a gain on the sale of publicly traded securities and within 60 days reinvests the entire sales proceeds in the stock of or a partnership interest in an SSBIC, the taxpayer may elect to postpone recognition of the gain. If the taxpayer reinvests only part of the proceeds of the sale of the publicly traded securities in the stock or a partnership interest in an SSBIC, the taxpayer must recognize the *lesser of* (1) the amount of gain realized or (2) the excess of the sales proceeds over the amount reinvested in the SSBIC.[58] The postponed gain may not exceed either the annual or lifetime limits discussed below.

Example 38: During the year, Bucknell, Inc. sells publicly traded stock for $600,000. Its adjusted basis in the stock is $125,000. The sale produces a $475,000 realized gain ($600,000 – $125,000). Within 60 days of the sale, Bucknell invests $460,000 of the $600,000 proceeds in an SSBIC and files an election on its tax return to postpone the gain to the extent allowed under the tax law. Bucknell must recognize *at least* $140,000 of its realized gain that it failed to reinvest in an SSBIC ($600,000 – $460,000). Annual and lifetime limits apply to determine whether any of the $335,000 of remaining gain ($475,000 – $140,000) must be recognized.

---

[56] Code Sec. 1044(a).
[57] Code Sec. 1044(c)(1).

[58] Code Sec. 1044(a).

Annual and lifetime limits. An individual taxpayer may elect to annually postpone up to $50,000 of gain, subject to a lifetime maximum of $500,000.[59] These limits are halved for married taxpayers who file separate returns. C corporations can elect to annually postpone up to $250,000 of gain, subject to an aggregate $1 million limit. The tax laws treat all C corporations that are members of a controlled group of corporations as one corporation.[60] (See ¶ 804 for the definition of a controlled group.)

Example 39: Continuing with Example 38, because Bucknell's $335,000 remaining gain exceeds the $250,000 annual limit allowed to corporations, Bucknell will be allowed to exclude $250,000 of the realized gain but will be required to recognize an additional $85,000 of gain ($335,000 realized gain – $250,000 annual limit). Thus, Bucknell's total recognized gain will be $225,000 ($140,000 + $85,000). Another way to compute the recognized gain is to subtract the postponed gain from the realized gain ($475,000 – $250,000 = $225,000). Bucknell's $1 million aggregate limit is reduced by the $250,000 it excludes in the current year. If Bucknell has never before postponed gain by investing in an SSBIC, its remaining aggregate limit to use in subsequent tax years equals $750,000 ($1,000,000 – $250,000).

 Planning Pointer: Code Sec. 1044 is available only to individuals and C corporations.

.02 Reduction of Basis

To ensure that the postponed gain is eventually recognized (and not permanently excluded), the basis in the stock of or partnership interest in an SSBIC is reduced by the postponed gain.[61] However, for purposes of calculating the exclusion of gain available to individuals on the sale of Section 1202 stock (which includes SSBIC stock held for more than five years) (see ¶ 806), the adjusted basis of the SSBIC stock is not reduced by the postponed gain.[62] This provision prevents deferred gain invested in Code Sec. 1202 stock from being taxed.

Example 40: Fagan Corporation, a C corporation, purchased publicly traded bonds in 20X1 for $2 million. In prior yearns, Fagan postponed under Code Sec. 1244 a total of $450,000 of gain on the sale of publicly traded securities by investing in the stock of an SSBIC. In 20X3, Fagan sells the bonds for $2.4 million and realizes a $400,000 gain ($2,400,000 – $2,000,000). Within 60 days after selling the bonds, Fagan invests $3 million in the stock of an SSBIC. Because the $400,000 realized gain exceeds the annual maximum gain deferral of $250,000 for C corporations, Fagan must recognize at least $150,000 of the gain ($400,000 – $250,000). However, Fagan can elect to postpone $250,000 of the $400,000 realized gain because it invested more than the proceeds from the sale in an SSBIC within 60 days of the sale. Because the aggregate postponed gain of $700,000 ($450,000 in prior years + $250,000 in the current year) does not exceed the aggregate limit of $1 million, Fagan can postpone recognition of the remaining $250,000 gain. The postponed gain reduces the basis in the stock of the SSBIC to $2.75 million ($3,000,000 – $250,000).

Example 41: Dawn Foster operates a business as a sole proprietorship. In 20X1, Dawn purchased stock in a publicly traded corporation for $460,000. In 20X3, she sells the stock for $550,000 and realizes a $90,000 gain ($550,000 – $460,000). Within 60 days of the sale, Dawn pays $550,000 for stock in an SSBIC. She elects to defer $50,000 of the gain (the annual limit for individual taxpayers) and reduces her basis in the stock in the SSBIC. Dawn's basis in the stock in the SSBIC is $500,000 ($550,000 – $50,000). However, Dawn's basis in the stock for the purpose of calculating the gain eligible for the exclusion under Code Sec. 1202 is the $550,000 that she paid for the stock. In

---

[59] Code Sec. 1044(b).
[60] Code Sec. 1044(b)(4).

[61] Code Sec. 1044(d).
[62] Code Sec. 1044(d).

order to meet the provisions of Code Sec. 1202, Dawn will have to hold the stock for at least five years.

Example 42:   Continuing with Example 41, Dawn sells the stock in the SSBIC in 20X5 for $1 million. Because she did not hold the stock in the SSBIC for more than five years, her realized and recognized gain equals $500,000 ($1,000,000 – $500,000).

Example 43:   Assume the same facts as in Example 42, except that Dawn purchased the stock in the SSBIC on February 8, 2009 and sold it more than five years later for $1 million. Because Dawn held the stock in the SSBIC for more than five years, it qualifies as Section 1202 stock, and her realized gain from the sale equals $450,000 ($1,000,000 – $550,000). She may exclude $225,000 of her gain.

 GAAP vs. Code: On the company's financial statements, all realized gains from the sale of stock are included in net income. Corporations that elect to postpone gain on the sale of publicly traded securities by reinvesting the proceeds in SSBICs, must subtract out the postponed gain from net income when reconciling net income to taxable income in the year the stock is sold. Because the amount of postponed gain reduces the corporation's basis in the SSBIC, in the year the SSBIC stock is sold, the amount of gain reported on the tax return will exceed the amount included in the calculation of net income. Accordingly, the difference in the amount of the gain must be added to net income when reconciling net income to taxable income in the year in which the corporation sells the SSBIC stock.

.03 Making the Election

Taxpayers make the election to roll over (postpone) gain on the sale of publicly traded stock by attaching a statement to the tax return and filing the return on or before its due date (including extensions). The statement must show (1) how the postponed gain was calculated, (2) the SSBIC in which the investment was made, (3) the date on which the investment was made, and (4) the basis of the stock or the partnership interest in the SSBIC.[63]

¶ 808 Like-Kind Exchanges

When property held for productive use in a trade or business or for investment is exchanged solely for like-kind property that is to be held either for productive use in a trade or business or for investment, no gain or loss may be recognized.[64] If property received in exchange consists not only of like-kind property but also other property or money, any gain has to be recognized to the extent of the sum of such money and the fair market value of such other property.[65] However, no loss may be recognized.[66]

.01 Like-Kind Exchange Requirements

A like-kind exchange occurs when a taxpayer transfers property and receives in exchange property of "like-kind" that is to be held either for productive use in a trade or business or for investment. Property of "like-kind" refers to the nature or character of the property and not to its grade or quality.[67] The various types of property that are never considered to be like-kind are listed in Figure 8-3.

---

[63] Reg. § 1.1044(a)-1(b).
[64] Code Sec. 1031(a)(1).
[65] Code Sec. 1031(b).

[66] Code Sec. 1031(c).
[67] Reg. § 1.1031(a)-1(b).

Figure 8-3 Property Never Considered Like-Kind[68]

- Property used by a taxpayer for personal purposes;
- Real property located outside the United States;
- Personal property used predominately outside the United States;
- Partnership interests;
- Stocks, bonds, notes, and other securities or evidences of indebtedness or interest (however, the term "stocks" does not include shares in a mutual ditch, reservoir, or irrigation company if at the time of the exchange the mutual ditch, reservoir, or irrigation company is an organization described in Code Sec. 501(c)(12)(A) and the shares in that company have been recognized by the highest court of the state in which the company was organized or by applicable state statute as constituting or representing real property or an interest in real property[69]);
- Inventory;
- Certificates of trust or beneficial interests;
- Choses in action; and
- Livestock of different sexes.

With respect to exchanges of real property (other than real property located outside the United States), any other business or investment real property qualifies as like-kind property.[70] Thus, the exchange of land for an office building qualifies as like-kind property, as would the exchange of a vacant lot for a warehouse or an apartment building.

With respect to tangible personal property, like-kind property must be of like kind or like class. Personal property that has the same use qualifies as property of like class.[71] For example, a like-kind exchange occurs when a business trades in a truck as a part of the consideration for the purchase of a new truck. For property to be of a "like class," it must be within the same *General Asset Class* or within the same *Product Class*.[72] Property cannot be classified within more than one General Asset Class or within more than one Product Class. Furthermore, property that is classified within a General Asset Class cannot qualify as like-class property using the Product Class designations. Table 8-1 lists the various General Asset Classes.[73]

Table 8-1 General Asset Classes

Asset Class	Includes
00.11	Office furniture, fixtures, and equipment
00.12	Computers and peripheral equipment
00.13	Data handling equipment other than computers
00.21	Helicopters and airplanes (except those used in commercial or contract carrying of passengers or freight)
00.22	Automobiles and taxis
00.23	Buses
00.241	Light general purpose trucks
00.242	Heavy general purpose trucks

[68] Code Sec. 1031(a)(2), (e), (h).
[69] Code Sec. 1031(i), after amendment by the Heartland, Habitat, Harvest, and Horticulture Act of 2008.
[70] Reg. § 1.1031(a)-1(b).

[71] Reg. § 1.1031(a)-2(b)(1).
[72] Reg. § 1.1031(a)-2(b)(1).
[73] Reg. § 1.1031(a)-2(b)(2); Rev. Proc. 87-56, 1987-2 CB 674.

Asset Class	Includes
00.25	Railroad cars and locomotives (except those owned by railroad transportation companies)
00.26	Tractor units for use over the road
00.27	Trailers and trailer-mounted containers
00.28	Vessels, barges, tugs, and similar water-transportation equipment (except those used in marine construction)
00.4	Industrial steam and electric generation and/or distribution systems

Example 44: Hall Company exchanges a computer for Ruiz Company's color laser printer. The exchange qualifies as a like-kind exchange because both the computer and the color laser printer are in the same General Asset Class (00.12).[74]

Example 45: Gregory Company exchanges a heavy general purpose truck for Fisher Company's automobile. The exchange does not qualify as a like-kind exchange under the general asset class criterion because the heavy general purpose truck is in the 00.242 General Asset Class, and the automobile is in the 00.22 General Asset Class. Because the properties are included in a General Asset Class, the taxpayer cannot classify the properties as like class using product class designations. Therefore, the exchange does not qualify as a like-kind exchange.

A "Product Class" consists of depreciable tangible personal property described in a six-digit product class within Sectors 31, 32, and 33, of the North American Classification System (NAICS) Manual, prepared under the auspices of the Office of Management and Budget.[75] This manual is available online at *http://www.census.gov/eos/www/naics*. If the last digit of an NAICS code for a product class is "9" (a miscellaneous category), the product class is not considered a product class for the like-kind exchange rules.[76]

Example 46: Rhodes Company exchanges a grader for Flowers Company's scraper. Neither property is listed in a General Asset Class (see Table 8-1), but both properties are in the same Product Class (NAICS Code 333120). Therefore, the properties are of like class, and the exchange qualifies as a like-kind exchange.[77]

Example 47: Michaels Company exchanges a stamping machine for Hammer Company's drill press. Neither property is listed in a General Asset Class (see Table 8-1). Because both types of property are classified in Product Class code 333517, the exchange is considered a like-kind exchange.

.02 Time Frame for Taking Possession of Like-Kind Property

Although direct exchanges of like-kind property fall under the nonrecognition rules for like-kind exchanges, the exchange of the like-kind properties does not have to be simultaneous. Often taxpayers wishing to engage in like-kind exchanges do not have specific properties in mind for which to make a trade. Fortunately, there are specialized intermediaries who act as escrow agents and hold property until another party interested in completing an exchange can be found.

To qualify for a deferred like-kind exchange, the property the taxpayer receives in the exchange must be identified within 45 days of the date that the taxpayer transfers property to the other party. In addition, the taxpayer must receive the like-kind property by the *earlier of* (1) 180 days after the transfer of the like-kind property to the other party or (2) the due date (including extensions) of the

---

[74] Reg. § 1.1031(a)-2(b)(7), Ex. 1.
[75] Reg. § 1.1031(a)-2(b)(3).
[76] Reg. § 1.1031(a)-2(b)(3).
[77] Reg. § 1.1031(a)-2(b)(7), Ex. 3.

taxpayer's income tax return for the tax year in which the taxpayer transfers property.[78] If the exchange does not meet both conditions, the exchange will not qualify as a like-kind exchange, and any realized gain or loss will have to be recognized.

Example 48:   On June 20, 20X1, Harris Corporation transfers land held for investment to a qualified intermediary in anticipation of exchanging the land for another parcel of land that it will hold for investment. Harris uses the calendar year as its tax year, and accordingly, the due date of its 20X1 tax return is March 15, 20X2. Harris must take possession of the new land from the other party through the qualified intermediary no later than the *earlier of* (1) December 17, 20X1, which is 180 days after Harris transferred its land to the intermediary, or (2) the due date of Harris's 20X1 tax return. Therefore, Harris must receive like-kind property no later than December 17, 20X1.

Example 49:   O'Connor Corporation transfers an office building on December 16, 20X1, to a qualified intermediary. O'Connor uses the calendar year as its tax year. The 180-day period after the initial transfer ends on June 14, 20X2. If O'Connor does not extend the deadline for filing its income tax return, the like-kind property must be received no later than March 15, 20X2 (the *earlier of* June 14, 20X2, or March 15, 20X2).

Example 50:   Assume the same facts as in Example 49, except O'Connor Corporation is granted a six-month extension to file its 20X1 income tax return. O'Connor must receive the like-kind property no later than June 14, 20X2 (the *earlier of* June 14, 20X2, or the September 15, 20X2 extended due date), in order for the exchange to qualify as a like-kind exchange. By obtaining the extension to file its income tax return, O'Connor has three additional months (June 14 versus March 15) to receive the like-kind property for the exchange to qualify as a like-kind exchange.

Planning Pointer: If an exchange qualifies as a like-kind exchange, the like-kind exchange rules are mandatory. Most taxpayers prefer to recognize losses immediately because of the tax savings associated with reducing taxable income. Likewise, taxpayers typically prefer to defer the recognition of gains because of the time value of money. However, if the taxpayer is in a low tax bracket and expects to be in a much higher tax bracket in the future, the taxpayer may want to recognize the gain on the exchange. Also, if the taxpayer has expiring loss carryovers (for example, capital losses (¶ 901.01) or net operating losses (¶ 1001.01)), the taxpayer may want to recognize the gain in the year of the exchange to utilize the expiring carryovers.

To recognize a gain or loss on an exchange, a taxpayer can structure the transaction as a sale followed by a purchase of the new property. A taxpayer can modify the terms of an exchange of tangible depreciable personal property so that the property received is not of the same General Asset Class or the same Product Class as the asset given in the exchange. If the exchange is not a direct exchange, a taxpayer can recognize gain or loss by ensuring that the property to be received is not identified within 45 days after the initial transfer or is not timely received. A taxpayer also can negotiate to receive enough non-like-kind property in the exchange so that all realized gain will have to be recognized (see ¶ 808.03).

.03 Tax Consequences of a Like-Kind Exchange

The realized gain or loss on an exchange of like-kind property is not recognized. Instead, any gain or loss is postponed until the taxpayer disposes of the newly acquired like-kind property in a non-like-kind transaction.[79] To make sure that the postponed gain or loss is recognized, the tax laws

---

[78] Code Sec. 1031(a)(3).   [79] Code Sec. 1031(a)(1).

require the taxpayer to take a substituted basis in the newly acquired like-kind property. This is accomplished by decreasing the FMV of the like-kind property by any postponed gain and increasing the FMV of the like-kind property by any postponed loss.[80] The holding period of the like-kind property includes the holding period of the like-kind property given up in the exchange.[81]

Example 51: Rodgers & Moore, LLC exchanges a building worth $50,000 for land worth $50,000 owned by Gartner & Associates, LLP. Rodgers & Moore's adjusted basis in the building is $30,000; Gartner's basis in the land is $60,000. Each party uses the property in its business and neither property is located outside of the United States. Thus, the exchange qualifies as a like-kind exchange for both parties.

In determining the tax consequences of the exchange, each party first determines its realized gain or loss. As depicted in the diagram below, the FMV of the property received is the same for each party. Assume neither party incurred any selling expenses resulting from the exchange. Therefore, their realized gain equals the $50,000 amount realized, minus their respective adjusted basis in the property given up in the exchange. The result is a $20,000 realized gain for Rodgers & Moore and a $10,000 realized loss for Gartner.

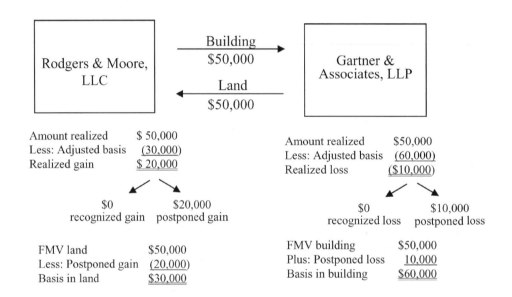

In this example, the like-kind exchange rules require that all realized gains and losses be postponed and reflected in the basis of the newly acquired like-kind property. Therefore, none of Rodgers & Moore's $20,000 realized gain is recognized, and its basis in the land is reduced to $30,000 ($50,000 – $20,000). Similarly, none of Gartner's $10,000 realized loss is recognized, and its basis in the building increases to $60,000 ($50,000 + $10,000). The holding period of the land acquired by Rodgers & Moore includes the holding period of the building. Thus, if Rodgers & Moore purchased the building in 1998, the land will be deemed to have been acquired in 1998. Similarly, Gartner's holding period in the building will begin on the date it acquired the land. Gartner's depreciable basis in the newly acquired building is its $60,000 basis after the exchange.

 Reason for the Rule: Under the wherewithal-to-pay principle, taxpayers are in the best position to pay tax when the property is sold or otherwise disposed and the proceeds

---

[80] Code Sec. 1031(d).

[81] Code Sec. 1223(1).

can be used to pay any tax due. If gain from a like-kind exchange were required to be recognized, taxpayers might be forced to sell the property in order to pay the taxes owed. Under the like-kind rules, recognition of the gain is postponed until the taxpayer has the wherewithal to pay the taxes on the gain.

Receipt of boot. If in an exchange the taxpayer receives property (including cash) that is not like-kind, the non-like-kind property is referred to as **boot**. When taxpayers receive boot in addition to like-kind property, any realized gain is recognized to the extent of the boot received. Thus, taxpayers recognize gain equal to the *lesser of* (1) the FMV of the boot received or (2) the amount of gain realized.[82] Receipt of boot in a like-kind exchange does not trigger a recognized loss on the exchange.[83]

Example 52: Assume the same facts as in Example 51, except that Gartner's land is worth only $42,000 and Gartner pays Rodgers & Moore $8,000 cash. Under this scenario, the tax consequences to the two parties are as follows:

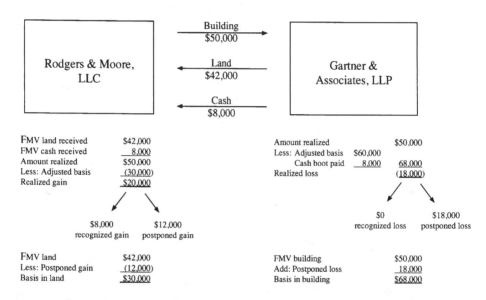

Because Rodgers & Moore receives boot on the exchange, the *lesser of* the FMV of the boot received ($8,000) or the realized gain ($20,000) is taxed, and the remainder of the realized gain is deferred and reflected in the basis of the like-kind property acquired in the exchange. The payment of cash boot by Gartner does not trigger recognition of any of its realized gain or loss.[84] However, see ¶ 803.03 for a discussion of instances when boot given results in gain recognition.

 Reason for the Rule: When taxpayers receive boot in an exchange, they have the ability to pay taxes due on the realized gain. Therefore, taxpayers recognize gain to the extent of the boot received.

The tax laws treat a person's release from liability as though the person received cash, which was then used to pay off the debt. Thus, the amount of liability from which a taxpayer is relieved in a like-kind exchange is treated as boot received and represents the taxpayer's wherewithal to pay tax

---

[82] Code Sec. 1031(b).
[83] Code Sec. 1031(c).

[84] Code Sec. 1031(a)(1).

on the recognized gain.[85] The party that assumes debt or takes property subject to a liability is treated as having given boot.

When the two parties assume one another's debts as part of the exchange, the party that is relieved of more debt than it assumes is treated as having received boot for the difference in the amount of debt.[86] Likewise, the party that assumes more debt than it is relieved of is treated as having paid boot for the net difference of the debt. However, debt incurred by a taxpayer does not reduce boot received as cash or non-like-kind property. Therefore, it is possible for both parties to receive boot in a like-kind exchange if one party receives cash and the other party is treated as having received boot by having been released from more debt than it assumed on the exchange.[87]

Example 53: Brock Company purchased land for investment purposes in 20X1 for $190,000 by making a down payment and signing a note secured by a mortgage. Smyth Company purchased land in 20X0 for $245,000 by making a down payment and signing a note secured by a mortgage. On August 27, 20X4, Brock and Smyth agree to exchange properties and to assume one another's outstanding mortgage with the consent of the lenders. On the date of the exchange, the FMV of Brock's land is $400,000 and the outstanding mortgage is $200,000; the FMV of Smyth's land is $360,000 and its outstanding mortgage is $160,000.

Because Brock and Smyth swap debt, it is first necessary to calculate the net amount of debt and determine which party is deemed to have paid boot and which party is deemed to have received boot. The net amount of debt exchanged is $40,000 ($200,000 – $160,000). Because Brock is relieved of $200,000 of debt and assumes only $160,000 of debt, Brock is treated as having received $40,000 boot. This amount is included in Brock's amount realized. On the other side of the transaction, Smyth, which has taken on $200,000 of debt in exchange for being relieved of $160,000 of debt, is treated as having paid $40,000 boot. Like the adjusted basis of the property given up in the exchange, any boot given is subtracted from Smyth's amount realized in determining its realized gain or loss from the exchange. The tax consequences of the exchange are illustrated below.

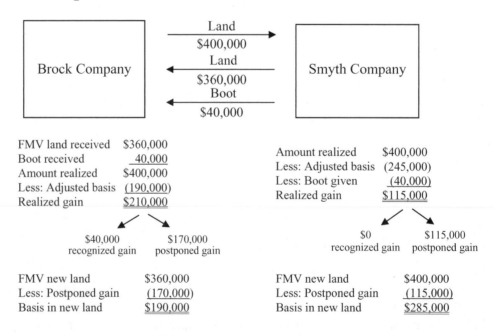

[85] Reg. § 1.1031(b)-1(c).

[86] Reg. § § 1.1031(b)-1(c), 1.1031(d)-2, Ex. 2.

[87] Reg. § 1.1031(b)-1(c); Reg. § 1.1031(d)-2, Ex. 2.

Both parties realize gain on the exchange. However, only Brock recognizes gain. Brock is treated as having the wherewithal to pay the tax on gain due to the boot (net release of debt) it received on the exchange. The remainder of Brock's gain is postponed and reduces the basis in the new land that it received from Smyth. Because Smyth did not receive any boot on the exchange, the entire $115,000 of realized gain is postponed, and the FMV of the land received from Brock is reduced by $115,000 when Smyth computes its basis in the land.

Example 54: In 20X1, Beck Company purchased land held for investment for $245,000 by making a down payment and signing a note for the remainder. In 20X0, Snyder Company paid $257,000 for land held for investment by making a down payment and signing a note for the remainder. On April 2, 20X4, Beck and Snyder exchange properties, each assuming the other's outstanding debt with the consent of the lenders. On the date of the exchange, Beck's property is worth $345,000, and its outstanding loan amount is $195,000. Snyder's property is worth $260,000, and its outstanding mortgage is $200,000. Snyder pays Beck $90,000 in cash to even up the exchange.

Because the two parties swap debt, only the net debt is considered boot. Because Snyder is relieved of $5,000 more debt than it assumes from the exchange, Snyder is treated as having received $5,000 boot on the exchange. Beck receives $90,000 boot in the form of the cash it receives from Snyder. The tax law does not allow these two types of boot to be netted against one another.[88]

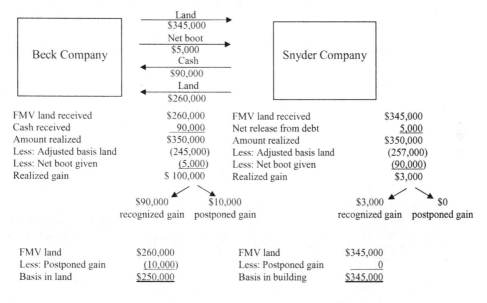

Each party's amount realized on the exchange is $350,000, and both parties realized a gain on the exchange. Because Beck received $90,000 cash from Snyder, Beck must recognize $90,000 of its $100,000 realized gain. Accordingly, Beck's basis in the land it receives in the exchange is reduced by the $10,000 of postponed gain. Snyder benefits from having been relieved of $5,000 more of debt than it assumes on the exchange. Therefore, it recognizes the entire $3,000 of realized gain. Because none of the gain is postponed, Snyder's basis in the new land is its $345,000 FMV at the time of the exchange.

 Reason for the Rule: Normally, the receipt of boot triggers the recognition of realized gain on a like-kind exchange. However, when one party takes on more debt than it is

---

[88] Reg. § 1.1031(d)-2, Ex. 2.

> relieved of, that party has less liquidity than before the exchange. The special rule allowing the parties to offset each other's debt prevents the party increasing its debt from having to recognize gain on a like-kind exchange when the only boot is debt relief.

Gain or loss on transfer of boot. Although boot typically is cash or involves the assumption of debt, boot can also consist of other types of non-like-kind property. When the FMV of the boot given is different from the transferor's adjusted basis in the boot, the transferor is treated as having sold the boot for its FMV. Consequently, any realized gain or loss on the sale of boot (any difference between its FMV and adjusted basis) is recognized by the transferor under the normal rules that govern gains and losses on the sale of property.[89]

 GAAP vs. Code: The revenue recognition principle governs the financial accounting rules regarding exchanges of similar assets. Under GAAP, gains from the exchange of similar assets must be postponed and subtracted from the basis of the similar property received on the exchange. Losses, on the other hand, are reported on the income statement. If a corporation receives monetary (cash) consideration as part of the exchange, the earnings process is considered to have been partially completed, and part of the realized gain is recognized on the income statement. These rules are similar to the tax laws requiring recognition of gain upon the receipt of boot. However, the amount of gain reported on the income statement is the proportion the amount of cash bears to the total FMV of the properties received in the exchange.[90] Thus, if a corporation receives a total consideration of $100,000 on the exchange, of which $20,000 is cash, 20 percent of the realized gain is reported on the income statement. By contrast, for tax purposes the *lesser of* the amount of realized gain or $20,000 has to be recognized.

.04 Special Rules for Like-Kind Exchanges between Related Parties

If a taxpayer exchanges like-kind property with a related person and before the date two years after the date of the last transfer that was part of the exchange either the related person disposes of the like-kind property or the taxpayer disposes of the property received from the related person that was of like kind to the property transferred by the taxpayer, any gain or loss not recognized on the original transfer has to be recognized.[91]

Such gain or loss is recognized in the tax year in which the like-kind property is subsequently sold. Thus, if related parties enter into a like-kind exchange transaction, they must each hold onto the like-kind property they receive for at least two years to take full advantage of the nonrecognition of gain or loss under Code Sec. 1031. The rules defining related parties presented earlier in the chapter also apply to like-kind exchanges (see ¶ 804 and Figure 8-2).

Exceptions are made for dispositions after the death of the taxpayer or the related person or in a compulsory or involuntary conversion (if the exchange occurred before the threat or imminence of such conversion). The taxpayer may also avoid gain or loss recognition by proving to the IRS that avoidance of federal income tax was not one of the principal purposes of the like-kind exchange or the disposition.

---

[89] Code Sec. 1001(c).

[90] "Accounting for Nonmonetary Transactions," *Opinions of the Accounting Principles Board No. 29* (Stamford, Conn.: FASB, 1973).

[91] Code Sec. 1031(f).

If there is a disposition within the two-year period, a basis adjustment is required. Any recognized gain is added, and any recognized loss is subtracted, from the basis of the like-kind property.

Example 55: In 20X2, Eagle Eye Corporation exchanges land used in its business for land held for investment by its sole shareholder Amanda Eagle. Eagle Eye realizes a $10,000 gain on the exchange of its land. Amanda realizes a gain of $12,000, but neither recognizes any gain because no boot was exchanged. In 20X3, Amanda sells her land to an unrelated party and recognizes a $14,000 gain. The sale of Amanda's land triggers recognition of the $10,000 gain by Eagle Eye in 20X3.

Example 56: Anzelt Corporation owns as an investment an apartment building (Building A) worth $1 million and with an adjusted basis of $100,000. Bakkert owns an apartment building (Building B) worth $1 million, but it has an adjusted basis of $900,000. Anzelt and Bakkert are members of the same controlled group. Therefore, they are related parties. The controlling shareholders of the two companies have decided they would like Anzelt to dispose of Building A because they are concerned about it holding its value in the long term. However, they would also like for Bakkert to sell its investment in the apartment building and invest the $1 million in its operations.

If Anzelt were to sell Building A, it could use the proceeds to purchase Building B (which is a much more promising investment in the long run) from Bakkert. However, it would recognize gain of $900,000 ($1 million – $100,000). Bakkert would recognize gain of $100,000 on the sale of Building B to Anzelt ($1,000,000 – $900,000 adjusted basis). Anzelt's basis in Building B would be its cost of $1 million.

Because the two corporations are related, they could exchange their respective properties and postpone recognition of their realized gain. Anzelt would have a basis of $100,000 in Building B; and Bakkert would have a basis of $900,000 in Building A as shown below.

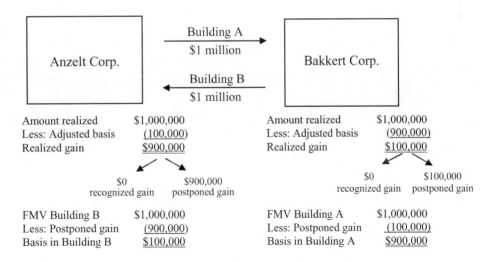

If Bakkert sells its apartment building within two years of the exchange, the related party rules will require Angell to recognize its postponed gain in the year Bakkert sells Building A.

The running of the two-year period is suspended for any period during which the holder's risk of loss with respect to the property is substantially diminished by the holding of a put with respect to the property, the holding by another person of a right to acquire the property, or a short sale or any other transaction.

Reason for the Rule: When like-kind property is exchanged, each party takes a substituted basis for the property it receives. Congress adopted the related-party restrictions because related parties were engaging in like-kind exchanges of high basis property for low basis property in anticipation of selling the low basis property to reduce or avoid the recognition of gain on the subsequent sale and accelerate a loss on retained property. Congress believed that if a related party exchange is followed shortly thereafter by a disposition of the property the related parties are, in effect, "cashing out" their investment, and the original exchange should be accorded nonrecognition treatment.[92]

¶ 809 Involuntary Conversions

If property (as a result of its destruction in whole or in part, theft, seizure, requisition, condemnation, or threat or imminence of its seizure, requisition, or condemnation) is compulsorily or involuntarily converted into property similar or related in service or use to the property converted, no gain may be recognized.[93] However, any loss may be recognized.[94]

If property is converted into money or into property not similar or related in service or use to the converted property and the taxpayer, during the replacement period, for the purpose of replacing the converted property purchases other property similar or related in service or use to the property converted, or purchases stock in the acquisition of control of a corporation owning such other property, the taxpayer may elect to recognize gain only to the extent that the amount realized on the conversion (regardless whether that amount is received in one or more taxable years) exceeds the cost of the replacement property or stock.[95]

 Reason for the Rule: To the extent the taxpayer reinvests the entire proceeds in qualified replacement property, the taxpayer is not considered to have the wherewithal to pay the tax on the gain realized.

 Planning Pointer: The taxpayer does not have to spend all of the cash received in an involuntary conversion on the qualified replacement property. The taxpayer's reinvestment also includes debt incurred in the process of acquiring qualified replacement property.

"Control" means the ownership of stock possessing at least 80 percent of the total combined voting power of all classes of stock entitled to vote and at least 80 percent of the total number of shares of all other classes of stock of the corporation.[96]

If property was received as the result of a compulsory or involuntary conversion, the basis of the property received is the same as the basis of the property converted decreased by the amount of any boot received by the taxpayer and increased by the amount of any gain (or decreased by the amount of any loss) recognized upon the conversion.[97] The basis of replacement property purchased is its cost, decreased by the amount of any gain not recognized. If the replacement property consists of more than one piece of property, the basis has to be allocated to the properties in proportion to their respective costs. The holding period of property received includes the holding period of the property converted.[98]

---

[92] Senate Finance Committee Report No. 101-56 on Section 7601 of the Omnibus Budget Reconciliation Act of 1987 (P.L. 101-239).

[93] Code Sec. 1033(a)(1).

[94] Reg. § 1.1033(a)-1(a).

[95] Code Sec. 1033(a)(2).

[96] Code Sec. 1033(a)(2)(E)(i); Reg. § 1.1033(a)-2(c)(1).

[97] Code Sec. 1033(b)(1).

[98] Code Sec. 1223(1).

Planning Pointer: Most people might assume that postponing gain is always in the taxpayer's best interest. However, it is important to look closely at the overall picture if the taxpayer has a choice between postponing and recognizing gain. If the taxpayer has carryovers that are about to expire (for example, charitable contributions (¶ 511), capital losses (¶ 901.01), net operating losses (¶ 1004.02) or tax credits (¶ 1103.02 and ¶ 1117)), recognizing the gain immediately may allow the taxpayer to avoid losing the tax benefits associated with the carryover amounts. This is especially important to consider if the taxpayer plans to sell the replacement property in the near future and would recognize gain anyway. It may also be advantageous to recognize the gain if the taxpayer is currently in a low tax bracket and is expected to be in a higher tax bracket in future tax years. In that event, the taxpayer may want to pay tax today at the lower tax rates rather than pay more tax in the future. Because the amount of postponed gain reduces the taxpayer's basis in the replacement property, more depreciation will be taken in upcoming (higher tax rate) years if the gain is recognized and the depreciable basis is the (unreduced) cost of the replacement property.

.01 Qualified Replacement Property

"Qualified replacement property" is property that is similar to or related in service or use to the property involuntarily converted.[99] Typically, the replacement property must have the same *functional use* as the property that was involuntarily converted. For example, if the property involuntarily converted was a warehouse, qualified replacement property would be another building with the same functional use (a storage facility for inventory). For property held as an investment, qualified replacement property would be property that will be used in similar investment endeavors. For example, if the taxpayer's investment in an apartment building is involved in an involuntary conversion, the owner can replace it with any other rental property, not just another apartment building. This special rule allows investors more flexibility in defining qualified replacement property.

A more flexible rule applies if tangible property held for productive use in trade or business or for investment located in a disaster area is compulsorily or involuntarily converted as a result of a federally declared disaster.[100] Tangible property of a type held for productive use in trade or business will be treated as property similar or related in service or use to the property converted.

If real property (not including stock in trade or other property held primarily for sale) held for productive use in a trade or business or for investment is compulsorily or involuntarily converted (as a result of its seizure, requisition, condemnation, or threat or imminence of its seizure, requisition, or condemnation), property of a like kind to be held either for productive use in a trade or business or for investment will be treated as property similar or related in service or use to the converted property.[101] Thus, the proceeds from a condemnation can be used to purchase any business or investment realty. This rule does not apply to the purchase of stock in the acquisition of control of a corporation owning such other property.[102]

Example 57: Steele Corporation's machine is destroyed in an accident. Steele receives insurance proceeds in excess of its basis in the machine and realizes an $8,000 gain. To defer the gain, Steele must invest the entire insurance proceeds in another similarly-functioning machine within the time allowed. In an involuntary conversion of personal property, the replacement asset must have the same function as the asset involuntarily converted.

Example 58: The office building of Drew Corporation is destroyed in a fire. Drew receives insurance proceeds that result in a $100,000 realized gain. To postpone the gain,

---

[99] Reg. § 1.1033(a)-1(a).
[100] Code Sec. 1033(h)(2).

[101] Code Sec. 1033(g)(1).
[102] Code Sec. 1033(g)(2).

Drew must reinvest the entire insurance proceeds in another office building within the time allowed. In an involuntary conversion of real estate used in a business, the replacement property must have the same function as the property involved in the involuntary conversion.

Example 59: Dan Breaux, LLC owns an investment in an apartment building that is completely destroyed by a tornado. The insurance company pays Breaux $500,000, which results in a realized gain of $240,000. To defer the gain, Breaux must reinvest the entire $500,000 proceeds in any type of investment real estate in which Breaux acts as the landlord and receives rental income from the property. The proceeds need not be used to purchase another apartment building.

Example 60: Wood Company's warehouse is condemned by the state under the power of eminent domain to use as a part of the right-of-way for a new highway. The state pays Wood the FMV of the property, and Wood realizes a gain on the condemnation. Wood can defer the gain by investing the entire amount received from the state in property of a like kind to be held either for productive use in trade or business or for investment.

.02 Replacement Period

To defer part or all of the gain realized on an involuntary conversion, the taxpayer must obtain qualified replacement property within a certain period of time.

The "replacement period" begins on the date that the converted property is disposed (or, if earlier, the date that the threat or imminence of seizure, requisition, or condemnation begins) and ends two years after the close of the first tax year in which any part of the gain upon the conversion is realized.[103]

A taxpayer may ask the IRS to extend the replacement period by filing an application before the end of the replacement period (or at a later time if the taxpayer can show to the IRS' satisfaction that the taxpayer had reasonable cause for not filing an application within the required period of time and the application was filed within a reasonable time after the expiration of the required period of time). The replacement period will not be extended unless the taxpayer can show reasonable cause for not replacing the converted property within the required period of time.

If real property (not including stock in trade or other property held primarily for sale) held for productive use in trade or business or for investment is compulsorily or involuntarily converted as the result of its seizure, requisition, condemnation, or threat or imminence of its seizure, requisition, or condemnation, the replacement period is extended for an additional year (to three years).[104]

Example 61: Zuckerman Industries paid $50,000 for land on September 16, 20X2. On October 6, 20X5, the state condemns the land under the power of eminent domain to build a new highway. The state pays Zuckerman $90,000 for the land on January 4, 20X6. Zuckerman's realized gain in 20X6 equals $40,000 ($90,000 – $50,000), and the company has until December 31, 20X9 (three years from December 31, 20X6), to purchase replacement business or investment realty. If Zuckerman reinvests at least $90,000 during this period, it can postpone the entire $40,000 of realized gain.

Example 62: Continuing with Example 61, assume that during 20X6, Zuckerman pays $75,000 for new land and does not plan to reinvest the remaining $15,000 in qualified replacement property prior to December 31, 20X9. Zuckerman recognizes a gain of $15,000 in 20X6 (the *lesser of* the $40,000 realized gain or $15,000) and defers $25,000 of the gain ($40,000 – $15,000). Its basis in the new land is $50,000 ($75,000 cost of replacement property – $25,000 postponed gain). The holding period includes the holding period of the land purchased on September 16, 20X2.

---

[103] Code Sec. 1033(a)(2)(B); Reg. § 1.1033(a)-2(c)(3).   [104] Code Sec. 1033(g)(4).

Example 63: Donna Underwood's business machine is destroyed by fire. An insurance company reimburses her $45,000 for the loss on September 5, 20X6. The machine originally cost $62,000, but Donna had deducted Section 179 and Modified Accelerated Cost Recovery System (MACRS) totaling $34,000 up until the time of the casualty. Thus, her adjusted basis in the machine was $28,000 ($62,000 – $34,000). Donna's realized gain equals $17,000 ($45,000 – $28,000) on the involuntary conversion. Donna has until December 31, 20X8 (two years after December 31, 20X6, the year in which she realized the gain), to purchase another similarly functioning machine for her business. As long as the new machine costs at least $45,000, all $17,000 of the realized gain can be postponed.

Example 64: Continuing with Example 63, assume that during 20X7 Donna purchases a similarly functioning machine for $50,000. Donna recognizes no gain on the involuntary conversion because the cost of the new machine exceeds the proceeds she received from the insurance company. Therefore, all of her realized gain of $17,000 is deferred, and her basis in the new machine is $33,000 ($50,000 – $17,000).

Example 65: Assume instead that Donna Underwood from Example 63 reinvests $40,000 in a new machine during the allowed period. Because Donna does not reinvest the entire proceeds, she will recognize $5,000 of the $17,000 realized gain ($45,000 – $40,000). The remaining $12,000 of realized gain ($17,000 – $5,000) will be postponed, and the basis of her new machine will be $28,000 ($40,000 – $12,000).

 GAAP vs. Code: For financial accounting purposes, realized gains and losses resulting from involuntary conversions are reported on the income statement.[105] Thus, when taxpayers postpone gain for tax purposes, the postponed gain must be subtracted from net income when reconciling net income to taxable income on the corporate tax return.

¶ 810 Installment Sales

An **installment sale** is a disposition of property where at least one payment is to be received after the close of the tax year in which the disposition occurs.[106] When taxpayers sell property in an installment sale that produces a loss, they generally recognize the loss in the year of the sale or the exchange.[107] Unless they elect otherwise, taxpayers generally must report income from an installment sale using the installment method of accounting.[108]

 Reason for the Rule: Under the installment method, taxpayers recognize the gain as they receive cash or its equivalent under the terms of the sale. That is when they are considered to have the wherewithal to pay the tax on the gain.

.01 Installment Method of Accounting

Under the installment method of accounting, the amount of any payment received during a tax year that has to be included in income is determined by multiplying the amount of the payment by the gross profit percentage.[109]

The gross profit percentage is determined by dividing the gross profit realized or to be realized by the total contract price.

---

[105] FASB Interpretation No. 30, *Accounting for Involuntary Conversions of Nonmonetary Assets to Monetary Assets.*

[106] Code Sec. 453(b)(1).

[107] Code Sec. 1001(c).

[108] Code Sec. 453(a).

[109] Code Sec. 453(c); Temp. Reg. § 15A.453-1(b)(2).

The term "gross profit" means the selling price less the adjusted basis. In the case of sales of real property by a person other than a dealer and casual sales of personal property, commissions and other selling expenses are added to basis.

The term "selling price" means the gross selling price, not reduced to reflect any existing mortgage or other encumbrances on the property (whether assumed or taken subject to by the buyer) or any selling expenses. Neither interest, whether stated or unstated, nor original issue discount is considered part of the selling price.

The term "contract price" means the selling price, reduced by that portion of any qualifying indebtedness assumed or taken subject to by the buyer that does not exceed the seller's basis in the property (increased by commissions and other selling expenses).

The term "qualifying indebtedness" means a mortgage or other indebtedness encumbering the property and indebtedness not secured by the property but incurred or assumed by the purchaser incident to the purchaser's acquisition, holding, or operation in the ordinary course of business or investment of the property. The term "qualifying indebtedness" does not include a taxpayer's obligation incurred incident to the disposition of the property (e.g., legal fees relating to the taxpayer's sale of the property) or an obligation functionally unrelated to the acquisition, holding, or operating of the property. Any obligation created subsequent to a taxpayer's acquisition of the property and incurred or assumed by the taxpayer or placed as an encumbrance on the property in contemplation of disposition of the property is not qualifying indebtedness if the arrangement results in accelerating recovery of the taxpayer's basis in the installment sale.

Example 66: Johnson Manufacturing sells land to Able Manufacturing for $150,000. The terms of the sale require Able to pay cash of $20,000 and issue an installment note that calls for five annual payments of $20,000 of principal plus interest at the market rate. In addition, Able assumes Johnson's $30,000 mortgage on the land with the consent of the lender. Johnson incurs $8,000 in selling expenses on the sale. Johnson purchased the land two years earlier for $82,000. Because Johnson will receive payments over more than one tax year, it will report the $60,000 gross profit from the sale over the next six years.

Gross sales price	$150,000
Less: Adjusted basis*	(90,000)
Gross profit from the sale	$ 60,000
Gross sales price	$150,000
Less: Debt assumed by buyer	(30,000)
Total contract price	$120,000

$60,000 gross profit ÷ $120,000 total contract price = 50% gross profit percentage

* Includes $8,000 of commissions paid on the sale of the land

In the year of the sale, Johnson's recognized gain equals $10,000 ($20,000 cash payment × 50%). Johnson will recognize $10,000 gain for each of the next five years as it collects each payment on the installment note ($20,000 × 50%). In addition, Johnson will include the interest it receives from the note in gross income. At the end of five years, Johnson will have recognized the entire $60,000 of gross profit from the sale ($10,000 in the year of the sale + $10,000 annually for five years).

If the amount of debt the buyer assumes exceeds the taxpayer's adjusted basis in the property, the seller adds the excess to the total contract price.[110] In these cases, the gross profit percentage will always be 100 percent. When the amount of the assumed debt exceeds the seller's adjusted basis in the property, the seller is deemed to have been paid cash equal to such excess amount in the year of the sale.

Example 67: Assume the same facts as in Example 66, except Johnson's remaining mortgage on the land is $100,000, and the terms of the sales agreement call for Able to assume the debt and pay Johnson $10,000 at the time of the sale and the rest of the purchase price in five installment payments of $8,000 each.

Gross sales price	$150,000
Less: Adjusted basis	(90,000)
Gross profit from the sale	$ 60,000

Gross sales price	$150,000
Less: Debt assumed by buyer	(100,000)
Plus: Excess of $100,000 debt assumed over $90,000 adjusted basis	10,000
Total contract price	$ 60,000

$60,000 gross profit ÷ $60,000 total contract price = 100% gross profit percentage

Because Johnson is relieved of $10,000 more of debt than its adjusted basis in the land, Johnson is deemed to have received a total of $20,000 cash from the buyer in the year of the sale ($10,000 down payment + $10,000 from excess release from debt). Johnson will recognize the entire $20,000 in the year of sale ($20,000 × 100%), and then recognize 100 percent of each $8,000 payment it receives over the next five years. At the end of five years, Johnson will have recognized the entire $60,000 of gross profit from the sale ($20,000 plus $8,000 annually for five years).

.02 Dispositions for Which the Installment Method of Account Cannot Be Used

The installment method of accounting cannot be used for any dealer disposition or any dispositions of personal property of a kind that is required to be included in the taxpayer's inventory if on hand at the close of the tax year.[111]

A "dealer disposition" includes any disposition of personal property by a person who regularly sells or otherwise disposes of personal property of the same type on the installment plan and any disposition of real property that is held by the taxpayer for sale to customers in the ordinary course of the taxpayer's trade or business.[112]

A "dealer disposition" does not include:[113]

- A disposition on the installment plan of any property used or produced in the trade or business of farming;

- A disposition in the ordinary course of the taxpayer's trade or business to an individual of a timeshare right to use or a timeshare ownership in residential real property for no more than six weeks per year, or a right to use specified campgrounds for recreational purposes, if the taxpayer elects to pay interest on the amount of deferred tax attributable to the use of the installment method; or

---

[110] Temp. Reg. § 15A.453-1(b)(2)(iii), (5), Ex. 3.

[111] Code Sec. 453(b)(2).

[112] Code Sec. 453(l)(1).

[113] Code Sec. 453(l)(2).

- A disposition in the ordinary course of the taxpayer's trade or business of any residential lot (but only if the taxpayer or any related person is not to make any improvements with respect to the lot) if the taxpayer elects to pay interest on the amount of deferred tax attributable to the use of the installment method.

.03 Disposition of an Installment Obligation

If an installment obligation is satisfied at other than its face value or distributed, transmitted (other than at death), sold, or otherwise disposed of, gain or loss has to be recognized.[114]

The amount of gain or loss realized is the difference between the taxpayer's basis in the obligation and either (1) the amount realized, if the obligation is satisfied at other than face value or is sold or exchanged or (2) the fair market value of the obligation at the time that it is distributed, transmitted, or disposed, if the obligation is distributed transmitted, or disposed otherwise than by a sale or exchange.

The basis of an installment obligation is the difference between the face value of the obligation (reduced by the amount of payments already received) and the amount of income that would be returnable if the obligation were satisfied in full.[115] The amount of income returnable is calculated by multiplying the unpaid balance by the gross profit ratio.

Example 68:   On December 4, 20X1, Lofton Enterprises sold land used in its business for $150,000. Its basis in the land was $60,000. Lofton received $50,000 cash and an installment note for $100,000 that calls for annual payments of $20,000 over the next five years beginning December 4, 20X2. The note also provides for Lofton to receive interest at the market rate on any outstanding balance of the note. Lofton's realized gain from the sale equals $90,000 ($150,000 amount realized less $60,000 adjusted basis), and its gross profit percentage is 60 percent ($90,000 ÷ $150,000). Accordingly, in 20X1, Lofton's recognized gain is $30,000 ($50,000 cash received × 60%). In each subsequent year, Lofton's recognized gain from the installment sale will equal $12,000 ($20,000 × 60%).

On January 9, 20X5, after having collected three of the five installment payments, Lofton sells the note for $29,000. At the time of the sale, the balance due on the principal of the note equals $40,000 ($100,000 minus three installments of $20,000 each), and the amount of deferred gain is $24,000 [$90,000 – $30,000 – ($12,000 × 3)]. Accordingly, the adjusted basis in the installment note equals $16,000 ($40,000 uncollected principal minus $24,000 of deferred gain). In 20X5, Lofton recognizes $13,000 of gain from the sale of the note ($29,000 amount realized minus $16,000 adjusted basis in the note).

 Reason for the Rule: When the taxpayer sells an installment note, the taxpayer has the wherewithal to pay the tax on the resulting gain.

.04 Installment Sales between Related Persons

If a taxpayer disposes of property to a related person (the "first disposition") and the related person disposes the property (the "second disposition") no more than two years after the first disposition (and before the taxpayer receives all payments with respect to the first disposition), the taxpayer will be treated as having received the amount realized with respect to the second disposition at the time of the second disposition.[116]

---

[114] Code Sec. 453B(a), (c).
[115] Code Sec. 453B(b).

[116] Code Sec. 453(e).

Planning Pointer: This provision will not be triggered if it is established to the satisfaction of the IRS that neither the first disposition nor the second disposition had as one of its principal purposes the avoidance of federal income tax.

The term "related person" means a person whose stock would be attributed under Code Sec. 318(a) (other than Code Sec. 318(a)(4)) or a person who bears a relationship described in Code Sec. 267(b) (see ¶ 804) to the person first disposing of the property.[117]

The amount treated as received by the person making the first disposition may not exceed the difference between the following amounts:

- The lesser of (1) the total amount realized with respect to the second disposition of the property occurring before the close of the tax year or (2) the total contract price for the first disposition; and

- The sum of (1) the aggregate amount of payments received with respect to the first disposition before the close of the tax year plus (2) the aggregate amount treated as received with respect to the first disposition for prior tax years by reason of the second disposition.

If the second disposition is not a sale or exchange, an amount equal to the fair market value of the property disposed will be treated as the amount realized.

The running of the two-year cutoff is suspended for any period during which the related person's risk of loss with respect to the property is substantially diminished by the holding of a put with respect to the property (or similar property), the holding by another person of a right to acquire the property, or a short sale or any other transaction.

.05 Electing Out of the Installment Method

If an installment sale is made, the default method of reporting the recognized gain is the installment method. However, taxpayers have the option of electing out of the installment method and instead recognizing the entire gain in the year of the sale. Such an election normally must be made by the due date (including extensions) of the tax return.[118] Once an election is made, it cannot be revoked without the IRS' permission.

GAAP vs. Code: For financial accounting purposes, any gain or loss realized on the sale of property is recognized immediately—with rare exceptions. The financial accounting rules require sellers of real estate to recognize all the profit in the year of sale provided the collection of the sales proceeds is reasonably assured or the seller can reasonably estimate the uncollectible amount. In addition, the terms of the sale must not require the seller to perform significant services after the sale.[119] Consequently, when taxpayers report a gain from an installment sale, the amount of net income must be adjusted each year for the difference between the gain reported on the income statement and the gain reported on the tax return.

¶ 811 Summary

Under the realization principle, taxpayers generally do not realize gains and losses from the sale of business or investment property until the property is disposed of in a taxable transaction. Realized gains and losses from the disposal of business and investment property are generally recognized; however, exceptions do exist.

---

[117] Code Sec. 453(f)(1).
[118] Code Sec. 453(d).

[119] "Accounting for Sales of Real Estate," *Statement of Financial Accounting Standards No. 66* (Stamford, Conn.: FASB, 1982).

Proper tax planning requires that taxpayers understand the circumstances under which realized gains can be excluded or postponed as well as the circumstances under which realized losses can be disallowed, either permanently or temporarily. Deferring gains is not always in the taxpayer's best interest. However, a good understanding of the tax laws will allow taxpayers to structure transactions to best serve their interests.

GLOSSARY OF TERMS INTRODUCED IN THE CHAPTER

Abandonment. The situation in which the owner of property permanently and intentionally relinquishes any claim to the property without receiving any consideration in return.

Adjusted basis. The initial basis of property adjusted upward for capital improvements and any deferred losses and downward for capital recoveries and deferred gains. Used in determining the realized gain or loss from the sale of property.

Amount realized. The sum of the cash, FMV of property, and release of liability received in a sale or an exchange of property, minus any selling expenses. Used in determining the realized gain or loss from the sale of property. *See also* Realized gain or loss.

Boot. A term tax practitioners use to describe non-like-kind property involved in a like-kind exchange. *See also* like-kind.

Condemnation. A legal action in which the government takes possession of property under the power of eminent domain.

Constructive ownership. A rule under which a taxpayer may be treated as owning stock that is actually owned by another person or entity in which the taxpayer has an ownership interest.

Exchange. A transaction in which two parties exchange property. Various types of boot (see definition above) may also constitute part of the proceeds.

Installment sale. A sale or exchange of property in which the seller receives payments in more than one tax year.

Involuntary conversion. An event caused by casualty, theft, or condemnation in which the taxpayer's property is damaged or destroyed.

Nonrecourse liability. A liability for which the seller is not personally liable, but for which the creditor can only look to property specified in the loan agreement for satisfaction of the debt.

Realized gain or loss. Measure of the taxpayer's true economic gain or loss resulting from the disposal of property in a sale, an exchange, or an abandonment.

Recognized gain or loss. The amount of the realized gain or loss that is reported on the tax return.

Recourse liability. Liability for which the seller is personally liable.

Unrealized gains and losses. The difference between the FMV of property and its adjusted basis at a time other than when the property has been disposed. Sometimes referred to as paper gains and losses because they represent the appreciation or decline in value of property that has yet to be sold.

Wash sale. A sale of securities (stocks and bonds) in which a taxpayer realizes a loss on the sale and then purchases the same or substantially identical securities within 30 days before or 30 days after the date of the sale. The tax laws do not allow taxpayers to recognize losses that result from wash sales.

CHAPTER PROBLEMS

Chapter 8 Discussion Questions

1. When computing realized gain or loss from the sale of property, why does the amount realized include the fair market value of property received?

2. When computing realized gain or loss, why does the amount realized include debt relief?

3. A business owns land used in its business. The land increased $100,000 in value this year. Why does the tax law not require the business to pay taxes on the increase in the value of the land? Explain.

4. Discuss what is meant by an exchange. How does it differ from a sale? How does the tax law treat the gains and losses on exchanges?

5. What is the income tax treatment of a holder of a call option or put option on common stock who allows the option to expire worthless? How does this treatment compare to stocks or bonds that become worthless?

6. Distinguish between unrealized, realized, and recognized gains and losses and explain their importance in computing taxable income.

7. What is a wash sale? How do the tax laws treat realized losses from a wash sale?

8. Discuss the annual and lifetime limits that individuals may exclude on the gain from the sale of publicly traded securities when they invest the proceeds in a specialized small business investment company (SSBIC). How do these limits differ from the annual and lifetime limits for a C corporation?

9. How do the tax laws treat losses on a sale between related parties? What happens to any disallowed loss?

10. What does "like class" mean in a like-kind exchange?

11. When a like-kind exchange is not simultaneous, what is the allowable time after the initial transfer to identify the property to be received in the exchange? Within what period must the taxpayer receive the like-kind property in a like-kind exchange?

12. May a taxpayer elect out of the like-kind exchange rules? If so, how? If not, can a taxpayer structure the transaction in a different manner so as to make the exchange taxable?

13. What is "boot" in a like-kind exchange? How is a release from debt treated when it is part of a like-kind exchange?

14. Do the tax laws allow like-kind exchanges between related parties? Explain.

15. What constitutes an "involuntary conversion," and how do the tax laws treat realized gains and losses resulting from an involuntary conversion of business property?

16. What constitutes "qualified replacement property" in an involuntary conversion?

17. In an involuntary conversion, what period does a taxpayer have in which to purchase qualified replacement property to avoid recognition of gain?

18. Sam Kinder sold land he used in his business in 20X1. The buyer gave him 10 percent down and a note for the remaining 90 percent due in 20X2. Sam realized a gain on the sale of the land. Does the sale qualify as an installment sale?

19. What is the meaning of "total contract price" with respect to an installment sale?

20. May a taxpayer elect out of the installment method of recognizing gain from an installment sale? If so, how?

Chapter 8 Problems

1. Tennison Company sells a machine used in its business. Tennison receives $18,000 in cash and a promissory note for $75,000 that bears interest at the market rate. Tennison incurs $500 in selling expenses. Compute Tennison's amount realized.

2. Roberts Company exchanged a truck used in its business for a new truck. The new truck was worth $58,000. Roberts Company paid $5,000 in cash for the new truck and signed a note for $36,000 that is secured by the new truck. The dealer agreed to pay $11,000 that Roberts still owed on the old truck. What is the amount realized by Roberts on the exchange of the old truck?

3. Jenkins Corporation sold equipment used in its business for cash. The amount realized was $80,000. The equipment originally cost $140,000, but it had an adjusted basis of $60,000 at the time of the sale. What is the gain or loss realized by Jenkins Corporation?

4. Lockwood Corporation purchased land. The contract sales price was $122,000 and Lockwood Corporation had to pay all of the closing costs, including the unpaid real estate taxes from the first of the year. The estimated real estate taxes for the year are $1,200. The date of sale was June 1. The closing costs other than the real estate taxes and prepaid items were $3,100. What is Lockwood Corporation's adjusted basis in the land?

5. Martin Company bought land with an FMV of $20,000, a building with an FMV of $70,000, and equipment with an FMV of $10,000 at an estate auction for a lump sum payment of $60,000. What is the basis of each asset?

6. Sanchez Company sold land for $100,000 to Belita Sanchez, who owns 60 percent of the outstanding stock of Sanchez. The company's adjusted basis in the land is $120,000.

   a. Compute the company's realized and recognized gain or loss on the sale of the land.

   b. What is Belita's adjusted basis in the land?

   c. If Belita sold the land for $90,000 two years after she purchased it, compute her realized and recognized gain or loss.

   d. If Belita sold the land for $105,000 two years after she purchased it, compute her realized and recognized gain or loss.

   e. If Belita sold the land for $145,000 two years after she purchased it, compute her realized and recognized gain or loss.

7. Warren Davis owns 20 percent of the outstanding stock of Davis Corporation. Warren's sister, Sara Smith, owns 30 percent of the stock; his cousin, Reggie Anderson, owns 20 percent of the stock; and his father, Ben Davis, owns 30 percent of the stock. Determine Warren's actual and constructive ownership in Davis Corporation under the related party rules.

8. Biggs Company bought 1,000 shares of RXA Corporation for $50,000 on May 10, 20X0. Biggs Company sold the 1,000 shares for $40,000 on July 14, 20X1. On July 28, 20X1, Biggs Company purchased 600 shares of RXA Corporation for $26,400.

   a. Calculate Biggs's realized and recognized gain or loss from the sale of the 1,000 shares sold.

   b. Compute Biggs's basis in the new shares purchased on July 28, 20X1.

9. Julie Waters sold qualified small business stock (Section 1202 stock) that she had owned for more than five years. She purchased the stock in the year 2007. She realized a gain of $400,000. Compute Julie's recognized gain.

10. Giese Corporation, a C corporation, sold publicly traded bonds for $897,000. Giese's adjusted basis in the bonds was $600,000. Two days after receiving the proceeds from the sale, Giese invested $750,000 in an SSBIC.

    a. How much gain must Giese recognize on the sale of the bonds?

    b. What is Giese's adjusted basis in the stock in the SSBIC?

11. Jeannie Lynne sold stock in a publicly traded corporation for $480,000 and realized a gain of $160,000. Within 60 days of selling the stock, she purchased stock in an SSBIC for $500,000.

    a. Calculate Jeannie's recognized gain if she elects to postpone as much gain as possible from the sale of the stock.

   b. Calculate her adjusted basis in the SSBIC stock.

   c. Calculate her adjusted basis in the SSBIC stock for purposes of determining the Code Sec. 1202 exclusion that could result if she holds the stock for at least five years.

12. Lopez Company transfers a computer used in its business that has an adjusted basis of $300 and an FMV of $1,000 to Greene Company and receives in exchange a laser printer with an FMV of $600 that it will use in its business and cash of $400.

   a. Calculate Lopez's realized and recognized gain or loss.

   b. What is Lopez's basis in the laser printer?

13. Wheeler Corporation transferred land to a qualified intermediary on March 1, 20X1, as a part of a like-kind exchange. The tax year for Wheeler Corporation is the calendar year.

   a. By what date must the land be identified that Wheeler Corporation will receive in the exchange?

   b. By what date must Wheeler Corporation actually receive the land?

14. Garrison Corporation transfers unimproved land to Rucker Corporation and receives in exchange improved land with an FMV of $600,000 and $250,000 of cash. Rucker's adjusted basis in the improved land is $750,000. Garrison's adjusted basis in the unimproved land is $400,000, and the FMV of the land is $900,000. At the time of the exchange Garrison's unimproved land is subject to a $200,000 mortgage that Rucker assumes. Rucker's improved land is subject to a mortgage of $150,000 that Garrison assumes.

   a. Compute Garrison's realized and recognized gain or loss on the exchange of the unimproved land and its basis in the newly acquired improved land.

   b. Compute Rucker's realized and recognized gain or loss on the exchange of the improved land and its basis in the newly acquired unimproved land.

15. Harris Corporation transfers unimproved land to Newman Corporation and receives in exchange improved land worth $850,000 and $100,000 of cash. Newman's improved land is subject to a $120,000 mortgage, which Harris assumes. Harris's unimproved land has an FMV of $830,000 and an adjusted basis to Harris of $700,000. The unimproved land is not subject to any mortgage at the time of the exchange. Newman's basis in the improved land is $770,000.

   a. Compute Harris's realized and recognized gain or loss on the exchange and its adjusted basis in the newly acquired improved land.

   b. Compute Newman's realized and recognized gain or loss on the exchange and its adjusted basis in the newly acquired unimproved land.

16. The business equipment of Connor Corporation was destroyed in a fire. The insurance company reimburses Connor $221,000. At the time of the fire, the adjusted basis in the equipment was $171,000. Two months after receiving the insurance proceeds, Connor Corporation purchases similarly functioning equipment that costs $215,000.

   a. Compute Connor's realized and recognized gain or loss from the casualty.

   b. What is Connor's basis in the new equipment?

17. Murray Corporation's office building is destroyed in a tornado. Murray receives $2 million in insurance proceeds. Murray's adjusted basis in the office building at the time of the tornado was $2,150,000. Within three months of receiving the insurance proceeds, Murray purchases a new office building at a cost of $1,950,000.

   a. Compute Murray's realized and recognized gain or loss from the casualty.

   b. What is Murray's basis in the new office building?

18. Tanger Company's warehouse is destroyed in a fire on October 4, 20X4. Tanger's adjusted basis in the warehouse at the time of the fire is $140,000. The insurance company reimburses Tanger $200,000 for the loss on January 14, 20X5. Tanger has a calendar year end.

a. How much must Tanger reinvest in qualified replacement property to avoid recognizing any gain on the involuntary conversion?

b. How long does Tanger have to reinvest in qualified replacement property?

c. What constitutes qualified replacement property?

d. How would your answers to a., b., and c. change if the warehouse were condemned by the government?

19. Walker Corporation sold land on the installment basis in 20X1. Walker Corporation received $70,000 in cash at the time of the sale and an installment note for $630,000 that called for seven annual payments of $90,000 of principal plus interest at 10 percent per year. In addition, the purchaser assumed a mortgage on the land in the amount of $100,000. Walker Corporation had an adjusted basis in the land of $450,000. Walker Corporation paid selling expenses of $70,000 in 20X1.

a. Compute Walker's gross profit percentage on the sale.

b. How much of the realized gain must Walker recognize in 20X1?

c. How much of the realized gain must Walker recognize each year from 20X2 through 20X8?

20. Cahill Corporation sells land on the installment basis. Cahill receives $50,000 in cash at the time of sale. The purchaser assumes a mortgage on the land in the amount of $400,000. Cahill also receives an installment note that calls for five annual payments of $50,000 of principal plus interest at the market rate. Cahill's adjusted basis in the land is $300,000. Cahill pays $20,000 in commissions on the sale.

a. Compute Cahill's gross profit percentage on the sale.

b. How much of the realized gain must Cahill recognize in the year of the sale?

c. How much of the realized gain must Cahill recognize each year for the next five years?

21. Sedita Company sold land on the installment basis to Benson Company. Sedita received $50,000 in cash and an installment note for $350,000 that calls for annual payments of $70,000 plus interest at the market rate for five years. Sedita had a basis in the land of $160,000. Calculate the gain realized by Sedita. Calculate the gain that Sedita has to recognize in the year of sale and in each of the next five years.

22. Carper Company sold land it held for investment for $100,000. Carper received in exchange $10,000 in cash and an installment note for $90,000 that calls for annual payments of $10,000 plus interest at the market rate for nine years. Carper had a basis in the land of $60,000. After collecting two installment payments, Carper sold the note for $62,000. Calculate the gain or loss that Carper realized on the sale of the installment note.

23. Orosz Company bought land for $10,000 cash and by signing a nonrecourse note for $90,000. Five years later, when the balance on the nonrecourse note was $50,000, Orosz sold the land to Reyes Company for $130,000 in cash. Reyes took the land subject to the nonrecourse liability with the consent of the lender. Calculate Orosz's gain or loss on the sale of the land.

24. Albright Company bought 800 shares of LoTech Company for $32,000 ($40 per share) on November 16, 20X6. On March 9, 20X7, Albright sold the 800 shares of LoTech for $22,400 ($28 per share). Soon thereafter, the shares of LoTech began to increase in value. On April 2, 20X7, Albright bought 1,000 shares of LoTech for $36,000 ($36 per share).

a. Calculate the gain or loss that Albright realized on the sale of the 800 shares of LoTech on April 2, 20X7.

b. How much of the realized gain or loss is recognized?

c. What is Albright's basis in the 1,000 shares of LoTech?

25. Grossman Company received land with a fair market value of $90,000 and $10,000 in cash from Francona Company. In exchange, Grossman transferred land to Francona that had an FMV of $100,000 and an adjusted basis of $130,000.

a. Calculate the gain or loss that Grossman realized on the exchange.

b. How much of Grossman's realized gain or loss is recognized?

c. What is Grossman's adjusted basis in the land it received from Francona?

Chapter 8 Review Problems

1. Benson Corporation purchased office furniture for $300,000 in 2013 at a bargain price at a bankruptcy auction. Benson did not claim a Code Sec. 179 deduction on the office furniture or bonus depreciation. In 2015, Benson Corporation exchanged the office furniture for new office furniture. The old office furniture was subject to a debt of $50,000, which the other party assumed. The fair market value of the new office furniture was $340,000, and it was subject to a debt of $40,000, which Benson assumed. Benson Corporation also received $60,000 cash in the exchange.

   For Benson Corporation, calculate the following:

   a. Depreciation allowed on the old office furniture under MACRS for 2013–2015 (assume the half-year convention applies).

   b. Benson's adjusted basis in the old furniture.

   c. The realized gain or loss on the exchange of the old office furniture.

   d. The recognized gain or loss on the exchange of the old office furniture.

   e. Benson's basis in the new office furniture.

2. In January 2013, Karen Sparks purchased land with a building situated on it for $320,000. It was determined that the building accounts for 62.5 percent of the FMV of the property and the land for the other 37.5 percent. Karen immediately began using the land and building in her business, which she operates as a sole proprietorship. On September 1, 2015, the building was completely destroyed in a fire. She received insurance proceeds of $500,000 on September 21, 2015. She built a new building on the land and used it for the same purpose. The new building cost $480,000. She began using it on December 22, 2015. She wants to defer as much gain as possible.

   Based on this information, determine the following:

   a. The initial basis in the land and in the original building.

   b. The depreciation on the building for years 2013–2015.

   c. The adjusted basis in the building at the time of the fire.

   d. Realized gain or loss on the involuntary conversion of the building.

   e. Recognized gain or loss on the involuntary conversion of the building.

   f. The adjusted basis in the new building.

Chapter 8 Research Question

Melton Company bought land for $100,000 that it held for a possible future plant site. Melton Company bought the property for a $20,000 cash payment and by signing a note secured by a mortgage on the land in the amount of $80,000.

Property values in the area increased significantly. When the land was worth, $300,000, Melton Company took out a new mortgage loan of $250,000 and paid off the $100,000 existing mortgage loan.

Property values in the area then decreased a great deal, and Melton Company could no longer make the payments on the mortgage. When Melton Company's land had a fair market value of $175,000, the lender foreclosed on the mortgage. The balance of the mortgage loan at the time of the foreclosure was $240,000. The mortgage loan was a recourse loan. Although the lender could have held Melton Company liable for any deficiency resulting from the foreclosure, the lender forgave the entire debt because of Melton Company's deteriorating financial condition. However, Melton Company was not bankrupt or insolvent.

How much gain or loss did Melton Company realize on the foreclosure? How much, if any, gain or loss must it recognize? How much gross income does Melton Company recognize as income from the discharge of indebtedness?

CHAPTER 9

Property Transactions: Character of Gain or Loss

CHAPTER CONTENTS

LEARNING OBJECTIVES

1. Understand when gain or loss on a sale or exchange will be treated as capital gain or loss or ordinary gain or loss.

2. Explain why the distinction between a capital gain or loss and an ordinary gain or loss is significant.

3. Understand the holding period for property and how it affects a taxpayer's tax when the property is sold or exchanged.

4. Describe the capital losses limitations that apply to corporate and noncorporate taxpayers.

5. Calculate the tax on net capital gain.

¶ 900 Introduction

In the previous chapter, the tax laws governing realized and recognized gains and losses were presented. Any gain that a taxpayer realizes represents income, but only recognized gains are included in gross income under federal income tax law. Realized losses are reported on the income tax return only to the extent that the tax laws allow them to be recognized.

Ultimately, all recognized gains and losses from the sale, exchange, or other disposal of property are treated either as ordinary gains and losses or as capital gains and losses. The distinction is important because preferential treatment is given to both capital gains and ordinary losses.

Recognized gains and losses may be characterized as any one of the following: ordinary gains and losses, short-term capital gains and losses, long-term capital gains and losses, Section 1231 gains and losses, or business casualty and theft gains and losses. The proper classification of recognized gains and losses is critical not only for determining the amount of losses taxpayers can deduct in a particular tax year, but also for calculating an individual taxpayer's federal income tax liability.

This chapter discusses the rules regarding the characterization of gains and losses and the loss limitation rules.

¶ 901 The Significance of Capital Gains and Losses

Although recognized gains and losses can be characterized in several ways, all recognized gains are ultimately treated either as capital gains or as ordinary income. Likewise, all recognized losses are treated either as capital losses or as ordinary losses. The distinction between capital and ordinary gains and losses is important for two reasons. First, the tax laws limit the amount of capital losses that can be deducted in a particular tax year. No such limits apply to ordinary losses. Second, lower tax rates apply to capital gains recognized by individual taxpayers. Ordinary income, however, is taxed at the taxpayer's marginal tax rate.

The lower tax rates for capital gains of individual taxpayers are limited to special instances in which an individual recognizes a "net capital gain." This occurs when the taxpayer's net long-term capital gains exceed net short-term capital losses (see ¶ 901.02). Typically, capital gains and losses result from the sale or exchange of a capital asset. However, capital gain treatment can be generated from the sale of certain other assets. The definition of what constitutes a capital asset and the various other ways in which capital gain treatment can be generated are discussed in this chapter (see ¶ 903 and ¶ 904). A long-term capital gain or loss generally results from the sale or exchange of a capital asset that the taxpayer held for more than one year.[1] For most property, the taxpayer's "holding period" begins on the day after the taxpayer acquires property and ends on the day the taxpayer disposes of the property.[2] However, special holding period rules may apply (see ¶ 901.03).

.01 Limitations on Capital Losses

The tax laws limit the amount of capital losses that can be deducted in a particular tax year. Different limitations apply to corporate and individual taxpayers. Flow-through entities are not subject to capital loss limitations because those entities are merely conduits through which capital gains and losses recognized by the business during the year are summarized and passed along to their owners. The owners of the flow-through entity are responsible for combining the capital gains and losses that are allocated to them from the flow-through entity with the other capital gains and losses that they recognize during the year.

Corporate taxpayers. When corporations recognize capital losses, the capital loss deduction in any one tax year is limited to the amount of capital gains included in gross income that year.[3] Any excess capital loss can be carried back three years and carried forward five years to offset capital gains in those tax years.[4] When a capital loss is carried back, it must be applied first to offset capital gains in the third preceding tax year. To the extent there are not sufficient capital gains to offset the loss in that year, the excess loss is carried to the second preceding year to offset capital gains in that year. Any remaining unutilized capital loss from the second preceding year carries over to the immediately preceding tax year and then carries forward for up to five tax years. A capital loss carryback cannot create or increase a corporation's net operating loss (see ¶ 1001).[5]

---

[1] Code Sec. 1222.
[2] Rev. Rul. 66-7, 1966-1 CB 188.
[3] Code Sec. 1211(a).

[4] Code Sec. 1212(a)(1).
[5] Code Sec. 1212(a)(1).

When capital gains and losses are reported on the corporation's tax return, short-term capital gains and losses are reported separately from long-term capital gains and losses. Although both short-term and long-term capital gains are taxed at the same rates for corporate taxpayers, the tax laws require that short-term capital losses first offset short-term capital gains and long-term capital losses first offset long-term capital gains.[6] This process is commonly referred to as the "netting process" of capital gains and losses. If netting the short-term and long-term gains and losses produces both a net gain and a net loss, then the net losses are used to offset the net gains. The netting process of capital gains and losses is illustrated in the examples that follow.

Example 1: Amblyn, a C corporation, recognizes the following capital gains and losses during 20X4:

Short-term capital gain	$10,000
Short-term capital loss	(4,000)
Long-term capital gain	12,000
Long-term capital loss	(16,000)

The first step in the netting process is to offset short-term capital losses against short-term capital gains. Then, long-term capital losses are offset against long-term capital gains.

Short-Term	*Long-Term*
$10,000	$12,000
(4,000)	(16,000)
$ 6,000	($ 4,000)

Because there is a net gain and a net loss remaining, the corporation uses the net loss to offset the net gain as follows.

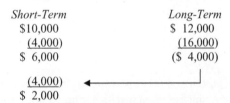

Short-Term	*Long-Term*
$10,000	$ 12,000
(4,000)	(16,000)
$ 6,000	($ 4,000)
(4,000)	
$ 2,000	

Amblyn has an overall gain. Therefore, the entire $22,000 of capital gain ($10,000 + $12,000) is included in its gross income, and the entire $20,000 of capital losses ($4,000 + $16,000) can be deducted from gross income in 20X4. Amblyn's taxable income increases by the $2,000 overall net short-term gain.

When a corporation's capital losses exceed its capital gains, the excess is carried back three years and forward five years to offset the *capital gains* that were recognized in those years. Even when the taxpayer's excess capital loss stems partly or entirely from a long-term capital loss, the amount carried over to another tax year is treated as a short-term capital loss in the carryover year.[7] Therefore, the capital loss carried back or forward from another tax year first offsets any short-term capital gains.

Example 2: Assume the same facts as in Example 1, except Amblyn suffers a $26,000 long-term capital loss instead of a $16,000 long-term capital loss during 20X4. Once again, the netting process begins by offsetting short-term capital losses against short-term capital gains, followed by offsetting long-term capital losses against long-term capital gains.

---

[6] Code Sec. 1222.   [7] Code Sec. 1212(a)(1).

Short-Term	Long-Term
$10,000	$12,000
(4,000)	(26,000)
$ 6,000	($14,000)

Because the initial netting of short-term and long-term capital gains and losses produces a net gain and a net loss, Amblyn uses $6,000 of the net long-term capital loss to offset its net short-term capital gain.

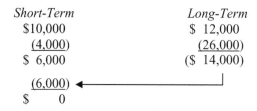

Short-Term	Long-Term
$10,000	$ 12,000
(4,000)	(26,000)
$ 6,000	($ 14,000)
(6,000)	
$ 0	

Amblyn's $30,000 ($4,000 + $26,000) in capital losses exceed its $22,000 ($10,000 + $12,000) of capital gains. Therefore, it can deduct only $22,000 of its capital losses in 20X4 and must carry back $8,000 of its capital losses ($30,000 – $22,000) to the third preceding tax year as a short-term capital loss.

Example 3: Continuing with Example 2, assume that on its 20X1 tax return (the third preceding tax year), Amblyn originally had reported the following capital gains and losses:

Short-Term	Long-Term
$15,000	$6,000
(2,000)	(5,000)
$13,000	$1,000

On Amblyn's 20X1 tax return, the entire $21,000 of capital gains ($15,000 + $6,000) were included in gross income, and the $7,000 of capital losses ($2,000 + $5,000) were deducted from gross income. Thus, Amblyn's 20X1 taxable income increased by $14,000 as a result of its capital gains and losses. When the $8,000 excess capital loss from 20X4 is carried back to 20X1 as a short-term capital loss, the netting process from 20X1 changes, as shown below:

	Short-Term	Long-Term
Carryback from 20X4	($ 8,000)	
	15,000	$6,000
	(2,000)	(5,000)
	$ 5,000	$1,000

When Amblyn adds the $8,000 short-term capital loss to the netting process, its taxable income is reduced by $8,000 ($14,000 overall net gain reported originally versus $6,000 overall net gain as recomputed). Amblyn files for a refund of the taxes paid on the $8,000 of capital gain by filing Form 1139, *Corporation Application for Tentative Refund*. If Amblyn's marginal tax rate in 20X1 was 35 percent, the IRS will refund Amblyn $2,800 ($8,000 × 35%), which represents the overpaid taxes for that year.

¶ 901.01

Example 4: Blyth Enterprises recognizes the following capital gains and losses during 20X4:

Short-term capital gain	$20,000
Short-term capital loss	(45,000)
Long-term capital gain	15,000
Long-term capital loss	(62,000)

Blyth begins the netting process by offsetting its short-term capital gains and losses, and then by offsetting its long-term capital gains and losses. This initial netting produces a $25,000 net short-term capital loss and a $47,000 net long-term capital loss.

Short-Term	*Long-Term*
$20,000	$15,000
(45,000)	(62,000)
($25,000)	($47,000)

Because there are no net gains to offset, Blyth's capital losses for 20X4 will be limited to its $35,000 ($20,000 + $15,000) of capital gains included in gross income. Blyth carries back the excess $72,000 loss ($62,000 + $45,000 – $35,000 utilized in 20X4) to 20X1. When it performs the netting process for 20X1, Blyth includes the $72,000 as a short-term capital loss carryback.

Example 5: Continuing with Example 4, assume that on its 20X1 tax return Blyth's netting of its capital gains and losses was as follows:

When Blyth reconstructs the netting process after including its $72,000 capital loss carryback from 20X4, only $4,000 of the loss carryback can be utilized to offset the excess capital gains recognized in that year. As shown below, $68,000 of the loss carryback was not utilized and must be carried over to 20X2 ($75,000 net short-term loss – $7,000 utilized to offset net long-term capital gains). Blyth will request a refund of taxes paid on the $4,000 of capital gains originally reported on its 20X1 tax return that were offset by the 20X4 capital loss carryback.

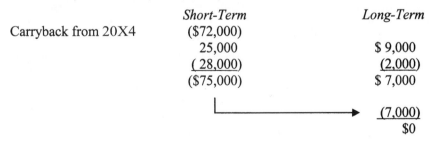

Example 6: Continuing with Example 5, assume that on its 20X2 tax return Blyth reported an $8,000 short-term capital loss, a $26,000 long-term capital gain, and a $6,000 long-term capital loss. (The netting process follows). On its 20X2 tax return, Blyth included the $26,000 capital gain in gross income and deducted the entire $14,000 from its gross income ($6,000 + $8,000). Thus, Blyth's 20X2 taxable income increased by $12,000 ($26,000 – $14,000) as a result of the capital gains and losses recognized in that year.

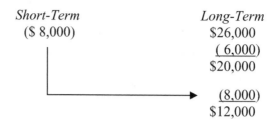

When Blyth includes its $68,000 capital loss carryover and reconstructs the netting process for 20X2, only $12,000 of the loss carryover can be utilized to offset the excess capital gains recognized in that year. As shown below, $56,000 ($76,000 – $20,000) of the loss carryover was not utilized and must be carried over to 20X3.

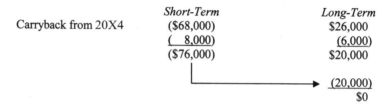

Blyth will include the $56,000 capital loss carryback as a short-term capital loss when it redoes the netting process from its 20X3 tax return. To the extent that the entire $56,000 capital loss carryback cannot be utilized on its 20X3 tax return, it will carry over any remaining loss to its 20X5 tax return. Blyth has a total of five years after 20X4 to fully utilize its capital loss recognized in 20X4. Thus, if in 20X9 Blyth still has any remaining capital loss carryover from 20X4, it should plan to sell property during the year to produce sufficient capital gain to absorb all of its capital losses (including any capital loss carryovers).

 GAAP vs. Code: On a corporation's income statement, a capital loss is deducted in the year the loss is realized. Therefore, in a year in which a corporation's capital losses exceed its capital gains, the excess loss will create a difference between net income and taxable income. This difference must be added back to net income when reconciling net income to taxable income. Likewise, when the capital loss carryover is utilized in a subsequent tax year, the amount used must be subtracted from net income during the reconciliation process in the carryover year.

Individual taxpayers. For individuals, the deduction for capital losses is limited to the capital gains included in gross income plus $3,000. (The limit is $1,500 for individuals who are married but file separate tax returns).[8] Any unused capital losses are carried forward indefinitely but may not be carried back. Unlike corporate taxpayers, whose capital loss carryovers are carried over as short-term capital losses, an individual taxpayer's capital loss carryovers retain their long-term and short-term nature. When an individual's capital losses exceed capital gains, the $3,000 deduction is taken first from net short-term capital losses. Any remaining amount needed to reach the $3,000 limit is taken from the long-term capital losses. Thus, as required of all taxpayers, individuals must properly classify each capital gain or loss as a short-term or a long-term capital gain or loss.

Example 7: In 20X6, Nan Jones has a net short-term capital gain of $10,000 and a net long-term capital loss of $24,000. Nan uses $10,000 of her long-term capital loss to offset her short-term capital gain (see below). This leaves Nan with an overall capital loss of $14,000 ($10,000 – $24,000). Nan uses $3,000 of the net capital loss to reduce her

---

[8] Code Sec. 1211(b).

ordinary income. She carries over to 20X7 a long-term capital loss of $11,000 ($14,000 – $3,000). She adds this amount to her other long-term capital gains and losses in 20X7.

	Short-Term	*Long-Term*
	$10,000	($24,000)
	(10,000)	
	$0	

As mentioned previously, the tax laws do not limit the number of years individual taxpayers can carry over a capital loss. However, if an unmarried taxpayer dies with an unused capital loss carryover, the capital loss carryover expires, and it cannot be used by any other taxpayer.[9] If a married taxpayer dies with a capital loss carryover from a joint return, the decedent's spouse can continue to use the capital loss carryover during his or her lifetime.

Example 8: Brenda Puckett was unmarried when she died in 20X6. At the time of her death, Brenda had a $23,000 capital loss carryover from 20X5. During 20X6, but prior to her death, Brenda did not recognize any capital gains or losses. On her final individual income tax return for 20X6, $3,000 of the capital loss carryover may be used to reduce ordinary income. The remaining $20,000 ($23,000 – $3,000) expires, and it cannot be deducted on Brenda's estate tax return or on any other income tax return.

Example 9: In 20X4, Don and Alma Smith, joint filers, incur a $46,000 net capital loss. They utilize $13,000 of the loss in 20X5, and carry over the rest to 20X6. Don dies during 20X6. Alma can utilize the $33,000 ($46,000 – $13,000) capital loss carryover in 20X6 first to offset any capital gains and then to reduce $3,000 of ordinary income. She can then carry over any remaining capital loss to 20X7 and future tax years.

 Spotlight: The carryover rules for capital losses are different for corporate and individual taxpayers in two ways. Excess losses for individual taxpayers are defined as capital losses in excess of capital gains plus $3,000. However, for corporate taxpayers, excess losses are defined as simply the excess of capital losses over capital gains. A second difference has to do with capital loss carrybacks and carryforwards. Corporations can carry back excess losses three years; individual taxpayers can only carry forward excess losses. The carryforward period for individuals is indefinite; for corporate taxpayers it is five years.

Other business entities. Flow-through entities (i.e., partnerships, S corporations, limited liability companies, and certain trusts) are not subject to capital loss limitations. Instead, these entities keep track of all short-term and long-term capital gains and losses during the year. At the end of the year the entity calculates its "net short-term capital gain or loss" and its "net long-term capital gain or loss" and reports these amounts, along with each owner's share of these net gains and losses, on the entity's tax return. The owners then report their respective amounts of net short-term and net long-term capital gain or loss in the netting process on their own income tax returns. Thus, any net long-term or net short-term capital loss that flows through from a flow-through entity to its owner is included in the owner's netting process along with other short-term and long-term capital gains and losses the owner recognizes during the year. Because the owners of these entities can be individuals, corporations, or other flow-through entities, when flow-through entities recognize capital gains and losses, they must also report which of the capital gains and losses are long-term and which are short-term.

---

[9] Rev. Rul. 74-175, 1974-1 CB 52.

.02 Special Tax Rates on Net Capital Gains of Individuals

Although progressive tax rates are applied to an individual's taxable income, net capital gain recognized by an individual taxpayer is taxed at a lower tax rate than ordinary income. **Net capital gain** is defined as the excess of the taxpayer's net long-term capital gains over its net short-term capital losses.[10] If the individual does not have a net long-term capital gain, then net capital gain equals zero. If the individual does not have a net short-term capital loss, then net capital gain equals the amount of its net long-term capital gain (if any).

The tax rate on ordinary income ranges from 10 to 39.6 percent for individual taxpayers.[11] For taxpayers in the 10- or 15-percent tax bracket, net capital gain is not taxed.[12] Taxpayers in the 25-, 28-, 33-, or 35-percent income tax bracket have to pay a 15 percent income tax on their net capital gain. Taxpayers in the 39.6 percent income tax bracket have to pay a 20 percent tax on their net capital gain.

Special rules apply to certain types of capital gains. Unrecaptured Section 1250 gain is taxed at a maximum 25-percent tax rate, and net capital gain on the sale of collectibles is taxed at a maximum 28-percent tax rate. (See ¶ 907 and ¶ 1306.01.) Generally, corporations do not receive any preferential tax rate treatment for net capital gains.

Medicare tax on unearned income. As discussed in ¶ 405.02, net investment income (including gain from the property other than property held in a trade or business) is subject to an additional 3.8 percent tax on the lesser of:[13]

1. Net investment income for the taxable year, or
2. The excess of the modified adjusted gross income (MAGI) for the year over the threshold amount ($250,000 for married filing jointly and surviving spouse; $125,000 for married filing separately; and $200,000 for head of household and single).

The tax also applies to estates and trusts with income in excess of the dollar amount with which the highest tax bracket begins.[14]

The tax is commonly referred to as the Net Investment Income Tax (NIIT).

Example 10: Chauncy Lee, III, a single taxpayer, had MAGI of $325,000, including net capital gains of $50,000 during 2015. Chauncy had no other investment income during the year. In addition to the regular capital gains tax of 15 percent, Chauncy must pay an additional $1,900 of NIIT (i.e., .038 × the lesser of ($325,000 – $200,000) or ($50,000)).

Example 11: Assume the same facts except that Chauncy's MAGI is only $240,000. His NIIT is an additional $1,520 (i.e., .038 × the lesser of ($240,000 – $200,000) or ($50,000)).

 Spotlight: The revenues from the NIIT go into the Supplemental Medical Insurance trust fund to help pay for the expansion of health care that is commonly referred to as "ObamaCare." Is the 3.8 percent tax: a proportional tax; a progressive tax through all income levels; or progressive, but proportional at certain income levels? In comparing Taxpayer A with $100,000 of net investment income with Taxpayer B who has $200 million of net investment income, is the effect of the tax regressive?

Example 12: Janice Jacks is a single taxpayer in the 35-percent tax bracket. In the current tax year, Janice sold the following capital assets:

---

[10] Code Sec. 1222(11).
[11] Code Sec. 1.
[12] Code Sec. 1(h).

[13] Code Sec. 1411(a)(1).
[14] Code Sec. 1411(a)(2).

Description	Gain (Loss)
Stock held 6 months	$6,000
Stock held 3 years	(3,000)
Land held 5 years	1,000
Land held 8 months	(1,000)

Janice begins the netting process by offsetting short-term capital losses against short-term capital gains. This yields a net short-term capital gain of $5,000. Long-term capital gains and losses are then netted to yield a $2,000 net long-term capital loss. The netting process is complete after the net long-term capital loss is used to offset the short-term gain.

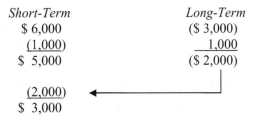

Short-Term	Long-Term
$ 6,000	($ 3,000)
(1,000)	1,000
$ 5,000	($ 2,000)
(2,000)	
$ 3,000	

Because Janice does not have a net long-term capital gain, her net capital gain is $0. Her $3,000 overall short-term capital gain increases her adjusted gross income (AGI) by that amount. From her AGI, Janice subtracts out her deductions from AGI (see ¶ 1304) to compute her taxable income. Her income tax liability is calculated by applying the progressive income tax rates for single taxpayers to her taxable income (see the Appendix at the back of this book).

Example 13: June Blakley is a single taxpayer. In 2015, she sold the following capital assets. Before considering these items, June's AGI is $94,850 and she has $10,000 of deductions from AGI.

Description	Gain (Loss)
Stock held 5 months	$5,000
Stock held 12 years	2,000
Land held 13 years	(1,000)
Land held 3 months	(2,000)

June's netting process begins by netting her short-term capital gains and losses to yield a $3,000 net short-term capital gain. She then nets her long-term capital gains and losses to yield a $1,000 net long-term capital gain.

Short-Term	Long-Term
$5,000	$2,000
(2,000)	(1,000)
$3,000	$1,000

Because June does not have a net short-term capital loss, her net capital gain is equal to her $1,000 net long-term capital gain. The capital gains and losses increase her AGI to $98,850 ($94,850 + $4,000 overall capital gains). From this amount, June subtracts out her deductions from AGI to compute her taxable income of $88,850 ($98,850 – $10,000). When she calculates the income tax on her taxable income, June backs out the $1,000 net capital gain and taxes it at 15 percent because her taxable income falls in the 25 percent tax bracket (see the tax rates for Single Individuals in the Appendix at the back of this book). She computes her 2015 tax liability as follows:

Tax liability on $87,850 ($88,850 – $1,000)	$17,756
Plus: Tax on net capital gain ($1,000 × 15%)	150
Total 2015 tax liability	$17,906

Example 14: Assume the same facts as in Example 13, except June's AGI after considering her capital gains and losses is $35,400, which puts her $25,400 taxable income ($35,400 – $10,000) in the 15-percent tax bracket (see the Appendix at the back of this book).

Tax liability on $24,400 ($25,400 – $1,000)	$3,199
Plus: Tax on net capital gain ($1,000 × 0%)	0
Total 2015 tax liability	$3,199

Example 15: Misty Jenkins is a single taxpayer. In 2015, she sold the following capital assets. Before considering these items, her AGI is $105,650 and she has $10,000 of deductions from AGI.

Description	Gain (Loss)
Stock held 5 months	($ 1,000)
Stock held 9 months	2,000
Land held 13 months	11,000
Land held 3 months	(6,000)

Misty's netting process begins by netting her short-term capital gains and losses to yield a $5,000 net short-term capital loss. She then uses the net short-term capital loss to offset the $11,000 net long-term capital gain. Misty's net capital gain is $6,000 ($11,000 net long-term capital gain in excess of $5,000 net short-term capital loss).

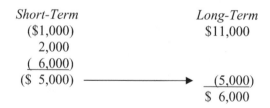

The $6,000 net capital gain increases Misty's AGI to $111,650 ($105,650 + $6,000). From this amount, she subtracts out her deductions from AGI to arrive at her taxable income of $101,650 ($111,650 – $10,000). When she calculates income tax on the taxable income, Misty backs out the $6,000 net capital gain and taxes it at 15 percent because her taxable income falls in the 28-percent tax bracket (see the Appendix at the back of this book). She then computes her 2015 tax liability as follows:

Tax liability on $95,650 ($101,650 – $6,000)	$19,853
Plus: Tax on net capital gain ($6,000 × .15)	900
Total 2015 tax liability	$20,753

Example 16: William Ledbetter, a single taxpayer, in 2015 had taxable income before including capital gains of $420,000. He had net capital gains of $20,000. His total tax is as follows:

Tax liability on $420,000	$122,689
Tax on $20,000 of capital gains × .20	4,000
NTIT $20,000 × .038	760
Total tax	$127,449

Gains and losses from the sale or exchange of property are not included in the calculation of net earnings from self-employment. Consequently, a net gain from the sale of business property increases the taxpayer's AGI (and the taxpayer's income tax liability) but does not increase the amount of self-employment tax a sole proprietor or partner owes during the year. Likewise, losses from the sale of business property reduce a taxpayer's AGI but do not reduce the self-employment taxes owed by a sole proprietor or partner.

Example 17: Owen Jacobs operates a research and marketing business as a sole proprietorship. During the year, Owen sells all rights to a patent he held for designing a new computer chip and recognizes a $25,000 long-term capital gain. Although the patent was obtained as a result of Owen's business, it is classified as a capital asset. Any gain or loss realized from the sale of a capital asset produces capital gain or loss. Owen therefore includes the $25,000 in gross income and reports it as long-term capital gain in his netting process for the year. If Owen recognizes any capital losses during the year, he can use up to $25,000 of the loss to offset his capital gain from the sale of the patent, and he can use another $3,000 to offset ordinary income. Because the $25,000 gain is not included in Owen's net earnings from self-employment, he does not have to pay self-employment taxes on the gain.

.03 Holding Periods

Reduced tax rates apply to certain long-term gains reported in an individual taxpayer's taxable income. Although the focus of this textbook is not individual income taxation, an understanding of the rules that govern individual taxpayers is necessary because an individual owner's allocated share of gains and losses from a flow-through entity are reported on the individual's income tax return. Thus, in addition to computing a taxpayer's recognized gain or loss (see Chapter 8), it is important to be able to determine the short-term or long-term nature of that gain or loss.

If, at the time property was sold, the taxpayer's holding period in the property was more than one year, the resulting gain or loss is usually long-term gain or loss. The taxpayer's **holding period** in property generally begins the day after the taxpayer acquires property and ends on the day the taxpayer disposes of the property.[15] When property is disposed of in a sale or exchange, the "disposal date" is the date of the sale or exchange. For stocks and bonds traded on an established exchange (like the New York Stock Exchange), the "trade date" with respect to a security is considered the date that the taxpayer acquires or disposes of a security. The actual delivery of the security is irrelevant for determining the taxpayer's holding period.[16]

If property is partially or completely destroyed in a casualty, the disposal date is the date of the casualty. If property is stolen, the disposal date is the date on which the taxpayer becomes aware of the theft. In the case of stocks or bonds that are considered worthless, the tax laws treat a worthless security as having been sold for $0 on the last day of the tax year in which it becomes worthless (see ¶ 802.01). This rule regarding the date of the deemed sale can affect whether the worthless security produces a short-term or a long-term loss.

Example 18: On March 5, 20X4, a taxpayer sells property for $30,000 that was purchased for $45,000 on January 22, 20X1. The taxpayer's capital loss of $15,000 ($30,000 – $45,000) is long-term because the asset was held for more than one year.

---

[15] Rev. Rul. 66-7, 1966-1 CB 188.   [16] Rev. Rul. 93-84, 1993-2 CB 225.

Example 19: A taxpayer purchases property for $31,600 on September 1, 20X1. The taxpayer's holding period begins on September 2, 20X1. The taxpayer sells the property for $40,000 on September 1, 20X2, and recognizes an $8,400 short-term gain ($40,000 – $31,600). Had the taxpayer held the asset for one more day, the gain would have been a long-term gain. To qualify as long-term gain, the taxpayer must have held the property for *more than* one year.

Example 20: Mike Faulkner purchases 500 shares of stock in NuHome Décor. The trade date is May 14, 20X1, but the shares are not credited to his brokerage account until May 17, 20X1. Mike's purchase date for the stock is May 14, 20X1, and his holding period begins on May 15, 20X1. If Mike sells the stock any time on or after May 15, 20X2, he will have held the shares for investment for more than one year, and his gain or loss will be classified as long-term capital gain or loss.

Example 21: Ivan Miller bought 200 shares of DotCom common stock for $8,000 on July 8, 20X1. The shares became worthless on April 6, 20X2, when the company declared bankruptcy. Ivan is deemed to have sold the 200 shares for $0 on December 31, 20X2. Therefore, his $8,000 loss is a long-term capital loss.

Properties having a transferred (substituted) basis. When a taxpayer acquires property in a nonrecognition exchange, the basis of the acquired property is the taxpayer's basis (with adjustments) in the transferred property (this basis is referred to as "substituted basis"), and the holding period of the taxpayer's acquired property includes the holding period of the transferred property. Nonrecognition exchanges include involuntary conversions (see ¶ 809) and like-kind exchanges (see ¶ 808). The taxpayer's holding period will also "tack on" when a realized gain from the sale of publicly traded stock is postponed when the taxpayer purchases stock in a specialized small business investment company (SSBIC) (see ¶ 806).[17]

Example 22: A corporation acquires land worth $100,000 in a like-kind exchange by giving up land also worth $100,000. The corporation's basis in the land it exchanged was $80,000, and accordingly, the corporation realizes a $20,000 gain on the exchange ($100,000 – $80,000). Because no boot was received in the exchange, the corporation's gain is postponed, and its basis in the new land is reduced to $80,000 ($100,000 FMV of the new land – $20,000 postponed gain). The corporation's holding period for the land it acquired in the like-kind exchange begins on the day of the holding period for the old land it exchanged.

Example 23: On May 2, 20X3, Bucknell, Inc. sells publicly traded stock in Bannister, Ltd. that it bought on January 21, 20X1. Bucknell's amount realized from the sale is $600,000. Its adjusted basis in the stock was $125,000. Bucknell's realized gain is $475,000 ($600,000 – $125,000). Within 60 days of the sale, Bucknell invests $460,000 of the $600,000 proceeds in Alpena Corporation, an SSBIC, and files an election on its tax return to postpone $335,000 of the gain. Bucknell's holding period in the Alpena stock includes its holding period in the Bannister stock, which began on January 22, 20X1.

Property acquired by gift. The transferred basis rules also apply in most instances when a taxpayer receives property as a gift. When a donor's basis in property carries over to the donee, the donor's holding period includes the donee's holding period.[18] However, if the FMV at the time of the gift is less than the donor's basis, that FMV becomes the basis to the donee, and a new holding period begins the day after the gift. If an individual receives property from a spouse (or a former spouse incident to their divorce), the property is treated as acquired by gift, and the spouse's (or former spouse's) basis in the property carries over and becomes the individual's basis in the property.[19]

---

[17] Code Sec. 1223.

[18] Reg. § 1.1223-1(b).

[19] Code Sec. 1041(b).

Example 24: On October 24, 20X1, Henry Waters gave to his daughter, Debra, 100 shares of HiFly Company stock, worth $5,000 at the time of the gift. Henry had purchased the 100 shares for $4,000 on May 2, 20X1. Debra takes her father's $4,000 basis in the shares, and her holding period begins on May 3, 20X1 (the day after Henry purchased the stock). Debra sells the shares on May 4, 20X2. Her gain or loss will be classified as a long-term capital gain or loss.

Example 25: Assume the same facts as in Example 23 except that the stock was worth only $3,500 at the time of the gift. Debra's holding period begins on October 25, 20X1.

Inherited property. The disposition of inherited property results in a long-term capital gain or loss, regardless of the actual time the taxpayer holds the property or the decedent had held the property.[20] Furthermore, the beneficiary's basis in inherited property is generally the FMV of the inherited property on the decedent's date of death. This basis is referred to as a "stepped up" basis because, if the property has appreciated in value, the basis to the heir is stepped-up from the decedent's basis to FMV. However, the personal representative of an estate may elect to value the estate six months later (as allowed) on the alternative valuation date. In that event the FMV on such date generally becomes the heir's basis. If the alternate valuation date is used and the property is sold after death, but before the alternate valuation date, the basis becomes FMV at the date of sale.

Example 26: Vance Enterprises inherits a parcel of land from one of its shareholders. The shareholder purchased the land on October 6, 20X0, for $16,250. The shareholder dies on November 23, 20X4, when the land is worth $28,100. The executor of the shareholder's estate does not use the alternative valuation date. If Vance Enterprises sells the land for $30,400 on October 24, 20X5, it will recognize a $2,300 long-term capital gain ($30,400 − $28,100), even though the corporation did not actually own the land for more than one year.

Spotlight: The special basis and holding period rules that govern gifted and inherited property are less likely to affect businesses than their owners. If an individual is an owner of a flow-through entity or operates a business as a sole proprietorship, all of the owner's tax items for the year (not just those of the business) are reported on the individual's income tax return. This would include any gains from the sale of gifted or inherited property plus losses on the sale of such property, assuming that the property is held as an investment. Accordingly, it is important to be aware of the special basis and holding period rules that apply to such property so that all tax aspects of an individual owner's tax return can be taken into consideration when tax planning for businesses and their owners.

¶ 902 Generating Capital Gains and Losses

Recognized gain or loss from the sale or exchange of a capital asset usually produces capital gain or loss. If the taxpayer's holding period for the capital asset exceeds one year, the recognized gain or loss is a **long-term capital gain or loss.** If the holding period is one year or less, a **short-term capital gain or loss** results (see ¶ 901.03).

In addition to selling a capital asset, there are other ways to generate capital gains and losses. For example, when a taxpayer recognizes a nonbusiness bad debt, the loss is recognized as a short-term capital loss, regardless of how long the debt that went bad was outstanding. (See ¶ 510.) Nonbusiness bad debts pertain primarily to individual taxpayers because the debts of business entities typically involve business bad debts, which are deductible as ordinary losses.

---

[20] Code Sec. 1223(9).

Example 27: Larry Mahan owns and operates a sole proprietorship. In 20X0, Larry loaned his friend Bill Eastin $5,000 so that Bill could start up his own business. The nature of Larry's loan is not related to his business. Bill defaults on the loan and declares bankruptcy in 20X3. Larry is entitled to take a short-term capital loss for the difference between the $5,000 loan amount and the amount he receives as a distribution from the bankruptcy court.

Although depreciable personal property and real property used in a trade or business are excluded from the definition of "capital asset,"[21] Code Sec. 1231 allows taxpayers to generate long-term capital gains by selling such property, but only when the property is held for more than one year (such property is referred to as "Section 1231 property"). When a taxpayer's gains ("Section 1231 gains") exceed its losses ("Section 1231 losses" from sales of Section 1231 property for a tax year, the Section 1231 gains are treated as long-term capital gains, and the Section 1231 losses are treated as long-term capital losses. When a taxpayer's Section 1231 losses exceed its Section 1231 gains for a tax year, the gains are treated as ordinary income, and the losses are treated as ordinary losses. Section 1231 benefits taxpayers by allowing them to treat net gain as capital gain and net loss as ordinary loss.

Example 28: Perry Corporation has the following gains and losses during the year:

Long-term capital loss	($15,000)
Section 1231 gain	30,000
Section 1231 loss	(10,000)

Perry has a net Section 1231 gain of $20,000 ($30,000 – $10,000). Because the net Section 1231 gain is treated as a long-term capital gain, Perry may deduct the entire $15,000 long-term capital loss. If the tax laws did not allow the net Section 1231 gain to be treated as a long-term capital gain, Perry would have no capital gains included in gross income and could not deduct any of its capital loss for the year.

¶ 903 Sale or Exchange of Capital Assets

The most straightforward way to generate capital gains and losses is to dispose of a capital asset in a taxable transaction. Although the term capital asset may conjure up images of buildings, equipment, machinery, and the like, for tax purposes, capital assets are specifically defined in the Internal Revenue Code (the "Code"). Although the general rule for classifying gains and losses from the sale of capital assets as long-term (held for more than one year) and short-term (held for one year or less) applies to most capital assets, special rules apply to the sale of certain assets.

.01 "Capital Asset" Defined

Code Sec. 1221 defines **capital assets** by exclusion, meaning that "capital asset" is defined as any property *except*:

1. Inventory and other property held primarily for sale to customers in the ordinary course of business.

2. Accounts or notes receivable acquired in the ordinary course of trade or business for services rendered or from the sale of inventory or other property held primarily for sale to customers in the ordinary course of business.

3. Supplies used in the ordinary course of business.

4. Depreciable property and land used in a trade or business.

5. Copyrights, literary, musical, and artistic compositions, letters and memorandums, and similar property held by the taxpayer whose personal efforts created such property; in the case of a letter, memorandum, or similar property, a taxpayer for whom the property was

---

[21] Code Sec. 1221(a)(2).

prepared or produced; or a taxpayer in whose hands the basis is determined in whole or part by reference to the basis of the property in the hands of a taxpayer previously described (however, certain taxpayers can elect to treat self-created musical works or copyrights of such works as capital assets[22]).

6. U.S. government publications (other than those purchased at the price at which offered for sale to the public) if held by the taxpayer who received the publication or a taxpayer who receives a transferred basis in the publication.

7. A commodities derivative financial instrument held by a commodities derivatives dealer, unless the instrument has no connection to the dealer's activities as a dealer and the instrument is clearly identified in the dealer's records as having no connection to the dealer's activities as a dealer.

8. Any hedging transaction clearly identified as such before the close of the day on which it was acquired, originated, or entered into.

The most common types of capital assets are properties held for investment or personal use (in the case of an individual taxpayer). Personal use assets should not be confused with tangible personal property (see ¶ 104.01). The former includes all assets that individuals possess and use in their personal lives. The latter consists of all tangible property other than real estate. Personal use assets include assets such as a taxpayer's home, automobile, furniture, and other personal belongings. A gain on the sale of a personal use asset is recognized as a capital gain, unless a tax law specifically excludes the gain from gross income. A loss on the sale or exchange of a personal use asset is not deductible unless it stems from a casualty or theft loss (see ¶ 1304.03).[23]

Example 29: Chris Riley owns and operates a business as a sole proprietorship. Chris owns the properties listed below:

        Vacation home

        100 shares of stock in Omega Company

        Automobile used entirely for personal use

        Inventory from his sole proprietorship

        Computer used in his sole proprietorship

        Among the property Chris owns, only the inventory and the computer are on the list of property that is specifically not a capital asset. The remaining items are capital assets. If any of these items is sold at a gain, the gain is reported in Chris's gross income. However, if Chris sells either his residence or his automobile at a loss, neither loss can be deducted because the items are Chris's personal belongings. When Chris sells the inventory, the gain or loss from the sale will be reported as ordinary income or loss. The tax law governing the tax treatment of a gain or loss on the sale of the computer is discussed at ¶ 904.

 Spotlight: Stocks and bonds are common types of capital assets. Thus, when bonds are sold at a gain, a capital gain results, even if the bonds sold are state or local government bonds ("municipal bonds"). Although the interest on municipal bonds is excluded from gross income (see ¶ 411.01), taxpayers recognize capital gain or loss on the sale or exchange of municipal bonds.

.02 Capital Assets Sold to a Related Person

If property is directly or indirectly sold or exchanged to a related person and the property is depreciable property in the hands of the transferee, any gain recognized by the transferor is treated

---

[22] Code Sec. 1221(b)(3).   [23] Code Sec. 165(c).

as ordinary income.[24] Appreciation in value included in the purchaser's (depreciable) basis will be taxed as ordinary income to offset the ordinary deductions the purchaser will take as the property is depreciated.

Example 30: Arden Wright sells to a related person artwork that he currently holds as an investment (a capital asset). The artwork is sold for its $25,000 FMV; Arden purchased the artwork for $5,000. The (related) purchaser plans to use the artwork as business property and depreciate the $25,000 depreciable basis. Thus, over the years, the purchaser will be taking ordinary deductions against gross income totaling $25,000. Because Arden sold the artwork to a related person, his $20,000 gain ($25,000 – $5,000) must be recognized as ordinary income on his tax return in the year of the sale.

Reason for the Rule: Code Sec. 1239 was enacted to prevent "related persons" from selling capital assets to one another at a capital gain and having the purchaser receive a stepped-up depreciable basis. Rather than deny the stepped-up basis to the purchaser (who does, in fact, pay the FMV for the property), the tax law instead requires the seller to report the gain as ordinary income. By taxing the gain as ordinary income, the seller loses out on the ability to use the gain to offset capital losses, and, in the case of an individual, the ability to have the gain taxed at a lower tax rate. Furthermore, the government's taxing of the gain on the stepped-up basis at the ordinary income rates more closely offsets the tax benefits the related purchaser will realize as the property is depreciated.

For purposes of this rule, "related persons" are defined as the following:[25]

- A person and a corporation if the person owns, *directly or indirectly*, more than 50 percent of the value of the outstanding stock of the corporation;

- A person and a partnership if more than 50 percent of the capital or profits interest in the partnership is owned directly or indirectly by or for that person;

- Two corporations that are members of the same controlled group (applying the rules from ¶ 804, except that more than 50-percent ownership is required instead of at least 80-percent ownership);

- A corporation and a partnership, if the same persons own both more than 50 percent of the value of the outstanding stock of the corporation and more than 50 percent of the value of the capital or profits interest in the partnership;

- Two S corporations, if the same persons own more than 50 percent of the value of the outstanding stock of each entity; and

- An S corporation and a C corporation, if the same persons own more than 50 percent of the value of the outstanding stock of each corporation.

.03 Patents

A "patent" is an intangible asset that gives its owner the exclusive right to profit commercially from a specified product or process for a limited number of years. By filing for a patent, the inventor discloses trade secrets regarding the product, but during the legal life of a patent, others are specifically prohibited from profiting from the patented invention.

Patents are capital assets. Thus, the sale of a patent normally produces capital gain or loss (unless the taxpayer is in the business of buying and selling patents or is holding the patent as inventory to sell to customers in the ordinary course of business).

---

[24] Code Sec. 1239(a).   [25] Code Sec. 1239(b).

If certain requirements are met, the tax laws treat gain or loss from the sale of patents as long-term capital gain or loss, regardless of how long the taxpayer has held the patent and regardless of whether the patent is a capital asset to the taxpayer.[26] The long-term capital gain treatment also applies to transfers of patent rights, even when the patent itself or the patent application for the invention does not yet exist.[27] One appellate court has held that secret formulas and trade names are similar enough to patents to warrant the special treatment accorded to patents.[28]

> **Spotlight:** A patent that meets the requirements of Code Sec. 1235 does not have to be held for more than a year to qualify for long-term capital gain treatment because the transfer by a holder of a patent is considered a sale or exchange of a capital asset held long-term. Thus, from the moment property capable of being patented is created, it is considered long-term capital gain property. The seller recognizes long-term capital gain on the sale, even if the seller is in the business of making inventions or buying and selling patents.[29]

To qualify for long-term capital gain treatment, the "holder" must sell *all substantial rights* in the patent or an undivided interest in all substantial rights in the patent. The holder of the patent is the individual whose efforts created the patent (the "inventor"). The holder can also be any other individual who acquired his or her interest in the property in exchange for consideration in money or money's worth paid to the creator prior to actual reduction to practice of the invention covered by the patent.[30] However, neither the employer of the inventor nor certain parties related to the inventor can qualify as the holder of the patent for this special rule.[31]

The main issue involving the sale of a patent is whether the sale is of *all substantial rights* in the patent. If a taxpayer sells less than all substantial rights in the patent, the taxpayer has sold a license to use the patent, and the sale of a right to use a patent results in ordinary income in the form of royalties.

Example 31: Ray Kelly works for a corporation. During the year, Ray invents a secret formula to which his employer holds the rights. The corporation sells the formula for a $100,000 gain. Because the employer of the inventor does not qualify as a holder of the patent, the employer recognizes $100,000 of ordinary income.

Transfer of all substantial rights. In determining whether a taxpayer has transferred *all substantial rights* to a patent, all of the facts and circumstances surrounding the transfer are examined, not merely the language used in the sales contract.[32] The sale of rights to a patent for a limited geographical area or for a limited time that is less than the remaining life of the patent does not qualify as the transfer of all substantial rights; it is instead treated as a license. If, however, the holder retains legal title or a lien on the patent to secure payment from the buyer, this alone will not cause the holder to recognize ordinary income instead of capital gain.[33] A holder may obtain capital gain treatment on the sale of a patent even though another person holds nonexclusive rights to use the patent.[34]

> **Planning Pointer:** When considering the sale of all substantial rights to a patent versus granting a license to use the patent, the holder of the patent should consider the preferential tax treatment accorded long-term capital gains over ordinary income.

---

[26] Code Sec. 1235(a).

[27] Reg. § 1.1235-2(a).

[28] *J.H. Pickren*, CA-5, 67-2 USTC ¶ 9477, 378 F2d 595.

[29] Reg. § 1.1235-2(d)(3).

[30] Code Sec. 1235(b)(2); Reg. § 1.1235-2(e).

[31] Code Sec. 1235(b).

[32] Reg. § 1.1235-2(b)(1).

[33] Reg. § 1.1235-2(b)(2).

[34] *D.C. MacDonald*, 55 TC 840, Dec. 30,665 (1971).

Example 32: Nancy Allegan patents a new design for a motorboat. She sells the right to both manufacture and sell the motorboat in Kazakhstan to Allegan Corporation. Nancy has not sold her patent but has rather granted a license to Allegan Corporation. Because the Code Sec. 1235 rules do not apply to payments received from Allegan, the payments give rise to ordinary income and not to long-term capital gain.

Related persons. The special rules that apply to patents do not apply to sales between the holder and certain related persons.[35] "Related persons" for purposes of the special rule for patents are very similar to those described in Figure 8-2 (see ¶ 804) by the rule that disallows losses between certain related parties. However, the ownership percentages for purposes of the special rule for patents is *25 percent or more* (instead of more than 50 percent), and siblings are not considered related to the holder of a patent. "Related persons" for purposes of Code Sec. 1235 include the following:

1. An individual and the individual's spouse, ancestors, or descendants;

2. An individual and a corporation in which the individual *directly or indirectly* owns 25 percent or more of the value of the outstanding stock;

3. Corporations that are members of the same controlled group;

4. A corporation and a partnership if the same person(s) own 25 percent or more of the outstanding value of the stock in the corporation and 25 percent or more of the capital or profits interests in the partnership;

5. An S corporation and another S corporation if the same person(s) own 25 percent or more of the value in the outstanding stock of each corporation;

6. An S corporation and a C corporation if the same person(s) own 25 percent or more of the value in the outstanding stock of each corporation;

7. An individual and a partnership in which the individual *directly or indirectly* owns more than 25 percent of the capital or profits interest; and

8. Two partnerships in which the same persons own, *directly or indirectly*, more than 25 percent of the capital or profits interest.

 Planning Pointer: If capital gain treatment is denied for the sale of a patent by an inventor because the transfer was made to a related person, the tax consequences of the transfer are determined under the general rules for determining gain or loss on the sale of property. Thus, if the property is a capital asset in the hands of the inventor, the gain can still be treated as long-term capital gain if the inventor holds the property for more than one year prior to selling it.

.04 Subdivided Realty

Taxpayers who purchase a large tract of real estate often find it easier to resell the land if they subdivide it into smaller parcels (lots). In addition, they may find that the sale of the land usually takes less time and is more lucrative if they engage in efforts that involve advertising and/or promoting the property. Unfortunately, when real estate owners undertake such efforts, they may no longer be considered merely investors but instead may be considered dealers in real estate. The distinction between property held as an investment and property held in the normal course of business is important because the sale of the former generates capital gain or loss, while the latter involves the sale of inventory, which generates ordinary income or loss.

Investor versus dealer in real estate. Normally, the determination as to whether an owner is an investor or dealer in real estate must be made based on the facts and circumstances of the case. To avoid having the IRS repeatedly challenge these types of issues, Congress enacted Code Sec.

---

[35] Code Sec. 1235(d).

1237, which provides that individuals, partnerships, and S corporations *will not* be treated as real estate dealers merely because real estate acquired as an investment or for use in a trade or business is later subdivided and sold in lots. Although the sale of the lots may resemble sales of inventory, the gain on the sale of subdivided realty *will not* automatically be considered ordinary income if the following three conditions are met:[36]

1. The taxpayer did not previously hold either the tract or any lot or parcel of the tract primarily for sale to customers in the ordinary course of trade or business (unless the tract would have been covered by Code Sec. 1237 at that time) and did not so hold any other real property in the same tax year in which the sale of the lot or parcel occurred. (This rule automatically excludes real estate dealers from being eligible for this special provision.)

2. The taxpayer made no substantial improvement that substantially enhanced the value of the lot or parcel sold while held by the taxpayer or pursuant to a contract of sale entered into between the taxpayer and the buyer. An improvement will be deemed made by the taxpayer if it was made by the taxpayer, the taxpayer's whole or half siblings, spouse, ancestors, or lineal descendants, by a corporation controlled by the taxpayer (by direct or constructive ownership of more than 50 percent of the corporation's voting stock), an S corporation that included the taxpayer as a shareholder, or by a partnership that included the taxpayer as a partner; a lessee, but only if the improvement constitutes income for the taxpayer; or federal, state, or local government, or any political subdivision, but only if the improvement increases the taxpayer's basis in the property (e.g., it is paid for by a special assessment).[37]

3. The lot or parcel is held by the taxpayer for a period of at least five years (unless the real property was acquired by inheritance or devise).

If these three conditions are satisfied and there is no other substantial evidence that a taxpayer holds real estate primarily for sale to customers in the ordinary course of the taxpayer's business, the taxpayer will not be considered to be a real estate dealer holding the real estate primarily for sale merely because the taxpayer has subdivided the tract into lots (or parcels) and engaged in advertising, promotion, selling activities, or the use of sales agents in connection with the sale of lots in the subdivision.[38] Such subdividing and selling activities will be disregarded in determining the purpose for which a taxpayer held real property whenever they are the only substantial evidence indicating that the taxpayer has ever held the real property sold primarily for sale to customers in the ordinary course of the taxpayer's business.

When other substantial evidence tends to show that the taxpayer held real property for sale to customers in the ordinary course of the taxpayer's business, the taxpayer's activities in connection with the subdivision and sale of the property sold will be taken into account in determining the purpose for which the taxpayer held both the subdivided property and any other real property.[39]

Substantial evidence may consist of the taxpayer's selling activities in connection with other property in prior years during which the taxpayer was engaged in subdividing or selling activities with respect to the subdivided tract, the taxpayer's intention in prior years (or at the time the property subdivided was acquired) to hold the tract primarily for sale in the taxpayer's business, the taxpayer's subdivision of other tracts in the same year, the taxpayer's holding other real property for sale to customers in the same year, or the taxpayer's construction of a permanent real estate office that that taxpayer could use in selling other real property.

If the only evidence of the taxpayer's purpose in holding real property consists of not more than one of the following, in the year in question, that fact will not be considered substantial other evidence.[40]

---

[36] Code Sec. 1237(a).
[37] Code Sec. 1237(a)(2); Reg. § 1.1237-1(c)(2).
[38] Reg. § 1.1237-1(a)(2).

[39] Reg. § 1.1237-1(a)(3).
[40] Reg. § 1.1237-1(a)(3).

- Holding a real estate dealer's license,
- Selling other real property that was clearly investment property,
- Acting as a sales representative for a real estate dealer, but without any financial interest in the business, or
- Merely owning other vacant real property without engaging in any selling activity whatsoever with respect to it.

Code Sec. 1237 does not apply if the taxpayer *substantially improves* the property and the improvements substantially increase the value of the lot sold.[41] Examples of substantial improvements include shopping centers and other commercial or residential buildings, hard surface roads, or utilities (such as sewers, water, gas, or electric lines).[42] However, surveying, filling, draining, leveling, and clearing operations as well as the construction of minimum all-weather access roads (including gravel roads when required by the climate) will not be considered substantial improvements. Erecting a temporary structure used as a field office will not be considered a substantial improvement.

An improvement will not be considered substantial if *all four* of the following conditions are met:[43]

1. The taxpayer has held the lot or parcel for at least 10 years. (The full 10-year period must elapse, whether the taxpayer inherited the property or not. Although the taxpayer must hold the property 10 years, the taxpayer need not hold the property for 10 years after it is subdivided.)

2. The improvement consists of the building or installation of water, sewer, drainage facilities (either surface, subsurface, or both), or roads, including hard surface roads, curbs, and gutters.

3. The IRS is satisfied that without the improvement the lot or parcel would not have been marketable at the prevailing local price for similar building sites.

4. The taxpayer elects not to capitalize the cost of the improvement to the basis of the lot or parcel sold or to the basis of any other property held by the taxpayer, and also agrees not to expense any such costs.

 Planning Pointer: As long as the taxpayer has owned the land for at least five years, subdividing the property will not prevent the taxpayer from being considered an investor in real estate. However, if the taxpayer substantially improves the property to enhance its marketability or price and then sells it before the full 10-year holding period has elapsed, the taxpayer risks being deemed a dealer in real estate and having to recognize all gain on the sale of the lots as ordinary income.

Character of the gain. Assuming Code Sec. 1237 applies, the tax law allows the taxpayer to treat the gain on the sale of all lots as long-term capital gain until *the tax year* in which the sixth lot or parcel is sold.[44] In that year and for all subsequent tax years, the gain from all sales of all lots or parcels is treated as ordinary income to the extent of five percent of the *selling price*; the remainder is long-term capital gain. In computing the number of lots or parcels sold, two or more contiguous lots sold to a single buyer in a single sale will count as only one parcel.[45]

Selling expenses cannot be deducted as ordinary business expenses, but they can be deducted from the five percent of the gain that otherwise would be considered ordinary income. Any selling expenses not offsetting the ordinary income reduce the gain from the sale or exchange that would otherwise be considered capital gain.[46]

---

[41] Code Sec. 1237(a)(2); Reg. § 1.1237-1(c)(1).
[42] Reg. § 1.1237-1(c)(4).
[43] Code Sec. 1237(b)(3); Reg. § 1.1237-1(c)(5)(i).

[44] Code Sec. 1237(b)(1); Reg. § 1.1237-1(e)(2).
[45] Reg. § 1.1237-1(e)(2)(i).
[46] Code Sec. 1237(b)(2); Reg. § 1.237-1(e)(2)(ii).

Example 33: In 20X0, Dwane Carter purchased a large tract of real estate for $50,000. In 20X6, he subdivided the tract into 20 lots of equal size and engaged in advertising, promotional, and selling activities in connection with the lots. Dwane sold two lots (lots numbers 1 and 2) during 20X7 for $8,000 each. He incurred $1,000 in total selling expenses in connection with the sale of the lots. Dwane's amount realized from the sale is $15,000 ($16,000 selling price minus $1,000 in selling expenses). His basis in each lot is $2,500 ($50,000/20) Because Dwane did not sell the sixth lot during 20X7, he will recognize $10,000 long-term capital gain from the sale ($15,000 – $5,000).

Example 34: Continuing with Example 33, in 20X8, Dwane sells another three lots (lots 3, 4, and 5) for a total of $35,000. He incurs $1,500 in selling expenses on the sale. Because Dwane did not sell the sixth lot in 20X8, he recognizes a $26,000 long-term capital gain ($35,000 – $1,500 – $7,500).

Example 35: Assume the same facts as in Example 34, except Dwane sells four lots (lots 3, 4, 5, and 6) in 20X8 for a total of $44,000 and incurs $2,000 in selling expenses on the sale. His amount realized on the sale is $42,000 ($44,000 – $2,000). Dwane's gain from the sale is $32,000 ($42,000 – $10,000). Because he sold the sixth lot during the year, five percent of the *sales price* ($44,000 × 5% = $2,200) must be recognized as ordinary income. However, the selling expenses are used first to reduce the amount taxed as ordinary income and then to reduce the amount taxed as long-term capital gain. Thus, of the $32,000 gain, $200 ($2,200 – $2,000) is taxed as ordinary income, and $31,800 ($32,000 – $200) is taxed as long-term capital gain.

Example 36: Continuing with Example 35, in 20X9 Dwane sells another five lots (lots 7–11) for a total of $50,000. He incurs $2,800 in selling expenses on the sale. Dwane's realized and recognized gain is $34,700 ($50,000 – $2,800 – $12,500). He does not recognize any ordinary income because the $2,800 of selling expenses exceeds five percent of the $50,000 selling price ($50,000 × 5% = $2,500). Thus, the entire $34,700 gain is taxed as long-term capital gain.

 Spotlight: Code Sec. 1237 does not apply to C corporations. Thus, no assumptions are made regarding the actions of a C corporation that subdivides realty and sells the lots individually. The determination of whether the C corporation acted as a dealer or as an investor must be made based on the facts and circumstances on a case-by-case basis.

.05 Section 1244 Stock

Because stock is a capital asset for most taxpayers, gains and losses on the sale of stock normally produce capital gains and losses. To encourage individuals to invest in smaller corporations, Code Sec. 1244 allows individual taxpayers each year to treat up to $50,000 of their losses on the sale of "Section 1244 stock" as ordinary losses.[47] Married couples who file a joint return are allowed to recognize up to $100,000 in ordinary losses on the sale of Section 1244 stock each year. Any recognized loss on the sale of Section 1244 stock that exceeds these amounts is treated as a capital loss. Only individuals are entitled to this ordinary loss treatment on the sale of Section 1244 stock.

 Spotlight: Section 1244 applies only to individuals who own stock directly and to individuals who are partners in partnerships that own stock. An individual who is a partner in a partnership at the time the partnership acquired the Section 1244 stock may

---

[47] Code Sec. 1244(a), (b).

> deduct an ordinary loss under Section 1244 if the partner's distributive share of partnership items reflects the loss sustained by the partnership.[48]
>
> The ordinary loss deduction is limited to the *lesser* of the partner's distributive share at the time of the issuance of the stock or the partner's distributive share at the time the partnership realized the loss. To claim a deduction under Section 1244, the individual, or the partnership sustaining the loss must have held the stock from the date of issuance (i.e., be the original owner of the stock).[49]
>
> A corporation, trust, or estate may not deduct an ordinary loss under Section 1244.[50] Individuals who are shareholders of an S corporation may not deduct an ordinary loss under Section 1244 on the sale of small business stock owned by the S corporation.[51]

Section 1244 stock is stock that satisfies the following requirements:[52]

- It is stock in a domestic corporation;
- At the time that the stock was issued, the issuing corporation was a small business corporation; and
- During the issuing corporation's five most recent tax years ending before the date that a loss on the stock was sustained, the issuing corporation derived more than 50 percent of its aggregate gross receipts from sources other than royalties, rents, dividends, interest, annuities, and sales or exchanges of stocks or securities. This requirement does not apply to a corporation if the amount of deductions (not counting net operating loss deductions and dividends received deductions) it has been allowed for the five-year period exceeds the amount of its gross income. Gross receipts from sales or exchanges of stock or securities are taken into account only to the extent of gains from such sales or exchanges.

A corporation is a "small business" if the aggregate amount of money and other property it has received for stock as a contribution to capital and as paid-in surplus does not exceed $1 million as of the time that the stock in question is issued.[53] Amounts received for the stock issued and all stock previously issued count toward the $1 million limitation. Property other than money that is received for stock is taken into account at its adjusted basis to the corporation for determining gain, reduced by any liability to which the property was subject or that was assumed by the corporation at the time that the corporation received the corporation.

If a corporation has not been in existence for five tax years ending before the date that the loss on the stock was sustained, substituted for that five-year period is the period of the corporation's tax years ending before that date or, if the corporation has not been in existence for one tax year ending before that date, the period that the corporation has been in existence before that date.[54]

Example 37: On November 14, 20X1, Dan and Sue Jones contributed $300,000 to a corporation in exchange for 1,000 shares of the corporation's common stock. The corporation qualifies as a small business under Code Sec. 1244. The Joneses sell all 1,000 shares in the corporation on December 12, 20X6, for $140,000. Their recognized loss from the sale is $160,000 ($140,000 – $300,000). The Joneses may deduct $100,000 of this loss as an ordinary loss under Code Sec. 1244. The remaining $60,000 loss is a long-term capital loss. If they did not sell or exchange any other capital assets during the year, they will be able to deduct $3,000 of the long-term capital loss against their ordinary income. They will carry over the remaining $57,000 loss as a long-term capital loss to the next tax year.

---

[48] Reg. § 1.1244(a)-1(b).
[49] Reg. § 1.1244(a)-1(b).
[50] Reg. § 1.1244(a)-1(b).
[51] *V.D. Rath*, 101 TC 196, Dec. 49,266 (1993).

[52] Code Sec. 1244(c).
[53] Code Sec. 1244(c)(3).
[54] Code Sec. 1244(c)(2).

Example 38: In exchange for 100 percent of the stock, Edgar Jones contributed equipment, building, and land to a corporation in a Code Sec. 351 transaction. The corporation assumed a $300,000 mortgage on the building. The FMV and adjusted basis of the property contributed was as follows:

	FMV	Adjusted Basis
Equipment	$200,000	$250,000
Building	1,100,000	800,000
Land	150,000	90,000
Total	$1,450,000	$1,140,000

For purposes of the $1 million limitation, the contributed capital is $840,000 ($1,140,000 – $300,000). Therefore, the corporation qualifies as a small business corporation.

Reason for the Rule: Congress wanted to encourage individuals to invest in small corporations to stimulate the economy and create jobs. Investments in small corporations are risky, especially newer ones. Although the lower tax rates on net capital gains and dividends are an incentive to buy stock, the favorable tax treatment in the event of a loss provides investors with an additional incentive to invest directly in small corporations.

Planning Pointer: The limit on deducting a loss on the sale or exchange of Code Sec. 1244 stock as an ordinary loss is an annual limit. Therefore, a taxpayer who would realize a loss on the sale of Code Sec. 1244 stock that exceeds the limit should consider selling the stock over two or more years. For example, in Example 37, the Joneses could have waited to sell some of their shares until the next tax year. That would have allowed them to deduct the entire $140,000 as an ordinary loss over two tax years. Furthermore, the $50,000/$100,000 annual limit is an aggregate limit applied to each tax return. It is not a limit that is applied on a per corporation basis. Thus, losses on sales of all Section 1244 stock make during the years are included in applying this annual limit.

¶ 904 Section 1231 Gains and Losses

Code Sec. 1221 specifically excludes depreciable property and land used in the taxpayer's trade or business from the definition of a capital asset. If these business properties are held for one year or less at the time they are disposed of, the recognized gain or loss is taxed as ordinary gain or loss. However, if these business properties are held for more than one year (exceptions exist for certain livestock), they fall under the definition of "Section 1231 property." When taxpayers sell Section 1231 property, it usually results in a Section 1231 gain or loss.

.01 Significance of Net Section 1231 Gains

A Section 1231 gain or loss is generally recognized when the taxpayer disposes of Section 1231 property. **Section 1231 property** consists of business property held long-term (more than one year). However, inventory, receivables, and supplies do not qualify as Section 1231 property. Section 1231 gains and losses typically result from sales or exchanges of Section 1231 property. However, they can also result from gains and losses on condemnations of business or investment property that the taxpayer holds for more than one year (see ¶ 809).[55] When accelerated depreciation methods are used to depreciate certain business assets, some of the Section 1231 gain may be recharacterized as ordinary income (see ¶ 904.02). However, because land is nondepreciable property, all recognized gains and losses from the sale or exchange of land that qualifies as Section 1231 property are always treated as Section 1231 gains and losses. Loss recognized on the sale of Section 1231 property is always **Section 1231 loss**, regardless of whether the Section 1231 property was depreciable or nondepreciable property.

When a taxpayer combines all Section 1231 gains and losses for the year and the result is a net Section 1231 loss, all Section 1231 gains and losses are treated as ordinary gains and losses.[56] If a net Section 1231 gain results, the net gain has the potential to be treated as a long-term capital gain.[57] However, the amount equal to any nonrecaptured Section 1231 losses from the previous five years must first be characterized as ordinary income (see ¶ 904.03). Any excess gain is then treated as long-term capital gain.

Example 39: During the year, Hale Co., Inc. sells the following five properties:

Property	Section 1231 Gain (Loss)
Equipment	($ 2,500)
Land	44,000
Machinery	(1,000)
Building	35,000
Truck	(6,400)
Net Section 1231 gain	$69,100

Because Hale has a net Section 1231 gain for the year, its taxable income will increase by $69,100 because of the gains and losses from these five transactions. The $69,100 net Section 1231 gain is added to Hale's long-term capital gain in the netting process of capital gains and losses (assuming that Hale does not have any nonrecaptured Section 1231 losses that recharacterize the gain as ordinary income). By allowing the net Section 1231 gain to be included as long-term capital gain in the netting process, the tax law potentially allows Hale to deduct more capital losses.

Example 40: Assume the same facts as in Example 39, except the land is sold for a $44,000 loss (instead of a $44,000 gain).

Property	Section 1231 Gain (Loss)
Equipment	($ 2,500)
Land	(44,000)
Machinery	(1,000)
Building	35,000
Truck	(6,400)
Net Section 1231 loss	($18,900)

Because Hale has a net Section 1231 loss for the year, all of the Section 1231 gains and losses are treated as ordinary gains and losses. Thus, Hale's taxable income is reduced by the $18,900 net loss. A net Section 1231 loss does not affect the amount of the taxpayer's capital gains and losses involved in the netting process.

---

[55] Code Sec. 1231(a)(3).

[56] Code Sec. 1231(a)(2).

[57] Code Sec. 1231(a)(1).

Spotlight: As illustrated in Examples 39 and 40, Code Sec. 1231 provides taxpayers with the "best of both worlds"—treating net Section 1231 gains as long-term capital gains and treating net Section 1231 losses as ordinary losses. By allowing taxpayers to increase the amount of long-term capital gains, the tax law allows individual taxpayers to pay a lower tax rate on their net Section 1231 gain. Although corporate taxpayers pay the same rate of tax on ordinary income and capital gains, the ability to count net Section 1231 gains as long-term capital gains helps corporations (as well as individuals) avoid being limited on the amount of capital losses they can deduct. Because corporations are allowed to carry back excess capital losses three years, any long-term capital gain recognized in the current year may benefit the corporation for the next three tax years to the extent the corporation incurs capital losses.

.02 Depreciation Recapture

If a taxpayer sells depreciable personal property held for more than one year and recognizes a gain, some or all of the gain may be treated as ordinary gain rather than as long-term capital gain under Section 1231. Due to the accelerated methods available to depreciate tangible personal property (Modified Accelerated Cost Recovery System (MACRS), Section 179, and additional first-year "bonus" depreciation), it is likely that much if not all of the gain on the sale of depreciable property may be due to depreciation deductions, rather than from an actual increase in the value of the property sold.

Section 1245 depreciation recapture. Any gain from the sale of tangible personal property that is attributable to depreciation (and not to an increase in the property's value) is taxed as ordinary income under Code Sec. 1245. Real property placed in service after 1986 is not subject to Code Sec. 1245 depreciation recapture.

The amount of **Section 1245 gain** is equal to the *lesser* of (1) the accumulated depreciation taken on the property or (2) the recognized gain. Accumulated depreciation includes all depreciation taken, including MACRS depreciation, bonus depreciation, and any Section 179 expense. Use of the alternative depreciation system (ADS), does not avoid the Code Sec. 1245 recapture provisions (i.e., the entire amount of straight-line depreciation taken is subject to recapture). Generally, the entire gain on Section 1245 property sales will be taxed as ordinary income. However, if the sales price of the property exceeds the basis before depreciation is deducted (usually the original basis if no adjustments other than depreciation have been made), then *some* of the gain will be Code Sec. 1231 gain.

Example 41: Cross Company sells a machine used in its business for $38,000. The company purchased the machine two years earlier for $40,000 and has claimed depreciation deductions (including Section 179) totaling $22,000. Thus, Cross's adjusted basis in the machine equals $18,000 ($40,000 – $22,000) and the recognized gain on the sale is $20,000 ($38,000 – $18,000). Cross must recognize all $20,000 of the gain as ordinary income under Code Sec. 1245 gain (the *lesser* of (1) $22,000 of depreciation taken or (2) $20,000 of recognized gain). Cross's Section 1231 gain is zero ($20,000 – $20,000).

Example 42: Assume the same facts as in Example 41, except that Cross sold the machine for $45,000. The recognized gain on the sale is $27,000 ($45,000 – $18,000). Cross must recognize $22,000 of the gain as ordinary income under Code Sec. 1245 gain (the *lesser* of (1) $22,000 of depreciation taken or (2) $27,000 of recognized gain). Cross's Section 1231 gain is $5,000 ($27,000 – $22,000). Notice that the $5,000 Section 1231 gain is equal to the excess of the sales price over the original basis.

> **Planning Pointer:** Self-employed taxpayers can benefit by claiming depreciation deductions and Section 179 expense in more ways than just the obvious time value of money. Depreciation and Section 179 expense reduce net earnings from self-employment and the amount of self-employment tax the owner pays. When these amounts are later recaptured on a sale or exchange of the property and taxed as ordinary income, they are not included in the taxpayer's self-employment income.

Section 1250 depreciation recapture. If a taxpayer sells depreciable real estate (such as a building) and realizes a gain, the gain is referred to as **Section 1250 gain** to the extent that the accumulated depreciation taken on the property exceeds what the accumulated depreciation would have been had the straight-line method been used. Because straight-line depreciation is the only method available under MACRS, Section 1250 recapture does not apply to the sale of real property placed in service after 1986. Furthermore, because pre-ACRS property (acquired before 1987) is by now fully depreciated, there is no excess depreciation to recapture on its sale. However, Code Sec. 1250 is relevant for two purposes:

- It applies to Section 291 gain (discussed next); and

- "Unrecaptured Section 1250 gain" affects the tax rate that is applied to individuals on the sale of depreciable real property (see ¶ 907).

Section 291 gain. Even though Section 1250 recapture no longer applies to depreciable realty placed in service after 1986, Code Sec. 291 requires C corporations to treat as ordinary income 20 percent of the gain that would result if the property were Section 1245 property over the amount of ordinary income recognized under Section 1250. Because Section 1250 gain is always zero for property placed in service after 1986, a corporation's **Section 291 gain** (ordinary income from the sale of real property) equals the *lesser* of (1) 20 percent of the accumulated depreciation taken on the property or (2) the recognized gain. Any gain not taxed as ordinary income is treated as Section 1231 gain.

Example 43: DuRite Corporation sells its office building for $500,000 in 20X0. DuRite purchased the building for $400,000, and the corporation has taken $80,000 of straight-line depreciation on the building over the years. Thus, its adjusted basis in the building at the time of the sale is $320,000 ($400,000 – $80,000). DuRite's recognized gain is $180,000 ($500,000 – $320,000). If the building were subject to Section 1245 recapture, its Section 1245 gain would be $80,000 (the *lesser* of the $80,000 accumulated depreciation taken or the $180,000 gain). Under Code Sec. 291, DuRite must recognize $16,000 ($80,000 × 20%) of the gain as ordinary income. The remaining gain of $164,000 ($180,000 – $16,000) is Section 1231 gain.

Example 44: Continuing with Example 43, in addition to selling the building, DuRite also realized the following gain and loss during 20X0:

Gain on the sale of business land held for 12 years	$88,000
Loss on the sale of a warehouse held for 3 years	(40,000)

DuRite computes its net Section 1231 gain or loss as follows:

	Section 1231 Gain (Loss)	Ordinary Gain (Loss)
Office building	$164,000	$16,000
Land	88,000	- 0 -
Warehouse	(40,000)	- 0 -
Total	$212,000	$16,000

DuRite's net Section 1231 gain will be treated as a long-term capital gain for purposes of determining the amount of capital losses DuRite can deduct from gross income in 20X0 (assuming the nonrecaptured Section 1231 gain rules do not apply, see ¶ 904.03.)

Example 45: Assume the same facts as in Example 44, except that the land was sold for a loss of $188,000 (instead of an $88,000 gain). Under this scenario, DuRite has a $64,000 net Section 1231 loss for the year, as shown below:

	Section 1231 Gain (Loss)	Ordinary Gain (Loss)
Office building	$164,000	$16,000
Land	(188,000)	- 0 -
Warehouse	(40,000)	- 0 -
Total	($ 64,000)	$16,000

Code Sec. 1231 does not limit the losses that DuRite can deduct. DuRite treats all Section 1231 gains and losses as ordinary gains and losses. Therefore, all of DuRite's $180,000 of gains for the year ($164,000 + $16,000) are included in gross income, and the entire $228,000 ($188,000 + $40,000) of losses for the year are deducted from gross income.

Depreciation recapture and nontaxable transactions. The general rule relating to the recognition of ordinary income upon the disposition of Section 1245 property does not apply if the property is disposed of in a like-kind exchange (see ¶ 808) or in an involuntary conversion (see ¶ 809). If any gain is recognized in a like-kind exchange or in an involuntary conversion of Section 1245 property, Section 1245 gain must be recognized to the same extent.

Example 46: Alan Starker, who operates a printing shop, trades a used printing press that has a market value of $50,000 for a newer, smaller press that has a market value of $25,000. In the exchange he also receives cash of $10,000 and undeveloped land having a market value of $15,000. Alan originally purchased the printing press for $60,000 and had taken $40,000 in depreciation over the years. Thus, Alan's basis in the old press is $20,000 ($60,000 – $40,000). Alan's realized gain on the exchange is $30,000 ($50,000 – $20,000); however, his recognized gain is limited to the $25,000 of boot received ($10,000 cash + $15,000 FMV of the non-like-kind property). If Alan had sold the printing press for $50,000 cash, he would have recognized the entire $30,000 as ordinary income under Section 1245. However, because Alan's recognized gain under Code Sec. 1031 is limited to $25,000 ($10,000 cash plus the $15,000 FMV of the non-like-kind property), he will recognize $25,000 of Section 1245 gain.

Depreciation recapture from an installment sale. In an installment sale, the taxpayer recognizes gain each year equal to the amount the taxpayer actually or constructively receives during the year multiplied by the gross profit percentage (see ¶ 810.01).[58] However, if the property sold is subject to depreciation recapture, the tax law requires that the *entire amount* of depreciation recapture be recognized as ordinary income in the year of sale, regardless of the amount of cash the taxpayer receives during the year.[59] The amount of the depreciation recapture is then added to the adjusted basis of the property to calculate the gross profit from the sale. The Section 1231 gain the taxpayer will recognize each year is equal to the gross profit percentage multiplied by the cash or its equivalent received as a down payment or as a payment on the principal of the installment note.[60]

Example 47: In 20X1, Anthony Samari paid $45,000 for equipment that he uses in his business. Over the years, Anthony claimed depreciation (including Section 179 expense)

---

[58] Code Sec. 453(c).
[59] Code Sec. 453(i).

[60] Reg. § 1.1245-6(d).

totaling $28,000. In 20X3 he sells the equipment for $60,000. The terms of sale require the buyer to make a $20,000 cash payment at the time of sale and to pay $20,000 on the principal of the installment note one year after the sale date and another $20,000 on the principal of the installment note two years after the sale date. The buyer also agreed to pay the accrued interest on each payment date. The payments to be made were evidenced by a $40,000 installment note that bears interest at the market rate. The tax consequences of the installment sale are as follows:

Cash paid at the time of sale	$20,000
Installment note	40,000
Amount realized	$60,000
Less: Adjusted basis ($45,000 – $28,000)	(17,000)
Realized gain	$43,000

Anthony recognizes $28,000 as ordinary income in the year of sale. The amount taxed as Section 1245 gain is the *lesser* of (1) the $28,000 of accumulated depreciation or (2) the $43,000 gain from the sale. He adds the $28,000 to the adjusted basis of the asset to calculate his gross profit on the installment sale. Anthony computes his gross profit and gross profit percentage from the installment sale as follows:

Selling price	$60,000
Less: Adjusted basis ($17,000 + $28,000)	(45,000)
Gross profit from the sale	$15,000

$$\text{Gross profit percentage} = \$15,000 \div \$60,000 = 25\%$$

In the year of the sale (20X3), Anthony recognizes a Section 1231 gain of $5,000 ($20,000 × 25%) from the cash received at the time of the sale. He also recognizes the $28,000 of Section 1245 gain (ordinary income). The $5,000 of Section 1231 gain will be offset against other Section 1231 gains and losses for the year. In 20X4, Anthony will recognize a Section 1231 gain of $5,000 ($20,000 × 25%), and in 20X5, he will recognize the remaining $5,000 of Section 1231 gain ($20,000 × 25%). Anthony will also recognize the interest from the note that the buyer pays. Over the three years, Anthony will recognize $43,000 of total gain as follows:

Character of the gain:

Section 1245 gain	$28,000
Section 1231 gain ($5,000 + $5,000 + $5,000)	15,000
Total gain recognized	$43,000

.03 Nonrecaptured Section 1231 Losses

If a taxpayer incurs a net Section 1231 loss for the year, the loss is treated as an ordinary loss. However, when the taxpayer has a net Section 1231 gain in a subsequent tax year, the net gain is normally treated as long-term capital gain. Like the depreciation recapture rules, which attempt to counteract the tax benefits associated with ordinary deductions in one year followed by preferential long-term capital gains in another, the tax laws require that net Section 1231 gain be recaptured as ordinary income to the extent that the taxpayer has "nonrecaptured Section 1231 losses" from the previous five tax years.[61]

Example 48: In the current year, a corporation has $55,000 of net Section 1231 gains. Over the past five tax years, the corporation has deducted net Section 1231 losses as ordinary losses, and the amount of nonrecaptured net Section 1231 losses at the beginning of the year is $35,000. Although the entire $55,000 of net Section 1231 increases the taxpayer's taxable income, the corporation is taxed on the first $35,000 of the gain as ordinary income. It can then treat the remaining $20,000 of net Section 1231 gain ($55,000 – $35,000) as long-term capital gain. Therefore, $20,000 of the gain can be used to offset capital losses in the current year. If the corporation's capital losses in the current year are less than its capital gains, the excess capital gain can be used to offset excess capital losses recognized over the next three years when such excess losses are carried back three tax years.

Reason for the Rule: Before the Deficit Reduction Act of 1984, a taxpayer's net Section 1231 gain was treated as a long-term capital gain. Good tax planners advised their clients to claim their Section 1231 losses in one tax year and their Section 1231 gains in another tax year. Taxpayers who did this could recognize all of their Section 1231 losses as ordinary losses and all their Section 1231 gains as long-term capital gains. Congress decided to minimize the benefits of this tax planning strategy by requiring taxpayers to treat net Section 1231 gains as ordinary income to the extent of their net Section 1231 losses recognized in the previous five years.

The Section 1231 look-back provision requires that net Section 1231 gain in the current year be recognized as ordinary income to the extent of the taxpayer's nonrecaptured net Section 1231 losses from the previous five years. Any remaining net Section 1231 gain can be treated as a long-term capital gain. The look-back provision requires that in any year in which a taxpayer reports a net Section 1231 gain it must determine how much of the net Section 1231 losses in the previous five years have not yet been "paid back" through the recharacterization of net Section 1231 gain as ordinary income. These net Section 1231 losses from the last five tax years that have not been "paid back" are called **nonrecaptured net Section 1231 losses**. The calculation of nonrecaptured net Section 1231 losses is illustrated in the McMillan example below.

Example 49: McMillan, Inc. has recognized the following net Section 1231 gains and losses over the past five years. McMillan's first year of operations was 20X1.

Year	Net Section 1231 Gain (Loss)
20X1	$12,000
20X2	(14,200)
20X3	3,700
20X4	(18,900)
20X5	5,200

In 20X1, McMillan reports a net Section 1231 gain of $12,000. Because 20X1 is McMillan's first year of operations, there are zero nonrecaptured Section 1231 losses. Therefore, the entire $12,000 is treated as long-term capital gain.

In 20X2, the company has a net Section 1231 loss of $14,200. This amount is deducted as an ordinary loss from McMillan's gross income in 20X2. Because McMillan benefits from being able to deduct this amount against income that is

---

[61] Code Sec. 1231(c).

taxed at the ordinary income tax rates, the $14,200 becomes McMillan's nonrecaptured Section 1231 loss at the end of 20X2.

In 20X3, McMillan reports a $3,700 net Section 1231 gain. This gain is taxed as ordinary income to counteract the ordinary deduction it received in the prior tax year. Because McMillan "pays back" $3,700 of its prior net Section 1231 losses, its nonrecaptured Section 1231 loss at the end of 20X3 is reduced to $10,500 ($14,200 – $3,700).

In 20X4, McMillan reports an $18,900 net Section 1231 loss and deducts this amount as ordinary loss. McMillan's nonrecaptured Section 1231 losses for the past five years increase to $29,400 ($10,500 + $18,900).

In 20X5, the company reports a $5,200 net Section 1231 gain. The entire gain is taxed as ordinary income under the look-back provision, and McMillan's nonrecaptured Section 1231 losses are reduced to $24,200 ($29,400 – $5,200).

McMillan's nonrecaptured Section 1231 losses are summarized as follows:

Year	Amount of Net Section 1231 Gain (Loss)	Amount of Nonrecaptured Section 1231 Losses
20X1	$12,000	$ 0
20X2	(14,200)	14,200
20X3	3,700	10,500
20X4	(18,900)	29,400
20X5	5,200	24,200

If in 20X6 McMillan has a net Section 1231 gain of $29,800, only the first $24,200 of this gain will be treated as ordinary income. The remaining $5,600 ($29,800 – $24,200) will be treated as a long-term capital gain. The company's nonrecaptured Section 1231 losses will be zero at the end of 20X6.

Planning Pointer: If a taxpayer recognizes Section 1231 gains and had no nonrecaptured net Section 1231 losses in the previous five years, the taxpayer may treat the net Section 1231 gain as a long-term capital gain. Net section 1231 losses incurred in subsequent years will be deductible as ordinary losses. Therefore, a good tax-planning strategy for taxpayers who have no nonrecaptured net Section 1231 losses is to first sell Section 1231 assets that create gains and then, the following tax year, sell any Section 1231 assets that will produce losses. This point is illustrated in Example 46.

Example 50: Frank Adams operates a farming business as a sole proprietor. His long-term capital gains are taxed at 15 percent. His ordinary income is taxed at 25 percent. Frank is considering selling a tractor and a parcel of land used in his farming business. Based on good estimates of their FMVs, Frank concludes that the sale of his tractor will result in an $8,000 Section 1231 loss, and the sale of his farmland will result in a $12,000 Section 1231 gain. These are the only assets Frank will be selling during the year.

If Frank sells both assets in the current year, he will have a net Section 1231 gain of $4,000 ($12,000 – $8,000), which will be taxed as a long-term capital gain. His tax associated with the net gain will be $600 ($4,000 × 15%). However, if Frank waits to sell the tractor until the next tax year, he will report a $12,000 net Section 1231 gain in the current year, which will be taxed as a long-term capital gain. His tax associated with that gain will be $1,800 ($12,000 × 15%). In the next year Frank will report an $8,000 net Section 1231 loss that he can fully deduct as an ordinary loss.

His tax savings from the loss will be $2,000 ($8,000 × 25%). When the tax consequences for the two years are combined, Frank will save $200 in taxes ($2,000 reduction in taxes in the second year – $1,800 taxes owed in the first year).

When the two alternatives are compared, Frank will pay $600 in taxes under the first scenario but save $200 in taxes under the second scenario. This $800 difference in tax liability is due to the tax benefits of deducting losses as ordinary losses and taxing gains as long-term capital gains.

 Planning Pointer: In Example 50, Frank was able to engage in effective tax planning by selling Section 1231 property at a gain the year before he sold Section 1231 property at a loss. If the situation were reversed and Frank had sold the loss property first, the Section 1231 look-back provision would have taxed the subsequent Section 1231 gain as ordinary income.

¶ 905 Business Casualty and Theft Gains and Losses

When business property is involved in a casualty or theft, the amount of the loss depends on whether the business property is partially or completely destroyed.[62] For completely destroyed business property, the amount of the loss is the taxpayer's adjusted basis in the property minus any insurance reimbursement. If the insurance proceeds exceed the taxpayer's adjusted basis in the property, a casualty gain results. For partially destroyed business property, the amount of the loss is measured as the *lesser* of (1) the taxpayer's adjusted basis in the property or (2) the decrease in the property's FMV. Any insurance reimbursement the taxpayer receives is subtracted from the lesser of the two amounts. (see ¶ 802.02). If the insurance proceeds exceed the taxpayer's adjusted basis in the partially destroyed business property, a casualty gain results.

Gains and losses from business property involved in a casualty or theft are treated as ordinary gains and losses if the business property was held for no more than one year. A loss recognized on a casualty or theft of business property held for more than one year is treated as a "business casualty or theft loss." A gain recognized on a casualty or theft of business property held for more than one year is subject to the same depreciation recapture rules as discussed previously in the chapter (see ¶ 904.02). After the appropriate amount of the gain from business property involved in a casualty or theft has been taxed as ordinary income, any remaining gain is treated as a "business casualty or theft gain."

Example 51: Anniston's corporate warehouse is completely destroyed by a fire. Anniston purchased the warehouse for $300,000. It had taken depreciation deductions over the years of $100,000. The insurance company reimburses Anniston $250,000 for its loss. Because the amount of the reimbursement ($250,000) exceeds the taxpayer's $200,000 ($300,000 – $100,000) adjusted basis in the warehouse, Anniston recognizes a $50,000 business casualty gain ($250,000 – $200,000). Although Code Sec. 1250 depreciation recapture does not apply to realty placed in service after 1986, C corporations are required to recognize as ordinary income under Code Sec. 291 the *lesser* of (1) 20 percent of the $100,000 depreciation taken on the property or (2) the $50,000 gain. Thus, of the $50,000 gain, Anniston must recognize $10,000 as ordinary income ($50,000 × 20%) and $40,000 ($50,000 – $10,000) as business casualty and theft gain.

Example 52: A taxpayer has three casualty and theft events during the year that involve business property held for more than a year. The first involves an automobile, the second involves the taxpayer's office building, and the third involves computer equipment.

---

[62] Reg. § 1.165-7(b).

The taxpayer's adjusted basis in each type of property, each type of property's FMV before and after the casualty or theft, and any insurance proceeds are:

Property	Adjusted Basis	FMV Before	FMV After	Insurance Proceeds
Automobile	$ 2,000	$ 7,000	$ 0	$ 6,500
Office building	180,000	220,000	190,000	28,000
Computer	1,500	1,000	0	0

Because the automobile is completely destroyed in the casualty (evidenced by the $0 FMV after the event) the amount of the casualty loss is measured as the adjusted basis ($2,000) minus the amount of the insurance reimbursement ($6,500). When the insurance proceeds are subtracted from the adjusted basis, a casualty loss does not result. Thus, the taxpayer recognizes a gain to the extent that the insurance proceeds exceed its adjusted basis in the property, or $4,500 ($6,500 – $2,000). However, to the extent that this gain is attributable to depreciation (and not a decline in the value of the automobile), the gain will be taxed as ordinary income under Code Sec. 1245.

Because the office building is partially destroyed by the casualty, the amount of the casualty loss is measured as the excess of the *lesser* of the adjusted basis of the property ($180,000) or its decline in value ($220,0000 – $190,000 = $30,000) over the $28,000 of insurance proceeds. Therefore, the taxpayer's business casualty loss equals $2,000 ($30,000 – $28,000). Because the computer equipment was stolen, the theft loss is measured as its adjusted basis ($1,500) minus the amount of the insurance reimbursement ($0).

All business casualty and theft gains and losses are netted against one another at the end of the year. If a net business casualty and theft loss results, the business casualty and theft gains and losses are treated as ordinary gains and losses.[63] If, however, the taxpayer has a net business casualty and theft gain, the gains and losses are treated as Section 1231 gains and losses, and the net gain is added to the taxpayer's other Section 1231 gains and losses.[64]

Example 53:   Continuing with Example 52, assuming that the taxpayer's entire $4,500 gain on the automobile is taxed as ordinary income under Code Sec. 1245, the taxpayer's business casualty and theft loss for the year equals $3,500 ($2,000 + $1,500). This net business casualty and theft loss is deducted as an ordinary loss from the taxpayer's gross income.

¶ 906 Review of the Netting Process

All gains and losses are taxed either as ordinary gains and losses or as capital gains and losses. The netting process of gains and losses from the disposal of long-term business property and capital assets is used to determine the taxpayer's ordinary versus capital gains or losses. When completing the taxpayer's income tax return, this netting process starts with computing the taxpayer's recognized gain or loss for each property disposed of during the year (see Chapter 8). Once the taxpayer's recognized gain or loss is determined, it is important to apply the rules from this chapter to determine the character of the recognized gain or loss. Initially gain or loss can be classified into one of the following five categories:

1. Casualty or theft gains and losses from long-term business property (Note that condemnations of business property and property held for the production of income are automatically Code Sec. 1231 items, and are *not* included with casualty gains and losses);

2. Section 1231 gain or loss (after Code Secs. 1245, 1250, and 291 have been considered and the ordinary income component of any gain has been removed);

---

[63] Code Sec. 1231(a)(4).   [64] Code Sec. 1231(a)(3)(A)(ii).

3. Short-term capital gain or loss;

4. Long-term capital gain or loss; and

5. Ordinary income (includes all depreciation recapture, Section 1231 gains recharacterized as ordinary income due to nonrecaptured Section 1231 losses, and gains and losses from short-term property that is not a capital asset).

The netting process is illustrated in Figure 9-1. In order to make sure that all capital gains and losses are properly recorded and the rules of the netting process are followed, the netting process must begin with the netting of business casualty and theft gains and losses, followed by the netting of Section 1231 gains and losses, and then the netting of capital gains and losses.

Figure 9-1 Summary of the Netting Process

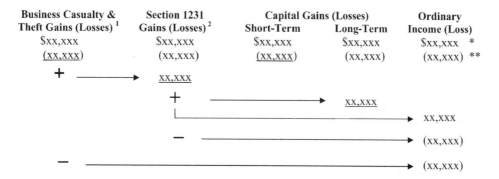

*In addition to ordinary income derived from business profits, interest, or dividend income, etc., amounts in this column include any depreciation recapture under Code Secs. 1245, 1250, or 291 resulting from the sale, exchange, or destruction of Section 1231 property. The column also includes any gain from the sale or exchange of business property held short-term (one year or less) or from casualty gains involving short-term business property.

**In addition to ordinary losses resulting from business activities, this amount includes losses from the sale of business property held short-term as well as casualty and theft losses involving business property held short-term.

[1] The amounts reported reflect only the gains and losses from business property damaged or destroyed in a casualty or theft. Business gains reported in this column are shown after any depreciation recapture associated with the casualty or theft gain has been removed and placed in the far right column as ordinary income (designated by an asterisk "*"). If a net business casualty and theft gain results, the net gain is included in the column along with other Section 1231 gains and losses. If a net business casualty and theft loss results, the net loss reduces ordinary income.

[2] The amounts reported are Section 1231 gains and losses from the sale or exchange of Section 1231 property, as well as gains and losses resulting from the condemnation of business property. Any amounts representing depreciation recapture of Section 1231 property are not included in this column but instead are reported in the far right column as ordinary income (designated by an asterisk "*"). If a net Section 1231 gain results, the gain is either ordinary income (to the extent of nonrecaptured Section 1231 losses) or long-term capital gain. Because a net Section 1231 loss reduces ordinary income, it is shown as a negative amount in the ordinary income (loss) column.

Example 54: After taking into consideration the depreciation recapture rules, Basken, a C corporation, has the following casualty and theft gains and losses resulting from business property held for more than one year:

Business casualty gain	$54,000
Business casualty loss	(36,000)
Theft loss	(6,000)

Basken's net business casualty and theft gain equals $12,000 ($54,000 – $36,000 – $6,000). It treats the $12,000 as Section 1231 gain and adds this amount to its other Section 1231 gains and losses for the year.

Example 55: Continuing with Example 54, during the year Basken has a Section 1231 gain of $15,000 and a Section 1231 loss of $4,000. Basken's net Section 1231 gain of $23,000 is computed as follows:

Section 1231 gain	$15,000
Section 1231 loss	(4,000)
Business casualty gain treated as Section 1231 gain	12,000
Net Section 1231 gain	$23,000

If Basken has $5,000 of nonrecaptured Section 1231 losses from the last five years, it treats $5,000 of its net Section 1231 gain as ordinary income and treats the remaining $18,000 ($23,000 – $5,000) as long-term capital gain in the netting process of capital gains and losses. Thus, to the extent that Basken incurs capital losses during the year, the $18,000 can be used to offset those losses.

Example 56: Continuing with Example 55, during the year Basken has a long-term capital loss of $6,000 and a short-term capital loss of $3,000. Basken's netting of capital gains and losses is as follows:

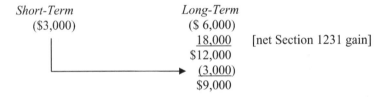

Basken is able to use the $18,000 net Section 1231 gain that is treated as long-term capital gain to reduce its $9,000 total capital losses for the year. The $9,000 excess of capital gains increases Basken's taxable income by $9,000 for the year.

Example 57: George Restin is in the 25 percent tax bracket. He has the following gains and losses during the year (after taking into consideration the depreciation recapture rules):

Section 1231 gain	$25,000
Section 1231 loss	(9,000)
Business casualty gain treated as Section 1231 gain	12,000
Net Section 1231 gain	$28,000

In addition to those gains and losses, George also has $30,000 of long-term capital losses during the year. If George has no nonrecaptured Section 1231 losses from the last five years, the entire $28,000 is treated as long-term capital gain in the netting process of capital gains and losses. Because George is an individual taxpayer, he is allowed to deduct up to $3,000 of capital losses in excess of capital gains. Therefore, his capital losses are limited to the $28,000 of long-term capital gain (from net Section 1231 gains) plus $3,000, or $31,000. Therefore, George will be allowed to deduct the entire $30,000 capital loss on his individual income tax return. When

George includes the $28,000 of long-term capital gain in his gross income and deducts the $30,000 capital loss from gross income, his AGI will decrease by $2,000 ($28,000 − $30,000).

Example 58: Assume the same facts as in Example 57, except George does not have any other capital gains or losses during the year except those that result from his net Section 1231 gain. George's AGI will increase by the $28,000 gain. However, when George computes the tax on his taxable income, the maximum tax rate on his $28,000 net capital gain ($28,000 net long-term capital gain in excess of $0 short-term capital losses) will be 15 percent (see ¶ 405.02).

.01 Netting Process for Flow-Through Entities

The netting process applies only to individual and corporate taxpayers. Because flow-through entities do not pay income taxes, the tax consequences of the gains and losses recognized by those entities are determined on the owners' income tax returns. Because different rules apply to individual and corporate taxpayers and because the limitations that apply to capital losses must be applied independently for each taxpayer, flow-through entities are responsible for summarizing the various categories of gains and losses they recognize during the year. This includes not only their net short-term capital gain (loss) and net long-term capital gain (loss) but also the amount of net Section 1231 gain (loss) and net business casualty and theft gain (loss).

When a flow-through entity sells property at a gain and the property is subject to depreciation recapture, the amount recaptured is determined by the entity and separated from the remaining gain. Gains and losses from business casualties and thefts, Section 1231 property, and capital assets must be kept separate from ordinary income because the owners include their respective shares of the gains and losses in their own netting process on their income tax returns. Because all taxpayers pay tax on ordinary income at the regular tax rates, amounts set aside for depreciation recapture are combined with the other items of ordinary income or loss recognized by the entity.

¶ 907 Long-Term Capital Gains for Individual Taxpayers

Individuals and corporations use a similar netting process to determine the tax consequences of gains and losses on the sale of business and investment property. Capital losses are netted against capital gains, and long-term gains and losses are separated from short-term gains and losses during the netting process. Corporate taxpayers pay the same rate of tax on all types of income, including gains from the sale of property, whereas the tax rates on long-term capital gains for individual taxpayers can be taxed at 0, 15, 20, 25, or 28 percent, depending on the type of asset sold and the taxpayer's tax bracket.

Gains from the sale of small business stock that qualify for the Code Sec. 1202 exclusion (see ¶ 806) plus gains and losses on the sale of collectibles held for more than one year are taxed at a maximum 28-percent tax rate (instead of the lower 0, 15, or 20 percent tax rate). **Collectibles** include antiques, stamps, coins, rugs, artwork, alcoholic beverages, gems, and metals.[65]

As discussed previously, after Section 1231 gains and losses are netted against one another any net Section 1231 gain is taxed as ordinary income to the extent of nonrecaptured Section 1231 losses for the past five years. Any excess gain is treated as long-term capital gain. Consequently, when individual taxpayers sell depreciable real business property at a gain, the Section 1231 gain may end up being taxed at the lower capital gain tax rate. Often, the reason depreciable property is sold at a gain is because its adjusted basis has been significantly reduced by depreciation expense.

To the extent that gain on the sale of depreciable real property is due to depreciation (and not appreciation in value), such gain is subject to a maximum 25-percent tax rate (instead of the lower 0- or 15- or 20-percent tax rate).[66] The gain taxed due to depreciation of real property is known as

---

[65] Code Sec. 1(h)(5)(A).   [66] Code Sec. 1(h)(1).

unrecaptured Section 1250 gain. The amount of this gain equals the *lesser* of (1) the amount of the recognized gain or (2) the amount of accumulated depreciation taken on the property.[67]

Example 59: Joe Ackers, a single taxpayer, sells an apartment building for $440,000. Joe purchased the building years ago for $300,000, and over the years, he deducted MACRS totaling $100,000. Joe's adjusted basis in the building is $200,000 ($300,000 – $100,000), and his gain on the sale equals $240,000 ($440,000 – $200,000). Because Joe took depreciation deductions totaling $100,000 with respect to this property, $100,000 of the gain is unrecaptured Section 1250 gain, which is taxed at a maximum 25-percent tax rate. The remaining $140,000 of gain ($240,000 – $100,000) is taxed at a maximum 20 percent rate if Joe's marginal tax rate is 39.6 percent). The amount taxed as long-term capital gain represents the gain due to appreciation during Joe's ownership of the building ($440,000 – $300,000 cost basis).

 Spotlight: The 25-percent maximum tax rate applies only to *gains* from the sale of depreciable realty. When depreciable realty is sold at a loss, the loss is treated as a Section 1231 loss. When Section 1231 losses exceed Section 1231 gains, the net Section 1231 loss is deducted against ordinary income and is not part of the netting process involving capital gains and losses.

¶ 908 Summary

The process of computing the correct amount of recognized gain or loss (Chapter 8), along with the process of determining the character of that gain or loss (Chapter 9), are critical to correctly calculating a taxpayer's taxable income and income tax liability. Both corporate and individual taxpayers are limited on the amount of capital losses they can deduct in any given tax year. The best way to ensure that capital losses are not limited is to generate sufficient capital gains during the tax year.

Capital gains are generated through the sale of capital assets and in several other ways. The most common way is through the sale of Section 1231 (long-term business) property. The tax laws governing Section 1231 property are, for the most part, taxpayer-friendly. However, the depreciation recapture and Section 1231 look-back rules counteract the tax benefits associated with taking ordinary deductions, thereby making it more difficult for taxpayers to generate capital gains from the sale of business property.

GLOSSARY OF TERMS INTRODUCED IN THE CHAPTER

Capital asset. Any property other than property listed in Code Sec. 1221. In general, a capital asset is either an asset held for investment or a personal-use asset.

Collectibles. Works of art, antiques, rugs, metals, gems, stamps, coins, and other similar items of tangible personal property. If held more than a year, collectibles are subject to a maximum 28-percent tax rate when sold.

Holding period. Time period that generally begins the day after a taxpayer acquires property and ends on the day the taxpayer disposes of the property. Used to determine whether a recognized gain or loss is short-term or long-term.

Long-term capital gain or loss. A capital gain or loss on a capital asset held for more than one year.

---

[67] Code Sec. 1(h)(6).

Medicare tax on unearned income. Commonly referred to as the Investment Income Tax (NIIT). A tax at the rate of 3.8 percent levied on the net investment income of high income taxpayers.

Net capital gain. The excess of a net long-term capital gain over any net short-term capital loss. Relevant to individual taxpayers because it is subject to reduced tax rates.

Net long-term capital gain. The excess of long-term capital gains over long-term capital losses.

Net long-term capital loss. The excess of long-term capital losses over long-term capital gains.

Net short-term capital gain. The excess of short-term capital gains over short-term capital losses.

Net short-term capital loss. The excess of short-term capital losses over short-term capital gains.

Nonrecaptured net Section 1231 losses. The net Section 1231 losses recognized in the previous five tax years that have not previously caused a net Section 1231 gain to be treated as ordinary income.

Section 291 gain. Ordinary income recognized on the sale of depreciable real property that is sold by a C corporation.

Section 1231 gain. The gain on the sale, exchange, or condemnation of Section 1231 property other than ordinary gain due to depreciation recapture.

Section 1231 loss. A loss on the sale, exchange, or condemnation of Section 1231 property.

Section 1231 property. Land or depreciable property used in a business and held for more than one year.

Section 1244 stock. Stock issued by a domestic corporation in exchange for money or property at a time the corporation does not have more than $1 million in paid-in capital. The corporation must also meet an active business requirement unless it is a new corporation.

Section 1245 gain. The (ordinary income) gain that results from depreciation recapture on depreciable personal property held for more than one year. The amount of gain is equal to the *lesser* of the amount of the gain or the accumulated depreciation taken on the property.

Section 1250 gain. The (ordinary income) gain on the sale of depreciable real property that is recaptured as ordinary income. The amount recaptured is the *lesser* of the amount of the gain or the excess of the depreciation taken over the amount that would have been allowed under the straight-line method.

Short-term capital gain or loss. A capital gain or loss on a capital asset held for one year or less.

Unrecaptured Section 1250 gain. A term applicable only to individual taxpayers. The portion of the gain on the sale of depreciable realty that is taxed at a maximum 25-percent tax rate.

CHAPTER PROBLEMS

Chapter 9 Discussion Questions

1. How is net capital gain calculated? What tax rates apply to net capital gains recognized by individual taxpayers?

2. Discuss the significance of a capital gain or loss.

3. a. What are the tax consequences to an individual who has an overall capital loss of $8,000?

   b. What are the tax consequences to a corporate taxpayer that has an overall net capital loss of $8,000?

4. a. What tax treatment applies to a capital loss carryover when an unmarried individual dies?

   b. What tax treatment applies to a capital loss carryover when a married individual dies and the couple files a joint return?

5. What is the tax treatment of a nonbusiness bad debt?

6. What rules apply to the recognition of a loss on a worthless security?

7. Why is equipment used in the taxpayer's business not considered a capital asset?

8. Under what circumstances will the gain on the sale of land be an ordinary gain, a capital gain, or a Section 1231 gain?

9. a. How long must a taxpayer hold a capital asset for the gain on its sale or exchange to be a long-term capital gain?

   b. How is the holding period determined if the taxpayer received the asset by inheritance?

   c. How is the holding period determined if the taxpayer received the asset in a like-kind exchange?

10. How do the tax laws treat the gain on the sale of a capital asset to a related person?

11. What special rule applies to the sale of a patent? What is the difference between a sale of a patent and a licensing of the right to use the patent?

12. Sharon Moss bought a tract of land in 20X1 as an investment. In 20X3, she subdivided the land into 20 lots but made no further improvements on them. In 20X7, she sold nine lots for a total of $315,000. The adjusted basis of each lot is $5,000. The total selling expense for the nine lots was $3,510. How are the gains on the lots and their selling expense treated for income tax purposes?

13. How much of a loss on the sale of Section 1244 stock may an unmarried individual recognize as an ordinary loss? How much of a loss on the sale of Section 1244 stock may a married couple recognize as an ordinary loss on a joint return? What is the tax treatment of any loss recognized on the sale of Section 1244 stock that exceeds the amount the taxpayer may recognize as an ordinary loss?

14. Discuss how taxpayers receive "the best of both worlds" with respect to Code Sec. 1231.

15. The gain on the sale of an asset used in a business can be comprised of both a Section 1245 gain and a Section 1231 gain. Can a loss on the sale of business property be comprised of both a Section 1245 loss and a Section 1231 loss?

16. Does an individual who operates a business as a sole proprietorship include capital gains and losses recognized on the sale or exchange of business property in calculating the net profit or loss from the business?

17. Does a taxpayer recognize ordinary income on the sale of depreciable personal property if the straight-line method (under ADS) is used?

18. Is depreciation recapture on the sale of depreciable realty placed in service after 1986 relevant to C corporations?

19. Explain the rationale of Congress when it enacted the depreciation recapture rules of Code Sec. 1245?

20. If a taxpayer sells a depreciable asset on the installment basis, what effect does Section 1245 recapture have on the amount of gain that must be recognized in the year of sale?

Chapter 9 Problems

1. Higgins Corporation realized the following capital gains and losses during 20X6:

Short-term capital gain from the sale of land held for investment	$10,000
Short-term capital loss from the sale of common stock	(18,000)
Long-term capital gain from the sale of corporate bonds	6,000
Long-term capital loss from the sale of common stock	(4,000)

Determine the effects of these transactions. Assume that Higgins Corporation had a net long-term capital gain of $1,000 in 20X3, a net long-term capital gain of $1,500 in 20X4, and a net short-term capital gain of $2,500 in 20X5.

2. Skagway Co., Inc. recognizes the following capital gains and losses during 20X4:

Short-term capital gain	$ 10,000
Short-term capital loss	(33,000)
Long-term capital gain	15,000
Long-term capital loss	(44,000)

On its 20X1 tax return, Skagway's netting of its capital gains and losses produced a net capital gain of $7,000.

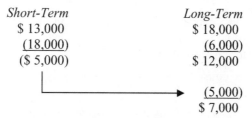

Compute Skagway's capital loss carryback to 20X1 and determine its capital loss carryover to 20X2.

3. Answer the same questions posed in Problem 2, except assume that the taxpayer is Damon Skadden, an individual taxpayer.

4. Roger Dales has $10,000 of ordinary income. In addition, Roger has a $5,000 long-term capital loss and a $500 short-term capital gain. How much of the capital loss can be used against ordinary income? What happens to the remaining loss?

5. Tony Rogers recognizes the following capital gains and losses during 2015:

Short-term capital gain from the sale of stock held for investment	$20,000
Short-term capital loss from the sale of land held as an investment	(22,000)
Long-term capital gain from the sale of corporate bonds	20,000
Long-term capital loss from the sale of common stock	(14,000)

Compute Tony's net capital gain. If Tony's taxable income (before considering the above items of gain or loss) is $55,000, what would be his 2015 tax liability? Tony's filing status is single.

6. Mark and Sara Hopkins are married and file a joint return. In 20X1, they invested $600,000 in NuTech Company. The stock qualifies as Section 1244 stock. On December 17, 20X6, they sold all of their NuTech Company stock for $100,000. They did not realize any other capital gains or losses during 20X6. What are the tax effects of the sale of the stock? If they

called you just before they sold all of their NuTech Company stock, what advice would you give them that would provide them with a more favorable tax result?

7. Hank Jarbee bought 1,000 shares of WentLo Company for $20,000 on November 6, 20X5. The company declared bankruptcy on February 5, 20X6. The bankruptcy case was closed on October 12, 20X6, and at that time the court informed the shareholders that their shares were worthless. What is the tax effect of Hank's loss?

8. A taxpayer purchases land held as an investment for $280,000 on January 5, 20X1. The taxpayer sells the land for $300,000 on January 5, 20X2. Compute the amount and character of the taxpayer's gain or loss.

9. Assume the same facts as in Problem 8, except the land was used in the taxpayer's trade or business. Compute the amount and character of the taxpayer's gain or loss.

10. A C corporation purchased an office building on January 1, 20X1, for $225,000 (not including the land on which the building was located). On January 1, 20X7, the corporation sells the building for $375,000. Depreciation of $93,750 was taken on the building using MACRS. Compute the amount and character of the recognized gain or loss from the sale.

11. Carla Anderson loaned her friend Debbie Jarvis $1,000 for personal purposes on May 8, 2014. On November 16, 2015, Debbie declared bankruptcy. Carla has learned that her loan is worthless. What is the tax effect to Carla?

12. Three years ago, Roswell Copying purchased a color copier for $80,000 and expensed it under Code Sec. 179 in the year it was placed in service. In the current year, Roswell traded in the old copier for a newer, smaller model worth $15,000. In exchange for the new copier, the manufacturer took Roswell's old copier and gave Roswell $5,000 cash. Compute the amount and nature of Roswell's gain or loss from the exchange.

13. Terrance Vincent sold a capital asset to a corporation in which he owned 60 percent of the value of the outstanding shares of stock. Terrance paid $50,000 for the asset three earlier, and the sales price to the corporation is $120,000.

    a. What are the tax consequences if the property is a capital asset in the hands of the corporation?

    b. What are the tax consequences if the property is depreciable Section 1231 property in the hands of the corporation?

    c. How would your answer to parts a. and b. change if Terrance owned 50 percent of the value of the outstanding shares in the C corporation?

14. John Adner, a farmer, subdivided an unimproved tract of land that he acquired approximately 20 years ago. In 20X1, he sold four lots for $10,000 each. The basis of each lot is $2,000, and the selling expenses are $400 per lot.

    a. What is the gain or loss on these transactions, and how will these transactions be taxed?

    b. If John sells five lots in 20X2 at the same price with selling expenses of $400 per lot, what will be the gain or loss, and how will these transactions be taxed?

15. Joan Miller purchased equipment for $50,000 and placed it in service in her business. Two years later, she sold the equipment after having claimed $33,000 in depreciation and Section 179 expense. Calculate the amount and character of Joan's recognized gain or loss assuming that the amount realized from the sale is:

    a. $12,000.

    b. $45,000.

    c. $60,000.

16. Finley Enterprises sold an apartment building in 2015 for $1 million. Finley purchased the building years ago for $780,000. Over the years, it claimed straight-line depreciation of $200,000 on the building. Finley has no other Section 1231 gains or losses or capital gains

or losses during 2015. Finley does not have any nonrecaptured net Section 1231 losses from prior years. What are the tax consequences from the sale of the apartment building?

17. Cavanaugh Inc. sold a machine in 20X5. The terms of the sale stipulate that Cavanaugh is to receive a cash payment of $10,000 at the time of the sale and an installment note that calls for four annual payments of $20,000 on principal plus interest at 10 percent beginning one year after the date of sale. Cavanaugh purchased the machine in 20X1 for $59,000 and at the time of the sale had claimed $40,000 in depreciation and Section 179 expense. The machine was subject to a mortgage of $14,000, which the buyer assumed. Based on this information, calculate:

a. Cavanaugh's realized gain or loss;

b. Cavanaugh's gross profit from the sale, total contract price, and gross profit percentage;

c. The amount and character of the gain recognized in 20X5; and

d. The amount and character of the gain to be recognized in each year from 20X6 though 20X9.

18. Max Wyatt has a $2,000 short-term capital gain on the sale of common stock, a $6,000 short-term capital loss on the sale of land held for investment, a $5,000 long-term capital loss on the sale of land held for investment, a $4,000 Section 1245 gain from the sale of depreciable equipment, and a $10,000 long-term capital gain on the sale of common stock.

a. What is Max's net short-term capital gain or loss?

b. What is Max's net long-term capital gain or loss?

c. What is Max's net capital gain?

19. For 20X6, Brandon Manufacturing has a net Section 1231 gain of $28,000. Brandon reported the net Section 1231 gains or (losses) for the previous five years shown below. None of the losses ever caused a net Section 1231 gain in any year before 20X1 to be treated as an ordinary gain.

20X1	($14,000)
20X2	(7,000)
20X3	9,000
20X4	6,000
20X5	(2,000)

How much of the $28,000 Section 1231 gain realized in 20X6 is treated as ordinary income? How much is treated as a long-term capital gain?

20. After taking into consideration the depreciation recapture rules, Danik, Inc., a C corporation, has the following gains and losses resulting from business property held for more than one year:

Business casualty gain	$53,000
Business casualty loss	(22,000)
Theft loss	(6,000)
Section 1231 gain	5,000
Section 1231 loss	(14,000)

As of the beginning of the year, Danik's nonrecaptured Section 1231 losses are $12,000. Discuss the tax consequences of these gains and losses on Danik's corporate tax return.

21. Fuente Company sold its warehouse for $1,000,000. The company paid $1,400,000 for the building several years ago and over the years had properly claimed $216,000 of depreciation using the straight-line method. What is the amount and character of Fuente's gain or loss?

22. Two years ago, Drew Corporation (a C corporation) purchased 3,000 shares of stock in Nuco Corporation directly from Nuco for $300,000 in cash. The total capital of Nuco at that

time was $900,000. Drew holds the shares in Nuco as an investment. Calculate the amount and character of the loss assuming that Drew sold all 3,000 shares for $180,000. What if the stock had been held by Frank Drew, a single individual, rather than by Drew Corporation?

23. Sara Lantz began to invest some of her excess cash from the income generated from her sole proprietorship in stamps to hold as an investment. She sold one of her stamp collections during the year for $20,000. She had purchased the collection three years ago for $12,000. She is in the 28-percent marginal tax bracket for ordinary income. Sara did not sell or exchange any other capital assets during the current year. How much will her income tax liability increase because of the sale of this stamp collection?

24. Nathan Pace realized a net Section 1231 gain of $8,000 on the sale of land used in his business. He had no nonrecaptured Section 1231 losses from previous tax years. He realized a $20,000 short-term capital gain on the sale of bonds he held for investment. Nathan realized a $5,000 long-term capital loss on the sale of stock held for investment. He did not sell or exchange any other capital assets during the year. What is his net capital gain? If he is in the 25-percent marginal tax bracket for ordinary income, how much additional tax will he pay due to these gains and loss?

25. Brenda Sizemore bought land in her own name for $6,000 on March 1, 20X7. She died in an accident on November 29, 20X7. At the date of her death, the land was worth $7,000. Her living trust specified that Sizemore Corporation was to receive the land in the event of her death. Her executor did not elect the alternate valuation date. Sizemore Corporation received the land from the trustee on December 15, 20X7, when it had a fair market value of $7,100. The corporation sold the land on February 11, 20X8, for $7,500. What is the amount and character of Sizemore Corporation's gain on the sale of the land?

Chapter 9 Review Problems

1. Years ago, Robert Reese purchased land for an investment at a cost of $50,000. In the current year, when his land was worth $150,000, he exchanged his land for other land that he would hold for investment. The new land had an FMV of $120,000. He also received $30,000 in cash.

   a. What is Robert's amount of realized gain or loss?

   b. What is the amount and character of Robert's recognized gain or loss?

   c. What is Robert's basis in the newly acquired land?

2. Howard Corporation had equipment destroyed in a fire. The equipment had an original cost of $400,000, and it had accumulated depreciation recorded to the date it was destroyed of $140,000. Howard Corporation collected $325,000 in insurance proceeds and 10 days later bought equipment with the same functional use for $300,000.

   a. What is Howard's adjusted basis in the old equipment?

   b. What is Howard's realized gain or loss?

   c. What is the amount and character of Howard's recognized gain or loss?

   d. What is Howard's basis in the new equipment?

Chapter 9 Comprehensive Review Question

Kyle Brown bought computer equipment (five-year property) for his business on May 1, 2012, at an auction for a bargain price of $200,000. He immediately placed the equipment in service in his business. He claimed $20,000 of Section 179 expense on the computer equipment and began depreciating the remaining $180,000 using MACRS and the half-year convention.

On June 16, 2014, he sold the property on an installment basis. He received $40,000 cash on the date of sale. The buyer assumed Kyle's $50,000 debt on the property and gave Kyle a $210,000 installment note that called for $30,000 payments each year on principal plus interest for seven years beginning on June 16, 2015. The note carried interest at the market rate. Kyle's nonrecaptured net Section 1231 losses are $2,000 at the beginning of 2014.

a. Compute Kyle's adjusted basis in the five-year property at the time of the sale.

b. Compute the gross profit, total contract price, and gross profit percentage.

c. What is the amount and character of the gain recognized in 2015?

d. What is the amount and character of the gain recognized in 2016?

Chapter 9 Research Question

Bruce Wilson won $2 million in the state lottery. The lottery pays out the prize money in 20 annual installments of $100,000 each. After receiving three $100,000 installments, Bruce sold the remaining $1.7 million of payments for $1 million, reported the $1 million as a long-term capital gain on his tax return, and paid tax on that amount at the 15-percent tax rate. Bruce's tax return has been selected for audit by the IRS. Is he likely to prevail on his treatment of the $1 million sale of his future lottery payments as a long-term capital gain?

PART IV:
Calculating Tax Liability and Taxes Owed

CHAPTER

10

NOLs, AMT, and Other Business Taxes

LEARNING OBJECTIVES

1. Understand what a net operating loss (NOL) is, how it is calculated, and how it can be used to offset taxable income for other tax years.

2. Be able to explain the purpose of the alternative minimum tax (AMT), calculate the tax, and plan for it.

3. Understand what corporations are subject to the accumulated earnings tax and how the tax is calculated.

4. Understand what corporations are subject to the personal holding company tax and how the tax is calculated.

¶ 1000 Introduction

After corporate or individual taxpayers compute their taxable income, they calculate their regular income tax liability using the applicable progressive income tax rates. Taxpayers reporting negative taxable income do not have any regular income tax liability and may be allowed to carry all, or a portion of, the negative amount to other tax years and deduct it against gross income generated in those years. The amount taxpayers are allowed to carry over to other tax years is known as a "net operating loss" (NOL), which may be a different amount from the amount of negative taxable income reported on the taxpayer's income tax return. How NOLs are calculated and how they can be used to offset gross income in other tax years are discussed in this chapter.

Besides regular income taxes, C corporations may be subject to several additional taxes enacted to address issues that arose over time when Congress felt it was necessary to take corrective action to ensure a more accurate determination of the proper taxes owed. These taxes include the alternative minimum tax (AMT), the accumulated earnings tax, and the personal holding company (PHC) tax. Although the accumulated earnings tax and the PHC tax apply only to C corporations, individuals may be subject to the AMT.

The AMT is an alternative method of calculating income tax. It has its own definitions of exclusions from or deductions against gross income. The AMT is an add-on income tax that represents the excess of a taxpayer's tentative minimum tax (computed under special AMT rules) over the taxpayer's regular income tax (computed using the rules discussed in Chapters 1–9). The AMT was enacted to prevent taxpayers from taking advantage of exclusions and deductions available under the regular tax system to such an extent that their income tax obligation was eliminated or reduced to very little. For the most part, the exclusions and deductions allowed under the AMT system are less generous than those allowed in the regular income tax system. Consequently, taxpayers who take advantage of the exclusions and deductions incorporated into the regular income tax system may find themselves subject to the AMT. The AMT applies to both corporate and individual taxpayers.

The accumulated earnings tax is a penalty tax developed to keep corporations from avoiding the second layer of taxation by retaining previously taxed earnings in the corporation beyond the reasonable needs of the business in lieu of distributing these earnings as dividends. The PHC tax, another penalty tax, is designed to prevent individual taxpayers from gaining a tax advantage by shifting their investment portfolios into corporate form. Each of these taxes will be discussed in this chapter.

NET OPERATING LOSSES

The Internal Revenue Code (the "Code") taxes income from all sources except those items specifically identified as exclusions from their gross income. As discussed in Chapters 5 through 9, businesses can deduct from their gross income various expenditures associated with generating income. However, because the life of a business is arbitrarily divided into tax years for reporting gross income and expenses, the taxable income or loss reported on the tax return for any particular year may not accurately reflect the overall, long-term performance of a business. Consequently, if the government did not allow taxpayers to offset losses from one tax year against profits in another, businesses could owe taxes on net profits from years of good performance without deriving any tax benefits from net losses generated in years of weaker performance. That situation might deter taxpayers from starting new businesses because losses in early years are common.

The NOL rules were enacted to ease the unduly drastic consequences of taxing income strictly on an annual basis.[1] They were designed to permit a taxpayer to offset gross income from profitable years with losses from unprofitable years. The current tax law generally allows taxpayers to carry back a NOL to the previous two tax years and then to carry forward any unutilized NOL for up to 20 years.

¶ 1001 Tax Treatment of NOLs

The tax laws allow NOLs generated from carrying on a trade or business to offset gross income generated in other tax years. A NOL may arise from losses generated either by a corporation or by an individual engaged in a trade or business. Because flow-through entities, such as partnerships and S corporations, do not pay income taxes, they do not generate NOLs that need to be carried over to other tax years. Instead, any operating losses from such entities are passed on to their owners and may result in a NOL on the owner's income tax return.

.01 Carryover Provisions

The current tax law generally allows taxpayers to carry back a NOL to the two previous tax years. Any amounts not utilized in those years can be carried forward to the following 20 years.[2] When a NOL is carried back, the NOL must first be offset against gross income from the second preceding tax year before it can be carried over to the first preceding year. Any unutilized losses during the carryback period are carried over sequentially for 20 years, or until fully utilized.

 Reason for the Rule: Because a carryback requires amending a tax return that has already been filed with the IRS, the carryback period typically is limited to tax years for which the statute of limitations for amendment by the taxpayer has not yet expired. Because the carryforward goes into years for which the taxpayer has not yet filed returns, the carryforward period tends to be longer.

Special carryback and carryover rules for certain types of losses. There are special carryback and carryover rules for certain types of net operating losses (e.g., a casualty loss, farming loss, specified liability loss, excess interest loss, loss attributable to a federally declared disaster, bad debt loss of a commercial bank, or loss sustained by a real estate investment trust).

Taxpayers can elect to forego the entire carryback period[3] An election must be made by the due date (including extensions) of the return for the year of the loss. An election can be made on the tax return. Once made, an election is irrevocable.

Example 1: A taxpayer generates a NOL in 2015. The taxpayer carries back the NOL to 2013. To the extent the NOL is not fully utilized in 2013, the taxpayer carries over the NOL to 2014. Any NOL not utilized in 2014 is carried over to offset gross income on the taxpayer's 2016 through 2035 tax returns until fully utilized. Alternatively, the taxpayer can elect to forego the carryback period and carry forward the entire NOL to 2016. Any NOL not utilized in 2016 would be carried forward to 2017 through 2035.

¶ 1002 Calculating a Corporation's NOL

Simply put, a NOL is the excess of allowed deductions over gross income. Whenever a corporation reports negative taxable income, it may have incurred a NOL. All expenses deducted on the corporate tax return are business related, but one adjustment that must be made to negative taxable income is to add back any NOL deduction from another tax year. Without this adjustment, the taxpayer would be taking a double deduction for the same NOL. Also, the tax law does not allow the domestic production activities deduction to create or increase a taxpayer's NOL.

---

[1] Code Sec. 172.
[2] Code Sec. 172(b)(1).
[3] Code Sec. 172(b)(3).

Example 2: In 2015, Centrol Corporation reports a negative taxable income of $50,000. Included in this calculation is a NOL deduction of $30,000 carried over from 2014. In calculating Centrol's 2015 NOL deduction, the NOL carried over from 2014 is disregarded. Centrol's NOL from 2014 remains $30,000, and its NOL for 2015 is $20,000 (assuming no adjustment for the domestic production activities deduction must be made).

.01 The DRD and the NOL

The dividends received deduction (DRD) is not a typical deduction because it is computed as a percentage of dividends and is not the result of an expenditure made by the taxpayer. Nonetheless, the tax law does not require corporations to add back to negative taxable income any of the DRD when computing their NOL for the year. Consequently, the DRD can produce or contribute to a corporation's NOL.

The DRD is equal to 70, 80, or 100 percent of dividend income, depending on the corporation's percentage ownership of stock in the corporation paying the dividends (see ¶ 412.02). Only corporations that are part of an affiliated group (in which the corporation's ownership is at least 80 percent) are allowed to deduct 100 percent of the dividends included in income. For corporations that are not part of an affiliated group, the DRD is limited to 70 percent or 80 percent of taxable income.

If a corporation computes its DRD using the applicable 70 or 80 percent of dividends received and if deducting the full DRD causes the corporation to sustain a NOL for a tax year, the taxable income limit on the DRD does not apply in computing the corporation's NOL. Accordingly, the full DRD can contribute to the taxpayer's NOL for the year.

Example 3: Abbet, Inc. owns less than 20 percent of the stock in Bahara. During 2015, Bahara pays Abbet a $100,000 dividend. Abbet's taxable income is computed as follows:

Dividend income	$100,000
Ordinary income	40,000
Less: Business expenses	(80,000)
Taxable income before DRD	$ 60,000
Less: DRD ($100,000 × 70%))	(70,000)
Taxable loss	($ 10,000)

Deducting 70 percent of the dividends received produces a taxable loss; therefore, the taxable income limit on DRDs does not apply, and Abbet's DRD equals $70,000 (70 percent of the dividends received). Because Abbet's negative taxable income is not due to a NOL carryover from another tax year, its NOL for the year equals $10,000.

Example 4: Mavelton owns less than 20 percent of the stock in Reiter, Inc. During 2015, Mavelton receives $100,000 of dividends from Reiter. In addition, Mavelton reports $40,000 of income and $50,000 of deductions from business operations. Mavelton computes its 2015 taxable income as follows:

Dividends received	$100,000
Business income	40,000
Less: Business expenses	(50,000)
Taxable income before DRD	$ 90,000
Less: DRD (limited to 70% of $90,000)	(63,000)
Taxable income	$ 27,000

Because Mavelton owns less than 20 percent of the stock in Reiter, its DRD cannot exceed 70 percent of the $100,000 of dividends it receives during the year. However, if Mavelton were to deduct the full $70,000 ($100,000 × 70%) against its taxable income, it would not create a tax loss. Therefore, the DRD is computed as the *lesser* of 70 percent of (1) the dividends received or (2) the taxable income before the DRD. Mavelton reduces its taxable income by $63,000 ($90,000 × 70%).

Planning Pointer: When a corporation's DRD is limited by the taxable income limitation, the amount by which the DRD is reduced is lost and will never create a tax benefit to the corporation. For example, in Example 4, Mavelton's DRD normally would be $70,000 ($100,000 × 70%). Thus, the taxable income limitation effectively increases Mavelton's taxable income by $7,000 ($70,000 – $63,000), and Mavelton ends up paying more income tax as a result of the limitation.

A corporation can avoid losing the full benefit of the DRD by (1) accelerating income to the year and/or postponing deductions to a subsequent year, or (2) accelerating sufficient deductions and/or postponing sufficient income to create a NOL and avoid the taxable income limitation on the DRD.

For example, if Mavelton could accelerate $20,001 of deductions into the current year, its taxable income before the DRD would be $69,999 ($90,000 – $20,001). If Mavelton subtracted the full $70,000 DRD from that amount, a NOL would result. Thus, Mavelton's taxable loss for the year would equal $1 ($69,999 – $70,000 DRD). Mavelton would reduce its 2015 taxable income by an additional $27,001, and its tax liability in 2015 would be reduced to zero. Assuming a 15-percent tax rate, the tax savings from these deductions would equal $4,050 ($27,001 × 15%). Normally a taxpayer with a 15-percent marginal tax rate would expect $3,000 in tax savings from a $20,001 deduction ($20,001 × 15%); therefore, accelerating expenses into the current year would result in an additional $1,050 ($4,050 – $3,000) in tax savings.

Example 5: Continuing with Example 4, in 2017 Mavelton incurs a $30,000 NOL that it carries back to 2015.

Taxable income before DRD and NOL deduction	$90,000
Less: DRD (no change, still limited to 70% of $90,000)	(63,000)
Taxable income before NOL carryback	$27,000
Less: NOL deduction (limited to taxable income)	(27,000)
Taxable income	$ 0

Because the taxable income is less than the NOL carryback, the NOL deduction is limited to the taxable income, and the $3,000 difference between the $30,000 NOL carryback and the $27,000 taxable income may be carried over to a subsequent year.

¶ 1003 Calculating an Individual Taxpayer's NOL

As discussed in Chapters 1 and 4, the calculation of an individual taxpayer's taxable income includes both business and nonbusiness deductions. Included in the tax laws are deductions from adjusted gross income (AGI) for various personal expenses (itemized deductions) as well as "free" deductions like the standard deduction and personal exemption. Because the tax laws governing NOLs are intended to allow businesses to deduct operating losses against gross income generated in other tax years, when an individual taxpayer reports negative taxable income it is necessary to determine what amount of the loss is due to business deductions and what amount is due to personal deductions.

With few exceptions, an individual's deductions from AGI (which include the taxpayer's personal and dependency exemptions plus the *greater* of the taxpayer's standard deduction or itemized deductions) are not permitted to generate an individual taxpayer's NOL that can be used to offset gross income in other tax years. Furthermore, any reductions to taxable income that result from the domestic production activities deduction (see ¶ 509) or NOL carryovers are added back to an individual's taxable income in computing the NOL generated during the year. Capital losses in excess of capital gains that are deducted in computing taxable income are limited when computing the individual's NOL.

¶ 1004 Utilizing a NOL

Like other business deductions, a NOL carryover is a deduction from gross income. The NOL deduction is applied against income in general and is not restricted to offsetting only business income. A taxpayer's **NOL deduction** is the total of the NOL carryforwards and carrybacks to the tax year. Each carryback and carryforward is separately computed under the rules described at ¶ 1002 and ¶ 1003 and then is combined with the others into one total NOL deduction.[4]

Example 6: For 2015, a corporation has income totaling $110,000 and deductions of $50,000. The corporation has an unused NOL from 2014 of $40,000 that originated in 2013. This amount is carried over to 2015 and becomes the corporation's NOL deduction for 2015. The NOL deduction reduces the corporation's taxable income to $20,000 ($110,000 – $50,000 – $40,000).

A NOL generally can be carried back two years. If taxable income for the carryback years is not sufficient to absorb the entire loss, any remaining NOL can be carried forward for 20 years following the year it is generated. Alternatively, the taxpayer can elect to forego the carryback period and just carry forward the NOL for the next 20 years.

When a corporation carries a NOL back or forward, the corporation must modify its taxable income. The excess of the NOL carryover over the corporation's modified taxable income is the amount of NOL that can be carried over to the subsequent tax year.

Example 7: A corporation reports negative taxable income of $25,000 in 2015. The corporation carries back the NOL to 2013, when it reported taxable income of $14,000. Because the amount of the NOL exceeds the taxable income from 2013, the corporation carries over the $11,000 excess ($25,000 – $14,000) to 2014.

Example 8: Lax Corporation incurs a NOL of $100,000 for calendar year 2015. After carrying the NOL back to its two previous tax years, Lax carries forward a $30,000 NOL to 2016. In 2016, Lax reports $500,000 of gross income and business expenses of $540,000. Lax's taxable income for 2016 is computed as follows:

Gross income	$500,000
Less: Business expense	(540,000)
Taxable income before NOL deduction	($ 40,000)

Because Lax's taxable income before any NOL deduction is negative, it is unable to utilize any of the NOL carryover from 2015. Lax carries forward to 2017 the $30,000 NOL from 2015 and the $40,000 NOL from 2016. The combined $70,000 NOL will be

---

[4] Code Sec. 172(a); Reg. § 1.172-1.

deducted against Lax's gross income in 2017. To the extent that Lax can utilize any of the $70,000, it will be deemed to utilize the NOL carryover from 2015, followed by the NOL carryover from 2016.

.01 Modified Taxable Income

A NOL carried back to a previous tax year is used to offset gross income in that year. Accordingly, taxable income is reduced as well. The amounts for several exclusions and deductions taken on the tax return are based on a percentage of taxable income. For example, both individual and corporate taxpayers are limited as to the amounts they can deduct for charitable contributions. Therefore, the question may be raised as to whether these items must be recomputed when determining the extent to which a NOL carryover can be utilized.

Modified taxable income for corporate taxpayers. A corporation's taxable income is used both in determining the amount of the charitable contribution deduction (see ¶ 511) and the dividends received deduction (DRD) (see ¶ 412.02). However, in the process of recomputing the taxable income in a carryback year, the tax laws specifically state that the taxpayer does not have to recompute these deductions. Instead, the NOL is deducted after both the DRD and the charitable contribution deduction have been taken into consideration. The NOL is utilized in the carryback year to the extent that it does not reduce taxable income below $0. Any excess NOL represents the taxpayer's NOL carryover to the next subsequent tax year.[5]

Corporations can claim a refund of taxes attributable to a NOL carryback on Form 1139, *Corporation Application for Tentative Refund,* or on an amended Form 1120, *U.S. Corporation Income Tax Return.* Filing Form 1139 produces the quickest refund. The difference between the tax originally paid in the carryback year and the tax on the taxable income recomputed with the NOL deduction may be claimed as a refund.

If the recomputed taxable income is zero or negative, the entire tax originally paid is refunded. For example, Mavelton from Example 5 would be entitled to a refund for the entire amount of taxes paid in 2015. When taxable income is reduced to less than zero after the entire NOL carryover is taken into consideration, a portion of the NOL may remain for carryover to the next subsequent year. For example, in Example 5, Mavelton has a $3,000 NOL carryover to a subsequent year.

Example 9: Assume the same facts as in Example 5, except that in 2017, Mavelton incurs a $20,000 NOL that it carries back to 2015.

Taxable income before DRD and NOL deduction	$90,000
DRD (no change, still limited to 70% of $90,000)	(63,000)
Taxable income before NOL carryback	$27,000
NOL deduction	(20,000)
Taxable income	$ 7,000

Here, Mavelton is able to fully absorb the NOL carryback in 2015. When filing its claim for a refund for 2015, Mavelton will request a refund of the difference between the taxes it paid on $27,000 of taxable income and the taxes it would have paid on $7,000 of taxable income.

Example 10: In 2015, Cablenet, Inc. reports taxable income of $100,000 before taking into consideration a $25,000 charitable contribution. Cablenet's charitable contribution for 2015 is limited to $10,000 ($100,000 × 10%). After deducting its charitable contribution, Cablenet reports taxable income of $90,000, which results in an $18,850 tax liability.

---

[5] Code Sec. 172(b)(2); Reg. § 1.172-5(a)(2)(iii).

Cablenet carries forward the unutilized $15,000 charitable contribution to 2016 ($25,000 – $10,000). In 2016, Cablenet reports sufficient taxable income to fully utilize the carryover.

In 2017, Cablenet reports a $210,000 net operating loss, which it carries back to 2015—the first available carryback year. When determining how much of the NOL is utilized in the carryback year, Cablenet does not recompute the DRD or the charitable contribution deduction. Therefore, the starting point in the calculation is taxable income before the NOL deduction.

Taxable income before NOL deduction	$90,000
NOL deduction (limited to taxable income)	(90,000)
Taxable income	$ 0

Cablenet uses $90,000 of the NOL from 2017 to offset its 2015 taxable income to zero. Because there is no tax liability on $0 taxable income, Cablenet files an amended return for 2015 or Form 1139 to claim a refund for the $18,850 of taxes it paid that year. Cablenet carries forward the remaining $120,000 NOL ($210,000 – $90,000) to 2016 and recomputes its taxable income (without recomputing its DRD or charitable contribution deduction) and its tax liability in that year.

 Spotlight: The tax law specifically requires that modified taxable income be computed without recalculation of the DRD or charitable contribution deductions. This rule prevents taxpayers from losing out on the tax benefits of any charitable contribution carryovers. In Example 10, Cablenet was able to fully utilize the $15,000 charitable contribution carryover from 2015 in 2016. Thus, between 2015 and 2016, Cablenet generated tax savings from making a $25,000 charitable contribution in 2015.

If Cablenet had been required to recompute its charitable contribution limit in 2015 after the NOL deduction, none of the $25,000 contribution would have been deductible because recomputed taxable income would have been $0. Cablenet would have been able to utilize $100,000 of the NOL (to reduce original taxable income of $100,000 to $0) and carry forward $110,000 ($210,000 – $100,000) to 2016. It also would have carried forward the full $25,000 charitable contribution to 2016 because none of it would have been deducted in 2015. Because the charitable contributions can be carried forward only five years (see ¶ 511.04), Cablenet may have some difficulty utilizing the full $25,000 carryover. If the tax laws required that Cablenet recompute the taxable income limitation for 2016 after deducting the NOL carryover from 2015, it is likely that its charitable contribution deduction would be limited. Because we know that Cablenet generated a NOL in 2017, only 2018, 2019, and 2020 would remain to absorb the charitable contribution carryover.

Modified taxable income for individual taxpayers. Because both personal and business expenses are deducted on an individual's income tax return, the computation of modified taxable income is more complicated for individual taxpayers. For several items that are deductible on the individual tax return, the amount of the deduction depends on the taxpayer's AGI for the year. For example, medical expenses, personal casualty and theft losses, and miscellaneous itemized deductions are all deductible as itemized deductions. However, only amounts that exceed a certain percentage of the AGI can be deducted. When carrying back a NOL from another tax year, the taxpayer's deductions for such items must be recomputed.

.02 Carryback and Carryover Periods

When applying a NOL to the allowed carryback years, the taxpayer must start by carrying the NOL to the second preceding tax year. To the extent that the NOL is not fully utilized in that year, it is carried over to the immediately preceding tax year. Any NOL that cannot be utilized in the carryback period is carried forward to the year immediately following the loss year, then to the second year following the loss year, and then to subsequent tax years until the loss is used up or the carryover period expires, whichever occurs first.[6] If the taxpayer elects to forego the carryback period, the NOL must first be applied to the first tax year following the year the NOL is generated before it can be deducted in the second subsequent year.

Example 11: A corporation generates a $52,000 NOL in 2015. The corporation's modified taxable income is computed as follows:

2013	$ 9,000
2014	4,000
2016	13,000
2017	12,000
2018	80,000

The $52,000 loss is first carried back to 2013. After offsetting the $9,000 of modified taxable income in that year, the corporation carries the remaining $43,000 ($52,000 – $9,000) over to 2014 and uses it to offset the $4,000 of modified taxable income in that year. The $39,000 ($43,000 – $4,000) of remaining NOL is then carried forward to 2016, 2017, and 2018 until it is entirely used up.

Carryovers from multiple periods. If a taxpayer has NOLs for more than one year and each is carried to the same tax year, the NOLs are applied in the order in which they occurred. This ensures that the oldest carryovers (those expiring first) are utilized first.

.03 Deriving Tax Benefits from a NOL

Because a NOL deduction reduces the taxpayer's gross income, tax savings are derived when a NOL is carried over to a previous or to a subsequent tax year. Like all deductions, the tax savings produced depend on the taxpayer's marginal tax rate. For example, in Example 11 the $52,000 NOL is carried over to multiple tax years. Although the taxpayer must wait until filing the tax returns for the carryforward years to derive the tax savings from the NOL deductions, assuming that the taxpayer generates sufficient taxable income in the carryover period the taxpayer eventually will realize the tax benefits of the NOL.

Example 12: Continuing with Example 11, by utilizing the $52,000 NOL generated in 2015 by carrying back the NOL to 2013 and 2014, the taxpayer can file a claim for a refund of taxes paid in those years of $1,350 and $600, respectively. When the corporation carries forward the remaining NOL to 2016 through 2018, it will generate additional tax savings in those years.

Year	Tax Savings
2013	$1,350 ($9,000 × 15%)
2014	600 ($4,000 × 15%)
2016	1,950 ($13,000 × 15%)
2017	1,800 ($12,000 × 15%)
2018	3,950 [($9,000 × 25%) + ($5,000 × 34%)]
Total tax savings	$9,650

---

[6] Code Sec. 172(b).

Alternatively, the taxpayer could elect to forego the carryback period and could carry over the NOL to 2016 through 2018. This would produce total tax savings of $10,950.

Year	Tax Savings	
2016	$ 1,950	($13,000 × 15%)
2017	1,800	($12,000 × 15%)
2018	7,200	[($22,000 × 25%) + ($5,000 × 34%)]
Total tax savings	$10,950	

Planning Pointer: The decision whether to waive the carryback of a NOL depends on the taxpayer's particular situation. For example, if the taxpayer expects substantially more gross income in future years, a waiver would be useful because the taxpayer's marginal tax rate would be higher. The additional tax savings in those later years would need to be weighed against the (perhaps lower) immediate tax benefits derived from filing a claim for a refund of taxes from the two carryback years.

For example, the taxpayer in Example 12 would generate greater tax savings ($10,950 versus $9,650) by electing to forego the carryback period because its marginal tax rate in 2018 is higher than the 15-percent tax rate in 2013 and 2014. However, the additional tax savings will not be realized for three years. Because the marginal tax rate in the third carryforward year is not known with certainty at the time the election must be made, the taxpayer must weigh the possibility of generating additional tax savings against the certain refund amount generated in the carryback period.

ALTERNATIVE MINIMUM TAX

Many provisions in the Code allow taxpayers to reduce their total income by investing or participating in activities that produce income that is excluded from gross income or in activities that produce expenses that reduce taxable income. By properly investing in these types of activities, taxpayers can reduce their tax liability to relatively low amounts when compared to their total economic income. The **alternative minimum tax (AMT)** was enacted to enhance equity in the income tax system by ensuring that all taxpayers pay at least some minimum income tax each year.

Statistics indicated that many individual and corporate taxpayers were taking such effective advantage of deductions and credits afforded to them under the regular federal income tax system that they were often able to reduce or eliminate their federal income tax obligations. Before the Tax Reform Act of 1969, some high-income taxpayers who could take advantage of tax preferences paid a significantly lower effective tax rate on their economic income than did other taxpayers. In some instances, millionaires paid little or no tax. In an attempt to curb this practice, Congress enacted a minimum tax system with more restrictive rules for calculating what deductions and exclusions are allowed. Taxpayers calculate their tax liability under both the regular tax system and the alternative tax system and pay the higher of the two taxes.

¶ 1005 Taxpayers Subject to the AMT

Both C corporations and individuals may be subject to the AMT. The calculation of the AMT is similar for both types of taxpayers. However, because personal deductions are permitted on the individual tax return, differences exist in the calculation of corporate and individual AMT. Only certain larger corporations are subject to the corporate AMT, and only those whose tax liability under the AMT system exceeds their regular tax liability actually pay AMT. All individuals are subject to the AMT when their regular income tax liabilities are less than the amount of tax computed using the AMT system.

.01 Corporate Taxpayers Subject to the AMT

Large corporations are subject to the AMT; small corporations are not. A corporation is not subject to the AMT in its first year of existence.[7] After the first year, a corporation qualifies as a small corporation and is not subject to the AMT if:

1. Its *average* annual gross receipts for its first three years after 1993 but before the current year did not exceed $5 million and

2. Its *average* annual gross receipts for all subsequent three-year periods before its current tax year did not exceed $7.5 million.[8]

For the average annual gross receipts test, gross receipts in the first year must be annualized if the corporation was in existence for fewer than 12 months during its first year.[9]

Example 13: A calendar year corporation is incorporated on October 5, 2015. The corporation will qualify as a small corporation in 2015 regardless of its gross receipts for the year. To qualify as a small corporation in 2016, its *average* annual gross receipts for 2015 and 2016 must not exceed $5 million. The corporation's gross receipts for 2015 must be computed on an annualized basis in accordance with Code Sec. 448(c) (3) (B).

Once a corporation qualifies as a small corporation, it will continue to be exempt from the AMT for as long as the *average* of its gross receipts for the prior three-year period does not exceed $7.5 million. Once a corporation fails to qualify as a small corporation, it cannot qualify in any subsequent tax year.

Example 14: Brownett Corporation, a calendar year taxpayer, has been in existence since January 1, 2009. To qualify as a small corporation in 2015, Brownett's *average* gross receipts for the three tax years from 2009–2011 must have been $5 million or less, and its *average* gross receipts for the periods 2010–2012, 2011–2013, and 2012–2014 must have been $7.5 million or less. If Brownett qualifies as a small business in 2015, it will continue to qualify as a small business for 2016 as long as its *average* gross receipts for the period 2013–2015 are $7.5 million or less. If it fails to qualify as a small business in 2015, it cannot qualify as a small corporation in 2015 or in any subsequent tax year.

.02 Individual Taxpayers Subject to the AMT

Technically, all individuals are required to compute their income tax liability under both the regular and the AMT systems and pay the higher of the two tax amounts. In reality, most taxpayers pay sufficient tax under the regular tax system to avoid being subject to the AMT. When the AMT was first introduced in 1969, only 155 individuals had to pay the tax. However, because of reductions in the regular tax rates and the addition of deductions and credits to the regular income tax system over the years, now millions of individuals have to pay the AMT.

---

[7] Code Sec. 55(e)(1)(C).
[8] Code Sec. 55(e).

[9] Code Secs. 55(e)(1)(D) and 448(c)(3)(B).

¶ 1006 The Corporate AMT Formula

The AMT is an add-on tax that taxpayers owe in addition to regular income taxes if the income tax computed under the AMT system exceeds the income tax they owe under the regular tax system. The AMT system is like any other tax system in which a tax rate is applied to a tax base. The tax base used in the AMT system is called the **AMT base**. This amount is analogous to taxable income in the regular income tax system. The AMT rate for corporations is 20 percent of the AMT base.

Example 15: A corporation subject to the AMT has an AMT base of $60,000. The minimum amount of income tax it will owe for the year is $12,000 ($60,000 × 20%). If its regular income tax exceeds that amount, the corporation will not owe any AMT.

The AMT base is computed by subtracting an exemption amount from the **alternative minimum taxable income (AMTI)**. The AMT exemption is $40,000 for corporations with AMTI that does not exceed $150,000. For corporations with AMTI in excess of $150,000, the AMT exemption is reduced by 25 percent of the excess.[10] The AMT exemption is zero for corporations with AMTI of $310,000 or more.

Example 16: A corporation subject to the AMT has $120,000 of AMTI. Because this amount does not exceed $150,000, its AMT exemption equals $40,000. Thus, the corporation's AMT base is $80,000 ($120,000 – $40,000). The minimum amount of income tax it will owe for the year is $16,000 ($80,000 × 20%). If the corporation's regular income tax exceeds this amount, it will not owe any AMT.

Example 17: A corporation subject to the AMT has $220,000 of AMTI. Because this amount exceeds $150,000, the corporation's initial AMT exemption is reduced to $22,500.

Initial exemption		$40,000
AMTI	$220,000	
	(150,000)	
	$ 70,000	
	× 25%	(17,500)
AMT exemption		$22,500

The corporation's AMT base equals $197,500 ($220,000 – $22,500), and the minimum amount of income tax the corporation will owe for the year is $39,500 ($197,500 × 20%). If the corporation's regular income tax is $23,000, its AMT will be $16,500 ($39,500 – $23,000). Through the regular income tax system the taxpayer pays $23,000. When the $16,500 of AMT is added to this amount, the taxpayer pays a total of $39,500, which is equal to the minimum amount of income tax owed as computed under the AMT system.

Example 18: A corporation subject to the AMT has $320,000 of AMTI. Because this amount exceeds $310,000, its AMT exemption is $0. The corporation's AMT base equals $320,000, and the minimum amount of income tax it will owe for the year is $64,000 ($320,000 × 20%). If the corporation's regular income tax is less than this amount, it will owe the difference as AMT.

Many of the tax rules governing the calculation of AMTI are the same as those used in computing taxable income. Therefore, the calculation of AMTI involves adjusting the taxpayer's taxable income for various adjustments and preferences.[11] The calculation of the corporate AMT is shown in Figure 10-1.

---

[10] Code Sec. 55(d)(3).   [11] Code Sec. 55.

Figure 10-1 Calculation of Corporate AMT

	Corporate taxable income
+	Tax preferences
±	AMT adjustments
±	ACE adjustment*
=	AMTI
–	AMT exemption
=	AMT base
×	20% (corporate AMT rate)
=	Tentative minimum tax
–	Regular income tax
=	AMT (only if a positive amount)

*Note: The adjusted current earnings (ACE) adjustment is discussed at ¶ 1009.

Example 19: A corporation reports taxable income of $200,000 and owes regular income tax on this amount of $61,250. Included in taxable income are tax preference items totaling $100,000, negative AMT adjustments totaling $20,000, and a $40,000 positive ACE adjustment. The corporation computes its AMT as follows:

Corporate taxable income	$200,000
Plus: Tax preferences	100,000
Less: Negative AMT adjustments	(20,000)
Plus: Positive ACE adjustment	40,000
AMTI	$320,000
Less: AMT exemption	(0)
AMT base	$320,000
20% (corporate AMT rate)	× 20%
Tentative minimum tax	$ 64,000
Regular income tax	(61,250)
AMT (only if a positive amount)	$ 2,750

Example 20: A corporation reports taxable income of $300,000 and owes regular income tax on this amount of $100,250. Included in taxable income are tax preference items totaling $40,000, positive AMT adjustments totaling $20,000, and a $30,000 negative ACE adjustment. The corporation computes its AMT as follows:

Corporate taxable income	$300,000
Plus: Tax preferences	40,000
Plus: Positive AMT adjustments	20,000
Less: Negative ACE adjustment	(30,000)

AMTI	$330,000
Less: AMT exemption	(0)
AMT base	$330,000
20% (corporate AMT rate)	× 20%
Tentative minimum tax	$ 66,000
Regular income tax	(100,250)
AMT (only if a positive amount)	$ 0

¶ 1007 Tax Preferences

Tax preferences are deductions and exclusions that are allowed when calculating taxable income but not allowed when calculating AMTI. Because these deductions and exclusions are taken away in the AMT system, tax preferences are always added back to taxable income in arriving at a taxpayer's AMTI. Figure 10-2 provides a list of tax preferences that must be added to taxable income when computing AMTI.[12]

Figure 10-2 AMT Tax Preferences

1. Percentage depletion in excess of the adjusted basis in the property,

2. Excess intangible drilling costs, and

3. Tax-exempt interest on specified private activity bonds.

In an effort to encourage domestic oil and gas production, Congress enacted tax incentives that allow domestic oil and gas companies to immediately expense intangible drilling costs that would normally be capitalized expenditures and to take percentage depletion—a deduction that has no connection to actual expenses. To the extent that these two deductions result in "excessive" deductions, the amounts deducted represent tax preference items that must be added back to taxable income when computing AMTI.

.01 Percentage Depletion

If the percentage depletion deduction taken when computing taxable income exceeds the taxpayer's adjusted basis in the property at the end of the tax year (computed before reduction of the basis by the depletion deduction), the difference is a tax preference added back to taxable income when computing AMTI. The preference item is computed separately for each piece of depletable property. Excess percentage depletion is not considered a tax preference item with respect to independent oil and gas producers and royalty owners.[13]

Example 21: An oil and gas company (not an independent producer) deducts $70,000 for percentage depletion on its tax return. Its adjusted basis in the property (before the depletion deduction) was $50,000. To compute AMTI, the taxpayer adds back $20,000 to taxable income.

.02 Intangible Drilling Costs

Operators of domestic oil, gas, or geothermal wells may elect to currently deduct intangible drilling and development costs (IDCs) rather than capitalize and recover them through depletion or

---

[12] Code Sec. 57.

[13] Code Sec. 57(a)(1).

depreciation.[14] (See ¶ 501.03 and ¶ 707.) Excess IDCs are treated as a tax preference item to the extent that the excess exceeds 65 percent of the net income from oil, gas, and geothermal properties. "Excess IDCs" equal the amount of the IDCs the taxpayer deducted in computing taxable income over the amount that would have been deducted if such amount had been capitalized and amortized ratably over a 120-month period. Alternatively, the taxpayer can elect to compute the deduction for IDCs under the AMT system using the amounts that would have been allowed through cost depletion (in lieu of amortization over 120 months).

Example 22: Marquette Oil Company incurs $120,000 of IDCs with respect to oil wells that are placed in service in July 20X0. Marquette elects to deduct the entire amount of the IDCs when computing its regular taxable income. If Marquette had amortized its IDCs over 120 months, it would have been allowed a $6,000 deduction in 20X0 ($120,000/120 months × 6 months). Therefore, it has excess IDCs of $114,000 ($120,000 immediately expensed minus the $6,000 amortized amount). If Marquette has net income from oil, gas, and geothermal properties of $150,000 in 20X0, 65 percent of its net income equals $97,500 ($150,000 × 65%). Thus, its IDC that exceeds 65 percent of the net income from the property is $16,500 ($114,000 − $97,500). Therefore, Marquette Oil must add back to taxable income a tax preference of $16,500 when computing its AMTI for 20X0.

.03 Tax-Exempt Interest from Private Activity Bonds

Chapter 4 explained that the tax laws allow as an exclusion the interest earned from state and local government bonds (more commonly referred to as "municipal bonds"). (See ¶ 412.01.) However, tax-exempt interest from these bonds ("municipal interest") is a preference item when the interest is paid on a *specified private activity bond*. Under the AMT system, a specified private activity bond is a type of private activity bond issued after August 7, 1986, that pays interest that can be excluded from gross income for regular tax purposes.[15] Although interest paid with respect to a private activity bond usually has to be included in gross income for regular tax purposes, an exception is made for interest payable with respect to a private activity bond that is a *qualified bond*.

A bond is a **private activity bond** if it satisfies both the private business use test and the private security or payment test or it satisfies the private loan financing test.[16] A bond issue satisfies the private business use test if more than 10 percent of the proceeds from the issue are to be used for any private business use.[17] A bond issue satisfies the private security or payment test if payment of the principal of, or the interest on, more than 10 percent of the proceeds from the issue are (under the terms of the issue or any underlying arrangement) directly or indirectly (1) secured by any interest in property used or to be used for a private business use or payments in respect of such property or secured by any interest to be derived from payments (whether or not to the issuer) in respect of property, or borrowed money, used or to be used for a private business use or (2) to be derived from payments (whether or not to the issuer) in respect of property, or borrowed money, used or to be used for a private business purpose.[18]

The private business use and private security or payment tests will be treated as satisfied if the tests would be satisfied if "5 percent" were satisfied for "10 percent" and only taken into account are issue proceeds to be used for any private business use that is not related to any government use of the proceeds, the disproportionate related business use of the issue proceeds, and payments, property, and borrowed money with respect to any use of proceeds previously described.[19] A private activity bond is a qualified bond if the proceeds are used for certain specified purposes (e.g., to build an airport, sewage facility, finance owner-occupied residences, or student loans).[20]

---

[14] Code Sec. 263(c); Reg. § 1.612-4.

[15] Code Sec. 57(a)(5)(C).

[16] Code Sec. 141(a).

[17] Code Sec. 141(b)(1).

[18] Code Sec. 141(b)(2).

[19] Code Sec. 141(b)(3).

[20] Code Sec. 141(e).

A private activity bond is a "qualified bond" if the proceeds are used for certain specified purposes (i.e., the bond is an exempt facility bond, qualified mortgage bond, qualified veterans' mortgage bond, qualified small issue bond, qualified loan bond, qualified redevelopment bond, or qualified 501(c)(3) bond).[21]

Certain types of bonds are excluded from the definition of "specified private activity bond":

- Qualified 501(c)(3) bond (a bond whose proceeds are used to benefit a charitable Code Sec. 501(c)(3) organization or governmental unit).

- Certain housing bonds (i.e., an exempt facility bond whose proceeds are used to provide qualified residential rental projects, qualified mortgage bond, or qualified veterans' mortgage bond).

In the AMT system, interest from specified private activity bonds does not qualify for the exclusion allowed for qualified private activity bonds. Thus, any interest from specified private activity bonds received during the year is added back to taxable income when computing AMTI. Interest incurred in connection with an investment in tax-exempt bonds is not deductible in the regular income tax system (see ¶ 505). In the AMT system, interest expense associated with private activity bond investments can be used to offset the interest income. Thus, only the difference represents a tax preference item.[22]

Example 23: A corporation receives $10,000 of interest from a *specified private activity bond.* The corporation paid $500 in interest on a temporary loan to purchase the bonds. For computing taxable income, the $10,000 is not included in gross income, and the $500 is not deductible from gross income. For computing AMTI, the $10,000 is taxable and the $500 is deductible. Accordingly, the taxpayer's tax preference amount is $9,500 ($10,000 – $500).

 Spotlight: Private activity bonds are issued by or on behalf of municipalities to provide financing for projects of private business users. Investors typically purchase the bonds from the municipality, and then the municipality loans the proceeds to private users for completion of their projects, such as airports, certain residential rental projects, and the like.

¶ 1008 AMT Adjustments

AMTI is computed by making certain adjustments to a taxpayer's taxable income in addition to tax preferences. Like tax preference items, AMT adjustments are intended to eliminate the tax advantages of items that, in the aggregate, reduce the taxpayer's taxable income to such an extent that the government considers the taxpayer to be paying too little in income tax relative to the taxpayer's economic income. However, unlike preference items, which always increase AMTI, AMT adjustments can be positive or negative.

Figure 10-3 lists some of the more common AMT adjustments required when calculating corporate AMTI.[23] Although these adjustments also apply to individuals, the list of AMT adjustments for individual taxpayers is more extensive due to the number of personal expenses they are allowed to deduct from AGI.

---

[21] Code Sec. 141(e).
[22] Code Sec. 57(a)(5).

[23] Code Sec. 56.

Figure 10-3 AMT Adjustments

- Adjusted current earnings,
- Depreciation on realty and personal property,
- Gain or loss from property with an AMT adjusted basis,
- Amortization of certified pollution control facilities,
- Amortization of mining exploration and development costs,
- Amortization of circulation expenditures,
- Long-term contracts,
- Domestic production activities deduction, and
- NOL recomputed using AMT income and deductions.

AMT adjustments typically require using a different method for computing a deduction. If the deduction is accelerated on the tax return (as it typically is with such items), in later years the deduction allowed for computing AMTI will be greater. These types of differences are known as **timing differences.** The distinguishing feature of timing differences is that they reverse themselves over time.

With respect to income items, if the recognition of income occurs earlier for the AMT than under the regular income tax system, a positive adjustment will be necessary in the year the income is recognized under the AMT system. In the year the item is included in taxable income, it must be subtracted from taxable income to compute AMTI.

.01 AMT Adjustment for Depreciation

One area in which timing differences cause AMT adjustments is depreciation. AMT rules may require recovery periods that are similar to or different from those the regular tax system requires. In addition, the same or different depreciation methods may apply under the AMT system.

For example, if the tax laws governing the calculation of taxable income allow for more accelerated methods of depreciation than those allowed under the AMT system, then in the earlier years of an asset's recovery period depreciation expense deducted in computing taxable income will be greater than that allowed in computing AMTI. Thus, in the earlier years, the difference between these two depreciation amounts must be added back to taxable income to arrive at AMTI. In the later years of the asset's recovery period, the opposite will occur, and the necessary adjustment will be a subtraction from taxable income.

Example 24: Assume that the following rules apply to the depreciation of an asset. For purposes of computing taxable income, the tax laws allow property to be depreciated over five years using the double declining balance (DDB) method, switching to the straight-line (SL) method when that method produces greater deductions. Under the AMT system, depreciation is allowed over the same five years, but the straight-line method must be used. Both methods require taxpayers to use the half-year convention to depreciate five-year property. (See ¶ 702.01.)

Under each tax system, depreciation during the six tax years for property costing $50,000 would be as follows:

Year	Regular Tax System*	AMT System**	Required Adjustment
1	$10,000	$ 5,000	$5,000
2	16,000	10,000	6,000
3	9,600	10,000	(400)

Year	Regular Tax System*	AMT System**	Required Adjustment
4	5,760	10,000	(4,240)
5	5,760	10,000	(4,240)
6	2,880	5,000	(2,120)
	$50,000	$50,000	$ 0

* These amounts were computed using the column for 5-year property from Table 7A in the Appendix to Chapter 7.

** These amounts were computed using the column for 5-year property from Table 7F in the Appendix to Chapter 7.

As you can see from this example, during the earlier years of the recovery period, a positive adjustment is required. The $11,000 of positive adjustments required during the first two years of the recovery period is reversed by the negative adjustments in the last four years.

Now assume that the tax laws governing the depreciation of an asset under the regular income tax and under the AMT systems allow for the same depreciation methods, but the recovery periods are longer under the AMT system. Up to the last year in which the property is depreciated under the regular income tax system, the amount deducted against taxable income will exceed the amount deducted in computing AMTI. Accordingly, a positive adjustment will be necessary in those years. However, once the property has been fully depreciated for regular income tax purposes, the amount allowed in the AMT system must be subtracted from taxable income to properly calculate AMTI.

Example 25: Assume that the following rules apply to the depreciation of an asset. For computing taxable income, the tax laws allow property to be depreciated over three years using the straight-line method. For computing AMTI, the property must be depreciated over five years using the straight-line method. Both methods require taxpayers to use the half-year convention when depreciating property.

Depreciation during the respective recovery periods for property costing $30,000 would be as follows:

Year	Regular Tax System*	AMT System**	Required Adjustment
1	$ 5,000	$ 3,000	$2,000
2	10,000	6,000	4,000
3	10,000	6,000	4,000
4	5,000	6,000	(1,000)
5	0	6,000	(6,000)
6	0	3,000	(3,000)
	$30,000	$30,000	$0

* These amounts were computed using the column for 3-year property from Table 7F in the Appendix to Chapter 7.

** These amounts were computed using the column for 5-year property from Table 7F in the Appendix to Chapter 7.

As you can see from this example, until the year in which the property is fully depreciated under the regular tax system positive adjustments are needed. In the year the property is fully depreciated and in all subsequent tax years, negative adjustments to taxable income will be required.

Under the Modified Accelerated Cost Recovery System (MACRS), taxpayers have the option of using regular (accelerated) MACRS, straight-line MACRS, or the alternative depreciation system (ADS) to depreciate personal property. (See ¶ 702.) Taxpayers that qualify can also elect to expense some or all of their personal property under Code Sec. 179. (See ¶ 702.03.) The AMT system also allows Code Sec. 179 immediate expensing, but it prohibits taxpayers from using the 200-percent (double) declining balance method and instead requires that taxpayers depreciate personal property using the 150-percent declining balance or the straight-line methods and use the same recovery periods allowed under regular MACRS. Thus, an AMT adjustment is required when 3-, 5-, 7-, or 10-year property is depreciated using the double declining balance method.

Because MACRS uses only the SL method to depreciate real property, fewer adjustments are required to real property depreciation for AMT purposes. In the regular income tax system, real property placed in service after 1986 is depreciated using regular MACRS over 27½, 31½, or 39 recovery periods, depending on whether the property is residential and, in the case of commercial realty, when the property was placed in service. (See ¶ 703.) Under the AMT system, real property placed in service after 1986, but before 1999, is depreciated using the SL method over a 40-year recovery period. This is the same depreciation that is allowed under the ADS. Consequently, unless ADS was used to depreciate real property placed in service after 1986 and before 1999, an adjustment is required each year when computing AMTI. The tax laws were changed so that real property placed in service after 1998 is now depreciated using the same method under both the regular income tax system and the AMT system. Thus, no AMT adjustment is required for real property placed in service after 1998.

Table 10-1 outlines the differences in depreciation methods under the regular income tax system and the AMT system and discusses the types of adjustments that are needed each year.

Table 10-1 Comparison of Allowable Depreciation Methods

Description	Regular Tax System	AMT System	Required Adjustment
Real property placed in service after 1986, but before 1999	Under regular MACRS, taxpayers use the straight-line (SL) method over 27½, 31½, or 39 years, depending on the type of property. Under ADS, taxpayers depreciate real property over 40 years using the SL method.	Taxpayers must depreciate real property over 40 years using the SL method.	If regular MACRS is used, positive adjustments are required to taxable income until the end of the regular MACRS recovery period. Negative adjustments will be required for all subsequent years. If ADS is used under the regular tax system, no adjustments will be needed.
Real property placed in service after 1998	Same as for real property placed in service after 1986, but before 1999.	Same as the regular depreciation system.	No adjustments required.

Description	Regular Tax System	AMT System	Required Adjustment
Personal property	Taxpayers can use regular (DDB) MACRS, SL MACRS, or ADS. (See ¶ 702.)	Taxpayers must use 150% declining balance using the same recovery periods as allowed under MACRS.	If the double declining balance method under MACRS is used, positive adjustments will be required during the earlier recovery periods, and negative adjustments will be required during the later periods.

Special rule for bonus depreciation. Bonus depreciation taken with respect to property does not have to be added back to AMTI.[24]

Example 26: DuMont Enterprises placed an office building in service on June 5, 1998. The building cost $500,000; under MACRS, it is depreciated using the SL method over 39 years. To compute AMTI, the building must be depreciated over 40 years. From 1999 through 2015, depreciation under each of these methods is as follows:

Year	Regular Tax System*	AMT System**	Required Adjustment
1998	$ 6,945	$ 6,771	$174
1999–2015	$12,821 a year	$12,500 a year	$321

*For 1999–2015, this amount equals $500,000/39. For 1998, the depreciation is allowed for the last 6½ months of the year, so depreciation equals $12,821/12 × 6.5.

**For 1999–2015, this amount equals $500,000/40. For 1998, the depreciation is allowed for the last 6½ months of the year, so depreciation equals $12,500/12 × 6.5.

.02 Adjusted Gain or Loss

When calculating the amount of gain realized from the disposition of depreciable property that was subject to AMT adjustments, the adjusted basis must be determined for purposes of the AMT using the amount of depreciation taken into account for computing AMTI. Thus, the amount of gain will differ for regular and for AMT purposes. This difference will result in an adjustment to taxable income when computing AMTI.

If the amount of gain included in taxable income is greater than the gain computed under the AMT system, the amount of gain is a negative adjustment to taxable income. Likewise if the loss included in taxable income is less than the loss computed under the AMT system, the amount of loss is a negative adjustment to taxable income. Positive adjustments are required if the gain is greater or the loss is smaller under the AMT system.

Example 27: Continuing with Example 26, assume that on February 19, 2015, DuMont sells the office building for $700,000. The depreciation deduction for regular tax purposes for 2015 would equal $1,603 ($500,000/39 × 1.5/12). For computing AMTI, depreciation expense would be $1,563 ($500,000/40 × 1.5/12). Thus, the $40 difference ($1,603 – $1,563) would be reported as a positive adjustment to taxable income in 2015. During

---

[24] Code Sec. 168(k)(2)(G).

the years 1999 to 2015, DuMont will have reported positive AMT adjustments totaling $5,497 ($174 + ($321 × 16) + $40).

DuMont's adjusted basis in the office building as well as its realized and recognized gain under both the regular income tax and the AMT systems are computed as follows:

	Regular Tax System		AMT System	
Amount realized		$700,000		$700,000
Less:				
Cost	$500,000		$500,000	
Accumulated depreciation	(213,684)*	(286,316)	(208,334)**	(291,666)
Recognized gain		$413,684		$408,334

*$6,945 + ($12,821 × 16 years) + $1,603

**$6,771 + (12,500 × 16 years) + $1,563

The $5,350 ($413,684 – $408,334) less gain recognized under the AMT system must be reported as a negative adjustment to taxable income. This amount is equal to the cumulative positive adjustments made over the years when depreciation was taken on the building. Thus, the timing differences resulting from depreciation reverse themselves at the time the asset is sold or fully depreciated, whichever occurs first.

Although the above example illustrates the adjustments required on the sale of depreciable property, similar rules apply to all sales of property. To the extent that the adjusted basis of the property under the regular tax system and the adjusted basis under the AMT system differ, so too will the amount of gain or loss reported under each system.

.03 Amortization Required for Certain Costs

For purposes of computing taxable income, the tax laws allow taxpayers to immediately expense circulation costs.[25] Alternatively, corporations may elect to amortize (expense) their circulation costs over three years. **Circulation costs** are amounts paid or incurred to establish, maintain, or increase the circulation of a newspaper, magazine, or other periodical. When a corporation immediately expenses its circulation costs for regular income tax purposes, the AMT rules do not allow the corporation to expense its circulation costs. Consequently, the fully expensed circulation costs is a positive adjustment to taxable income when computing AMTI. However, if the corporation elects to amortize its circulation costs for regular tax purposes, the AMT rules allow the same deduction for computing AMTI.[26] Hence, no adjustment is necessary.

The costs associated with certified pollution control facilities and mining exploration and development normally are capitalized because the taxpayer benefits from such expenditures beyond the current year. However, when computing taxable income, these costs may be deducted immediately. When computing AMTI, these costs must be capitalized and amortized ratably over a 10-year period (in the case of mining exploration and development costs) or depreciated using ADS (in the case of certified pollution control facilities). Under ADS, the costs of the certified pollution control facility are depreciated using the SL method over the facility's class life. (See ¶ 702.01.)

---

[25] Code Sec. 173.　　　　　　　　　　　　　　[26] Code Sec. 56(b)(2).

.04 Long-Term Contracts

In very limited situations involving real estate construction contracts, taxpayers may be allowed to compute taxable income using the completed contract method. (See ¶ 309.02.) For purposes of computing AMTI, the percentage of completion method must be used for all long-term contracts other than certain home construction contracts.[27] The completed contract method is allowed for home construction contracts for computing both the regular tax and the AMT. All other differences between the amount of income from a long-term contract recognized during the year for regular tax purposes and that recognized under the percentage of completion method for AMT purposes result in an adjustment to taxable income. When the amount included in AMTI exceeds the amount included in taxable income, a positive adjustment to taxable income is required.

Example 28: In 2013, a corporation enters into a long-term contract to construct a building that it reasonably expects to complete within two years. The corporation is eligible to use the completed contract method under the regular income tax system. The taxpayer recognizes the entire $50,000 in 2015, the year in which the construction is completed. Under the percentage of completion method, the corporation would recognize $20,000 in 2013, $20,000 in 2014, and $10,000 in 2015. For computing the AMTI, the following adjustments must be made to taxable income:

Year	Regular Income Tax	AMT	AMT Adjustment
2013	$ 0	$20,000	$20,000
2014	0	20,000	20,000
2015	50,000	10,000	(40,000)

.05 Recomputed Deductions Using the AMT System

The deduction for domestic production activities (see ¶ 509) uses amounts and limits based on the regular income tax system. Taxpayers who take a deduction for domestic production activities must recompute their deduction using the AMT system rules.[28] If the deduction allowed in calculating regular taxable income is larger than the deduction allowed in calculating AMTI, the excess must be added to taxable income as a positive adjustment when computing AMTI. On the other hand, if the deduction taken in the calculation of taxable income is less than the deduction under the AMT system, a negative adjustment to taxable income would need to be made.

Taxpayers that have a NOL for a tax year must recompute the NOL using the AMT system. The NOL calculated under the AMT system can be carried back and forward in the same manner as regular NOLs. This rule ensures that to the extent the NOL is attributable to accelerated depreciation, depletion, or other favorable provision under the regular income tax system, such amounts cannot be used to reduce a taxpayer's AMTI.

¶ 1009 ACE Adjustment

Preference items and AMT adjustments apply both to corporations and to individuals. Corporations alone are required to make an adjustment based on their **adjusted current earnings** (ACE). The calculation of ACE closely resembles the calculation of **current earnings and profits** (current E&P), which is the amount (together with accumulated E&P) from which corporations pay dividends to their shareholders (see ¶ 1204). E&P attempts to measure a corporation's ability to pay dividends from its current year earnings. Accordingly, many of the tax incentives incorporated into the regular and AMT systems are not included in the calculation of E&P.

Generally, a corporation's ACE exceeds its AMTI because the ACE rules are more restrictive with respect to allowable exclusions and deductions. The AMT rules require a C corporation to increase its AMTI by 75 percent of the amount by which its ACE exceeds its unadjusted AMTI

---

[27] Code Sec. 56(a)(3).   [28] Code Sec. 199(d)(6).

(AMTI computed without regard to the ACE adjustment and the AMT NOL deduction). This adjustment is known as the ACE adjustment.

If a corporation's unadjusted AMTI exceeds its ACE, AMTI is reduced by 75 percent of the difference. However, the AMTI is reduced only to the extent that the aggregate amount of the negative ACE adjustments used against positive ACE adjustments from prior years does not exceed the aggregate positive ACE adjustments from prior years.[29]

Example 29: Handell, Inc., a calendar year corporation, has an unadjusted AMTI equal to $330,000 each year from 2013 to 2015. Handell's ACE and ACE adjustments during those years are as follows:

Year	ACE	AMTI	Difference	ACE Adjustment
2013	$400,000	$330,000	$ 70,000	$52,500
2014	330,000	330,000	0	0
2015	140,000	330,000	(190,000)	(52,500)

In 2013, ACE exceeds its unadjusted AMTI by $70,000 ($400,000 – $330,000). Therefore, 75 percent of this amount ($52,500) must be included as an ACE adjustment when computing its AMTI in 2013. In 2014, there is no increase (or decrease) to AMTI because the difference between ACE and the unadjusted AMTI is zero. In 2015, Handell's unadjusted AMTI exceeds its ACE by $190,000 ($330,000 – $140,000), creating a potential negative adjustment to the AMTI equal to $142,500 ($190,000 × 75%). Because the aggregate increases to the AMTI for prior years (i.e., 2013) equal $52,500, only $52,500 of the potential $142,500 negative adjustment can reduce Handell's AMTI in 2015.

Example 30: Assume the same facts as in Example 29, except that in 2015 Handell's unadjusted AMTI once again is $330,000, but its ACE for 2015 equals $360,000. Because Handell's ACE exceeds its unadjusted AMTI by $30,000 ($360,000 – $330,000), 75 percent of the $30,000 ($22,500) must be included as a positive ACE adjustment when computing the AMTI in 2015. If, in 2016, Handell's unadjusted AMTI exceeds its ACE, 75 percent of the difference, up to $22,500, can be used as a negative adjustment to AMTI.

.01 Concept of E&P

Earnings and profits (E&P) will be discussed in more detail in Chapter 12; however, the basic concepts, which are important to understanding ACE, are discussed here. As a corporation earns income and pays expenses, current E&P attempts to capture the corporation's capacity to distribute amounts to shareholders without returning any portion of their investment in the corporation. Such distributions are classified as dividends. Unlike the regular income tax system or the AMT system, in which exclusions and deductions are included for various social, economic, and political reasons, the calculation of current E&P focuses on how much an item of income or expense affects the corporation's ability to pay dividends to its shareholders.

For example, interest from state and local municipal bonds ("municipal interest") generally is excluded from gross income. However, interest paid on specified private activity bonds is included in the calculation of the AMTI. Although most types of municipal interest are exempt from both the regular income tax and AMT, the reality is that when a corporation receives the interest that amount can be distributed to the shareholders. Thus, both taxable and tax-exempt interest are included in the calculation of E&P.

Example 31: A corporate taxpayer receives $150,000 of municipal interest, which includes $40,000 of interest from specified private activity bonds. Taxable income under the regular

---

[29] Code Sec. 56(g).

income tax system is $400,000. Under the AMT system, only the municipal interest on specified private activity bonds is taxable. Therefore, the corporation's AMTI equals $440,000 ($400,000 + $40,000). However, all municipal interest is included in current E&P. Thus, the taxpayer's current year E&P equals $550,000 ($400,000 + $150,000).

As discussed in previous chapters, some expenditures are not deducted from gross income. These include federal income taxes paid during the year; bribes, fines and penalties that violate public policy; and 50 percent of meals and entertainment expenses (M&E). Although there are valid reasons why the government does not allow these amounts to be deducted when calculating the regular income tax and AMT, these expenditures nonetheless affect the corporation's ability to pay dividends. Accordingly, these amounts are deducted in computing a corporation's E&P.

Example 32: In its first year of operations, a corporation reports business income of $100,000 and incurs $60,000 of ordinary and necessary business expenses. The corporation also incurs $2,000 in M&E and $5,000 in penalties for activities that violate public policy. The corporation computes its $39,000 taxable income and $33,000 of current year E&P as follows:

Business income		$100,000
Less: Operating expenses	$60,000	
50% of M&E	1,000	(61,000)
Taxable income		$ 39,000
Taxable income		$ 39,000
Less: Nondeductible portion of M&E	$ 1,000	
Nondeductible penalties	5,000	(6,000)
Current year E&P		$ 33,000

Although the corporation reports $39,000 of taxable income, if it distributes more than $33,000 to its shareholders the excess will represent a return to shareholders of some of their investment in the corporation. The tax consequences of dividend and return of capital distributions is discussed in Chapter 12 (see ¶ 1204).

.02 Calculating ACE

Although the concepts behind the ACE are similar to the concepts involved in the calculation of current E&P, differences exist between the two calculations. For example, current E&P attempts to measure a corporation's capacity to pay dividends from current period earnings; the ACE calculation is intended to measure pretax income before any distributions. Thus, although federal and foreign income taxes are not deducted in computing taxable income or AMTI, these amounts reduce a corporation's dividend-paying capacity and therefore reduce E&P. However, neither of these items nor any dividends paid during the year is considered when computing a corporation's ACE. (E&P is discussed in greater detail in Chapter 12, which discusses corporate distributions.)

The starting point for calculating ACE is AMTI. Differences between the amounts of income and deduction items taken into account when calculating AMTI and the amounts taken into account when calculating ACE are handled as positive and negative adjustments to AMTI. Thus, if an item of income is excluded from AMTI but is included in ACE, the amount is a positive adjustment to AMTI. Likewise, if a deduction is allowed in computing AMTI, but not in computing ACE, the deductible amount would be added back to AMTI for purposes of computing the corporation's ACE. On the other hand, an expense that is not deductible for computing AMTI but is deductible for computing ACE would be a negative adjustment to AMTI.

Some ACE adjustments reflect timing differences that eventually reverse themselves. For example, if the AMT allows a greater deduction for an item than is allowed under the provision governing the ACE calculation, the excess amount is a positive adjustment to AMTI. However, in the year that the deduction for computing ACE exceeds the deduction allowed for computing AMTI, the difference will be a negative adjustment.

Positive adjustments for exclusion items. Items that are excluded from gross income for computing AMTI but that are included in determining ACE must be reported as positive adjustments and added to AMTI when computing a corporation's ACE. Deductions related to an exclusion that normally are not deducted in computing AMTI offset a positive ACE adjustment. For example, AMTI is increased by interest on tax-exempt bonds and reduced by any interest expense associated with financing the bonds. However, this rule does not apply to interest on specified private activity bonds because such amounts have already been reflected in AMTI.[30] ACE does not include interest from certain housing bonds (i.e., an exempt facility bond whose proceeds are used to provide qualified residential rental projects, qualified mortgage bond, or qualified veterans' mortgage bond).

Example 33: A corporate taxpayer receives $130,000 of municipal interest, which includes $60,000 of interest from specified private activity bonds. Taxable income under the regular income tax system is $600,000. The taxpayer incurs $10,000 of interest expense on municipal bonds other than specified private activity bonds. Because this expense relates to property that produces tax-exempt income, the $10,000 is not deductible under the regular income tax system.

Under the AMT system, the interest on specified private activity bonds is taxable. Accordingly, the corporation's AMTI equals $660,000 ($600,000 + $60,000). The $10,000 of interest expense is not deductible because the income from the bonds to which the interest pertains is exempt from the AMT. However, $720,000 ($600,000 + $130,000 − $10,000) represents the corporation's capacity to pay dividends from current year's earnings. Accordingly, this amount is included in the corporation's ACE. When computing the corporation's ACE, $60,000 ($720,000 − $660,000) would be shown as a positive adjustment to AMTI.

Positive adjustments for deduction items. As a general rule, no deduction from ACE is allowed for an item that is not deductible for purposes of computing a corporation's E&P. The deduction for domestic production activities is not based on expenditures but instead is computed as a percentage of domestic production activity income. However, a special rule makes it deductible when computing a corporation's ACE.[31]

Like the domestic production activities deduction, the dividends received deduction (DRD) does not reduce the corporation's ability to pay dividends. Although it would make sense that this deduction would not be allowed in computing the ACE, corporations that own at least 20% of another corporation's stock and thus qualify for the 80- or 100-percent DRD for dividends received from that corporation subtract the DRD when computing their ACE. However, corporations that are "portfolio investors" with respect to another corporation because they own less than 20 percent of the stock in that corporation must add back the amount of their (70-percent) DRD to AMTI when computing their ACE.[32] The DRD was discussed in Chapter 4 (see ¶ 412.02).

Other expenses allowed in the calculation of AMTI that are not recognized as deductions in computing a corporation's ACE include deductions for circulation costs (amortized over three years for AMTI) and organizational expenses (either expensed (up to $5,000) or amortized over 180 months for AMTI). Any amounts deducted from AMTI for these items are positive adjustments to AMTI when computing a corporation's ACE for the year.

---

[30] Code Sec. 56(g)(4)(B).
[31] Code Sec. 56(g)(4)(C)(v).

[32] Code Sec. 56(g)(4)(C)(ii).

Example 34: Amica Corporation began its business operations on March 1, 2015. Amica Corporation incurred $80,000 of organizational costs, but because this amount exceeds $55,000 it cannot immediately expense any of the costs (see ¶ 503). Instead, it elects to amortize the costs over 180 months. Amica files its first tax return using a calendar year-end. On its 2015 tax return, Amica deducts $4,444 ($80,000/180 × 10 months) as amortization of its organizational costs. Although this amount is also allowed for purposes of computing AMTI, it is not deductible in computing Amica's ACE. Thus, the $4,444 must be added back to Amica's AMTI in 2015 when computing its ACE.

Adjustments for timing differences. Some differences between the calculation of ACE and AMTI stem from timing differences, which eventually reverse themselves. Required adjustments due to timing differences are listed in Table 10-2.

Table 10-2 ACE Adjustments Due to Timing Differences

Item	AMTI System	ACE Calculation
Depreciation of personal property	Taxpayers must use 150% DB using the same recovery periods as allowed under MACRS. (See ¶ 1008.01.).	Personal property must be depreciated using ADS. (See ¶ 702.01.)[a] The difference between the AMTI amount and the ACE amount is a timing difference. In years when the AMTI deduction is greater, a positive ACE adjustment results. In years when ADS expense is greater, a negative ACE adjustment results.
Depletion	Percentage depletion in excess of the adjusted basis of the property is added back to AMTI. (See ¶ 1007.01.)	With the exception of independent oil and gas producers, taxpayers must use cost depletion.[b] Therefore, the excess of the amount deducted against taxable income minus any depletion preference item used in computing AMTI over the ACE amount is a positive ACE adjustment, and accordingly, it is added to AMTI when computing ACE.
Installment sale method	Allowed for computing AMTI.	Income from installment sales is reported in the year of the sale.[c] Therefore, in the first year, a positive ACE adjustment will occur, followed by negative ACE adjustments in years in which installment method gain is reported in AMTI.
Intangible drilling and development costs (IDCs)	IDCs are usually expensed immediately in computing taxable income, but in computing AMTI, they are amortized over 120 months and result in a preference item only if the excess of the amount expensed over the amortized amount exceeds 65 percent of the net income from the property. (See ¶ 1007.02.)	IDCs are amortized over 60 months.[d] The ACE adjustment equals the difference between the amount deducted in determining AMTI and the amortized amount allowed for the ACE calculation. When the deduction allowed in computing AMTI exceeds the deduction allowed in computing ACE, the adjustment is positive; when the ACE deduction exceeds the AMTI deduction, the adjustment is negative.

Item	AMTI System	ACE Calculation
LIFO	Last-in, first-out (LIFO) or first-in, first-out (FIFO) can be used to compute inventory costs.	LIFO must be used.[e] Therefore, the excess of the inventory amount reported on the balance sheet using FIFO over the inventory amount using the LIFO method is a positive ACE adjustment if the taxpayer uses the FIFO method to calculate regular taxable income.

[a] Code Sec. 56(g)(4)(A).

[b] Code Sec. 56(g)(4)(F)

[c] Code Sec. 56(g)(4)(D)(iv).

[d] Code Sec. 56(g)(4)(D)(i).

[e] Code Sec. 56(g)(4)(D)(iii).

Example 35: An oil and gas company (not an independent producer) deducts $70,000 for percentage depletion on its 2015 tax return. Its adjusted basis in the property (before the depletion deduction) was $60,000. If the cost method had been used, the taxpayer's depletion deduction would have been $35,000.

For AMT purposes, the taxpayer's depletion deduction would be limited to the taxpayer's basis in the property. Consequently, the taxpayer adds back to taxable income the $10,000 excess of percentage depletion over the taxpayer's basis in the property ($70,000 – $60,000) to arrive at AMTI. For computing the corporation's ACE, the $25,000 difference between the deduction used in computing AMTI ($60,000) and the deduction using the cost depletion method ($35,000) is included as a positive ACE adjustment for the year. This amount is added to AMTI in the calculation of the corporation's ACE.

Example 36: A corporation sells land for $500,000, resulting in a $150,000 profit. The terms of the sale require that the buyer pay $200,000 at the time of the sale and $100,000 annually for each of the next three years. The corporation reports the gain on the installment method. On its tax return for the year of the sale, the corporation recognizes a $60,000 gain ($200,000/$500,000 × $150,000). In each of the next three years, $30,000 of gain is recognized ($100,000/$500,000 × $150,000). Under the ACE calculation, the entire $150,000 of gain is recognized in the year of the sale. The AMT adjustment required each year is as follows:

Year	AMTI	ACE	Adjustment to AMTI
1	$60,000	$150,000	$90,000
2	30,000	0	(30,000)
3	30,000	0	(30,000)
4	30,000	0	(30,000)

The $90,000 positive ACE adjustment in the first year is reversed in years 2 to 4 with negative adjustments of $30,000 in each of the three years.

¶ 1010 Minimum Tax Credit

Certain tax credits can be used to offset the AMT, and certain tax credits cannot. Tax credits are discussed in detail in Chapter 11. However, we discuss one tax credit here: the **minimum tax credit**. Code Sec. 53 provides that the amount of AMT paid by a corporation in one year can be used to offset the corporation's regular tax liability for a subsequent year. However, the minimum tax credit, in combination with other tax credits (see Chapter 11) cannot be used by a corporation to reduce its regular tax liability below the tentative minimum tax in that subsequent tax year. A corporation may not use a minimum tax credit to offset any future AMT liability.

The amount of AMT paid by an individual can offset the individual's regular tax liability for a subsequent tax year only to the extent that the AMT is attributable to timing differences (as opposed to exclusions).

Minimum tax credits may be carried forward indefinitely but never back.

Example 37: In 2015, Reyas Inc. reports $16,000 of AMT stemming from specified private activity bond interest that was exempt from regular income tax. The $16,000 can be used to reduce the taxpayer's regular income tax liability to the extent that it exceeds the taxpayer's AMT liability for a subsequent tax year.

Example 38: In 2015, Dreyfus Tools, Inc. pays $16,000 in AMT. In 2016, the taxpayer's regular income tax liability is $149,000, and its tentative minimum tax is $135,000. Dreyfus can use $14,000 of its minimum tax credit to reduce its total 2016 taxes to $135,000 ($149,000 – $14,000). Dreyfus can carry over the remaining $2,000 ($16,000 – $14,000) of minimum tax credit to 2017 and subsequent tax years.

¶ 1011 Individual AMT

Individuals are subject to an alternative minimum tax (AMT) when the amount of their tentative minimum tax exceeds the amount of regular income taxes owed.[33] The formula for computing the AMT is similar to that which corporations use to calculate AMT. Individual taxpayers are subject to the same tax preferences as corporations. Figure 10-4 shows the calculation of individual AMT.

Figure 10-4 Calculation of Individual AMT

	Taxable income
±	Tax preferences and adjustments
=	AMTI
–	AMT Exemption
=	AMT tax base
×	AMT rates
=	Tentative Minimum Tax
–	Regular income tax
=	AMT (if positive amount)

.01 AMT Preferences and Adjustments for Individual Taxpayers

Individuals do not have an ACE adjustment. However, individuals have a number of additional adjustments that must be taken into consideration when computing AMTI due to the many personal expenses deductible on the individual tax return. Table 10-3 summarizes the adjustments that an individual taxpayer must make to taxable income.

---

[33] Code Sec. 55.

Many of these adjustments have been discussed in Chapter 10; however, a few adjustments that are unique to individual taxpayers are listed in Table 10-3. For example, individuals are allowed to reduce taxable income by a standard deduction or itemized deductions, plus personal exemptions (see ¶ 104.07). Some itemized deductions are not allowed in computing AMTI. Likewise, neither the standard deduction nor deduction for personal exemptions is allowed in the calculation of AMTI. Instead, a larger AMT exemption is allowed.[34] The standard deduction (except to the extent attributable to a disaster loss deduction) and personal exemptions are added back to regular taxable income as positive adjustments in computing AMTI.

Table 10-3 Summary of AMT Preferences and Adjustments

Item	*Adjustment Necessary to Taxable Income*
Standard deduction*	Added back to taxable income.
Personal exemptions	Added back to taxable income.
State and local income taxes	Added back to taxable income.
State and local real property taxes	Added back to taxable income.
State and local personal property taxes	Added back to taxable income.
Miscellaneous itemized deductions	Added back to taxable income
MACRS depreciation	Same rules as for a corporation. (See ¶ 1008.01.)
Circulation costs	Same rules as for corporations. (See ¶ 1008.03.)
Research and experimental expenditures	Individuals must amortize these costs over 10 years. (See discussion that follows.)
Mining exploration and development costs	Same rules as for corporations. (See ¶ 1008.03.)
Long-term contracts	Same rules as for corporations. (See ¶ 1008.04.)
Pollution control facilities	Same rules as for corporations. (See ¶ 1008.03.)
Gain excluded on the sale of Section 1202 stock	Add back seven percent of the exclusion to taxable income. (0 percent for stock acquired after September 27, 2010 and before January 1, 2015)
Incentive stock options	Excess of FMV over the option price at date of exercise is added back to taxable income.
Passive activity losses	Net losses from passive activities, including tax shelter farm activities, are not allowed.
Intangible drilling costs	Same rules as for corporations. (See ¶ 1007.02.)
Alternative tax net operating loss	Recompute NOL using AMT rules and make any necessary adjustments to taxable income.

* Except to the extent attributable to a disaster loss deduction or motor vehicle sales tax deduction

Deductions from AGI. No deduction for personal and dependency exemptions is allowed in computing AMTI.[35] Thus, these amounts are added back to regular taxable income as positive adjustments to taxable income when computing AMTI. Many itemized deductions are not allowed or are further limited in the AMT system.

---

[34] Code Sec. 56(b)(1)(E).

[35] Code Sec. 56(b)(1)(E).

Research and experimental expenditures. As discussed in Chapter 5, when computing taxable income, businesses have the following three options for handling research and experimental expenses. (See ¶ 507.01.)

1. Deduct the costs in full in the year incurred,

2. Capitalize and amortize the costs over a period of 60 months, or

3. Capitalize the costs, but do not amortize them.

For the AMT system, individual taxpayers must amortize these expenditures over ten years.[36] Therefore, the difference between the amount deducted under the regular income tax system and amount deducted under the AMT system results in an adjustment to taxable income when computing an individual's AMTI.

Gain on the sale of small business stock. Individual taxpayers can exclude up to 50 percent of the gain on the sale of Section 1202 qualified small business stock held for at least five years (75 percent in the case of Section 1202 qualified small business stock acquired after February 17, 2009, and on or before September 27, 2010, and 100 percent in the case of stock acquired after September 27, 2010, and before January 1, 2015, see ¶ 806). Consequently, only half of the gain is subject to regular income tax (25 percent of the gain if the Section 1202 stock was acquired after February 17, 2009, and on or before September 27, 2010, and none of the gain if the stock was acquired after September 27, 2010, and before January 1, 2015). For purposes of computing AMTI, 7 percent of the amount of gain excluded from the disposition of qualified small business stock is treated as a tax preference item and added to AMTI.[37] Under a special rule, none of the gain excluded from the disposition of qualified small business stock acquired after September 27, 2010, and before January 1, 2015, is treated as a tax preference item.[38]

.02 AMT Exemption for Individual Taxpayers

The AMT exemption for individual taxpayers varies depending on the taxpayer's filing status. The initial AMT exemption for individuals is as follows for a tax year beginning in 2015:

Unmarried individuals (other than surviving spouses)	$53,600
Married filing jointly and surviving spouses	$83,400
Married filing separately	$41,700

For individuals whose AMTI exceeds a specified amount ($79,450 for married individuals filing a separate return; $119,200 for unmarried individuals (other than surviving spouses), and $158,900 for married individuals filing a joint return and surviving spouses), the exemption amount is reduced by $.25 for every dollar of excess[39]

Example 39: A married couple that files a joint return as AMTI equal to $200,000 in 2015. Because this amount exceeds the threshold ($158,900), their $83,400 exemption has to be reduced by $10,275 [($200,000 − $158,900) × 25%]. Thus, their AMT exemption amount is reduced to $73,125 ($83,400 − $10,275).

.03 AMT Tax Rates for Individual Taxpayers

The tax structure of the individual AMT is a two-tier progressive tax. For a tax year beginning in 2015, the first $185,400 ($92,700 if the taxpayer is married and filing a separate return) of AMT tax base is taxed at a 26 percent rate. Any excess over that amount is taxed at 28 percent. Net capital gain and qualified dividend income are subtracted from the AMT base because they are taxed at the same rate for purposes of both the regular tax and AMT. However, because gain on the sale of collectibles (such as coins and stamps) and net gain from sales of small business stock may be taxed

---

[36] Code Sec. 56(b)(2).
[37] Code Sec. 57(a)(7).
[38] Code Sec. 1202(a)(4).
[39] Code Sec. 55(d)(3).

for regular tax purposes at a rate exceeding the AMT rate, any such gain is taxed at the taxpayer's normal AMT rate.

¶ 1012 Tax Planning for the AMT

Although the AMT system is more restrictive than the regular tax system, it remains possible that by choosing the right strategies and investments taxpayers can reduce their tax liabilities under both the regular tax system and the alternative minimum tax system. For example, although tax-exempt interest from specified private activity bonds is subject to the AMT, all other types of state and local government bonds remain exempt both from the regular tax and from the AMT for individual taxpayers. Municipal interest (other than from specified private activity bonds) increases a corporation's tentative minimum tax if its ACE exceeds its AMTI.

For taxpayers subject to the AMT, the impact of the AMT on the taxpayer's marginal tax rate must be considered in determining the tax savings of a deduction or costs associated with additional income. For example, if a corporation is in the 15-percent tax bracket for regular tax purposes but is subject to the AMT due to the extensive preferences and adjustments taken in computing taxable income, the corporation's federal marginal tax rate for tax planning is 20 percent. State and local income taxes (both regular tax and AMT) must be considered as well.

ACCUMULATED EARNINGS TAX

The accumulated earnings tax is imposed on C corporations that accumulate profits in excess of the reasonable needs of the corporation. Because a corporation's after-tax profits are taxed a second time when distributed to shareholders in the form of a dividend, the board of directors may be hesitant to distribute profits. Accumulation of profits often results in higher stock prices because the cash retained by the corporation adds value to the company. Instead of receiving periodic dividend payments, taxpayers could sell their shares of stock for a higher price, thereby generating capital gains. In addition to the lower capital gain rates that apply to individual taxpayers, capital gains generated by both individual and corporate taxpayers can be used to offset capital losses.

Historically, dividend income has been taxed at an individual taxpayer's ordinary income rates, thereby making capital gains more attractive than dividend income. The reduced tax rates now applied to qualified dividends have taken some of the "sting" out of receiving dividend distributions; however, the fact that capital gains can be offset by capital losses remains an attractive feature of generating capital gain over dividend income. In addition, capital gains are taxed only when the stock is sold, whereas dividend income is taxed in the year it is received. Accordingly, being able to defer the tax consequences of the second level of taxation is another reason for not distributing corporate profits. Although the accumulated earnings tax has almost always been applied to closely held corporations, its application is not limited to those corporations.[40]

¶ 1013 Corporations Subject to the Accumulated Earnings Tax

The **accumulated earnings tax** applies only if a corporation is formed or continues to exist for the purpose of preventing individual shareholders from paying tax on the profits of the corporation by allowing E&P to accumulate.[41] The accumulated earnings tax, however, does not apply to personal holding companies because such companies are subject to their own penalty tax (see ¶ 1015).

A presumption of tax-avoidance intent arises when a corporation accumulates E&P in excess of the reasonable needs of its business. However, this presumption can be overcome by a preponderance of evidence that the accumulation was not motivated by a desire to avoid the income tax on the

---

[40] Code Sec. 532(c) and *Technalysis Corp.*, 101 TC 397, Dec. 49,378 (1993).

[41] Code Sec. 532(a); Reg. § 1.532-1.

part of the shareholders of the corporation.[42] A presumption of tax-avoidance intent also arises when a corporation is found to be a mere holding or investment company.[43] Thus, the burden of disproving the allegation that it has accumulated earnings beyond its reasonable needs rests upon the corporation.[44] The circumstances that tend to negate the presumption of tax-avoidance intent include:

- The fact that little or no tax savings were achieved as a result of the corporation's accumulation of earnings and profits,
- The fact that the corporation's accumulation of earnings was for the reasonable needs of the business,
- The absence of loans to shareholders or the payment of their personal expenses by the corporation,
- The absence of investments that have no reasonable connection with the business, and
- A good dividend-paying record.

¶ 1014 Calculating the Accumulated Earnings Tax

Assuming that the IRS can prove that a corporation was formed or continues to exist for the purpose of preventing individual taxpayers from paying tax on the corporation's profits, the accumulated earnings tax equals 20 percent of the corporation's accumulated taxable income.

The calculation of "accumulated taxable income" starts with a corporation's taxable income, which is adjusted to reflect the corporation's current year earnings (the result is called "adjusted taxable income"). The adjusted taxable income is then reduced by the dividends paid deduction and the accumulated earnings credit.

The "dividends paid deduction" generally is the amount of dividends the corporation paid during the tax year. The corporation can elect to treat dividends paid during the first 2½ months of the following year as dividends paid in the current year. However, those dividends are then not eligible for the dividends paid deduction in the following year.[45] The **accumulated earnings credit** is the amount of current year earnings considered to be for the reasonable needs of the business. The formula for computing the accumulated earnings tax is shown in Table 10-4.

Table 10-4 Calculating the Accumulated Earnings Tax

Taxable income	$xxx,xxx
Plus/minus: Adjustments	xx,xxx
Adjusted taxable income	$xxx,xxx
Less: Dividends paid deduction	(xx,xxx)
Less: Accumulated earnings credit	(xx,xxx)
Accumulated taxable income	$xxx,xxx
Accumulated earnings tax rate	× 20%
Accumulated earnings tax	$ xx,xxx

---

[42] Code Secs. 532 and 533; Reg. §§ 1.532-1 and 1.533-1.

[43] Code Sec. 533(b).

[44] *Iowa School of Men's Hairstyling, Inc.,* 64 TCM 1114, Dec. 48,591(M), TC Memo. 1992-619; *MYCO Industries, Inc.,* 63 TCM

2355, Dec. 48,068(M), TC Memo. 1992-147; *Yates Petroleum Corporation,* 63 TCM 2347, Dec. 48,067(M), TC Memo. 1992-146.

[45] Code Secs. 561 and 563(a) and (d); Reg. §§ 1.561-1, 1.563-1, and 1.563-3.

Example 40: Dodge and Company reports taxable income of $550,000 during 2015 and has $200,000 of positive adjustments to taxable income to reflect current earnings. Dodge uses the calendar year. On October 5, 2015, Dodge distributes $45,000 of dividends to its shareholders, and on February 18, 2016, it distributes $90,000. Its accumulated earnings credit is $250,000. Assuming that Dodge elects to treat the dividends paid on February 18, 2016, as paid in 2015, its accumulated earnings tax is computed as follows:

Taxable income		$550,000
Plus: Adjustments		200,000
Adjusted taxable income		$750,000
Less: Dividends paid deduction	$135,000	
Accumulated earnings credit	250,000	(385,000)
Accumulated taxable income		$365,000
Accumulated earnings tax rate		× 20%
Accumulated earnings tax		$ 73,000

.01 Adjustments to Taxable Income

Several adjustments to taxable income are made to calculate accumulated taxable income. These adjustments attempt to provide a more accurate measure of a corporation's earnings for the year that can be distributed to shareholders. The required adjustments to taxable income include:[46]

1. A negative adjustment for amounts paid for federal income taxes and certain foreign income taxes accrued during the year. These amounts are not deducted when calculating taxable income, but they reduce a corporation's capacity to pay dividends.

2. A negative adjustment for any charitable contributions made during the year that were disallowed because of the 10-percent taxable income limitation. Although the charitable contribution deduction is limited when computing taxable income, the entire amount contributed reduces a corporation's ability to pay dividends.

3. A negative adjustment for any capital losses in excess of capital gains because these losses affect a corporation's dividend-paying capacity.

4. A positive adjustment for any DRD and/or NOL deduction taken when calculating taxable income. The NOL deduction related to a previous tax year does not affect a corporation's ability to pay dividends from current year earnings. The DRD reduces the amount of dividends taxed under the regular tax system, but the deduction does not reduce the corporation's ability to distribute the full amount of dividends received during the year to its shareholders.

5. A negative adjustment for any net capital gain (excess of net long-term capital gain over net short-term capital loss) for the tax year, reduced by the taxes attributable to the net gain.

6. A positive adjustment for any charitable contribution carryover from a previous tax year deducted in arriving at taxable income. The contribution to which this deduction relates reduced the corporation's ability to pay dividends out of the prior year's earnings and was taken into consideration in the year in which the contribution was made. (See the explanation in item number 2. above.)

7. A positive adjustment for any capital loss carryover from a previous tax year that offsets capital gains in the current year. The capital loss from another tax year affected the corporation's ability to pay dividends out of earnings in the year in which the loss was incurred.

---

[46] Code Sec. 535(b); Reg. § 1.535-2.

8. A positive adjustment for the recovery of any amount deducted in a prior tax year for purposes of calculating accumulated taxable income (but not for purposes of calculating taxable income) to the extent that the amount recovered reduced the corporation's accumulated earnings tax for the prior tax year.[47]

Many of the adjustments involve deductions that either are limited for the purpose of calculating taxable income or are nondeductible but reduced the amount available to be distributed to shareholders because these amounts were paid by the corporation. Examples include the deduction for federal income taxes and the limitations that are applied to charitable contributions and capital losses. Other adjustments, like the requirement that the NOL deduction and the DRD be added back to taxable income, are necessary because they reduce taxable income but are not associated with a cash outflow that reduced the corporation's ability to pay dividends to its shareholders.

Example 41: Dawning Corporation reports business profits of $100,000 during 2015. Dawning made charitable contributions during the year totaling $50,000. It received dividends from another domestic corporation of $100,000; Dawning owns five percent of the stock in the corporation. Dawning Corporation's dividends paid deduction is $10,000, and its accumulated earnings credit is $35,000.

Business profits		$100,000
Dividend income		100,000
		$200,000
Less: Charitable contribution deduction (limited to $200,000 × 10%)		(20,000)
DRD ($100,000 × 70%)		(70,000)
Taxable income		$110,000
Regular tax on $110,000 taxable income		$ 26,150
Taxable income		$110,000
Less: Excess charitable contributions	$30,000	
Federal income tax	26,150	(56,150)
Adjusted taxable income		$ 53,850
Less: Dividends paid deduction	$10,000	
Accumulated earnings credit	35,000	(45,000)
Accumulated taxable income		$ 8,850
Accumulated earnings tax rate		× 20%
Accumulated earnings tax		$ 1,770

.02 Accumulated Earnings Credit

Accumulated earnings and profits (accumulated E&P) represent the corporation's dividend-paying ability from previous years' E&P. It represents the amount of E&P the corporation has generated over the years that has not been distributed. A corporation is not subject to the accumulated earnings tax if its accumulated E&P does not exceed an amount that the corporation needs to retain to cover the reasonable needs of the business. At a minimum, the tax laws allow corporations to retain $250,000 of accumulated E&P ($150,000 for personal service corporations

---

[47] Code Sec. 111(d); Reg. § 1.111-1(c).

(PSCs), which are corporations engaged in performing services in the fields of health, law, engineering, architecture, accounting, actuarial science, performing arts, or consulting).

The accumulated earnings credit is intended to measure the amount of current year E&P the corporation needs to hold onto in addition to its accumulated E&P to meet the reasonable needs of the business. The accumulated earnings credit is the amount by which the *greater* of (1) the corporation's foreseeable reasonable financial needs or (2) $250,000 ($150,000 for PSCs) exceeds the corporation's accumulated E&P at the beginning of the year.[48] Only the greater of the two amounts over the amounts already retained from previous years (beginning balance in accumulated E&P) is allowed as a credit against adjusted taxable income when computing the current year's accumulated earnings tax. If the corporation can show that its reasonable needs exceed $250,000, it will be able to retain a total of that amount in accumulated E&P.

Example 42: A corporation has accumulated E&P of $50,000 at the beginning of 2015. Its adjusted taxable income for 2015 is $330,000. The corporation paid $20,000 of dividends during 2015. Assuming that the corporation cannot establish the need for more than $250,000 of accumulated earnings, its accumulated earnings credit for the year equals $200,000 ($250,000 – $50,000). The corporation's accumulated taxable income for 2015 is computed as follows:

Adjusted taxable income	$330,000
Less: Dividends paid deduction	(20,000)
Accumulated earnings credit	(200,000)
Accumulated taxable income	$110,000

Assuming that the IRS can show that the corporation was formed or continues to exist to avoid taxation of profits to individual shareholders, its accumulated earnings tax for 2015 equals $22,000 ($110,000 × 20%). This tax is paid in addition to the regular income tax and AMT that the corporation owes for the year.

> **Planning Pointer:** A corporation with individual shareholders that has accumulated E&P in excess of $250,000 should be prepared to justify its reasons for needing to hold onto those accumulated earnings. If no reason exists, the corporation should consider distributing its excess earnings before 2½ months after the close of the tax year to avoid any possibility of being assessed the accumulated earnings tax.

Reasonable accumulations. Accumulations that are considered reasonably necessary to meet the needs of a business include accumulations for business expansion or plant replacement, debt retirement, acquisition of a business through purchase of stock or assets, working capital, investments or loans to suppliers or customers necessary to the maintenance of the corporation's business, and some stock redemptions.[49]

Unacceptable grounds for having excess accumulations include loans to shareholders and expenditures for their personal benefit, loans to relatives or friends of shareholders or to others that have no reasonable connection with the business, loans to a sister corporation, investments that are not related to the business, and accumulations to provide against unrealistic hazards.[50]

Example 43: A corporation has taxable income in year 2015 of $200,000, but its adjusted taxable income is $233,850. The corporation paid $86,000 in dividends during 2015. Accumulated E&P at the beginning of 2015 equals $250,000 and the corporation cannot show a need for accumulations in excess of the $250,000 allowed without justifying its

---

[48] Code Sec. 535(c).
[49] Reg. § 1.537-2(b).

[50] Reg. § 1.537-2(c).

reasonable needs. The corporation's $29,570 accumulated earnings tax for 2015 is computed as shown below. The corporation owes this amount in addition to the regular income tax and any AMT it owes during the year.

Adjusted taxable income		$233,850
Less: Dividends paid deduction	$86,000	
Accumulated earnings credit	0	(86,000)
Accumulated taxable income		$147,850
		× 20%
Accumulated earnings tax		$ 29,570

Example 44: Assume the same facts as in Example 43, except the corporation can demonstrate that its reasonable needs for accumulations of E&P are $400,000. Under this scenario, the corporation would not be subject to any accumulated earnings tax.

Adjusted taxable income		$233,850
Less: Dividends paid deduction	$ 86,000	
Accumulated earnings credit ($400,000 – $250,000)	150,000	(236,000)
Accumulated taxable income		$ 0

Spotlight: Unlike the regular income tax or the AMT, enforcement of the accumulated earnings tax often requires the IRS to reach a decision about the reasonable needs of a corporation. Thus, unsophisticated management may not be aware of a potential accumulated earnings tax liability until an IRS agent in the course of an audit brings the liability to management's attention.

PERSONAL HOLDING COMPANY TAX

In addition to the regular corporate income tax and the AMT, a special tax is imposed on any C corporation that is classified as a personal holding company (PHC). This tax is imposed to prevent individuals from holding investments in corporations whose income is taxed at a lower rate. The PHC tax is 20 percent of a corporation's undistributed PHC income.[51]

Reason for the Rule: When the PHC tax was originally enacted in 1934, the maximum corporate tax rate was 13.5 percent and the top individual tax rate was 63 percent. The difference in these two rates created huge incentives for individuals to form closely held corporations to hold personal investments that would be taxed at much lower tax rates. When the individual needed access to the investments in the corporation, the corporation could be liquidated on a tax-free basis under the tax laws in effect at the time. Today, the difference between the top tax rate for individuals and corporations is not as large, and a PHC can no longer be liquidated free of tax. Thus, even though the PHC rules continue to exist, the advantages of forming a PHC have diminished significantly over time.

---

[51] Code Sec. 541.

¶ 1015 Personal Holding Company Defined

A C corporation is a **personal holding company (PHC)** if (1) at any time during the last half of the tax year, more than 50 percent of the corporation's stock is owned, *directly or indirectly*, by five or fewer individuals and (2) at least 60 percent of the corporation's adjusted ordinary gross income for the tax year is PHC income.[52]

A corporation is excluded from this definition if it is a bank, life insurance company, surety company, foreign corporation, small business investment company, or a corporation that is subject to court jurisdiction in a federal or state bankruptcy, receivership, foreclosure, or similar proceeding; under some circumstances a lending or finance company may also be exempt.[53]

.01 Stock Ownership Requirement

A corporation meets the stock ownership requirement of being a PHC if at any time during the last half of its tax year more than 50 percent in value of its outstanding stock was owned, *directly or indirectly*, by or for five or fewer individuals. Corporations with a considerably greater number of shareholders may also meet the test when the constructive ownership rules are applied.[54] These rules were first introduced in Chapter 8 with the discussion of the related party rules (see ¶ 804). Two of the more common constructive ownership rules are:

1. Stock owned by a corporation or partnership is considered owned proportionately by its shareholders or partners.

2. An individual is considered to own the stock owned by family members (only siblings, spouse, ancestors, or lineal descendants) or by a partner.

.02 Income Requirement

A corporation meets the income requirement for being a PHC if at least 60 percent of its adjusted ordinary gross income for the tax year is PHC income.[55] The purpose of this requirement is to determine whether the income of the corporation is weighted with certain types of passive or investment income so as to indicate that the corporation has no substantial purpose other than to hold income-producing properties for its shareholders.

The ordinary gross income of a PHC is gross income reduced by capital gains and gains from sales or disposition of property used in a trade or business.[56] "Adjusted ordinary gross income" is ordinary gross income minus certain deductions associated with rents, mineral royalties, working interests in oil and gas wells, and certain interest income.[57]

PHC income includes the portion of a corporation's adjusted ordinary gross income that consists of: (1) dividends, interest, and royalties; (2) rents; (3) mineral, oil, and gas royalties; (4) copyright royalties; (5) produced film rents; (6) amounts received by a corporation for the use of its property; (7) compensation under personal services contracts; and (8) estate or trust income.[58]

Example 45: Gamma Corporation, which meets the stock ownership requirement of a PHC, owns a department store, some rental property, and some securities. Its adjusted ordinary gross income for the tax year is $110,000, consisting of gross income from the mercantile business of $40,000, adjusted rental income of $25,000, dividend income of $35,000, and interest income of $10,000. Gamma is a PHC because its $70,000 of PHC income (rents of $25,000 + dividends of $35,000 + interest of $10,000) represents at least 60 percent of its adjusted ordinary gross income of $110,000 ($70,000/$110,000 = 63.6%).

---

[52] Code Sec. 542(a).
[53] Code Sec. 542(c).
[54] Code Sec. 544; Reg. §§ 1.544-1–1.544-7.
[55] Code Sec. 542(a)(1).

[56] Code Sec. 543(b)(1).
[57] Code Sec. 543(b)(2).
[58] Code Sec. 543(a).

¶ 1016 Undistributed Personal Holding Company Income

The amount subject to the PHC tax is a personal holding company's **undistributed personal holding company income**. This amount is determined by applying certain adjustments to a personal holding company's taxable income and subtracting a dividends paid deduction.[59] A 20 percent tax rate is assessed on undistributed PHC income.[60] The adjustments to taxable income include many of the adjustments necessary for the accumulated earnings tax. (See ¶ 1014.01.)

As in the calculation of the accumulated taxable income, dividends paid during the year are deducted in computing a personal holding company's undistributed PHC income. This includes dividends paid during the first 2½ months of the following year that the taxpayer elects to treat as paid in the current year.[61] This deduction makes it possible for a corporation that has not been able to avoid PHC status to avoid payment of the penalty tax on its undistributed PHC income.

Example 46: A PHC's taxable income for 2015 is $200,000, computed without taking into account the deductions for charitable contributions or for dividends received deduction (DRD). The PHC made contributions of $45,000 to a charitable organization during the year. It also received $100,000 of dividends from other domestic corporations in which it owned five percent of the stock. The PHC paid $70,000 of dividends to its shareholders in 2015, and it paid an additional $14,000 of dividends prior to March 15, 2016. The PHC elects to treat the dividends paid before March 15, 2016, as paid during 2015.

Taxable income		$200,000
Less: Charitable contribution deduction		
($200,000 × 10%)	$20,000	
DRD ($100,000 × 70%)	70,000	(90,000)
Taxable income		$110,000
Regular tax on $110,000 taxable income		$ 26,150
Taxable income		$110,000
Add: DRD		70,000
Deduct: Excess charitable contribution deduction	$25,000	
Federal income taxes paid	26,150	
Dividends paid during year	70,000	
Dividends paid before March 15, 2016	14,000	(135,150)
Undistributed PHC income		$ 44,850
		× 20%
Personal holding company tax		$ 8,970

¶ 1017 Summary

If after applying the tax laws discussed in Chapters 1 to 9, an individual or corporate taxpayer has negative taxable income, the taxpayer may have a NOL that can be used to offset gross income in other tax years. If taxable income results, regular income taxes must be paid by individual and corporate taxpayers, and for some taxpayers, AMT might be due. In addition to income taxes, the

---

[59] Code Sec. 545.
[60] Code Sec. 541.

[61] Code Secs. 561(b), 563.

accumulated earnings tax and the PHC tax are penalty taxes corporations will want to avoid because they are imposed in addition to the income taxes corporations pay during the year.

GLOSSARY OF TERMS INTRODUCED IN THE CHAPTER

Accumulated earnings and profits. The amount of E&P a C corporation has generated over the years that has not been distributed as of the beginning of its current tax year.

Accumulated earnings credit. A credit taken as part of the calculation of the accumulated earnings tax. The amount of the credit is the amount by which the *greater of* (1) the corporation's foreseeable reasonable financial needs or (2) $250,000 ($150,000 for personal service corporations) exceeds the corporation's accumulated E&P at the beginning of the year.

Accumulated earnings tax. A penalty tax imposed on C corporations formed or that continue to exist for the purpose of preventing individual shareholders from paying tax on the profits of the corporation by allowing E&P to accumulate. The amount of the tax is 20% of a corporation's accumulated taxable income.

Adjusted current earnings (ACE). An adjustment made to taxable income to compute alternative minimum taxable income. The ACE is similar to current earnings and profits. ACE differs from current E&P in that current E&P attempts to measure the corporation's capacity to pay dividends from current period earnings, while the ACE calculation is intended to measure pretax income before any distributions.

Alternative minimum tax (AMT). A tax enacted to enhance equity in the income tax system by ensuring that all taxpayers pay at least some minimum income taxes each year. It is imposed in addition to the regular tax.

Alternative minimum taxable income (AMTI). AMTI is calculated to determine whether a taxpayer owes the alternative minimum tax. AMTI is determined by making certain adjustments to regular taxable income. *See also* Alternative minimum tax.

AMT base. The tax base used in the AMT system; determined by subtracting the exemption amount from the alternative minimum taxable income. This amount is analogous to taxable income in the regular income tax system. *See also* Alternative minimum tax *and* Alternative minimum taxable income.

Circulation costs. Amounts paid or incurred to establish, maintain, or increase the circulation of a newspaper, magazine, or other periodical.

Current earnings and profits. A C corporation's earnings and profits for its current tax year. A corporate tax concept that attempts to capture a corporation's capacity to pay dividends from its current year's earnings.

Minimum tax credit. The amount of alternative minimum tax paid in one year that can be used to offset a taxpayer's regular tax liability for a subsequent tax year. *See also* Alternative minimum tax *and* Timing differences.

Net operating loss deduction. The total of a taxpayer's net operating loss carryforwards and carrybacks to a tax year.

Personal holding company (PHC). Any corporation for which (1) at any time during the last half of the tax year, more than 50 percent of the corporation's stock is owned, *directly or indirectly*, by five or fewer individuals and (2) at least 60 percent of the corporation's adjusted ordinary income for the year is PHC income.

Personal holding company income. Eight specific types of ordinary income, including: (1) dividends, interest, and royalties; (2) rents; (3) mineral, oil, and gas royalties; (4) copyright royalties; (5) produced film rents; (6) amounts received by a corporation for the use of its property; (7) compensation under personal services contracts; and (8) estate or trust income.

Personal service corporation (PSC). For purposes of the accumulated earnings tax, a corporation whose principal function is the performance of services in the field of health, law, engineering, architecture, accounting, actuarial science, the performing arts, or consulting. Personal service corporations are entitled to a lower accumulated earnings credit than other corporations.

Private activity bond. A bond issued by a state or other municipality from which more than 10 percent of the proceeds are used to finance private business activities. Interest paid on these bonds is exempt from regular income tax if the issuer has complied with certain limitations concerning the volume of the bonds issued and the use of the bond proceeds.

Tax preference. A deduction or exclusion allowed in the calculation of regular taxable income that is not allowed in the calculation of alternative minimum taxable income.

Timing difference. In the alternative minimum tax system, a difference in the treatment of an item for determining regular taxable income and alternative minimum taxable income that reverses itself over time.

Undistributed personal holding company income. The amount subject to the personal holding company tax, determined by applying certain adjustments to the taxable income of the corporation.

CHAPTER PROBLEMS

Chapter 10 Discussion Questions

1. A taxpayer has a net operating loss. In looking over the past several tax returns and the anticipated future growth of his business, the taxpayer believes it would be advantageous from a tax perspective to utilize its NOL in future tax years. Can this be done, and if so what steps must the taxpayer take?

2. Sig and Tom are equal partners in a partnership that reports an ordinary loss of $17,000. Is this loss a NOL? Who is entitled to the loss?

3. Under what circumstances can the dividends received deduction create or increase a corporation's NOL?

4. Are all taxpayers subject to the AMT? Discuss.

5. If a corporation fails to qualify as a small corporation in 2015 for purposes of the alternative minimum tax (AMT), what, if anything, can it do in 2016 to avoid being subject to the AMT?

6. What role does "tentative minimum tax" play in the calculation of the AMT?

7. The maximum corporate AMT exemption amount is $40,000. At what point does a corporation subject to the AMT have a $0 exemption?

8. What two AMT tax preferences relate to owners and/or produces of oil and gas property?

9. AMT preferences items are always positive adjustments to taxable income for purposes of computing AMTI. Explain.

10. AMT adjustments resulting from timing adjustments may be positive or negative. Explain.

11. Do taxpayers that experience a net operating loss (NOL) for the tax year need to recompute the NOL for AMT purposes?

12. While corporate earnings and profits (E&P) attempt to measure a corporation's capacity to pay dividends from current period earnings, what is the adjusted current earnings (ACE) calculation intended to measure?

13. When can AMT paid in one year be carried forward as a credit against regular tax in a subsequent year?

14. Is the AMT tax rate the same for corporate and individual taxpayers?

15. Which taxpayers are subject to the accumulated earnings tax and under what circumstances does it apply?

16. Which party (the corporation or the IRS) has the burden of proving that earnings and profits are not being accumulated for a tax avoidance purpose?

17. How is the accumulated earnings credit computed?

18. What might constitute "reasonable needs of the business" for purposes of computing the accumulated earnings credit?

19. What is a personal holding company (PHC)?

20. What tax law changes have contributed to the decline in the attractiveness of personal holding companies?

Chapter 10 Problems

1. In 2015, Acme Corporation reports negative taxable income of $350,000, including a net operating loss (NOL) carryforward from 2014 of $70,000. What is Acme's NOL for 2015?

2. An individual taxpayer reports a $19,000 NOL in 2015. To which tax years can this NOL be applied? How would your answer change if the taxpayer were a C corporation, rather than an individual?

3. Failing Corporation incurred a NOL of $90,000 for the calendar year 2015. Failing carried this loss back to 2013. In 2013, Failing had $400,000 of gross income and business expenses of $325,000. Included in the business expenses was a deduction for a charitable contribution of $3,000. In addition, a NOL of $40,000 from 2014 had been carried back to 2013. What is the Failing's NOL to be carried forward from 2013?

4. The Simplex Machine Corporation presents you with the following profit and loss statement of its operations for 2015 and requests that you prepare its tax return.

Sales	$570,000
Less: Cost of goods sold	(480,000)
Gross profit	$ 90,000
Less: Operating expenses	(110,000)
	($ 20,000)
Section 1231 gain from sale of building	4,000
Taxable income (loss)	($ 16,000)

Simplex Machine's taxable income for 2013 and 2014 was $9,000 and $33,000, respectively.

a. Compute the NOL, if any, for the Simplex Machine Corporation for 2015, its NOL deduction, if any, for 2013 and 2014, and the amount, if any, of its NOL for 2015 that it can carry forward to subsequent tax years.

b. What else should you do for your client once you apply the loss to the prior years' income?

5. A corporation generates a $72,000 NOL in 20X6. The corporation's modified taxable income for the following years is as follows.

20X1	$ 19,000
20X2	25,000
20X3	3,000
20X4	10,000
20X5	12,000
20X7	22,000
20X8	21,000

NOL 12,000 (handwritten annotation next to 20X5/20X7)

a. Compute the corporation's NOL carryover to 20X9 assuming that the corporation does not elect to forego the NOL carryback.

b. Compute the corporation's NOL carryover to 20X9 assuming the corporation elects to forego the NOL carryback.

6. Assume that the marginal tax rate of the corporation in Problem 5 is 15 percent from 20X1–20X5 and 34 percent from 20X7–20X9. Compute the total tax savings generated from the NOL assuming (a) that the corporation does not forego the carry back period, and (b) the corporation elects to forego the carry back period. For purposes of this calculation, assume that any remaining NOL carryover is utilized in 20X9.

7. For the prior tax year, XYZ Corp. had an asset with a basis of $20,000, for both regular tax and AMT purposes, with respect to which a $700 depreciation deduction was calculated for regular tax purposes but a $500 depreciation deduction was calculated for AMT purposes. What will be the basis for determining gain in the current year under both the regular tax system and the AMT system?

8. ACME Corporation sells a piece of equipment with an adjusted tax basis of $300,000 for $400,000. The terms of the sale have ACME receiving $100,000 at the time of the sale and $100,000 annually over the next three years. ACME does not elect out of the installment method. Compute the positive or negative adjustments that must be made to AMTI in each of the four years for purposes of computing ACME's adjusted current earnings.

9. A corporation's taxable income and AMTI are $130,000 and $280,000, respectively. Assuming the corporation is subject to the AMT, compute the corporation's total income tax liability for the year.

10. A calendar-year corporation's first tax year is 20X1. Its unadjusted AMTI is $150,000 each year from 20X1–20X3. The corporation's ACE during those years is $200,000, $120,000, and $100,000, respectively. Compute the ACE adjustment in each of these three years 20X1–20X3.

11. A corporate taxpayer receives $50,000 of municipal interest, which includes $10,000 of interest from specified private activity bonds. What amount of the $50,000 interest is included in the corporation's taxable income, alternative minimum taxable income, and current year earnings and profits (E&P)?

12. A corporation in the retail industry with calendar-year end has $300,000 in taxable income in 2015. This figure includes $1,000 for an installment sale made in 2012; the total gain from the sale was $5,000. The taxable income reflected $30,000 in depreciation, $20,000 of which represented the excess of accelerated depreciation over straight-line. The corporation received $10,000 of tax-exempt interest from a specified private activity bond. No nondeductible expenses were related to this income. The corporation's ACE equaled $800,000. Determine the corporation's alternative minimum tax for 2015.

13. Widget Corporation has taxable income of $500,000 for the current year. There are net positive adjustments to taxable income for purposes of the accumulated earnings tax of $50,000. Widget paid dividends during the year of $45,000, and its accumulated earnings credit is $200,000. Calculate Widget's accumulated earnings tax for the year.

14. A retail hardware store was organized on January 1, 2015. Its taxable income in the first year is $300,000. It makes no distributions to its shareholders during that year or during the

first 2½ months of the second year. The only adjustments to taxable income for purposes of the accumulated earnings tax is for federal income taxes paid on its taxable income.

   a. Will the corporation be subject to the accumulated earnings tax for the first tax year?

   b. Assuming that the corporation has the same taxable income the second year and that it makes no distributions during the second year or the first 2½ months of the third year, will it be subject to the accumulated earnings tax for the second year?

   c. If the corporation had distributed $115,000 to shareholders in its first year of existence and nothing in the second year, would it be subject to the accumulated earnings tax for the second year?

15. West Corporation had taxable income of $200,000 in 2015 and $250,000 for 2016. How much, if any, of the 2015 income must the West Corporation distribute in order to be sure to avoid the accumulated earnings tax for 2016 if it cannot justify taking more than the minimum credit? Assume that the only adjustment to taxable income for purposes of the accumulated earnings credit is for its federal tax paid.

16. The Axel Construction receives 90 percent of its gross income during the tax year from interest on industrial bonds and dividends on railways stocks. Dan Majors owns 20 percent of Axel, Dan's son owns 10 percent, and the son's wife owns five percent. The rest of the shares are owned by 13 unrelated employees each of whom own five percent. Is Axel Construction a personal holding company? Explain.

17. A corporation that meets the stock ownership requirement of a personal holding company (PHC), owns a hardware store, residential rental property, and some corporate stocks and bonds. Its adjusted ordinary gross income for the tax year is $180,000, consisting of gross income from the mercantile business of $50,000, adjusted rental income of $35,000, dividend income of $55,000, and interest income of $40,000. Is the corporation a PHC?

18. Assume the same facts as in Problem 17, except that the corporation's dividend income is $5,000. Assume all other income items and amounts remain the same. Is the corporation a PHC?

19. A personal holding company's taxable income for 2015 is $200,000, which includes a $90,000 dividends received deduction. The PHC has a $13,000 charitable contribution carryover due to its current year contributions being subject to the taxable income limitation. It paid $45,000 of dividends to its shareholders in 2015 and an additional $26,000 of dividends on March 19, 2016. The PHC elects to treat dividends paid within the first 2½ months of 2016 as paid during 2015. Compute the company's PHC tax for 2015.

20. Assume the same facts as in Problem 19, except that the PHC makes a dividend distribution on March 15, 2016. Compute the company's PHC tax for 2015. Comment on the difference between the answers to Problems 19 and 20.

21. Godsey Corporation has a net operating loss of $60,000 for its 2015 tax year. For its 2013 tax year, its taxable income was $55,000 and its modified taxable income was $45,000. For its 2014 tax year, its taxable income was $35,000 and its modified taxable income was $30,000. For its 2016 tax year, it expects its taxable income to be $30,000 and its modified taxable income to be $25,000. For its 2017 tax year, it expects its taxable income to be $120,000 and its modified taxable income to be $100,000. Based on this information, how should the corporation treat its NOL for 2015, and how much will it save if it follows your recommendation?

22. Jernigan Corporation, which uses the calendar year as its tax year, started business on December 1, 2013. Its gross receipts for 2013 totaled $500,000. Its gross receipts for 2014–2016 were $4,500,000, $4,900,000, and $6,000,000, respectively. Will the corporation be subject to the AMT in 2016? Explain your answer.

23. Hoffman, Inc. had to pay $50,000 in AMT for its 2015 tax year. If its taxable income for 2016 is $170,000 and it is not subject to the AMT that year, how much tax will it owe?

24. For her 2015 tax year, Rosie Longo, who is unmarried, received $75,000 in wages (her only source of AGI for the year). During the year she exercised an incentive stock option and purchased 100 shares of her company's stock (with a fair market value of $40 per share) for $10 per share. She took the standard deduction and personal exemption. What is her tentative minimum tax for the year? Does she owe any AMT?

25. Hyman, Inc. has four shareholders. John Hyman owns 20% of the corporation's stock. Mae Ritter, who is not related to John, owns 15% of the corporation's stock. The Bracket Partnership owns the remaining 65% of the corporation's stock. That partnership consists of John and four unrelated partners, who each owns the same interest in the partnership. Does John satisfy the stock ownership requirement for a personal holding company?

Chapter 10 Review Problems

1. After an investigation by the IRS, the following facts were discovered from the books and records of the Shady Tree Nursery, which began business on January 1, 2013.

	2013	2014	2015	2016
Gross profit on sales	$100,000	$210,000	$160,000	$70,000
Net capital gains			5,000	
Net capital losses		(5,000)		(3,000)
Gross income	$100,000	$205,000	$165,000	$67,000
Business expenses	(130,000)	(155,000)	(145,000)	(87,000)
Net income per books	($ 30,000)	$ 50,000	$ 20,000	($20,000)

a. In computing taxable income for 2014 and 2016, are the net capital losses deductible?

b. Compute the taxable income for 2014 after taking into account any net operating loss carrybacks and carryforwards from 2013 and 2016.

2. A personal holding company's taxable income for 2015 is $250,000, computed before taking into account the charitable contributions deduction and the dividends received deduction. Included in the $250,000 is $120,000 of dividends it received from other domestic corporations in which it owns 25 percent of the stock. The PHC makes contributions of $55,000 to a charitable organization during the year. It paid $75,000 of dividends to its shareholders in 2015 and an additional $40,000 of dividends on March 8, 2016. What amount of PHC tax does it owe for 2015?

3. A calendar year corporation has $100,000 in taxable income for 2015. In calculating its alternative minimum tax (AMT), it has positive adjustments and tax preferences of $140,000 and $60,000, respectively. Its adjusted current earnings for the year are $500,000.

a. Compute the corporation's 2015 AMT.

b. What would have been the corporation's AMT given its average gross receipts for all three-tax-year periods ending before its current tax year was below $5 million?

Chapter 10 Comprehensive Review Question

For its tax year ended December 31, 2015, Beneficial Corporation had the following income and expenses:

Income:

Sales	$4,000,000
Interest income ($100,000 of tax-exempt interest other than from specified private activity bonds)	200,000
Short-term capital gain	50,000

Expenses:

Cost of goods sold	$2,000,000
Wages	400,000
Interest expense	50,000
Depreciation*	150,000
Charitable contributions	100,000
Miscellaneous	500,000

* Under GAAP, depreciation expense is $100,000; for purposes of AMT depreciation is $125,000.

Beneficial's QPAI for purposes of the domestic production activities deduction is $600,000. Compute Beneficial's 2015 regular income tax liability and its AMT.

Chapter 10 Research Question

You are approached by a corporation with a long-standing dispute with the IRS. The corporation incurred alternative minimum tax net operating losses in the years subsequent to the enactment of the corporate alternative minimum tax in 1986. The corporation seeks to carryforward these AMT net operating losses so that it can obtain tax refunds for subsequent tax years. The IRS contends that these AMT net operating losses must first be carried back and applied against regular tax in the years prior to the enactment of the corporate AMT. Determine whether you can find any authority on this issue that would support the taxpayer's or the IRS's position.

CHAPTER 11

Tax Credits

CHAPTER CONTENTS

LEARNING OBJECTIVES

1. Understand what a tax credit is and how it differs from a tax deduction.

2. Learn the distinction between a refundable tax credit and a nonrefundable tax credit.

3. Be able to explain what credits available to businesses are and how they are calculated.

4. Be able to describe the limitations that apply to business tax credits and explain the rules that allow tax credits that cannot be utilized in one tax year to be carried over to other tax years.

5. Understand how tax credits can reduce a business's transaction costs.

¶ 1100 Introduction

As discussed in Chapter 1, the federal government often uses tax laws to encourage certain types of behavior. One tool used to accomplish this is the **tax credit**, which is an amount by which the government allows a taxpayer to reduce its tax liability. This chapter reintroduces the concept of a tax credit and reviews the advantages of tax credits over tax deductions.

This chapter introduces the various tax credits available to businesses and discusses the requirements and limitations that apply to some of the more commonly used ones. Most credits available to businesses are computed individually and then grouped together as part of the general business credit. A separate limitation applies to the general business credit each year. The limitations on and treatment of any unutilized credits are discussed.

Because tax credits reduce a taxpayer's tax liability, anyone involved in making decisions on behalf of a business needs to understand how tax credits can be used to reduce transaction costs. What otherwise might be considered an unattractive endeavor might become attractive when available credits are taken into consideration.

 GAAP vs. Code: Financial reporting has no equivalent to a tax credit. A tax credit is a tax concept only.

¶ 1101 Tax Savings Generated from a Tax Credit vs. a Tax Deduction

A tax credit is an amount that is subtracted from a taxpayer's tax liability. Thus, the tax savings derived from a $1 tax credit equals $1.

Example 1: Berglund Thermometers, Inc. had a gross income of $200,000, deductions of $106,000, and a business tax credit of $10,000. Burglund's taxable income equals $94,000 ($200,000 – $106,000), and its tax liability using the corporate income tax rates is $20,210. The $10,000 tax credit is subtracted from Berglund's tax liability, thereby reducing its taxes owed by $10,000.

By contrast, a tax deduction reduces a taxpayer's taxable income. The tax savings derived from a $1 tax deduction equals $1 multiplied by the taxpayer's marginal tax rate, which is the rate of tax paid on the last dollar included in taxable income. Therefore, all other things being equal, the tax benefits of a tax credit always outweigh the tax savings produced by a tax deduction.

Example 2: Assume the same facts as in Example 1, except that instead of a $10,000 tax credit Berglund has additional tax deductions of $10,000. The additional deductions reduce Berglund's taxable income to $84,000. Because Berglund's taxable income falls into the 34-percent tax bracket, its tax liability will be reduced by $3,400 ($10,000 × 34%). Hence, the $10,000 tax savings from the $10,000 tax credit illustrated in Example 1 outweigh the $3,400 tax savings produced by the $10,000 tax deduction illustrated here.

Because the tax savings derived from a deduction vary with the taxpayer's marginal tax rate, taxpayers in higher tax brackets benefit more from tax deductions than those in lower tax brackets. Therefore, tax deductions favor higher-income taxpayers. Tax credits, on the other hand, benefit all taxpayers equally. Consequently, tax credits often are seen as a fairer way to offer tax incentives to taxpayers.

Example 3: Godsey Handles, Inc. and Arbuckle Co. are each entitled to a $50,000 depreciation deduction and a $10,000 business tax credit. Godsey's taxable income falls in the 25-percent tax bracket; Arbuckle's falls in the 34-percent tax bracket. The $10,000 tax credit reduces each company's respective tax liability by $10,000. The $50,000 depreciation deduction reduces Godsey's tax liability by $12,500 ($50,000 × 25%), but Arbuckle's tax liability by $17,000 ($50,000 × 34%). The $4,500 difference is due to the nine-percent difference in the companies' marginal tax rates ($50,000 × 9% = $4,500 additional tax savings to Arbuckle).

Recall that the government takes an all-inclusive approach to defining gross income but allows deductions for expenses only by legislative grace. Thus, when the government allows businesses to deduct expenses from gross income, less tax revenues are generated and the government in essence subsidizes a portion of the company's expenditures. By contrast, when the entire amount of an expenditure is offered as a tax credit, the actual cost of the item is paid for by the government. Therefore, most tax credits are computed as a percentage of the actual expenditure. In some instances when the government allows a portion of the cost to be taken as a tax credit, it then allows the remainder to be deducted from gross income.

Example 4: As discussed in Chapter 6, the tax laws allow businesses to deduct wages they pay their employees as an ordinary and necessary business expense against their gross income. In the current year, Roland Enterprises (whose taxable income falls in the 35-percent tax bracket) pays an employee wages totaling $20,000. Roland's tax savings from those wages equals $7,000 ($20,000 × 35%). Accordingly, Roland's actual out-of-pocket cost for the wages paid to the employee is only $13,000 ($20,000 – $7,000).

Example 5: Assume the same facts as in Example 4, except that the tax laws allow businesses to take a tax credit equal to 40 percent of the first $10,000 of first-year wages paid to a long-term family assistance recipient. Any wages not taken as a credit can be deducted from the taxpayer's gross income. Accordingly, if Roland hires a long-term family assistance recipient and pays that individual $20,000 in the first year, Roland's tax credit will equal $4,000 ($10,000 × 40%). Roland will then be able to deduct the remaining $16,000 ($20,000 – $4,000) from its gross income, thereby generating an additional tax savings of $5,600 ($16,000 × 35%). Roland's total tax savings from hiring this employee would be $9,600 ($4,000 + $5,600), and its actual out-of-pocket costs with respect to the wages would be $10,400 ($20,000 – $9,600).

Examples 4 and 5 illustrate how a company's understanding of the tax laws can generate additional cash flows by reducing the amounts the company pays in federal income taxes. Comparing the cash savings in the two scenarios, Roland can reduce its out-of-pocket costs for this worker by $2,600 ($13,000 – $10,400) by hiring a long-term family assistance recipient instead of a worker who is not a long-term family assistance recipient. Another way to compute the $2,600 of cash savings is to compare the tax savings of hiring a long-term family assistance recipient ($9,600) with that of hiring someone who is not a long-term family assistance recipient ($7,000).

¶ 1102 Types of Tax Credits

Tax credits can be business or personal. They can also be refundable or nonrefundable. A **refundable tax credit** can reduce a taxpayer's tax liability to zero and produce a refund for any amount of the credit in excess of the taxpayer's tax liability. A **nonrefundable tax credit** can only reduce a taxpayer's tax liability to zero.

Most tax credits are nonrefundable. For example, amounts taxpayers prepay toward their current year's tax liability, whether through withholdings or by making estimated tax payments, reduce the amount of taxes taxpayers owe when filing their annual income tax returns and are refunded to the extent not needed to cover their current year tax liability (see ¶ 410). Most other refundable tax credits are personal credits available only to individual taxpayers.

.01 Business vs. Personal Tax Credits

Tax incentives, whether they are offered as exclusions, deductions, or credits, are used by governments to encourage and reward taxpayers for making certain types of decisions. **Business tax credits** are a way governments reward businesses by subsidizing a portion of the expenditures they incur when participating in certain types of activities. An example of a business tax credit is the work opportunity credit, which was illustrated in Example 5. This credit rewards businesses that hire members of a targeted group by reducing the company's tax liabilities. Business tax credits are available to all types of business entities, including corporations, sole proprietorships, and flow-through entities.

Personal tax credits are available only to individual taxpayers. Like business tax credits, many personal tax credits subsidize certain types of expenditures. However, a few personal credits are available without any corresponding cash expenditures. For example, the federal government allows an earned income credit to taxpayers who report relatively low amounts of earned income on their individual income tax returns. It also allows a $1,000 tax credit for each qualifying child of a taxpayer whose income does not exceed a specified amount. Most personal tax credits are nonrefundable. However, a few are refundable. Because the focus of this book is how taxes impact business decisions, the details regarding the various personal credits are beyond the scope of this chapter. However, the more common personal tax credits available to individual taxpayers are listed in Figure 11-1.

Figure 11-1 Personal Tax Credits

Nonrefundable Personal Credits
- Lifetime Learning credit
- Child and dependent care credit,
- Adoption expenses credit,
- Credit for the elderly and the disabled,
- Elective deferrals and IRA contributions credit,
- Mortgage interest credit,
- Nonbusiness energy property credit,
- Residential energy efficient property credit,
- Alternative motor vehicle credit for new qualified fuel cell motor vehicles, and
- Qualified plug-in electric drive motor vehicle credit.

Refundable Personal Credits
- Credit for prepayment of taxes,
- Credit for overpayment of social security taxes,
- Earned income credit, and
- Health insurance costs credit.

Partially Refundable Personal Credits
- Child tax credit, and
- American Opportunity credit.

The nonbusiness energy property credit does not apply with respect to property placed in service after December 31, 2014. The residential energy efficient property credit does not apply to property placed in service after December 31, 2016.

Reason for the Rule: As mentioned in Chapter 1, the standard deduction and personal exemption are intended to reduce the taxable income of lower-income taxpayers to zero or near zero. Because nonrefundable tax credits are of little or no value to taxpayers with little or no taxable income, some personal tax credits, like the earned income credit and the child tax credit, were made refundable so that taxpayers with little or no taxable income can benefit from them. Because the earned income tax credit is available only to taxpayers who report taxable earned income to the federal government on their income tax returns, the earned income tax credit serves the purposes of reallocating wealth to lower-income taxpayers, encouraging lower-income taxpayers to earn more money, and increasing tax compliance by lower-income taxpayers by requiring them to file an annual tax return in order to claim the credit.

.02 The Motivation Behind Offering Tax Credits

Offering tax credits to individuals and businesses serves many purposes. Some tax credits, like the refundable tax credit for prepaid income taxes, exist to prevent taxpayers from overpaying taxes that they owe. Other examples include the foreign tax credit and the credit for overpayment of social security taxes.

When income included in taxable income is taxed by both the United States and a foreign country, the federal government allows a tax credit for the taxes paid to the foreign country to ensure that the taxpayer is taxed only once on the income. The foreign tax credit is available to all types of taxpayers, including individuals and all business entities.

The tax credit for overpayment of social security taxes is necessary because the tax laws require employers to withhold the 6.2-percent social security tax on the first $118,500 of income earned during a tax year beginning in 2015. Thus, employees who have more than one employer during 2015 and earn more than $118,500 will overpay their social security tax. The refundable credit for overpayment of social security taxes ensures that any excess social security tax withheld during the calendar year will be refunded to workers when they file their income tax returns.

Although a few tax credits exist to ensure that taxpayers are refunded any taxes they overpay during the year, most tax credits exist to encourage businesses to make certain types of decisions. For example, the federal government offers tax incentives for businesses to hire certain groups of economically disadvantaged workers. It also helps subsidize the costs businesses incur in rehabilitating a historical structure or providing access to individuals with a physical disability. Such credits are the focus of this chapter.

¶ 1103 General Business Credit

Numerous tax credits are available to businesses. With the exception of the foreign tax credit (discussed in ¶ 1116), tax credits aimed at businesses are components of what is known as the **general business credit**. As with deductions, each business credit is subject to its own set of eligibility requirements and limitations. Each credit that is part of the general business credit is computed separately, and then the various credits are aggregated to compute a taxpayer's general business credit for that tax year.

In addition to the limits imposed on each separate credit, Congress also limits the amount that taxpayers can claim as a general business credit in any one tax year. Although the general business credit is a nonrefundable credit, any amount of general business credit that cannot be taken in any one tax year can be carried over to other tax years. Unused general business credits can be carried back one year and forward for up to 20 years.[1]

---

[1] Code Sec. 39(a).

Reason for the Rule: The limitation prevents taxpayers from being able to entirely offset their income tax liabilities in any given tax year. However, the generous carryover provisions help ensure that taxpayers will eventually utilize the tax credits in tax years when they have sufficient amounts of tax liabilities.

.01 Calculating the General Business Credit

Businesses are allowed a nonrefundable general business credit equal to the sum of the following amounts:

1. The current year general business credit;
2. The general business credit carried forward from prior tax years to the current tax year; and
3. The general business credit carried back to the current tax year from a subsequent tax year.[2]

Example 6: Taggert Company claimed a $20,000 general business credit on its 2015 corporate tax return. During 2016, Taggert Company generates a $50,000 general business credit. However, due to the limitations imposed on the amount of general business credit allowed in any one year, only $35,000 of the credit is allowed. Taggert carries back the $15,000 of disallowed general business credit to 2015 and recomputes its taxes owed in that year using a $35,000 recomputed general business credit ($20,000 current year [2015] credit + $15,000 credit carried back from 2016).

Example 7: Assume the same facts as in Example 6, except that when Taggert reapplies the general business credit limitations in 2015, $3,000 of the general business credit is disallowed. Taggert carries forward the $3,000 to 2017 and adds it to any general business credit generated in that year.

Like many credits, the credits that comprise the general business credit were enacted to encourage certain types of behavior. The various types of activities and behaviors that the government was hoping to encourage include (1) hiring certain types of workers; (2) conserving and exploring new sources of energy; (3) conducting research in specified areas; and (4) assisting in economic development. Other business tax credits were enacted to subsidize businesses for certain socially or economically desirable expenditures made during the year. Figure 11-2 summarizes the various tax credits that comprise the general business credit.

Figure 11-2 Tax Credits That Comprise the General Business Credit

Tax Credits Aimed at Encouraging Employers to Hire Certain Workers
- Work opportunity credit,
- Employer wage credit for employees who are active duty members of the uniformed services,
- Empowerment zone employment credit, and
- Indian employment credit.

Tax Credits Aimed at Encouraging Conservation of Energy and Reduction of Greenhouse Gases
- Alternative motor vehicle credit,
- Plug-in electric drive motor vehicle credit

---

[2] Code Sec. 38(a).

- Alternative fuel vehicle refueling property credit,
- Home builder's credit for new energy efficient homes,
- Energy credit,
- Electricity produced from certain renewable resources credit,
- Credit for producing fuel from a nonconventional source,
- Alcohol used as fuel credit,
- Biodiesel and renewable diesel used as fuel credit,
- Low sulfur diesel fuel production credit,
- Renewable electricity and refined coal production credit,
- Carbon dioxide sequestration credit,
- Qualifying advanced coal project credit,
- Qualifying gasification project credit,
- Advanced energy project credit,
- Advanced nuclear power facilities production credit,
- Enhanced oil recovery credit, and
- Marginal oil and gas well production credit.

Tax Credits Aimed at Rewarding Research in Certain Areas

- Research credit,
- Orphan drug credit, and
- Qualifying therapeutic discovery project credit.

Tax Credits to Encourage Economic Development

- Empowerment zone employment credit, and
- New markets credit.

Tax Credits Used to Subsidize Businesses for Certain Expenditures during the Year

- Employer social security tax credit,
- Employer wage credit for employees who are active duty members of the Uniformed Services,
- Rehabilitation credit,
- Low-income housing credit,
- Disabled access credit,
- Employer-provided child care credit,
- Small employer pension plan start-up cost credit,
- Small employer health insurance credit,
- Distilled spirits credit,
- Railroad track maintenance credit,
- Mine rescue team training credit,
- Agricultural chemicals security credit, and
- Advanced nuclear power facility credit.

The work opportunity credit, employer wage credit for employees who are active duty members of the uniformed services, empowerment zone employment credit, Indian employment credit, home builder's credit for new energy efficient homes, alcohol used as fuel credit, biodiesel fuels credit, research credit, new markets tax credit, credit for electricity produced from renewable resources, railroad track maintenance credit, and mine rescue team training credit expire December 31, 2014.

¶ 1103.01

The alternative fuel vehicle refueling property credit does not apply to any property placed in service after December 31, 2014. The alternative motor vehicle credit is available only for new qualified fuel cell motor vehicles purchased no later than December 31, 2014. Note, however, that Congress has been extending these credits from year to year.

.02 Overall Limitations on the Amount of the General Business Credit

The amount of a taxpayer's general business credit for any tax year is limited to the amount by which the taxpayer's net income tax exceeds the *greater* of (1) the taxpayer's tentative minimum tax for the tax year or (2) 25 percent of the amount by which the taxpayer's net regular tax liability exceeds $25,000.[3]

Tentative minimum tax was introduced in Chapter 10. When a taxpayer's tentative minimum tax exceeds the taxpayer's regular tax liability, the excess represents the taxpayer's alternative minimum tax (AMT) for the year. "Regular tax liability" is the tax liability computed on taxable income using the applicable progressive income tax rates. **Net regular tax liability** is the taxpayer's regular tax liability minus certain tax credits like the foreign tax credit and personal tax credits (in the case of an individual, including a sole proprietor).[4] **Net income tax** equals the sum of the net regular tax liability and any AMT minus the same tax credits used in computing net regular tax liability. Thus, the difference between net income tax and net regular tax liability is usually the taxpayer's AMT for the year.

Example 8: For 2015, Norris Machine Shop calculates $170,000 of regular tax liability on its taxable income and takes a $10,000 foreign tax credit. Norris's tentative minimum tax equals $120,000. Because this amount does not exceed its regular tax liability, Norris is not subject to AMT in 2015.

For the purposes of computing the limitation on its general business credit, net regular tax liability equals $160,000 ($170,000 regular tax liability – $10,000 foreign tax credit). Because Norris is not subject to AMT in 2015, net income tax also equals $160,000 ($170,000 regular tax liability + $0 AMT – $10,000 foreign tax credit). If in 2015 Norris generates a total general business credit of $50,000, it will be allowed to reduce its 2015 tax liability by $40,000 as calculated below. The $10,000 ($50,000 – $40,000) that Norris is not allowed to use in 2015 can be carried back to 2014. If not fully utilized in 2014, the remaining credit can be carried forward from 2016 through 2035, and it can be applied against the company's income tax liability in those years.

Net income tax	$160,000
Less: The *greater of* (1) $120,000 or	
(2) $33,750 [25% × ($160,000 – $25,000)]	(120,000)
General business credit allowed in 2014	$ 40,000

Example 9: For 2015, McMurray, Inc. had a regular tax liability and a tentative minimum tax of $175,000 and $210,000, respectively. Because the amount of tentative minimum tax exceeds the taxpayer's regular tax liability, McMurray reports the $35,000 excess as AMT on its 2015 tax return. McMurray has no foreign tax credit in 2015. McMurray's net income tax is $210,000 ($175,000 regular tax + $35,000 AMT). In 2015, McMurray generated a total general business credit of $20,000, but, as shown below, the company cannot utilize any of the credit in 2015. The $20,000 can be carried back to 2014. If not utilized in that year, any unused credit can be applied against its income tax liability from 2016 through 2035.

---

[3] Code Sec. 38(c).   [4] Code Sec. 38(c)(1).

Net income tax	$210,000
Less: The *greater of* (1) $210,000 or	
(2) $37,500 [25% × ($175,000 – $25,000)]	(210,000)
General business credit allowed in 2015	$ 0

Modification of the limitation for certain credits. The limitation is modified for certain credits so that they can be used to offset all or a portion of the alternative minimum tax. For example, in applying the limitation to the empowerment zone employment credit, only 75 percent of the tentative minimum tax is used. In the case of a specified credit (i.e., the alcohol used as fuel credit, the credit for electricity produced from certain renewal resources, the employer tax credit for FICA paid on tips, the railroad track maintenance credit, the employer health insurance credit, the energy credit, the rehabilitation credit, and the work opportunity credit), the tentative minimum tax is treated as zero. After making these adjustments in calculating the limitation, the limitation has to be reduced by the amount of other credits allowed for the tax year that are components of the general business credit.

.03 Carryback and Carryforward of Unused Credit

The entire amount of an unused credit is first carried to the prior tax year. To the extent that an unused credit cannot be used in the prior tax year, it is carried to each of the other 20 tax years in the carryforward period.[5]

Example 10:   After applying the annual limitation to the general business credit on its 2015 tax return, Warden Dormers, Inc. had an excess general business credit of $25,000 that it carried back to 2014. In 2014, Warden's regular income tax liability and its net income tax were $200,000, and its tentative minimum tax was $180,000. Warden's 2014 general business credit (before considering the $25,000 carryback) was $17,500. The amount of general business credit that Warden is entitled to take for 2014 is recomputed to $20,000.

Net income tax	$200,000
Less: The *greater of* (1) $180,000 or	
(2) $43,750 [25% × ($200,000 – $25,000)]	(180,000)
Recomputed general business credit for 2014	$ 20,000

For 2014, Warden is allowed a general business credit of $20,000. However, because it has already claimed a $17,500 credit on its originally filed corporate tax return, Warden can only utilize $2,500 ($20,000 – $17,500) of the general business credit carried back to 2014. The remaining $22,500 ($25,000 – $2,500) of the excess general business credit from 2015 will be carried forward and utilized in 2016 through 2035.

The first-in, first-out method (FIFO) is used to determine the order in which credits are carried back and forward. The oldest credits are used first in determining the amount of a taxpayer's general business credit for a tax year.[6] Allowing taxpayers to use the FIFO rule to utilize carryovers reduces the risk that a taxpayer will lose the benefit of a general business credit because the carryover period has expired.

---

[5] Code Sec. 39(a)(1).   [6] Code Sec. 39(a).

Example 11: Kendell-Jenkins, Inc. generates a $20,000 general business credit for 2015. Kendell-Jenkins has general business credit carryforwards from prior tax years as follows:

Year	Amount
2010	$11,000
2011	7,500
2012	16,000
2013	2,000
2014	5,000
	$41,500

Kendell-Jenkins's total general business credit for 2015 equals $61,500 ($20,000 current year business credit + $41,500 carryforward from prior tax years). After computing the limitation imposed on the general business credit, Kendell-Jenkins determines that its allowable general business credit for 2015 is $36,000. Using the FIFO method, the $36,000 credit for 2015 consists of the $11,000 carried over from 2010; the $7,500 carried over from 2011; $16,000 carried over from 2012; and $1,500 from 2013. The amount of general business credit unused at the end of 2015 totals $25,500 ($61,500 − $36,000 utilized in 2015). This carryforward amount is attributable to the following years:

Year	Amount
2013	$ 500
2014	5,000
2015	20,000
	$25,500

 Planning Pointer: Taxpayers entitled to a tax refund after carrying any unused general business credit back to the previous tax year can obtain a quick refund by filing Form 1139, *Corporation Application for Tentative Refund,* or Form 1045, *Application for Tentative Refund* (for individuals, estates, and trusts). These forms are filed in lieu of filing an amended income tax return.

.04 Claiming the General Business Credit

Taxpayers must file Form 3800, *General Business Credit,* if they claim more than one of the credits included in the general business credit or if one of the credits (not including the low-income housing credit) is from a passive activity. Taxpayers carrying over credits from other tax years must also file Form 3800 in order to compute the correct amount of general business credit for the year.

BUSINESS TAX CREDITS AIMED AT ENCOURAGING EMPLOYERS TO HIRE CERTAIN WORKERS

The federal government provides tax incentives for businesses to hire certain workers (such as individuals having difficulty finding work). By offering tax credits to businesses that hire such workers, the amount of taxes the federal government collects is reduced, but the savings the government derives from no longer having to provide assistance to these individuals exceeds the loss in revenues. Two tax credits the federal government uses to encourage employers to hire certain workers are the empowerment zone employment credit and the work opportunity credit.

¶ 1104 Empowerment Zone Employment Credit

Empowerment zones are specific geographic areas within the United States that the federal government has identified as being in need of revitalization. Forty empowerment zones have been designated by the federal government. The period for which the designation will remain in effect ended on December 31, 2014. However, Congress has been extending the credit from year to year.

Employers that hire individuals who both live and work in an empowerment zone are entitled to tax credits for a portion of the wages paid to those workers. Employers can determine whether their business or an employee's residence is located in an empowerment zone by using the RC/EZ/EC address locator at *egis.hud.gov/ezrclocator*.

.01 Calculating the Amount of the Credit

Only wages paid to workers who both live *and* work in an empowerment zone qualify for the **empowerment zone employment credit**. Each calendar year, up to $15,000 of qualified zone wages paid to (in the case of a cash basis taxpayer) or incurred for (in the case of an accrual basis taxpayer) each qualified empowerment zone employee are eligible for the credit.[7] The employer's credit equals 20 percent of qualified zone wages paid to or incurred for qualified empowerment zone employees during a calendar year (up to $15,000 per qualified employee).[8]

Only qualified zone wages paid or incurred in the calendar year that ends with or within the employer's tax year can be used to compute the employer's empowerment zone employment credit. If the employer uses a calendar year-end, then all qualified zone wages paid during the employer's tax year (up to the $15,000 limit) are used in computing the credit. However, employers that use a fiscal year-end can use only qualified zone wages paid during the calendar year ending within the fiscal year to compute their credit for the fiscal year.

Example 12: Deschamp Window Blinds, Inc. uses a fiscal year that ends on March 31. For the tax year that began on April 1, 2014, and ended on March 31, 2015, only qualified zone wages paid or incurred during the 2014 calendar year can be used in computing Deschamp's credit during that fiscal year. Any qualified zone wages paid or incurred during the 2015 calendar year will be included in the calculation of Deschamp's tax credit for the fiscal year ending March 31, 2016.

The $15,000 limit is reduced by the amount of wages paid or incurred during the year that are used to compute the work opportunity credit (discussed in ¶ 1105).[9] Furthermore, an employer's wage expense deduction must be reduced by the amount of any credit taken during the year.

Example 13: During 2014, Deschamp Window Blinds, Inc. (from Example 12) paid $20,000 of qualified zone wages to Jorge Calahan and $11,000 of qualified zone wages to Rosa Gonzalez. Jorge's services were provided in an empowerment zone where he also resides; Rosa's were provided in an empowerment zone where she resides. Deschamp's empowerment zone employment credit for the fiscal year ended March

---

[7] Code Sec. 1396(a), (b).
[8] Code Sec. 1396(c)(2).

[9] Code Sec. 1396(c)(3).

31, 2015, equals $5,200 ($15,000 × 20% = $3,000 for Jorge's wages; $11,000 × 20% = $2,200 for Rosa's wages). Deschamp reduces its wage deduction by $5,200 on its tax return for the fiscal year ended March 31, 2015.

Reason for the Rule: The empowerment zone employment credit was enacted because Congress believed federal tax incentives could play a role in revitalizing economically distressed urban and rural areas.[10] Congress hoped the credit would lead to revitalization in distressed areas by expanding business and employment opportunities and would help alleviate both economic and social problems, including those caused by crime and narcotics.

.02 Qualified Zone Wages

Qualified zone wages include wages paid or incurred by an employer for services performed by an employee while working as a qualified zone employee.[11] A **qualified zone employee** is an employee who performs substantially all of his or her services for an employer within an empowerment zone and whose principal residence while performing such services is located within an empowerment zone. Usually employees must work for the employer for at least 90 days to have their wages qualify for the credit; however, the wages of employees who are unable to complete 90 days of employment due to becoming disabled or to being fired for cause constitute qualified zone wages. Wages paid to or incurred for employees who are related to the employer are never considered qualified zone wages.[12]

.03 Claiming the Credit

Employers claim the empowerment zone employment credit by completing and filing Form 8844, *Empowerment Zone and Renewal Community Employment Credit*. Although the credit is part of the general business credit, a special (slightly higher) tax liability limit applies. Accordingly, the allowed credit is calculated on Form 8844, not on Form 3800 with the other general business credits generated during the year.[13]

¶ 1105 Work Opportunity Credit

Employers that hire workers from a targeted group of individuals may receive a **work opportunity credit** for a portion of the wages they pay those workers during their first year of employment (and second-year wages in the case of long-term family assistance recipients).[14] No credit is to be allowed with respect to employees hired after December 31, 2014.[15] However, Congress has been extending this credit from year to year.

Reason for the Rule: The work opportunity credit was enacted to give employers an incentive to provide jobs and training for economically disadvantaged individuals, many of whom are underskilled and/or undereducated.[16]

.01 Qualifying for the Credit

Employers are entitled to a work opportunity credit for a portion of the qualified first-year wages (and second-year wages in the case of long-term family assistance recipients) they pay to eligible workers during the year. Eligible workers are individuals from one of the targeted groups

---

[10] House Ways and Means Committee Report No. 103-11, H.R. 2141 (May 19, 1993), at 353.

[11] Code Sec. 1396(c)(1).

[12] Code Secs. 1396(d).

[13] Code Sec. 38(c)(2)(A).

[14] Code Sec. 51(a).

[15] Code Sec. 51(c)(4)(B).

[16] Senate Finance Committee Report on the Small Business Job Protection Act of 1996 (June 19, 1996), at 32.

that have been identified as having a particularly high unemployment rate or other special employment needs.[17] To qualify for the credit, the worker must have performed services for the employer for no fewer than 120 hours during the year, cannot be related to the employer, and cannot have previously worked for the employer.[18]

Employers can qualify for the work opportunity credit by hiring individuals from the following targeted groups:[19]

1. *Qualified IV-A recipient.* Any individual who has been a member of a family receiving Temporary Assistance for Needy Families (TANF) for any nine months during the 18-month period leading up to the individual's hiring date.

2. *Qualified veteran.* Any veteran who (1) has been a member of a family receiving assistance under a supplemental nutrition assistance program under the Food and Nutrition Act of 2008 for at least a three-month period ending during the 12-month period ending on the hiring date; (2) is entitled to compensation for a service-connected disability and either is hired no more than one year after being discharged or released from active duty in the U.S. Armed Forces or has been unemployed during the one-year period ending on the hiring date for periods aggregating at least six months; (3) has been unemployed during the one-year period ending on the hiring date for periods aggregating at least four weeks but fewer than six months; or (4) has been unemployed during the one-year period ending on the hiring date for periods aggregating at least six months.

3. *Qualified ex-felon.* Any individual who has been convicted of a felony and who, as of the hiring date, is not more than one year past the date of release from prison or the date of the conviction.

4. *Designated community resident.* An individual who is at least age 18 but under age 40 on the hiring date and who has his or her principal place of abode within an empowerment zone, enterprise community, renewal community, or rural renewal county.

5. *Vocational rehabilitation referral.* Any individual who has a physical or mental disability that results in a substantial handicap to employment and who has been referred to the employer upon completion of (or while receiving) rehabilitative services pursuant to an individualized written plan for employment under a state plan for vocational rehabilitation services, a vocational rehabilitation program, or an individual work plan developed and implemented by an employment network pursuant to the Social Security Act.

6. *Qualified summer youth employee.* Any person age 16 or 17 on the date hired who performs services for the employer between May 1 and September 15. A qualified summer youth employee cannot have worked for the employer during any period before the 90-day period prior to being hired. In addition, the youth must reside within an empowerment zone, enterprise community, or renewal community, as designated by the federal government.

7. *Qualified Supplemental Nutrition Assistance Program Benefits Recipient.* Any individual at least 18 but younger than 40 on the hiring date who is a member of a family that either (1) received assistance under a supplemental nutrition assistance program under the Food and Nutrition Act of 2008 for the six-month period ending on the hiring date or, (2) in the case of a member of a family who ceased to be eligible for such assistance under Section 6(o) of the Food and Nutrition Act of 2008, received such assistance for at least three months during the five-month period ending on the hiring date.

8. *Qualified Supplemental Security Income (SSI) recipient.* Any individual who has been receiving SSI benefits for any month ending within the 60-day period leading up to the hiring date.

9. *Long-term family assistance recipient.* Any individual who (1) is a member of a family that has received Temporary Assistance for Needy Families (TANF) for a period ending on the hiring date that has lasted at least 18 months, (2) is a member of a family that has received

---

[17] Code Sec. 51(b).
[18] Code Sec. 51(i).

[19] Code Sec. 51(d).

TANF for at least 18 months and was hired within two years after the end of the earliest such 18-month period, or (3) is a member of a family that ceased to be eligible for TANF because of a limitation on the maximum period such assistance is payable and was hired within two years after the family's eligibility ceased.

.02 Calculating the Amount of the Credit

The amount of the work opportunity credit equals 40 percent of up to $6,000 ($10,000 in the case of a long-term family assistance recipient; $12,000 in the case of an individual who is a qualified veteran because the individual is entitled to compensation for a service-connected disability and was hired no more than one year after being discharged or released from active duty in the U.S. Armed Forces; $14,000 in the case of an individual who is a qualified veteran because the individual has been unemployed for periods aggregating at least six months during the year ending on the hiring date; and $24,000 in the case of an individual who is a qualified veteran because the individual is entitled to compensation for a service-connected disability and has been unemployed for periods aggregating at least six months during the one-year period ending on the hiring date) of an employee's qualified first-year wages for workers who provide at least 400 hours of service during their first year.[20]

The percentage drops to 25 percent for workers who perform between 120 and 400 hours of service.[21] No credit is available for an individual who has worked fewer than 120 hours.[22] For summer youth employees, only the first $3,000 of qualified first-year wages are used in computing the credit, and the credit is equal to 25 percent of those wages.[23]

Qualified first-year wages include all eligible wages paid (in the case of a cash basis employer) or incurred (in the case of an accrual basis employer) during the first year that begins on the date the individual is hired (the "hiring date").[24]

An additional credit equal to 50 percent of up to $10,000 of an employee's qualified second-year wages is provided for hiring a long-term family assistance recipient.[25] Qualified second-year wages include all eligible wages paid or incurred with respect to a long-term family assistance recipient during the second year following the individual's hiring date.

Example 14: Tiles, Inc. paid $8,000 in wages to Ana Hoffman during her first year of employment. Ana is a qualified IV-A recipient. Thus, $6,000 of Ana's first-year wages are used in computing Tiles's work opportunity credit. If Ana works at least 400 hours during her first year, Tiles will be able to take credit equal to $2,400 ($6,000 × 40%) as part of the general business credit.

Example 15: Tiles, Inc. paid $3,500 in wages to Norman Godsey, a qualified summer youth employee. Only $3,000 of Norman's wages are eligible for the work opportunity credit. Assuming Norman worked at least 120 hours for Tiles during the summer, Tiles can claim a $750 ($3,000 × 25%) work opportunity credit for the wages it paid Norman during the summer months.

Example 16: Lairs Pest Control paid $9,000 in qualified first-year wages and $11,500 in qualified second year wages to a qualified long-term family assistance recipient. Because the qualified worker is a long-term family assistance recipient, up to $10,000 of qualified wages paid during each of the worker's first two years qualify for the work opportunity credit. For the worker's first year, Lairs's work opportunity credit equals $3,600 ($9,000 × 40%). For the worker's second year, the credit equals $5,000 ($10,000 × 50%).

---

[20] Code Sec. 51(a).
[21] Code Sec. 51(i)(3)(A).
[22] Code Sec. 51(i)(3)(B).
[23] Code Sec. 51(d)(7)(B)(ii).
[24] Code Sec. 51(b)(2).
[25] Code Sec. 51(e)(1).

Example 17: Oday Flowers, Inc. paid $4,000 in wages to Lorraine Arnette, who worked 390 hours during her first year of employment. Lorraine is a qualified SSI recipient. Oday's work opportunity credit with respect to Lorraine's first-year wages equals $1,000 ($4,000 × 25%). If Lorraine had worked another 10 hours during her first year, Oday's work opportunity credit would have increased to $1,600 ($4,000 × 40%).

When an employee's first year of employment spans two of the employer's tax years, the employer can take the credit over those two tax years. (Likewise, in the case of long-term family assistance workers, if the employee's first and second year wages span three of the employer's tax years, the employer can take the credit over those three tax years.) However, only the wages earned in each of those years are allowed in computing that year's work opportunity credit. Furthermore, an employer's wage expense deduction must be reduced by the amount of the work opportunity credit.[26]

Example 18: On November 14, 2014, Eloise Meyers was hired by Jakelin Enterprises, a calendar year taxpayer. Eloise is a qualified food stamp recipient. Eloise's first-year wages were $11,200, of which $1,100 was received during 2014. Jakelin is entitled to a work opportunity credit equal to $440 ($1,100 × 40%) in 2014 and a credit equal to $1,960 [($6,000 − $1,100 = $4,900) × 40%] in 2015. During 2014, Jakelin paid $1,100 in qualified first year wages, which resulted in a $440 tax credit. Jakelin can deduct the remaining $660 ($1,100 − $440) of wages paid to Eloise in computing its 2014 taxable income.

Example 19: Lairs Pest Control (from Example 16) paid $9,000 of qualified first year wages to a long-term family assistance recipient. Of this amount, $2,000 was paid during 2013 and the rest ($7,000) in 2014. Lairs also paid $11,500 in qualified second years wages, of which $2,700 were paid in 2014 and the rest ($8,800) in 2015. Lairs is entitled to take an $800 work opportunity tax credit in 2013 ($2,000 × 40%). In 2014, Lairs's work opportunity credit equals $4,150 (($7,000 first year wages paid in 2014 × 40% first year rate) + ($2,700 second year wages paid in 2014 × 50% second year rate)). Its work opportunity credit for 2015 will equal $3,650 (($10,000 maximum − $2,700 paid in 2014) × 50%).

Of the $2,000 of qualified wages paid in 2013, Lairs can deduct $1,200 ($2,000 − $800) as wage expense in computing its taxable income. Likewise, of the $9,700 of qualified wages paid in 2014, Lairs can deduct $5,550 in computing its 2014 taxable income ($9,700 − $4,150). Finally, of the $8,800 of qualified wages paid in 2015, Lairs will be able to deduct $5,150 as wage expense ($8,800 − $3,650).

.03 Coordination with the Empowerment Zone Employment Credit

When a worker's wages qualify for the work opportunity credit and for the empowerment zone employment credit, the tax laws do not permit the same wages to be used in computing both credits. Thus, any of an eligible worker's wages used in computing the work opportunity credit must reduce both the worker's qualified zone wages as well as the $15,000 limitation used in computing the employer's empowerment zone employment credit.[27]

The empowerment zone employment credit is based on wages paid to qualified workers during a given calendar year, and the credit is available each year as long as qualified zone wages continue to be paid to the qualified zone employee.

---

[26] Code Sec. 280C(a).   [27] Code Sec. 1396(c)(3).

Planning Pointer: The wages eligible for the empowerment zone employment credit ($15,000) exceed the $6,000, $10,000, $12,000, and $14,000 limits (but not the $24,000 limit in the case of an individual who is a qualified veteran because the individual is entitled to compensation for a service-connected disability and has been unemployed for periods aggregating at least six months during the one-year period ending on the hiring date) for first-year wages that are eligible for the work opportunity credit. However, the percentage of wages that qualify for the work opportunity credit (40 percent) exceeds that allowed for the empowerment zone employment credit (20 percent). Accordingly, when a worker's wages qualify for *both* credits, employers will benefit by using the first $6,000 (or, if applicable, $10,000, $12,000, $14,000 or $24,000) of the employee's qualified wages in the calculation of the work opportunity credit and then reducing the amount of wages eligible for the empowerment zone employment credit by the wages used in computing the work opportunity credit.

Example 20: On October 5, 2014, Raskin Enterprises hired John Sanchez, a qualified IV-A recipient whose wages qualify both for the empowerment zone employment credit and for the work opportunity credit. John lives and works in an empowerment zone. During John's first year of employment (October 5, 2014–October 4, 2015), Raskin paid him $13,500 in total wages, of which $3,200 were paid in 2014. During 2015, John's wages were $16,000. Raskin files its corporate tax return using the calendar year.

The $3,200 of wages paid during the 2014 calendar year qualify for both credits, Raskin would be better off using those wages to claim a $1,280 work opportunity credit ($3,200 × 40%), rather than a $640 ($3,200 × 20%) empowerment zone credit. In computing its 2014 taxable income, Raskin must reduce its wage expense deduction by the $1,280 credit taken in that year.

In 2015, the first $2,800 ($6,000 – $3,200) of wages paid to John qualify for both credits. Thus, on its 2015 tax return, Raskin should claim a $1,120 work opportunity credit ($2,800 × 40%) and reduce the wages eligible for the empowerment zone employment credit by the $2,800 of wages used in computing the work opportunity credit. Raskin's empowerment zone employment credit for 2015 would equal $2,440 ($15,000 maximum qualified wages – $2,800 = $12,200 × 20%). Raskin would then reduce its 2015 wage deduction by the total $3,560 ($1,120 + $2,440) tax credits taken in that year.

In Example 20, had Raskin chosen to use the entire wages paid to John Sanchez in computing its empowerment zone employment credit, its tax credit for 2014 would have been $640, and its 2015 tax credit would have been $3,000 ($15,000 × 20%). Accordingly, the tax credits over the two years would have totaled $3,640 ($640 + $3,000). In Example 20, Raskin took the work opportunity credit on the first $6,000 of the worker's first-year wages and then reduced the amount of wages eligible for the empowerment zone employment credit. Raskin's tax credits over the same two tax years totaled $4,840 ($1,280 + $3,560). Thus, by using its understanding of the tax laws, Raskin claimed an additional $1,200 ($4,840 – $3,640) in tax credits. However, because the amounts taken as a tax credit reduce the amounts that can be deducted as wage expense, the true tax savings can be measured only after determining the difference in taxes Raskin will pay under each scenario.

Assuming Raskin's taxable income for each of the two years falls in the 35-percent tax bracket, the $1,200 additional wage expense that Raskin would take if all wages were used in computing the empowerment zone and renewal community employment credit would produce an additional $420 in tax savings ($1,200 × 35%) over the approach used in Example 20. Thus, Raskin's actual tax savings would be $780 ($1,200 additional tax credit – $420 additional tax liability due to less wage expense deduction). Hence, Raskin is still better off using the planning technique illustrated in Example 20 to reduce its taxes owed to the federal government over the two tax years.

.04 Claiming the Credit

Employers file Form 5884, *Work Opportunity Credit*, with their federal income tax return to claim the work opportunity credit. The amount of the credit is included as part of the general business credit on Form 3800, *General Business Credit*. To claim the credit for an employee's wages, an employer must request and be issued a certification for the employee from the state employment security agency. If an employer does not receive the certification by the day that an employee begins work, the employer must complete Form 8850, *Pre-Screening Notice and Certification Request for the Work Opportunity Credit*, on or before the individual is offered a job and submit this form to the state employment security agency no later than 28 days after the employee begins to work for the employer.[28]

TAX CREDITS AIMED AT ENCOURAGING CONSERVATION OF ENERGY

¶ 1106 Energy Credits

Several tax credits aimed at encouraging taxpayers to conserve energy and reduce greenhouse gases are available to individuals and businesses. Although the details of these credits are beyond the scope of this textbook, the types of credits the tax laws provide include:

- Credit for the use or production of qualified biodiesel and renewable diesel,
- Alcohol used as fuel credit,
- Enhanced oil recovery credit,
- Renewable electricity and refined coal production credit,
- Credit for small business refiners of low-sulfur diesel fuels,
- Credit for producing oil and natural gas from qualified marginal wells,
- Alternative motor vehicle credit,
- Qualified plug-in electric drive motor vehicle credit,
- Alternative fuel vehicle refueling property credit,
- Home builder's credit for new energy efficient homes,
- Energy credit,
- Electricity produced from certain renewable resources credit,
- Credit for producing fuel from a nonconventional source,
- Enhanced oil recovery credit,
- Advanced nuclear power facilities production credit,
- Carbon dioxide sequestration credit,
- Qualifying advanced coal project credit,
- Qualifying gasification project credit, and
- Advanced energy project credit.

The home builder's credit for new energy efficient homes, alcohol used as fuel credit, biodiesel fuels credit, and credit for electricity produced from renewable resources expired December 31, 2014. The alternative fuel vehicle refueling property credit does not apply to any property placed in service after December 31, 2014. The alternative motor vehicle credit is available only for new qualified fuel cell motor vehicles purchased no later than December 31, 2014. Note, however, that Congress has been extending these credits from year to year.

---

[28] Code Sec. 51(d)(13).

TAX CREDITS AIMED AT REWARDING RESEARCH IN CERTAIN AREAS

¶ 1107 Tax Credit for Increasing Research Activities

Employers who conduct research and experimentation may qualify for a nonrefundable **research activities credit**, which is part of the general business credit.[29] This credit is not available with respect to any amounts paid or incurred after December 31, 2014. However, Congress has been extending this credit from year to year.

 Reason for the Rule: The research activities credit was enacted in 1981 based on concerns that the United States' lead in research and development had diminished and on a belief that from research and development come technological advances that are essential to increased productivity and competitiveness.[30] Congress hoped that giving businesses the research activities credit as a tax incentive would encourage businesses to increase the amounts they spend on qualified research activities.

The research activities credit is different from the deduction allowed for research and experimental expenditures (discussed in Chapter 5). The research activities credit is intended to reward businesses that conduct research in specific areas and those that increase the amounts they spend each year on specified research and development activities. Some research expenditures qualify for both the research activities tax credit and the deduction for research and experimental expenditures. In these situations, the taxpayer has the option of taking the full amount as a deduction and then reducing the allowable credit to 65 percent of the amount otherwise allowed to be taken. Alternatively, the taxpayer may take a credit for these expenditures and then reduce the amount of its deduction (or amortizable amount) by the amount of the credit taken.[31]

Example 21: Biotechnologies, Inc. incurred $200,000 in expenditures during the year that qualify for both the research activities credit and the deduction for research and experimental expenditures. Biotechnologies' marginal tax rate is 35 percent. The computed amount of the tax credit available for these expenditures is $40,000. Biotechnologies has the option of deducting the entire $200,000 in computing its taxable income and reducing the amount of its credit to $26,000 ($40,000 × 65%). This would generate tax savings equal to $96,000 ($200,000 × 35% plus $26,000). Alternatively, Biotechnologies can choose to take the full $40,000 tax credit and reduce its research and experimental expenditures deduction to $160,000 ($200,000 – $40,000). This latter option would generate the same $96,000 in total tax savings ($160,000 × 35% plus $40,000).

 Planning Pointer: As illustrated in Example 21, taxpayers with a marginal tax rate of 35-percent generate the same tax savings under both options. Only taxpayers with a marginal tax rate of less than 35 percent will generate greater tax savings by electing to take the full tax credit and reduce the amount eligible for the deduction. It is not a coincidence that the 35-percent "indifference" rate corresponds to the highest corporate tax rate (not including the three- and four-percent surtaxes that are imposed in addition to the top 35-percent tax rate in order to eliminate the tax benefits of the lower tax rates).

---

[29] Code Sec. 41.
[30] Senate Finance Committee Report No. 97-144 (July 6, 1981), at 120.

[31] Code Sec. 280C(c).

.01 Calculating the Amount of the Credit

The research activities credit is the sum of the (1) incremental credit, (2) university basic research credit, and (3) qualified energy research credit. Each credit is 20 percent of qualifying expenditures.[32]

Incremental credit. The "incremental credit" is intended to reward businesses that increase the amounts spent on research activities. The amount of the credit equals 20 percent of the amount by which a business's qualified research expenses for the tax year exceeds its base amount. (The base amount is discussed in ¶ 1107.04.) Alternatively, businesses can elect to compute an alternative simplified credit amount.[33]

Example 22: Tann Communications, Inc. incurred $80,000 of qualified research expenses during its most recent tax year. If Tann's base amount is $50,000, its incremental credit for the year equals $6,000 ($80,000 – $50,000 = $30,000 × 20%).

Example 23: Martin Enterprises incurred $100,000 of qualified research expenses during its most recent tax year. If Martin's base amount is $90,000, its incremental credit for the year equals $2,000 ($100,000 – $90,000 = $10,000 × 20%).

Instead of computing the incremental credit using 20 percent of the excess of qualified research expenses over the base amount, taxpayers have the option of electing an alternative simplified credit:[34]

Alternative simplified credit. A business' alternative simplified credit is equal to 14 percent of its qualified research expenses in excess of 50 percent of the average of its qualified research expenses for the three preceding tax years for which the credit is being determined. If a taxpayer had no qualified research expenses for any of the three preceding tax years, the credit is six percent of the taxpayer's qualified research expenses for the tax year. An election applies to the tax year for which it is made and all subsequent tax years unless revoked with the IRS' consent.[35]

Example 24: Pickard Telecommunications, Inc. incurred $500,000 in qualified research expenses during 2014. The average of its qualified research expenses for 2011, 2012, and 2013 was $300,000. Its alternative simplified research credit is $42,000, computed as follows:

$$14\% \times [\$500,000 - (50\% \times \$300,000)] = \$49,000$$

Example 25: Helget Industries, Inc. had $60,000 of qualified research expenses during the year. It had no qualified research expenses for one of the three preceding years. Its alternative simplified credit is 6% × $60,000 = $3,600.

University basic research credit. The university basic research credit equals 20 percent of the difference between basic research payments and the qualified organization base period amount. Like the incremental credit, this component of the research activities credit is available to businesses that increase their research expenditures during the year. Basic research includes any original investigation for the advancement of scientific knowledge that does not have a specific commercial objective. Expenditures paid or incurred for research conducted outside the United States or research conducted in the social sciences, the arts, or humanities do not qualify for the university basic research credit, regardless of the amount spent on the research.[36]

Qualified energy research credit. The qualified energy research credit equals 20 percent of amounts paid or incurred by the taxpayer (including contributions) in carrying on any trade or business during the tax year with an energy research consortium. Unlike the other two components

---

[32] Code Sec. 41(a).
[33] Code Sec. 41(a)(1).
[34] Code Sec. 41(c)(5).

[35] Code Sec. 41(c)(5)(C).
[36] Code Sec. 41(e)(7).

of the research activities credit, the amount of the qualified energy research credit is not dependent on the company increasing its research expenditures over prior tax years.

An "energy research consortium" is an organization that satisfies each of the following requirements.[37]

- It is either a tax-exempt public charity (as defined in Code Sec. 501(c)(3)) organized and operated primarily to conduct energy research or an organization operated primarily to conduct energy research in the public interest;

- It is not a private foundation;

- During the calendar year in which the organization's tax year begins, at least five unrelated persons provide amounts to the organization for energy research; and

- No single person provides 50 percent or more of the total amounts provided to the organization for energy research during the calendar year.

.02 Qualified Research

"Qualified research" for purposes of the research activities credit includes (1) research with respect to which expenditures qualify for the research and experimentation deduction (discussed in ¶ 507.01) and (2) research undertaken for the purpose of discovering information that is technological in nature whose application is intended to be useful in the development of a taxpayer's new or improved business component.[38] Substantially all (defined as 80 percent or more) of the research activities must constitute elements of a process of experimentation relating to a new or improved function, performance, reliability, or quality.

Research will *not* be treated as conducted for a qualified purpose if it relates to style, taste, cosmetic, or seasonal design factors.[39] Other disbursements that do not constitute qualified research expenditures include any efficiency survey; activity relating to management function or technique; marketing research, testing, or development (including advertising or promotions); routine data collection; or routine or ordinary testing or inspection for quality control.

Research is "undertaken for the purpose of discovering information" if it is intended to eliminate uncertainty concerning the development or improvement of a business component. "Uncertainty" exists if the information available to the taxpayer does not establish the capability or method for developing or improving the business component or the appropriate design for the business component.[40] Information is "technological in nature" if the process of experimentation used to discover the information fundamentally relies on the principles of the physical or biological sciences, engineering, or computer science. A taxpayer may employ existing technologies and may rely on existing principles of the physical or biological sciences, engineering, or computer science to satisfy this requirement.[41]

Example 26: Odom Shelving, Inc. decides it wants to manufacture shelving in a different color. Odom researches the available colors and surveys its customers to determine which color they prefer. The research does not constitute qualified research because it relates to style, taste, cosmetic, or seasonal design factors.

Example 27: After selecting a color for its shelving, Odom Shelving from Example 26 determines that it cannot use its existing painting-spraying machine because the new color has characteristics that differ from those of the paints it previously used. Odom consults with the manufacturer of its paint-spraying machine and learns that a new nozzle is needed. Odom purchases the nozzle and performs tests to ensure the nozzle will satisfy the company's needs. Odom's research does not constitute qualified research because the company did not conduct a process of evaluating alternatives to elimi-

---

[37] Code Sec. 41(f)(6).
[38] Code Sec. 41(d).
[39] Reg. § 1.41-4(a)(6).

[40] Reg. § 1.41-4(a)(3).
[41] Reg. § 1.41-4(a)(4).

nate uncertainty regarding the modifications required for painting the shelving. Instead, the manufacturer eliminated any uncertainty by informing Odom of the nozzle that was needed. Odom's testing of the new nozzle falls into the category of routine or ordinary testing or inspection for quality control.

Example 28: Perrault Food Grinders, Inc. decided to manufacture a smaller version of its grinder. Because a smaller version of the blade the company uses for its current model was not commercially available, it developed a blade that it could manufacture using its current production line. Perrault engages in a systematic trial-and-error process of analyzing blade designs and materials to determine what design and material would be best. The research constitutes qualified research because the appropriate design and material were uncertain when Perrault began its research activities. Perrault went through the process of identifying and evaluating alternatives, and the process of evaluating alternatives was technological in nature.

Research conducted after commercial production of a business component begins does not constitute qualified research; nor does research related to the adaptation of an existing business component to a particular customer's requirement or need. Expenses incurred in connection with computer software developed primarily for internal use do not qualify for the research activities credit.

Expenditures do not qualify if they are related to research that reproduces an existing business component (in whole or in part) from a physical examination of the business component itself or from plans, blueprints, detailed specifications, or publicly available information with respect to the business component. Research usually must be conducted within the United States, Puerto Rico, or any U.S. possession to be eligible for the research activities credit. Expenditures paid or incurred for research in the social sciences, the arts, or humanities do not qualify for the credit.

.03 Qualified Research Expenses

"Qualified research expenses" are the sum of (1) in-house research expenses and (2) contract research expenses paid or incurred by the taxpayer during the tax year in carrying on a trade or business of the taxpayer.[42] *In-house research expenses* include wages paid to or incurred for the services of an employee who is engaged in qualified research or in the direct supervision or direct support of research activities that constitute qualified research. In-house research expenses also include amounts paid or incurred for supplies and amounts paid to another person or incurred for the right to use computers to conduct qualified research.[43] *Contract research expenses* are 65 percent of any amount a taxpayer pays to any person (other than a taxpayer's employee) or incurs for qualified research. However, if the amounts are paid to or incurred for an eligible small business, an institution of higher education, or a federal laboratory, 100 percent of such amounts are considered in computing the research activities credit.[44]

A "small business" is one whose average number of employees did not exceed 500 during either of the two preceding calendar years. A small business is an *eligible small business* if the taxpayer does not directly or indirectly own 50 percent or more of the outstanding value or voting shares of its stock (if the business is a corporation) or 50 percent or more of the business's capital and profits interests (if the business is not a corporation).[45]

.04 Base Amount

For purposes of the research activities credit, the "base amount" equals a fixed-base percentage multiplied by the average annual gross receipts of the taxpayer for the previous four tax years. In no

---

[42] Code Sec. 41(b)(1).
[43] Code Sec. 41(b)(2).

[44] Code Sec. 41(b)(3)(D).
[45] Code Sec. 41(b)(3)(D)(ii).

event may the base amount be less than 50 percent of the taxpayer's qualified research expenses for the credit year.[46]

Example 29: In the current year, Sidhu Cloths, Inc. incurred $30,000 in qualified research expenditures. Sidhu's fixed-base percentage is two percent, and its average annual gross receipts for the four prior tax years was $1 million. Two percent of Sidhu's average annual gross receipts equals $20,000 ($1,000,000 × 2%). Because this amount is not less than $15,000 (50% of the $30,000 qualified research expenditures), Sidhu's base amount for the year is $20,000.

Example 30: Assume the same facts as in Example 29, except that Sidhu's qualified research expenditures for the current year are $45,000 (instead of $30,000). Because 2 percent of Sidhu's average annual gross receipts ($20,000) is less than 50 percent of its current year's expenditures ($45,000 × 50% = $22,500), Sidhu's base amount for the year is $22,500.

Fixed-base percentage. The calculation of the fixed-base percentage depends on how long the taxpayer has been in business. The maximum fixed-base percentage is 16 percent.[47] The actual computation of the fixed-base percentage can be quite involved, and it is beyond the scope of this discussion. However, as a rule, the fixed-base percentage is calculated by dividing the taxpayer's aggregate qualified research expenses for tax years beginning after December 31, 1983, and before January 1, 1989, by the taxpayer's aggregate gross receipts for those tax years.

Example 31: Eccles Imaging, Inc. had $270,000 in qualified research expenses for tax years beginning after 1983 and before 1989. During that same period, its aggregate gross receipts were $3 million. Eccles' fixed-base percentage is nine percent ($270,000 ÷ $3,000,000).

Code Sec. 41(c)(3) provides a series of complex rules for determining a company's fixed base percentage if the company was not in existence for at least three years from 1984–1988.

.05 Claiming the Credit

Taxpayers can claim the credit by filing Form 6765, *Credit for Increasing Research Activities*. Because this credit is part of the general business credit, amounts reported on Form 6765 flow through to Form 3800, *General Business Credit*, and they are used in determining the taxpayer's general business credit for the current year.

¶ 1108 Orphan Drug Credit

The tax laws allow a larger tax credit for research conducted in the clinical testing of drugs for rare diseases and conditions. This credit, often called the "orphan drug credit," is similar to the research activities credit in that both in-house and contract research expenses are allowed in computing the credit. However, for the purposes of computing the orphan drug credit, 100 percent of contract research expenses are allowed (up from 65 percent for the research activities credit). The calculation of the credit is similar to the research activities credit, except that the credit is equal to 50 percent of qualified clinical testing expenses (up from 20 percent for the incremental credit).[48]

Because expenses that qualify for the orphan drug credit also qualify for the research activities credit, any expenses used in computing the orphan drug credit cannot be used in computing a taxpayer's research activities credit. However, such amounts are included in a company's base amount when computing its incremental research activities credit.[49]

Example 32: In 2015, Biogene Company incurred $200,000 in the clinical testing of a drug for a rare disease. Biogene also incurred $50,000 in other qualified research expenses.

---

[46] Code Sec. 41(c).
[47] Code Sec. 41(c)(3).

[48] Code Sec. 45C(a).
[49] Code Sec. 45C(c).

Biogene's orphan drug credit for 2015 equals $100,000 ($200,000 × 50%). Because the entire $200,000 is used to compute its orphan drug credit, it cannot use any of this amount to compute its research activities credit. Accordingly, Biogene will compute its research activities credit based on the $50,000 of other qualified research expenses it incurred during 2015.

The orphan drug credit is computed on Form 8820, *Orphan Drug Credit,* and the amount of the credit is transferred to Form 3800, *General Business Credit,* where it is used to compute the taxpayer's general business credit.

TAX CREDITS AIMED AT ENCOURAGING ECONOMIC DEVELOPMENT

Although discussed earlier in this chapter as a credit aimed at encouraging employers to hire certain workers, the empowerment zone employment credit also exists to provide tax incentives for businesses to relocate to distressed urban and rural areas that the federal government believes are in dire need of revitalization.[50] As previously mentioned, Congress hoped that by enacting this credit businesses would expand to those areas and bring with them employment opportunities that would help alleviate both economic and social problems. The new markets credit is another tax credit aimed at encouraging economic development in low-income communities.

¶ 1109 New Markets Credit

Taxpayers that invest in a qualified community development entity may be entitled to a new markets credit.[51] The **new markets credit** is a nonrefundable credit that is part of the general business credit. Congress has not authorized any investments after 2014, but it has been authorizing such investments from year to year.

 Reason for the Rule: The new markets credit was enacted as part of the Community Renewal Tax Relief Act of 2000 to encourage taxpayers to invest in CDEs, whose primary mission is to serve or provide investment capital for low-income communities and low-income individuals.[52]

A **qualified community development entity** (qualified CDE) is a domestic corporation or partnership whose primary mission is to serve, or provide investment capital for, low-income communities or low-income persons. During its first six years, a qualified CDE must use at least 85 percent of the cash it raises to make qualified low-income community investments. After the sixth year, a qualified CDE need only use 75 percent of its cash to make qualified low-income community investments.[53] In addition, a qualified CDE must maintain accountability to the residents of low-income communities by including them as representatives on any governing board of the entity or on any advisory board to the entity. Finally, a qualified CDE must be certified as such by the Community Development Financial Institutions (CDFI) Fund of the Department of the Treasury.[54]

An equity investment in a qualified CDE is an investment in the stock of a qualified CDE (in the case of a corporation) or an investment in a capital interest of a qualified CDE (in the case of a partnership). The taxpayer must pay cash to purchase its investment in a qualified CDE, although the taxpayer may borrow the funds to generate the cash necessary to purchase the investment.[55]

---

[50] House Ways and Means Committee Report No. 103-11, H.R. 2141 (May 19, 1993), at 353.

[51] Code Sec. 45D(a).

[52] Joint Committee on Taxation, *General Explanation of Tax Legislation Enacted in the 106th Congress* (J.C.T. Rep. No. JCS-2-01), at 122 and 123.

[53] Reg. § 1.45D-1(c)(5).

[54] Code Sec. 45D(c).

[55] Code Sec. 45D(b)(1); Rev. Rul. 2003-20, 2003-1 CB 465.

.01 Calculating the Amount of the Credit

The amount of the credit equals the applicable percentage multiplied by the amount invested in a qualified CDE. The applicable percentage is five percent for the first three credit allowance dates and six percent for the next four credit allowance dates. The "credit allowance date" is the date on which the investment initially was made and each of the next six anniversaries of that date.[56]

Example 33: On July 1, 2015, Creekmore Illustrators, Inc. paid $100,000 for a qualified equity investment in a CDE. Creekmore (a calendar year corporation) is entitled to a new markets credit equal to $5,000 (5% × $100,000) for 2015 and will be entitled to another $5,000 credit on its 2016 and 2017 tax returns. The company will be entitled to a $6,000 (6% × $100,000) credit on its 2018–2021 tax returns.

.02 Claiming the Credit

Taxpayers can claim the credit by filing Form 8874, *New Markets Credit*. The new markets credit is part of the general business credit. Accordingly, any credit generated on Form 8874 is transferred to Form 3800, *General Business Credit*, and used to compute the taxpayer's general business credit for the year. The taxpayer's basis in its investment in the CDE is reduced by the new markets credit taken with respect to that investment.[57]

Example 34: Continuing with Creekmore Illustrators from Example 33, over the seven years Creekmore will receive tax credits equal to $39,000 ($5,000 for each of the first three years + $6,000 for each of the next four years). If these amounts were considered as reducing Creekmore's cost in its investment in the CDE, its out-of-pocket costs would effectively be reduced to $61,000 ($100,000 – $39,000). However, because Creekmore must reduce its basis in the CDE by the $39,000 of tax credits taken, the $39,000 will eventually be taxed when Creekmore disposes of the investment. Until then, Creekmore will have the use of the amounts it receives from the tax savings generated by the tax credits.

.03 Recapture of the Credit

If, at any time during the seven-year period beginning on the date of the taxpayer's investment in the qualified CDE, (1) the entity ceases to be a qualified CDE, (2) the taxpayer's investment is redeemed by the qualified CDE, or (3) the proceeds from the investment are not substantially used by the qualified CDE to make qualified low-income community investments, the taxpayer's tax liability must be increased by an amount equal to the amount by which the taxpayer's general business credit would have been reduced if there had been no new markets credit, plus interest at the federal government's underpayment rate.[58]

TAX CREDITS USED TO SUBSIDIZE BUSINESSES FOR CERTAIN EXPENDITURES MADE DURING THE YEAR

¶ 1110 Employer Social Security Credit

Tips constitute income and therefore are taxable to the recipient. However, because most tips are paid in cash, they are difficult for the government to trace (and therefore to tax). Consequently, compliance with this tax law is extremely low. To combat this, the government has enacted tax laws requiring certain businesses to impute the amount of tips their employees earn and include those amounts as employee wages on their employees' Form W-2s.

---

[56] Code Sec. 45D(a); Reg. § 1.45D-1(b).
[57] Code Sec. 45D(h).

[58] Code Sec. 45D(g).

As discussed in Chapter 6, employers must withhold federal, state, and FICA taxes from their employees' wages. In addition, employers are required to match any amounts withheld for FICA taxes. Normally, employers deduct their matching FICA contributions as ordinary and necessary business expenses. However, to encourage businesses to comply with the tax laws requiring them to impute tips on behalf of their employees, the federal government allows employers to take a tax credit equal to 100 percent of any Social Security tax that they pay with respect to tips that an employee receives for serving food and beverages, but only to the extent that the tips exceed the amount necessary to bring the employee's wages above the minimum wage.[59]

 Reason for the Rule: By allowing employers to take a tax credit for 100 percent of the amounts they pay toward FICA on employees' tip income, the federal government encourages employers to report their employees' tips as taxable wages.

Although by allowing the tax credit (versus deduction) the government is subsidizing a much larger portion of the employer's cost for FICA matching, in return, the tips the employer reports are subject to the employee's portion of FICA as well as state, local, and federal income taxes. Hence, the government is willing to pay businesses for their efforts to increase employees' compliance by allowing the businesses a tax credit instead of a tax deduction for their share of the FICA on tip income.

¶ 1111 Rehabilitation Credit

Businesses are entitled to a **rehabilitation credit** for costs associated with the substantial rehabilitation of a certified historic structure or other depreciable building that was originally placed in service prior to 1936.[60]

 Reason for the Rule: The rehabilitation credit is intended to encourage businesses to rehabilitate and modernize older structures rather than build new structures or relocate their businesses to new structures. The credit is also intended to encourage the preservation of historic structures. Congress believed that a tax incentive was needed because businesses otherwise would be deterred from rehabilitating older or historic buildings because of the extra costs of undertaking such rehabilitation and because the social and aesthetic values of rehabilitating and preserving older structures are not necessarily taken into consideration when businesses decide whether to rehabilitate an older structure or to move a new structure.[61]

.01 Calculating the Amount of the Credit

The rehabilitation credit is the sum of (1) 20 percent of the qualified rehabilitation expenditures with respect to any certified historic structure and (2) 10 percent of the qualified rehabilitation expenditures with respect to any qualified rehabilitated building that is not a certified historic structure.[62]

Example 35: Bourn Leasing, Inc. purchased an apartment building that is a qualified rehabilitated building that is not a certified historic structure. During the year, Bourn made $100,000 in qualified rehabilitation expenditures with respect to five of the apartments and made the apartments available to renters by the end of the year. Bourn is entitled to a rehabilitation credit of $10,000 ($100,000 × 10%).

[59] Code Sec. 45B(b).
[60] Code Sec. 47.

[61] Joint Committee on Taxation, *General Explanation of the Tax Reform Act of 1986* (J.C.T. Rep. No. JCS-10-87), at 149.
[62] Code Sec. 47(a).

.02 Expenditures Qualifying for the Rehabilitation Credit

An expenditure qualifies for the rehabilitation credit if it is a qualified rehabilitation expense with respect to a qualified rehabilitated building.[63] Qualified rehabilitation expenditures are capital in nature and relate to depreciable residential or nonresidential realty. In addition, the expenditure must be incurred in connection with the rehabilitation of a qualified rehabilitation building.[64]

Qualified rehabilitated building. A certified historic structure is a **qualified rehabilitated building** if, sometime after purchasing the building, the taxpayer pays or incurs substantial expenditures to rehabilitate it. A building is a certified historic structure if it is listed in the National Register or if it is located in a registered historic district and is certified by the Secretary of the Interior as being of historic significance to the district.[65]

A building that is not a certified historic structure is considered a qualified rehabilitated building only if it was originally placed in service before 1936 and if some time after purchasing the building the taxpayer pays or incurs substantial rehabilitation expenditures. Once the rehabilitation is completed, at least 50 percent of the building's original external walls must still be external walls; at least 75 percent of its original external walls must have been retained as either internal or external walls; and at least 75 percent of its internal structural framework must have been retained.[66]

Example 36: Samuel Industries paid $200,000 for a building that is not a certified historic structure. The building was originally placed in service in 1940. Because the building is not a certified historical structure and it was not first placed in service before 1936, any expenditure the company makes to rehabilitate the building will not qualify for the rehabilitation credit.

Substantially rehabilitated. A building must be substantially rehabilitated after the taxpayer purchases it for the rehabilitation expenditures to qualify for the credit. A building has been "substantially rehabilitated" if during any 24-month period ending within the taxable year in which the property is placed in service the qualified rehabilitation expenditures exceed the *greater* of (1) $5,000 or (2) the adjusted basis of the building and its structural components. The adjusted basis of a building is determined as of the beginning of the 24-month period or the beginning of the holding period for the building, whichever is later.[67]

Example 37: Tarrik Inc. pays $100,000 for a building that is a certified historic structure. During the next 24-months, Tarrik incurs $50,000 in costs associated with rehabilitating the building. Because the $50,000 costs do not exceed $100,000 (the *greater* of Tarrik's adjusted basis or $5,000), the building is not considered to have been substantially rehabilitated.

Example 38: On May 5, 2013, Rycline Industries pays $200,000 for a building that is not a certified historic structure. Rycline is a calendar year taxpayer. The building was originally placed in service in 1923. Rycline places the property in service on October 9, 2015. Between August 10, 2013, and August 9, 2015, Rycline incurs $250,000 to rehabilitate the building. Because the $250,000 exceeds $200,000 (the *greater* of Rycline's adjusted basis or $5,000), the building is considered to have been substantially rehabilitated.

.03 When Expenditures May Be Taken Into Account

As a rule, qualified rehabilitation expenditures with respect to any qualified rehabilitated building are taken into account for the tax year in which the qualified rehabilitated building is placed in service.[68] This tax year must also contain the end of the 24-month period used to determine whether the building placed in service was substantially rehabilitated.

---

[63] Code Sec. 47(a).
[64] Code Sec. 47(c)(2).
[65] Code Sec. 47(c)(3).

[66] Code Sec. 47(c)(1).
[67] Code Sec. 47(c)(1)(C)(i).
[68] Code Sec. 47(b)(1).

Example 39: Rycline Industries from Example 38 will claim a $25,000 rehabilitation credit ($250,000 × 10% for buildings that are not certified historic structures) as part of its general business credit on its 2015 tax return.

Example 40: On May 5, 2013, Northeastern Company (a calendar year taxpayer) paid $50,000 for a building that qualifies as a certified historic structure. From May 6, 2013, until August 28, 2015, Northeastern incurred $75,000 to rehabilitate the building. The building is placed in service on August 31, 2015. Because the rehabilitation expenditures exceed $50,000 (the *greater* of $5,000 or its $50,000 adjusted basis), Northeastern can take a $15,000 rehabilitation credit ($75,000 × 20% credit for certified historic structures) as part of its general business credit on its 2015 tax return.

.04 Claiming the Credit

Businesses can claim the rehabilitation credit on Form 3468, *Investment Credit*. The rehabilitation credit is one of the components of the nonrefundable investment credit.[69] Other credits that make up the investment credit are the energy credit, the qualifying advanced coal project credit, the qualifying gasification project credit, and qualifying advanced energy project credit. The aggregate of these investment credits is reported as part of the general business credit on Form 3800, *General Business Credit*. Taxpayers claiming the rehabilitation credit must reduce their basis in the property by the amount of the credit.[70]

.05 Recapture of the Credit

If a taxpayer disposes of rehabilitated property, or if such property otherwise ceases to be investment credit property with respect to the taxpayer, within five years after it was placed in service, the taxpayer's tax liability is increased by an amount equal to the recapture percentage times the original credit taken. The recapture percentages, listed in Table 11-1, reflect the equivalent of the amount by which the taxpayer's general business credit would have been reduced if no credit for rehabilitation expenditures had been allowed.[71] Taxpayers file Form 4255, *Recapture of Investment Credit*, when property ceases to qualify as investment credit property within five years after it was placed in service. Amounts recaptured are added back to the adjusted basis of the building.[72]

Table 11-1 Recapture Percentages for the Rehabilitation Credit

Period of Time After Property Was Placed in Service That It Ceases To Be Investment Credit Property	*Recapture Percentage*
Within 1 full year	100%
More than 1 but within 2 years	80%
More than 2 but within 3 years	60%
More than 3 but within 4 years	40%
More than 4 but within 5 years	20%
More than 5 years	0%

Example 41: On its 2013 tax return, Oday Tambourines took a $10,000 rehabilitation credit for a building with a total cost basis of $180,000. Oday Tambourines placed the building in service on April 1, 2013. Oday reduced its basis in the building to $170,000 ($180,000 – $10,000) and began depreciating the building using this depreciable basis and the

---

[69] Code Sec. 46.
[70] Code Sec. 50(c)(1).
[71] Code Sec. 50(a).
[72] Code Sec. 50(c)(2).

cost recovery rules from Chapter 7. On February 2, 2015, Oday sold the building for $300,000. Because Oday disposed of the property within two years after it was placed in service, the amount of additional income tax that Oday must pay in 2015 is $8,000 (80% × $10,000). Oday increases its adjusted basis in the building by $8,000.

> **Reason for the Rule:** The recapture provisions prevent taxpayers from taking undue advantage of the investment credit. However, because in the year the credit is taken the taxpayer's adjusted basis in the building was reduced by the full amount of the credit, it is only fair that any amounts recaptured be added back to the building's basis, thereby reducing the amount of realized gain (or increasing the amount of loss) upon its disposition.

¶ 1112 Low-Income Housing Credit

Taxpayers who purchase or substantially rehabilitate residential rental property used for low-income housing may take a **low-income housing credit**.[73] The nonrefundable credit is part of the general business credit.

> **Reason for the Rule:** Congress enacted the low-income housing credit as part of the Tax Reform Act of 1986 because it believed that tax incentives (for example, accelerated depreciation) in existence at the time were not effective in providing affordable housing for low-income individuals. In particular, these subsidies were not linked to the number of units serving low-income persons; they were not targeted to persons of truly low income; and they did not limit the amount of rent that low-income individuals could be charged.[74] Through the provisions enacted in the low-income housing credit, Congress addressed these issues and provided tax incentives that it hoped would make providing affordable housing to low-income persons and families an attractive investment for businesses.

.01 Calculating the Amount of the Credit

The amount of the low-income housing credit is the applicable percentage of the qualified basis of each qualified low-income building.[75] The amount of the low-income housing credit may be taken each year for a total of 10 years, beginning with the tax year during which the building is placed in service or, at the building owner's election, the following tax year. If the taxpayer elects to start the 10-year period in the year subsequent to the year in which the building is placed in service, such election is irrevocable.[76]

Example 42: In 2015, McIlwain Real Estate Investors, LLC purchased a residential building and began renting it to low-income persons. At the time the building was placed in service, the applicable percentage was eight percent, and the qualified basis was $1 million. McIlwain will include an $80,000 ($1,000,000 × 8%) low-income housing credit as part of its 2015 general business credit. Because McIlwain is a flow-through entity, its owners will report their respective shares of the general business credit on their respective income tax returns.

Example 43: McIlwain Real Estate Investors, LLC from Example 42 is able to take an $80,000 low-income housing credit each year from 2015 to 2024. Alternatively, McIlwain can

---

[73] Code Sec. 42.

[74] Joint Committee on Taxation, *General Explanation of the Tax Reform Act of 1986* (J.C.T. Rep. No. JCS-10-87), at 152.

[75] Code Sec. 42(a).

[76] Code Sec. 42(f).

irrevocably elect to forego taking any credit in 2015 and instead take an $80,000 credit each year from 2016 to 2025.

Qualified low-income building. A "qualified low-income building" is a residential rental building that is part of a qualified low-income housing project during the 15-year compliance period. A "qualified low-income housing project" is a residential rental property project that satisfies either of the following tests:[77]

1. *20-50 test.* This test is satisfied if 20 percent or more of the residential units in the project are rent-restricted and are occupied by individuals whose income is 50 percent or less of the area median gross income.

2. *40-60 test.* This test is satisfied if 40 percent or more of the residential units in the project are rent-restricted and are occupied by individuals whose income is 60 percent or less of the area median gross income.

Applicable percentage. The "applicable percentage," which the IRS redetermines each month, is the percentage that will yield a credit over the 10-year credit period with a present value equal to 70 percent of the qualified basis of new buildings that are not federally subsidized and 30 percent of the qualified basis of existing buildings and new buildings that are federally subsidized. The applicable percentage must be a minimum of nine percent for a new building that is not federally subsidized if the housing credit dollar amount was allocated to the building before January 1, 2015. A new building will be treated as federally subsidized if, at any time during the tax year or any prior tax year, there is or was outstanding any state or local obligation paying tax-exempt interest whose proceeds are or were used (directly or indirectly) with respect to the building or its operation.[78]

 Planning Pointer: Owners of federally subsidized buildings can take advantage of the higher credit percentage by electing to reduce their eligible basis by the balance of the loan or by the proceeds of the obligation.

Qualified basis. The "qualified basis" of any qualified low-income building is an amount equal to the applicable fraction times the eligible basis of the building. The "applicable fraction" is the *smaller* of the unit fraction or the floor space fraction. The *unit fraction* is the fraction whose numerator is the number of low-income units in the building and whose denominator is the number of residential rental units (whether or not occupied) in the building. The *floor space fraction* is the fraction whose numerator is the total floor space of the low-income units in the building and whose denominator is the total floor space of the residential rental units (whether or not occupied) in the building.[79]

The "eligible basis" of a building varies depending on whether it is a new or existing building. For a new building, the eligible basis is its adjusted basis as of the close of the first tax year in the credit period. For an existing building, the eligible basis is its adjusted basis as of the close of the first tax year in the credit period provided (1) the taxpayer purchased the building; (2) at least 10 years have elapsed since the building was last placed in service by the previous owner; (3) the building was not previously placed in service by a party related to the taxpayer; and (4) a low-income housing credit is allowed with respect to the building. If any of these conditions is not met, the eligible basis of the existing building will be zero.[80]

.02 Claiming the Credit

The credit is claimed by filing Form 8586, *Low-Income Housing Credit.* Because the low-income housing credit is part of the general business credit, the credit computed on Form 8586 is

---

[77] Code Sec. 42(c)(2), (g), and (i)(1).
[78] Code Sec. 42(b)(2) and (i)(2).
[79] Code Sec. 42(c)(1)(D).
[80] Code Sec. 42(d).

transferred to Form 3800, *General Business Credit*, when computing the business's general business credit for the year.

.03 Recapture of the Credit

If a building is not owned and operated as low-income housing for 15 years, a portion of the credit usually must be recaptured. However, no recapture will be required when a building is disposed of before the end of the compliance period if it is reasonably expected that the building will continue to be operated as a qualified low-income building for the remainder of the compliance period. The amount of the credit that must be recaptured is the sum of the difference between the amount of the credit taken and the amount that would have been allowed if the credit had been spread over 15 years instead of 10 years plus interest from the dates the recaptured credits were claimed. The interest rate used is the rate paid on overpayment of taxes.[81]

Example 44: Garoutte Investors, LLC placed a qualified low-income building in service and started taking a $1.5 million credit in annual installments of $150,000. After claiming the credit for six years, the company ceased operating the building as a low-income building. If the credit had been taken over 15 years, the company would have been able to take a $100,000 credit each year. Therefore, $50,000 for each year the credit was claimed, or $300,000 ($50,000 × 6 years), must be recaptured. Interest (using the federal government's overpayment rate) will be charged from the date each recaptured $50,000 credit was claimed until the date the credit was recaptured.

¶ 1113 Disabled Access Credit

Eligible small businesses may take a disabled access credit for amounts paid or incurred to enable them to comply with applicable requirements under the Americans with Disabilities Act of 1990.[82] The nonrefundable credit is part of the general business credit.

> **Reason for the Rule:** Congress enacted this credit as part of the Revenue Reconciliation Act of 1990 because it was concerned that complying with the requirements included in the Americans with Disabilities Act of 1990 would impose a severe financial burden on certain small businesses.[83]

.01 Eligible Small Business Defined

A business qualifies as an "eligible small business" if during the preceding tax year it met either of the following conditions: (1) its gross receipts did not exceed $1 million or (2) it employed no more than 30 full-time employees. A "full-time employee" is an employee who works at least 30 hours per week for 20 or more calendar weeks during the tax year.[84]

Example 45: During the previous tax year, Riggers, Inc. reported gross receipts totaling $1,150,000 and employed 31 individuals full-time. Riggers does not qualify as an eligible small business because in its previous tax year its gross receipts exceeded $1 million and it employed more than 30 full-time individuals.

Example 46: During the previous tax year, Collins, Inc. had gross receipts of $1,200,000 and employed 29 full-time individuals. Even through Collins's gross receipts in the previous tax year exceeded $1 million, in that year it did not have more than 30 full-time employees. Accordingly, Collins qualifies as an eligible small business in the current year.

---

[81] Code Sec. 42(j).
[82] Code Sec. 44(a).

[83] Senate Finance Committee Report, S. 3209 (October 13, 1990), at 71.
[84] Code Sec. 44(b).

.02 Computing the Amount of the Credit

The amount of the disabled access credit equals 50 percent of the amount by which the eligible access expenditures during the tax year of an eligible small business exceed $250 but do not exceed $10,250.[85] Thus, when eligible expenditures equal or exceed $10,250, the maximum credit allowed is $5,000 ($10,250 – $250 = $10,000 × 50%). The adjusted basis of the building is increased by the amount by which the expenditures exceed the taxpayer's disabled access credit.[86]

Example 47: Christiansen Lighting is an eligible small business that made $10,000 of eligible access expenditures during the tax year. Christiansen may take a disabled access credit equal to $4,875 [($10,000 – $250 = $9,750) × 50%]. Christiansen increases the basis in its building by $5,125, the amount by which its eligible capital expenditures exceed the disabled access credit ($10,000 – $4,875) and will depreciate this amount using the MACRS rules discussed in Chapter 7.

Example 48: Davidson & Sons is an eligible small business. During the year, Davidson made $15,000 of eligible access expenditures. Davidson's disabled access credit equals the maximum $5,000 because its eligible access expenditures exceed $10,250. Davidson increases its basis in the building by $10,000 ($15,000 – $5,000) and can depreciate this amount under MACRS.

.03 Eligible Access Expenditures

"Eligible access expenditures" are amounts paid or incurred by an eligible small business to enable it to comply with applicable requirements under the Americans with Disabilities Act of 1990. They include ordinary and necessary expenditures paid or incurred for any of the following purposes:[87]

- Removal of architectural, communication, physical, or transportation barriers that prevent a business from being accessible to, or usable by, individuals with disabilities, but not if the amounts are paid or incurred in connection with a facility first placed in service after November 5, 1990;

- Provision of qualified interpreters or other effective methods of making aurally delivered materials available to individuals with hearing impairments;

- Provision of qualified readers, taped texts, and other effective methods of making visually delivered materials available to individuals with visual impairments;

- Acquisition of or modification of equipment or devices for individuals with disabilities; or

- Provision of similar services, modifications, materials, or equipment.

.04 Claiming the Credit

Taxpayers can claim the credit by filing Form 8826, *Disabled Access Credit*. Because the disabled access credit is part of the general business credit, amounts reported on Form 8826 are transferred to Form 3800, *General Business Credit*.

As mentioned in Chapter 5, businesses normally can elect to currently deduct up to $15,000 each year of such expenses as qualified architectural and transportation barrier removal expenses.[88] If a disabled access credit is taken, the amount of any deduction must be reduced by the amount of the credit taken. Because taxpayers are almost always better off taking a tax credit rather than a tax deduction, the tax savings (and therefore cash flow) will be greater when the disabled access credit is taken and the deduction is reduced.

Example 49: Cable Corporation incurs $22,000 in costs to install wheelchair ramps at the entrances to its office building. Cable has the option of expensing $15,000 of its costs in

---

[85] Code Sec. 44(a).

[86] Code Sec. 44(d)(7).

[87] Code Sec. 44(c).

[88] Code Sec. 190.

the current year or taking a $5,000 disabled access credit and deducting $10,000 of the remaining costs in the current year. In both scenarios, the excess $7,000 ($22,000 – $15,000) will be added to the basis in the building and depreciated under MACRS. Assuming that Cable's marginal tax rate is 35 percent, if it were to choose to deduct $15,000 in the current year its tax savings would equal $5,250 ($15,000 × 35%). If Cable were to take the $5,000 disabled access credit, the tax savings from the $10,000 deduction ($15,000 maximum – $5,000 credit taken) would be $3,500 ($10,000 × 35%) and its total tax savings would equal $8,500 ($3,500 + $5,000). The additional tax savings from taking the credit equals $3,250 ($8,500 – $5,250). Because the $7,000 in excess of the $15,000 eligible for immediate expensing will be depreciated under MACRS in either scenario, the tax savings from the depreciation deductions is the same and consequently is not relevant for purposes of considering the tax advantages of taking the credit over the $15,000 deduction.

¶ 1114 Employer-Provided Child Care Credit

Employers are allowed a nonrefundable **employer-provided child care credit** when they provide employee child care and child care resource and referral services.[89] The credit is part of the general business credit.

 Reason for the Rule: The credit was enacted as part of the Economic Growth and Tax Relief Act of 2001 to encourage employers to provide child care for their employees.

.01 Calculating the Amount of the Credit

The amount of the credit is the sum of 25 percent of qualified child care expenditures and 10 percent of qualified child care resource and referral expenditures.[90] The amount of the credit cannot exceed $150,000.[91]

Example 50: P. Mackey, Inc. made $30,000 of qualified child care expenditures and $10,000 of qualified child care resource and referral expenditures during its tax year. Its employer-provided child care credit equals $8,500 [($30,000 × 25%) + ($10,000 × 10%)].

Qualified child care expenditures. Twenty-five percent of a taxpayer's qualified child care expenditures are used to compute the employer-provided child care credit. "Qualified child care expenditures" are amounts paid or incurred for any of the following purposes:[92]

- Acquisition, construction, rehabilitation, or expansion of property to be used as part of a qualified child care facility of the taxpayer if the property is depreciable (or amortizable) and if the property is not part of the principal residence of the taxpayer or any employee of the taxpayer;

- Payment for operating costs of a qualified child care facility of the taxpayer, including expenses for training employees, scholarship programs, and the provision of increased compensation to employees with higher levels of child care training;

- Provision of child care services to the taxpayer's employees under a contract with a qualified child care facility.

A qualified child care facility has as its principal purpose providing child care assistance. The facility must meet the requirements of all applicable laws and regulations of the state and local government where it is located, including the licensing of the facility as a child care facility, and it cannot be the principal residence of the person who operates the facility. Enrollment in the facility

---

[89] Code Sec. 45F.
[90] Code Sec. 45F(a).
[91] Code Sec. 45F(b).
[92] Code Sec. 45F(c)(1).

must be open to the taxpayer's employees during the tax year, and at least 30 percent of the enrollees must be dependents of the taxpayer's employees. Finally, a qualified child care facility cannot discriminate in favor of the taxpayer's highly compensated employees.[93]

Example 51: Kehoe Tack Boards, Inc. sets aside part of its building for child care. The child care facility is open to the children of all employees, and only employees and their dependents can use the facility. However, special teachers were brought in for the children of the owners and top executives (all of whom are highly compensated). Because the facility discriminates in favor of highly compensated employees, it is not a qualified child care facility. Therefore, the costs incurred in operating the facility do not qualify for the employer-provided child-care credit.

Qualified child care resource and referral expenditures. Ten percent of the taxpayer's qualified child care resource and referral expenditures are used in computing the employer-provided child care credit. "Qualified child care resource and referral expenditures" are amounts paid or incurred under a contract to provide child care resource and referral services to a taxpayer's employee.[94] Such services will not be qualified if the contract discriminates in favor of highly compensated employees to provide child care for their employees.

.02 Claiming the Credit

Taxpayers can claim the credit by filing Form 8882, *Credit for Employer-Provided Child Care Facilities and Services*. Because this credit is part of the general business credit, the amount computed on Form 8882 is transferred to Form 3800, *General Business Credit*.

Because qualified child care expenditures include amounts paid or incurred to acquire, construct, rehabilitate, or expand property, any credit allowed for qualified child care expenditures with respect to such property must reduce the taxpayer's basis in the property. Furthermore, if an expenditure used to qualify an employer for the credit is otherwise a deductible expenditure (for example, wages paid to workers to operate the facility), the amount of the employer's deduction for that expenditure must be reduced by the amount of the credit taken.[95]

Example 52: In 2015, Kambell Company pays wages totaling $40,000 to workers who operate its child care facility. Because the costs are qualified child care expenditures, Kambell is eligible for a $10,000 tax credit ($40,000 × 25%) on its 2015 tax return. In computing its taxable income, Kambell must reduce its wage expense deduction by $10,000.

Thus, on its 2015 tax return, Kambell can only deduct $30,000 of the wages it paid to the workers of its child care facility.

.03 Recapture of the Credit

If a recapture event occurs with respect to any qualified child care facility during any of the 10 tax years after the facility was placed in service, the employer's tax liability is increased by an amount equal to the applicable recapture percentage (as shown in Table 11-2), multiplied by the amount by which the general business credit for all prior tax years would have decreased if the taxpayer's qualified child care expenditures had been zero.[96] The recapture provision is similar to the provisions that apply to the low-income housing and rehabilitation tax credits.

Cessation of the operation of a facility as a qualified child care facility constitutes a recapture event, unless the cessation is due to a casualty loss and the loss is restored by reconstruction or replacement within a reasonable period. Disposition of the taxpayer's interest in the qualified child care facility is also a recapture event, unless the person acquiring the taxpayer's interest agrees in writing to assume the taxpayer's recapture liability. The applicable recapture percentage depends on when the recapture event occurs, as shown in Table 11-2.

---

[93] Code Sec. 45F(c)(2).
[94] Code Sec. 45F(c)(3).
[95] Code Sec. 45F(f).
[96] Code Sec. 45F(d).

Table 11-2 Applicable Recapture Percentages for the Employer-Provided Child Care Credit

Recapture Event Occurs in	Applicable Recapture Percentage
Years 1-3	100%
Year 4	85%
Year 5	70%
Year 6	55%
Year 7	40%
Year 8	25%
Year 9 or 10	10%
Year 11 or thereafter	0%

Example 53: Lockridge Shoes, Inc. took a $50,000 employer-provided child care credit in 2011 for a qualified child care facility that it constructed and operated. In 2012, Lockridge took a $20,000 credit for operating expenses; in 2013, it took a $30,000 credit for operating expenses. In 2014, the company closed the facility because it had become too costly to operate. If its credit for the previous years had been zero, its general business credit would have been reduced by $100,000 ($50,000 + $20,000 + $30,000). Because the recapture event took place in year 4, the applicable recapture percentage is 85 percent. Thus, the recapture amount equals $85,000 ($100,000 × 85%).

¶ 1115 Small Employer Health Insurance Credit

Certain small employers can take the small employer health insurance credit to reimburse themselves for a portion of their cost to provide health insurance for their employees.[97] The credit is part of the general business credit for eligible small employers who are not tax-exempt eligible small employers and is a refundable credit for tax-exempt eligible small employers.

.01 Eligible Small Employer

An employer is an "eligible small employer" for a tax year if it satisfies all of the following requirements:

- It has no more than 25 full-time equivalent employees for the tax year.
- Its average annual wages do not exceed an amount equal to twice the specified dollar amount ($25,800 for calendar year 2015).
- It pays at least 50 percent of the health insurance premiums of each employee.

An employer is a "tax-exempt eligible small employer" if it is an eligible small employer and is a tax-exempt charitable organization.

.02 Amount of the Credit

The amount of the credit for eligible small employers is 50 percent of the lesser of the following amounts:

- The aggregate amount of premium paid for qualified health plans offered through an Exchange.

---

[97] Code Sec. 45R.

- The aggregate amount of premiums payments it would have made if each employee had enrolled in a qualified health plan that had a premium equal to the average premium for the small group market in the rating area in which its employees enroll for coverage).

The amount of the credit for tax-exempt eligible small employers is the lesser of the following amounts:

- An amount determined the same way as for eligible small employers except that the credit percentage is 35 percent.
- The amount of the employer's payroll taxes during the calendar year in which its tax year began.

.03 Phaseout of the Credit

The amount of the credit has to be phased out if an employer has more than 10 employees and/or its average annual wages exceed $25,800 (for a tax year beginning in 2015):

- The amount of the credit has to be reduced by a fraction whose numerator is the total number of full-time employees in excess of 10 and whose denominator is 15. An employer with 25 or more full-time employees is not entitled to any credit.
- The amount of the credit has to be reduced by a fraction whose numerator is the employer's average annual wages in excess of a specified dollar amount ($25,800 for a tax year beginning in 2015) and whose denominator is the specified dollar amount. If an employer's average annual wages are $51,600 more for a tax year beginning in 2015, it will not be eligible for any credit.

.04 Claiming the Credit

Employers can claim the credit by filing Form 8941, *Credit for Small Employer Health Insurance Premiums*. Employers can claim the credit for only two consecutive tax years.

TAX CREDIT FOR FOREIGN INCOME TAXES PAID

¶ 1116 Foreign Tax Credit

When U.S. businesses receive income from a foreign country, the foreign-source income may be subject to income tax both by the foreign country and by the United States. To reduce the possibility of double taxation on the same income, U.S. citizens and residents and certain nonresident taxpayers are permitted to take a **foreign tax credit (FTC)** for income, war profits, and excess profits taxes (collectively referred to as income taxes) that they paid or accrued to a foreign country or to a U.S. possession during the tax year.[98]

 Reason for the Rule: U.S. citizens and residents are taxed on their worldwide income, meaning that they are taxed on all income that they receive from both U.S. and foreign sources. U.S. businesses and residents are permitted to take a tax credit or a deduction for foreign income taxes they paid so that they will not be taxed on the same income twice (once by the foreign country and a second time by the United States).

.01 Election To Take a Deduction Instead of a Credit for Foreign Income Taxes Paid

In lieu of claiming a tax credit for foreign taxes paid, taxpayers can instead take a deduction for the foreign taxes paid or accrued.[99] For businesses, this deduction would offset business profits and, therefore, reduce the taxpayer's tax liability by the amount of the deduction times the taxpayer's

---

[98] Code Sec. 901(a).   [99] Code Sec. 164(a)(3).

marginal tax rate. However, any foreign taxes paid by an individual taxpayer are considered personal taxes and, therefore, must be taken as itemized deductions (deductions from AGI). Thus, foreign taxes that result from profits earned by sole proprietors do not reduce their sole proprietorship's profits or their adjusted gross income. Payment of such taxes can reduce a sole proprietorship's taxable income only if the total amount of the taxpayer's itemized deductions exceeds the standard deduction amount.

As a rule, taxpayers benefit more by taking a credit for foreign income taxes paid because each dollar of the credit reduces the taxpayer's tax liability by one dollar. However, the amount of foreign tax credit that taxpayers can claim is limited to the ratio of their income from foreign sources to total income. Therefore, under certain circumstances taxpayers may be better off taking a deduction for foreign taxes paid instead of a credit. For example, if the rate of tax on the foreign income was high and the taxpayer's foreign income was a small proportion of the taxpayer's U.S. income, the tax benefits to taking a deduction may outweigh the amount of the tax credit.

Example 54: Elkin Teak Floors, Inc. paid $1,000 in foreign taxes during the year. Because of limitations on the foreign tax credit, the company's credit for the year is only $10. Elkin's taxable income falls in the 34-percent tax bracket. If Elkin elects to deduct the $1,000 in foreign taxes paid rather than to take the credit, it will save $340 (34% × $1,000) in income taxes for the year. This amount exceeds the $10 foreign tax credit it could take by $330.

Planning Pointer: Taxpayers may take a credit for all qualified foreign taxes that they paid or accrued during the year or they may take a deduction for all qualified foreign taxes that they paid or accrued during the tax year. They may *not* take a credit for some foreign taxes and a deduction for other foreign taxes. However, taxpayers who claim a foreign tax credit one year may claim a foreign tax deduction the next year, and vice versa.

.02 Taxpayers Eligible for the Credit

U.S. citizens and residents and domestic corporations are eligible to take a credit for the amount of foreign income tax paid or accrued during the tax year to any foreign country or to a U.S. possession. Partners, S corporation shareholders, and beneficiaries of a trust or estate are allowed a credit for their proportionate share of foreign income tax paid by their partnership, corporation, estate, or trust to a foreign country or to a U.S. possession.[100] Nonresident alien individuals and foreign corporations engaged in a trade or business within the United States are allowed a credit for foreign income tax paid or accrued (or deemed paid or accrued) to any foreign country or U.S. possession with respect to income effectively connected with the conduct of their trade or business within the United States.[101]

Example 55: Bracken Inc., a U.S. corporation, paid $20,000 in foreign income taxes during the year. Because the company is a U.S. corporation, Bracken is eligible for the foreign tax credit.

Example 56: Elkins Company is incorporated under the laws of a foreign country. During the year, the company engaged in business within the United States and had $100,000 of income effectively connected with that business. Half of that income was considered foreign-source income and was taxed by a foreign country. Elkins can take a foreign tax credit for the foreign income taxes it paid.

---

[100] Code Sec. 164(a)(3).   [101] Code Sec. 906(a).

.03 Taxes Eligible for the Foreign Tax Credit

Not every amount that a business pays to a foreign government qualifies for the foreign tax credit. A business is allowed a credit for income taxes paid or accrued to a foreign country or to a U.S. possession.[102] To be eligible for the foreign tax credit or deduction, a foreign tax must be a levy whose predominant character is that of an income tax in the U.S. sense. A penalty, fine, interest, or customs duty is not considered a tax. A foreign levy is not considered a tax to the extent that a person subject to the levy receives (or will receive), directly or indirectly, a specific economic benefit from the foreign country in exchange for payment pursuant to the levy.[103] In some instances, foreign income taxes paid by an entity in which the taxpayer owns an interest are "deemed" to have been paid by the taxpayer. Foreign taxes "deemed" to have been paid are also eligible for the credit.[104]

Taxes deemed paid. If a domestic (U.S.) corporation, other than an S corporation, owns at least 10 percent of the voting stock of a foreign corporation from which it receives dividends, the domestic corporation will be "deemed" to have paid a portion of the foreign corporation's foreign income taxes paid. However, the amount of deemed taxes cannot be attributable to dividends distributed by the foreign corporation in prior tax years.[105] The calculation of a deemed payment can be expressed as follows:

$$\begin{matrix} \text{Foreign taxes "deemed" paid by the domestic shareholder (corporation)} \end{matrix} = \begin{matrix} \text{Foreign income taxes actually paid by the foreign corporation} \end{matrix} \times \frac{\text{Dividends paid to the domestic (corporation) shareholder}}{\text{Foreign corporation's post-1986 undistributed earnings}}$$

Example 57: Pulido Inc., a U.S. corporation, owns 30 percent of the voting stock of Outright, Inc., a foreign corporation. When Pulido receives a dividend from Outright, it will be deemed to have paid a portion of Outright's foreign income taxes.

When a U.S. taxpayer claims a foreign tax credit or deduction for deemed taxes paid under this special rule, the corporation must add the amount of the foreign taxes to the dividend income it received from the foreign corporation. Thus, although the deemed taxes may result in a higher foreign tax credit, additional income taxes will be owed on the additional dividend income reported by the taxpayer.

Example 58: Domestics, Inc., a U.S. corporation, owns 40 percent of the voting stock of First-Tier, a foreign corporation. During 2015, First-Tier pays a $20,000 dividend to Domestics. As of the end of 2015, First-Tier has $100,000 of post-1986 undistributed earnings and has paid $40,000 in foreign income taxes. The $20,000 of dividends paid to Domestics during the year represents 20 percent ($20,000/$100,000) of First-Tier's post-1986 accumulated earnings. Thus, Domestics is deemed to have paid 20 percent of First-Tier's $40,000 of foreign income taxes, or $8,000 ($40,000 × 20%). If Domestics includes this amount as foreign taxes paid during the year in computing its tax credit, it will report $28,000 of dividend income from First-Tier on its 2015 tax return ($20,000 + $8,000).

.04 Limitations on the Amount of the Credit

A taxpayer's foreign tax credit is limited to the portion of its U.S. income tax liability that is attributable to foreign income being taxed by both the United States and a foreign government.[106] The overall limitation can be expressed as follows:

---

[102] Code Sec. 901(b).

[103] Reg. § 1.901-2(a)(2)(ii).

[104] Code Sec. 903.

[105] Code Sec. 902; Reg. § 1.902-1(a).

[106] Code Sec. 904(a).

$$\text{U.S. Income tax (before any FTC)} \quad \times \quad \frac{\text{Taxable income from foreign sources}}{\text{Worldwide taxable income}}$$

The taxpayer's credit is the *lesser* of the foreign taxes paid or the calculated amount of the overall limitation.

Example 59: Seale Clothes, Inc. had a total taxable income of $1 million and a pre-credit U.S. income tax of $340,000. Its taxable income from foreign sources was $400,000, and it paid $175,000 in foreign income tax during the year. The maximum amount of foreign income tax credit Seale can take is $136,000.

$$\$340,000 \quad \times \quad \frac{\$400,000}{\$1,000,000} \quad = \quad \$136,000$$

Because only 40 percent ($400,000/$1,000,000) of Seale's worldwide income came from foreign sources, only 40 percent of its U.S. income tax liability is attributable to foreign income. Consequently, the maximum amount of foreign tax credit that Seale Clothes can take is $136,000 (the *lesser* of the $175,000 foreign taxes paid or the $136,000 overall limitation).

> **Reason for the Rule:** The overall limitation prevents taxpayers from using foreign tax payments to reduce their U.S. tax liability on income from U.S. sources. Permitting taxpayers to use the foreign tax credit to reduce the U.S. income tax on their U.S. income would give foreign countries the right to tax income earned in the United States.[107]

Example 60: Murdell Distributors, Inc. paid $500,000 in foreign income taxes on $1 million in foreign-source income and owed $680,000 in U.S. income tax on its $2 million of taxable income from both U.S. and foreign sources. If Murdell had only the $1 million in taxable income from U.S. sources, its U.S. income tax liability would have been $340,000 (using the tax rates from Table 4-1 at ¶ 405.01). If Murdell were permitted to take a credit and reduce its U.S. tax liability by the full $500,000 paid in foreign income taxes from its U.S. tax liability, its U.S. income taxes would be reduced to $180,000 ($680,000 – $500,000). Accordingly, if no limitation were imposed on the amount of foreign tax credit, Murdell would pay $160,000 ($340,000 – $180,000) less in taxes to the U.S. government than it would have paid without its foreign activities.

A second limitation based on the aggregate of separate limitations also applies. The calculation of these separate limitations is quite involved and beyond the scope of this discussion. However, when taxpayers report different types of foreign-source income, the taxes attributable to each category of income will be limited to the amount of taxable income from that activity.[108]

Special rule for individuals. If the entire amount of an individual's gross income for a tax year from sources outside the United States consists of qualified passive income (including most types of interest and dividends), all of the income and taxes paid on it were reported to the individual on a qualified payee statement, and the amount of creditable foreign taxes paid or accrued by the individual during the tax year does not exceed $300 ($600 if married and filing a joint return), the

---

[107] Joint Committee on Taxation, *General Explanation of the Tax Reform Act of 1986* (J.C.T. Rep. No. JCS-10-87), at 854.

[108] Code Secs. 901(b) and 904.

individual can elect not to have the foreign tax credit limitation rules apply.[109] If an election is made, the individual cannot carry over any excess credit to or from the election year.[110]

.05 Foreign Tax Credit Carryback and Carryover

The amount of foreign income taxes not allowed as a credit because of the overall and separate limitations can be carried back one year and carried forward 10 years.[111] Foreign income tax payments in excess of the limitations are deemed paid in the prior (or subsequent) tax year.

Example 61:   Because of the overall and separate limitations, Benton Document could not take a credit for $50,000 in foreign income taxes that it paid. Benton adds the $50,000 to its foreign income taxes paid for the prior tax year. After applying the overall and separate limitations to the recomputed amount of foreign income taxes, Benton is able to increase its foreign tax credit for its prior tax year by $5,000. Benton can carry forward the $45,000 ($50,000 – $5,000) that it could not use for its prior tax year for up to 10 subsequent tax years.

Foreign income tax payments carried back to the prior tax year or carried forward to a subsequent tax year cannot be deducted for that year. The deduction for foreign taxes is allowed only in the year in which the foreign taxes are paid or incurred.

.06 Claiming the Credit

Corporations claim the foreign tax credit by completing Form 1118, *Foreign Tax Credit— Corporations*, and attaching it to their income tax return. A separate form must be completed for each separate category of income against which a separate limitation is applied. The foreign tax credit is not part of the general business credit. The credit from Form 1118 is reported directly on Form 1120, *U.S. Corporation Income Tax Return*. Corporations that elect to take the deduction report the amount of foreign taxes paid during the year on Form 1120.

Individuals usually must complete Form 1116, *Foreign Tax Credit* (Individual, Estate, or Trust), and attach it to their income tax return to claim the credit. A separate form must be completed for each separate category of income against which a separate limitation is applied. Individuals who choose to take a deduction for foreign taxes paid report the deduction on Schedule A, *Itemized Deductions*. Individuals do not have to file Form 1116 and instead can claim the credit on Form 1040 if they elected to be exempt from the foreign tax credit limitation rules.

Flow-through entities report both the amount of foreign-source income as well as the amount of taxes accrued or paid during the year on the entities' tax returns. The owners then use their respective shares of these amounts to compute the amount of the foreign tax credit they are allowed to claim on their own tax returns.

¶ 1117 Summary

Whenever a business calculates the financial cost of a proposed transaction, it should consider whether a tax credit is available to offset some or all of its costs. Tax credits are available to reimburse a business for the additional costs that may be required to train an individual who has had trouble finding employment. Tax credits also are available to encourage businesses to reduce their use of oil and natural gas, conduct research, invest in economically disadvantaged areas, and rehabilitate older structures.

Each of the tax credits discussed in this chapter illustrates the many ways businesses can reduce the overall costs of certain expenditures by having the federal government, in essence, subsidize a portion of their expenditures. Accordingly, knowledge about which expenditures qualify for a tax credit and the requirements for each of the credits is needed for good tax planning.

---

[109] Code Sec. 904(k).
[110] Code Sec. 904(k)(1); Reg. § 1.904(j)-1(b)(1).

[111] Code Sec. 904(c).

GLOSSARY OF TERMS INTRODUCED IN THE CHAPTER

Business tax credit. Tax credit used by governments to reward businesses for participating in certain types of activities by subsidizing a portion of the expenditures that they incur by participating in those activities.

Disabled access tax credit. A nonrefundable credit that eligible small businesses may take for amounts paid or incurred to enable them to comply with applicable requirements under the Americans with Disabilities Act of 1990.

Employer-provided child care credit. A nonrefundable income tax credit for employers who provide employees with child care and child care resource and referral services.

Empowerment zones. Specific geographic regions within the United States that the federal government has identified as being in need of revitalization.

Empowerment zone employment credit. A nonrefundable tax credit for employers who hire individuals who both live *and* work in an empowerment zone.

Foreign tax credit (FTC). A nonrefundable income tax credit for income, war profits, and excess profits taxes paid or accrued to a foreign country or to a U.S. possession during the tax year.

General business credit. A combination of business credits, each of which is computed under its own set of rules.

Low-income housing credit. A nonrefundable income tax credit for taxpayers who purchase or substantially rehabilitate residential rental property used for low-income housing.

Net income tax. Term used in the alternative minimum tax system. The sum of the net regular tax liability and any alternative minimum tax minus the same tax credits used in computing net regular tax liability.

Net regular tax liability. Term used in the alternative minimum tax system. A taxpayer's regular tax liability minus certain tax credits, such as the foreign tax credit and personal tax credits.

New markets credit. A nonrefundable income tax credit for taxpayers who make a qualified equity investment in a qualified community development entity. See also *Qualified community development entity.*

Nonrefundable tax credit. A tax credit that can only reduce a taxpayer's income tax liability.

Personal tax credit. A tax credit available only to individuals.

Qualified community development entity (qualified CDE). A domestic corporation or partnership whose primary mission is serving, or providing investment capital for, low-income communities or low-income persons.

Qualified rehabilitated building. A building that is a certified historic structure or a building that originally was placed in service before 1936 and with respect to which the taxpayer paid or incurred substantial rehabilitation expenditures.

Qualified zone employee. An employee who performs substantially all of his or her services for an employer within an empowerment zone and whose principal residence while performing such services is located within an empowerment zone.

Qualified zone wages. Wages paid or incurred by an employer for services performed by an employee while working as a qualified zone employee.

Recapture of a tax credit. If a taxpayer ceases to use property for the purposes that qualified the property for a tax credit, all or a portion of the credit may have to be added to the taxpayer's tax liability for the year that the property ceased to be used for the qualified purpose.

Refundable tax credit. A credit that can reduce a taxpayer's tax liability to zero and produce a refund for any amount of the credit in excess of the taxpayer's tax liability.

Rehabilitation credit. A nonrefundable credit available for substantially rehabilitating a depreciable building that was placed in service before 1936 or that qualifies as a certified historic structure. *See also* Substantially rehabilitated *and* Qualified rehabilitated building.

Research activities credit. A nonrefundable income tax credit for conducting qualified research.

Tax credit. Amount that reduces a taxpayer's tax liability. Can be either refundable or nonrefundable.

Work opportunity credit. A nonrefundable income tax credit for employing individuals from certain targeted groups.

CHAPTER PROBLEMS

Chapter 11 Discussion Questions

1. What is a tax credit?

2. How does a tax credit differ from a tax deduction in terms of affecting a taxpayer's tax liability?

3. Why are the various tax credits combined into a general business credit?

4. How many years can a general business credit in excess of the annual limitation be carried back and carried forward?

5. Whom can an employer hire if the employer wants to qualify for the empowerment zone employment credit?

6. When will a member of a targeted group be ineligible for the work opportunity credit?

7. What is the work opportunity credit for hiring a long-term family assistance recipient?

8. What role does the state employment security agency have in determining whether an employer qualifies for the work opportunity credit?

9. When does research constitute "qualified research," thereby entitling a business to a research activities credit?

10. How is the base amount calculated for purposes of determining the research activities credit, and what is the minimum base amount?

11. What types of expenditures qualify for the new markets credit?

12. Expenditures to rehabilitate what types of buildings can qualify for the rehabilitation credit?

13. A taxpayer pays $250,000 for a certified historical structure originally placed in service in 1948. Over the next 20 months, the taxpayer spends $180,000 rehabilitating the building. Does the taxpayer qualify for the rehabilitation credit?

14. What does "recapture a credit" mean?

15. For how many years may a taxpayer take a low-income housing credit, and for how many years must the property be owned and operated as low-income housing?

16. What businesses may be eligible to take a disabled access credit?

17. What types of expenditures are eligible for the disabled access credit?

18. What types of expenditures qualify for the employer-provided child care credit?

19. What limitations are placed on the amount of a taxpayer's foreign tax credit?

20. What happens to foreign tax payments for which no foreign tax credit is allowed?

Chapter 11 Problems

1. Hoang Skis, Inc. has a tentative general business credit of $60,000. Its net income tax is $250,000, its tentative minimum tax is $200,000, and its net regular tax liability is $250,000. How much of its tentative general business credit can it take for the tax year?

2. For the tax year, Carlson, Inc., had regular tax of $100 million, tentative minimum tax of $80 million, and current year general business credit components of $50 million. What is Carlson's general business credit for the tax year?

3. During the tax year, Reimer Office Designers, Inc. made $200,000 of qualified rehabilitation expenditures with respect to two qualified rehabilitated buildings, one of which qualified as a certified historic structure. Of the qualified rehabilitation expenditures, $120,000 was made with respect to the certified historic structure. What is the company's rehabilitation credit for the tax year?

4. Pizzo Nursing Homes, Inc. took a $100,000 rehabilitation credit for a building and sold the building 18 months after it was placed in service. How much of the credit has to be recaptured?

5. In 2004, Allgood Tubing, Inc. hired Pedro Urrutia and Shane Earhart as full-time employees. At the time, Pedro was 19 and lived in an empowerment zone, and Shane was a veteran who had been unemployed for seven months during the year prior to his hiring date. Allgood paid Pedro $15,000 and Shane $16,000 during their respective first year of employment. What amount of work opportunity credit may Allgood take for these two employees?

6. After having success with its hiring of Pedro and Shane, Allgood Tubing, Inc. from Problem 5 hired Rachelle Bleich and Herman Weinstock. Rachelle, age 16, was hired to work full time from May 30 to September 1. Rachelle lives in an empowerment zone. Herman has a mental disability that was a substantial handicap to his employment, but he was referred to Allgood after he successfully completed rehabilitative services under a state vocational rehabilitation program. During the employees' first year of employment, Allgood paid Rachelle $3,500 and Herman $10,000. What amount of work opportunity credit may Allgood take with respect to these employees?

7. Lemelle Mufflers, Inc. qualified for the work opportunity credit by employing Candy Macedo, a long-term family assistance recipient. She was hired on June 1, 2014. From June 1, 2014, through December 31, 2014, Lemelle paid Candy $9,000 and took a work opportunity credit based on that amount. From January 1, 2015, through May 31, 2015, Lemelle paid Candy $10,000 in wages. For the remainder of 2015, the company paid Candy $15,000 in wages. What is the amount of its work opportunity credit for 2015?

8. Chew Plastic Balls, Inc. paid Roberto Haycraft $20,000 of qualified zone wages during 2014 for his services in an empowerment zone. What is the amount of empowerment zone employment credit the company may take with respect to Roberto's wages?

9. In 2004, Izzi Sheet Metal, Inc. had $60,000 of qualified research expenses for the year, and its base amount was $30,000. What is Izzi's research activities credit for the year?

10. Assume the same facts as in Problem 9, except that Izzi decided to calculate its alternative simplified credit. Its average qualified research expenses for the three preceding tax years was $40,000. What is its alternative simplified credit?

11. Sayer Music Systems, Inc. had a fixed-base percentage of three percent and average annual gross receipts for its previous four tax years of $3 million. What is its base amount for the current tax year for purposes of determining its research activities credit?

12. Sudduth Precision Imagers, Inc. made a $200,000 qualified equity investment in a qualified community development entity on October 1, 2014. What amount of new markets credit will it be entitled to in 2017?

13. A taxpayer has research expenditures in the current year of $800,000 that qualify for the increased research expenditure credit. The taxpayer does not elect the alternative simplified credit. The applicable aggregate qualified research expenses are $400,000 and the applicable aggregate gross receipts are $2,000,000. The average annual gross receipts for the four preceding tax years are $3,000,000. There are no university basic research payments. Compute the credit for increased research expenditures.

14. Clifton Investors, LLC was eligible for a low-income housing credit of $900,000. After 10 years, the company ceased using the property as low-income housing. What amount, if any, of the credit has to be recaptured?

15. Norwood Compactors, Inc., an eligible small business, made $8,000 of eligible disabled access expenditures for the tax year. What is the amount of disabled access credit that it may take?

16. Jahn Heating, Inc. pays $50,000 of qualified child care expenditures and $20,000 of qualified child care resource and referral expenditures during its tax year. What is the amount of its employer-provided child care credit?

17. Dutcher Garden Tillers, Inc. took a $50,000 employer-provided child care credit in 2015 for a qualified child care facility that it constructed that year. If the company were to sell the facility in 2020, how much of that credit taken in 2015 would have to be recaptured? Could the company do anything to avoid having to recapture the credit?

18. Fenton Millers, Inc., a U.S. C corporation, owns 15 percent of the voting stock of Beane Millers, Inc., a foreign corporation. Beane distributed a $30,000 dividend to Fenton. The amount of post-1986 foreign income taxes paid by Beane was $100,000, and the amount of the company's post-1986 undistributed earnings at the end of the year during which the dividend was paid was $200,000. What amount, if any, of the foreign income taxes paid by Beane can be taken as a foreign tax credit by Fenton?

19. Lenz Jewelers, Inc. is a U.S. corporation. Its total taxable income for the year is $750,000, its taxable income from foreign sources is $150,000, and its pre-foreign tax credit income tax is $255,000. Applying the overall limitation, what is the maximum amount of the company's foreign tax credit for the year? What happens to any excess?

20. A taxpayer has worldwide income of $200,000 and a tentative U.S. tax liability of $65,000. The taxpayer earned $40,000 in a foreign country. Compute the maximum allowable foreign tax credit.

21. Bracken Batteries, Inc. is thinking about opening a manufacturing plant in an empowerment zone and asks you what its after-tax cost will be if it hires individuals who live in the empowerment zone. It plans to pay each of these individuals $20,000 a year. Its marginal tax bracket is 34 percent.

22. Torrey Trucks, Inc. hired a long-term family assistance recipient on January 1, 2013, and on January 1, 2014, hired a veteran entitled to compensation for a service-connected disability who had been discharged six months earlier. Both employees qualify Torrey Trucks for a work opportunity credit. If it pays each one qualified wages of $25,000 in 2014, what is its work opportunity credit for that year?

23. Pulido Power Tools, Inc. had $300,000 in qualified research expenses during 2014. The average of its qualified research expenses for the prior three years was $200,000. What is its alternative simplified credit?

24. Seale Coffee Roasters, Inc. invested $100,000 in a qualified community development entity in 2014. What is the total amount of new markets credit to which it will be entitled?

25. Benton Linens, Inc. spent $75,000 during its tax year to operate a qualified child care facility for its employees. The company also paid $5,000 to a business to provide child care referral

services to the company's employees. How much is its employer-provided child care credit for the year?

Chapter 11 Review Problems

1. Salter Technological Solutions, Inc. incurred $50,000 in qualified research expenses during 2014. Its base amount is $30,000. How much of its expenses can the company deduct, and how much can it take as a credit?

2. A corporation that uses the calendar year hires a new employee on March 1, 2012. The employee works for the corporation full-time and is paid the following amounts during the first two years of employment. The corporation's marginal tax rate is 35 percent.

Time Period	Amount Paid
3/1/12 – 12/31/12	$ 7,500
1/1/13 – 2/28/13	2,450
3/1/13 – 12/31/13	8,000
1/1/14 – 2/28/14	2,500
Total wages paid	$20,450

Compute the tax savings that the corporation would generate for 2012–2014 if the employee qualifies for the work opportunity credit (other than as a long-term family assistance recipient or qualified veteran). Determine the amount of the company's out-of-pocket costs for the $20,450 wages that it pays this employee during the first two years of employment. What percentage of the $20,450 gross wages paid is the actual cash paid by the company (net of tax savings)?

Chapter 11 Comprehensive Review Question

Stella Clay, Inc. purchased a manufacturing plant for $1 million and made $500,000 in improvements. A few years later it constructed a child care facility in the plant for $200,000 and took an employer-provided child care credit with respect to those expenditures. Over the next five years, it spent $300,000 on operating expenses and took an employer-provided child care credit for those expenditures. In the sixth year after opening the child care facility, Stella sold the manufacturing plant (including the child care facility), and the buyer refused to assume liability for any recapture tax. As of the date of the sale, Stella had taken $250,000 in depreciation deductions. If the amount realized from the sale is $1,750,000, compute the amount and character of the corporation's gain or loss on the sale.

Chapter 11 Research Question

Stephen Aguilera, who owns a business, wants to save fuel costs by purchasing motor vehicles that run on batteries for himself and his employees. He remembers reading about a tax credit for such vehicles and asks you how much the credit is. Using the CCH *Standard Federal Tax Reporter*, determine the credit.

PART V:

Business Entity Issues and Tax Planning

CHAPTER 12

Corporate Formation, Distributions, and Other Corporation-Related Tax Issues

CHAPTER CONTENTS

LEARNING OBJECTIVES

1. Understand how a transfer of property to a corporation in exchange for stock is taxed.

2. Be able to explain how distributions by corporations to their shareholders are taxed.

3. Understand what constructive dividends and stock dividends are and how they are taxed.

4. Be able to discuss the differences between book income and taxable income.

5. Understand what Schedules M-1, M-2, and M-3 are and how they are completed.

¶ 1200 Introduction

When a corporation is formed, property is often transferred to the corporation in exchange for stock. Such a transaction usually is tax-free if the transferor, or two or more transferors as a group, control the corporation following the transfer. However, under certain situations gain has to be recognized. Those situations and what constitutes "control" are discussed in this chapter.

Many C corporations regularly distribute cash or other property to their shareholders. They usually make these distributions because shareholders expect to share in the profits of the corporation. However, corporations are sometimes forced to make distributions to avoid triggering additional taxes, such as accumulated earnings or personal holding company taxes. (See ¶ 1013 and ¶ 1015.)

A distribution of money or property has tax consequences for the corporation as well as for its shareholders. A distribution of property from a corporation to its shareholders can be treated as a dividend or as a return of capital. When a shareholder receives a distribution that is a return of capital, the distribution can be tax-free, a capital gain, or both, depending on the shareholder's basis in the stock at the time of the distribution. This chapter explains how to determine which type of distribution is being made and what the tax consequences of the distribution are. This chapter also discusses the tax consequences of distributions of stock dividends and the concept of constructive dividends. Finally, the differences between the financial reporting rules and the tax laws and the reconciliation of net income with taxable income are reviewed.

FORMATION OF A CORPORATION

¶ 1201 Transfer of Property to a Controlled Corporation

Although property may be transferred to a corporation in exchange for the corporation's stock at any time, such a transaction occurs most frequently when a corporation is being formed. As a general rule, the transferor will not have to recognize any gain realized when property is transferred in exchange for stock provided that the transferor, or the transferor and one or more other persons transferring property to the corporation, control the corporation following the transfer.[1] However, there are situations when the transferor will have to recognize gain:

- The transferor receives "boot" in addition to stock.
- The corporation assumes "excess liabilities."

 Spotlight: A loss realized on the transfer of property to a controlled corporation is never recognized.

The exchange of securities other than stock issued by a controlled corporation is not tax-free.

.01 "Control" Defined

A transferor has **control** of a corporation if the transferor or the transferor and one or more other transferors as a group own stock possessing at least 80 percent of the total combined voting power of all classes of stock entitled to vote and at least 80 percent of the total number of shares of all other classes of stock of the corporation.[2] Control must exist immediately after the exchange.[3] "Immediately after the exchange" does not necessarily require simultaneous exchanges by two or more persons, but comprehends a situation where the rights of the parties have been previously defined and the execution of the agreement proceeds with an expedition consistent with orderly procedure.[4] If control exists, it is immaterial whether the stock received by two or more transferors is in the same proportions as the transferors' interests in the properties before the exchange or whether the transferor, if a corporation, distributes the stock received.[5]

Example 1: Kelvin Labate transferred land to a newly formed corporation for $260,000 of common stock and $140,000 of nonvoting preferred stock. The land had a fair market value of

---

[1] Code Sec. 351(a).
[2] Code Sec. 368(c).
[3] Code Sec. 351(a).

[4] Reg. § 1.351-1(a)(1).
[5] Reg. § 1.351-1(a)(1), (b)(1).

$400,000 and an adjusted basis of $200,000. Robin Harsch transferred machinery with a fair market value of $100,000 and an adjusted basis of $150,000 for $60,000 of common stock and $40,000 of nonvoting preferred stock. After the transfers, Kelvin and Robin possessed more than 80 percent of the combined voting power of all classes of stock entitled to vote and more than 80 percent of the total number of the shares of all other classes of stock. As a result, Kelvin does not recognize any gain (even though he received stock worth $200,000 more than the adjusted basis of the property transferred), and Robin cannot recognize any of the $50,000 loss that she realized on the transfer.

.02 Excepted Transactions

Under certain circumstances, stock will not be treated as having been issued in return for property (and thus not eligible for tax-deferred treatment).

Stock for property of relatively small value. Stock or securities issued for property that has a value less than 10 percent of the value of the stock and securities already owned (or to be received for services) by the transferor will not be treated as having been issued in return for property if the primary purpose of the transfer is to enable other transferors to qualify for tax-deferred treatment under Code Sec. 351.[6]

Stock for services rendered. Stock issued for services rendered is never considered issued for property.[7]

.03 "Boot"

If a transferor receives money or property other than the controlled corporation's stock (such property is referred to as **"boot"**) in addition to stock, the transferor will have to recognize gain to the extent of the amount of money and the fair market value of the other property received.[8] If the property transferred to the corporation is depreciable by the corporation, any gain recognized will be treated as ordinary income.[9] No loss can be recognized by the transferor.

Example 2: Roxanna Niland transferred property with a fair market value of $50,000 and an adjusted basis of $40,000 to a controlled corporation for stock worth $45,000 and $5,000 in cash. Roxanna has to recognize $5,000 of her gain.

Multiple assets transferred. If more than one asset is transferred to a controlled corporation, the amount of cash and fair market value of property received from the corporation has to be allocated to each transferred asset in proportion to its fair market value.[10]

Property subject to a liability. When property transferred to a corporation is subject to a liability, the amount of the liability is not treated as boot unless the amount of debt exceeds the transferor's adjusted basis in the property.[11]

Example 3: Gary Shirtzinger transferred property to a controlled corporation. The property had a fair market value of $500,000 and an adjusted basis of $225,000. It was subject to a $150,000 mortgage. In return, he received stock worth $350,000. Because the debt is not considered boot, Gary does not have to recognize any of the $125,000 gain that he realized.

Liabilities in excess of basis. A liability will be treated as boot to the extent that the sum of the amount of liabilities assumed and the amount of liabilities on property taken subject to a liability exceeds the adjusted basis of the property transferred to the corporation.[12]

---

[6] Reg. § 1.351-1(a)(1); Rev. Proc. 77-37, 1977-2 CB 568.
[7] Code Sec. 351(d); Reg. § 1.351-1(a)(1).
[8] Code Sec. 351(b).
[9] Code Sec. 1239.

[10] Rev. Rul. 68-55, 1968-1 CB 140.
[11] Code Sec. 357(a), (c).
[12] Code Sec. 357(c), (d).

Example 4: Assume the same facts as in the previous example except that the property transferred was subject to a $300,000 mortgage. Gary has to recognize $75,000 of his $125,000 gain.

.04 Basis in Property Received

Following an exchange of stock for property, both the corporation and the transferor have to determine their basis in the property that they receive.

Corporation's basis. As a general rule, a corporation's basis in property acquired in a tax-deferred exchange for stock is the transferor's adjusted basis in the property plus any gain recognized by the transferor on the exchange.[13] However, the corporation's basis cannot be increased above the fair market value of the property by reason of any gain recognized to the transferor as a result of the assumption of a liability.[14]

Transferor's basis. A transferor's basis in stock acquired in a tax-deferred exchange is the same as the transferor's adjusted basis in the property transferred, with the following adjustments:[15]

Decreases

- The amount of any money received by the transferor.

- The fair market value of any property other than stock received by the transferor.

- The amount of any liability assumed by the corporation from the transferor.

- Any loss recognized on the exchange.

Increases

- The amount of any gain recognized.

- Any amount treated as a dividend.

 Spotlight: Although a liability to which transferred property is subject (such as a mortgage) is not treated as boot, it is treated as money received by the transferor for purposes of determining the transferor's basis in property received in the exchange.[16]

Example 5: Lori Forquer transferred property with a fair market value of $50,000 and an adjusted basis of $20,000 to a controlled corporation in exchange for stock worth $50,000. Lori's basis in the stock is $20,000.

Example 6: Assume the same facts as in the previous example except that Lori received stock worth $45,000 plus $5,000 in cash. Her basis in the stock is $20,000 ($20,000 minus the $5,000 in cash received plus the $5,000 of gain that she has to recognize).

Example 7: Dominic Kjos transferred land to a controlled corporation in exchange for stock. The land had a fair market value of $500,000. Its adjusted basis was $200,000, and it was subject to a $150,000 mortgage. Dominic's basis in the stock received is $50,000 (his adjusted basis of $200,000 minus the $150,000 mortgage).

The basis of any property other than stock received by the transferor is its fair market value.[17]

---

[13] Code Sec. 362(a).
[14] Code Sec. 362(d).
[15] Code Sec. 358(a)(1).

[16] Code Sec. 358(d)(1).
[17] Code Sec. 358(a)(2).

CORPORATE DISTRIBUTIONS

When a corporation distributes money or other property to its shareholders, the corporation must classify the distribution either as a dividend or as a return of capital. A distribution may be treated as a dividend, tax-free return of capital, or capital gain. A **dividend** is a distribution of current or accumulated **earnings and profits (E&P)** by a C corporation to its shareholders.[18] The concept of E&P was introduced in Chapter 10 (see ¶ 1009.01). It represents a corporation's ability to make distributions to shareholders from the corporation's current or accumulated profits. (See ¶ 1207.)

Dividends usually are paid in cash, but they may be paid in other property, such as land or equipment. Distributions of noncash property are known as **property distributions**. Distributions of stock in the corporation making the distribution are not considered property dividends, but instead are stock dividends. (See ¶ 1206.) Thus, in this chapter, the term "property distribution" or a wording that suggests a distribution of property refers to a distribution from the corporation of property that is not cash and is not the corporation's own stock.

¶ 1202 Calculating the Amount of a Distribution

When a corporation distributes cash or other property to its shareholders, the amount of the distribution equals the sum of (1) the money distributed and (2) the fair market value (FMV) of any property distributed (determined as of the date of the distribution).[19] When a corporation makes a distribution to its shareholders, to the extent the corporation has current or accumulated E&P, the distribution is considered to have come from E&P. A *proportional* distribution from current or accumulated E&P is treated as a dividend distribution.

When a property distribution is treated as a dividend, the shareholder recognizes ordinary income equal to the FMV of the property. The shareholder's basis in the property received is equal to the FMV of the property. When a corporation distributes appreciated property to its shareholders, it must recognize gain equal to the amount it would have recognized if it had sold the property for its FMV immediately prior to the distribution.[20] A corporation does not recognize a loss when it distributes property that has declined in value.

Example 8: Pacer Trucking has $50,000 in current and accumulated E&P at the time it distributes $10,000 to its owners. The distribution is treated as a dividend because it was distributed from Pacer's current and accumulated E&P.

Example 9: Image Consultants distributes to its sole shareholder, Al Jones, 100 shares of stock that it owns in Prince Enterprises. Image's current and accumulated E&P equals $100,000. The FMV of the 100 shares on the date distributed is $40,000. Because the property distributed is not shares of Image's own stock and is made from Image's current and accumulated E&P, the distribution is treated as a $40,000 property distribution.[21] Al reports the $40,000 as dividend income on his income tax return, and his basis in the Prince Enterprises stock will be $40,000.

Example 10: Faulk Furnishings distributes a $15,000 dividend to each of its two shareholders. It distributes $15,000 cash to shareholder A and property worth $15,000 to shareholder B. Faulk is treated as having made a $30,000 proportional distribution to its shareholders. Each shareholder reports $15,000 of dividend income in its gross income.

Example 11: Continuing with Example 10, Faulk's basis in the property distributed is $12,000. Because appreciated property is distributed, Faulk recognizes $3,000 of gain ($15,000 – $12,000) on the distribution. Shareholder B's basis in the property it receives from the distribution is $15,000.

---

[18] Code Sec. 316(a).
[19] Code Sec. 301(b)(1).

[20] Code Sec. 311(b)(1).
[21] Code Sec. 301(d).

Example 12: Assume the same facts as in Example 11, except that Faulk's basis in the property distributed is $26,000. Because property that had declined in value is distributed, Faulk does not recognize a loss on the distribution. Shareholder B's basis in the property received is $15,000.

 Planning Pointer: Corporations should not distribute property that has declined in value because that will cost them the opportunity to deduct their loss. If Faulk from Example 12 had sold the property for its $15,000 FMV, it would have recognized an $11,000 loss ($15,000 − $26,000). Assuming it could deduct the loss, its tax liability would have decreased by its marginal tax rate times $11,000. If Faulk's marginal tax rate were 35 percent, its tax savings from the loss would equal $3,850 ($11,000 × 35%). Faulk could have then distributed the $15,000 proceeds from the sale as a cash dividend. In both scenarios, the shareholder receives property worth $15,000. However, the $11,000 decline in value (and the associated tax savings) is lost if the property is distributed instead of the cash.

.01 Reduction for Liabilities

If the property distributed is subject to a liability, the amount of a distribution must be reduced (but not below zero) by the amount of any liability (1) to which the property is subject or (2) that the shareholder assumes in connection with the distribution.[22]

Example 13: Electronic Supplies distributes equipment with an FMV of $10,000 to its sole shareholder. The equipment is subject to a $6,000 liability. The amount of the distribution equals $4,000 ($10,000 minus the $6,000 liability to which the equipment is subject).

¶ 1203 Tax Consequences of Dividend Distributions

How a shareholder is taxed on dividend income depends on whether the shareholder is a corporate or a noncorporate shareholder. When a partnership, S corporation, or other flow-through entity is a shareholder in a C corporation, any dividends it receives from the corporation are passed through to its owners and are taxed to the owners.

.01 Corporation Making the Distribution

Corporations are not entitled to any deduction when they make a dividend distribution. However, they must reduce their E&P by the amount of the distribution.

When a corporation distributes appreciated property to its shareholders, it must recognize gain equal to the amount it would have recognized if it had sold the property for its FMV immediately prior to the distribution.[23] A corporation does not recognize a loss when it distributes property that has declined in value.

.02 Corporate Shareholders

When a corporation owns stock in another corporation, only a portion (ranging from 0% to 30%) of the dividend it receives is taxable. Table 12-1 summarizes the amount of the dividends received deduction, which varies depending on a recipient's ownership of the corporation paying the dividends.[24] (See ¶ 412.02.)

---

[22] Code Sec. 301(b)(2).
[23] Code Sec. 311(b)(1).

[24] Code Sec. 243.

Table 12-1 Summary of Dividends Received Deduction Rates

Ownership (by vote and value)	Dividends Received Deduction	Percentage Taxed in Gross Income
Less than 20%	70%	30%
At least 20% but less than 80%	80%	20%
At least 80%	100%	0%

Example 14: Liscana Enterprises receives $5,000 in dividends from Windows Framing, Inc. Liscana currently owns 10 percent of the outstanding shares in Windows. Because Liscana does not own at least 20 percent of the stock, it receives a 70-percent dividends received deduction. Therefore, it is taxed on only 30 percent of the dividends it receives from Windows. $1,500 of the dividends it receives ($5,000 – $3,500 dividends received deduction) is taxed like any other income the corporation earns during the year.

Example 15: Duke Steel receives $50,000 in dividends from Ketchun Equipment. Duke's ownership in Ketchun represents 25 percent of Ketchun's shares. Because Duke owns at least 20 percent but not more than 80 percent of the stock of Ketchun, it is taxed on only 20 percent of the dividends it receives from Ketchun. Of the taxable dividends Duke receives, $10,000 ($50,000 – $40,000 dividends received deduction) is taxed like any other income at Duke's marginal tax rate.

Reason for the Rule: The dividends received deduction is designed to prevent triple taxation of a corporation's income. When a corporation earns income, the income is taxed for the first time. When the corporation distributes income to its shareholders, the income is taxed a second time when reported as dividend income on the shareholder's tax return. Without this deduction, a corporation's income could be taxed at least three times: once when earned by the corporation, a second time when distributed to corporate shareholders, and a third time when the corporate shareholders distribute the income to their shareholders. If any of the shareholders were themselves corporations, in the absence of the dividends received deduction, the income would then be taxed a fourth time. The stacking of layers of taxation in this manner could potentially be unlimited without the dividends received deduction.

When a property distribution is treated as a dividend, the shareholder recognizes ordinary income equal to the FMV of the property. The shareholder's basis in the property received is equal to the FMV of the property.

.03 Individual Shareholders

How dividends received by individual taxpayers are taxed depends on whether the dividend is qualified dividend income. **Qualified dividend income** means dividends received during the tax year from a U.S. corporation or qualified foreign corporation.[25] To qualify as qualified dividend income, the stock with respect to which the dividends were paid must have been held by the taxpayer for more than 60 days during the 121-day period beginning 60 days before the ex-dividend date. A foreign corporation is a "qualified foreign corporation" if the corporation is incorporated in a U.S. possession, the corporation is eligible for the benefits of a comprehensive income tax treaty

---

[25] Code Sec. 1(h)(11)(B).

with the United States, or the stock of the corporation with respect to which the dividend is paid is readily tradable on an established securities market in the United States.

A dividend that is not qualified dividend income is taxed like other ordinary income using the progressive income tax rates (ranging from 10 percent to 39.6 percent) that apply to individuals. Qualified dividend income is taxed at the same rates as net capital gains to individual taxpayers.[26] For taxpayers in the 10- or 15-percent tax bracket, qualified dividend income is not taxed. Taxpayers in the 25-, 28-, 33-, or 35-percent income tax bracket have to pay a 15 percent income tax on their qualified dividend income. Taxpayers in the 39.6 percent income tax bracket have to pay a 20 percent tax on their qualified dividend income. A taxpayer whose modified adjusted gross income exceeds $200,000 ($250,000 if the taxpayer is married and filing a joint return or a surviving spouse and $125,000 if the taxpayer is married and filing a separate return) has to pay an additional 3.8 percent Medicare contribution tax on qualified dividend income (as well as other net investment income).

Example 16: Elijah Coppersmith received $1,000 in dividends from a U.S. corporation. Because Elijah is taxed at the 15-percent rate, he will pay $0 on the dividends. If Elijah had received $1,000 of nonqualified dividends, his tax on the dividends would have been $150 ($1,000 × 15%).

Example 17: Boyd Willet receives $1,000 in dividends from a U.S. corporation. Because Boyd is in the 35-percent tax bracket, the tax he owes on the dividend income is $150 ($1,000 × 15%). If Boyd had $1,000 in nonqualified dividends, his tax on the dividend income would have been $350 ($1,000 × 35%).

> **Reason for the Rule:** Prior to the Jobs and Growth Tax Relief Reconciliation Act of 2003 (P.L. 108-27), dividends received by noncorporate shareholders were taxed as ordinary income at rates that ranged up to 39.6 percent. Congress reduced the tax on dividends received by noncorporate taxpayers for three reasons. First, it believed the reduction of the tax on dividends (and thus the cost of capital needed by corporations to finance new investments) would increase national investment, output, productivity, employment, and real wages. Second, it believed the tax rate reduction would reduce the incentive of corporations to finance their operations with debt (and its tax-deductible interest) rather than equity and would thus reduce the risk of corporate bankruptcies during economic downturns. Third, Congress believed that taxing dividend income at a higher rate than income from capital gains encouraged corporations to retain earnings rather than to distribute them as dividends, even though shareholders might have an alternative use for the funds that could offer a higher rate of return than that earned on retained earnings.[27]

When a property distribution is treated as a dividend, the shareholder recognizes ordinary income equal to the FMV of the property. The shareholder's basis in the property received is equal to the FMV of the property.

¶ 1204 Distributions Treated as Dividends vs. Return of Capital

Corporations are responsible for letting their shareholders know the extent to which a distribution constitutes a dividend versus return of capital. A distribution of cash or property to shareholders is treated as a dividend to the extent that the distribution is made out of current or accumulated earnings and profits (E&P). **Current E&P** refers to E&P that the corporation generates in the current year. **Accumulated E&P** refers to E&P generated in prior tax years that the corporation

---

[26] Code Sec. 1(h)(11)(A).

[27] House Ways and Means Committee Report No. 108-94 (May 8, 2003), pp. 30, 31.

has not distributed to its shareholders. Therefore, as long as a corporation has current and/or accumulated E&P at the time of a distribution, the distribution is treated as a dividend.

Any portion of a distribution that is not considered a dividend is treated as a return of capital. When shareholders receive a **return of capital distribution**, it is a tax-free return of their investment in the stock and thus reduces their adjusted basis in the stock (but not below zero).[28] To the extent shareholders receive a return of capital distribution in excess of their adjusted basis in stock, they are treated as having realized gain from the sale or exchange of their stock. The gain is "capital gain" if the stock is a capital asset to the shareholder (which it will be unless the shareholder is a dealer in stock). The capital gain is "long-term capital gain" if the shareholder held the stock for more than one year as of the date of the distribution. The capital gain is "short-term capital gain" if the shareholder held the stock for one year or less on the date of the distribution.

Example 18: Demere Air Cylinders distributes $100 per share to each of its shareholders. Of this amount, $60 per share is from current or accumulated E&P. One of its shareholders, Santos Martell, owns 100 shares of stock in Demere. His adjusted basis in those shares is $50 per share, or $5,000. Santos includes $6,000 ($60 per share × 100 shares) of the distribution as ordinary dividend income on his current year income tax return. The remaining $40 per share reduces his adjusted basis in each share of stock to $10 ($50 – $40). Santos's basis in his 100 shares will be $1,000 ($10 × 100) after the distribution.

Example 19: Continuing with Example 18, Boyd Milden also owns 100 shares of stock in Demere as an investment. Boyd's adjusted basis in each share is $30. Boyd includes $6,000 ($60 × 100 shares) in gross income as a dividend. The remaining $40 per share is treated as a return of capital distribution. The first $30 per share reduces Boyd's basis in each share to $0. The excess $10 per share that he receives ($40 – $30) is treated as gain from the sale or exchange of the stock. Because the stock is a capital asset for Boyd, his $1,000 gain ($10 × 100 shares) is capital gain. If Boyd held the stock for more than one year on the date of the distribution, his capital gain would be long-term capital gain. If he held the stock for one year or less, his capital gain would be short-term capital gain.

Example 20: Continuing with Example 19, assume that Boyd sells his 100 shares of Demere for $4,500. Because Boyd's basis in the stock is $0, he will recognize a $4,500 capital gain ($4,500 – $0). Whether the gain will be treated as short-term or long-term capital gain depends on how long Boyd held the stock prior to selling it. (See ¶ 901.03.)

How a shareholder's original basis is determined depends on how the stock was acquired. If the shares were purchased, then the original basis of the stock is its purchase price plus any purchase costs (such as commissions and transfer fees). The purchase price includes amounts paid in cash and the fair market value (FMV) of any other property transferred. If the shares are acquired in return for services rendered, then the original basis of the stock is the FMV of the stock received. This amount corresponds to the amount taxed to the shareholder upon receipt of the stock. The basis of property transferred to a corporation for stock in a tax-deferred exchange under Code Sec. 351 is discussed in ¶ 1201.04.

Example 21: Deedra Stasiuk purchased 100 shares of stock for $5,000 (including commissions and transfer fees). Deedra's original basis in those shares is $5,000. Her basis in each share is $50 ($5,000 ÷ 100).

Example 22: Fidel Brech performed accounting services for a corporation in return for two shares of stock with an FMV of $100. His original basis in those two shares of stock is $100. His original basis in each share is $50 ($100 ÷ 2).

---

[28] Code Sec. 301(c).

Example 23: Rod Zinkievich is one of three individuals who contributed cash and other property to a newly formed corporation in exchange for 100 percent of the stock in the corporation. Rod contributed $10,000 plus land with an FMV of $500,000 and an adjusted basis of $200,000 in return for 10,000 shares in the corporation. Rod's original basis in the 10,000 shares is $210,000 ($10,000 + $200,000). His basis in each share is $21 ($210,000 ÷ 10,000).

Special rules apply to stock acquired by gift, inheritance, or divorce. If stock is acquired from a spouse or from a former spouse incident to a divorce, then the taxpayer's original basis is the same as the transferor spouse's basis in the stock. If the shares are inherited, then the taxpayer's original basis in the stock usually is its FMV at the time of the decedent's death.

When the taxpayer is gifted stock, the donor's basis in the stock generally becomes the donee's (taxpayer's) basis. If the FMV of the gifted property at the time of the gift exceeds the donor's adjusted basis in the stock, then a portion of any gift tax paid on the transfer by the donor is added to the donee's basis. However, when the FMV of the gifted property at the time of the gift is less than the donor's adjusted basis in the stock, the donee's basis cannot be determined until the donee sells the stock. If the donee subsequently sells the stock for more than the donor's basis, then the donee's basis is the donor's basis. If the donee subsequently sells the stock for less than the FMV of the stock at the time of the gift, then the donee's basis is the FMV of the stock at the time of the gift. If the donee sells the stock for an amount greater than the FMV at the time of the gift but less than the donor's basis, then the donee's basis in the stock is equal to the amount realized from the sale.

Example 24: When Ileen Oflaherty divorced her husband Bernie, he gave her 100 shares of stock. The shares had an FMV of $5,000. Bernie's adjusted basis in the shares was $3,000. Ileen's original basis in the shares is $3,000. Her original basis in each share is $30 ($3,000 ÷ 100).

Example 25: Alvaro Amacker inherited 100 shares of stock from his uncle Miguel. The shares had an FMV of $6,000 at the time of Miguel's death. Miguel's adjusted basis in the shares was $1,000. Alvaro's original basis in the share is $6,000. His original basis in each share is $60 ($6,000 ÷ 100).

Example 26: Laveta Berver's mother Janice gifted her with 100 shares of stock. At the time of the gift, the 100 shares had an FMV of $4,000. Janice's adjusted basis in the shares was $2,000. Laveta's original basis in the shares is $2,000. Her original basis in each share is $20 ($2,000 ÷ 100).

Basis of stock is adjusted for certain events that occur after its acquisition. For example, basis is adjusted when there is a nondividend distribution (described later in this section) or a stock split or additional contributions are made to a corporation's capital.

Example 27: Lavenia Cockrel acquired 100 shares of stock for $3,000. Her original basis in each share is $30 ($3,000 ÷ 100). Three years after her purchase, the company declared a stock split, and Lavenia received 100 additional shares. Lavenia's original basis does not change, but her basis in each share becomes $15 ($3,000 ÷ 200 total shares).

Example 28: Same facts as in Example 27 except that Lavenia received a $1,000 return of capital distribution. This distribution reduced her basis in the 200 shares to $2,000 ($3,000 – $1,000 tax-free return of capital), and her basis in each share became $10 ($2,000 ÷ 200).

Example 29: Same facts as in Example 27 except that Lavenia contributed an additional $1,500 to the corporation to help finance a new business operation. She received no additional shares for the contribution. Her contribution increases her basis in the 200 shares to $3,500 ($2,000 + $1,500), and her basis in each share becomes $17.50 ($3,500 ÷ 200).

.01 Distributions That Do Not Exceed Current Year E&P

Corporate distributions are considered to be made from the most recently accumulated E&P. Thus, a distribution is considered to come first from the current year's E&P. Once all current E&P has been exhausted, any remaining amount of the distribution is considered to be paid from accumulated E&P.[29] If a corporation generates sufficient current E&P to cover all distributions made during the year, the distributions will be considered to have come from current E&P, and current E&P is reduced accordingly. Any remaining current year E&P is then added to the corporation's accumulated E&P to determine its accumulated E&P for the next tax year. As long as the corporation has current E&P, a distribution may be treated as having come from current E&P, even if the corporation has a deficit balance in its accumulated E&P.

Example 30: Shune Automobile Parts has $20,000 in current year E&P and $10,000 in accumulated E&P. Shune distributes $12,000 during the year. Because its total distribution did not exceed its current E&P, the entire amount of the distribution is treated as a dividend distributed out of current E&P. Shune reduces its current E&P by $12,000, and the remaining $8,000 ($20,000 – $12,000) of current year E&P is added to its accumulated E&P. For the following year, Shune's accumulated E&P will equal $18,000 ($8,000 + $10,000).

Example 31: McClour Wall Plaques has a $15,000 deficit in its accumulated E&P at the beginning of its tax year. During the year the company generates $10,000 of E&P and distributes $10,000 to its shareholders. The $10,000 distribution will be treated as a dividend (out of current year E&P), even though the corporation still has negative accumulated E&P for the prior years it has been in existence.

 Reason for the Rule: In Example 31, McClour's $10,000 distribution is considered to come from its current year E&P, even though its combined current and accumulated E&P are a negative amount. The distribution is taxed to the shareholders as a dividend because the Internal Revenue Code (the "Code") defines dividends as distributions out of either accumulated earnings *or* current year earnings.[30]

.02 Distributions When Current Year E&P Has a Negative Balance

If a corporation has a deficit in E&P for the tax year in which a distribution is made but has a positive balance in accumulated E&P, the current year deficit is prorated as of the day the distribution is made and subtracted from the corporation's accumulated E&P before determining the source of the distribution.[31]

Example 32: Klement Building Blocks, a calendar year corporation, has $15,000 in accumulated E&P at the beginning of its tax year. During the year, its current E&P is negative $21,900. On January 5, Klement distributes $14,500 to its sole shareholder, whose adjusted basis in the Klement stock is $16,000. Of the corporation's $21,900 negative current E&P, only $300 ($21,900/365 days × 5 days) is attributable to the portion of the year from January 1 to January 5. This allocation of current E&P deficit reduces Klement's accumulated E&P to $14,700 ($15,000 – $300). Therefore, the entire $14,500 distribution will be treated as a taxable dividend to the shareholder because the distribution does not exceed Klement's accumulated E&P at the time of the distribution.

Example 33: Assume the same facts as in Example 32, except the distribution was made on November 30 instead of January 5. As of November 30, $20,040 ($21,900/365 × 334

---

[29] Reg. § 1.316-2(a).

[30] Code Sec. 316(a)(2).

[31] Rev. Rul. 74-164, 1974-1 CB 74.

days) of the corporation's current year negative E&P must be taken into consideration when determining Klement's accumulated E&P. Because accumulated E&P on November 30 is negative ($15,000 – $20,040), none of the distribution is treated as a dividend. Instead, it is treated as a return of capital. Because the shareholder's adjusted basis in its stock is greater than the amount of the distribution, the shareholder recognizes no income or gain on the return of capital. The shareholder's adjusted basis in the stock immediately following the distribution will be reduced to $1,500 ($16,000 – $14,500 tax-free return of capital).

.03 Distributions in Excess of Current Year E&P

If current year E&P is not sufficient to cover the amounts distributed during the year, the distribution is considered to come first from current year E&P and then from accumulated E&P. Even when the corporation has a deficit balance in accumulated E&P, distributions are considered to have been made first from current year E&P. Any distribution in excess of current E&P is treated as a return of capital and is tax free to the shareholder to the extent of the shareholder's basis in the stock. Any excess is taxed as capital gain.[32]

Example 34:   Olman Corporation has $20,000 in current year E&P and a $15,000 deficit balance in accumulated E&P. The company distributes $25,000 during the year. The first $20,000 of the distribution is treated as coming from current E&P. This amount is taxed as dividend income. Because the distributions exceed Olman's current E&P and because Olman has a deficit in accumulated E&P, the remaining distribution is treated as a return of capital to the shareholders and is tax free to them to the extent of their respective bases in the stock. Any return of capital distribution in excess of a shareholder's basis is taxed as a capital gain. Olman's accumulated E&P at the beginning of the next year remains a $15,000 deficit.

If the amount of a corporation's distributions with respect to its stock for a year exceeds the corporation's current and accumulated E&P, it is necessary to determine first what part of each distribution is made from current E&P at the time of the distribution. Any part of the distribution that does not come from current E&P is considered a distribution from accumulated E&P. Any distribution that is not from either current or accumulated E&P is not a dividend but is instead considered a return of capital, which will be tax free to the shareholders to the extent of their respective adjusted bases in the stock. Return of capital distributions in excess of adjusted basis are taxed as capital gains.

To determine what portion of a distribution was made from current E&P that existed at the time of the distribution, it is necessary to first determine the percentage of the distributions for the year that came from current E&P. This is computed by dividing current E&P by the total distributions for the year. This percentage is then multiplied by each distribution made during the year.[33]

Example 35:   Bassinet, Inc. has current year E&P of $10,000 and accumulated E&P of $16,000. During the year, Bassinet distributes $20,000 to each of its shareholders, Fred and Alice. Fred and Alice each own 50 percent of the stock in Bassinet. Fred's basis in his shares of stock is $10,000; Alice's basis in her shares of stock is $5,000.

Date	Total Distribution
April 1	$ 5,000
September 1	15,000
December 1	20,000
	$40,000

---

[32] Code Sec. 301(c).   [33] Reg. § 1.316-2(b).

Because Bassinet's total distributions ($40,000) exceed its current and accumulated E&P ($26,000), it must determine how much of each distribution comes from current E&P. Of the total amounts distributed during the year, $10,000 is deemed to have come from current E&P. Thus, 25 percent ($10,000/$40,000) of each distribution is considered to have come from current E&P.

Date	Amount		Current E&P
April 1	$ 5,000	× 25% =	$ 1,250
September 1	15,000	× 25% =	3,750
December 1	20,000	× 25% =	5,000
	$40,000		$10,000

Of the $5,000 distributed on April 1, $1,250 is considered to come from current E&P and the rest ($3,750) from accumulated E&P. This reduces Bassinet's accumulated E&P to $12,250 ($16,000 – $3,750). With respect to the September 1 distribution of $15,000, $3,750 is considered to come from current E&P and $11,250 from accumulated E&P ($15,000 – $3,750). After the September 1 distribution, Bassinet's accumulated E&P have been reduced to $1,000 ($12,250 – $11,250). Thus, of the $20,000 distribution on December 1, $5,000 is considered to come from current E&P and $1,000 from accumulated E&P. Bassinet will have a zero balance in its accumulated E&P. The remaining $14,000 ($20,000 – $5,000 – $1,000) of the December 1 distribution is treated as a return of capital to the shareholders. A summary of the allocation of each distribution between dividend and return of capital is shown below.

Date	Dividend	Return of Capital
April 1	$ 5,000	$ 0
September 1	15,000	0
December 1	6,000	14,000
	$26,000	$14,000

Of the $20,000 distribution that each shareholder receives during the year, a total of $13,000 is considered to come from current and accumulated E&P ($26,000 × 50%). The shareholders report this amount as dividend income on their respective income tax returns. The remaining $7,000 distribution ($14,000 × 50%) is treated as a return of capital. Because Fred's basis in his stock is $10,000, the entire $7,000 is treated as a tax-free return of his investment in Bassinet, and his basis in the stock is reduced to $3,000 ($10,000 – $7,000). Because Alice's basis in her stock is $5,000, only $5,000 of her $7,000 return of capital is treated as a tax-free return of her investment in Bassinet. Thus, her basis in the stock is reduced to $0. The $2,000 excess is taxed as a capital gain.

In the previous example, $10,000 ($1,250 + $3,750 + $5,000) of the $40,000 in distributions is considered to have come from current E&P and $16,000 from accumulated E&P ($3,750 + $11,250 + $1,000). This same result would have occurred without allocating each distribution between current and accumulated E&P by treating each distribution as coming first from current E&P until exhausted and then from accumulated E&P. However, when stock is sold during the year, it is important to allocate each distribution between current and accumulated E&P to determine what portion of each distribution represents a taxable dividend versus what portion is a return of capital to each shareholder receiving a distribution during the year.

Example 36: Assume the same facts as in Example 35, except on August 16 of the current year, Alice sells her shares of stock in Bassinet to Julia for $9,000. Because Fred's ownership in Bassinet remains the same throughout the year, he still reports $13,000 as dividend income on his tax return and treats the remaining $7,000 of the distribution as a tax-free return of capital. However, Alice is entitled only to her share of the April 1 distributions ($5,000 × 50%) and not to later distributions. Accordingly, the entire $2,500 distribution Alice receives during the year is a taxable dividend because the April 1 distributions to Fred and Alice do not exceed Bassinet's current and accumulated E&P as of that date. Alice reports a $4,000 capital gain from the sale of her stock to Julia ($9,000 amount realized – $5,000 basis in the stock).

As the owner of 50 percent of the stock as of August 16, Julia receives her share of the September 1 and December 1 distributions from Bassinet. All $15,000 of the September 1 distribution is paid from current and accumulated E&P. Julia's share of this amount is $7,500. Of the $20,000 distribution on December 1, only $6,000 is considered a dividend distribution. Julia's share of this amount is $3,000. Therefore, Julia will report a total of $10,500 ($7,500 + $3,000) as dividend income for the year. Her share of the $14,000 return of capital is $7,000. That reduces her basis in the Bassinet stock to $2,000 ($9,000 – $7,000). The allocation of each distribution between dividend and return of capital (RofC) is summarized below.

	Fred		Alice		Julia	
Date	Dividend	RofC	Dividend	RofC	Dividend	RofC
April 1	$ 2,500	$ 0	$2,500	$0		
Sept. 1	7,500	0			$ 7,500	$ 0
Dec. 1	3,000	7,000			3,000	7,000
	$13,000	$7,000	$2,500	$0	$10,500	$7,000

¶ 1205 Constructive Dividends

Before making a dividend payment, a C corporation's board of directors usually declares that it will be paying a dividend to shareholders of record as of a specific date. However, a **constructive dividend** may occur when a corporation confers an economic benefit on a person in that person's capacity as a shareholder. The corporation must have conferred the benefit in order to distribute available earnings and profits without expectation of repayment.[34]

.01 The Need for the Constructive Dividend Rules

A constructive distribution is treated like all other distributions. It is considered a dividend distribution to the extent that it comes from the corporation's current and/or accumulated E&P. The constructive dividends rules were enacted to prevent corporations and their shareholders from avoiding tax on a corporation's earnings at the corporate or the shareholder level (or both) by disguising dividends as another form of payment. Examples 37 to 39 illustrate the possible abuse that might occur and the need for the constructive dividends rules.

Example 37: Pecelli Distributors has E&P of $300,000 for the year and pays a federal income tax of $100,250 to the IRS on its taxable income. It distributes $100,000 to its sole shareholder, Renee Pecelli, and she pays $15,000 in tax on the dividend income ($100,000 × 15%). When the corporation's $39,000 federal income tax liability on the $100,000 distributed ($100,000 × 39%, Pecelli's marginal tax rate) is added to Renee's $15,000 tax on that same $100,000, a total of $54,000 in federal income tax is paid on the $100,000 earned by the corporation.

Example 38: Assume the same facts as in Example 37, except that Renee is also an employee of Pecelli and, instead of paying her a dividend, the company increases the compensa-

---

[34] *T.J. Welle*, 140 T.C. No. 19, CCH Dec. 59,576 (2013).

tion it pays Renee for the year by $100,000. Renee must pay tax on the additional compensation at a higher rate of tax than that imposed on dividends because compensation is taxed at a higher rate than qualified dividend income. In this case, Renee's tax on that additional $100,000 of compensation is $35,000 ($100,000 × 35%, Renee's marginal tax rate). However, because compensation paid to employees is deductible by a corporation, the $100,000 in additional compensation paid to Renee reduces the corporation's taxable income for the year by $100,000. Thus, the $100,000 escapes tax at the corporate level, and only $35,000 in federal income tax is paid on the $100,000 Pecelli paid to Renee. Overall, $19,000 in federal income tax is saved ($54,000 – $35,000).

Example 39: Assume the same facts as in Example 38, except that instead of increasing Renee's compensation Pecelli increases the amount of nontaxable fringe benefits (see ¶ 602) provided to her by $20,000. Because the fringe benefits are nontaxable to Renee, she receives $20,000 in benefits without having to pay any tax on the benefits. At the same time, the $20,000 in benefits paid by the company reduces the company's taxable income by $20,000. As a result, no tax is paid at either the corporate or shareholder levels on the $20,000.

.02 Identifying a Constructive Dividend

Whether a constructive dividend has been paid depends on the particular facts and circumstances of a transaction. Sometimes a transaction inadvertently results in a constructive dividend. Other times it is found that a transaction was intentionally designed to disguise a dividend as a different type of payment so tax at the corporate and/or shareholder levels could be avoided. Whether intentional or unintentional, when the economic substance of a transaction indicates that it is the payment of a dividend the transaction will be recharacterized as a constructive dividend. Examples of transactions that may be recharacterized as constructive dividends include:

1. *Unreasonable compensation.* A constructive dividend may occur when a C corporation pays an unreasonable amount of compensation to a shareholder-employee.

2. *Payment of a shareholder's personal expenses.* A constructive dividend may result when a corporation pays a shareholder's personal expenses.

3. *Use of a corporation's property by a shareholder or person related to a shareholder.* A constructive dividend may result when a corporation allows a shareholder or a shareholder's relative to use corporate property for personal purposes without having to pay the fair rental value for the use of the property.

4. *Payment of an amount owed by a shareholder.* A constructive dividend may result when a corporation pays an amount owed by a shareholder.

5. *Loan by a corporation to a shareholder.* A constructive dividend may result when a corporation makes a loan to a shareholder on terms that would not be expected following arm's-length negotiations.

6. *Bargain sale of property to a shareholder.* A constructive dividend may result when a corporation sells property to a shareholder at a bargain price.

7. *Overpaying for a shareholder's property.* A constructive dividend may result when a corporation purchases property from a shareholder for more than its FMV.

8. *Services provided by a corporation to a shareholder.* A constructive dividend may result when a corporation provides services to a shareholder without expectation of repayment. The amount of the constructive dividend equals the cost of the services (minus any amount paid by the shareholder) but does not include any foregone profit.[35]

Example 40: Samuelson Corporation has $100,000 in earnings for the year. Rather than pay tax on those earnings and have its sole shareholder and CEO, Samantha (Sam) Davis, pay a

---

[35] *T.J. Welle*, 140 T.C. No. 19, CCH Dec. 59,576 (2013).

second tax on those earnings when they are distributed to her as a dividend, the corporation increases Sam's compensation by $100,000 for the year. If Sam's total compensation is unreasonably high, the corporation will be treated as having made a constructive dividend to Sam equal to the amount by which her compensation exceeds what would be deemed reasonable.

Example 41: Assume the same facts as in Example 40, except that Samuelson pays $50,000 to remodel the family room in Sam's home. The $50,000 will be treated as a constructive dividend to Sam except to the extent that the corporation and Sam can show a business purpose for the remodeling and business use of the family room.

Example 42: Assume the same facts as in Example 40, except that Samuelson purchases a ship for $100,000 and leaves it in Sam's exclusive possession. The $100,000 will be treated as a constructive dividend to Sam except to the extent that the corporation and Sam can show a business purpose for the purchase and a business use for the ship.

Example 43: Assume the same facts as in Example 40, except that Samuelson pays $50,000 for the college tuition and living expenses of Sam's daughter. The $50,000 payment will be treated as a constructive dividend to Sam.

Example 44: Assume the same facts as in Example 40, except that Sam makes a $100,000 loan to Samuelson. Interest at the rate of eight percent per year is payable on the loan. The corporation was not required to make any repayments at any specified intervals, and it was not required to provide any security for repayment. Given these facts, it is likely that the loan will be treated as a contribution of capital to the corporation, and interest payments to Sam will be treated as constructive dividends.

Example 45: Assume the same facts as in Example 40, except that Samuelson makes an interest-free demand loan of $100,000 to Sam. Sam will be treated as making interest payments to the corporation, and the corporation will be treated as transferring those amounts back to Sam as constructive dividends.[36] If, as is likely, the interest payments are treated as nondeductible personal interest, the net tax effect to Sam will be that she will be required to include the entire amount of the deemed interest in her taxable income as a dividend without any offsetting deduction for the interest payment.

Example 46: Assume the same facts as in Example 40, except that Samuelson purchases a motor vehicle for $30,000 and then sells it to Sam for $5,000. The company will likely be treated as having made a $25,000 constructive dividend to Sam ($30,000 – $5,000).

Example 47: Assume the same facts as in Example 40, except that Samuelson pays $600,000 for a parcel of land that Sam owned and that had been appraised as having an FMV of $500,000. The corporation will be treated as having made a constructive dividend of $100,000 to Sam.

Example 48: Cassessee Contractors constructed a home for John Cassessee, one of its shareholders. John reimbursed Cassessee Contractors for its costs but not for its foregone profit. John did not receive any constructive dividend.

 Planning Pointer: The preceding examples should not cause tax planners to discourage corporations and their shareholders from entering into the types of transactions described in the examples. Changes in some of the facts can avoid characterization of a transaction as a constructive dividend. For example, if a shareholder loans money to a corporation on terms that would be expected in any arm's-length negotiation between

---

[36] Code Sec. 7872.

unrelated parties (such as adequate interest and security for repayment), then the interest payments will not be recharacterized as constructive dividends, and the corporation will be able to deduct the payments when calculating its taxable income. The parties can achieve their original goal—avoiding the corporate level of tax on some of the corporation's income—without triggering the constructive dividend rules.

¶ 1206 Stock Dividends

The term used to describe a C corporation's distribution of its own stock to its shareholders is **stock dividend**. Shareholders are not taxed on stock dividends provided that the stock dividend does not alter their interests in the corporation. If the shareholders' ownership percentages in their corporation do not change following a stock dividend, the stock dividend will be excluded from the shareholders' gross incomes.[37] When a stock dividend is not taxable to the shareholders, it does not affect the corporation's E&P.

Example 49: Rugg Equipment distributes one share of its own stock to the holder of each of its outstanding shares of stock. Following the distribution, each shareholder owns twice as many shares of Rugg as each owned prior to the distribution. No amount of the distribution is included in a shareholder's gross income. Ruggs's E&P is not reduced by the nontaxable stock dividend.

 Reason for the Rule: A stock dividend that does not alter ownership interests or transfer assets to shareholders is considered a mere bookkeeping change, not income.[38] Because no corporate assets are paid out, the distribution merely gives each stockholder more pieces of paper to represent the same interest in the corporation.

When stock dividends alter the shareholders' interests in a corporation, the FMV of the stock distributed is taxable to the shareholders to the extent that the distribution is made out of current or accumulated E&P of the corporation. Taxable stock dividends also occur when a disproportionate distribution (see below) is made to shareholders.[39]

.01 Distributions in Lieu of Money or Other Property

If a corporation gives its shareholders the option of electing to receive cash or other property in lieu of stock, all shareholders receiving a distribution will be treated as having received a taxable dividend to the extent that the distribution is made from the corporation's accumulated or current E&P. Any distribution not treated as a dividend is treated as a return of capital.[40]

Example 50: A corporation offers its shareholders one share of its stock for each share they currently own, or $10 for each share of stock. Because shareholders have the option of receiving cash in lieu of stock, the stock dividend will be treated as a distribution of property and will be taxed as a dividend to the extent of the corporation's current and/or accumulated E&P.

 Reason for the Rule: If a corporation with only common stock outstanding gives each shareholder the option of receiving either an additional share of common stock or cash,

---

[37] Code Sec. 305(a).

[38] Senate Finance Committee Report No. 91-552 (November 21, 1969), 1969 United States Code Congressional and Administrative News, p. 2182.

[39] Code Sec. 305(b).

[40] Code Sec. 305(b)(1).

> the shareholders who receive stock are in the same position as if they had received a cash dividend and purchased additional stock with the proceeds.[41]

.02 Disproportionate Distributions

If a corporation's distribution of its stock results in some shareholders receiving money or other property and other shareholders increasing their proportionate interests in the assets or E&P of the corporation, the distribution will be treated as a dividend to the extent that it is made from the corporation's current or accumulated E&P.[42]

Example 51: Variety Merchandise has two classes of stock, Class A common stock and Class B preferred stock. The company declares a stock dividend payable to its Class A shareholders and a cash dividend to its Class B preferred stock shareholders. Because the distribution does not increase the proportionate interests of the Class A shareholders in the E&P of the company, it is not considered a disproportionate distribution.

Example 52: Pulos Trailers, Inc. pays a cash dividend to the owners of its Class A common stock and one share of its stock to the owners of each share of its Class B common stock. Because the result of the distribution is that some shareholders (Class A) receive cash and other shareholders (Class B) increase their proportionate interests in the E&P of the corporation, the distribution is treated as a dividend to the extent that the distribution comes from the corporation's current or accumulated E&P.

.03 Distributions of Common and Preferred Stock

If common stock is distributed to some common stock shareholders and preferred stock is distributed to other common stock shareholders, the distribution will be treated as a dividend to the extent of the corporation's current and accumulated E&P.[43]

Example 53: Sebert Novelties, Inc. distributed preferred stock to some common stock shareholders and common stock to other common stock shareholders. Both of the distributions will be treated as dividends to the extent of the corporation's accumulated and current E&P.

.04 Shareholders' Basis Adjustments and Holding Period

If a corporation distributes a taxable stock dividend, the shareholder's basis in the stock is the FMV of the stock on the date of the distribution. This is the same amount that the shareholder reports as dividend income from the stock dividend. When a shareholder receives a taxable stock dividend, the holding period begins on the date that the dividend is distributed to the shareholder.

Shareholders that receive a nontaxable stock dividend must allocate their basis in their stock prior to the distribution (their "old stock") between their old stock and their new stock in proportion to the FMV of each on the date that the stock is distributed.[44] If the stock distributed is the same class as the stock with respect to which the distribution was made (e.g., common stock was distributed to common stock shareholders), the new basis of each share is determined by dividing the aggregate basis of the old shares by the total number of old and new shares.

Example 54: Kathlyn Ross owns 100 shares of the single class of stock of Mins Glass. Kathlyn's basis in the stock is $6,000. On August 1, Mins issues a stock dividend of one share for each two shares that a shareowner already owns. Because the shares distributed are identical to the shares Kathlyn already owns, she allocates her $6,000 basis to the

---

[41] Senate Finance Committee Report No. 91-552 (November 21, 1969), 1969 United States Code Congressional and Administrative News, p. 2182.

[42] Code Sec. 305(b)(2).

[43] Code Sec. 305(b)(3); Reg. § 1.305-4.

[44] Code Sec. 307(a).

total number of shares after the distribution. Prior to the distribution, Kathlyn's basis per share was $60 ($6,000/100). After the distribution, her basis per share is $40 ($6,000/150).

If the stock dividend is made in a different class of stock (for example, a common stock dividend on preferred stock, or a preferred stock dividend on common stock), the shareholder's new basis calculation becomes more complicated. In such situations, the basis of the stock with respect to which the dividend was paid must be allocated to the old stock and new stock based on the *respective FMV* of each class of stock on the date of the distribution.

Example 55: Chemists Supplies distributes one share of preferred stock for each five shares of common stock that its shareholders own. Dom Lanzarin, who owns 100 shares of common stock, receives 20 shares of preferred stock. Dom's basis in his 100 shares of common stock was $4,000 ($40 per share). The FMV of the common stock on the date of distribution was $60 per share. The FMV of the preferred stock was $15 per share.

	FMV	Relative FMV	New Basis
Common	$6,000	$6,000/$6,300 = 95.24%	$3,810
Preferred	300	$300/$6,300 = 4.76%	190
Total FMV	$6,300		$4,000

The FMV of the 100 shares of common stock and the 20 shares of preferred stock are computed. The FMV of the common shares is $6,000 (100 shares × $60); the FMV of the preferred shares is $300 (20 shares × $15). By comparing the FMV of each type of stock to the FMV of all types of stock Dom owns, the relative FMV percentage of each type of stock can be determined. Because the FMV of the common shares represents 95.24 percent of the FMV of both types of shares, that percentage of Dom's $4,000 basis is allocated to his common shares ($4,000 × 95.24% = $3,810). When he does the same calculations for the preferred shares, he allocates a total of $190 of the $4,000 original basis to those shares.

If nontaxable stock dividends are received, the shareholder's holding period for the stock received includes the holding period for the stock with respect to which the distribution was made.

Example 56: Shelly Larran acquired 100 shares of stock on July 1, 2011. On August 8, 2015, Shelly receives a stock dividend with respect to her 100 shares. Her holding period in the shares she receives on August 8 runs from July 2, 2011.

¶ 1207 Keeping Track of E&P

Because only distributions from current or accumulated E&P are treated as dividend distributions, each time a corporation makes a distribution to its shareholders it must know the amount of its current and accumulated E&P.

In many ways, E&P resembles the retained earnings of a company. However, the calculation of retained earnings is determined under the rules that govern generally accepted accounting principles (GAAP), whereas E&P is computed under the tax laws enacted by Congress.

E&P is used as a gauge of a corporation's ability to pay dividends without refunding the shareholders' investment in the corporation's stock. Therefore, the calculation of E&P differs in many ways from the calculation of taxable income. However, because many items included in the calculation of taxable income are also included in the calculation of E&P, the starting point for computing E&P is taxable income. From taxable income, various adjustments are made for those items treated differently for purposes of computing taxable income than for computing E&P. In making these adjustments, corporations must use the same basic method of accounting for calculating their E&P that they use for calculating their taxable income.[45]

Example 57: A corporation uses the accrual method of accounting to report its income and expenses. It must use the accrual method of accounting to report its income and expenses for purposes of determining its E&P.

The required adjustments to taxable income may be positive or negative. Positive adjustments include income not reported on the tax return that increases the corporation's ability to pay dividends as well as deductions taken on the tax return that do not reduce the corporation's ability to pay dividends. Negative adjustments to taxable income include income reported on the tax return that does not increase the corporation's ability to pay dividends as well as expenses that cannot be deducted on the tax return that reduce the amount of dividends a corporation can pay.

.01 Adjustments Due to Permanent Differences

Differences between amounts reported in taxable income and those reported in E&P result from the different rules that govern how the two amounts are computed. If one method includes an item of income, whereas the other method never recognizes it, a permanent difference results. Likewise, permanent differences occur when one method allows an expense to be deducted, but the other method never allows a deduction for it. Permanent differences between the two methods can result in positive or negative adjustments to taxable income, depending on whether the item disallowed results in lower or higher taxable income in relation to the corporation's E&P.

Negative adjustments resulting from permanent differences. Many expenses not deductible against gross income reduce a corporation's ability to pay dividends. Such amounts must be subtracted from taxable income to arrive at a corporation's E&P for the year. For example, federal income taxes cannot be deducted when calculating taxable income, but when a corporation pays $50,000 in federal income taxes the payment reduces the amount that can be distributed to shareholders. Likewise, penalties, fines, and other expenditures that violate public policy are not deductible in computing taxable income, but they reduce the amount of profits available to be distributed to shareholders.

Example 58: Wedge Photo pays $40,000 in federal income tax for the year. Although Wedge Photo cannot reduce its taxable income by this amount, the payment reduces the amount of money available to the corporation for making distributions to shareholders without refunding their investment in the corporation's stock. Therefore, the company must reduce its E&P by the $40,000 of federal income tax paid.

Losses disallowed for tax purposes affect a corporation's ability to pay dividends. For example, a corporation cannot deduct a loss resulting from a sale to a related party. However, when a corporation realizes a loss on the sale or exchange of an asset, that indicates the amount realized from the transaction was less than the corporation's adjusted basis in the property. Thus, the loss reduces the corporation's ability to pay dividends. Accordingly, losses from related party transactions are deducted in computing E&P. These disallowed losses are negative adjustments to taxable income. Figure 12-1 provides a list of negative adjustments to taxable income.

Figure 12-1 Negative Adjustments Due to Permanent Differences

- Federal income taxes paid;
- Disallowed losses from related party transactions;
- Life insurance premiums paid for a policy benefiting the corporation;

---

[45] Reg. § 1.312-6.

- Interest and expenses relating to tax-exempt income;
- Nondeductible, unreasonable amount of compensation paid to officers;
- Disallowed portion of meals and entertainment;
- Disallowed deduction for gifts in excess of $25; and
- Nondeductible fines and other penalties that violate public policy.

Example 59: Kalan Enterprises gifts $55 to each of its 100 top customers. On its tax return, the deduction is limited to $2,500 ($25 × 100). However, its dividend-paying capacity is reduced by $5,500 ($55 × 100). Thus, the $3,000 difference is a negative adjustment to taxable income when computing the corporation's E&P.

Example 60: Macro Services, Inc. incurs $20,000 in meal and entertainment expenses for the year, but it can deduct only half of such expenses on its tax return. However, the entire $20,000 paid reduces Macro's ability to pay dividends to its shareholders. Therefore, it must subtract the disallowed portion of the expenses ($10,000) from taxable income when computing its current year E&P.

Positive adjustments due to permanent differences. The tax laws allow certain types of income to be excluded from federal income tax. These amounts, known as "exclusions," are not included in the calculation of taxable income, but they increase a corporation's ability to pay dividends. For example, interest on state and local government bonds is specifically excluded from gross income. However, when a corporation receives $15,000 of interest from such a bond, its ability to distribute earnings to its shareholders increases by $15,000. Accordingly, this amount is a positive adjustment to taxable income when computing E&P.

Other examples of positive adjustments include tax-exempt life insurance proceeds and federal income tax refunds. When computing E&P, a corporation's organizational expenditures are never deductible. For tax purposes, taxpayers may elect to currently deduct up to $5,000 of their start-up expenses (a dollar figure reduced by the amount of start-up expenditures exceeding $50,000) and amortize remaining expenditures over 180 months. (See ¶ 503.) These and other permanent differences are listed in Figure 12-2.

Figure 12-2 Positive Adjustments Due to Permanent Differences

- Municipal bond interest,
- Federal income tax refunds,
- Amortization or deduction of organizational expenses,
- Any deduction related to construction period carrying charges, and
- Circulation expenditures deducted from gross income.

Example 61: Culkin Tractors has $1,000 in interest on a state bond that was not included in its taxable income but was included in its E&P because it increased the corporation's economic capacity to make distributions. Although the income was not taxable to the corporation, it will be taxed as a dividend when it is distributed to a shareholder.

Example 62: A corporation receives $15,000 of tax-exempt interest on a municipal bond and a $5,000 federal income tax refund. Although neither amount is included in the corporation's gross income, each amount increases the amount of funds available to the corporation to make distributions and therefore increases the corporation's E&P.

¶ 1207.01

Not all amounts excluded from gross income that increase the amount of assets available to make distributions increase a corporation's E&P. Items excluded from gross income that increase a corporation's capital, but not its income, do not increase a corporation's E&P. Such items include contributions to capital.

Example 63: Fuqua Decorators was organized as a corporation on April 1. At that time, five individuals transferred a total of $100,000 to the corporation in return for stock in the corporation. Although the capital contributed to the corporation increased the amount available for it to make distributions, any distribution of that $100,000 to the corporation's shareholders would be a return of the capital contributed to the corporation, not a distribution of any income the corporation earned. Therefore, the $100,000 is not included in the calculation of the company's E&P.

 Reason for the Rule: E&P is a measure used to determine what portion of a distribution consists of income earned by a corporation that should be taxed when received by a shareholder. Amounts that increase a corporation's capital but do not constitute income are not included in E&P.

.02 Adjustments Due to Timing Differences

Up to this point, the discussion concerning adjustments to taxable income has been about permanent differences in the way the regular income tax system and the E&P rules handle a particular item. Some expenses are allowed under both sets of rules, but the two rules differ as to how quickly the item is expensed. For example, both the federal income tax laws and the rules governing the calculation of E&P allow certain assets to be depreciated. The income tax laws allow personal property to be depreciated under the Modified Accelerated Cost Recovery System (MACRS) (see ¶ 702.01). Furthermore, some corporations are eligible to expense some or all of the cost of personal property under Code Sec. 179. These accelerated methods of depreciation were incorporated into the income tax laws to make it more attractive for businesses to invest in such assets.

When computing E&P, the cost of depreciable property is recovered using the alternative depreciation system (ADS) over specified periods (see Table 7-2 at ¶ 702.01 and ¶ 703), and the cost of property expensed under Code Sec. 179 is instead expensed ratably over five years. Thus, in years in which tax depreciation is higher than allowed under the E&P rules (typically the early years), a positive adjustment to taxable income is required. In the later years of the asset's life, when depreciation allowed for E&P is greater than tax depreciation, a negative adjustment is required.

Because different methods are used to depreciate property for purposes of determining corporate taxable income than for determining E&P, the adjusted basis in depreciable property will differ. Thus, when depreciable property is sold, the gain or loss reported on the tax return must be compared to the gain or loss recognized for computing E&P. The difference between these two amounts will result in either a positive or a negative adjustment to taxable income.

Other examples of timing differences involve intangible drilling costs and mining exploration and development costs. For tax purposes, these costs are generally expensed in the year they are incurred. For E&P purposes, intangible drilling costs are deducted ratably over 60 months, and mineral exploration and development costs are deducted ratably over 120 months. Table 12-2 summarizes the more common timing differences that require adjustments to taxable income.

Table 12-2 Adjustments Due to Timing Differences

Description of the Item	Discussion
Installment sales	For tax purposes, gain from an installment sale is recognized as the cash is received. For E&P purposes, the gain is earned in the year of the sale. Thus, in the year of the sale, a positive adjustment to taxable income will be required. In subsequent tax years when the cash is received, a negative adjustment will be required.
Depreciation of personal property	The differences between the depreciation taken under the two methods results in a timing difference. The difference will reverse itself as the property is depreciated or when the property is sold.
Capital losses in excess of capital gains	In the year the loss is disallowed, a negative adjustment to taxable income must be made. In a subsequent year when the carryover loss is allowed, a positive adjustment must be made.
Charitable contributions in excess of the 10-percent limit	In the year the charitable deduction is limited, a negative adjustment to taxable income is necessary. In the year in which the charitable contribution carryover is utilized, a positive adjustment to taxable income must be made.
Intangible drilling costs	In the first year, a positive adjustment must be made, but for the next five years negative adjustments are required.
Mining exploration and development costs	In the first year, a positive adjustment must be made, but for the next 10 years negative adjustments are required.

Example 64: Kovar Shipping sells stock for a $60,000 capital loss. Because corporations can deduct capital losses only to the extent of capital gains, Kovar cannot deduct the $60,000 loss on its tax return and instead must carry the loss over to the next year. However, the loss reduces the corporation's capacity to pay dividends and therefore must be subtracted from taxable income to accurately reflect the corporation's E&P.

Example 65: Bartek Moving purchases a delivery truck on September 1, 2015, for $45,000 and depreciates it under general MACRS. The truck weighs more than 6,000 pounds and is not subject to the luxury automobile depreciation limits. Bartek's depreciation deduction for federal income tax purposes is computed using the five-year column from Table 7A in the Appendix to Chapter 7. Depreciation for computing E&P is calculated using ADS, which depreciates trucks over five years using the straight-line (SL) depreciation method (see Table 7F in the Appendix to Chapter 7).

Year	MACRS Depreciation	E&P Depreciation
2015	$ 9,000 ($45,000 × 20%)	$4,500 ($45,000 × 10%)
2016	14,400 ($45,000 × 32%)	9,000 ($45,000 × 20%)
2017	8,640 ($45,000 × 19.2%)	9,000 ($45,000 × 20%)

Because Bartek's depreciation deduction for 2015 using MACRS exceeds the depreciation deduction under ADS (for purposes of computing E&P) by $4,500 ($9,000 – $4,500), the difference must be added back to taxable income. In 2016, the $5,400 difference ($14,400 – $9,000) must also be added back to taxable income when computing the company's E&P for the year.

In 2017, Bartek uses $9,000 of depreciation to compute E&P compared to $8,640 of depreciation deducted in computing taxable income. Because its depreciation using ADS exceeds its depreciation deduction on the tax return, the corporation must subtract an additional $360 ($9,000 – $8,640) from its taxable income when computing its E&P for 2017.

Effect of sale of property on E&P. When a corporation sells an asset, the gain or loss realized will increase or decrease the corporation's E&P. The amount of gain or loss realized for the purpose of determining the adjustment to a corporation's E&P may differ from the amount of gain or loss realized in computing a corporation's taxable income because property may have a different adjusted basis for purposes of determining E&P than it does for purposes of determining taxable income. When computing gain for E&P, adjusted basis using E&P depreciation deductions must be used.

Example 66: On January 1, 2015, Katch Oils, a calendar year taxpayer, purchased a delivery truck for $45,000 and expensed the entire cost. As a result, the truck's adjusted basis for tax purposes is $0. On January 1, 2017, Katch sells the delivery truck for $30,000 and reports a $30,000 gain on its tax return.

To compute E&P each year, Katch expenses the Section 179 property over five years. Accordingly, it deducts $9,000 each year. When the truck is sold, Katch's total depreciation deductions are $18,000 ($9,000 × 2 years). Katch's adjusted basis in the truck for E&P equals $27,000 ($45,000 – $18,000), and its E&P gain equals $3,000 ($30,000 – $27,000).

In 2015, Katch makes a $36,000 positive adjustment to taxable income. This amount is the difference between the depreciation expense reported on the tax return ($45,000) and the expense allowed for E&P ($9,000). In 2016, the entire $9,000 deducted against E&P requires a $9,000 negative adjustment to taxable income. In 2017, Katch makes a negative adjustment to taxable income equal to the difference between the $30,000 gain reported on the tax return and the $3,000 gain included in E&P.

Year	Positive Adjustment	Negative Adjustment
2015	$36,000	
2016		$ 9,000
2017		27,000
	$36,000	$36,000

As this example illustrates, the initial $36,000 difference between these two depreciation methods reverses itself as the property is depreciated or at the time the property is subsequently sold.

Although realized gains and losses generally do not affect a corporation's E&P until they are recognized, an exception is made for installment sales. A corporation's E&P is computed as if the corporation did not use the installment method to report gain from the sale.

Example 67: Scheve Foods sold vacant land with an adjusted basis of $100,000. The proceeds from the sale were $250,000, payable in five equal annual installments. The entire $150,000 gain ($250,000 – $100,000) is included in E&P in the year of the sale, even though for tax purposes the gain is recognized over the next five years.

.03 Items Requiring No Adjustment to E&P

Certain items of income whose recognition is deferred to a subsequent tax year do not increase a corporation's E&P in the year the gain is realized, but only in the year in which the gain is finally recognized. That is because an increase in E&P in the year of realization could result in the income being taxed twice to the shareholders as dividend income if E&P were also increased in the year income was recognized. Items that do not increase E&P include gains from like-kind exchanges and the involuntary conversion of property. Income from the discharge of indebtedness that is excluded from gross income does not increase E&P to the extent that the amount discharged is applied to reduce the corporation's basis in assets.

Example 68: Gramm, Inc. exchanges an office building with an FMV of $500,000 and an adjusted basis of $200,000 for an office building with an FMV of $600,000. As part of the exchange, Gramm transfers $100,000 to the other party. No amount of Gramm's $300,000 realized gain ($500,000 – $200,000) is recognized because the transaction qualifies as a like-kind exchange. However, recognition of that gain is only deferred, and Gramm's basis in its new office building is reduced by the postponed gain ($600,000 – $300,000 = $300,000). If Gram subsequently sells the office building for $600,000, it will have to recognize the $300,000 of postponed gain ($600,000 – $300,000). If the company were required to include that $300,000 in E&P at the time the gain was realized (but unrecognized) and a second time when the new office building was sold and the gain was recognized, E&P would include $600,000 instead of $300,000, the actual increase in the corporation's ability to pay dividends from previously taxed profits.

Example 69: Stalling, Inc. does not recognize any income when $50,000 of its debt is discharged in bankruptcy. The tax laws require Stalling to apply the $50,000 to reduce the basis of the assets it retains following its bankruptcy. Thus, when Stalling sells those assets, it will realize $50,000 more in gain than it would have realized absent the discharge of indebtedness. If both the $50,000 discharge of indebtedness income and $50,000 gain realized from the sale of assets were included in the corporation's E&P, the shareholders could be taxed on $50,000 of income that the corporation never actually earned.

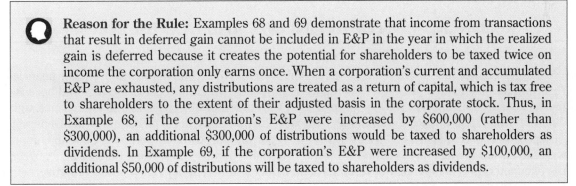

Reason for the Rule: Examples 68 and 69 demonstrate that income from transactions that result in deferred gain cannot be included in E&P in the year in which the realized gain is deferred because it creates the potential for shareholders to be taxed twice on income the corporation only earns once. When a corporation's current and accumulated E&P are exhausted, any distributions are treated as a return of capital, which is tax free to shareholders to the extent of their adjusted basis in the corporate stock. Thus, in Example 68, if the corporation's E&P were increased by $600,000 (rather than $300,000), an additional $300,000 of distributions would be taxed to shareholders as dividends. In Example 69, if the corporation's E&P were increased by $100,000, an additional $50,000 of distributions will be taxed to shareholders as dividends.

.04 Effects of Distributions on E&P

As a general rule, when C corporations distribute money or property with respect to their stock, they must decrease their E&P (but not below zero) by the sum of the following amounts:[46]

1. The amount of money distributed,

2. The principal amount of any obligations of the corporation that are distributed,[47]

3. The adjusted basis of property (other than appreciated property) distributed, and

4. The FMV of appreciated property distributed.

---

[46] Code Sec. 312(a).   [47] Code Sec. 312(c).

For purposes of reducing E&P for property distributions, the adjusted basis of property (in the case of distributions other than of appreciated property) is its adjusted basis for purposes of computing E&P.[48] When a C corporation distributes appreciated property, its E&P is increased by the gain it recognizes on such distribution. After E&P is increased by the gain, it is reduced by the FMV of the property distributed.

Example 70: Hahl Engines distributes equipment with an FMV of $10,000 and an adjusted basis of $2,000 to its sole shareholder. Hahl increases its E&P by the $8,000 gain it recognizes (the difference between the FMV of the equipment and its adjusted basis). Hahl then reduces its E&P by the $10,000 FMV of the equipment. Because of the distribution, the company's E&P is reduced by $2,000, which is the amount of the adjusted basis of the property distributed.

When a corporation makes a nontaxable distribution of its own stock, the corporation does not reduce its E&P. However, if a corporation makes a distribution that results in a taxable dividend the corporation's E&P must be reduced by the taxable amount of the distribution.[49]

Example 71: Machine Coolants declares a stock dividend and distributes two shares of stock for each share of stock held by a shareholder. Because the distribution is nontaxable, the company does not reduce its E&P.

Example 72: Medical Alarms has two classes of common stock outstanding: Common Stock A and Common Stock B. The company distributes $10 per share to the owners of Common Stock A outstanding and distributes one share of its own stock to the owner of each share of Common Stock B. Because this is a disproportionate distribution, the FMV of the stock distributed to the Common Stock B shareholders must be included in their gross income. As a result, the company must reduce its E&P by both the amount of cash and the FMV of the stock distributed.

RECONCILIATION OF NET INCOME AND TAXABLE INCOME

Larger C corporations are required to maintain two sets of accounting records: one for financial reporting purposes and a second for tax reporting purposes. Different records are required because financial statements and tax returns are prepared with different objectives and in compliance with different rules. For financial accounting purposes, corporations need to comply with Generally Accepted Accounting Principles (GAAP). For tax reporting purposes, corporations need to comply with the *tax laws*, which are different from the financial reporting rules. Most differences between the two methods of computing net earnings stem from the different objectives of the two governing bodies in charge of the rules.

The GAAP rules have been written to provide users of financial statements with the most relevant and reliable information about the activities and financial position of a business. When writing the tax laws, Congress is concerned with raising revenues for the federal government and with maintaining certain economic, social, or political agendas. (See ¶ 106.)

Corporations with total receipts of at least $250,000 *and* at least $250,000 in total assets at the end of the year are required to reconcile any disparities between their **net income per books** and their **taxable income per return** (before any net operating loss (NOL) or dividends received deduction (DRD)).

---

[48] Code Sec. 312(b).   [49] Reg. § 1.312-1(d).

¶ 1208 Differences between Book Income and Taxable Income

The different rules for reporting income for financial accounting purposes and for tax purposes result in differences in a corporation's net income and taxable income. These differences can be characterized as permanent differences and timing differences.

.01 Permanent Differences

Permanent differences result when certain items of income or expenses reported for financial accounting purposes are *never* reported for tax purposes. They can also occur when deductions taken on the tax return are *never* reported in net income. When the item results in more net income than taxable income, the item must be subtracted from net income in order to reconcile net income with the taxable income reported on the company's tax return. For example, interest from state and local government bonds is exempt from federal income tax. However, the interest is included in the calculation of net income. Thus, the amount of municipal interest must be subtracted from net income in order to reconcile net income (per books) and taxable income (per return). When the item results in less net income than taxable income, the item must be added to net income in order to reconcile it with taxable income reported on the corporation's tax return.

Example 73: Bolles Forklifts receives $2,000 of tax-exempt interest during the year. The tax-exempt interest increases the company's net income by $2,000 but is excluded from the company's taxable income. In order to reconcile the amount reported in net income with that reported in taxable income, the $2,000 must be subtracted from net income.

The permanent differences between the calculation of taxable income and net income are included in Table 12-3.

Table 12-3 Permanent Differences Between Taxable Income and Net Income

Item	Tax Return	Financial Reporting
Municipal interest (see ¶ 412.01.)	Not taxable*	Included
Life insurance proceeds	Not taxable**	Included
Expenses related to tax-exempt investments (see ¶ 505.)	Not deductible	Deductible
Federal income taxes paid	Not deductible	Deductible
Premiums paid for life insurance in which the corporation is named as a beneficiary	Not deductible	Deductible
Fines and penalties (see ¶ 501.04.)	Not deductible	Deductible
Meals and entertainment (see ¶ 605.)	50% limitation	Entirely deductible
Unreasonable compensation (see ¶ 601.02.)	Not deductible	Deductible
Loss on the sale of property to a related party (see ¶ 804.)	Not deductible	Deductible
Depletion expense (see ¶ 705 and ¶ 706.)	The greater of percentage or cost depletion	Cost depletion

Item	Tax Return	Financial Reporting
Organizational and start-up costs (see ¶ 503.)	Up to $5,000 deductible immediately or amortizable over 180 months	No deduction
Intangible assets with an infinite life (see ¶ 708 and ¶ 709.)	Amortizable over 15 years	No deduction
Business gifts (see ¶ 512.)	Deduction limited to $25	Entirely deductible
Domestic production activities deduction (see ¶ 509.)	Deductible	No deduction
Dividends received deduction (see ¶ 412.02 and ¶ 508.)	Deductible	No deduction
Net operating loss deduction (see ¶ 1002.)	Deductible	No deduction

* Interest may be taxable if it is paid with respect to a private activity bond that is not a qualified bond, an arbitrage bond, or a bond not in registered form.

** Life insurance proceeds may be taxable to a certain extent if the transfer for value rule applies or the policy is on the life of an employee.

Example 74: Howell Industries incurs $10,000 of meals and entertainment expenses during the year. Howell reduces its net income by the $10,000 but can reduce its taxable income by only $5,000. When reconciling its net income with its taxable income, Howell must add back the disallowed meals and entertainment.

For tax purposes, corporations can deduct the *greater* of percentage depletion (subject to the taxable income limitations) or cost depletion. For financial accounting purposes, only the cost depletion method can be used. Although differences in these two methods are usually timing differences that will reverse themselves over time, if the amount deducted for percentage depletion exceeds the corporation's adjusted basis in the property, a permanent difference results. Any excess deducted on the tax return requires a negative adjustment to net income to reconcile net income with taxable income on the corporate tax return.

Example 75: A corporation owns oil and gas property that it fully depleted by the beginning of the year. During the year, gross income from the property was $250,000, and percentage depletion equals $37,500 ($250,000 × 15%). (See ¶ 706.) Because the property is fully depleted, cost depletion is zero. Accordingly, no amount is subtracted when computing net income on the income statement. On its tax return, the corporation deducts $37,500 as depletion expense (the *greater* of $0 or $37,500). The $37,500 difference is a permanent difference.

.02 Timing Differences

Timing differences result when income and expenses are reported for tax purposes in a different tax year than they are reported for financial accounting purposes. Timing differences originate in one tax year but reverse themselves in a subsequent tax year. For this reason, in the year of its creation the difference is often called an **originating difference**. In the subsequent year(s) when the difference is reversed, it is called a **reversing difference**.

Example 76: Scribb Equipment purchases equipment costing $10,000 on July 1, 2015. Scribb deducts depreciation expense over the years in accordance with the tax laws (on its tax return) and GAAP (on its financial statements) as shown below.

Year	Tax Depreciation	Book Depreciation	Difference
2015	$ 2,000	$ 1,000	$1,000
2016	3,200	2,000	1,200
2017	1,920	2,000	(80)
2018	1,152	2,000	(848)
2019	1,152	2,000	(848)
2020	576	1,000	(424)
	$10,000	$10,000	$ 0

During 2015 and 2016, depreciation deductions on the tax return exceed depreciation taken against net income. However, the differences reverse from 2017 through 2020 when book depreciation exceeds tax depreciation. Nonetheless, the total amount of depreciation deductions that Scribb takes from 2015 to 2020 is the same. Therefore, the differences merely involve timing.

Four basic types of timing differences create differences between a corporation's net income and its taxable income:

1. Income is included in net income but not in taxable income during the same year.

2. Income is included in taxable income but not in net income during the same year.

3. Amounts are deducted when calculating net income but are not deducted when calculating taxable income for the same year.

4. Amounts are deducted when calculating taxable income but are not deducted when calculating net income for the same year.

The differences are summarized in Tables 12-4 and 12-5.

Table 12-4 Differences between Net Income and Taxable Income Due to the Timing of Gains and Other Income

Item	Originating Difference	Reversing Difference
Installment sales (see ¶ 309.01 and ¶ 810.)	In the year of the sale, the entire gain is included in net income, but only a portion of the gain is reported on the tax return. This difference will require a negative adjustment to net income.	In each subsequent tax year as payments are received, gain is recognized on the tax return. This will require a positive adjustment to net income.
Gains from involuntary conversions (see ¶ 809.)	Gain from an involuntary conversion is not taxable if the proceeds are reinvested in qualified replacement property. This will require a negative adjustment to net income in the originating year.	Because the adjusted basis of the replacement property for tax purposes is reduced by the postponed gain, the originating difference is reversed through differences in depreciation taken on the replacement property or when the property is eventually sold.
Gains from like-kind exchanges (see ¶ 808.)	Gain is recognized on the income statement to the extent that the earnings process has been completed. Gain is recognized on the tax return to the extent of boot received. Any difference between the two amounts will need to be shown as an adjustment to net income in the year of the exchange.	Because the basis of the like-kind property received is reduced by any postponed gain, any originating difference will be reversed either through differences in depreciation deductions taken with respect to the like-kind property or when the property is subsequently sold.
Income received in advance (see ¶ 307.01.)	Can be taxed in the year received or over no more than two tax years. Income is included in net income in the year it is earned.	When income is eventually taxed in the second tax year, a positive adjustment to net income will be needed.
Long-term contracts (see ¶ 309.02.)	If the completed contract method is used for financial accounting purposes, each year until the final year gain reported on the tax return (under the percentage-of-completion method) will result in an originating difference due to higher taxable income being reported.	When the project is completed, the entire gain is reported in net income. Thus, in the final year, net income will be greater than taxable income, and a positive adjustment to net income is required.
Rollover of gain from the sale of publicly traded securities (see ¶ 807.)	Gain from the sale of publicly traded securities can be postponed for tax purposes if the proceeds are invested in a specialized small business investment company (SSBIC). A negative adjustment to net income is required in the year that publicly traded stock is sold.	Because the tax basis in the SSBIC stock is adjusted for any postponed gain, this difference will reverse itself when the corporation sells the SSBIC stock.

Item	Originating Difference	Reversing Difference
Unrealized gain on marketable securities (see ¶ 801.)	GAAP requires that unrealized gains and losses on marketable trading securities be reported on the income statement in the year in which the unrealized gain or loss occurs. This causes a difference between the calculation of net income and taxable income.	Any remaining unrealized gain or loss previously reported on the income statement will be reversed in the year that the securities are sold.

Example 77: On December 20, 2015, Kraft Dyes sells a parcel of land for $150,000. The adjusted basis of the land is $50,000. The terms of the contract call for five annual payments of $30,000 beginning on January 20, 2016. Kraft uses the calendar year as its tax year.

For 2015, the company must include its entire $100,000 gain ($150,000 – $50,000) in its net income. However, because none of the proceeds is received in 2015, none of the gain is included in taxable income. Kraft will report a $100,000 negative adjustment to net income when it reconciles its net income to taxable income on its corporate tax return. From 2016 to 2020, Kraft will report $20,000 of the gain in taxable income each year ($100,000/5 years). The amounts will be reported as positive adjustments to net income in those years.

Example 78: On November 1, 2015, Rennell, Inc. receives a $36,000 payment for rent covering the three-year period beginning on November 1, 2015, and ending on October 31, 2018. Rennell uses the calendar year as its tax year. In 2015, Rennell includes $2,000 ($36,000/36 × 2 months) in income on both its tax return and on its financial statements. In 2016, it reports $12,000 in net income ($36,000/36 × 12 months). It must include the remaining rents ($34,000) in gross income on its tax return because taxpayers cannot defer prepaid amounts beyond the subsequent tax year (see ¶ 307.01).

In 2016, Rennell must add the $22,000 difference to net income when it reconciles net income with taxable income. In 2017 and 2018, Rennell will report $12,000 and $10,000, respectively, as negative adjustments to net income.

Table 12-5 Differences between Net Income and Taxable Income Due to the Timing of Losses and Deductions

Item	Originating Difference	Reversing Difference
Depreciation (see ¶ 702.)	When accelerated methods of depreciation are used to depreciate property for tax purposes, the amounts deducted in the earlier years of an asset's life will result in originating differences that will need to be subtracted from net income.	In the latter years of an asset's life, depreciation expense on the income statement will exceed depreciation deducted on the tax return.
Depletion (see ¶ 705 and ¶ 706.)	For tax purposes, corporations deduct the *greater* of percentage depletion or cost depletion. On the income statement, depletion expense must be computed using the cost method. When the amount of percentage depletion taken on the tax return exceeds the amount deducted on the income statement, the corporation will be required to make a negative adjustment to net income. However, any difference due to depletion expense on the tax return exceeding the adjusted basis of the property is a permanent, not a timing, difference (see Table 12-4 and Example 68).	In years in which the depletion taken on the income statement exceeds that which is deducted on the tax return, the difference will be a positive adjustment to net income.
Intangible assets with finite lives (see ¶ 708 and ¶ 709.)	Any differences between the amortization of such assets over their useful lives for financial accounting purposes and over 15 years for tax purposes will result in timing differences.	Any difference between the amortization methods is a timing difference that will eventually be reversed.
Research and experimentation costs (see ¶ 507.)	If the corporation elects to amortize these costs over 60 months (rather than to expense them immediately), the expense reported on the income statement in the year the costs are incurred will exceed the amount deducted on the tax return. This difference will require a positive adjustment to net income.	In each subsequent year as the costs are amortized on the tax return, a negative adjustment will be required to net income when reconciling it to taxable income on the corporate tax return.
Wash sale transactions (see ¶ 805.)	In the year in which a wash sale occurs, the loss disallowed for tax purposes will require a positive adjustment to net income	Because the adjusted basis of the stock for tax purposes is increased by the postponed loss, when the stock is subsequently sold a negative adjustment to net income will be required.

Item	Originating Difference	Reversing Difference
Losses from like-kind changes (see ¶ 808.)	Losses from like-kind exchanges must be recognized on the income statement but must be postponed for tax purposes. Thus, the postponed loss will be a positive adjustment to net income in the year of the exchange.	Because for tax purposes the adjusted basis of the like-kind property received is increased by any postponed loss, the originating difference will be reversed through differences in depreciation expense taken on the like-kind property or when such property is subsequently sold.
Bad debts (see ¶ 510.)	Because the direct write-off method, which is the only acceptable method for tax purposes, is not allowed for financial accounting purposes, differences in timing for writing off bad debt expenses will require an adjustment to net income.	As amounts estimated to be bad debts on the financial statement become actual bad debts, the originating differences will reverse and require an adjustment to net income.
Charitable contributions and capital losses (see ¶ 511 and ¶ 901.01.)	When these deductions are limited on the tax return, an originating difference will require a positive adjustment to be made to net income.	As these carryover amounts are utilized, the originating differences will be reversed and a negative adjustment to net income will be required.

Example 79: W.R. Leasing uses the calendar year as its tax year. During 2015, it sells for $10,000 stock that has an adjusted basis of $15,000. W.R. has no capital gains for 2015. On its 2015 income statement, W.R. reduces its net income by the $5,000 loss ($10,000 – $15,000) but cannot utilize the loss on its 2015 tax return. This $5,000 originating difference will be reversed in the tax year in which the $5,000 capital loss carryover is utilized.

Example 80: Damkor Fixtures uses the calendar year as its tax year. During 2015, Damkor exchanges equipment with an adjusted basis of $10,000 for like-kind equipment worth $8,000. Damkor must reduce its 2015 net income by the $2,000 loss ($8,000 – $10,000), but it must postpone the loss for tax purposes. Damkor increases its tax basis in the new equipment by the $2,000 postponed loss. This will cause Damkor's tax depreciation on the new equipment to be greater than its book depreciation over the asset's depreciable life. Any part of the originating difference not reversed through depreciation deductions will be reversed when the property is eventually sold and different bases for the property are used for book versus tax purposes.

¶ 1209 Schedules M-1 and M-3

C corporations whose total receipts are at least $250,000 *and* whose total assets are at least $250,000 at the end of the year are required to reconcile the net income reported on their income statement with the taxable income reported on their income tax returns (before any NOL deduction or DRD). This reconciliation is reported either on Schedule M-1 or on Schedule M-3, both of which are part of the U.S. corporate income tax return.

A corporation's *total receipts* are the sum of the corporation's gross receipts or sales (not reduced by returns and allowances or by the cost of goods sold), dividends (not reduced by the dividends received deduction), interest, gross rents, gross royalties, capital gain net income, net gain or loss from sales of business property, and other income reported on the corporation's income tax return.

.01 Schedule M-1

C corporations whose total receipts are at least $250,000 *and* whose total assets are at least $250,000 but less than $10 million are required to complete Schedule M-1, *Reconciliation of Income (Loss) Per Books With Income Per Return*. C corporations with total assets of $10 million or more on the last day of a tax year must complete Schedule M-3 instead of Schedule M-1. Schedule M-1 is part of Form 1120, *U.S. Corporation Income Tax Return*. Corporations complete Schedule M-1 to reconcile their financial accounting net income or loss for the year with their taxable income or loss (before any NOL deduction or DRD) reported on their federal income tax returns.

Example 81: Coffee Roasting, Inc. has gross receipts of $235,000, returns and allowances of $5,000, and cost of the goods sold of $50,000. It has also earned $5,000 of interest income and $10,000 of dividend income (all of which is eligible for the 70-percent DRD). Its total gross receipts equal $250,000 ($235,000 + $5,000 + $10,000). It also has $300,000 in total assets at the end of the tax year. Coffee Roasting will be required to complete Schedule M-1 of its corporate income tax return.

Reason for the Rule: Schedule M-1 is designed to help the IRS identify matters that require extended examination. Small corporations have been exempted so that they can use record keeping based on their checkbook or cash receipts and disbursements journal instead of additional accounting methods solely for tax reporting.[50]

Schedule M-1 starts by adding to net income or loss as reported on the income statement all items that result in positive adjustments to net income (lines 2–5). These are items for which the amount of income recognized on the tax return exceeds that reported in net income or for which the expenses deducted on the income statement exceed those reported on the tax return. Positive adjustments from both permanent and timing differences are reported in the first part of Schedule M-1.

The second half of Schedule M-1 takes into account the negative adjustments to net income (lines 7–8). These include items of income that are included in net income but are not recognized for tax purposes and expenses that are allowed on the tax return but not deducted in computing net income. Negative adjustments stemming from both permanent and timing differences are reported on the bottom half of Schedule M-1. Any NOL deduction or DRD is not included as an adjustment because net income is reconciled to taxable income or loss on the tax return before either of these items is deducted. After all positive and negative adjustments to net income have been made, the result must equal the corporation's taxable income before any NOL deduction or DRD.

---

[50] IRS News Release IR-2002-48 (April 10, 2002).

Schedule M-1 Reconciliation of Income (Loss) per Books With Income per Return

1. Net income (loss) per books $_____

2. Federal income tax per books _____

3. Excess of capital losses over capital gains _____

4. Income subject to tax not recorded on books this year (itemize) _____

5. Expenses recorded on books this year not deducted on this return (itemize):

    a. Depreciation $_____

    b. Charitable contributions _____

    c. Travel and entertainment _____

    d. _____ _____

6. Add lines 1 through 5 $_____

7. Income recorded on books this year not included on this return (itemize):

    Tax-exempt interest $_____

    _____ _____

    _____ _____ $_____

8. Deductions on this return not charged against book income this year (itemize):

    a. Depreciation $_____

    b. Charitable contributions _____

    _____ _____

    _____ _____ _____

9. Add lines 7 and 8 $_____

10. Line 6 minus line 9. The result should be the same as taxable income before any NOL or dividends received deductions $_____

Example 82: In 2015, Lotan Containers reports net income per books of $365,600 and taxable income of $410,000. Lotan does not show any deduction for an NOL or dividends received deduction on its tax return. Lotan's federal income tax for 2015 is $139,400. The taxable income reflects $3,000 more than the amount reflected in net income due to differences in adjusted basis used to compute the gains for book and tax purposes. The difference in adjusted basis stems from accelerated depreciation taken to depreciate the property for tax purposes (versus straight-line for financial statement purposes). Taxable income also includes an additional $40,000 in depreciation expense over the amount used in determining its net income. Items reflected in the net income but not on the tax return include $12,000 of charitable contributions in excess of the 10-percent taxable income limit, $10,000 of interest expense incurred on amounts borrowed to purchase tax-exempt bonds, $30,000 of tax-exempt interest, and $50,000 of nontaxable insurance proceeds. Lotan's completed Schedule M-1 is shown below.

Schedule M-1 Reconciliation of Income (Loss) per Books with Income per Return

1.	Net income (loss) per books			$365,600
2.	Federal income tax per books			139,400
3.	Excess of capital losses over capital gains			_____
4.	Income subject to tax not recorded on books this year (itemize): Additional gain due to accelerated depreciation			3,000
5.	Expenses recorded on books this year not deducted on this return (itemize):			
	a.	Depreciation	$_____	
	b.	Charitable contributions	12,000	
	c.	Travel and entertainment	_____	
	d.	Interest to carry tax-exempt bonds	10,000	22,000
6.	Add lines 1 through 5			$530,000
7.	Income recorded on books this year not included on this return (itemize):			
	a.	Tax-exempt interest	$30,000	
	b.	Insurance proceeds	50,000	
	c.	_____		80,000
8.	Deductions on this return not charged against book income this year (itemize):			
	a.	Depreciation	$40,000	
	b.	Charitable contributions	_____	
	c.	_____	_____	
	d.	_____		40,000
9.	Add lines 7 and 8			$120,000
10.	Line 6 minus line 9. The result should be the same as taxable income before any NOL or dividends received deductions			$410,000

.02 Schedule M-3

Schedule M-3, *Net Income (Loss) Reconciliation for Corporations With Total Assets of $10 Million or More,* is required for all corporations with $10 million or more in assets. Schedule M-3 is an expanded version of Schedule M-1. Effective for tax years ending December 31, 2014 and later, corporations with at least $10 million but less than $50 million in total assets at tax year end have to complete Part I of Schedule M-3 but may complete Schedule M-1 in lieu of Parts II and III of Schedule M-3. Corporations with at least $50 million in total assets must complete Schedule M-3 in lieu of Schedule M-1. Other C corporations may voluntarily file Schedule M-3 in lieu of Schedule M-1.

 Reason for the Rule: Schedule M-3 was developed to increase the transparency of corporate tax returns by making the differences between financial accounting net income and taxable income more transparent and help the IRS determine whether a return should be audited (and, if so, what portions of the return should be audited).[51] Schedule M-3 is also intended to address two problems with Schedule M-1: (1) no

---

[51] IRS News Release 2004-14 (January 28, 2004).

uniform reporting requirement regarding the definition of book income and (2) no uniform disclosure requirements for reporting differences between financial accounting net income and taxable income.[52]

Schedule M-3, which is divided into three parts, requires more detail regarding the source of the differences between net income and taxable income. Unlike Schedule M-1, which has 10 numbered lines, Schedule M-3 has more than 100 numbered lines.

Part I: The corporation identifies the source of its financial statement information among the following: an SEC Form 10-K income statement; a certified audited income statement; an income statement prepared by the corporation; or the corporation's books and records.

Part II: The corporation reconciles net income (or loss) reported on its income statement with the taxable income (or loss) reported on its U.S. income tax return.

Part III: The corporation reconciles expenses and other deductions reported on its income statement with expenses and other deductions reported on its U.S. income tax return.

Spotlight: The information provided on Schedule M-1 and on Schedule M-3 helps the federal government identify areas in which corporations use different methods to compute net income and taxable income. While some of these differences result from differences in the requirements in the two sets of rules used to report the information, some differences result from actions of the corporation to (legally) avoid paying income taxes.

The SEC and the IRS Commissioner have discussed whether corporations should be required to provide investors with a side-by-side presentation of tax reporting and financial reporting and whether corporate income tax returns should be made public. During a March 14, 2006, speech at the National Press Club, the IRS Commissioner was quoted as saying, "If we are not willing to operate the two systems by the same set of rules, it makes sense to discuss whether corporate tax returns should be (made) public." In response to these discussions, a spokesperson for the National Taxpayers Union commented that allowing such disclosure "would be one of the most radical departures in tax history" as tax return information "is often regarded as the most private in American society."[53]

¶ 1210 Schedule M-2

C corporations that are required to complete Schedule M-1 or Schedule M-3 are also required to complete Schedule M-2, *Analysis of Unappropriated Retained Earnings Per Books.* Schedule M-2, which is part of the U.S. corporate income tax return, requires that corporations explain changes in their unappropriated retained earnings per their books during the year.

Reason for the Rule: Schedule M-2 is another tool the IRS uses to ensure compliance with the tax laws.

---

[52] 2004 ARD 019-5 (January 29, 2004).

[53] "SEC, IRS May Seek Tax Data Disclosure," *L.A. Times,* May 2, 2006.

Schedule M-2 Analysis of Unappropriated Retained Earnings per Books

1.	Balance at beginning of year	$_____
2.	Net income (loss) per books	_____
3.	Other increases (itemize):	
	_____	
	_____	_____
4.	Add lines 1, 2, and 3	$_____
5.	Distributions:	
	a. Cash	_____
	b. Stock	_____
	c. Property	_____
6.	Other decreases (itemize):	
	_____	
	_____	_____
7.	Add lines 5 and 6	$_____
8.	Balance at end of year (line 4 less line 7)	$_____

The analysis begins with the balance of the unappropriated retained earnings per books at the beginning of the year. This amount is then adjusted for the items that affect retained earnings during the year. The amount resulting from these calculation is the corporation's unappropriated retained earnings per books at the end of the current year. This amount should agree with the retained earnings reported on the corporation's balance sheet.

Example 83: On January 1, 2015, the unappropriated retained earnings per books for Kenniston Frozen Custards were $1.2 million. At the end of the year, the unappropriated retained earnings were $915,000. The corporation's net income per books for 2015 was $365,000. During the year, Kenniston paid a cash dividend of $150,000 and transferred $500,000 to its appropriated retained earnings account to cover the projected liability of a products liability claim made against the company for which there was no insurance coverage. Schedule M-2 would be completed as follows.

Schedule M-2 Analysis of Unappropriated Retained Earnings per Books

1.	Balance at beginning of year	$1,200,000
2.	Net income (loss) per books	365,000
3.	Other increases (itemize):	
	_____	
	_____	_____
4.	Add lines 1, 2, and 3	$1,565,000
5.	Distributions:	
	a. Cash	150,000
	b. Stock	
	c. Property	_____

6. Other decreases (itemize):
    Appropriated retained earnings   500,000

7. Add lines 5 and 6 $ 650,000
8. Balance at end of year (line 4 less line 7) $ 915,000

¶ 1211 Summary

As a general rule, a person who transfers property to a corporation in exchange for stock will not have to recognize any gain realized if that person, or that person and one or more other persons transferring property to the corporation, control the corporation following the transfer. However, gain has to be recognized if the transferor receives boot in addition to stock or the corporation assumes excess liabilities.

When a C corporation distributes cash or other property to its shareholders, the distribution is treated as a dividend to the extent of the corporation's accumulated and current E&P. Sometimes a corporation will be deemed to have made a constructive distribution with respect to its stock. That may occur, for example, if a corporation pays a shareholder-employee an unreasonable amount of compensation or lets a shareholder use corporate property for personal purposes.

As a rule, when a C corporation distributes any of its own stock, no amount of the distribution has to be included in a shareholder's gross income unless the distribution is in lieu of money or other property or is a disproportionate distribution. In such instances, the distribution is taxable to the shareholders as a dividend to the extent that it is paid out of the corporation's current or accumulated E&P.

When large corporations file their U.S. income tax, they are required to reconcile the net income or loss reported on their financial statements with the taxable income or loss reported on their tax return. Differences result because of timing and permanent differences between the methods used to report net income on the books and those used to report taxable income on the tax return.

GLOSSARY OF TERMS INTRODUCED IN THE CHAPTER

Accumulated earnings and profits. The amount of E&P a C corporation has generated over the years that has not been distributed as of the beginning of its current tax year.

Boot. Cash and other property added to an exchange to equalize the value of exchanged items. When made part of an otherwise nontaxable exchange, the portion of realized gain equal to the value of the boot will have to be recognized.

Constructive dividend. A payment to or for the benefit of a shareholder that is treated as a dividend even though it may not be denoted as such by the corporation.

Control. Persons control a corporation if they own stock possessing at least 80 percent of the total combined voting power of all classes of stock entitled to vote and at least 80 percent of the total number of shares of all other classes of stock of the corporation. Code Sec. 368(c).

Current earnings and profits. A C corporation's earnings and profits for its current tax year. A corporate tax concept that attempts to capture a corporation's capacity to pay dividends from its current year's earnings.

Dividend. A distribution of current and/or accumulated earnings and profits by a C corporation to its shareholders.

Earnings and profits (E&P). A tax term used to reflect a C corporation's economic capacity to make a distribution from corporate earnings that is not a return of a shareholder's capital. It is computed by making adjustments to the corporation's taxable income.

Net income per books. The net income a corporation reports for financial accounting purposes.

Originating difference. The initial difference that occurs in the year in which a timing difference is created. *See also* Reversing difference *and* Timing difference.

Permanent difference. The condition that exists when items of income or expense are reported for financial accounting purposes but *never* for tax purposes, or vice versa.

Qualified dividend income. Dividend income that is taxed to an individual taxpayer at a rate lower than the taxpayer's marginal tax rate. The dividends must be paid on stock of a U.S. corporation or a qualified foreign corporation that the individual held for more than 60 days during the 121-day period beginning 60 days before the ex-dividend date.

Return of capital distribution. A distribution of cash or other property from a corporation that is not made from current or accumulated earnings and profits.

Reversing difference. Timing difference that occurs in a year subsequent to the year in which the originating difference occurred. *See also* Originating difference *and* Timing difference.

Schedule M-1. Part of Form 1120, *U.S. Corporation Income Tax Return*; it requires corporations to reconcile their net income for financial accounting purposes with their taxable income. Must be filed by corporations with total receipts and total assets of at least $250,000 (but total assets less than $10 million) at the end of the year.

Schedule M-2. Part of Form 1120, *U.S. Corporation Income Tax Return*; it requires corporations to explain changes during the year in their unappropriated retained earnings. Must be filed by corporations that file Schedule M-1 or Schedule M-3.

Schedule M-3. An expanded version of Schedule M-1. Effective for tax years ending December 31, 2014 and later, corporations with at least $50 million in total assets must complete Schedule M-3 in lieu of Schedule M-1. Corporations with at least $10 million but less than $50 million in total assets at tax year end have to complete Part I of Schedule M-3 but may complete Schedule M-1 in lieu of Parts II and III of Schedule M-3.

Stock dividend. A dividend payable in shares of the distributing corporation's own stock.

Taxable income per return. A corporation's taxable income, as reported on the U.S. federal income tax return.

Timing difference. Difference that results when income and expenses are reported in one year for financial accounting purposes and in a different year for tax purposes. *See also* Originating difference *and* Reversing difference.

CHAPTER PROBLEMS

Chapter 12 Discussion Questions

1. What is a dividend?

2. How are dividends received by a C corporation taxed?

3. How are dividends received by an individual taxed?

4. If a corporation distributes property other than money or stock in the distributing corporation to a shareholder, what is the shareholder's basis in that property?

5. If the amount of a C corporation's distribution exceeds the amount of its current and accumulated E&P, how is the distribution taxed?

6. How is the amount of a distribution to a shareholder calculated?

7. Zeff Polishing distributes shares of its own stock to its shareholder, Kim Zeff, as a nontaxable stock dividend. Kim originally acquired her shares of Zeff stock on February 1, 2015, and Zeff Publishing distributed the stock to Kim on September 1, 2015. When does her holding period in the new stock begin?

8. Why do corporations have to calculate their E&P for tax purposes?

9. What is the starting point for determining a corporation's E&P for tax purposes?

10. When may a corporation be treated as having paid a constructive dividend?

11. Why was the concept of a constructive dividend developed?

12. Pegboard Hooks distributes one share of its common stock to the holder of each of its outstanding shares of common stock. How is the distribution taxed?

13. Industry Leaders has two classes of common stock, Class A and Class B. On January 1, 2015, Industry Leaders distributes one share of Class A common stock to the owner of each outstanding share of Class A stock. On October 15, 2017, the company distributes a cash dividend of $1 per share to the owner of each share of Class B stock. How is each distribution taxed?

14. How does payment of a dividend affect a corporation's taxable income?

15. How does a payment of a dividend affect a corporation's E&P for tax purposes?

16. Why can a corporation's net income for financial accounting purposes differ from its taxable income?

17. What is meant by a "timing difference" in the reporting of income and expenses for financial accounting and tax accounting?

18. What is meant by a "permanent difference" in the reporting of income and expenses for financial accounting and tax accounting?

19. What is Schedule M-1, and who must complete it?

20. What is Schedule M-2, and who must complete it?

Chapter 12 Problems

1. Lamonte Absorbents has two shareholders, each of whom owns an equal share in the corporation. Lamonte has $50,000 in accumulated and current E&P. During the year it distributes $5,000 in cash to one shareholder and property with an adjusted basis of $2,000 and a FMV of $5,000 to its other shareholder. What amount of its distribution constitutes a dividend?

2. A U.S. corporation distributes $80 in cash to the owner of each of its shares. Of that $80, $60 is distributed from the corporation's current or accumulated E&P. If Sheila Pano owns 100 shares, each with an adjusted basis of $80, how is she taxed on the distribution?

3. Assume the same facts as in Problem 2, except Tommie Mu owns 150 shares of stock, each with an adjusted basis of $15. How is he taxed on the distribution?

4. A calendar year corporation has a $10,000 deficit (negative) E&P at the beginning of the year. During the year, the company's E&P is $8,000. On November 30, it distributes $5,000 to its shareholders. How much of the distribution is treated as a dividend? How much is treated as a return of capital?

5. A calendar year corporation has current year E&P of $15,000 and accumulated E&P of $10,000. It distributes $30,000 to its shareholders during the year. The $30,000 was

distributed as follows: $10,000 on April 1 and $20,000 on December 1. How much of each distribution is treated as a dividend, and how much is treated as a return of capital?

6. At the beginning of its calendar tax year a corporation has $10,000 in accumulated E&P. During the year, it reports negative E&P of $18,250. On April 30, the company distributes $10,000. How much of the distribution is treated as a dividend, and how much is treated as a return of capital?

7. Assume the same facts as in Problem 6, except the corporation made an additional distribution of $2,000 on May 10. How much of the distribution is treated as a dividend, and how much is treated as a return of capital?

8. A calendar year corporation has $4,000 of accumulated E&P at the beginning of the year. Its current year E&P is $10,000. On June 30, the corporation distributes $15,000 to the owners of its common stock. How is the distribution taxed?

9. Broc Exercise Equipment distributes $500 in cash and an elliptical exerciser with an FMV of $600 to one of its shareholders. Broc's adjusted basis in the exerciser is $100. What is the amount of the distribution?

10. Riven Printing distributes $5,000 cash and 100 shares of its stock (with an FMV of $4,000) to its sole shareholder, Roman Riven, who agreed as part of the distribution to assume a $5,000 loan obtained by the corporation. What is the amount of the distribution?

11. A corporation has taxable income of $50,000. The company received $1,000 of tax-exempt interest and made $2,000 of charitable contributions in excess of the deduction limit. It also paid federal income taxes of $7,500. Based on these facts, what is the corporation's E&P for tax purposes for the year?

12. A corporation has taxable income of $100,000. During the year it makes an installment sale of equipment and includes $5,000 of its $20,000 gain in its taxable income. During the year it paid $10,000 in meal and entertainment expenses that it could not deduct from its taxable income and incurred federal income taxes of $22,250. At the end of the year, the company paid a $20,000 dividend to its shareholders. Based on these facts, what is the corporation's current year E&P?

13. Abel Blackhurst owns 100 shares of common stock in his mother's company, Blackhurst Machines. His adjusted basis in the shares is $4,500. The company distributes to each of its shareholders one share of common stock for every two the shareholder owns. Abel is issued another 50 shares of common stock. The common stock had an FMV of $60 per share at the time of the distribution. What is Abel's basis in the 50 shares distributed to him and in the 100 shares he already owned?

14. Elijah Soro owns 100 shares of common stock, each with an adjusted basis of $40, in Dowe Magazine Racks. Dowe distributes one share of common stock for every 10 shares of common stock a shareholder owns. On the date of the distribution, each share of the common stock had an FMV of $50. What is Elijah's adjusted basis in his stock?

15. Kady Switches distributes one share of preferred stock to the owner of each share of its Class A common stock and one share of common stock to the owner of each share of its Class B common stock. Each share of preferred stock had an FMV of $40 on the date of the distribution, and each share of common stock had an FMV of $30 on the date of the distribution. Aubrey Kady receives 100 shares of common stock. The FMV of the common and preferred stock distributed did not exceed the corporation's accumulated and current E&P. How is Aubrey taxed on the distribution?

16. Sage Paper sells land with an adjusted basis of $150,000 for $300,000. Payment of the purchase price is to be made over five years, with the first payment due the year after the sale. How much income does the company have to include in its net income, and how much income does the company have to include in its taxable income for the year of the sale?

17. One of a corporation's motor vehicles is destroyed in a casualty, and the corporation reinvests the insurance proceeds in another motor vehicle during the same year as the

casualty. Its basis in the destroyed motor vehicle was $0 for income tax purposes and $18,000 for financial accounting purposes; the insurance proceeds were $20,000. How does this event affect the corporation's net income and taxable income?

18. A corporation incurs $15,000 in federal income tax for the year. It incurs $1,000 in expenses with respect to tax-exempt income and pays $3,000 in premiums on a life insurance policy that names the corporation as the beneficiary. How do these expenditures affect its net income for financial accounting purposes and taxable income?

19. On January 1, 2015, Hansbrough Corporation has unappropriated retained earnings per its books of $980,000. During the year, it reports net income of $411,300 and taxable income on its tax return of $380,000. On the tax return, it shows a dividends received deduction of $120,000. Federal income taxes for the year were $129,200. Because Hansbrough took accelerated depreciation deductions on its machinery, its taxable income included $5,000 more in gain from the sale of the machinery than its net income included. The corporation's tax depreciation exceeds its book depreciation by $32,000.

During the year, the corporation received $25,000 in tax-exempt interest and paid $9,500 in interest on a loan obtained to purchase the tax-exempt bonds. The corporation also received $10,000 from a life insurance policy naming the corporation as the beneficiary. These three items are reflected in net income but not in taxable income. The corporation made charitable contributions that exceeded the 10-percent limitation by $12,000.

During 2015, Hansbrough paid a cash dividend of $120,000 and transferred $300,000 from its unappropriated retained earnings per books to its appropriated retained earnings per books to cover an unsettled tort claim. Using this information, complete Schedule M-1 for the corporation.

20. Assume the same facts as in Problem 19. Complete Schedule M-2 for the corporation. What are the corporation's unappropriated retained earnings per books as of December 31, 2015?

21. At the beginning of its 2016 tax year, Harness Hostels, Inc. had $10,000 in accumulated earnings and profits. Its earnings and profits for the year were a negative $32,850. On January 31, 2016, the company distributed $10,000 to its two shareholders, Billy Harness and his sister Tawny Harness, who each owned 50 percent of the corporation. Billy's adjusted basis in his shares was $6,000. How is he taxed on the distribution?

22. The facts are the same as in Problem 21 except that the distribution was made on April 30. How is Billy taxed on the distribution?

23. Warden Communications, Inc. permitted its sole shareholder, Mabel Warden, to use one of its hospitality suites free of charge. The hospitality suite had a fair rental value of $150 a day, and Mabel used it for 50 days during the year. The company had $15,000 in earnings and profits for its current year and $50,000 in accumulated earnings and profits. Mabel received a cash distribution of $10,000 during the year. If her adjusted basis in her stock is $15,000, how will she be taxed on amounts she received during the year from the corporation?

24. Bourn Office Furniture, Inc. offered its shareholders the option of receiving one share of its stock for each share that they currently owned or the fair market value of such shares ($25 per share). Dean Bourn chose to receive 100 shares. What amount of taxable distribution, if any, did he receive?

25. Allgood Textiles, Inc. started the year with $200,000 in accumulated earnings and profits. During the year, it earned $75,000 from its business operations, received a $2,000 federal income tax refund, received a $10,000 contribution to capital from its shareholders, paid $13,750 in federal income taxes, and could not deduct $1,000 of its meal expenses. What is the amount of its accumulated earnings and profits at the end of the year?

Chapter 12 Review Problems

1. Bauk Printing uses the calendar year. Bauk purchases a digital printer for $140,000 and places it in service on April 1, 2015. The company estimates that the digital printer will have a useful life of 10 years and no salvage value. If it uses MACRS and the half-year convention to compute its depreciation deduction, how will the purchase affect its net income and its taxable income in 2015? In 2019?

2. Desmond Photocopying and Supplies, Inc. exchanges an old photocopying machine (with an adjusted basis of $0 and an FMV of $5,000) plus $3,000 in cash for a new photocopying machine. Desmond's book value in the machine is $4,000. The FMV of the new machine is $8,000. How does this exchange affect the company's taxable income and its net income for financial accounting purposes for the tax year of the exchange? What is its adjusted basis in the new photocopying machine?

Chapter 12 Comprehensive Review Question

Wahlgren Reed Furniture, Inc. is an accrual method taxpayer that uses the calendar year as its tax year. Its gross sales for 2015 were $500,000, and its cost of goods sold was $150,000. In addition to its gross sales, at the end of the year it received $50,000 in advance payments for furniture to be constructed in January 2017. It received $6,000 in interest on a municipal bond, and it paid $5,000 in interest on a loan obtained to purchase the municipal bond.

In 2014, it purchased machinery with an estimated useful life of 10 years for $5,000. Wahlgren uses MACRS and the half-year conversion to depreciate the machinery. The machine has no salvage value.

Wahlgren had $6,000 of capital losses and $2,000 of capital gains for the year. Wahlgren paid $15,000 in research and experimental expenditures on October 1, 2015, and elected to amortize the expenditures over 60 months. It paid $3,000 in premiums for life insurance insuring a key employee and naming the corporation as the beneficiary. It paid $10,000 for meals and entertainment during the year. It received $20,000 in dividends from a U.S. corporation; it owned five percent of the stock of that corporation. Its qualified production activities income was $250,000. (Assume that Wahlgren has sufficient W-2 wages to take the full amount of the deduction based on the applicable percentage for 2015.) Based on these facts, what are its net income and taxable income for the year?

Chapter 12 Research Question

Tashia Dux is the sole shareholder of Dux Digital Cameras. Her daughter Elena is the sole shareholder of Dux Photographic Lenses. Dux Digital Cameras loans Dux Photographic Lenses $100,000 to help Dux Photographic Lenses develop a new lens that Dux Digital Cameras could use for its cameras. No interest was payable on the loan, no security was provided, and no repayments were scheduled. Has Dux Digital Cameras paid a constructive dividend? See *R. Fenn, Jr.*, 40 TCM 559, Dec. 37,040(M), TC Memo. 1980-229.

CHAPTER 13

Sole Proprietorships, Partnerships, LLPs, and LLCs

CHAPTER CONTENTS

LEARNING OBJECTIVES

1. Learn about the differences in how incorporated and unincorporated businesses are taxed.

2. Understand which business deductions reduce a sole proprietor's income taxes.

3. Understand the concept of self-employment taxes.

4. List the tax and nontax aspects of flow-through entities.

5. Describe how a partnership is formed and the tax implications to both the partnership and its partners when property is contributed to the partnership.

6. Illustrate the tax consequences of partnership operations and the allocation of income and deductions to the partners.

7. Distinguish between a partner's capital account and the partner's tax basis in the partnership interest and demonstrate how each is calculated.

8. Describe limited liability companies and explain how those entities are treated for tax purposes.

¶ 1300 Introduction

Sole proprietorships are a popular form of doing business, especially among owners just starting a new business. The popularity of forming a business as a sole proprietorship stems, in large part, to the lack of the formality that other types of business entities require. Sole proprietorships involve businesses with a single owner. However, unlike shareholders of a corporation that enjoy limited liability from the activities of the corporation, owners of a sole proprietorship are generally liable for both the contractual debts incurred by the business plus any liabilities caused by the actions of the owners or their employees when representing the business.

As the business grows and becomes successful, there may come a point when additional funding is needed beyond what can be raised either though borrowing or from the owner's own personal assets. In these situations, the business owner may find it necessary to raise additional capital by taking in new owners. If these new owners are merely investors in the business who are interested in sharing in the profits of the business but have no interest in being involved in its day-to-day operations, then incorporating the business may make sense. By holding a majority interest in the corporation's stock, the business owner can still manage and control the direction of the business, while at the same time protecting himself or herself and the other shareholders from the liabilities of the business. Unfortunately, incorporation comes at a steep price, as the profits of an incorporated business that operates as a C corporation are subject to double taxation.

Business owners that wish to avoid being taxed twice on the business's profits may consider operating the business either as a partnership or as an S corporation. These business entities are called flow-through entities because the business entity does not pay tax on the profits it generates, but instead its profits "flow through" to the owners. Although a flow-through entity does not pay tax, it is required to file an annual income tax return that summarizes the business's gross income, deductions, gains, losses, and credits for the year and provides both the IRS and the owners with information regarding the items and amounts to be reported on the owners' respective income tax returns. S corporations are the focus of Chapter 14. This chapter discusses the tax laws that govern income taxation of partnerships.

A partnership is a business entity with at least two owners (partners). Tax laws unique to partnerships include: (1) the tax consequences of forming the partnership; (2) the reporting of business operations, including the allocation of partnership profits and losses to the partners; and (3) making sure that the partnership items of income, gain, deduction, and loss are taxed one time. These areas are the focus of discussion for this chapter. The rules discussed in this chapter also pertain to limited liability partnerships (LLPs) and limited liability companies (LLCs) that choose to be taxed as partnerships. LLCs and LLPs are governed under the state laws of the states in which they are formed. Although the Internal Revenue Code (the "Code") does not specifically recognize these two business entities, the federal government now allows LLPs and LLCs to be taxed as partnerships using the partnership rules discussed in this chapter.

This chapter begins with a discussion of the similarities and differences of sole proprietorships to a corporation. Then it will present how the income and expenses of a sole proprietorship are reported on the tax return. The chapter will then show an overview of the taxation of partnerships and their partners. In the overview, the tax concerns of forming and operating a partnership are introduced. The chapter continues with a discussion of these issues and concludes with a discussion of LLCs and LLPs.

¶ 1301 Sole Proprietorship vs. a Corporation

Unlike a corporation, which is a separate business entity for tax purposes, the activities of a sole proprietorship are reported on the owner's individual income tax return. Consequently, the income, deductions, gains, and losses from the sole proprietorship are included among the owner's personal items of income, deduction, gain, and loss in calculating the owner's taxable income. Furthermore, individual tax rates are used to compute the sole proprietor's tax liability. Although the tax rates for individuals are also progressive, they vary depending on the taxpayer's filing status.

Like corporations, individuals may be subject to alternative minimum tax (AMT); however, because taxable income is calculated differently for individuals and corporations, so too is AMT. Like corporations, a variety of tax credits are available to individuals to reduce their regular and AMT income tax liabilities. However, in addition to the business credits and the foreign tax credit described in Chapter 11, many personal tax credits are available to individual taxpayers. Most personal credits are nonrefundable, but some can create a refund when the amount of the credit exceeds the individual's tax liability.

The most important distinguishing feature of a business operated as a sole proprietorship is the owner's responsibility for both the employer and employee portions of FICA taxes on any profits generated by the business. These amounts, known as self-employment taxes when paid by sole proprietors, are reported directly on the owners' individual tax returns and are added to their regular income tax liabilities. The calculation of self-employment tax begins with computing net profit or loss from the business. Although most of the business income, deductions, gains, and losses discussed in Chapters 4 through 9 are reflected on the sole proprietor's income tax return, some of these amounts are not part of the calculation of net profit from the business but are reported elsewhere on the individual's income tax return.

As with corporations, the owners of sole proprietorships must select a method of accounting for the business. Sole proprietors can use either the cash or accrual method and have the option of selecting different accounting methods if they have multiple businesses. Generally, the cash method requires that income be reported in the tax year it is actually or constructively received and deductions be taken in the tax year in which they are paid (see ¶ 306). The accrual method generally requires that income be taxed in the period in which the business has the right to receive it, and deductions be taken in the year in which they are incurred (see ¶ 307). For businesses where inventory is a material income producing item, the tax laws require that sole proprietors use the accrual method of accounting for sales and the cost of goods sold of the business, but allows them to use the cash method for other items of income and deduction for the business. The combined use of these two methods is referred to as the hybrid method of accounting (see ¶ 309).

.01 Certain Business-Related Expenses Not Deductible as Business Expenses

Every business, whether operated as a corporation, partnership, or sole proprietorship, incurs expenses in the normal process of generating profits. For the most part, the deductions discussed in Chapters 5 through 9 are available to all business entities, including sole proprietorships. When a business is operated as a corporation, there is usually little doubt that all expenses relate to business activities. However, when a business is operated as a sole proprietorship, it becomes important that proprietors keep their business activities separate and distinct from their personal activities to avoid any confusion as to what is a valid business expense versus a nondeductible personal expense.

Certain items reported by individual taxpayers on the individual tax return are automatically considered personal expenses. For example, charitable contributions are always considered a personal expense, as are state, local, and foreign income taxes an individual pays during the year. Fortunately, the tax laws allow these expenses to be deducted as itemized deductions, so the tax benefits are not necessarily lost. However, because these amounts cannot be used in the computation of net profit or loss from the business, they do not reduce the owner's self-employment taxes. Furthermore, since itemized deductions are only deductible if the total of all itemized deductions exceeds the standard deduction amount, the possibility exists that some, if not all, of the tax benefits associated with these expenses could be lost.

Example 1: Bev Thomas operates a sole proprietorship business. During 2015, Bev generates $100,000 of business income and $30,000 of deductible business expenses. Also during 2015, Bev donates $10,000 to a local charity from her business checking account.

Because Bev's business is operated as a sole proprietorship, the $10,000 charitable contribution is deducted as an itemized deduction. Assuming Bev's other itemized deductions exceeded the standard deduction amount, the full $10,000 will reduce Bev's taxable income; however, her self-employment taxes will be based on the $70,000 ($100,000 – $30,000) of net profit from her business that is included in AGI. If the charitable contribution was Bev's only itemized deduction and she was a single taxpayer, the additional tax deduction resulting from her charitable contribution would be $3,700, which is the amount by which the $10,000 charitable contribution exceeds her $6,300 standard deduction amount for 2015.

Deficiency interest. When errors are subsequently discovered in the calculation of taxes owed to the government, the IRS charges interest on the back taxes owed. This interest, referred to as "deficiency interest," is normally deductible if assessed as a result of an income tax deficiency arising from business activities (see ¶ 505.01). Thus, when a corporation pays deficiency interest, it is deducted against its business profits. However, when deficiency interest is imposed on an individual taxpayer, the interest is always considered nondeductible personal interest, even when the deficiency stems from errors made in computing net profits from a sole proprietor's business.[1] Unfortunately, this is one area of the tax law where operating a business as a sole proprietorship has its disadvantages.

Example 2: A business makes an error in computing its 2013 taxable income. The error is discovered early in 2015 and results in an additional $50,000 of taxes owed. The IRS charges $14,000 of interest on the back taxes, which the business pays in 2015. If the business is operated as a corporation, the $14,000 would be deducted as interest expense on the 2015 corporate tax return. Assuming the corporation is in the 34-percent tax bracket, the corporation reduces its taxes that year by $4,760 ($14,000 × 34%), and the true cost to the corporation for the interest charged is $9,240 ($14,000 – $4,760). If the business is operated as a sole proprietorship, the $14,000 is nondeductible personal interest, and, therefore, the true cost to the business for the interest charged is the full $14,000.

Hobby activities. In order to deduct expenses paid or incurred in carrying on a trade or business, it goes without saying that the taxpayer must already be carrying on a trade or business. Unless the facts and circumstances indicate that a taxpayer entered into or continued the activity with the objective of making a profit, it is considered an activity not engaged in for profit, or what is commonly referred to as a hobby.

The tax consequences of having an activity treated as a hobby can be quite severe. First, any income that the activity generates is included in the individual's gross income under the Code's all-inclusive approach to defining income. Second, expenses related to the activity are limited to the amount of gross income from the hobby activity, and any excess expenses cannot be carried over to any other tax year. Third, the deductible expenses are treated as miscellaneous itemized deductions subject to the two-percent AGI floor.[2]

Example 3: John Baron is a professional musician who also raises Black Angus cattle. John's AGI from sources other than the cattle activity is $50,000. During the year, John paid $1,500 for feed for the cattle and raised $1,000 from the sale of cattle. If the activity is deemed a business, the entire $1,500 would be deductible against the $1,000, and John's AGI would decrease to $49,500 ($50,000 + $1,000 – $1,500). However, if the activity is considered a hobby, John's expenses would be limited to $1,000 and would be deductible as miscellaneous itemized deductions that are subject to the two-percent AGI floor. However, the $1,000 from the sale of the cattle would be included in John's gross income, causing his AGI to increase to $51,000.

---

[1] Temp. Reg. § 1.163-9T.   [2] Code Sec. 183.

The tax laws presume that if an activity generates a profit in any three of five consecutive years, it is one that has a profit motive and as such, the IRS has the burden of proving that the activity is instead a hobby.[3] Activities that fail to generate a profit during any three of five consecutive years will automatically be considered a hobby and the burden of proving that the activity is actually a business rests with the taxpayer. (The time frame for generating a profit is two of seven years for activities related to horse racing and breeding.) Although the party with the burden of proof often has the more difficult task, it does not mean that it cannot be done. The Tax Court held in one case that despite 12 consecutive years of losses, the taxpayers established a profit motive in connection with the operation of their ski lodge.[4] A list of nine factors the courts use in making its determination of whether an activity should be treated as a business or as a hobby are listed below.[5]

1. The manner in which the taxpayer carried on the activity,

2. The expertise of the taxpayer or the taxpayer's advisors,

3. The time and effort expended by the taxpayer in carrying on the activity,

4. The expectation that assets used in the activity may appreciate in value,

5. The success of the taxpayer in carrying on other similar or dissimilar activities,

6. The taxpayer's history of income or loss with respect to the activity,

7. The amount of occasional profit, if any, which is earned,

8. The financial status of the taxpayer, and

9. Whether elements of personal pleasure or recreation are involved.

 Reason for the Rule: In almost all income tax matters, the burden of proof rests with the taxpayer claiming the exclusion, deduction, or tax credit, so normally the burden of proving that an activity was entered into for a profit motive would rest with the taxpayer. However, Congress realized that many businesses struggle to earn a profit during the first few years, and it wanted to give businesses a few years to "get on their feet" before judging whether the activity was entered into for a profit motive. Although any activity can generate profits, only those considered to be business endeavors can use business expenses to offset the income generated from the activity. Nonetheless, when an activity generates profits in any three of five consecutive years, the tax laws shift the burden of proof over to the IRS to prove that the activity is not a business endeavor.

 Spotlight: Because many hobbies generate some income and may occasionally turn a profit, it is not always easy to distinguish a business from a hobby. Some activities, such as raising cattle or horse breeding, can be either. Therefore, the determination must be made on a case-by-case basis. Two Tax Court decisions involving similar fact situations resulted in different outcomes. In one case, the Tax Court held that one horse breeding venture was operated for profit,[6] and, in the other, it held that no profit motive existed.[7]

.02 Expenses Paid or Incurred in Carrying on a Trade or Business

Assuming an activity is considered a trade or business, business profit or loss will be added to gross income. If there is income from business, then gross income will increase, thus also increasing the AGI. The reverse is also true. If there is a loss from business, gross income will decrease and consequently AGI will decrease. As previously mentioned, certain business-related expenses may be deducted from the gross income to arrive at AGI (thus, called above the line deductions). However, losses on the sale of business property and certain expenses sole proprietors

---

[3] Code Sec. 183(d).

[4] *T. Allen*, 72 TC 28, Dec. 35,977 (1979).

[5] Reg. § 1.183-2(b); *L.D. Boyer*, 69 TC 521, Dec. 34,900 (1977).

[6] *T. Engdahl*, 72 TC 659, Dec. 36,167 (1979).

[7] *S. Golanty*, 72 TC 411, Dec. 36,111 (1979).

pay or incur on their own behalf are not part of the calculation of net profit or loss from the business. The tax laws regarding these items are discussed later on in the chapter. The remainder of this section focuses on some special rules that pertain to the expenses that sole proprietors deduct in the calculation of net profit of loss from their businesses.

Schedule C. Net profits from a sole proprietorship are computed on Schedule C, *Profit or Loss from Business*. This profit or loss is transferred to page 1 of the owner's Form 1040 and included in the calculation of the owner's total income. Any net profit from Schedule C is also transferred to Schedule SE, *Self-Employment Tax*, and becomes the starting point for calculating the sole proprietor's self-employment taxes for the year. A list of business expenses that sole proprietors deduct against business profits on Schedule C is shown in Figure 13-1.

Figure 13-1 List of Business Expenses Deducted on Schedule C

- Advertising,
- Car and truck expenses,
- Commissions and fees,
- Contract labor costs,
- Contributions to employees' benefit plans,
- Depletion,
- Depreciation, amortization, and Section 179 expense deduction,
- Employee benefit programs,
- Insurance (other than health),
- Interest,
- Legal and professional services,
- Meals and entertainment (subject to a 50-percent limitation),
- Office expense,
- Rent,
- Repairs and maintenance,
- Supplies,
- Travel,
- Utilities,
- Wages (less employment tax credits), and
- Other expenses (education, dues, etc.).

As the list in Figure 13-1 shows, many of the expenses discussed in Chapters 5 through 7 are reported on Schedule C. For example, advertising, interest, taxes, rent, and wage expense are each listed as deductions against gross income from the business, along with many other business expenses. Amounts sole proprietors pay for employee benefit programs (such as health care coverage) and contributions to pension and profit-sharing plans are reported on Schedule C. Note, however, that only amounts they pay on behalf of their employees can be deducted against business income. Contributions owners make to their own retirement plans, and premiums they pay for their own health care coverage are above the line deductions on Form 1040.

Example 4: Jay Reynolds operates his business as a sole proprietorship. The business earns gross income of $100,000 during the year before considering the following expenses.

Advertising	$ 5,000
Rent	6,700
Contributions to employees' retirement plans	1,760
Contributions to Jay's retirement plan	2,640
Employee benefits (health insurance for employees)	8,500
Jay's health insurance premiums	6,000
Charitable contributions	1,000
Wages paid to employees	30,000
Payroll taxes	3,600
Total business expenses	**$65,200**

Because Jay operates his business as a sole proprietorship, he deducts the charitable contributions as an itemized deduction. He deducts the contributions made to his own retirement plan and amounts paid for his own health insurance premiums for AGI, but cannot use these amounts to calculate the profits from his business. Jay's net profit from his business will be computed on Schedule C as follows.

Gross income from the business		$100,000
Business expenses:		
Advertising	$ 5,000	
Rent	6,700	
Employees' retirement plan contributions	1,760	
Employee benefits	8,500	
Wages paid to employees	30,000	
Payroll taxes	3,600	(55,560)
Net profit from the business		$ 44,440

Jay will include the $44,440 net profit from his business in his gross income. He will then deduct for AGI the $2,640 contributions he made to his own retirement plan and the $6,000 of premiums he paid for his own health insurance. Jay also will be able to deduct the employer's share (one-half) of the self-employment taxes for AGI. Jay calculates his self-employment tax using the $44,440 of profits from his business.

In contrast, if Jay operated the business as a corporation, the entire $65,200 of business expenses would have been deducted against business profits. In addition, any wages paid to Jay as an employee (plus the employment taxes assessed on those wages) would be deducted by the corporation. The corporation would also withhold social security and Medicare taxes on wages paid to Jay.

Although the tax laws that apply to most deductions are the same for all business entities, because the activities of businesses operated as sole proprietorships are reported on the owner's individual tax return, some additional rules may apply. These rules are the focus of the discussion that follows.

Bad debts. An individual can have a business bad debt if the nature of the loan is related to the sole proprietor's business.[8] As with all other business entities, business bad debts of a sole proprietorship are deductible against the income from the business. Business bad debts generally result from credit sales of goods or services to customers, as well as loans to suppliers, clients,

---

[8] Code Sec. 165; Reg. § 1.166-5(b).

employees, or distributors. Sole proprietors who use the cash method for their business activities cannot deduct a bad debt for uncollectible accounts receivable since those amounts were never included in gross income.

Example 5: Arthur Nelson is an attorney who reports his business activities using the cash method. During 2015, Arthur bills a client for $10,000 who subsequently files for bankruptcy and has the entire debt discharged in 2016. As a cash basis taxpayer, Arthur does not report any income during 2015 when the invoice is sent and will not be entitled to a bad debt deduction when the debt is discharged by the bankruptcy court in 2016.

Example 6: Referring to Example 5, if Arthur reports his income using the accrual method of accounting, he would report the $10,000 as income for 2015 when the income was earned and then be entitled to a bad debt deduction during 2016 when the debt is discharged.

A business bad debt is one that is closely related to a taxpayer's trade or business. A nonbusiness bad debt is a debt which comes about from a debt incurred or acquired in some manner other than through a trade or business (see ¶ 510). When a sole proprietor loans money to friends or relatives for use in their respective businesses, the loan still constitutes a nonbusiness loan to the sole proprietor. When a nonbusiness bad debt becomes worthless, the loss will be recognized as a short-term capital loss.[9] Individual taxpayers can deduct capital losses to the extent of any capital gains included in gross income plus $3,000[10] (see ¶ 901.01).

Example 7: Jan Russell makes a *bona fide* loan to a friend for $10,000 so that her friend can start her own business. The friend later files for bankruptcy. In the year that the loan becomes worthless, Jan would be entitled to a nonbusiness bad debt deduction. Assuming Jan has no other capital gains or losses in that year, her loss deduction would be limited to $3,000 and the remaining $7,000 would carry forward to the next tax years.

Transportation expense. Sole proprietors who use their personal automobile for business can deduct the business portion of their automobile expenses from business income on Schedule C. As discussed in Chapter 6, the owner's transportation expense deduction can be computed using either the actual expense method or the standard mileage rate ($.575 per mile in 2015).[11] Any business-related parking and tolls also can be deducted. Sole proprietors have the option of using the standard mileage rate to reimburse their employees as well as to deduct amounts for the business use of their own personal automobiles. However, the actual method must be used by sole proprietors who use five or more automobiles simultaneously for business[12] (see ¶ 607.01).

Example 8: John Harris is a self-employed attorney who used his personal automobile for travel between his office and the courthouse. For 2015, John properly documents the 10,000 business-related miles his automobile was driven during the year. The total miles during the year were 15,000 miles. John's actual operating expenses include $7,600 for gas, oil, insurance, repairs, maintenance, and depreciation, plus $500 for business-related parking and tolls. Because John used his automobile 66.67 percent of the time for business (10,000/15,000), he is allowed to deduct $5,567 (($7,600 × 66.67%) + $500) against his business income on Schedule C. Had John elected to use the standard mileage rate, his deduction would have been $6,250 ((10,000 × $.575) + $500).

 Spotlight: The Internal Revenue Service (IRS) released Notice 2014-79 establishing the optional standard mileage rates effective January 1, 2015, at 57.5 cents per mile for

---

[9] Code Sec. 166(d)(1)(B).
[10] Code Sec. 1211.

[11] Notice 2014-79, IRB 2014-53, December 10, 2014.
[12] Notice 2014-79, IRB 2014-53, December 10, 2014.

> business miles driven. The rate is established based upon a study of the fixed and variable costs of operating an automobile. Thus, while the price of gasoline is a significant factor in the mileage rate, other operating costs are included in the calculation which can be a moderating factor when considering volatile gasoline prices.[13]

Depreciation and Section 179 expense. The rules for calculating depreciation from Chapter 7 apply to all business entities, including sole proprietorships. Individuals starting out a business may find it financially beneficial to take their own personal assets and convert them into business property. When personal-use property, such as part of the owner's home or the owner's personal automobile or furniture, is converted to business use, the amount that can be depreciated is the *lesser* of the property's fair market value (FMV) on the date of the conversion or its adjusted basis.[14]

Example 9: Alan Landon operates a sole proprietorship. On June 15, 2015, Alan decides to convert his SUV from personal use to business use. The SUV cost Alan $42,000 when he acquired it in 2014. On June 15, 2015, the SUV had a FMV of $36,000. Alan can depreciate the SUV using a $36,000 depreciable basis.

Another issue unique to businesses operated as sole proprietorships is the owner's use of listed property. **Listed property** is property that is easily used for both business and personal use, and includes automobiles, computers, and peripheral equipment. When listed property is not used more than 50 percent of the time for business, the tax laws prohibit the taxpayer from taking Section 179 or accelerated depreciation on the business use of the property.[15] Thus, listed property that is not used primarily for business must be depreciated using the alternative depreciation system (ADS). Recall from Chapter 7 that ADS uses the straight-line method of depreciation over slightly longer recovery periods. See Table 7-2 at ¶ 702.

Also recall from Chapter 7 that depreciation expense taken on an automobile is subject to annual limits. The amounts provided in Table 7G (see ¶ 726) represent the limits for automobiles used 100 percent for business. For purposes of depreciating automobiles used less than 100 percent for business, the luxury automobile limits from the table must be reduced to reflect the portion of business use during the year.

Example 10: Joanne Smith operates her business as a sole proprietorship. During 2014, Joanne acquires a new automobile for $14,000 and uses it 40 percent of the time for business. The half-year convention applies. Since the business use percentage for the automobile does not exceed 50 percent, Joanne uses Table 7F from Chapter 7 to depreciate her automobile using ADS over a five-year recovery period. The maximum depreciation allowed in 2014 for an automobile used 40 percent for business is $1,184 ($2,960 × 40%). Since Joanne's ADS depreciation deduction of $560 ($14,000 × 40% business use × 10% ADS first year recovery rate) does not exceed $1,184, she can deduct $560 on her Schedule C.

Example 11: Assume the same facts in Example 10, except that the business use percentage of the automobile is 80 percent. Joanne would be entitled to use regular (accelerated) MACRS to depreciate the automobile. She uses the recovery percentages from the column for 5-year property in Table 7-3 at ¶ 702 to compute the MACRS depreciation deduction on the automobile of $2,240 ($14,000 × 80% × 20%). Since this amount does not exceed 80 percent of the first year limit for luxury automobiles placed in service during 2014 ($2,960 × 80% = $2,368), Joanne would deduct $2,240 for depreciation expense on her Schedule C in 2014.

---

[13] Notice 2014-79, IRB 2014-53, December 10, 2014
[14] Reg. § 1.167(g)-1 and Reg. § 1.168(i)-4(b).

[15] Code Secs. 280F and 179; Temp. Reg. §§ 1.280F-1T–1.280F-6T.

In determining whether listed property is used primarily for business, for transportation vehicles, usage should be based on mileage driven during the year. For other types of listed property, hours used during the year is appropriate. If listed property originally used primarily for business is later used 50 percent or less of the time for business, then any depreciation taken over the years in excess of what would have been allowed under ADS must be included in gross income in the year the property is no longer used primarily for business.

Example 12: Continuing with Example 11, if Joanne's business use drops to 40 percent in 2015, she would be required to begin depreciating the 40 percent business use using ADS starting in 2015. In addition, she would be required to go back and recalculate what her depreciation deduction would have been had she elected to use ADS on the 80-percent business use in 2014 and recapture the excess of the amount she deducted ($2,240) and the amount that would have been allowed under ADS. She adds this excess to her income reported on Schedule C in 2015.

Interest and taxes. Most of the rules discussed in Chapter 5 with respect to the deduction for interest and taxes also apply to sole proprietorships and are deducted on Schedule C. However, any interest an individual taxpayer pays on a tax deficiency, even one that stems from mistakes made on Schedule C, represents nondeductible personal interest. Also, any state, local, or foreign income taxes paid by an individual are considered personal taxes; however, these taxes can be deducted as itemized deductions on the individual's tax return. Federal income taxes are not deductible by any taxpayer or business entity, including sole proprietors and individuals. Individuals, like all taxpayers, can chose to take a foreign tax credit in lieu of a deduction for any foreign income taxes paid during the year. The rules discussed in Chapter 11 regarding the limits that apply to the foreign tax credit apply to individual taxpayers as well as corporate taxpayers.

Example 13: A business generates profits totaling $30,000 during the year. The state in which the business operates taxes profits at a rate of six percent. Accordingly, $1,800 ($30,000 × 6%) is paid to the state government for state income taxes. If the business is operated as a corporation, then the $1,800 is deducted in computing corporate taxable income in the year the taxes are paid. If the corporation is in the 25-percent tax bracket, the corporation's tax liability is reduced by $450 ($1,800 × 25%) as a result of the deduction. Alternatively, if the business is operated as a sole proprietorship, then the owner deducts the $1,800 of taxes as an itemized deduction in the year the taxes are paid. If the taxpayer's itemized deductions do not exceed the standard deduction amount, then no tax benefit will be derived from this deduction. Furthermore, the $1,800 cannot reduce business profits on Schedule C and, therefore, will not reduce the owner's self-employment taxes owed on business profits.

Home office deduction. Sole proprietors that rent office space can deduct amounts they pay to their landlords as rent expense on Schedule C. As another option, sole proprietors can convert a part of their personal residences into an office and use it regularly and exclusively for business. They can then deduct the costs associated with that part of their home on Schedule C against the gross income from the business,[16] including a portion of any home mortgage interest, real estate taxes, and utilities paid during the year. They also can deduct depreciation on the portion of the taxpayer's home that represents an office. Although residences are considered residential realty, the portion of the home that is being depreciated is an office, and, as such, the home office is nonresidential realty that must be depreciated over 39 years under MACRS.[17] Furthermore, since the office is personal property being converted to business use, the depreciable basis for the office is the lesser of the FMV of the home or its adjusted basis at the time it is converted to an office, multiplied by the percentage of the square footage of the home that represents the home office.

---

[16] Code Sec. 280A(c)(1).

[17] Code Secs. 168(b)(3)(A), 168(c), and 168(d)(2).

Spotlight: For tax years starting on, or after, January 1, 2013 (filed beginning in 2014), a sole proprietor may now have a simpler option for computing the business use of his or her home.[18] This new simplified option can significantly reduce recordkeeping burden by allowing a qualified taxpayer to multiply a prescribed rate by the allowable square footage of the office in lieu of determining actual expenses. Standard deduction of $5 per square foot of home used for business (maximum 300 square feet) will be used to calculate home office deduction.

Example 14: Tony Johnson operates a business as a sole proprietorship. On March 2, 2015, Tony converts one of his bedrooms into a home office. The size of the bedroom is 196 square feet; his entire home is 2,000 square feet. Tony purchased the home in 1995 for $130,000, and at the time he converted the space to an office, it was worth $200,000. Of these amounts, $20,000 is associated with the costs of the land. On his 2015 tax return, Tony will deduct 9.8 percent (196/2,000) of the expenses related to his home, including his mortgage interest, real estate taxes, utilities, and insurance as business expenses. Tony also will be able to depreciate 9.8 percent of the $110,000 basis in his home (the *lesser* of (1) $130,000 minus $20,000 for the land, or (2) $200,000 minus $20,000) over 39 years starting on March 15, 2015, under the mid-month convention.

Individual taxpayers deduct home mortgage interest and real estate taxes as itemized deductions. Thus, the portion of these amounts they deduct as home office expenses cannot be deducted as itemized deductions. Also, the tax law does not allow home office expenses, other than for mortgage interest, real estate taxes, and casualty losses, to generate a loss from the business. Any amounts not deductible in the current tax year due to this limitation can be carried over to subsequent tax years and deducted as home office expenses when the sole proprietor generates enough profits to cover these amounts.[19]

Example 15: Continuing with Example 14, assume that in 2015, Tony's home mortgage interest and real estate taxes are $8,400 and $2,200, respectively. Tony will be able to deduct $823 ($8,400 × 9.8%) and $216 ($2,200 × 9.8%), respectively, on Schedule C to offset his business profits. He can then deduct the remaining $7,577 ($8,400 – $823) and $1,984 ($2,200 – $216) as itemized deductions.

Example 16: Continuing with Examples 14 and 15, assume that Tony generates business income of $13,000 and has $6,000 of business expenses in 2015. After subtracting out the business portion of his mortgage interest and real estate taxes, Tony's net profits equal $5,961 ($13,000 – $6,000 – $823 – $216). Therefore, Tony's other deductible home office expenses (for utilities, insurance, depreciation, etc.) cannot exceed this amount.

Example 17: If Tony opted to use the simplified method in Example 14, he would calculate his home office deduction by multiplying 196 square feet with $5, which is $980.

.03 Other Business Expenses as Above the Line Deductions

Once net profits from the business are calculated, sole proprietors calculate the amount of self-employment taxes owed on those profits. They also can then determine the amount they are allowed to contribute and deduct to their own retirement plans.

Deduction for one-half of self-employment taxes. Self-employment taxes represent both the 7.65 percent employer and 7.65 percent employee contributions to FICA.[20] In 2015, the maximum net earnings subject to the social security portion is $118,500, whereas all net earnings from self-employment are subject to the Medicare tax.[21] Because one-half of these amounts represent the

---

[18] Rev. Proc. 2013-13, January 15, 2013.

[19] Code Sec. 280A(c)(5).

[20] Code Sec. 1401.

[21] Code Secs. 3101, 3111, and 3121.

employer's responsibility, self-employed taxpayers can deduct one-half of their self-employment taxes as an above the line deduction. If the one-half of self-employment taxes were allowed to be deducted as a business expense on Schedule C, they would reduce the amount of net profits subject to self-employment tax; however, this would create additional problems in how the tax is calculated. Therefore, the tax laws require that the one-half of self-employment taxes be deducted as an above the line deduction to arrive at AGI. However, when computing the amount of self-employment taxes owed for the year, only 92.35 percent (100 percent minus the 7.65 percent employer share of FICA taxes) of net profits from the business are subject to self-employment tax.[22] This 92.35 percent of net profits from the business is referred to as **net earnings from self-employment**. Self-employed taxpayers with at least $400 of net earnings from self-employment are subject to self-employment taxes on their earnings.[23]

Spotlight: For 2011 and 2012, the rate of the old age, survivors, and disability insurance (OASDI) tax on self-employment income is reduced by two percent, to 10.4 percent. The rate of the employee's OASDI portion of the payroll tax under Code Sec. 3101(a) is also reduced by two percent, to 4.2 percent. The employer's share of OASDI remains at 6.2 percent. However, the rate reduction is not taken into account in determining the self-employment income deduction allowed for determining the amount of the net earnings from self-employment for the tax year. Thus, the deduction for 2011 and 2012 remains at 7.65 percent of self-employment income. These rates went back to 12.4 percent and 6.2 percent for self-employment income and employee's OASDI, respectively, for 2013 and thereafter.

Example 18: Grace Williams, a sole proprietor, reports a net profit from her business of $40,000. Grace's self-employment tax is calculated below.

Net profit from the business	$40,000
	× 92.35%
Net earnings from self-employment	$36,940
Self-employment tax rate	× 15.3%
Self-employment tax	$ 5,652

When Grace files her tax return, she will add the $5,652 of self-employment taxes to her regular income taxes. In computing her taxable income and regular income tax liability, Grace's will deduct one-half of self-employment taxes ($2,826) as an above the line deduction.

Reason for the Rule: Since one-half of self-employment taxes that sole proprietors pay represent the employer's share of FICA taxes, it is appropriate that one-half of these taxes be deducted. However, since the calculation of self-employment taxes starts with net profits of the business, the calculation of the self-employment taxes becomes more complicated if the deduction for one-half of these taxes were required in determining net profits from the business. Using only 92.35 percent of these profits in the calculation of self-employment taxes attempts to solve this issue by subtracting from 100 percent of business profits the 7.65 percent of the employer's share of FICA taxes.

Since only the first $118,500 of earnings during 2015 is subject to social security taxes (otherwise known as OASDI), sole proprietors who also earn wages as an employee during the year

---

[22] Code Secs. 164(f) and 1402(a)(12).   [23] Code Secs. 1402(b)(2) and 6017.

will have already contributed towards the social security portion of FICA. Consequently, the amounts they and their employers have already contributed to FICA need to be considered in the calculation of the 12.4 percent component of self-employment tax. Accordingly, when computing the OASDI component of the self-employment tax, the 12.4 percent is applied to the *lesser* of (1) 92.35 percent of net profit from the business or (2) the excess of the maximum earnings subject to OASDI over the taxpayer's social security wages.

Example 19: Glen Smith is an employee of a construction corporation and has taxable wages subject to FICA of $64,200 in 2015. Glen also operates a sole proprietorship that generates profits totaling $50,000 during the year. Glen's self-employment tax is $7,059.

Net profit from the business	$50,000
	× 92.35%
Net earnings from self-employment	$46,175
Maximum earnings subject to OASDI	$118,500
Less: Social security wages	(64,200)
Remaining earnings subject to OASDI	$54,300
Lesser of: net earnings from self-employment or the remaining earnings subject to OASDI	$46,175
OASDI rate	× 12.4%
OASDI component of self-employment tax	$ 5,726
Net earnings from self-employment	$46,175
Medicare rate	× 2.9%
Medicare component of self-employment taxes	$ 1,339
Total self-employment tax ($5,726 + $1,339)	$ 7,065
Deduction for one-half of self-employment tax	$ 3,532.50

Sole proprietor's health insurance premiums. Self-employed individuals can deduct against their business profits on Schedule C health insurance premiums they pay for their employees' health coverage.[24] However, amounts they pay for their own health insurance premiums are deductible as an above the line deduction but do not reduce their net profits from the business.[25] Any amounts paid during months when sole proprietors are eligible to participate in any employer-sponsored health plan (including their spouses' plans) are not deductible as above the line item.[26]

 Spotlight: In 2010 only, the deduction for health insurance costs of self-employed individuals can be taken into account in determining an individual's net earnings from self-employment. Thus, self-employed persons may deduct the cost of health insurance

---

[24] Reg. § 1.132-1(a).
[25] Code Sec. 162(l)(4).
[26] Code Sec. 162(l)(2)(B) and *C. Reynolds*, 79 TCM 1376, Dec. 53,721(M), TC Memo. 2000-20.

> costs incurred in 2010 for themselves their spouses, their dependents, and any child of the taxpayer who as of the end of the tax year has not attained age 27 in the calculation of their 2010 self-employment tax.

Example 20: John Martin operates a sole proprietorship. During the year, John pays insurance premiums on the policy that covers himself and his two employees. The amount of the premiums for each covered individual is $10,000. John can deduct the $20,000 of premiums paid for his two employees as a trade or business expense on Schedule C. He can also deduct the $10,000 of premiums paid for his own policy as an above the line deduction. John will pay less self-employment tax due to the $20,000 deduction taken on Schedule C for health insurance premiums paid on behalf of his employees. He will pay less income taxes as a result of reducing his taxable income by $30,000 ($20,000 + $10,000).

Contributions to the sole proprietor's own retirement plan. Self-employed persons can deduct contributions they make to their own qualified retirement plans, provided that those plans are also made available to all eligible employees.[27] Many self-employed individuals establish defined contribution or Simplified Employee Pension (SEP) plans because of the larger amounts they can contribute (and deduct). However, for sole proprietors who have employees, these plans generally require the owners to make contributions on behalf of their employees as well, so many sole proprietors may offer 401(k) plans and Savings Incentive Match Plans for Employees (SIMPLE). The rules regarding the amounts that employers and employees can contribute annually to each of these plans are essentially the same as those discussed in Chapter 6 (see ¶ 603).

A sole proprietor also must follow the rules regarding participation of the employees of the business. Contributions to a plan must be separated between those contributions on behalf of the employee and sole proprietor. The contributions on behalf of the employee are deductible in arriving at the net profits from the business and, therefore, reduce the taxpayer's self-employment taxes. Sole proprietors' contributions to their own retirement plans are deductible as a deduction for AGI but do not reduce the net income from the business for purposes of the self-employment tax.

Example 21: Justin Church is self-employed and has one employee. Justin contributes $8,000 to the company's retirement plans during the year: $5,000 for himself and $3,000 for his employee. Net profit from the business before considering these contributions equals $55,000. Justin's gross income from sources other than his sole proprietorship total $10,000. After deducting the retirement contributions, net profit from the business equals $52,000 ($55,000 – $3,000). This amount will be included in Justin's gross income, which increases it to $62,000 ($52,000 + $10,000). The $5,000 Justin contributes to his own retirement plan reduces his AGI to $47,000 ($52,000 – $5,000) but does not affect the amount of net profit from his sole proprietorship. Thus, the $8,000 Justin contributes to the company's retirement plans reduce his taxable income and his income tax liability, but only the $3,000 that he contributes to his employee's plan reduces his self-employment tax.

Qualified moving expenses. Amounts employers pay or reimburse their employees for qualified moving expenses are not taxable to employees and are deducted by the employer. Qualified moving expenses were discussed in Chapter 6 and include costs incurred in relocating employees and their families to the new location. It also includes the costs of lodging en route as well as 23 cents per mile for moves that take place during 2015 (see ¶ 602.04).[28]

Qualified moving expenses are for moves that pass both the time and mileage tests. The *mileage test* is met if the employee's commute to the new job would be increased by at least 50 miles.

---

[27] Code Secs. 401–404.

[28] Code Secs. 162 and 217(b)(1) and Notice 2013-80, IRB 2013-52, December 6, 2013.

Thus, the distance between the employee's current residence and the location of the new job must be 50 miles farther than the distance between the employee's current residence and the location of the old job. The *employment test* is met if the employee is employed full-time in the new location for at least 39 of the first 52 weeks after the move. It is not necessary that the 39 weeks be consecutive or with the same employer.[29]

Any amounts an employer reimburses its employees for moving expenses that do not qualify as deductible moving costs are taxable as additional wages to the employee and are deductible as such by the employer. Hence, these additional wages would be subject to income and FICA tax withholding and the employer would be responsible for its share of FICA tax and any unemployment taxes on those wages.

Sole proprietors can also deduct qualified moving expenses they pay for their own moves. However, the sole proprietor must pass the distance test and a more stringent time test. In addition to being employed full-time in the new location at least 39 of the first 52 weeks following the move, sole proprietors must also be employed full-time for 78 of the first 104 weeks following the move.[30]

Example 22: Norman Stockington is self-employed. In May 2015, Norman moves to a new town 1,000 miles away. Norman paid $3,500 to a moving company to move his household goods and personal effects. He drove himself and his family to the new location traveling 1,000 miles and incurring $150 for lodging and $110 for meals during the trip.

On his 2015 tax return, Norman deducts $3,880 for AGI ($3,500 + $150 + $230 for mileage at $.23 a mile). This amount reduces his AGI but does not affect his net profits reported on Schedule C. Furthermore, as a self-employed individual, Norman will be required to be employed full-time at the new location 39 of the first 52 weeks and 78 out of the first 104 weeks after the move.

Losses from the sale of property. In Chapter 9, the calculation of gain or loss on the disposal of business property was discussed. These same rules apply to sole proprietors. Although the netting of Section 1231 gains and losses and capital gains and losses is similar to that discussed in Chapter 9 (see ¶ 904), these amounts are not reflected on Schedule C, but are included in the calculation of total income. Individual taxpayers are allowed to deduct up to $3,000 of net capital losses against ordinary income, and any excess retains its short-term or long-term character and can be carried forward indefinitely. (Recall that corporations can only offset capital losses against capital gains, and any excess loss is carried back three years and forward five years as a short-term capital loss.) (See ¶ 901.01.)

Example 23: Gwen Wolfe operates a small retail shop as a sole proprietorship. During the 2015 tax year, Gwen realizes gains and losses from the disposition of business assets and investments as follows.

Loss from sale of business equipment (held 4 months)	($ 5,000)
Gain from sale of business land (held 3 years)	8,000
Loss from sale of stock (held 6 months)	(40,000)
Gain from sale of stock (held 2 years)	25,000

The business property held short-term is deducted against Gwen's ordinary income. The business land held long-term is the only Section 1231 property sold during the year. Assuming no nonrecaptured Section 1231 losses from the last five years, the $8,000 of Section 1231 gain is treated as long-term capital gain, thus making Gwen's total long-term capital gain $33,000 ($25,000 + $8,000). When Gwen nets the $40,000 of net short-term capital loss against the $33,000 of net long-term

---

[29] Code Sec. 217(c) and Reg. § 1.217-2.   [30] Code Sec. 217(f).

capital gain, she ends up with a $7,000 net short-term capital loss. Gwen is allowed to deduct $3,000 of this loss against her other income in computing her gross income. The remaining $4,000 ($7,000 – $3,000) is carried over to 2016 and netted against short-term capital gains and losses generated that year.

.04 Passive Activity Losses

A provision enacted in the Tax Reform Act of 1986 limits the deductibility of losses resulting from certain trades or businesses, as well as and rental activities. Deductions from a passive activity, including expenses such as interest attributable to acquiring or carrying on an interest in a passive activity, generally may not be deducted from other income for the tax year to the extent that the deductions exceed income from all of the taxpayer's passive activities. The effect of this rule is to prohibit the offsetting of passive losses against income that can be termed "nonpassive," such as compensation for services, portfolio income (interest, dividends, royalties, and gain from the sale of property held for investment), and income from a trade or business in which the taxpayer materially participates. Likewise, credits from passive activities generally are limited to the tax allocable to such activities.[31]

Example 24: Katie Harris has three business activities that are classified as passive activities for the 2015 tax year. In addition, she has income in the form of compensation for services of $50,000, business income of $20,000 from a business activity considered "nonpassive" and interest income of $3,000. The taxable income or (loss) from each passive activity is as follows:

A	$15,000
B	(9,000)
C	(8,000)

For 2015, the net passive activity loss of $2,000 (the $15,000 of passive income from Activity A minus the $17,000 of passive losses from Activities B and C) cannot be used to reduce Katie's other income of $73,000 stemming from compensation for services, "nonpassive" business income, and interest income.

 Reason for the Rule: Prior to the enactment of the Tax Reform Act of 1986, taxpayers could fully deduct losses from rental activities and from trades or businesses, regardless of the level of participation of the taxpayer in the activity. This gave rise to a significant number of tax shelters, which allowed taxpayers to deduct losses from activities in which they had little or no participation against wages and investment income. The Tax Reform Act of 1986 added Code Sec. 469, which limits taxpayers' ability to deduct losses from most rental activities and from trades or businesses in which they do not materially participate.

The passive activity loss rules are applied at the individual taxpayer level and extend to virtually every business or rental activity whether reported on Schedule C, Profit or Loss from Business (Sole Proprietorships); Schedule F, Profit or Loss from Farming; or Schedule E, Supplemental Income or Loss (Rental Activities), as well as to flow through income and losses from partnerships, S corporations, and trusts. The passive loss limitations also apply to personal service corporations. They also apply to closely held C corporations, but have a limited application.

Deductions from passive activities for the tax year that exceed passive income may not be deducted in that year, but instead, the excess (passive activity loss) is "suspended" and carried forward to offset passive activity income generated in future years. Similarly, credits from passive

---

[31] Code Sec. 469.

activities that exceed the tax liability allocable to passive activities for the tax year must be suspended and utilized to offset tax liability associated with passive activities in future years.

Example 25: Continuing with Example 24, Katie would be able to carry forward the nondeductible portion of the passive activity losses to 2016. If in 2016 the three passive activities produced a net passive activity income of $5,000, the $2,000 suspended loss would be allowed as a deduction reducing her taxable income from these activities in 2016 to $3,000 ($5,000 less $2,000).

To fully deduct losses from a trade or business, the taxpayer must participate in the activity on a regular, continuous, and substantial basis. This is known as the **material participation**. Both losses and income from businesses in which the taxpayer materially participates are treated as "nonpassive" and generally all losses are fully deductible. For activities other than rental realty, the tax law provides seven tests to measure whether a taxpayer's participation in a trade or business is material. The four most common tests are quantitative in nature and are based upon a taxpayer's hours of participation during the tax year. These four tests are listed in Table 13-1.

Table 13-1 Tests for Material Participation by the Taxpayer

1. Participation in the activity for more than 500 hours during the tax year.

2. Participation constitutes substantially all of the participation in the activity of all individuals (including the taxpayer and nonowners) for the tax year.

3. Participation in the activity for more than 100 hours during the tax year, and the taxpayer's participation is not less than the participation of any other person.

4. The activity is a significant participation activity for the tax year, and the taxpayer's aggregate participation in all significant participation activities during the year exceeds 500 hours. A *significant participation activity* is one in which the taxpayer has more than 100 hours of participation during the tax year but fails to satisfy any other tests for material participation. A rental activity may not be included in the significant participation activity test. If the sum of all the time spent in the significant participation activities exceeds 500 hours, then all such activities of the taxpayer are considered "nonpassive."

Example 26: Jason Johnson has six separate businesses in which he participates. The numbers of hours he participated and the hours his other employee, Sandy Smith, participated in the activities during the current tax year are as follows. Sandy is Jason's only employee.

Business	Jason's Hours	Sandy's Hours
A	615	1,100
B	82	0
C	135	50
D	385	435
E	215	375

All of the business activities would constitute material participation and would be considered "nonpassive" activities, thereby allowing any loss resulting from them to be deductible against income from "nonpassive" sources. Business A is "nonpassive" because Jason participated for more than 500 hours and passes the Test 1 from Table 13-1. His participation in Business B is "nonpassive" because his participation constitutes substantially all the participation of all employees for the tax year (Test 2) and would not meet the requirement for any of the other tests because his participation is less than 100 hours (the threshold hours for Tests 3 and 4). Jason's participation in Business C is deemed material because his participation was more than 100 hours and Sandy did not participate for more hours than him (Test 3). Jason's participation in Businesses D and E do not meet the requirements of Test 3 because of the number of hours Sandy participated in the businesses; however, they do meet the criteria for significant participation activities with a cumulative participation in excess of 500 hours.

A rental activity is generally considered to be a passive activity, regardless of the extent of the taxpayer's participation in the activity. Thus, classification of an activity expected to produce losses as a rental activity is generally disadvantageous to those persons who would otherwise have materially participated had the activity been a trade or business. To compensate for this possible inequity, a more stringent, two-prong, material participation test applies to rental activities. First, the taxpayer must participate in the rental activity for at least 750 hours during the year. Second, the taxpayer's hours of participation in all rental activities during the year must be more than the taxpayer's participation in all other activities during the year.[32]

Taxpayers not meeting the material participation test for rental activities generally cannot deduct losses from such activities in excess of income from passive activities. However, up to $25,000 of rental losses may be deducted by anyone whose modified adjusted gross income (MAGI) does not exceed $100,000. MAGI is AGI calculated without including certain items of income and deduction, such as other passive activity losses and the deduction for IRA contributions.[33] To qualify for this special deduction, the taxpayer must meet the **active participation** test with respect to the rental activity, own at least a 10 percent interest in the activity, and not be a limited partner. The $25,000 exception is phased out at the rate of $.50 for every dollar of MAGI over $100,000. Thus, when a taxpayer's MAGI exceeds $150,000, the no loss deduction is allowed.

 Planning Pointer: Taxpayers wanting to take advantage of the $25,000 real estate loss deduction need to satisfy both the active participation and MAGI components of the test. While active participation is not as stringent as material participation, the taxpayer is required to participate in making management decisions, such as selecting tenants, or arranging for services for the property in a significant and bona fide sense, such as arranging for repairs. To meet the active participation test, the taxpayer must fulfill the requirements both in the year the loss arose and in the year the loss is deducted. The MAGI component requires taxpayers to project their income and deductions from other sources and plan to keep their MAGI under $100,000, when possible.

Example 27: Daryl Williams has an AGI of $118,000 after deducting $2,000 for an IRA contribution, but before any deduction for a $20,000 rental real estate loss. The rental activity is one in which Daryl actively participates and he does not have any other passive activity losses. Under the general rules for the passive activity loss deduction the $20,000 would not be deductible, however, since Daryl's $120,000 of MAGI ($118,000 + $2,000) is less than $150,000, the special rule for allowance of losses from rental real estate applies. The $20,000 of excess MAGI ($120,000 – $100,000) reduces the amount of the possible loss deduction by $10,000 ($20,000 × $.50). Daryl's loss deduction will be $15,000, which is the *lesser* of the $20,000 of rental real estate loss or $15,000 ($25,000 – $10,000 phase-out for excess MAGI).

Any unused suspended loss deductions are allowed in full when the taxpayer disposes of the entire interest in the activity in a fully taxable transaction. Suspended credits are not allowed on disposition of a taxpayer's interest in an activity. A taxpayer may be involved in several activities,

---

[32] Code Sec. 469(c)(7).   [33] Code Sec. 469(i)(3)(F).

and, to compute the passive activity loss (if any) for a tax year, the income and deductions from all passive activities must be aggregated. Nevertheless, for some purposes it is necessary to account for the net income or loss of each activity separately. One major reason for separating an activities and allocating losses and income among activities is to be able to determine the tax treatment upon disposition of an interest in an activity.

Example 28: On January 1, 2014, John Olsen pays $500,000 for an investment in a restaurant and hires a full-time manager and staff. As an owner he does not participate in the restaurant and his interest in the restaurant is passive. John has no other passive activities. Assume that for 2014, John's loss from the restaurant is $100,000. The loss is not deductible in 2014, and must be suspended until 2015. In 2015, John realizes $60,000 of taxable income from the restaurant, which continues to retain its status as a passive activity to John. Accordingly, John would report no net income or loss from the restaurant for 2015 and would have a suspended loss carry forward to 2016 of $40,000 ($100,000 loss from 2014 less a $60,000 profit in 2015). On January 1, 2016, John disposes of his entire interest in the restaurant at a passive activity gain of $25,000. The $25,000 gain would be applied against the $40,000 loss carry forward to 2016 leaving $15,000 to be deductible in 2016 against "nonpassive" trade or business income and portfolio income.

 Planning Pointer: When a taxpayer is faced with continuing passive activity losses from a trade or business, there can be devastating results from the inability to deduct the losses on the taxpayer's tax return. There are a few potential courses of action that can be taken to have the passive losses become deductible. First, the taxpayer can acquire an investment that generates passive income. Since passive losses can be deducted against passive income, this will allow the taxpayer to absorb the passive losses that would otherwise not be currently deductible. Second, the taxpayer can become a material participant in the activity. If a taxpayer has substantial losses from a passive activity, it could be worthwhile to increase the level of the taxpayer's involvement to that of a material participant. Finally, the taxpayer can dispose of the entire interest in the passive activity since any suspended losses can be deducted in the year of complete disposition in a taxable transaction.

¶ 1302 Tax and Nontax Aspects of Partnerships

Flow-through entities are a popular form for operating a business, primarily because of the single layer of taxation on profits. Unlike the profits of a C corporation, which are taxed first at the entity level and again when distributed to shareholders as dividends, flow-through entities are not treated as separate taxable entities, and accordingly, their profits are taxed a single time to the owners. Although both partnerships and S corporations are flow-through entities, the income taxation of partnership profits is the primary focus of this chapter and the income taxation of S corporation profits is the focus of Chapter 14.

.01 Responsibility for Partnership Liabilities

The shareholders of a C corporation are not responsible for the liabilities of the corporation. The shareholder's liability is limited to the shareholder's basis in the shares of stock it owns in the corporation plus any indebtedness owed to the shareholder by the corporation. Although an S corporation is a flow-through entity and is taxed differently than a C corporation, the owners of an S corporation are shareholders, and they are accorded the same protection from the corporation's liabilities as are shareholders of a C corporation.

The owners of a partnership are partners, and the rules regarding the liability of partners depend upon the classification of the partnership as either a general partnership or a limited partnership. A **general partnership** arises from an agreement among two or more partners to operate a business for profit. In a general partnership all the partners are classified as "general partners," each of whom has unlimited liability for the debts of the partnership. The liabilities can be those that come about from the operations of the business or from the negligence of the other partners as it relates to the operations of the business. The formation of a general partnership is fairly easy and only requires that the partners come to an agreement regarding the terms and conditions that surround the operation of the partnership. It is recommended that this agreement be made in writing and signed by the partners; however, verbal partnership agreements can exist and can be respected (see ¶ 1304.01).

Example 29:   Paul Stone and Mary Brice are general partners operating a retail store as a general partnership. The partnership has outstanding invoices to its vendors for $10,000. Both Paul and Mary are liable for the entire $10,000 that the partnership owes its vendors.

Example 30:   Brent Meyers and Trina Williams are physicians who operate a medical practice as a general partnership. One of Mary's patients is suing the partnership for negligence. If the patient prevails, as general partners both Brent and Trina will be liable for any amounts for which the partnership is liable but cannot satisfy.

When a partnership operates as a **limited partnership**, some partners have limited liability with respect to the debts of the partnership. The partners with limited liability are called "limited partners." When a limited partnership is formed, the federal tax laws require that there be at least one general partner responsible for the actions of the partnership. The general partner or partners are subject to unlimited liability and manage the day-to-day operations of the partnership. Limited partners do not participate in the management of the partnership, and their liability for partnership debts is limited to the amount they have invested in the partnership plus any guarantees the limited partners may have extended to the partnership. Amending a partnership agreement to give original limited partners a voice in the management of the partnership has been held to convert the limited partners to general partners.[34]

A limited partnership does not come into existence with the same ease or lack of formality with which a general partnership may be formed. Forming a limited partnership requires a certificate of limited partnership to be filed with the appropriate state government office. The filing of the certificate of limited partnership along with the requirement that the name of the partnership include a term such as "LP" or "Limited Partnership" gives notice to potential creditors of the partnership that not all partners are unlimitedly liable for the business's debt.

Example 31:   A retail store operates as a limited partnership in which P.G. Giles, Incorporated is the general partner and Mary Wright is a limited partner. The partnership currently has $10,000 in outstanding invoices to its vendors. Mary's capital account balance is $2,000, which represents the amount she has invested in the limited partnership. P.G. Giles's capital account balance is $5,000, which represents its investment in the limited partnership. As the general partner, P.G. Giles is liable for the entire $10,000 in liabilities despite the fact that it only has $5,000 in its capital account. As a limited partner, Mary is liable to the extent of the $2,000 in her capital account.

 Reason for the Rule: After all partners' capital accounts have been used to satisfy a partnership's liabilities, creditors' only remaining recourse is to go after the general partners to satisfy any outstanding loan amounts. When the general partner is a corporation, the possibility exists that all of the owners could be protected from the partnership's debts because the shareholders of a C corporation enjoy limited liability from the debts of the corporation. Thus, the general partner is really only liable for the

---

[34] *Financial Dynamics, Ltd.* (DC Fla.) 80-2 USTC ¶ 9585.

partnership's debts to the extent of the corporation's net assets. By requiring a limited partnership to be formally registered as an "LP" or "Limited Partnership," potential creditors are forewarned that they may have limited avenues for satisfying amounts loaned to the partnership.

.02 Single Level of Taxation

The most appealing feature of a flow-through entity is the single layer of taxation. All flow-through entities are required to file an annual income tax return reporting their activities during the year regarding gross income, deductions, gains, losses, and tax credits. The entity is then required to allocate those items among its owners so the owners can include those amounts on their respective income tax returns. These allocated amounts are deemed to be taxed to the owners on the last day of the entity's tax year, regardless of the amounts that have been distributed to the owners.

Example 32: Alan Kraig owns a one-fifth interest in Tillman partnership. Both Alan and Tillman use a calendar year-end. During 2015, Tillman reports profits of $35,000, of which Alan's share is $7,000. Also during 2015, Tillman distributes $7,000 to Alan. Alan only includes the $7,000 share of profits on his 2015 individual income tax return, which causes his adjusted gross income (AGI), taxable income, and tax liability to increase. The $7,000 distribution is not taxed to Alan because it is the same $7,000 that was reported by Alan as income and on which Alan has already paid tax.

Example 33: Assume the same facts as in Example 32, except Tillman distributes $3,000 to Alan during 2015 (instead of $7,000). Alan still reports his $7,000 distributive share of partnership profits on his 2015 income tax return. The $3,000 represents part of the $7,000 distributive share of previously taxed profits.

.03 Responsibility for Making Accounting Elections

As discussed throughout this textbook, the amount and timing of gross income and deductions can vary depending upon the accounting method and other elections made by the taxpayer. For example, the time when gross income is reported and when expenses are deductible against gross income depends largely on the method of accounting the taxpayer uses, such as the cash or accrual methods of accounting discussed in Chapter 3. If the taxpayer sells property and receives the proceeds over more than one tax year, the gain from the sale is normally recognized over more than one year. However, at the election of the taxpayer, the entire gain from the installment sale can be taxed in the year of the sale (see ¶ 309.01). If the taxpayer realizes a gain from an involuntary conversion of business or investment property, at the taxpayer's election, the gain can be postponed by investing the entire proceeds in qualified replacement property within a specified period of time (see ¶ 809.01). When tangible personal property is purchased and placed in service in a trade or business, at the taxpayer's election, the property may be immediately expensed under Code Sec. 179 to the extent that the tax laws provide (see ¶ 702.03). With a C corporation, the entity reporting the activities is also the one that is responsible for paying the tax on the profits. Therefore, having the corporate entity make these and other elections does not raise any issues. However, with respect to flow-through entities, the issue arises as to which party should make such elections—the entity reporting the activities or the owners, who are ultimately affected by the elections made.

 Planning Pointer: The election to expense qualified Code Sec. 179 property is made at the partnership level. The amount of the deduction and the reduction in such are applied at both the partnership and partner levels.[35] Once the partnership calculation is

---

[35] Code Sec. 179(d)(8).

made, the partner's allocable share is added to the partner's tax return to calculate the amount each partner is entitled to deduct. In the case of a partner who has Code Sec. 179 elections in place in other pass through entities or from a sole proprietorship, that partner may not be able to take advantage of the entire amount of expense allocated to them.

For example, if Marc owns a 50 percent interest in three partnerships, all of which elect to expense the maximum $500,000 for 2015 under Code Sec. 179, his total Code Sec. 179 expense would be $750,000 ($500,000 × 50% × 3). Marc would not be able to take advantage of the excess deduction of $250,000 ($750,000 – $500,000) due to the limitations applied at the partner level. Because the excess is not due to the taxable income limitation, the $250,000 excess cannot be carried over to a future tax year, but is instead permanently lost. Thus, it is critical that there be coordination between the elections made at the partnership and partner levels for electing to expense property under Code Sec. 179 in order to maximize potential tax savings.

The American Recovery and Reinvestment Act of 2009 extended the 50-percent first-year bonus depreciation deduction on qualified new property acquired and placed in service through December 31, 2009. The bonus depreciation is taken on top of the regular depreciation reported for the year the property is placed into service. Unlike the Code Sec. 179 expensing allowance referred to above, there is no taxable income limitation or investment limitation on the bonus allowance at either the partnership or partner level as illustrated in the previous example.

 Spotlight: The American Taxpayer Relief Act extends through 2013 enhanced Section 179 small business expensing. The Section 179 dollar limit for 2012 and 2013 is $500,000 with a $2 million investment limit. The rule allowing off-the-shelf computer software is also extended.

 Spotlight: The Creating Small Business Jobs Act of 2010 (P.L. 111-240) extended the 50-percent bonus depreciation for one year to apply to qualifying property acquired by a taxpayer after December 31, 2007, and placed in service before January 1, 2011. Further, the Section 179 annual dollar limit is increased to $500,000 for tax years beginning in 2010 and 2011 while the investment limit is increased to $2 million for tax years beginning in 2010 and 2011. The ability to revoke an expensing election without the IRS's consent has also been extended to tax years beginning in 2011. Similarly, the allowance of expensing for off-the-shelf computer software is extended for software placed in service in tax years beginning in 2011.

 Spotlight: The Tax Relief, Unemployment Insurance Reauthorization, and Job Creation Act of 2010 extended the bonus depreciation for two more years to apply to qualifying property acquired after December 31, 2007, and placed in service before January 1, 2013. In the case of property with a longer production period and certain noncommercial aircraft the bonus depreciation will apply until December 31, 2013. Further, the bonus depreciation allowance rate is increased from 50 percent to 100 percent for qualified property acquired after September 8, 2010, and before January 1, 2012, and placed in service before January 1, 2012 (or before January 1, 2013, for longer period production property and certain noncommercial aircraft).

The tax laws require that most elections affecting the calculation of gross income and the timing of expenses be made by the partnership.[36] Thus, the partnership makes the elections regarding which accounting period and which overall accounting method to use to report partnership items. Other elections made by the partnership include the depreciation method used to expense real and tangible personal property and the election not to use the installment sale method. The partnership also makes the election to immediately expense intangible drilling and development costs or research and development expenditures or to postpone gain from an involuntary conversion when qualified replacement property is purchased within the specified time period.[37] These elections, once made, are binding on the partners of the partnership, and the methods used by the partnership apply to all of its partners.[38] All other elections are made individually by each partner. For example, each partner decides whether to deduct or take a tax credit for foreign taxes paid during the year. A list of the elections made by the partnership is shown in Figure 13-2.

Figure 13-2 List of Elections Made at the Partnership Level

- The accounting period used to report partnership activities (see ¶ 302.01), including the election to use a tax year other than a required tax year under Code Sec. 444 (see ¶ 302.02)
- The accounting method used to compute partnership income (see ¶ ¶ 306–308)
- The depreciation method used to expense depreciable property, including any election to expense tangible personal property under Code Sec. 179 (see ¶ 702.03)
- The election to opt out of using the installment method (see ¶ 309.01 and ¶ 810.04)
- The option to expense intangible drilling and developments costs (see ¶ 501.03)
- The election to deduct research and experimentation expenditures (see ¶ 507)
- The election to deduct up to $5,000 of a partnership's organizational and start-up costs and then amortize the rest over 180 months[39]
- The election to postpone gain from an involuntary conversion (see ¶ 809.01)

 Spotlight: The Creating Small Business Jobs Act of 2010 (P.L. 111-240) temporarily increased the amount allowed as deduction for start-up expenses for tax years beginning in 2010. The amount of trade or business start-up expenses that may be deducted by a taxpayer is increased from $5,000 to $10,000. In addition, the threshold limit for reducing the deduction (but not below zero) is increased from $50,000 to $60,000. Thus, a taxpayer that pays or incurs $70,000 or more of start-up expenses in 2010 before their active trade or business begins may not claim a current expense deduction for the expenses. Any start-up expenses that are not currently deductible must continue to be amortized ratably over a 180-month period (15 years) beginning with the month in which the active trade or business begins.

¶ 1303 Why Study Partnership Taxation?

The single layer of taxation on profits makes any flow-through entity a popular business entity choice. The tax laws governing the taxation of partnerships are one of the most complex areas of tax law. However, the flexibility in the types and number of owners that partnerships can have and the ability of the partners to decide how to allocate partnership profits and losses give partnerships an edge over S corporations. Unfortunately, the one disadvantage of operating a business as a

---

[36] Code Sec. 703(b).

[37] *Demirjian*, 72-1 USTC ¶ 9281, 457 F2d 1.

[38] Code Sec. 703(b); Reg. § 1.703-1(b).

[39] Code Sec. 709(b); Reg. § 1.709-1(b)(1) and § 1.709-2(c).

partnership has been the requirement that every partnership have at least one general partner with unlimited liability. In the last three decades, all 50 states have come to recognize limited liability companies (LLCs) as an alternative to partnerships. In an LLC, all owners (called members) have limited liability for the general debts of the business entity, and there is no requirement that any owner be ultimately responsible for the entity's debts. More recently, the federal government has come to accept limited liability partnerships (LLPs) as a business entity that can be taxed as a partnership. Like LLCs, all partners in an LLP have limited liability from the partnership's debts. Since the owners of LLCs and LLPs have limited liability similar to that offered by corporations (but unlike with corporations, the profits are taxed only one time), these entities have become the latest trend of business entity choice.

As the information presented in Table 13-2 shows, in 2010, the number of partnership tax returns filed increased 2.5 percent from 3,168,728 for 2009 to 3,248,481. However, a closer look at the table shows that traditional general partnerships displayed a continuing pattern of decline over this same period of time. Since 2001, the number of partnerships has increased at an average annual rate of 4.7 percent. The majority of this growth has been from partnerships classified as limited liability companies (LLC). The number of partners increased by 6.1 percent, from 21,141,979 for 2009 to 22,428,047 for 2010, and has grown 9 out of the last 10 years. More than half (56.6 percent) of all partnerships have only two partners, while 44 percent of all partners are related to partnerships with more than 100 partners.

Table 13-2 Partnership Tax Returns Filed by Type of Entity[40]

Year	Total Number of Returns (000's)	Domestic General Partnerships (000's)	Domestic Limited Partnerships (000's)	Domestic Limited Liability Companies (000's)	Domestic Limited Liability Partnerships (000's)	Other (000's)
1993	1,468	1,176	275	17	——	——
1994	1,494	1,163	283	48	——	——
1995	1,581	1,167	295	119	——	——
1996	1,654	1,116	311	221	——	5
1997	1,759	1,069	329	349	——	13
1998	1,855	945	343	470	26	71
1999	1,937	898	354	589	42	52
2000	2,058	872	349	718	53	64
2001	2,132	815	369	809	69	70
2002	2,242	780	377	946	78	61
2003	2,375	757	379	1,092	88	58
2004	2,547	725	402	1,270	89	61
2005	2,764	729	414	1,465	100	56
2006	2,947	718	433	1,630	109	57
2007	3,094	693	426	1,818	110	47
2008	3,146	670	411	1,898	120	47
2009	3,169	624	397	1,969	118	60
2010	3,248	590	375	2,090	142	51

[40] IRS Statistics of Income Bulletin, Fall 2012, Partnership Returns, 2010.

¶ 1304 Forming a Partnership

Since a partnership involves two or more owners, forming a partnership requires a little more formality than forming a sole proprietorship. The first step in forming a partnership is for the partners to enter into a **partnership agreement**, which provides, among other things, how the partners will share in the partnership's profits and losses. Although there is no requirement that the partnership agreement be in writing, as with any contract, it is highly recommended that the partners enter into a written partnership agreement to avoid any disputes in the future over any of the partnership arrangements.

After a partnership agreement has been established, the partners must contribute capital (assets) to the partnership so the partnership can begin operations. Often the partners will contribute cash to the partnership in exchange for a partnership interest; however, sometimes property other than cash or services is contributed.

.01 Partnership Agreement

The partnership agreement is a contract between the parties that usually establishes how the partnership's income, gains, losses, deductions, and credits will be allocated among the partners. These allocated amounts are known as the partner's **distributive shares** of partnership items. If the partnership agreement does not specify each partner's distributive share of such items, the partners' shares are determined according to each partner's interest in the partnership, taking all the facts and circumstances into consideration. Although the partnership agreement normally controls the allocation of partnership items, the allocations provided in the agreement are disregarded if they lack substantial economic effect. Partnership agreements are interpreted under the law of the state in which the entity is formed.

 Spotlight: A partnership agreement may be an oral or written understanding between the partners and need not even be referred to as a partnership agreement for it to be a binding agreement. Since the partnership agreement is considered to be the governing instrument for tax allocation purposes as well as the contract to be relied upon by the partners for the effective management of the partnership, its importance cannot be overstated.[41] Provisions that are commonly included in a partnership agreement that have tax implications include: (1) initial capital contributions by the partners; (2) method of accounting; (3) fiscal year of the partnership; (4) determination of the partnerships profit or loss for the tax year; (5) division of profits and losses amongst the partners; and, (6) maintenance of partners capital accounts. This chapter addresses each of these provisions, as well as other topics that should be considered in drafting a partnership agreement.

The partnership agreement also contains many nontax-related provisions that govern the operations of the partnership. For example, the partnership agreement will specify who will manage the partnership operations, including how disputes among the various partners will be resolved. The agreement may restrict the partners' abilities to transfer their partnership interests, or it may provide a formula to determine the amount at which one partner will buy out another partner should a partner retire or otherwise decide to leave the partnership. The partnership agreement also states how partners will distribute the partnership assets upon dissolution of the partnership.

---

[41] Code Sec. 704(a).

.02 Contributions of Property

Before any business can begin operations, it must first generate capital. Typically, the partners contribute property (including cash) to the partnership in exchange for a capital interest in the partnership. A partner's interest in the partnership is similar to a shareholder's shares of stock in a corporation. It represents the partner's ownership rights in the partnership. A capital interest in a partnership is an asset that a partner can sell for cash or for another consideration, provided the terms of the sale do not violate any limitations specified in the partnership agreement. As with the disposal of any asset, the partner recognizes gain or loss on the sale equal to the difference between the amount realized and the partner's adjusted basis in the partnership interest.

When a partner contributes money or property to a partnership solely in exchange for an interest in the partnership, no gain or loss is recognized by either the partner or the partnership.[42] Instead, the realized gain or loss is deferred (postponed) and will be recognized at a later point in time. Nonrecognition of gain, however, does not extend to the contribution of services. If the partner performs services for the partnership in exchange for an interest in the partnership, the partner includes the fair market value (FMV) of the partnership interest received as gross income.[43] When the FMV of a partnership interest a partner receives exceeds the FMV of the property the partner contributes to the partnership, the difference represents the value of the services rendered by the partner in exchange for a capital interest in the partnership. Thus, the difference between the FMV of the partnership interest received and the value of the property contributed to the partnership is the amount of taxable services the partner reports in gross income.

Example 34: Joan Andrews and David Busbee agree to form an equal partnership. Each contributes $5,000 of property in exchange for his or her respective partnership interests. Joan contributes $5,000 cash; David contributes $5,000 worth of property with an adjusted basis of $3,000. Although David realizes a $2,000 gain ($5,000 – $3,000) on the transfer, neither the partnership nor the partners recognize any gain or loss on the exchange.

Example 35: Jessica Adams owns and operates a business as a sole proprietorship. Three years earlier she hired Eric DuPree and promised to make him a 50-percent partner in her business if he was still employed at the end of three years. At the end of three years, Eric is still working for Jessica, and in accordance with their agreement, a partnership is formed with net assets (total assets minus total liabilities) of $150,000. David's share of those net assets equals $75,000 ($150,000 × 50%). Upon formation of the partnership, David receives $75,000 in exchange for no consideration other than his prior services, and accordingly, the $75,000 is taxable to him as ordinary income.

Example 36: Erica Harris and Jeff Jenkins form an equal partnership. In exchange for her interest, Erica contributes $50,000 cash. In exchange for his 50-percent interest, Jeff performs services for the partnership and contributes $20,000 cash. Since Jeff receives a 50-percent capital interest in the partnership, the FMV of the amounts he contributed must be the same as the $50,000 Erica contributes in exchange for her 50-percent interest. Therefore, in order to receive a 50-percent interest in the partnership, Jeff must have contributed services worth $30,000. Thus, Jeff will report the $30,000 of services rendered in gross income and will pay tax on that amount at the ordinary income (marginal) tax rates.

Profits-only interest in the partnership. In the previous three examples, each partner received a share of the partnership's capital in exchange for contributing property, services, or both. When a partner has an interest in the future profits the partnership generates as well as an interest in the partnership's assets upon his liquidation from or dissolution of the partnership, the partner has a **capital and profits interest**. If the partner is entitled to a share of future partnership profits but does not have an ownership interest in the partnership capital, the partner receives a **profits**

---

[42] Code Sec. 721.

[43] Reg. § 1.721(1)(b)(1).

only interest. A partner with a profits interest does not receive anything upon the dissolution of the partnership beyond any previously taxed profits that have yet to be distributed to the partner.

The receipt of a profits interest in exchange for the contribution of services is taxable upon receipt only if the FMV of the profits interest is determinable. Thus, if an individual contributes past services in exchange for a profits interest, and the profits interest has only speculative value, the individual recognizes income only as the profits are received.[44] According to the IRS, a partner's receipt of a profits interest is not taxable unless *any* of the following circumstances exists:

1. The interest relates to a substantially certain and predictable stream of income from partnership assets, such as from a high-grade lease of real property,

2. Within two years of receipt, the partner disposes of the profits interest, or

3. The interest is a limited partnership interest in a publicly traded partnership.[45]

Example 37: Edwina Stewart is admitted as a partner in the ABC partnership. Edwina does not contribute anything to the partnership in exchange for her interest, but she nonetheless receives 15 percent of partnership profits in exchange for remaining with the partnership. During the year the partnership's profits are $200,000, and in accordance with the partnership agreement Edwina is allocated $30,000 of the partnership income. Edwina will be taxed during the current year on the $30,000 distributive share of the partnership profits. However, neither she nor the partnership will be taxed on the value of her interest in the partnership (i.e., her right to future profits).

Example 38: Sally Jensen is given a 20-percent interest in the future profits from the operation of an apartment building that has guaranteed leases that have produced a $150,000 profit for the past 10 years. The building will produce the same profit for the next 10 years, which will complete the terms of the guaranteed leases. Sally is taxed on the value of the partnership interest based upon the predictable nature of the income.

> **Spotlight:** Receipt of a profits-only interest differs from a capital and profits interest in that the owner of the latter is entitled to a portion of the partnership assets upon dissolution of the partnership. For example, Eric DuPree from Example 35 was taxed on $75,000 because that amount represented the FMV of the 50-percent capital and profits interest he received in the partnership due to past services he rendered to Jessica's business. Thus, if Eric were to sell his 50-percent capital and profits interest immediately upon becoming a partner, his interest should be worth $75,000 because the purchaser would be buying a claim to half of the $150,000 FMV of partnership assets. Contrast this to Examples 37 and 38, in which Edwina and Sally have no claim to partnership assets. Should either Edwina or Sally decide to sell her profits-only partnership interest, the buyer would be purchasing only an interest in the future profits of the partnership. In Example 37, a high degree of uncertainty exists regarding the value of Edwina's future profits, and accordingly, she is not taxed until her distributive share of partnership profits is realized.

.03 Partnership's Basis and Holding Period in Contributed Property

The contributing partner's realized gain or loss from the contribution of property in exchange for a partnership interest is not recognized but is merely deferred and eventually must be taxed. One way this is accomplished is by requiring that the partnership use as its basis in the contributed property the contributing partner's basis in the property.[46] Thus, when the partnership sells the property, the unrealized gain or loss will be recognized by the partnership and taxed to the partners.

---

[44] *W.G. Campbell*, CA-8, 91-2 USTC ¶ 50,420.

[45] Rev. Proc. 93-27, 1993-2 CB 343, clarified by Rev. Proc. 2001-43, 2001-2 CB 191.

[46] Code Sec. 723.

Example 39: Jay Morrill contributes land that is worth $50,000 to a partnership. Jay's adjusted basis in the land is $33,000. In return for the land, Jay receives a one-third interest in the partnership. Jay realizes $17,000 gain ($50,000 – $33,000); however, he does not recognize any gain on the exchange. The partnership takes Jay's $33,000 basis in the land. If the partnership later sells the land for $50,000, it will both realize and recognize a $17,000 gain ($50,000 – $33,000). Thus, Jay's $17,000 gain is merely postponed.

Example 40: Daria Monroe and Monica Edwards form an equal general partnership. Each partner contributes $100,000. Daria contributes $100,000 cash; Monica contributes land worth $100,000. Monica's adjusted basis in the land is $140,000. The partnership's basis in the cash is $100,000; its basis in the land is $140,000. Monica does not recognize the $40,000 loss ($100,000 FMV less $140,000 basis) upon transfer of the land to the general partnership.

If the partner contributes nonbusiness property to the partnership (such as a personal automobile or other personal belonging), the basis of the property to the partnership is the *lesser* of (1) the FMV of the property at the time of contribution or (2) its adjusted basis to the contributing partner.[47]

Example 41: Jake Matthews contributes his personal automobile to a partnership in exchange for a 10-percent capital and profits interest in the partnership. The automobile is worth $15,000 at the time he contributes it to the partnership. Jake paid $35,000 for the automobile, and since it is a personal asset, this amount represents his adjusted basis in the property. Although the general rule stipulates that the partnership take Jake's $35,000 basis in the automobile, the special rule governing the contribution of a partner's personal belongings limits the partnership's basis to $15,000 (the *lesser* of $15,000 FMV or $35,000 adjusted basis). This amount also represents Jake's basis in his partnership interest.

Reason for the Rule: Almost all personal belongings individuals own decline in value over time. Since personal belongings cannot be depreciated, their adjusted basis usually is their cost. Thus, when these personal belongings are sold, the realized loss cannot be recognized on the tax return (see ¶ 803). If the partnership tax laws allowed individuals to contribute their personal belongings to a partnership and to follow the general rule and allow the partnership's basis in those assets to be the (higher) adjusted basis, then the partnership would benefit from the partner's realized loss on the property contributed. For example, if in Example 41, the partnership were to immediately sell Jake's automobile for its $15,000 FMV, no gain or loss would be recognized by the partnership. However, if the tax laws had permitted the partnership to use Jake's $35,000 adjusted basis in the automobile, it would recognize a $20,000 loss ($15,000 – $35,000). This, in effect, would allow the partnership (and the partners) to benefit from the $20,000 realized loss on the exchange of a personal belonging for a partnership interest which would not have been deductible if sold by Jake outside the partnership.

The holding period of property contributed to the partnership includes the period during which the contributing partner held the property.[48] This holding period determines whether any gain upon a sale will be treated as long-term or short-term gain.

.04 Partner's Tax Basis and Holding Period in the Partnership Interest

A partnership interest represents an investment in a partnership, and like any other investment, it is important to keep track of its tax basis. When an interest in a partnership is sold, the partner recognizes gain or loss for the difference between the amount realized from the sale and the

---

[47] *L.Y.S. Au*, CA-9, 64-1 USTC ¶ 9447, 330 F2d 1008.   [48] Code Sec. 1223(2); Reg. § 1.723-1.

adjusted basis of the partnership interest. The partner's tax basis in the partnership interest is also used to ensure that the profits of the partnership are taxed only one time.

The contributions a partner makes to a partnership represent the partner's investment in the partnership. Therefore, contributions the partner makes to the partnership are included in the calculation of the partner's basis in the partnership interest. As partnership income and gain is allocated (and taxed) to the partner, the partner's basis in the partnership is increased by these amounts. Likewise, the partner's allocable share of partnership deductions and losses reduces the partner's tax basis in the partnership interest. When the partnership makes distributions to its partners, the partners reduce their basis in the partnership interest as they receive a tax-free return of capital to the extent of their basis in the partnership interest. The only time a partner is taxed on a distribution from the partnership is when the amount of cash distributed exceeds the partner's basis in the partnership interest.[49]

When a partner sells its partnership interest, the partner only recognizes gain to the extent that the amount realized from the sale exceeds its adjusted basis in the partnership interest. Thus, to the extent that a partner's share of allocated partnership profits has not been distributed at the time the partner sells the interest in the partnership, a higher adjusted basis will cause the partner to recognize less gain or a greater loss from the sale.

Example 42: Kelly Moore and Julie Costas are equal partners in JK general partnership. To form the partnership, each partner contributed $10,000. Kelly and Julie's initial basis in their respective partnership interests is $10,000. During the first year of operations, JK reports taxable profits of $4,000, which it allocates 50 percent to each partner. Each partner's basis in the partnership interest increases by $2,000, to $12,000 ($10,000 + $2,000). If Kelly sells his interest in JK for $12,000, he will not recognize any gain, thus ensuring that the $2,000 of partnership profits is not taxed a second time and that he receives a tax-free return of his original $10,000 investment.

Example 43: Continuing with Example 42, if JK distributes $8,000 to Julie at the beginning of the second year, this amount reduces the basis in her partnership interest to $4,000 ($12,000 – $8,000), but she does not recognize gain on the distribution. The $8,000 distribution she receives represents the previously taxed partnership profits ($2,000) and a tax-free return of part of the amount she contributed to JK ($6,000).

The partner's tax basis is calculated differently from the partner's capital account. The **partner's capital account** keeps track of what the partner is entitled to receive upon dissolution of the partnership. Initially, the partner's capital account includes the *value* of the property the partner contributes to the partnership because this amount represents the partner's contribution of assets to the partnership relative to the other partners. The partner's capital account is increased by the partner's allocable shares of partnership income and gain, as determined in accordance with the partnership agreement. Likewise, the partner's capital account is decreased by the partner's allocable shares of partnership deduction and loss, as well as the *value* of property distributed to the partner, as determined in accordance with the partnership agreement. The partner's capital account is often referred to as the partner's "book" basis.

Example 44: Isabel Anderson and Miranda Bates form a 50-50 general partnership. Isabel contributes property that has an adjusted basis of $20,000 and a value of $50,000. Miranda contributes $50,000 cash. For book purposes, each partner contributes property worth $50,000, and therefore this amount represents each partner's capital account balance. If the partnership were to dissolve, each partner would be entitled to 50 percent of the partnership net assets, as determined by their respective capital account balances.

---

[49] Code Sec. 731.

Initial basis. When a partner contributes property (including cash) to a partnership in exchange for an interest in the partnership, the partner's initial (tax) basis in a partnership interest is the amount of money contributed plus the partner's adjusted basis of any property contributed.[50] When a partner contributes services to the partnership in exchange for a partnership interest, the taxable amount of those services increases the partner's basis in the partnership interest. The partner's capital account (book basis) is computed using the FMV of the contributed property and the taxable services rendered. Because a property's *value* often is different from the taxpayer's adjusted (tax) basis in the property, the partner's basis in the partnership interest is often different from the balance in the partner's capital account.

Example 45: Continuing with Example 44, for tax purposes, Isabel's basis in her partnership interest is $20,000 (the adjusted basis in the property she contributes), while Miranda's basis in her partnership interest is $50,000. The tax and book balances of each account are shown below. In both cases, the partnership's assets are equal to its liabilities and the partners' capital. However, the rules for computing the account balances are different.

Assets	Tax Basis	Book Basis	Partner's Capital	Tax Basis	Book Basis
Cash	$50,000	$ 50,000	Isabel	$20,000	$ 50,000
Property	20,000	50,000	Miranda	50,000	50,000
	$70,000	$100,000		$70,000	$100,000

Example 46: Jim Chan, Mary Dunn, and Charles Edger form an equal three-member general partnership. In exchange for their respective one-third interests, Jim contributes $150,000 in cash; Mary contributes $75,000 in cash plus stock worth $75,000; and Charles contributes land worth $150,000. Mary's adjusted basis in the stock is $45,000; Charles's adjusted basis in the land is $160,000. Each partner contributes property worth $150,000 in exchange for his or her one-third interest in the partnership, and therefore, each partner's capital account balance is credited for $150,000. Although each partner contributed property worth equivalent amounts, the tax bases of their interests differ.

Jim's basis in his partnership interest is $150,000, the amount of cash he contributes. Mary's basis is $120,000 ($75,000 cash plus $45,000 adjusted basis of the stock). Charles's basis is $160,000 (adjusted basis of the land). Thus, if the three partners were to sell their interests to three other individuals for $150,000 each, Jim would not report any gain or loss ($150,000 – $150,000); Mary's gain would be $30,000 ($150,000 – $120,000); and Charles's loss would equal $10,000 ($150,000 – $160,000).

Assets	Tax Basis	Book Basis	Partner's Capital	Tax Basis	Book Basis
Cash	$225,000	$225,000	Jim	$150,000	$150,000
Stock	45,000	75,000	Mary	120,000	150,000
Land	160,000	150,000	Charles	160,000	150,000
	$430,000	$450,000		$430,000	$450,000

Example 47: Ed Rentara and Jessica Sampson form an equal general partnership. In exchange for his 50-percent interest, Ed contributes $20,000 cash and stock worth $30,000. Ed's adjusted basis in the stock is $25,000. In exchange for her 50-percent interest, Jessica performs services for the partnership and contributes land worth $40,000. Jessica's

---

[50] Code Sec. 722; Reg. § 1.722-1.

adjusted basis in the land is $45,000. Ed contributes $50,000 in exchange for his 50-percent interest ($20,000 cash + $30,000 FMV of property). Therefore, in order for Jessica to receive the same 50-percent interest in partnership capital, she must have contributed $50,000 as well. Since the property Jessica contributes is worth $40,000, the services she contributes must be worth $10,000. Thus, Jessica reports the $10,000 of services rendered in gross income and will pay tax on that amount at her ordinary income (marginal) tax rates.

Neither Ed nor Jessica recognizes any gain or loss on the contribution of property to the partnership solely in exchange for his or her partnership interest. Ed's (tax) basis in his partnership interest is $45,000 ($20,000 cash + $25,000 adjusted basis in the stock). Jessica's (tax) basis in her partnership interest is $55,000 ($45,000 adjusted basis in the land + $10,000 recognized as ordinary income for her services rendered).

 Spotlight: The tax laws governing the partner's basis in a partnership interest are similar to the tax laws that govern the taxpayer's basis in property received in a like-kind exchange. In a like-kind exchange, any realized gain or loss is postponed and reflected in the taxpayer's basis in the newly acquired property (see ¶ 808.03). Thus, when the taxpayer later sells the like-kind property, the postponed gain or loss is recognized. The tax laws operate similarly to "hide" the partner's realized (but unrecognized) gain or loss on the contribution of property to a partnership in exchange for a partnership interest. As illustrated in Example 47, Jessica receives a partnership interest worth $50,000 in exchange for property and services of which her basis is $55,000 (property with an adjusted basis of $45,000 + $10,000 of taxable services). Thus, Jessica's realized loss on the exchange is $5,000 ($50,000 – $55,000). The tax laws do not allow her to recognize this loss but instead postpone it until later by allowing her to take the $55,000 as her basis in the partnership. Thus, if Jessica were to immediately turn around and sell her partnership interest she would recognize a $5,000 loss.

Liabilities associated with contributed property. Since the partners are ultimately responsible for the debt of the partnership, when contributed property is transferred subject to indebtedness or when a partner's indebtedness is assumed by the partnership, the contributing partner's basis in the partnership interest is reduced by the amount of the indebtedness assumed by the other partners. Likewise, the noncontributing partners' bases in their partnership interests increase by their respective amounts of partnership debt for which they are now responsible.[51]

A partner's basis in a partnership interest cannot be reduced below zero. Therefore, if the debt assumed by the other (noncontributing) partners exceeds the contributing partner's adjusted basis in the property, the basis of that partner's interest is reduced to zero, and the excess of the debt assumed by the other partners over the contributing partner's basis for the property is taxable to the contributing partner. Generally, the excess is taxed as capital gain.[52] However, the amount of the taxable excess does not increase the contributing partner's basis.

Figure 13-3 Initial Basis of Contributing Partners

The initial basis of a contributing partner is calculated as follows:

Money Contributed by Partner

Plus: Partner's adjusted basis in contributed property

Plus: Taxable amount of partner's services contributed to the partnership

---

[51] Code Sec. 752; Reg. § 1.752-1.   [52] Code Sec. 731(a).

Plus:	Amount of existing partnership indebtedness assumed by the contributing partner
Minus:	Amount of indebtedness assumed by noncontributing partners of indebtedness transferred to the partnership by the contributing partner
Equals:	Initial Basis of Contributing Partner

Example 48: Fred Ackers contributes land worth $105,000 to a general partnership in exchange for a one-third interest in the partnership. The other partner, Jeff Rowley, contributes $120,000 cash in exchange for a two-thirds interest in the partnership. Fred's basis in the land is $55,000, and the land is subject to a $45,000 mortgage that the partnership assumes. Prior to contributing the property, Fred was entirely responsible for the $45,000 mortgage associated with the land. After the contribution, all liabilities of the partnership are borne by the partnership (and ultimately, its partners), and Fred's share of the mortgage held by the partnership is $15,000. Jeff's responsibility is $30,000. By contributing the land to the partnership, Fred's responsibility for the mortgage decreases by $30,000 ($45,000 – $15,000). Each partner's basis in his partnership interest is shown below:

Fred

Adjusted basis in the land contributed	$ 55,000
Less: Liabilities assumed by other partners	(30,000)
Fred's initial basis in his partnership interest	$ 25,000

Jeff

Cash contributed	$120,000
Plus: Share of partnership liabilities	30,000
Jeff's initial basis in his partnership interest	$150,000

Example 49: Assume the same facts as in Example 48, except that Fred's basis in the land is $20,000. Fred reduces his basis in the partnership interest by the $30,000 decrease in his responsibility for the mortgage; however, the tax laws do not allow his basis to fall below zero. Fred is taxed on the $10,000 excess ($30,000 – $20,000). Each partner's basis in his partnership interest is shown below:

Fred

Adjusted basis in the land contributed	$ 20,000
Less: Liabilities assumed by the other partners	(30,000)
Fred's initial basis in his partnership interest	$ 0

Jeff

Cash contributed	$120,000
Plus: Share of partnership liabilities	30,000
Jeff's initial basis in his partnership interest	$150,000

Allocating the debt among the various partners depends on whether the debt assumed by the partnership is a recourse or nonrecourse debt. If the debt assumed is a recourse debt, each partner's share of the assumed liability is that portion of the liability for which he or a related person[53] bears

---

[53] Reg. § 1.752-4(b).

the economic risk of loss.[54] A nonrecourse debt is usually shared in the same ratio as the partnership profits.[55]

A **nonrecourse debt** gets its name from the fact that the lender has no recourse (no ability to collect the debt) directly from the borrower in the event the borrower defaults on the loan. Instead, the lender has recourse against property, called **collateral**, that can be used to satisfy the debt in the event the borrower defaults on the loan. If a lender makes a nonrecourse loan and the borrower defaults on the loan, the lender can use the collateral to satisfy the remaining balance on the loan. If the collateral is not sufficient to satisfy the entire loan amount, the lender has no further recourse (hence the term, nonrecourse debt) and is out of pocket for any remainder of the debt.

Example 50: A partnership acquires land costing $200,000 by making a down payment of $20,000 and taking out a nonrecourse loan for $180,000. The land is used as collateral for the loan. After making several payments on the loan, the partnership defaults on the loan when the loan balance is $160,000. The lender takes possession of the land and sells it for $150,000. The lender uses the entire $150,000 of proceeds to satisfy $150,000 of the $160,000 outstanding balance. Because the loan was nonrecourse debt, the lender cannot go back to the partnership for the remaining $10,000 owed on the debt. The lender will incur a $10,000 loss on the amount of debt that it cannot collect.

With a **recourse debt**, the lender can proceed directly against the debtor for any debt on which the debtor has defaulted. Typically, if property is pledged as collateral for a recourse debt, the lender will first look to the collateral to satisfy the debt and will then try to attach the debtor's other assets. In the case of a partnership, if the collateral is insufficient to satisfy a recourse debt or if no property is pledged as collateral on the debt, the lender can go after the partnership assets (and accordingly, the partners) to satisfy the debt. In the case of a limited partnership, the limited partners would be liable to satisfy their portions of the debt for the amount equal to their capital account balances in the partnership plus any loans they have made to the partnership. The general partners of a partnership have unlimited liability with respect to the debts of the partnership, and thus, should the partnership assets be insufficient to satisfy the recourse debt, the general partners' assets other than their interests in the partnership are at risk for satisfying any remaining portion of the partnership's debt.

Example 51: Assume the same facts as in Example 50, except the $180,000 loan is structured as a recourse debt. The partnership defaults and $150,000 of the outstanding loan amount is satisfied with the proceeds from the sale of the property. Because the debt was structured as a recourse debt, the lender is able to require that the remaining $10,000 be satisfied using other partnership assets. If the partnership is unable to satisfy the remainder of the debt, the lender will have recourse to go after the general partner's personal assets.

If the debt assumed is a recourse debt, each partner's share of the assumed liability is that portion of the liability for which the partner bears the economic risk of loss. To determine each partner's economic risk of loss for recourse debt, a "constructive sale and liquidation" is deemed to take place, and the resulting loss is allocated among the partners in accordance with the loss allocation provisions in the partnership agreement. The losses are then applied against the partner's capital account balances. The negative balances in the partner's capital accounts represent the partner's risk of economic loss. Thus, the steps taken to determine a partner's risk of economic loss are as follows:

1. The partnership is deemed to sell all of its assets (including cash) for $0 and the resulting loss (based on the book value of the assets) is then allocated to each of the partners in accordance with each of their loss allocation ratios.

2. The allocated loss reduces each partner's respective capital account balances.

3. The resulting negative balances in the partners' capital accounts represent each partner's share of economic loss with respect to the recourse debt.[56]

---

[54] Reg. § 1.752-2.
[55] Reg. § 1.752-3.

[56] Reg. § 1.752-2.

Example 52: Tim Roberts and Chip Frasier form a general partnership. The partnership agreement provides that Tim and Chip will share profits equally, but they will share partnership losses 60/40. Tim contributes $100,000 in cash; Chip contributes land worth $140,000 that is subject to a recourse mortgage of $40,000. Chip's adjusted basis in the land is $70,000. Chip's lender agrees to release Chip from liability for the mortgage and to substitute the partnership as the obligor. Both partners contribute property worth $100,000. Although the property Chip contributes is worth $140,000, it is contributed along with a $40,000 liability, which reduces the total value of his contribution to $100,000 ($140,000 − $40,000). Thus, each partner's "initial capital account balance" (the amount each partner would be entitled to upon the dissolution of the partnership) is $100,000.

By contributing the encumbered property to the partnership, Chip is discharged from personal responsibility for the $40,000 liability; however, through his 50-percent ownership interest in the partnership, he will be responsible for a portion of the $40,000 recourse mortgage. To determine Tim and Chip's respective shares of the $40,000 recourse debt, each partner is allocated his share of the economic risk of loss from the $40,000. This amount can be determined by going through the calculations of a hypothetical sale of all of the partnership's assets for $0 and then allocating the loss (calculated based on the book value of the assets) among the partners. The resulting negative balances in each partner's capital account represent each partner's economic risk of loss from the property. If the partnership were to sell all of its assets, including cash, for $0, the partnership would realize a $240,000 loss (based on book value) which would be allocated 60 percent to Tim and 40 percent to Chip.

Asset	Sales Price	Book Value	Loss
Cash	$0	$100,000	($100,000)
Land	0	140,000	(140,000)
			($240,000)

Tim's initial capital account balance	$100,000
Tim's distributive share of $240,000 loss	(144,000)
Tim's economic risk of loss	($ 44,000)
FMV of property Chip contributes	$140,000
Less: Personal release of liability	(40,000)
Chip's initial capital account balance	$100,000
Chip's distributive share of $240,000 loss	(96,000)
Chip's economic risk of loss	$ 4,000

The hypothetical liquidation shows that if all of the partnership assets were sold for $0, the entire $40,000 recourse debt would be borne by Tim. Therefore, Tim's adjusted (tax) basis in his partnership interest is $140,000 ($100,000 cash contributed plus his $40,000 share of the recourse liability). Chip's adjusted (tax) basis in his partnership interest is $30,000 ($70,000 adjusted basis in the property contributed minus $40,000 of the liability assumed by the partnership plus his $0 share of the recourse liability). The allocation of the mortgage among the partners is the proportion of the liability, if any, for which each partner or related person bears the economic risk of loss. The ratio at which the partners agree to share partnership income is irrelevant when allocating recourse debt between the two partners.

Example 53: Assume the same facts as in Example 52, except that the debt is a nonrecourse liability. Nonrecourse debt is allocated in accordance with the partner's profit-sharing ratio. Thus, Tim and Chip would each add $20,000 ($40,000 × 50%) of the nonrecourse debt to his basis in his interest in the partnership.

Partnership interest acquired from another partner. If a partner acquires an interest in the partnership by purchasing it from a partner, rather than from the partnership itself, a different rule applies to determine the partner's initial basis in the partnership interest.[57] The purchasing partner receives an initial basis in the interest equal to its cost to the partner, including the selling partner's share of partnership liabilities assumed by the purchasing partner.

Holding periods. The holding period of a partner's interest determines the nature of the gain (or loss) as long-term or short-term. Gain or loss from the sale or other disposition of a partnership interest held by a partner for over one year generally qualifies as long-term capital gain or loss. Partnership interests held one year or less generally give rise to short-term capital gain or loss.[58] If a partner pays cash to a partnership in exchange for a partnership interest, the partner's holding period for the interest begins as of the time the partner acquires the interest. In the case of a contribution of property, if the contributed property was a capital asset or a Code Sec. 1231 asset in the hands of the contributing partner, the holding period of the contributed property carries over to the acquired partnership interest.[59] Thus, an interest acquired from a partnership in exchange for contributing property that is a capital asset or a Code Sec. 1231 asset not only takes the adjusted basis of the contributing property but also takes its holding period.

¶ 1305 Reporting Partnership Operations

Once the partners have entered into a partnership agreement and assets have been contributed to the partnership, the partnership is ready to begin operations. Like any other business, a partnership must select a tax year and an overall accounting method. A partnership is not a taxpaying entity, but nonetheless it is required to keep track of its gross income, gains, deductions, and losses using the accounting method it has selected. It then files an income tax return reporting these items in accordance with its tax year. It also allocates the items among its partners in accordance with the terms of the partnership agreement.

.01 Required Tax Year

As first discussed in Chapter 3, a partnership's required tax year is the one that best conforms to the tax year of its partners, as determined using a series of rules prescribed in the Code. The first rule requires that a partnership adopt the year-end of its majority partners. If a partnership does not have a majority of partners with the same year-end, the tax laws require that the partnership adopt the year-end of *all* its principal partners. For partnerships that do not have either a majority of partners or all principal partners with the same year-end, then the tax laws require that the partnership use as its year-end the tax year that produces the least aggregate deferral of income. Although a partnership's required tax year is determined by sequentially following these three sets of rules, the tax laws allow a partnership to have a tax year other than its required tax year if it (1) establishes to the IRS's satisfaction a business purpose for that requested tax year, (2) elects a particular tax year as allowed under Code Sec. 444 (see ¶ 302.02), or (3) elects to use a 52- to 53-week tax year that ends with reference to its required tax year or a tax year elected under Code Sec. 444.[60] (See ¶ 302.02.)

---

[57] Code Sec. 742 and Code Sec. 1011.
[58] Code Sec. 1222.

[59] Code Sec. 1223(1).
[60] Reg. § 1.706-1(b)(2)(ii).

Reason for the Rule: When a partnership computes taxable income, each of the partners includes their allocated share of partnership income, gain, loss, deduction, or credit from the partnership tax year ending within or with the partner's tax year. Without the rules outlined in ¶ 1404, when a partnership's tax year ended on January 31, a calendar-year partner's income from the partnership would be reported by the partner in his tax year ending on December 31 of that same year, thereby resulting in an 11-month deferral of income recognition and payment of tax. To prevent this deferral of income and payment of tax, a provision of the Tax Reform Act of 1986 added the "least aggregate deferral of income" rule to the Code. When combined with the majority partner's and principal partners' year-end tests, the ability to defer the payment of tax through the selection of a tax year end has been substantially curtailed.

Majority partners' year-end. This rule provides that the partnership's tax year must conform to the year-end used by its partners that own a majority interest in the partnership. The **majority partners rule** only applies if a partner, or group of partners, owns more than a 50-percent interest in partnership capital *and* profits. This test is applied annually on the first day of the partnership's tax year.[61] If a partnership's required tax year is determined under the majority partners rule, the partnership must use the year-end of that used by those partners, unless the partnership makes an election under Code Sec. 444 to use a different year-end or the partnership can prove a natural business year.

Example 54: ABC partnership is formed on April 6, 2015, when Klatten Industries and Joanna McNeal contribute property in exchange for an 80-percent and a 20-percent interest in capital and profits, respectively. Klatten uses a June 30 year-end; Joanna uses the calendar year-end. Since Klatten is a majority partner in ABC, the partnership's required tax year is a June 30 fiscal year.

Example 55: Assume the same facts as in Example 54, except that on June 30, 2015, Klatten Industries sells half of its interest in ABC (equal to 40 percent of its interest in the capital and profits of ABC) to Jeremy Odam, a calendar year taxpayer. As of July 1, 2015, Klatten no longer owns a majority interest in ABC. Instead, Joanna and Jeremy now collectively own 60 percent (20% + 40%) of ABC. Thus, effective July 1, 2015, ABC's required year-end changes to a calendar year. ABC is required to file a short year income tax return for the period July 1, 2015, to December 31, 2015.

Example 56: Assume the same facts as in Example 55, except Klatten Industries sells its one-half interest in ABC to a corporation that uses a March 31 fiscal year. As of July 1, 2015, ABC no longer has a majority partner because its three partners, each with a different year-end, now own 20 percent, 40 percent, and 40 percent, respectively. The majority interest rule does not apply to ABC, and it must decide if its required tax year is determined under the principal partners rule.

Principal partners' year-end. The second of the conformity rules is the principal partner rule, which applies only when partners having the same year-end do not own a majority interest in partnership capital and profits. The **principal partner rule** requires that the partnership adopt a tax year used by *all* of its principal partners. A **principal partner** is a partner that has at least a five-percent interest in the profits *or* capital of the partnership. The principal partner rule does not apply unless ALL partners who own at least a five-percent interest in capital *or* profits have the same year-end. If neither the majority interest nor the principal partners rules applies, the partnership's required tax year is the tax year that results in the least aggregate deferral of income.[62]

Example 57: Hensley, Inc. and Ingram Enterprises both use a fiscal year that ends on September 30. Each corporation owns a 20-percent interest in the DEF partnership. Each of the

---

[61] Code Sec. 706(b)(1)(B)(i), (4).

[62] Code Sec. 706(b)(1)(B)(ii)(3).

remaining partners in DEF owns less than a five-percent interest in DEF. Hensley and Ingram are the only two principal partners of DEF, and since they have the same year-end, DEF's required tax year is the fiscal year that ends on September 30.

Example 58: Assume the same facts as in Example 57, except Angela Lenox is admitted to the partnership as a partner owning a five-percent profits-only interest in DEF. Angela uses a calendar year-end. Since Angela owns at least a five-percent interest in capital *or* profits, DEF's principal partners no longer all have the same year-end. Accordingly, DEF's required tax year is no longer the year-end of its principal partners. Instead, it must now determine which year-end results in the least aggregate deferral of partnership income.

Least aggregate deferral of income. When the partnership and its partners do not use the same tax year, the tax laws require that each partner's allocable share of partnership items be reported in that partner's tax year that includes the year-end of the partnership. If the tax year of a partner is different from that of the partnership, the partner's share of the partnership taxable income is to be reported as if the entire amount were received by the partner on the closing date of the partnership tax year.

Example 59: Tom Reynolds (a calendar year taxpayer) is a partner in JKL partnership. JKL uses an approved January 31 year-end. Tom reports his share of JKL's income for the year ended January 31, 2015, on his 2015 calendar year individual income tax return. Thus, even though $11/12$ths of JKL's income was earned during 2014 (February 1, 2014–December 31, 2014), all of JKL's income for the 2014–2015 fiscal year is reported on Tom's 2015 calendar year tax return that includes JKL's January 31, 2015 year-end.

When a partnership cannot determine its required tax year using either the majority interest or the principal partners rule, that fact indicates that its partners use a variety of year-ends. The government's goal in this situation is to have the partnership use as its year-end the one that produces the shortest time for the government to wait to tax the income earned by the partnership. This method, called the **least aggregate deferral of income rule**,[63] involves performing a test using each of the year-ends of its partners and determining which of those year-ends, on average, will allow the government to collect taxes on the partnership income the most quickly. Using each of its partners' tax years as possible tax years, the number of months of deferral is measured and then weighted in accordance with the percentage of ownership of the partners using that particular year-end. The sum of the weighted deferrals for each tax year is compared. The tax year with the shortest (least) aggregate deferral is the partnership's required tax year.

Example 60: RST partnership has three equal partners. Robbins, Inc. uses a March 31 year-end; Schutsler, Inc. uses a July 31 year-end; and Terry Teranto uses a calendar year-end. Since no one partner or group of partners owns more than 50 percent of the capital and profits of RST, and since the three principal partners have a different year-end, RST's required year-end is determined using the year-end that produces the least aggregate deferral of income. In determining which of these three possible year-ends meets this requirement, the deferral period for each partner using each of the year-ends is determined. The deferral period is the number of months from the selected year-end until the partner's year-end. These deferral periods are then weighted by the partner's percentage of ownership in RST (one-third for each partner in this example). The sum of the deferrals for each of the partners for a particular year-end equals the aggregate deferral for that possible year-end.

---

[63] Code Sec. 706(b)(1)(B)(iii) and Temp. Reg. § 1.706-1T.

If March 31 were used as RST's year-end

Partner	Months of Deferral			Weighted Deferral Period
Robbins	0	×	1/3	0
Schutsler	4 (April–July)	×	1/3	1.33
Terry	9 (April–December)	×	1/3	3.00
Aggregate deferral using a March 31 year-end				4.33

If July 31 were used as RST's year-end

Partner	Months of Deferral			Weighted Deferral Period
Robbins	8 (August–March)	×	1/3	2.67
Schutsler	0	×	1/3	0
Terry	5 (August–December)	×	1/3	1.67
Aggregate deferral using a July 31 year-end				4.34

If December 31 were used as RST's year-end

Partner	Months' Deferral			Weighted Deferral Period
Robbins	3 (January–March)	×	1/3	1.00
Schutsler	7 (January–July)	×	1/3	2.33
Terry	0	×	1/3	0
Aggregate deferral using a December 31 year-end				3.33

The least of the three weighted aggregate deferrals is 3.33, which corresponds to using a December 31 year-end. Thus, RST's required tax year is a calendar year.

Example 61: Assume the same facts as in Example 60, except Robbins's ownership in RST is 40 percent; Schutsler's ownership is 40 percent; and Terry's ownership is 20 percent. To determine RST's required tax year, the aggregate deferral periods are computed as follows:

If March 31 were used as RST's year-end

Partner	Months of Deferral			Weighted Deferral Period
Robbins	0	×	40%	0
Schutsler	4 (April–July)	×	40%	1.6
Terry	9 (April–December)	×	20%	1.8
Aggregate deferral				3.4

If July 31 were used as RST's year-end

Partner	Months of Deferral			Weighted Deferral Period
Robbins	8 (August–March)	×	40%	3.2
Schutsler	0	×	40%	0
Terry	5 (August–December)	×	20%	1.0
Aggregate deferral				4.2

If December 31 were used as RST's year-end

Partner	Months of Deferral			Weighted Deferral Period
Robbins	3 (January–March)	×	40%	1.2
Schutsler	7 (January–July)	×	40%	2.8
Terry	0	×	20%	0
Aggregate deferral				4.0

The least of the three aggregate deferrals is 3.4, which corresponds to a March 31 fiscal end. Thus, RST's required year-end is the fiscal year that begins on April 1 and ends on March 31, unless it shows that it has a business purpose for using another year-end or elects a different year-end under Code Sec. 444.

Natural business year. Although the Code prescribes various rules that must be followed to determine a partnership's required tax year, a partnership is allowed to select a different tax year if it can establish to the IRS's satisfaction that a business purpose exists for using the requested tax year. A business purpose exists if the partnership's tax year coincides with its natural business year, which is a tax year in which the partnership receives at least 25 percent of its gross receipts in the last two months.[64] However, to demonstrate a natural business year, the 25-percent gross receipts test must be met for the preceding three consecutive 12-month periods ending with the desired year-end.[65] If more than one tax year exists in which the 25-percent gross receipts test can be met for the previous three years, the tax year that produces a higher percentage of gross sales during the last two months is the business's natural business year. (See ¶ 304.01.)

Example 62: M&N partnership currently uses a June 30 year-end. M&N wants to change to a March 31 fiscal year. M&N would like the change to become effective after the short tax year July 1, 2015, through March 31, 2016. During the last 12-month period ending on the desired year-end (April 1, 2015, to March 31, 2016), the partnership's gross receipts were $300,000, and its gross receipts for February 2016 and March 2016 total $90,000. Thus, gross receipts for the last two months are 30 percent of the total gross receipts for the desired March 31 fiscal year ($90,000/$300,000). When M&N performs this same calculation for the 12-month periods ending March 31, 2015, and March 31, 2014, its percentage of gross receipts in the last two months is 31 and 27 percent, respectively. Since the percentages are at least 25 percent, M&N passes the gross receipts test. However, M&N cannot adopt a March 31 year-end unless it can show that no other tax year would produce a greater percentage of gross receipts in the last two months. Thus, M&N would need to perform this test for each of the 11 other possible tax years before it can determine whether it can adopt March 31 as its tax year.

Section 444 election. A partnership may elect a different tax year under Code Sec. 444, provided that the selected year-end does not result in a deferral of income more than three months over the partnership's required tax year. In Example 61, RST is required to use a March 31 fiscal year-end; however, RST can elect to use either a December 31, January 31, or February 28 year-end because none of these year-ends would cause a deferral of partnership income of more than three months. (The deferral period from December 31 to March 31 is exactly three months).

---

[64] Code Sec. 706(b)(1)(C).   [65] Rev. Proc. 2002-38, 2002-1 CB 1037.

For the privilege of electing a tax year other than its required tax year, the partnership must prepay to the government an amount that represents the tax on the deferred income that the owners will not report until a later year.[66] The exact amount that must be prepaid is calculated using Form 8752, *Required Payment or Refund Under Section 7519*.

Example 63: Refer back to Example 61, in which RST's required year-end is March 31. Under Code Sec. 444, RST can elect to use a calendar year, provided it agrees to prepay (keep on reserve with the IRS) any taxes associated with the profits generated from January 1 to March 31 of its tax year. Each year the partnership computes its estimated tax liability for those three months of the year. If the estimate for the year is higher than the amount currently on reserve with the IRS, it must file Form 8752 and pay the additional taxes owed. If the estimate for the year is less than the taxes on reserve with the IRS, RST can request a refund by filing Form 8752.

.02 Permissible Accounting Methods

As a rule, a partnership may elect to use any method of tax accounting that clearly reflects its income and that is regularly used in keeping its books and records. The permissible methods of accounting introduced in Chapter 3 include the cash receipts and disbursements method, the accrual method, and the hybrid method (see ¶¶ 306–308). However, a partnership usually cannot use the cash method of accounting if one of the following applies:

1. The partnership has at least one corporate partner, average annual gross receipts of more than $5 million, and it is not a farming business or

2. The partnership is a tax shelter as defined in Code Sec. 448(d)(3).

In addition to selecting an overall accounting method, partnerships are also required to abide by the special methods of accounting for certain items, such as installment sales, long-term contracts, and research and development expenditures, as discussed in Chapter 3 (see ¶ 309).

.03 Calculating Partnership Income

At the end of each tax year, a partnership (including an LLP or an LLC that elects to be taxed as a partnership) is required to file Form 1065, *U.S. Partnership Income Tax Return*. On Form 1065, the partnership provides a summary of all income, gains, deductions, losses, and credits generated during the tax year using the appropriate methods of accounting. The various partnership items are then allocated among the partners in accordance with the partnership agreement, and each partner is issued a Schedule K-1, *Partner's Share of Income, Deductions, Credits, etc.*, which reports each partner's distributive shares of the various partnership items.

The partners include the amounts reported on their respective Schedule K-1s on their income tax returns for the year that includes the last day of the partnership's tax year, regardless of whether any or all of the income was distributed to them during the year.[67] Even if restrictions exist that prevent a partner from withdrawing its share of partnership income, the partner must include the amounts reported on Schedule K-1 in the tax year that contains the day of the partnership's year-end.[68] If the partnership has more than one closing date within a partner's tax year, the partner's distributive shares from more than one partnership period are included in the partner's return.[69]

Example 64: AB partnership has two equal partners, A and B. During its tax year ending August 31, 2015, AB generates profits of $200,000. Of this amount, $50,000 was distributed to each partner during the year, and the remaining $100,000 was retained in the partnership. Although A and B receive only $50,000 each from the partnership during the year, each must report its entire $100,000 distributive share of the

---

[66] Code Secs. 444(c)(1), 7519.
[67] Code Sec. 706(a).

[68] Reg. § 1.702-1; *J.A. Basqe*, SCt, 73-1 USTC ¶ 9250, 410 U.S. 441.
[69] Code Sec. 706.

partnership income on its own respective income tax return for the tax year that includes August 31, 2015.

Example 65: CDE partnership currently uses a fiscal year ending June 30. Carla Tucker is a calendar year taxpayer who is a partner in CDE. On July 1, 2014, CDE performs the required tests for its year-end and determines that it must change to an October 31 year-end effective November 1, 2015. Thus, CDE will file its normal 12-month income tax return for the period from July 1, 2014, to June 30, 2015, and it will then file a short period return for the period from July 1, 2015, to October 31, 2015. CDE's next income tax return will be for the period from November 1, 2015, to October 31, 2016. As a calendar year taxpayer, Carla will report on her 2015 individual income tax return her distributive share of partnership items for CDE's tax returns that end during Carla's 2015 tax year (June 30, 2015, and October 31, 2015). On her 2016 income tax return, Carla will report her distributive share of partnership items reported on CDE's tax return for the year ending October 31, 2016.

Guaranteed payments. If any partner is paid amounts from the partnership that are determined *without regard* to the profits generated by the partnership during the year, such amounts are referred to as **guaranteed payments.** Although partners are not considered employees of the partnership, guaranteed payments is the closest thing to salary or wage payments that a partnership can make to any of its partners. However, guaranteed payments can be made for services provided other than personal services.

Guaranteed payments are ordinary income to the partner and can be deducted by the partnership if made for services that are not capital in nature. Thus, if a partner rents out a building that it owns to the partnership for $10,000 a month, the landlord partner is guaranteed to be paid $120,000 ($10,000 × 12 months) over the course of the partnership's tax year, regardless of how well or poorly the partnership performs during the year. The tax laws require that the partner report and pay tax on the rental income it receives from the partnership and that the partnership deduct the rental expense paid to the partner from its gross income for the year. Consequently, the amount of partnership profits that are allocated to the partners is reduced by $120,000.

Example 66: GHI partnership is owned equally by three partners. In addition to being a one-third partner in GHI, Hugh Dunkin performs accounting and tax services for GHI. GHI agrees to pay Hugh $20,000 a year for his services, regardless of the partnership's performance during the year. During the year, the GHI's profits (not including the amounts paid to Hugh for his accounting and tax services) are $140,000. When reporting its activities on Form 1065, GHI deducts the $20,000 of guaranteed payments made to Hugh during the year and reports an overall profit of $120,000 ($140,000 – $20,000). Each partner's distributive share of these profits is $40,000 ($120,000/3), which is reported on each partner's respective Schedule K-1. In addition, GHI reports the $20,000 guaranteed payment on Hugh's Schedule K-1. When Hugh completes his individual income tax return for the year that includes GHI's year-end, he will include both the $20,000 of guaranteed payments and the $40,000 of partnership profits in his gross income and pay taxes on those amounts.

 Spotlight: Since partners are not considered employees of the partnership, the partnership does not withhold tax from amounts paid to partners for personal services rendered to the partnership. When a general or limited partner performs personal services for the partnership and receives a guaranteed payment from the partnership, the partner is required to pay self-employment taxes on such income. In addition, ordinary income that is allocated to an individual who is a general partner is also considered earnings subject to self-employment tax. (The calculation of ordinary income is discussed in the next part of this section). These earnings from self-employment are added to an individual partner's other sources of self-employment income and self-employment taxes are then calculated on these amounts using the rules discussed earlier in this chapter. (See ¶ 1301.03.) Sole proprietors can deduct one-half of their self-employment tax as an above line deduction.

Ordinary income versus separately stated items. At the end of the tax year, the partnership totals up its various items of income, loss, deduction, gain, and credit. It then separates out those items that are treated differently by different taxpayers.[70] For example, when a partnership makes a charitable contribution, it determines the amount that is deductible under the tax laws described in Chapter 5 (see ¶ 511.02). However, since the tax laws apply different charitable contribution limits to corporate and individual taxpayers, it would be inappropriate to deduct charitable contributions against partnership gross income.

Example 67: Albert Shaffer is a partner in ABC partnership. During the year, ABC contributes to various qualified public charities. Albert's share of those contributions is $1,000. During that same year, Albert personally contributes $5,000 to a qualified public charity. When preparing his individual income tax return, Albert's total charitable contributions for the year are $6,000 ($5,000 + $1,000). Since these amounts were contributed to qualified public charities, he applies the 50-percent AGI limit to determine how much of the $6,000 he can deduct as an itemized deduction on his income tax return. (See ¶ 511.04.)

Example 68: Continuing with Example 67, Byron Industries is also a partner in ABC. Byron's share of ABC's charitable contributions is $2,500. Bryon adds this amount to any contributions it makes to qualified charitable organizations for the year and applies the 10-percent taxable income limitation to determine how much it can deduct from its gross income on its corporate tax return. (See ¶ 511.04).

In addition to separately stating items for which the tax laws are different for corporate and individual taxpayers, any item for which the tax treatment *could* differ among two partners must be separately stated on the partnership tax return. For example, both corporate and individual taxpayers are limited in 2010 and 2011 to a total of $500,000 of Section 179 expense, subject to the taxpayer having sufficient taxable income (see ¶ 702.03). Since the amount of taxable income from the business differs among the partners, any Section 179 expense elected by the partnership during the tax year must be separated from the other partnership items, and each partner's respective share of Section 179 expense must be separately reported on the partner's Schedule K-1.

 Spotlight: The Creating Small Business Jobs Act of 2010 (P.L. 111-240) increased Section 179 dollar limit to $500,000 for tax years beginning in 2010 and 2011. The temporary rule which allows the revocation of the Section 179 election without special permission from the IRS is extended one additional year through tax years beginning before 2012.

Example 69: Morton, Inc. owns a 75-percent interest in MNO partnership. Because Morton is a majority partner, MNO's required tax year is the same as Morton's calendar year-end. During the year, MNO purchases Section 179 property and elects to expense the maximum $500,000 that is allowed in 2011. As a 75-percent partner in MNO, Morton's share of MNO's Section 179 expense is $375,000 ($500,000 × 75%). This amount flows through separately from ordinary income on Morton's Schedule K-1. When preparing its 2011 tax return, Morton adds the $375,000 to any Section 179 property it elects to expense during 2011, keeping in mind that it can only elect a

---

[70] Code Sec. 702 and Reg. § 1.702-1(a).

total of $500,000 of Section 179 expense for 2011. In addition, any amounts that Morton elects to expense in 2011 (including the $375,000 from MNO) can only be deducted if Morton's taxable income from the business is sufficient to absorb these amounts in 2011. Any amounts not deducted in 2011 are carried forward to Morton's 2012 tax year as Section 179 expense deduction in that year. (See ¶ 702.03.)

Figure 13-4 lists items that a partnership must state separately from the partnerships ordinary income or loss when preparing its tax return.

Figure 13-4 Separately Stated Items

- Guaranteed payments made to partners (see ¶ 1305.03).

- Gains and losses from sales or exchanges of capital assets held for one year or less (see ¶ 901).

- Gains and losses from sales or exchanges of capital assets held for more than one year (see ¶ 901), including a breakdown of those that may be subject to a maximum 28-percent tax rate (from the sale of collectibles and Section 1202 stock) and any unrecaptured Section 1250 gain subject to a maximum 25-percent tax rate.

- Gains and losses from sales or exchanges of Section 1231 property (see ¶ 904).

- All other items included in the calculation of investment income and investment expense that are necessary to compute an individual's investment interest expense limitation. This includes interest income, dividend income (keeping separate any amounts of qualified dividends that are eligible for the reduced tax rates applicable to individual taxpayers (see ¶ 907), and (investment) expenses for the production of income that are not business deductions.

- Rental income and royalties that may be used as passive income in computing an individual's passive loss limitation.

- Section 179 deduction (see ¶ 702.03).

- Charitable contributions (see ¶ 511).

- Any special allocations of income, gain, loss, or deduction under the partnership agreement (see ¶ 1305.04).[71]

- Foreign income taxes paid or accrued plus the partner's share of foreign-source income that the partner can use to compute its foreign tax credit (see ¶ 1117).

- Any tax credits generated by the partnership during the year (see Chapter 11).

- The partner's net earnings from self-employment. For general partners, this amount includes the partner's distributive share of ordinary income during the year plus any guaranteed payments the partner received for personal services rendered to the partnership.[72] A limited partner's distributive share of partnership income is not earnings from self-employment.[73]

- The partner's share of any alternative minimum tax (AMT) (see ¶ 1005), tax preference items (see ¶ 1007), and AMT adjustment items (see ¶ 1008) that are attributable to partnership operations during the year.

- Dividends for which there is a dividends received deduction available (see ¶ 1203.01).

The partnership need only separately track those items of income, deduction, gain, or loss that could be treated differently on the partners' own respective income tax returns. Items that are treated identically for all types of taxpayers can be lumped together and reported as one lump sum

---

[71] Reg. § 1.702-1.
[72] Code Sec. 1402(a).
[73] Code Sec. 1402(a)(13).

amount called "ordinary income (loss)." Therefore, amounts recognized as gross receipts or sales (net of any cost of goods sold) are included in the partnership's ordinary income (loss). Also included would be any gains or losses taxed as ordinary income from the disposal of property, which includes gains and losses from business property held short-term and any depreciation recapture on the sale or exchange of depreciable property. Likewise, salaries, wages, and amounts paid for employee benefit programs would be ordinary deductions included in the calculation of the partnership's ordinary income (loss). Also included in the calculation would be guaranteed payments made to partners (assuming the costs are not capital in nature), repairs, bad debts, interest, taxes, rent, depreciation expense (Modified Accelerated Cost Recovery System (MACRS) or alternative depreciation system (ADS)), depletion expense, and other similar ordinary deductions.

Example 70: Susie Reeser owns a 25-percent interest in QRST partnership. Both Susie and QRST use a calendar year-end. For the year ended December 31, 2015, QRST reports the following items of partnership income, gain, loss, deduction, and credit.

Gross sales	$400,000
Cost of goods sold	120,000
Wage expense	80,000
Depreciation recapture	5,000
Net Section 1231 gain	24,000
Equipment rental	18,000
Mortgage interest	10,000
Real estate taxes	5,000
MACRS depreciation	11,000
Contribution to employee retirement plans	3,000
Charitable contributions	10,000

On its partnership tax return, QRST lumps together all items that are taxed as ordinary income or loss without limitation to any partner as follows:

Gross profit (net of cost of goods sold)			$280,000
Depreciation recapture			5,000
Less:	Wage expense	(80,000)	
	Rent expense	(18,000)	
	Interest	(10,000)	
	Taxes	(5,000)	
	MACRS depreciation	(11,000)	
	Retirement plan contributions	(3,000)	(127,000)
Ordinary income of the partnership			$158,000

QRST then allocates the $158,000 of ordinary income to its partners on their respective Schedule K-1s. On her personal income tax return, Susie includes $39,500 of ordinary income in her gross income ($158,000 × 25%).

In addition to allocating a 25-percent share of the ordinary income to Susie, QRST allocates 25-percent of its net Section 1231 gain and charitable contributions to her. Susie adds her $6,000 share ($24,000 × 25%) of the Section 1231 gain to the netting process on her income tax return to determine whether any of the gain can be considered long-term capital gain subject to a maximum 15-percent tax rate. Both the $39,500 ($158,000 × 25%) and $6,000 increase Susie's AGI. Susie then adds her $2,500 ($10,000 × 25%) share of QRST's charitable contributions to her own contributions and then applies the AGI limits to determine the amount she can deduct as an itemized deduction.

> **Planning Pointer:** Since amounts allocated to partners are not subject to withholding, partners will need to make sure that the proper amount of taxes are prepaid to the federal and state governments during the year. If an individual partner (or partner's spouse if filing a joint return) is also an employee, the partner (or partner's spouse) can arrange to have additional amounts withheld from wages to cover the additional taxes owed on partnership income. In all other cases, the partner will need to make quarterly estimated payments to avoid any underpayment penalties. (See ¶ ¶ 409.01 and 409.02.) In addition to income taxes, individual partners must also consider any self-employment taxes that will be assessed on income allocated from the partnership that is considered self-employment income. This includes any guaranteed payments for personal services, as well as a general partner's distributive share of ordinary income.

Character of gain or loss from the sale of contributed property. Normally, the character of the gain or loss recognized by the partnership depends on the type of property sold and the partnership's holding period of the property. For example, if a partnership purchases a capital asset and sells it for a gain after holding it for nine months, the partnership will report a short-term capital gain on its tax return and will allocate the short-term capital gain among its partners on their respective Schedule K-1s. However, special rules apply to the character of the gain or loss recognized on the sale or other disposition of contributed property. "Contributed property" is property the partnership acquires as a contribution from a partner in exchange for a capital and profits interest in the partnership. When a partnership sells contributed property, the nature and character of the gain or loss is sometimes determined by the character and holding period of the property in the hands of the contributing partner.[74] These special rules apply to the sale of unrealized receivables, inventory, and capital loss property.

An **unrealized receivable** includes any right to income for services or goods that are not capital assets that have not been previously recorded in gross income under the contributing partner's method of accounting.[75] Thus, if a cash method partner contributes to a partnership amounts due from customers, the receivables are unrealized receivables because those amounts have yet to be reported in income. The amounts will be recognized as ordinary income as they are collected by the partnership, regardless of the partnership's method of accounting.[76]

Example 71: In exchange for a capital and profits interest in ABC partnership, Anthony Ryan contributes $50,000 of accounts receivable he had obtained in the course of operating his sole proprietorship. Anthony used the cash method of accounting in his sole proprietorship, and therefore, had not reported these accounts receivable in his gross income prior to contributing them to ABC. Thus, Anthony's basis in the accounts receivable is $0, which becomes ABC's basis in the receivables. When ABC collects the $50,000 from Anthony's former clients, it will include the $50,000 in its gross income as part of partnership profits for the year.

If the contributed property is inventory in the hands of the contributing partner, then for five years after the date the partner contributes the property to the partnership, any gain or loss recognized from the sale of the property will be taxed as ordinary income or loss to the partnership. This rule applies regardless of whether the property is inventory in the hands of the partnership. After five years, the character of the gain is determined based on how the property is used by the partnership.[77]

---

[74] Code Sec. 724.

[75] Code Sec. 751(c) and Reg. § 1.751-1(c).

[76] Code Sec. 724(a).

[77] Code Sec. 724(b).

Example 72: On April 29, 2015, Frank Simmons contributes inventory from his sole proprietorship in exchange for a 30-percent capital and profits interest in EFG partnership. At the time of the contribution, the FMV of the inventory is $50,000. Frank's basis in the inventory is $22,000. EFG's basis in the inventory also is $22,000. If EFG sells the inventory within five years of April 29, 2015, the gain will be taxed as ordinary income or loss to EFG.

Example 73: Continuing with Example 72, Frank is a real estate developer, and the property he contributes to EFG is land that was inventory in his business. If EFG is in the real estate business, the land will be inventory to the partnership and any gain or loss upon its sale will always produce ordinary income or loss.

Example 74: Assume the same facts as in Example 73, except EFG is a law firm and it uses the land as an employee parking lot. If EFG sells the land in 2015 for $60,000, it will recognize $38,000 of ordinary income ($60,000 – $22,000). If, however, EFG sells the land for $60,000 after five years have passed, it will recognize $38,000 of Section 1231 gain.

Example 75: Assume the same facts as in Example 74, except that EFG holds the land as an investment. The $38,000 gain on the sale of the land will be characterized as long-term capital gain if EFG waits more than five years to sell the land.

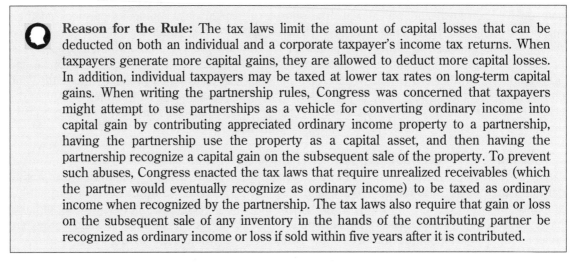

Reason for the Rule: The tax laws limit the amount of capital losses that can be deducted on both an individual and a corporate taxpayer's income tax returns. When taxpayers generate more capital gains, they are allowed to deduct more capital losses. In addition, individual taxpayers may be taxed at lower tax rates on long-term capital gains. When writing the partnership rules, Congress was concerned that taxpayers might attempt to use partnerships as a vehicle for converting ordinary income into capital gain by contributing appreciated ordinary income property to a partnership, having the partnership use the property as a capital asset, and then having the partnership recognize a capital gain on the subsequent sale of the property. To prevent such abuses, Congress enacted the tax laws that require unrealized receivables (which the partner would eventually recognize as ordinary income) to be taxed as ordinary income when recognized by the partnership. The tax laws also require that gain or loss on the subsequent sale of any inventory in the hands of the contributing partner be recognized as ordinary income or loss if sold within five years after it is contributed.

For property that was a capital asset in the hands of the contributing partner, any loss on the disposal of the property by the partnership within five years is a capital loss to the extent that the adjusted basis of the property to the contributing partner exceeded the property's FMV immediately before the contribution.[78] This special rule applies only if property that had declined in value is contributed to the partnership and within five years is sold by the partnership at a loss.

Example 76: On March 8, 2015, Dottie Britten contributes land worth $50,000 in exchange for a capital and profits interest in XYZ partnership. Prior to contributing the land, Dottie held it as an investment. Her basis in the land is $130,000, which becomes XYZ's basis in the land and Dottie's adjusted basis in XYZ. The land is Section 1231 property in the hands of XYZ. If XYZ sells the land for less than its $130,000 basis within five years of March 8, 2015, it will recognize the first $80,000 of loss as a capital loss. Any additional loss would be characterized as a Section 1231 loss.

Example 77: Continuing with the Example 76, assume that XYZ sells the land for $100,000 on January 15, 2015. XYZ recognizes a $30,000 capital loss ($100,000 – $130,000).

---

[78] Code Sec. 724(c).

Example 78: Assume the same facts as in Example 77, except XYZ sells the land for $30,000. XYZ recognizes a $100,000 loss ($30,000 – $130,000), of which the first $80,000 is a long-term capital loss. The remaining $20,000 ($100,000 – $80,000) loss is recognized as a Section 1231 loss.

Example 79: Assume the same facts as in Example 78, except XYZ sells the land for $160,000. XYZ recognizes a $30,000 gain ($160,000 – $130,000), which XYZ recognizes as a Section 1231 gain.

> **Reason for the Rule:** Because of the tax laws that limit the amount of capital losses that can be deducted on both an individual and a corporate taxpayer's income tax return, Congress was concerned that taxpayers might attempt to use partnerships as a vehicle for converting capital losses into ordinary losses. To prevent abuses in this area, Congress requires that the partnership recognize a capital loss on the sale of contributed property that was a capital asset in the hands of the contributing partner. However, the amount of the loss that must be characterized as a capital loss is limited to the amount by which the adjusted basis of the property to the contributing partner exceeds the property's FMV at the time it is contributed to the partnership.

.04 Allocating Partnership Items

The partners are liable for the tax on the partnership income, regardless of whether the income is actually distributed to them.[79] For the most part, the allocation of any item of income, gain, loss, deduction, or credit among the partners is controlled by the partnership agreement. If the partnership agreement does not provide for the allocation of any item, the partner's distributive share of each item will be determined by reference to the partner's interest in the partnership, after taking into account all facts and circumstances. The partner's distributive share of each item will be determined by the partner's interest in the partnership if the partnership agreement lacks substantial economic effect.[80]

Example 80: Eric Brown owns 25 percent of ABCD partnership. The partnership agreement calls for all depreciation expense and dividend income to be allocated to Eric. As a 25-percent partner in ABCD, Eric normally would be allocated 25 percent of these items. However, if the allocation of 100 percent of these items has substantial economic effect, then the allocation will be respected, and ABCD will be allowed to allocate these items in accordance with the terms in the partnership agreement.

Special allocations. To determine whether an allocation specified in the partnership agreement has **substantial economic effect**, it is first necessary to determine whether the allocation has economic effect and then determine whether that effect is substantial.[81] An allocation in the partnership agreement has *economic effect* if (1) the partnership maintains separate capital accounts in accordance with prescribed regulatory rules for each partner; (2) upon liquidation of the partnership or any partner's interest in the partnership, liquidating distributions are required to be made in accordance with positive capital account balances of the partners; and (3) each partner with a deficit balance in his or her capital account following the liquidation must restore the deficit (negative) balance.[82] Normally, an economic effect will be deemed *substantial* if (1) a reasonable possibility exists that the allocation will substantially affect the dollar amount of the partners' shares of the partnership's tax items independently of tax consequences and (2) the partner to whom an allocation is made actually receives the economic benefit or bears the economic burden corresponding to the allocation.[83]

---

[79] Code Sec. 701; Reg. § 1.701-1.
[80] Code Secs. 704(a) and (b), 706(d); Reg. § 1.706-1(c)(2).
[81] Reg. § 1.704-1(b)(2).

[82] Reg. § 1.704-1(b)(2)(ii)(b).
[83] Reg. § 1.704-1(b)(2).

The rules governing what constitutes substantial economic effect are very complex and beyond the scope of this chapter; however, it is important to note that if certain conditions are met, partnership items can be specially allocated among the partners. For example, assuming the requirements of substantial economic effect are met, a partner that owns a 40-percent interest in capital and profits may be allocated none of one item—the partnership's tax-exempt income, for example—and instead be allocated 100 percent of another partnership item, such as dividend income. Any specially allocated items must be separately stated on the partners' Schedule K-1s and are not included as part of the partnership's ordinary income or loss.

Reason for the Rule: Much of the complexity of the tax rules surrounding partnerships stems from Congress's concern that partners may use the partnership to manipulate the reporting of income or loss, thus distorting their tax liabilities. For example, there is a requirement that each partnership allocation of a tax item must have substantial economic effect. This is designed to prevent the allocation of income to partners with tax losses that the income would offset or the allocation of deductions to partners with high incomes for whom the loss allocations would have more value due to their higher income tax brackets. In these situations, the total tax liabilities of all the partners could be less if the partnership were to allocate income among partners for the sole purpose of reducing taxes without any business purpose or consequence to any of the partners.

Required allocations. The tax laws require that certain partnership items be allocated to the partners in a particular manner, despite the allocations that may be specified in the partnership agreement. Like special allocations, these required allocations are separately stated on the partner's Schedule K-1. Although the tax laws surrounding these required allocations are extremely complex and beyond the scope of this introductory chapter on partnership taxation, a brief discussion of a couple of the required allocations provides an idea of how the rules work.

When a partner contributes appreciated property to the partnership, the amount of the appreciation represents realized gain that neither the partner nor the partnership immediately recognizes. Instead, the contributing partner's adjusted basis in the contributed property becomes the partnership's basis in the property and is added to the partner's basis in the partnership interest. By having both parties take a "substituted basis" (and by the special allocation rules discussed in the paragraphs that follow), the tax laws ensure that the contributing partner eventually recognizes (and pays tax on) the gain. This occurs either when the partnership sells the property or when the partner sells the partnership interest.

When a partnership sells property, the recognized gain or loss is normally allocated among the partners in accordance with the terms in the partnership agreement (assuming the allocation has substantial economic effect). However, when contributed property is sold, the realized gain or loss must be allocated to the contributing partner to the extent of any deferred gain or loss to the contributing partner.[84] Any remaining gain or loss is allocated in accordance with the partnership agreement.

Example 81: David Cotton contributes land worth $100,000 in exchange for a one-third capital and profits interest in ABC partnership. ABC plans to use the land as a parking lot for its employees, thus making the land Section 1231 property in the hands of the partnership. David purchased the land several years earlier as an investment for $30,000. Thus, when David contributes the land to ABC, he realizes a $70,000 gain ($100,000 − $30,000); however, recognition of the gain is postponed, and both David's basis in his ABC partnership interest and ABC's basis in the land are $30,000. Furthermore, David's long-term holding period for the land carries over and becomes the holding

---

[84] Code Sec. 704(c)(1)(C).

period for both David's interest in ABC and ABC's holding period in the land. If David immediately sells his partnership interest for $100,000, he will recognize a $70,000 ($100,000 – $30,000) long-term capital gain.

Example 82: Assume the same facts as in Example 81, except David does not sell his interest in ABC. Instead, ABC sells the land for $100,000, and the partnership recognizes a $70,000 Section 1231 gain ($100,000 – $30,000). The tax laws require that ABC allocate the entire gain to David, which will cause his basis in ABC partnership to increase to $100,000 ($30,000 + $70,000). If David then sells his partnership interest, the increase to his partnership basis will ensure that the $70,000 gain from the sale of the land is not taxed a second time.

Example 83: Assume the same facts as in Example 82, except ABC sells the land for $120,000. The partnership recognizes $90,000 of Section 1231 gain ($120,000 – $30,000). The tax laws generally require that ABC allocate the first $70,000 of gain to David. The remaining $20,000 gain ($90,000 – $70,000) is then allocated among the partners in accordance with the partnership agreement.

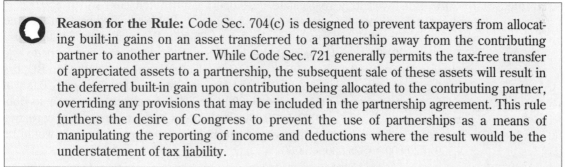

Reason for the Rule: Code Sec. 704(c) is designed to prevent taxpayers from allocating built-in gains on an asset transferred to a partnership away from the contributing partner to another partner. While Code Sec. 721 generally permits the tax-free transfer of appreciated assets to a partnership, the subsequent sale of these assets will result in the deferred built-in gain upon contribution being allocated to the contributing partner, overriding any provisions that may be included in the partnership agreement. This rule furthers the desire of Congress to prevent the use of partnerships as a means of manipulating the reporting of income and deductions where the result would be the understatement of tax liability.

When a partnership purchases a depreciable asset, the cost of the asset is depreciated over a number of years, and the depreciation expense is allocated among the partners. When a partner contributes depreciable property in exchange for an interest in the partnership, the partner's adjusted basis in the property becomes the partnership's tax basis, and accordingly, becomes the depreciable basis in the property. If the adjusted basis is less than the FMV of the contributed property, the partnership's total depreciation deductions will be less than they would have been had the partnership purchased the property for its FMV. This, in turn, means the partners will be allocated less depreciation than normally would have been allocated to them if the partnership had acquired the property for its FMV. Since the contributing partner is responsible for this difference, the tax laws require that the depreciation expense be specially allocated to the noncontributing partners to make up for any difference in total depreciation expense.[85]

Example 84: Amber Trane contributes depreciable property worth $50,000 in exchange for a 50-percent interest in AB partnership. Amber's basis in the property is $40,000. AB's basis in the depreciable property is $40,000, and therefore over the years AB will deduct depreciation expense totaling $40,000. The tax laws require that depreciation expense be allocated to the other partners to compensate for the $10,000 ($50,000 – $40,000) of depreciation that AB will never deduct because it uses Amber's substituted basis. In accordance with this rule, over the years the noncontributing partners would be entitled to 50 percent of the depreciation ($25,000) based upon the FMV at the date of contribution ($50,000). Amber would be entitled to $15,000 in depreciation expense, the actual depreciation allowed ($40,000) less the amount allocated to the noncontributing partners ($25,000).

---

[85] Code Sec. 704(c)(1)(A).

Character of allocated items. The character of the gain or loss recognized by the partnership retains it character when it flows through to the partners. Thus, if property that is Section 1231 property to the partnership is sold at a gain, then each partner's share of Section 1231 gain is allocated to each partner, regardless of the character the property sold would have had in the hands of the partner. Similarly, when the partnership sells contributed property and is required to recognize ordinary income or loss (in the case of unrealized receivables or inventory) or capital loss (in the case of a capital asset), the character of the income or loss recognized by the partnership flows through to the partners in accordance with the allocation rules described in this chapter.

Example 85: ABC partnership owns 100 shares of common stock that is a capital asset in the hands of ABC. The partnership has owned the stock for several years. ABC sells the stock at a gain of $10,000, which is treated as long-term capital gain. If this gain were not reported separately from ABC's other income and deductions, it would be treated as ordinary income and could not be used to offset capital losses generated on its partners' own tax returns. Thus, it is important that ABC separately state this long-term capital gain on the partnership tax return and on the partners' Schedule K-1s.

Example 86: In 2010, Bob Everett (a real estate developer) contributed land worth $50,000 in exchange for a 50-percent interest in BD partnership. Bob's adjusted basis in the land was $30,000. In 2015, BD sells the land for $75,000. BD realizes a $45,000 gain ($75,000 – $30,000) on the sale of the land. Since the land was inventory to the contributing partner and was sold within five years after it was contributed to BD, the $45,000 gain is ordinary income to BD. The tax laws require that the first $20,000 of the deferred gain upon contribution ($50,000 – $30,000) be allocated entirely to Bob. The remaining $25,000 ($45,000 – $20,000) is allocated to the partners in accordance with the terms in the partnership agreement. Bob's total share of the gain would be $32,500 ($20,000 + ($25,000 × 50%)).

Example 87: Assume the same facts as in Example 86, except the land is sold for $40,000. BD recognizes $10,000 of ordinary income ($40,000 – $30,000), which must be entirely allocated to Bob since it represents deferred gain from the contribution of the asset to the partnership.

Example 88: On January 5, 2011, Clint Wix contributes land held as an investment in exchange for a one-third interest in WXY partnership. The land is worth $100,000. Clint's basis in the land is $120,000, which becomes WXY's basis in the land. The land is Section 1231 property in the hands of WXY. In 2015, WXY sells the land for $90,000 and recognizes a $30,000 loss ($90,000 – $120,000). Because the property was sold within five years after it was contributed, the first $20,000 of the loss ($120,000 – $100,000) must be allocated to Clint and will be characterized as a capital loss. The remaining $10,000 of the loss is allocated to the partners in accordance with the terms of the partnership agreement and will be characterized as a Section 1231 loss. (The partnership is only required to recognize a capital loss to the extent that the contributing partner's adjusted basis in the property exceeded the FMV of the property at the time it was contributed to the partnership.)

¶ 1306 Keeping Track of a Partner's Interest in the Partnership

The adjusted basis in property is the mechanism used to make ensure that the amount that represents a return of the taxpayer's investment is tax-free to the taxpayer when the property is sold (see ¶ 802.02). This same principle applies to the partner's basis in a partnership interest. The partner's basis in the partnership interest is also used to ensure that the profits of the partnership are not taxed a second time when distributed to the partners. The amount of the partner's basis in the partnership interest also determines the maximum amount of any allocated loss from the partnership that the partners can deduct on their respective income tax returns.[86]

The initial basis of the partner's interest in the partnership was discussed at ¶ 1304.04. The tax law normally increases the partner's basis in the partnership interest by the adjusted basis of the property and taxable services that the partner contributes to the partnership in exchange for an interest in partnership capital and profits (minus the partner's net release of any debt associated with the contributed property). These same rules also apply to any subsequent contributions a partner makes to the partnership. The tax law then requires that the partner's basis in the partnership interest be increased by the partner's allocable share of partnership income and gain items to ensure that the taxable profits and gains of the partnership are taxed only one time or, in the case of tax-exempt income, never taxed at all. Likewise, the tax law requires that the partner's basis in the partnership interest be decreased by the partner's allocable share of partnership deduction and loss items to ensure that the partners only benefit once from those items (or that in the case of nondeductible expenses, the partner never benefits at all).

.01 Increases to Basis

After the partner's initial partnership tax basis has been determined, the basis of the partner's interest is increased by the partner's distributive share of partnership items of income and gain. The partner's basis is not only increased by the partner's share of taxable partnership income and gain but also by the partner's share of tax-exempt income. The partner's basis in the partnership interest is also increased by any additional contributions the partner makes during the year using the rules described in ¶ 1305.04.

Example 89: Mark Witherspoon contributes $10,000 in exchange for a 10-percent interest in MNO partnership. During its first year of operations, MNO allocates $5,000 of ordinary income and $1,000 of tax-exempt income to Mark. Mark's basis in his partnership interest increases by the $6,000 of taxable and tax-exempt income he is allocated during the year. Assuming MNO does not make any distributions to Mark during the year, Mark's basis in MNO at the end of the first year is $16,000 ($10,000 + $6,000).

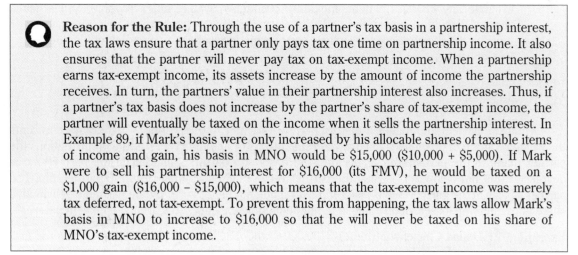

Reason for the Rule: Through the use of a partner's tax basis in a partnership interest, the tax laws ensure that a partner only pays tax one time on partnership income. It also ensures that the partner will never pay tax on tax-exempt income. When a partnership earns tax-exempt income, its assets increase by the amount of income the partnership receives. In turn, the partners' value in their partnership interest also increases. Thus, if a partner's tax basis does not increase by the partner's share of tax-exempt income, the partner will eventually be taxed on the income when it sells the partnership interest. In Example 89, if Mark's basis were only increased by his allocable shares of taxable items of income and gain, his basis in MNO would be $15,000 ($10,000 + $5,000). If Mark were to sell his partnership interest for $16,000 (its FMV), he would be taxed on a $1,000 gain ($16,000 – $15,000), which means that the tax-exempt income was merely tax deferred, not tax-exempt. To prevent this from happening, the tax laws allow Mark's basis in MNO to increase to $16,000 so that he will never be taxed on his share of MNO's tax-exempt income.

Increase in partner's share of partnership liabilities. One distinctive feature of operating a business as a partnership is that a partnership's owners are ultimately responsible for the debts of the partnership. Thus, the tax laws allow partners to include as part of the tax basis in their partnership interests their respective shares of partnership liabilities. This is done by treating the partner's share of partnership liabilities the same as if the partner had made a cash contribution to

---

[86] Reg. § 1.704-1(d).

the partnership.[87] Thus, when the partnership takes on additional liabilities, each partner's tax basis in the partnership interest increases accordingly.

A partner's share of partnership recourse liabilities generally is determined by the ratio for apportioning partnership losses. If, however, none of the partners has personal liability (a nonrecourse debt), the liability generally is shared by all partners, including any limited partners, in the same proportion as they share profits.[88] However, if a partner personally guarantees a nonrecourse liability, the liability is allocated to the guarantor partner to the extent of the guarantee. For example, if the general partner of a limited partnership personally guarantees a nonrecourse loan assumed by the partnership, the general partner's tax basis is increased by the amount of the loan. The tax basis of the other (nonguaranteeing) partners is not affected by this particular loan.

Example 90: Art Myers and Ken Norman form AK equal partnership. AK takes out a loan from the bank for $100,000. Art and Ken's bases in their respective partnership interests are increased by $50,000 ($100,000 × 50%).

Example 91: Brian Michaels and Jeannie Richards are equal partners in BJ partnership. During the year, BJ's liabilities increased from $200,000 to $260,000. Accordingly, each partner is treated as having contributed $30,000 cash at the end of the tax year, which represents each partner's one-half share of the $60,000 increase in partnership debt ($260,000 – $200,000). Brian and Jeannie increase their respective bases in their partnership interests by $30,000 at the end of the partnership's tax year.

 Spotlight: Since a partner's basis cannot be reduced below zero, allowing the tax basis in the partnership to be increased by the partner's share of partnership debts makes it less likely that the partner will be taxed on cash distributions or limited on the amount of partnership losses that it can deduct. A partner faced with not being able to deduct a loss as a result of lack of basis can have the partnership increase its debt at year end which increases basis at the partner level and thus permits a tax deductible loss from what would have been a nondeductible loss. The ability to utilize debt to increase basis also can create a problem when the partnership debts are reduced. Partnerships must evaluate any change in debt, including accounts payable, notes payable, and other accrued liabilities, before the end of the year to make certain they have not inadvertently created a circumstance where partnership losses become nondeductible due to a lack of basis.

.02 Decreases to Basis

When the partnership makes a distribution to a partner, the distribution generally represents the partner's share of previously taxed partnership profits or amounts representing contributions the partner made to the partnership. Therefore, the basis of a partner's interest in the partnership is decreased (but not below zero) when the partner receives a distribution from the partnership. The partner's basis in the partnership is also reduced (again, not below zero) by the partner's distributive share of partnership losses, deductions, and nondeductible expenses that are not capital in nature.[89]

Example 92: Donna Chapel contributes $100,000 to the ABCD equal partnership. During the first year, Donna's share of the partnership taxable income is $25,000, but only $10,000 is actually distributed to her. At the end of the year, Donna includes her $25,000 distributive share of partnership income on her individual income tax return. Her basis in ABCD at the end of the first year is $115,000. This amount represents Donna's initial investment in ABCD ($100,000) plus $15,000 ($25,000 – $10,000) of previously taxed partnership income that has not yet been distributed to her.

---

[87] Code Sec. 752(a).
[88] Reg. § 1.752-3(a).

[89] Code Sec. 733.

Contributions to the partnership	$100,000
Plus: Allocable share of partnership income	25,000
Less: Distributions made during the year	(10,000)
Tax basis at the end of the year	$115,000

Example 93: At the beginning of the year, Antwon Nasim's basis in his partnership interest is $100,000. Antwon's share of the partnership's ordinary loss for the year is $40,000, and his share of tax-exempt municipal bond interest is $3,000. The partnership distributes $33,000 to Antwon during the tax year. Antwon's basis at the end of the year is computed as follows:

Tax basis at the beginning of the year	$100,000
Plus: Allocable share of tax-exempt income	3,000
Less: Distributions made during the year	(33,000)
Less: Allocable share of partnership loss	(40,000)
Tax basis at the end of the year	$ 30,000

Example 94: Continuing with Example 93, during the subsequent tax year, Antwon contributes an additional $20,000 to the partnership in exchange for an interest in partnership capital and profits. His share of the partnership ordinary income for the year is $25,000, and his share of separately stated Section 1231 losses is $6,000. Also during the year the partnership paid and incurred a nondeductible fine. Antwon's allocable share of the fine was $2,000. The partnership distributes $40,000 to Antwon during the tax year. Antwon's basis at the end of the year is computed as follows:

Tax basis at the beginning of the year	$30,000
Plus: Additional contribution	20,000
Plus: Allocable share of partnership income (loss)	25,000
Less: Distributions	(40,000)
Less: Allocable share of Section 1231 loss	(6,000)
Less: Allocable share of nondeductible expenditures	(2,000)
Tax basis at the end of the year	$27,000

Reason for the Rule: When a partnership pays an expense that is not deductible, its assets decrease by the amount of the expense. This, in turn, reduces the value in the partnership assets. If a partner's tax basis does not decrease by the partner's share of the nondeductible expense, the partner will eventually benefit from the nondeductible expense (either by recognizing less gain or more loss on the sale of the partnership interest or by being able to have additional basis from which to receive tax-free distributions).

Decrease in partner's share of partnership liabilities. As previously discussed, if the partnership's liabilities increase during the year, the tax law treats the increase as though the partners made additional cash contributions to the partnership. The reverse happens when the partnership's liabilities decrease during the year. A decrease in partnership liabilities is treated as though the partnership made a cash distribution to the partners for their respective shares in the decrease in partnership liabilities.[90]

Example 95: Daryl Tristin and Glen Ackers are equal partners in DG partnership. During the year, DG's liabilities decreased from $300,000 to $160,000. Because of the $140,000 decrease ($300,000 – $160,000) in partnership liabilities, each partner is deemed to have received a $70,000 cash distribution from the partnership. The cash distribution reduces the partner's basis in the partnership interest. If the cash distribution exceeds the partner's basis in the partnership interest, the partner recognizes gain for the amount of the excess.

> **Spotlight:** Allocating partnership liabilities, both recourse and nonrecourse liabilities, requires the partnership to recognize differences in the allocation due to the two types of liabilities. The partnership is also required to report to partners their shares of the allocated liabilities on their Schedule K-1s, including the breakdown between recourse and nonrecourse, to help in facilitating the calculation of each partner's basis in capital and to allow the IRS to know the amounts of the different categories of liabilities. In the case of a general partnership, each partner's share of the partnership's recourse liabilities is that partner's share of the economic risk of loss relating to that liability computed as if the partnership were liquidated and all the assets were of no value.[91] (See ¶ 1304.04.) Special rules apply in cases in which partners guarantee all or part of the debt. Generally, a guarantee creates an economic risk of loss, and a partner's basis is increased to the extent of that risk.[92] In the case of a limited partnership, the limited partners are, by definition, liable generally only to the extent of their original contributions to the partnership. Therefore, a limited partner generally cannot increase his or her basis in a partnership interest because of recourse debt, unless he or she guarantees all or part of the debt.

.03 Ordering Rules

The tax law never allows a partner's tax basis to go below zero. A partner never recognizes gain or loss from the allocation of losses and deductions in excess of the partner's basis in the partnership interest. The only time a partner recognizes gain from a distribution from the partnership is when the amount of the cash distribution exceeds the partner's basis in the partnership interest.[93] Since both distributions and the partner's share of partnership losses and deductions reduce the partner's basis in the partnership interest, it is necessary to establish an order in which items of income, gain, deduction, and loss are taken into account in determining a partner's basis.

The tax law requires that, at the end of the year, all items that increase a partner's basis be taken into account first. Such items include the partner's distributive share of partnership taxable income, tax-exempt income, and gain. Also taken into account are any contributions the partner made to the partnership during the year, including any cash contributions the partner was deemed to have made due to an increase in partnership liabilities. Any taxable services the partner provided in exchange for a capital interest in the partnership are also taken into account.

After the partner's basis in the partnership interest is as high as it can be made, the tax law next requires that the partner's basis be reduced by any distributions by the partnership, including deemed cash distributions due to a decrease in partnership liabilities during the year.[94] If the amount of the cash distributions during the year exceeds the partner's basis in the partnership interest, the excess is a taxable gain to the partner.[95]

---

[90] Code Sec. 752(b).
[91] Reg. § 1.752-2(a), Reg. § 1.752-2(b).
[92] Reg. § 1.752-2(e).

[93] Code Sec. 731(a).
[94] Rev. Rul. 66-94, 1966-1 CB 166.
[95] Code Sec. 731(a)(1).

After the distributions have been subtracted from the partner's basis, the last items taken into consideration are the partner's allocable share of partnership losses, deductions, and nondeductible (but not capitalized) expenditures.[96] To the extent that these items exceed the partner's remaining basis in the partnership interest, they are carried over to the next tax year.[97]

Example 96: Richard purchases a partnership interest for $5,000. During the current tax year, Richard receives a $3,000 cash distribution from the partnership. At the end of the tax year, Richard's distributive share of partnership losses is $6,000. The distribution reduces Richard's basis in the partnership interest to $2,000 ($5,000 – $3,000). Thus, only $2,000 of Richard's share of partnership losses is deductible on Richard's income tax return in the current year. His basis in the partnership is reduced to zero. The $4,000 disallowed loss is carried forward to the next tax year. Richard will be allowed to deduct the suspended loss when he generates sufficient basis in his partnership interest to absorb the loss.

Amount paid for partnership interest	$5,000
Less: Distributions	(3,000)
	$2,000
Less: Allocable share of partnership losses	(6,000)
Tax basis at the end of the year	$ 0

Example 97: Florena Santiago, a partner of FGH partnership, has an $80,000 basis in her partnership interest at the beginning of the year. During the year, Florena's share of partnership losses is $40,000 and the partnership distributes $50,000 to her. Florena's basis in her partnership interest at the end of the year is $0, and $10,000 of her partnership loss ($40,000 – $30,000) will be suspended until her basis in the partnership interest increases.

Basis at beginning of year	$80,000
Less: Cash distributions	(50,000)
	$30,000
Less: Distributive share of losses (cannot reduce basis below zero)	(40,000)
Adjusted tax basis at the end of the year	$ 0

Example 98: On May 5, 2015, Jade Avery contributes $10,000 in exchange for a 50-percent partnership interest in JK partnership. During 2015, JK has $3,000 of ordinary income, of which Jade's allocable share is $1,500. JK also distributes $2,000 to Jade. Her share of partnership liabilities is $1,000. Jade increases her basis in JK by the $1,500 of partnership income and the $1,000 representing her share of partnership liabilities. She then reduces her tax basis in JK by the $2,000 distribution. Jade's basis in JK at the end of 2015 is $10,500.

Initial basis	$10,000
Plus: Allocable share of partnership income	1,500
Plus: Share of partnership liabilities	1,000
Less: Distributions during 2015	(2,000)
Tax basis at the end of 2015	$10,500

---

[96] Rev. Rul. 66-94, 1966-1 CB 166.   [97] Code Sec. 704(d).

Example 99: Continuing with Example 98, in 2016 JK generates a $5,000 loss, of which Jade's distributive share is $2,500. Also during 2016 JK distributes $3,000 to Jade, and at the end of the year, Jade's share of partnership liabilities is $200 (down from $1,000 at the beginning of the year). Jade's $4,200 basis at the end of 2016 is computed as follows:

Tax basis at the beginning of 2016	$10,500
Less: Decrease in share of partnership liabilities	(800)
Less: Distributions during 2016	(3,000)
Tax basis for purposes of loss limitations	$ 6,700
Less: Allocable share of partnership loss	(2,500)
Tax basis at the end of 2016	$ 4,200

Example 100: Continuing with Example 99, in 2017 JK generates a $15,000 loss, of which Jade's distributive share is $7,500. JK distributes $500 to Jade during 2017, and her share of partnership liabilities at the end of 2017 is $2,000 (up from $200 at the beginning of the year). Jade's zero basis at the end of 2017 is computed as follows:

Tax basis at the beginning of 2017	$4,200
Plus: Increase in share of partnership liabilities	1,800
Less: Distributions during 2017	(500)
Tax basis for purposes of loss limitations	$5,500
Less: Allocable share of partnership loss	(7,500)
Tax basis at the end of 2017	$ 0

Jade's losses for 2017 are limited to her $5,500 tax basis in JK after taking into consideration all increases and her distributions during the year. Jade's tax basis in JK at the end of 2017 is $0. She carries over to 2018 the $2,000 ($7,500 – $5,500) disallowed loss from 2017. The suspended loss will be deductible once Jade's tax basis in JK increases.

Example 101: Continuing with Example 100, in 2018 JK generates $10,000 of ordinary income, of which Jade's distributive share is $5,000. JK distributes $2,000 to Jade during 2018, and Jade's share of partnership liabilities at the end of 2018 is $1,200 (down from $2,000 at the beginning of the year). On her income tax return, Jade includes her $5,000 distributive share of partnership income and the $2,000 suspended loss from 2017. Jade's basis at the end of 2018 is computed as follows:

Tax basis at the beginning of 2018	$ 0
Plus: Allocable share of partnership income	5,000
Less: Distributions during 2018	(2,000)
Less: Decrease in share of partnership liabilities	(800)
Tax basis for purposes of loss limitations	$2,200
Less: Release of suspended losses from 2017	(2,000)
Tax basis at the end of 2018	$ 200

Figure 13-5 summarizes items for which a partner's basis in its partnership interest is adjusted upward or downward.

Figure 13-5 Summary of Adjustments Made to a Partner's Basis

A partner's basis is adjusted upward for the following items:

- The partner's distributive share of partnership ordinary income plus all separately stated items of income and gain,
- The partner's distributive share of tax-exempt partnership income, and
- Contributions the partner makes to the partnership, including the partner's share of increases to partnership liabilities (treated as cash contributions).

A partner's basis is adjusted downward (but never below zero) by the following items:

- Distributions made to the partner from the partnership, including the partner's share of any decrease in partnership liabilities (treated as a cash distribution),
- The partner's distributive share of partnership losses and deductions, and
- The partner's distributive share of nondeductible partnership expenditures.

¶ 1307 Impact of Distributions to Partners

A "distribution" is a payment, either in money or other property, made by a partnership to a partner. Partnership distributions fall into two categories: (1) those made in complete liquidation of a partner's interest in the partnership and (2) all other partnership distributions.[98] The latter type of distribution is also known as a "current distribution."[99] Liquidating distributions, disproportional distributions, and distributions involving noncash property can involve very complex tax laws, and accordingly, are beyond the scope of this introductory chapter on partnership taxation. All distributions described in this chapter are assumed to be current distributions in the form of cash that the partnership makes proportionally to each of its partners.

Current distributions do not completely liquidate a partner's interest in a partnership. They include distributions of the current profits of the partnership, pro rata distributions of the partners' capital interests, and disproportionate distributions that reduce the distributees' proportionate interests in the partnership. An advance or drawing of money or property against a partner's distributive share of income is treated as a current distribution made to the partner on the last day of the partnership tax year. No prorating of profits to the withdrawal dates is necessary.[100] A partner who receives a current cash distribution recognizes a taxable gain only to the extent that the amount of cash received exceeds the basis of the partner's partnership interest.[101] The ordering rules described in ¶ 1306.03 are used to determine how the cash distribution is taken into consideration in determining a partner's tax basis in the partnership interest. If there is a gain, it is considered a gain from the sale or exchange of the partner's interest and is usually taxed as a capital gain. Losses are never recognized on a current distribution since the partner still retains an interest in the partnership and there is no closed transaction (no sale of distributed property) from which a loss can arise.[102]

¶ 1308 Limited Liability Companies (LLCs) and Limited Liability Partnerships (LLPs)

The tax laws generally do not allow businesses that provide professional services (for example, law firms, medical practices, and CPA firms) to shield themselves from the liabilities of the business by incorporating their businesses and hiding behind corporate partners. Thus, many of these

---

[98] Code Sec. 731.
[99] Reg. § 1.761-1(d).
[100] Reg. § 1.731-1(a)(1)(ii).

[101] Code Sec. 731(a)(1); Reg. § 1.731-1(a)(1).
[102] Reg. § 1.731-1(a)(2).

businesses operate as general partnerships in which each and every partner is personally responsible for the actions of the partnership and of each of its individual partners acting on behalf of the partnership.

In 1977, Wyoming became the first state to authorize the limited liability company (LLC) as a business entity. In an LLC, the owners (called "members") are protected from most debts of the entity, much as limited partners are protected in a limited partnership. However, unlike the limited partnership rules that require that at least one general partner be responsible for the partnership's liabilities beyond those covered by the limited partners, in an LLC all members have limited liability. The tax laws generally prohibit professional services firms (for example, law firms or CPA firms) from operating as limited partnerships, and accordingly, most states' LLC laws prohibit these firms from operating as LLCs. In 1991, Texas became the first state to authorize the limited liability partnership (LLP) as a business entity. Today, most states recognize LLCs and LLPs as legal business entities.

 Planning Pointer: The Code and the IRS have made converting from a general partnership to an LLC taxed as a partnership a tax-friendly option. The conversion is considered a tax-free conversion from one partnership to another with the contribution of assets to the new partnership considered a tax-free transaction governed by Code Sec. 721 (see ¶ 1304.02). In addition, the treatment is the same whether the resulting LLC is formed in the same state or in a different state from the converting partnership. After the conversion, the tax year of the converting partnership does not close with respect to any or all of the partners, and the resulting LLC operates under the same taxpayer identification number as the general partnership had previously.[103]

The Code does not specifically address the taxation of LLCs and LLPs, except to acknowledge that at the entity's election, they can be treated for income tax purposes either as a corporation or as a partnership. Much like a corporation or limited partnership, the LLC is formed and operates in conformity with the law of the state in which it is organized. To form an LLC, articles of organization, much like articles of incorporation, must be filed with the appropriate state office. The owners of an LLC are referred to as members. The members are similar to partners, and when the LLC is taxed as a partnership, they are treated as a partner would be in a partnership. The determination of the interests and responsibilities of the members can be found in the "operating agreement" of the LLC, an agreement similar to the partnership agreement (See ¶ 1304). While an LLC operates under state law to limit claims of liability by third parties against the members to the amount of the members' investment in the LLC plus any guarantees of LLC debt by the member, along with that benefit come responsibilities to comply with the statute. For example, most statutes require the name of the LLC to be distinctive, including at the end of the name such terms as "LLC" or "Limited Liability Company." While the operating agreement cannot waive such conditions as the name requirement, other default provisions within the statutes can be overridden by the agreement of the partners. Figure 13-6 lists the advantages and disadvantages of limited liability companies.

Figure 13-6 LLC Advantages and Disadvantages

LLC advantages:

- The primary advantage of a two-or-more member LLC is that the entity is not subject to federal income tax as a corporation if it elects to be treated as a partnership; it thus avoids the double taxation of the C Corporation.

- A member of an LLC has no personal liability for the entity's debts, while at the same time it receives tax advantages similar to those of a limited partner.

---

[103] Rev. Rul. 84-52.

- LLCs can have a single owner, but the tax consequences of a single member LLC are similar to those of a sole proprietorship.

- Members of an LLC have the freedom to allocate entity tax items in the same manner that partners do in partnerships. As will be discussed in Chapter 14, shareholders in an S corporation must allocate income, deductions, and other items on a *pro rata* basis.

- LLC members have the right to participate in the management of the LLC, while limited partners who participate in management risk losing their limited liability status.

- As will be discussed in Chapter 14, S corporations have restrictions on the number and type of shareholders they can have. These limits and restrictions do not apply to LLCs, and therefore, LLCs provide more flexibility in this regard.

- Members of an LLC can make tax-free contributions of property for interests in the LLC at any time (similar to partnerships). As mentioned previously in Chapter 12, shareholders of a C corporation can make tax-free contributions of property to a C corporation in exchange for stock and securities only if they own at least 80 percent of the stock in the corporation after the exchange.

LLC disadvantages:

- The Code does not specifically address LLC issues as such. The only real authority in this area is the acceptance that LLCs with two or more members can elect to be taxed as partnerships, even if they offer limited liability to all of their members.

- A single member LLC is disregarded for tax purposes. Although a single member LLC is treated as a sole proprietorship, the member continues to be protected from lawsuits in state court.

- State LLC statutes are not uniform, thereby raising jurisdictional issues. For example, if an LLC is organized in California but does business in another state, which state's statutes will control? Jurisdictional issues always have been a part of U.S. law, but with LLCs being relatively new entities, there is substantial uncharted territory to be explored.

.01 Entity Classification

An LLC files Form 8832, *Entity Classification Election*, to elect a business entity classification.[104] If the LLC does not file the Form 8832, an entity with two or more members will automatically be classified as a partnership. However, an LLC is more like a corporation than a partnership in that members of the LLC have limited liability with respect to the LLC's debts and to any claims against the LLC. In addition, all members of an LLC are eligible to participate in the management of the LLC, unlike a limited partner in a partnership. A single member LLC will be disregarded for federal tax purposes and will be treated as a sole proprietorship for federal income tax purposes.

 Spotlight: While the complexities of the tax rules governing partnerships require a careful study of the tax laws, the number of businesses filing partnership tax returns continues to increase. Since 2001, the number of partnerships has increased at an average annual rate of 4.7 percent. The majority of this growth has been from partnerships classified as limited liability companies (LLC). See Table 13-2. However, this increase was not the result of an increase in traditional general or limited partnerships but instead was the result of the increasing number of LLPs and LLCs that chose to be taxed as partnerships. In fact, the number of general partnerships decreased from the 1,176,000 partnership returns filed in 1993 to 590,000 filed in 2010. The increase in filing

---

[104] Reg. § 301.7701-1, -2, -3.

of partnership tax returns has come from LLCs and LLPs which increased from 17,000 in 1993 to 2,232,000 in 2010.

¶ 1309 Summary

The taxation of pass-through entities allows taxpayers the opportunity to enter into business ventures with options ranging from ease of formation (general partnerships) to limited liability either for a select group of partners (limited partners) or for all the members of the firm (LLCs). To understand the differences and make an informed selection requires a review of the tax and nontax considerations for the formation of a general partnership, limited partnership, LLC, or LLP. With the option to be taxed as a partnership for any of these four business entities, the selection process can generally proceed without concern over any significant tax differences among the entities.

GLOSSARY OF TERMS INTRODUCED IN THE CHAPTER

Active participation. A requirement for a taxpayer to be able to take advantage of the exception permitting a $25,000 real estate loss deduction under the passive activity loss rules. A taxpayer must own at least a 10-percent interest in the rental activity, not be a limited partner, and participate in making management decisions.

Capital and profits interest. The term used to describe a partner's interest in a partnership when the partner has an interest in the future profits the partnership generates as well as an interest in the partnership's assets upon liquidation of the partner's interest or dissolution of the partnership.

Collateral. Property offered by the borrower that the lender can use to satisfy the debt in the event the borrower defaults on the loan.

Current distributions. Distributions from a partnership to a partner that do not completely liquidate the partner's interest in the partnership.

Distributive share. A partner's allocated share of partnership income, gains, losses, deductions, and credits as specified in either the partnership agreement or in accordance with each partner's interest in the partnership.

General partnership. A business entity that arises from an agreement among two or more persons, all of whom have unlimited liability for the debts of the partnership, to operate a business for profit.

Guaranteed payments. Amounts paid from the partnership to a partner that are determined *without regard* to the profits generated by the partnership during the year.

Least aggregate deferral of income rule. The last of three tests used to determine a partnership's required tax year. It involves performing a test using each of the year-ends of its partners and determining which of those year-ends, on average, will allow the government to collect taxes on the partnership income the most quickly. *See also* Majority partners rule *and* Principal partner rule.

Limited partnership. A business entity that arises from an agreement among two or more partners to operate a business for profit in which one or more of the partners has limited liability with respect to the debts of the partnership and at least one partner is responsible for the debts of the partnership.

Listed property. Certain personal property susceptible to both business and personal use. Examples include passenger automobiles, computers, and cellular telephones.

Majority partners rule. The first of three tests used to determine a partnership's required tax year. It requires that a partnership adopt the year-end of the partner, or group of partners, that owns more than a 50-percent interest in partnership capital *and* profits. *See also* Least aggregate deferral of income rule *and* Principal partner rule.

Material participation. A taxpayer who participates in a trade or business on a regular, continuous, and substantial basis is considered to materially participate in the trade or business. The tax law provides seven tests to measure whether a taxpayer's participation in a trade or business is material.

Net earnings from self-employment. The amount from which self-employment taxes of a sole proprietor are based. It equals 92.35 percent of net profits reported on Schedule C.

Nonrecourse debt. The type of debt arrangement in which the lender has no recourse (no ability to collect the debt) directly from the borrower in the event the borrower defaults on the loan.

Passive activity loss. A loss from a rental property or a trade or business activity in which the owner does not materially participate.

Partner's capital account. An account on the partnership books that keeps track of what a partner is entitled to receive upon the liquidation of the partner's interest or upon dissolution of the partnership.

Partnership agreement. A written or oral agreement among the partners in a partnership that provides, among other things, how the partners will share in the partnership's profits and losses and how the assets of the partnership will be divided upon dissolution of the partnership.

Principal partner. A partner that has at least a five-percent interest in the profits *or* capital of the partnership.

Principal partner rule. The second of three tests used to determine a partnership's required tax year. If the majority interest rule does not apply, this rule requires that a partnership adopt the tax year of *all* of its principal partners. *See also* Least aggregate deferral of income rule *and* Majority partners rule.

Profits only interest. The term used to describe a partner's interest in a partnership when the partner is entitled to a share of future partnership profits but does not have an ownership interest in the capital of the partnership.

Recourse debt. The type of debt arrangement in which the lender can proceed directly against the borrower for any debt on which the borrower defaults.

Substantial economic effect. The standard that must be met before allocations of partnership items can be made to the partners as specified in the partnership agreement.

Unrealized receivable. Any right to income for services or goods that are not capital assets that have not been previously recorded in gross income under the taxpayer's method of accounting.

CHAPTER PROBLEMS

The following questions and problems relate to the discussion in Chapter 13, Sole Proprietorships, Partnerships, LLPs, and LLCs, which begins at ¶ 1300 in *Part V: Business Entity Issues*.

Chapter 13 Discussion Questions

1. What is the tax base used to compute the self-employment tax, and what is the self-employment tax rate?

2. A sole proprietor is generally permitted to deduct losses from their trade or business in the tax year in which they occur. If the trade or business is determined to be a passive activity, how does this impact the year in which the loss is deductible? Under what circumstances may the sole proprietor be able to classify the trade or business as a nonpassive activity?

3. How are gains and losses on the disposition of business assets treated by the sole proprietor different than by a C corporation?

4. Distinguish between a business and nonbusiness bad debt and the difference in the tax treatment between them?

5. Explain the increase in the number of partnership tax returns filed with the Internal Revenue Service over the past decade.

6. Discuss the nontax differences between a general partnership, limited partnership, and limited liability company.

7. Are the following elections made at the partner or partnership level?

   a. Election to expense property under Code Sec. 179.

   b. Replacement of property under involuntary conversion rules.

   c. Use of foreign taxes as a deduction or credit.

8. What methods of accounting are available to the partnership and how is the method used by the partnership selected?

9. A partnership has 10 partners, each of whom owns a 10-percent interest in partnership capital and profits. Four of the partners use the calendar year, and the other partners all have different fiscal years. How is the required tax year of the partnership determined?

10. How does the partnership agreement affect the operations of a partnership?

11. How does a contribution of a personal asset to the partnership by a partner differ from the contribution of a business asset by the partner?

12. Under what circumstances does the contribution of services to a partnership in exchange for a partnership capital interest constitute taxable income to the contributing partner?

13. How is the partner's initial basis in a partnership interest determined if the property contributed is subject to a recourse liability that the partnership assumes?

14. How is the partner's initial basis in a partnership interest determined if the property contributed is subject to a nonrecourse liability that the partnership assumes?

15. Which of the following is a separately stated item for partnership reporting, and why?

   a. Business bad debts

   b. Charitable contributions

   c. Gains and losses from sales or exchanges of capital assets held for one year or less

   d. Real estate taxes

16. What are guaranteed payments to partners and how are they treated by the partnership and the partner?

17. What constitutes an unrealized receivable in the hands of the partnership? What rules are associated with it?

18. How does a change in liabilities owed by the partnership at the end of a tax year affect the basis of a partner's interest in the partnership?

19. If a partnership distributes only cash to its partners in a current distribution, do the partners recognize gain or loss on the distribution?

20. How is the character of the gain or loss from the sale of property contributed to the partnership by one of its partners determined?

21. How is the concept of double taxation as discussed in reference to C corporations eliminated or mitigated through the use of a partnership?

22. In what order are increases and decreases to a partner's basis in the partnership determined at the end of the year?

23. When a partnership does not distribute the entire net income of the partnership for the tax year, does a partner have the option to exclude the income from his or her tax return and report it when it is received?

24. Does a limited liability company have an agreement similar to the partnership agreement? What is it and what are the similarities and differences?

Chapter 13 Problems

1. Leona Henderson, a part-time employee of the City School System, also operates a business as a swimming instructor. In 2015, Leona's salary is $10,000. She also gives private lessons from which her income is $20,000. Compute:

    a. The maximum amount of net self-employment earnings that she can earn in 2015 that will be subject to the social security component of the self-employment tax.

    b. Leona's self-employment tax for 2015.

    c. The amount Leona will deduct as employer's share of her self-employment tax.

2. George Hampton is a self-employed computer programmer with no employees. George has the following income and expenses related to the operating of his business:

Gross billings to customers during 2015	$150,000
Collections on billings during 2015	160,000
Bad debts on 2014 billings	10,000
Advertising expense	5,000
Commissions and fees paid	25,000
Insurance	8,000
Office expense	9,000
Taxes and licenses	10,000
Repairs and maintenance	20,000
Contribution to self-employed retirement plan	15,000
Payment of health insurance for George	12,000
Mileage driven using personal automobile for business	15,000 miles

    a. Calculate the net profit or loss from the trade or business assuming that George uses the cash method of accounting. Assume all expenses listed above were expenses both paid and incurred during 2015.

    b. Calculate George's 2015 self-employment tax.

    c. What other amounts are deductible for AGI that are not allowable in calculating the net profit or loss of the business?

3. Linda Sullivan converted her personal automobile to business use on July 1, 2015. At the time of purchase of the automobile (April 1, 2014) the purchase price was $22,800, and at the date of conversion to business use, the fair market value was $12,000.

    a. What is the amount that would be used to calculate depreciation for business purposes for the automobile?

    b. If the property is used 65 percent for business, what would be the maximum amount of depreciation that Linda could claim as a deduction for 2015?

    c. If the property is used 35 percent for business, what would be the maximum amount of depreciation that Linda could claim as a deduction for 2015?

    d. If Linda used the automobile for 6,000 properly documented business mileage and incurred $300 in parking fees and tolls, what would be the transportation deduction if she elects to use the standard mileage rate method?

4. John Church has a business operated out of his home. The business portion of the home consists of a room (400 square feet), which is used regularly and exclusively to see clients and the only location at which he operates his business. His home has a total of 2,000 square feet. For 2015, John incurs the following expenses related to his home.

Real estate taxes	$5,500
Qualified mortgage interest	7,500
Utilities	4,800
Depreciation	6,000
Insurance	500

a. If the net income from John's business is $45,000 prior to the deduction of home office expenses, what amount will he be able to deduct against the net profits from his business?

b. How do the expenses related to business use of the home affect the computation of the self-employment tax?

c. How much is John entitled to as a deduction from AGI related to these home office expenses?

d. If John were an employee and the home office was related to his employment, how would the deduction be taken on his 2015 tax return?

5. Samantha Dolan operates a small consulting business as a sole proprietor. During 2015, she has the following transactions related to the business.

Customer sales on account	$75,000
Collections from 2015 credit sales	55,000
Collections from 2014 credit sales	18,000
Business bad debts	8,000
Operating expenses incurred during 2015	44,000
Operating expenses from 2015 paid in 2015	33,000
Operating expenses from 2014 paid in 2015	10,000

a. Calculate the net income or loss from Samantha's business using the accrual method of accounting.

b. Calculate the net income or loss from Samantha's business using the cash method of accounting.

c. What accounts for the difference in the two net incomes and how does this benefit or cause a problem for a trade or business?

6. Donald Maxwell is a Certified Public Accountant who is a partner in a national CPA firm and has several other business ventures. The businesses and the hours of participation are as follows:

Description of Business	Hours worked by Donald	Hours worked by other employees	Income or (loss) from the business for 2015
Commercial real estate rental property	50	500	($25,000)
Italian ice retail store	250	2,845	15,000
Collectable train mail order sales business	185	-0-	(6,000)

With regards to the rental property, Donald is actively involved in the selection of tenants and handling of maintenance issues. Donald has an AGI of $500,000 before considering any of the above businesses.

a. Which of the above businesses are considered to be passive activities?

b. What will Donald's AGI be after considering the income and losses from these three other activities?

c. What happens to any losses not deductible in 2015?

d. How would your answer to part b. differ if Donald's AGI were $90,000 before considering any of the three activities?

e. How would your answer to part b. differ if Donald's AGI were $140,000 before considering any of the three activities?

7. Flo Wolfe has seven separate businesses in which she participates, none of which involve rental property. The numbers of hours she participated and the hours of participation of her three employees in the activities during the current tax year are as follows:

Business	Flo's Hours	Employee A	Employee B	Employee C
A	115	0	0	330
B	55	0	0	25
C	525	0	0	850
D	270	200	600	200
E	215	1,900	1,600	750
F	77	0	0	0

Indicate which of the business activities would be considered to be passive activities for the current tax year.

8. Adam, Brian, and Cynthia are equal partners in ABC partnership. In exchange for their one-third interests, Adam contributes $90,000; Brian contributes business property worth $90,000 with an adjusted basis of $60,000; and Cynthia contributes a capital asset with a fair market value and adjusted basis of $90,000.

a. How much gain is recognized by each of these partners on the contribution of property to ABC partnership?

b. What is each partner's basis in his or her respective partnership interests?

c. What is the partnership's basis in each of these assets?

9. Nicole O'Conner and Jonathan Rix form NJ Partnership. In exchange for equal interests in NJ, each contributes the following property. Jonathan also performs services for NJ.

Nicole:

	Adjusted Basis	FMV
Cash	$600,000	$600,000
Inventory (held 3 months)	70,000	150,000

Jonathan:

	Adjusted Basis	FMV
Office equipment (held 18 months)	$400,000	$600,000

a. How much gain or loss is recognized by the partners and the partnership at formation because of the contributions?

b. What is each partner's basis in his or her partnership interest at formation?

c. What is NJ Partnership's basis and holding period at formation for each asset contributed to it?

10. The ABC partnership agreement provides for guaranteed payments for services rendered of $70,000, $64,000, and $60,000 for Adam, Brian, and Cynthia, respectively. After the guaranteed payments are deducted, the partnership agreement calls for sharing of profits and losses as follows: Adam, 40 percent; Brian, 35 percent; and Cynthia, 25 percent. Each

partner is a general partner. If net profits before the guaranteed payments are $176,000, what amount of income from the partnership should each partner report on his or her individual income tax return?

11. Katie and Grace operate their business as a calendar-year partnership. They share profits and losses equally. During 2014, the partnership had a $16,000 loss and in 2015 it reported a $20,000 profit. At the beginning of 2014, Katie's adjusted basis in her partnership interest was $5,000. The partnership made no distributions during 2014 or 2015, and Katie made no additional contributions.

    a. What is the adjusted basis of Katie's partnership interest at the end of 2014?

    b. What is Katie's basis in her partnership interest in 2015?

12. Timothy Nesbith owns a 40-percent interest in capital and profits of TNT partnership. Timothy and TNT both have calendar year-ends. Timothy's basis in his TNT interest at the beginning of 2015 is $140,000. For 2015, TNT has $600,000 of ordinary income and $100,000 of dividend income from stocks it holds in various corporations. TNT also makes $150,000 of contributions to qualified charitable organizations. During 2015, TNT distributes $280,000 to Timothy. In 2016, TNT reports $250,000 of ordinary loss, and distributes $100,000 to Timothy.

    a. What is Timothy's basis in his TNT at the end of 2015?

    b. How much of the TNT loss may Timothy deduct on his 2016 individual income tax return?

    c. What is Timothy's basis in TNT at the end of 2016?

13. Samuel Todd became a member of the STX partnership when it was organized in 2009. At that time he contributed $45,000 in cash and land worth $20,000. He had purchased the land for $15,000. His share of the partnership earnings (loss) and the amounts withdrawn for the years 2009 to 2015 are as follows:

Year	Share of Profit (Loss)	Amounts Withdrawn
2009	$18,000	$12,000
2010	12,000	15,000
2011	(6,000)	0
2012	25,000	15,000
2013	35,000	30,000
2014	15,000	10,000
2015	(15,000)	5,000

What is Samuel's basis in STX's partnership interest at the end of 2015?

14. Nancy Carter contributes property with a fair market value of $150,000 to a new partnership in exchange for a 50-percent interest in the partnership. The property has an adjusted basis of $45,000 and is subject to an $80,000 (nonrecourse) mortgage that is assumed by the partnership. What is Nancy's basis in her partnership interest?

15. ABCD Partnership begins business on January 19, 2015. ABCD consists of four partners, Albert, Brandon, Carol, and Daryl. Consider the following independent situations:

    a. Albert, who uses a fiscal year ending on September 30, owns a 60-percent interest in ABCD. Brandon, Carol, and Daryl have fiscal years ending June 30. Brandon owns a 20-percent interest, and Carol and Daryl own a 10-percent interest each. What is ABCD's required tax year?

    b. Albert uses a fiscal year ending June 30, and he owns a 47-percent interest in ABCD. Brandon uses a fiscal year ending June 30 and owns 47 percent of the partnership. Partners Carol and Daryl use fiscal years ending May 31, and each owns a 3-percent partnership interest. What is ABCD's required tax year?

c. May ABCD adopt a tax year other than the one required in a. or b. without declaring a business purpose for the selection of the year? If so, how may it do so, and what tax year(s) can it use?

16. A partnership has three equal partners. One partner uses a March 31 year-end. The second partner uses a June 30 year-end, and the third partner uses an October 31 year-end. Discuss the possible tax years the partnership can select.

17. A sole proprietor offers an employee the chance to become a partner. If the employee works an additional two years, the sole proprietor has agreed to transfer half the business to the employee. The employee meets the requirement and receives half ownership in the capital and profits of the partnership. What is the tax effect on the employee at the time the promise is made? At the time the transfer occurs?

18. Danielle Jefferson and Waylon Evans form an equal partnership. In exchange for her interest, Danielle contributes $30,000 of cash and property worth $70,000. Danielle's adjusted basis in the property is $50,000. In exchange for his 50-percent interest, Waylon performs services for the partnership and contributes $40,000 cash.

   a. What amount of gain or loss does each partner recognize on the exchange of his or her contributions for a 50-percent share in the partnership?

   b. What is each partner's basis in his or her respective partnership interest?

   c. What is the partnership's interest in the property Danielle contributes to the partnership?

19. Justin contributes land worth $100,000 to a general partnership in exchange for a 50-percent interest in JM partnership. Mike contributes $50,000 cash in exchange for a 50-percent interest in JM. Justin's basis in the land is $60,000, and the land is subject to a $50,000 mortgage, which the partnership assumes. The partnership agreement allocates profits equally between the partners and allocates losses 45 percent to Justin and 55 percent to Mike. These allocations have substantial economic effect.

   a. Compute the tax consequences to each partner on the receipt of his respective partnership interest, including each partner's basis in the respective partnership interests assuming that the $50,000 mortgage is nonrecourse debt.

   b. Compute the tax consequences to each partner on the receipt of his respective partnership interest, including each partner's basis in the respective partnership interests assuming that the $50,000 mortgage is recourse debt.

20. Ahmeek partnership is owned equally by four partners. John Barley, a partner in Ahmeek, receives a guaranteed payment of $30,000 a year in exchange for services. During the year, Ahmeek's profits (not including the amounts paid to John for his accounting and tax services) are $150,000. How much income does each partner recognize for the year?

21. Angela Peterson owns a 25-percent interest in Ishpeming Partnership. Both Angela and Ishpeming use a calendar year-end. For the year ended December 31, 2015, Ishpeming reports the following items of partnership income, gain, loss, deduction, and credit.

Gross sales	$380,000
Cost of goods sold	110,000
Wage expense	90,000
Depreciation recapture	8,000
Net Section 1231 gain	60,000
Casualty loss	7,000
Interest	12,000
Real estate taxes	8,000
MACRS depreciation	14,000
Business bad debt	8,000
Charitable contributions	20,000

Calculate Angela's distributive share of partnership ordinary income and separately stated items. How does she report these items on her individual income tax?

22. What is the amount and character of gain/loss recognized by the partnership in the following situations?

a. A partner contributes inventory from his sole proprietorship to a partnership in exchange for an interest in the partnership. At the time of the contribution, the FMV of the inventory is $60,000. The partner's basis in the inventory is $22,000. The property is a capital asset in the hands of the partnership, which sells it for $60,000 within five years of the contribution.

b. In 2002, a real estate developer contributes land (with a basis of $36,000 and a fair market value of $40,000) to a manufacturing LLC in which he is a member. The land was inventory to the real estate developer. The LLC uses the land as an employee parking lot. The LLC sells the land in 2015 for $50,000.

c. A partner contributes property with a basis of $4,000 and a fair market value of $6,000 to a partnership. The property is inventory in the hands of both the partner and the partnership. The partnership sells the property after five years for $8,000.

23. How is the gain and loss from the sales in Problem 15 allocated among the partners?

24. How much gain or loss is recognized by the partnership in the following transactions?

a. Jeri Holden contributes land worth $80,000 in exchange for a capital and profits interest in a partnership. Prior to contributing the land, Jeri held it as an investment. Jeri's basis in the land is $160,000. The partnership uses the land in its trade or business and then sells it within five years for $100,000.

b. How does the answer in a. change if the partnership sells the land for $70,000?

c. How does the answer in a. change if the partnership sells the land for $170,000?

25. Andrew Springer has a partnership interest with a basis of $20,000. The partner receives a $24,000 current cash distribution that is proportional. What are the tax consequences of the distribution to Andrew?

26. A partner contributes $15,000 in exchange for a 50-percent partnership interest in a partnership. During the tax year, the partnership has $8,000 of ordinary income, of which the partner's allocable share is $4,000. The partnership also distributes $3,000 to the partner. Her share of partnership liabilities is $2,000. What is her tax basis in her partnership interest at the end of the year?

27. A partner purchases a partnership interest for $6,000. During the current tax year, the partner receives a $2,000 cash distribution from the partnership. At the end of the tax year, the partner's distributive share of partnership losses is $8,000. What portion of the partner's share of losses is deductible in the current year? What happens to any portion that is not deductible? What is the partner's tax basis in the partnership at the end of the year?

28. Phyllis and Sally are equal partners in the income and losses of the PS Partnership. The partnership's balance sheet at the end of the current year is as follows:

Cash	$100,000
Inventory	160,000
Land (Collateral for Third Mortgage Corp Mortgage Payable)	150,000
Total Assets	$410,000

Note Payable—First Bank (recourse note)	$100,000
Mortgage Payable—Third Mortgage Corp. (nonrecourse mortgage)	150,000
Capital—Phyllis	110,000
Capital—Sally	50,000
Total Liabilities and Capital	$410,000

a. If both Phyllis and Sally are general partners, what is the maximum amount of the partnership's liabilities each would be liable to repay in the event of a default by the partnership?

b. If Phyllis is a general partner and Sally is a limited partner, what is the maximum amount of the partnership liabilities each would be liable to repay in the event of a default by the partnership?

c. If Phyllis and Sally had registered the partnership as a limited liability company (LLC), what is the maximum amount of the liabilities each would be liable to repay in the event of a default by the partnership?

d. Phyllis and Sally ask you to calculate their respective share of the year end liabilities from the partnership Balance Sheet to be included in the basis of their respective partnership interests. Assume that the liabilities shown in the problem represent the entire amount of liabilities of the partnership and land with a book value of $150,000 is used as collateral for the nonrecourse liability to Third Mortgage Corporation. Further assume that the partnership capital accounts represent the year end adjusted basis in their capital after allocating the current year's profit and before any allocation of partnership liabilities.

29. Bob Sanford and Michelle Thomas form an equal general partnership. Bob contributes $65,000 in cash and land with a FMV of $35,000 and an adjusted basis of $50,000 in exchange for his 50 percent interest. Michelle contributes services of $20,000 and equipment with a FMV of $80,000 and adjusted basis of $40,000 in exchange for her 50 percent interest.

a. What amount of gain or loss must Bob recognize as a result of his contributions to the partnership?

b. What amount of gain or loss must Michelle recognize as a result of his contributions to the partnership?

c. What is Bob's initial basis in his partnership interest?

d. What is Michelle's initial basis in his partnership interest?

30. Referring to the facts in Problem 22, the partnership depreciates the equipment contributed by Michelle utilizing MACRS depreciation over a seven-year life. Over the life of the equipment, how much of the depreciation expense will be allocable to Bob and Michelle?

31. Sarah Austin is a 25 percent general partner in the SBS partnership with a basis in her capital account of $50,000 as of the first day of the 2015 tax year. During 2015, SBS sustained a $60,000 tax loss and Sarah withdrew $20,000 from the partnership. During 2015, the amount of partnership liabilities remains unchanged.

a. Compute Sarah's tax basis in her capital account at December 31, 2015.

b. What amount may Sarah deduct as a loss on her 2015 tax return?

c. During 2016, the SBS partnership sustains a loss of $80,000 and reduces its liabilities (all recourse) by $40,000 over the prior year. Compute Sarah's tax basis in her capital account at December 31, 2016.

d. What amount may Sarah deduct as a loss on her 2016 tax return?

32. Janet Miller and Terry Wood form a general partnership. As part of the general partnership agreement, Janet and Terry will share profits equally and losses 75 percent and 25 percent, respectively. Terry has an initial contribution to the capital of the partnership of $20,000 cash and land with a FMV of $80,000 (adjusted tax basis $50,000) and the partnership assumes a mortgage against the land of $50,000 which the lender releases Terry from

liability and adds the partnership as mortgagee. After the reduction in FMV of the land by the amount of the mortgage assumed and the cash contribution, Terry's contribution has a net FMV of $50,000 for her 50 percent interest ($20,000 + $80,000 – $50,000 mortgage). Janet contributes $50,000 in cash for her 75 percent interest in the partnership.

a. How much of the $50,000 is allocated to Janet in the determination of her tax basis if the debt is nonrecourse debt to the partners?

b. How much of the $50,000 is allocated to Janet in the determination of her tax basis if the debt is recourse debt to the partners?

Chapter 13 Review Problems

1. Cheryl has been operating a small gift shop as a supplemental source of income since 2010 in space rented from a local shopping mall operator. Information regarding her income and deductions in 2015 is as follows:

Business income and expenditures

Sales revenue	$200,000
Cost of goods sold	150,000
Health insurance Cheryl paid in addition to coverage provided by her employer	4,800
Contribution to employees' retirement plans	2,000
Home office expenses (excludes real estate taxes and mortgage interest listed above)—the office is 200 of the 2,000 total square feet of the residence	7,500
Cost of automobile used for business (acquired 1-1-13)	12,000
Operating expenses of automobile (insurance, gas, oil, and repairs)	8,600
Business tolls and parking fees	340
Business miles—8,000; total miles—20,000	
Salary and wages paid to employees	30,000
Taxes and licenses	5,000
Rent expense for equipment	16,000

Calculate Cheryl's business income and self-employment taxes for 2015.

2. Schedule K-1, Form 1065, filed by the ABC Partnership discloses the following amounts attributable to a partner for the year:

Ordinary income	$33,000
Guaranteed payments to partners—salaries and interest	20,500
Charitable contributions	200
Net long-term capital gain	1,500

Indicate the total amount of ordinary income from the partnership that the partner should report on his individual income tax return.

3. Clark Huber, a calendar-year taxpayer, is a member of a partnership with a tax year ending on October 31. During the partnership year ended October 31, 2015, Clark is paid a guaranteed payment for services rendered of $12,500 a month for each of the 12 months, and his distributive share of partnership ordinary income was $50,000. How much must Clark report on his 2015 return as ordinary income from the partnership? How much of this amount is subject to self-employment tax if Clark is a general partner?

Chapter 13 Comprehensive Review Question

A has a one-fourth and B a three-fourths interest in a partnership that operates a toy manufacturing company. The partnership files its partnership return on the calendar-year basis. The partnership books disclose the following information for the current calendar year:

Sales	$235,000
Returns and allowances	10,000
Opening inventory	50,000
Purchases	50,000
Cost of labor and supplies	105,000
Closing inventory	61,000
Royalties received for use of a patent	1,100
Salaries	26,000
Guaranteed payments to partners ($8,400 to each)	16,800
Rent paid	17,000
Interest expense on business debt (other than payments to partners)	550
Taxes	8,500
Bad debt written off	1,000
Repairs	3,000
Depreciation	2,470
Light, postage, stationery, etc.	1,680
Net long-term capital gain	600
Dividends	200

Compute the partnership income and the partners' distributive shares of items that are required to be separately stated.

Chapter 13 Research Questions

1. Jennifer Woods is 32 years old and for the last six years has been employed as a manager by Ski USA, a distributor of ski equipment and boots. In the past two years as a professional bicycle racer she has participated in approximately 50 races annually. Although she has won some of the races in which she was entered, Jennifer has incurred annual expenses that far exceed her annual income from racing. Jennifer trains extensively on a daily basis; she has sponsors who have provided her with the bicycles, clothing, and, occasionally, entry fees required for participation in these races. Otherwise she pays her own expenses which include the costs of bicycle repairs, transportation, lodging, and most entry fees. During racing season, she works a lighter schedule at Ski USA and also utilizes her vacation time. The National Bike Racing Association ranked Jennifer in two events—the dual slalom and downhill races—for which she wears a full-face helmet, chest protector, knee protection, elbow pads, goggles, and heavy-duty clothing. Jennifer wants to know if she was correct in deducting her expenses against the winnings from the races in which she has won prize money and the sponsorship income she has received.

2. Taylor Tamblyn is a partner in three partnerships. Earlier in the year, Taylor received her Schedule K-1s from her partnerships and discovered that she had been allocated amounts under Code Sec. 179 of $300,000, $154,000, and $72,000, respectively. Taylor is familiar with Code Sec. 179 and knows that she will not be able to deduct more than $500,000 on her 2014 tax return. What alternatives are available for the excess section 179 expense Taylor was allocated in 2014? By what amount is her basis in each partnership reduced by the allocation of section 179 expense? See Rev. Rul. 89-7, 1989-1 CB 178; Code Sec. 179(b)(1).

3. Florena Santiago is a general partner in Santiago and Johnston Partnership (SJ) with a 50-percent interest in profits and losses. SJ files partnership tax returns on a calendar year basis and uses the cash receipts and disbursements method of accounting. At the close of the current taxable year at issue, SJ had liabilities for accrued expenses of $100,000 and accounts payable of $250,000. At the end of the prior tax year, SJ had liabilities for accrued expenses of $160,000 and accounts payable of $285,000. Florena had a basis in her

partnership interest at the end of the prior tax year of $50,000 excluding any allocation of partnership liabilities. What are the tax ramifications of the Santiago and Johnston Partnership having a $210,000 loss for the current tax year on Florena's basis and deductibility of losses? See Code Sec. 752 and Revenue Ruling 88-77, 1988-2 CB 128.

CHAPTER

14

S Corporations

CHAPTER CONTENTS

LEARNING OBJECTIVES

1. Understand the advantages and disadvantages of operating a business as an S corporation and be able to compare S corporations to other types of business entities.

2. Learn about the requirements for qualifying to elect S corporation status.

3. Understand how an S corporation can terminate its S status and the tax consequences of doing so.

4. Understand how an S corporation's taxable income is calculated and how S corporation shareholders are taxed on their share of the corporation's profits.

5. Understand how distributions by an S corporation to its shareholders are taxed.

6. Learn about the special taxes that apply to S corporations that were C corporations prior to electing S status.

¶ 1400 Introduction

For federal income tax purposes, a corporation generally is treated as an entity separate from its shareholders. Taxable income of the corporation is taxed when earned by the corporation and again when distributed to its shareholders. Shareholders of a corporation enjoy limited liability for the debts and other activities of the corporation, thereby making corporations a widely used business entity choice. As discussed in Chapter 13, partnerships are also considered separate entities distinct from their owners. However, taxable income earned by a partnership is taxed directly to the owners, regardless of whether any amounts are distributed to them during the year. Although limited partners in a limited partnership enjoy limited liability similar to that of corporate shareholders, the limited partnership rules require that at least one partner (general partner) be responsible for the debts of the partnership.

In an ideal world, business owners would like to operate a business that enjoys the corporate aspects of limited liability but pay only a single level of taxation. In addition, they would like any corporate losses to be passed through to them so that they can deduct the losses on their own income tax returns.

S corporations combine the corporate aspects of limited liability with the tax advantages of a partnership. They provide business owners the "best of both worlds," by combining the limited liability aspects of a corporate entity with the single layer of taxation associated with a partnership. For many years S corporations were the only entity choice that shared these two features. Today, business owners can achieve similar results by organizing their businesses as limited liability companies (LLCs) or limited liability partnerships (LLPs) and electing to have them treated as partnerships for tax purposes (as discussed in Chapter 13).

Nonetheless, S corporations continue to be a popular corporate entity choice. During the IRS's 2013 fiscal year, 4,566,000 S corporation returns were filed (accounting for 67 percent of all corporate returns filed).[1]

S corporations get their name because they are corporations that have elected to be taxed under Subchapter S of Chapter 1 of the Code. A C corporation is a corporation other than an S corporation. A C corporation gets its name because many of the provisions that apply specifically to these types of corporations are located in Subchapter C of Chapter 1 of the Code.

Many of the tax laws presented in this textbook also pertain to S corporations.[2] This chapter focuses on the areas where an S corporation and its owners are treated differently from other types of business entities. It begins with an overview of the history of the S corporation. The chapter then presents the rules for how corporations can elect S status, and continues by discussing how S corporations calculate taxable income and allocate it to their shareholders. The tax consequences of distributions from an S corporation are discussed, as are other features that distinguish an S corporation from other types of business entities.

¶ 1401 The History Behind the S Corporation

Closely held businesses that operate in corporate form often are not much different in their economic character and operation than closely held businesses that operate as partnerships. Recognizing this, in 1953 President Eisenhower proposed that:

> Small businesses should be able to operate under whatever form of organization is desirable for their particular circumstances, without incurring unnecessary tax penalties. To secure this result, I recom-

---

[1] IRS Data Book, 2013, Table 2, at *http://www.irs.gov/pub/irs-soi/13databk.pdf.*   [2] Code Sec. 1371(a).

mend that corporations with a small number of active stockholders be given the option to be taxed as partnerships and that certain partnerships be given the option to be taxed as corporations.[3]

In drafting what was to become the Internal Revenue Code of 1954, the Senate Finance Committee accepted President Eisenhower's recommendation and proposed legislation that would allow small corporations that are essentially partnerships to enjoy the advantages of the corporate form of organization without subjecting themselves to the tax disadvantages of the corporate form.[4] The House Ways and Means Committee rejected the proposal of the Senate Finance Committee, but the Conference Committee accepted it, and provisions allowing corporations to be taxed as partnerships and partnerships to be taxed as corporations were included in the 1954 Code.

The Technical Amendments Act of 1958 amended the Code by adding Subchapter S, which preserves the corporate character of corporations for tax purposes but permits certain small corporations to pass through their income to their shareholders so that their income will be taxed only at the shareholder level. Congress enacted Subchapter S to minimize the effect of federal income taxes on the choice of form of organization by business owners and to permit the incorporation and operation of certain small businesses without incurring a second level of taxation on business income.[5]

The Subchapter S Revision Act of 1982 modified and simplified the rules relating to eligibility for Subchapter S status and the operation of S corporations. Many of the tax rules for S corporations were modified to make them more like the rules that govern the taxation of partnerships. Congress adopted a partnership approach to the tax treatment of items of income because it believed that partnership-like rules provide a simpler and more rational taxing scheme than the modified corporate rules adopted by the Technical Amendments Act of 1958.[6]

¶ 1402 Advantages and Disadvantages of Operating a Business as an S Corporation

There are tax and nontax advantages and disadvantages to operating a business as an S corporation. For example, S corporation shareholders, like C corporation shareholders, enjoy limited liability. But the taxable income of an S corporation, unlike the taxable income of a C corporation, is taxed only once. Also, S corporations are not subject to many of the taxes that apply to C corporations, including the accumulated earnings tax, personal holding company tax, and alternative minimum tax.

The main disadvantage of operating a business as an S corporation is that several restrictions exist as to the type and number of shareholders that an S corporation may have. Also, S corporations that were previously C corporations are subject to LIFO recapture tax. They also may be subject to a tax on excess passive investment income and built-in gains. Finally, S corporation shareholders may be taxed on fringe benefits they receive from the corporation. These advantages and disadvantages of operating a business as an S corporation are summarized in Table 14-1.

---

[3] President Eisenhower's Budget Message of January 1953, Tax Recommendation § 16.

[4] Senate Finance Committee Report to Accompany H.R. 8300 (June 18, 1954).

[5] H.R. Rep. No. 97-826 (September 16, 1982), at 5.

[6] S. Rep. No. 97-640 (September 29, 1982), at 6.

Table 14-1 Advantages and Disadvantages of Operating a Business as an S Corporation

Advantages	Discussion
Limited liability	Similar to C corporations and LLCs.
Single level of taxation	Similar to partnerships, as well as LLCs that elect to be taxed as partnerships.
Corporate losses flow through to shareholders	Similar to partnerships, as well as LLCs that elect to be taxed as partnerships.
No accumulated earnings tax, personal holdings tax, or alternative minimum tax	These additional taxes are imposed on C corporations.
Free transferability of stock	Unless specifically prohibited from doing so in accordance with a binding agreement among the shareholders.
Distributive share of S corporation income is not subject to self-employment tax	Unlike a general partnership where both a partner's distributive share of profits and guaranteed payments for services are subject to self-employment tax, S shareholders who work for the corporation are employees, and only their wages are subject to employment taxes.

Disadvantages	Discussion
Limit on the number of shareholders	No such restriction exists for C corporations.
Restrictions on who can be a shareholder	No such restrictions exist for C corporations.
Can have only a single class of stock	No such restriction exists for C corporations.
Flow-through percentage is pro rata	Partnerships (and LLCs that elect to be taxed as partnerships) can allocate items as specified in the partnership (membership) agreement.
Tax on built-in gains and excess passive investment income	An S corporation that was once a C corporation may be required to pay tax on its recognized built-in gains and may be subject to tax on excessive amounts of passive investment income that it earns during the year.
LIFO recapture tax	A corporation that used the last-in, first-out (LIFO) method for its inventory before it elected S status is required to include its LIFO recapture amount in gross income in its final C corporation tax year.
Tax on fringe benefits	Shareholders who own more than two percent of the corporation's outstanding stock are taxed on the fringe benefits they receive from the S corporation.

¶ 1403 Corporations That Can Elect S Status

A corporation is an S corporation if it is a small business corporation that elects to be treated as an S corporation.[7] A corporation is a "small business corporation" if it satisfies each of the following five requirements.[8]

1. It is a domestic corporation,
2. It is not an ineligible corporation,
3. It has no more than 100 shareholders,
4. It has only permitted shareholders, and
5. It has only one class of stock.

A domestic corporation is a corporation organized or created in the United States or under the laws of the United States or the District of Columbia.[9] Corporations that are ineligible for S status include financial institutions that use the reserve method of accounting for bad debts, insurance companies, corporations that have elected the Puerto Rico and possession tax credit, and Domestic International Sales Corporations (DISCs) or former DISCs.[10]

For tax years beginning before 1997, a corporation could not elect S status if it was a member of an affiliated group. However, an S corporation may now elect to treat a wholly owned subsidiary as a **qualified Subchapter S subsidiary (QSub)**.[11] A QSub is a domestic corporation that is not an ineligible corporation. A QSub is not treated as a separate corporation. Instead, all of its assets, liabilities, and items of income, deduction, and credit are treated as assets, liabilities, and items of income, deduction, and credit of the S corporation.

.01 Permitted Shareholders

Individuals other than nonresident aliens, estates, eligible trusts, and certain tax-exempt organizations are *permitted shareholders* of an S corporation.[12] A corporation cannot elect S status if it has as a shareholder a nonresident alien, corporation, partnership, LLC, LLP, or ineligible trust.[13] A **nonresident alien** is an individual who is not a U.S. citizen or resident.[14] U.S. citizens and residents are treated similarly because they both pay U.S. income tax on their worldwide income. Permanent resident aliens ("green card" holders) are considered U.S. residents, as are some foreign citizens who become U.S. residents for tax purposes due to their extended stays in the United States.[15]

Example 1: A corporation has three individuals (all U.S. citizens) and a partnership as its shareholders. Because the corporation has a partnership as a shareholder, it cannot elect to be taxed as an S corporation.

Example 2: A corporation has as one of its shareholders a citizen and resident of France. Because the company has a nonresident alien as a shareholder, it may not elect to be taxed as an S corporation.

If a shareholder's spouse is a nonresident alien and the spouse is treated as having an ownership interest in a corporation's stock either because of community property laws or the laws in effect in a foreign country, the corporation cannot qualify as an S corporation. However, a nonresident alien married to a U.S. citizen or resident can elect to be treated as a U.S. resident for federal income tax purposes.[16] This allows the spouse to be treated as a U.S. resident for purposes of determining whether a corporation can be an S corporation. However, as long as the election is in effect, the spouse will be required to pay U.S. income tax on all worldwide income earned during the year.

---

[7] Code Sec. 1361(a).
[8] Code Sec. 1361(b).
[9] Code Sec. 7701(a)(4), (10).
[10] Code Sec. 1361(b)(2); Reg. § 1.1361-1(d).
[11] Code Sec. 1361(b)(3).

[12] Code Sec. 1361(b)(1), (c)(2)(A).
[13] Reg. § 1.1361-1(f).
[14] Code Sec. 1361(b)(1)(C); Reg. § 1.1361-1(g); Code Sec. 7701(b)(1)(B).
[15] Code Sec. 7701(b).
[16] Code Sec. 6013(g).

Example 3: Billy Renteria, a U.S. citizen, marries Anna, a nonresident alien. Billy is the sole shareholder of a C corporation. The Renterias decide to move to Anna's country of residence. Under the law of the foreign country where Billy and Anna live, the stock is considered jointly owned by Billy and Anna. Because Anna (a nonresident alien) is considered to own stock in Billy's company, the corporation does not qualify for S corporation status.

Example 4: Assume the same facts as in Example 3, except that Billy and Anna elect to treat Anna as a U.S. resident. Anna will be required to pay U.S. income taxes on her worldwide income, and the corporation may qualify as an S corporation.

An estate may be a shareholder of an S corporation while the estate is being administered.[17] The process of settling an estate can take time, and during the administration period the income earned by the estate is subject to income tax. Accordingly, the income, deductions, and credits that flow through to the estate as a shareholder in an S corporation are taxed to the estate.

Trusts as S corporation shareholders. A **trust** is a legal arrangement established by a person (often referred to as the "trustor" or "grantor") who transfers legal title to property to an individual, institution, or organization (the "trustee") made responsible for managing and administering the property for the benefit of others (the "beneficiaries").

The following five types of trusts can be shareholders of an S corporation.[18]

- Qualified Subchapter S trusts,

- Electing small business trusts,

- Qualified grantor trusts,

- Testamentary trusts, but only for the two-year period beginning on the day stock is transferred to the trust,[19] and

- Qualified voting trusts.

Note that foreign trusts are not eligible S corporation shareholders.[20] A trust is a foreign trust unless one or more U.S. persons have authority to control all substantial decisions of the trust and a court within the United States can exercise primary supervision over administration of the trust.[21]

Qualified Subchapter S trust. A trust is a **qualified Subchapter S trust (QSST)** if all of its income is required to be distributed each year to its one income beneficiary who is a U.S. citizen or resident. That beneficiary must make a timely election to have the trust treated as a QSST, and the terms of the trust must stipulate that:[22]

- There be only one income beneficiary of the trust during the life of the current income beneficiary,

- Any trust principal distributed during the life of the current income beneficiary be distributed only to the income beneficiary,

- The current income beneficiary's income interest in the trust terminates upon the earlier of the termination of the trust or upon the death of the income beneficiary, and

- All trust assets be distributed to the current income beneficiary if the trust terminates during that beneficiary's lifetime.

If spouses are income beneficiaries of the same trust and they file a joint income tax return and they are both U.S. citizens or residents, then the spouses will be treated as one beneficiary.

---

[17] Code Sec. 1361(b)(1)(B).
[18] Code Sec. 1361(b)(1)(B), (c)(2), (d).
[19] Reg. § 1.1361-1(h)(1).

[20] Reg. § 1.1361-1(h)(2).
[21] Code Sec. 7701(a)(30)(E).
[22] Reg. § 1.1361-1(j)(1).

Planning Pointer: QSSTs are useful in estate planning because they can manage S corporation stock gifted or bequeathed to someone who needs a trust to manage his or her property (such as a minor or individual with a disability). A QSST election must be made within the 2½-month period beginning on the day that stock is transferred to the trust. An election, once made, may be revoked only with the IRS's consent.

Electing small business trust. An **electing small business trust (ESBT)** may be a shareholder of an S corporation.[23] A trust cannot be an ESBT if it is a QSST, a tax-exempt trust, or a charitable remainder annuity trust or unitrust. Any other trust may qualify as an ESBT, but only if no interest in the trust was acquired by purchase and the trust makes a timely election to be treated as an ESBT.[24] In addition, the trust cannot have as a beneficiary any person other than:

- An individual,
- An estate,
- A charitable organization, or
- A state, the District of Columbia, a U.S. possession, or any political subdivision thereof, but only if such entity holds a contingent interest in the trust and is not a potential current beneficiary.

Example 5: Valerie Marra contributed 100 shares of S corporation stock to a trust for the benefit of her three children. Income from the stock was to be accumulated for her children until they reached age 21. The trustee may elect to treat the trust as an ESBT.

 Reason for the Rule: The Small Business Job Protection Act of 1996 added ESBTs to the list of permissible shareholders because Congress believed that a trust providing for income to be distributed to (or accumulated for) a class of individuals should be allowed to hold S corporation stock.[25]

Qualified grantor trust. A grantor trust may be a shareholder of an S corporation, provided that the grantor is a U.S. citizen or resident.[26] The grantor is treated as the "deemed owner" of the trust assets and is responsible for paying the taxes owed on the trust income. A grantor trust that continues to exist after its deemed owner's death can be a shareholder of an S corporation for two years after the date of the deemed owner's death.[27]

Example 6: Vivian Briggs, a U.S. citizen, created a grantor trust for her own benefit and transferred all of her shares of stock in an S corporation to the trust. Vivian retained the right to revoke the trust at any time and to invest trust assets herself. The trust is a grantor trust and can be a shareholder of the S corporation.

Example 7: Assume the same facts as in Example 6, except that Vivian dies in 2015. The trust can remain a shareholder of the S corporation for two years after her death. This gives the personal representative of Vivian's estate time to transfer the S corporation stock held by the trust to someone that is a permitted shareholder of an S corporation.

Testamentary trust. A trust with respect to stock transferred to it pursuant to the terms of a will may be an S corporation shareholder, but only for the two-year period beginning on the day that the stock is transferred to the trust.

Qualified voting trust. A trust created primarily to exercise the voting power of S corporation stock transferred to it can be an S corporation shareholder if the beneficial owners are treated as the

---

[23] Code Sec. 1361(b)(1)(B), (c)(2); Reg. § 1.1361-1(h)(1)(vi).
[24] Code Sec. 1361(e); Reg. § 1.1361-1(m).
[25] H.R. Rep. No. 104-586 (May 20, 1996), at 82.
[26] Code Sec. 1361(c)(2)(A)(i); Reg. § 1.1361-1(h)(1)(i).
[27] Code Sec. 1361(c)(2)(A)(ii); Reg. § 1.1361-1(h)(1)(ii).

owners of their respective portions of the trust under the grantor trust rules in the Code. In addition, the trust must have been created pursuant to a written trust agreement entered into by the shareholders that delegates to one or more trustees the right to vote; requires all distributions with respect to the stock to be paid to, or on behalf of, the beneficial owners of that stock; requires that title and possession of that stock be delivered to the beneficial owners when the trust terminates; and terminates, pursuant to its terms or state law, on or before a specific date or event.

Traditional and Roth IRAs. Neither a traditional nor Roth IRA may be a shareholder of an S corporation.[28]

.02 100 Shareholder Limit

A corporation that wants to elect and retain S corporation status can at no time have more than 100 shareholders. Accordingly, it is important to be able to determine who is considered a shareholder for purposes of this rule. Ordinarily, the person who is taxed on the dividends paid by the corporation will be considered a shareholder of the corporation.[29]

 Spotlight: Over the years, the number of permitted shareholders has increased. When the S corporation provisions were originally enacted, only corporations with 10 or fewer shareholders could elect S status. In the past 30 years, Congress has increased this limit several times. The Small Business Job Protection Act of 1996 increased the limit to 75 shareholders. The American Jobs Creation Act of 2004 increased the number of permitted shareholders to 100. By increasing the shareholder limit, Congress hoped it would facilitate corporate ownership by additional family members, employees, and capital investors.[30] This strategy seems to have worked. The number of S corporation returns has risen from 724,749 in 1985 to 4,566,000 in 2013.[31]

Stock owned by spouses (and their estates) is treated as owned by one shareholder.[32]

Example 8: Todd Rales and his spouse each own stock in a corporation. The couple counts as one shareholder for purposes of determining the number of shareholders that an S corporation has.

Example 9: Larry Theriot and his spouse each own stock in a corporation and count as one shareholder for purposes of calculating the number of the corporation's shareholders. Larry dies during 2015, and his shares of stock pass to his estate. The estate and Larry's surviving spouse count as one shareholder for purposes of determining the number of shareholders the S corporation has.

Members of a family. All members of a family (and their estates) are treated as one shareholder.[33] Members of a family must be within six generations of one another and all have the same *common ancestor*. Members of a family include the common ancestor, any lineal descendant of that common ancestor, and any spouse or former spouse of that common ancestor or any such lineal descendant.[34] For purposes of this rule, any legally adopted child, any child who is lawfully placed with an individual for legal adoption, and any eligible foster child of an individual is considered a child of the individual. An "eligible foster child" is an individual placed with the taxpayer by an authorized placement agency or by a judgment, decree, or other order of any court of competent jurisdiction.

---

[28] Reg. § 1.1361-1(h)(1)(vii); *Taproot Administrative Services, Inc.*, 133 TC 202, CCH Dec. 57,950 (2009) (Roth IRA), affd CA-9, 2012-1 USTC ¶ 50,256, 679 F3d 1109.

[29] Reg. § 1.1361-1(e)(1).

[30] H.R. Rep. No. 104-586 (May 20, 1996), at 82.

[31] "IRS Launches Study of S Corporation Reporting Compliance," IRS News Release, IR-2005-76, July 25, 2005; IRS Data

Book, 2013, Table 2, at *http://www.irs.gov/pub/irs-soi/13databk.pdf.*

[32] Code Sec. 1361(c)(1)(A); Reg. § 1.1361-1(e)(2).

[33] Code Sec. 1361(c)(1)(B).

[34] Code Sec. 1361(c)(1)(B).

Although an individual may be a member of more than one family, each family (not all of whose members are also members of the other family) will be treated as one shareholder. The estate, grantor trust, or testamentary trust of a deceased family member will be considered to be a family member during the period in which the estate or trust holds stock in the S corporation.

Example 10: Mattie and Mark Gourley own stock in an S corporation. Mark's father, as well as the Gourley's four children and nine grandchildren also own stock in the S corporation. These 16 individuals will be treated as one shareholder for purposes of calculating the number of shareholders the corporation has because they all have a common ancestor (Mark's father) and the members are not more than six generations apart.

Example 11: Jonathan and Martha Schindler adopted Lisa as their daughter. For purposes of determining who the members of Jonathan's family are, Lisa will be treated as a natural born child. Lisa's spouse and children will all be treated as members of Jonathan's family.

Special stock ownership rules. If stock is owned by joint tenants or tenants in common, each of the tenants is considered a shareholder. This rule does not apply to spouses who own stock as joint tenants or tenants in common because the tax law treats spouses as one shareholder. When a nominee, custodian, guardian, or agent holds stock in an S corporation, the person for whom stock is being held is considered the shareholder of the corporation.[35]

Example 12: Joan Wistrom and her daughter own stock in an S corporation as joint tenants. Both Joan and her daughter are treated as shareholders for purposes of determining whether a corporation has more than 100 shareholders.

Example 13: Dora Hardiman owns stock in a corporation on behalf of her son as his guardian. The son, not Dora, is considered a shareholder in the corporation.

Example 14: Lucretia Lemont holds stock for her son George under the Uniform Transfers to Minors Act. George, not Lucretia, is considered the shareholder.

When stock of an S corporation is owned by an eligible trust, the party treated as the shareholder depends on the type of trust.[36] In the case of a QSST, the income beneficiary is treated as the shareholder. For ESBTs, each potential current beneficiary is treated as a shareholder. If for any period there is no potential current beneficiary, the ESBT will be treated as the shareholder. A "potential current beneficiary" includes any person who at any time during the period is entitled to, or at the discretion of any person may receive, a distribution of trust principal or income. A person will not be treated as a potential current beneficiary solely because that person holds any future (contingent) interest in the trust.

If stock is held by a grantor trust, then the deemed owner of the trust is treated as the shareholder. When the deemed owner of a grantor trust dies, the estate of the deemed owner generally is treated as the shareholder starting on the day of the deemed owner's death. The estate ordinarily will cease to be treated as the shareholder when the stock is transferred to the beneficiary, or, if earlier, on the expiration of the two-year period beginning on the day of the deemed owner's death.

If stock is held by a testamentary trust, the estate is treated as the shareholder until the stock is transferred by the trust or on the expiration of the two-year period beginning on the day that stock is transferred or deemed distributed to the trust. If the stock is held by a qualified voting trust, then each beneficial owner of the stock is treated as a shareholder with respect to the owner's proportionate share of the stock held by the trust. The rules governing who is considered a shareholder when a trust owns stock in an S corporation are summarized in Table 14-2.

---

[35] Reg. § 1.1361-1(e)(1).

[36] Code Sec. 1361(c)(2); Reg. § 1.1361-1(h)(3).

If stock is held by a decedent's estate, the decedent's estate, not the beneficiaries of the estate, is considered the shareholder.[37]

Table 14-2 Persons Treated as Shareholders of a Trust

Type of Trust	*Person(s) Considered To Be Shareholders*
QSST	The sole income beneficiary.
ESBT	Each potential current beneficiary.
Grantor trust	The deemed owner during the owner's lifetime. Upon the death of the deemed owner, the estate is generally considered to be a shareholder.
Testamentary trust	Estate of the testator for two years after the stock is transferred to the trust.
Qualified voting trust	Each beneficial owner of the stock.

Example 15: Robert Riddick owns stock in an S corporation. Robert transfers some of his stock in the company to an ESBT and names his children, Gladys and Michael, as beneficiaries. Although the stock is held in trust, the stock is treated as owned by Gladys and Michael. Because Robert, Gladys, and Michael are members of a family, they are treated as one shareholder for purposes of determining the number of shareholders of the S corporation.

Example 16: S corporation stock is held in trust. Meri Eger is entitled to all of the income from the trust. Her friend, Chelsea, is entitled to all remaining trust assets after Meri dies. Chelsea also is entitled to receive distributions of trust principal at the discretion of the trustee. An election was made to treat the trust as an ESBT. Because both Meri and Chelsea are potential current beneficiaries of the trust, each is treated as a shareholder of the S corporation.

Example 17: Assume the same facts as in Example 16, except that Chelsea is not entitled to receive any distributions of trust principal. Because Chelsea is not a potential current beneficiary, she is not considered a shareholder of the S corporation.

Example 18: Gerardo Hildenbrand dies and bequeaths his S corporation stock to his two children. Until the stock is distributed to his two children, the estate is considered the shareholder of the S corporation.

A person will be counted as only one shareholder of a corporation even though that person may be treated as a shareholder by direct ownership and indirectly through one or more trusts permitted to be shareholders of an S corporation.[38]

Example 19: Rita Lyons owns stock in Tomei, Inc., an S corporation. She also is a potential current beneficiary of an ESBT that owns stock in Tomei. Rita counts as one shareholder of the S corporation.

Example 20: Damon Romain owns stock in R.W. Hoists, an S corporation. Damon's spouse is a potential current beneficiary of an ESBT that owns stock in R.W. Hoists. Damon and his spouse are considered one shareholder of the S corporation.

---

[37] Reg. § 1.1361-1(e)(1).

[38] Reg. § 1.1361-1(m)(4)(vii).

Reason for the Rule: Due to the limitation on the number of shareholders an S corporation can have, Congress did not want taxpayers to be able to circumvent the shareholder limit by establishing trusts with multiple beneficiaries and having those trusts own stock in an S corporation. Accordingly, Congress specifically limits the types of trusts that can own stock in an S corporation and includes provisions in the tax law to be sure that each beneficiary counts as a shareholder.

.03 Single Class of Stock

A corporation cannot qualify as an S corporation if it has more than one class of stock.[39] As a general rule, a corporation will be treated as having only one class of stock if all of its outstanding shares of stock confer identical rights to distribution and liquidation proceeds. Differences in voting rights among shares of stock of a corporation are ignored for purposes of determining whether a corporation has more than one class of stock. Also, a corporation will not be considered to have more than one class of stock merely because there are differences in the timing of distributions.

Example 21: All of the outstanding shares of an S corporation give the owners identical rights to distribution and liquidation proceeds. However, some shares give their owner the right to vote on corporate matters, while others do not. Because all shares confer identical rights to distribution and liquidation proceeds, the corporation will be considered to have only one class of stock, even though some shares are voting and others are nonvoting.

Example 22: All of the outstanding shares of stock of an S corporation give the owners identical rights to distribution and liquidation proceeds. However, the corporation is required to withhold income tax from distributions made to some shareholders but not others. These differences will not cause the corporation to be treated as having more than one class of stock.

In an attempt to circumvent the single class of stock rule, S corporations may be tempted to disguise a second class of stock as debt. An instrument, obligation, or arrangement issued by a corporation, regardless whether it is designated as debt, will be considered as a second class of stock if both of the following requirements are satisfied.

1. The instrument, obligation, or arrangement constitutes equity or otherwise results in the holder being treated as the owner of stock under general principles of federal tax law, and

2. A principal purpose of issuing or entering into the instrument, obligation, or arrangement was to circumvent the rights to distribution or liquidation proceeds conferred by the outstanding shares of stock or to circumvent the limitation on eligible shareholders.

Example 23: Papuel Gaskets wants to elect S corporation status but currently has 101 shareholders. Papuel enters into an agreement to redeem for $10,000 all 500 shares of stock owned by one of its shareholders, Alvin Seo. At the same time, Alvin agrees to loan the company $10,000. The terms of the loan do not set a schedule for repayment of the loan or require any security for the loan. Had Alvin continued as a shareholder, the company would have been obligated to pay Alvin $10,000 of dividends. Under these circumstances, the loan is equivalent to stock. If it can be established that a principal purpose of the loan was to circumvent the limit on shareholders, the loan will be treated as a second class of stock.

Straight debt will not be treated as a second class of stock, even though it is considered equity under general principles of federal tax law. **Straight debt** is a written, unconditional promise to pay

---

[39] Code Sec. 1361(c)(4); Reg. § 1.1361-1(l).

a sum certain in money on demand or on a specified date, but only if it satisfies each of the following three requirements.

1. It does not provide for an interest rate or payment dates that are contingent on profits, the borrower's discretion, the payment of dividends with respect to common stock, or similar factors.

2. It cannot be converted (directly or indirectly) into stock or any other equity interest of the corporation.

3. It is held by an individual (other than a nonresident alien), estate, trust eligible to be an S corporation shareholder, or a person who is actively and regularly engaged in the business of lending money.

If the rate of interest is unreasonably high, an appropriate portion of the interest may be recharacterized as a payment that is not interest. However, such a recharacterization will not make the obligation a second class of stock.

¶ 1404 Electing S Corporation Status

To be treated as an S corporation, an eligible corporation must elect to be treated as such.[40] This election applies both to newly formed corporations as well as to existing C corporations that want to convert to S corporations. A corporation can make an election to be an S corporation by filing Form 2553, *Election by a Small Business Corporation*. An election is not valid unless all of the corporation's shareholders at the time of the election consent to the election. A shareholder's consent may be made directly on Form 2553 or on a separate statement. Once a shareholder consents to an election, it is binding and cannot be withdrawn. The corporation does not need to obtain the consent of those who become shareholders after an election has been made, even if the effective date is not until the beginning of the subsequent tax year.

If an election is made by the 15th day of the third month of a tax year and is intended to be effective for that entire year, then each person who is a shareholder at the time of the election plus anyone who was a shareholder during the portion of the year prior to the election must consent to the election. If consent is not obtained, the election will be effective beginning on the first day of the following year.[41] If the election is to be effective for the following tax year, the consent is needed only from the shareholders at the time the election is made.

Example 24: A calendar year C corporation elects S corporation status on March 15, 2016. If the corporation wants the election to take effect retroactive to January 1, 2015, then it must obtain the written consent of each shareholder as of March 15, 2015, plus anyone who was a shareholder during the period from January 1, 2015, until March 14, 2015. If the corporation fails to obtain the consent of any shareholders who sold their shares during the first 2½ months of 2015, the election will take effect on January 1, 2016.

 Reason for the Rule: Items of income, gain, deduction, loss, and credit generated by an S corporation flow through to its shareholders on a pro rata basis. Income generated by a C corporation is taxed to the corporation and taxed to the shareholders only when distributed in the form of a dividend. Thus, beginning on the day that a corporation's S election becomes effective, its shareholders become responsible for the taxes owed on any income or gain the corporation generates. Accordingly, a corporation that files an S election during the first 2½ months of the tax year can make the election retroactive to January 1 only if it obtains the consent of all who owned stock in the corporation during that year. Shareholders who sold their shares during the year but before the election

---

[40] Code Sec. 1362(a); Reg. § 1.1362-1(a).   [41] Code Sec. 1362(b); Reg. § 1.1362-6(a)(2).

> have to agree to pay tax on their respective shares of S corporation taxable income. Anyone who purchases stock after the election becomes effective will be aware of the corporation's intention to become an S corporation.

If stock is owned by spouses as community property or if the income from the stock is community property, each spouse must consent to the election.[42] If stock is owned by tenants in common, joint tenants, or tenants by the entirety, each tenant must consent to the election. If stock is owned by a minor, the minor's consent must be made by the minor's legal representative (or by a parent of the minor if no legal representative has been appointed).

In the case of an ESBT, both the trustee and anyone who is treated under the grantor trust rules as owner of the portion of the trust consisting of the corporation must consent to the S corporation election. For all other trusts permitted to be shareholders of an S corporation, only the person treated as the shareholder must consent to the election. However, if spouses have a community interest in trust property, both spouses must consent to the election. In the case of an estate, consent must be obtained from the estate's executor or personal representative.

¶ 1405 Termination of S Status

An election of S status is effective for the entire tax year for which it is made and for all succeeding tax years until the election is terminated.[43] A corporation's S status can be terminated voluntarily or involuntarily. Normally if a corporation's S status is terminated, the corporation must wait at least five years before re-electing S status.[44] However, if the corporation can show that the termination was involuntary, the IRS may allow the corporation to retroactively reinstate its S status as if the terminating event never occurred.[45] (See ¶ 1405.02.)

.01 Voluntary Revocation of an S Election

A corporation may terminate its S status at any time by revoking its election.[46] To revoke an S election, a corporation must file a statement with the IRS stating that it intends to revoke its S election and informing the IRS of the numbers of outstanding shares of S stock that it had at the time of the revocation.[47] An S election may be revoked only with the consent of the shareholders who own more than one-half of the number of outstanding shares of the corporation's stock at the time of the revocation.

Example 25: An S corporation decides to revoke its S election. The corporation has outstanding 60,000 shares of Class A voting common stock and 40,000 shares of Class B nonvoting common stock. Thus, to revoke its S election, shareholders owning at least 50,001 shares must consent to the revocation. If shareholders owning 25,000 shares of Class A stock and 26,000 shares of Class B stock consent to the revocation, the corporation will be able to revoke its S election because shareholders owning more than 50 percent of the corporation's outstanding stock consented to the revocation.

A revocation may specify a date in the future for the revocation to become effective. If no such date is specified, a revocation will be effective retroactive to the first day of the tax year if the revocation is made within the first 2½ months of the tax year. If the revocation is made after the first 2½ months of the tax year and no future date is specified, then the revocation will be effective on the first day of the following tax year.

---

[42] Code Sec. 1362(b)(2).
[43] Reg. § 1.1362-1(b).
[44] Code Sec. 1362(d).

[45] Code Sec. 1362(f).
[46] Code Sec. 1362(d)(1); Reg. § 1.1362-2(a).
[47] Reg. § 1.1362-6(a)(3).

Example 26: On March 15, 2015, a calendar year S corporation files a statement with the IRS to revoke its S election. If the statement does not specify a future date on which the revocation is to take effect, the corporation's S status will be revoked retroactively to January 1, 2015.

Example 27: Assume the same facts as in Example 26, except that the corporation files the statement to revoke its S election on March 16, 2015. If the statement does not specify a future date on which the revocation is to take effect, the corporation's S status will be revoked effective January 1, 2016.

 Spotlight: To elect S status (and thus subject the corporation to a single layer of taxation), the tax laws require that all affected shareholders consent to the election. However, to revoke the corporation's S election (and thus subject the corporation to double taxation), only a majority of the corporation's shareholders must consent.

A corporation may rescind a revocation at any time before it becomes effective. To rescind a revocation, a corporation must file a statement to the effect with the IRS service center where the revocation was made.[48] A rescission may be made only with the consent of each person who consented to the revocation and by each person who has become a shareholder of the corporation within the period beginning on the first day after the date that the revocation was made and ending on the date on which the rescission is made.

Example 28: Continuing with Example 27, anytime prior to January 1, 2016, the S corporation can rescind its revocation. However, to do so all shareholders who consented to the revocation plus any who purchased stock since March 16, 2015, must agree to rescind the revocation.

.02 Involuntary Revocation of an S Election

An S corporation may accidentally revoke its S status by either no longer qualifying as a small business corporation or by having excess passive investment income for three consecutive years. The latter situation only applies to corporations that were formerly C corporations that have undistributed accumulated earnings and profits (E&P) from their C corporation years.

Corporation ceases to be a small business corporation. A corporation's S election terminates if it ceases to be a small business corporation.[49] An S corporation ceases to be a small business corporation if a C corporation, partnership, nonresident alien, or other nonpermitted shareholder becomes a shareholder in the corporation. An S corporation also ceases to be a small business corporation if it issues a second class of stock or if the number of shareholders exceeds 100. When an S corporation no longer qualifies as a small business corporation, its S corporation tax year closes on the day before the terminating event.

Example 29: On June 5, 2015, an S corporation ceased to be a small business corporation because the number of its shareholders increased to 101. The corporation's S status terminates, and its S corporation tax year ends, on June 4, 2015. The corporation reverts to a C corporation beginning on June 5, 2015.

 Planning Pointer: If at any time during its existence a nonpermitted shareholder owns stock in an S corporation or if the number of shareholders of the S corporation exceeds 100, the corporation's S status is terminated and the corporation reverts back to being a C corporation. Thus, to avoid losing S status, shareholders of an S corporation should formally agree not to transfer shares of stock in their corporation to someone other than

---

[48] Reg. § 1.1362-6(a)(4).   [49] Code Sec. 1362(d)(2); Reg. § 1.1362-2(b).

a permitted shareholder and not to transfer shares without the permission of the other shareholders.

Excess passive investment income. A corporation's S election terminates if the corporation has accumulated E&P and reports excess passive investment income for three consecutive tax years. An S corporation can have accumulated E&P either from its years as a C corporation or because it acquired a C corporation with accumulated E&P. "Excess passive investment income" is defined as passive investment income that exceeds 25 percent of the corporation's gross receipts for the year.[50]

Gross receipts generally include the total amount that a business receives or accrues (depending on the corporation's method of accounting). It is not reduced by returns and allowances, cost of goods sold, or any deductions. Gross receipts from dispositions of capital assets (other than stock and securities) are taken into account only to the extent of the capital gain net income from the dispositions. Gross receipts from the sale or exchange of stock or securities are taken into account only to the extent of the gains from the dispositions. **Passive investment income** includes gross receipts derived from royalties, rents, dividends, interest, and annuities.

The termination of a corporation's S status because of excessive passive investment income is effective on the first day of the tax year that begins after the third consecutive tax year in which the S corporation had excessive passive investment income.[51]

Example 30: Eppini Real Estate Holdings is an S corporation that uses the calendar year as its tax year. Eppini has $100,000 in accumulated E&P from its years as a C corporation and from 2015–2017, it reports the following gross receipts and passive investment income.

Tax Year	Passive Investment Income (PII)	Gross Receipts	Percentage of Gross Receipts from PPI
2015	$115,000	$450,000	25.56%
2016	$105,000	$400,000	26.25%
2017	$140,000	$500,000	28.00%

Because Eppini's passive investment income exceeds 25 percent of its gross receipts for each of these three consecutive years, its S election terminates effective January 1, 2018.

Reason for the Rule: Accumulated E&P represent profits of a C corporation that have previously been taxed to the corporation but have not been taxed at the shareholder level. When a C corporation with accumulated E&P elects to be taxed as an S corporation, its accumulated E&P avoid double taxation until the S corporation distributes these amounts to its shareholders. The excess passive investment income rule was enacted to prevent corporations with accumulated E&P from converting "a regular corporation's operating company into a holding company whose income is not subject to a corporate level tax, without the imposition of any shareholder tax on accumulated E&P as would occur if the corporation was liquidated."[52]

Relief from an inadvertent termination. A corporation may be treated as continuing as an S corporation during a period specified by the IRS even though its S status terminated because the

---

[50] Code Sec. 1362(d)(3); Reg. § 1.1362-2(c).

[51] Code Sec. 1362(d)(3)(A).

[52] H.R. Rep. No. 97-826 (September 16, 1982), at 6.

corporation ceased to be a small business corporation or had excessive passive investment income.[53] In order to receive this treatment, each of the following three requirements must be satisfied.

1. The IRS determines that the circumstances resulting in termination were inadvertent,

2. Within a reasonable period of time after the corporation discovered the circumstances resulting in termination, steps were taken to correct the problem, and

3. The corporation and each person who was a shareholder at any time during the period that the IRS permits the corporation to continue as an S corporation agree to make adjustments the IRS may require that are consistent with the treatment of the corporation as an S corporation.[54]

The IRS is more likely to accept an S corporation's request to disregard an inadvertent termination if it believes that the terminating event was not reasonably within the corporation's control and was not part of a plan to terminate the corporation's S status. If the terminating event took place without the corporation's knowledge, notwithstanding its due diligence to safeguard itself against such an event, it tends to establish that the termination was inadvertent.[55]

.03 Treatment of S Termination Year

In the year that an S corporation terminates its S status, the portion of the tax year ending on the day before the effective date of the termination is treated as a short tax year for which the corporation was an S corporation (the "**S short year**"). Starting with the day of the terminating event, the remaining portion of the year is treated as a short tax year for which the corporation was a C corporation (the "**C short year**").[56] There is no S termination year when a corporation's S status is terminated because it had excessive passive investment income because such termination is effective as of the first day of the corporation's tax year.

Computing short year taxable income. The amount of each item of income, gain, loss, deduction, and credit is allocated pro rata between the S short year and C short year on a daily basis unless the corporation elects otherwise. If the pro rata allocation rules do not apply, then the corporation must allocate its items of income, gain, deduction, loss, and credit on the basis of its normal tax accounting method. In such a situation, the corporation's items are allocated to shareholders who owned stock in the corporation during the period that the items were generated. A corporation's election to allocate S termination year income on the basis of its normal tax accounting method may be made only with the consent of each person who is a shareholder at any time during the S short year and each person who is a shareholder on the first day of the C short year.[57]

Corporation's tax for its C short year. A corporation's tax for its C short year is the portion of the tax on annualized taxable income that relates to the period in which the business is taxed as a C corporation. The first step in computing this tax is to annualize the corporation's taxable income for the C short year. This can be accomplished by dividing taxable income for the C short year by the number of days in the C short year and multiplying this amount by the number of days in the year (365). Next, tax is computed on the annualized taxable income and then multiplied by a percentage that represents the portion of the year that the corporation is taxed as a C corporation.[58]

Example 31: On July 6, 2016, the number of shareholders of Freedberg Automotive increases to over 100. Freedberg, a calendar year corporation, has an S short year that ends on July 5, 2016, and a C short year that begins on July 6, 2016. Freedberg's taxable income for its C short year was $500,000. The first step in calculating its tax for its C short year is to annualize its taxable income for its C short year by dividing its taxable income for its C short year by the number of days in the C short year and then multiplying this amount by 365 (($500,000/179) × 365 = $1,019,553). Using the

---

[53] Code Sec. 1362(f).
[54] Code Sec. 1362(f).
[55] Reg. § 1.1362-4(b).

[56] Code Sec. 1362(e); Reg. § 1.1362-3(a).
[57] Reg. § 1.1362-3(b)(1).
[58] Code Sec. 1362(e)(5).

corporate income tax rates schedule, Freedberg's annual tax on that amount would be $346,648. Because the company is taxed as a C corporation for 179 days during 2016, its C short year tax liability is $170,000 ($346,648/365 × 179).

¶ 1406 Allocating S Corporation Items

S corporations, like partnerships, do not pay federal income tax on their taxable income.[59] Instead, an S corporation's shareholders are taxed on their pro rata share of the S corporation's income, gains, losses, deductions, and credits. S corporations are required to compute and report their taxable income on Form 1120S, *U.S. Income Tax Return for an S Corporation*. Because the activities of the S corporation flow through to its shareholders, some items of income, gain, deduction, loss, and credit must be separately stated from S corporation taxable income so that any limit that applies to the items at the shareholder-level can be applied on the shareholders' respective income tax returns.[60]

Most S corporations use a calendar year-end, but an S corporation may use a fiscal year if it establishes a business purpose for doing so. An S corporation also may select as its tax year a year end that does not defer recognition of income by its shareholders for more than three months, but only if the corporation agrees to pay an amount representing the tax on the deferral provided for its shareholders. This election under Code Sec. 444 is the same that applies to partnerships. (See ¶ 302.02.)

No carryovers arising for a tax year for which a corporation is a C corporation may be carried to a tax year for which the corporation is an S corporation. However, if the S corporation reverts to C status before the end of the year carryover period, it may be able to utilize the carryovers on its C corporation income tax return.[61]

Example 32: In 2015, Folts Gutters and Downspouts, a C corporation, reported a $15,000 net operating loss, which would normally carry over to each of the following 20 tax years. If Folts elects S status, it will not be able to utilize any remaining net operating loss during its years as an S corporation. If Folts reverts back to a C corporation prior to 2035 (when its net operating loss expires), it may be able to utilize its net operating loss carryover.

S corporations make most of the elections affecting the computation of their taxable income and, consequently, the taxable income of their shareholders.[62] For example, they make elections regarding which accounting method and depreciation method to use, whether and how much to elect to expense under Code Sec. 179, and whether to deduct intangible drilling and development costs. The decision whether to reinvest the proceeds from an involuntary conversion in qualified replacement property to defer recognition of realized gain is also made at the entity level. However, the decision whether to deduct or take a credit for foreign income taxes paid or accrued by the S corporation is made at the shareholder level. Accordingly, the amount of foreign income taxes paid or accrued by the S corporation must be reported separately from other items on the S corporation's income tax return.

 Spotlight: The S corporation rules require that items of income, gain, loss, deduction, and credit be allocated to shareholders on a pro rata basis. Unlike partnerships and limited liability companies that elect to be taxed as partnerships, S corporations cannot specially allocate these items.

---

[59] Code Sec. 1363(a); Reg. § 1.1363-1(a)(1).
[60] Code Sec. 1363(b).

[61] Code Sec. 1371(b)(1).
[62] Code Sec. 1363(c)(1); Reg. § 1.1363-1(c)(1).

.01 Separately vs. Nonseparately-Stated Items

For the same reasons that a partnership is required to separately state certain items of income, gain, deduction, loss, or credit on its tax return, an S corporation must separately state certain items on Schedule K-1, *Shareholder's Share of Income, Deductions, Credits, and Other Items* of Form 1120S.[63] A list of items of income, gain, deduction, loss, or credit that an S corporation must separately state is provided in Table 14-3.

---

[63] Code Sec. 1366(a)(1).

Table 14-3 Separately Stated Items of an S Corporation

Separately Stated Item	*Reason for Stating Separately*
Income or Loss:	
Net short-term capital gains and losses; net long-term capital gains and losses; net gains and losses from the sale of collectibles; unrecaptured Section 1250 gain; net Section 1231 gains and losses	For purposes of computing the net capital gain taxed at a maximum 5-, 15-, 20-, 25-, or 28-percent tax rate. See ¶ 1306.01.
Taxable and tax-exempt interest income; qualified and nonqualified dividend income; investment expenses (other than interest)	For purposes of computing the investment interest expense limitation that applies to individual taxpayers.
Net income or loss from rental real estate activities; net income or loss from other rental activities; royalty income	For purposes of computing the limitation on losses from passive activities. See IRS Publication 925.
Recoveries of tax benefit items	For purposes of determining whether the taxpayer benefited from deducting these items. See ¶ 313.
Deductions:	
Code Sec. 179 expenses	For purposes of applying the taxable income limitation. See ¶ 702.03.
Charitable contributions	For purposes of applying the 20-, 30-, and 50-percent limits that apply to individual taxpayers. See ¶ 1304.03.
Investment interest expense	For purposes of computing the investment interest expense limitation that applies to individual taxpayers.
Circulation expenditures, research and experimentation expenditures, intangible drilling costs, and mining exploration costs	Various tax preference items used in computing an individual's alternative minimum tax.
Post-1986 depreciation adjustment, adjusted gain or loss, depletion, gross income, and deductions from oil, gain and geothermal properties, and other AMT items	For purposes of computing tax adjustments necessary to compute an individual's alternative minimum taxable income.
Tax Credits:	
Various business tax credits discussed in Chapter 11, including the low-income housing credit, work opportunity credit, and credit for increasing research activities.	For purposes of computing the general business credit limitation on the shareholder's income tax return.
Foreign taxes paid or accrued; gross income from foreign sources	For purposes of applying the formula for the foreign tax credit. See ¶ 1116.

Nonseparately stated items include the corporation's gross income from its business operations and its business deductions. Nonseparately stated items are those items of income, deduction, gain, or loss that are treated and taxed as ordinary income to all types of shareholders. Furthermore, nonseparately stated items are not subject to any limitations applied at the shareholder-level. The corporation's deductions are subtracted from its gross income from business operations, and the resulting ordinary income or loss is passed through to shareholders pro rata as one lump sum amount.

.02 Treatment of Organizational Expenditures

Recall from Chapter 5 that the tax law allows corporations to elect to deduct up to $5,000 of their organizational expenditures for the tax year in which they begin business. The $5,000 amount is reduced dollar-for-dollar when the total organizational costs exceed $50,000. Thus, no current deduction is allowed to corporations that incur more than $55,000 in organizational costs. At the taxpayer's election, any costs not currently expensed may be amortized ratably over a 180-month period, starting in the month in which the business begins.[64] If the election is not made, these expenses are capitalized and recovered in the year the corporation is liquidated (see ¶ 503). These rules apply to both C corporations and S corporations.

Organizational expenses are capital expenditures incident to the creation of a corporation. Examples include legal services to organize the corporation, accounting services, fees paid to the state of incorporation, expenses of temporary directors, and expenses for organizational meetings of directors and shareholders. Expenditures that do not qualify as organizational expenditures include commissions, professional fees, and printing costs to issue or sell stock or other securities, expenditures to transfer assets to a corporation, or expenses connected with the reorganization of a corporation.

As with other business entities, S corporations may make an election to amortize organizational expenses in a statement attached to their first tax return. The statement and return must be filed by the due date (including extensions) for filing that first tax return.

Example 33: An S corporation incurs $18,000 in organizational expenses. Because these amounts do not exceed $50,000, the entire $18,000 can be deducted in arriving at taxable income in the first year of operations.

.03 Corporate Preference Items

If the S corporation was a C corporation for any of the three tax years immediately preceding its current tax year, it must adjust certain items before taking them into account in determining its taxable income. These adjustments result in the same amount of tax being collected as if the corporation had continued as a C corporation.

Gain on the disposition of Section 1250 property. When a corporation disposes of depreciable real property, 20 percent of the difference between the amount that would be treated as ordinary income if the property were Section 1245 property and the amount treated as ordinary income under Code Sec. 1250 is treated as ordinary income.[65] When an individual sells Section 1250 property for a gain, the gain is treated as Section 1231 gain, assuming that the straight-line method was used to depreciate depreciable property. Consequently, when Section 1250 property is sold by an S corporation, the shareholders will include their pro rata share of the gain on their tax return. Because no shareholders of an S corporation are C corporations, the portion of the gain that would have been taxed as ordinary income is now likely to be taxed as Section 1231 gain. For individual taxpayers, net Section 1231 gain often is treated as long-term capital gain, which is taxed at a lower rate than ordinary income.

---

[64] Code Sec. 1363(b)(3).

[65] Code Sec. 291(a)(1).

To prevent corporations from converting ordinary income into Section 1231 gain, if an S corporation sells such property during the first three years after converting from a C corporation, then the S corporation must characterize a portion of the gain as ordinary income using the same rules that would have applied if it were still a C corporation.[66] This ordinary income is passed through and taxed as such to the S corporation's shareholders.

Example 34: Immediately after converting to S status, an S corporation sells an office building for $1 million. Its adjusted basis in the office building is $300,000. It had depreciated the building using the straight-line method. Total depreciation deductions were $80,000. Accordingly, none of its $700,000 gain ($1,000,000 – $300,000) is recaptured as ordinary income under Code Sec. 1250. However, had the property sold been Section 1245 property, all $80,000 of depreciation taken would have been recaptured as ordinary income. Therefore, 20 percent of this amount, or $16,000, represents gain that flows through to shareholders as ordinary income. The remaining $64,000 of the gain ($80,000 – $16,000) flows through to the shareholders as Section 1231 gain.

Percentage depletion for iron ore and coal. A corporation's percentage depletion deduction for iron ore and coal is reduced by 20 percent of the difference between its percentage depletion deduction for the tax year and the adjusted basis (determined without regard to the depletion deduction for the tax year) of the property at the close of the tax year.

Amortization of pollution control facilities. An S corporation must reduce the amortizable basis of a certified pollution control facility by 20 percent before calculating its amortization deduction.

Mineral exploration and development costs. The S corporation may deduct only 70 percent of its domestic exploration costs. It capitalizes the remaining 30 percent of such costs and may amortize them over the 60-month period beginning with the month during which the costs were paid or incurred. The amount amortized is treated as additional depreciation and is subject to recapture as ordinary income when the corporation disposes of the property.

¶ 1407 Tax Consequences to Shareholders

S corporation shareholders must report on their federal income tax returns their pro rata shares of each item of their corporation's separately stated income, gain, loss, deduction, and credit, regardless of the amounts distributed to them during the year.[67] They also must report their respective nonseparately computed income or loss, irrespective of any distributions made to them during the year. A shareholder's pro rata share of corporate items is reported to the shareholder on Schedule K-1, *Shareholder's Share of Income, Deductions, Credits, and Other Items*, for Form 1120S.

.01 Pro Rata Share

The tax laws normally require that S corporation income, gain, deduction, loss, and credit be allocated to shareholders on a pro rata basis. However, the pro rata allocation rules do not apply if at any time during the S termination year there is a change in ownership of 50 percent or more of the issued and outstanding shares of stock of the corporation.[68] A shareholder's pro rata share of any S corporation item for a tax year is determined by applying the following four steps:[69]

Step 1: Divide the amount of an item by the number of days in the corporation's tax year. This amount represents the per-day amount for that item.

Step 2: Divide the per-day amount by the number of outstanding shares on that day. This amount represents the per-share, per-day amount for that item.

---

[66] Code Sec. 1363(b)(4).
[67] Code Sec. 1366(a); Reg. § 1.1366-1(a)(1).

[68] Reg. § 1.1362-3(b).
[69] Code Sec. 1377(a)(1); Reg. § 1.1377-1(a)(1).

Step 3:   Multiply the number of the shareholder's shares on the per-day amount by the amount assigned to that day. Then multiply this amount by the number of days that the shareholder owned that exact number of shares.

Step 4:   Repeat Step 3 for each different number of shares that the shareholder held during the year. When finished, the sum of these amounts equals the shareholder's pro rata share of the item.

If there is no change in a corporation's shareholders or their ownership interests during a year, a shareholder's pro rata share of an item may be calculated by multiplying the amount of the item by the shareholder's percentage ownership.

Example 35: Candida Rensch owns 15 percent of the shares of stock of an S corporation during the entire year. Her pro rata share of the corporation's $10,000 interest income for the year is $1,500 ($10,000 × 15%).

Example 36: William Reese owned 100 shares of stock in an S corporation from January 1, 2016, until May 24, 2016. This represented 10 percent of the 1,000 total shares of stock outstanding in the S corporation. On May 25, 2016, William purchased 275 additional shares and increased his ownership percentage to 25 percent of the 1,500 shares outstanding. William's pro rata share of the corporation's $30,000 dividend income for the year is $5,724.26.

Step 1: $30,000/365 = $82.19 (per-day amount)

Step 2: $82.19/1,000 shares = $.08219 (per-share, per-day amount from January 1, 2016–May 24, 2016)
$82.19/1,500 shares = $.05479 (per-share, per-day amount from May 25, 2016–December 31, 2016)

Step 3: $.08219 × 100 shares × 144 days = $1,183.54
$.05479 × 375 shares × 221 days = $4,540.72

Step 4: $1,183.54 + $4,540.72 = $5,724.26

Election to terminate tax year following termination of shareholder's interest. If a shareholder's entire interest in an S corporation is terminated during the S corporation's tax year and the corporation and all affected shareholders agree, then the S corporation may elect to determine the shareholder's share of a corporation's separately and nonseparately stated items as if the corporation's tax year ended on the day that the shareholder's entire interest in the corporation terminated.[70] "Affected shareholders" are those shareholders whose interest is terminated and all shareholders to whom the shareholder has transferred shares during the tax year. If the shareholder has transferred shares to the corporation, affected shareholders include all persons who were shareholders during the tax year.[71]

Example 37: Archie Osaki, a shareholder of a calendar tax year S corporation, sells all of his shares of stock in the corporation on June 1. On September 1, the corporation disposes of a building and recognizes $1 million of gain. If all affected shareholders agreed to determine Archie's share of this gain as if the corporation's tax year ended on June 1, none of the gain from the sale of the building will be included in Archie's gross income.

Election to terminate tax year following qualifying disposition. If there is a qualifying disposition of stock, a corporation may elect to determine each shareholder's pro rata share of the corporation's separately and nonseparately stated items as if the corporation's tax year consisted of two separate tax years, the first of which ended at the close of the day on which the qualifying disposition occurred.[72] A "qualifying disposition" includes:

---

[70] Code Sec. 1377(a)(2); Reg. § 1.1377-1(b)(1).
[71] Reg. § 1.1377-1(b)(2).

[72] Reg. § 1.1368-1(g).

- A shareholder's disposition of 20 percent or more of the outstanding stock of the corporation in one or more transactions during any 30-day period during the corporation's tax year.

- A redemption treated as an exchange under Code Secs. 302(a) or 303(a) of at least 20 percent of the corporation's outstanding stock from a shareholder in one or more transactions during any 30-day period during the corporation's tax year.

- Issuance of an amount of stock equal to or greater than 25 percent of the previously outstanding stock to one or more new shareholders during any 30-day period during the corporation's tax year.

.02 When Income Must Be Reported

S corporation shareholders must include their pro rata share of their corporation's items of income, gain, loss, deduction, and credit and their pro rata share of their corporation's nonseparately computed gain or loss for their tax year with or within which their corporation's tax year ends.[73]

Example 38: Jayne Sloan is a shareholder of an S corporation. Jayne uses a calendar year-end. The corporation's tax year ends on September 30. For the fiscal year ending September 30, 2015, Jayne's pro rata share of the corporation's taxable income was $30,000. She must include that $30,000 in her taxable income for 2015, even though the corporation earned a portion of that amount during the last three months of 2014.

.03 Character of Items Constituting a Shareholder's Pro Rata Share

As a general rule, the character of any item of income, gain, loss, deduction, or credit included in a shareholder's pro rata share is determined at the entity level and retains that character in the shareholder's hands.[74] When it is necessary to determine the amount or character of a shareholder's gross income, the shareholder's gross income will include the shareholder's pro rata share of the corporation's gross income.[75]

Example 39: Robin Matus is a shareholder in an S corporation. Robin is an art dealer; the corporation is not. During the year, the corporation sells artwork held as an investment for a $1,000 gain. Robin's pro rata share of the corporation's gain from the sale of the artwork will be characterized as capital gain even though Robin is a dealer in the property that was sold.

 Planning Pointer: Guaranteed payments that a partnership makes to a partner are usually subject to self-employment tax, as are a general partner's distributive share of partnership income. By contrast, S corporation shareholders who work for the corporation are treated as employees and their wages are subject to employment taxes, but a shareholder's distributive share of the S corporation profits is not subject to employment taxes.[76]

.04 Limits on the Deductibility of Losses

An S corporation shareholder may deduct the shareholder's pro rata share of the corporation's items of loss and deduction only to the extent that the amount of those items does not exceed the sum of the adjusted basis of the shareholder's stock in the S corporation plus the adjusted basis of any S corporation indebtedness to the shareholder (see ¶ 1409).[77] A shareholder's aggregate amount of items of loss and deduction for a tax year in excess of the sum of the adjusted basis of the shareholder's stock in the S corporation and the adjusted basis of any indebtedness of the S

---

[73] Code Sec. 1366(a); Reg. § 1.1366-1(a)(1).
[74] Code Sec. 1366(b); Reg. § 1.1366-1(b)(1).
[75] Code Sec. 1366(c); Reg. § 1.1366-1(c)(1).

[76] *A.R. Durando*, CA-9, 95-2 USTC ¶ 50,615, 70 F3d 548; Rev. Rul. 59-221, 1959-1 CB 225.
[77] Code Sec. 1366(d)(1); Reg. § 1.1366-2(a)(1).

corporation to the shareholder retains its character and is treated as incurred by the corporation in the next tax year (and subsequent tax years) with respect to the shareholder.[78]

Example 40:   Suzan Resendes is a shareholder of an S corporation. Suzan's pro rata share of the corporation's loss for the tax year is $10,000. At the end of that year, Suzan's adjusted basis in her stock (before taking into account her share of the corporation's loss) is $6,000. She is not owed any money by the corporation. Suzan can deduct a $6,000 loss for the year, and her adjusted basis in the stock is reduced to zero. The remaining $4,000 ($10,000 – $6,000) of Suzan's loss is disallowed for the year.

Example 41:   Continuing on with Example 40, in the next tax year, Suzan's pro rata share of the corporation's income increases her adjusted basis in her stock to $3,000 (before taking into account the $4,000 loss disallowed the previous year). Suzan may deduct $3,000 of the $4,000 loss carried over from the previous tax year. The loss once again reduces her adjusted basis in the stock to $0. She then carries over the $1,000 loss to the next tax year.

Example 42:   Van Eisler is a shareholder of an S corporation. Van's pro rata share of the corporation's loss for the tax year is $20,000. At the end of that year, his adjusted basis in the stock (before taking into account his share of the corporation's loss) is $8,000. The corporation owes Van $15,000 from a loan he made the corporation in a previous tax year. Van can deduct the $20,000 loss for the year. The first $8,000 of loss reduces his adjusted basis in the stock to zero. The remaining $12,000 loss ($20,000 – $8,000) reduces his basis in the indebtedness owed to him to $3,000 ($15,000 – $12,000).

If S corporation stock is transferred by a shareholder to the shareholder's spouse or to the shareholder's former spouse incident to their divorce, any suspended loss or deduction with respect to that stock carries over to the transferee and is treated as incurred by the corporation with respect to the transferee in the subsequent tax year.

Passive activity losses. If an S corporation shareholder does not materially participate in the corporation's business activities, the shareholder may deduct the shareholder's pro rata share of losses only to the extent of the amount of the shareholder's passive activity income.[79] Passive activity income includes income other than from portfolio sources (interest, dividends, capital gains) or income from a business in which the taxpayer materially participates.

At-risk limitation. S corporation shareholders with sufficient adjusted basis to take advantage of their pro rata share of their corporation's loss nevertheless will be denied a deduction for the loss to the extent that the loss exceeds their amount at risk in a corporate activity.[80] An S corporation shareholder is considered at risk for all of the following amounts:

- The amount of money and the adjusted basis of other property contributed to the S corporation.

- The shareholder's share of net income retained by the S corporation.

- Amounts borrowed by the shareholder for use in the activity if the shareholder is personally liable for repayment of the amount borrowed or the amount borrowed is secured by the shareholder's property (other than property used in the activity). A shareholder's at-risk amount is also increased by the amount of qualified nonrecourse financing secured by real property used by the corporation.

---

[78] Code Sec. 1366(d)(2); Reg. § 1.1366-2(a)(2).

[79] Code Sec. 469.

[80] Code Sec. 465.

¶ 1408 Adjustment of Shareholder's Basis in Stock

A shareholder's adjusted basis in the stock of an S corporation determines the extent to which a distribution made by the corporation to the shareholder is taxable, as well as the amount of losses that shareholders may claim in a given year. A shareholder's adjusted basis in the stock is also used to determine the shareholder's realized gain or loss upon the disposition of the stock.

As previously discussed, the tax term "basis" is used to describe a taxpayer's investment in property. With respect to stock, original basis is the basis of stock at the time it is acquired, and adjusted basis is the taxpayer's original basis adjusted for certain events that occur after the stock is acquired. A shareholder's original basis includes the amount the shareholder pays to acquire the stock. An S corporation shareholder may acquire stock from an S corporation in exchange for cash or property other than cash, or through other means, such as by gift or inheritance.

Once the shareholder's original basis from the acquisition of the S corporation stock has been determined, the shareholder's basis is adjusted to reflect a variety of transactions and events that occur with respect to the operations of the S corporation. For example, a shareholder's basis in S corporation stock is increased by the shareholder's pro rata share of income and gain (including tax-exempt interest), and is decreased by the shareholder's pro rata share of deductions, losses, excess depletion, and any noncapital, nondeductible expenses. A shareholder's basis in S corporation stock is also decreased by any distributions the corporation makes to the shareholder.

Example 43: During 20X0, Tammi Subaugh pays $5,000 for 100 shares of stock in an S corporation. During 20X0, Tammi is allocated a total of $1,000 of separately and non-separately stated income and gain. Her adjusted basis in her shares of stock increases by $1,000 to $6,000 ($5,000 + $1,000).

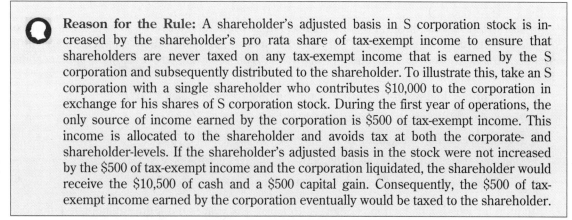

Reason for the Rule: A shareholder's adjusted basis in S corporation stock is increased by the shareholder's pro rata share of tax-exempt income to ensure that shareholders are never taxed on any tax-exempt income that is earned by the S corporation and subsequently distributed to the shareholder. To illustrate this, take an S corporation with a single shareholder who contributes $10,000 to the corporation in exchange for his shares of S corporation stock. During the first year of operations, the only source of income earned by the corporation is $500 of tax-exempt income. This income is allocated to the shareholder and avoids tax at both the corporate- and shareholder-levels. If the shareholder's adjusted basis in the stock were not increased by the $500 of tax-exempt income and the corporation liquidated, the shareholder would receive the $10,500 of cash and a $500 capital gain. Consequently, the $500 of tax-exempt income earned by the corporation eventually would be taxed to the shareholder.

After making all positive adjustments to a shareholder's basis, the basis in the S corporation stock decreases (but not below zero) by the following amounts in the following order:[81]

1. The amount of nontaxable distributions to the shareholder,

2. The shareholder's pro rata share of the corporation's noncapital, nondeductible expenses plus the corporation's deduction for depletion for any oil and gas property (to the extent that the deduction does not exceed the shareholder's proportionate share of the adjusted basis of such property),

3. The shareholder's pro rata share of the corporation's loss (if any) and any separately stated items of loss and deduction, and

4. Any amount of loss or deduction allowed at the end of the post-termination transition period.[82]

---

[81] Code Sec. 1367(a)(2); Reg. § 1.1367-1(c), (f).   [82] Code Sec. 1366(d)(3)(C).

Example 44: Jonas Sturman is a shareholder of an S corporation. At the beginning of the year, Jonas's adjusted basis in his stock was $2,000. On April 10, he receives a $1,300 distribution from the corporation. His pro rata share of the corporation's income for the year is $400, and his pro rata share of the corporation's separately stated items of loss and deduction for the year is $1,500. Jonas's basis in his stock is adjusted as follows.

Beginning basis in S stock	$2,000
Plus: Pro rata share of income	400
	$2,400
Less: Distribution	(1,300)
	$1,100
Less: Pro rata share of separately stated items of loss and deduction	(1,500)
Ending basis in S stock	$ 0

A shareholder's basis cannot be reduced below zero. Jonas's remaining $400 loss ($1,500 − $1,100) is treated as incurred the next tax year. If Jonas is able to increase his basis in the stock, either through additional contributions or his pro rata shares of next year's S corporation income, he may deduct the loss in that year.

 Spotlight: A distribution during the tax year reduces a shareholder's adjusted basis for purposes of determining the amount of loss that a shareholder may deduct.

Shareholders must reduce their adjusted basis in S corporation stock by their pro rata share of noncapital, nondeductible expenses. A corporation's noncapital, nondeductible expenses are those items for which no loss or deduction is allowable. The following are examples of noncapital, nondeductible expenses.[83]

- Illegal bribes, kickbacks, and other nondeductible payments (see ¶ 501.04).
- Nondeductible fines and penalties (see ¶ 501.04).
- Expenses and interest relating to tax-exempt income (see ¶ 505).
- Disallowed losses from transactions between related persons (see ¶ 804).
- The disallowed portion of meal and entertainment expenses (see ¶ 605).

An item for which a deduction is deferred to a later tax year is not a noncapital, nondeductible expense. For example, postponed losses resulting from like-kind exchanges do not reduce a shareholder's adjusted basis in S corporation stock.

Special rule for charitable contributions. As a general rule, when an S corporation makes a charitable contribution each shareholder's basis in stock is reduced by the shareholder's pro rata share of the fair market value of the contributed property. However, for charitable contributions made in tax years beginning before January 1, 2015, a shareholder's basis is reduced by the shareholder's pro rata share of the adjusted basis of the contributed property.

¶ 1409 Adjustment to Basis of Indebtedness to Shareholder

Unlike partners, who increase their basis in their partnership interests by their allocable share of partnership liabilities, S corporation shareholders do not increase the adjusted basis of their stock

---

[83] Reg. § 1.1367-1(c)(2).

by their share of the general liabilities of the corporation. However, S corporation shareholders keep track of their basis in any amounts they personally loan to the corporation. After the adjusted basis in their shares of S corporation stock has been reduced to zero, shareholders can use any basis they have in the corporation's debt to them to deduct any losses of the corporation that flow through to them.[84] The shareholder's original basis in an S corporation's indebtedness to the shareholder is the amount the shareholder loans to the corporation. This amount may be adjusted for the shareholder's pro rata share of the S corporation's losses, deductions, nondeductible expenses, and depletion to the extent such items exceed the shareholder's adjusted basis in the shareholder's S corporation stock at the time of allocation.

Spotlight: Indebtedness to a shareholder must be bona fide.[85] Whether indebtedness is bona fide is determined under general federal tax principles and depends on all of the facts and circumstances.

Planning Pointer: A shareholder does not obtain basis of indebtedness in an S corporation merely by guaranteeing a loan or acting as a surety, accommodation party, or in any similar capacity relating to a loan.[86] When a shareholder makes a payment on bona fide indebtedness of the S corporation for which the shareholder has acted as guarantor or in a similar capacity, then the shareholder may increase the shareholder's basis of indebtedness by the amount of that payment.

After making each of the adjustments that increase the adjusted basis in stock, basis reductions for any distributions are taken into consideration. After this, the shareholder's pro rata share of corporate deductions, losses, nondeductible expenses, and excess depletion are applied to the remaining adjusted basis of the shareholder's stock. If the shareholder's basis is reduced to zero, any excess corporate deductions, losses, nondeductible expenses, and excess depletion are applied to reduce (but not below zero) the shareholder's basis in any indebtedness of the corporation to the shareholder.[87] It is important to note that distributions do not reduce a shareholder's basis in indebtedness. Instead, these amounts reduce a shareholder's adjusted basis in the shareholder's S corporation stock to zero. Any excess is taxed as a capital gain.

Example 45: Barb Jendro is a shareholder of an S corporation. In April 2015, Barb loans the corporation $10,000. At the end of the corporation's 2014 tax year, Barb's adjusted basis in her stock in the corporation was $3,000. Her pro rata share of the corporation's losses, deductions, and nondeductible expenses for 2015 equals $3,500. The $3,500 reduces the adjusted basis of Barb's shares to $0, and the remaining $500 ($3,500 – $3,000) reduces her basis in the indebtedness to $9,500 ($10,000 – $500). Barb is allowed to deduct on her 2015 tax return her entire pro rata share of losses and deductions because she has sufficient basis in her stock and indebtedness to absorb those losses.

If a shareholder's adjusted basis in the S corporation's indebtedness to the shareholder is decreased by corporate deductions, losses, nondeductible expenses, and excess depletion, any subsequent amounts of the shareholder's pro rata share of income and gain items will be applied first to increase the shareholder's basis in indebtedness owed the shareholder by the S corporation.[88] Once the shareholder's basis in the indebtedness is restored to the amount loaned, any excess increases the shareholder's basis in the S corporation stock.

---

[84] Code Sec. 1367(b)(2)(A); Reg. § 1.1367-2(b).
[85] Reg. § 1.1366-2(a)(2)(i).
[86] Reg. § 1.1366-2(a)(2)(ii).

[87] Code Sec. 1367(b)(2)(A); Reg. § 1.1367-2(b).
[88] Code Sec. 1367(b)(2)(B); Reg. § 1.1367-2(c).

Example 46:   Malcolm Caraveo is a shareholder of an S corporation. At the end of the corporation's 2015 tax year, Malcolm's adjusted basis in his S stock is reduced to $0, and his adjusted basis in indebtedness owed by the corporation to him is reduced from $5,000 to $2,000 due to S corporation losses and deductions allocated to him in 2015. At the end of the 2016 tax year, Malcolm's pro rata share of the corporation's taxable income equals $5,000. Malcolm's adjusted basis in the indebtedness is restored to the $5,000 that the corporation owes him, and the remaining $2,000 of Malcolm's pro rata share of the corporation's net income ($5,000 – $3,000) increases his adjusted basis in his shares of stock in the corporation to $2,000 ($0 + $2,000).

¶ 1410 Distributions to Shareholders

The tax consequences of distributions of property made by an S corporation to its shareholders depends on the adjusted basis of the shareholders' stock in the corporation and whether or not the S corporation has any accumulated E&P.[89] Shareholders who receive a distribution during the year must wait until the end of the year to determine how the amount they receive will be taxed.

.01 Accumulated Adjustments Account

An S corporation's accumulated E&P should be distinguished from its **accumulated adjustments account (AAA)**. The former represents the amount of the corporation's earnings as a C corporation that has been taxed only at the corporate level. The latter measures the accumulated undistributed net income of a corporation while it has been an S corporation.[90] Because the earnings of an S corporation are taxed each year to its shareholders, regardless of whether any of those earnings are distributed to the shareholders during the year, the amounts in the AAA represent undistributed, previously-taxed S corporation earnings. Normally, distributions from an S corporation are treated as first coming from AAA, and then from accumulated E&P. Consequently, the shareholders normally enjoy tax-free distribution of previously taxed earnings before receiving a dividend distribution from corporate accumulated E&P.

 Planning Pointer: S corporations with accumulated E&P must maintain an AAA to determine how distributions are taxed to their shareholders. Corporations without accumulated E&P are not required to maintain an AAA, but it is recommended that they do so because should they engage in a transaction, such as a merger with an S corporation that has accumulated E&P, they will know the balance in their AAA.

On the first day that a corporation is an S corporation, the balance of its AAA is zero. Subsequently, it is adjusted by the following amounts in the following order.[91] Through these adjustments, it is possible for a corporation's AAA to be reduced below zero.

Step 1:   AAA is first increased by the corporation's nonseparately and separately stated items of income and gain (other than tax-exempt income). It is also increased by the amount by which the corporation's deductions for depletion exceed the basis of its property (other than oil or gas property) subject to depletion.

Step 2:   AAA is decreased, but only to the extent it is increased in Step 1, by the corporation's nonseparately and separately stated items of loss and deduction, including depletion on oil and gas property, and the amount of noncapital, nondeductible expenses, other than federal taxes attributable to any year in which the corporation was a C corporation and expenses related to tax-exempt income.

Step 3:   AAA is decreased (but not below zero) by the amount of distributions (other than dividend distributions) to shareholders made during the year.

---

[89] Code Sec. 1368.

[90] Code Sec. 1368(e); Reg. § 1.1368-2(a).

[91] Code Sec. 1368(e); Reg. § 1.1368-2.

Step 4:   AAA is decreased by the remaining amounts of loss and deduction items, nondeductible expenses (other than federal taxes attributable to when the corporation was a C corporation and expenses related to tax-exempt income), and shareholders' depletion deductions not already applied to decrease AAA in Step 2.

Step 5:   Finally, AAA is adjusted (whether negative or positive) for distributions in redemption of shareholders' stock.

.02 S Corporations with No Accumulated E&P

If an S corporation has no accumulated E&P, its distribution of property to its shareholders with respect to their stock is a nontaxable distribution of previously-taxed S corporation earnings to the extent that the amount of the distribution does not exceed the adjusted basis of the shareholder's stock. Once a distribution reduces the shareholder's basis in the stock to $0, any additional distribution is treated as gain from the sale or exchange of property.[92] Because stock is a capital asset for most taxpayers, such gain will be taxed as capital gain. The length of time that the shareholder has owned the stock will determine whether the gain will be recognized as short-term or long-term capital gain.

Example 47:   Quentin Sabino is a shareholder of an S corporation. Quentin's adjusted basis in his stock is $4,000. On June 1, the corporation distributes $5,000 to Quentin. The distribution is a nontaxable distribution to the extent that it does not exceed Quentin's $4,000 adjusted basis in his stock. The remaining $1,000 ($5,000 – $4,000) is treated as capital gain.

.03 S Corporations with Accumulated E&P

If an S corporation has accumulated E&P at the end of its tax year, a distribution made during the year by the corporation with respect to its shareholders is taxed as follows:[93]

1. The amount of a distribution that does not exceed the amount of the corporation's AAA is a nontaxable distribution of previously-taxed S corporation earnings. The distribution from AAA reduces the shareholder's adjusted basis in the stock accordingly.

2. The amount of a distribution that exceeds the amount of the corporation's AAA is treated as a dividend to the extent of the corporation's accumulated E&P. Distributions from accumulated E&P do not affect a shareholder's adjusted basis in stock.

3. Any remaining distribution is a nontaxable return of capital to the extent that it does not exceed the shareholder's adjusted basis in the shareholder's S corporation stock (after it has been reduced by the distribution from AAA in the first step). Any excess distribution is treated as capital gain.

Example 48:   Rod Heldenbrand owns 25 percent of the shares of an S corporation that once was a C corporation. Rod's adjusted basis in those shares is $10,000. On April 1, the corporation distributes $48,000 to its shareholders. Rod's share of the distribution is $12,000 ($48,000 × 25%). The corporation has $14,000 of accumulated E&P carried over from its C corporation years. The balance in its AAA at the end of the tax year is $28,000.

Under the normal ordering rules, the first $28,000 of the distribution is deemed to come from AAA, which is reduced to $0. Because this amount represents previously-taxed S corporation earnings, Rod's $7,000 share ($28,000 × 25%) of this amount is a tax-free distribution. This amount reduces Rod's basis in his S corporation stock to $3,000 ($10,000 – $7,000).

Of the remaining $20,000 distributed from the corporation ($48,000 – $28,000), $14,000 is deemed to come from accumulated E&P, which is taxed as a dividend to

---

[92] Code Sec. 1368(b); Reg. § 1.1368-1(c).   [93] Code Sec. 1368(c); Reg. § 1.1368-1(d).

the shareholders. Rod includes his $3,500 share of this amount ($14,000 × 25%) as dividend income on his personal income tax return. Rod's basis in his S corporation stock is not affected by the dividend distribution. The remaining $1,500 distribution ($12,000 – $7,000 – $3,500) is not taxable to Rod and reduces his adjusted basis in the stock to $1,500 ($3,000 – $1,500).

Election to distribute accumulated E&P first. With the consent of all shareholders who receive a distribution during the tax year, an S corporation may elect to treat a distribution as coming first from its accumulated E&P and then from its AAA.[94] To the extent that the distribution comes from accumulated E&P, it is taxed as a dividend to the shareholders. Once accumulated E&P is reduced to zero, the distribution is then considered to come from the corporation's AAA. Amounts distributed from AAA are nontaxable distributions to shareholders of previously-taxed S corporation earnings. Any amount distributed after the corporation's accumulated E&P has been reduced to $0 is applied against the shareholder's adjusted basis in the S corporation stock. Any remaining distribution after the shareholder's basis in the S stock is reduced to zero is taxed as capital gain to the shareholder.

A corporation makes the election by attaching a statement to a timely filed original or amended Form 1120S. An election, which applies to all distributions made during the year for which it is made, is irrevocable and effective only for the tax year for which it is made. Therefore, if the amount of the distribution is not sufficient to eliminate the corporation's accumulated E&P, another election must be made in a subsequent tax year if the corporation wants to elect to distribute accumulated E&P prior to AAA.

 Planning Pointer: By making an election, a corporation can eliminate its accumulated E&P and avoid the tax on excessive passive investment income (see ¶ 1412). Furthermore, for S corporations that tend to have excessive amounts of passive investment income year-after-year, reducing the corporation's accumulated E&P to zero will prevent the corporation from involuntarily terminating its S election (see ¶ 1405.02).

Example 49: Dean Motta owns 20 percent of the shares of an S corporation that once was a C corporation. Dean's adjusted basis in those shares is $20,000. On June 11, the corporation distributes $50,000 to its shareholders. Dean's share of the distribution is $10,000 ($50,000 × 20%). The corporation has $24,000 of accumulated E&P carried over from its C corporation years. The balance in the corporation's AAA at the end of the tax year is $33,000. The shareholders of the S corporation elect to treat the $50,000 distribution as first having come from accumulated E&P.

The first $24,000 of the distribution is deemed to come from accumulated E&P, which is taxed as a dividend to the shareholders. Dean includes his $4,800 share of this amount ($24,000 × 20%) in his gross income on his personal income tax return. The remaining $26,000 of the distribution ($50,000 – $24,000) is deemed to come from AAA, which results in a tax-free distribution to shareholders. The AAA balance at the end of the year is reduced to $7,000 ($33,000 – $26,000).

Dean's adjusted basis in the shares is not affected by the $4,800 dividend distribution. However, his $5,200 share of the $26,000 distribution from AAA ($26,000 × 20%) reduces his basis to $14,800 ($20,000 – $5,200).

.04 Distributions of Property Other Than Cash

When an S corporation distributes property to its shareholders, the property is valued at its FMV, which becomes the shareholder's basis in the property. The corporation recognizes gain to

---

[94] Code Sec. 1368(e)(3); Reg. § 1.1368-1(f)(2).

the extent that the FMV of the property distributed exceeds the corporation's basis in the property.[95] The gain recognized by the corporation flows through to the shareholders on a pro rata basis. The character of the gain (ordinary income, Section 1231 gain, or capital gain) depends on the asset being distributed.

An S corporation does not recognize loss on a distribution of property if the FMV of the property is less than the corporation's adjusted basis in the property. The shareholder's basis in the distributed property is its (lesser) FMV. Thus, recognition of any loss is deferred until the shareholder subsequently sells the property.

 Reason for the Rule: If the basis to the shareholder of appreciated property were its FMV and the tax law did not require that the corporation recognize the gain and allocate it pro rata to its shareholders, the appreciation would escape tax.

.05 Distributions During the Post-Termination Transition Period

If a corporation distributes cash (but not property) with respect to its stock during the post-termination transition period, the distribution will be a nontaxable distribution of previously taxed S corporation earnings to the extent of the balance in the corporation's AAA.[96] After the post-termination transition period ends, the AAA disappears, and distributions are taxed under the rules applicable to C corporation distributions (i.e., distributions are taxed as dividends to the extent of the corporation's current and accumulated E&P).

The **post-termination transition period** is the period that begins on the day after the last day of the corporation's last tax year as an S corporation and generally ends one year later or (if later) on the due date for filing a tax return for the corporation's last year as an S corporation.

Instead of treating a distribution as coming first from the corporation's AAA, a corporation may elect to treat the distribution as coming first from the corporation's accumulated E&P (thus making the distribution taxable as a dividend to the extent of the corporation's accumulated E&P).[97] All shareholders to whom distributions are made during the post-termination transition period (whether or not the distribution is a cash distribution) must consent to the election for it to be valid.

Example 50: Saginaw Corporation, a calendar-year taxpayer, elects to terminate its Subchapter S status effective January 1, 20X0. As of that date, it has an AAA of $30,000. On December 31, 20X0, it has a total of $40,000 current and accumulated E&P. On March 1 of that year, it distributes $50,000 in cash to its shareholders. Of the $50,000 distribution, $30,000 is treated as coming from Saginaw's AAA; consequently, this portion of the distribution is not taxed to the shareholders and reduces each shareholder's respective basis in the Saginaw stock. The remaining $20,000 distribution is treated as a dividend and is taxable to the shareholders to the extent of Saginaw's current and accumulated E&P.

Example 51: Assume the same facts as in Example 50, except that Saginaw elects to treat distributions in its post-termination transition period as coming first from accumulated E&P. Under this scenario, $40,000 of the distribution will be taxable to the shareholders as dividend income, and $10,000 will not be taxable but will be applied to reduce the shareholders' basis in their stock.

---

[95] Code Secs. 311(b) and 1371(a).
[96] Code Sec. 1371(e)(1).

[97] Code Sec. 1371(e)(2); Reg. § 18.1371-1.

Planning Pointer: Shareholders can use the post-termination transition period to increase their basis in stock or debt so that they can claim losses and deductions that were suspended because they did not have sufficient basis in their stock or debt.

¶ 1411 Fringe Benefits for Shareholders

Unlike a C corporation, an S corporation cannot provide certain shareholder-employees with tax-free fringe benefits. Shareholders that own more than two-percent of the stock in an S corporation are treated like partners for purposes of determining how the fringe benefits that they receive are taxed.[98] Other shareholder-employees are treated as employees and can be provided tax-favored fringe benefits. A "two-percent shareholder" is a person who actually or constructively owns on any day during the corporation's tax year more than two percent of the corporation's outstanding stock or stock representing more than two percent of the total combined voting power of all of the corporation's stock.[99]

Employee fringe benefits paid or furnished by an S corporation to a two-percent shareholder-employee in consideration for services rendered are treated like partnership guaranteed payments.[100] They are deducted by an S corporation as a trade or business expense. Two-percent shareholders are treated as self-employed individuals and must include the value of fringe benefits in their gross income unless an exclusion is available to self-employed individuals. Two-percent shareholders may be entitled to a deduction for the amount included in their gross income (e.g., if the payment was for health care premiums).

Example 52: Pettway Heaters, Inc., an S corporation, paid $4,000 of Cesar Dole's health insurance premiums. Cesar owns 10 percent of the shares of Pettway. Because Cesar is a two-percent shareholder, Pettway deducts the $4,000 as a business expense. Cesar must include the $4,000 payment in his gross income but may offset that amount by taking a $4,000 deduction from AGI for his self-employed health insurance premiums.

¶ 1412 Corporate Tax on Excess Passive Investment Income

If an S corporation has accumulated E&P at the close of a tax year and more than 25 percent of its gross receipts for the year came from passive investment income, then the corporation is taxed at the top corporate tax rate (currently 35 percent) on its excess net passive income.[101]

 Reason for the Rule: This "sting tax" is similar to the personal holding company tax imposed on C corporations and is intended to prevent C corporations otherwise subject to the personal holding company tax from avoiding that tax by electing S corporation status. An S corporation is subject to this sting tax for having excess passive investment income until it distributes all of its accumulated E&P from its years as a C corporation.

Example 53: Hermon Toys is an S corporation with accumulated E&P from its years as a C corporation. In 2015, more than 25 percent of its gross receipts consisted of passive income, and its excess net passive income was $100,000. The corporation's tax on passive investment income equals $35,000 ($100,000 × 35%).

.01 Amounts Subject to Passive Investment Income Tax

The amount subject to the 35-percent passive income tax (excess net passive income) is determined by multiplying a corporation's net passive income for the tax year by a fraction whose numerator is the amount by which the corporation's passive investment income for the tax year exceeds 25 percent of the corporation's gross receipts for the tax year and whose denominator is the

---

[98] Code Sec. 1372(a).
[99] Code Sec. 1372(b).

[100] Rev. Rul. 91-26, 1991-1 CB 184.
[101] Code Sec. 1375(a).

corporation's passive investment income for the tax year.[102] The amount subject to the passive investment income tax can be stated as:

$$\text{net passive income} \times \frac{\text{passive investment income} - (25\% \times \text{gross receipts})}{\text{passive investment income}}$$

where:

"Net passive income" = passive investment income – allowable deductions directly connected with the production of such income (other than the dividends received and net operating loss deductions.[103]

Passive investment income includes gross receipts derived from royalties, rents, dividends, interest, and annuities.[104] Passive investment income does not include interest on any obligation acquired in the ordinary course of the corporation's trade or business or from its sale of inventory. Passive investment income also does not include any recognized built-in gain or loss of the S corporation for any tax year during the recognition period.[105] (See ¶ 1413.)

"Gross receipts" generally includes the total amount received or accrued under the method of accounting used by a corporation in computing its taxable income.[106] Gross receipts are not reduced by returns and allowances, cost of goods sold, or deductions. If capital assets (other than stock and securities) are disposed of, gross receipts from such dispositions are taken into account only to the extent of the corporation's capital gain net income from the disposition. Gross receipts from sales or exchanges of stock and securities are taken into account only to the extent of gains from such sales. Losses are not taken into consideration when computing gross receipts.

The amount of an S corporation's excess net passive income for any tax year may not exceed the amount of the corporation's taxable income for that year (determined without regard to the dividends received or net operating loss deductions).

Example 54: McQuiller Elevators, Inc. is an S corporation with accumulated E&P. Its gross receipts for the year are $2 million, and its passive investment income is $625,000. McQuiller's deductions related to passive investment income equal $25,000, making net passive income $600,000. Its excess net passive income of $120,000 is computed as follows.

$$\$600,000 \times \frac{[\$625,000 - (0.25 \times \$2,000,000)]}{\$625,000} = \$120,000$$

McQuiller's excess passive investment income tax for the year equals $42,000 ($120,000 × 35%).

Waiver of the tax. The IRS may waive imposition of the tax on excess passive investment income if the S corporation establishes to the IRS's satisfaction that:[107]

- The corporation determined in good faith that it had no accumulated E&P at the close of the tax year, and

- During a reasonable period of time after it was determined that the corporation did, in fact, have accumulated E&P, the corporation distributed those amounts.

---

[102] Code Sec. 1375(b)(1).
[103] Code Sec. 1375(b)(2).
[104] Code Sec. 1375(b)(3).

[105] Code Sec. 1375(b)(4).
[106] Code Sec. 1375(b)(3).
[107] Code Sec. 1375(d).

Planning Pointer: Only S corporations with accumulated E&P are subject to the tax on excess passive investment income. Corporations that are subject to this tax for three consecutive years automatically lose their S election beginning with the next tax year (see ¶ 1405.02). S corporations that have been subject to the tax for two consecutive years can keep from losing their S status by making an election to treat distributions during the third year first from accumulated E&P and then distributing enough during the year to eliminate the balance in the accumulated E&P account.

.02 Deduction for the Tax

Each item of passive investment income that is allocated to shareholders is reduced by its proportionate share of the excess passive income tax. That amount is calculated by multiplying the amount of the tax by a fraction whose numerator is the net amount of the item and whose denominator is the corporation's total passive investment income for the tax year.[108] This reduction in amount taxed to shareholders is consistent with the amount of after-tax income that normally would increase a C corporation's earnings and profits for the year in which the income is earned.

Example 55: An S corporation generates $10,000 of interest income during the year. The corporation is subject to the tax on excess passive investment income, and the portion of the tax that relates to interest income is $55. When allocating the interest income to its shareholders at the end of the year, the corporation will allocate a total of $9,945 ($10,000 – $55).

¶ 1413 Corporate Tax on Built-In Gains

When a C corporation sells appreciated property, it normally recognizes gain, which is taxed to the corporation and is included in the corporation's accumulated E&P until distributed to the shareholders in the form of a dividend.

To prevent corporations from escaping tax at the entity-level for unrealized gains from periods during its C corporation years, S corporations that were once C corporations are taxed at the highest corporate tax rate (currently 35 percent) on any net recognized **built-in gain** for any tax year beginning during the recognition period.[109] The recognition period is the 10-year (120-month) period generally beginning with the first day of the first tax year for which a corporation was an S corporation.[110]

Special rules for 2009–2014. If the first tax year that a corporation was an S corporation, began in 2009 or 2010, the recognition period ends after seven years. If the first tax year that a corporation was an S corporation began in 2011, 2012, 2013, or 2014, the recognition period ends after five years.

Installment sales. If an S corporation sells an asset within the recognition period and reports income from the sale using the installment method, payments received, whether within the recognition period or not, are subject to the built-in gains tax to the extent that they are built-in gains.

In addition to taxing the S corporation on its net recognized built-in gain, the recognized gain is allocated pro rata to its shareholders, thereby imposing a tax on the gain at the shareholder-level as well. However, each item subject to recognized built-in gain is reduced by its proportionate share of the built-in gains tax.[111] This is consistent with the amount of after-tax gain that normally would increase a C corporation's earnings and profits in the year of the sale.

---

[108] Code Sec. 1366(f)(3); Reg. § 1.1366-4(c).
[109] Code Sec. 1374(a), (b).

[110] Code Sec. 1374(d)(7); Reg. § 1.1374-1(d).
[111] Code Sec. 1366(f)(2); Reg. § 1.1366-4(b).

> **Reason for the Rule:** This tax was enacted by the Tax Reform Act of 1986 to prevent C corporations from avoiding double taxation on sales and distributions of appreciated property by converting to an S corporation.[112]

Example 56: At the time a corporation elects S status, it has a capital asset with an adjusted basis of $100,000 and a FMV of $400,000. If the corporation had sold the asset as a C corporation, it would have paid tax on the $300,000 of capital gain ($400,000 – $100,000). If the after-tax gain were distributed to the shareholders, that amount would be taxed to the shareholders as a dividend.

If the corporation waits until after it converts to an S corporation to sell the asset, without the built-in gains tax rules the $300,000 gain would be allocated pro rata to its shareholders and taxed to them as capital gain (and perhaps long-term capital gain) on their respective income tax returns. The gain would increase the S corporation's AAA by $300,000, which could be distributed tax-free to the S corporation's shareholders.

Because of the built-in gain tax rules, if within 10 years of electing S status (seven years if the corporation first became an S corporation in a tax year beginning in 2009 or 2010 and five years if the corporation first became an S corporation in a tax year beginning in 2011, 2012, 2013, or 2014) the corporation sells appreciated property from its C corporation years, such appreciation is subject to built-in gains tax. Accordingly, when the S corporation sells the property, the $300,000 gain is subject to built-in gains tax equal to 35 percent of the gain ($300,000 × 35% = $105,000). The amount of gain that is allocated to the shareholders is reduced by the gain taxed to the corporation. Thus, the gain of $195,000 ($300,000 – $105,000) would be allocated pro rata to the shareholders. Accordingly, any appreciation resulting from the C corporation years is subject to tax at both the corporate and shareholder levels.

.01 Calculating the Built-In Gains Tax

Only appreciation generated during a corporation's existence as a C corporation is subject to the built-in gains tax. Accordingly, if property with an adjusted basis of $100,000 is sold for $500,000, any amount of gain resulting from appreciation while the corporation is an S corporation is not subject to the built-in gains tax. The built-in gains tax is limited to the amount of the corporation's taxable income. Thus, any built-in gain that is triggered during years in which the S corporation has little or no taxable income is carried over to tax years in which the S corporation produces higher levels of taxable income. Even though net operating loss and capital loss carryovers from a corporation's C tax years cannot be utilized to offset taxable income generated by the S corporation, the tax laws allow these carryover amounts to offset the corporation's built-in gain.[113] The specific details of the calculation of these limits are beyond the scope of this chapter.

> **Planning Pointer:** By waiting 10 years (seven years if the corporation first became an S corporation in a tax year beginning in 2009 or 2010 and five years if the corporation first became an S corporation in a tax year beginning in 2011, 2012, 2013, or 2014) before selling any appreciated assets it owned while it was a C corporation, an S corporation can avoid the tax on built-in gains altogether.

---

[112] Joint Committee on Taxation, *General Explanation of the Tax Reform Act of 1986*, (J.C.T. Rep. No. JCS-10-87), at 337.

[113] Code Sec. 1374.

¶ 1414 Corporate Tax on LIFO Recapture Amount

In times of rising prices, the last-in, first-out (LIFO) method produces a higher deduction of cost of goods sold and lower basis in ending inventory. If a C corporation uses the LIFO method to determine which items of inventory were sold during the year before its S election becomes effective, the corporation must include the LIFO recapture amount in its gross income for its last tax year as a C corporation. If a C corporation transfers LIFO inventory assets to an S corporation in a nonrecognition transfer and the S corporation takes the C corporation's basis in the transferred inventory assets, the C corporation must include the LIFO recapture amount in its gross income for the year of the transfer.[114]

The "recapture date" is the day before the effective date of the S election if the tax is triggered by the S election. If the tax is triggered by a transfer of assets, the recapture date is the date of the transfer.[115] The recapture amount is determined as of the end of the recapture date if that date is the day before the effective date of the S election. The recapture amount is determined as of the moment before the transfer if the recapture date is the date of a transfer.

 Reason for the Rule: Congress enacted this tax because it was concerned that corporations using the LIFO method could avoid the tax on built-in gains to the extent that they did not invade LIFO layers during the 10-year period following their conversion to S corporation status.[116]

The **LIFO recapture amount** is the difference between the amount of the corporation's inventory assets under the first-in, first-out (FIFO) method and the amount of the corporation's inventory assets under the LIFO method.[117] If a corporation uses the retail method to value its inventories, it must use that method to value its inventory assets. Otherwise, the corporation must use the lower of cost or FMV to value its inventory assets.[118]

Example 57: Lion Plastics, Inc. elects to become an S corporation beginning on January 1, 2016. Lion uses the calendar year and the LIFO method to value its inventory. Lion includes the LIFO recapture amount in its 2015 gross income on its final C income tax return. If the value of its inventory under the FIFO method is $1 million as of the end of 2015 and the value of its inventory under the LIFO method is $750,000, the LIFO recapture amount that it must include in its gross income for its 2015 tax year equals $250,000 ($1,000,000 – $750,000).

Any increase in a corporation's tax caused by including the LIFO recapture amount in the corporation's gross income is payable in four equal installments.[119] The first installment is due by the due date (not including extensions) for the corporation's last year operating as a C corporation (or year of the transfer if the tax is triggered by a transfer), and the other installments are due by the due date (not including extensions) for the corporation's (or the transferee corporation's) next three tax years. The IRS does not charge interest on these payments.

Appropriate adjustments must be made to the basis of a corporation's inventory to reflect the amount included in the corporation's gross income.[120] Basis is adjusted by collapsing any LIFO layers and adding the LIFO recapture amount to the LIFO value of the ending inventory as of the end of the taxpayer's last tax year as a C corporation.[121]

---

[114] Code Sec. 1363(d)(1); Reg. § 1.1363-2(a).

[115] Reg. § 1.1363-2(c).

[116] H.R. Rep. No. 100-391 (October 26, 1987), at 1097-1098.

[117] Code Sec. 1363(d)(3).

[118] Code Sec. 1363(d)(4)(C).

[119] Code Sec. 1363(d)(2); Reg. § 1.1363-2(d).

[120] Code Sec. 1363(d)(1).

[121] Rev. Proc. 94-61, 1994-2 CB 775 (Q&A-2).

¶ 1415 Summary

Business owners have a variety of legal entities to choose from for operating their business. In deciding which form of entity to select, one of the factors they should consider is which entity will save them the most in taxes. Because income earned by a flow-through entity is taxed to its owners instead of to the business, flow-through entities are popular types of business. One type of flow-through business is the S corporation. However, only certain businesses can elect S status.

The rules for distinguishing nonseparately and separately stated items are very similar to those that govern partnerships. However, unlike partnerships, which are allowed to specially allocate various items to their partners, all items from an S corporation are allocated to shareholders on a pro rata basis. Shareholders of an S corporation are shielded from the liabilities of the business.

S corporations continue to be more popular than C corporations. However, before electing S status, a C corporation needs to keep in mind the various taxes that may apply after it converts to an S corporation. Some of these taxes can be avoided if the corporation distributes its accumulated E&P prior to electing S status.

Glossary of Terms Introduced in This Chapter

Accumulated adjustments account (AAA). Measures the accumulated undistributed net income of a corporation while it has been an S corporation.

Built-in gains. All unrealized gain that arose on assets during the time that a corporation was taxed as a C corporation.

Built-in gains tax. A tax imposed on built-in gains that are recognized during an S corporation's first 10 years of existence after converting from a C corporation (7 years if the corporation first became an S corporation in a tax year beginning in 2009 or 2010 and 5 years if the corporation first became an S corporation in a tax year beginning in 2011, 2012, 2013, or 2014).

C corporation. A corporation other than an S corporation that is treated as a separate tax entity from its shareholders. The income of a C corporation is subject to two layers of taxation.

C short year. In the S termination year, the portion of the year beginning on the effective date of the termination of the corporation's S status.

Electing small business trust (ESBT). A trust that is eligible to be a shareholder of an S corporation at the election of the trustee and any person treated under the grantor trust rules as the owner of the portion of the trust consisting of the corporation's stock. Such a trust may have multiple beneficiaries, but no person or entity other than an individual, estate, or certain types of charitable organizations may be a beneficiary.

Excess passive investment income tax. A tax imposed on an S corporation with accumulated E&P if more than 25 percent of its gross receipts are derived from passive investment income.

Grantor trust. A trust whose income is taxed to its grantor under the grantor trust rules of Code Sec. 671 et seq. One example of a grantor trust is a revocable trust, which is a trust that can be revoked by its grantor.

LIFO recapture amount. Used in computing the LIFO recapture tax. Equals the difference between the amount of the corporation's inventory assets under the first-in, first-out (FIFO) method and the amount of the corporation's inventory assets under the LIFO method.

Nonresident alien. An individual who is not a U.S. citizen or resident.

Passive investment income. Gross receipts derived from royalties, rents, dividends, interest, and annuities.

Post-termination transition period. Generally the one-year period that starts one day after a corporation ceases to be an S corporation.

Pro rata share. The portion (based on ownership percentage) of each item of an S corporation's taxable income that a shareholder is required to take into account when calculating the shareholder's taxable income.

Qualified Subchapter S subsidiary (QSub). A domestic corporation 100-percent owned by an S corporation that the S corporation has elected to treat as a QSub.

Qualified Subchapter S trust (QSST). One of the types of trusts that can be a shareholder of an S corporation if the beneficiary elects to qualify the trust as a shareholder. All of the income of the trust must be distributed to one individual, who must be a U.S. citizen or resident. Any trust principal distributed during the income beneficiary's lifetime can be distributed only to that income beneficiary.

S corporation. An S corporation is a flow-through entity. Only corporations that satisfy certain requirements can elect to be taxed as S corporations. An S corporation gets its name because it is a corporation that has elected to be taxed under Subchapter S of Chapter 1 of the Code.

S short year. In the S termination year, the portion of the year ending before the effective date of the termination of the corporation's S status.

S termination year. The year that a corporation's status as an S corporation terminates.

Straight debt. A written, unconditional promise to pay a sum certain in money on demand or on a specified date. It will not be treated as a second class of stock, even though it is considered equity under general principles of federal tax law, if it satisfies the following requirements: (1) it does not provide for an interest rate or payment dates contingent on profits, the borrower's discretion, the payment of dividends with respect to common stock, or similar factors; (2) it cannot be converted (directly or indirectly) into stock or any other equity interest of the corporation; and (3) it is held by an individual (other than a nonresident alien), estate, trust eligible to be an S corporation shareholder, or a person who is actively and regularly engaged in the business of lending money.

Testamentary trusts. Trusts created from a decedent's will that come into existence upon the death of the grantor.

CHAPTER PROBLEMS

Chapter 14 Discussion Questions

1. What is an S corporation?
2. What are the advantages of operating a business as an S corporation?
3. What corporations qualify as a small business corporation, and why is this status significant?
4. Who can be a shareholder of an S corporation?
5. Dominic Rutigliano, a U.S. citizen who lives in Freedonia, owns 100 shares of stock in a corporation. Dominic is married to a citizen of Freedonia, whose laws applicable to assets owned by married persons are similar to those of an American community property state. Can the corporation elect S status? If not, is there anything that can be done to allow the corporation to elect S status?

6. When will a corporation be treated as having one class of stock?

7. Under what circumstances will debt be considered a second class of stock?

8. Under what circumstances may a corporation's S status terminate?

9. How can an S corporation revoke its S election?

10. Who pays tax on an S corporation's taxable income that is not distributed to shareholders?

11. What are the basic rules for computing an S corporation's taxable income?

12. Why is it important to determine a shareholder's adjusted basis in the stock of an S corporation?

13. What amounts increase or decrease a shareholder's basis in S corporation stock?

14. How is a shareholder's basis in an S corporation's indebtedness to the shareholder affected by the S corporation's income, gain, loss, deduction, and credit?

15. What is an accumulated adjustments account?

16. What happens to income previously taxed to shareholders after a corporation converts from an S corporation to a C corporation?

17. Under what circumstances may an S corporation be subject to the tax on excess passive investment income?

18. Under what circumstances may an S corporation have to pay the tax on built-in gains?

19. Under what circumstances may a corporation have to pay the LIFO recapture tax?

20. If a LIFO recapture tax has to be paid, when does it have to be paid, and who has to pay it?

Chapter 14 Problems

1. The stock in an S corporation is owned by 105 different persons. Among its shareholders are Bree Corlew, Bree's mother, Bree's two children, her brother, and one of her nephews. Based on these facts, how many shareholders does the corporation have for purposes of determining whether it can elect S status?

2. Deland Ice Cream has 103 shareholders. Two of the shareholders are Portia Merchant and her husband, Bassanio. A third shareholder is an electing small business trust (ESBT). The income beneficiaries of the ESBT are Samantha Beno and her husband, Joshua. The Benos's son is entitled to all remaining trust assets after his parents die and is entitled to distributions of trust principal at the trustee's election. Samantha, Joshua, and their son do not own any stock in the corporation except through the ESBT. How many shareholders does the corporation have for purposes of determining whether it can elect S status?

3. Kohen Pipe is eligible to be an S corporation and has decided that it wants to become an S corporation starting with its 2016 tax year. If the corporation uses the calendar year as its tax year, when can it make an election that will be effective for its 2016 tax year?

4. Robin Cottone, one of the shareholders of McCrady Sandals, Inc., wishes to have the corporation revoke its S election. Robin owns 100 shares of the corporation's voting stock. Kelvin Kotlone owns 50 shares of the corporation's voting stock and 150 shares of the corporation's nonvoting stock. Kelvin's spouse, Amy, owns 50 shares of the corporation's voting stock and 50 shares of the corporation's nonvoting stock. The rest of the stock is owned by Alton Snide and his spouse, Margaret, who each own 75 shares of the corporation's voting stock. How many other shareholders must Robin convince to consent to the revocation?

5. Booster Seats, Inc. is an S corporation using the calendar year as its tax year. In 2013, Booster had gross receipts of $500,000 and passive investment income of $200,000. In 2014, it had gross receipts of $550,000 and passive investment income of $137,500. In 2015, it had gross receipts of $600,000 and passive investment income of $155,000. For each of those years it had accumulated E&P. Can Booster continue to be an S corporation for 2016? Explain.

6. Alene Harledge's pro rata share of her S corporation's loss for the tax year was $10,000. Her adjusted basis in her shares of stock in the corporation was $6,500, and her adjusted basis in a loan she made to the corporation was $1,000. How much of her pro rata share of the loss may Alene deduct?

7. Machinery Slides, an S corporation, has $1 million of taxable income for its 2015 tax year, which began November 1, 2015, and ended October 31, 2016. Vernell Teachout is its sole shareholder. Machinery Slides earns $200,000 of its taxable income in November and December of 2015, $800,000 from January 1–October 31, 2016, and $300,000 from November 1, 2016–December 31, 2016. How much taxable income must Vernell include in his gross income on his 2016 tax return?

8. Shandra Flohr's adjusted basis in her shares of stock of an S corporation was $20,000 at the beginning of the year. Shandra's share of the corporation's separately and nonseparately computed income for the year was $25,000. She received a distribution of $20,000 during the year, and her share of separately stated items of loss and deduction was $10,000. What is Shandra's adjusted basis of her shares of stock at the end of the year?

9. Samantha Presley owns 1,000 shares of stock in an S corporation. At the beginning of the year, her adjusted basis in her shares of stock was $30,000. Her share of the corporation's income for the year is $10,000 (which includes $3,000 of tax-exempt interest). She received a distribution of $20,000 during the year, and her share of separately stated items of loss and deduction is $22,000. What is Samantha's adjusted basis of her share of stock at the end of the year?

10. Rina Heart owns 200 shares of stock in an S corporation. The adjusted basis in her shares was $25,000 at the beginning of the year. During the year, Rina's share of the corporation's income was $10,000, and she received an $8,000 distribution from the corporation. If Rina's share of the corporation's separately stated items of loss and deduction is $15,000, what is her adjusted basis of her shares at the end of the year?

11. Lena Susa owns 100 shares of stock in Algee Roofing Company, an S corporation. The adjusted basis in her shares was $5,000 at the beginning of 20X1. During 20X0, Lena had loaned $10,000 to the corporation, which still remains owed to Lena. Lena's share of the corporation's income for 20X1 was $20,000, and her share of the corporation's separately stated items of loss and deductions was $24,000. Also during 20X1, Lena received a distribution of $8,000 from the corporation. Compute Lena's adjusted basis of her stock and her indebtedness at the end of 20X1.

12. Assume the same facts as in Problem 11, except that in 20X2, Lena's share of the S corporation's income is $30,000, her share of separately stated items of loss and deduction is $25,000, and she receives a $6,000 distribution during the year. Compute Lena's adjusted basis of her stock and indebtedness at the end of 20X2.

13. An S corporation with no accumulated E&P distributes $10,000 to one of its shareholders, Darius Camelo. Darius's adjusted basis in his shares of stock in the corporation was $6,000 prior to the distribution. How will Darius be taxed on the distribution?

14. Marcel Morles is a shareholder of an S corporation. On August 10, the corporation distributes $20,000 to Marcel. Of this distribution, $5,000 came from the corporation's accumulated E&P. Marcel's adjusted basis in his shares is $10,000. What amount must Marcel include in his gross income, and how is it characterized?

15. An S corporation paid the health insurance premiums for two of its employees, Jonathon Tremmel and Sam Fussler. The premiums were $4,000 for Jonathon and $5,000 for Sam. Jonathon owns 100 of the corporation's 1,000 outstanding shares of stock; Sam owns 20 shares. How are the premium payments taxed to the corporation and its two employees?

16. An S corporation has accumulated E&P and therefore is subject to the tax on excess passive investment income. If its excess net passive income for the year is $50,000, how much excess passive investment income tax does it owe?

17. An S corporation has accumulated E&P and therefore is subject to the tax on excess passive investment income. If the corporation's gross receipts are $4 million, its passive investment income is $1,500,000, and deductions related to passive investment income are $300,000, how much tax will it pay on its excess net passive income?

18. Selsor Data Processing converted from a C corporation to an S corporation on January 1, 2015. At the time it converted to an S corporation, Selsor had $50,000 of accumulated E&P. On January 1, 2015, it owned a motor vehicle with a FMV of $10,000 and an adjusted basis of $5,000. On January 13, 2018, the company sold the motor vehicle for $6,000. At that time, the motor vehicle's adjusted basis was $0. What is the company's recognized built-in gain from the sale?

19. Coated Fabrics converted from a C corporation to an S corporation on January 1, 2016. At the time it converted to an S corporation, Coated Fabrics had $100,000 of accumulated E&P. On July 3, 2016, it sold a building that it had owned while it was a C corporation. The sale price was $300,000. On January 1, 2016, the FMV of the building was $280,000, and its adjusted basis was $100,000. Assuming that it has sufficient taxable income during 2016 and recognizes sufficient taxable gain on the sale, what amount of built-in gains tax will the corporation have to pay?

20. Copper Tubing, Inc., a corporation that had been using the LIFO method to value its inventory, elects to be an S corporation, effective January 1, 2016. The value of its inventory under the FIFO method is $450,000 at the beginning of 2015 and $500,000 at the end of 2015. The value of its inventory under the LIFO method is $150,000 and $200,000, respectively at the beginning and end of 2015. Compute Copper's LIFO recapture amount.

21. Shane Earhart and his spouse own shares of stock in an S corporation. Shane not only owns stock in his own name but also holds stock for his son George under the Uniform Transfers to Minors Act. Dustin Blakeslee and Dina Briant own stock as joint tenants. An ESBT with four potential current beneficiaries also holds stock in the corporation. How many shareholders is the S corporation treated as having?

22. Jillian McSweeney sold her 30-percent interest in an S corporation on April 30. The corporation, which uses the calendar year as its tax year, had $36,000 in income from business operations. Most of this income was earned in December. $5,475 of its gross income was earned before Jillian sold her shares. What is Jillian's pro rata share of the corporation's income from business operations?

23. Pocock Data Processing, Inc. is an S corporation with $2,000 of accumulated E&P and an AAA with a balance of $15,000. If the corporation makes a $3,000 distribution to Earl Pocock and elects to distribute accumulated E&P before AAA, how will the distribution be taxed?

24. Haycraft Housewares, Inc. terminated its S status. At the time that it terminated its S status, the corporation had $10,000 of accumulated E&P and $30,000 in its AAA. Two months after the effective date of its S status termination, Haycraft Housewares distributed $4,000 in cash and property with a fair market value of $5,000 to Ricardo Haycraft. How will those distributions be taxed?

25. Lemelle China, Inc. elected S status. While it was a C corporation, it used LIFO to value its inventory. On the day before the effective date of its S election, its inventory was valued at $80,000 under LIFO. If the company had used FIFO to value its inventory, its inventory would have been valued at $120,000. Before calculating the value of its inventory using FIFO, the corporation had determined that its taxable income for its last year as a C corporation was $260,000. How much additional federal income tax will the corporation have to pay?

Chapter 14 Review Problems

1. Cotterman Stains, Inc. converts from an S corporation to a C corporation, effective January 1, 2015. At the time of the conversion, it had an accumulated adjustments account (AAA) of $30,000 and $10,000 of accumulated E&P. Cotterman retains the calendar year as its tax year. During 2015, the company had $300,000 of gross income from its business operations and $200,000 of deductions. It sold for $50,000 a capital asset with an adjusted basis of $20,000. Darius Baulch owns 25 percent of the shares of stock in the company. His shares have an adjusted basis of $40,000. During the year, the corporation distributes cash and property to its shareholders with respect to their stock. It distributes to Darius $57,500 in cash. Based on these facts, how are Darius and the corporation taxed for 2015?

2. Larita Goetze owned 25 percent (1,000 shares) of the stock of Sun Lamps, Inc., an S corporation. Her adjusted basis in the shares at the beginning of the year was $40,000. On March 31, she sold her shares for $60,000. The corporation's net income for the three months ending March 31 was $30,000. Its net income for the remainder of the year was $300,000 (including a gain of $200,000 on the sale of some property). None of the corporation's income was distributed to Larita during the year. Compare how Larita will be taxed if an election is made to calculate Larita's share of the corporation's income as if the corporation's tax year ended on March 31 and how Larita will be taxed if no such election is made.

Chapter 14 Research Question

An S corporation's election terminated because a shareholder transferred stock to a trust not qualifying as an eligible shareholder. Under what circumstances is it possible for the corporation to retain its S corporation status through the "inadvertent termination" procedures?

CHAPTER 15

Income Tax Planning for Business

CHAPTER CONTENTS

LEARNING OBJECTIVES

1. Learn the objectives of income tax planning for a business.
2. Become familiar with basic income tax planning tactics.
3. Learn what planning can be done with respect to compensation.
4. Understand what tax planning can be done when a closely held business is disposed.

¶ 1500 Introduction

The overall objective of tax planning is to structure financial transactions to maximize a taxpayer's after-tax wealth. The following should not necessarily be the objectives of tax planning:

1) To minimize taxes. Although in many instances, after-tax wealth is maximized by minimizing taxes, this is not always the result.

Example 1: In order to offset $50,000 of capital gains, Smith sells stock in December of the current year to create 50,000 of capital losses. Two months later the stock has doubled in value.

2) To achieve nontax objectives. Although tax planning can sometimes achieve nontax objectives, it is unrealistic to expect to accomplish these goals through tax planning.

Example 2: Alisha Harding is advised by her estate planner to minimize estate taxes by making gifts to her children. However, Harding wants to retain power over her children through her ability to change her will. Good tax planning will not necessarily help her achieve her nontax objective (control).

Is tax planning ethical? Accounts of individual and corporate tax planning in the media might cause one to wonder.

Media reports about inequities in the tax system may cause some to think that "tax avoidance" is illegal *per se* or at the least unethical. However, it is well established that taxpayers may arrange their personal and business affairs to pay the least amount of federal income taxes that are legally required. Judge Learned Hand, who is generally acknowledged to be one of the most influential Federal judges in the history of our country, said:

> Anyone may arrange his affairs so that his taxes shall be as low as possible; he is not bound to choose that pattern which best pays the treasury. There is not even a patriotic duty to increase one's taxes. Over and over again the Courts have said that there is nothing sinister in so arranging affairs as to keep taxes as low as possible. Everyone does it, rich and poor alike and all do right, for nobody owes any public duty to pay more than the law demands.[1]

¶ 1501 Basic Income Tax Planning Tactics

If one may analogize income tax planning to roads, there are several primary roads leading to the destination of after-tax wealth maximization. They include:

- Avoiding the recognition of income;
- Deferring tax by deferring income;
- Deferring tax by accelerating deductions;
- Selection of the tax entity;
- Selection of accounting methods;
- Converting ordinary income into capital gains;
- Smoothing year-to-year taxable income;
- Shifting income from high tax jurisdictions to low tax jurisdictions; and
- Lowering marginal tax rates by spreading income among various business entities or among family members.

Each road will be discussed in some detail. Not all roads lead in the same direction (i.e., two or more of the tactics may be at cross-purposes).

.01 Avoiding the Recognition of Income

Recall from the discussion in Chapter 3 that income for financial purposes is generally recognized when considered earned. If transactions can be structured or converted so as to avoid the recognition of income (i.e., having to report the item as income), the tax savings can be considerable. Examples of methods to increase financial income and/or cash flow and still avoid income recognition include:

1) *Borrow money against appreciated assets.* With the exception of borrowing against certain types of life insurance policies, borrowing money does not create a taxable event.

Example 3: Grace Brothers, Inc wishes to redeem the stock of a retiring stockholder at a cost of $500,000. The corporation does not have that much cash above its working capital needs. However, it has many appreciated assets, among them an office building that cost $300,000 and has a mortgage paid down to $100,000 but appraises at $1,200,000. Borrowing the $500,000 by taking out a second mortgage against the office building would require much less cash than would funding the stock redemption out of an after-tax gain on the sale of assets.

---

[1] *Gregory v. Helvering,* 293 U.S. 465, 35-1 USTC ¶ 9043, 55 S.Ct. 266 (1935).

Partnerships, individuals, estates, trusts, and S corporations are all subject to limitations on interest deductions if the funds are used to acquire property held for investment purposes (C corporations are not subject to investment interest limitations).

2) *Invest in tax-exempt bonds.* Assume that a 10-year AAA rated corporate bond yields four percent, while a comparably high-quality municipal bond, which is tax-exempt, yields three percent. A taxpayer in the 35% tax bracket who invests in the corporate bonds would have an after-tax yield of only 2.6 percent, less than the municipal bond. If the taxpayer is a resident of the state where the municipality is located, the bonds may be "double exempt" (i.e., the interest may also be exempt from state income taxes).

3) *Use life insurance policies.* Premiums paid on life insurance policies are not deductible if the payer is the beneficiary. However, policy proceeds are generally excludable from income. Borrowing against the cash value of a policy generally is free of income tax consequences.

Example 4: Heady Heating & Air, Inc. took out a $1,000,000 whole-life insurance policy on James Heady, its president and majority stockholder. After paying net premiums of $230,000, the corporation collected the face value upon the death of James. The entire $1,000,000 is free of income tax. The corporation then used the proceeds to redeem stock from the estate of James Heady, thus providing the estate with liquidity to settle claims, pay estate taxes, and bestow bequests.

4) *Take compensation from the business in the form of fringe benefits.* The benefit of owner/employees receiving after-tax income cannot be overstated. Therefore, the use of the following fringes (discussed in more detail later in ¶ 1502) is highly desirable:

- Health and accident policies;
- Employer-provided group-term life insurance;
- Meals and lodging;
- Child care facilities;
- Educational assistance programs;
- No-cost fringes;
- Qualified employee discounts;
- Working condition fringes;
- Pension and profit-sharing plans

5) *Plan with respect to social security benefits.* Recipients of social security may be subject to marginal income tax rates that in effect are 50 percent or even 85 percent higher than the rate schedule. This is so because joint filers who have provisional income (AGI plus some adjustments) above $32,000 must include as much as 50 percent of their social security benefits in income. When provisional income exceeds $44,000 on a joint return, as much as 85 percent of the benefits may be taxed. The comparable income levels for those not filing joint returns are $25,000 and $34,000. Note that none of the income levels are adjusted for inflation. For taxpayers in the social security "bubbles," it may pay to replace high-yielding securities with low-yielding growth securities. Another strategy that may work for cash basis taxpayers is to time the collection of income with the objective of staying below the $32,000 or $44,000 level in year one and reporting enough income in year two so as to get above the social security bubble (so that all the social security benefits in year two are subject to 50 percent or 85 percent inclusion in income).

Example 5: Hank Higgins and his wife Eliza expect to have AGI from rental and investment income of $40,000 in both 2015 and 2016. Their social security benefits (ignoring the modest inflation adjustment) will be $28,000 each year. Hank will also do some consulting work for his former employer in December of both years for $18,000 each year. He could collect the 2015 fee in 2016, or collect both fees in 2016. If he includes the fee in income both years, then $23,800 ($28,000 × .85) of his social security benefits will be taxed each year. However, if he delays collecting the 2015 fee until 2016 (thus reporting $36,000 of fees in 2016), only $14,500 of social security benefits will be taxed in 2015. Taxable social security benefits in 2016 would still be $23,800. Thus, the tax on $9,300 of income ($23,800 – $14,500) would be saved.

6) *Exclude gain on the sale of a personal residence.* Taxpayers may exclude up to $250,000 ($500,000 on a joint return) of the gain on the sale of a principal residence, provided that residency and ownership tests are met.[2] This provision is often helpful to executives of a company who are transferred to another location.

.02 Defer Tax by Deferring Income

Deferring tax by deferring income has one definite and one possible benefit. The definite benefit arises from the time value of money concept (i.e., that a dollar paid in tax one or more years from the current year is worth less than a dollar paid in the current year).

Example 6: A taxpayer in the 35 percent bracket is able to defer the recognition of $80,000 of income for three years. Assuming a 10 percent discount rate, the present value of the $28,000 of tax ($80,000 × .35) to be paid in three years is only $21,037.

The possible benefit is that the deferral may postpone recognition of the income to years in which the recipient is in a lower tax bracket.

Example 7: Jeff Rosen, a taxpayer in the 35 percent bracket, has a deferred compensation agreement providing for the payment of $20,000 in the year following his retirement. If his marginal rate drops from 35 percent to 28 percent after retirement, he saves $1,400 in tax.

Examples of ways to defer tax by deferring income include:

1) *Use of nontaxable exchanges.* As discussed in Chapter 8, gain or loss need not be recognized when property held for productive use in a trade or business or for investment is exchanged for like-kind property. Because the definition of "like-kind" is very broad for realty, many uses of nontaxable exchanges are possible.

Example 8: Dixon Brothers, Co., Inc. needs a distribution center in the southern suburbs of the city. Fortunately, the owner of a suitable building is willing to trade the building for some highly appreciated vacant land that Dixon Brothers has been holding for possible plant expansion. The nontaxable exchange defers gain on the vacant land until the replacement property (the distribution center) is sold.

2) *Utilize involuntary conversion rules where applicable.* When involuntary conversions of assets occur, taxpayers may have an unenviable combination of taxable income and an economic loss. This happens when the insurance recovery is more than the tax basis of the asset but less than the property's fair market value. This set of circumstances makes the elective deferral of gains on involuntary conversions especially helpful. To defer gain, qualified replacement property must be acquired within a specified time period. Refer to ¶ 809 for a discussion of these rules.

Example 9: Wainright Inc.'s office building was destroyed by fire. The building had a basis of $140,000, but a fair market value of $400,000. The insurance recovery was $320,000. Absent an election to defer gain, the company would have a tax of $63,000 (.35 × ($320,000 – $140,000). Thus, the after-tax insurance proceeds would be only $257,000 ($320,000 – $63,000). However, replacing the building within the required time at a cost of at least $320,000 would postpone indefinitely the realized gain of $180,000.

---

[2] *See* Code Sec. 121.

3) *Consider making installment sales.* Recognition of gain can be deferred by structuring a sale as an installment sale. The installment method is not available for dealer dispositions or for dispositions of personal property held as inventory. If the total of all deferred payments at the end of a year exceeds $5 million, a "tax" that in effect represents interest on the tax that is deferred may have to be paid. The "tax" is computed by multiplying the deferred payments outstanding in excess of $5 million by the underpayment rate in effect for the month in which the taxable year ends.[3] However, this rule does not apply to sales of personal use property and farm property, regardless of the amount deferred.[4] Because the underpayment rate has been low, the cost of deferring income for installment sales above $5 million has been relatively modest. Refer to ¶ 810 for a more detailed discussion of installment sales rules.

4) *Utilize deferred compensation plans for owners/employees.* Deferred compensation plans are covered in more detail in ¶ 1502.03. Strategic use of deferred compensation plans can yield significant tax savings for a business and increased compensation for executives of the business. "Qualified" plans have three advantages: employer contributions are not currently taxed to the employee but are currently deductible to the employer, and the plan itself is exempt from taxation (therefore the earnings are not taxed until made available to the employee). Examples of qualified plans include: traditional pension plans; profit sharing plans; stock bonus plans; 401(k) plans; Keogh plans; IRAs, both traditional and ROTH, SIMPLE retirement plans, and Simplified Employee Pensions (SEPS). Nonqualified plans typically take the form of deferred compensation plans or restricted property plans (usually restricted stock). Employers receive a tax deduction in the year that nonqualified plans become taxable to the employee.

Example 10: In 2013 New Tech Co. granted Manoj Kerala, the CEO, 1,000 shares of restricted stock. The stock will be issued on December 31, 2015, contingent on the completion of continuous service in the company through that date. At the time of grant the stock was selling for $30 per share. It was worth $90 per share when issued to Manoj. Manoj has $90,000 of ordinary income in 2015. New Tech Co. has a deduction of $90,000 for its tax year encompassing that date.

.03 Defer Tax by Accelerating Deductions

The objective here is to structure a transaction so that the expense or loss deduction falls into an earlier tax year than it might otherwise. There are a number of expense acceleration tactics available for both businesses and individual taxpayers. These tactics include:

1) *Use of the Code Sec. 179 expense election and the Bonus Depreciation.* These deductions are discussed in chapter 7. The ability to expense $500,000 per year (for 2014) of depreciable tangible personal property saves recordkeeping costs as well as accelerating deductions. The phase-out as acquisitions exceed $2,000,000 (in 2014) eliminates the expense election for medium-sized and large businesses. However, the bonus depreciation (50 percent in 2014) has no such phase-out. Note that Congress has been renewing the annual dollar limit and investment limit for Code Sec. 179 and bonus depreciation from year to year.

2) *Minimize nonbusiness use of listed property.* As discussed in ¶ 702, the modified accelerated depreciation system (MACRS) allows taxpayers to depreciate personal property over short time periods using accelerated rates. In order to qualify for MACRS, including the Code Sec. 179 deduction and bonus depreciation, the business use of listed property (automobiles, light trucks, entertainment property, recreation property, amusement property, computers or peripheral equipment, and cellular phones) must exceed 50 percent. Otherwise, the alternative depreciation system (ADS) must be used. ADS generally requires a longer life than MACRS and straight-line depreciation must be used.

Example 11: Roy Hayes, a self-employed businessman, purchased a computer in January 2015 for $5,000. In 2015 he used the computer for business use only 45% of the time. Roy must

---

[3] Code Sec. 453A(c).   [4] Code Sec. 453A(b)(3).

use straight-line depreciation and the ADS life to depreciate the computer. Thus his depreciation is only $225 ($5,000 × .45 /5 × .5) Had he upped the business use to over 50%, say 55%, he could have used the Code Sec. 179 deduction and/or the bonus depreciation on the business portion. Even without using either, his MACRS depreciation would have been $550 ($5,000 × .55/5 × .5 × 2).

3) *Realize capital and Code Sec. 1231 losses to offset capital and Code Sec. 1231 gains.* Businesses and their owner/employees should, during the last quarter of their tax year, review their completed capital and Code Sec. 1231 transactions. If there are net gains, they should consider if any assets having a basis in excess of fair market value should be sold.

Example 12: Blue Mountain Ski Resort, Inc., a C corporation, has a fiscal year ending November 30. In June 2015 the corporation sold for development some land which it had been holding to build an additional lodge. It realized a Code Sec. 1231 gain of $2 million from the sale. Blue Mountain also owns stock representing a minority interest in Blue Mountain Condos, Inc. The stock has an adjusted basis of $4,500,000, but the downturn in the economy has caused the value of the stock to fall to $3 million. Selling the stock before November 30, 2015 would, assuming a 35 percent tax rate, reduce its FYE 2015 tax by $525,000 ($1,500,000 × .35).

4) *Prepay expenses (if cash basis taxpayer).* There are some limitations on the deductibility of prepayments (see ¶ 306.02 for details). However, this remains an excellent method for cash basis taxpayers to defer tax.

Example 13: The law firm of Tort and Tort, PC, a calendar year corporation, uses the cash basis method of tax accounting. It generally purchases four months of office supplies in early January. This year, because of unusually large revenues, it decides to purchase the supplies in December.

5) *Accelerate the incurrence of expenses (if accrual basis taxpayer).* Accrual basis taxpayers have much less flexibility with respect to expense acceleration than do cash basis taxpayers. As discussed in ¶ 306 and ¶ 307, cash basis taxpayers can (subject to the constraint of the constructive receipt doctrine) control the timing of when income is received. Cash basis taxpayers can also accelerate or delay the payment of expenses. By contrast, accrual basis taxpayers generally report income when earned and expenses when incurred. However, certain expenses of accrual basis taxpayers can be accelerated by incurring the expense at an earlier date. For example, before the end of the tax year an accrual business could take such steps as scheduling repair expenses, doing advertising campaigns, paying accrued bonuses to related taxpayers (assuming that this was agreeable to the related taxpayer), charging off partially worthless bad debts, and so on. However, when seeking to accelerate deductions for accrual basis taxpayers, it is important to keep in mind that both the all events test and the economic performance test must be met for an expense to be deductible. (See ¶ 307.02 for details.)

6) *Owners/employees can prepay itemized deductions.* Estimated state income taxes (typically the last installment is due in January) can be prepaid in December. Charitable contributions (e.g., church tithes) can be prepaid. The entire year's property taxes can be paid before year end. Medical bills can be paid, and discretionary medical costs can be incurred and paid before the end of the year. Another tactic that can be used if the taxpayer's itemized deductions are just below the standard deduction is to bunch as much as possible of two or more years of itemized deductions into one tax year. The goal of bunching is to be able to itemize the year that the deductions are bunched and to take the standard deduction the other year. In that way, the total two-year deduction can often be increased.

Example 14: Maria Cortez, a single individual, without prepayment would have approximately $5,800 of itemized deductions in both 2015 and 2016. She has already paid one-half of her property taxes on her residence (due in June 2015). Assume her standard deduction will be $6,000 in both 2015 and 2016. Maria is considering paying $1,500 of property taxes in December 2015 instead of June 2016. She is also considering paying six months of her pledge to her church amounting to $1,200 in December 2015. The effect of those two prepayments would be to move $2,700 ($1,500 + $1,200) of itemized deductions from 2016 to 2015. The effect of the prepayments is shown below:

	If prepayments are *not* made			If prepayments *are* made		
	2015	2016	Total	2015	2016	Total
Standard deduction	$6,000	$6,000	$12,000	$6,000	$6,000	$12,000
Itemized deductions	5,800	$5,800	$11,600	8,500	3,100	11,600
Greater of the two	$6,000	$6,000	$12,000	$8,500	$6,000	$14,500

Thus, bunching of itemized deductions can create an additional $2,500 ($14,500 – $12,000) of deductions for Maria over the two-year period.

.04 Selection of Tax Entities

In many instances, selection of a tax entity is not discretionary (i.e., circumstances may dictate the use of a particular entity). There are also many nontax considerations to consider when selecting an entity (e.g., limited or unlimited liability, ease of transfer of ownership, and so on). However, with respect to tax considerations, each type of entity has benefits and drawbacks.

Partnerships. Partnerships have the advantage of a greater flow through of loss deductions than do either C or S corporations. Partnership debt increases basis, while S corporation debt is available for loss absorption only if it is owed to the particular shareholder. There is no loss flow through from C corporations to shareholders. Partnerships also have more flexibility with respect to allocation of profits and losses. As long as the allocation has economic substance, profits may be allocated in a different ratio than the ratio of partnership capital. Losses may be allocated in a different manner than profits, again subject to the economic substance constraint. Partnerships are also able to elect basis revision upon the sale or liquidation of a partnership interest. This can have the effect of a stepped-up basis in partnership assets. There is no comparable election for C or S corporations.

Example 15: Ian Vestor is considering investing in two fast food restaurants. The equipment in both restaurants has been largely expensed. The fair market value of the assets in both is $400,000, but their basis is only $160,000. Restaurant A is organized as a partnership; restaurant B is an S corporation. Vestor would pay $100,000 for one-fourth ownership. If the partnership makes a Code Sec. 743 adjustment, his share of the basis of the partnership assets in Restaurant A will be $100,000. However, his share of the basis of the assets in Restaurant B, the S corporation, will be only $40,000 ($160,000 × .25) even though he pays $100,000 for one-fourth of the stock.

A primary drawback of partnerships is the lack of fringe benefits available to the partner/employee. Because a partner is generally not treated as an employee for income tax purposes, fringe benefits such as group-term life insurance are not available. The complexity of keeping track of the inside and outside bases is another disadvantage of the partnership entity.

S corporations. S corporations retain the characteristics (and certain advantages) of the corporate entity while achieving much of the conduit (flow through) advantages of the partnership. Thus, the double tax is all but eliminated (built-in gains and excessive passive income can be subject to tax at the corporate level in certain instances). Net operating losses, typically experienced by new businesses, can flow through to the shareholders and give them immediate tax benefits.

Another important advantage of S corporations as opposed to C corporations is that the basis of S corporation stock increases as the S corporation earns income. Thus, the seller of S corporation stock will likely have a much smaller gain than if it had been organized as a C corporation. Sellers of

S corporation stock have an advantage over sellers of partnership interests when the business has assets that would create ordinary income if sold. Because S corporation stock is a capital asset, it generates capital gain or loss when sold. By contrast, the sale or liquidation of a partnership interest can create some ordinary income to the seller if the partnership holds ordinary income assets.

A major drawback of S corporations, when compared to C corporations, is the lack of fringe benefits available to those shareholders who own more than two percent of the stock. In some instances the tax savings from fringe benefits may outweigh income tax rate differentials.

Example 16: Hickock Family, Inc. owns and operates a large cattle ranch. The corporation owns the ranch house and purchases all of the food for its employee/shareholders. The value of the meals and lodging is $18,000 per year. If the corporation elects S status, the family members will not be able to exclude the value of the meals and lodging from their gross income. As a C corporation, the meals and lodging could be excluded from the employee/shareholders' gross income.

An S corporation also may not be appropriate if the corporation needs to retain earnings for expansion and the shareholders need to receive distributions of those earnings to pay their tax on the earnings.

S corporations are subject to several restrictions making them much less flexible than C corporations. There can be no preferred stock in S corporations. S corporations have a 100 shareholder limit. S corporations cannot be members of an affiliated group except as parents to C corporations or qualified subsidiaries. These restrictions can limit business expansion possibilities.

Corporations and partnerships cannot own stock in S corporations. This may act as a constraint on the raising of capital. However, S corporations can be partners in a partnership and can own stock in other corporations.

Limited Liability Companies (LLCs). LLCs are very attractive entities because they combine the strength of the corporate entity (limited liability) with the strength of the partnership entity (flow through). Therefore, an LLC has the advantages and drawbacks of a partnership without the drawback of unlimited liability.

A partner's share of partnership losses is deductible only to the extent that the partner's investment is "at risk." Because an LLC member is at risk only to the extent of his or her capital investments, the member's share of the company's debt, although increasing tax basis, does not increase the amount that the member has at risk.

C corporations. C corporations can pay fringe benefits to employee/shareholders. The highest marginal tax rate of C corporations (39 percent) is slightly less than the highest marginal rate (39.6 percent) of individuals. Note, however, that an additional 3.8 percent tax is imposed on the net investment income of joint filers with adjusted gross income in excess of $250,000 ($200,000 for single filers). In addition the Medicare tax increases by 0.9 percent for wages above $200,000. Therefore, the generous rate for the first $50,000 of C corporation income (15 percent) may result in a lower effective tax rate for small C corporations than the marginal tax rate of its shareholders. Of course this advantage will only hold true to the extent that the earnings are retained in the business rather than paid out as dividends.

The drawbacks of C corporations as compared with S corporations are as follows:

- C corporation income is taxed once when earned and a second time when distributed as dividends. The double tax is a serious disadvantage if distributions in the form of taxable dividends need to be made to shareholders;

- The absence of the flow through of losses to shareholders makes the C corporation disadvantageous for a company's first years of existence if losses are expected or even possible;

¶ 1501.04

- If the retention of earnings cannot be justified, the accumulated earnings tax may be assessed;

- Closely held C corporations and personal service C corporations are subject to certain of the passive loss limitations as well as most of the at-risk limitations. Therefore, the C corporation entity has little advantage over S corporations or partnerships in this respect.

.05 Selection of Accounting Methods

The accounting method used by a business can affect the timing of when income and deductions are recognized for tax purposes. Thus, when a business has a choice, the selection of accounting methods is an important factor in income tax planning. A listing of all of the elective accounting methods is outside the scope of this discussion. Hence, the focus is on: cash vs. accrual vs. hybrid; the installment sales method; LIFO inventory; MACRS depreciation rates and lives; and long-term construction.

Cash vs. Accrual vs. Hybrid. If businesses have a choice of accounting methods, the cash method is almost always superior to the accrual or hybrid methods. Income deferral opportunities for cash basis businesses are considerable because revenue is not taxed until actually or constructively received.

Example 17: Kirk Newberry, an attorney, selects the cash basis method for year 0, the year in which he opens his practice. His receivables at the end of his first year of practice were $40,000. The receivables grew as his practice increased so that by the end of year 40, his year of retirement, they amounted to $90,000. Assuming an eight percent discount rate, the present value in year 0 of one dollar of tax to be paid in year 40 on his receivables is less than five cents (.046). If his combined federal and state income tax rate were 40 percent in year 0, the present value of the $16,000 of tax deferred until year 40 would be only $736.

Opportunities for accelerating expense deductions are also much greater for cash basis businesses. Generally, expenditures for items that will either be used up or expire by the end of the year following the year of prepayment are deductible in the year paid. (See Chapter 3 for details). The cash basis method is not without drawbacks. In most instances the relationship between revenue deferrals and expense accelerations to cash inflows and outflows is direct (i.e., revenue deferrals carry the cost of delayed cash inflows, and expense prepayments require early cash outflows). Thus, tax planning through use of the cash method may be limited if cash flow needs are great.

Accrual method. The accrual method, in which the taxpayer generally recognizes income when earned, affords far fewer tax planning opportunities than does the cash method. Few entities would likely use the accrual method if they had a choice. However, most C corporations are required to use the accrual method (see ¶ 305.01 for details). The accrual method does afford some flexibility with respect to the timing of billing of customers and the amount received on advance payments.

Hybrid method. The hybrid method (discussed in ¶ 308) entails the use of the accrual method to account for purchases and the sale of goods and the cash basis method for non-sales revenue and expenses not related to the cost of goods sold. The hybrid method contains more flexibility than does the accrual method, especially with respect to acceleration of expenses.

LIFO inventory method. Under the LIFO inventory method (last in, first out), the latest purchases are costed out (see ¶ 410.02 for details). The use of LIFO represents good tax planning because LIFO minimizes gross profit when the cost of replacement inventory is rising.

Drawbacks to the LIFO method of accounting include:

- The financial statement conformity requirement. Many companies, especially publicly-held companies, are reluctant to use LIFO for book purposes because of the adverse effect on earnings per share (when inventory replacement costs are rising, which is generally the case, LIFO results in a higher cost of goods sold and a lower gross profit than other methods).

- Increased recordkeeping costs. Computers have reduced this drawback. However for small companies the extra cost of keeping track of the various LIFO layers is significant.
- Impact of LIFO layers. If for whatever reason a company on LIFO is forced to reduce inventory, the LIFO layers that will be taken to cost of goods sold will be of units that have a low tax basis. The effect may be to dramatically increase taxable income.

Given those drawbacks, why adopt LIFO? In times of even moderate inflation, LIFO results in significant tax savings because early acquired, low cost goods are retained in inventory and not costed out.

Long-term construction. Under the completed contract method, income and expenses are not recognized until the contract is completed. Thus, its use defers recognition of income. Although Congress has restricted the use of the completed contract method, it may still be used by small businesses in a number of instances (for details see ¶ 309.02).

A modification of the completed contract method, the "percentage of completion-capitalized cost method," may be used for residential construction contracts that do not qualify for the completed contract method. The completed contract method or the modified completed contract method, if available for use, can defer income for as many as several years. Its use is generally very advantageous to taxpayers.

Example 18: Luxury Builders, Inc. enters into a contract in October 2015 to build four expensive houses. The contract price is $6 million, and the estimated cost of construction at the time the contract is entered into is $5 million. The contract was completed in March 2016. Costs incurred were as follows:

2015	$600,000
2016	$3,000,000
2017	$1,400,000

If the percentage of completion method is used, the taxable income for the three years would be:

Year	Revenue Recognized	Costs Incurred	Taxable Income
2015	$720,000	$600,000	$120,000
2016	3,600,000	3,000,000	600,000
2017	1,680,000	1,400,000	280,000

However, if the completed contract method is utilized, the entire $1,000,000 of taxable income is deferred until 2017 (the year of completion).

Installment sales method. Under the installment sales method, income is recognized (often over several years) as the installment sales proceeds are collected. Therefore, as discussed in ¶ 15.02, the installment sales method is an effective method to defer income

.06 Selection of the Tax Year

Certain entities are not granted very much latitude in selection of their tax year. Individuals are required to use a calendar year unless they keep a set of books, which few individuals do. Sole proprietors are required to use the same tax year for their business as they use for their other income and expenses. Partnerships, S corporations, and personal service corporations are generally required to use a calendar year. Of the various exceptions to the calendar year requirement, the only exception that contains much of a tax advantage is the "natural business year" exception. If a partnership, S corporation, or personal service corporation has a seasonal business and qualifies under the natural business year exception, no deposit of tax need be made with the IRS (see ¶ 304.01 for a discussion of the natural business year). Hence, owners of these entities can defer receipt of income.

Example 19: Sam's Ski Shop, Inc., an S corporation, has a natural business year-end of April 30. Sam, the sole shareholder, is on the calendar year. Sam has a permanent deferral of eight months of S corporation earnings.

C corporations, unless they are personal service corporations, may use any fiscal year they wish as long as the year ends on the last day of a month or is a 52-53 week year. However, the first year cannot exceed 12 months. Because C corporations do not allow flow through of income or losses, the deferral possibilities for fiscal years are rather minimal. However, for small C corporations, the selection of the year-end for the first partial year can yield tax savings.

Example 20: Allegany Computers, Inc. begins business on June 1, 2015. It expects to have taxable income of approximately $100,000 per year for the first several years. However, the corporation does not reach $50,000 of taxable income until January 31, 2016. If it selects a January 31 year-end, the tax on its income from June 1, 2015 through January 31, 2016 will be only $7,500. It can benefit from the low tax rate on the first $50,000 of taxable income by closing its tax year on January 31.

.07 Converting Ordinary Income Into Capital Gains

Capital gains receive a substantial tax advantage under current law. Capital assets held more than 12 months are taxed, depending on an individual's income, at 28 percent, 25 percent, 20 percent, 15 percent, or zero percent (for individuals with a marginal tax rate below 25 percent). Note, however, capital gains and other net investment income received by individuals, estates, and trusts is subject to a special 3.8 percent tax. See ¶ 901.02 for details and examples. Ordinary income is taxed at a maximum rate of 39.6 percent.

Three tax planning strategies will be discussed regarding converting ordinary income to capital gains: taking advantage of instances under current law when capital gains are preferred over ordinary income; converting ordinary income into capital gains; and optimizing the timing of capital gains and losses.

When capital gains are preferred. Under current law, individuals are taxed at favorable tax rates on their long-term capital gains. Also, individuals can deduct up to $3,000 of their capital losses against their ordinary income each year. C corporations can deduct capital losses only to the extent of their capital gains. Therefore, if a tax entity has already experienced net capital losses for the year, the netting feature of capital gains makes them preferable to ordinary income.

Example 21: Spoon-feed, Inc., a corporation in the 39 percent tax bracket, has a net capital loss to date in 2016 of $50,000. The corporation is planning to sell a small branch building that it has held for slightly less than one year for a taxable gain of $55,000 (ordinary income because the building is a not a capital asset). The building has been depreciated using the straight-line method. Therefore, all of the gain can qualify as Code Sec. 1231 gain if the sale is delayed until the building has been held for more than one year. Assuming that the corporation has no other Code Sec. 1231 transactions, the corporation will be able to fully offset its $50,000 capital loss against its $55,000 gain.

The tax savings to the corporation would be $19,500 ($50,000 × .39).

How to convert ordinary income into capital gains. There are several ways that businesses and their employee/owners can convert ordinary income into capital gains.

Code Sec. 1231 gains. Depreciable property used in a trade or business and real property used in a trade or business are potentially eligible for Code Sec. 1231 treatment. The key to generating maximum Code Sec. 1231 treatment is to:

- Meet the holding period requirement (usually one day over a year), if gains are desirable; and

- Do not meet the holding period requirement if losses are desirable.

Example 22: Deespose, LLC purchased land for a plant site, but changed circumstances dictated a sale of the land. Because land prices were appreciating, the company was able to sell the land for $1,500,000, even though the company had paid only $1,200,000 eleven months earlier. Holding the land for an additional month would convert the ordinary income into Code Sec. 1231 gains, which would flow through to the LLC members.

Example 23: Drayage Company, a one-member LLC, already has a Code Sec. 1231 gain of $300,000 in the current year. The company wishes to sell a warehouse that it expects to bring $650,000. Its adjusted basis in the warehouse is $900,000. The warehouse has been held for only 11 months. The company anticipates no other gains or losses during the current year and has no unrecaptured Code Sec. 1231 losses. Selling the warehouse before the 12 months and one-day holding period is met would result in a Code Sec. 1231 gain of $300,000 and an ordinary loss of $250,000. Thus the owner would have $300,000 of capital gains taxed at a maximum rate of 20 percent along with an ordinary deduction of $250,000. However, if the warehouse is held for more than a year, the loss would be a Code Sec. 1231 loss rather than an ordinary loss, and the result would be only $50,000 of gain that would taxed at a favorable long-term capital gain tax rate.

Cutting of timber. The cutting of timber may, at the election of the taxpayer, be given Code Sec. 1231 treatment (i.e., by treating the cutting as a taxable disposition).[5] This election is generally advantageous unless sale of the timber is not contemplated until subsequent tax years. In that event, Code Sec. 1231 treatment would be achieved at the expense of accelerating income into earlier tax years.

Example 24: Clear Cutting, LLP has four equal partners, all in the 35% tax bracket. In 2015 Clear Cutting plans to harvest and sell timber with an income tax basis of $300,000. It harvests the timber in January but does not sell the timber until May 2015. As of January 1, 2015 (the required date of measurement), the timber has a FMV of $800,000. However, the ultimate sales price amounts to $860,000. Clear Cutting elects to treat the cutting as a Code Sec. 1231 transaction. Assume that neither the partnership nor the partners have any unrecaptured Code Sec. 1231 losses in the past five years and that they have no Code Sec. 1231 losses in 2015. The Code Sec. 1231 $500,000 gain ($800,000 – $300,000) flows through to the partners as capital gain. After the election, their basis in the timber becomes $800,000. Therefore, they have an additional $60,000 ($860,000 – $800,000) of ordinary income. Assuming that all partners are in the 35 percent tax bracket, the tax savings that each partner gains from the Code Sec. 1231 election is $25,000 ($125,000 × (.35–.15)).

Subdivided realty. Noncorporate businesses may in certain instances receive capital gain on the sale of part or all of subdivided realty. The essential requirements are:

- Not be a dealer in real estate;

- Not have made substantial improvements to the property; and

- Held the property for at least five years.

See ¶ 903.04 for a more detailed discussion of the rules regarding subdivided realty.

---

[5] Code Sec. 631(a).

Conversion opportunities for employee/shareholders. Conversion opportunities for employee/shareholders are two-fold: they can convert ordinary income into capital gains and extract earnings from the corporation while avoiding the ordinary income treatment that dividends usually bring. Incentive stock options (discussed in more detail in ¶ 1502.02) are a good vehicle for accomplishing the first objective because the employee can receive capital gain treatment upon the sale of the stock.[6] Of the several qualification requirements for incentive stock options, two act as restrictions to prevent large grants to employee/shareholders:

- The recipient of the option, at the time of the grant, must not own more than 10 percent of the combined voting power of all classes of stock; and

- The total FMV of stock options that is exercisable in one year cannot exceed $100,000 per employee.

The not-more-than-10-percent ownership requirement is especially restrictive for closely held corporations. This restriction is made even stricter because attribution rules also apply (i.e., stock owned by spouses and certain blood relatives, as well as entities in which the employee has an interest, is considered owned by the employee).[7] The $100,000 ceiling limits the amount of benefit to corporate executives.

Notwithstanding the restrictions listed above, incentive stock options are an excellent device for rewarding valuable employees.

Corporate distributions. Distributions from a corporation to shareholders can be in the form of liquidating distributions (i.e., a distribution of money, stock, or property in conjunction with the winding up of the corporation). Alternatively, the distribution could be an ordinary distribution (i.e., *not* in conjunction with a liquidation). Prior to 1987 a judicial doctrine known as the General Utilities rule enabled corporations to avoid taxable gains or losses on certain liquidating distributions to stockholders. Now a liquidating distribution results in a double tax (gain recognized is taxed to the distributing corporation and to the distributee stockholder).

An ordinary distribution in the form of cash generally creates ordinary income to the shareholder. However, recall from ¶ 405.02 that recipients of qualified dividends are entitled to capital gains treatment. If a corporation has positive cash flow (and thus the funds to pay a dividend), but has no earnings and profits (E & P), distributions are generally treated as a nontaxable return of capital until basis is exhausted. The excess will be taxed as capital gains.

Example 25: Black Mining has a deficit in both current and accumulated earnings and profits. In the current year the corporation made an ordinary distribution of $400,000, one-fourth of which was received by Big Sam, who has owned the stock for two years. Sam's basis in his stock immediately before the distribution was $70,000. Of Sam's distribution, $70,000 is treated as a nontaxable return of capital. The remaining $30,000 is a long-term capital gain.

Stock redemptions. A stock redemption occurs when a corporation acquires its own stock from a shareholder in exchange for cash or property. If the redeeming corporation uses cash to redeem its own stock, it does not have a taxable event. However, if the redemption takes the form of property, then gains (but not losses) are recognized by the redeeming corporation.[8] This is so whether the redemption is treated as an exchange or as a dividend with respect to an individual. The acquisition qualifies as a redemption regardless of whether the stock is actually canceled or retired, or merely held as treasury stock.[9]

Depending on several factors (discussed below), stock redemptions are treated as either exchanges (thus qualifying for capital gain or loss treatment) or as dividends. In the past, exchange treatment has generally been a more favorable alternative for shareholders. If considered an

---

[6] Code Sec. 422.

[7] Code Sec. 424(d).

[8] Code Sec. 311(b).

[9] Code Sec. 317(b).

exchange, not only are any gains from the redemption subject to capital gains tax rates (likely lower than the taxpayer's marginal income tax rate), but the gain is reduced by the basis in the stock. However, if the stockholder has a net operating loss, dividend treatment may enable the corporation to get rid of all or part of its E & P at no cost to the stockholder.

 Planning Pointer: The very favorable 20 percent (or lower) rate on qualified dividends has lessened the advantages of exchange treatment. If the shareholder has a low basis in the stock, the difference between exchange treatment and dividend treatment may be minimal.

There are four instances in which redemptions from a living taxpayer are treated as exchanges, rather than as dividends.[10]

1. The redemption is "not equivalent to a dividend." This criterion is somewhat vague and subjective and therefore is not usually relied upon to get exchange treatment.

2. The redemption is substantially disproportionate. This is a mechanical test. The objective here is to make the redemption not be pro rata among the shareholders.

3. The redemption completely terminates the shareholder's interest.

4. The redemption is from a noncorporate shareholder in partial liquidation of the corporation.

Example 26: Cash Rich, Inc., with E & P of $2 million, redeems stock of Sam Rich, in a redemption that qualifies as disproportionate. Sam receives cash of $400,000. The basis of his stock that is redeemed is $160,000. Sam has held the stock for three years. Because the stock redemption qualifies as disproportionate, the redemption is treated as an exchange. Therefore, Sam has a LTCG of $240,000 ($400,000 – $160,000).

Example 27: Assume the same facts as in Example 26 except that the redemption does not qualify as disproportionate. Sam has $400,000 of dividend income. In neither case does the corporation recognize income from the redemption.

Stock redemptions to pay death taxes. Stock redemptions to pay estate taxes are yet another way to convert what might otherwise be ordinary income into capital gain. The estate of a decedent having as its primary asset an interest in a closely held corporation is not likely to be liquid. Often the corporation has more cash than the decedent. To help mitigate this liquidity problem, Congress has enacted several helpful laws, one of which is Code Sec. 303. If a corporation redeems stock that is included in the gross estate of a decedent, at least part of the redemption may be treated as a sale or exchange, thus achieving capital gain or loss treatment. Given that there will also generally be little gain or loss (the adjusted basis of the stock to the decedent will be FMV at date of death), this redemption feature can provide significant tax planning advantages.

Example 28: K Bucket died during the current year. Included in his gross estate is stock in Big Buckets, Inc., valued at $800,000 at Bucket's death. In a redemption that qualifies as an exchange, the corporation redeems the stock several months after Bucket's death when the value of the stock is $850,000. The estate has only a $50,000 gain, and that is taxed as a long-term capital gain.

Example 29: Assume the same facts as in Example 28, except that the redemption does not qualify as a stock redemption. Also assume that the corporation has E & P at least equal to $850,000. The estate has ordinary income of $850,000.

---

[10] Code Sec. 302(b).

.08 Optimizing the Timing of Capital Gains and Losses

There are several general rules concerning the optimal combination of capital gains and losses that apply to individual taxpayers. In many instances, their capital gains and losses will flow through from their interest in LLCs, partnerships, and S corporations.

1. If possible, let long-term gains stand alone, so as to maximize the amount eligible for preferential treatment.

Example 30: Stephanie Crowder, in the 35 percent bracket, has already realized a long-term capital gain of $3,000. She also has securities that she has held for two months. Toward the end of her tax year, Stephanie has a paper loss of $3,000 on those securities. She could sell the securities this year, or wait until next year. In any case Stephanie does not plan on additional dispositions of capital assets. If she sells the loss securities in the current year, her net capital gains tax for both years is zero. However, if Stephanie waits until the next year to sell the loss securities, she pays tax of $450 in the current year ($3,000 × .15), but has a tax savings in the next year of $1,050 ($3,000 × .35). Thus, by isolating the long-term capital gains, Stephanie saves $600 ($1,050 − $450).

2. If loss property is sold to offset capital gains, it is preferable for individuals and flow through entities to sell long-term capital loss property over short-term loss property. The short-term capital loss property could then be sold in the next tax year (before the more than one-year holding period is met) and be deducted first against short-term capital gains. This reduces the amount of losses offsetting long-term capital gains.

Example 31: Near the end of his tax year, Mike Jenrod had $27,000 of long-term capital gains realized. An S corporation of which he owns 100 percent has two capital assets, each of which if sold would create a loss of approximately $25,000. Asset A has been held for five months; Asset B has been held for 22 months. Because he owns all of the stock, all of the losses will flow through to him. Next year Mike expects to have both short-term and long-term capital gains of about $30,000. His tax results for the current year would be just as favorable if the S corporation sold the stock held for five months as if the corporation sold the stock held for 22 months (in either instance the net gains eligible for preferential treatment would be $2,000). However, by selling the stock held for 22 months this year, the loss on the sale of the stock held for five months, if realized early in the next year, would offset the $30,000 of expected short-term capital gains. That would enable the expected $30,000 long-term capital gains to be isolated and thus eligible for the favorable tax rate on long-term capital gains.

3. If possible, offset short-term capital gains against existing long-term capital losses, rather than using long-term capital gains to offset the long-term losses. This preserves the preferential treatment for long-term capital gains.

Example 32: Near the end of the year Chun Zhao has already realized $16,000 of long-term capital losses. She has two batches of stock, each of which would result in a $14,000 gain if sold. One batch has been held for five months; the other batch has been held 21 months. Chun's tax results for the current year will be identical regardless of which batch is sold. However, for the next tax year, it would be ideal to be assured of a long-term gain without having to hold the stock for an additional period of time. Hence, the stock held for five months should be sold during the current year, and the 21-month stock held.

4. If property is sold to create a $3,000 capital loss deduction, it is generally preferable to sell short-term capital loss property rather than long-term capital loss property. Then, if later in the tax year both short-term and long-term capital gains are realized, the capital loss offsets income taxed at ordinary rates (short-term capital gains) rather than offsetting income taxed at preferential rates (long-term capital gains).

5. If possible, offset long-term capital losses against existing short-term capital gains. Here the reasoning is similar to Rule #3. However, realizing some kind of capital losses (short-term if necessary) is important because short-term capital gains standing alone will be taxed at ordinary rates.

Example 33: Xavier Robinson picked a good stock (Half Dollar Value) that appreciated $30,000 in just three months after its purchase. He sold the stock in June 2015 to "take the profit off the table." By December of 2015 Xavier has an unrealized capital loss of $34,000 on Neckbook, a stock he purchased in May 2014 and an unrealized capital loss of $35,000 on Outtel, stock that he acquired in November 2015. He also has an unrealized capital gain of $40,000 on Bruckers, a stock that he acquired in 2012, and an unrealized capital gain of $36,000 on Free State, a stock he acquired in December 2015. He plans to sell both the Bruckers and the Free State stock in early 2016. Assume that the price of all Xavier's stock remains unchanged. If Xavier offsets the short-term capital gain on the Half Dollar stock by selling the Neckbook stock, he can then, in early 2016, sell the Outtel stock and realize a short-term capital loss. That loss can be offset against the short-term gain on the Free State stock. The result is to leave the Bruckers stock isolated as a long-term capital gain and thus eligible for preferential treatment. Had Xavier instead sold the Outtel stock in 2015 and the Neckbook stock in 2016, the long-term capital loss on the Neckbook stock would offset all but $6,000 of capital gain, thus losing $34,000 of preferential treatment.

.09 Smoothing Year-to-Year Taxable Income

The idea of smoothing year-to-year taxable income is to stay in the same tax bracket each year (i.e., to equalize year-to-year marginal tax rates).

Example 34: Elena Barchas estimated her taxable income toward the end of the year 2015 and discovered that she was $20,000 below the beginning of the 33 percent bracket. Thus her highest marginal rate is 28 percent. She expects to have sufficient income in 2016 to place her well into the 33 percent bracket. She has traditionally received in January of each year a $15,000 bonus from the C corporation of which she is the majority shareholder. Accelerating the January 2016 bonus into December 2015 would save her $750 ($15,000 × (.33 − .28)) of federal income tax.

The advantage of smoothing income is sometimes lessened (even completely negated) because the tax planning tactic: deferring tax.

Example 35: Assume the same fact as in the previous example and also that Elena can invest in stock that can earn a 12 percent return. Accelerating the income to 2016 would cost her $504 ($15,000 × .28 × .12) of return. In this example the loss of deferral significantly reduces the tax savings from smoothing.

On the other hand, smoothing and tax deferral will sometimes work in the same direction and increase tax savings.

Example 36: Henry Odom, a cash basis surgeon, estimated his taxable income toward the end of the year 2015 and discovered that he was only a few dollars below the beginning of the 35 percent bracket. Henry has about $40,000 that he could bill early enough to collect the receivable in 2015. Henry plans on closing his practice for two months in 2016 to do some mountain climbing in Tibet. Therefore, he expects his 2016 income to be considerably below the start of the 35 percent bracket. Henry believes he can invest any deferred tax in stock that would return 10 percent. By smoothing his income, Henry can save $800 ($40,000 × (.35 – .33)). The $800 dollar one-year deferral, if invested at 10 percent, yields a total tax planning savings of $880.

.10 Lowering Marginal Tax Rates by Spreading Income (Family Tax Planning)

Spreading income among family members may achieve other objectives in addition to lowering marginal tax rates. The wealth and income distributor may wish to decrease estate and gift taxes, provide for the education of children or grandchildren, or have some assurance that heirs will have adequate income should the distributor die.

Means of shifting income. Income may be shifted to lower-bracket family members by:

- Paying salaries and bonuses to family members;

- Transferring family interests to family members by gift, either outright or through trusts or custodial arrangements, or via interest-free loans.

Paying salaries to dependent "children". In this and later discussions about spreading income among family members, the term "children" includes other dependent relatives, such as grandchildren, foster children, nieces, nephews, and others for whom the dependency deduction can be taken.[11] Payments made to dependent children are deductible if performed for work in a trade or business, rental or other income-producing or investment activities. The deductibility of such payments is subject to the ordinary, necessary, and reasonable requirements that apply to any business deduction.[12] The income will be earned income to the child; thus the child can take the standard deduction ($6,300 in 2015) against the earned income. Any wages above the maximum standard deduction will be taxed at the child's tax rates (this is true even if the child is under 18). Another advantage of paying wages to children is that the wages may be used for some of the child's support without the income being taxed back to the parents. Generally, care should be taken to ensure that the child does not spend so much for his or her support that the dependency deduction is lost to the parents. Another advantage of paying children wages is that wages paid by a parent to a child under 18 are not subject to FICA taxes.[13] It is important to keep the wages at a reasonable rate and to maintain good records of time worked by the child.

Example 37: Adamo and Agense De Luca own and operate a pizza restaurant sufficiently profitable to put them in the 35 percent tax bracket. They employed Claretta, their unmarried 17-year old daughter, for 600 hours during 2015 and paid her $6,000 in wages. Claretta saved $1,500 of the wages for college and spent the remaining $4,500 for her own support. Her parents contributed $6,000 toward her support. Her parent may take a $6,000 deduction against their pizza shop revenue and claim her as a dependent (assuming the dependency tests in addition to the support test are met). Claretta has gross income of $6,000. However, she may offset her income with the standard deduction, thus leaving her with no taxable income resulting from the wages. Note that the family unit would have saved taxes even for wages paid to Claretta in excess of the standard deduction. Wages above that level would be taxed to Claretta at the lowest rate but would save her parents $.35 for every dollar paid in wages to her.

Transferring an interest in a family business. Transferring an interest in a family business can be another effective method of shifting income to a family member in a lower income tax bracket. Transferring an interest in either a C corporation, an LLC, or a partnership, including a family limited partnership, can shift income. However, a transfer of a corporate interest is fairly similar to other gifts; hence it will be discussed later in this chapter in conjunction with other gifts. Only the partnership entity will be discussed here.

---

[11] *See* Code Sec. 152(c) and (d) for the definitions of "qualifying child" and "qualifying relative."

[12] *See* ¶ 501.01 and ¶ 501.02 for a discussion of these tests.
[13] Code Sec. 3121(b)(3).

A self-employed parent could form a partnership and give a portion of the partnership to the children. If the business performs personal services, it is generally not possible to spread income among family members via a partnership arrangement.[14] However, "a person shall be recognized as a partner . . . if he owns a capital interest in a partnership in which capital is a material income-producing factor, whether or not such interest was derived by purchase or gift from any other person."[15] Capital ordinarily is a material income-producing factor if the operations of the business necessitate either substantial inventories or a substantial investment in plant, machinery, or other equipment.

When a "family" partnership interest is transferred by purchase, the transaction is considered to be a gift by the seller. "Family" for this purpose includes only spouses, ancestors, lineal descendants, and any trusts for the primary benefit of such persons.[16] In that event the share of the partnership income reported by the donee (e.g., child) must be determined by reducing the partnership income by reasonable compensation attributable to services the donor (e.g., parent) provides to the partnership. In addition, the donee's share of partnership income cannot be proportionately greater than the donee's share attributable to the donor's capital interest.[17]

Example 38: Melissa Green sold a 50 percent capital interest in her floral shop to her son, Andrew. The resulting partnership had taxable income of $140,000. Reasonable compensation for Melissa's work in the floral shop in the current year amounted to $60,000. Andrew did not work in the shop. In determining each partner's distributive share of income, the $60,000 must be deducted. Andrew's share of the remaining $80,000 cannot exceed his 50 percent interest. Thus, the greatest amount of partnership income that can be allocated to Andrew is $40,000. The remaining $100,000 ($60,000 + $40,000) must be allocated to Melissa.

 Spotlight: Suppose that in Example 38 an unlimited amount of partnership income could be allocated to Andrew. Under what circumstances would that constitute good tax planning? Why do you think that Code Sec. 704 prohibits allocating an unlimited amount of partnership income to the donee relative? Why do you think siblings are not subject to this rule, but grandchildren are?

Gifts to children. Gifts to children may be made outright, in trust, or under the Uniform Gifts to Minors Act (UGMA) or Uniform Transfers to Minors Act (UTMA). Outright gifts are advantageous in that the income may be used for the child's support without it being taxed to the parent. An obvious drawback is that the parent may lose control over the property. Also, depending on the type of property and the maturity of the child, the minor may be unable to look after the property or to dispose of the property. However, a gift under UGMA or UTMA enables the parent to exercise control as custodian. A drawback of a UGMA or UTMA gift is that any income used for support of the child will then be taxed back to the parent. Trusts have been a basic part of family tax planning for many years. However, trusts do not have to have much taxable income before their marginal income tax rate hits 39.6 percent.

Making interest-free loans. Interest-free loans to family members generally constitute what is termed a "gift loan." When a gift loan is made, the foregone interest is treated as if the lender had made a gift of the interest to the borrower and the borrower had paid the interest back to the lender. Thus, the lender is considered to have made a gift, subject to the gift tax laws, and received interest income. The borrower is considered to have received a gift (not subject to income tax, and also has a potential deduction for interest expense (subject to the various limitations and restrictions on the deduction of interest expense).[18] This required interest income imputation largely removes the advantages of gift loans.

---

[14] This precept was established by several judicial decisions, e.g., *Lucas v. Earl*, 2 USTC ¶ 496, 281 US 111 (1930).

[15] Code Sec. 704(e)(1).

[16] Code Sec. 704(e)(3).

[17] Code Sec. 704(e)(2).

[18] Code Sec. 7872(a)(1).

Pros and cons of various types of gift property to children. Children under the age of 18 are subject to the notorious "kiddie tax." The kiddie tax also applies to children ages 19-23 who are in college if they do not have earned income in excess of one-half of the total amount spent on their support. Imposition of the kiddie tax results in the child's investment income (e.g., interest, dividends, rents, royalties, capital gains) in excess of $2,100 (in 2015) being taxed at the parent's rates.

Example 39: Alfred Affluent and his wife Audie are in the 35 percent tax bracket. They transfer stock yielding dividend income of $3,600 in 2015 to their 16-year old daughter Mindy. Assuming Mindy has no other investment income and no earned income, the first $1,050 of her investment income will go untaxed (shielded by her $1,050 standard deduction). The next $1,050 will be taxed at her rate (10 percent). However, the remaining $1,500 will be taxed at the parent's rate of 35 percent.

Because of the kiddie tax, the appropriate type of property to gift children depends on their age and whether or not they are in college. Children whose income is subject to the kiddie tax should generally be given property that produces little current taxable income but is expected to appreciate in value. The objective is to defer the recognition of income until the child has reached 18 (or 24 if a college student). Thus, the following types of gift property are attractive:

- High-growth, low dividend paying stock—the greatest part of the return, capital gains, can be deferred;

- Series EE bonds—the discount (interest) is not recognized until the bonds mature;

- Market discount bonds—the holder can defer recognition of the discount until the bonds mature or are disposed of;

- Stock in a closely held C corporation—the dividend rate can be controlled by the parent/donor/majority shareholder.

Gifts to children reaching age 18 (or 24 if a college student). Once the kiddie tax no longer applies, children are taxed at their rates, not their parent's rates). Because the children's rates are usually less than the parent's rates, a considerable amount of income-yielding assets can be given before the income tax savings potential is exhausted. The gifts should generally be of high-yielding assets. If a child was previously given property which has appreciated (e.g., common stock) or which has deferred income attached to it (e.g., Series EE bonds), the assets can be sold with a minimum of tax due. Dividend payments on closely held stock can be increased.

Example 40: Rahul Kapoor's daughter Rhea graduated from college in May 2015 at the age of 22 and began work full-time. Rahul is in the 39.6 percent tax bracket. However, Rhea does not expect to get above the 15 percent bracket for the year 2015. Rahul makes a gift to Rhea in June 2015 of $400,000 of corporate bonds yielding 3 percent annually. Rhea expects to collect about $6,000 of dividends from the bonds in 2015. She will owe tax of $900 ($6,000 × .15). Had Rahul retained the bonds, his tax would have been $2,376 ($6,000 × .396).

Planning Pointer: Two caveats apply to gifts made to children who have reached age 18. Parents may justifiably be reluctant to take full advantage of the income tax savings potential of gifts because:

- To do so might require a transfer of more assets than advisable. The parents may believe that they will need the assets eventually, or the parents may not wish their child to have that amount of assets under the child's control; and

- The parents may not wish to pay the gift tax due on large gifts.

¶ 1502 Other Tax Planning Issues

.01 Compensating Employees and Employee/Owners

The main tax planning objectives of compensating employees and employee/owners are to give employers a deduction for the compensation and to exclude as much of the compensation as possible from the employee's gross income. No planning other than retirement planning is possible for sole proprietorships because the business entity is not separate from the owner. Partnerships also provide few tax planning opportunities because for income tax purposes partners are generally not considered employees of the partnership. This discussion will focus on C corporations and S corporations.

C corporations. Salaries, wages, and bonuses paid to C corporation employees in the form of cash, property, or stock are taxable to the employee and deductible by the corporation. However, certain other payments on behalf of employees, known as fringe benefits, can be deducted by the employer and excluded from the employee's gross income.

The essential trade-off between cash salaries and fringe benefits, from the perspective of the employee, is the reduced freedom in spending the compensation versus the reduced income tax burden. Fringe benefits other than retirement plans (which are discussed later in this chapter) include:

- *Employee achievement awards.*[19] A limited amount ($400 for nonqualified plans and $1,600 for qualified plans) may be excluded from gross income if the award is for either a safety achievement or for length of service and is paid in the form of tangible personal property (e.g., a watch).

- *Group-term life insurance.*[20] Premiums paid on the first $50,000 of coverage are deductible to the employer and excludable by the employee. The plan cannot discriminate in favor of highly-paid employees.

- *Medical, health, and disability insurance.*[21] Premiums paid by an employer can be deducted by the employer and excluded from gross income by the employee. Such insurance is not subject to the anti-discrimination requirements (unless the payments are made under an employer's self-insured plan).

 Spotlight: In terms of revenue lost to the U.S. treasury, the exclusion for employer-provided health insurance is the 500 pound gorilla of fringe benefits. Which income groups do you think most benefit from this exclusion?

- *Meals and lodging.*[22] The value of meals furnished an employee may be excluded from gross income if furnished for the convenience of the employer on the business premises. The value of lodging may be excluded from gross income if it is furnished for the convenience of the employer and the employee is required to live on the premises as a condition of employment.

- *Educational assistance plans.*[23] If the educational assistance plan is nondiscriminatory, up to $5,250 of payments or reimbursements for tuition, fees, books, equipment and supplies may be excluded from an employee's gross income. If the education is job-related, the exclusion may be available even if the plan does discriminate in favor of highly-paid employees or those who are partial owners.

---

[19] *See* Code Sec. 74.
[20] *See* Code Sec. 79.
[21] *See* Code Sec. 105.

[22] *See* Code Sec. 119.
[23] Code Sec. 127.

- *Child or dependent care assistance programs.*[24] Up to $5,000 of qualifying day care services for certain dependents is excludable, provided that there is a written, nondiscriminatory plan.

- *Adoption assistance programs.*[25] Up to $13,400 (for a tax year beginning in 2015) of payments made by employers or reimbursements to the employee to enable the employee to adopt a child are excludable, if there is a written, nondiscriminatory plan.

- *Code Sec. 132 fringes.* This code section authorizes the following fringe benefits:

  — No additional cost services. This applies when the employer incurs no substantial additional costs. Examples include hotel accommodations by a hotel and airline tickets from an airline.

  — Qualified employee discounts. These are discounts for services that do not exceed 20 percent of the price at which the services are offered to customers and discounts for property that do not exceed the gross profit percentage of the price at which the property is offered to customers.

  — Working condition fringes. This is any property or service provided to an employee to the extent that if the employee paid for the item it would be deductible as either a business expense under Code Sec. 152 or as depreciation under Code Sec. 167. Examples include the value of use by an employee of a company car used for business purposes or the provision of a bodyguard for the employee.

  — *De minimis* fringes. These are property or services that are so small in value as to make accounting for them unreasonable or administratively impractical. Examples include company picnics, occasional supper money or cab fare, and holiday gifts of property with a low value. On-premises athletic facilities (e.g., pools, gyms) also qualify as *de minimis*.

  — Qualified transportation fringes. These benefits qualify:

    • Transportation in a commuter highway vehicle from the employee's residence to work;

    • Transit passes; and

    • A limited amount for qualified parking.

  — Qualified moving expense reimbursements. These are amounts received by an individual directly or indirectly from an employer as payment for (or reimbursement of) expenses that would be deductible as moving expenses if directly paid or incurred by the employee.

  — Qualified retirement planning services. The value of retirement planning services provided to the employee is not taxable.

  — Qualified military base realignment and closure fringe. Payments under the authority of Section 1013 of the Demonstration Cities and Metropolitan Development Act of 1966.

The benefit to employees of providing compensation in the form of fringe benefits instead of cash salary can be considerable, as evidenced by the following examples:

Example 41: John Jones and his brother James Jones are both majority owners of C corporations that employ several workers. John pays his workers $40,000 yearly in cash wages but offers no fringe benefits. James pays his workers $35,000 in cash wages. However, his corporation has a non-discriminatory health and accident plan that pays premiums averaging $5,000 per employee. The employees pay the remaining premiums. Assuming James's employees are in the 15% tax bracket, they save $750 ($5,000 × .15) as a result of the health and accident fringe benefit.

Example 42: Michael Amoretti and has wife are in the 25% tax bracket. Michael currently has a job paying $50,000 in cash wages. He has been offered a job as manager of an apartment complex. The nature of the job requires Michael and his wife to live in an apartment on the premises. The FMV of the rent-free apartment is $12,000 per year. Michael

---

[24] *See* Code Sec. 129. [25] *See* Code Sec. 137.

has been offered $37,000 cash wages plus free use of the apartment. Because the lodging qualifies as an excludable fringe benefit, if Michael takes the job his after tax income will increase from $37,500 ($50,000 × .75) to $39,750 (($37,000 × .75) + $12,000).

Example 43: The employees of Y-Cell Corporation eat lunch in the company cafeteria. The FMV of the meals amounts to $6.00 per day (about $1,500 per year) per employee. However, the company charges only $3.50 per meal (enough to cover its variable costs). The $2.50 per meal ($625 per year) qualifies as a *de minimis* fringe benefit. Y-Cell also provides free membership in the company gym, the FMV of which is $750 per year. This also qualifies as a *de minimis* fringe. Several employees occasionally are asked to work past closing time. On those days they are given supper money and money for a cab ride to their home. Both the supper money and the cab fare qualify as *de minimis* fringes.

Example 44: Becky Banders works as a ticket agent for We Fly High Airlines. Her employer owns several resort hotels on the island of Maui. Becky vacations by flying free on the airline and by staying free in the hotel. Assuming that there were vacant seats on the plane and empty hotel rooms, Becky's free trips qualify as no cost fringes.

Example 45: Robert Retail is a regional manager for J-Mart, a large discount chain. J-Mart furnishes Robert a company car to use to travel to the stores in his jurisdiction. Robert also, along with other J-Mart employees gets a 15% discount on all goods sold in the stores. Use of the company car is a working condition fringe,[26] and the discount is a qualified employee discount.

.02 The Role of Stock Options

A stock option is a contract whereby the owner of the stock grants to the acquirer of the option the right to purchase the stock at a fixed price (the exercise price) within a specified time period. Employees benefit from the grant of stock options by their employers by exercising the option at a time when the FMV of the stock exceeds the exercise price. Employers may grant employees incentive stock options or nonqualified stock options. Both types play a valuable role in tax planning. Both types also carry risks as well as benefits for employees. The table below compares the income tax effects of incentive options and nonqualified options.

Type of Stock Option	Effect on Employer	When Taxed To Employee	How Taxed to Employee
Nonqualified—Readily ascertainable FMV	Deduction on grant date equal to FMV -exercise price	Income on grant date equal to FMV-exercise price	Ordinary income
Nonqualified—No readily ascertainable FMV	Deduction on exercise date equal to FMV-exercise price	Income on exercise date equal to FMV-exercise price	Ordinary income

---

[26] However, note that to the extent that Robert uses the car for personal purposes he will have gross income.

Type of Stock Option	Effect on Employer	When Taxed To Employee	How Taxed to Employee
Incentive stock options	No deduction	If holding period requirements are satisfied, income when stock is sold equal to sales price minus exercise price	Long-term capital gain

.03 Incentive Stock Options

Incentive stock options represent another way to convert employee compensation that would otherwise be taxed as ordinary income into capital gains. Two requirements must be met by the employee however:[27]

- None of the stock can be disposed of within two years of the grant date or within one year after the exercise date; and

- The stock option recipient must be an employee of the company during the entire time period beginning on the grant date and ending three months before the exercise date.

Failure to meet both of the requirements results in the option being treated as if it were a nonqualified stock option (discussed later in this section).

If both requirements are met, the employee is not subject to the regular income tax until the date that the stock is disposed. However, the alternative minimum tax (AMT) may apply during the year in which the option is exercised.[28] The appreciation in value as of the exercise date is an adjustment for AMT purposes (i.e., it increases alternative minimum taxable income). The employer cannot deduct from taxable income the value of an option that qualifies as an incentive option.

Requirements that an incentive stock plan must meet. For a plan to qualify as an incentive stock plan, several requirements must be met:[29]

- The shareholders must approve the plan within 12 months before or after the plan is adopted;

- The option must be granted within ten years of the date that the plan is adopted or the plan is approved, whichever date is earlier;

- The option must not be exercisable more than ten years from the date of grant;

- The option price must not be less than the FMV of the stock on the grant date (i.e., there must be no bargain element at the time of grant);

- The option must not be transferable except by will or the laws of descent, and must be exercisable during the employee's lifetime only by the employee; and

- The individual at the time of grant must not own more than ten percent of the combined voting power of all classes of the corporation's stock.

Additional limitations and exceptions include:[30]

- The total FMV of stock options than can be exercised in one year cannot exceed $100,000; and

- The ten percent shareholder rule does not apply if the option price is at least 110% of the FMV of the stock subject to the option at the time that the option is granted and the option cannot be exercised for five years from the date that the option is granted.

---

[27] Code Sec. 422(a).
[28] Code Sec. 56(b)(3).

[29] Code Sec. 422(b).
[30] Code Sec. 422(c)(5) and (d).

Example 46: On May 1, 2014, Brenda Miles is granted an incentive stock option by her employer, Big Lots, Inc. Stock options in Big Lots are traded on an established options exchange. The option permits her to purchase 300 shares of stock at $50 per share, the FMV on the grant date. Brenda exercises the option on December 10, 2015 when the FMV has risen to $80 per share. On December 11, 2016 Brenda sells the stock for $90 per share. She has been employed by Big Lots during the entire time period. Brenda has no taxable income at either the grant or the exercise date. However, in 2015, the year of exercise, she has an AMT adjustment of $9,000 ($300 × ($80 – $50). In 2016 Brenda has a long-term capital gain of $12,000 (300 × $90) – (300 × $50). Big Lots is not entitled to a deduction for the stock option.

Example 47: Assume the same facts as in the previous example except that Brenda sells the stock on December 10 instead December 11. Because she disposed of the stock within one year of the exercise date, the stock option does not qualify as an incentive option, but rather is treated as a nonqualified option. Hence, Brenda has ordinary income on December 10, 2016 of $12,000, and Big Lots has a $12,000 compensation deduction in 2016.

Example 48: John Greer is the founder of Neck Book, Inc. Although the corporation is publicly-held, John owns 25 percent of the voting stock. No other employee owns more than ten percent of the voting power of the corporation. The corporation's shareholders approve an incentive stock plan, and the first batch of options is granted on July 1, 2014 at which time the FMV is $200 per share. John can be granted incentive stock options so long as the exercise price is at least $220 per share. All the other employees can have an option price of $200.

As previously mentioned, incentive stock options have the considerable advantage of converting ordinary income into capital gains for the employee. However, a potential pitfall for employees who exercise incentive stock options is that the bargain element at the time of exercise is an AMT adjustment. If the price of the stock falls after the exercise date, the employee may be left with a hefty AMT bill and no wherewithal to pay the tax.

Example 49: Hortense Hardluck has been the CFO of a start-up company for several years. In 2013, as part of an incentive stock option plan, Hortense was granted an option to purchase 10,000 shares of stock in the company at the price of $30 per share. In August 2015 the company went public, and Hortense exercised the options when the stock was selling for $120 per share. However, by April 2016 competition from another company had driven the stock value down to $6 per share. Hortense has an AMT adjustment of $900,000 (10,000 × ($120 –30)). Assuming an AMT tax rate of 28%, Hortense might owe as much as $252,000 in additional income tax as a result of exercising the option. Selling the stock to raise money to pay the tax, however, would yield her only $60,000 (10,000 × $6). Hortense may be able to recover some of that AMT tax in later years in the form of a tax credit if her regular income exceeds her AMTI.

> **Spotlight:** Prior to the economic recession of 2008-2009, many employees, especially those working for high-tech companies in Silicon Valley, exercised incentive stock options and incurred a hefty AMT. The resulting collapse in stock prices left them with a large tax bill and no means to pay. Many taxpayers were saddled with additional interest and penalties adding up to thousands of dollars. Some of the taxpayers formed a group called "Reform-AMT" and lobbied Congress for relief. Their efforts were rewarded when Congress, as part of The Emergency Economic Stabilization Act of 2008, eliminated the AMT liability on incentive stock options exercised before 2008. However, the AMT applies to incentive stock options exercised from 2008 onward.

1. Do you think relief provisions affecting only a subgroup of taxpayers are fair or unfair? Why?

2. Subjecting the bargain element in an incentive stock option to the AMT in effect taxes unrealized gains. What problems do taxpayers face when unrealized gains are taxed?

.04 Nonqualified Stock Options

Nonqualified stock options result in ordinary income to the employee and give the employer a deduction for compensation. The timing of the income and deduction recognition, however, depends on whether the option has a "readily ascertainable fair market value." If the option has a readily ascertainable FMV (i.e., the option is traded on an established options exchange), the income to the employee (FMV at the date of the grant minus exercise price) and the corresponding deduction by the corporation are recognized on the grant date. However, in many instances the option will not have a readily ascertainable FMV. For example, the option may be granted by a privately held company or by a publicly held company with such low stock trading volume that there is no market for its stock options. In that event, the grant date does not trigger any income or deduction recognition. Instead, the bargain element at the date of exercise (the FMV of the stock less the option price) is included in an employee's gross income.

Example 50: Arjun Banerjee is employed by a Fortune 50 company with options traded on the Chicago Board of Trade and elsewhere. On April 16, 2013, he is granted a nonqualified stock option to purchase 500 shares of stock at $28 per share. The stock is selling for $32 per share on the grant date. Arjun exercises the option on January 10, 2014 when the stock is selling for $36 per share. He sells the stock on January 11, 2015 for $42 per share. Arjun recognizes $2,000 (500 × ($32 − $28)) of ordinary income on the grant date in 2013. His employer takes a deduction for $2,000 of compensation in 2013. No income or deduction is recognized on the exercise date. Arjun's basis in the stock is $16,000 ((500 × $28) + $2,000), and his holding period begins on January 11, 2014. Upon sale of the stock in 2015, Arjun has a long-term capital gain of $5,000 ((500 × $42) − $16,000). The sale of stock has no tax impact on his employer.

Example 51: Assume the same facts except that Arjun works for Blue Patch, a small start-up company, and the options have no readily ascertainable FMV. The grant date in 2013 is not a taxable event to either Arjun or his employer Blue Patch. However, in 2014 Arjun recognizes $4,000 of ordinary income (500 × ($36 − $28)), and Blue Patch takes a deduction for $4,000 at the date of exercise. Arjun's basis is $18,000 ($4,000 + (500 × $28)). In 2015 Arjun has a long-term capital gain of $3,000 ((500 × $42) − $18,000).

Pros and cons of the two types of options. Incentive stock options offer the employee the best opportunity to receive compensation in the form of long-term capital gains. However, the AMT issue represents a potential pitfall for those who exercise incentive stock options. In addition, the employer receives no tax benefit from incentive stock options.

Nonqualified stock options create fewer capital gains for the employee but are not subject to the AMT. Nonqualified stock options enhance the cash flow of employers because such options give employers an income tax deduction without any corresponding payment in cash or property.

Another drawback of nonqualified stock options from the standpoint of the employee is that the employee has taxable income without any corresponding increase in cash. This is especially evident if the employer's stock options have a readily ascertainable value because income must be recognized at the grant date, which in some cases may precede the exercise of the option by several years. One method of delaying the recognition of income from nonqualified stock options is to place restrictions on the employee's ability to exercise the options.

.05 Other Nonqualified Plans

Nonqualified plans other than stock options usually take on one of two forms: deferred compensation plans or restricted property plans. In both, the purpose is to defer taxation to the employee and create a deduction for the employer.

.06 Deferred Compensation Plans

The purpose of a deferred compensation plan is to provide income for key employees without taxing them currently on that income. In addition to key executives, deferred compensation plans are commonly given to entertainers and professional athletes.

 Spotlight: The NFL staged a lock-out from March to July of 2011. Football players were not paid salaries during the lock-out. However, the lock-out did not prevent football players from receiving their deferred compensation. The Sports Business Daily Global Journal reported that Mario Williams, defensive end of the Houston Texans, received a deferred payment of $4.25 million in March 2011.

.07 Nonqualified Deferred Compensation Plans

Because a plan is nonqualified, it need not meet nondiscrimination or minimum benefit rules. Hence, the plan can be limited to key executives. A typical scenario would be an employment contract that calls for, in addition to yearly salary, bonus, and fringe benefits, the payment of a lump sum or a certain amount per year at the end of a term of service, or at retirement. If (as is almost always true) the employee is on the cash basis of accounting, deferred compensation will not be taxed until received, provided that the following two tax doctrines applicable to cash basis taxpayers are avoided:

1. *Cash equivalency doctrine.* Even if the employee has not actually received a payment in cash or property, "notes or other evidences of indebtedness received in payment for services constitute income in the amount of their fair market value at the time of transfer."

2. *Constructive receipt.* If the employee has power over disposition and control of the asset (the deferred compensation), that payment is delayed is irrelevant (i.e., the compensation will be taxed when constructively received).

Employees are naturally interested in having some assurance that their deferred compensation will be paid to them. "Rabbi Trusts" are often used for this purpose. A "rabbi trust" is an irrevocable trust established to pay the deferred compensation. In order to avoid constructive receipt, the trust must be subject to the claims of the employer's creditors.

There are several restrictions on nonqualified deferred compensation plans.[31] If during the taxable year a nonqualified deferred compensation plan fails to meet "distribution rules," "acceleration of benefit rules," or "election rules," all previously deferred compensation is includible in income to the extent that is it not subject to a substantial risk of forfeiture. In addition to the income acceleration, a penalty tax of 20 percent plus interest is levied on plans that fail to meet the rules.

.08 Funded Nonqualified Plans

Funded nonqualified plans are included in the income of the employee for the tax year in which the contribution is made if the contribution is substantially vested at that time.[32] If, on the other hand, there is a substantial risk of forfeiture, the contribution is not taxed until the forfeiture is lifted.

---

[31] Code Sec. 409A.

[32] Reg. § 1.402(b)-1(a)(1).

A "substantial risk of forfeiture" exists when rights in property transferred are conditioned, directly or indirectly, upon the future performance (or refraining from performance) of substantial services by any person, or the occurrence of a condition related to a purpose of the transfer, and the possibility of forfeiture is substantial if the condition is not satisfied.[33]

Example 52: Valley Sales establishes a trust in Sept. 2015 for the benefit of children of employees. The trust instrument provides that any child of the employee enrolled full-time at a college or university will receive an annual cash grant of $10,000 at the end of each academic year in which the student completes a year of study in good academic standing. John Chambers, an employee, has a child enrolled in college for the 2015–2016 academic year. John is not subject to tax on the grant in 2015 because there is a substantial risk of forfeiture.

.09 Unfunded Deferred Compensation Plans

Recipients of unfunded deferred compensation plans in essence have only the written contract or agreement that promises future payment as evidence of the intent to pay the compensation The employer cannot sign a note payable to the employee because that would constitute funding under the cash equivalency rule.

Amounts contributed to unfunded plans are not taxed to the employee until distributed to the employee. The employer also receives a deduction at that time. Although the plan is not funded, the employer can record the deferred liability on the books; appropriate retained earnings for that purpose; and even set up a special bank account out of which to pay the compensation. None of those actions cause the plan to be treated as funded.

 Planning Pointer: Deferred compensation plans that provide forfeitable benefits not only achieve income deferral for the employee but also can motivate the employee to continue in employment with the firm or to achieve certain predetermined management goals (e.g., increases in revenue or earnings per share). Because forfeitable plans can be funded, this can remove anxiety and uncertainty on the part of the employee. Unfunded plans, on the other hand, need not have any restrictions or forfeitures in order to defer taxation. The downside of unfunded plans from the perspective of the employee is that the employee may not be able to collect any of the deferred compensation if the company experiences financial difficulties.

 Spotlight: The risk of an unfunded deferred compensation plan not paying off is more than just academic. In 2010 Forbes Magazine reported that when the Texas Rangers baseball team went into bankruptcy its largest unsecured creditor was baseball player Alex Rodriguez. A-Rod was owed $24.9 million in deferred compensation. Can you think of a funded plan with a substantial loss of forfeiture that would have protected A-Rod?

.10 Restricted Property Plans

Unless an employee elects otherwise, the FMV of restricted property is included in the gross income of the employee during the first tax year in which the rights of the employee become substantially vested.[34] Property is substantially vested when it is either transferable or not subject to a substantial risk of forfeiture.[35] A substantial risk of forfeiture exists if the person's rights to full enjoyment of the property depend on the future performance of substantial services.[36] A require-

---

[33] Reg. § 1.83-3(c)(1).
[34] Code Sec. 83(a); Reg. § 1.83-1(a)(1).

[35] Reg. § 1.83-3(b).
[36] Code Sec. 83(c)(1).

ment that property be returned if the employee is discharged for cause is not a substantial risk of forfeiture.[37]

A requirement that property be returned to the employer if the employee accepts a job with a competing firm will not ordinarily be considered a substantial risk of forfeiture unless the particular facts and circumstances indicate to the contrary. Factors that may be taken into account in determining whether a covenant not to compete constitutes a substantial risk of forfeiture are the age of the employee, the availability of alternative employment opportunities, the likelihood of the employee obtaining such other employment, the degree of skill possessed by the employee, the employee's health, and the practice (if any) of the employer to enforce such covenants.

Example 53: On December 10, 2015 Macro-hard, Ltd., transfers 10,000 shares of its stock to William Fence, an employee of the corporation. At the time of transfer the stock is selling for $50 per share. The terms of the transfer provide that if Fence leaves the company for any reason for three years, he is required to relinquish the stock to Macro-hard. Because William must perform substantial services to the company before the restriction is lifted, the restricted stock is subject to a substantial risk of forfeiture.

An individual who performs services may elect to include in gross income, for the tax year in which restricted property is received, the excess of the FMV of the property over the cost (if any) of the property.[38] If this election is made and the property is later forfeited, *no* deduction is permitted.

Example 54: Assume in the previous example that William lacks confidence in both the company's prospects and in the likelihood that he will stay the required three years. Therefore, William forgoes the election. By December 2018, when the restrictions have been lifted, the stock has risen to $60 per share. Therefore, William reports compensation income of $600,000 ($60 × 10,000). Macro-hard takes a deduction for $600,000 during its year-end encompassing December 2018.

Example 55: Assume the same facts as in the preceding example except that William is very bullish on the company's prospects and has no intention of leaving the company. Therefore, he elects to report compensation income in 2015, the year of the stock grant. William reports $500,000 of compensation income ($50 × 10,000), and Macro-hard takes a deduction for the same amount. However, assume the stock has risen in value to $110 per share by December 2018 when the restrictions are lifted. William now has stock with an income tax basis of $500,000, but with a FMV of $1,100,000 ($110 × 10,000).

 Planning Pointer: The decision to make an election should not be taken lightly. The reward for making the election is reduced recognizable income if the property appreciates rapidly after the transfer but before the restrictions are lifted. The recipient of the restricted property would also need the financial resources to pay the tax. The risks are twofold:

1. The income must be reported early. Unless the property appreciates rapidly, the time value of money works against the taxpayer; and

2. If the property is forfeited, the taxpayer has reported taxable income without receiving anything of value.

.11 Utilizing Retirement Plans for Employees and Employee/Owners

Tax law regarding retirement plans is among the more detailed and complicated aspects of federal income tax. Detailed coverage of retirement plans is beyond the scope of this book.

---

[37] Reg. § 1.83-3(c)(2).   [38] Code Sec. 83(b).

However, because retirement planning is an integral part of business tax planning, some basic aspects of retirement plans will be discussed.

Employers have a variety of retirement plans from which to choose: pension, profit-sharing, stock bonus plans, and other qualified deferred arrangements (Code Sec. 401), employee annuities (Code Sec. 403), and individual retirement arrangements, including simplified employee pensions (Code Sec. 408). Providing a retirement plan for employees acts as an incentive for employees to stay with the employer.

.12 The Two Basic Types of Plans

Retirement plans fall into one of two categories, "defined benefit plans" and "defined contribution plans." Defined benefit plans (traditional pensions) provide a specified benefit to employees, usually based on a combination of their salary and their number of years in service. The required contribution to defined benefit plans depends on actuarial assumptions about a number of factors, including estimated earnings of the plan and the life expectancy of the employees.

Example 56: Wilbur Watson, an assembly worker in an auto parts plant, is covered by a defined benefit plan. The terms of the plan call for Wilbur, after reaching age 60 and 30 years of service, to retire at a pay equal to 60 percent of his highest wages. The amount that his employer needs to contribute to the plan each year will depend on a number of actuarial variables.

Defined contribution plans (e.g., employee annuities; profit-sharing plans) call for a specified contribution. The amount that an employee eventually receives depends on how well those contributions are invested.

Example 57: Cyndie Brueler is an employee of Mega State University. Mega State contributes eight percent of Cyndie's salary to a 403(b) annuity. An additional four percent is withheld from Cyndie's salary.

 Spotlight: The number of employees covered by defined benefit plans (traditional pensions) has been shrinking. Most of the workers still covered by defined benefit plans are union workers. Another trend is the freezing of plans (i.e., current workers do not accumulate additional benefits, and new employees are not covered, but instead may be enrolled in a defined contribution plan). Who bears the risk when employees are shifted from defined benefit plans to defined contribution plans? Why?

.13 Qualified Plans

Plans that are "qualified" have several advantages: employer contributions are not currently taxed to the employee, the employer is entitled to a deduction for contributions, the plans are funded, and the plan itself is exempt from taxation (therefore, the earnings are not taxed until made available to the employee). However, plans must meet strict criteria to be qualified. An overall objective of the requirements is to prevent plans from disproportionately benefiting highly-paid employees. The major requirements are:

- Minimum coverage rules (the plan must not discriminate in favor of highly compensated employees);

- Minimum participation rules (generally at least 40 percent of eligible employees must participate);

- Minimum vesting rules. Employees must have an irrevocable right to the benefits after certain time periods have passed;

- Distribution requirements. Distributions must begin by no later than April 1 of the calendar year following the year in which the employee becomes 70½ years of age, or the calendar year in which the employee retires, if that is later; and

- Funding requirements. Failure to properly fund a retirement plan may subject the employer to interest, an excise tax, or possible civil action. The actual funding requirements depend on the type of plan.

.14 Profit-Sharing and Stock Bonus Plans

Profit-sharing plans permit employees to share profits earned by the company. Payments made to the designated trustee of the plan may be made from either current or accumulated profits. Allocations are often based on salary. It is also typical to give some weight to length of service. Forfeitures may be used to decrease the employer's contribution, but more typically are allocated to the remaining employees.

Employees may make voluntary contributions to the plan. The plan may also provide for a choice between receiving an amount in cash (taxed currently as compensation), or having it contributed to the profit-sharing plan (deferring tax).

Advantages of profit-sharing plans. The main advantage of a profit-sharing plan is the flexibility afforded the employer contributions. Because there is no requirement to contribute a fixed amount, contributions may be reduced or eliminated in loss or low-profit years. From the viewpoint of the employee, forfeiture allocations can provide a substantial benefit to an employee who remains with the company over a long term, especially if there is high turnover.

Stock bonus plans. Stock bonus plans are similar to profit-sharing plans except that the contributions are not necessarily dependent on profits (although they could be). Another obvious difference is that the benefits are distributable in stock of the employer company rather than in cash.

.15 Employee Stock Ownership Plans

An employee stock ownership plan (ESOP) is a defined contribution plan that is designed to invest primarily in employer securities. ESOPs can be very advantageous to both employers and employees:

1. The employer may contribute its own stock and take a deduction based on the FMV of the stock at the time of contribution. Because the company incurs no out of pocket cost in contributing its own stock, a tax deduction is created without any outward cash flow.

2. The corporation may take a deduction for certain dividends paid to the ESOP on shares held by it.[39] Generally, to be deductible, the dividends must either be distributed to the employee participants or must be used to make payments on loans used by the ESOP to buy employer securities. If certain criteria are met, C corporations may deduct, at the election of the plan participants or their beneficiaries, dividends paid to an ESOP that are reinvested in the employer's stock.

3. Shareholders may sell stock to an ESOP and elect to defer their gain on the sale by acquiring qualified replacement property within a certain time period. Qualified replacement property is generally any security issued by a domestic operating corporation except for securities of the company whose stock is being sold. Several additional requirements must be met to qualify for this deferral of gain.[40]

Example 58: After consulting with retirement plan specialists, Valley Equipment, a small manufacturing company, set up an ESOP and contributed stock with a FMV of $300,000 to the plan. The resulting income tax deduction saved the company approximately $100,000 in federal and state income taxes. The company used the $100,000 savings

---

[39] *See* Code Sec. 404(k).   [40] *See* Code Sec. 1042.

to fund employee 401(k) plans. The result was a considerable increase in employee satisfaction at no out-of pocket cost to Valley Equipment.

.16 Deferred Arrangements—401(k) Plans

A 401(k) plan is a qualified cash or deferred compensation arrangement included in a profit-sharing or stock bonus plan.[41] Participants in 401(k) plans may choose either to receive compensation in the form of cash or to defer receipt of compensation.

The employer may make annual contributions in the form of a bonus. More commonly, the arrangement may involve a salary reduction. In either case, the employee in effect agrees to defer a portion of his or her compensation and to have it contributed to the plan by the employer. Employers often match a specified percentage of an employee's contributions.

The amount of compensation deferred is not currently taxed as income to the employee, and the employer receives a deduction for the same amount. Although contributions are not subject to income taxation, they are subject to FICA taxes.[42]

Annual limits. The limit on the amount of elective contributions that may be made to an employee's account in 2015 is $18,000. An additional $6,000 can be contributed as catch-up for employees over age 50. The limit on total contributions (elective deferral plus additional contributions made by the employer) is limited in 2015 to the lesser of the employee's compensation or $53,000, and is reduced by contributions to other qualified plans.

Advantages of 401(k) plans. 401(k) plans give employees flexibility to decide (within the annual limits) between current cash payments and retirement savings. Although certain other plans also offer some flexibility, qualified money purchase plans and defined benefit plans are much more rigid with respect to the trade-off between current and deferred compensation.

Distributions from 401(k) plans. Funds may not be withdrawn from 401(k) plans unless one of the following applies:[43]

- The employee reaches age 59½;
- The employee becomes permanently disabled;
- The employee no longer works for the employer sponsoring the plan;
- The individual is the beneficiary of a deceased employee;
- The employee is eligible for a qualified reservist distribution;
- The plan is terminated; or
- The employee can demonstrate financial hardship to the IRS.

SIMPLE IRA plans. Qualifying small employers are eligible to offer this plan. To qualify, the employer must have no more than 100 employers earning $5,000 or more in compensation. The SIMPLE IRA is a combination of elective salary reduction contributions by the employee and employer contributions. The employer must make matching contributions or fixed contributions.[44] The maximum that an employee can defer is $12,500 in 2015.

¶ 1503 Income Tax Planning Implications of Disposal of a Closely Held Business

In this discussion, the term "disposal" is used in its broadest sense. Thus, sales, liquidations, gifts, and transfers at death will be considered disposals of the business interests. The disposal of business interests in sole proprietorships, partnerships, and corporations will all be examined for their tax planning implications.

---

[41] Code Sec. 401(k)(1).
[42] Code Sec. 3121(v).

[43] Reg. § 1.401(k)-1(d).
[44] Code Sec. 408(p).

.01 Disposal of a Sole Proprietorship

For tax purposes the disposal of a sole proprietorship is not considered to be the disposal of the business as a whole, but rather as the disposition of the individual assets (both tangible and intangible), making up the business. If disposal is through a sale or taxable exchange to nonrelatives, the primary considerations are the advisability of a sale or exchange and, assuming a sale or exchange is advisable, the timing and characteristics of the income recognition. If the assets of the business have appreciated considerably, advisability of the sale or exchange may hinge in part on the loss of the stepped-up basis[45] feature of transfers at death.

Example 59: Robert Fletcher's ranch, operated as a sole proprietorship, has assets with a basis of $600,000 but a FMV of $2,000,000. Having a terminal illness, he decides to sell the ranch. Ten months later Robert dies. If Robert had retained the ranch, its basis to the heirs upon his death would have been stepped-up to its FMV. Thus, the income tax on the $1,400,000 of gain could have been avoided (the heirs could sell the ranch and recognize little or no gain.

On the other hand, nontax reasons may outweigh the advantage of a stepped-up basis. This may be especially true if a good part of the value of the business consists of intangible assets such as goodwill.

Example 60: Kevin Crumb owns a sole proprietorship with assets having a basis of $1,000,000 and a FMV of $1,800,000. Crumb is known to his customers as an extremely honest, efficient, and competent businessman. Of the total value of his business, approximately $500,000 is attributable to goodwill. His accountant estimates that the total federal and state income taxes from sale of the business would amount to approximately $320,000. Kevin dies suddenly intestate (without a will). His estate drags on for some time and the business, rudderless without him, quickly deteriorates. By the time the administrator is able to sell the business, the goodwill has evaporated and the purchaser is even able to knock down the price of the tangible assets from $1,300,000 to $1,100,000. Although a sale before death would have cost $320,000 in income taxes, this is dwarfed by the $700,000 loss in value of the business (the $500,000 of goodwill and the $200,000 loss of the tangible assets).

If a sale is considered advisable, the timing and recognition of the income (the gains) have tax planning implications. The sale or taxable exchange of the business will likely push the seller into a higher tax bracket. Regular income tax, but perhaps not the AMT, can be reduced by making an installment sale.

Changing the characteristics of income, if possible, is important because long-term capital gains are given preferential treatment. The characteristics of gains from the sale of a sole proprietorship can sometimes be altered through the timing of the sale and through contract allocations.

The sale should be timed to ensure that highly appreciated tangible assets have met the required holding period so as to qualify for Code Sec. 1231 (and ultimately, capital gain) treatment. Contract allocations of the sales price of the individual assets may be disregarded by the IRS if deemed unrealistic. Both parties to the sale are required to sign Form 8594, *Asset Acquisition Statement Under Section 1060* (which details the allocation of the sales price).[46]

Generally, it is to the seller's favor to allocate a maximum to such intangibles as goodwill, patents, leaseholds, franchises, trademarks, and trade names because capital gain treatment will usually result from such allocations. The value assigned to a covenant not to compete must be reported as ordinary income. High allocations to such ordinary income assets as receivables, inventory, and prepaid expenses should be avoided. With respect to fixed assets, land and buildings

---

[45] The basis of most assets transferred at death is stepped up (or down to FMV at date of death. (See Code Sec. 1014).

[46] Code Sec. 1060(b); Reg. § 1.1060-1(e)(1)(ii).

should carry a high value. However, high allocations to depreciable personal property will result in ordinary income to the extent of potential depreciation recapture.

Buyers have different objectives. Buyers want to be able to write off (depreciate or amortize) assets as soon as possible. Thus, buyers prefer that tangible personal property such as machinery and equipment be assigned a high value because of their short MACRS recovery period. Next the buyer will likely want to assign a high value to the intangibles in the business that qualify as Code Sec. 197 intangibles because the buyer can amortize those intangibles over a 15-year life.[47] Commercial buildings on the other hand have a 39-year life, and land is not depreciable. Hence the buyer will not be interested in assigning a high value to those assets. Appraisals should be obtained for tangible property to help support contract allocations.

Example 61: George Wilson operates Wilson's Machine Shop. Midwest Custom, Inc. offers to buy George's business. The basis and FMV of the machine shop assets as determined by appraisals and negotiation by the two parties are:

Asset	Basis	FMV	Type of Gain (Loss)
Receivables	$40,000	$37,000	($3,000) Ordinary
Prepaid expenses and supplies	$25,000	$21,000	($4,000) Ordinary
Machinery & Equipment	$200,000	$280,000	$80,000 Ordinary
Covenant not to compete	-0-	$75,000	$75,000 Ordinary
Goodwill	-0-	$200,000	$200,000 (LTCG)
Building	$300,000	$360,000	$60,000 (Code Sec. 1231)
Land	$70,000	$110,000	$40,000 (Code Sec. 1231).

George would receive $73,000 of ordinary income, $200,000 of LTCG, and $100,000 of Code Sec. 1231 gains, which, assuming he has no unrecaptured Code Sec. 1231 losses, would be treated as additional LTCG. Note that if more of the contract price is assigned to goodwill and less to the covenant not to compete, George will have more LTCG and less ordinary income (thus better off), but the buyer will be equally well off (both intangible are amortizable over 15 years). If more of the contract price is assigned to the building and less to the land, George will be equally well off, but the buyer will be able to take a larger depreciation deduction.

.02 Disposal of a Partnership Interest

Partnerships are more likely to have management that can preserve the value of the business after the death of a partner. In addition, partnerships may have existing agreements to purchase the interest of a decedent. Thus the drawbacks of a transfer at death may be less than might occur in a sole proprietorship. A partnership interest is a capital asset. However, when a partnership interest is sold or liquidated, the gain to the partner will be ordinary income to the extent of the partner's share of certain partnership assets. If a partnership interest is liquidated and the liquidating distribution is in the form of property, the partner may have some flexibility in the timing and reporting of income from the liquidating proceeds.[48]

.03 Disposal of an Interest in a Corporation

The ease of transferability of stock somewhat enhances the advisability of transferring appreciated stock at death rather than during the owner's lifetime. However, the value of any closely held business, regardless of the entity, will be decreased to some extent by the death of the principal owner/manager. If the focus is solely on the shareholder, the form of disposal (selling the stock,

---

[47] See ¶ 708 and ¶ 709 for a discussion of Code Sec. 197 intangibles and other intangibles.

[48] As is noted in Chapter 13, liquidating distributions and sales of partnership interests involve complex tax laws that are beyond the scope of the introductory chapter on partnerships in the text.

taking an in-kind liquidation, or having the corporation sell the assets) has no effect on the characteristics of income to the shareholder (in all three instances the shareholder will have capital gain). Such analysis however, ignores the double tax that may result. Selling the stock will not trigger the double tax. An in-kind liquidation or sale of the assets will generate the double tax if the entity is a C corporation. Of course buyers may prefer to purchase the assets instead of the stock, thus avoiding any hidden or contingent liabilities.

Some flexibility with respect to the timing of the income may be possible. Stock can be sold on a piecemeal basis (probably only feasible if the sale is to a relative), or on the installment method. Liquidating proceeds can be distributed in installments, thus taking advantage of the cost recovery benefit rule governing installment proceeds.

Example 62: Mary Landis owns 80 percent of Landis, Inc. Her two sons own the other 20 percent. Mary's 80 percent interest has a basis of $300,000, but a FMV of $700,000. In 2015 Mary agrees to sell her stock on the installment basis, with four equal yearly payments of $175,000, plus interest. By doing so, Mary defers income and possibly avoids the 3.8 percent tax on investment income.

¶ 1504 Summary

This discussion of tax planning has included basic tax planning tactics, such as avoiding the recognition of income and deferring tax by deferring income or accelerating deductions. Also discussed are planning issues surrounding the selection of tax entities, accounting methods, and the selection of tax years.

There are various methods for converting ordinary income into capital gains to obtain preferential tax rates. Marginal rates can be lowered by smoothing income from year to year and by spreading income among family members.

Employee compensation requires tax planning. Retirement plans are important in planning for businesses. Family tax planning for the disposal of closely held businesses is a crucial consideration for any business from both a tax planning perspective as well as overall business succession issues.

GLOSSARY OF TERMS INTRODUCED IN THE CHAPTER

Avoiding the recognition of income. Structuring or converting transactions so that the income realized from the transaction is not recognized for the year of the transaction.

Deferring tax by accelerating deductions. Structuring transactions so that the expense or loss deduction falls into an earlier tax year than it otherwise would.

Deferring tax by deferring income. Structuring transactions to defer the reporting of income for one or more tax years.

Double exempt bonds. State or local bonds that are exempt from federal and state taxation to residents of that state.

Kiddie tax. A tax imposed at the parents' rates on children under the age of 18 or under age 24 in college.

Smoothing income. Arranging the recognition of income and expenses so as to, as much as possible, equalize marginal income tax rates from year to year.

Tax planning. Structuring financial transactions to maximize the taxpayer's after-tax wealth.

CHAPTER PROBLEMS

Chapter 15 Discussion Questions

1. What is the objective of tax planning?

2. Which of the basic tax planning tactics is achieved by investing in tax-exempt securities?

3. How is the time value of money concept related to deferring income and accelerating deductions?

4. Which type of taxpayer, cash or accrual, has the most potential to accelerate expense deductions? Why?

5. Which type of entity has the most potential for deductible losses to flow through to the owners? The least potential?

6. Which type of entity provides the most tax benefit to employees from the use of fringe benefits?

7. Name a drawback of the cash basis method.

8. If the U.S. were to experience deflation, which inventory method, LIFO or FIFO would result in the least taxable income? Assume the quantity of inventory is increasing from year to year.

9. Which type of entity has the most flexibility for the selection of a tax year?

10. Is the maximum utilization of the preferential rate for long-term capital gains maximized when existing long-term capital gains are offset by capital losses? Explain.

11. If a taxpayer already has long-term capital losses, should he or she sell long-term or short-term capital gain property to offset the capital losses? Assume capital losses exceed the $3,000 yearly limit.

12. What is the objective of income smoothing?

13. How does spreading income among family members lower marginal tax rates?

14. Why is paying a salary to dependent children generally a better family tax planning strategy than gifting income producing securities?

15. At what age is a child of the taxpayer not subject to the "kiddie tax?" Does it matter if the child is in college?

16. What two requirements must be met for meals and lodging to be excluded from an employee's income?

17. Under what circumstances can the value of a company car furnished to an employee be excluded from income?

18. Edgar Employee exercised an incentive stock option in 2014. He sold the stock in 2015 before meeting the required holding period for incentive stock options. What are his tax consequences? His employer's tax consequences?

19. What AMT trap exists for employees who exercise incentive stock options? Explain.

20. Rebecca Withers was granted a nonqualified stock option in 2014 to acquire 1,000 shares of stock for $20 per share. The options had a readily determinable value of $30 per share at the time of grant. She exercised the options in 2015 when the stock was selling for $36 per share. What are her tax consequences (if any) in 2014? 2015?

21. What election is available to recipients of restricted property? What are the potential risks and rewards of making such an election?

22. Explain the difference between defined benefit and defined contribution plans.

23. List benefits of an ESOP.

24. Does the owner of a sole proprietorship get capital gain treatment on the sale of the business? Explain.

25. The owners of a corporation may prefer to sell their stock rather than the assets of the business. However, a prospective purchaser may prefer to acquire the assets. Explain the viewpoint of each.

Chapter 15 Problems

1. Terrance Silva is the sole owner of a corporation that uses the cash-basis method of accounting. Terrance usually receives a $20,000 bonus in December from the corporation. However, Terrance is already in the 35% bracket and anticipates that his marginal tax bracket will drop to 33% next year, even if he defers receiving the bonus until January. Terrance believes he can invest any tax savings to get a 6% return. How much in total will Terrance gain if he defers the bonus until January?

2. Three brothers, all of whom live in different states, all have the opportunity to purchase double exempt municipal bonds.

Brother	Federal tax rate	Bond Yield	State Tax rate
Don	.28	3.5%	4%
Ethan	.33	3.0%	9%
Fred	.35	3.25%	6%

Determine what yield each would need in a corporate bond to be equivalent to the double exempts. If they do invest in the double exempts, which of the basic tax planning strategies are they utilizing?

3. Two retired executives, Alan Affluent and Wilbur Wealth, are considering stock investments. They each have provisional income sufficiently high that each additional dollar of income (up to $5,000) will result in 50% of their social security benefits being included in income. Alan plans to buy public utility stock which he anticipates will return $4,000 in dividends and $1,000 in capital gains. Wilbur wants to purchase stock in a tech company that will pay only $1,000 in dividends but for which he expects to have an unrealized gain on stock appreciation of $4,000. Which retiree is engaged in the better tax planning? Support your answer.

4. Helen Whitman currently is in the 29% (combined federal and state) tax bracket. She can defer the tax on $20,000 of income for two years. However, she expects to be in the 33% bracket two years from now. Determine the pre-tax interest and post-tax yield she would need for the deferral aspect to outweigh the higher tax rate if she chooses to defer recognition of the income.

5. Provide three examples of ways for taxpayers to defer tax by accelerating deductions.

6. Bao Wang and her brother Chen plan to open a software company and wonder which form of entity they should select.

   a. Which form of entity should they *not* select if being able to immediately benefit from operating losses is the most important consideration?

   b. Which form of entity should they select if being able to pay themselves in fringe benefits is the most important consideration?

   c. Which form of entity should they select if flexibility with respect to division of profits and losses is the most important consideration?

7. Name three drawbacks of the LIFO inventory method.

8. Timberline Company owned timber with an adjusted basis of $260,000 that on January 1, 2015 had a FMV of $400,000. By March 10, when they harvest the timber, its value had risen to $450,000. They elect to treat the cutting of the timber as a Code Sec. 1231 transaction. They sell the timber on July 7 for $445,000. What is their total gain on the sale of the timber? How much of the gain (if any) is Code Sec. 1231 gain? Ordinary income? Capital gain?

9. Mountain Realty redeems 800 shares of stock owned by Roger Wilder. The corporation has E & P of $800,000. Immediately before the redemption, Roger owned 1,000 shares with an adjusted basis of $200,000. Mountain Realty pays Roger $500,000 for the 800 shares redeemed.

   a. Assuming the redemption is treated as disproportionate, how much gain does Roger have from the redemption? What kind of gain?

   b. Assuming the redemption does not qualify as disproportionate, how much gain does Roger have from the redemption? What kind of gain?

   c. What is the answer to question b. if the corporation has zero E & P?

10. In November 2015 Ivan Investor realized a long-term capital loss of $40,000 on the sale of stock. He has no other realized gains or losses in 2015. Ivan has an unrealized gain of $40,000 on stock in Fast Boom, Inc., which he has owned for two months. He also has unrealized gain of $40,000 on stock in Zeon Oil, which he has held for two years. Should he in 2015:

   a. Sell the Fast Boom stock;

   b. Sell the Zeon Oil stock; or

   c. Leave the $40,000 capital loss standing alone.

Explain your answer.

11. In June 2015 Sam Speculate realized a short-term capital gain of $50,000 on the sale of stock. He has no other realized gains or losses in 2015. Sam has $45,000 of unrealized short-term capital losses on stock A and $48,000 of unrealized long-term capital losses on stock B. Should he in 2015:

   a. Sell stock A;

   b. Sell stock B; or

   c. Leave the $50,000 short-term capital gain standing along.

Explain your answer.

12. E.N. Vestor has, as of December 2015, $3,000 of long-term capital losses. E.N. also has a stock in Z Co. held 9 months on which he has an unrealized gain of $5,000. Should he, in December 2015:

   a. Sell enough stock to offset the capital loss;

   b. Sell all of the stock in Z Co.; or

   c. Leave the capital loss standing alone.

Explain your answer.

13. Adolopho Perez estimated his taxable income toward the end of 2015 and learned that he was $30,000 below the beginning of the 33% bracket, making his highest marginal rate 28%. He expects that his 2016 income will place him about $50,000 above the beginning of the 35% bracket. He could accelerate to 2015 a $25,000 bonus normally paid to him in 2016.

   a. Assuming Adolopho can invest any tax deferred and earn a 8% pre-tax return, determine whether or not he should accelerate receiving the bonus.

   b. Assuming Adolopho can earn only a 3% pre-tax return, determine whether or not he should accelerate receiving the bonus.

Show your computations.

14. Karim Busiri has three children, all dependents: Chione, age 24 and a full-time college student with no earned income; Edfu, age 17; and Fenuku, age 11. Karim is in the 35% tax bracket. At the beginning of 2015, Karim transfers taxable bonds to the three children, resulting in interest income to: Chione, $8,000; Edfu, $1,000; and Fenuku, $1,000. He also paid Edfu $5,000 for work done in connection with rental properties that Karim owns.

    a. Determine how much income tax Karim and his family saved as a result of the above transactions.

    b. Would you have recommended additional transfers of bonds? If so, to whom, and how much?

15. Assume the same facts as problem 14.

    a. How much would Karim and family have saved if Chione were age 23 at the end of 2015?

    b. How would you have changed the transfer of bonds, still assuming Chione was only age 23 at the end of 2015.

16. Randy Stiller owns three successful businesses: a chain of four auto parts stores; a software company, and a consulting engineering firm. All three businesses are organized as one-person LLCs (permitted in his state). Randy is in the highest marginal tax bracket and is considering transferring an interest in the businesses to his two adult children, both of whom are in the 15% bracket and do not work in the businesses. Give your opinion as to which (if any) of the businesses are good vehicles in which to transfer a partnership (LLC) interest. Explain your answer.

17. List five fringe benefits that are not miscellaneous fringes.

18. John and Martha Miller are the owners of the Aspen Ridge ranch. They are considering transferring ownership of the ranch house, the machinery, and the livestock to a corporation owned by them and their family. The ranch land, including all the ranch building except for the ranch house, would continue to be owned by John and Martha.

    a. What type of corporation (C or S) would you recommend if fringe benefits are a major consideration? Why?

    b. In order to exclude meals and lodging, will John and Martha need to live on the premises? What about their two ranch hands?

    c. John and Mary would like the corporation to provide health insurance coverage for them, as employees of the corporation. Can they exclude their two full-time ranch hands from the health insurance coverage?

19. I.M. Worker was granted an incentive stock option on April 10, 2013 to purchase 500 shares of stock at the option price of $60 per share, the FMV at the time of the grant. I.M exercised the option on May 1, 2014, at which time the FMV was $75 per share. I.M. sold the stock on June 10, 2015 for $100 per share.

Determine the AMT adjustments (if any) and the income recognized (if any) for the years 2013–2015.

20. Jeans R Us is a successful clothing chain, organized as a C corporation. The corporation is considering offering both incentive and nonqualified stock options.

What are the pros and cons of each type of stock option? Which do you believe would be a better choice for mid-level management? For top executives?

21. In 2011 the Diamond Corp. transferred 5,000 shares of restricted stock to Tom, one of its vice presidents, and 5,000 shares of restricted stock to Harry, another vice president. At the time of the transfers, the stock was selling for $20 per share. The terms of the transfer provide that if either Tom or Harry leaves the company for any reason during the next two years, they must relinquish the stock to the company. Tom elects to include the value of the stock in his gross income for 2011. Harry forgoes the election. In 2013 both fulfill the restrictions, at which time the stock is selling for $24 per share. In 2015 both sell the stock for $40 per share. Determine the amount of income (if any) that Tom and Harry have in 2011, 2013, and 2015.

22. In 2014 River Road Corp. purchased stock on the open market for $70 per share and held the stock as treasury stock. In 2015 the corporation contributed the stock to an ESOP that it

set up. At that time the FMV of the stock was $90. Determine how much, if any, River Road Corp. may deduct for its contribution of the stock to the ESOP.

23. a. List five requirements that must be met for a retirement plan to be qualified.

b. Which of the five requirements are most designed to prevent plans from being "top heavy?"

c. Which requirement(s) provides protection from employees losing their benefits if they leave the company?

24. Knotty Pines, Inc. has three employees, all of whom participate in the company's 401(k) plan. In 2015 Allan, age 33, earned $40,000; Bob age 53, earned $46,000, and Carl, age 62, earned $55,000. Alan also had $8,000 contributions made on his behalf by another employer. Determine how much each employee can elect to defer, and how much in total can be deferred (employee contributions plus employer contributions).

25. a. What kind of gain(s) or loss(es) does the owner of a sole proprietorship have upon the sale of the business?

b. What kind of gain(s) or loss(es) does a partner in a partnership have upon the sale of the partnership interest assuming:

   i. The partnership has only capital assets; or

   ii. The partnership has a mix of ordinary income assets and capital assets.

c. What kind of gain(s) or loss(es) does a corporate shareholder have upon the sale of stock representing a 100% ownership in the corporation assuming:

   i. The corporation has only capital assets; or

   ii. The corporation has a mix of ordinary income assets and capital assets.

Chapter 15 Review Problems

1. Roger Kolters is the owner of Midwest Manufacturing, a sole proprietorship. The FMV and adjusted basis of the assets in the business are as follows:

Asset	FMV	Basis
Receivables	$100,000	$108,000
Prepaid expenses & supplies	$80,000	$85,000
Equipment	$300,000	$120,000
Covenant not to compete	$50,000	$ -0-
Goodwill	$150,000	$ -0-
Building	$500,000	$410,000
Land	$130,000	$70,000
Total	$1,310,000	$793,000

Assume that Roger contracts to sell the business for $1,310,000, prior to the sale uses cash in the business to pay off all liabilities, and that the sales contracts allocates the value to each asset as show above.

a. Determine the type of gains and losses Roger has from the sale of the business.

b. How would you change the allocation of the sales price among the various assets to obtain more favorable tax treatment for Roger?

c. How would you change the allocation of the sales price among the various assets to obtain more favorable tax treatment for the purchaser?

Chapter 15 Research Question

Hector Avilas, a new client, is a cash basis farmer in California. He comes to you for advice on two issues:

1. Hector markets walnuts through a cooperative. In Oct. 2015 he delivered walnuts to the cooperative with the understanding that they would hedge the crop and then pay him the going market rate established on November 1, an amount that would have given him $200,000. The cooperative, however, was unable to effect a hedging strategy until November 8, at which time the walnuts were worth only $150,000. In an attempt to settle the controversy, the cooperative on December 15 cut a check to Hector for $155,000. However, Hector refuses to cash the check because he is afraid that to do would damage his ability to collect more from the cooperative. Hector asks you whether he has to report the $150,000 as income in 2015.

2. Hector also delivered $90,000 of soybeans to the local elevator. Although the elevator customarily pays the customer upon delivery, Hector requested that it not cut a check to him until January 3. Hector asks you whether he has to report the $90,000 as income in 2015.

Research aids: Reg. § 1.451-2; *C.A. Miller*, TC Summary Opinion 2002-94; and *Mary J. Hineman, Executrix of the Estate of J. A. Hineman*, 51-2 USTC ¶ 9403, 99 FSupp 582.

PART VI:
U.S. Taxation of International Transactions

Chapter 16   Taxation of International Transactions

CHAPTER 16

Taxation of International Transactions

LEARNING OBJECTIVES

1. Describe the difference between the U.S. system of worldwide taxation and a territorial system.

2. Know who is taxed on "inbound" and "outbound" transactions.

3. Have a working knowledge of "income effectively connected with a U.S. trade or business" as well as "FDAP" income.

4. Know about the four ways that double taxation of outbound transactions is mitigated.

5. Be aware of the rules that establish residency both inside and outside the United States.

6. Be able to distinguish between U.S. source and foreign source income.

7. Know what types of income received by nonresident aliens and foreign corporations is subject to the flat 30-percent rate.

¶ 1600 Introduction

The United States taxes its citizens, residents, and domestic corporations on their worldwide income (this is referred to as a "residential system of taxation"). However, most countries tax only income received from a source within the country (a "territorial system of taxation"). Some observers believe that our worldwide system of taxation is outmoded in this modern world of many international transactions. However, proposals to change to a territorial system have been rejected.

Obviously, income earned or received in the United States by a U.S. citizen or resident is subject to tax. However, the taxation of cross-border transactions depends on whether the transaction is an "inbound" or an "outbound transaction."

¶ 1601 Inbound Transactions

The term "**inbound transactions**" refers to transactions by non-U.S. persons (i.e., nonresident aliens, foreign corporations, and foreign pass-through entities) within the United States. Because these entities are not citizens or residents of the United States, they are not subject to U.S. tax on their worldwide income.

To the extent that non-U.S. persons have income derived from the United States, they may be subject to U.S. tax. For example, Honda Corporation exports autos to the United States and also has auto factories in the United States. Its executives may work in the United States but may never become U.S. residents. Because they have engaged in inbound transactions, both the Honda Corporation and its foreign workers present in the United States are subject to U.S. taxation.

To be subject to U.S. tax, foreign persons and foreign corporations must have sufficient "nexus" with the United States. In general usage, the word "nexus" means a connection, tie, or link.[1] In tax law, the term delineates the minimum amount of presence that a person or entity must have before that person or entity becomes subject to taxation.

The objectives of *subjecting* inbound transactions to taxation and *enforcement and collection* of taxes on those transactions are different for foreign persons than for U.S. persons. Therefore, the taxation rules also differ, especially with respect to tax rates and withholding requirements, as discussed later in this chapter.

 Spotlight: A considerable portion of income derived from inbound transactions is subject to withholding at the source. Why do you think this is so, and what objectives of the Treasury are fulfilled by withholding at the source? Are there comparable rules (with comparable objectives) anywhere in the taxation of U.S. source income earned by U.S. citizens or residents?

¶ 1602 Income Effectively Connected with a U.S. Trade or Business

Income that is **effectively connected** with the conduct of a trade or business is taxed to nonresident aliens and foreign corporations at the regular U.S. tax rates.[2] Because other income received from U.S. sources is taxed much differently, it is important to be able to determine whether income is effectively connected.

Two tests are applied to determine whether gains, profits, income and certain other gains are effectively connected: the **Asset-Use Test** and the **Business Activities Test**. However, the following items of income, gain, or loss from sources outside the United States will nonetheless be treated as effectively connected with the conduct of a trade or business within the United States if the

---

[1] *Webster's New 20th Century Dictionary*, Unabridged, 2nd ed., p. 1210.   [2] Code Sec. 871(b).

foreign corporation or nonresident alien has an office or other fixed place of business in the United States to which the item is attributable (i.e., has nexus) and the item consists of:[3]

- Rents or royalties for the use of intangible property derived in the active conduct of the trade or business;

- Interest, dividends, and amounts received for the provision of guarantees of indebtedness if the item either is derived in the active conduct of a banking, financing or similar business within the United States or is received by a corporation whose principal business is trading in stocks or securities for its own account; or

- Income derived from the sale or exchange (outside the United States) through the office or other fixed place of business of stock in trade or other property of a kind that would properly be included in the taxpayer's inventory if on hand at the close of the tax year or property held by the taxpayer primarily for sale to customers in the ordinary course of the taxpayer's trade or business. Excluded is income from property sold or exchanged for use, consumption, or disposition outside the United States if the taxpayer's office or other fixed place of business in a foreign country participated materially in the sale.

Income or gain that is equivalent to any item of income or gain previously described will be treated in the same manner as that item.

.01 Asset-Use Test

The asset-use test determines whether the income, gain, or loss is derived from assets used in, or held for use in, the conduct of a trade or business within the United States.[4] The asset-use test ordinarily is applied in making a determination with respect to income, gain, or loss of a passive type where the trade or business activities as such do not give rise directly to the realization of the income, gain, or loss. However, even in the case of such income, gain, or loss any activities of the trade or business that materially contribute to the realization of such income, gain, or loss are also taken into account as a factor in determining whether the income, gain, or loss is effectively connected with the conduct of a trade or business in the U.S.[5]

Ordinarily, an asset is to be treated as used in, or held for use in, the conduct of a trade or business within the United States if the asset is:[6]

- Held for the principal purpose of promoting the present conduct of the trade or business in the United States;

- Acquired and held in the ordinary course of the trade or business conducted in the United States (e.g., an account or note receivable arising from that trade or business); or

- Otherwise held in a direct relationship to the trade or business conducted in the United States.

In determining whether an asset is held in a **direct relationship to the trade or business conducted in the United States**, the principal consideration is whether the asset is needed in that trade or business.[7] The asset must be held to meet the present needs of the trade or business rather than its anticipated future needs. An asset held to meet the operating expenses of the trade or business qualifies. However, an asset held for future diversification into a new trade or business, for expansion of a trade or business outside the United States, for future plant replacement, or for future business contingencies will not be considered needed in the trade or business conducted in the United States.

---

[3] Code Sec. 864(c)(4)(B).
[4] Reg. § 1.864-4(c)(1).
[5] Reg. § 1.864-4(c)(2)(i).
[6] Reg. § 1.864-4(c)(2)(ii).
[7] Reg. § 1.864-4(c)(2)(iv)(a).

An asset is presumed to be held in a direct relationship to the trade or business if:[8]

- It was acquired with funds generated by that trade or business;
- The income from the asset is retained or reinvested in that trade or business; and
- Personnel who are present in the United States and actively involved in the conduct of the trade or business exercise significant management and control over the investment of the asset.

Example 1: 3Z Company,[9] a foreign corporation, manufacturers its products in Finland. However, the company maintains a branch in the United States to import and distribute its product in the United States. The branch's cash needs vary considerably during the year. Hence, 3Z frequently purchases U.S. Treasury Bills when it has a temporary cash surplus. The Treasury Bills are held to meet the present needs of the business. Therefore, they are held in a direct relationship to 3Z's business. The interest income derived from the Treasury Bills is effectively connected income.

.02 Business Activities Test

The business-activities test ordinarily applies in making a determination with respect to income, gain, or loss that, even though generally of the passive type, arises directly from the active conduct of the taxpayer's trade or business in the United States.[10]

This test is of primary significance, for example where:

- Dividends or interest are derived by a dealer in stock or securities;
- Gain or loss is derived from the sale or exchange of capital assets in the active conduct of a trade or business by an investment company;
- Royalties are derived in the active conduct of a business consisting of the licensing of patents or similar intangible property; or
- Service fees are derived in the active conduct of a servicing business.

Example 2: Willhelm Distributors,[11] a German corporation, has a branch in the United States that acts as an importer and distributor of merchandise. By reason of the activities of that branch, Willhelm is engaged in business in the United States. It also carries on a business in which it licenses patents to unrelated persons in the United States for use in the United States. The businesses of the licenses in which these patents are used have no direct relationship to the business carried on in Willhelm's branch in the United States. However, the merchandise marketed by the branch is similar in type to that manufactured under its patents. The negotiations and other activities leading up to the consummation of these licenses are conducted by employees of Willhelm who are not connected to the branch. Further, the U.S. branch does not otherwise participate in arranging for the licenses. Royalties for these licenses are not effectively connected for that year with the conduct of its business because the activities of the business are not a material factor in the realization of such income.

¶ 1603 Income Not Effectively Connected with a U.S. Trade or Business

Income of a nonresident alien or foreign corporation that is not effectively connected is generally subject to a flat rate (30 percent unless a tax treaty specifies a lower rate). The non-resident alien withholding (NRA withholding) rate of 30 percent applies to income from sources within the U.S. that is either:[12]

- Gain from the disposition of timber, coal, and iron ore, or from the sale or exchange of patents, copyrights, and similar intangible property; or
- Fixed or determinable, annual or periodical ("FDAP") income.

---

[8] Reg. § 1.864-4(c)(2)(iv)(b).
[9] Adapted from Reg. § 1.864-4(c)(2)(v), Example 1.
[10] Reg. § 1.864-4(c)(3)(i).

[11] Adapted from Reg. § 1.864-4(c)(3)(ii), Example 2.
[12] Code Secs. 871(a) and 1441(b).

.01 FDAP Income

FDAP income (fixed or determinable, annual or periodical income) is essentially all kinds of income, except for capital gains from the sale of personalty and realty. Income that is effectively connected with U.S. source income is not FDAP income. The term also does not include income that is excluded from the definition of gross income (e.g., municipal bond interest). Taxpayers generally are not allowed to deduct any expenses attributable to FDAP income. However, foreign corporations with FDAP income are allowed a deduction for charitable contributions.[13]

The following is a non-exhaustive list of FDAP income:[14]

- Portfolio income such as interest and dividends;
- Salaries, wages, commissions, and other forms of compensation for personal services;
- Alimony;
- Rental income from real property (unless an election, described below, is made to treat the income as effectively connected with the conduct of a trade or business within the United States);
- Timber, coal and iron ore royalties;
- Pensions and annuities;
- Prizes and awards, including scholarships and fellowships;
- 85 percent of social security benefits received;
- Gambling winnings (unless from wagers placed on blackjack, baccarat, craps, roulette, or big-6 wheel).
- The distributable net income (DNI) of certain estates or trusts that has FDAP income;
- Distributions from partnerships that constitutes FDAP income, and in certain instances the includible amount of income, whether distributed or not; and
- Other fixed or determinable annual or periodical gains, profits, and income.

Rental income from realty. Nonresident aliens generally have a choice with respect to rental income from realty. They may either have it treated as passive income (subject to the flat 30 percent rate), or they may elect to treat the income as effectively connected with a U.S. trade or business.[15]

Exception for certain interest and dividends. The flat 30 percent tax is not imposed on the following items of income received by a nonresident alien individual or generally by a foreign corporation:[16]

- Interest on deposits held by banks if the interest is not effectively connected with the conduct of a trade or business in the United States;
- The active foreign business percentage (active foreign business income divided by gross income) of any dividend or interest paid by an 80/20 company (i.e., a corporation with at least 80 percent of its gross income consisting of active foreign business income);
- Income derived by a foreign central bank of issue from banker's acceptances; and
- Dividends paid by foreign corporations which are treated as being U.S. source income.

Portfolio debt instruments. In general, portfolio interest received by a nonresident alien individual or a foreign corporation from U.S. sources is exempt from the flat 30 percent tax.[17] "Portfolio interest" is interest (including original issue discount) paid on an obligation that is in registered form and with respect to which the United States person required to withhold tax receives a statement that the beneficial owner is not a United States person (or is not required to

---

[13] Code Sec. 882(c)(1)(B).

[14] *See* Code Sec. 871(a); Reg. § 1.871(b) and (c).

[15] Code Sec. 871(d)(1).

[16] Code Sec. 871(i), (l).

[17] Code Secs. 871(h) and 881(c).

receive such a statement). Portfolio interest does not include interest received by a 10-percent shareholder or contingent interest.

Rents and royalties: capital gains from rents and royalties. As mentioned previously, a nonresident alien who has income from real property located in the United States that is held for the production of income generally may elect to treat all of the income as being effectively connected with a trade or business in the United States.[18] Included are rents or royalties from mines, wells, or other natural deposits as well as timber, coal, and iron ore royalties. A gain from the sale of real property that produces such income is also eligible for the election. If the election is *not* made, no deductions are allowed, and the gross income is taxed at the flat 30 percent rate.

An election is made by attaching a statement to that effect to the relevant tax return.[19] The statement must include a schedule of all real property owned in the United States; an indication of the extent to which the taxpayer has direct or beneficial ownership of each item of real property; the location of the property; a description of any substantial improvements; and an identification of any tax year or years in which a revocation of the election or a new election has been made.

 Spotlight: The rules for rent and royalties, which allow no deductions if treated as FDAP income, may seem harsh, and one's first impulse might be to always make the election. Can you think of instances when not making the election would be advantageous?

Example 3: Maria de Cordoba, a nonresident alien, has rental property in the United States that generated $300,000 in revenue in 2015. Expenses related to the rental property amounted to $240,000. Maria has other U.S. source income that would place her in the 35-percent bracket whether or not she makes the election to treat the income as U.S. source income. If Maria does not make the election, she pays a tax of $90,000 on the rental income ($300,000 × .30). However, if she makes the election, her tax on the rental income is $21,000 (.35 × ($300,000 – $240,000)).

Example 4: Anah Kerem, a nonresident alien, has property in the United States that is subject to a net lease (all expenses paid by the tenant). His revenue from the property in 2015 is $150,000. Anah has other U.S. source income that places him in the 35-percent bracket. If Anah does not make the election, his tax on the rental income will be $45,000 ($150,000 × .30). However, if he does make the election, his tax will be $52,500 ($150,000 × .35).

Capital transactions. Net capital gains of a nonresident alien that are "effectively connected" with the trade of a U.S. trade or business are taxed the same as for U.S. citizens or residents. However, certain net capital gains of nonresident aliens are exempt from U.S. taxation. To be exempt from tax, the following criteria must be met:[20]

- The nonresident alien is present in the United States for fewer than 183 days during the tax year;

- The gains are *not* included in the definition of fixed or determinable, annual or periodical (FDAP) income); and

- The gains are *not* U.S. property gains under Code Sec. 897 (i.e., are *not* sales of realty located in the United States).

Note that a taxpayer present in the United States for at least 183 days during the tax year is likely considered a resident of the United States (see ¶ 1605). Therefore, sales and exchanges of capital assets are taxed in the same manner as for a U.S. citizen or resident.

---

[18] Code Sec. 871(d)(1).
[19] Reg. § 1.871-10(d)(1).

[20] Reg. § 1.871-7(d)(2)(ii).

Gambling winnings. If a nonresident alien's gambling activities constitute a trade or business, then gambling winnings are considered to be effectively connected income. Otherwise, gambling winnings are FDAP income and are subject to the flat 30 percent rate. However, winnings from wagers placed in blackjack, baccarat, craps, roulette, and big-6 wheel are exempt.[21]

¶ 1604 Deductions Allowed Nonresident Aliens

In general, nonresident alien individuals may take deductions only for expenses related to income that is effectively connected with a U.S. trade or business.[22] However, there are several exceptions:[23]

- **Losses.** A deduction is allowed (1) for a loss incurred in any transaction entered into for profit, though not connected with a trade or business, if any profit would have been taxable as income from sources within the United States, and (2) for a loss of property not connected with a trade or business or a transaction entered into for profit if the loss arises from a casualty or theft and the loss is of property located within the United States.

- **Charitable contributions.** A deduction is allowed for charitable contributions.

- **Personal exemption.** Only one personal exemption is allowed unless the taxpayer is a resident of Canada or Mexico or a national of the United States.

- **Student loan interest expense.** An individual is allowed a deduction for interest paid during the tax year on any qualified education loan.[24]

¶ 1605 Filing Requirements for Nonresident Aliens

Filing requirements for resident aliens are identical to that of U.S. citizens. However, in many instances nonresident aliens need not file a return because tax on FDAP income is withheld at the source.

Example 5: Roberto Sivertino is single and is a citizen and resident of Uruguay. His only U.S. source income in 2015 was $4,000 of dividend income, of which $1,200 of federal income tax was withheld at the source. Roberto owes no additional tax and need not file a return.

Nonresident aliens are required to file either Form 1040NR, *U.S. Nonresident Alien Income Tax Return*, or Form 1040NR-EZ, *U.S. Income Tax return for Certain Nonresident Aliens With No Dependents*, if they:[25]

- Engaged in a U.S. trade or business; or
- Received income from U.S. sources and not all of the tax owed was withheld from that income; or
- Are a representative or agent responsible for filing the return of a nonresident alien who engaged in a U.S. trade or business or received income from U.S. sources and not all of the tax owed was withheld; or
- Represent a deceased person who would have had to file either of those forms; or
- Represent an estate or trust that has to file either of those forms; or
- Owe any special taxes, received a distribution from a health savings account, or had net earnings from self-employment and resided in a country with whom the United States has an international Social Security agreement; or
- Want to claim a refund of overwitheld or overpaid tax; or
- Claim the benefit of any deductions or credits (e.g., by electing to treat income from real property as effectively connected income); or
- Want to elect to treat certain FDAP income as effectively connected income.

---

[21] Code Sec. 871(j).
[22] Code Sec. 873(a).
[23] Code Sec. 873(b); Reg. § 1.873-1.

[24] Code Sec. 221.
[25] Reg. § 1.6012-1(b); IRS Publication 519, *U.S. Tax Guide for Aliens*; Instructions for Form 1040NR.

Nonresident aliens who are required to file must divide their income into three baskets:[26]

- Income effectively connected;

- U.S. income not effectively connected (generally FDAP income) that is taxed; and

- U.S. income exempt by treaty.

Recall that effectively connected income of a nonresident alien is taxed at U.S. rates and that certain deductions are allowed. This income and deductions are reported on pages one and two of Form 1040NR. FDAP income, however, is reported on Schedule NEC of Form 1040NR. The income is reported in various columns representing the applicable rates. The tax on FDAP income is computed on Schedule NEC, *Tax on Income Not Effectively Connected With a U.S. Trade or Business*, then carried to Form 1040NR and added to the tax on effectively connected income. U.S.-source income exempt by treaty is reported on Schedule OI-*Other Information* and entered on page one of Form 1040NR as an information amount, rather than an amount subject to tax.

Example 6:   Humberto Higgins is single and a citizen and resident of the United Kingdom. In 2015 Humberto worked 160 days in the United States for a domestic corporation and received a salary of $30,000, from which $2,400 of federal income tax was withheld. He worked the remainder of the year in Liverpool and received a salary of $40,000. Humberto also received $200 of interest income on a U.S. corporate bond while working in the U.S. Sixty dollars of federal income tax was withheld from the interest income. He had no other income or deductions for AGI. His itemized deductions allowed for U.S. tax purposes amounted to $6,000, and he is allowed the $3,950 exemption. Thus, his taxable income from effectively connected sources is $20,050 ($30,000 − $6,000 − $3,950). His tax on the $20,050 is $2,554. From that he would deduct credits of $2,460 ($2,400 + $60). Humberto would owe additional tax of $94 ($2,554 − $2,460).

¶ 1606 Outbound Transactions

Outbound transactions involve **U.S. Persons** (i.e., domestic corporations, domestic pass-throughs, citizens, or residents that either conduct business abroad or invest abroad). Under our worldwide system of taxation, such income is fully subject to U.S. taxation. However, the *timing* of the taxation of the income may depend on how the U.S. Person organizes the foreign operations. If the foreign entity is organized as a branch of a domestic entity, all of the foreign-derived income is subject to taxation. As discussed below, if the foreign entity is organized as a foreign corporation, at least part of the earnings may be deferred.

 Planning Pointer: The fact that earnings of a foreign branch are taxed immediately (no deferral possibilities) can be an advantage. It is not uncommon for foreign operations to experience losses for the first several years. Organizing the foreign operation as a branch allows the losses from the branch to be deducted against income from the domestic entity.

Qualified dividends from foreign corporations. Certain dividends from foreign corporations may qualify for the maximum 20 percent rate of taxation that applies to qualified dividends paid from a domestic corporation. A foreign corporation is a qualified corporation (i.e., one whose dividends qualify for the lower rate) if:[27]

---

[26] Instructions for Form 1040NR.   [27] Code Sec. 1(h)(11)(C).

1. It is incorporated in a possession of the United States, or

2. It is eligible for benefits of a comprehensive income treaty with the United States that the IRS determines satisfactory and that includes an exchange of information program, or

3. The stock with respect the dividend is paid is readily tradable on an established securities market in the U.S.

Because additional tax must be paid to the country of origin, our worldwide system of taxation can appear to be quite punitive. However, in addition to the reduced tax rate for qualified dividends, there are four major ways in which the potential double taxation is mitigated.

.01 Deferral of Taxation of Earnings of Controlled Foreign Corporations

As part of our worldwide system of taxation, the Internal Revenue Code provides that a United States Person is generally subject to tax on income, regardless of where the income is earned or received. The term "United States Person" includes citizens or residents of the United States, domestic corporations, domestic partnerships, domestic estates, and most domestic trusts.[28]

Note, however, that a foreign corporation, even if controlled by a U.S. corporation, is not a United States Person. Therefore, unless the foreign corporation has U.S. source income or a permanent establishment in the United States, it is not subject to U.S. taxation. However, U.S. shareholders in foreign corporations are subject to U.S. tax on their share of the profits of the foreign subsidiary. Generally, those profits are taxed to U.S. shareholders only when the earnings are expatriated to the United States. Unless the controlled corporation has Subpart F income (or U.S. source income), its income is not taxed until or unless the income is repatriated.

Example 7: Big Brother, Inc. sets up a wholly owned subsidiary, Little Sister Co., in France. In the current year Little Sister Co. earns $50 million and remits $10 million to Big Brother, Inc. in the form of a dividend. Big Brother is subject to U.S. tax only on the $10 million remitted to it. Tax on the remaining $40 million is deferred until or unless it is repatriated to Big Brother.

 Planning Pointer: A basic aspect of tax planning for international transactions is to move income from high-taxed jurisdictions to low-taxed jurisdictions. Locating a subsidiary in a low-tax foreign country achieves that objective as long as the earnings remain in the foreign country. However, as discussed below, Congress has placed limitations on the ability to defer earnings.

Subpart F rules. As discussed above, unless the foreign corporation has U.S. source income or a permanent establishment in the United States, it is not subject to U.S. taxation. However, U.S. shareholders in foreign corporations can be subject to U.S. tax on their share of the profits of the foreign subsidiary. Prior to 1962, the U.S. tax code had no such provision. In the two decades following World War II, many U.S corporations, realized that being able to avoid tax on a foreign subsidiary was a valuable tax loophole. Eager to avoid high corporate tax rates, U.S. corporations began setting up foreign subsidiaries as a way to avoid U.S. taxation of the profits earned in foreign countries. In response, Congress began passing laws meant to close this loophole. Over the years and after many amendments to the tax code, the taxation of U.S. shareholders in controlled foreign corporations evolved into Subpart F of the Internal Revenue Code, thus giving rise to the expression **Subpart F income.** Because a main thrust of these laws is to prevent deferral of taxation on overseas earnings, Code Secs. 951–965 of Subpart F are called **Anti-Deferral rules.** A summary of these very complicated rules is presented below. Other rules designed to prevent the deferral of passive investment income are covered in Code Secs. 1291–1298. Coverage of those rules is outside the scope of this text.

---

[28] Code Sec. 7701(a)(30).

Subpart F rules apply to U.S. Persons who control a foreign corporation (thus the term CFCs). A corporation is a CFC if the U.S. shareholders own, directly or indirectly, more than 50 percent of either the total combined voting power of all classes of voting stock or the total value of the corporation's stock.[29]

A CFC does not necessarily have Subpart F income. However, to the extent that a CFC does have Subpart F income, U.S. shareholders are required to include in income each year as a deemed dividend their pro rata share of the CFC's Subpart F income.[30] Thus, Subpart F income is not deferred. When Subpart F income is distributed, it is treated as previously taxed income.

Example 8: Kansas Instruments owns 100 percent of the stock of Poland Tech. Both are on the calendar year. In 2015 Poland Tech had taxable income of $50 million from the production and sale of microchips and $5 million of interest income. Poland Tech made no distributions in 2015, but in early 2016 it distributed $55 million to Kansas Instruments. Assume that the interest income is Subpart F income. In 2016 all of the $50 million earned income is taxed to Kansas Instruments as distributed (taxation of the income was deferred from 2015). However, the $5 million received that is attributable to the interest income was taxed to Kansas Instruments in 2015. Therefore, when received in 2016, the income is treated as previously taxed income.

Subpart F income is defined as the sum of:[31]

- Insurance income;

- Foreign base company income (FBCI);

- Income generated by international boycott;

- The sum of illegal payments made, directly or indirectly, to foreign governments; and

- In general, income derived from foreign countries that the U.S. does not recognize.

Of the items listed, only FBCI will be discussed here.

What FBCI consists of. "Foreign base company income" includes foreign personal holding company income, foreign base company sales income, foreign base company services income, and foreign base company oil-related income.[32]

The term "foreign personal holding company income," like personal holding company income, includes passive income such as interest, dividends, royalties, rents, and annuities. The term also includes:[33]

- Gains from the sale of assets generating passive income;

- Certain commodity transactions;

- Certain foreign currency gains and losses;

- Income from notional principal contracts;

- Certain payments in lieu of dividends; and

- Certain personal service contracts.

Importance of FBCI. As noted above, FBCI consists in large part of passive income. Recall that a basic element of tax planning is to move income from a high-tax area to a low-tax area. It is much easier to shift the location of passive income than it is to shift earned income. Thus, an important objective of the Subpart F rules is to prevent the deferral of passive income.

---

[29] Code Sec. 957(a).
[30] Code Sec. 951(a).
[31] Code Sec. 952(a).

[32] Code Sec. 952(a).
[33] Code Sec. 954(c)(1).

.02 Foreign Earned Income Exclusion and Housing Allowance

Taxpayers who are residents or citizens of the United States often work in foreign countries. Unless exempted by a tax treaty, their earned income (e.g., salaries and wages) is subject to tax in both the foreign country and the United States. To mitigate the effects of what could be punitive rates of taxation, the United States has a limited foreign earned income exclusion, as well as a housing cost exclusion (or deduction).

 Reason for the Rule: The foreign earned income exclusion enables corporations and other business entities with foreign operations to employ U.S citizens and resident aliens. Without the exclusion, the resulting punitive level of income taxes would require extremely high levels of compensation, and that in turn would discourage using U.S. employees.

Foreign earned income exclusion. The exclusion is an alternative to another mitigation of the double tax, the foreign tax credit (discussed below). Taxpayers may use one, but not both of these two mitigation provisions. The foreign income exclusion is claimed by an election, which is made by filing Form 2555, *Foreign Earned Income* or Form 2555-EZ, *Foreign Earned Income Exclusion*.[34] Taxpayers may revoke an election but, once revoked, the taxpayer may not make another election before the sixth tax year after the year of revocation.[35]

The foreign earned income exclusion is adjusted annually for inflation.[36] For a tax year beginning in 2015, the maximum exclusion is $100,800, computed daily.[37] When spouses determine their respective amounts of foreign earned income, community property laws are not taken into account (i.e., the earned income of a spouse is solely attributable to that spouse).[38]

Foreign earnings received for work done in a prior year must be attributed to the prior year.[39] However, such amount may be excluded to the extent the maximum exclusion was not taken for the prior year. An exception to the above attribution rule applies if:[40]

- The period for which the payment is made is a normal payroll period of the employer that regularly applies to the employee;
- The payroll period includes the last day of the employee's tax year (normally December 31);
- The payroll period does not exceed 16 days; and
- The payment is part of a normal payroll period that is distributed before the end of the next payroll period and at the same time, in relation to the payroll period, that the payroll normally would be distributed.

Example 9: Ann Bonders met the criteria to take the foreign income exclusion for the entire year of 2015. She received during the year a salary of $96,000 for services rendered in 2015, and elected the foreign income exclusion on her 2015 return. On January 10, 2016, she received a bi-monthly salary of $4,000 for the last half of December 2015. Because she met the four requirements shown above, the payment for services rendered in the last part of December 2015 but received in 2016 will be attributed to 2015 (and thus eligible for the 2015 foreign earned income exclusion).

Example 10: Assume the same facts as the previous example, except that Ann in 2015 received $95,000 for services rendered in 2015, was paid monthly, and received her December 2015 pay check for $7,500 on January 12, 2016. Because Ann does not meet the exception (the payroll period was monthly), she must attribute the $7,500 to the year 2016.

---

[34] Code Sec. 911(a)(1).
[35] Code Sec. 911(e).
[36] Code Sec. 911(b)(2)(D)(ii).
[37] Rev. Proc. 2014-61, 2014-47 IRB 860.

[38] Code Sec. 911(b)(2)(C).
[39] Code Sec. 911(b)(2)(B).
[40] Reg. § 1.911-3(e).

The term "foreign earned income" is defined as "earned income" received by an individual from sources within a foreign country or countries.[41] "Earned income" includes salaries and wages or professional fees for personal services actually rendered.[42] The term does not include pensions, annuities, payments to employees of the U.S. government, nonqualified annuities, and deferred compensation.[43] It also does not include amounts paid to a taxpayer that in substance represent a distribution of earnings or profits rather than a reasonable allowance as compensation. If a taxpayer is engaged in a trade or business in which both personal services and capital are material in producing income, the amount allowed as personal compensation cannot exceed 30 percent of the net profits of the business.[44]

Example 11: Smith, a U.S. citizen formed a wholly-owned corporation to produce software in Thailand. The corporation has no U.S. source income or Subpart F income. Capital is not a material factor in production of income in Smith's corporation. In the current year the corporation had net income before a salary to Smith of $80,000. The corporation paid out the entire $80,000 to Smith in the form of a salary, and he elected to exclude the entire amount. Upon audit, the IRS asserted that $30,000 of the payment represented a constructive dividend to Smith. Therefore, he was entitled to exclude only $50,000.

Example 12: Ontre P. Neuer, a U.S. citizen, established an auto supply store in Ghana. He operated the business as a sole proprietor. In the current year the total profit from the auto supply store amounted to $150,000. Ontre's foreign income exclusion cannot exceed $45,000 ($150,000 × .30).

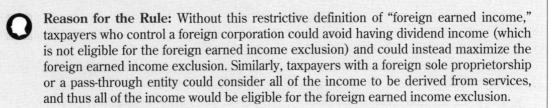

Reason for the Rule: Without this restrictive definition of "foreign earned income," taxpayers who control a foreign corporation could avoid having dividend income (which is not eligible for the foreign earned income exclusion) and could instead maximize the foreign earned income exclusion. Similarly, taxpayers with a foreign sole proprietorship or a pass-through entity could consider all of the income to be derived from services, and thus all of the income would be eligible for the foreign earned income exclusion.

The election of the foreign earned income exclusion can be made only by a **qualified individual**. To qualify the individual must have a **tax home** in a foreign country and:[45]

- Be a citizen of the United States who has been a bona fide resident of a foreign country(s) for an uninterrupted period including an entire tax year; or

- Be a citizen or resident of the United States who, during any 12 consecutive months, has been present in a foreign country(s) for at least 330 full days (the 330 days need not be consecutive).[46]

Example 13: Ted Travelor's employer transferred him to Thailand in 2013. Ted arrived in Thailand on November 30, 2013, and did not leave until February 10, 2015. The transfer was regarded as temporary, and Ted did not establish a permanent residence there. However, because Ted met the 330 days/12 month rule, he is entitled to a full exclusion up to $99,200 for 2014, and a partial exclusion for 2013 and 2015. His maximum exclusion for the year 2013 is $8,022 ($97,600 × 30/365). His maximum exclusion for 2015 is $11,047 ($100,800 × 40/365).

---

[41] Code Sec. 911(b)(1)(A).
[42] Code Sec. 911(d)(2)(A).
[43] Code Sec. 911(b)(1)(B).

[44] Code Sec. 911(d)(2)(B).
[45] Code Sec. 911(d)(1).
[46] Code Sec. 911(d)(1).

The residency test or number of days present test may be waived to the extent that the Secretary of State determines that it was necessary for the individual to leave the foreign country due to war or civil unrest.[47] The IRS publishes in the Internal Revenue Bulletin a list of the affected countries and the time periods for which the waiver qualifies. The instructions to Form 2555, *Foreign Income Exclusion*, and Form 2555-EZ, *Foreign Earned Income Exclusion*, contain instructions on how to claim the waiver.

A "tax home" is as defined in Code Sec. 162 (which determines whether one is away from home on business). Generally, if the taxpayer's abode is in the U.S., he or she does not have a tax home in a foreign country.[48]

 Spotlight: It is important to know that the income tax implications for a U.S. taxpayer living abroad differ according to the permanence of the stay. A taxpayer who is abroad on a temporary or short-term (less than one-year) assignment is generally not entitled to the foreign income exclusion. However, taxpayers away from their tax home can deduct many of their living costs as travel expenses.

How to meet the residency test. Generally, to meet the bona fide residency test a taxpayer must go to the foreign country to work for an indefinite or extended period. Going to a foreign country to work on a particular job or for a specified period of time would tend to indicate that one is not a resident of the foreign country. Taxpayers do not have to change their domicile to be a resident of the foreign country. They may have the intention to reside in the U.S. on a permanent basis but can still establish residency in the foreign country if the facts indicate so. Factors that support claiming residency include:

- Moving the family, furniture, and pets;
- Opening foreign bank accounts;
- Speaking the foreign language;
- Getting a foreign driver's license; and
- Joining foreign civic associations.

Foreign housing cost exclusion and deduction. Taxpayers who meet the foreign income exclusion tests listed above may also qualify for an exclusion or a deduction (both cannot be taken) if they reside abroad in a high-cost living area. Taxpayers whose housing costs are paid (directly or indirectly) by an employer may, if they qualify, take the exclusion. Self-employed taxpayers are not entitled to the exclusion but may deduct their housing cost amount when calculating their AGI. Note, however, that the result to the self-employed taxpayer is very similar to that of the employee. Both employees and self-employed taxpayers take the exclusion/deduction on Form 2555, *Foreign Earned Income* or Form 2555-EZ, *Foreign Earned Income*.

Taxpayers can exclude the **housing cost amount** from their gross income. The housing cost amount is equal to the excess of the taxpayer's housing expenses over the "base housing amount."[49] The **base housing amount** is determined by multiplying the maximum foreign income exclusion by 16 percent.[50] In the year 2015, the base housing amount is $16,128 ($100,800 × .16), or $44.19 per day. The amount of housing expenses that can be taken into consideration generally cannot exceed 30 percent of the maximum foreign earned income exclusion, applied on a daily basis.[51] For 2015, the maximum daily limitation is $82.85 (($100,800/365) × .3). However, the maximum housing expenses used in determining the excess amount is increased by the IRS for certain expensive living areas. The instructions to Form 2555, *Foreign Earned Income* contain tables showing the expensive areas along with the daily allowed housing amount.

---

[47] Code Sec. 911(d)(4).
[48] Code Sec. 911(d)(3).
[49] Code Sec. 911(c)(1).
[50] Code Sec. 911(c)(1)(B).
[51] Code Sec. 911(c)(2)(A).

Example 14: Lucy Sky moved to India on December 31, 2014, and remained there for all of 2015. Her employer paid her housing costs for the year 2015, which amounted to $22,000. The amount of housing costs she may use for purposes of computing the foreign housing allowance exclusion is the lesser of $22,000 or $30,240 ($100,800 × .30). Therefore, her housing exclusion is $5,872 ($22,000 – ($100,800 × .16)).

Example 15: Assume the same facts as in the previous example except that Lucy's reimbursed housing costs were $32,000. Her housing exclusion is $14,112 ($30,240 – ($100,800 × .16)).

Example 16: Lou Wong moved to Beijing, China on June 30, 2015 and established residence there. His employer, Out Here, Inc. reimbursed him $42,000 for his housing costs for the partial year, 184 days in 2015. Lou's housing costs were $228.26 per day ($42,000/184). The base housing amount is $44.19 per day for 2015. However, Beijing is a high-cost area. The designated daily limit in 2014 was $195.07. Assuming no change in 2015, his housing exclusion would be $27,762 ($195.07 – $44.19) × 184).

Impact of tax treaties. The United States has a number of tax treaties with foreign countries. The objective of tax treaties is to reduce the potential for double taxation. Publication 901, *U.S. Tax Treaties*, lists tax treaties and summarizes many of them. Under these treaties, U.S. citizens and residents subject to taxes imposed by a foreign country are entitled to certain deductions, exemptions, credits, and reductions in tax rates. U.S. citizens not residing in the United States generally are not entitled to treaty benefits. Common benefits of tax treaties include:

- Personal service income received for personal services performed in a treaty country by a U.S. resident in the treaty country for a limited number of days may be exempt from that country's income tax.

- Payments received by U.S. residents for the first two or three years that they teach or do research in a treaty country may be exempt from that country's income tax.

- Nongovernment pensions and annuities received by U.S. residents may be exempt from the treaty country's income tax.

- Investment income received by U.S. residents from a treaty country may be exempt from that country's income tax or taxed at a reduced rate.

For example, a treaty with Germany generally exempts from German income tax income received for personal services of U.S. residents, provided that three requirements are met:[52]

- The U.S resident is in Germany for no more than 183 days during the calendar year;

- The income is paid by, or on behalf of, an employer who is not a resident of Germany;

- The income is not borne by a permanent establishment that the employer has in Germany.

However, income that U.S. entertainers and athletes receive in Germany is subject to German income tax if their gross receipts exceed $20,000 for a calendar year.[53]

¶ 1607 Foreign Tax Credit

U.S. citizens and residents and domestic corporations are eligible to take a credit for the amount of foreign income tax paid or accrued during the tax year to any foreign country or U.S. possession.[54] Nonresident alien individuals and foreign corporations engaged in a trade or business within the United States are allowed a credit for foreign income tax paid or accrued to any foreign country or U.S. possession with respect to income effectively connected with the conduct of their trade or business within the United States.[55]

---

[52] U.S.-Germany Income Tax Treaty, Article 15.
[53] U.S.-Germany Income Tax Treaty, Article 17.

[54] Code Sec. 901(a), (b)(1).
[55] Code Sec. 901(a), (b)(4).

The purpose of the credit is to mitigate the effect of double taxation. The credit is taken in lieu of the deduction. However, taxpayers may elect to take the deduction instead. Because the credit results in a dollar-for-dollar reduction of taxes, the credit generally provides more benefits than the deduction. However, the credit is subject to limitations that sometimes result in the deduction providing more tax benefit.

The foreign tax credit is discussed in detail in ¶ 1116.

¶ 1608 Tax Status of Nonresident Aliens and Foreign Corporations

As previously mentioned, the United States taxes its citizens, residents, and domestic corporations on their worldwide income but taxes only certain income received by foreign persons and foreign corporations. Nonresident aliens and foreign corporations are generally taxed only on certain income from U.S. sources and foreign source income that is effectively connected with a U.S. trade or business.[56] Therefore, the distinction between U.S. and foreign persons is critical in determining what kind of income is taxed and what tax rates and withholding rates apply.

.01 Who Is a U.S. Person?

A **U.S. person** is defined as:[57]

- A citizen or resident of the U.S.;
- A domestic partnership or a domestic corporation;
- All estates except for foreign estates;
- Any trust, if a court within the U.S. can exercise primary supervision over its administration and at least one U.S. person has authority to control all substantial decisions of the trust; and
- Any other person who is not a foreign person (e.g., a domestic limited liability company (LLC)).

.02 Who Is a Foreign Person?

Foreign persons include:
- Nonresident individuals;
- Foreign corporations and foreign partnerships;
- Foreign trusts and estates; and
- Any other persons who are not U.S. persons.

.03 Who Is a U.S. Citizen?

The U.S. Code specifies who is entitled to citizenship, both at birth and through the naturalization process. The following are citizens at birth:[58]

- A person born in the United States;
- A person born outside the United States and its outlying possessions if both of the person's parents are U.S. citizens and at least one parent resided in the United States or one of its outlying possessions before that person's birth;
- A person born outside the United States and its outlying possessions if at least one parent is a U.S. citizen who was physically present in the United States or one of its outlying possessions for a continuous period of one year prior to the person's birth and the other parent is a national but not a U.S. citizen;
- A person born in an outlying U.S. possession if at least one parent is a U.S. citizen who has been physically present in the United States or one of its outlying possessions for a continuous period of one year at any time prior to the person's birth; or

---

[56] Code Sec. 871(a), (b); Reg. § 1.871-1(a).
[57] Code Sec. 7701(a)(30).
[58] 8 U.S.C. § 1401.

- A person born outside the geographical limits of the United States and its outlying possessions if one of the person's parents is an alien and the other is a U.S. citizen who was physically present in the United States or its outlying possessions prior to that person's birth for a period or periods totaling no fewer than five years (at least two of which were after attaining the age of 14).

Eligible individuals may apply for naturalization. The applicable form is N-400, *Application for Naturalization*. Individuals may qualify for naturalization if:

- They have resided continuously within the United States for at least five years (and were physically present in the United States for at least half that time) after being lawfully admitted for permanent residence;[59]

- They are married to a U.S. citizen, they have resided continuously within the United States for at least three years after being lawfully admitted for permanent residence, their spouse has been a U.S. citizen during all of that period, and they have been physically present in the United States for periods totaling at least one and a half years;[60]

- They have served honorably in the U.S. armed forces for a period or periods aggregating one year;[61] or

- At least one parent is a U.S. citizen, by birth or naturalization, the U.S. citizen parent either has been physically present in the United States or its outlying possessions for a period or periods totaling no fewer than five years (at least two of which were after attaining age 14) or has a U.S. citizen parent who has been physically present in the United States or its outlying possessions for a period or periods totaling no fewer than five years (at least two of which were after attaining age 14), they are under age 18, they are residing outside the United States in the legal and physical custody of their U.S. citizen parent, and they are temporarily present in the United States pursuant to a lawful admission (which they are maintaining).[62]

.04 Determination of Residency Status

Residency may be determined under an applicable tax treaty. However, if there is no applicable treaty, Code Sec. 7701(b) and the regulations determine residency. An alien individual is treated as a resident if one of the following three conditions is met:[63]

1. The individual is a lawful permanent resident of the United States at any time during the calendar year;

2. The individual meets the substantial presence test; or

3. The individual elects to be treated as a resident alien.

An alien is a resident alien if at any time during the year the alien is a **lawful permanent resident**. A lawful permanent resident is someone who has been granted the privilege of residing permanently in the United States (issued a green card).[64]

The **substantial presence test** is met if the individual has been present in the United States on at least 183 days during a three-year period that includes the current year.[65] For purposes of the 183-day test, each day of presence in the current year is counted as a full day, each day of presence in the first preceding year is counted as one-third of a day, and each day of presence in the second preceding year is counted as one-sixth of a day. Fractional days are not rounded up for this purpose.

If an individual is not physically present for more than 30 days during the current calendar year, the substantial presence test will not be applied for that year.[66] However, an individual need not be present for more than 30 days during either of the two preceding years.

---

[59] 8 U.S.C. § 1427.
[60] 8 U.S.C. § 1430.
[61] 8 U.S.C. § 1439.
[62] 8 U.S.C. § 1433(a).

[63] Code Sec 7701(b).
[64] Reg. § 301.7701(b)-1(b)(1).
[65] Code Sec. 7701(b)(3); Reg. § 301.7701(b)-1(c)(1).
[66] Reg. § 301.7701(b)-1(c)(4).

Example 17: Jack Hofstedder, an alien individual, is present in the United States for 175 days during the current year. He was present in the United States for 18 days in the first preceding year, and 24 days in the second preceding year. To determine the substantial presence test, he adds 175 + 6 + 4 = 185. Therefore, the substantial presence test is met.

Example 18: Kimberly Wong, an alien individual, was present the entire year in both 2013 and 2014. In 2015, the current year, she was present for 27 days. Because she was present for fewer than 31 days in the current year, the substantial presence test is not met.

.05 Rules for First and Last Years of Residency

An alien individual will not be considered a U.S. resident during any portion of a calendar year if:[67]

- Such portion is after the last day on which the individual was present in the United States;
- During such portion the individual has a closer connection to a foreign country than to the United States; and
- The individual is not a resident of the United States at any time during the next calendar year.

Example 19: Jacques Fournier, a citizen of France, has never been a U.S. resident. He comes to the United States on February 2, 2015, to attend a seminar on International Accounting Standards. He returns to France on February 17, 2015. He can establish a closer connection to France for that period. On May 1 he moves to the United States and establishes residency. He returns to France on November 30. He can establish a closer connection to France for the remainder of 2015 and does not return to the United States in 2016. His residency starting date for 2015 is May 1, and his termination date is November 30.

.06 Closer Connection Exception to the Substantial Presence Test

An alien individual who meets the substantial presence test may nevertheless be considered a nonresident alien if:[68]

- The individual is present in the United States for fewer than 183 days during the current year;
- The individual maintains a "tax home" in a foreign country during the current year; and
- The individual has a closer connection to the foreign country in which he or she maintains a tax home.

As previously mentioned, an individual's "tax home" is the location of his or her regular or principal (if more than one regular) place of business.[69] If an individual has no regular or principal place of business, the individual's tax home is the individual's regular place of abode in a real and substantial sense.

An individual will be considered to have a closer connection to a foreign country than to the United States if the individual has maintained more significant contacts with the foreign country than with the United States.[70] In determining whether an individual has maintained more significant contacts with a foreign country than the United States, the facts and circumstances to be considered include, but are not limited to, (1) the location of the individual's permanent home; (2) the location of the individual's family; (3) the location of personal belongings, such as automobiles, furniture, clothing and jewelry owned by the individual and his or her family; (4) the location of social, political, cultural or religious organizations with which the individual has a current relationship; (5)

---

[67] Code Sec. 7701(b)(2)(B).
[68] Code Sec. 7701(b)(3)(B); Reg. § 301.7701(b)-2(a).

[69] Reg. § 301.7701(b)-2(c)(1).
[70] Reg. § 301.7701(b)-2(d)(1).

the location where the individual conducts his or her routine personal banking activities; (6) the location where the individual conducts business activities (other than those that constitute the individual's tax home); (7) the location of the jurisdiction in which the individual holds a driver's license; (8) the location of the jurisdiction in which the individual votes; (9) the country of residence designated by the individual on forms and documents; and (10) the types of official forms and documents filed by the individual, such as Form 1078, *Certificate of Alien Claiming Residence in the United States*, Form W-8, *Certificate of Foreign Status*, or Form W-9, *Payee's Request for Taxpayer Identification Number*.

Example 20: Chancy Witherspoon, a citizen of the United Kingdom, was in the United States for 270 days in 2014. He was present in the United States for 150 days in 2015. Throughout 2015, Chancy maintained a tax home in which he had a closer connection to the United Kingdom. He was not granted a green card and returned to his home in Bristol before the end of 2015. Chancy did have a substantial presence in the United States in 2015 because he was present at least 183 days in the three-year period including 2015 (270/3) + 150 = 240 days. However, Clancy is not considered a resident of the United States in 2015 because he meets the closer connection exception.

If an individual's residency starting date does not fall on the first day of the tax year, or an individual's residency termination date does not fall on the last day of the tax year, his or her income tax is computed under the rules of Reg. § 1.871-13.[71] Under those rules, the individual's tax year is treated as comprised of two separate periods, one consisting of the time during which the individual was a resident of the United States and the other consisting of the time during which the individual was not a U.S. resident.[72]

.07 Election to Claim Residency Status

A nonresident alien may elect residency status, provided that the individual:[73]

- Is not a U.S. resident under the green card or substantial presence test for the current calendar year (the "election year");

- Was not a U.S. resident for the calendar year immediately preceding the election year;

- Is a U.S. resident under the substantial presence test for the calendar year immediately following the election year;

- Is present in the U.S. for at least 31 consecutive days during the election year; and

- Is present in the United States for at least 75 percent of the days in the period beginning with the first day of the 31-day period and ending with the last day of the election year.

An election is made on an individual's tax return for the election year but may not be made before the individual has met the substantial presence test with respect to the calendar year immediately following the election year.[74] An election, once made, remains in effect for the election year unless revoked with the IRS' consent.[75]

.08 Residency Start and Termination Dates

If an alien individual becomes a resident of the United States during the year, he or she will be treated as a resident only for the portion of the year that begins on the "residency starting date."[76]

The residency starting date depends on which test a taxpayer satisfies to qualify as a U.S. resident.[77]

---

[71] Reg. § 301.7701(b)-4(c)(2).
[72] Reg. § 1.871-13(a)(1).
[73] Code Sec. 7701(b)(4)(A).
[74] Code Sec. 7701(b)(4)(E).

[75] Code Sec. 7701(b)(4)(F).
[76] Code Sec. 7701(b)(2)(A)(i).
[77] Code Sec. 7701(b)(2); Reg. § 301.7701(b)-4.

Substantial presence test. If an alien meets the substantial presence test for residency, the residency starting date is the first day during the calendar year that the individual is present in the United States. However, an individual may be present in the United States for up to 10 days without triggering the residency starting date if the individual can establish that, during that period, the individual's tax home was in a foreign country and the individual maintained a closer connection to that foreign country than to the United States. An individual must include days of presence for purposes of determining whether the individual meets the substantial presence test even though the days may be disregarded for purposes of determining the individual's residency starting date.

Example 21:   Hans DeJong, a citizen of the Netherlands, came to the United States on May 4, 2015 to participate in a business discussion with the U.S. branch of his company. He returned to Rotterdam on May 11. Hans can establish a closer connection to the Netherlands for the time in May that he was in the United States. On June 15 he moved to the United States and established residency for the remainder of 2015. His residency starting date is June 15.

Green card test. If an individual is a lawfully permanent resident of the United States at any time during the calendar year but does not meet the substantial presence test, the residency starting date is the first day in the calendar year on which the individual was present in the United States while a lawful permanent resident.

Election of residency. If an individual elected to be a resident, the residency starting date is the first day during the calendar year on which the individual is treated as a resident of the United States.

Example 22:   Ana Tamayo, a citizen of Brazil, moved to the United States as a U.S. resident on September 1, 2014, and remained until November 2 before returning to Sao Paulo. She came back to the United States on July 20, 2015, and was a U.S. resident through the remainder of 2015. Ana's starting date for U.S residency in 2015 is considered to be January 1.

Residency termination date. The termination date for aliens who were U.S. residents in the prior tax year, but who were not U.S. residents during any part of the current tax year is December 31 of the prior tax year, unless the individual qualifies for an earlier termination date.[78]

Example 23:   Thiago Garcia, a citizen of Argentina, was a U.S. resident from January 1, 2015 until he moved back to Buenos Aires on December 31, 2015. Thiago was not a U.S. resident during any time in 2016. His residency termination date is December 31, 2015.

Often, however, aliens will qualify for an earlier termination date than December 31. The earlier termination date depends on whether the alien's residency was met by the substantial presence test, the green card test, or both tests.[79]

Substantial Presence Test—the residency termination date is the last day during the calendar year that the individual was physically present in the United States if the individual establishes that for the remainder of the calendar year the individual's tax home was in a foreign country and the individual maintained a closer connection to that foreign country than to the United States.

Green Card Test—the termination date is the first day that the individual is no longer a permanent resident of the United States if the individual establishes that for the remainder of the calendar year the individual's tax home was in a foreign country and the individual maintained a closer connection to that foreign country than to the United States.

Both Tests—the later of the two dates above.

---

[78] Reg. §301.7701(b)-4(b)(1).   [79] Code Sec. 7701(b)(2)(B); Reg. §301.7701(b)-4(b).

Example 24: Krishna Swati moved to the United States in 2013 and received a green card that year. She resided in the United States until October 30, 2015, when she moved back to Delhi and established residency there. Krishna returned to the United States on December 10 to finish up some work, and left the United States on December 14. Her termination date is December 14, 2015.

.09 Distinguishing Between Foreign and Domestic Businesses and Fiduciaries

A sole proprietorship is not separate from its owner for income tax purposes. However, corporations, partnerships, and fiduciaries (estates and trusts) are subject to the entity concept (i.e., the entity is separate from its owners for income tax purposes). Therefore, it is important to know what distinguishes foreign entities from domestic entities.

Foreign vs. Domestic corporations and partnerships. The term **domestic**, when applied to corporations and partnerships, means that the entity has been created or organized in the United States, or under the law of the United States, or of any state, unless, in the case of partnerships, the regulations specify otherwise.[80] Foreign corporations are defined in the tax code in a negative sense. The term **foreign** when applied to a corporation or partnership means a corporation or partnership which is not domestic."[81] The regulations, however, provide a list of business entities that, if formed in the various countries delineated, are considered to be foreign businesses.[82] The regulations list, for example, in the United Kingdom, a Public Limited Company, and in Germany, Aktiengesellschaft.

Foreign vs. Domestic fiduciaries. Trusts and estates are often referred to as fiduciaries because of the fiduciary responsibility that the trustees of trusts and executors of the estates are required by the laws of the states to exercise. Trusts are considered domestic trusts if:[83]

- A court within the United States is able to exercise primary supervision over its administration; and

- One or more "U.S. persons" have the authority to control all substantial decisions of the trust.

Note that a "U.S. person" does not have to be an individual. The term includes domestic partnerships, domestic corporations, and domestic trusts and estates.[84]

Example 25: The Young Family trust, formed under the laws of Utah, has Zion National Bank, a domestic corporation, as its trustee. The trust qualifies as a domestic trust.

A "foreign trust" is any trust that is not a domestic trust.[85] Domestic estates are also defined in a negative sense. A "domestic estate" is one that is not a foreign estate.[86] A "foreign estate" is an estate whose income from sources outside the United States that income is not effectively connected with a U.S. trade or business is not subject to U.S. income tax.[87]

¶ 1609 Determining Sources of Income

As previously mentioned, nonresident alien persons (the term includes individuals, corporations, partnerships, and estates and trusts) are generally taxed only if they have certain kinds of U.S. source income. Sourcing income is also important for residents and citizens of the United States because of the foreign tax credit and other ways in which non-U.S. source income is treated for tax purposes. Therefore, knowing what sources from which the income is derived is essential in determining U.S. income tax.

---

[80] Code Sec. 7701(a)(4).
[81] Code Sec. 7701(a)(5).
[82] Reg. §301.7701-2(b)(8)(i).
[83] Code Sec. 7701(a)(30)(E).

[84] Code Sec. 7701(a)(30).
[85] Code Sec. 7701(a)(31)(B).
[86] Code Sec. 7701(a)(30)(D).
[87] Code Sec. 7701(a)(31)(A).

The Internal Revenue Code contains U.S. source rules, foreign source rules, and mixed source rules. As is true of most Code Sections however, not all situations are covered. Therefore, it is also important to look at the regulations that cover sourcing rules. In some instances, there may be no specific sourcing rules. In that event, the general principles governing revenue and expense recognition apply. With respect to income, the following table summarizes general sourcing rules for some of the more common sources of income. However, the table should not be used as a final determinant in deciding from what source the income is derived. A more detailed discussion of the more common sources of income follows.

Type of Income	Relevant Factor
Interest	Residence of payer
Dividends	Whether the corporation paying the dividend is U.S. or foreign or has income effectively connected with a U.S. business
Personal service income	Country where services were performed
Rents	Location of property producing the income
Royalties from natural resources	Location of property producing the income
Royalties from intellectual property	Country where the property is used
Sales of real property	Country where property is located
Sales of inventory purchased for resale	Country where sold
Sales of inventory produced by seller	Allocated based on location of production activity and source of sales activity income
Sales of other personal property	Generally the tax home of the seller
Sales of natural resources (e.g., oil)	Allocated between U.S. sources and foreign sources according to FMV of product at export terminal
Pension distributions attributable to contributions	Where services that earned the pension were performed
Investment earnings on pension contributions	Location of pension fund

.01 Determining Taxable Income from Sources Outside the United States

Against gross income from sources outside the United States, deductions are allowed for expenses, losses, and other deductions that are properly apportioned or allocable to such income.[88] In addition a deduction is allowed for a ratable part of any other expenses, losses, or deductions that cannot definitely be allocated to some item or class of gross income.

.02 Special Rules for Determining the Source of the Income

Some income is derived from sources partly within and partly without the United States (i.e., the income is from mixed sources). Code Sec. 863(a) gives authority to the Treasury to promulgate regulations governing the allocation or apportionment to sources within or without the United States. Special rules exist for mixed-source income, debt guarantees, transportation income, space and ocean activities, international communications income, and natural resources.

Mixed source rules. The following items of income are treated as mixed-source income:[89]

- Income from services rendered partly within and partly without the United States;

- Gains resulting from the sale or exchange of inventory property produced within the United States and sold or exchanged without the United States or produced outside the United states but sold or exchanged within the United States; and

- Gains derived from the purchase of inventory property within a U.S. possession and its sale or exchange within the United States.

---

[88] Code Sec. 862(b).

[89] Code Sec. 863(b).

Ways of allocating cross border sales. The regulations to Code Sec. 863 provide three methods for allocating cross border sales:

The 50/50 method. The 50/50 method is the default method (used unless another method is elected).[90] Under this method, 50 percent of the taxpayer's gross income is considered attributable to production activity, and the remaining 50 percent of gross income is considered attributable to sales activity.

Example 26: Mr. Tea, Inc.,[91] a U.S. Corporation, produces electric teapots in the United States. Mr. Tea sells the teapots for $15 to an unrelated distributor in a foreign country. Mr. Tea's cost of goods sold is $7, and its gross income is $8 per teapot. Under the 50/50 method, $4 of gross income per teapot is considered attributable to production and $4 is considered attributable to sales.

Income attributable to production activity is sourced to the location of the taxpayer's production assets.[92] Income attributable to sales activity is sourced to the location of the sale.[93]

The IFP method. The **independent factory price method (IFP)** may be elected by a taxpayer if an IFP can be fairly established.[94] An IFP is considered fairly established if the taxpayer regularly sells part of its output to wholly independent distributors or to other selling concerns in such a way as to reasonably reflect the income earned from production.

If the taxpayer elects the IFP method, the amount of the gross sales price equal to the IFP is treated as attributable to production activity. The excess of the sales price over the IFP is then treated as attributable to sales activity. Note that a different IFP must be applied to sales in other geographic markets if the markets are substantially different.[95]

Example 27: National Grain Co.,[96] a U.S. corporation, purchases wheat in the United States and processes it into flour. National Grain sells the flour to an unrelated foreign wholesale distributor for $50 per unit. The cost of goods sold, all attributable to production, is $40 per unit. National Grain does not engage in significant sales activity. Therefore, the $10 per unit of gross income is all attributable to the production activity. The gross income attributable to sales activity is zero.

Example 28: Assume the same facts as in the previous example, except that National Grain Company also sells flour in the foreign company to an unrelated retailer for $55 per unit. The flour is substantially identical to the flour sold to the distributor. Therefore, the IFP fairly established in the sales to the distributor must also be used to determine the amount attributable to production activity in the sale to the retailer. Thus, $50 of the gross sales price per unit is attributable to production activity, and the remaining $5 is attributable to sales activity. Therefore, $10 of the gross income per unit is attributable to production and $5 is attributable to sales activity.

Books and records method. Taxpayers may elect to allocate their gross income between production and sales activities using the books and records method.[97] To use this method, a taxpayer must establish to the satisfaction of the IRS that the taxpayer, in good faith and unaffected by considerations of tax liability, will regularly employ in its books of account a detailed allocation of receipts and expenditures that clearly reflects the amount of income from production and sales activities. If a taxpayer receives permission to use this method, but does not comply with a material condition set forth by the IRS, permission to use the method may be revoked.

---

[90] Reg. § 1.863-3(b)(1).
[91] Adapted from Reg. § 1.863-3(b)(2)(ii), Example.
[92] Reg. § 1.863-1(c)(1).
[93] Reg. § 1.863-3(c)(2).

[94] Reg. § 1.863-3(b)(2).
[95] Id.
[96] Adapted from Reg. § 1.863-3(b)(2)(iv), Example 1.
[97] Reg. § 1.863-3(b)(3).

.03 Interest Income

As mentioned previously, generally the residence of the payer determines whether interest income is U.S. source income or foreign source income. Therefore, generally income from the U.S. government, the District of Columbia, and interest on debt issued by U.S. residents or domestic corporations is U.S. source income.[98] However, there is a bank deposit exception. Interest on deposits with a foreign branch of a domestic corporation or domestic partnership is not U.S. source income if the branch is engaged in the commercial banking business.[99]

.04 Dividend Income

Dividends paid by domestic corporations are treated as U.S. source income.[100] If any of the four exceptions below are met however, the dividends are not U.S. source income.[101]

- Dividends paid by a domestic corporation that has elected to claim the possession tax credit (a credit that provides an incentive for U.S. corporations to have operations in Puerto and U.S. possessions);
- Dividends from a foreign corporation where less than 25 percent of the gross income from all sources for the three-year period ending with the close of its taxable year preceding the declaration of the dividends was effectively connected with the conduct of a trade or business within the United States. If at least 25 percent of a corporation's gross income was effectively connected with the conduct of a trade or business within the United States, a portion of the dividend is treated as U.S. source income. That amount is the dividend multiplied by a fraction whose numerator is the amount of the foreign corporation's gross income that is effectively connected with a U.S. trade or business and whose denominator is the foreign corporation's gross income from all sources;

Example 29: Forp Co., a foreign corporation, had $250 million in gross income from its U.S. business and $1.2 billion gross income from its European operations during the calendar years 2012–2015. The company declared a dividend of $60 million in early 2016. None of the dividends are U.S. source income.

Example 30: Assume the same facts as in the previous example except that gross income from U.S. sources during that period was $600 million. Of the $60 million in dividends paid, $20 million ($60 million × ($600 million/$1,800 million)) is U.S. source income.

- Dividends from foreign corporations from earnings and profits accumulated while a domestic corporation; or
- Certain dividends from DISCS or former DISCS (discussion of these now expired export incentives are outside the scope of this course)

.05 Compensation for Personal Services

Personal services performed in the United States generally constitute U.S. source income. However, if the following three criteria are met, the income is not considered from a U.S. source:[102]

- The services are provided by a nonresident alien who is temporarily present in the United States for fewer than 91 days during the tax year;
- The compensation for the services does not exceed $3,000; and
- The compensation is for labor or services performed as an employee of, or under contract with (1) a nonresident alien, foreign corporation, or foreign partnership that is not engaged in business in the United States, or (2) a U.S. citizen or resident, domestic corporation, or domestic partnership, if the labor or services are performed for an office or place of business maintained in a foreign country or a U.S. possession by that individual, corporation, or partnership.

---

[98] Code Sec. 861(a)(1).
[99] Code Sec. 861(a)(1)(A)(i).
[100] Code Sec. 861(a)(2)(A).

[101] Code Sec. 861(a)(2).
[102] Code Sec. 861(a)(3).

Spotlight: The above exception to the definition of personal services was added in 1966, effective in 1967. In January 1967 the consumer price index (CPI) expressed in 1982 dollars was 32.9. In November 2014, the CPI was 236.151. Thus, if adjusted for inflation, the $3,000 threshold listed above would be more than $21,500! Can you see why much of the tax code is adjusted for inflation? Why do you think this provision has not been adjusted for inflation?

.06 Rents and Royalties

Rentals or royalties from property located in the United States or from any interest in such property is U.S. source income.[103] Such items include rentals or royalties for the use of or for the privilege of using in the United States, patents, copyrights, secret processes and formulas, goodwill, trademarks, trade brands, franchises, and other like property.

.07 Sales of Real Property

Gains, profits, and income from the disposition of a "United States real property interest" are U.S. source income.[104] In general, a "United States real property interest" means an interest, other than an interest solely as a creditor, in either:[105]

- Real property located in the United States or the Virgin Islands; or

- A domestic corporation, unless the corporation was at no time a United States real property holding corporation during the shorter of the period during which the taxpayer held the interest or the five-year period ending on the date that the interest was disposed.

A corporation is a "United States real property holding corporation" if the fair market value of its United States real property interests equals or exceeds 50 percent of the sum of the fair market value of its United States real property interests, its interests in real property located outside the United States, and any of its other assets used or held for use in a trade or business.

If any class of stock is regularly traded on an established securities market, stock of that class will be treated as a United States real property interest only in the case of a person who, at some time during the shorter of the period during which the person held the interest or the five-year period ending on the date that the person disposed of the interest, held more than five percent of that class of stock.

.08 Sales of Personal Property

Generally, income from the sale of personal property is sourced to the United States if the seller is a United States resident and is sourced outside the United States if the seller is a nonresident.[106] The term "United States resident" means any individual who is a United States citizen or resident alien and does not have a tax home in a foreign country or is a nonresident alien and has a tax home in the United States.[107]

Exceptions are made for:

- Inventory property.

- Depreciable personal property.

- Intangibles.

---

[103] Code Sec. 861(a)(4).
[104] Code Sec. 861(a)(5).
[105] Code Sec. 897(c); Reg. § 1.897-1(c).

[106] Code Sec. 865(a).
[107] Code Sec. 865(g)(1)(A).

Sales of inventory property. Income from the sale of inventory property *purchased* by the taxpayer for resale is generally sourced according to where the seller's rights, title, and interest in the property are transferred to the buyer.[108] Thus, income from the sale of inventory in the United States is U.S. source income, regardless of where the inventory was purchased.

As discussed previously, income from the sale of inventory property *produced* by the taxpayer in the United States and sold outside the United States as well as inventory produced outside the United States and sold in the United States is mixed source income, and must be allocated between U.S. sources and foreign sources.[109]

Depreciable personal property. The portion of the gain from the sale of depreciable property that is attributable to previously claimed depreciation deductions is considered to be from U.S. sources if the deductions were taken against U.S. source income.[110] Gain attributable to previously claimed depreciation that was taken against foreign source income is considered to be from foreign sources. Gain in excess of depreciation taken is sourced according to the general source rules for noninventory personal property.

Example 31: Juan Rodríguez. a nonresident alien who maintains his tax home in Costa Rica, sold equipment used in his business for $50,000. The equipment cost Juan $45,000, and he has taken $30,000 of depreciation on the equipment, $18,000 of which was taken against U.S. source income. Of his total gain of $35,000, $18,000 is U.S. source income, $12,000 is foreign source income, and the remaining $5,000 is sourced according to Juan's tax home. In this instance the remaining $5,000 of gain is foreign source income.

Intangibles. To the extent that any gain from the sale or exchange of an intangible (i.e., a patent, copyright, secret process or formula, goodwill, trademark, trade brand, franchise, or other like property) does not exceed the depreciation adjustments with respect to the intangible, the portion of that gain that is U.S. source income is determined by multiplying the gain by a fraction whose numerator is the amount of United States depreciation adjustments with respect to the property and whose denominator is the total amount of depreciation adjustments.[111] To the extent that payments are contingent on the productivity, use, or disposition of the intangible, the source of the payments is determined as if the payments were royalties. If the property is located or used within the United States, the gain is U.S. source income. If the property is located or used outside the Untied States, the gain is foreign source income. To the extent that payments are not contingent on the productivity, use or disposition of the intangible, gain will be treated as U.S. source income if the seller is a United States resident and foreign source income if the seller is a nonresident.

Stock of affiliates. If a U.S. resident sells stock in an affiliate that is a foreign corporation, the gain is considered foreign source income if:[112]

- The sale occurs in a foreign country in which the affiliate is engaged in an active trade or business; and

- More than 50 percent of the gross income of the affiliate for the three-year period ending with the close of the affiliate's taxable year immediately preceding the year in which the sale occurred was derived from the conduct of such trade or business.

.09 Sales of Natural Resources

Income from the sale of an interest (other than an interest solely as a creditor) in a mine, well, or other mineral deposit located in the United States or the Virgin Islands or in a domestic corporation that cannot establish that it was not a United States real property holding corporation

---

[108] Code Sec. 865(b).
[109] Code Sec. 863(b)(2).
[110] Code Sec. 865(c).

[111] Code Sec. 865(d).
[112] Code Sec. 865(f).

during the shorter of the period during which the seller held the interest or the five-year period ending on the date of the sale is U.S. source income.[113]

Once natural resources (e.g., oil; ore; crops; timber) are extracted from the ground or otherwise severed from the ground, they are no longer real property.[114] The income from the sale of such natural resources is allocated between U.S. sources and foreign sources according to the FMV of the product at the export terminal.[115]

.10 Pension and Annuity Distributions

Distributions received by a nonresident alien from a domestic pension, annuity, stock bonus, profit sharing, or annuity plan for services performed both inside and outside the United States constitute mixed-source income. The portion of the pension payment that is considered to be from U.S. sources is determined by multiplying the pension payments by a fraction.[116] The numerator of the fraction is:

- The employer contributions for services performed in the United States; plus
- The earnings of the pension plan attributable to the employee

The denominator of the fraction is:

- The employer contributions for services performed in the United States; plus
- The earnings of the pension plan attributable to the employee; plus
- The employer contributions for services performed outside the United States.

Example 32: Angus McLendon, a citizen and resident of Scotland, worked a number of years, both in the United States and Scotland, for a U.S. corporation. He retired in 2015 with a yearly pension of $40,000. Employer contributions attributable to work in the United States and Scotland were $180,000 and $100,000 respectively. Earnings of the plan attributable to Angus were $120,000. The portion of the pension considered to be from U.S. sources is $30,000 ($40,000 × ($180,000 + $120,000)/($180,000 + $120,000 + $100,000)).

¶ 1610 Source Rules for Deductions

Once gross income has been allocated between U.S. and foreign sources, deductions are allocated to the class of gross income to which they are directly related.[117]

A class of gross income may consist of one or more items of gross income enumerated in Code Sec. 61, namely:[118]

1. Compensation for services;
2. Gross income derived from businesses;
3. Gains from dealings in property;
4. Interest;
5. Rents;
6. Royalties;
7. Dividends;
8. Alimony and separate maintenance payments;
9. Annuities;
10. Income from life insurance and endowment contracts;
11. Income from discharge of indebtedness;

---

[113] Code Sec. 861(a)(5).
[114] Reg. § 1.897-1(b)(2).
[115] Reg. § 1.863-1(b).

[116] Rev. Proc. 2004-37, 2004-1 CB 1099.
[117] Code Sec. 861(b); Reg. § 1.861-8(a)(2).
[118] Reg. § 1.861-1(a)(3).

12. Distributive shares of partnership income;

13. Pensions;

14. Income in respect of a decedent (IRD); and

15. Income from an interest in an estate or trust.

A deduction will be considered definitely related to a class of gross income if it is incurred as a result of, or incident to, an activity or in connection with property from which that class of gross income is derived.[119] If a deduction is incurred as a result of, or incident to, an activity or in connection with property, which activity or property generates, has generated, or could reasonably have been expected to generate gross income, the deduction will be considered definitely related to that gross income as a class whether or not there is any item of gross income in the class that is received or accrued during the tax year and whether or not the amount of deductions exceeds the amount of the gross income in the class.

Although most deductions will be definitely related to some class of a taxpayer's gross income, some deductions are ratably apportioned to all gross income because they are related to all gross income or are treated as not definitely related to any gross income.[120] Deductions that are ratably apportioned include:[121]

- Certain interest expense;

- Real estate taxes on a personal residence or sales tax on items purchased for personal use;

- Medical expenses;

- Charitable contributions; and

- Alimony.

Deductions that are supportive in nature (e.g., overhead, general and administrative expenses, and supervisory expenses) may be allocated and apportioned along with the deductions to which they relate.[122] However, it is equally acceptable to attribute supportive deductions directly to the activities or property that generate the gross income.

Sometimes, for purposes of a Code provision (e.g., for purposes of determining effectively connected taxable income or applying the foreign tax credit limitations), deductions have to be apportioned within a class of gross income between the statutory grouping of gross income (or among the statutory groupings) and the residual grouping of gross income.[123]

If a class of gross income to which a deduction has been allocated consists entirely of a single statutory grouping or the residual grouping, there is no need to apportion that deduction.[124] However, if a deduction is allocated to a class of gross income included in one or more statutory groupings, it must be apportioned among the statutory groupings and, if necessary, the residual grouping. Examples of bases and factors that should be considered in apportioning a specific deduction include, but are not limited to, a comparison of units sold; the amount of gross sales or receipts; the cost of goods sold; profit contribution; expenses incurred, assets used, salaries paid, space utilized, and time spent that are attributable to the activities or properties giving rise to the class of gross income; and the amount of gross income.

The taxable income of each member of an affiliated group within each statutory grouping is determined by allocating and apportioning the expenses of each member according to apportionment fractions that are computed as if all members of the affiliated group were a single corporation.[125] Specifically, such expenses must be allocated to a class of gross income that takes into account gross income that is generated, has been generated, or could reasonably have been

---

[119] Reg. § 1.861-1(b)(2).

[120] Reg. § 1.861-1(b)(1).

[121] Reg. § 1.861-8(e)(9).

[122] Temp. Reg. § 1.861-8(b)(3).

[123] Reg. § 1.861-8(a)(2).

[124] Temp. Reg. § 1.861-1T(c)(1).

[125] Temp. Reg. § 1.861-14T(c).

expected to have been generated by the members of the affiliated group. If the expenses relate to the gross income of fewer than all members of an affiliated group, then those expenses must be apportioned as if those fewer members were a single corporation.

Example 33: Gold, Inc.[126] owns all of the stock of both Copper Co. and Silver, Inc. All are domestic corporations. Gold, Inc. incurs general training program expenses of $100,000 in 2015. Employees of all three companies participated in the programs. In 2015 Gold, Inc. had U.S. source gross income of $2,000,000 and foreign source general limitation income of $500,000. Copper Co. had U.S. source gross income of $1,500,000 and foreign source general limitation income of $800,000. Silver, Inc. had U.S. source gross income of $3,000,000 and foreign source general limitation income of $400,000. The training expenses incurred by Gold, Inc. are not definitely related solely to specific income-producing activities or property of Gold, Inc. Therefore, the training expenses are allocable to all of the gross income, both foreign and domestic.

The amount allocable to foreign source general limitation income is $20,732 ($100,000 × ($500,000 + $800,000 + $400,000)/($2,500,000 + $2,300,000 + $3,400,000)).

The amount allocable to U.S. source income is $79,268 ($100,000 × ($2,000,000 + $1,500,000 + $3,000,000)/($2,500,000 + $2,300,000 + $3,400,000)).

.01 Special Allocation Rules

The Code contains no reference to special allocations of deductions. However, the Code authorizes the Treasury Department to determine taxable income by processes or formulas of general apportionment."[127]

The Treasury has promulgated special allocation rules for the following expenses and deductions:

- Research and development expenses (R&D);
- Stewardship expenses;
- Legal and accounting fees;
- Income taxes;
- Losses on sale or exchange of property;
- Net operating losses (NOLs);
- Interest expense; and
- Charitable contributions.

R&D expenses. The regulations governing the allocating and apportioning of **research and development expenses (R&D)** incorporate the belief that research and experimentation is an inherently speculative activity, that findings may contribute unexpected benefits, and that the gross income derived from successful research and experimentation must bear the cost of unsuccessful research and experimentation.[128] Expenditures for R&D ordinarily are considered deductions that are definitely related to all income reasonably connected with the relevant broad product category or categories of the taxpayer. Therefore, the expenses are allocable to all items of gross income as a class related to that product category.[129]

Legally mandated R&D is allocated differently. If there is not a reasonable expectation that more than a *de minimis* gross income will be generated outside of a single geographic source, the R&D is allocated exclusively to the jurisdiction imposing the requirement.[130]

---

[126] Adapted from Temp Reg. § 1.861-14T(j), Example 2.
[127] Code Sec. 863(b).
[128] Reg. § 1.861-17(a)(1).

[129] Id.
[130] Reg. § 1.861-17(a)(4).

There are two permissible methods of apportionment of R&D that is not legally mandated R&D: the sales method and the optional gross income method.

- **Sales method**—An amount equal to 50 percent of the R&D is apportioned exclusively to the statutory grouping of gross income (or the residual grouping of gross income) that arises from the geographic source where the R&D expenditures that account for more than 50 percent of the amount of such deduction were performed.[131]

- **Optional gross income method**—An amount equal to 25 percent of the R&D is apportioned exclusively to the statutory grouping of gross income (or the residual grouping of gross income) that arises from the geographic source where the R&D expenditures that account for more than 50 percent of the amount of such deduction were performed.[132]

Under the sales-based apportionment method, the research expenses remaining after the 50 percent exclusive apportionment is made are apportioned between U.S. and foreign source income in the proportion that the sales from the product category that resulted in the income bears to the total sales from the product category.[133]

Taxpayers have two options for apportioning remaining research expenses under the gross income method:[134] Under Option 1, taxpayers may apportion research expenses remaining after the optional gross income method has been used ratably on the basis of gross income between the statutory groupings (or among the statutory groupings) of gross income and the residual grouping of gross income in the same proportions that the amount of gross income in the statutory grouping (or groupings) and the amount of gross income in the residual grouping bear, respectively, to the total amount of gross income, if the amount of research expenses ratably apportioned to the statutory grouping (or groupings in the aggregate) is not less than 50 percent of the amount that would have been so apportioned if the taxpayer had used the sales method and the amount of research expenses ratably apportioned to the residual grouping is not less than 50 percent of the amount that would have been so apportioned if the taxpayer had used the sales method.

Taxpayers who cannot use Option 1 can do either of the following:

- If the amount of research expenses ratably apportioned to the statutory grouping (or groupings) is less than 50 percent of the amount that would have been apportioned if the taxpayer had used the sales method, the taxpayer may apportion 50 percent of the amount of research and experimental expense that would have been apportioned to the statutory grouping (or groupings in the aggregate) under the sales method to such statutory grouping (or to such statutory groupings in the aggregate and then among such groupings on the basis of gross income within each grouping) and apportion the balance of the amount of research and experimental expenses to the residual grouping.

- If the amount of research expenses ratably apportioned to the residual grouping is less than 50 percent of the amount that would have been so apportioned if the taxpayer had used this sales method, the taxpayer may apportion 50 percent of the amount of research expenses that would have been apportioned to the residual grouping under the sales method to such residual grouping and apportion the balance of the amount of research expenses to the statutory grouping (or to the statutory groupings in the aggregate and then among such groupings ratably on the basis of gross income within each grouping).

Taxpayers may choose to use either the sales method or the optional gross income method for their original return for their first tax year to which they need to make an apportionment.[135] Use of either of the methods constitutes a binding election to use the method chosen for that year and for four tax years thereafter. A taxpayer may not revoke an election of a method without the IRS' prior consent.

---

[131] Reg. § 1.861-17(b)(1)(i).
[132] Reg. § 1.861-17(b)(1)(ii).
[133] Reg. § 1.861-17(c)(1).

[134] Reg. § 1.861-17(d).
[135] Reg. § 1.861-17(e).

Example 34: Digs and Hattan, Inc.[136] manufactures and distributes small gasoline engines. D&H Ltd. is a wholly owned foreign subsidiary. It also manufactures and sells the engines. During 2015 Digs and Hattan incurred research expenditures of $600,000 to invent and patent a new gasoline engine. All of the research was done in the U.S. Domestic sales of the new engine totaled $50 million in 2015. Sales by D&H, Ltd. of the engine were $30 million. Digs and Hattan had gross income in 2015 of $16 million, of which $14 million is U.S. source income, $1 million is foreign source royalties from D&H, Ltd., and $1 million is U.S. source interest income.

For purposes of applying the foreign tax credit limitation, the statutory grouping is general limitation gross income from sources without the United States, and the residual grouping is gross income from sources within the United States. The apportionment is to be based on sales. Because more than 50 percent of the R&D was performed in the United States, 50 percent of the $600,000 deduction, or $300,000, is apportioned exclusively to gross income from U.S. sources. Of the remaining $300,000, $112,500 ($300,000 × ($30 million/($30 million + $50 million)) is apportioned to the statutory grouping (sources within the foreign country). The amount apportioned to the residual grouping is $187,500 ($300,000 × ($50 million/($30 million + $50 million))). The total amount apportioned to the residual grouping is $487,500 ($300,000 + $187,500).

Example 35: Assume the facts as in the previous example except that the apportionment is made using the optional gross income method. The exclusive apportionment to the residual grouping of gross income equals $150,000 ($600,000 × .25). The amount apportioned to the statutory grouping (sources within the foreign country) is $30,000 ($450,000 × ($1 million/($14 million + 1 million))). The amount apportioned to the residual grouping is $420,000 ($450,000 × ($14 million/($14 million + $1 million))). The total amount apportioned to the residual grouping is $570,000 ($150,000 + $420,000).

Stewardship expenses. Stewardship expenses, which result from overseeing functions undertaken for a corporation's own benefit as an investor in a related corporation, are considered definitely related and allocable to dividends received, or to be received, from the related corporation.[137] Stewardship expenses may result from either "duplicative activities" or "shareholder activities." "Duplicative activities" are activities that duplicate an activity to be performed or that may reasonably be expected to be performed by a controlled corporation. "Shareholder activities" are activities whose sole effect is either to protect the renderer's capital investment in the recipient or to facilitate compliance by the renderer with legal, reporting, or regulatory requirements applicable to the renderer or to both.

If a corporation has a foreign or international department that exercises overseeing functions with respect to related foreign corporations and, in addition, the department performs other functions that generate other foreign-source income (such as fees for services rendered outside of the United States for the benefit of foreign related corporations, foreign-source royalties, and gross income of foreign branches), some part of the deductions with respect to that department are considered definitely related to the other foreign-source income. In some instances, the operations of a foreign or international department will also generate United States source income (such as fees for services performed in the United States). Permissible methods of apportionment with respect to stewardship expenses include comparisons of time spent by employees weighted to take into account differences in compensation, or comparisons of each related corporation's gross receipts, gross income, or unit sales volume, assuming that stewardship activities are not substantially disproportionate to such factors.

---

[136] Adapted from Reg. § 1.861-17(h), Example 1.

[137] Reg. § 1.861-8(e)(4)(ii).

Legal and accounting fees. Fees for legal and accounting services are ordinarily considered to be definitely related and allocable to specific classes of gross income or to all of a taxpayer's gross income, depending on the nature of the services rendered.[138] For example, accounting fees for the preparation of a study of costs to manufacture a specific product will ordinarily be definitely related to the class of income derived from (or that could reasonably have been expected to be derived from) that specific product.

Income taxes. Generally the deduction for: state; local and foreign income; war profits; and excess profit taxes is considered to be definitely related and allocable to the gross income on which the state income taxes are imposed.[139] In allocating and apportioning the deduction, the income upon which the state income tax is imposed is determined by reference to the laws of the state. For example, if the state imposes tax on income that includes foreign source income, the portion of the state income tax attributable to such foreign source income is definitely related and allocable to foreign source income.

Example 36: Zalon, Inc.[140] is a domestic corporation that has branches in three states. In 2015 the company earns $500 million, of which $100 million is foreign source general limitation income and $400 million is U.S. source income. The three branches each determine the taxable income in their state by making adjustments to Zalon's federal taxable income. They then apportion the adjusted taxable income on the basis of the relative amount of Zalon's payroll, property, and sales within each state compared to the worldwide payroll, property, and sales. Zalon is determined to have taxable income of $225 million, $200 million, and $25 million in the three states respectively. The respective tax rates are 4 percent, 6 percent, and 10 percent respectively. Hence, Zalon's state income tax amounts to $9 million, $12 million, and $2.5 million, for a total of $23.5 million. Because none of the states exempt foreign source income in making the calculations, the state income tax must be apportioned between foreign source general limitation gross income and U.S. source income. The three states together tax $450 million ($225 + 200 + 25). However, that amount exceeds Zalon's U.S. source income of $400 million. Therefore, the state income taxes are deemed to be taxed on $400 million of U.S. source income and $50 million of foreign source general limitation income. Of the total state income tax of $23.5 million, $2,611,111 ($23.5 million × ($50 million/$450 million) is apportioned to foreign source income. The remaining $20,888,889 is apportioned to U.S. source income.

Example 37: Assume the same facts as in the previous example except that state *A* specifically exempts foreign source income from taxation. All of *A*'s taxes will therefore be allocable to U.S. source income. States *B* and *C* impose tax on $225 million of Zalon's income, of which only $175 million ($400 million – 225 million is deemed to be from U.S. sources. Therefore, the amount of state income taxes apportioned to foreign source income is $3,222,222 (($12 million + $2.5 million) × ($50 million/225 million)). The remaining $11,277,778 is apportioned to U.S. source income.

Losses on sales or exchanges of property. The source rules for losses on the sale or exchange of property depend on whether the property is realty, personal property other than stock, or stock.

Losses on sale of realty. Nonresident aliens and foreign corporations who dispose of U.S. realty are taxed as if they were engaged in a U.S. trade or business and as if the losses were effectively connected to a U.S. trade or business.[141] Partnership assets are considered to be owned proportionately by its partners and used or held by the partners in the same trade or business as the partnership.[142]

---

[138] Reg. § 1.861-8(e)(5).
[139] Reg. § 1.861-8(e)(6).
[140] Adapted from Reg. § 1.861-8(g), Example 25.

[141] Code Sec. 897(a)(1).
[142] Code Sec. 897(c)(4)(B).

Losses on sales or exchanges of personal property other than stock. The loss rules described below do not apply to inventory.[143] Generally, losses on the sale of personal property other than stock are allocated to the class of gross income to which gain from a sale of such property would give rise in the hands of a seller. Therefore, loss recognized by a U.S. person on the sale of a bond generally is allocated to U.S. source income. These sourcing rules also apply to bad debts and to losses on property that is marked to market.[144]

Losses of a U.S. person on sales of property that is attributable to an office or other fixed place of business in a foreign country generally are allocated to reduce foreign source income if gains on such sales are taxed by the foreign country and the highest marginal rate of tax on such gains in the foreign country is at least 10 percent.[145] Such losses will be foreign source losses regardless if any gain would have been sourced under the depreciation recapture rules of Code Sec. 865(c), the intangible source rules for contingent payments under Code Sec. 965(d)(1)(B), or the goodwill rules of Code Sec. 865(d)(3).[146]

Example 38: On January 1, 2014, Batell, Inc.,[147] a domestic corporation, paid $500,000 for computer chip making equipment for use in its plant in the Philippines. The computer chips produced were sold both in the U.S. and foreign countries. On April 4, 2016, Batell sold the equipment for $140,000. Depreciation for the time period up through the date of sale amounted to $308,000, of which $200,000 was allocated to U.S. source income and $108,000 to foreign source general limitation income. Because gain attributable to depreciation recapture would have been general foreign source income had the equipment been sold at a gain, all of the loss is allocated against foreign source general limitation income.

If a U.S. citizen or resident alien has a foreign tax home, a loss on the sale of personal property will be allocated to foreign source income if a gain on the sale of such property would have been taxable by a foreign country and the highest marginal rate of tax on such gains in the foreign country is at least 10 percent.[148]

A partner's distributive share of loss recognized by a partnership with respect to personal property is allocated as if the partner recognized the loss.[149] If the losses are attributable to a partnership's office or fixed place of business, the office or fixed place of business is considered to be an office of the partner.

Loss with respect to a contingent debt instrument is generally allocated to the class of gross income with respect to which interest income from the instrument would give rise.[150]

Exceptions to the loss rules. These loss rules with respect to personal property other than stock do not apply to:[151]

- Foreign currency transactions;
- Inventory;
- Interest equivalents and trade receivables;
- Unamortized bond premium; and
- Accrued but unpaid interest.

Rules for stock losses. In general, losses from the sale of stock are allocated in the same manner as are gains from the sale of stock (reciprocal-to-gain rule).[152] For example, loss recognized by a resident of the United States on the sale of stock generally would be allocated to reduce U.S. source income. However, a loss on the sale of stock by a U.S. resident that is attributable to an office

---

[143] Reg. § 1.865-1(c)(2).
[144] Reg. § 1.865-1(a)(1).
[145] Reg. § 1.865-1(a)(2).
[146] Reg. § 1.865-1(b)(2).
[147] Adapted from Reg. § 1.865-1(e), Example 1.

[148] Reg. § 1.865-1(a)(3).
[149] Reg. § 1.865-1(a)(5).
[150] Reg. § 1.865-1(b)(2).
[151] Reg. § 1.865-1(c)(1)-(5).
[152] Reg. § 1.865-2(a)(1).

or other fixed place of business in a foreign country is allocated to reduce foreign source income, if:[153]

- A gain on the sale of the stock would been taxed by the foreign country, and
- The highest marginal income tax rate in the foreign country on such gains is at least 10 percent.

If a U.S. citizen or resident alien has a foreign tax home, the loss reduces foreign source income provided that the above two requirements are met.[154] Special rules (outside the scope of this text) apply to bona fide residents of Puerto Rico.

Exceptions to general rules for stock losses. Three exceptions exist to the above stock loss rules:[155]

- The rules do not apply to losses from stock that constitutes inventory;
- The rules do not apply to losses from stock in an S corporation; and
- The taxpayer included in income a dividend recapture amount with respect to the stock at any time during the recapture period.

Dividend recapture amounts. A dividend recapture amount includes:[156]

- Actual dividends;
- Certain dividends that are foreign personal holding company dividends; and
- Earnings from certain investments in U.S. property by controlled foreign corporations that result in an inclusion of Subpart F income.

The recapture period is the 24-month period preceding the date that a taxpayer recognizes loss with respect to the stock.[157] The recapture period is increased by any period of time in which the taxpayer has diminished its risk of loss from holding the stock through the use of options or other positions or by hedging the assets of the corporation.[158]

If the dividend recapture rule applies, the loss from the sale of stock is allocated and apportioned on a proportionate basis to the same class of income or the statutory or residual grouping to which the dividend recapture amount was assigned. This required allocation may reduce the foreign tax credit.

Example 39: Sam, Inc.[159] is a domestic corporation. It is a shareholder of Far East Co., a foreign corporation. Far East Co. has never owned any property in the U.S. that would give rise to Subpart F income. On July 6, 2015, it distributes $5 million in dividends to Sam, Inc. The dividend gives rise to a $250,000 foreign withholding tax, and Sam, Inc. is deemed to have paid an additional $1.25 million of foreign income tax with respect to the dividend. On April 10, 2016, Sam, Inc. sells its shares of Far East Co., and recognizes an $8 million loss. In 2016 Sam, Inc. has $20 million of foreign source income that is general limitation income. Sam, Inc. also has $25 million of foreign source capital gain income that is passive income and $18 million of U.S. source income. The $5 million dividend paid in 2015 is a dividend recapture amount. Therefore, $5 million of the $8 million loss must be allocated to the foreign source general limitation income. The remaining $3 million loss is allocated to U.S. source income. After the allocation, Sam, Inc. has $15 million of general limitation foreign source income and $25 million of foreign source passive income. Note that because the loss reduces the foreign source income, the fraction of income from foreign sources is reduced and the limitation on the foreign tax credit will be lower than otherwise.

---

[153] Reg. § 1.865-2(a)(2).
[154] Reg. § 1.865-2(a)(3).
[155] Reg. § 1.865-2(b).
[156] Reg. § 1.865-2(d)(2).

[157] Reg. § 1.865-2(d)(3).
[158] Reg. § 1.865-2(d)(3). These risks are described in Code Sec. 246(c)(4).
[159] Adapted from Reg. § 1.865-2(b)(1)(iv), Example 1.

Exceptions to the dividend recapture rules exist for *de minimis* amounts (dividend recaptures of less than 10 percent of the recognized loss).[160] In addition, the passive-basket dividend exception generally exempts dividend recapture of amounts that would be treated as passive income.[161] Passive income of a nonresident alien individual that is *not* connected with a U.S. trade or business but is received from U.S. sources is generally taxed at a flat 30 percent rate or, if lower, the applicable treaty rate.[162]

Net operating losses. Net operating losses (NOLs) are subject to special ordering rules.[163] The NOLs must be allocated between foreign source losses and domestic losses using a seven-step approach. Discussion of these detailed rules is outside the scope of this text.

Interest expense. Money is a fungible asset (i.e. one dollar is equally as good as another dollar). Therefore, for allocation purposes, interest expense is generally considered to relate to all activities and property rather than to any specific reason for borrowing the money. However, there are three exceptions to this rule.

Interest expense is allocated on the basis of assets. Under the asset method, interest expense is apportioned to the various statutory groupings based on the average total value of assets within each grouping for the tax year in question.[164] Assets are characterized according to the source and type of income the assets generate. The value of assets within the statutory grouping and the residual grouping at the beginning and end of the tax year are determined by dividing the assets into the following three groups:

- Single category assets (these assets generate income exclusively within a single category grouping or the residual grouping);

- Multiple category assets (these assets generate income within more than one grouping); and

- Assets that produce no identifiable yield or that contribute equally to the generation of all of the taxpayer's income (e.g., assets used in general or administrative functions).

There are three permissible ways to value assets for this purpose: the tax book value method (the adjusted basis of the assets) the fair market value method; and an alternate tax book value method that uses straight-line depreciation and longer depreciable lives.

Example 40: Horn Saddles Co.[165] incurs interest expense in 2015 of $2 million. The company uses the tax value method to value its assets for purposes of apportioning the interest expense. The adjusted basis of its assets is $5 million, $4 million of which generates U.S. source income. The remaining assets of $1 million generate foreign source general limitation income. The interest apportioned to U.S. source income is $1.6 million ($2 million × ($4 million/$5 million)). The interest apportioned to foreign source general limitation income is $400,000 ($2 million × ($1 million/$5 million)).

Exceptions to the interest apportionment rules. There are three instances where the apportionment rules discussed above for interest expense are not used:[166]

- Qualified nonrecourse indebtedness—if the proceeds are used to purchase, construct, or improve property, the interest expense is directly allocated.

- Integrated financial transactions—allocated to the income that generates the transaction.

- Excess related person indebtedness—interest received on the excess related person indebtedness is allocated in proportion to the relative aggregate amount of related controlled foreign corporation obligations held by the related United States shareholder.

---

[160] Reg. § 1.865-2(b)(1)(ii).
[161] Reg. § 1.865-2(b)(1)(iii).
[162] Code Sec. 871(a)(1).
[163] Reg. § 1.904(g)-3.

[164] Temp. Reg. § 1.861-9T(g).
[165] Adapted from Temp. Reg. § 1.861-9T(g)(2)(v).
[166] Temp. Reg. § 1.861-10T(b), (c), and (e).

¶ 1611 Expatriation

Individuals who relinquish their U.S. citizenship or cease to be a lawful permanent resident of the United States and qualify as a "covered expatriate" are subject to a special tax.[167]

 Reason for the Rule: U.S. citizens and residents are taxed on their worldwide income. However, nonresidents need to pay U.S. tax only on U.S. source income. Thus, there is considerable incentive to change one's citizenship or residence to a foreign country with no or low income tax. Congress enacted a special tax on wealthy expatriates because they were concerned that wealthy individuals were relinquishing citizenship or residence before realizing significant gains on sales of businesses and investments.

.01 "Covered Expatriate" Defined

U.S. citizens who relinquish their citizenship and long-term U.S. residents who cease to be a lawful permanent resident of the United States qualify as a "covered expatriate" if they satisfy one of the following prerequisites:[168]

- Their average annual net income tax for the five tax years ending before their expatriation date was greater than $160,000 (in 2015);[169]

- Their net worth as of their expatriation date was $2,000,000 or more; or

- They failed to certify on Form 8854, *Initial and Annual Expatriation Statement*, under penalties of perjury that they have complied with all U.S. tax obligations for the five years preceding the date that they relinquished their citizenship or ceased to be a lawful permanent resident.

Dual citizens and certain minors do not qualify as a covered expatriate. A dual citizen is an individual who:[170]

- Became at birth a citizen of both the United States and another country and continues to be a citizen of the other country;

- As of the expatriation date continued to be a citizen of, and was taxed as a resident of, the other country; and

- Has been a U.S. resident for no more than 10 tax years during the 15-tax-year period ending with the tax year during which the expatriation date occurred.

Individuals also will not qualify as a covered expatriate if:[171]

- They relinquished their U.S. citizenship before age 18½; and

- They were a U.S. resident for no more than 10 tax years before the date that they relinquished their citizenship.

.02 Additional Tax on Expatriates

Covered expatriates are treated as having sold all of their property at its fair market value on the day before their expatriation date[172] and are required to file Form 8854, *Initial and Annual Expatriation Statement*. Covered expatriates may exclude $690,000 of their gain for a tax year beginning in 2015.[173]

This mark-to-market tax does not apply to deferred compensation, interests in nongrantor trusts, and specified tax deferred accounts.[174] Eligible deferred compensation is subject to withhold-

---

[167] Code Sec. 877A.
[168] Code Sec. 877A(g)(1).
[169] Rev. Proc. 2014-61, 2014-47 IRB 860.
[170] Code Sec. 877A(g)(1)(B)(i).

[171] Code Sec. 877A(g)(1)(B)(ii).
[172] Code Sec. 877A(a).
[173] Rev. Proc. 2014-61, 2014-47 IRB 860.
[174] Code Sec. 877A(c).

ing (at a 30 percent tax rate).[175] With respect to ineligible deferred compensation, the present value of a covered expatriate's accrued benefit is treated as having been received on the day before the expatriation date.[176] The taxable portion of distributions from nongrantor trusts are subject to withholding (at a 30 percent tax rate).[177] In the case of specified tax deferred accounts, the covered expatriate is treated as receiving a distribution of the covered expatriate's account on the day before the expatriation date.[178]

"Eligible deferred compensation item" means any deferred compensation item with respect to which the payor is a United States person or someone who elects to be treated as a United States person and the covered expatriate notifies the payor of the individual's status as a covered expatriate and makes an irrevocable waiver of any right to claim any reduction in withholding under any treaty.[179]

Covered expatriates may elect to defer payment of the additional tax until property is sold (but no later than the due date for the income tax return for the year of their death or the time that security provided for the property fails to be adequate).[180] An election may be made on a property-by-property basis. Interest is charged for the period that the tax is deferred.

Instead of the mark-to-market tax, individuals who expatriated on or before June 16, 2008 are liable for 10 years following their expatriation for an alternative tax computed like the alternative minimum tax, with certain modifications.[181]

¶ 1612 Summary

International taxation covers the issue of how the United States taxes two entirely different transactions: inbound transactions and outbound transactions. Inbound transactions are transactions incurred in the United States by nonresident aliens, foreign corporations, and pass-through entities that are otherwise not subject to U.S. taxation. Outbound transactions are transactions incurred outside the United States by U.S. citizens, resident aliens, domestic corporations, and domestic pass-through entities that, because of the worldwide system of taxation that the U.S. imposes, are subject to U.S. taxation.

GLOSSARY OF TERMS INTRODUCED IN THE CHAPTER

Asset-use test. A test to determine whether income is effectively connected.

Business activities test. A test to determine whether income is effectively connected.

Controlled foreign corporations. Foreign corporations that are controlled by U.S. stockholders. Shareholders are taxed of their share of the corporation's subpart F income.

Domestic corporation. A corporation organized under the laws of one of the 50 states in the United States.

Effectively connected income. Income received by nonresident aliens and foreign corporations from a trade or business conducted in the United States.

Expatriation. The act of giving up citizenship. Individuals who expatriate to avoid U.S. taxation may be subject to a special tax.

FDAP income. Fixed, determinable, and annual or periodical income.

---

[175] Code Sec. 877A(d)(1).
[176] Code Sec. 877A(d)(2).
[177] Code Sec. 877A(f)(1).
[178] Code Sec. 877A(e).
[179] Code Sec. 877A(d)(3).
[180] Code Sec. 877A(b).
[181] Code Sec. 877.

Foreign corporation. A corporation organized under the laws of a foreign country.

Foreign earned income exclusion. An alternative to the foreign tax credit available for certain foreign earned income received by individuals who are citizens or residents of the United States.

Foreign person. Nonresident individuals and foreign corporations, partnerships, trusts, and estates.

Foreign tax credit. A credit allowed to receivers of income from outbound transactions. Its purpose is to mitigate double taxation.

Inbound transactions. Transactions in the United States that are incurred by nonresident aliens and foreign corporations.

Nonresident alien. A person who is neither a citizen nor a resident of the United States.

Outbound transactions. Foreign transactions and investments by U.S. citizens, residents, and domestic corporations.

Passive income. Unearned income such as dividends and interest.

Resident alien. A person who is not a citizen of the United States, but who is a lawful resident of the United States.

Substantial presence test. One test that establishes residency. Generally met if the individual stays at least 183 days during the taxable year.

Tax treaties. Agreements reached by the United States with foreign countries. The objective of tax treaties is to reduce the potential for double taxation. U.S. citizens and residents subject to taxes imposed by a foreign country are entitled to certain deductions, exemptions, credits, and reductions in tax rates.

United States person. Citizens and residents of the United States as well as domestic: corporations, partnerships, estates, and most trusts.

CHAPTER PROBLEMS

Chapter 16 Discussion Questions

1. What is an inbound transaction? What taxpayers are potentially subject to the tax on inbound transactions?

2. Why is the term "effectively connected" important with respect to the taxation of inbound transactions?

3. What does the acronym FDAP stand for?

4. What is an outbound transaction? What taxpayers are potentially subject to the tax on outbound transactions?

5. How do domestic corporations avoid taxation on earnings of foreign subsidiaries? Are the earnings ever taxed?

6. Why does the U.S. tax law allow limited foreign income exclusion to individuals working abroad?

7. Is passive income received abroad eligible for the foreign earned income exclusion?

8. Is it necessary for a U.S. citizen to be a resident of a foreign country in order to claim the foreign earned income exclusion? Explain.

9. Jim Jordan, a U.S. citizen is transferred to Tokyo by his U.S. employer. Will Jim be potentially eligible to claim tax benefits in addition to the foreign earned income exclusion? Explain.

10. What is the primary objective of tax treaties the United States has with other countries?

11. Is it generally better for taxpayers to claim the foreign earned income exclusion or the foreign tax credit? Explain your answer.

12. Explain what happens to the portion of the foreign tax credit that a taxpayer is unable to use due to the limitation provisions.

13. Is the foreign tax credit ever recaptured? If so, under what circumstances?

14. Compare and contrast U.S. persons and foreign persons.

15. How is the substantial presence test met?

16. What are sourcing rules? Why are they important?

17. Name the three methods that may be used to allocate cross-border sales.

18. Give three examples of U.S. source income.

19. Name two methods of allocating R&D costs.

20. Explain how the dividend recapture works.

21. Why is a considerable amount of income from inbound transactions subject to withholding at the source?

22. Explain in what context the asset use and business activities are applied.

23. What two choices do nonresident aliens have with respect to rental income from realty that is located in the United States?

24. Name two deductions that nonresident aliens are allowed even if the deductions are not related to effectively connected income.

25. Who is a covered expatriate?

Chapter 16 Problems

1. New Tech, Inc. has a solely owned subsidiary in Belgium. In the current year the subsidiary had taxable income of $100 million and remitted $30 million to New Tech in the form of a dividend. New Tech has a marginal U.S. tax rate of 35 percent. How much U.S. tax does New Tech owe on the subsidiary's income? Assume that the subsidiary has no Subpart F income.

2. General Gills, a domestic corporation, owns 100 percent of the stock in a foreign subsidiary. In 2015, the subsidiary had $200 million of general source foreign limitation income and $20 million of Subpart F income. Both corporations are on the calendar year. On January 1, 2016, the subsidiary distributed all $220 million to General Gills. How much if any is taxed to General Gills in 2015? In 2016?

3. Joseph Smithson, a U.S. citizen resided in Finland for all of 2015 and earned $100,000 working for a Finland cell phone manufacturer. If Joseph elects the foreign earned income exclusion, how much of his salary is subject to U.S. tax?

4. Hank Raulson met the criteria to take the foreign income exclusion for all of 2015. Hank is paid monthly. He received $98,000 in 2015 and the remaining $8,000 of his 2015 pay (he was paid monthly) in January 2016. How much of his $106,000 in salary is eligible for the foreign income exclusion in 2015? Can any of the $106,000 be excluded in 2016?

5. Mary Diaz, a U.S. citizen, owns and operates a coffee shop in Chile. Her net income from the coffee shop in 2015 amounted to $80,000. How much foreign earned income exclusion could Mary take in 2015 assuming she meets the requirements?

6. Amanda Struthers, a U.S. citizen, moved to Columbia in late 2014 and remained there for all of the year 2015. Her employer paid $25,000 of housing costs for her in 2015. Assume she

was not in a high cost area. How much of her $25,000 housing costs can Amanda exclude from her 2015 income?

7. Assume the same facts as in Problem 6 except that Amanda's reimbursed housing costs in 2015 were $35,000. How much of her $35,000 housing costs can Amanda exclude from her 2015 income?

8. Manuel Portico is a U.S. citizen. All of his foreign source income in 2012 was general category income. His foreign tax credit for the years 2012 through 2016 are as follows:

Year	Foreign Taxes Paid	Limitation on the Credit	Unused Credit
2012	$5,500	$4,000	$1,500
2013	$4,000	$4,500	($500)
2014	$6,000	$4,800	$1,200
2015	$4,400	$4,700	($300)
2016	$5,000	$4,400	$600

What is the amount of Manuel's foreign tax credit carryforwards, and when do they expire?

9. Ben Anders, an alien individual, is present in the United States for 160 days in the current year. He was present for 36 days in the first preceding year and 30 days in the second preceding year.

For purposes of the substantial presence test, how many days is Ben deemed to be present in the U.S. during the current year? Has Ben met the substantial presence test for the current year?

10. Outell, Inc., a U.S. corporation, manufactures computer chips in the United States and sells them to an unrelated computer manufacturer distributor in South America. Relevant information is as follows:

Sales price: $3.00 per unit

Cost of sales: $2.00 per unit

Gross profit: $1.00 per unit

Allocate the gross income between U.S. and foreign sources using the 50/50 method.

11. Assume the same facts as in Problem 10, except that Outell, Inc. does no marketing of its product and that the IFP has been established at $3.00 per unit. Allocate the gross income between U.S. and foreign sources using the IFP method.

12. Assume the same facts as in Problem 11, except that Outell, Inc. also sells identical chips to an unrelated wholesaler for $3.50 per unit. Allocate the gross income between U.S. and foreign sources using the IFP method.

13. Tony, Co., a foreign corporation, had gross income from its Asia operations of $12 billion, and $2 billion of gross income from its U.S. business in the calendar years 2011–2014. In 2015 the company declared a $300 million dividend. How much, if any of the dividend is U.S. source income to Tony, Co.?

14. Assume the same facts as in Problem 13 except that the gross income from the U.S. business amounted to $8 billion. How much, if any of the dividend is U.S. source income to Tony, Co.?

15. Aussie and Audra Sanders are citizens and residents of Australia. During the current year both worked temporarily outside of Australia. Aussie gave a two-week seminar for a U.S. based pharmaceutical company. The seminar was given in Puerto Rico and Aussie was paid $5,000 for his services. Audra accompanied an Australian family on a three week vacation trip to the U.S., serving as nanny for the three children. She was paid $2,500 for her services. How much U.S. source income do the Sanders have?

16. Assume the same facts as in Problem 15, except that Aussie was paid only $3,000 for presenting the seminar. How much U.S. source income do the Sanders have?

17. Assume the same facts as in Problem 15 except that Audra's $2,500 compensation was for work as a temporary secretary for the Vice President of Union Pacific Railroad. How much U.S. source income do the Sanders have?

18. Karim Busiri, a citizen and resident of Egypt, owns a business that generates U.S. source income as well as foreign source income. During the current year he sold equipment used in the business for $90,000. The equipment cost Karim $100,000 and depreciation taken amounted to $40,000, $15,000 of which was taken against U.S. source income. What is his total gain, and how much of the gain is U.S. source income? Foreign source income?

19. Assume the same facts as in Problem 18, except the equipment was sold for $109,000. What is his total gain, and how much of the gain is U.S. source income? Foreign source income?

20. Brendon DeJong, a citizen and resident of South Africa, was employed by Diamonds Ur Us, a U.S. corporation, in both the United States and South Africa. He retired on January 1 of the current year and drew a yearly pension of $60,000 from a noncontributory defined benefit plan established by Diamonds Ur Us. Employer contributions over the years amounted to $280,000, of which $180,000 was attributable to services performed in the U.S. and $100,000 attributable to services performed in South Africa. The plan earnings attributable to Brendon were $150,000. Determine the portion of the $60,000 pension benefit that is attributable to U.S. sources.

21. Inverse Co., a domestic corporation, produces and sells athletic shoes both in the U.S. and abroad. In the current year the company had gross income from U.S. sources of $800 million and gross income from foreign sources of $400 million. Among other expenses, Inverse spent $60 million on advertising its shoes on the internet. The company also spent $20 million on advertising in U.S. magazines and newspapers. How much of Inverse Co.'s advertising expense is allocable to foreign source general limitation income? How much to U.S. source income?

22. Widgets, Inc. is a domestic corporation with two divisions in different states. State A's corporate tax rate is 5 percent; State B's corporate tax rate is 8 percent. In the current year Widgets has $400 million domestic income and $600 million foreign source general limitation income. Neither state exempts foreign source income from taxation. Widget's taxable income in the two states is $300 million and $200 million respectively, with taxes of $15 million and $16 million. Determine the portion of the $31 million state income taxes that is apportioned to foreign source general limitation source income.

23. Larst & Dumas Seed Company uses the sales method to allocate its R&D costs. During the current year the company incurred R&D of $2 million to develop a new soybean. All of the research was performed in the U.S. Soybean sales in the current year amounted to $80 million in foreign countries and $240 million in the U.S. Assuming that Larst & Dumas uses the sales method to allocate R&D, calculate the amount of R&D that should be apportioned to the statutory grouping (sources within the foreign country).

24. Big Wheels Co. is a domestic corporation that owned 100 percent of Little Spokes, a foreign corporation. On April 4, 2015, Little Spokes paid Big Wheels a dividend of $10 million. Later in 2015 Big Wheels sells all of its stock in Little Spokes at a loss of $25 million. In addition to the loss on the sale of the stock in Little Wheels, Big Wheels had in 2015 general limitation foreign source income of $40 million and U.S. source income of $60 million. Keeping in mind the dividend recapture rules, determine Big Wheels' foreign source passive income, general limitation foreign source income, and its U.S. source income for 2015.

25. Assume the same facts as in Problem 24 except that the dividend was paid in 2012. Keeping in mind the dividend recapture rules, determine Big Wheels' foreign source passive income, general limitation foreign source income, and its U.S. source income for 2015.

Appendix

TAX TERMS

This tax glossary defines the words and phrases most commonly used in talking about federal taxes. The language of federal taxation is the language of law, accounting and business. Many of the terms have precise, technical meanings as compared with their meanings in everyday use. These definitions are only adaptations of the full meanings prescribed by the law, regulations and rulings, which are discussed in the explanatory text.

12-month rule. A tax law that allows taxpayers to deduct a prepaid expense in full in the year it is paid provided that it creates (or facilitates the creation of) any right or benefit that does not extend beyond the *earlier* of (1) 12 months after the first date any right or benefit is realized or (2) the end of the tax year that follows the tax year in which the payment was made.

Abandoned spouse. A married individual who lives with a dependent child but had not lived with his or her spouse for the last six months of the year.

Abandonment. The situation in which the owner of property permanently and intentionally relinquishes any claim to the property without receiving any consideration in return.

Ability-to-pay concept. Taxes are imposed on taxpayers that are in the best position to pay the taxes by having them pay a greater share of their tax bases toward the tax burden.

Accountable plan. Requires employees to submit adequate documentation or receipts for any reimbursed expenses and any advances in excess of substantiated expenses must be returned to the employer.

Accrual method. Income is included in gross income when all events have occurred that fix the right to receive the item and its amount can be determined with reasonable accuracy. Expenses are deducted when all events have occurred that determine the liability exists, the amount of the liability can be determined with reasonable accuracy, and economic performance has occurred with respect to the liability.

Accumulated adjustments account (AAA). Measures the accumulated undistributed net income of a corporation while it has been an S corporation.

Accumulated earnings and profits. The amount of E&P a C corporation has generated over the years that has not been distributed as of the beginning of its current tax year.

Accumulated earnings credit. A credit taken as part of the calculation of the accumulated earnings tax. The amount of the credit is the amount by which the *greater of* (1) the corporation's foreseeable reasonable financial needs or (2) $250,000 ($150,000 for personal service corporations) exceeds the corporation's accumulated E&P at the beginning of the year.

Accumulated earnings tax. A penalty tax imposed on C corporations formed or that continue to exist for the purpose of preventing individual shareholders from paying tax on the profits of the corporation by allowing E&P to accumulate. The amount of the tax is 20% of a corporation's accumulated taxable income.

Action on decision. An IRS pronouncement that informs the public as to whether the IRS acquiesced to a court decision.

Ad valorem tax. A tax that uses the value of property as the tax base.

Adjusted basis. The tax equivalent to book value. Adjusted basis equals the initial cost basis of an asset (typically its purchase price) plus the cost of any improvements made to the asset minus the accumulated depreciation taken on the asset.

Adjusted current earnings (ACE). An adjustment made to taxable income to compute alternative minimum taxable income. The ACE is similar to current E&P. ACE differs from current E&P in that current E&P attempts to measure the corporation's capacity to pay dividends from current period earnings, while the ACE calculation is intended to measure pretax income before any distributions.

Adjusted gross income (AGI). An intermediate step between gross income and taxable income that only individuals calculate. Only certain types of deductions are subtracted from gross income when computing AGI.

Administrative convenience. When a tax law is enacted because it reduces administrative costs or taxpayers' compliance costs.

All-events test. A test used to determine when an accrual method taxpayer has to report income and can deduct or capitalize an expense.

All-inclusive approach. The method used to define gross income. Under this approach, all income is subject to income tax unless a provision in the tax laws allows it not to be taxed.

Alternative depreciation system (ADS). An alternative to depreciating property under general MACRS. Recovery periods tend to be longer, and use of the straight-line method is required.

Alternative minimum tax (AMT). A tax enacted to enhance equity in the income tax system by ensuring that all taxpayers pay at least some minimum income taxes each year. It is imposed in addition to the regular tax.

Alternative minimum taxable income (AMTI). AMTI is calculated to determine whether a taxpayer owes the alternative minimum tax. AMTI is determined by making certain adjustments to regular taxable income. *See also* Alternative minimum tax.

Amortization. The annual deduction taken to recover the cost of intangible assets over time.

Amount realized. The sum of the cash, FMV of property, and release of liability received in a sale or an exchange of property, minus any selling expenses. Used in determining the realized gain or loss from the sale of property. See also Realized gain or loss.

AMT base. The tax base used in the AMT system; determined by subtracting the exemption amount from the alternative minimum taxable income. This amount is analogous to taxable income in the regular income tax system. *See also* Alternative minimum tax *and* Alternative minimum taxable income.

Annotated tax service. A tax service that is organized by Code section rather than by topic. CCH's *Standard Federal Tax Reporter* is an example of an annotated tax service.

Announcements. IRS pronouncements that inform the public as to matters of general interest. They may provide guidance as to both substantive and procedural matters.

Applicable federal rate (AFR). A statutory federal rate of interest that is adjusted monthly and is published by the IRS. The rates are based on the average market yield on outstanding marketable obligations of the United States during the one-month period ending on the 14th day of the preceding month.

Asset-use test. A test to determine whether income is effectively connected.

Average tax rate. The total tax liability divided by the tax base. Used in determining the portion of the tax base that is paid in taxes.

Avoiding the recognition of income. Structuring or converting transactions so that the income realized from the transaction is not recognized for the year of the transaction.

Below market loan. A loan charging an interest rate below the market rate.

Blue book. An explanation of a tax act prepared by the staff of the Joint Committee on Taxation.

Book value. The financial accounting equivalent of adjusted basis (i.e., cost less accumulated depreciation).

Boot. A term tax practitioners use to describe nonlike-kind property involved in a like-kind exchange. Cash and other property added to an exchange to equalize the value of exchanged items. When made part of an otherwise nontaxable exchange, the portion of realized gain equal to the value of the boot will have to be recognized.

Built-in gains. All unrealized gain that arose on assets during the time that a corporation was taxed as a C corporation.

Built-in gains tax. A tax imposed on built-in gains that are recognized during an S corporation's first 10 years of existence after converting from a C corporation (7 years if the corporation first became an S corporation in a tax year beginning in 2009 or 2010 and 5 years if the corporation first became an S corporation in a tax year beginning in 2011, 2012, 2013, or 2014).

Business activities test. A test to determine whether income is effectively connected.

Business bad debt. A *bona fide* debt that is closely related to a taxpayer's trade or business. There must have been a business reason for entering into the debt arrangement.

Business tax credit. Tax credit used by governments to reward businesses for participating in certain types of activities by subsidizing a portion of the expenditures that they incur by participating in those activities.

C corporation. An incorporated business entity other than an S corporation that is treated as a separate tax entity from its shareholders. The income of a C corporation is subject to two layers of taxation.

C short year. In the S termination year, the portion of the year beginning on the effective date of the termination of the corporation's S status.

Calendar year. A tax year that begins January 1 and ends December 31.

Capital and profits interest. The term used to describe a partner's interest in a partnership when the partner has an interest in the future profits the partnership generates as well as an interest in the partnership's assets upon liquidation of the partner's interest or dissolution of the partnership.

Capital asset. Any property other than property listed in Code Sec. 1221. In general, a capital asset is either an asset held for investment or a personal-use asset.

Capital expenditure. An expenditure that creates an asset expected to benefit a business for more than one year.

Capital recovery doctrine. When taxpayers dispose of property, in determining the amount of gain included in gross income (or loss deductible from gross income) they are allowed to recover their investment in the property.

Cash receipts and disbursements method. A method of accounting under which a business is required to recognize income when it is received and may deduct expenses when they are paid.

Chief Counsel Advice (CCA). Written advice or instructions issued by the Office of Chief Counsel to field or service center employees of the IRS or Office of Chief Counsel.

Circulation costs. Amounts paid or incurred to establish, maintain, or increase the circulation of a newspaper, magazine, or other periodical.

Claim of right doctrine. A rule that requires taxpayers that receive money or other property under a claim of right without restriction to include the amount received in gross income for the year of receipt, regardless of the taxpayer's method of accounting.

Closely-held corporations. Corporations whose stock is held by a small number of shareholders, typically from the same family or a related group of individuals.

Collateral. Property offered by the borrower that the lender can use to satisfy the debt in the event the borrower defaults on the loan.

Collectibles. Works of art, antiques, rugs, metals, gems, stamps, coins, and other similar items of tangible personal property.

Completed contract method. A special method of accounting for long-term contracts. No income or expenses related to the contract are recognized until the contract is completed.

Condemnation. A legal action in which the government takes possession of property under the power of eminent domain.

Constructive dividend. A payment to or for the benefit of a shareholder that is treated as a dividend even though it may not be denoted as such by the corporation.

Constructive ownership. A rule under which a taxpayer may be treated as owning stock that is actually owned by another person or entity in which the taxpayer has an ownership interest.

Constructive receipt of income doctrine. A rule that requires cash method taxpayers to report gross income in the tax year during which amounts are credited to the business's account, set apart for the business, or otherwise made available without any substantial limitation or restriction. A business may be treated as having constructively received income even though it does not have actual possession of the income until after the end of the tax year.

Control. Persons control a corporation if they own stock possessing at least 80 percent of the total combined voting power of all classes of stock entitled to vote and at least 80 percent of the total number of shares of all other classes of stock of the corporation.

Controlled Foreign Corporations. Foreign corporations that are controlled by U.S. stockholders. Shareholders are taxed of their share of the corporation's subpart F income.

Cost depletion. One of two acceptable tax methods for expensing the costs of a natural resource. This method is similar to the units-of-production method of depreciation and is the only acceptable method of depletion for financial reporting.

Court of Appeals. The court to which decisions made by the U.S. Tax Court, a U.S. district court, or the U.S. Court of Federal Claims may be appealed. There are 13 Courts of Appeals: 12 geographical (11 numbered and one named) plus the Federal Court of Appeals.

Current distributions. Distributions from a partnership to a partner that do not completely liquidate the partner's interest in the partnership.

Current earnings and profits. A C corporation's earnings and profits for its current tax year. A corporate tax concept that attempts to capture a corporation's capacity to pay dividends from its current year's earnings.

Deduction. An expenditure made by a taxpayer that the government allows the taxpayer to use to reduce taxable income.

Deferring tax by accelerating deductions. Structuring transactions so that the expense or loss deduction falls into an earlier tax year than it otherwise would.

Deferring tax by deferring income. Structuring transactions to defer the reporting of income for one or more tax years.

Deficiency interest. The interest charged on tax deficiencies when taxpayers fail to pay the proper amount of taxes on their income tax returns.

Defined benefit plan. A type of retirement plan that promises participants specified benefits during retirement years and continuing until the death of the participant, and often until the death of the spouse of the participant.

Defined contribution plan. A type of retirement plan where the amounts are contributed to an employee's own account, and the amount available upon retirement depends on the performance of the investments in the account.

Depletion. The annual deduction taken to recover an investment in productive natural resources.

Depreciable cost. In financial accounting, it represents the portion of the cost of an asset that may be written off over the asset's useful life (i.e., the costs associated with the acquisition of the asset minus the estimated salvage value). *See also* Salvage value.

Depreciation. An annual deduction taken to recover the capitalized cost of business or income-producing property that is either tangible personal property or real property (other than land).

Determination letter. A written determination issued by an IRS District Director in response to a written request from a taxpayer or the taxpayer's authorized representative. A determination letter will be issued only when the question presented is specifically answered by a statute, a tax treaty, the regulations, a conclusion stated in a revenue ruling, or an opinion or court decision that represents the IRS's position.

Direct tax. A tax levied on the party who ultimately bears the burden of the tax.

Disabled access tax credit. A nonrefundable credit that eligible small businesses may take for amounts paid or incurred to enable them to comply with applicable requirements under the Americans with Disabilities Act of 1990.

Distributive share. A partner's allocated share of partnership income, gains, losses, deductions, and credits as specified in either the partnership agreement or in accordance with each partner's interest in the partnership.

District court. One of the trial courts to which taxpayers may appeal an IRS determination.

Dividend. A distribution of current and/or accumulated earnings and profits by a C corporation to its shareholders.

Dividends received deduction. The amount of dividend income received by a C corporation that is not subject to taxation. It can be 70, 80, or 100 percent of the dividend income.

Domestic corporation. A corporation organized under the laws of one of the 50 states in the United States.

Domestic production gross receipts (DPGR). The gross receipts the taxpayer derives from any lease, rental, license, sale, exchange, or other disposition of (1) qualifying production property, a significant part of which was manufactured, produced, grown, or extracted by the taxpayer within the United States; (2) any qualified film produced by the taxpayer; or (3) electricity, natural gas, or potable water produced by the taxpayer in the United States.

Double exempt bonds. State or local bonds that are exempt from federal and state taxation to residents of that state.

Dwelling unit. A house or apartment used to provide living accommodations; includes mobile homes and manufactured homes; does not include a unit in a hotel, motel, inn, or other establishment in which more than 50 percent of the units are used on a transient basis. *See also* Residential rental property.

Earnings and profits (E&P). A tax term used to reflect a C corporation's economic capacity to make a distribution from corporate earnings that is not a return of a shareholder's capital. It is computed by making adjustments to the corporation's taxable income.

Effectively connected income. Income received by nonresident aliens and foreign corporations from a trade or business conducted in the United States.

Electing small business trust (ESBT). A trust that is eligible to be a shareholder of an S corporation at the election of the trustee and any person treated under the grantor trust rules as the owner of the portion of the trust consisting of the corporation's stock. Such a trust may have multiple beneficiaries, but no person or entity other than an individual, estate, or certain types of charitable organizations may be a beneficiary.

Employer-provided child care credit. A nonrefundable income tax credit for employers who provide employees with child care and child care resource and referral services.

Employment tax. A tax imposed by the government on employee wages (FICA and FUTA) and on net earnings from a sole proprietorship (self-employment taxes).

Empowerment zone and renewal community employment credit. A nonrefundable tax credit for employers who hire individuals who both live *and* work in an empowerment zone.

Empowerment zones. Specific geographic regions within the United States that the federal government has identified as being in need of revitalization.

Estate tax. A wealth transfer tax assessed on a decedent's taxable estate.

Estimated tax payments. Amounts that C corporations and individuals with taxable income not subject to withholding must pay during the year in order to avoid an underpayment of tax penalty.

Excess passive investment income tax. A tax imposed on an S corporation with accumulated E&P if more than 25 percent of its gross receipts are derived from passive investment income.

Exchange. A transaction in which two parties exchange property. Various types of boot (see definition above) may also constitute part of the proceeds.

Excise tax. A tax on the production or consumption of specific goods or services, like tobacco products, alcohol, and gasoline.

Exclusion. An item of income that is not subject to taxation.

Expatriation. The act of giving up citizenship. Individuals who expatriate to avoid U.S. taxation may be subject to a special tax.

Externality. The positive or negative effect of a transaction that occurs to persons or businesses that are not part of that transaction.

FDAP income. Fixed, determinable, and annual or periodical income.

Fair market value (FMV). The amount that would induce a willing seller to sell and a willing buyer to buy certain property.

Federal Insurance Contributions Act (FICA). A program enacted under the Federal Social Security Act that established a federal unemployment insurance program (Medicare) and a program to provide old-age, survivors, and disability benefits to employees (social security). Contributions to this plan are shared by employers and employees through FICA and self-employment taxes.

Federal Unemployment Tax Act (FUTA). FUTA was enacted by Congress to finance the federal unemployment program. Contributions to this plan are funded entirely by employers. The tax base is employee wages up to $7,000; the tax rate equals 6.2 percent.

Final regulation. A proposed regulation that has been adopted as a regulation having the full force and effect of law.

Financial accounting. Rules used to determine how information, including income and expenses, should be reported on a business's financial statements.

Fiscal year. A tax year that ends on the last day of any month other than December.

Flat tax. *See* Proportional tax.

Flexible spending account (FSA). This type of account is offered to employees to cover their dependent care costs and/or medical costs. Employees can set aside each year up to $5,000 of their pre-tax wages from which they can pay qualified health costs (in the case of Health FSAs) or qualified child care costs (in the case of Dependent Care FSAs).

Flow-through entity. A business entity that does not pay taxes, but files a tax return reporting the amounts of gross income, deductions, and credits generated by the business during the year, and passes information along to its owners regarding their respective shares of such items. Examples include partnerships, S corporations, limited liability corporations, and limited liability partnerships.

Foreign corporation. A corporation organized under the laws of a foreign country.

Foreign earned income exclusion. An alternative to the foreign tax credit available for certain foreign earned income received by individuals who are citizens or residents of the United States.

Foreign person. Nonresident individuals and foreign corporations, partnerships, trusts, and estates.

Foreign tax credit (FTC). A credit allowed to receivers of income from outbound transactions. Its purpose is to mitigate double taxation.

Franchise tax. An annual tax on the privilege of doing business in the state.

GAAP (Generally Accepted Accounting Principles). The set of rules publicly-traded companies must adhere to when preparing financial statements.

General business credit. A combination of business credits, each of which is computed under its own set of rules.

General partnership. A business entity that arises from an agreement among two or more persons, all of whom have unlimited liability for the debts of the partnership, to operate a business for profit.

Gift tax. A wealth transfer tax the government imposes upon the transferor for transfers to nonspouses in excess of a certain amount each year.

Golsen **rule.** This rule provides that the U.S. Tax Court will follow a Court of Appeals decision that is squarely on point when appeal of the Tax Court's decision lies to that Court of Appeals.

Grantor trust. A trust whose income is taxed to its grantor under the grantor trust rules of Code Sec. 671 et seq. One example of a grantor trust is a revocable trust, which is a trust that can be revoked by its grantor.

Gross income. All income from whatever source derived, except as specifically excluded by a provision in the Internal Revenue Code or other tax law. Represents the income the government has chosen to tax.

Gross receipts. The total amount of money and the fair market value of any other property received for selling property or performing services.

Gross sales. The total amount of sales at invoice prices, not reduced by any discounts, returns, or allowances.

Guaranteed payments. Amounts paid from the partnership to a partner that are determined *without regard* to the profits generated by the partnership during the year.

Half-year convention. Averaging convention used for tax depreciation. Property put in service in a trade or business during a tax year is deemed to have been placed in service in the middle of the year.

Head of household. A filing status available to taxpayers who are not married and do not qualify as a surviving spouse but maintain a household for more than half of the tax year in which a qualifying child of the taxpayer or any other person who is a dependent of the taxpayer lives.

Holding period. Time period that generally begins the day after a taxpayer acquires property and ends on the day the taxpayer disposes of the property. Used to determine whether a recognized gain or loss is short-term or long-term.

Hybrid method. A method of accounting that combines elements of the cash and accrual methods of accounting.

Imputed interest. The "deemed" interest payments a borrower makes to a lender on a below market loan, including a loan involving original issue discount. *See also* Below market loan *and* Original issue discount.

Inbound transactions. Transactions in the United States that are incurred by nonresident aliens and foreign corporations.

Income. Broadly defined as increases in wealth that the taxpayer has realized.

Indirect tax. A tax levied on someone other than the one who ultimately bears the burden of the tax.

Inheritance tax. A tax levied on the beneficiary upon receipt of inherited property.

Installment method. A special method of accounting requiring taxpayers to recognize gain from an installment sale as payments are received rather than at the time the sale occurs.

Installment sale. A sale or exchange of property in which the seller receives payments in more than one tax year.

Intangible property. Personal property that has no physical characteristics. Examples include goodwill, patents, copyrights, mutual funds, stocks, and bonds.

Internal Revenue Code. The primary statutory source of federal tax law. It is set forth in Title 26 of the United States Code.

Interpretive regulation. A regulation that interprets the Code. It is promulgated pursuant to the Secretary of the Treasury's general authority to issue regulations.

Involuntary conversion. An event caused by casualty, theft, or condemnation in which the taxpayer's property is damaged or destroyed.

Itemized deductions. A deduction from adjusted gross income that consists of various personal expenses that the federal government allows individuals to deduct in lieu of a standard deduction.

Kiddie tax. A tax imposed at the parents'rates on children under the age of 18 or under age 24 in college.

Least aggregate deferral of income rule. The last of three tests used to determine a partnership's required tax year. It involves performing a test using each of the year-ends of its partners and determining which of those year-ends, on average, will allow the government to collect taxes on the partnership income the most quickly. *See also* Majority partners rule *and* Principal partner rule.

Legislative regulation. A regulation that defines a statutory term or prescribes a method for implementing a Code provision. It carries more weight than other types of regulations because it is promulgated pursuant to a specific grant of authority by Congress.

LIFO recapture amount. Used in computing the LIFO recapture tax. Equals the difference between the amount of the corporation's inventory assets under the first-in, first-out (FIFO) method and the amount of the corporation's inventory assets under the LIFO method.

Limited liability. When an owner's liability with respect to the business is limited to the amount the owner has invested in the business.

Limited liability company (LLC). A business entity that can be treated as a partnership for tax purposes and whose owners enjoy limited liability.

Limited liability partnership (LLP). A business entity that can be treated as a partnership for tax purposes, but whose owners enjoy some aspects of limited liability.

Limited partnership. A business entity that arises from an agreement among two or more partners to operate a business for profit in which one or more of the partners has limited liability with respect to the debts of the partnership and at least one partner is responsible for the debts of the partnership.

Listed property. Certain personal property susceptible to both business and personal use. Examples include passenger automobiles, computers, and cellular telephones.

Long-term capital gain or loss. A capital gain or loss on a capital asset held for more than one year.

Low-income housing credit. A nonrefundable income tax credit for taxpayers who purchase or substantially rehabilitate residential rental property used for low-income housing.

Majority partners rule. The first of three tests used to determine a partnership's required tax year. It requires that a partnership adopt the year-end of the partner, or group of partners, that owns more than a 50-percent interest in partnership capital *and* profits. *See also* Least aggregate deferral of income rule *and* Principal partner rule.

Marginal tax rate. The rate of tax on the last dollar of taxable income or the amount of taxes saved on an additional dollar of deduction.

Medicare tax on unearned income. Commonly referred to as the Investment Income Tax (NIIT). A tax at the rate of 3.8 percent levied on the net investment income of high income taxpayers.

Medicare taxes. The hospital insurance (HI) portion of the FICA tax.

Method of accounting. The rules that govern when a business must recognize income and when it may deduct expenses. It refers not only to the overall method of accounting that a taxpayer uses but also to a taxpayer's accounting treatment of any particular item.

Mid-month convention. Averaging convention used for tax depreciation. Property put in service in a trade or business during a tax year is deemed to have been placed in service in the middle of the month in which it was actually placed in service.

Mid-quarter convention. Averaging convention used for tax depreciation. Property put in service in a trade or business during a tax year is deemed to have been placed in service in the middle of the quarter in which it was actually placed in service.

Minimum tax credit. The amount of alternative minimum tax paid in one year that can be used to offset a taxpayer's regular tax liability for a subsequent tax year. *See also* Alternative minimum tax *and* Timing differences.

Modified Accelerated Cost Recovery System (MACRS). A system for recovering the cost of capital expenditures through periodic depreciation deductions. MACRS applies to depreciable tangible property placed in service after 1986.

Municipal interest. Interest from state and local government bonds (municipal bonds, or "muni" bonds for short).

Necessary expense. An expense that is appropriate or helpful to the continuation of the taxpayer's business.

Net capital gain. The excess of a net long-term capital gain over any net short-term capital loss. Relevant to individual taxpayers because it is subject to reduced tax rates.

Net earnings from self-employment. The amount from which self-employment taxes of a sole proprietor are based. It equals 92.35 percent of net profits reported on Schedule C.

Net income per books. The net income a corporation reports for financial accounting purposes.

Net income tax. Term used in the alternative minimum tax system. The sum of the net regular tax liability and any alternative minimum tax minus the same tax credits used in computing net regular tax liability.

Net long-term capital gain. The excess of long-term capital gains over long-term capital losses.

Net long-term capital loss. The excess of long-term capital losses over long-term capital gains.

Net operating loss deduction. The total of a taxpayer's net operating loss carryforwards and carrybacks to a tax year.

Net regular tax liability. Term used in the alternative minimum tax system. A taxpayer's regular tax liability minus certain tax credits, such as the foreign tax credit and personal tax credits.

Net short-term capital gain. The excess of short-term capital gains over short-term capital losses.

Net short-term capital loss. The excess of short-term capital losses over short-term capital gains.

New markets credit. A nonrefundable income tax credit for taxpayers who make a qualified equity investment in a qualified community development entity. See also *Qualified community development entity.*

News release. An IRS pronouncement issued to the media to announce items of general interest. They often are used to announce that an important new revenue ruling or revenue procedure is going to be released and set forth the text of that ruling or procedure.

Nonaccountable plan. Reimbursements paid through a system that does not meet the requirements for an accountable plan.

Nonbusiness bad debt. A *bona fide* debt that is not a business bad debt. *See also* Business bad debt.

Nonrecaptured net Section 1231 losses. Net Section 1231 losses recognized in the previous five tax years that have not previously caused a net Section 1231 gain to be treated as ordinary income.

Nonrecourse debt. The type of debt arrangement in which the lender has no recourse (no ability to collect the debt) directly from the borrower in the event the borrower defaults on the loan.

Nonrecourse liability. A liability for which the seller is not personally liable, but for which the creditor can only look to property specified in the loan agreement for satisfaction of the debt.

Nonrefundable tax credit. A tax credit that can only reduce a taxpayer's income tax liability.

Nonresident alien. An individual who is not a U.S. citizen or resident.

Notices. IRS pronouncements issued to the public to provide guidance involving substantive interpretations of the Code. They often are issued to provide taxpayers with guidance about recently enacted legislation or to alert taxpayers about pending regulations.

Ordinary expense. An expense that is customary and acceptable in the taxpayer's type of business.

Organizational costs. Certain costs incurred in the process of incorporating a business.

Original issue discount (OID). Additional interest income representing the difference between the amount due at maturity (i.e., the face value of an obligation) and the obligation's issue price. It is a function of the difference between the face rate associated with the bond and the current market interest rate.

Originating difference. The initial difference that occurs in the year in which a timing difference is created. *See also* Reversing difference *and* Timing difference.

Outbound transactions. Foreign transactions and investments by U.S. citizens, residents, and domestic corporations.

Partner's capital account. An account on the partnership books that keeps track of what a partner is entitled to receive upon the liquidation of the partner's interest or upon dissolution of the partnership.

Partnership. A flow-through entity that has at all times at least two owners, at least one of whom is responsible for the debts of the business.

Partnership agreement. A written or oral agreement among the partners in a partnership that provides, among other things, how the partners will share in the partnership's profits and losses and how the assets of the partnership will be divided upon dissolution of the partnership.

Passive income. Unearned income such as dividends and interest.

Passive investment income. Gross receipts derived from royalties, rents, dividends, interest, and annuities.

Patent. An intangible asset that gives its owner the exclusive right to commercially profit from a specified product or process for a limited number of years.

Per diem. Established amounts allowed by the IRS to be deducted in lieu of substantiation for an employee's lodging, meals, and incidental expenses or a sole proprietor's for meals and incidental expenses.

Percentage depletion. One of two acceptable tax methods for expensing the costs of a natural resource. Because the expense is calculated as a percentage of gross profits generated by the resource, over time the costs expensed can exceed the income tax basis of the property.

Percentage of completion method (PCM). A special method of accounting that applies to long-term contracts. Taxpayers include in their gross income each year a portion of the total contract price that corresponds to the portion of the total estimated contract costs actually incurred during the year.

Permanent difference. The condition that exists when items of income or expense are reported for financial accounting purposes but *never* for tax purposes, or vice versa.

Perquisites. Fringe benefits that represent privileges that businesses make available to their employees.

Personal and dependency exemptions. A deduction from adjusted gross income the government allows to individual taxpayers. A deduction is allowed for the taxpayer, the taxpayer's spouse (if filing a joint return), and the taxpayer's dependents.

Personal holding company (PHC). Any corporation for which (1) during the last half of the tax year, more than 50 percent of the corporation's stock is owned, *directly or indirectly*, by five or fewer individuals and (2) at least 60 percent of the corporation's adjusted ordinary income for the year is PHC income.

Personal holding company income. Eight specific types of ordinary income, including: (1) dividends, interest, and royalties; (2) rents; (3) mineral, oil, and gas royalties; (4) copyright royalties; (5) produced film rents; (6) amounts received by a corporation for the use of its property; (7) compensation under personal services contracts; and (8) estate or trust income.

Personal property. Property that is not real estate. *See* Tangible personal property *and* Intangible property.

Personal service corporation (PSC). For purposes of the accumulated earnings tax, a corporation whose principal function is the performance of services in the field of health, law, engineering, architecture, accounting, actuarial science, the performing arts, or consulting. Personal service corporations are entitled to a lower accumulated earnings credit than other corporations.

Personal tax credit. A tax credit available only to individuals.

Points. Term used to describe the prepaid interest that a lender charges in exchange for a lower interest rate to the borrower over the term of the loan.

Portfolio income. Income derived from investments, such as stocks, bonds, and mutual funds.

Post-termination transition period. Generally the one-year period that starts one day after a corporation ceases to be an S corporation.

Precedent. Refers to a principle in law of using the past decisions to assist in making current decisions.

Primary source of authority. Part of the tax law. Examples of primary sources include legislative authority (e.g., the Code, tax treaties, and Congressional reports), administrative authority (e.g., Treasury regulations and IRS rulings), and judicial decisions.

Principal partner. A partner that has at least a five-percent interest in the profits *or* capital of the partnership.

Principal partner rule. The second of three tests used to determine a partnership's required tax year. If the majority interest rule does not apply, this rule requires that a partnership adopt the tax year of *all* of its principal partners. *See also* Least aggregate deferral of income rule *and* Majority partners rule.

Private activity bond. A bond issued by a state or other municipality from which more than 10 percent of the proceeds are used to finance private business activities. Interest paid on these bonds is exempt from regular income tax if the issuer has complied with certain limitations concerning the volume of the bonds issued and the use of the bond proceeds.

Private letter ruling. A written statement issued by the IRS' Office of Associate Chief Counsel that interprets and applies the tax laws to a specific set of facts presented by a taxpayer. A letter ruling is issued at the request of a taxpayer and upon payment of a fee.

Private nonoperating foundation. A privately funded, tax-exempt, nonprofit organization that does not meet the requirements of a private operating foundation.

Private operating foundation. A privately funded organization that directly carries out its own activities and is required to spend at least 85 percent of its earnings carrying out its activities and to pass certain other tests.

Pro rata share. The portion (based on ownership percentage) of each item of an S corporation's taxable income that a shareholder is required to take into account when calculating the shareholder's taxable income.

Procedural regulation. A regulation that establishes procedure or practice requirements (such as prescribing how an election is made).

Profits-only interest. The term used to describe a partner's interest in a partnership when the partner is entitled to a share of future partnership profits but does not have an ownership interest in the capital of the partnership.

Progressive tax. A tax structure in which the average tax rate increases as the tax base increases.

Property tax. A tax assessed on property, including real property, tangible personal property, and intangible personal property.

Proportional tax. A tax structure in which the average tax rate does not change as the tax base changes (also referred to as flat tax).

Proposed regulation. A Treasury regulation that the Secretary of the Treasury proposes to issue.

Public charities. Charitable organizations such as churches, public universities, the Red Cross, and the United Way that receive their funding from the general public.

Public good. A government-provided good or service for which enjoyment of the good cannot be limited.

Publicly-held corporations. Corporations whose stock is traded on one of the U.S. stock exchanges, such as the American Stock Exchange, New York Stock Exchange, or NASDAQ.

Qualified charitable organization. A tax-exempt, nonprofit organization formed and operated exclusively for the purposes specified in Code Sec. 501(c)(3).

Qualified community development entity (qualified CDE). A domestic corporation or partnership whose primary mission is serving, or providing investment capital for, low-income communities or low-income persons.

Qualified dividend income. Dividend income that is taxed to an individual taxpayer at a rate lower than the taxpayer's marginal tax rate. The dividends must be paid on stock of a U.S. corporation or a qualified foreign corporation that the individual held for more than 60 days during the 121-day period beginning 60 days before the ex-dividend date.

Qualified personal service corporation (QPSC). A corporation is a "qualified personal service corporation" if its employees spend at least 95 percent of their time performing services in a qualifying field (i.e., health, law, engineering, architecture, accounting, actuarial science, performing arts, or consulting) and at least 95 percent of the value of its stock is held directly or indirectly by employees performing services in a qualifying field, retired employees who performed such services for the corporation, the estate of such an employee or retired employee, or any other person who acquired stock in the corporation by reason of the death of such an employee or retired employee (but only for the two-year period beginning on the date of that individual's death).

Qualified rehabilitated building. A building that is a certified historic structure or a building that originally was placed in service before 1936 and with respect to which the taxpayer paid or incurred substantial rehabilitation expenditures.

Qualified Subchapter S subsidiary (QSub). A domestic corporation 100-percent owned by an S corporation that the S corporation has elected to treat as a QSub.

Qualified Subchapter S trust (QSST). One of the types of trusts that can be a shareholder of an S corporation if the beneficiary elects to qualify the trust as a shareholder. All of the income of the trust must be distributed to one individual, who must be a U.S. citizen or resident. Any trust principal distributed during the income beneficiary's lifetime can be distributed only to that income beneficiary.

Qualified zone employee. An employee who performs substantially all of his or her services for an employer within an empowerment zone and whose principal residence while performing such services is located within an empowerment zone.

Qualified zone wages. Wages paid or incurred by an employer for services performed by an employee while working as a qualified zone employee.

Real property. Land and buildings (also referred to as real estate).

Realization principle. Gains and losses on property are not reported on the tax return until the year in which property is disposed of in a taxable transaction.

Realized gain or loss. Measure of the taxpayer's true economic gain or loss resulting from the disposal of property in a sale, an exchange, or an abandonment.

Recapture of a tax credit. If a taxpayer ceases to use property for the purposes that qualified the property for a tax credit, all or a portion of the credit may have to be added to the taxpayer's tax liability for the year that the property ceased to be used for the qualified purpose.

Recognized gain or loss. The amount of the realized gain or loss that is reported on the tax return.

Recourse debt. The type of debt arrangement in which the lender can proceed directly against the borrower for any debt on which the borrower defaults.

Recourse liability. Liability for which the seller is personally liable.

Refundable tax credit. A credit that can reduce a taxpayer's tax liability to zero and produce a refund for any amount of the credit in excess of the taxpayer's tax liability.

Regressive tax. A tax structure in which the average tax rate decreases as the tax base increases.

Rehabilitation credit. A nonrefundable credit available for substantially rehabilitating a depreciable building that was placed in service before 1936 or that qualifies as a certified historic structure. *See also* Substantially rehabilitated *and* Qualified rehabilitated building.

Research activities credit. A nonrefundable income tax credit for conducting qualified research.

Resident alien. A person who is not a citizen of the United States, but who is a lawful resident of the United States.

Residential rental property. Rental property for which 80 percent or more of the gross rental income is derived from the rental of dwelling units. *See also* Dwelling unit.

Return of capital distribution. A distribution of cash or other property from a corporation that is not made from current or accumulated earnings and profits.

Revenue procedure. A ruling issued by the IRS that involves a procedural issue.

Revenue ruling. An official interpretation by the IRS as to the application of the tax laws to a specific set of facts.

Reversing difference. Timing difference that occurs in a year subsequent to the year in which the originating difference occurred. *See also* Originating difference *and* Timing difference.

S corporation. A flow-through business entity that does not pay income taxes. An S corporation gets its name because it is a corporation that has elected to be taxed under Subchapter S of Chapter 1 of the Code. Only corporations that satisfy certain requirements can elect to be taxed as S corporations.

S short year. In the S termination year, the portion of the year ending before the effective date of the termination of the corporation's S status.

S termination year. The year that a corporation's status as an S corporation terminates.

Sales tax. A broad-based tax on the consumption of goods and services.

Salvage value. Term used in financial accounting. The amount that the owner of an asset believes an asset could be sold at the end of its useful life.

Schedule M-1. Part of Form 1120,*U.S. Corporation Income Tax Return*; it requires corporations to reconcile their net income for financial accounting purposes with their taxable income. Must be filed by corporations with total receipts and total assets of at least $250,000 (but total assets less than $10 million) at the end of the year.

Schedule M-2. Part of Form 1120, *U.S. Corporation Income Tax Return*; it requires corporations to explain changes during the year in their unappropriated retained earnings. Must be filed by corporations that file Schedule M-1 or Schedule M-3.

Schedule M-3. An expanded version of Schedule M-1. Effective for tax years ending December 31, 2014 and later, corporations with at least $50 million in total assets must complete Schedule M-3 in lieu of Schedule M-1. Corporations with at least $10 million but less than $50 million in total assets at tax year end have to complete Part I of Schedule M-3 but may complete Schedule M-1 in lieu of Parts II and III of Schedule M-3.

Secondary source of authority. A reference that explains, comments on, or updates primary sources of tax authority. Examples include topical and annotated tax services, treatises, journals, papers from tax institutes, newsletters, and citators.

Section 179 property. Property eligible for immediate expensing under Code Sec. 179. Section 179 property is tangible personal property that is depreciable under MACRS and is acquired by purchase for use in the active conduct of a trade or business.

Section 197 intangibles. Intangible assets for which amortization deductions may be taken under Code Sec. 197. Section 197 intangibles are intangibles listed in Code Sec. 197 that are acquired by the taxpayer and held in connection with the conduct of a trade or business or for the production of income.

Section 291 gain. Ordinary income recognized on the sale of depreciable real property sold by a C corporation.

Section 1231 gain. The gain on the sale, exchange, or condemnation of Section 1231 property other than ordinary gain due to depreciation recapture.

Section 1231 loss. A loss on the sale, exchange, or condemnation of Section 1231 property.

Section 1231 property. Land or depreciable property used in a business and held for more than one year.

Section 1244 stock. Stock issued by a domestic corporation in exchange for money or property at a time the corporation does not have more than $1 million in paid-in capital. The corporation must also meet an active business requirement unless it is a new corporation.

Section 1245 gain. The (ordinary income) gain that results from depreciation recapture on depreciable personal property held for more than one year. The amount of gain is equal to the *lesser* of the amount of the gain or the accumulated depreciation taken on the property.

Section 1250 gain. The (ordinary income) gain on the sale of depreciable real property that is recaptured as ordinary income. The amount recaptured is the *lesser* of the amount of the gain or the excess of the depreciation taken over the amount that would have been allowed under the straight-line method.

Self-employment tax. The employee and employer portions of FICA tax that are imposed on net earnings from self-employment.

Short tax year. A tax year lasting fewer than 12 months.

Short-term capital gain or loss. A capital gain or loss on a capital asset held for one year or less.

Smoothing income. Arranging the recognition of income and expenses so as to, as much as possible, equalize marginal income tax rates from year to year.

Social security taxes. The old-age, survivors, and disability insurance (OASDI) portion of the FICA tax.

Sole proprietor. The owner of an unincorporated business.

Standard deduction. A deduction from adjusted gross income that the federal government allows individual taxpayers to deduct in lieu of itemized deductions.

Start-up costs. Costs that normally would be currently deductible if they were incurred in connection with the operation of an existing trade or business and that are not organizational costs.

Stock dividend. A dividend payable in shares of the distributing corporation's own stock.

Straight debt. A written, unconditional promise to pay a sum certain in money on demand or on a specified date. It will not be treated as a second class of stock, even though it is considered equity under general principles of federal tax law, if it satisfies the following requirements: (1) it does not provide for an interest rate or payment dates contingent on profits, the borrower's discretion, the payment of dividends with respect to common stock, or similar factors; (2) it cannot be converted (directly or indirectly) into stock or any other equity interest of the corporation; and (3) it is held by an individual (other than a nonresident alien), estate, trust eligible to be an S corporation shareholder, or a person who is actively and regularly engaged in the business of lending money.

Substantial authority. An objective standard that is less stringent than the "more-likely-than-not" standard, but more rigorous than the "reasonable basis" standard.

Substantial economic effect. The standard that must be met before allocations of partnership items can be made to the partners as specified in the partnership agreement.

Substantial presence test. One test that establishes residency. Generally met if the individual stays at least 183 days during the taxable year.

Surviving spouse. A filing status available to taxpayers widowed during one of the two preceding tax years who have a dependent son or daughter living with them the entire year.

Tangible personal property. Property that has physical characteristics but is not real estate.

Tax accounting. Rules used to determine when income and expenses are recognized for tax purposes.

Tax authority. Established tax law that can be used to help in reaching a conclusion about a tax issue.

Tax avoidance. The art of reducing tax liability through legitimate means.

Tax base. Used in computing tax liability. It represents the amount subject to tax. The tax base is multiplied by the tax rate to determine the taxpayer's tax liability.

Tax benefit rule. A tax rule under which an amount recovered must be included in gross income for the year of the recovery if all or a portion of the expense deducted in a prior tax year is recovered in a subsequent tax year and if the deduction resulted in a tax benefit for the taxpayer.

Tax compliance research. The process of determining how an item of income already received, an expense already incurred, or a transaction already completed should be reported for tax purposes.

Tax credit. Amount that reduces a taxpayer's tax liability. Can be either refundable or nonrefundable.

Tax deferred. When income or gain is postponed to some future point in time but is eventually taxed.

Tax evasion. Understating taxes due the government through unlawful means.

Tax planning. Structuring financial transactions to maximize the taxpayer's after-tax wealth.

Tax planning research. The process of determining how best to plan for income not yet received, expenses not yet incurred, and transactions that have not yet occurred to achieve the most favorable tax consequences.

Tax preference. A deduction or exclusion allowed in the calculation of regular taxable income that is not allowed in the calculation of alternative minimum taxable income.

Tax treaties. Agreements reached by the United States with foreign countries. The objective of tax treaties is to reduce the potential for double taxation. U.S. citizens and residents subject to taxes imposed by a foreign country are entitled to certain deductions, exemptions, credits, and reductions in tax rates.

Tax year. The period of time over which taxable income is computed.

Taxable income. The difference between a taxpayer's gross income and the total deductions a taxpayer is allowed. The tax base used in the regular income tax system.

Taxable income limitation. A limitation that disallows any Section 179 expense from being deducted in the current year to the extent that it exceeds the aggregate of the taxpayer's taxable income derived from the active conduct of any trade or business.

Taxable income per return. A corporation's taxable income, as reported on the U.S. federal income tax return.

Technical advice memorandum (TAM). Written advice from the IRS on the interpretation and proper application of tax law, tax treaties, regulations, revenue rulings, notices, or other precedents to a specific set of facts. A TAM is requested by IRS personnel, not taxpayers. No fee is charged a taxpayer for a TAM.

Temporary regulation. A Treasury regulation issued to provide interim guidance to tax practitioners and the public until final regulations are issued. The rules contained in temporary regulations can be used as authority pending issuance of final regulations.

Testamentary trusts. Trusts created from a decedent's will and come into existence upon the death of the grantor.

Timing difference. Difference that results when income and expenses are reported in one year for financial accounting purposes and in a different year for tax purposes. In the alternative minimum tax system, a difference in the treatment of an item for determining regular taxable income and alternative minimum taxable income that reverses itself over time. *See also* Originating difference *and* Reversing difference.

Topical tax service. A tax service that is arranged by topic rather than by Code section. CCH's *Tax Research Consultant* is an example of a topical tax service.

Treasury regulations. The official interpretation of the Code by the Secretary of the Treasury.

U.S. Court of Federal Claims. One of the trial courts to which taxpayers may appeal an IRS determination.

U.S. Supreme Court. The last resort for those appealing a decision of a Circuit Court of Appeal and final authority as to what the Code means.

U.S. Tax Court. One of the trial courts to which taxpayers may appeal an IRS determination. Unlike the U.S. district court or U.S. Court of Federal Claims, there is no requirement that the taxpayer pay any alleged deficiency before the court will hear the taxpayer's appeal.

Undistributed personal holding company income. The amount subject to the personal holding company tax, determined by applying certain adjustments to the taxable income of the corporation.

Uniform capitalization (UNICAP) rules. The rules that require a taxpayer to capitalize certain costs as part of the cost of real or tangible personal property the taxpayer produces.

United States person. Citizens and residents of the United States as well as domestic: corporations, partnerships, estates, and most trusts.

Unrealized gains and losses. The difference between the FMV of property and its adjusted basis at a time other than when the property has been disposed. Sometimes referred to as paper gains and losses because they represent the appreciation or decline in value of property that has yet to be sold.

Unrealized receivable. Any right to income for services or goods that are not capital assets that have not been previously recorded in gross income under the taxpayer's method of accounting.

Unreasonable position. A tax return preparer can be penalized for preparing a return or claim of refund that understates tax liability if the understatement is due to an unreasonable position. If a position (other than a position with respect to a tax shelter or reportable transaction to which Code Sec. 6662A applies) is adequately disclosed, it will be considered unreasonable unless the preparer had a reasonable basis for it (*reasonable basis standard*). If a position (other than a position with respect to a tax shelter or reportable transaction to which Code Sec. 6662A applies) is not adequately disclosed, it will be considered unreasonable unless there is or was substantial authority for it (*substantial authority standard*). If a position is with respect to a tax shelter or reportable transaction to which Code Sec. 6662A applies, it will be considered unreasonable unless it was reasonable for the preparer to believe that it would more likely than not be sustained on its merits (*more-likely-than-not standard*).

Unrecaptured Section 1250 gain. A term applicable only to individual taxpayers. The portion of the gain on the sale of depreciable realty that is taxed at a maximum 25-percent tax rate.

Use tax. A tax charged by states on the consumption, use, or storage of goods and services that are not subject to sales tax.

User fee. A tax charged to those that use a government-provided good or service.

Wash sale. A sale of securities (stocks and bonds) in which a taxpayer realizes a loss on the sale and then purchases the same or substantially identical securities within 30 days before or 30 days after the date of the sale. The tax laws do not allow taxpayers to recognize losses that result from wash sales.

Wealth transfer tax. The tax a government imposes on transfers of wealth between two individuals. *See also* Estate tax, Gift tax, *and* Inheritance tax.

Wherewithal-to-pay concept. The principle that taxes income at the point at which the taxpayer has the greatest ability to pay the tax on realized income.

Work opportunity credit. A nonrefundable income tax credit for employing individuals from certain targeted groups.

Written determinations. A private letter ruling issued by the IRS's Office of Associate Chief Counsel in response to a taxpayer's request, a determination letter issued by an IRS Director in response to a taxpayer's request, a technical advice memorandum issued by the IRS's Office of Associate Chief Counsel at the request of an IRS field office, or a Chief Counsel Advice issued by the Office of Chief Counsel to field and service center employees of the IRS or Office of Chief Counsel.

2015 TAX RATE TABLES

Schedule X: Single Individuals

If taxable income is:	The tax is:
Not over $9,225	10% of the taxable income
Over $9,225 but not over $37,450	$922.50 + 15% of the excess over $9,225
Over $37,450 but not over $90,750	$5,156.25 + 25% of the excess over $37,450
Over $90,750 but not over $189,300	$18,481.25 + 28% of the excess over $90,750
Over $189,300 but not over $411,500	$46,075.25 + 33% of the excess over $189,300
Over $411,500 not over $413,200	$119,401.25 + 35% of the excess over $411,500
Over $413,200	$119,996.25 + 39.6% of the excess over $413,200

Schedule Y-1: Married Filing Jointly and Surviving Spouses

If taxable income is:	The tax is:
Not over $18,450	10% of the taxable income
Over $18,450 but not over $74,900	$1,845 + 15% of the excess over $18,450
Over $74,900 but not over $151,200	$10,312.50 + 25% of the excess over $74,900
Over $151,200 but not over $230,450	$29,387.50 + 28% of the excess over $151,200
Over $230,450 but not over $411,500	$51,577.50 + 33% of the excess over $230,450
Over $411,500 but not over $464,850	$111,324 + 35% of the excess over $411,500
Over $464,850	$129,996.50 + 39.6% of the excess over $464,850

Schedule Y-2: Married Individuals Filing Separately

If taxable income is:	The tax is:
Not over $9,225	10% of the taxable income
Over $9,225 but not over $37,450	$922.50 + 15% of the excess over $9,225
Over $37,450 but not over $75,600	$5,156.25 + 25% of the excess over $37,450
Over $75,600 but not over $115,225	$14,693.75 + 28% of the excess over $75,600
Over $115,225 but not over $205,750	$25,788.75 + 33% of the excess over $115,225
Over $205,750 not over $232,425	$55,662 + 35% of the excess over $205,750
Over $232,425	$64,989.25 + 39.6% of the excess over $232,425

Schedule Z: Heads of Households

If taxable income is:	The tax is:
Not over $13,150	10% of the taxable income
Over $13,150 but not over $50,200	$1,315 + 15% of the excess over $13,150
Over $50,200 but not over $129,600	$6,872.50 + 25% of the excess over $50,200
Over $129,600 but not over $209,850	$26,722.50 + 28% of the excess over $129,600
Over $209,850 but not over $411,500	$49,192.50 + 33% of the excess over $209,850
Over $411,500 not over $439,000	$115,737 + 35% of the excess over $411,500
Over $439,000	$125,362 + 39.6% of the excess over $439,000

CASE TABLE

References are to paragraph (¶) numbers.

FINDING LIST

References are to paragraph (¶) numbers.

Regulations

Proposed Regulations

Technical Advice Memoranda

Treasury Decisions

References are to paragraph (¶) numbers.

References are to paragraph (¶) numbers.

References are to paragraph (¶) numbers.

References are to paragraph (¶) numbers.

References are to paragraph (¶) numbers.

References are to paragraph (¶) numbers.

References are to paragraph (¶) numbers.

References are to paragraph (¶) numbers.

References are to paragraph (¶) numbers.

References are to paragraph (¶) numbers.

References are to paragraph (¶) numbers.

References are to paragraph (¶) numbers.

References are to paragraph (¶) numbers.

References are to paragraph (¶) numbers.

References are to paragraph (¶) numbers.

References are to paragraph (¶) numbers.